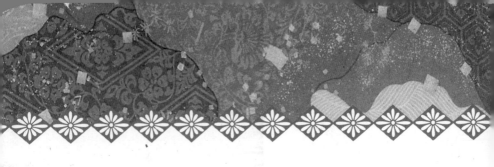

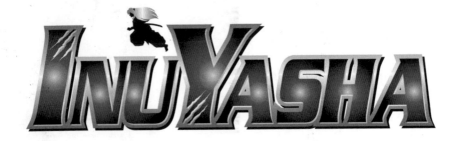

Story & Art by

Rumiko Takahashi

INUYASHA

Volume 6
VIZBIG Edition

Story and Art by RUMIKO TAKAHASHI

© 1997 Rumiko TAKAHASHI/Shogakukan
All rights reserved.
Original Japanese edition "INUYASHA"
published by SHOGAKUKAN Inc.

English Adaptation/Gerard Jones
Translation/Mari Morimoto
Transcription/David Smith
Touch-up Art & Lettering/Steve Dutro, Leonard Clark, Primary Graphix
VIZ Media Series Design/Yuki Ameda
VIZBIG Edition Design/Sean Lee
VIZ Media Series Editor (1st Edition)/Julie Davis
VIZ Media Series Editors (VIZ Media/Action Edition)/
Julie Davis, Avery Gotoh, Michelle Pangilinan
VIZBIG Edition Editor/Mike Montesa

The stories, characters and incidents mentioned in
this publication are entirely fictional.

No portion of this book may be reproduced or transmitted in any form or
by any means without written permission from the copyright holders.

Printed in China

Published by VIZ Media, LLC
P.O. Box 77010
San Francisco, CA 94107

10 9 8 7 6 5 4 3 2 1
First printing, February 2011

VIZBIG EDITION
www.viz.com

VIZ MEDIA

SHONEN SUNDAY
WWW.SHONENSUNDAY.COM

RATED
T+
FOR OLDER TEEN

PARENTAL ADVISORY
INUYASHA is rated T+ for Older Teen and is
recommended for ages 16 and up. This volume
contains fantasy violence and partial nudity.
ratings.viz.com

InuYasha

Volume 16
Kikyo's Plan

Volume 17
Tetsusaiga Reborn

Volume 18
Onigumo's Heart

Story & Art by

Rumiko Takahashi

Shonen Sunday Manga / VIZBIG Edition

CONTENTS

Cast of Characters 6

Volume 16: Kikyo's Plan

Scroll One: The Human Shield 11
Scroll Two: Turn Around 29
Scroll Three: The Light of the Shikon 47
Scroll Four: The Arrow Released 65
Scroll Five: Kikyo's Plan 83
Scroll Six: The Third Demon 101
Scroll Seven: Goshinki 119
Scroll Eight: Demon Blood 137
Scroll Nine: True Nature 155
Scroll Ten: The Ogre's Sword 175

Volume 17: Tetsusaiga Reborn

Scroll One: Tokijin 197
Scroll Two: Tetsusaiga Reborn 215
Scroll Three: Tokijin's Choice 233
Scroll Four: The Scent of Blood 251
Scroll Five: True Strength 269
Scroll Six: The Fourth One 287
Scroll Seven: Juromaru 305
Scroll Eight: Without Shields 323
Scroll Nine: Kageromaru 341
Scroll Ten: Two Against Two 359

Volume 18: Onigumo's Heart

Scroll One: The Enemy in the Earth 381
Scroll Two: Pulverized 399
Scroll Three: Kikyo's Crisis 417
Scroll Four: Onigumo's Heart 435
Scroll Five: Jealousy 453
Scroll Six: The Soil Shield 471
Scroll Seven: Where They First Met 489
Scroll Eight: Kagome's Heart 507
Scroll Nine: The Castle Ghost 529
Scroll Ten: Kohaku's Memory 547

Original Cover Gallery 565
Coming Next Volume 568

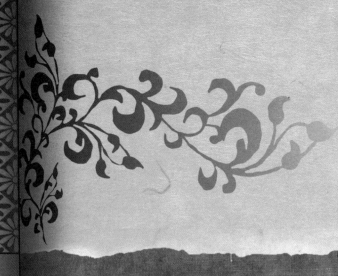

CAST OF CHARACTERS

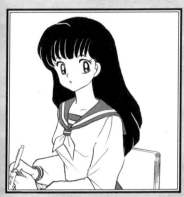

Kagome
A modern-day Japanese schoolgirl who is the reincarnation of Kikyo, the priestess who imprisoned Inuyasha for fifty years with her enchanted arrow. As Kikyo's reincarnation, Kagome has the power to see the Shikon Jewel shards, even ones hidden inside a demon's body.

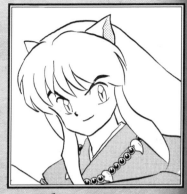

Inuyasha
A half-human, half-demon hybrid, Inuyasha has dog-like ears, a thick mane of white hair and demonic strength. He assists Kagome in her search for the shards of the jewel, mostly because he has no choice in the matter—a charmed necklace allows Kagome to restrain him with a single word.

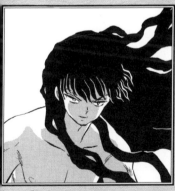

Naraku
This enigmatic demon is responsible for both Miroku's curse and for turning Kikyo and Inuyasha against each other.

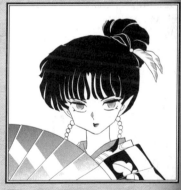

Kagura
Kagura was produced as a doppleganger from part of Naraku's body. Kagura inherited her abilities from a demon that controlled the wind.

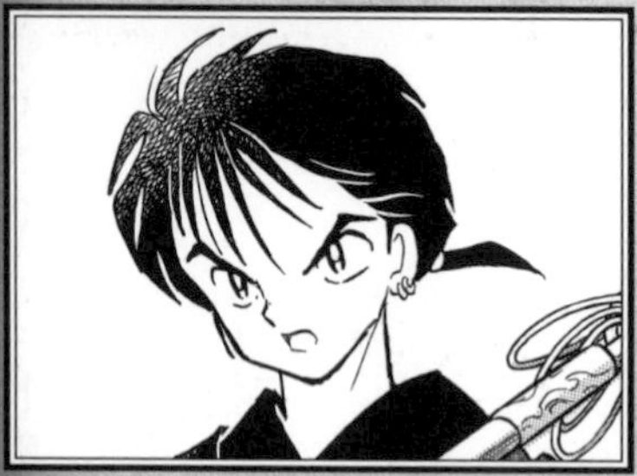

Miroku
An easygoing Buddhist priest of questionable morals. Miroku bears a curse passed down from his grandfather and is searching for the demon Naraku, who first inflicted the curse.

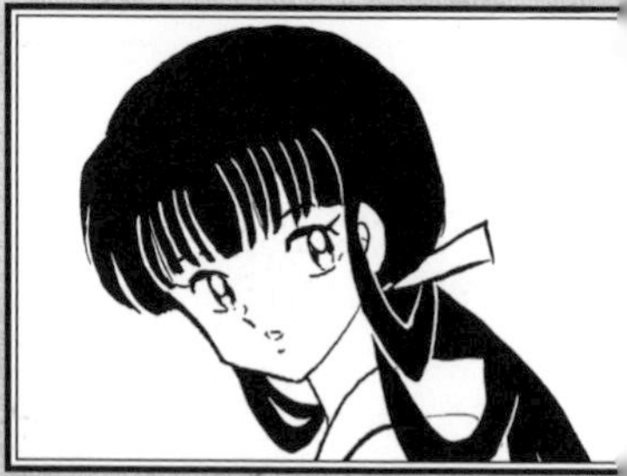

Kikyo
A village priestess who was the original protector of the Shikon Jewel. She died fifty years ago.

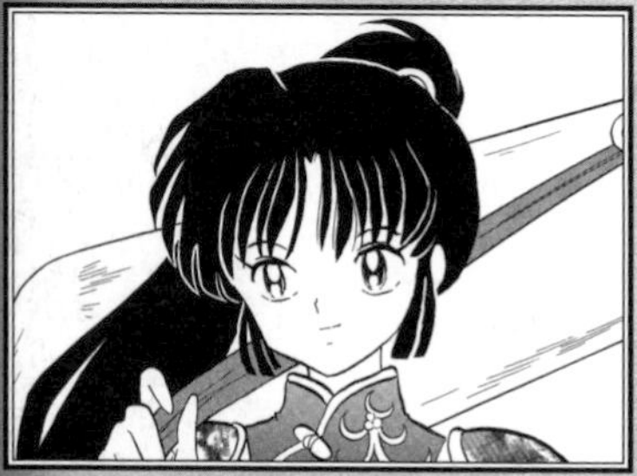

Sango
A proud Demon Slayer from the village where the first Shikon Jewel was born. Her clan and family lost, she fights on against the demonic Naraku along with Inuyasha.

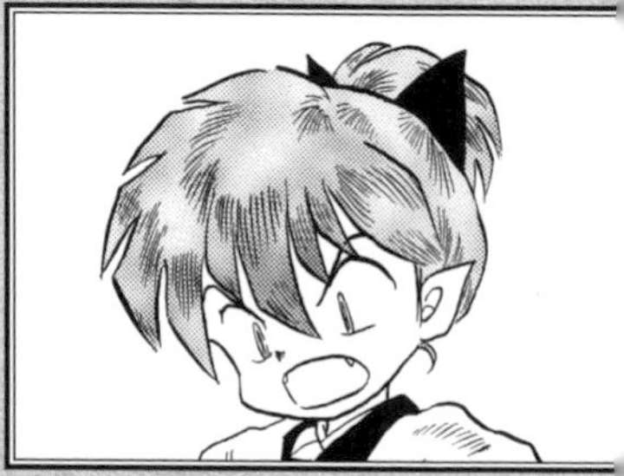

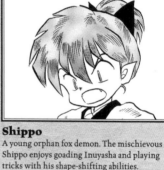

Shippo
A young orphan fox demon. The mischievous Shippo enjoys goading Inuyasha and playing tricks with his shape-shifting abilities.

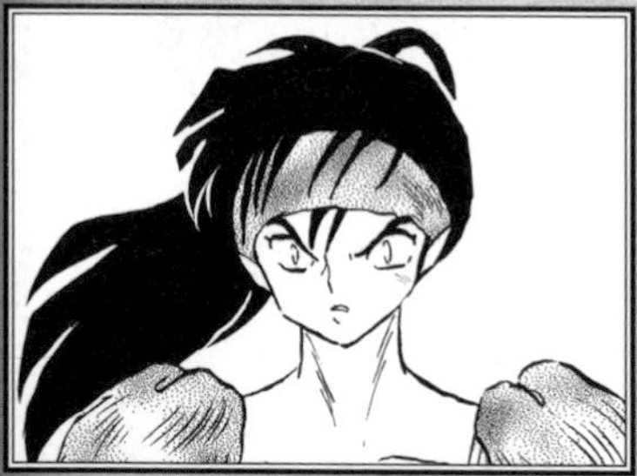

Koga
A wolf demon and leader of the wolf clan. Koga has Shikon shards in his legs, giving him super speed.

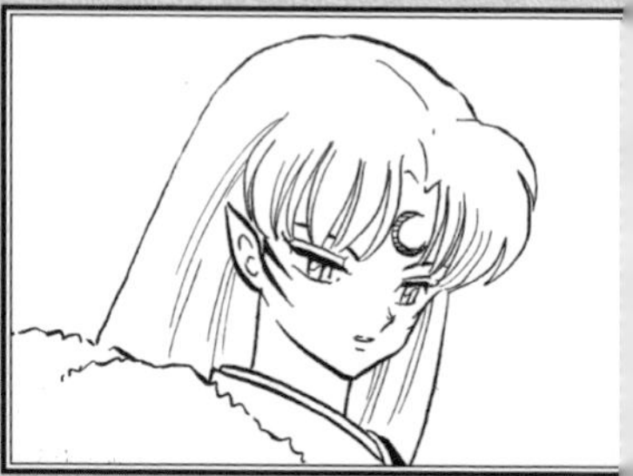

Sesshomaru
Inuyasha's half brother by the same demon father, Sesshomaru is a pureblood demon who covets the sword left to Inuyasha by their father.

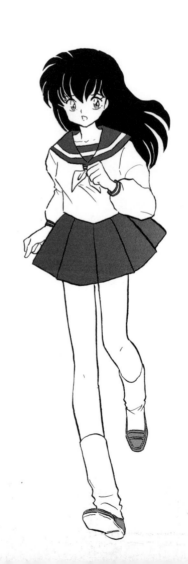

InuYasha

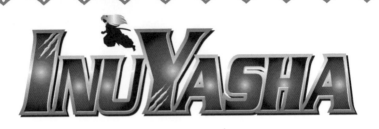

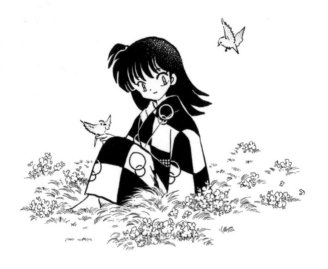

Volume 16

Kikyo's Plan

SCROLL ONE

THE HUMAN SHIELD

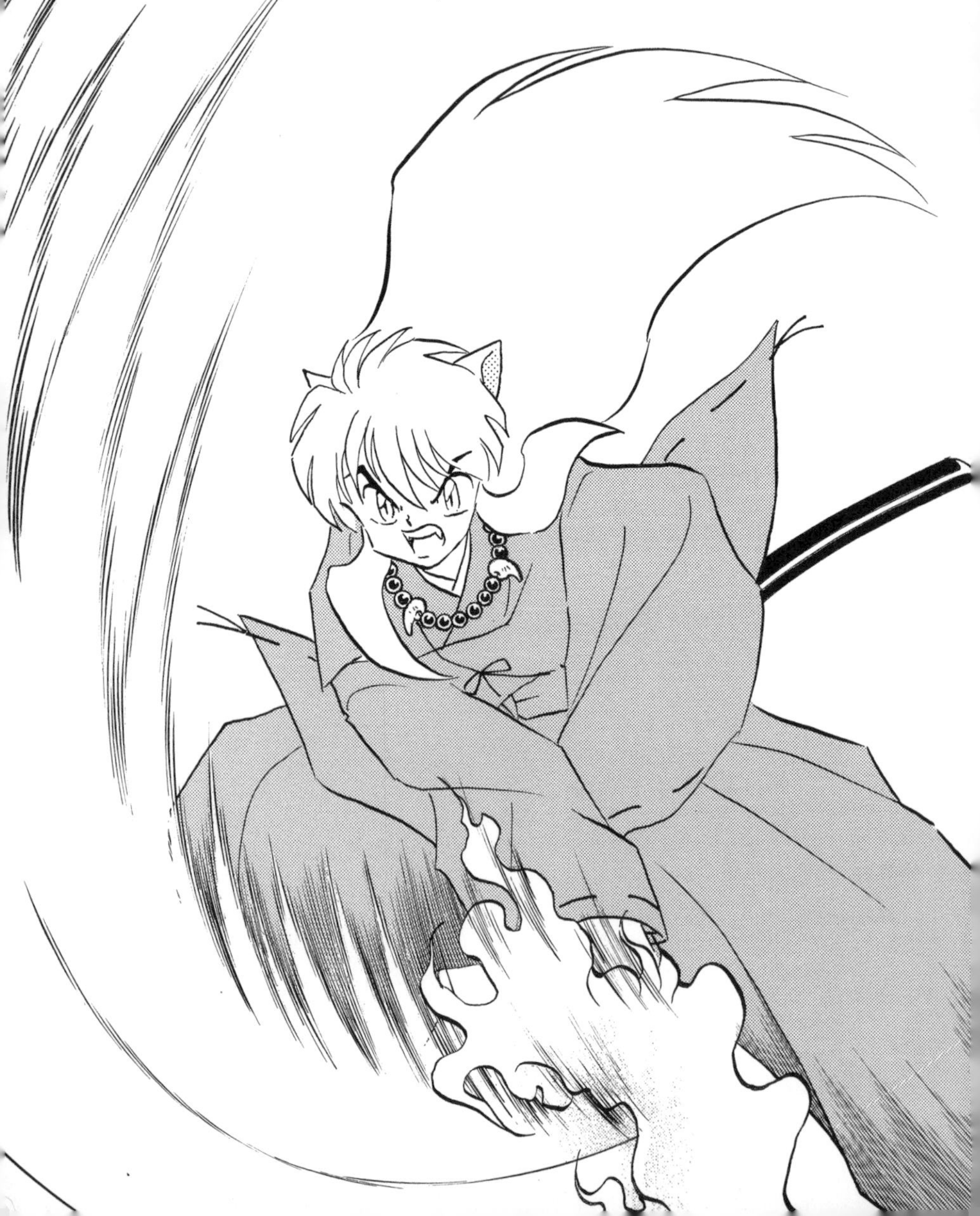

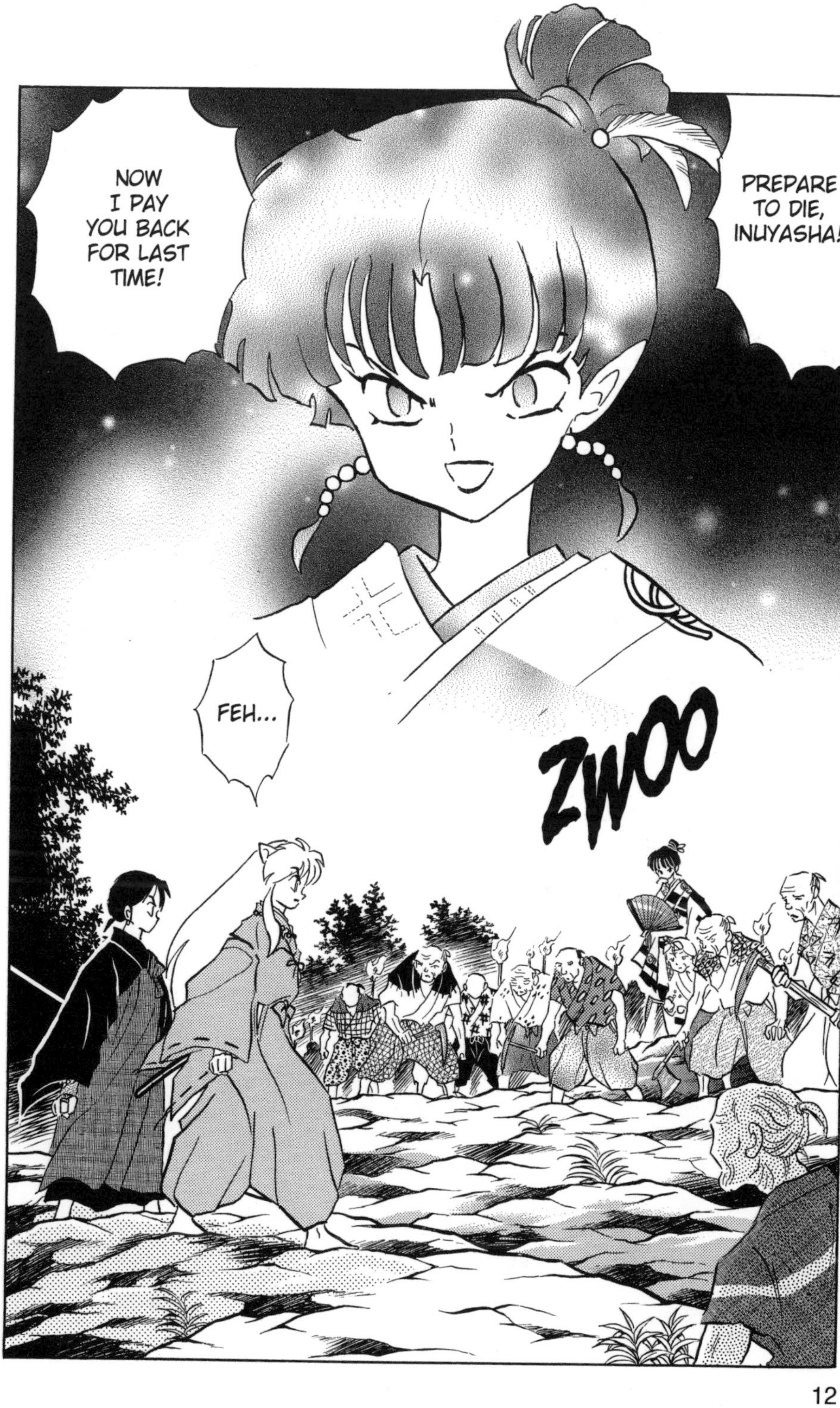
PREPARE TO DIE, INUYASHA!
NOW I PAY YOU BACK FOR LAST TIME!
ZWOO
FEH...

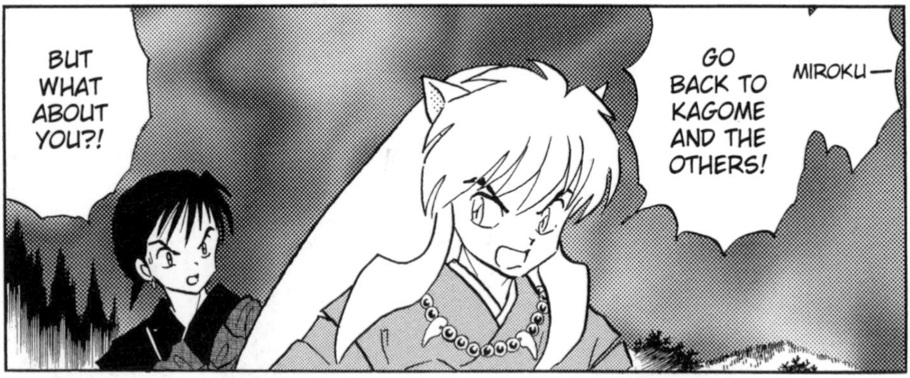
MIROKU—
GO BACK TO KAGOME AND THE OTHERS!
BUT WHAT ABOUT YOU?!
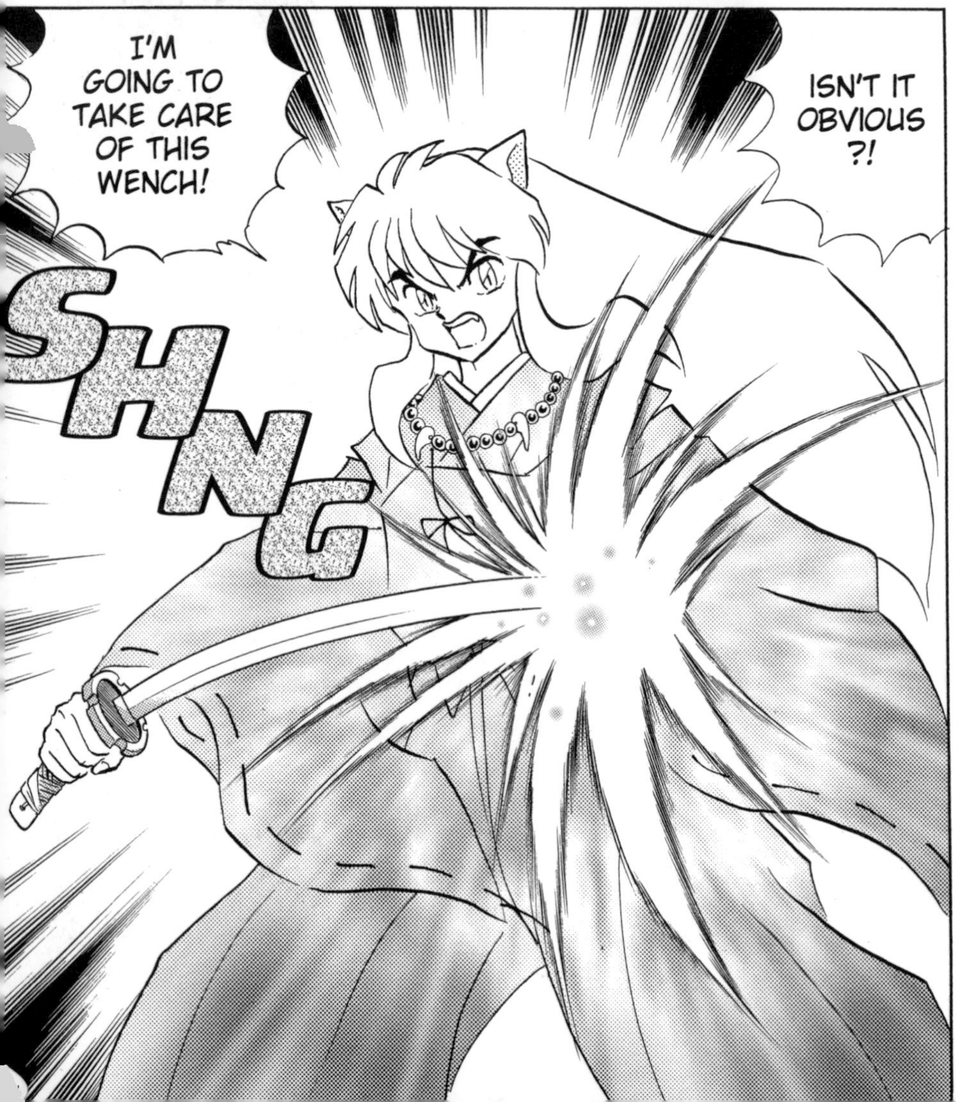
ISN'T IT OBVIOUS ?!
I'M GOING TO TAKE CARE OF THIS WENCH!
SHNG

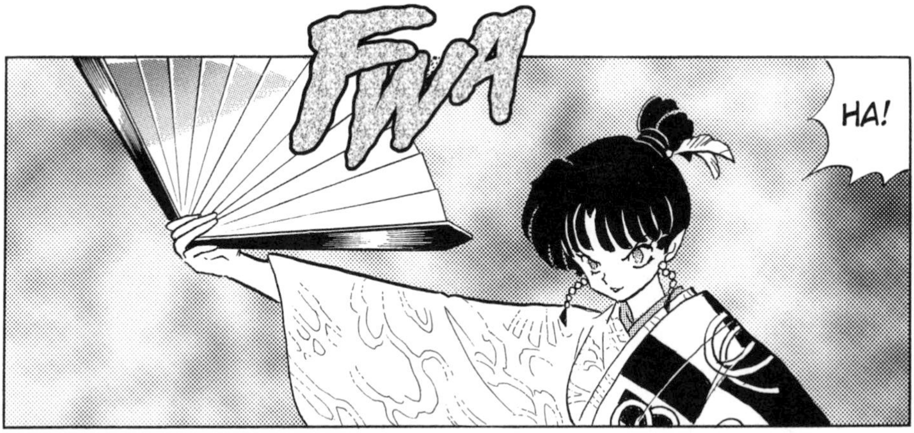
HA!
FWA

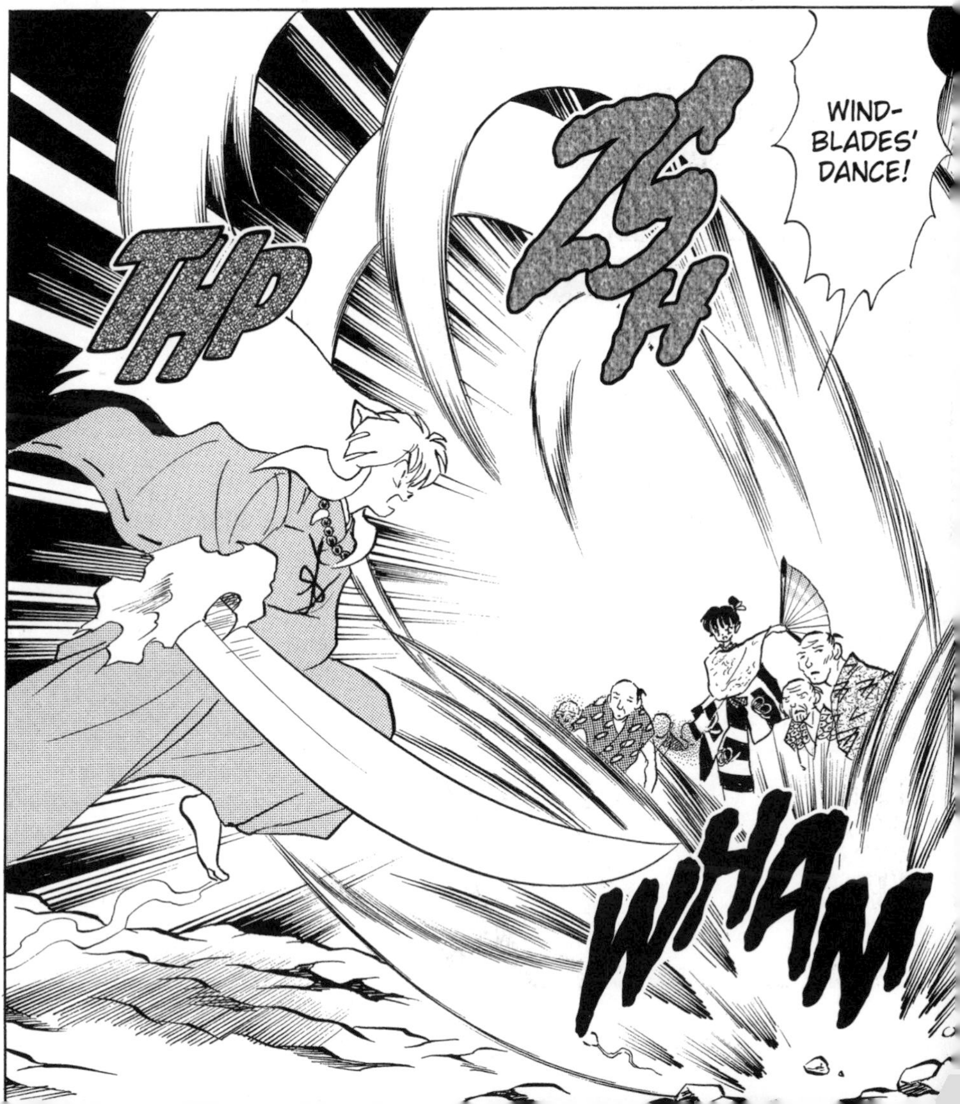
WIND-BLADES' DANCE!
ZSH
THP
WHAM

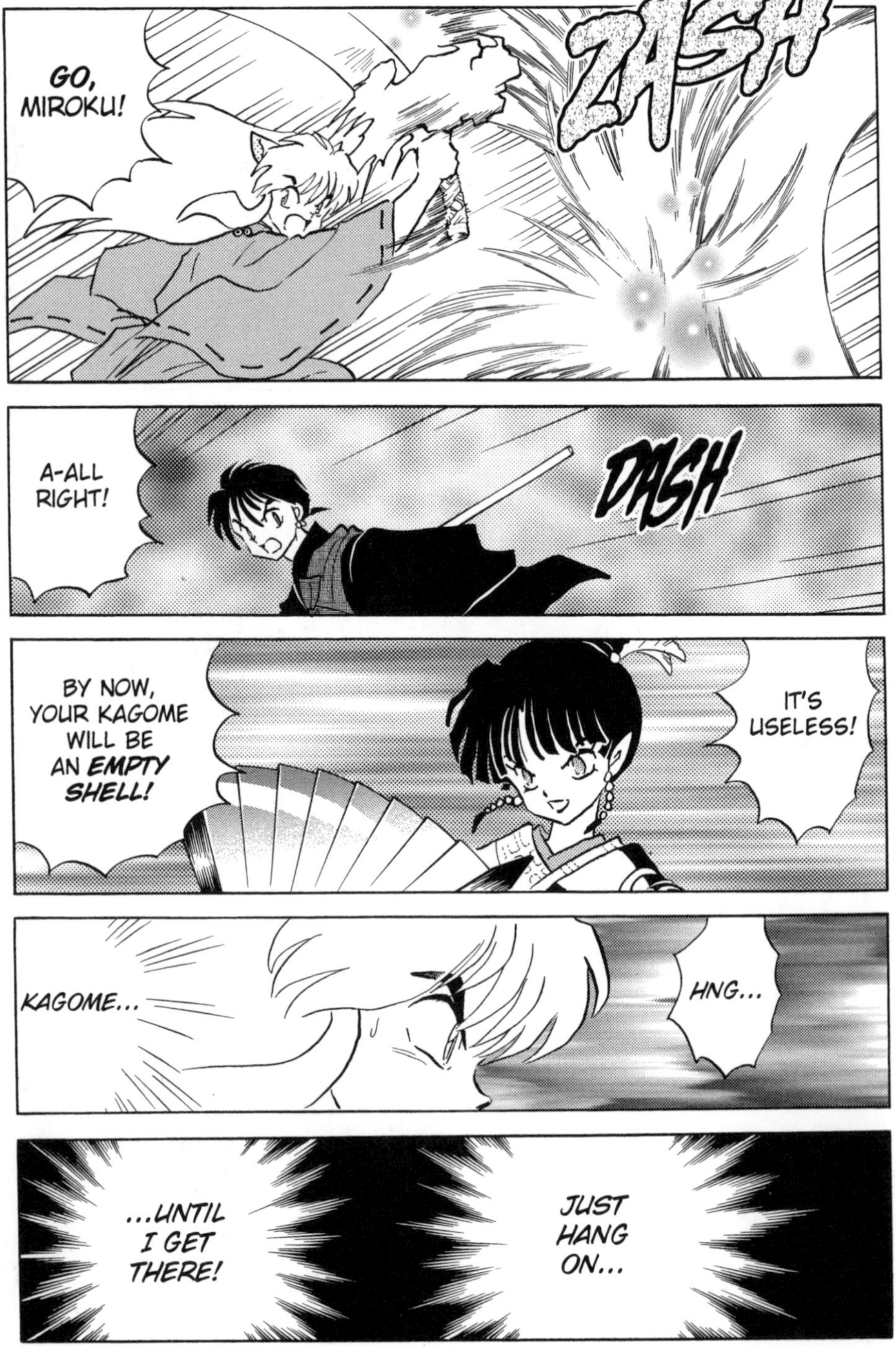
ZASH
GO, MIROKU!
DASH
A-ALL RIGHT!
IT'S USELESS!
BY NOW, YOUR KAGOME WILL BE AN EMPTY SHELL!
HNG...
KAGOME...
JUST HANG ON...
...UNTIL I GET THERE!

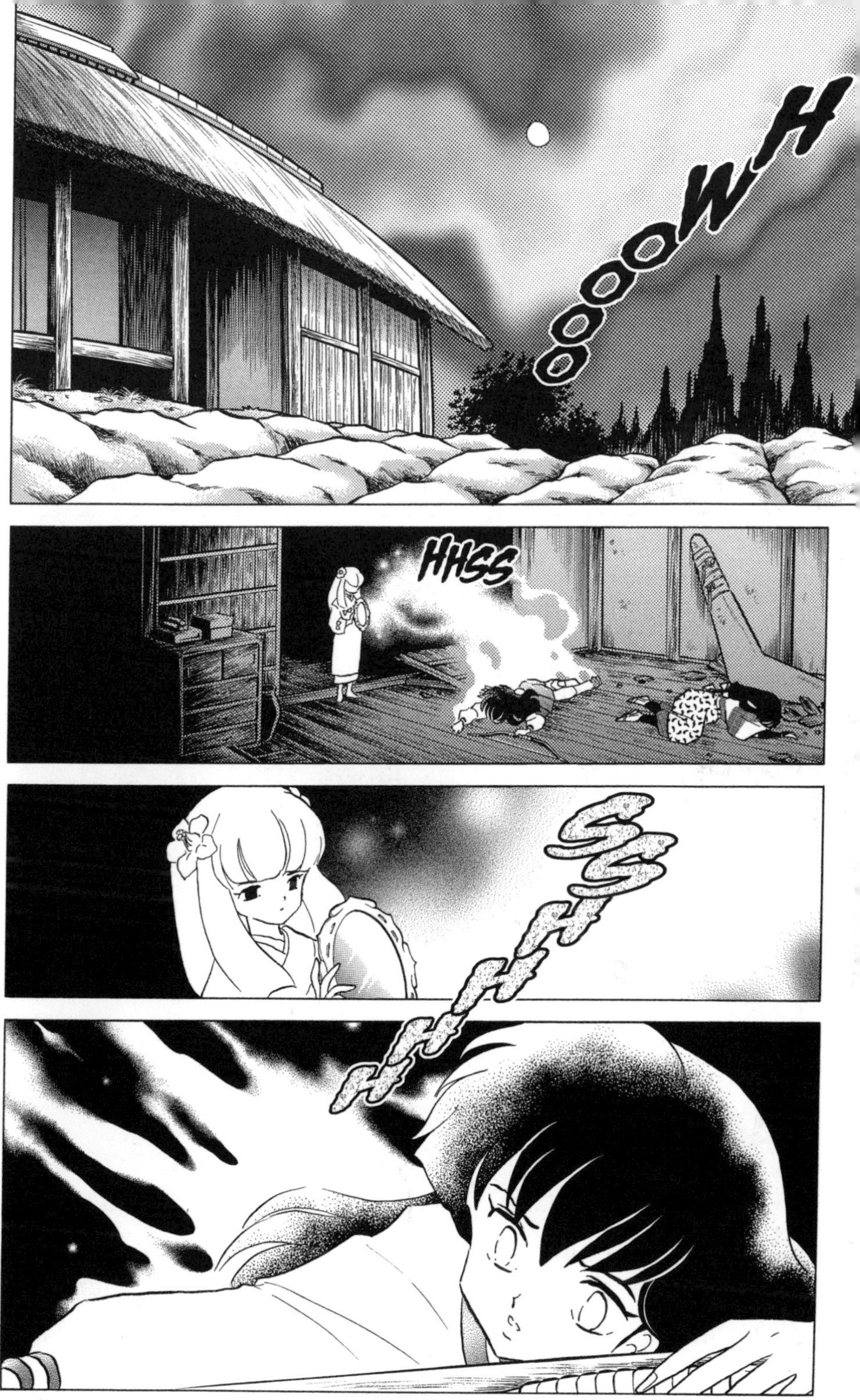
OOOOOWH
HHSS
SHHHHH

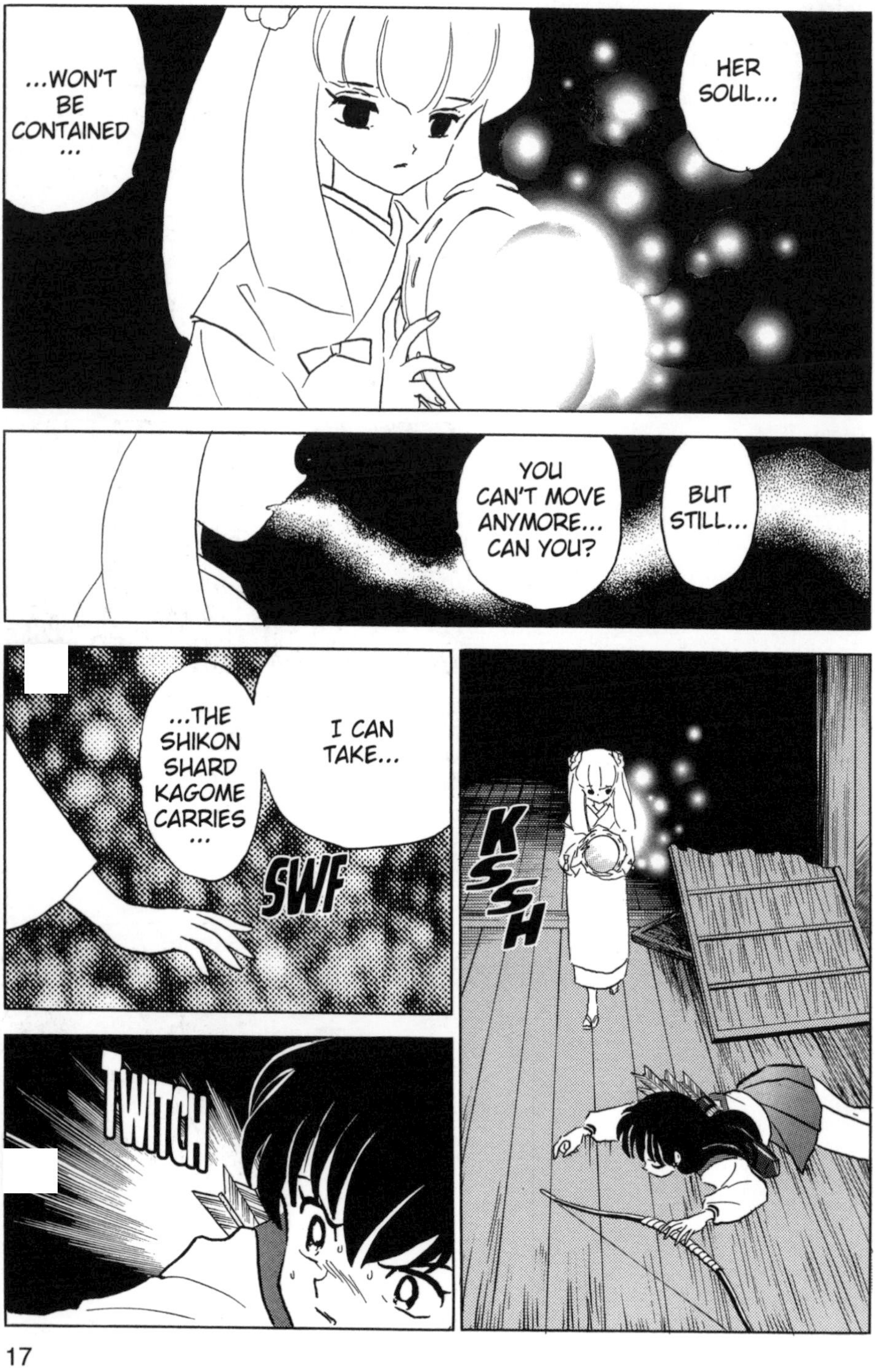
HER SOUL...
...WON'T BE CONTAINED...
BUT STILL...
YOU CAN'T MOVE ANYMORE... CAN YOU?
KSSH
I CAN TAKE...
...THE SHIKON SHARD KAGOME CARRIES...
SWF
TWITCH

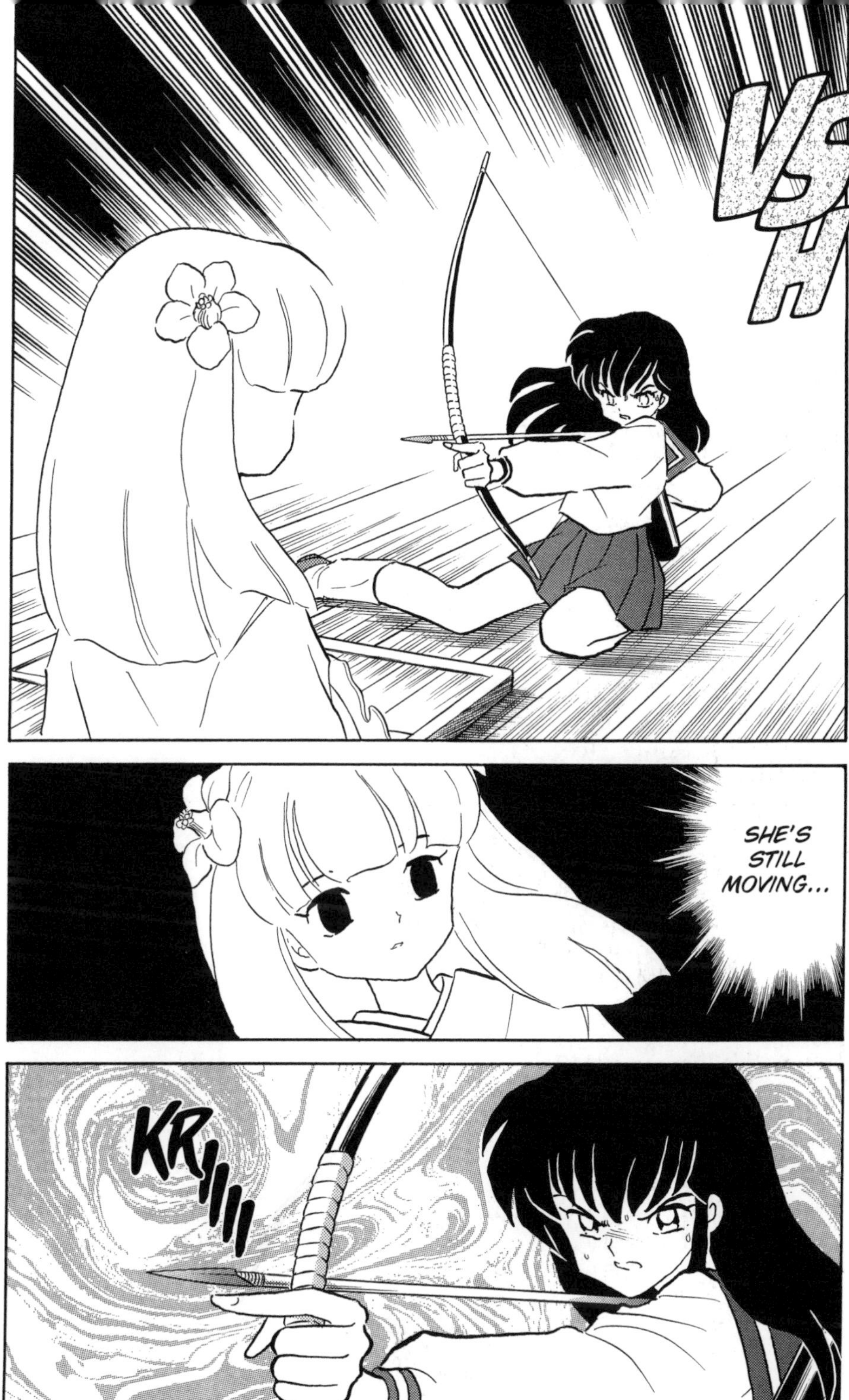
VSH
SHE'S STILL MOVING...
KRIIII

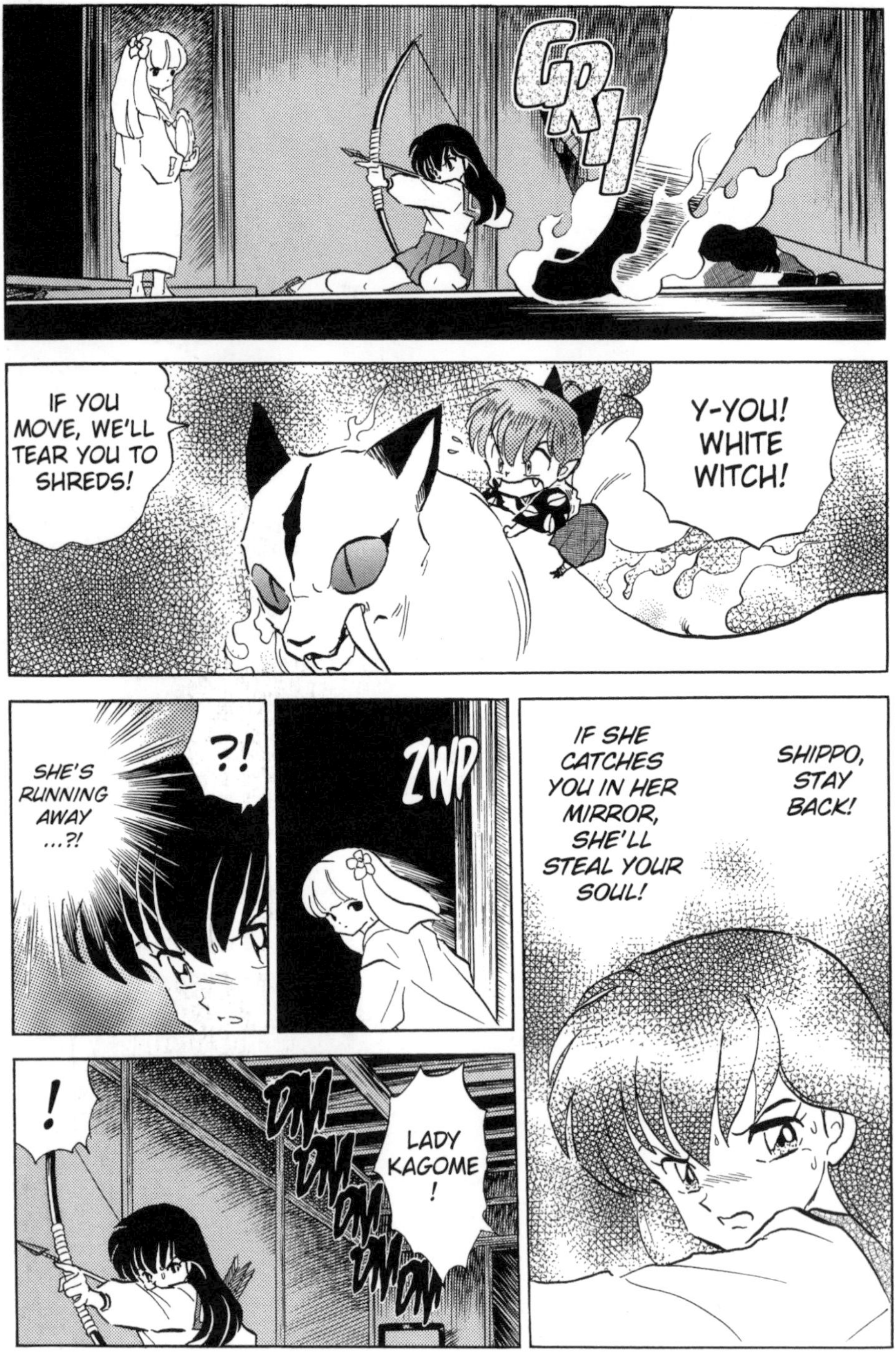
Y-YOU! WHITE WITCH!
IF YOU MOVE, WE'LL TEAR YOU TO SHREDS!
SHIPPO, STAY BACK!
IF SHE CATCHES YOU IN HER MIRROR, SHE'LL STEAL YOUR SOUL!
ZWP
?!
SHE'S RUNNING AWAY ...?!
LADY KAGOME!
!

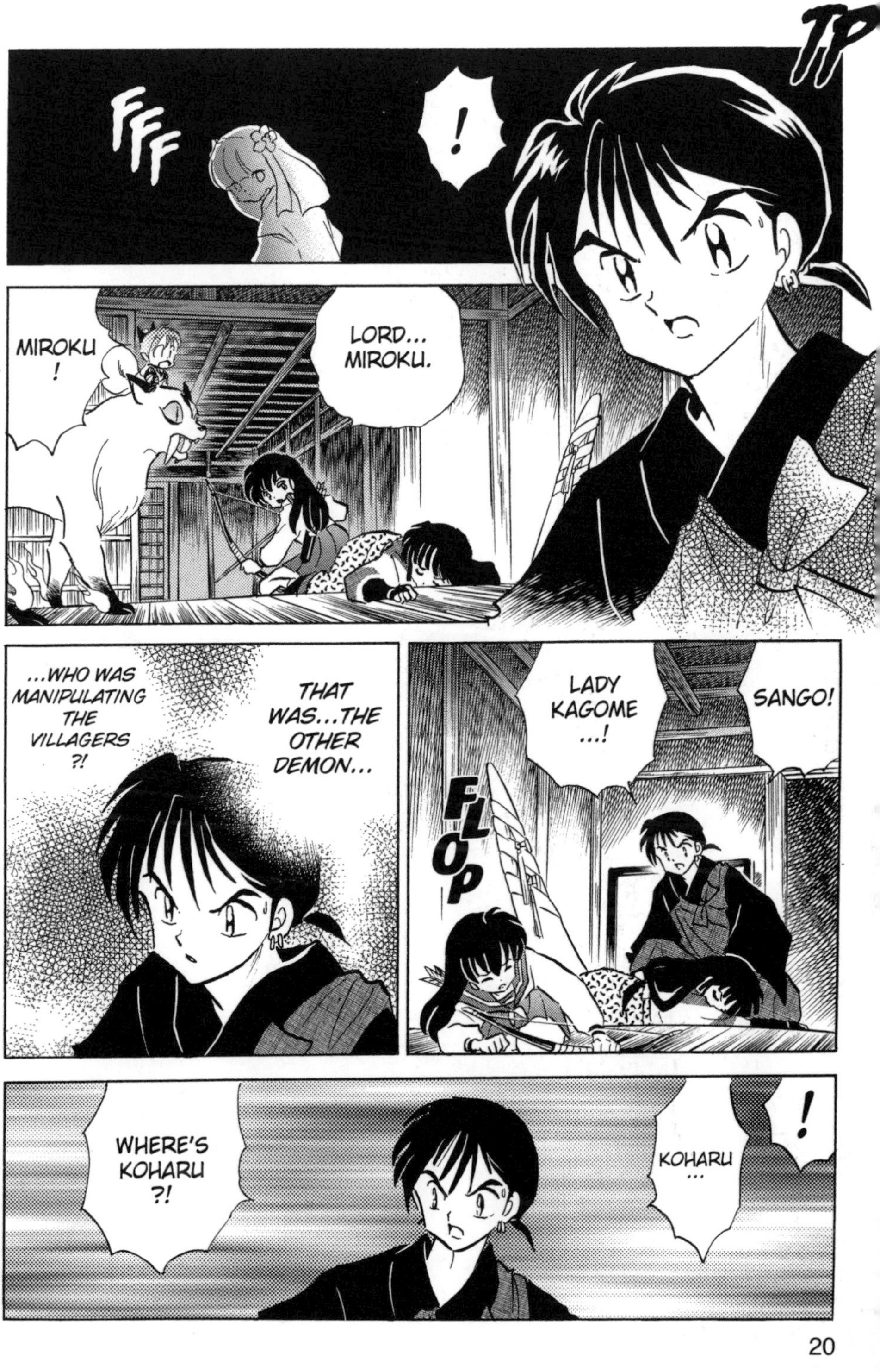
TP
!
FFF
LORD... MIROKU.
MIROKU!
SANGO!
LADY KAGOME ...!
FLOP
THAT WAS...THE OTHER DEMON...
...WHO WAS MANIPULATING THE VILLAGERS ?!
!
KOHARU ...
WHERE'S KOHARU ?!

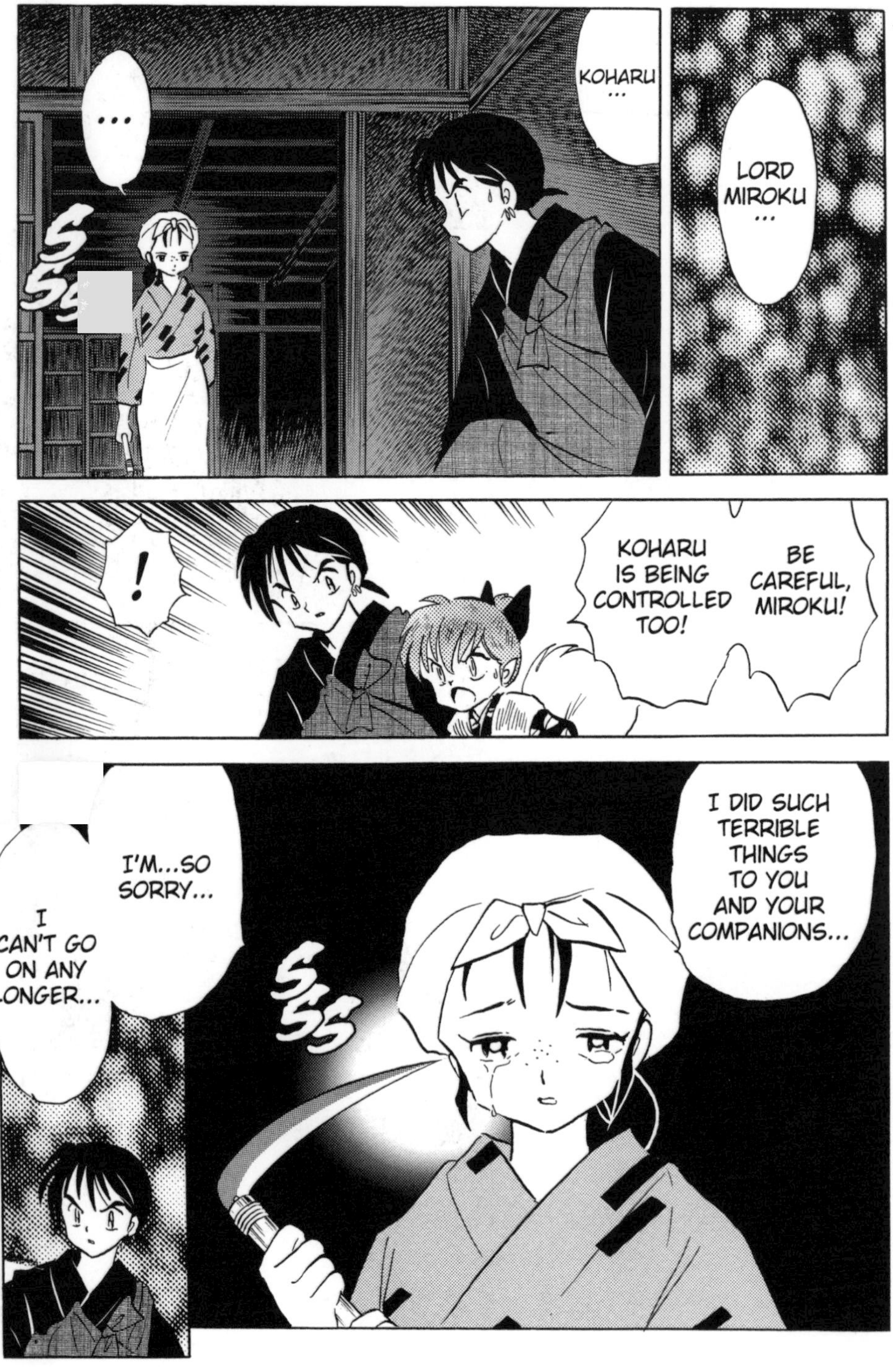
LORD MIROKU ...
KOHARU ...
...
SSS
BE CAREFUL, MIROKU!
KOHARU IS BEING CONTROLLED TOO!
!
I DID SUCH TERRIBLE THINGS TO YOU AND YOUR COMPANIONS...
I'M...SO SORRY...
SSS
I CAN'T GO ON ANY LONGER...

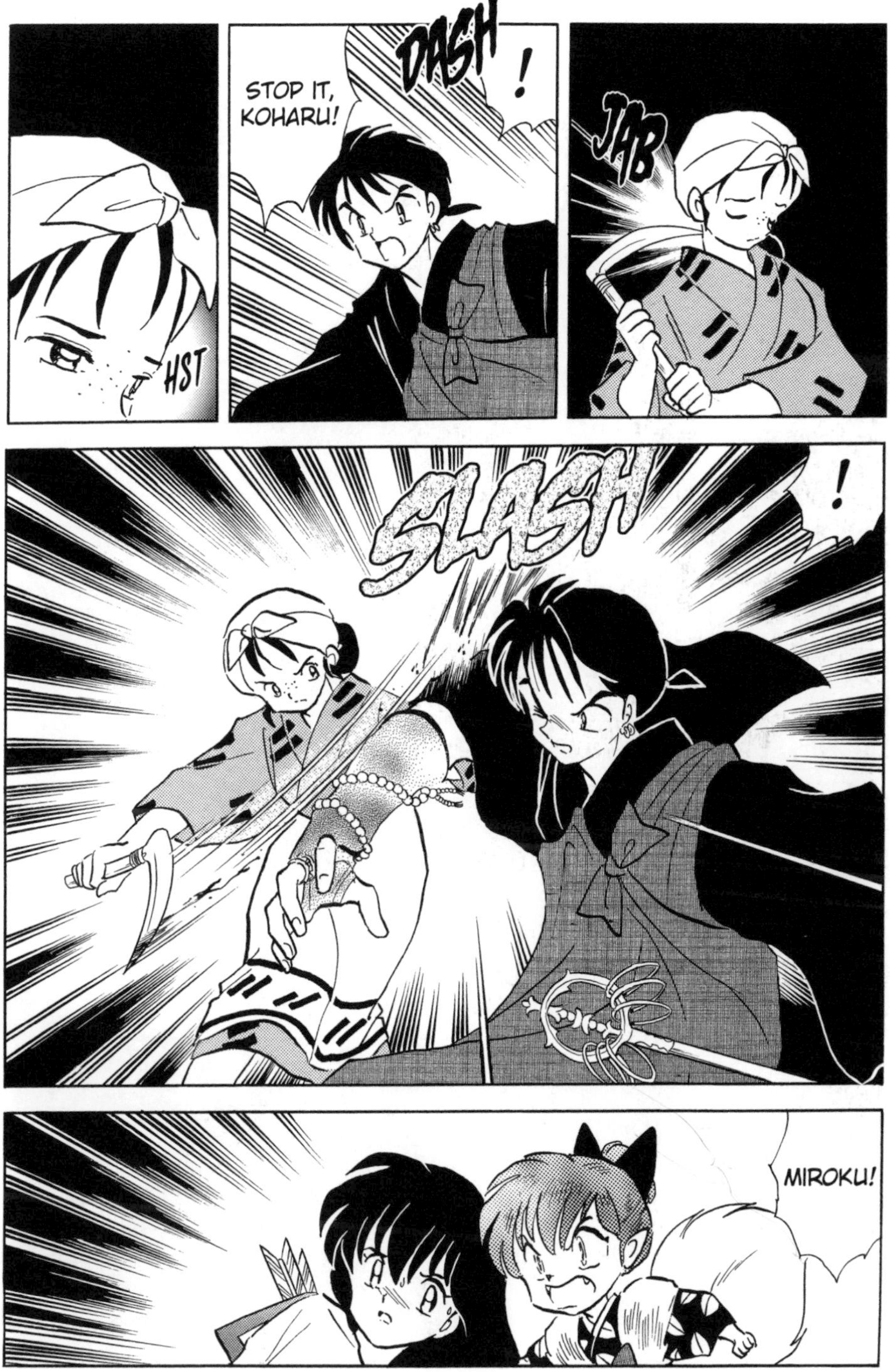
JAB
DASH
!
STOP IT, KOHARU!
HST
SLASH
!
MIROKU!

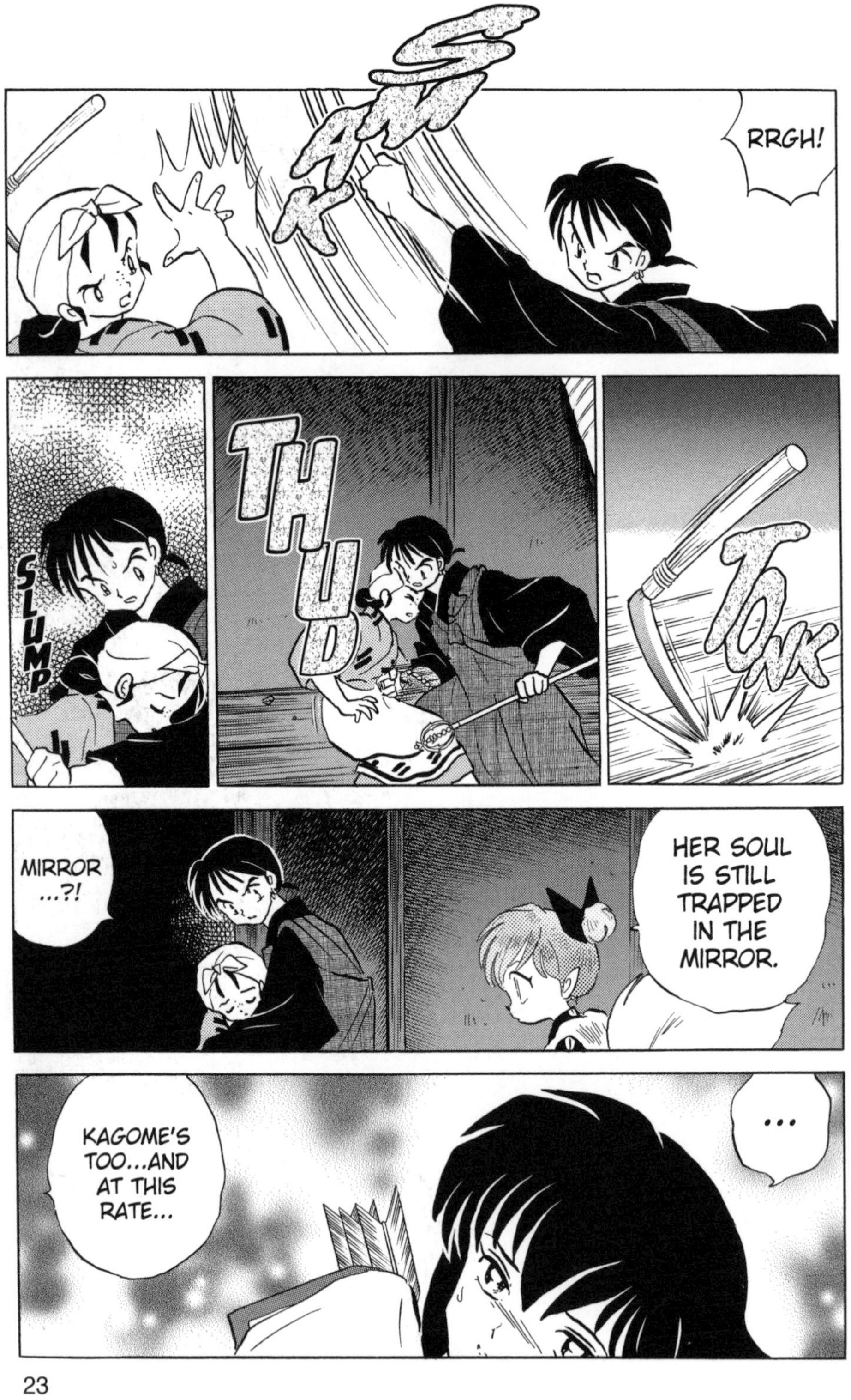
RRGH!
SWAK
TONK
THUD
SLUMP
HER SOUL IS STILL TRAPPED IN THE MIRROR.
MIRROR ...?!
...
KAGOME'S TOO...AND AT THIS RATE...

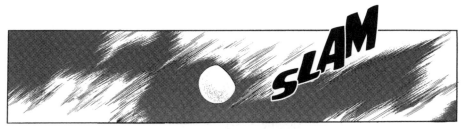

SLAM

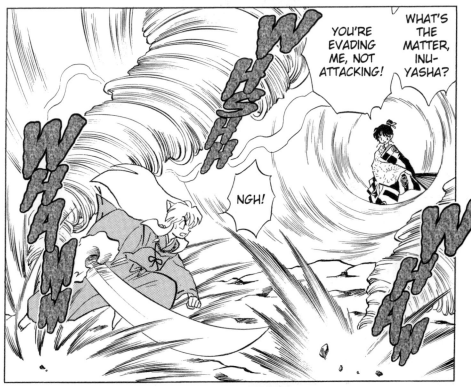

WHAT'S THE MATTER, INU-YASHA?

YOU'RE EVADING ME, NOT ATTACKING!

NGH!

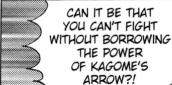

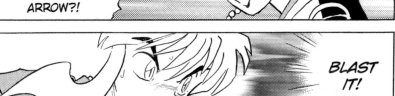

CAN IT BE THAT YOU CAN'T FIGHT WITHOUT BORROWING THE POWER OF KAGOME'S ARROW?!

BLAST IT!

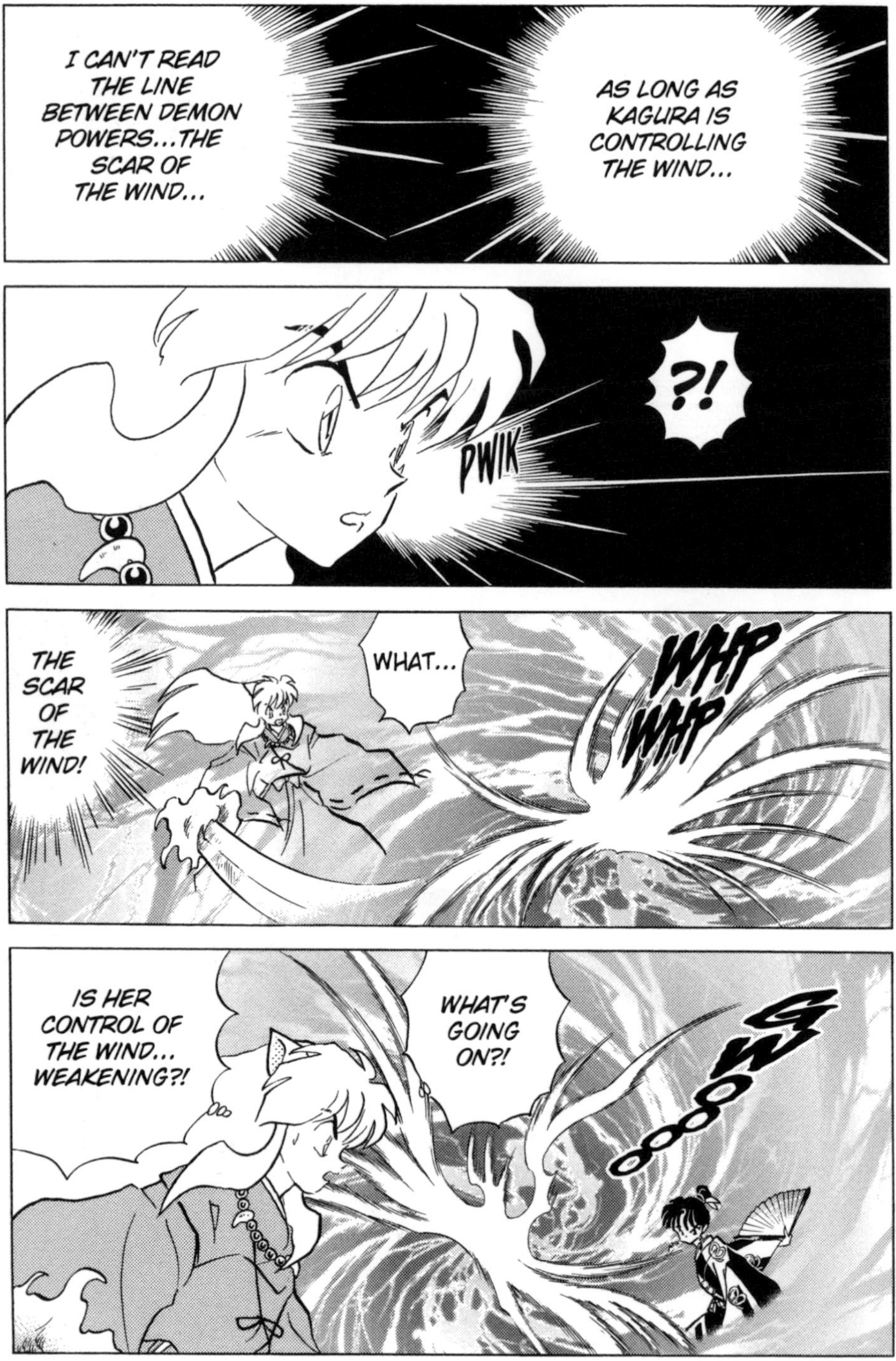
AS LONG AS KAGURA IS CONTROLLING THE WIND...
I CAN'T READ THE LINE BETWEEN DEMON POWERS...THE SCAR OF THE WIND...
?!
PWIK
WHP WHP
WHAT...
THE SCAR OF THE WIND!
GWOOOOO
WHAT'S GOING ON?!
IS HER CONTROL OF THE WIND... WEAKENING?!

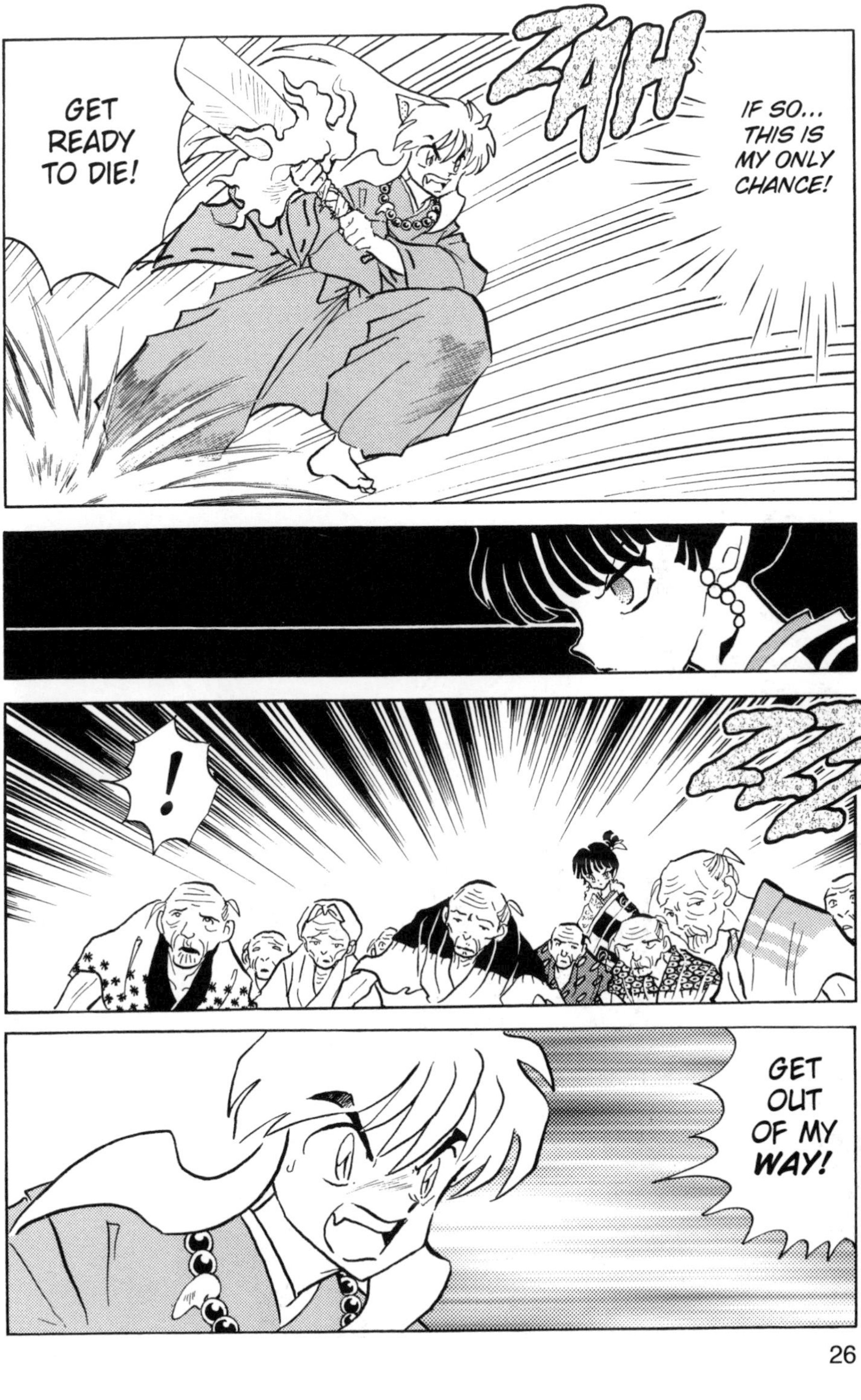

ZAH
IF SO... THIS IS MY ONLY CHANCE!
GET READY TO DIE!
!
GET OUT OF MY **WAY!**

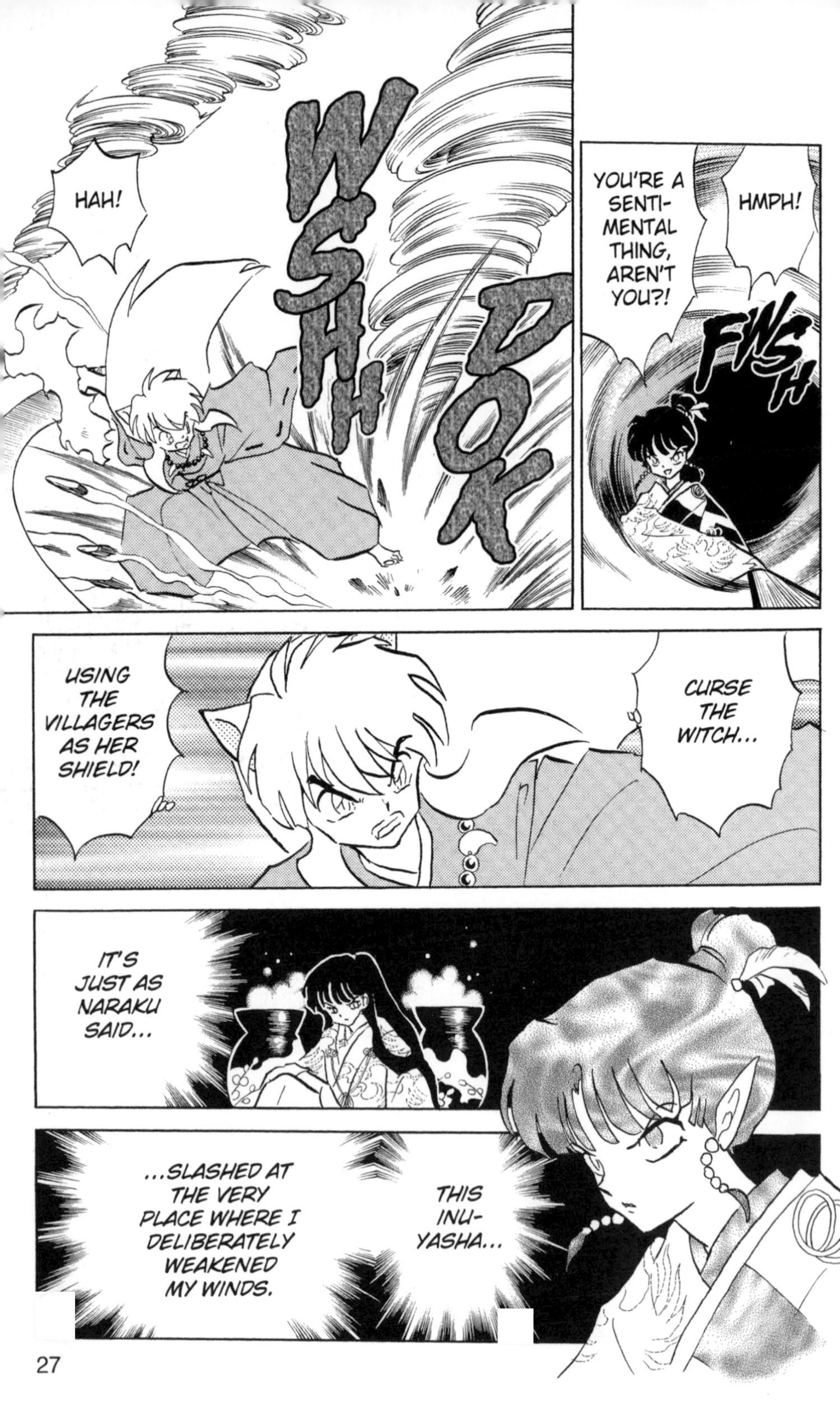
HMPH!
YOU'RE A SENTI-MENTAL THING, AREN'T YOU?!
FWSHH
WSHH
DOK
HAH!
CURSE THE WITCH...
USING THE VILLAGERS AS HER SHIELD!
IT'S JUST AS NARAKU SAID...
THIS INU-YASHA...
...SLASHED AT THE VERY PLACE WHERE I DELIBERATELY WEAKENED MY WINDS.

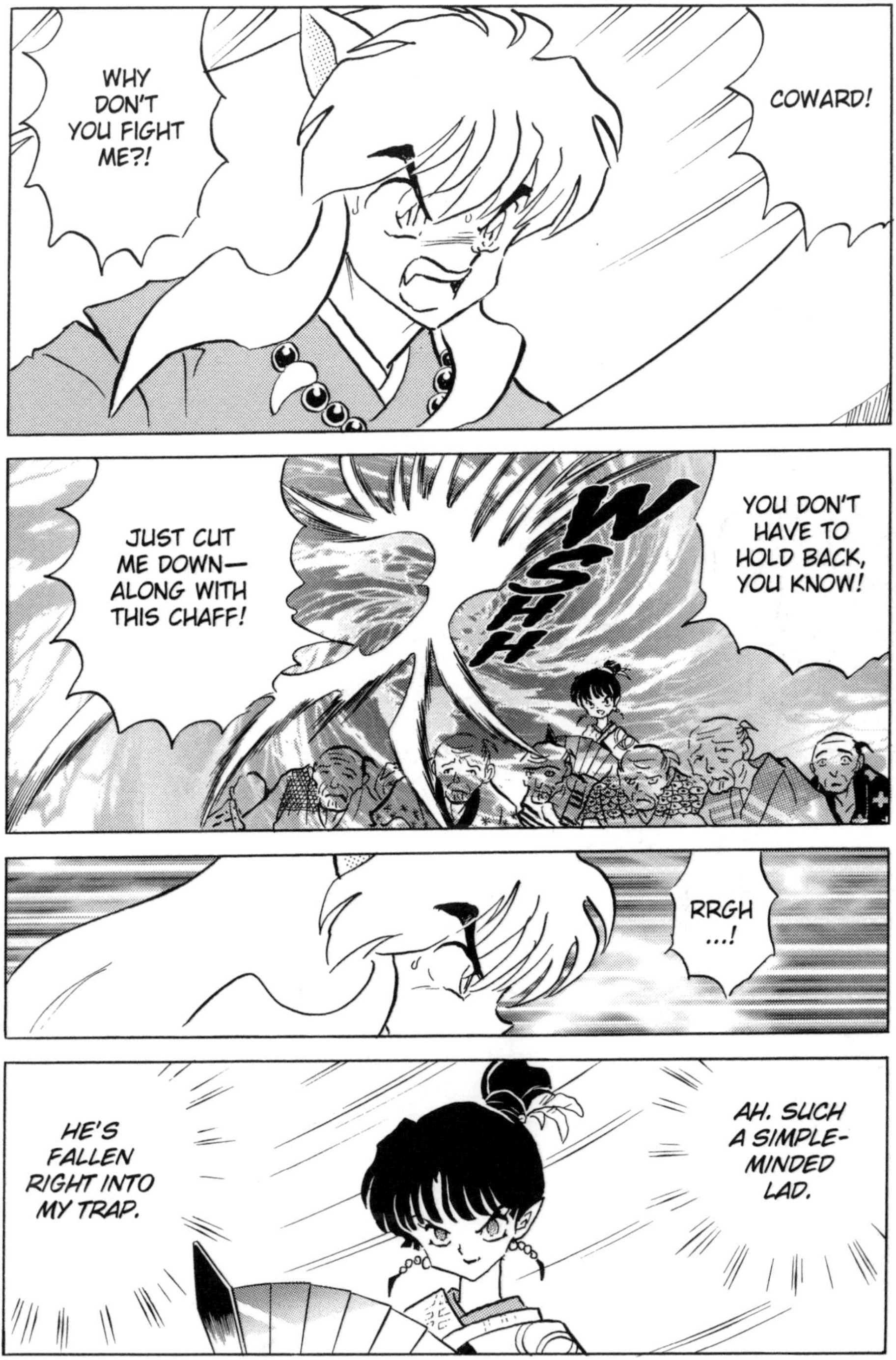
COWARD!
WHY DON'T YOU FIGHT ME?!
YOU DON'T HAVE TO HOLD BACK, YOU KNOW!
WSHH
JUST CUT ME DOWN— ALONG WITH THIS CHAFF!
RRGH ...!
AH. SUCH A SIMPLE-MINDED LAD.
HE'S FALLEN RIGHT INTO MY TRAP.

SCROLL TWO
TURN AROUND

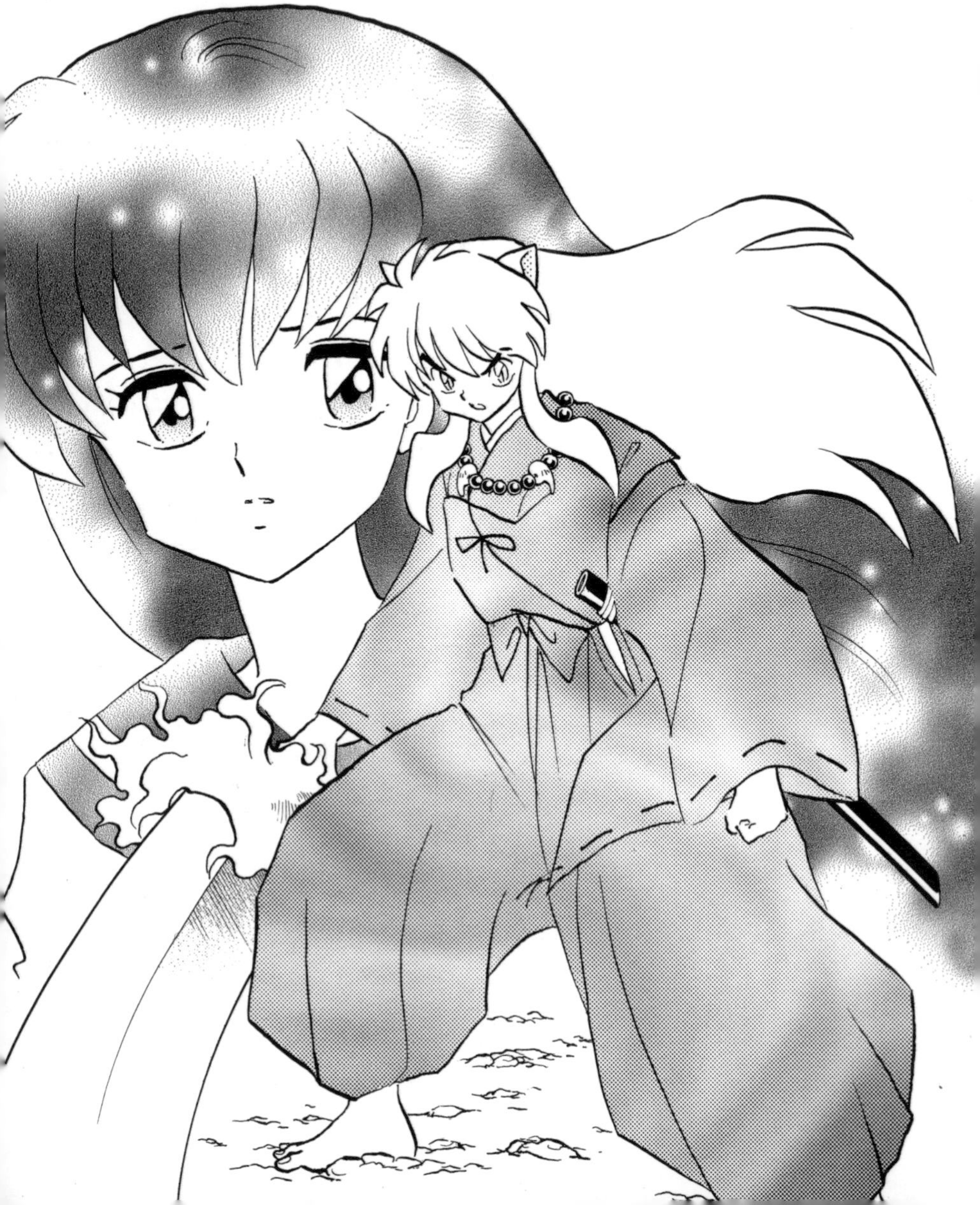

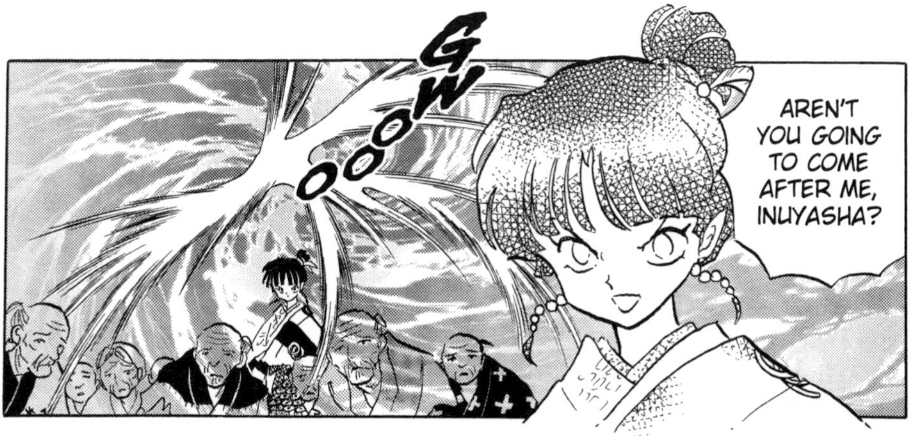
GWOOOOO
AREN'T YOU GOING TO COME AFTER ME, INUYASHA?

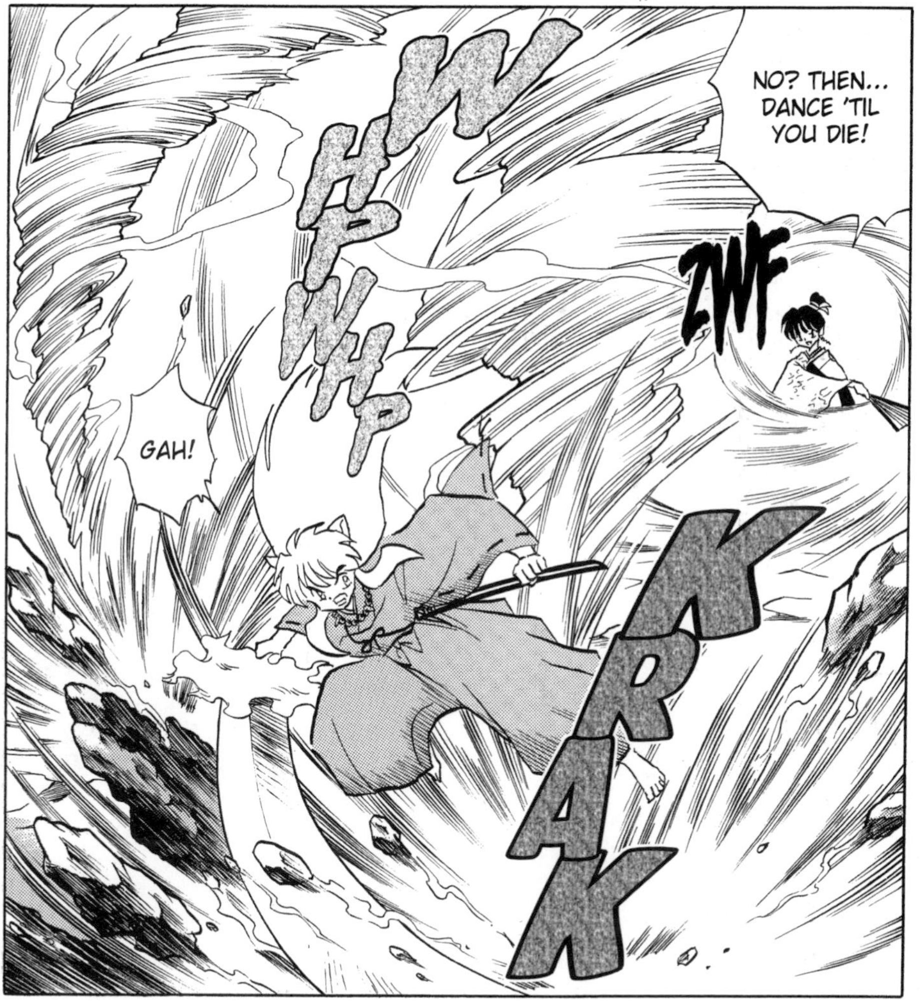
NO? THEN... DANCE 'TIL YOU DIE!
ZWF
WHP WHP
GAH!
KRAK

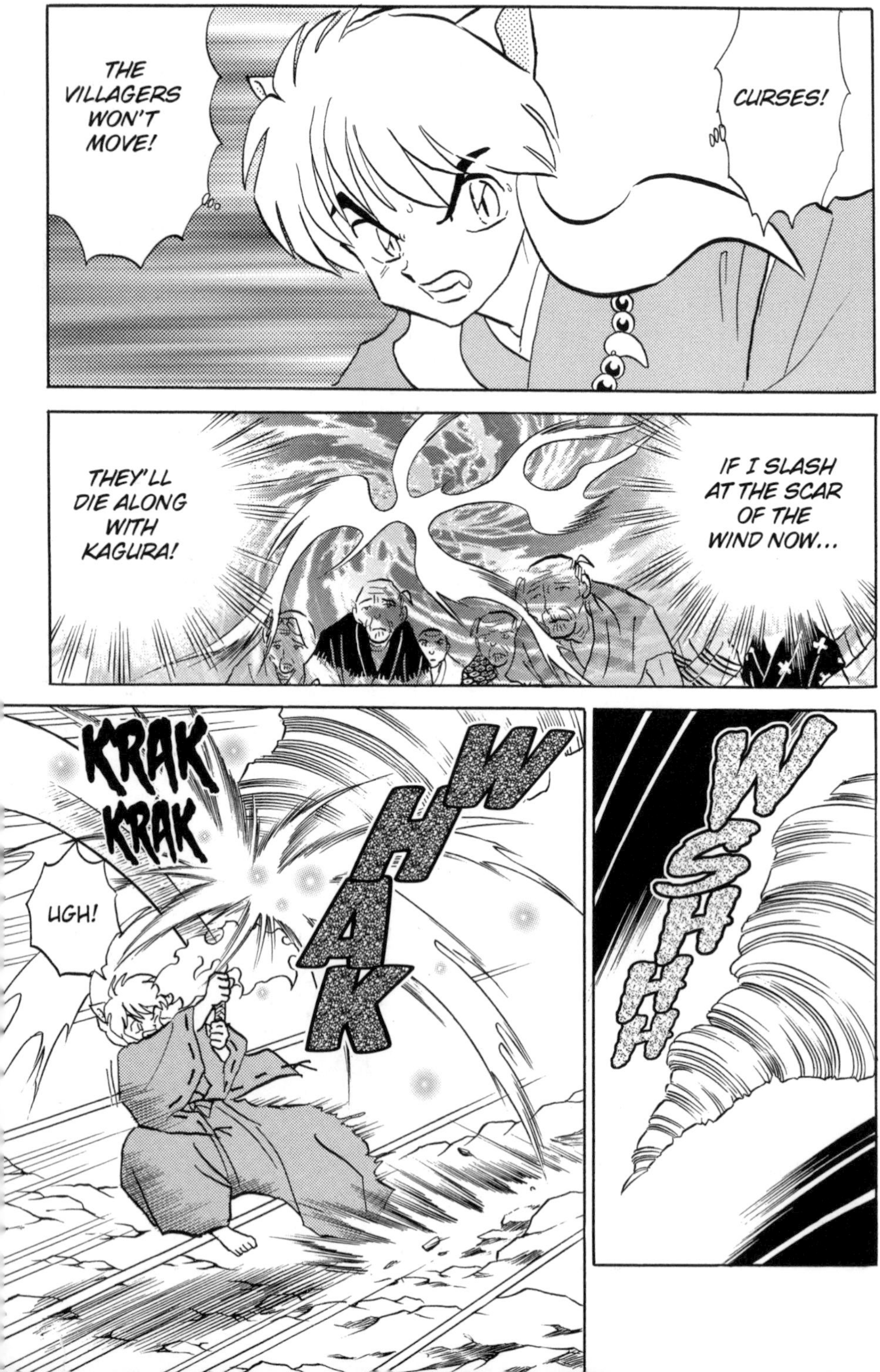
CURSES!
THE VILLAGERS WON'T MOVE!
IF I SLASH AT THE SCAR OF THE WIND NOW...
THEY'LL DIE ALONG WITH KAGURA!
WSHHH
WHAK
KRAK KRAK
UGH!

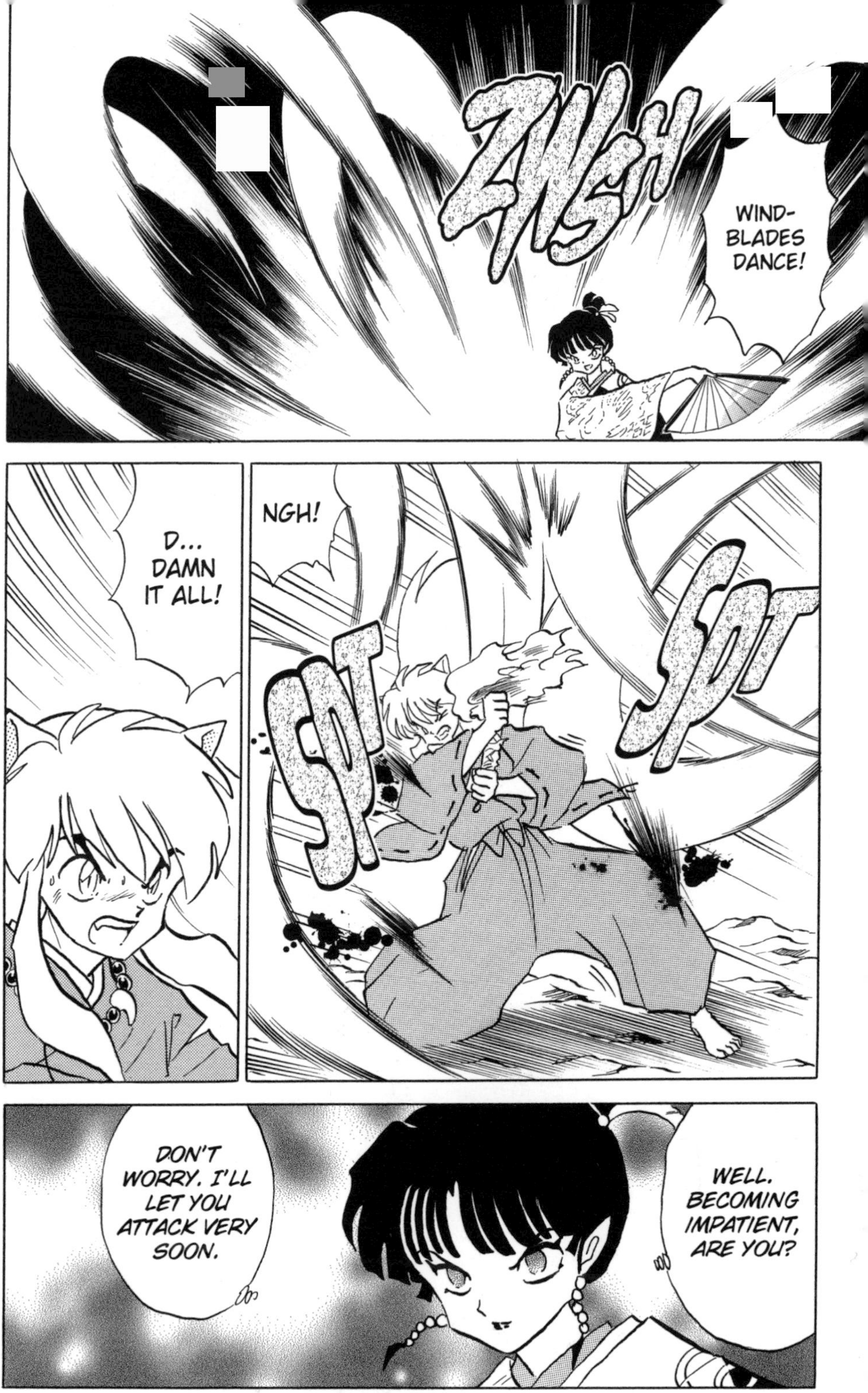
ZWNGH
WIND-BLADES DANCE!
NGH!
SPOT
SPOT
D... DAMN IT ALL!
WELL. BECOMING IMPATIENT, ARE YOU?
DON'T WORRY. I'LL LET YOU ATTACK VERY SOON.

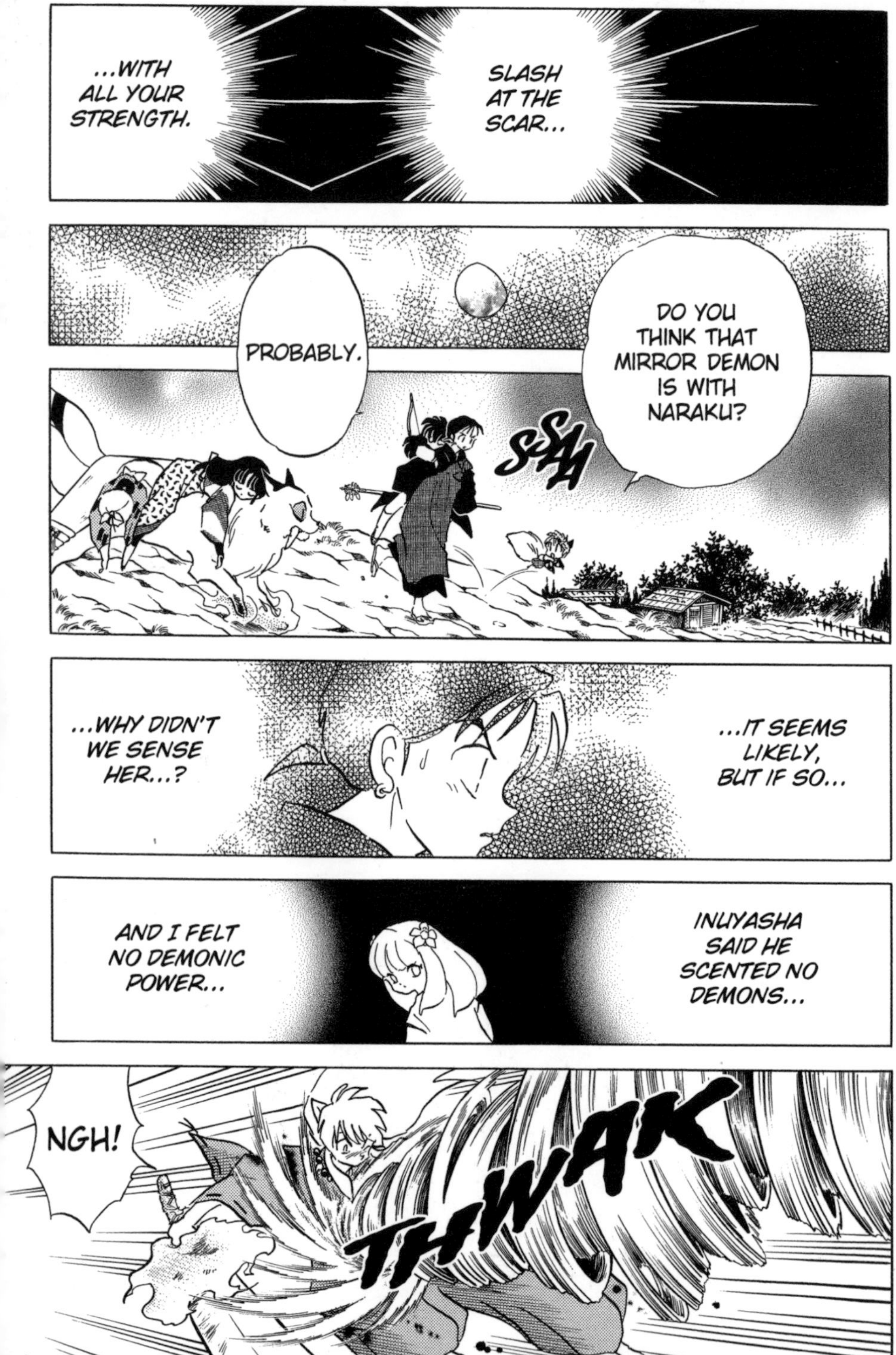
SLASH AT THE SCAR...
...WITH ALL YOUR STRENGTH.
DO YOU THINK THAT MIRROR DEMON IS WITH NARAKU?
SSAA
PROBABLY.
...IT SEEMS LIKELY, BUT IF SO...
...WHY DIDN'T WE SENSE HER...?
INUYASHA SAID HE SCENTED NO DEMONS...
AND I FELT NO DEMONIC POWER...
THWAK
NGH!

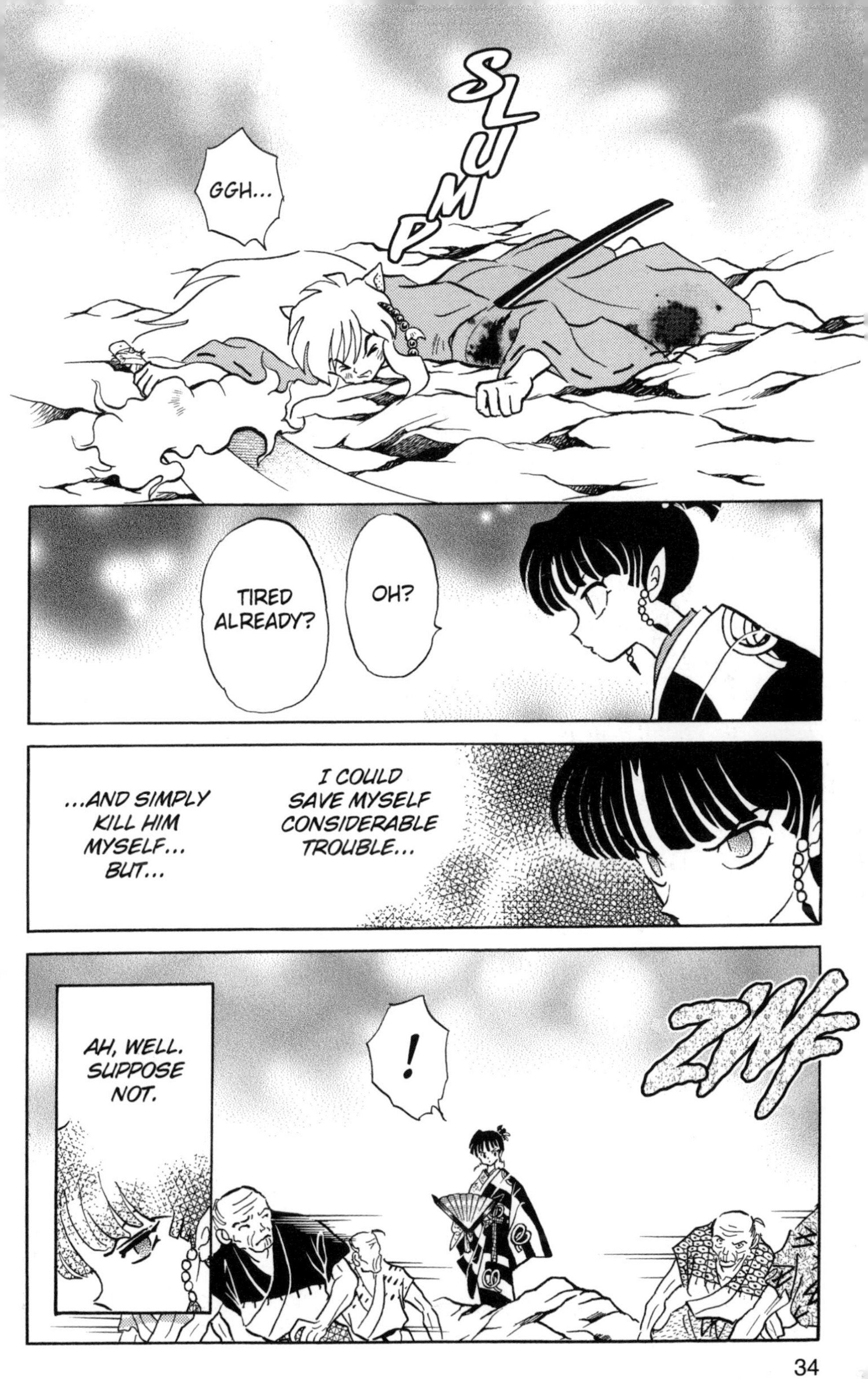
SLUMP
GGH...
OH?
TIRED ALREADY?
I COULD SAVE MYSELF CONSIDERABLE TROUBLE...
...AND SIMPLY KILL HIM MYSELF... BUT...
ZWF
!
AH, WELL. SUPPOSE NOT.

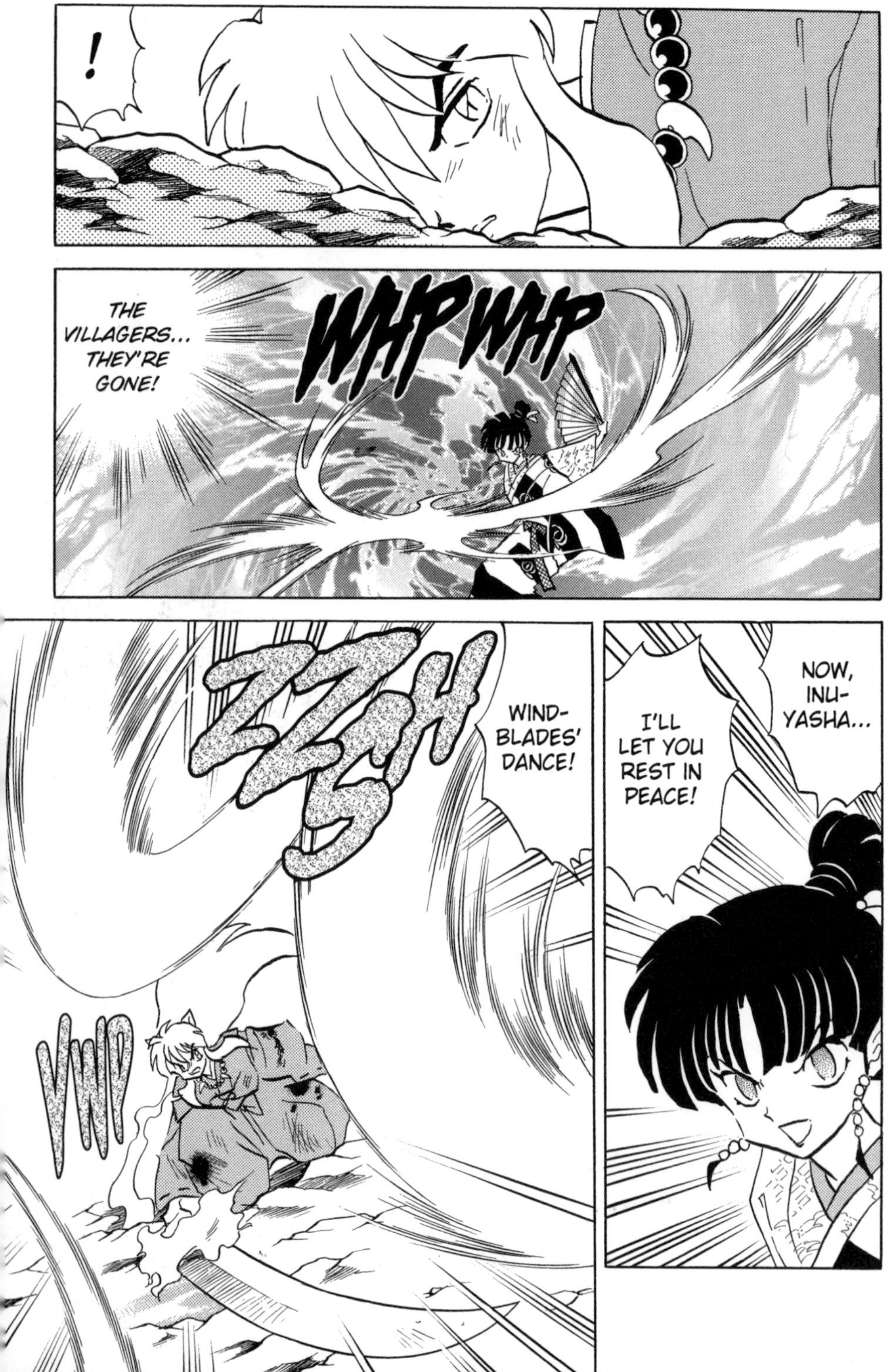
!
WHIP WHIP
THE VILLAGERS... THEY'RE GONE!
NOW, INU-YASHA...
I'LL LET YOU REST IN PEACE!
WIND-BLADES' DANCE!
ZZSH
VWIP

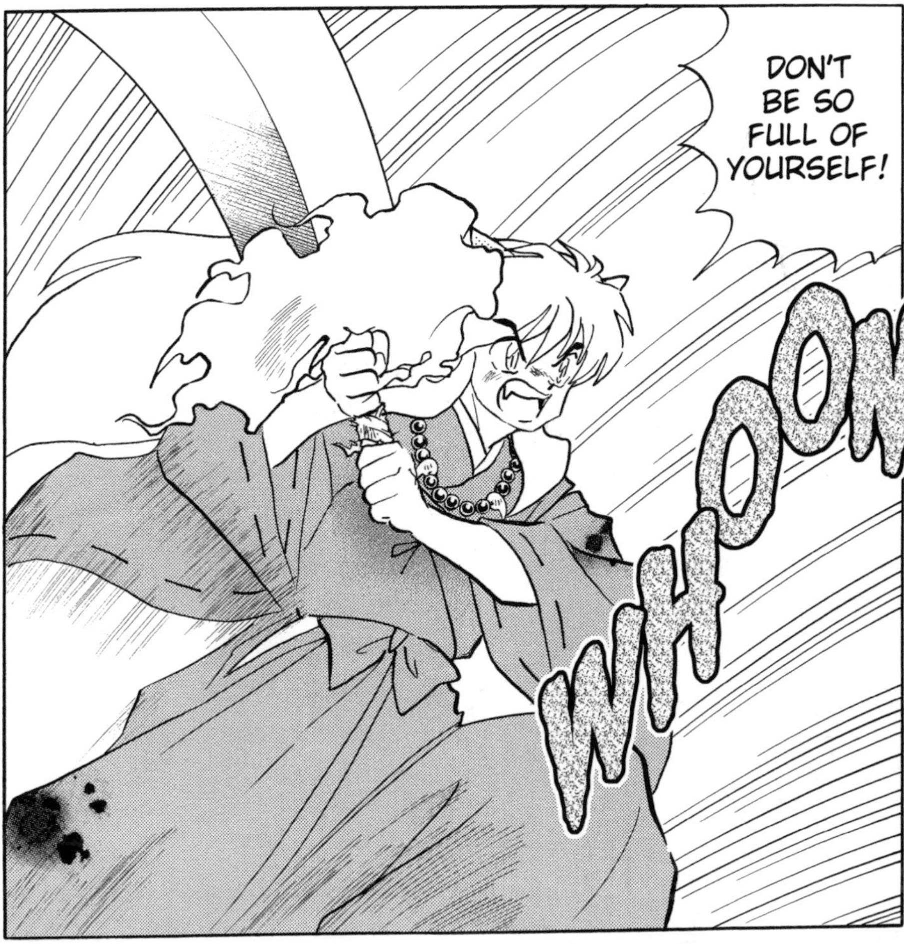
DON'T BE SO FULL OF YOURSELF!
WHOOOM
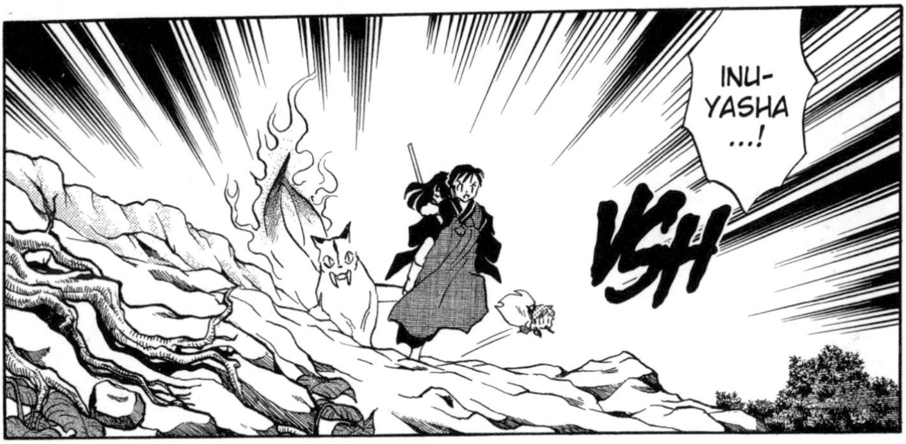
INU-YASHA ...!
VSH

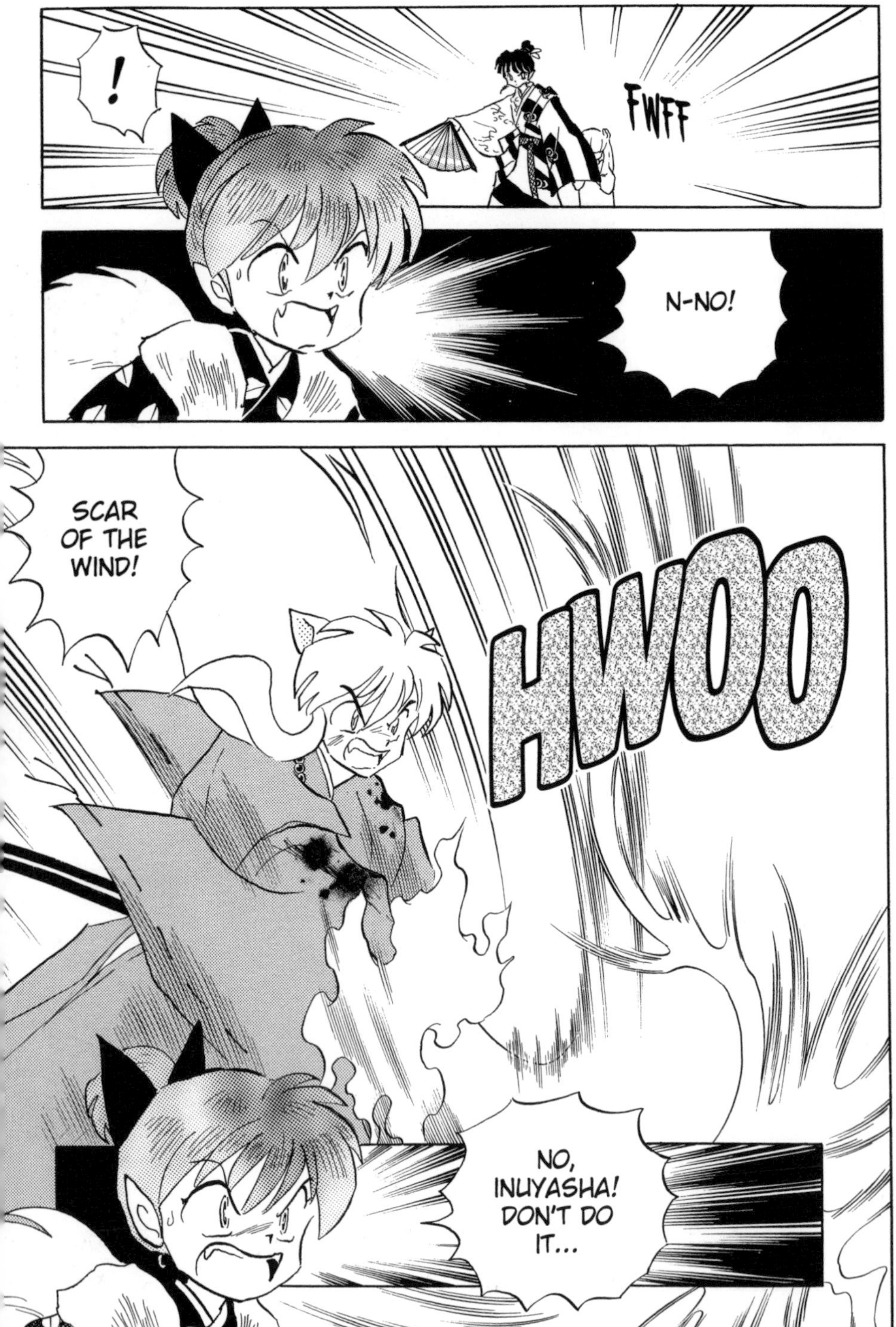
FWFF
!
N-NO!
SCAR OF THE WIND!
HWOO
NO, INUYASHA! DON'T DO IT...

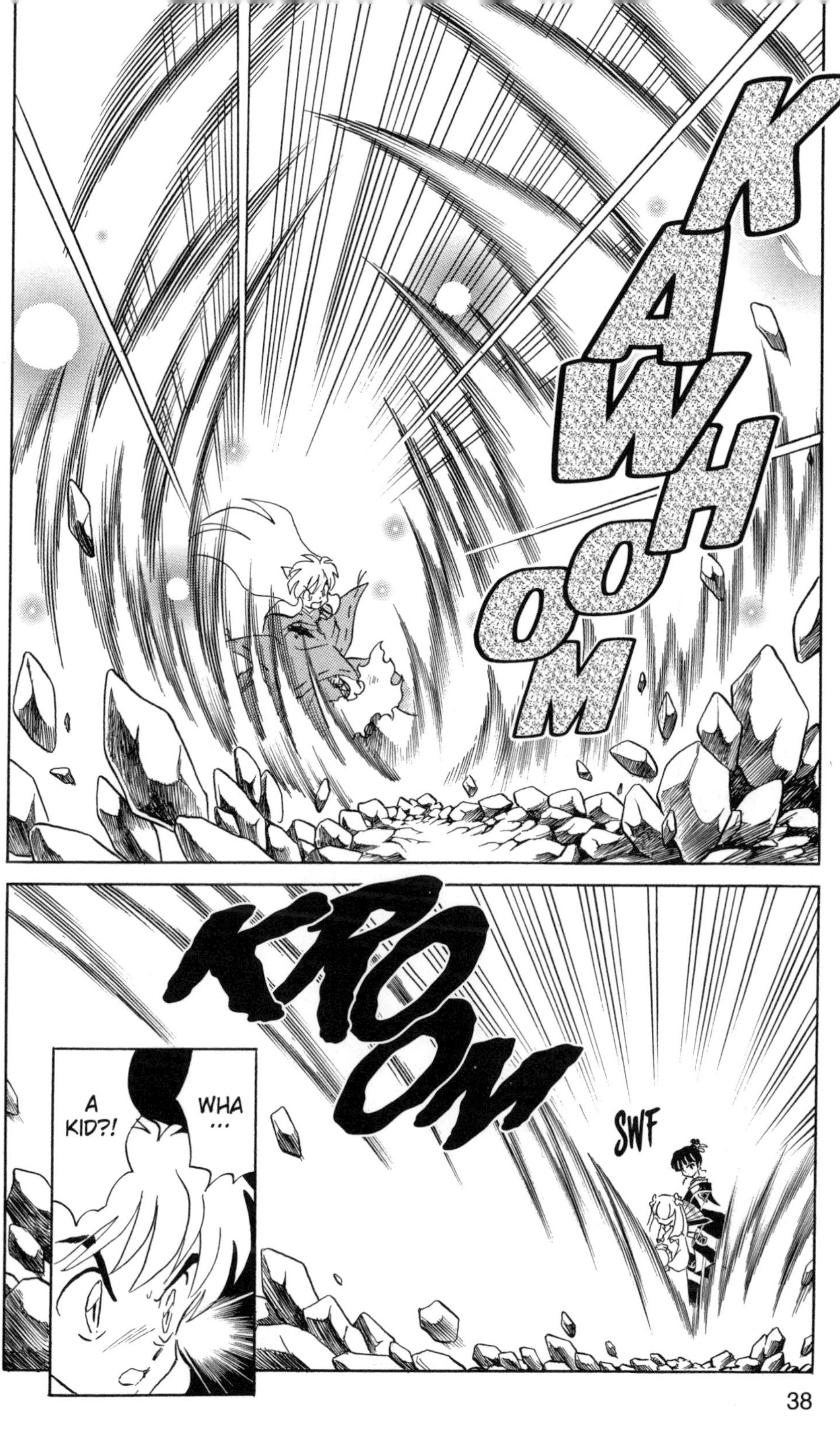
KAWHOOOM
KROOM
SWF
WHA...
A KID?!

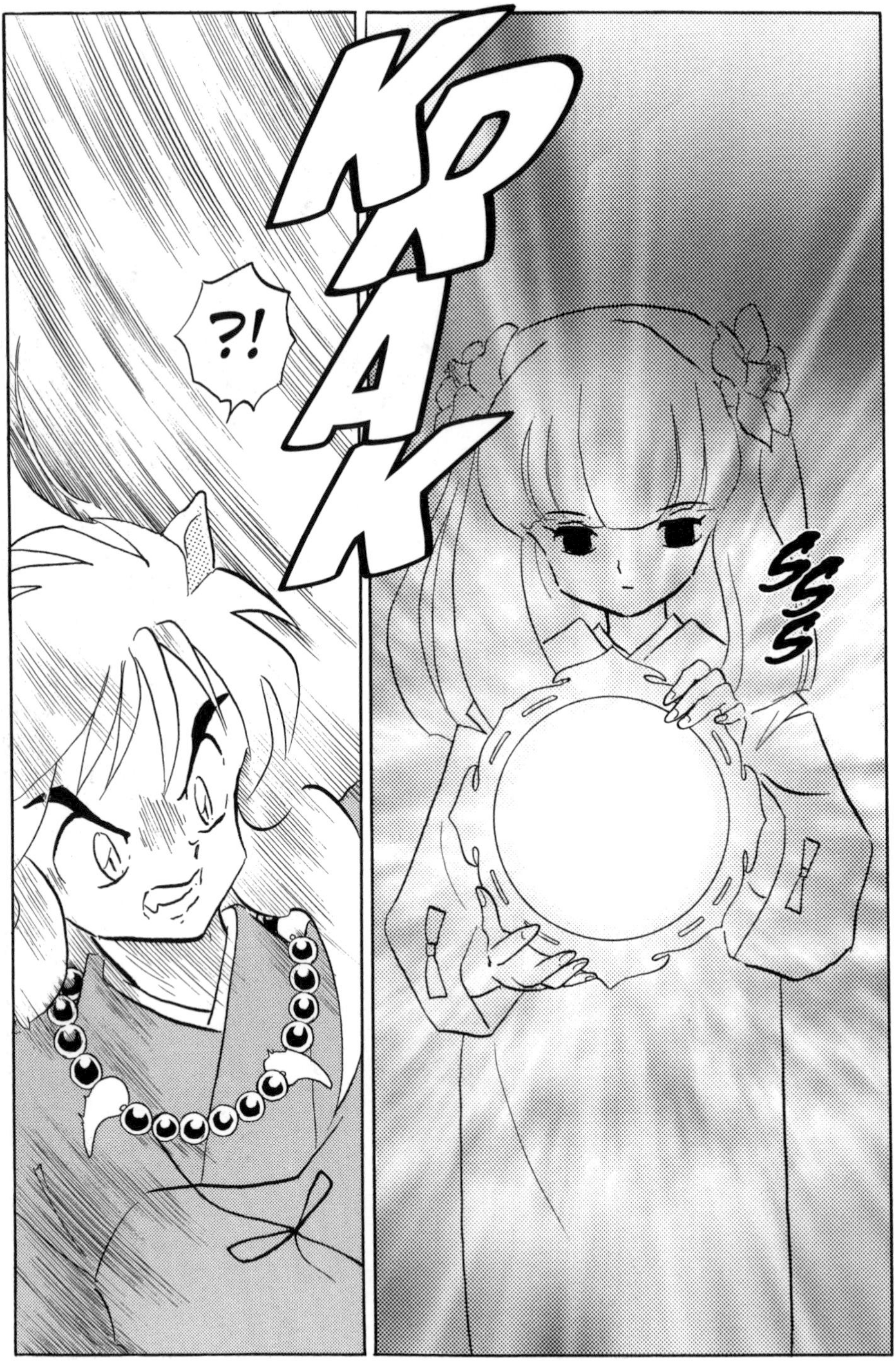
KRAAK
SSS
?!

11

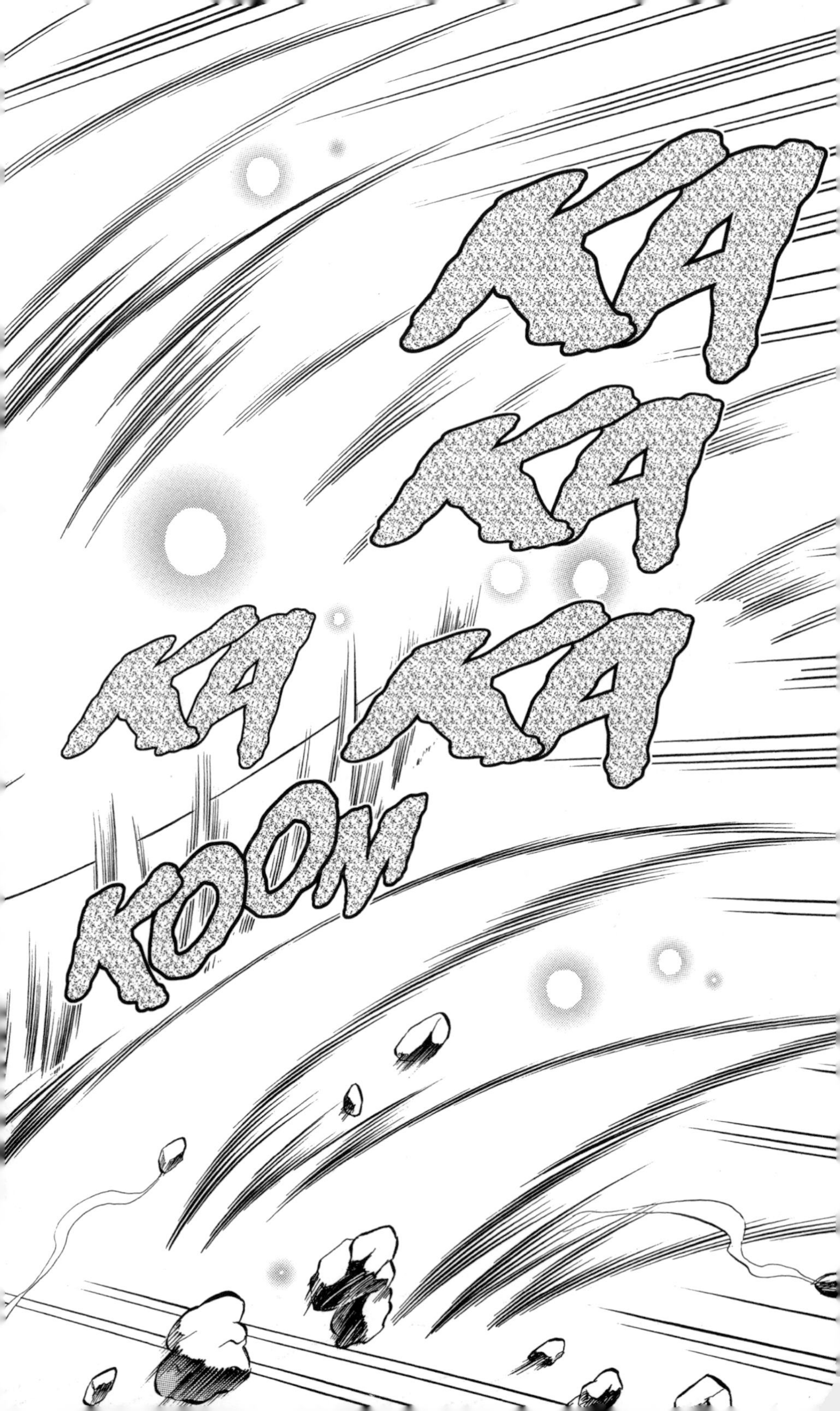
KA
KA
KA KA
KOOM

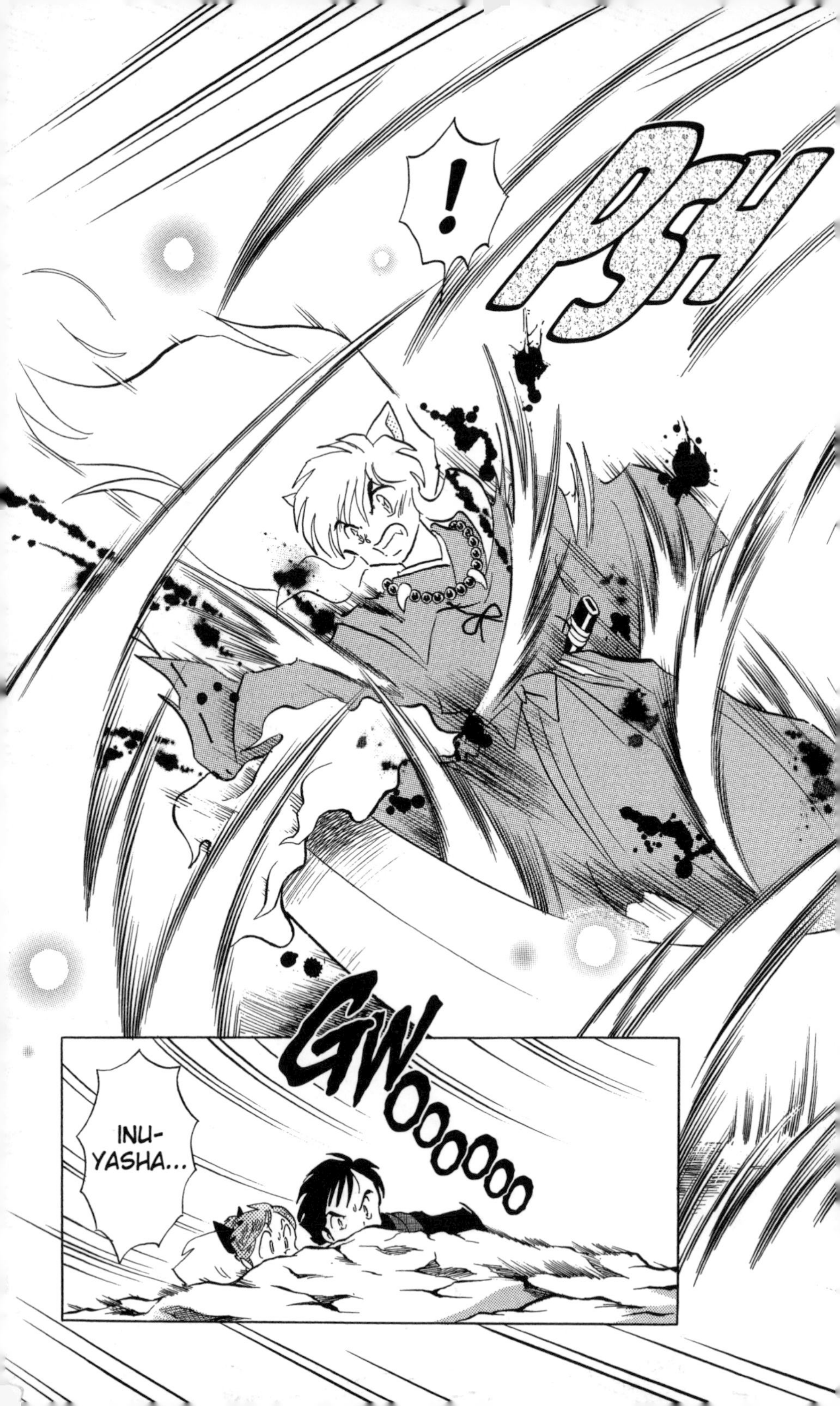

!
PSH
GWOOOOOO
INU-
YASHA...

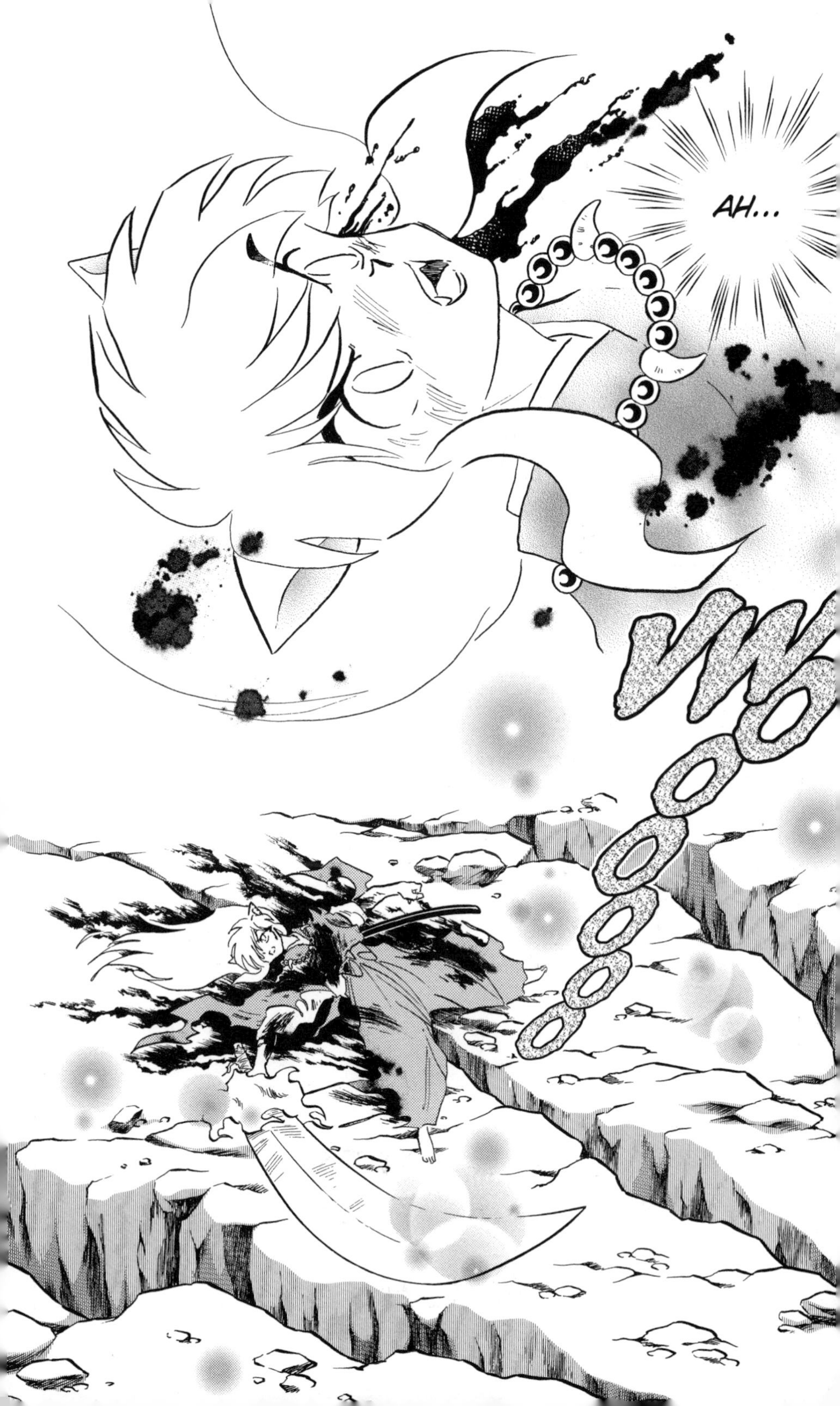
AH...
VWOOOOOOOO

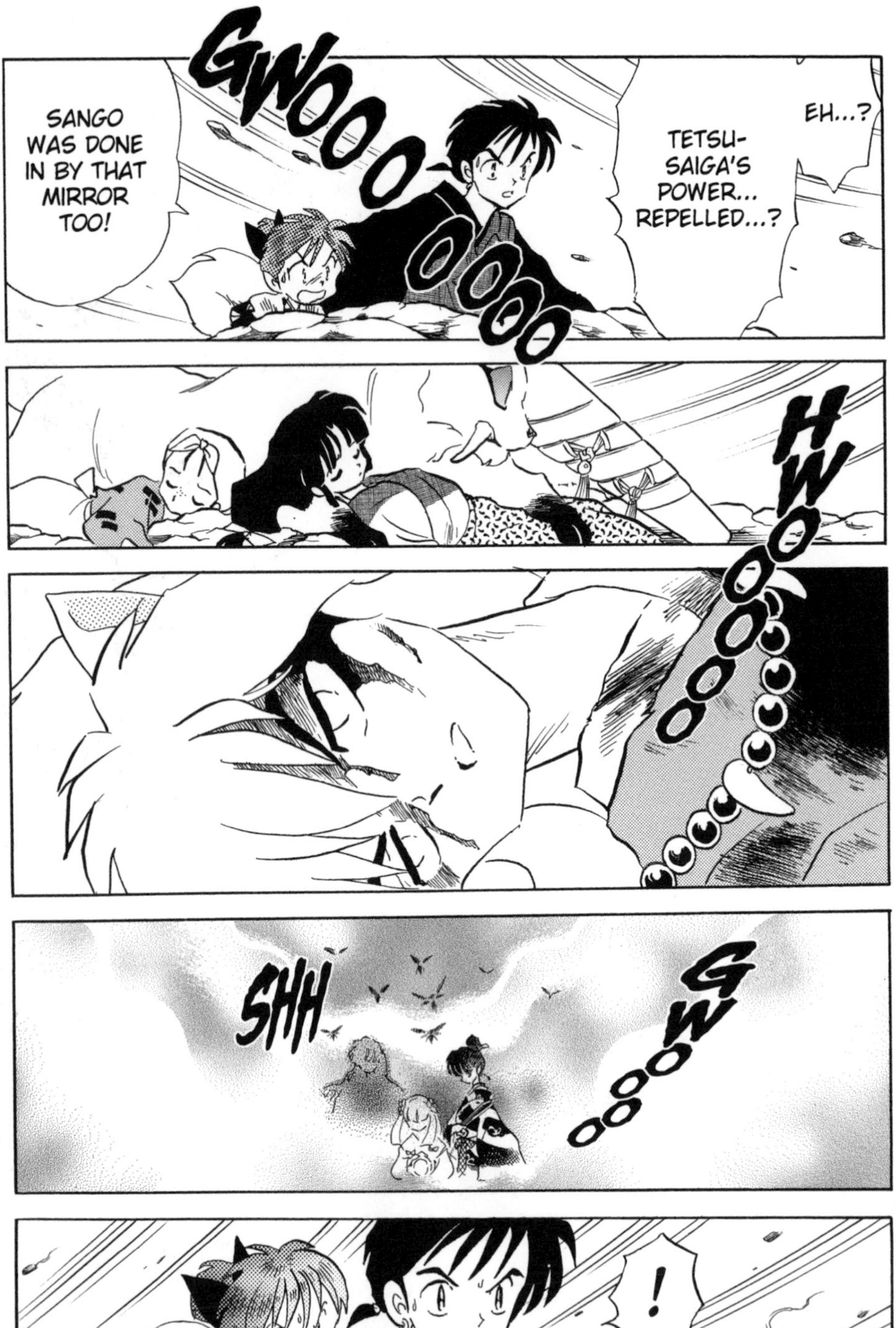
EH...?
TETSU-SAIGA'S POWER... REPELLED...?
SANGO WAS DONE IN BY THAT MIRROR TOO!
GWOOOOOOOO
HWOOOOOOOO
GWOOOOOO
SHH
!

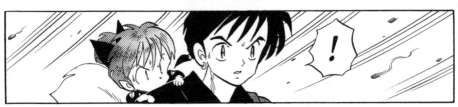

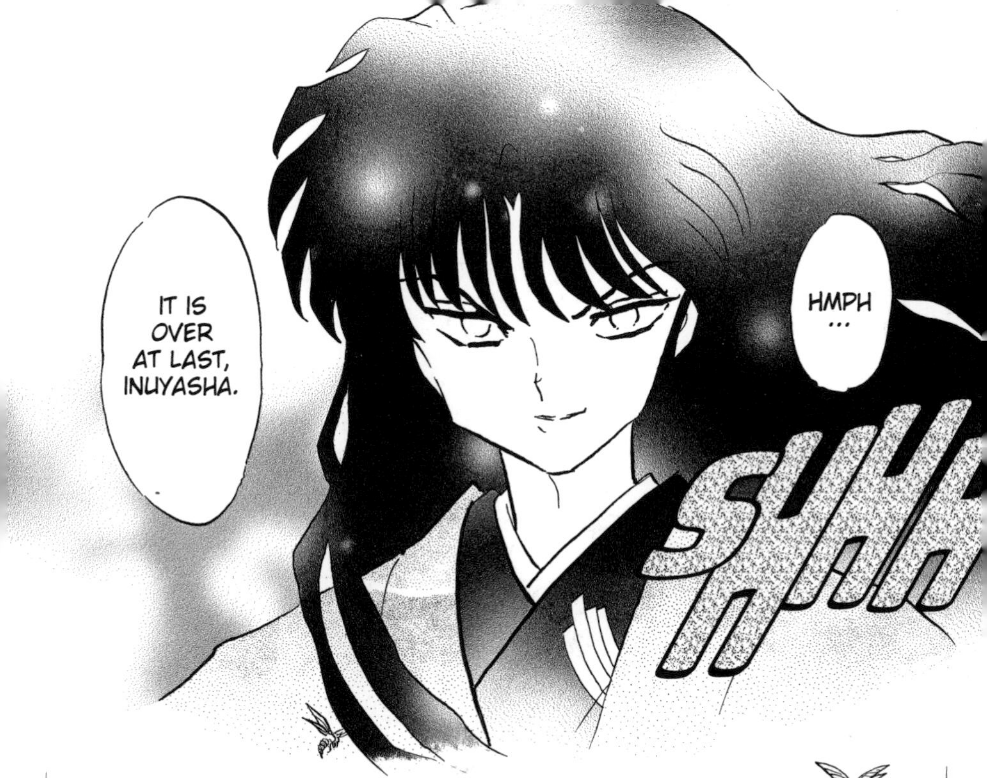
HMPH ...
IT IS OVER AT LAST, INUYASHA.
SHHH

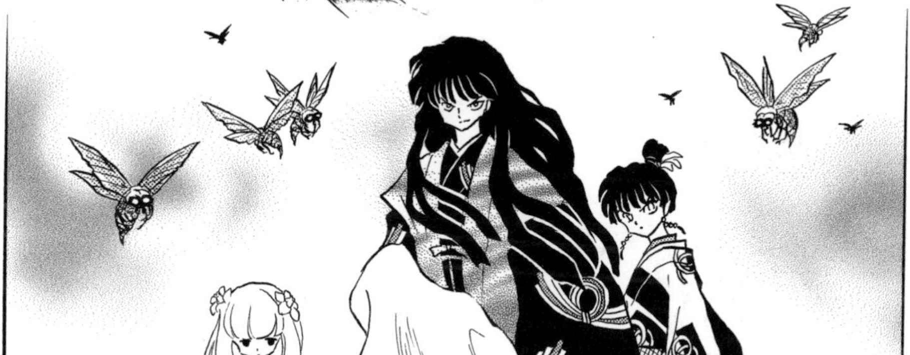

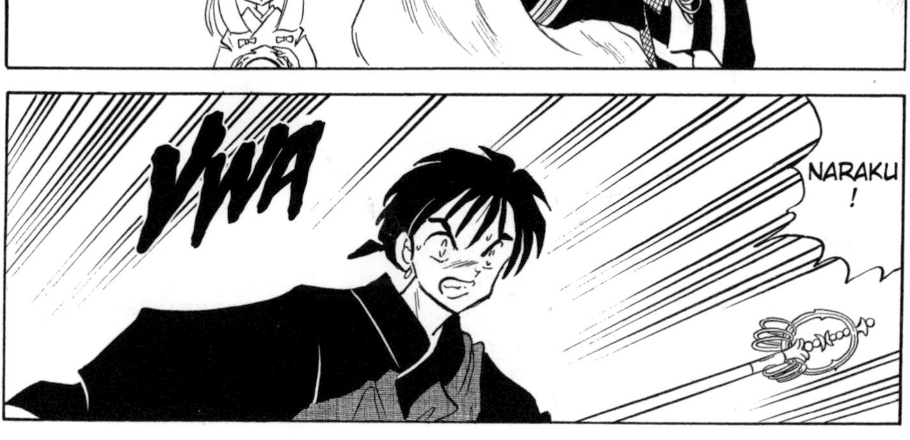
NARAKU !
VWA

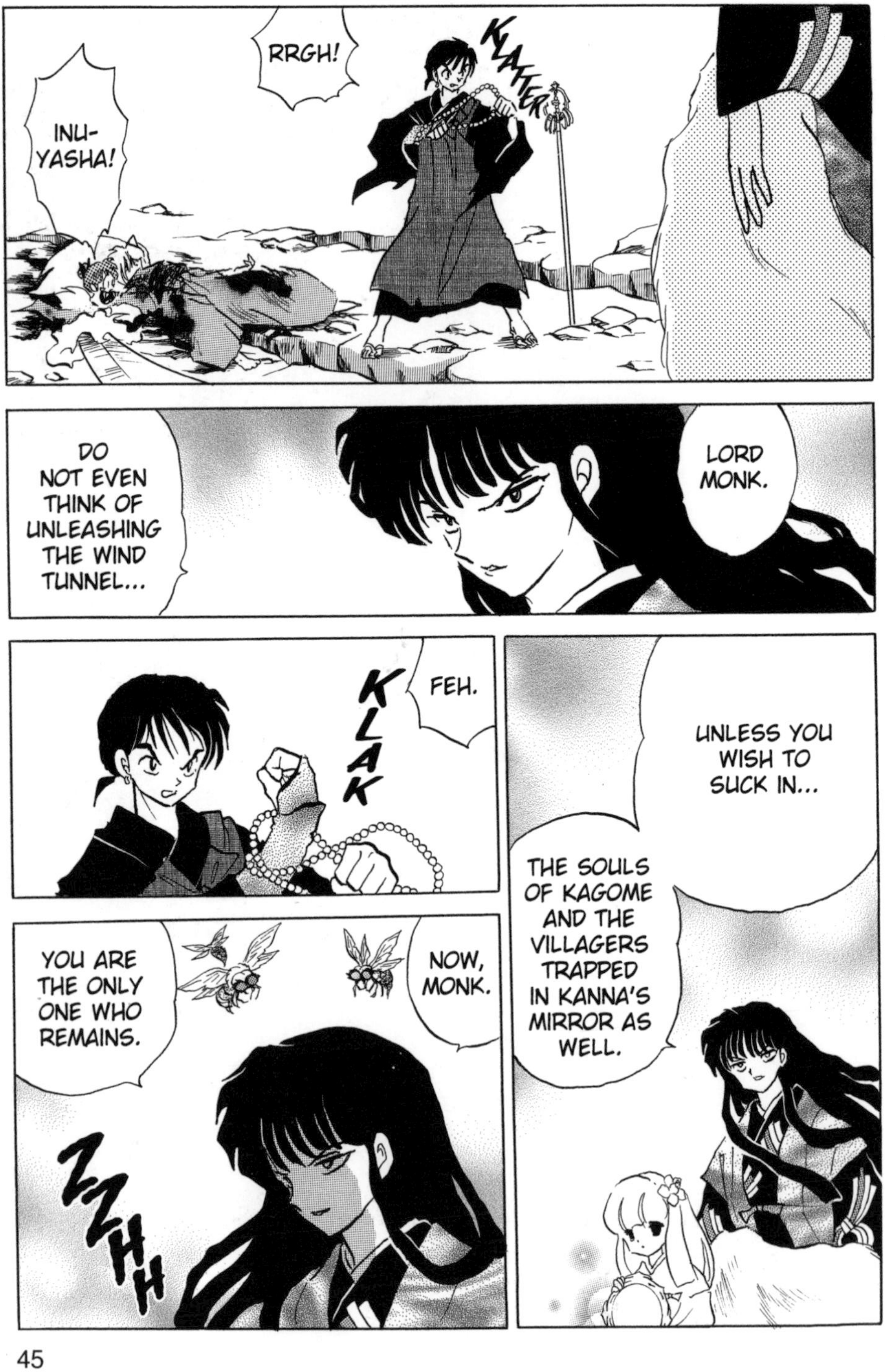
KLAKKER
RRGH!
INU-YASHA!
LORD MONK.
DO NOT EVEN THINK OF UNLEASHING THE WIND TUNNEL...
UNLESS YOU WISH TO SUCK IN...
THE SOULS OF KAGOME AND THE VILLAGERS TRAPPED IN KANNA'S MIRROR AS WELL.
FEH.
KLAK
NOW, MONK.
YOU ARE THE ONLY ONE WHO REMAINS.
ZZHH

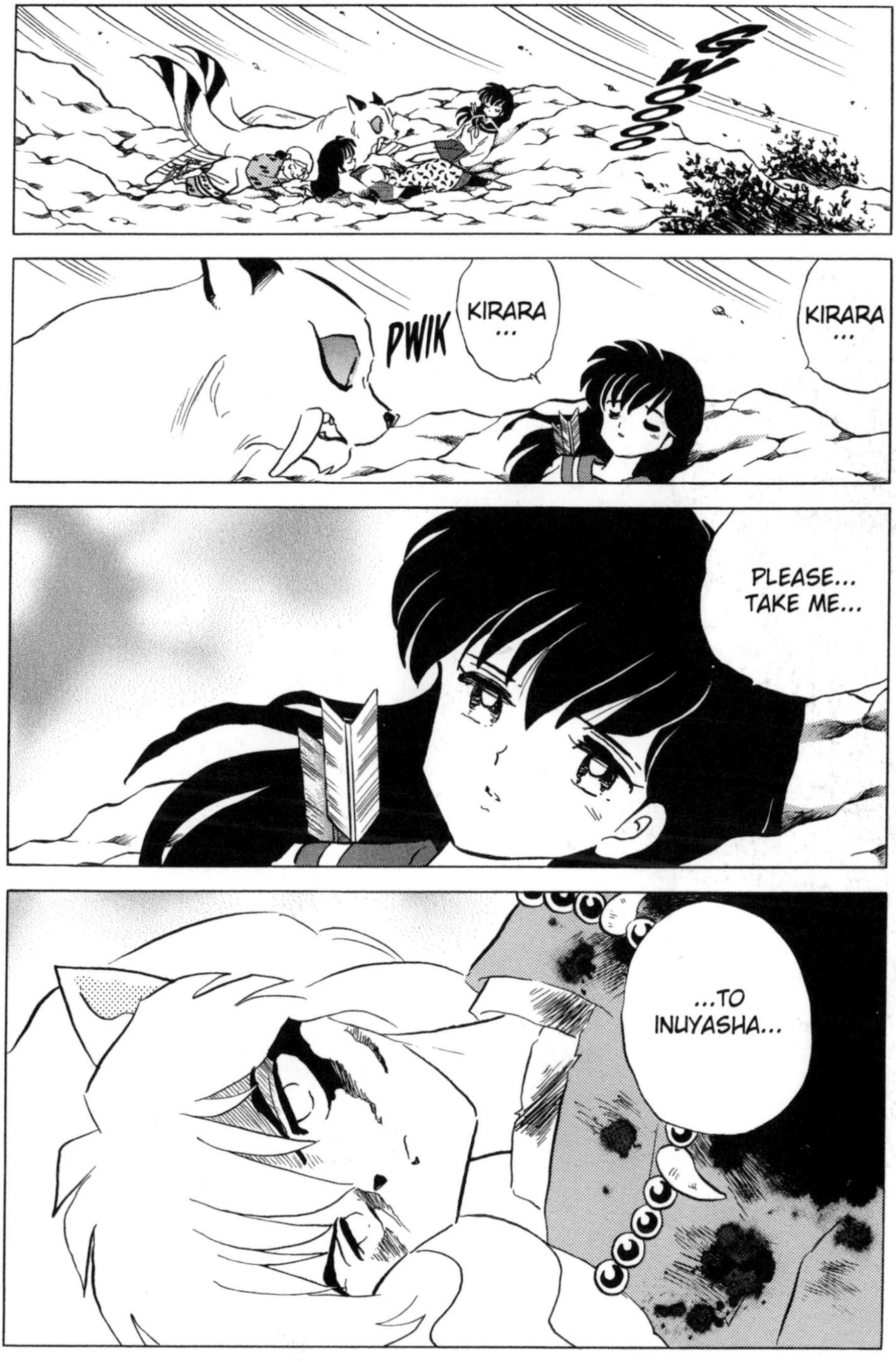
GWOOOO
KIRARA ...
KIRARA ...
PWIK
PLEASE... TAKE ME...
...TO INUYASHA...

SCROLL THREE
THE LIGHT OF THE SHIKON

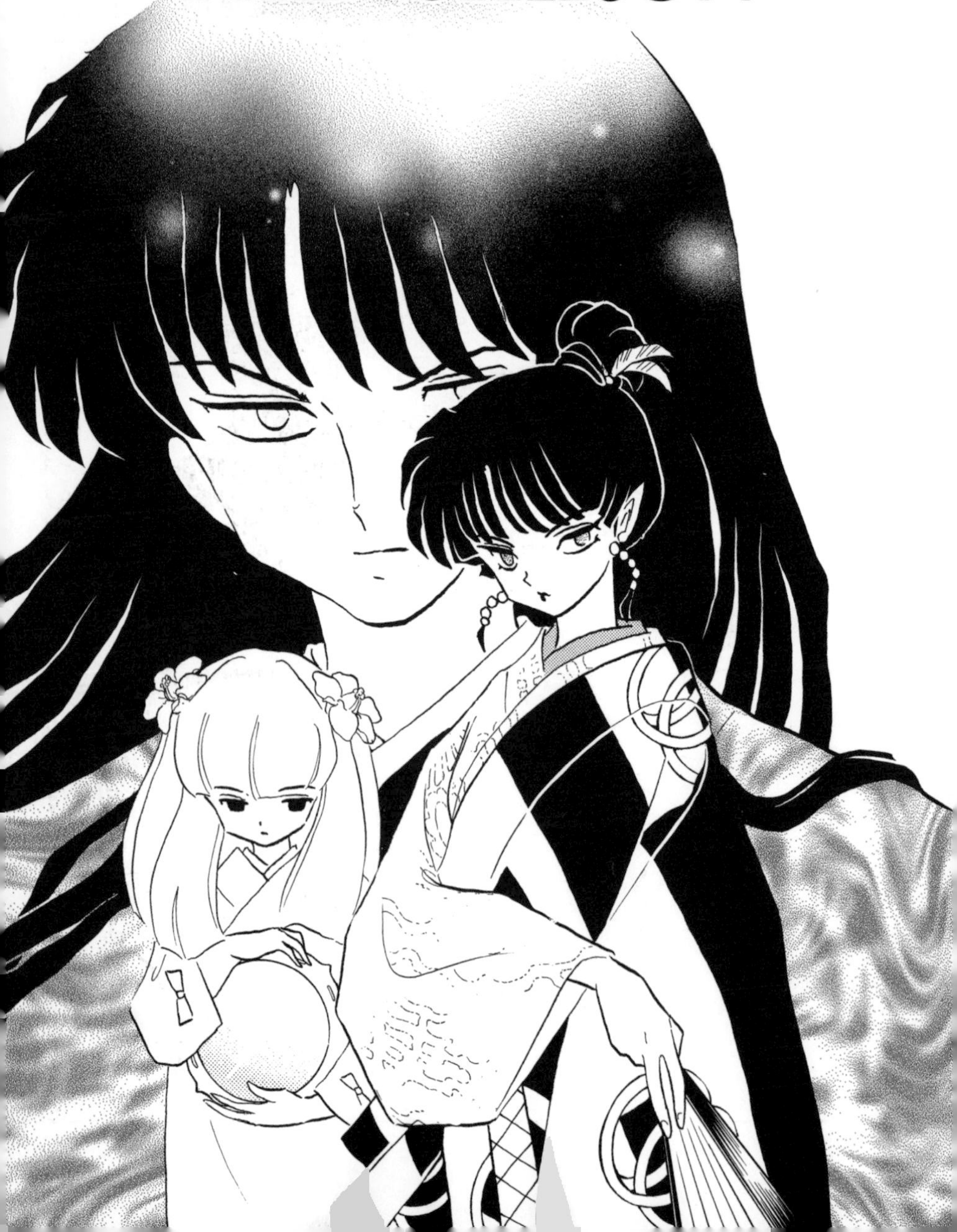

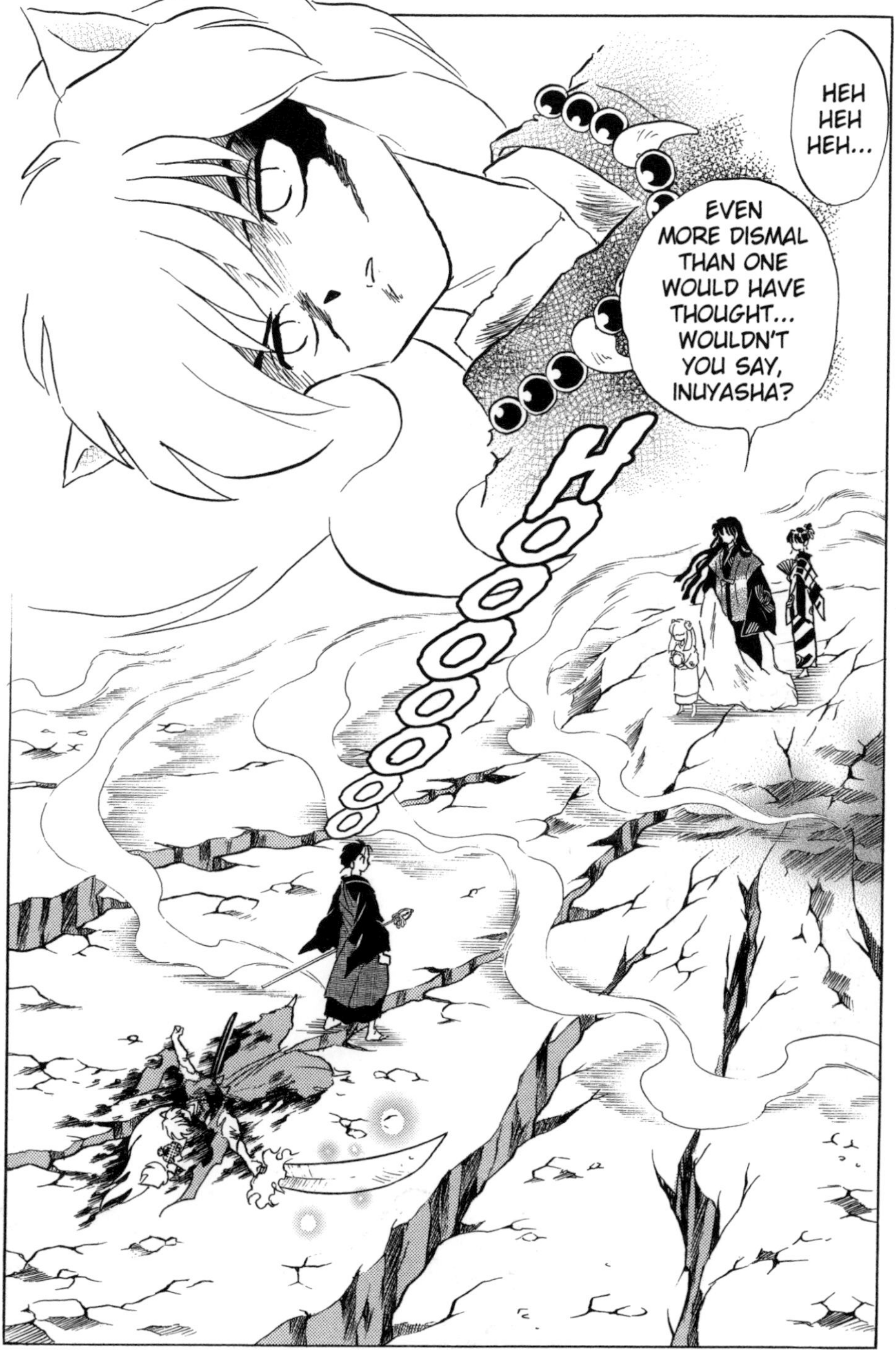
HEH HEH HEH...
EVEN MORE DISMAL THAN ONE WOULD HAVE THOUGHT... WOULDN'T YOU SAY, INUYASHA?
HOOOOOOOOO

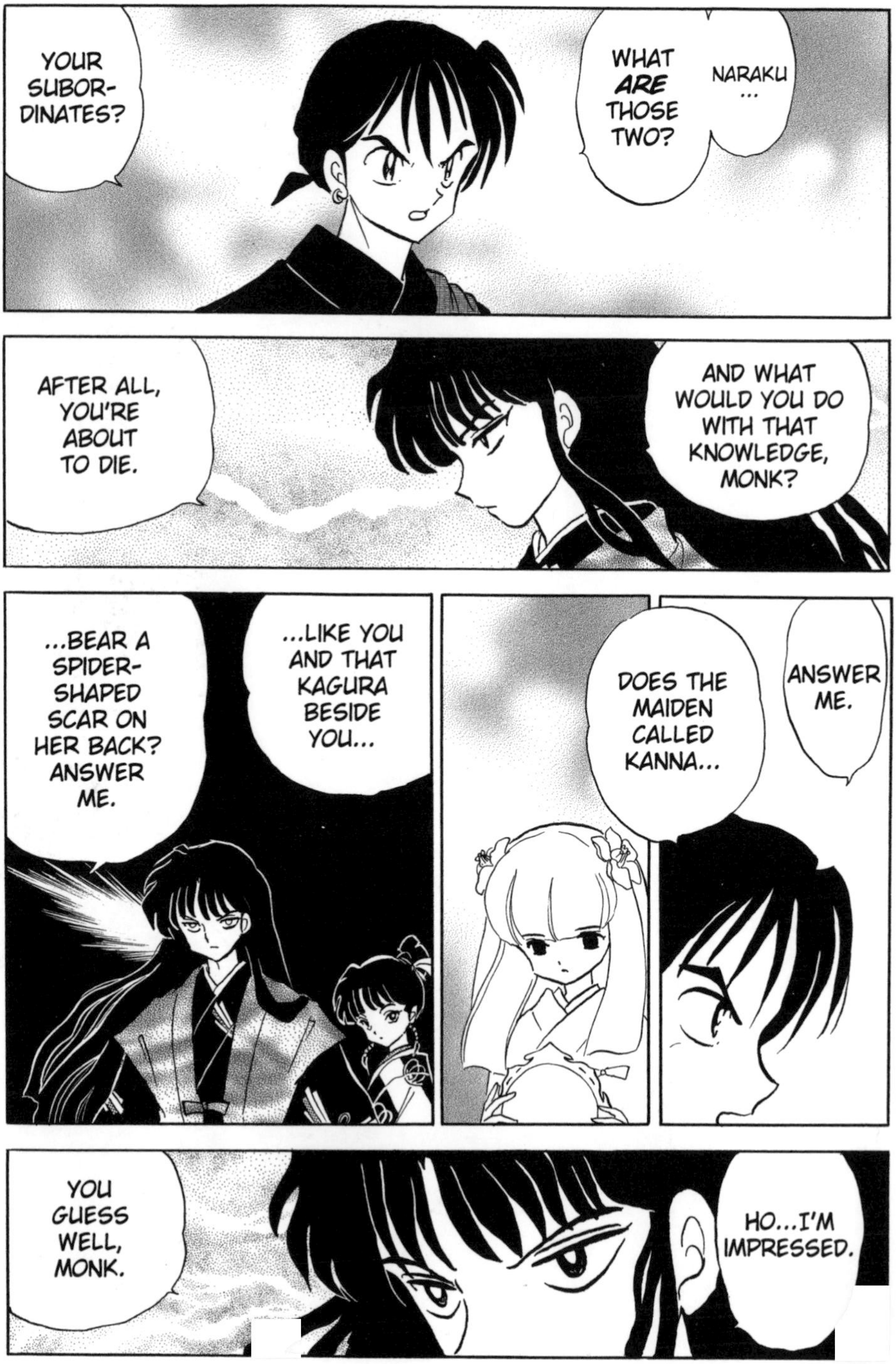
NARAKU...
WHAT *ARE* THOSE TWO?
YOUR SUBOR-DINATES?
AND WHAT WOULD YOU DO WITH THAT KNOWLEDGE, MONK?
AFTER ALL, YOU'RE ABOUT TO DIE.
ANSWER ME.
DOES THE MAIDEN CALLED KANNA...
...LIKE YOU AND THAT KAGURA BESIDE YOU...
...BEAR A SPIDER-SHAPED SCAR ON HER BACK? ANSWER ME.
HO...I'M IMPRESSED.
YOU GUESS WELL, MONK.

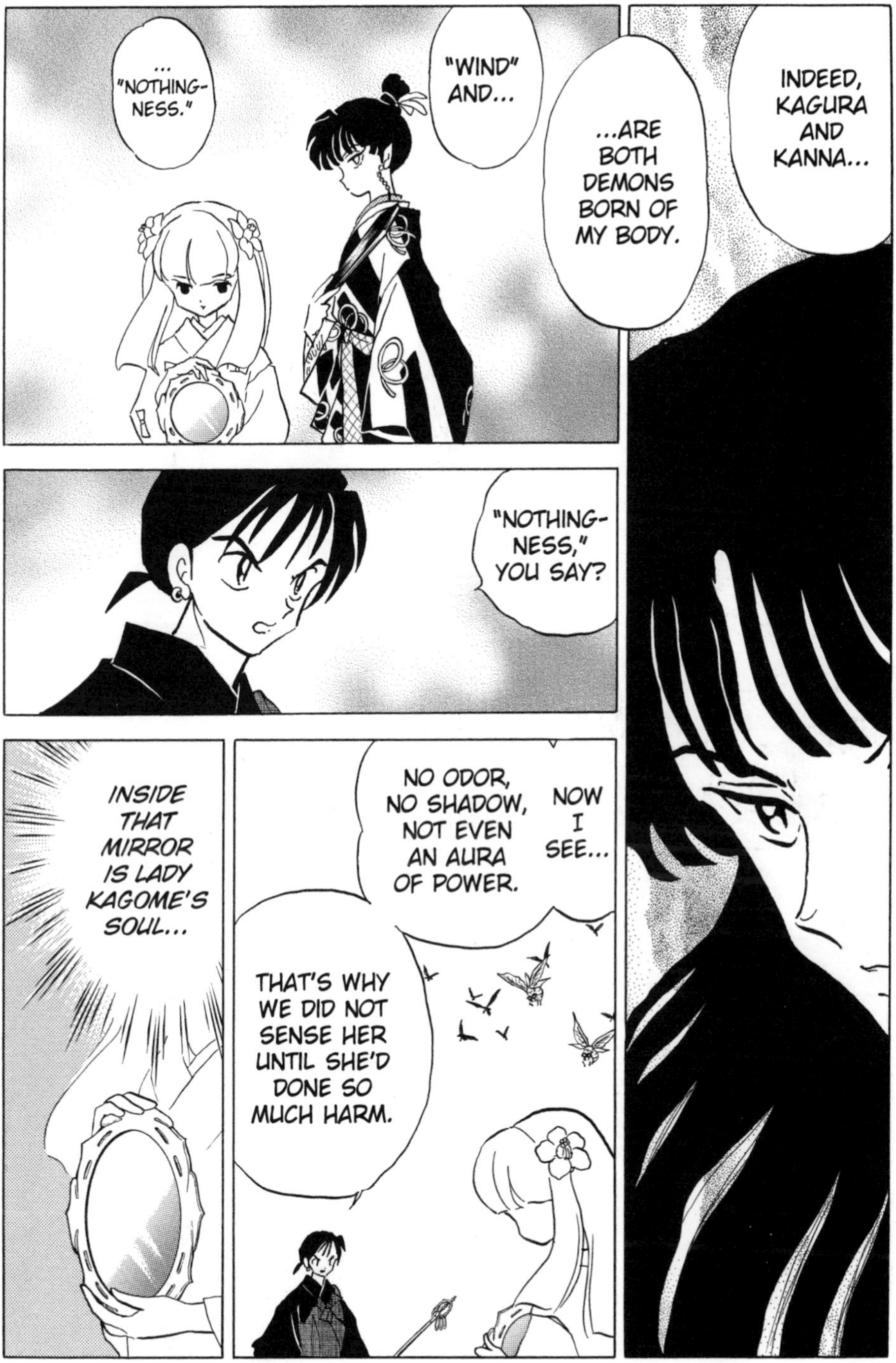
INDEED, KAGURA AND KANNA...
...ARE BOTH DEMONS BORN OF MY BODY.
"WIND" AND...
... "NOTHING-NESS."
"NOTHING-NESS," YOU SAY?
NOW I SEE...
NO ODOR, NO SHADOW, NOT EVEN AN AURA OF POWER.
THAT'S WHY WE DID NOT SENSE HER UNTIL SHE'D DONE SO MUCH HARM.
INSIDE THAT MIRROR IS LADY KAGOME'S SOUL...

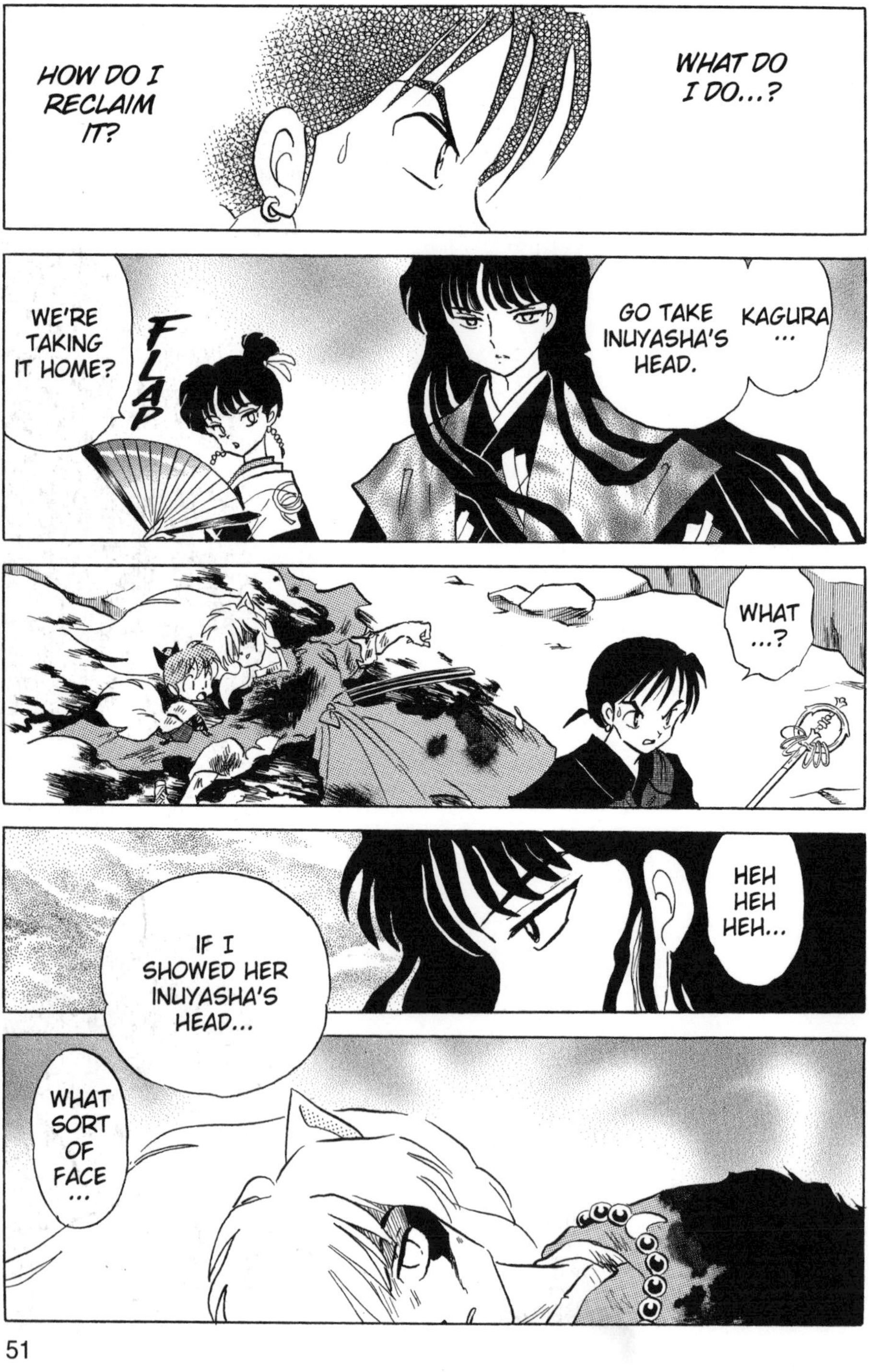
WHAT DO I DO...?
HOW DO I RECLAIM IT?
KAGURA ...
GO TAKE INUYASHA'S HEAD.
FLAP
WE'RE TAKING IT HOME?
WHAT ...?
HEH HEH HEH...
IF I SHOWED HER INUYASHA'S HEAD...
WHAT SORT OF FACE ...

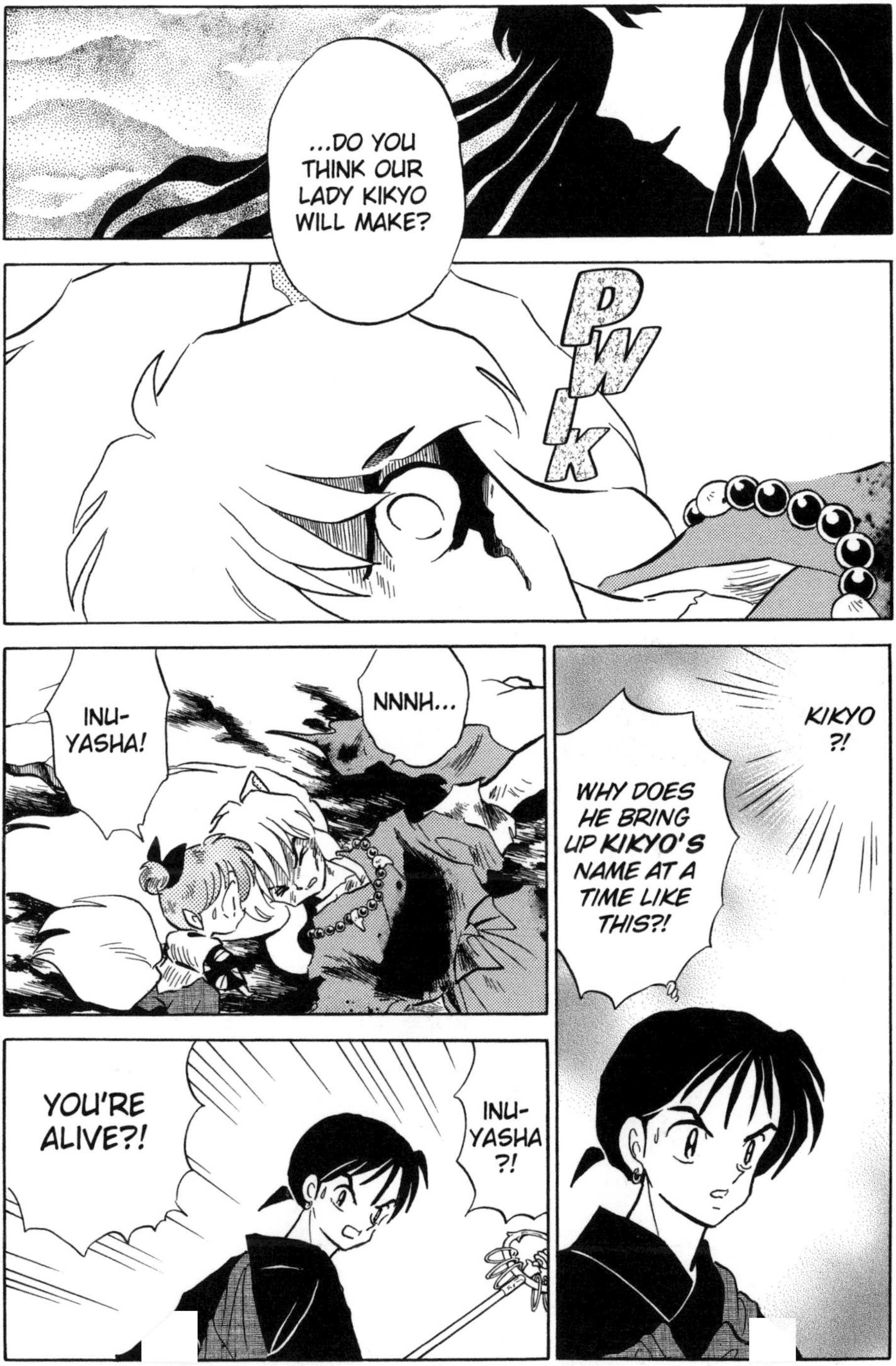
...DO YOU THINK OUR LADY KIKYO WILL MAKE?
PWIK
KIKYO ?!
WHY DOES HE BRING UP KIKYO'S NAME AT A TIME LIKE THIS?!
NNNH...
INU-YASHA!
INU-YASHA ?!
YOU'RE ALIVE?!

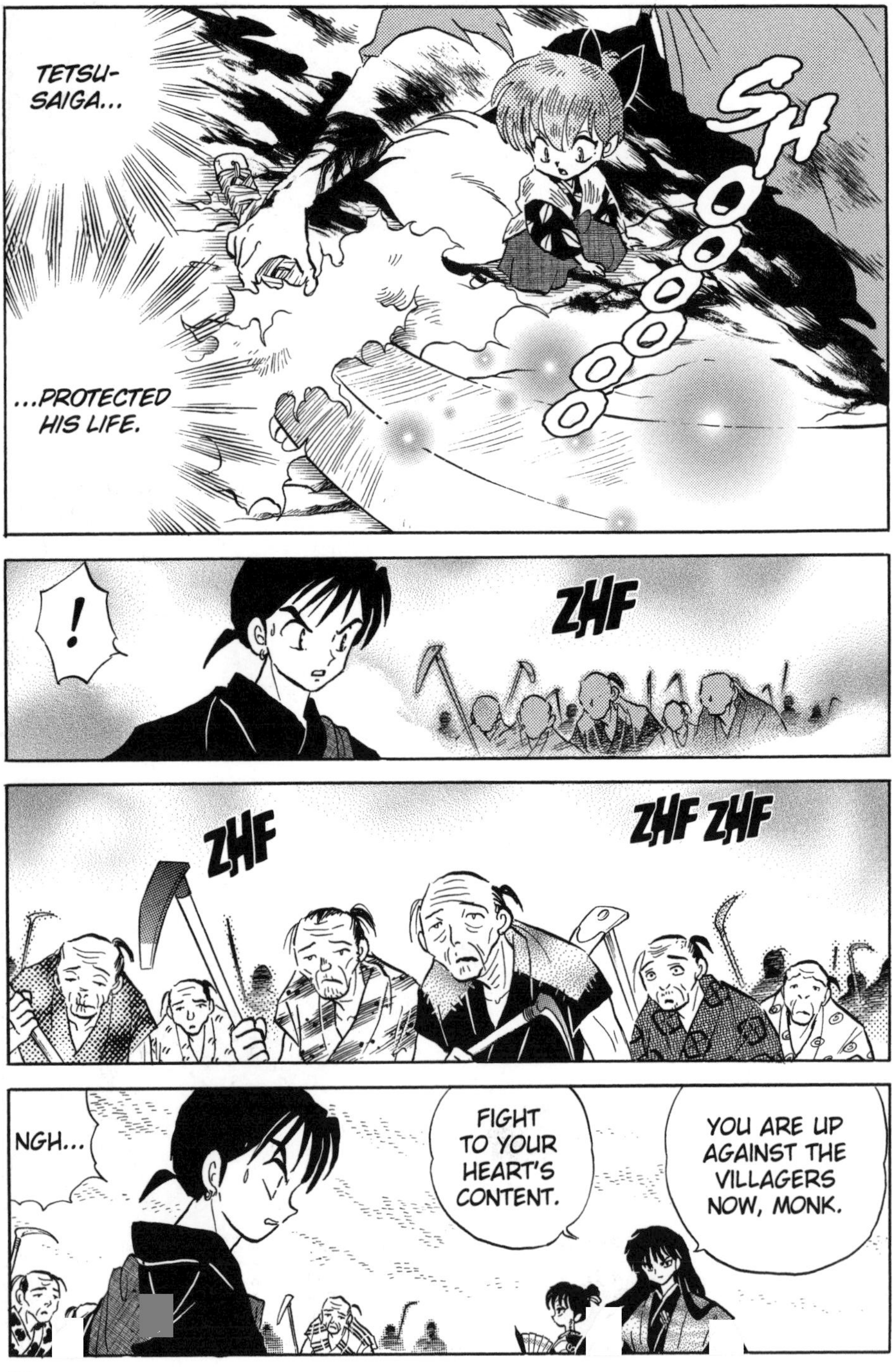
SHOOOOOOO
TETSU-SAIGA...
...PROTECTED HIS LIFE.
ZHF
!
ZHF ZHF
ZHF
YOU ARE UP AGAINST THE VILLAGERS NOW, MONK.
FIGHT TO YOUR HEART'S CONTENT.
NGH...

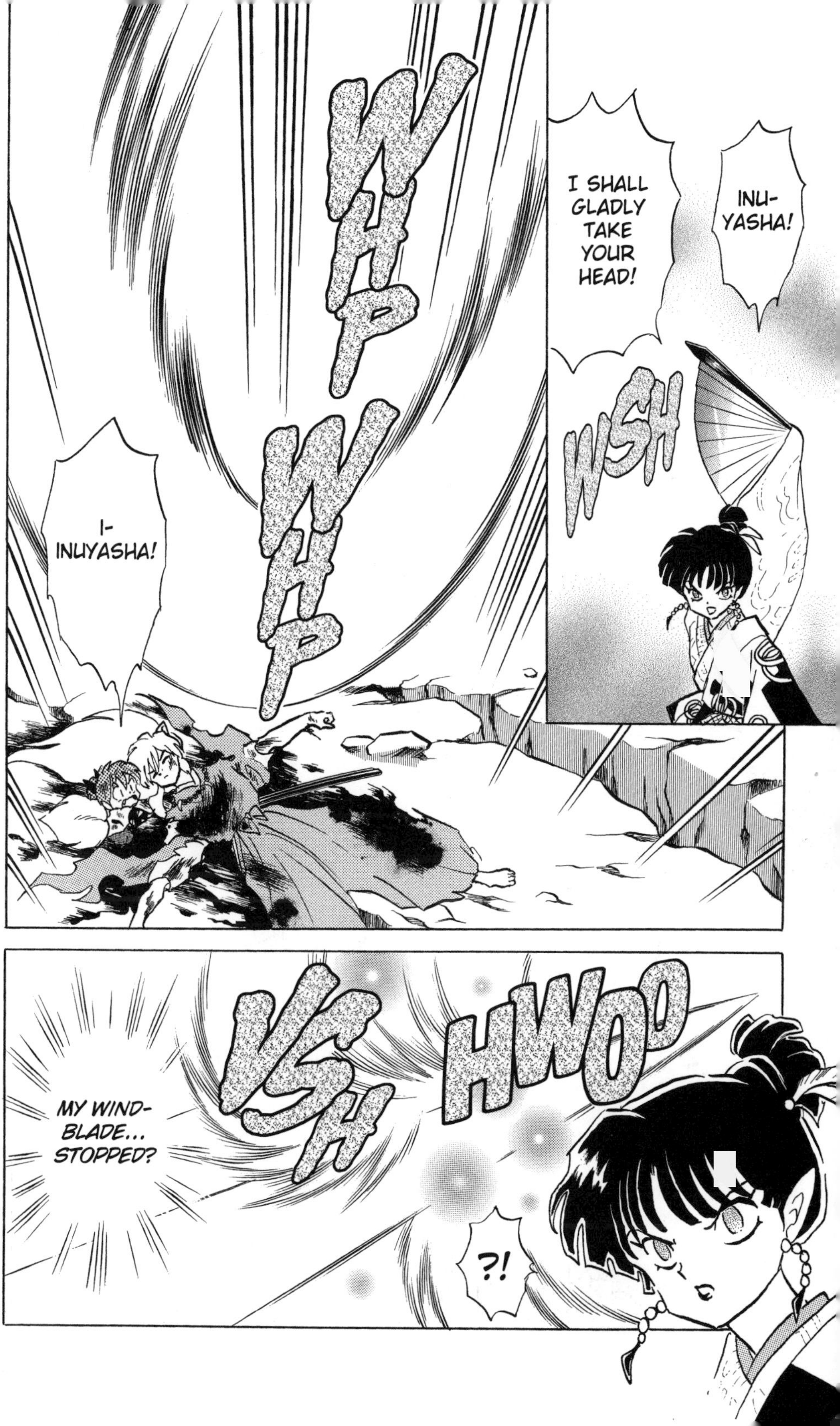
INU-YASHA!
I SHALL GLADLY TAKE YOUR HEAD!
WSH
WHP
WHP
I- INUYASHA!
HWOO
?!
VSH
MY WIND-BLADE... STOPPED?

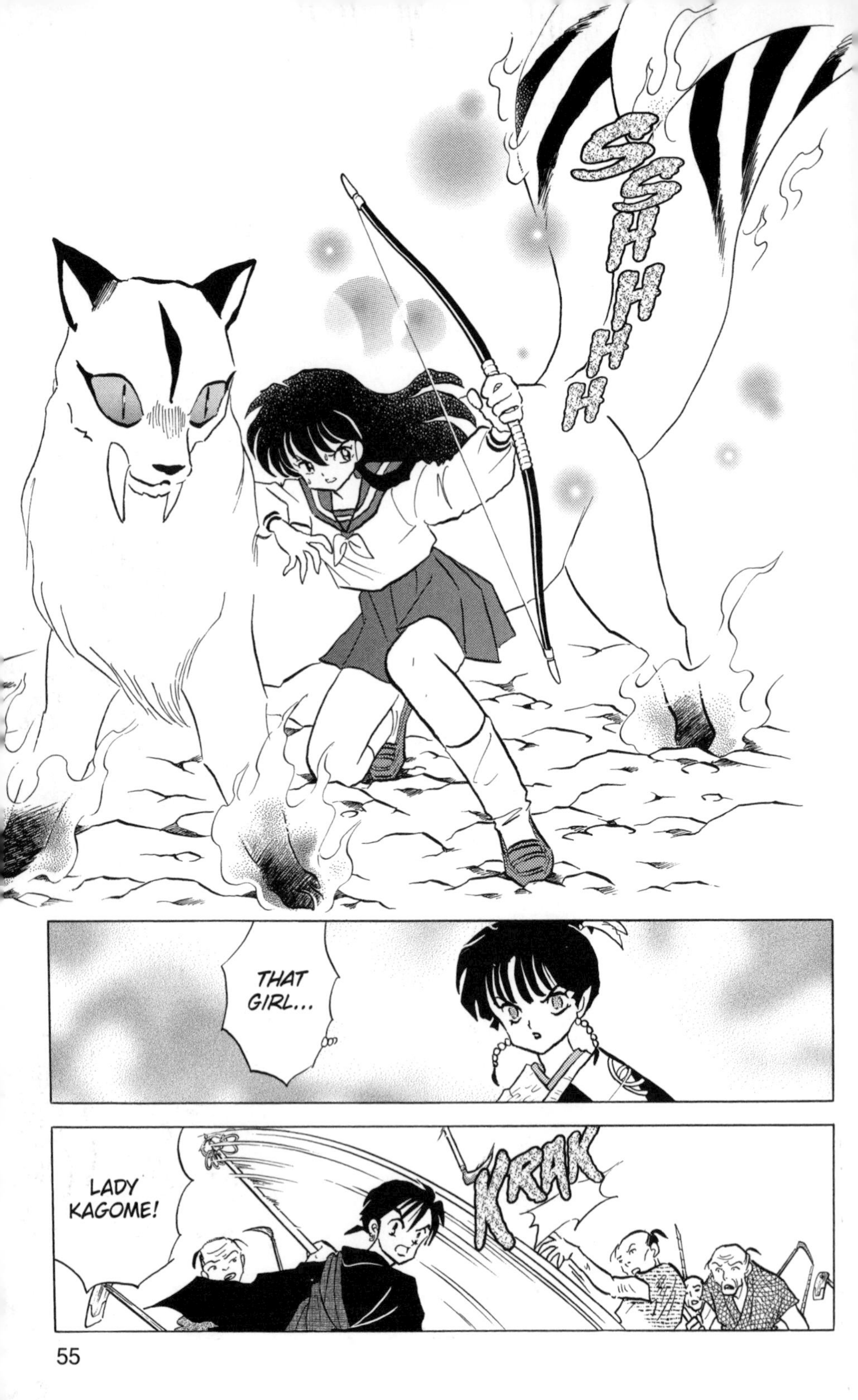
SSHHHH
THAT GIRL...
KRAK
LADY KAGOME!

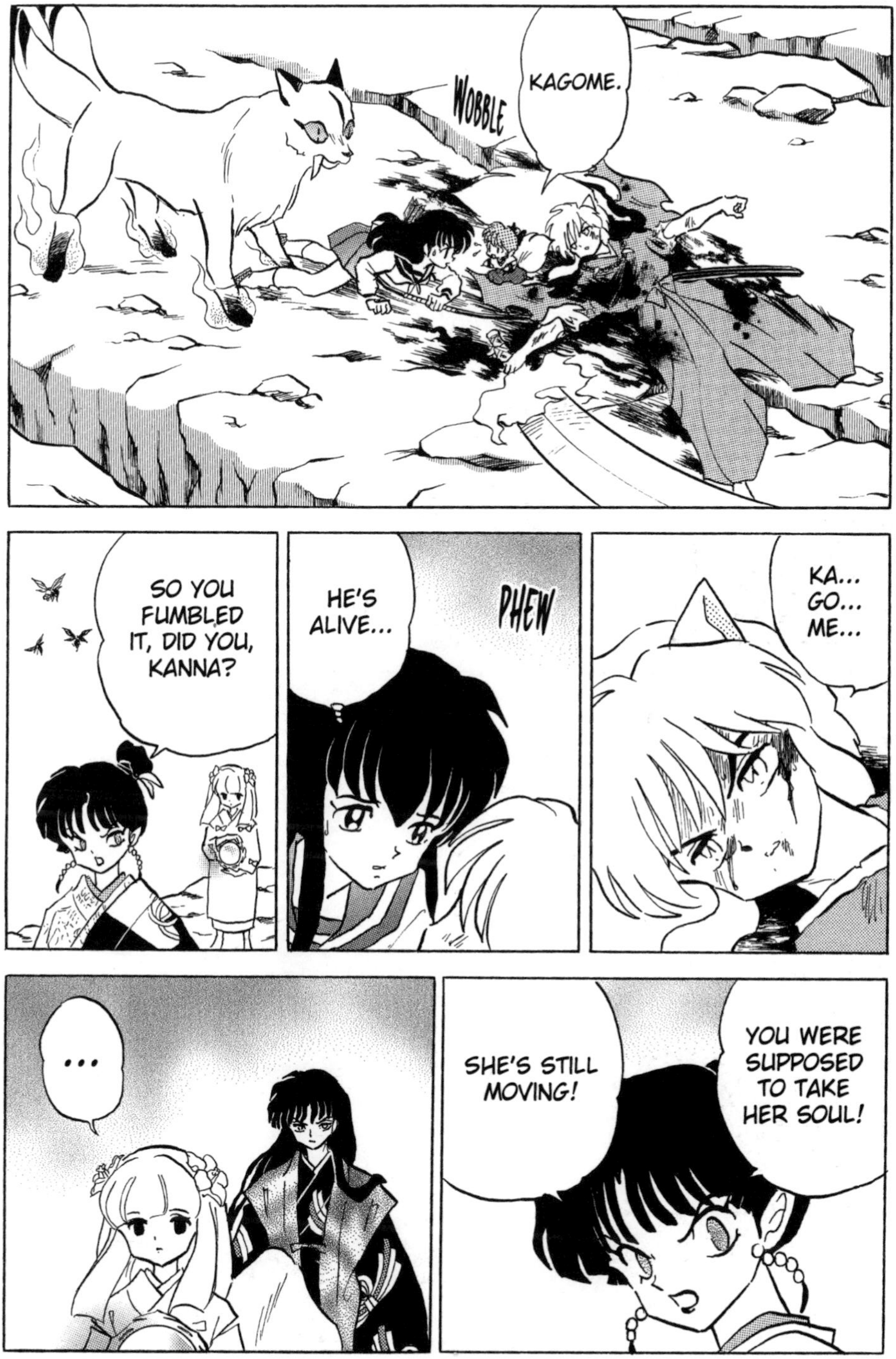
KAGOME.
WOBBLE
KA... GO... ME...
PHEW
HE'S ALIVE...
SO YOU FUMBLED IT, DID YOU, KANNA?
YOU WERE SUPPOSED TO TAKE HER SOUL!
SHE'S STILL MOVING!
...

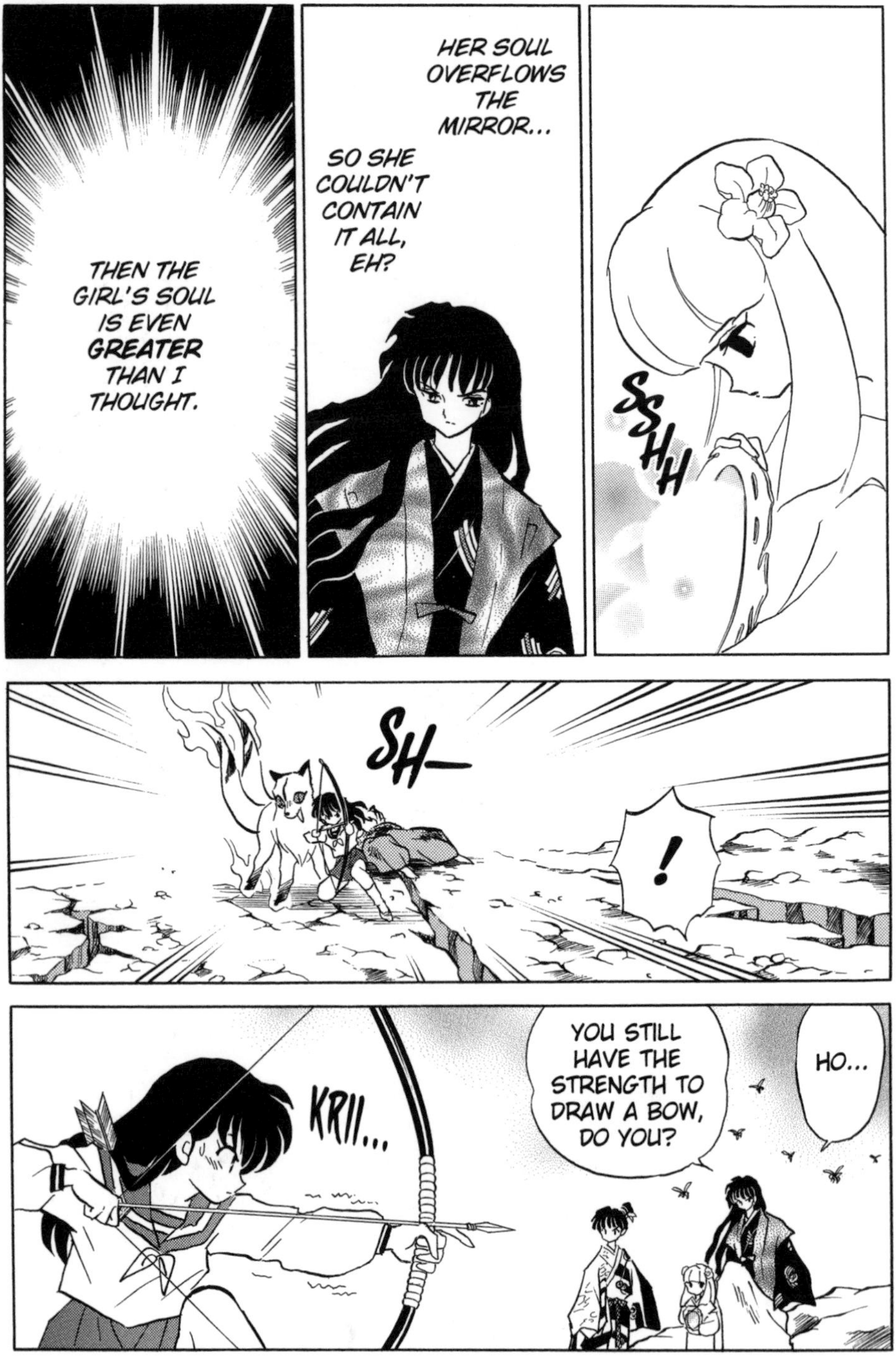
SSHH
HER SOUL OVERFLOWS THE MIRROR...
SO SHE COULDN'T CONTAIN IT ALL, EH?
THEN THE GIRL'S SOUL IS EVEN GREATER THAN I THOUGHT.
SH—
!
HO...
YOU STILL HAVE THE STRENGTH TO DRAW A BOW, DO YOU?
KRII...

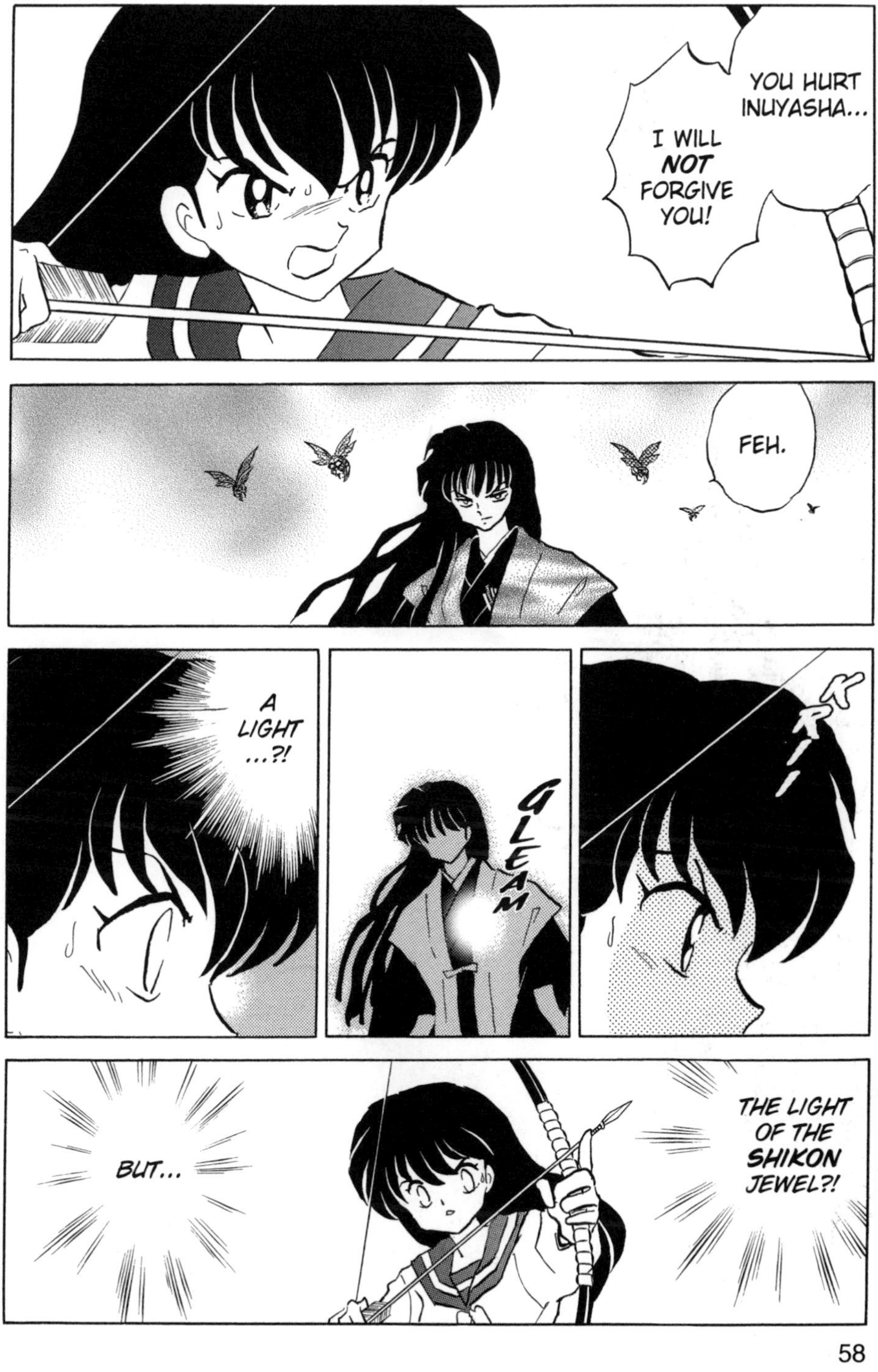
YOU HURT INUYASHA...
I WILL NOT FORGIVE YOU!
FEH.
KRIII
GLEAM
A LIGHT ...?!
THE LIGHT OF THE SHIKON JEWEL?!
BUT...

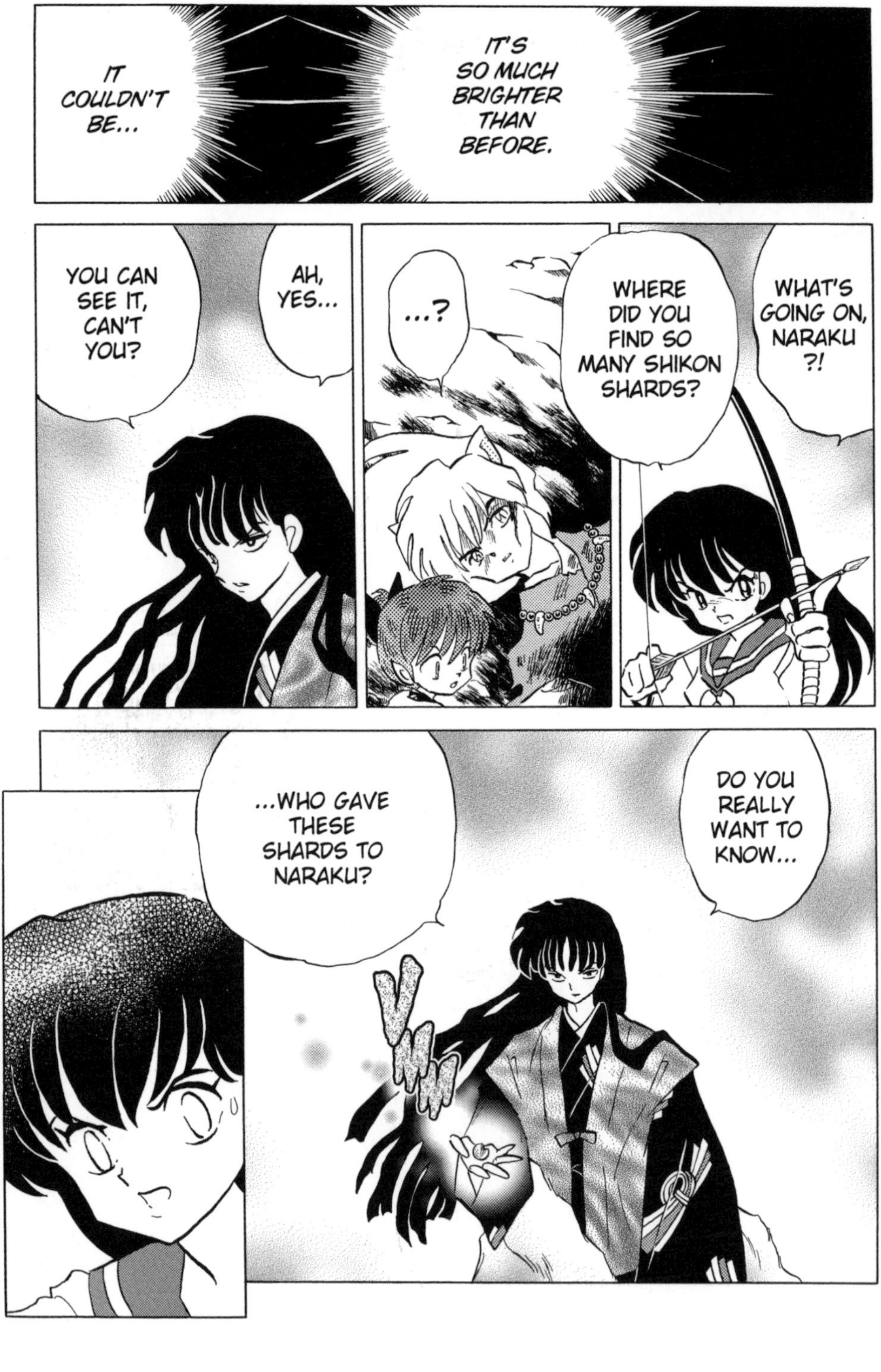
IT'S SO MUCH BRIGHTER THAN BEFORE.
IT COULDN'T BE...
WHAT'S GOING ON, NARAKU ?!
WHERE DID YOU FIND SO MANY SHIKON SHARDS?
...?
AH, YES...
YOU CAN SEE IT, CAN'T YOU?
DO YOU REALLY WANT TO KNOW...
...WHO GAVE THESE SHARDS TO NARAKU?
VWM

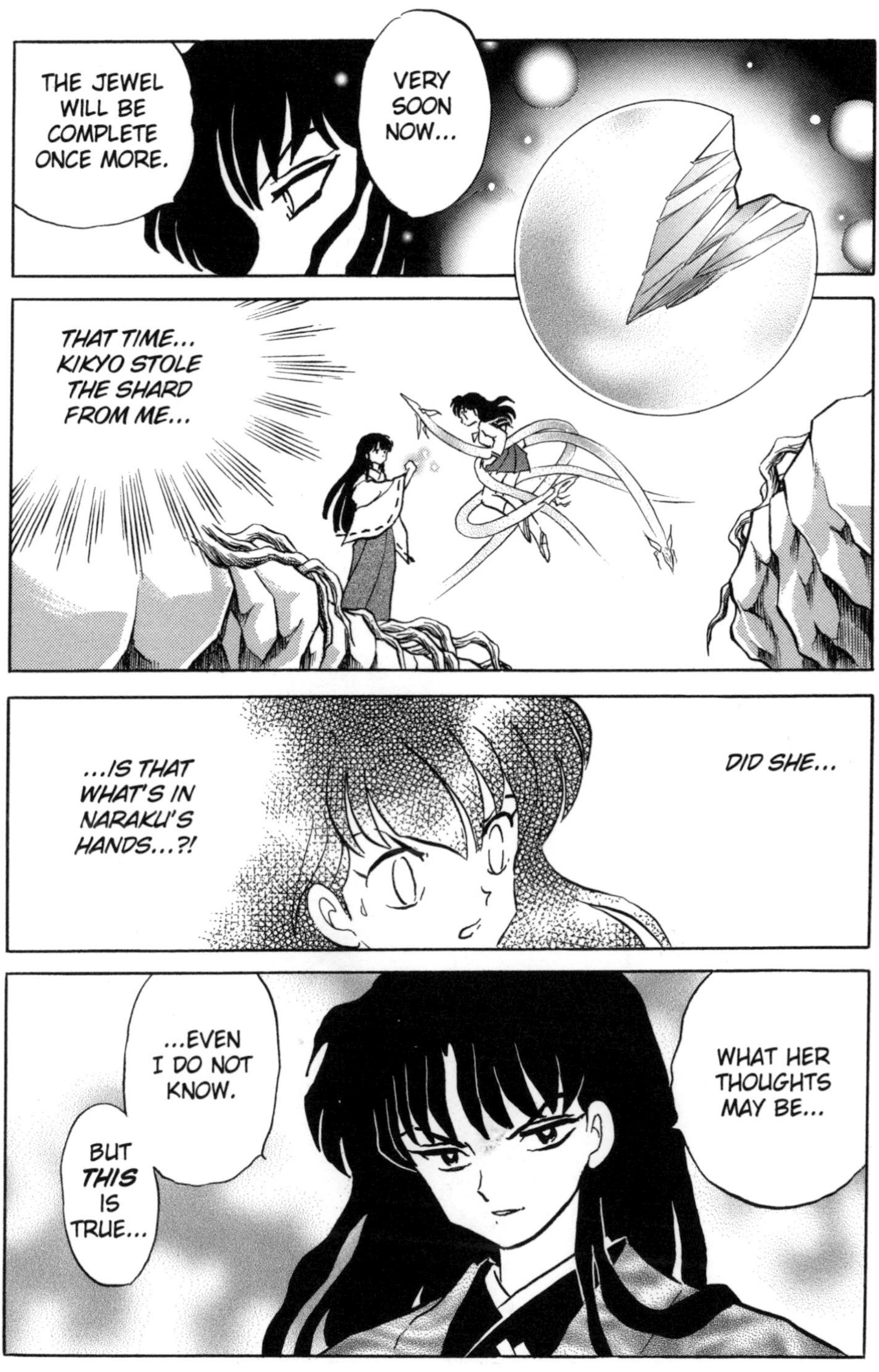
VERY SOON NOW...
THE JEWEL WILL BE COMPLETE ONCE MORE.
THAT TIME... KIKYO STOLE THE SHARD FROM ME...
DID SHE...
...IS THAT WHAT'S IN NARAKU'S HANDS...?!
WHAT HER THOUGHTS MAY BE...
...EVEN I DO NOT KNOW.
BUT THIS IS TRUE...

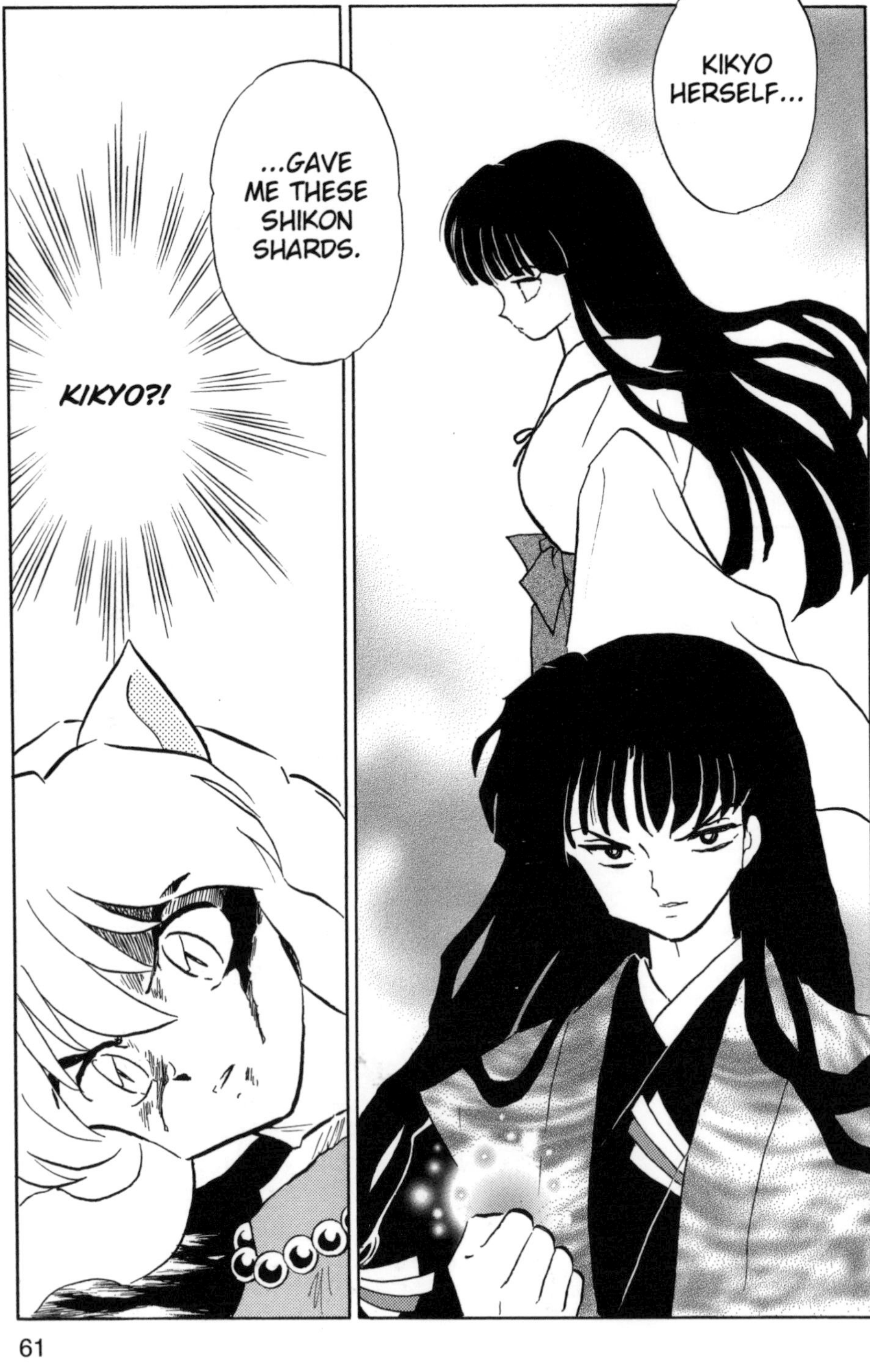
KIKYO HERSELF...
...GAVE ME THESE SHIKON SHARDS.
KIKYO?!

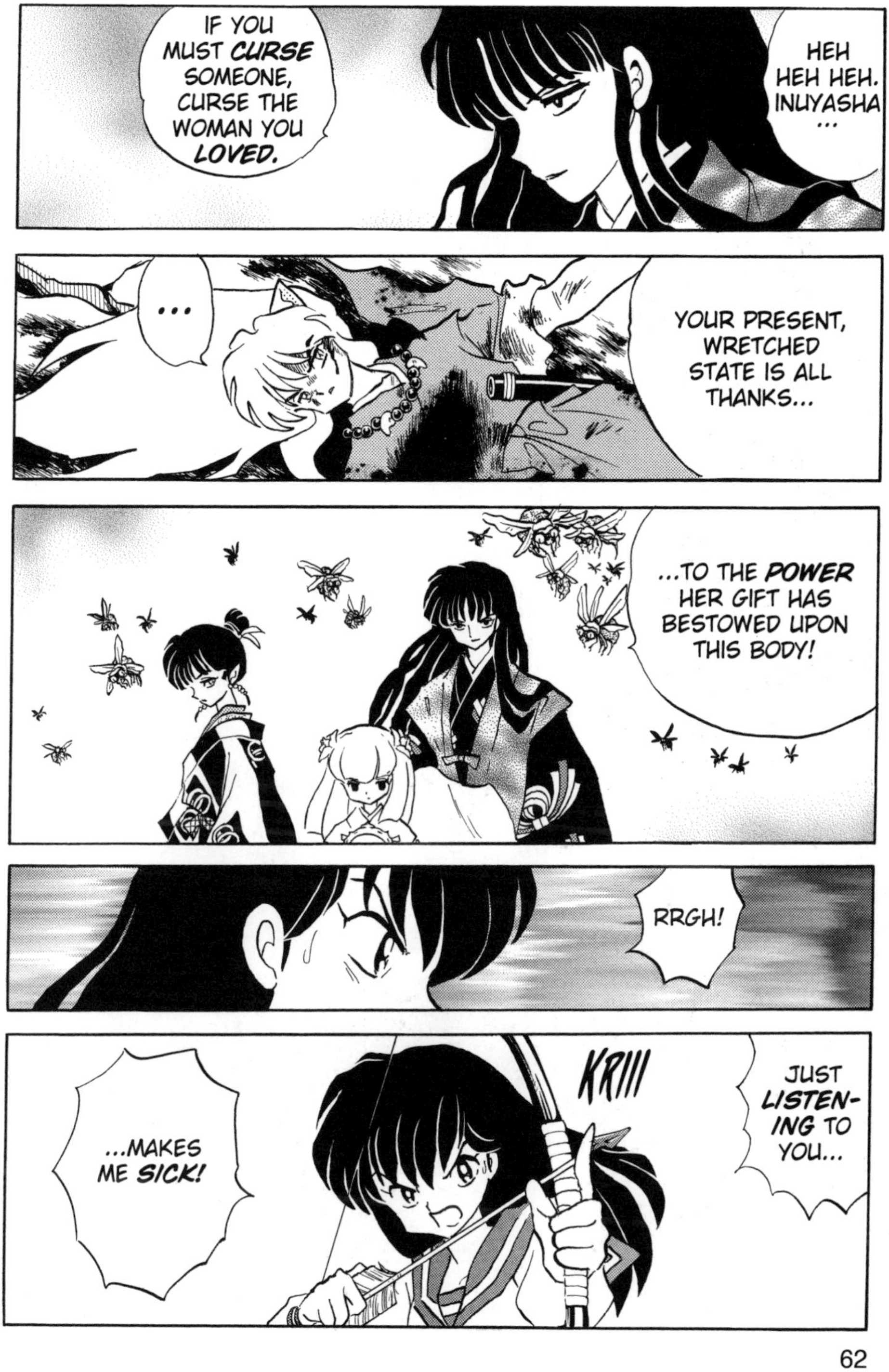
HEH HEH HEH. INUYASHA...
IF YOU MUST CURSE SOMEONE, CURSE THE WOMAN YOU LOVED.
YOUR PRESENT, WRETCHED STATE IS ALL THANKS...
...
...TO THE POWER HER GIFT HAS BESTOWED UPON THIS BODY!
RRGH!
JUST LISTENING TO YOU...
KRIII
...MAKES ME SICK!

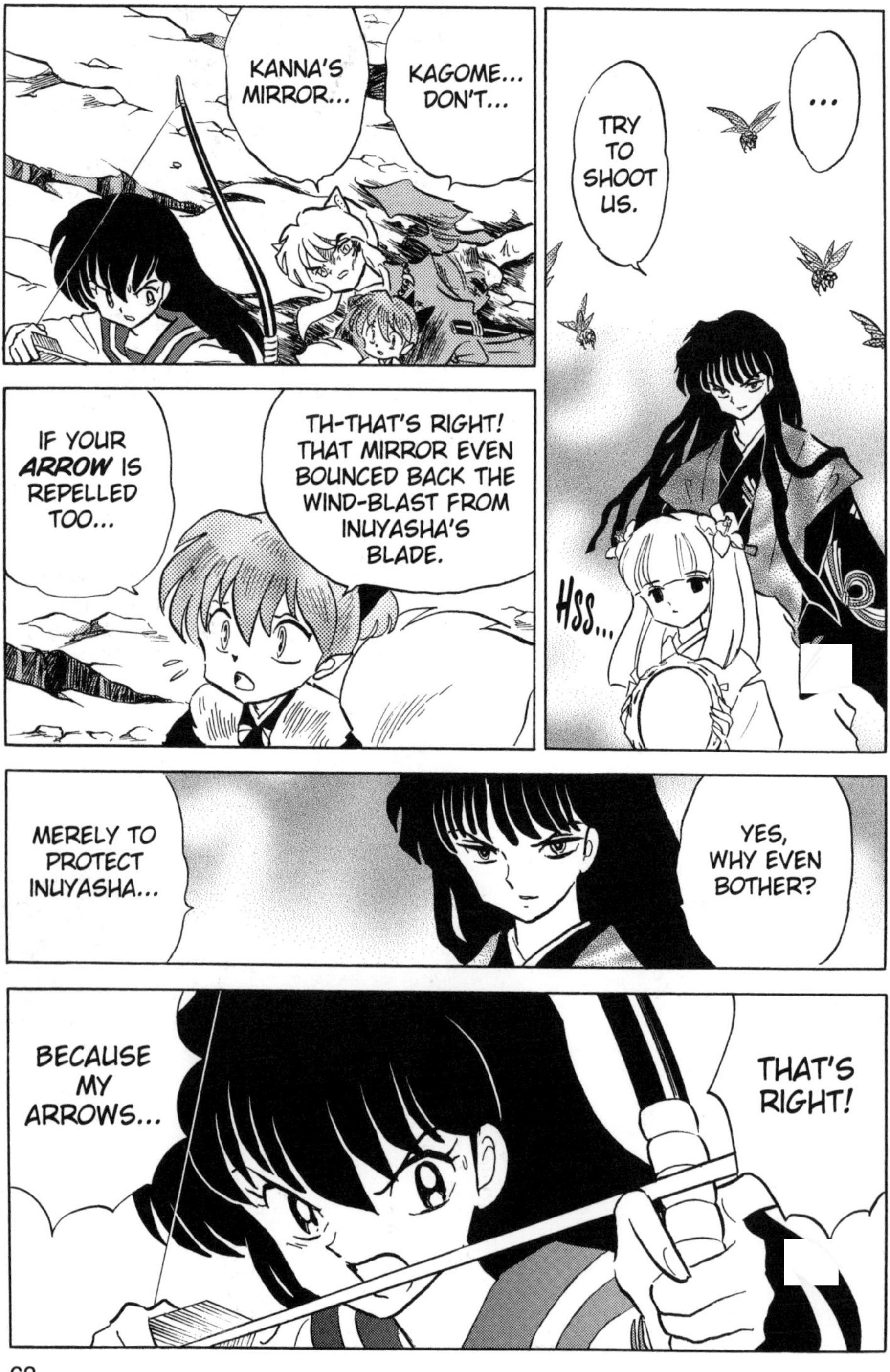
...
TRY TO SHOOT US.
HSS...
KAGOME... DON'T...
KANNA'S MIRROR...
TH-THAT'S RIGHT! THAT MIRROR EVEN BOUNCED BACK THE WIND-BLAST FROM INUYASHA'S BLADE.
IF YOUR *ARROW* IS REPELLED TOO...
YES, WHY EVEN BOTHER?
MERELY TO PROTECT INUYASHA...
THAT'S RIGHT!
BECAUSE MY ARROWS...

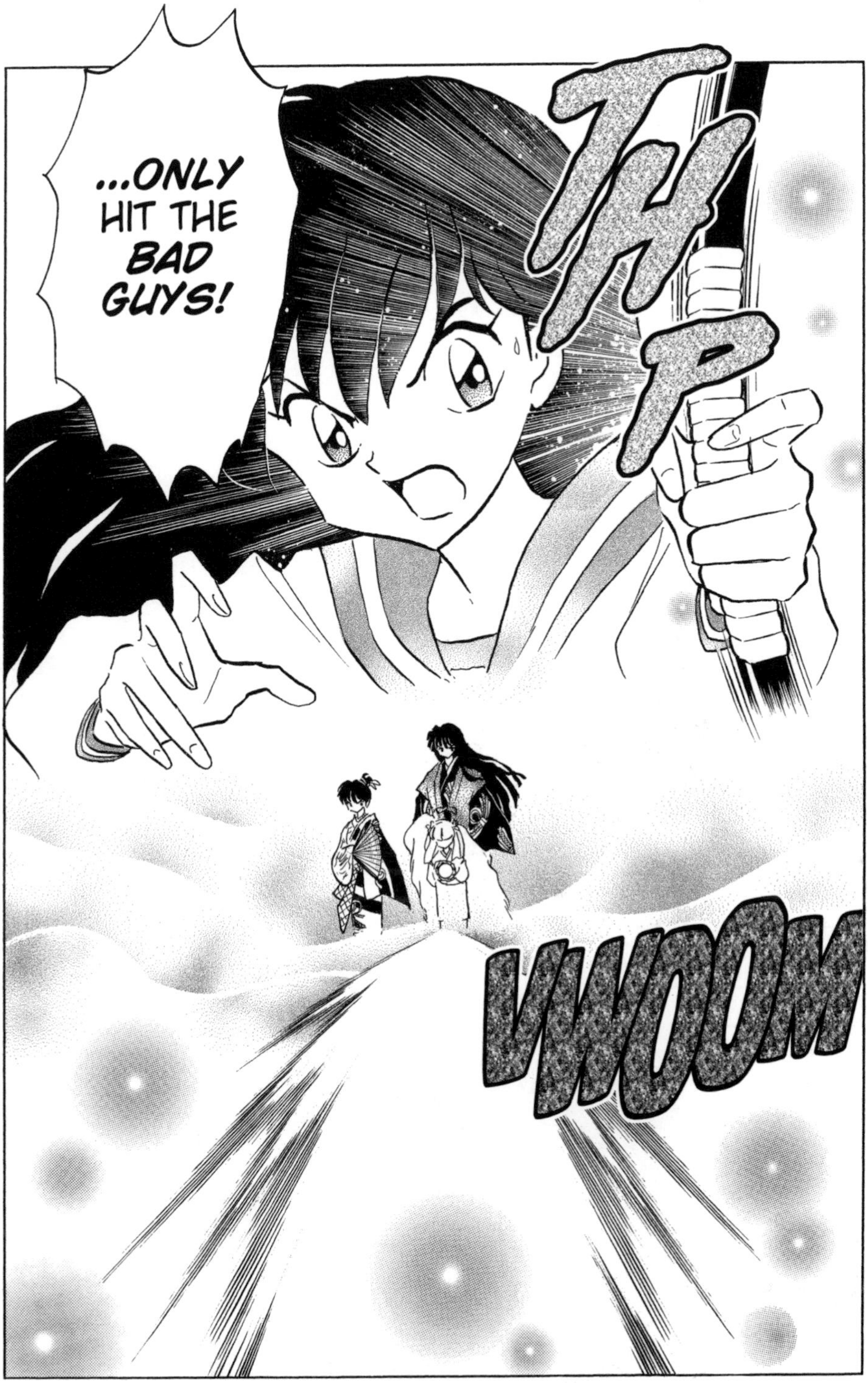
...ONLY HIT THE BAD GUYS!
THP
VWOOM

SCROLL FOUR
THE ARROW RELEASED

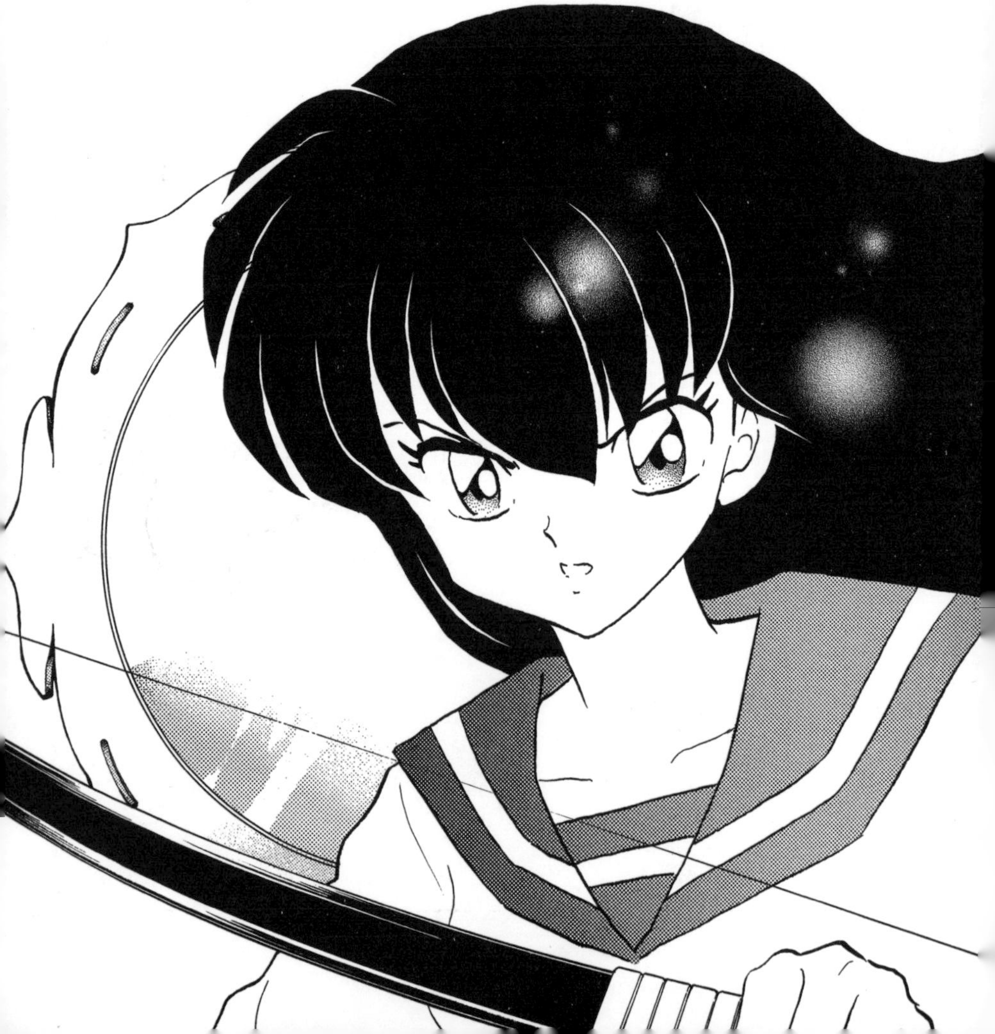

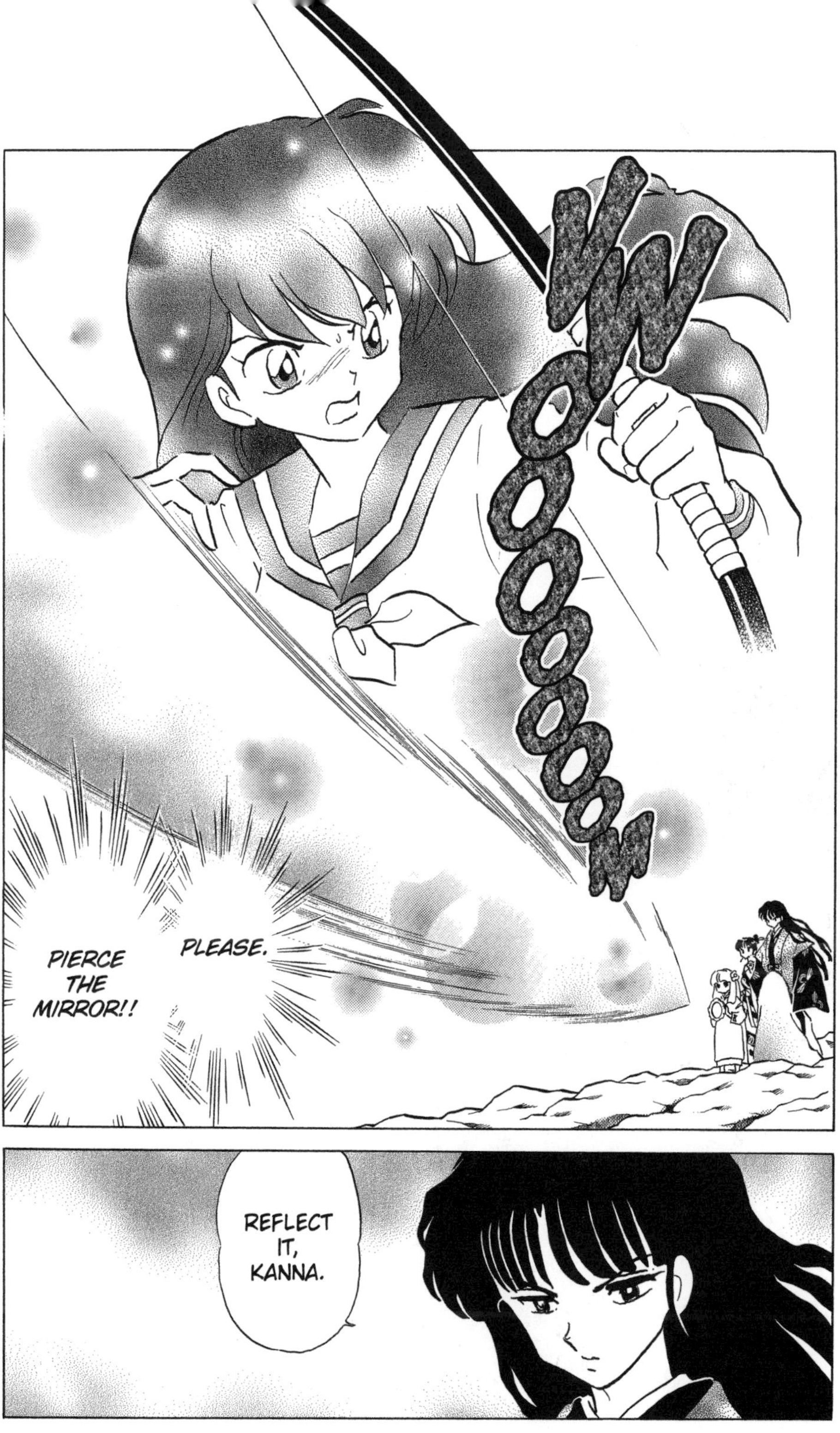
VWOOOOOOOOM
PLEASE.
PIERCE THE MIRROR!!
REFLECT IT, KANNA.

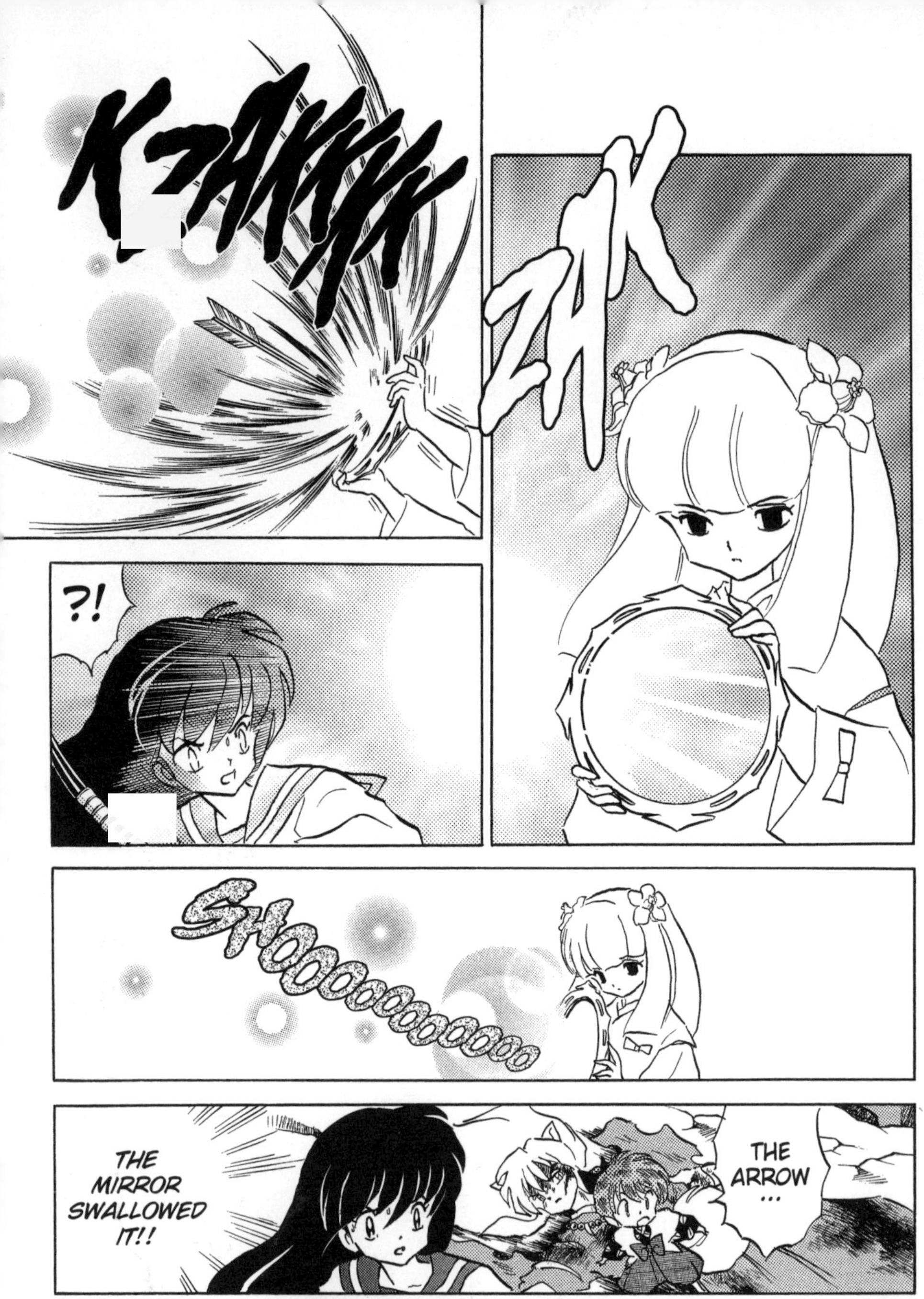
KRAKKKK
ZAK
?!
SHOOOOOOOOOOOOOO
THE ARROW ...
THE MIRROR SWALLOWED IT!!
...COULD NOT...

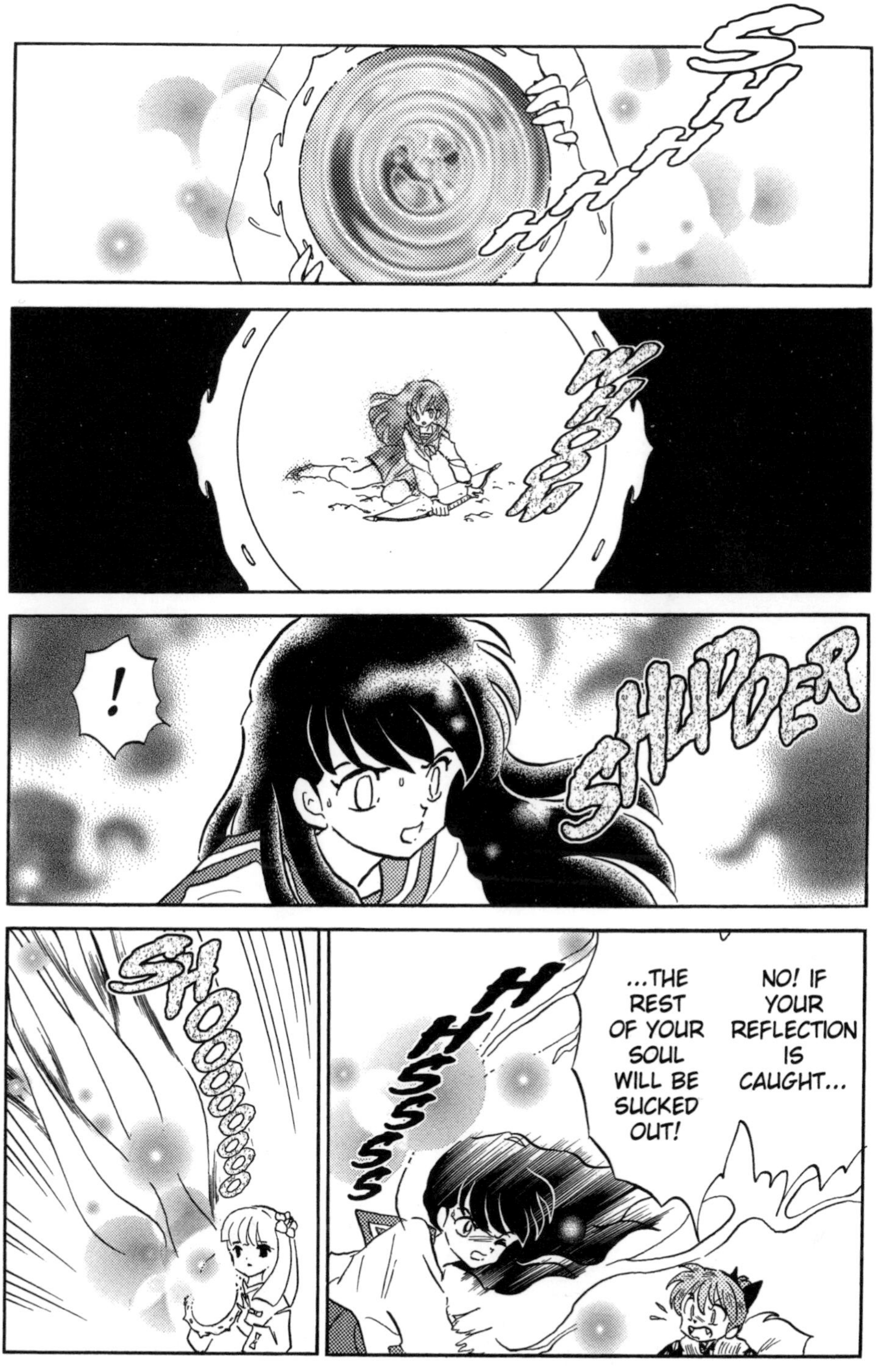
SHHHHH
WHOOSH
SHUDDER
!
NO! IF YOUR REFLECTION IS CAUGHT...
...THE REST OF YOUR SOUL WILL BE SUCKED OUT!
HHSSSSSS
SHOOOOOOOOO

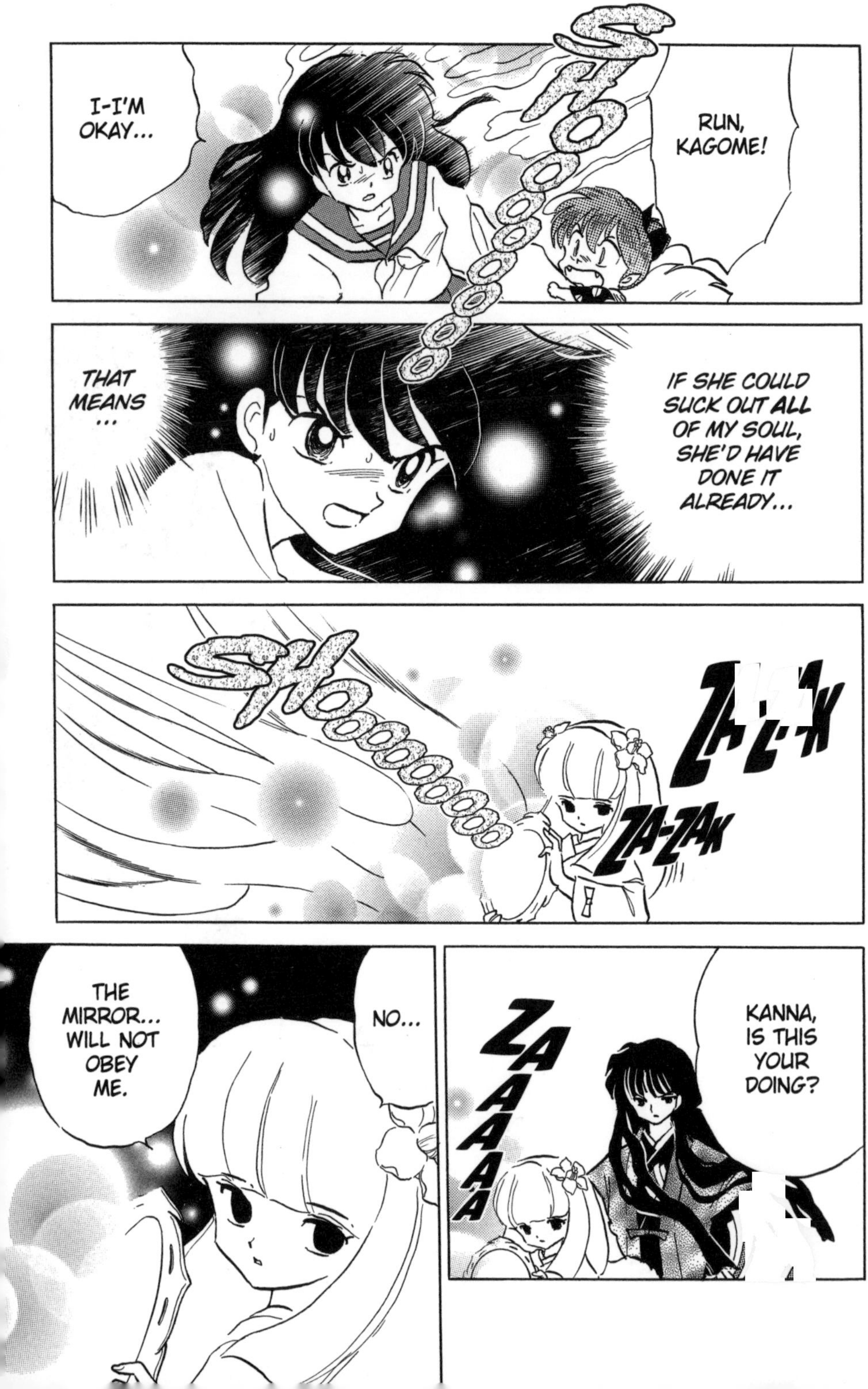
RUN, KAGOME!
SHOOOOOOOOO
I-I'M OKAY...
IF SHE COULD SUCK OUT **ALL** OF MY SOUL, SHE'D HAVE DONE IT ALREADY...
THAT MEANS ...
ZA-ZAK
SHOOOOOOOOOO
KANNA, IS THIS YOUR DOING?
ZAAAAAA
NO...
THE MIRROR... WILL NOT OBEY ME.

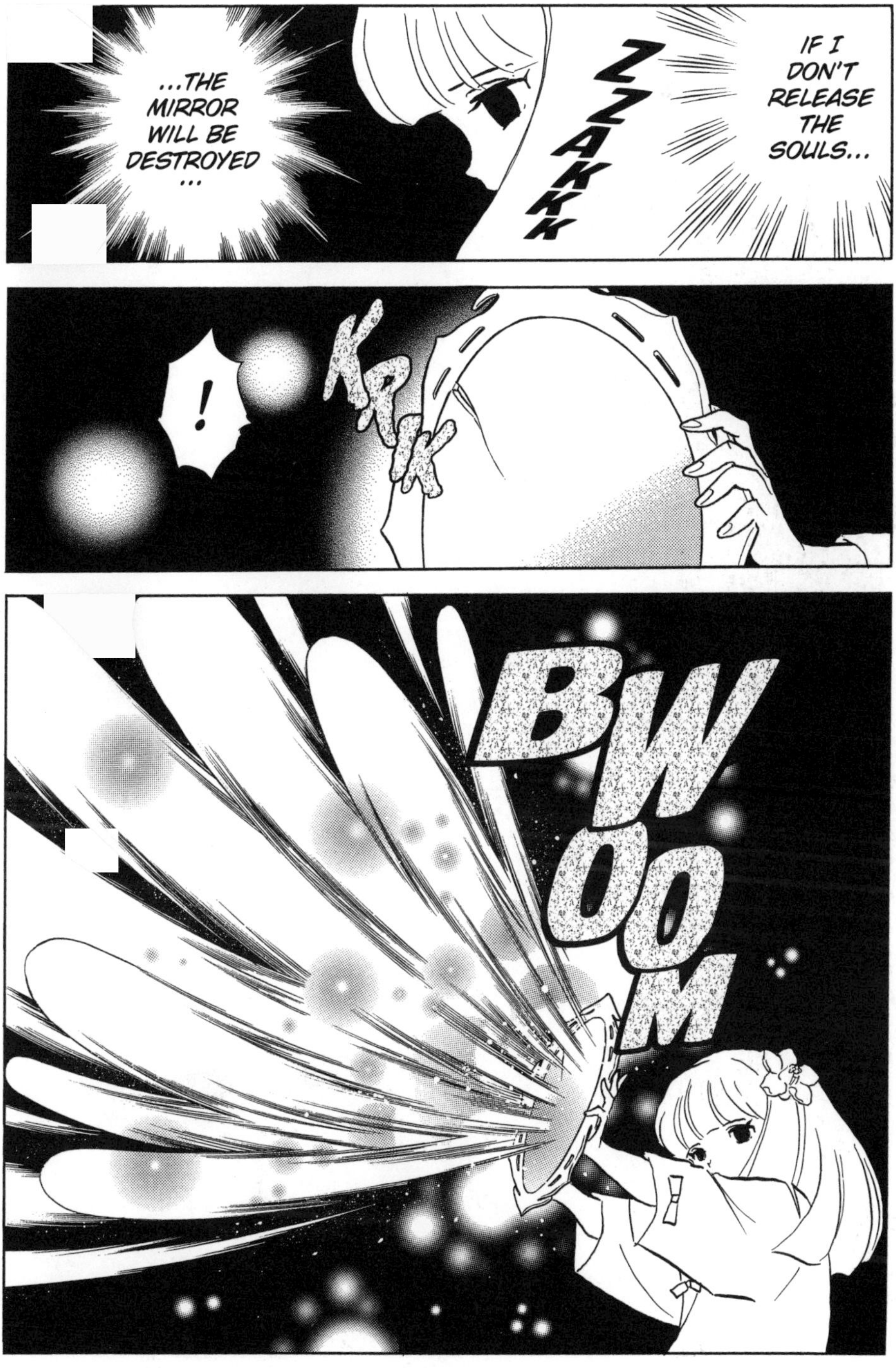
IF I DON'T RELEASE THE SOULS...
ZZAKKK
...THE MIRROR WILL BE DESTROYED ...
KRIK
!
BWOOM

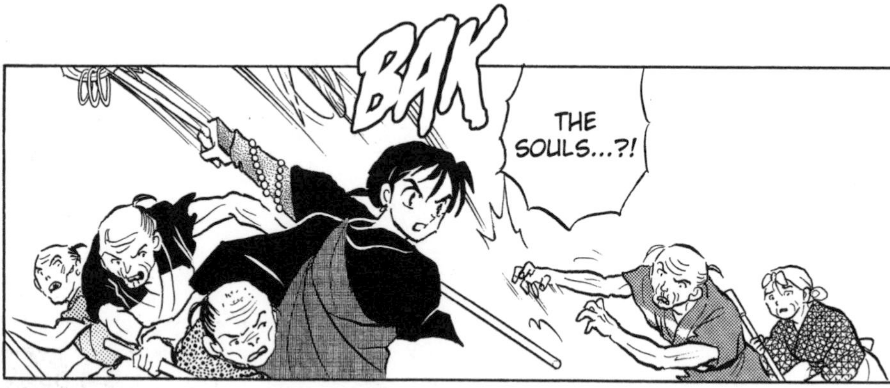
THE SOULS...?!
BAK
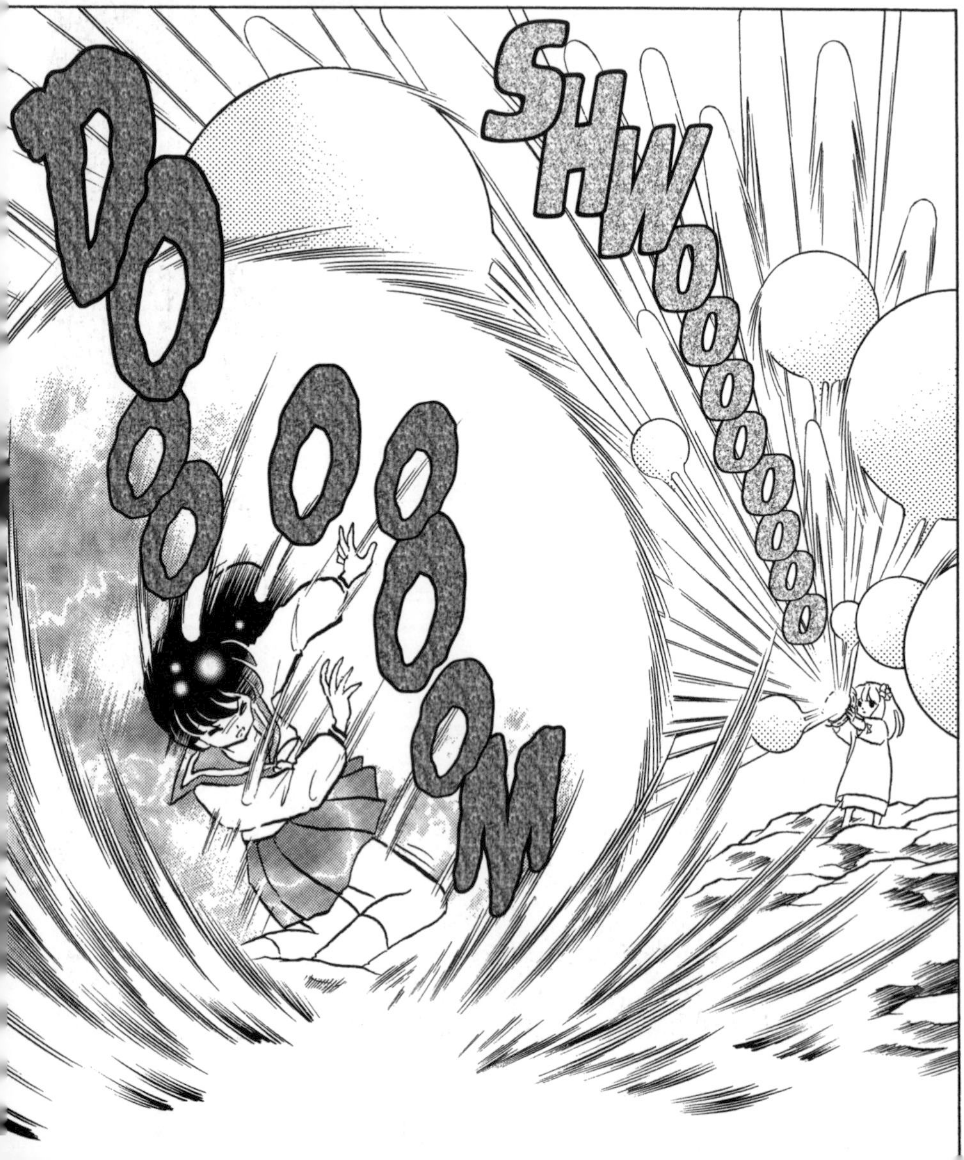
SHWOOOOOOOOO
DOOOOOOOOM

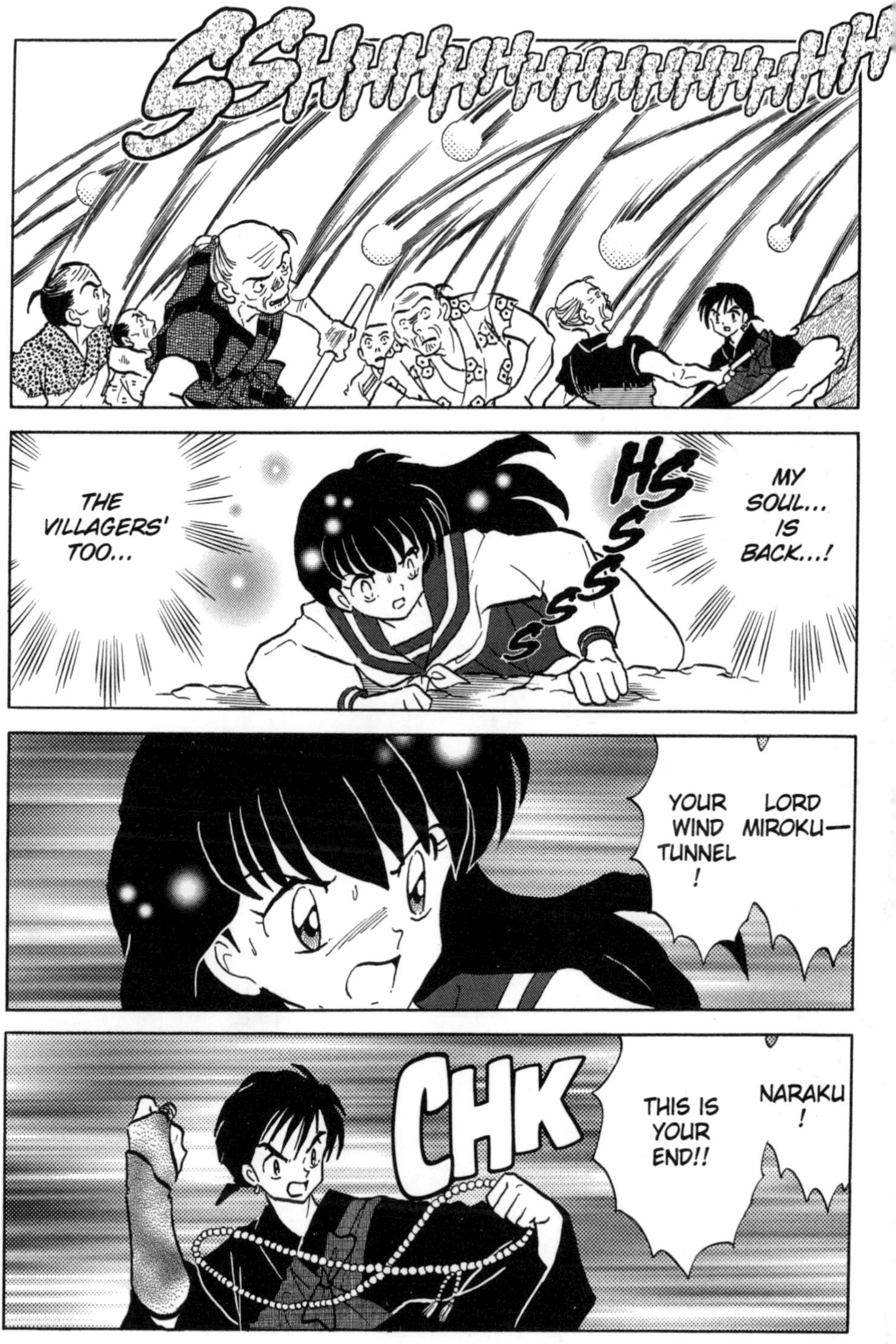
SSHHHHHHHHHHHHHH
MY SOUL... IS BACK...!
HSSSSSS
THE VILLAGERS' TOO...
LORD MIROKU—
YOUR WIND TUNNEL!
NARAKU!
THIS IS YOUR END!!
CHK

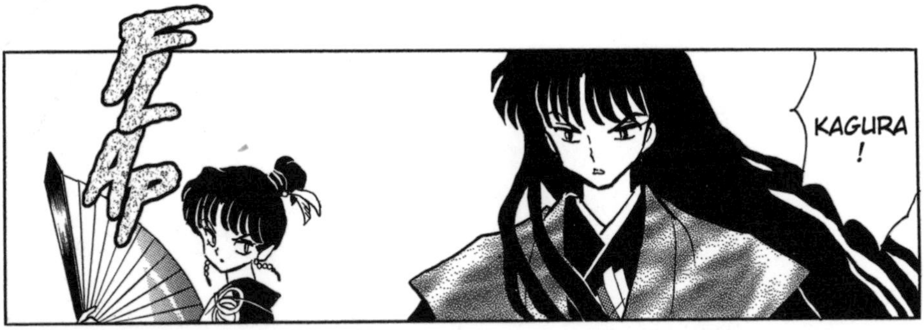
KAGURA!
FAP

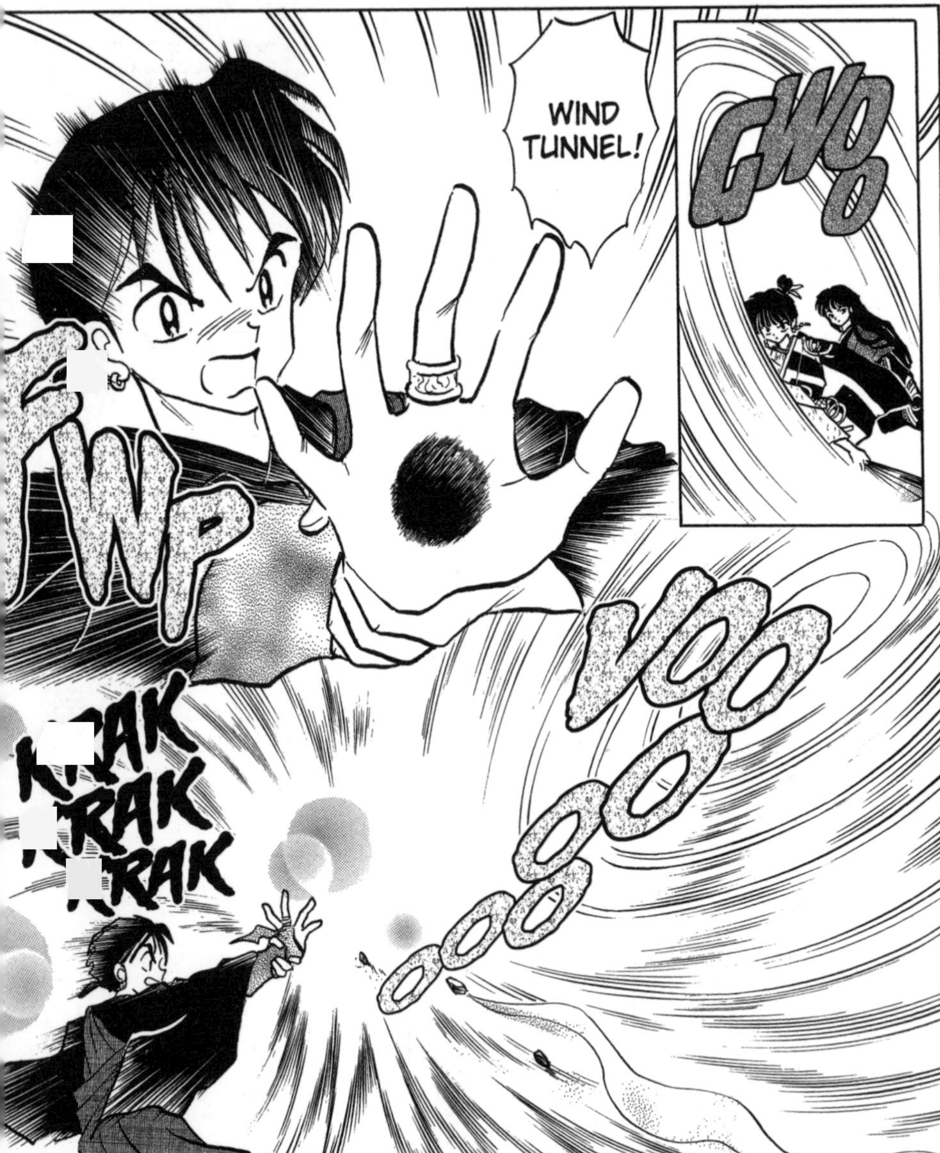
WIND TUNNEL!
GWOO
VOOOOOOO
WP
RAK
RAK
RAK

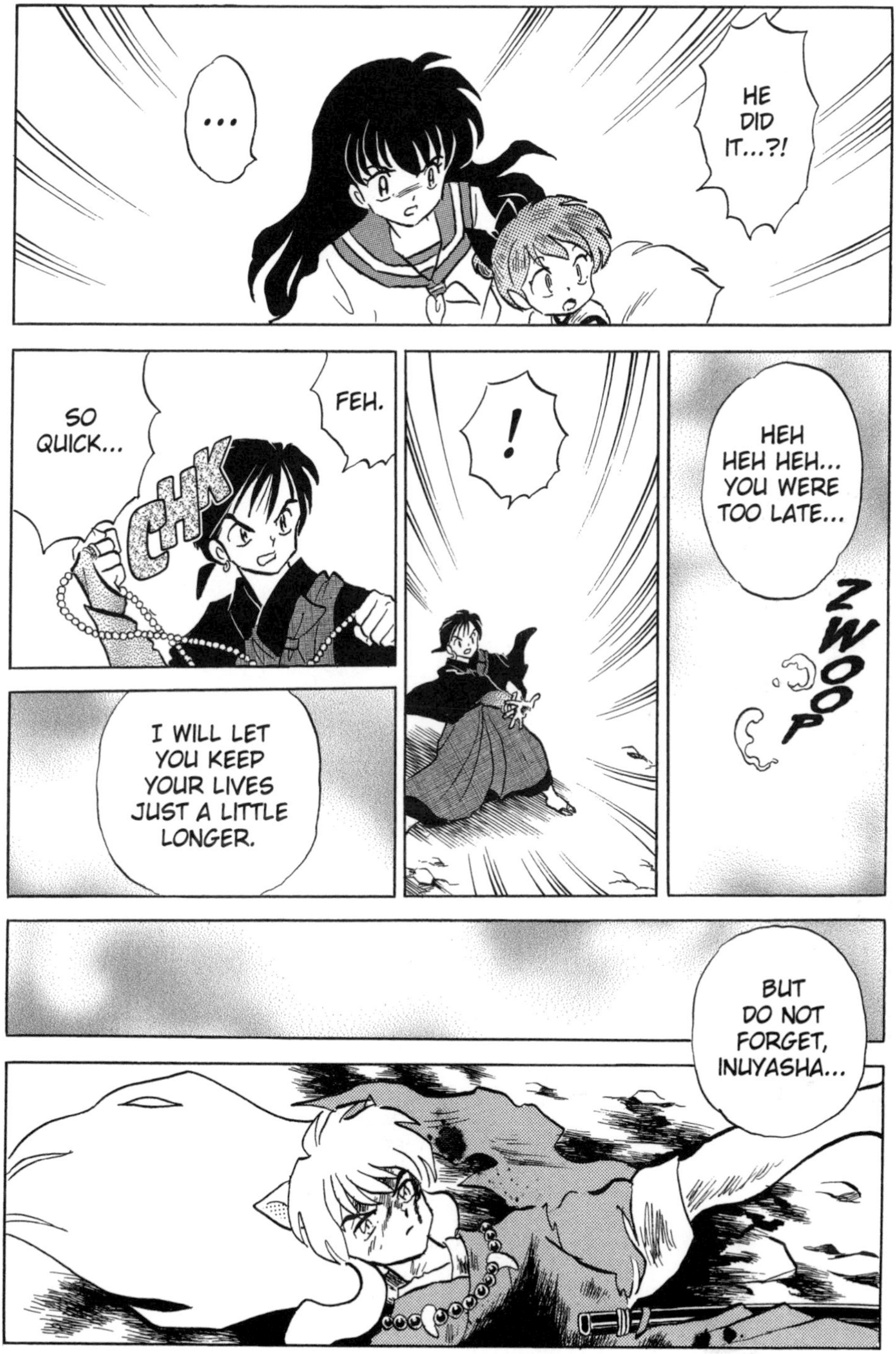
HE DID IT...?!
...
HEH HEH HEH... YOU WERE TOO LATE...
ZWOOP
!
FEH.
SO QUICK...
CHK
I WILL LET YOU KEEP YOUR LIVES JUST A LITTLE LONGER.
BUT DO NOT FORGET, INUYASHA...

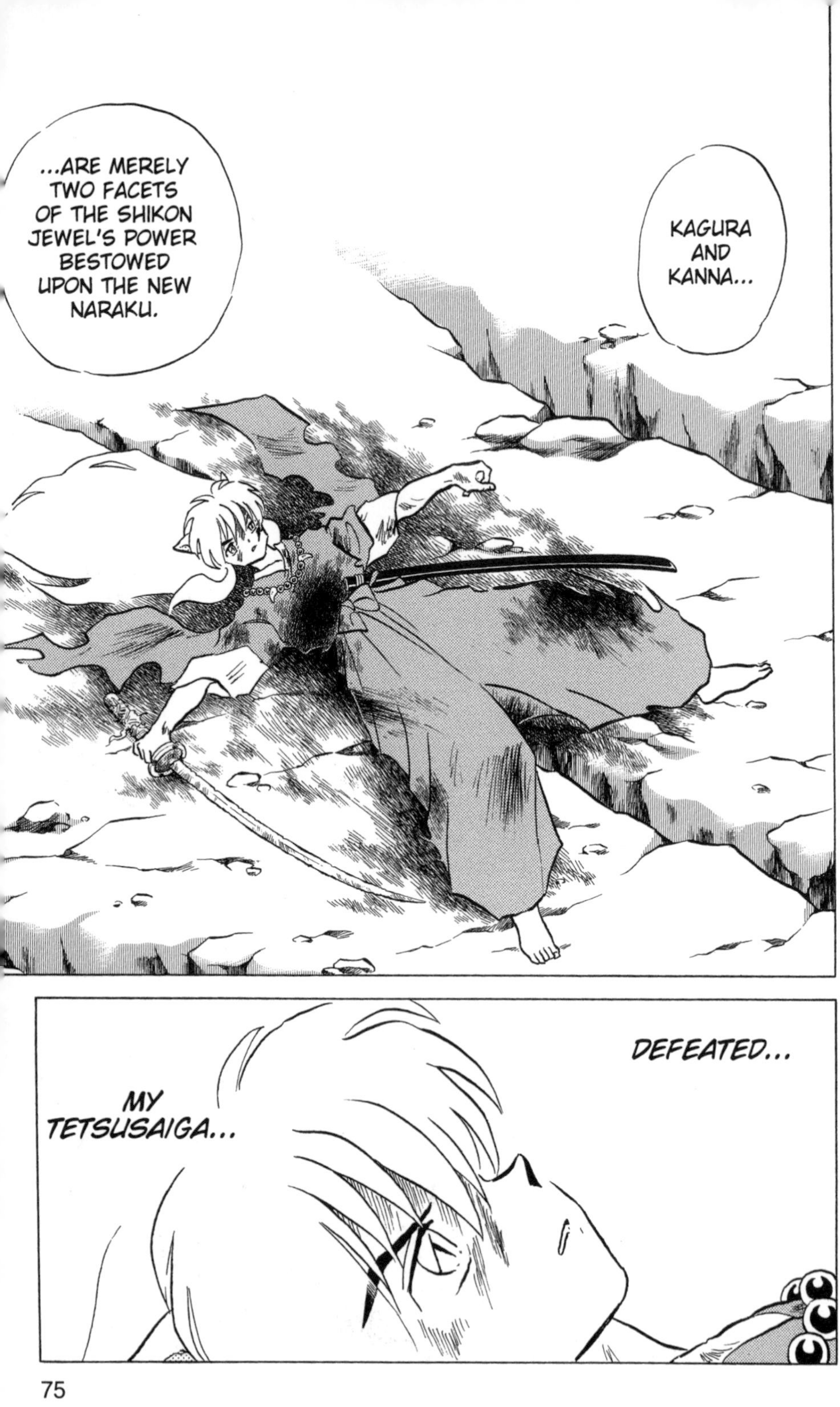
KAGURA AND KANNA...
...ARE MERELY TWO FACETS OF THE SHIKON JEWEL'S POWER BESTOWED UPON THE NEW NARAKU.
DEFEATED...
MY TETSUSAIGA...

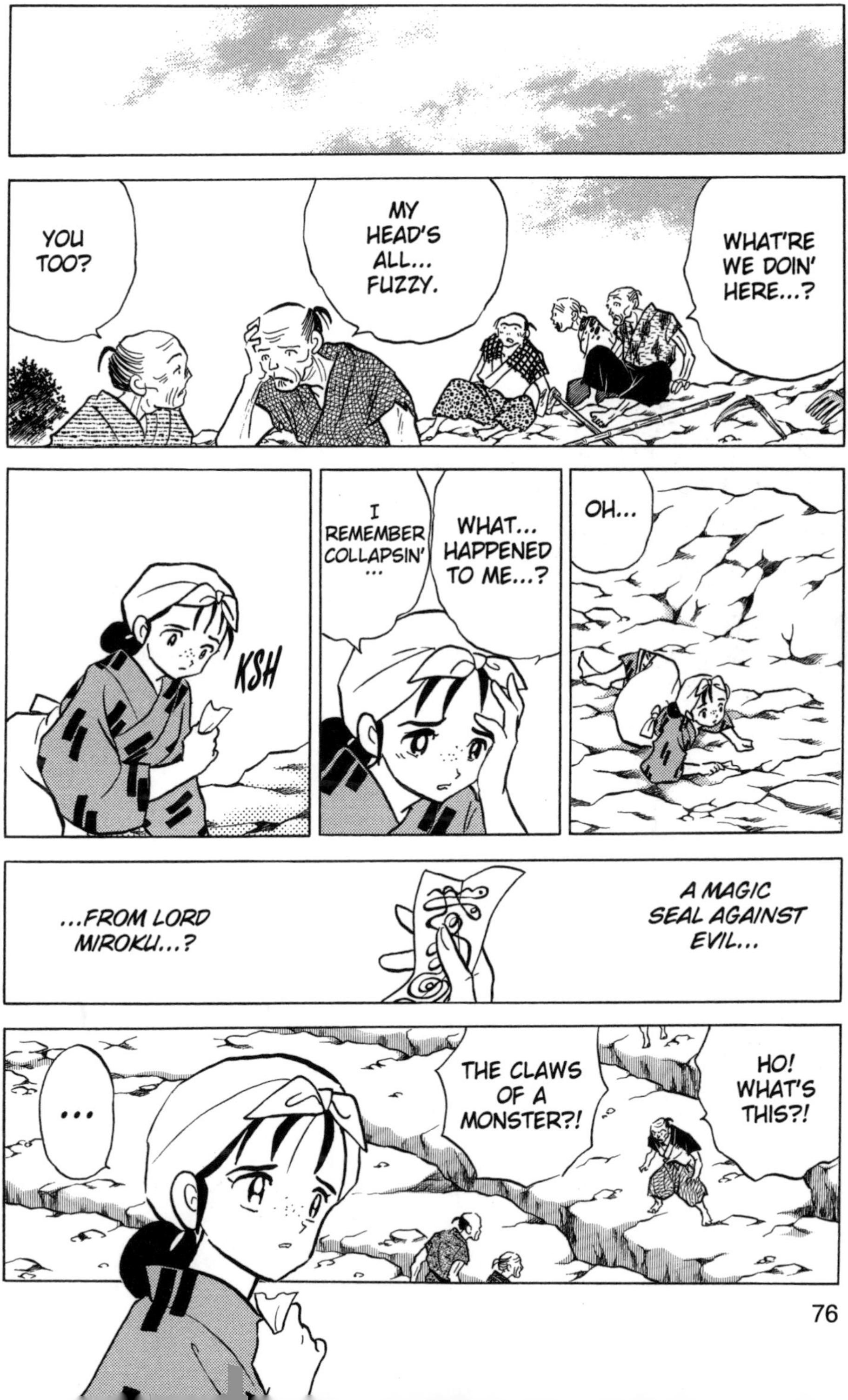

WHAT'RE WE DOIN' HERE...?
MY HEAD'S ALL... FUZZY.
YOU TOO?
OH...
WHAT... HAPPENED TO ME...?
I REMEMBER COLLAPSIN'...
KSH
A MAGIC SEAL AGAINST EVIL...
...FROM LORD MIROKU...?
HO! WHAT'S THIS?!
THE CLAWS OF A MONSTER?!
...

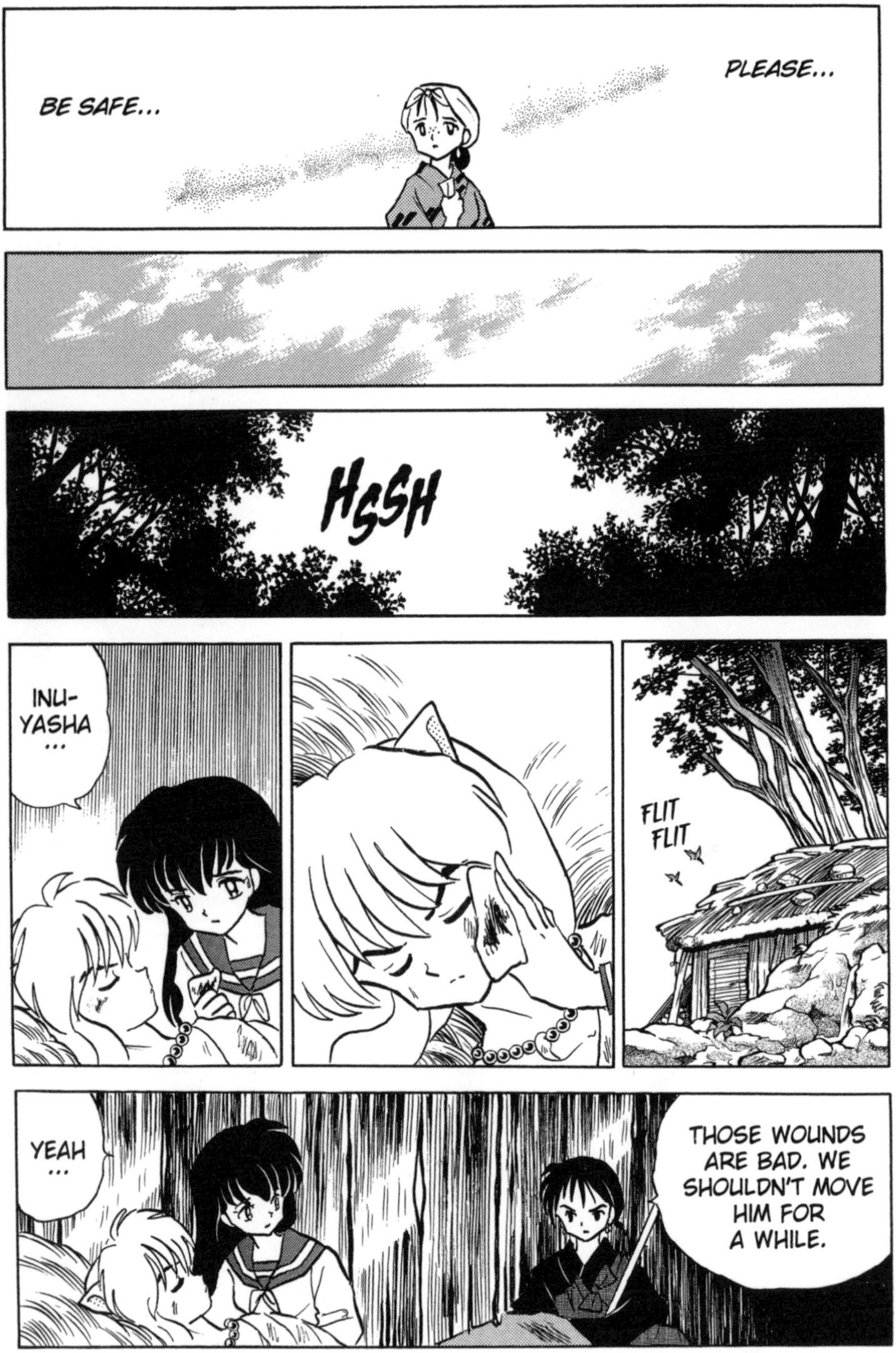
PLEASE...
BE SAFE...
HSSH
FLIT FLIT
INU-YASHA...
THOSE WOUNDS ARE BAD. WE SHOULDN'T MOVE HIM FOR A WHILE.
YEAH...

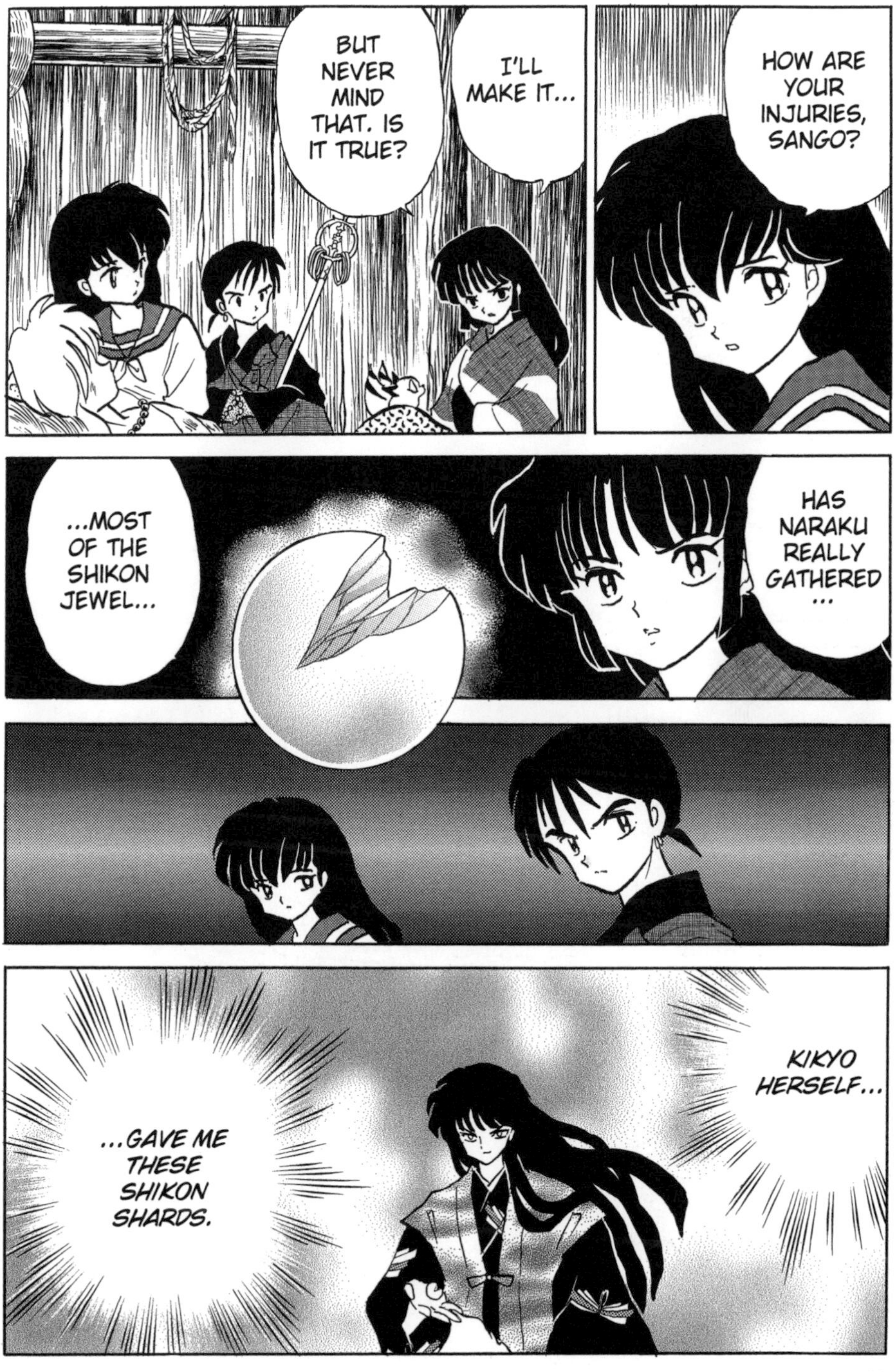
HOW ARE YOUR INJURIES, SANGO?
I'LL MAKE IT...
BUT NEVER MIND THAT. IS IT TRUE?
HAS NARAKU REALLY GATHERED...
...MOST OF THE SHIKON JEWEL...
KIKYO HERSELF...
...GAVE ME THESE SHIKON SHARDS.

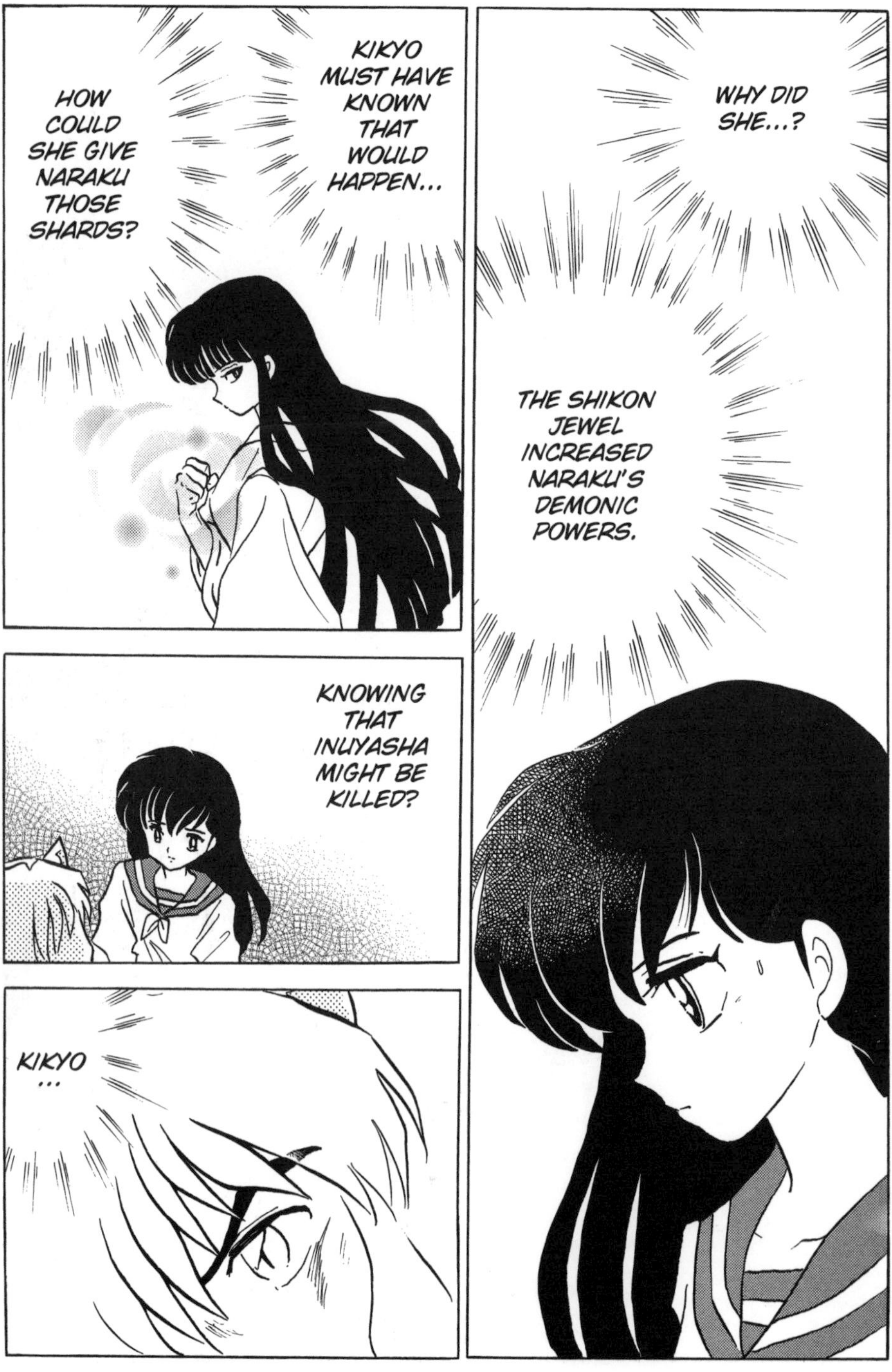
WHY DID SHE...?
THE SHIKON JEWEL INCREASED NARAKU'S DEMONIC POWERS.
KIKYO MUST HAVE KNOWN THAT WOULD HAPPEN...
HOW COULD SHE GIVE NARAKU THOSE SHARDS?
KNOWING THAT INUYASHA MIGHT BE KILLED?
KIKYO ...

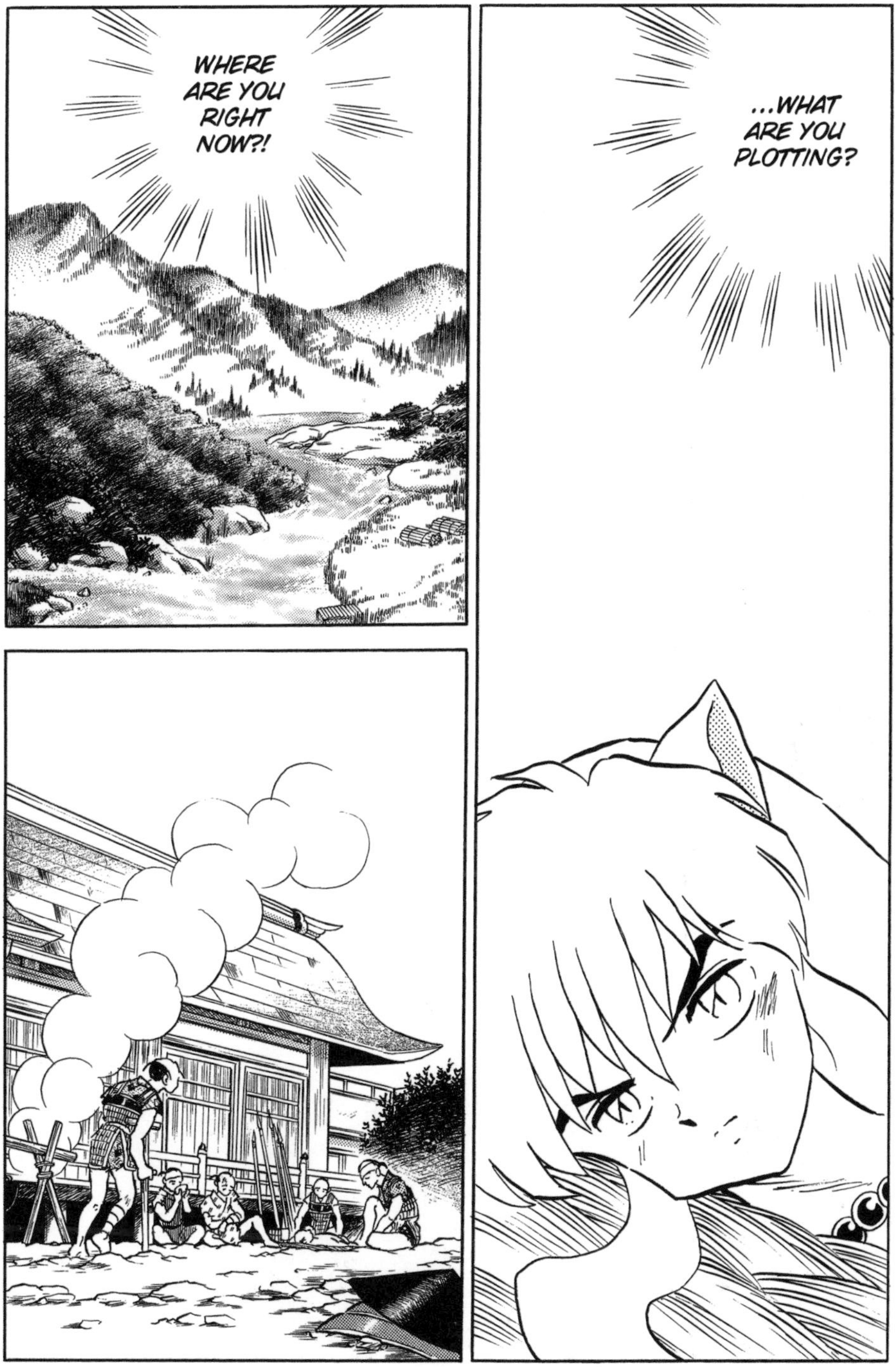
...WHAT ARE YOU PLOTTING?
WHERE ARE YOU RIGHT NOW?!

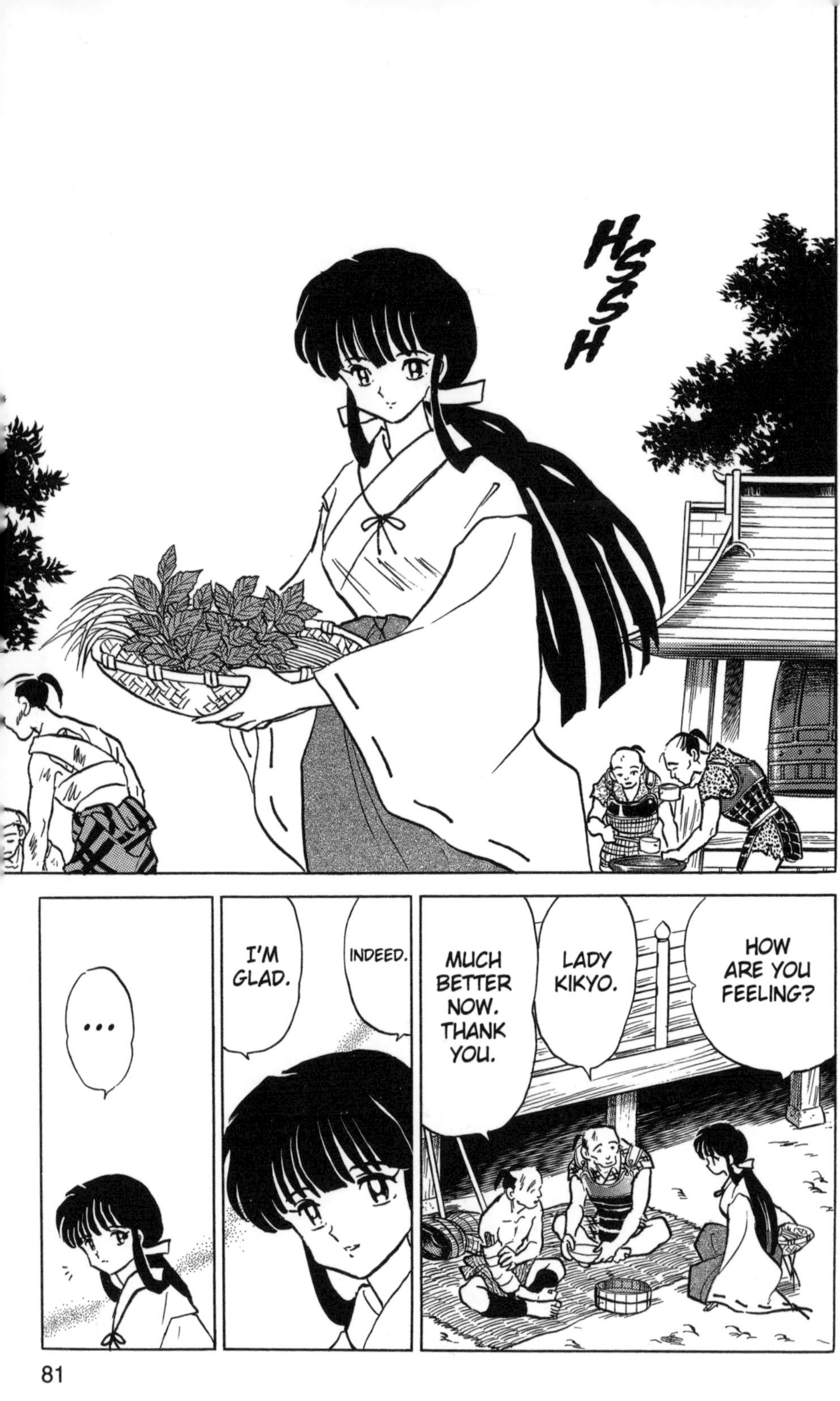
HSSH
HOW ARE YOU FEELING?
LADY KIKYO.
MUCH BETTER NOW. THANK YOU.
INDEED.
I'M GLAD.
...

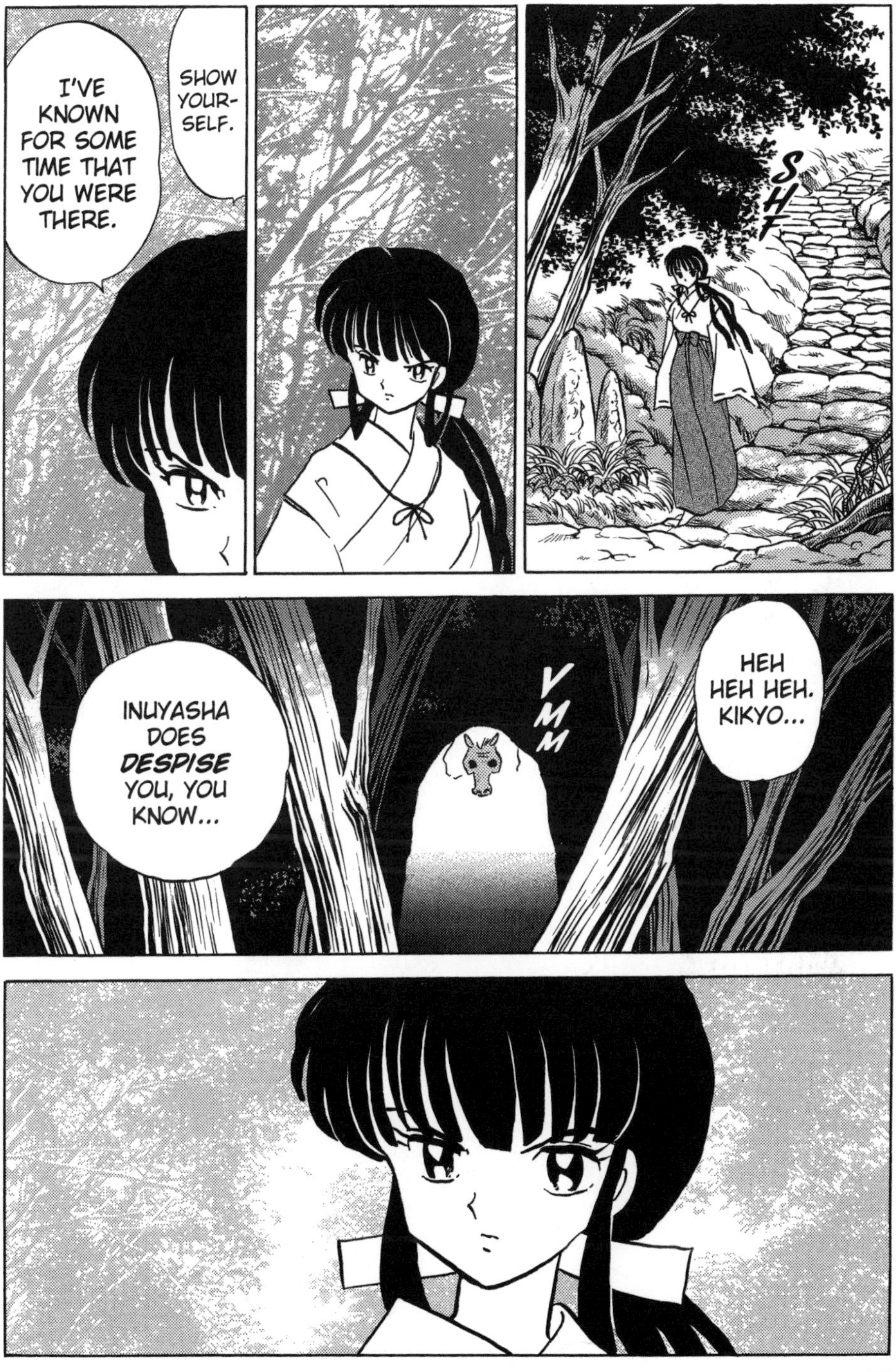
SHF
SHOW YOURSELF.
I'VE KNOWN FOR SOME TIME THAT YOU WERE THERE.
HEH HEH HEH. KIKYO...
VMM
INUYASHA DOES DESPISE YOU, YOU KNOW...

SCROLL FIVE
KIKYO'S PLAN

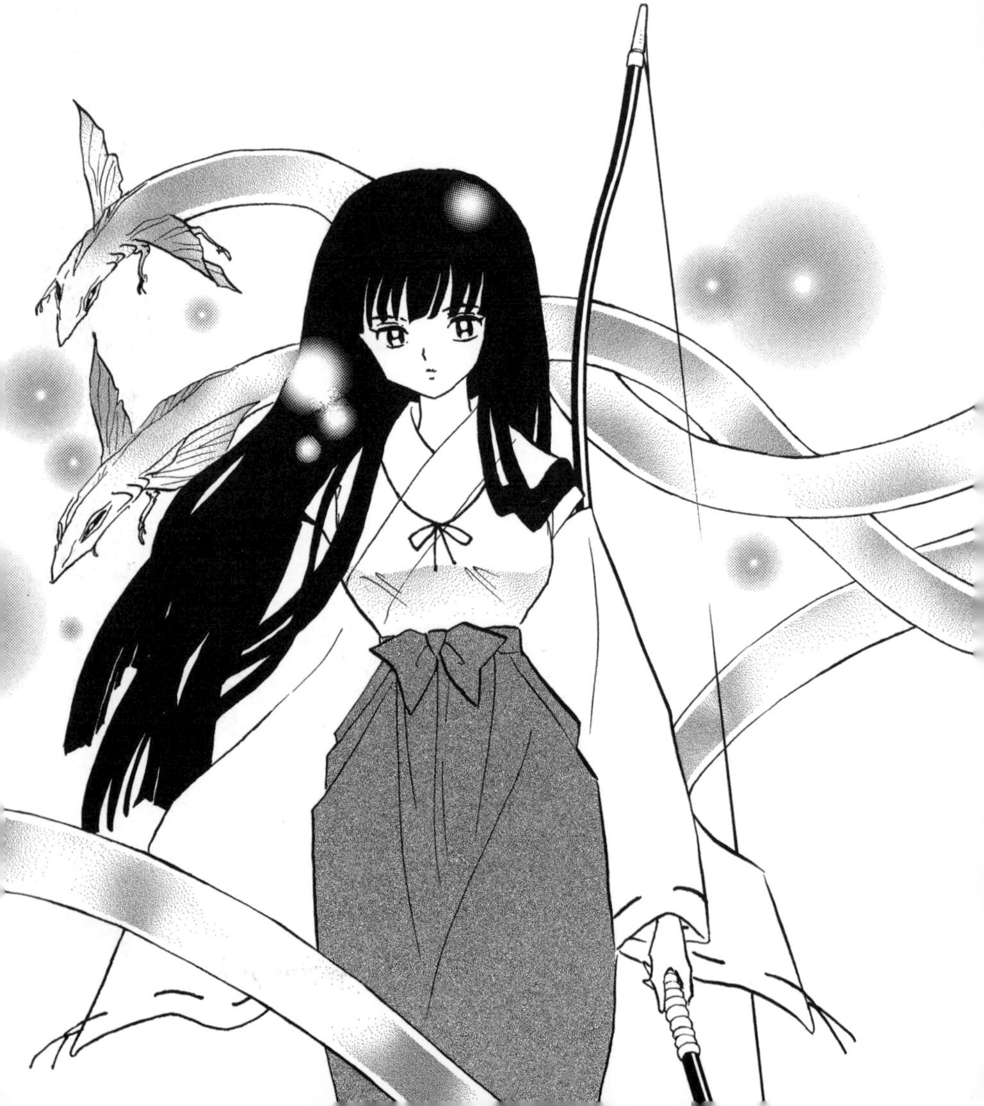

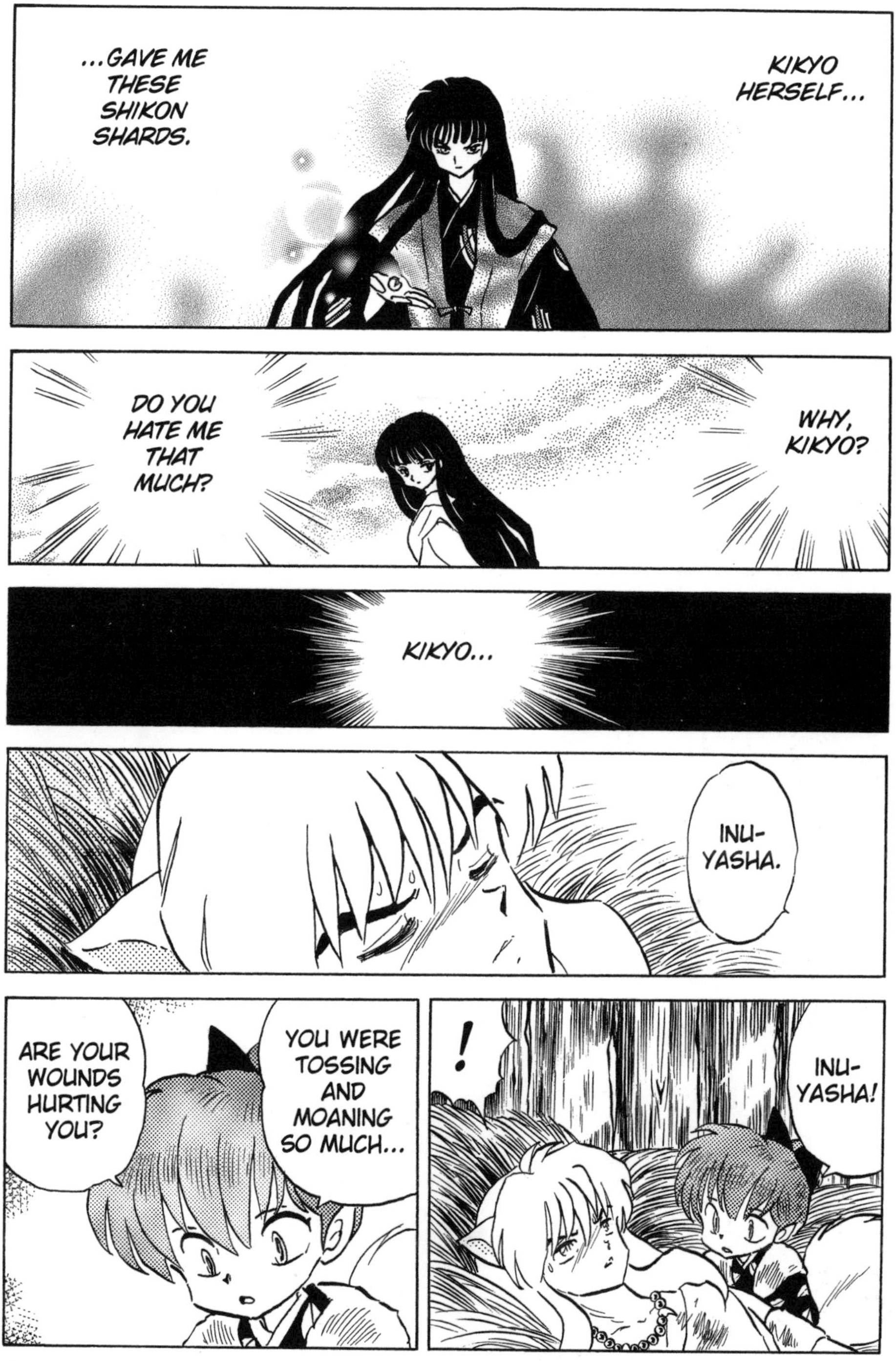
KIKYO HERSELF...
...GAVE ME THESE SHIKON SHARDS.
WHY, KIKYO?
DO YOU HATE ME THAT MUCH?
KIKYO...
INU-YASHA.
INU-YASHA!
!
YOU WERE TOSSING AND MOANING SO MUCH...
ARE YOUR WOUNDS HURTING YOU?

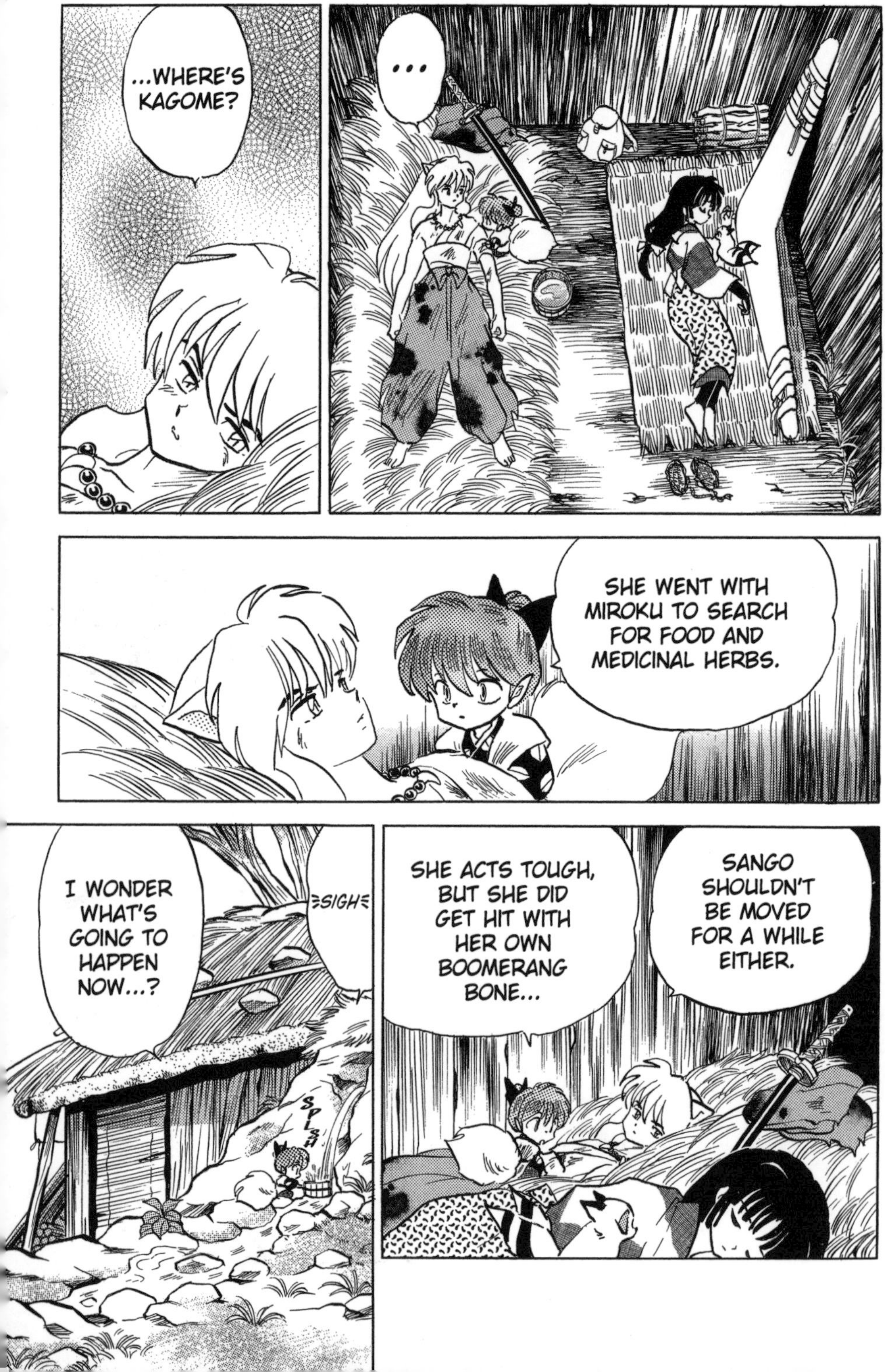
...
...WHERE'S KAGOME?
SHE WENT WITH MIROKU TO SEARCH FOR FOOD AND MEDICINAL HERBS.
SANGO SHOULDN'T BE MOVED FOR A WHILE EITHER.
SHE ACTS TOUGH, BUT SHE DID GET HIT WITH HER OWN BOOMERANG BONE...
SIGH
I WONDER WHAT'S GOING TO HAPPEN NOW...?
SPLSH

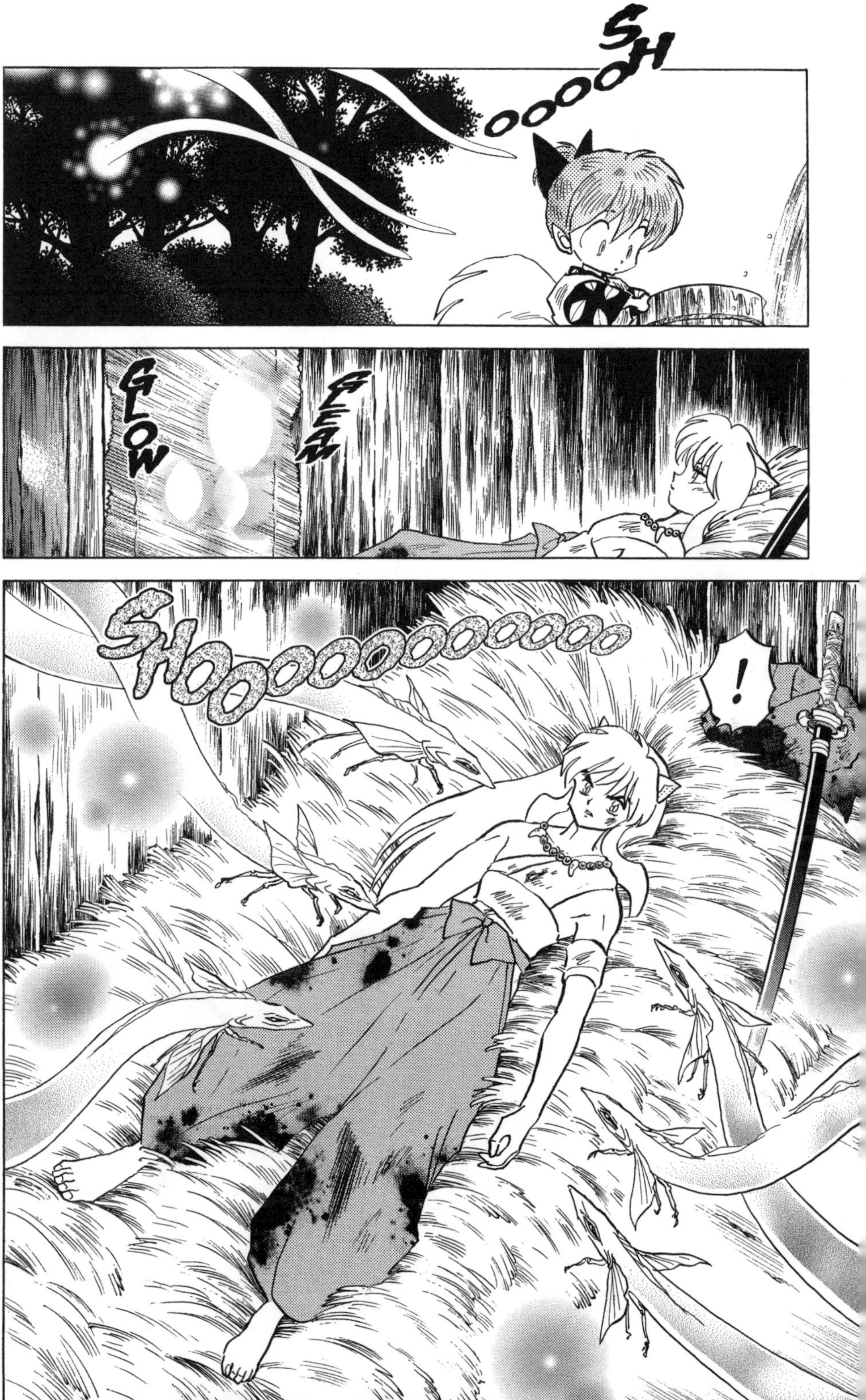
SHOOOOOH
GLEAM
GLOW
SHOOOOOOOOOOOOOO
!

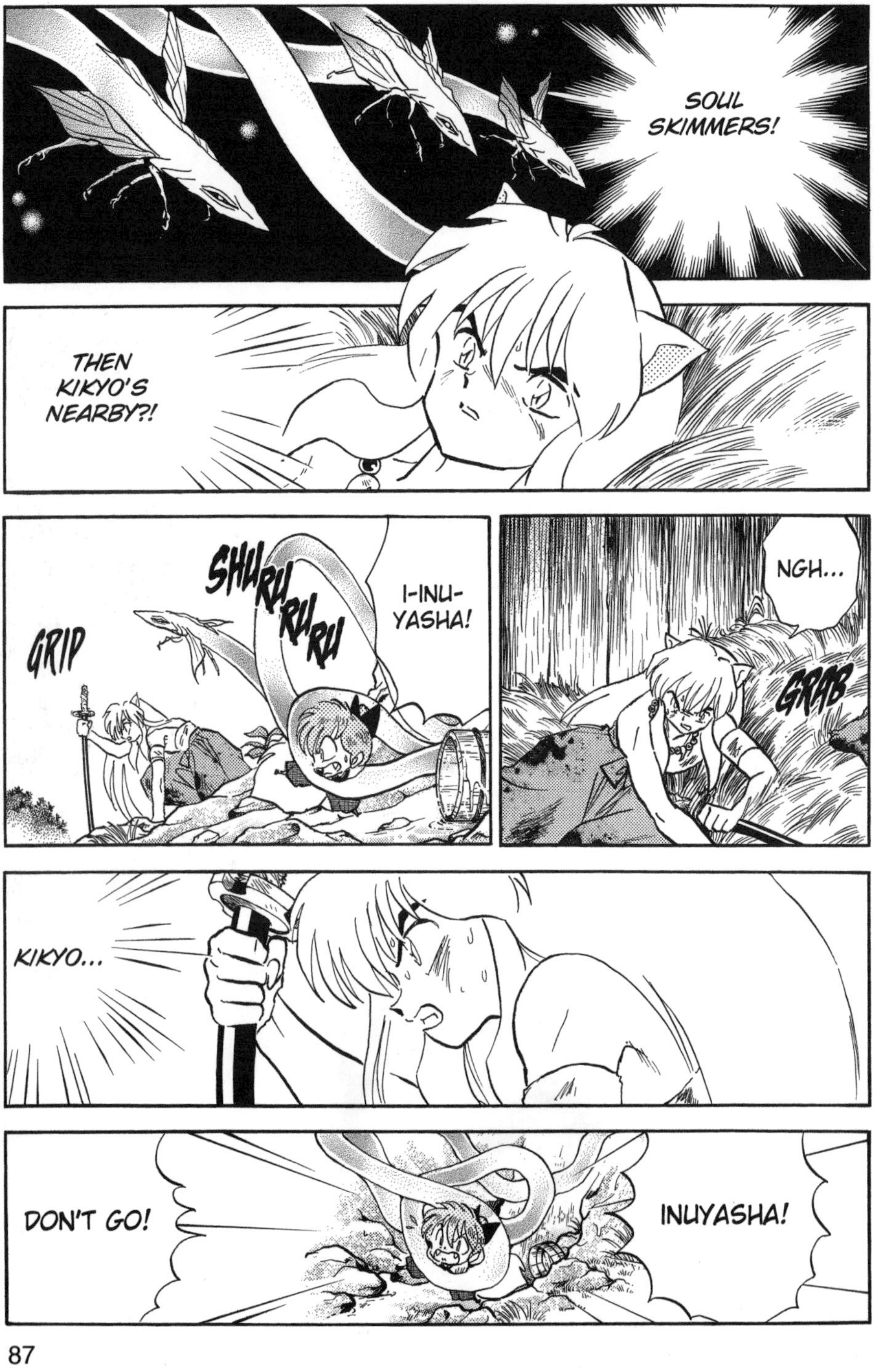
SOUL SKIMMERS!
THEN KIKYO'S NEARBY?!
NGH...
GRAB
I-INU-YASHA!
SHURURURU
GRIP
KIKYO...
INUYASHA!
DON'T GO!

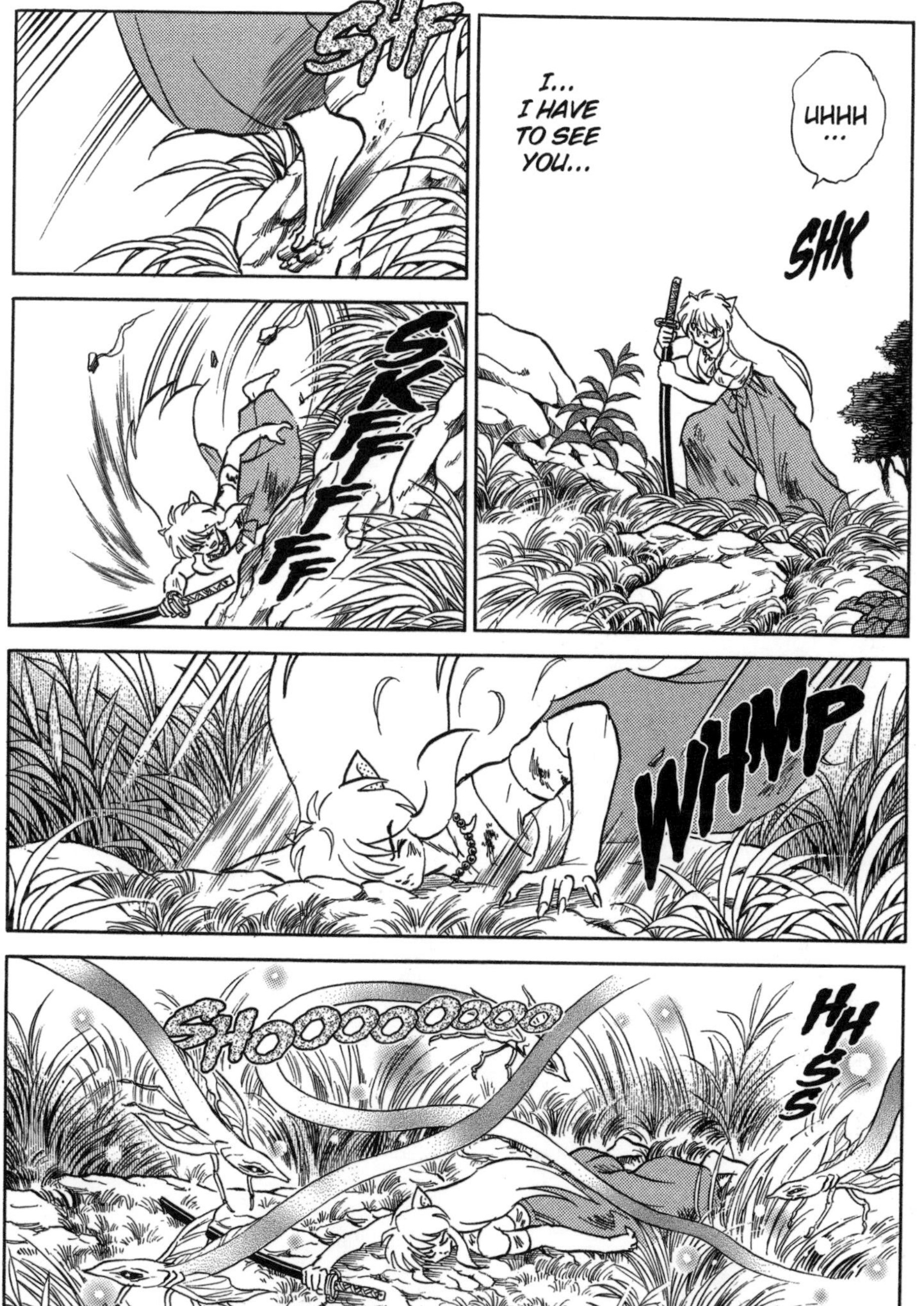
UHHH ...
I... I HAVE TO SEE YOU...
SHK
SHF
SKFFFFF
WHMP
HHISSS
SHOOOOOOOO

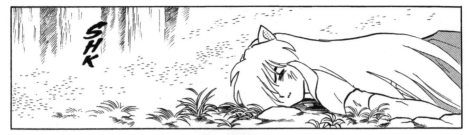

SHK

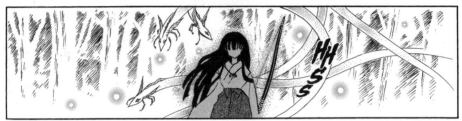

HHSS

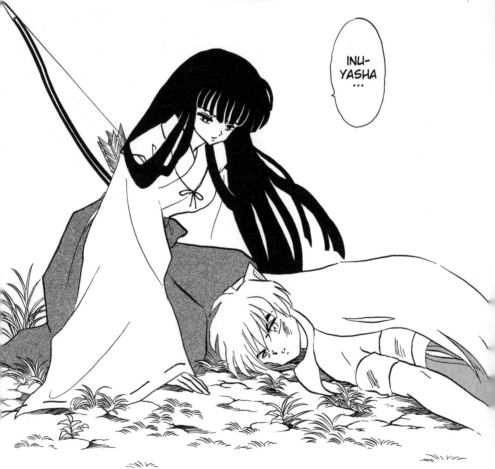

INU-
YASHA
...

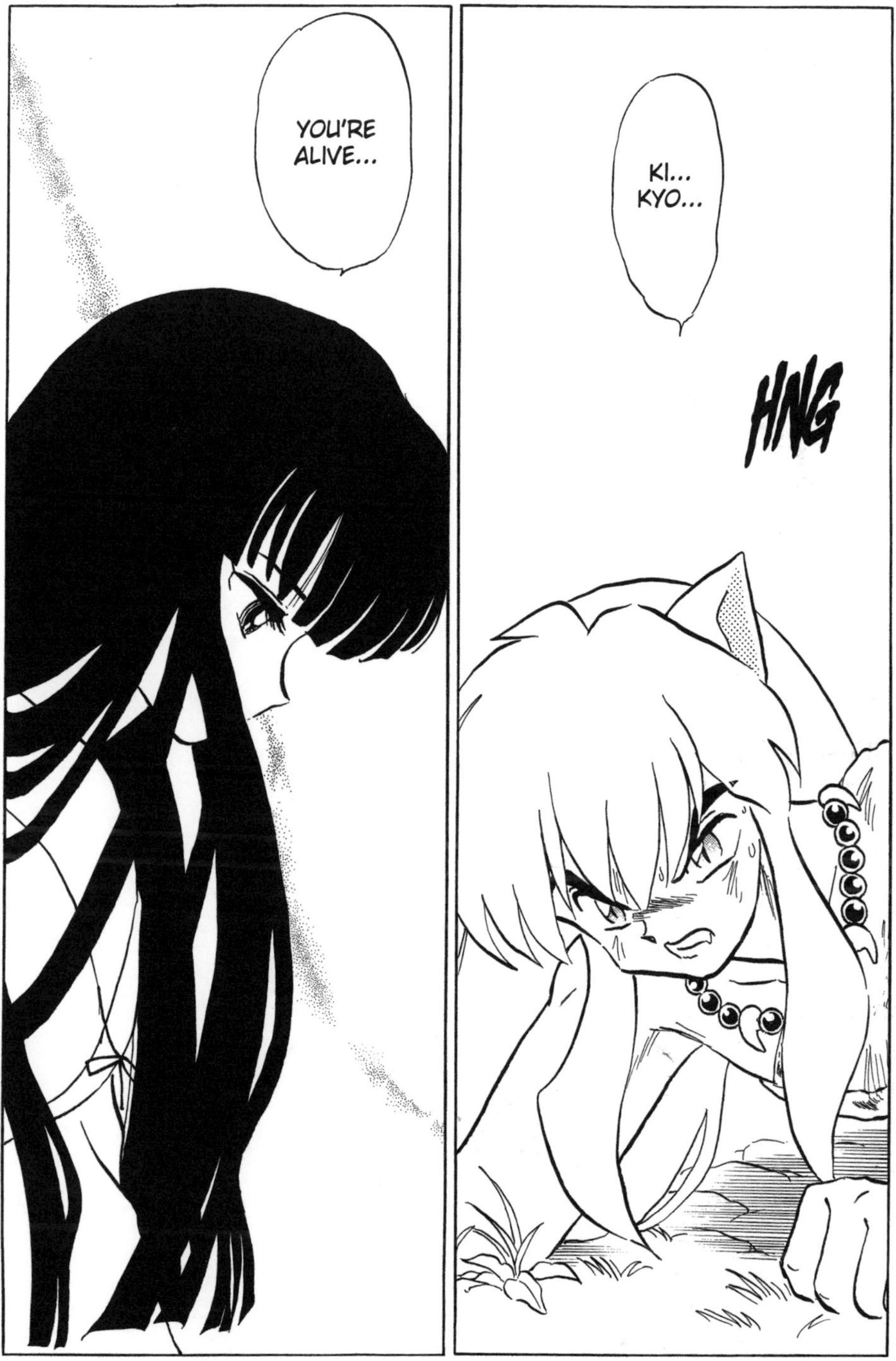
KI... KYO...
HNG
YOU'RE ALIVE...

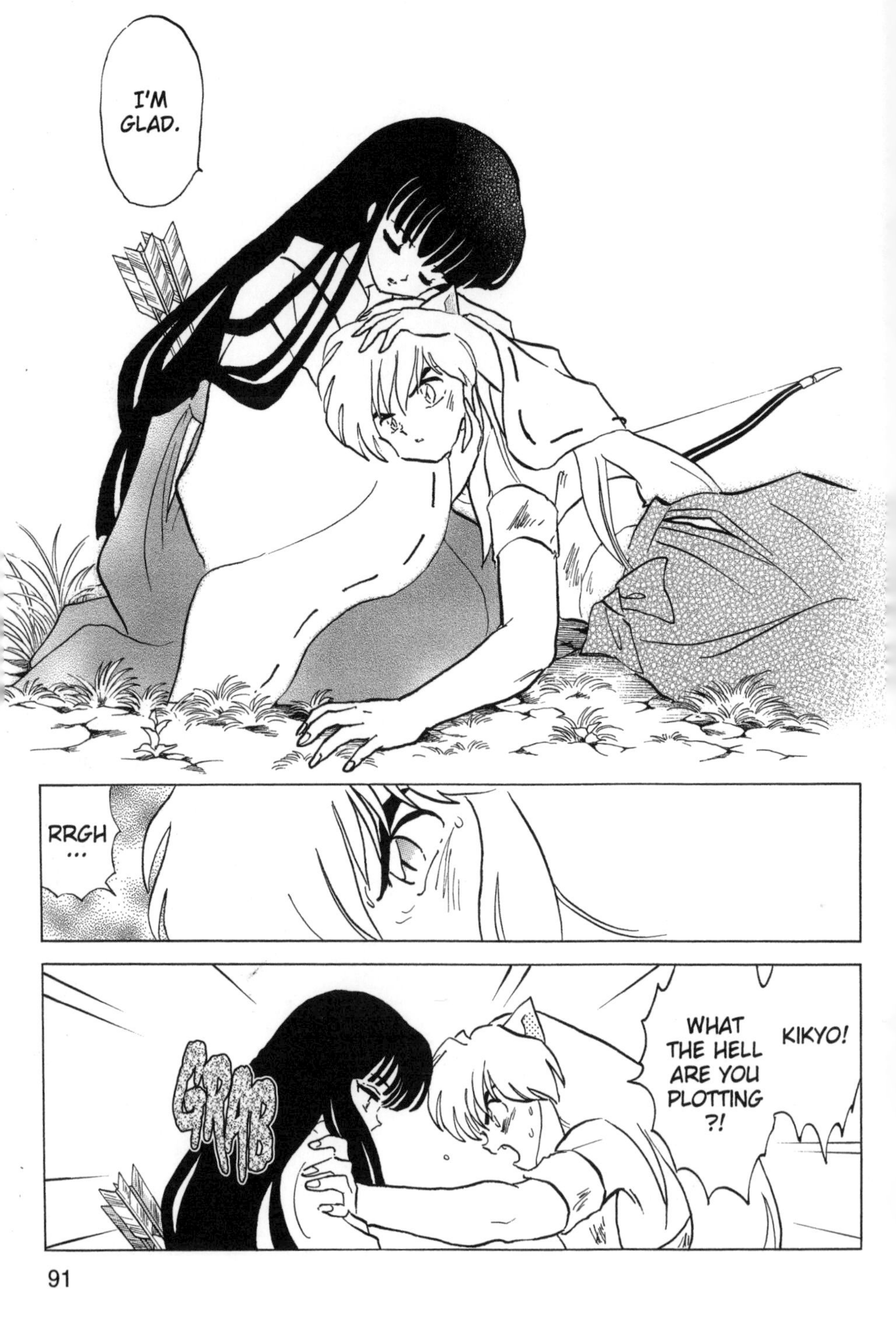
I'M GLAD.
RRGH ...
KIKYO!
WHAT THE HELL ARE YOU PLOTTING ?!
GRAB

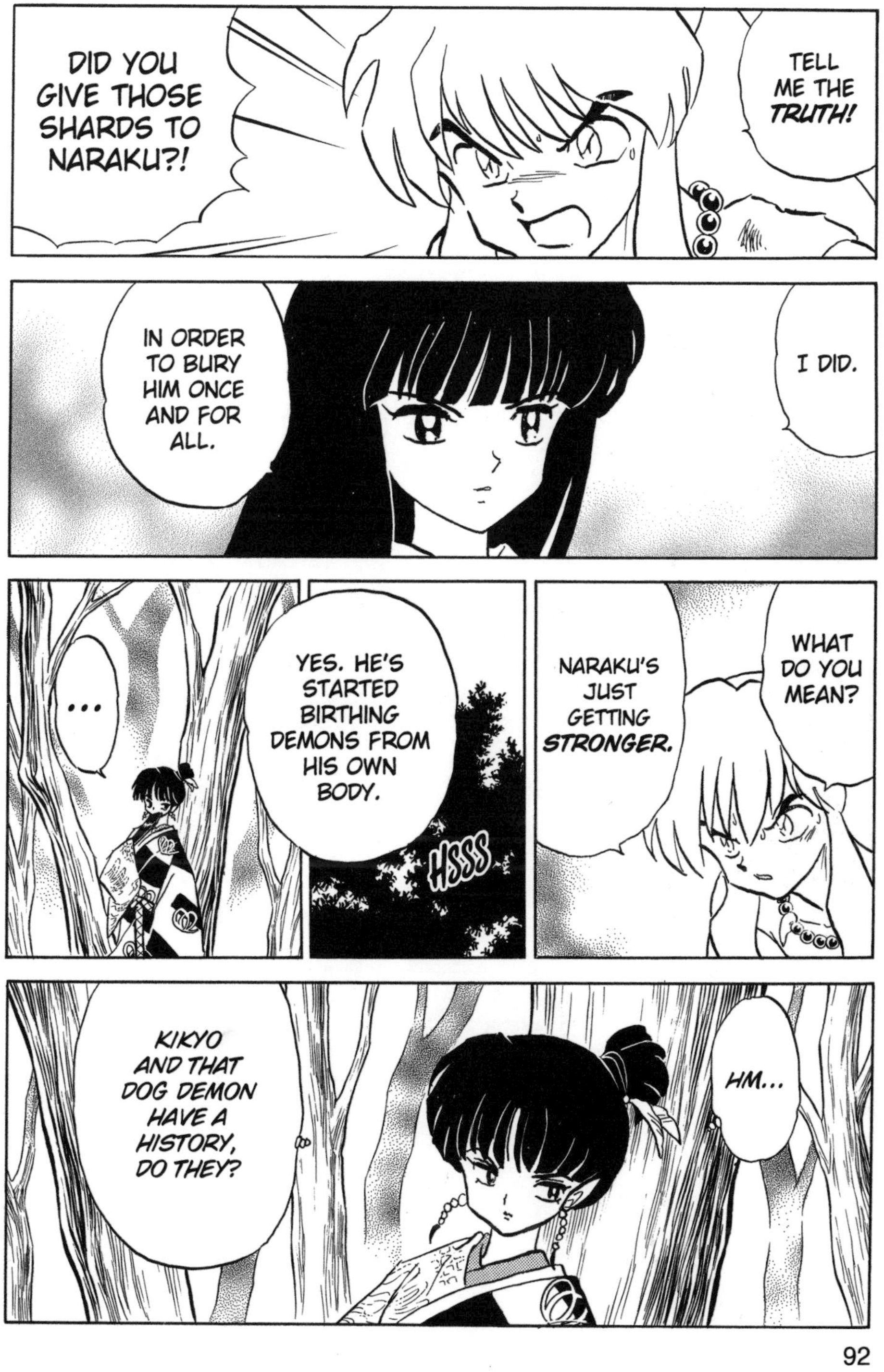
TELL ME THE *TRUTH!*
DID YOU GIVE THOSE SHARDS TO NARAKU?!
I DID.
IN ORDER TO BURY HIM ONCE AND FOR ALL.
WHAT DO YOU MEAN?
NARAKU'S JUST GETTING *STRONGER.*
YES. HE'S STARTED BIRTHING DEMONS FROM HIS OWN BODY.
HSSS
...
HM...
KIKYO AND THAT DOG DEMON HAVE A HISTORY, DO THEY?

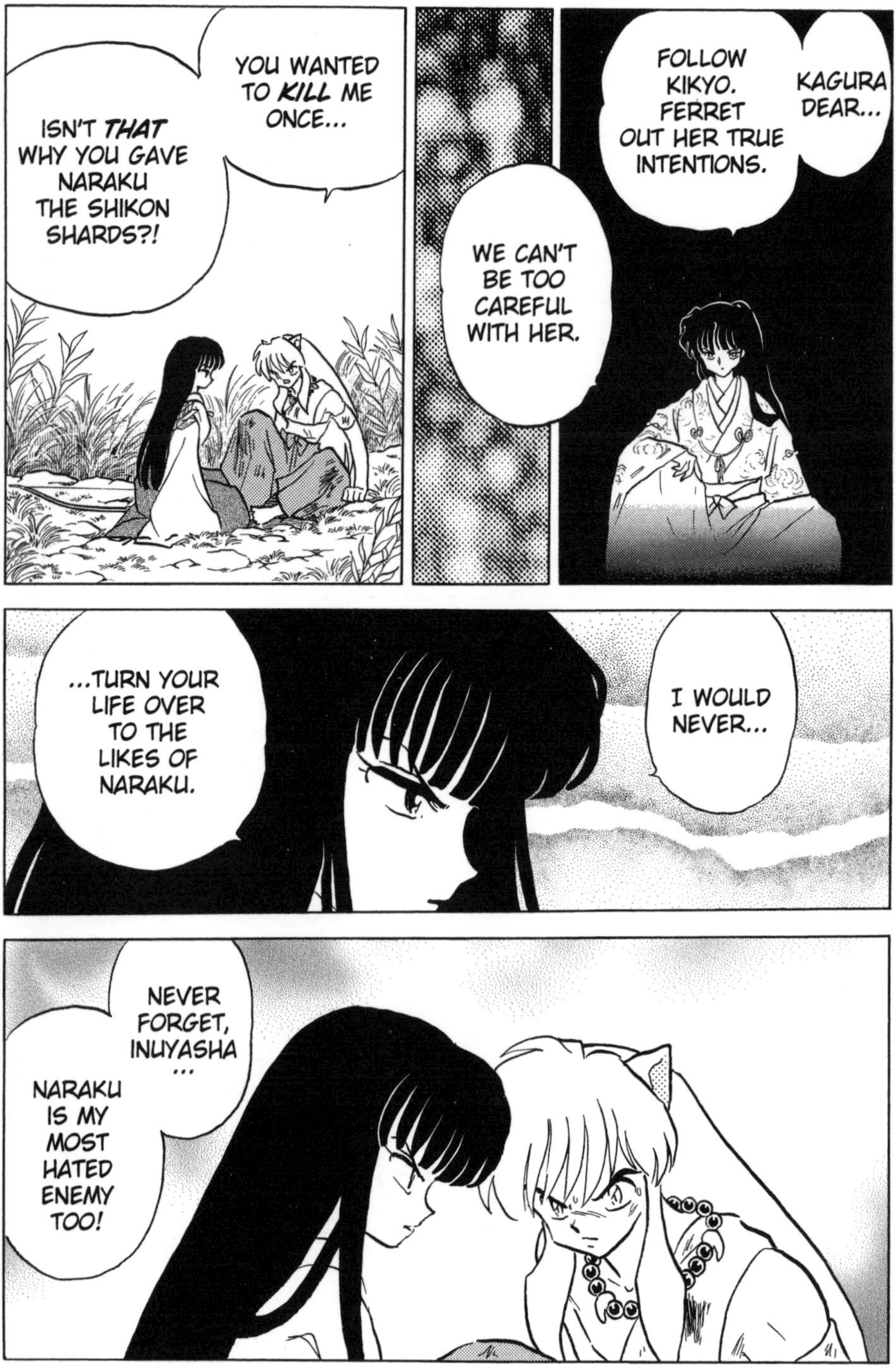
KAGURA DEAR...
FOLLOW KIKYO. FERRET OUT HER TRUE INTENTIONS.
WE CAN'T BE TOO CAREFUL WITH HER.
YOU WANTED TO *KILL* ME ONCE...
ISN'T *THAT* WHY YOU GAVE NARAKU THE SHIKON SHARDS?!
I WOULD NEVER...
...TURN YOUR LIFE OVER TO THE LIKES OF NARAKU.
NEVER FORGET, INUYASHA ...
NARAKU IS MY MOST HATED ENEMY TOO!

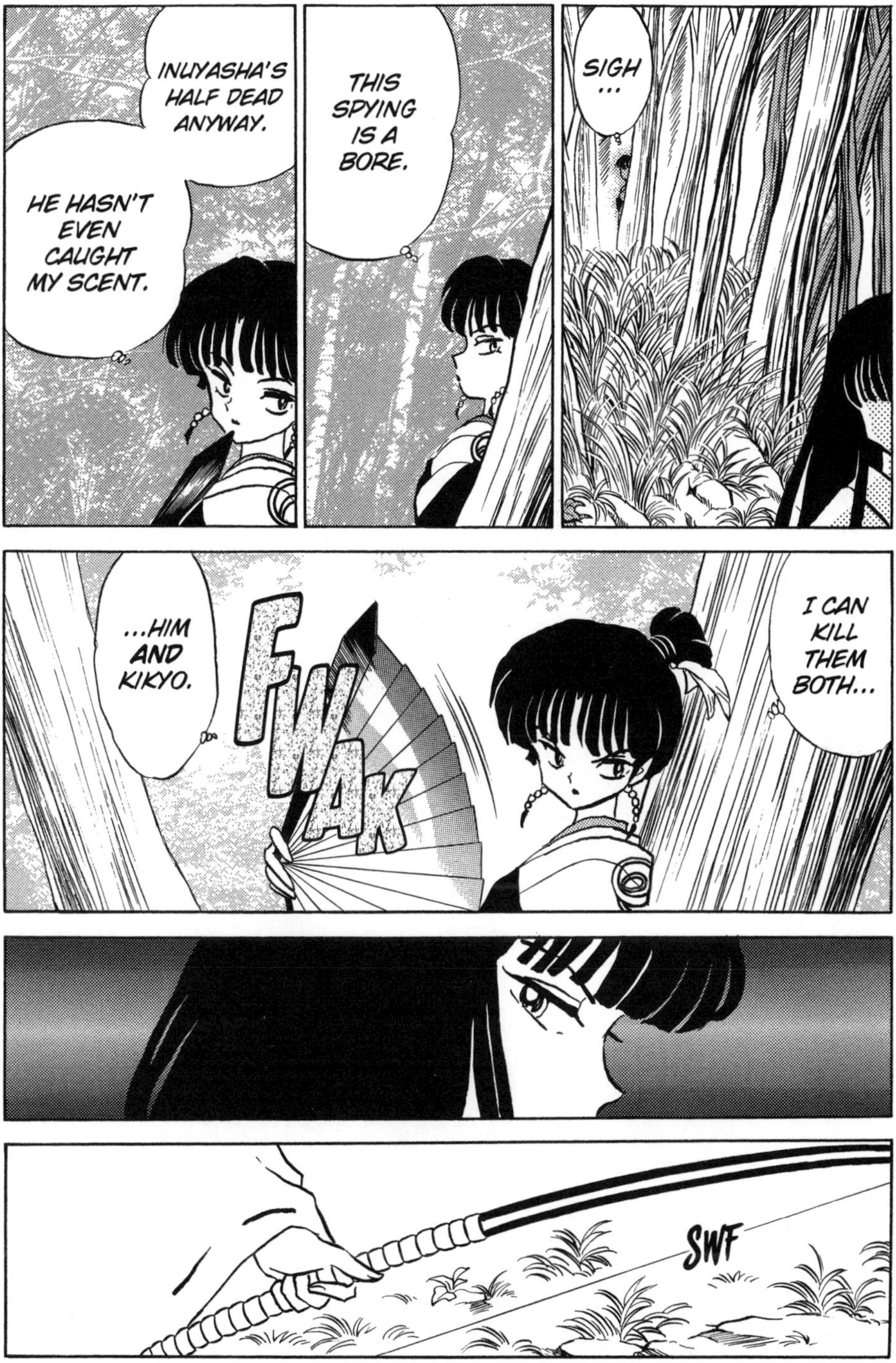
SIGH...
THIS SPYING IS A BORE.
INUYASHA'S HALF DEAD ANYWAY.
HE HASN'T EVEN CAUGHT MY SCENT.
I CAN KILL THEM BOTH...
...HIM AND KIKYO.
FWAK
SWF

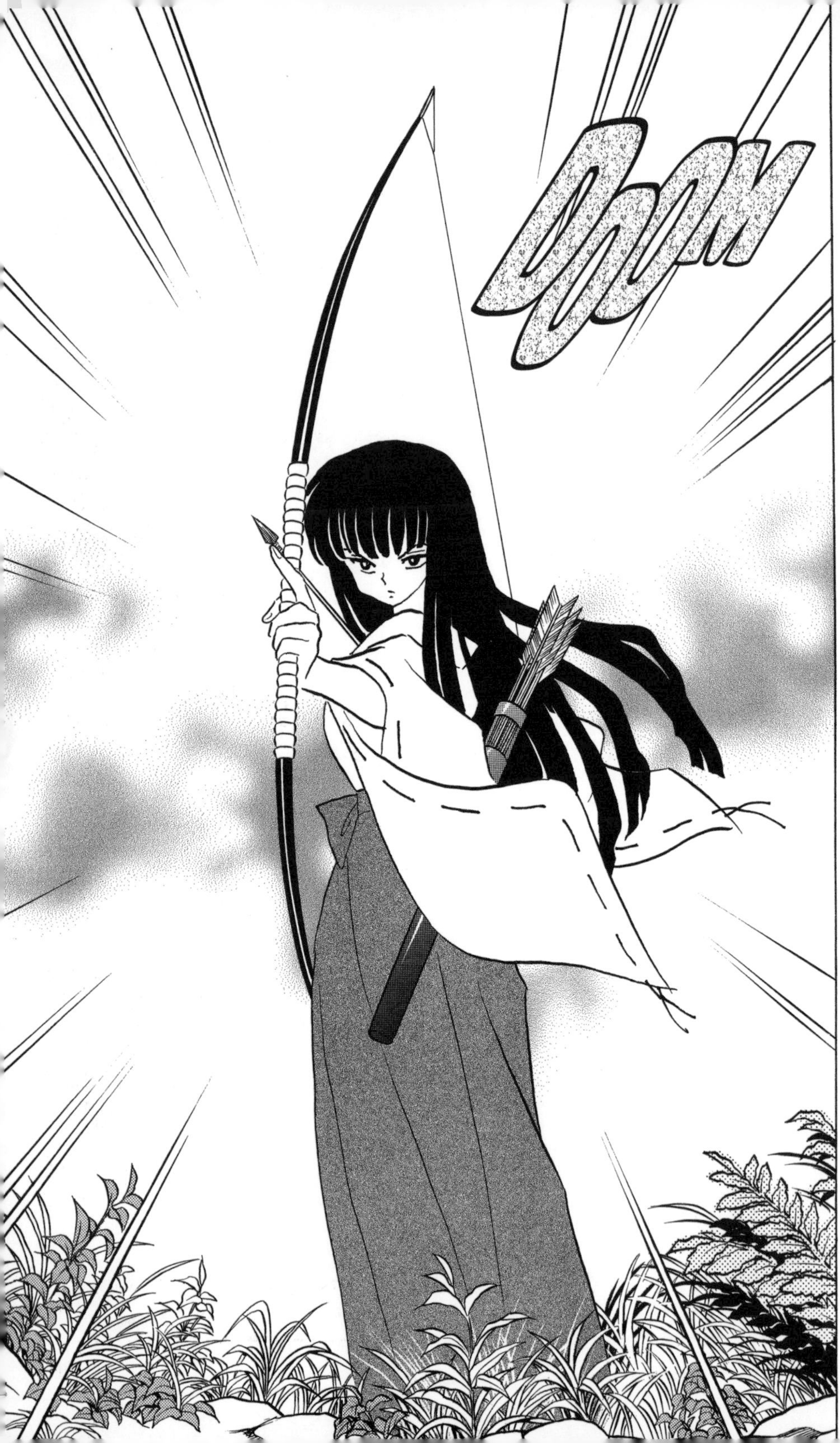
DOOM

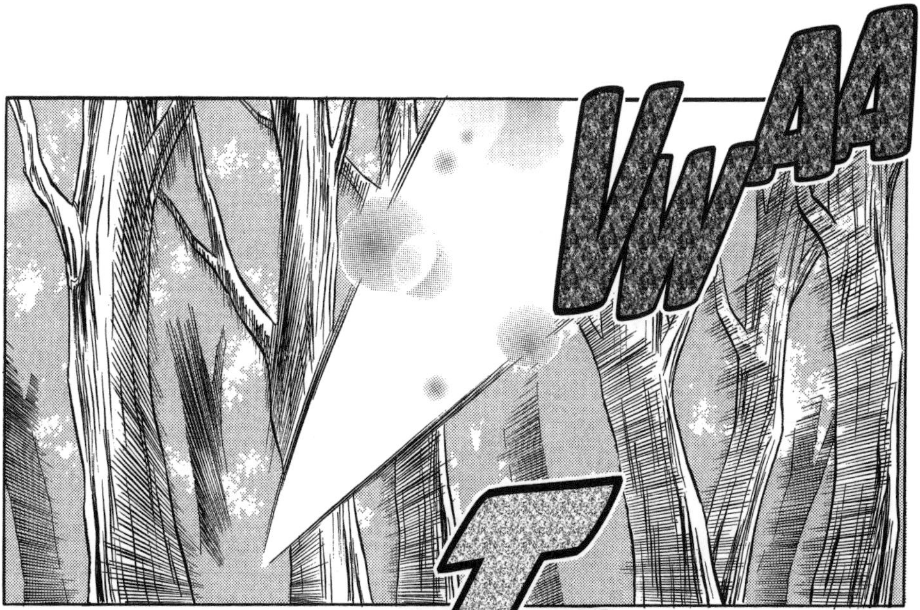
VWAA
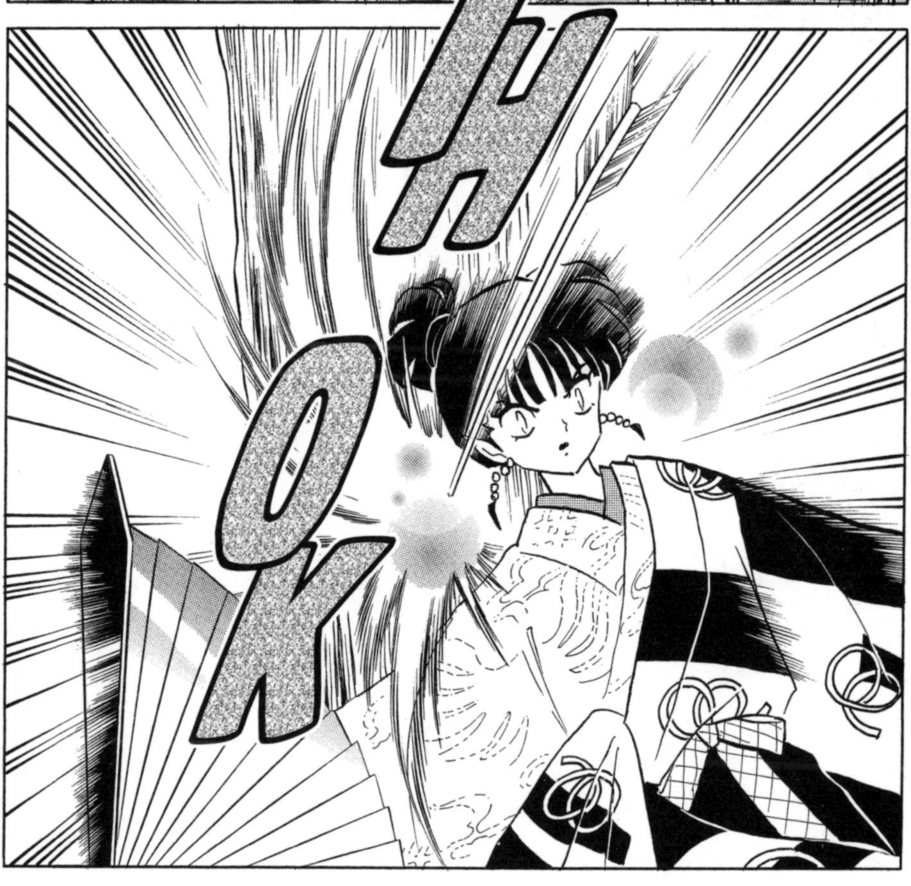
THOK

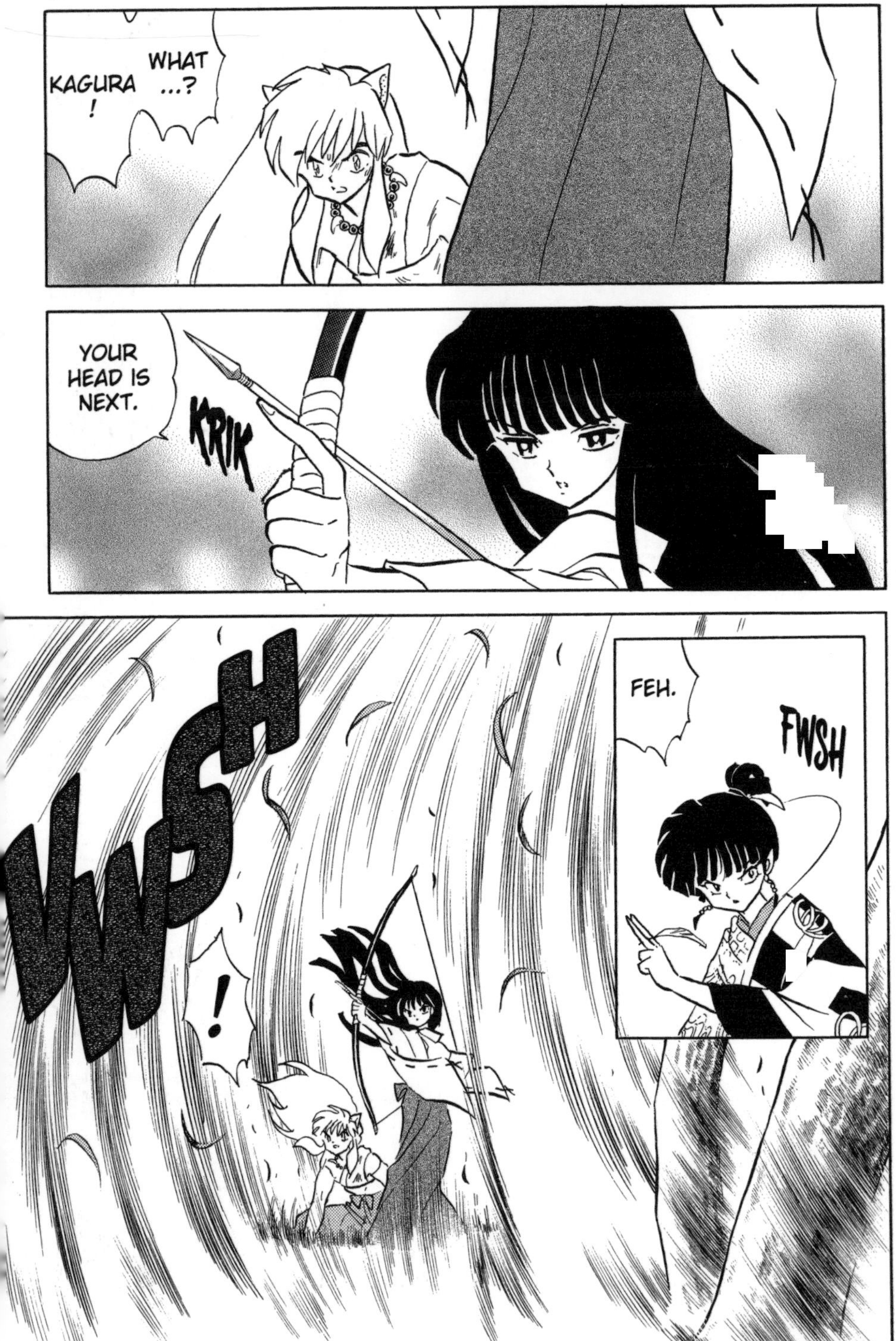
WHAT ...?
KAGURA !
YOUR HEAD IS NEXT.
KRIK
FEH.
FWSH
VWSH
!

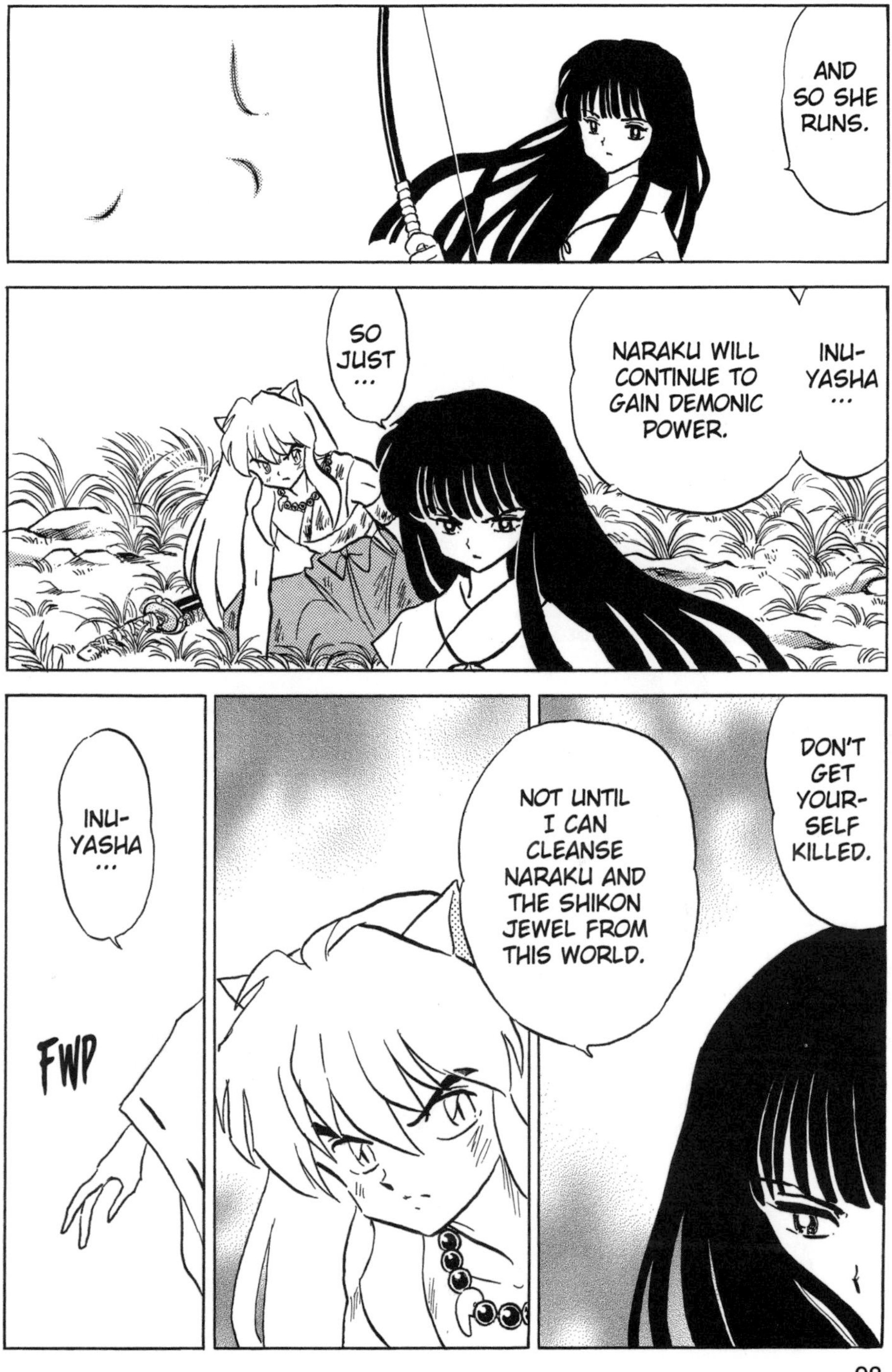
AND SO SHE RUNS.
INU-YASHA ...
NARAKU WILL CONTINUE TO GAIN DEMONIC POWER.
SO JUST ...
DON'T GET YOUR-SELF KILLED.
NOT UNTIL I CAN CLEANSE NARAKU AND THE SHIKON JEWEL FROM THIS WORLD.
INU-YASHA ...
FWP

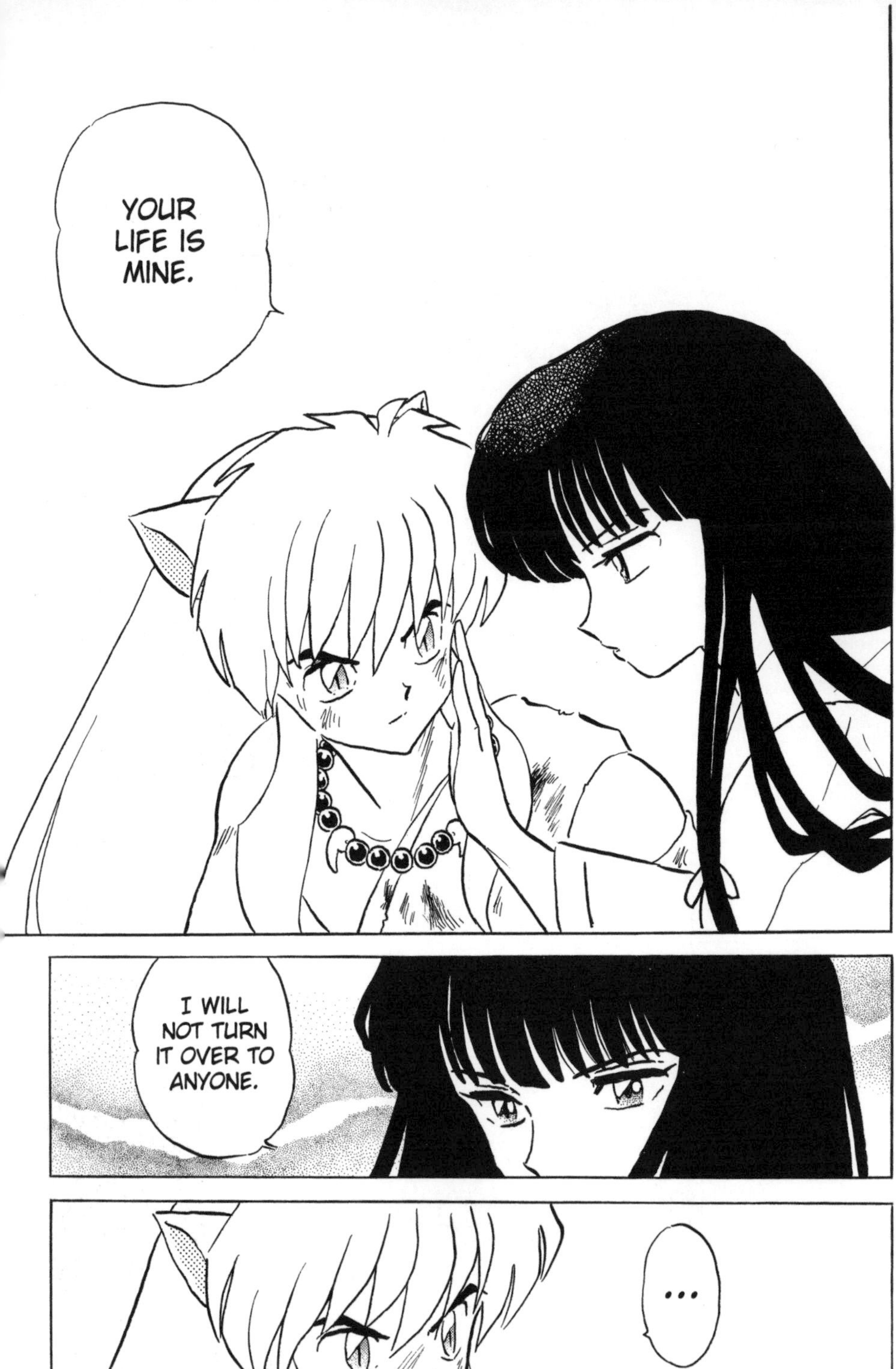
YOUR LIFE IS MINE.
I WILL NOT TURN IT OVER TO ANYONE.
...

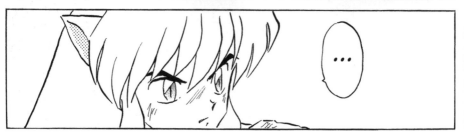

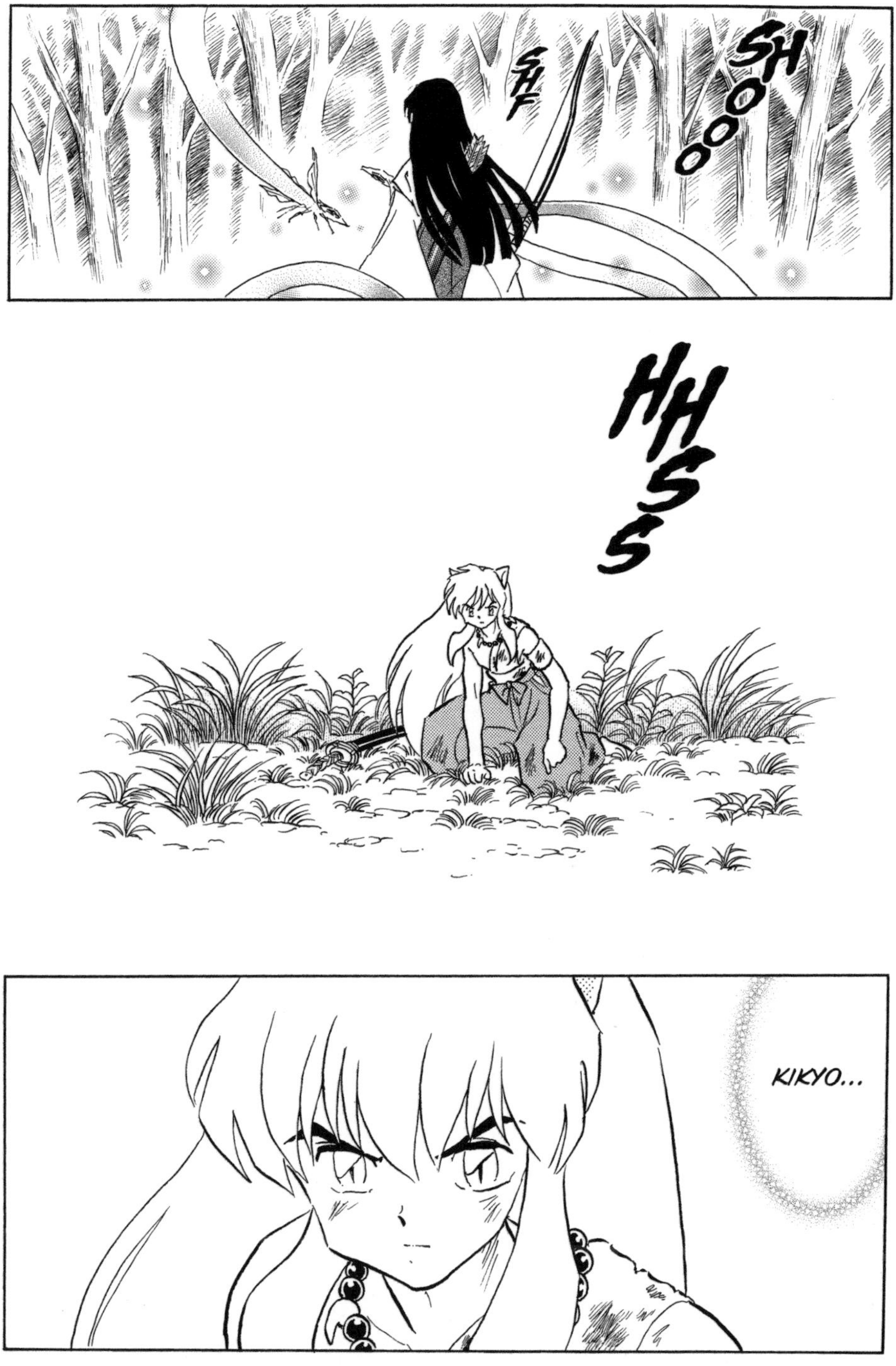
SHOOOO
SHF
HHSSS
KIKYO...

SCROLL SIX
THE THIRD DEMON

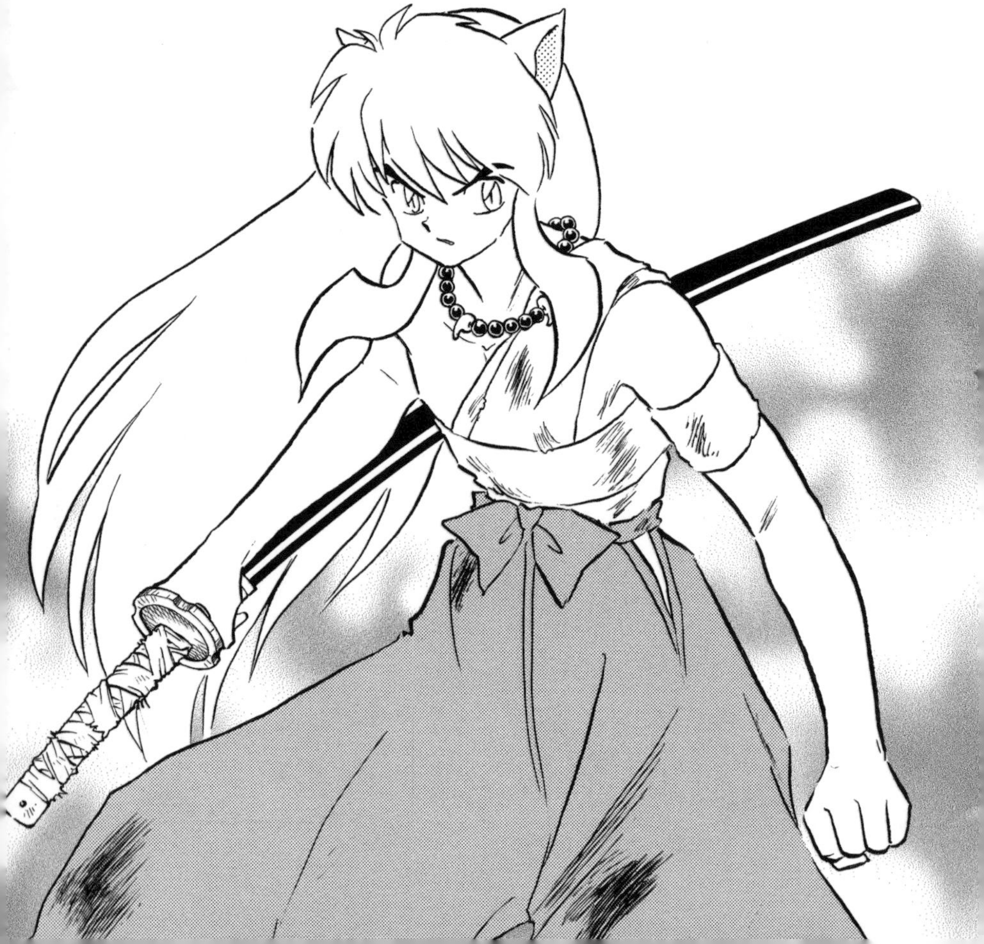

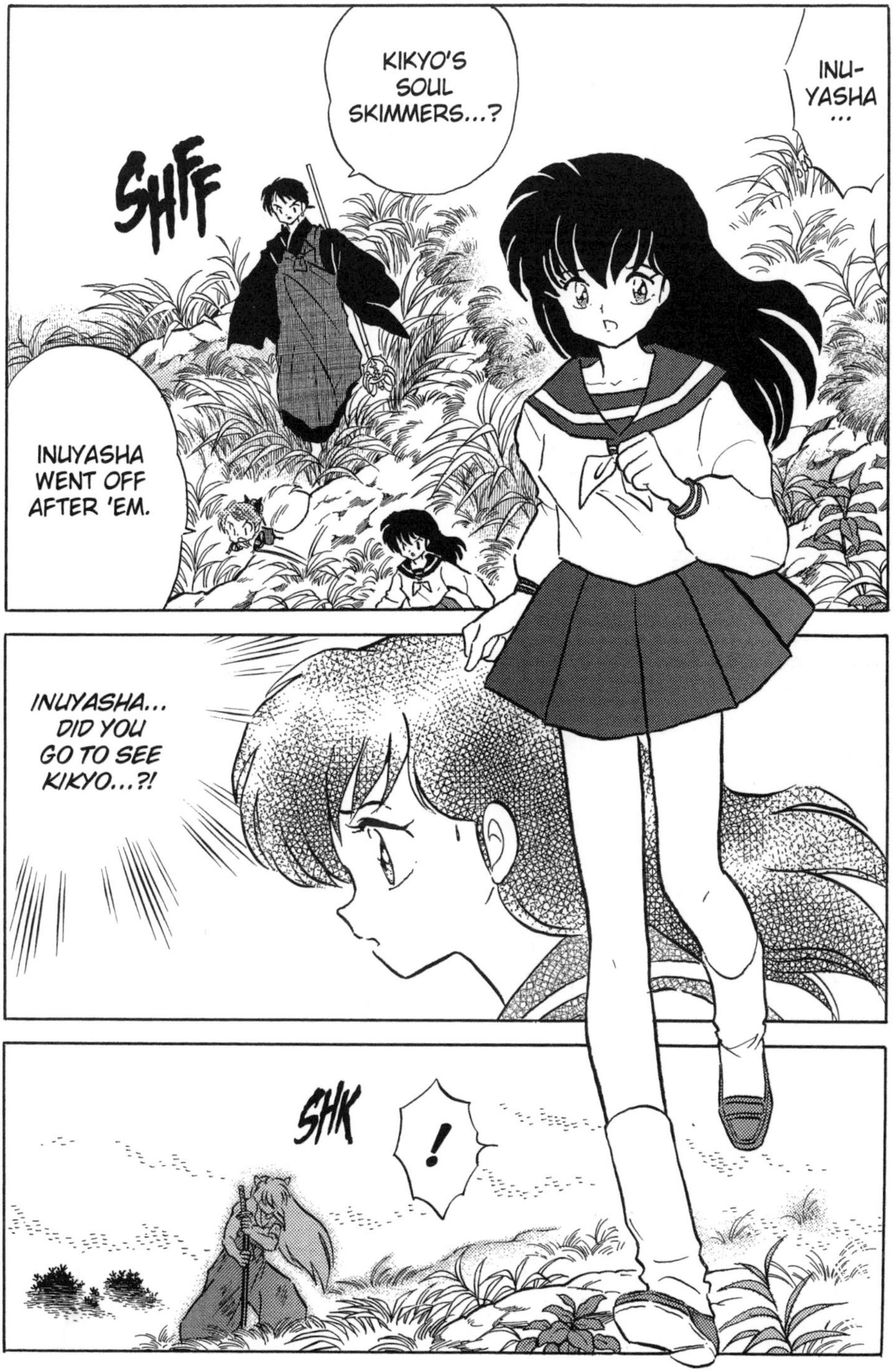
INU-YASHA...
KIKYO'S SOUL SKIMMERS...?
SHFF
INUYASHA WENT OFF AFTER 'EM.
INUYASHA... DID YOU GO TO SEE KIKYO...?!
!
SHK

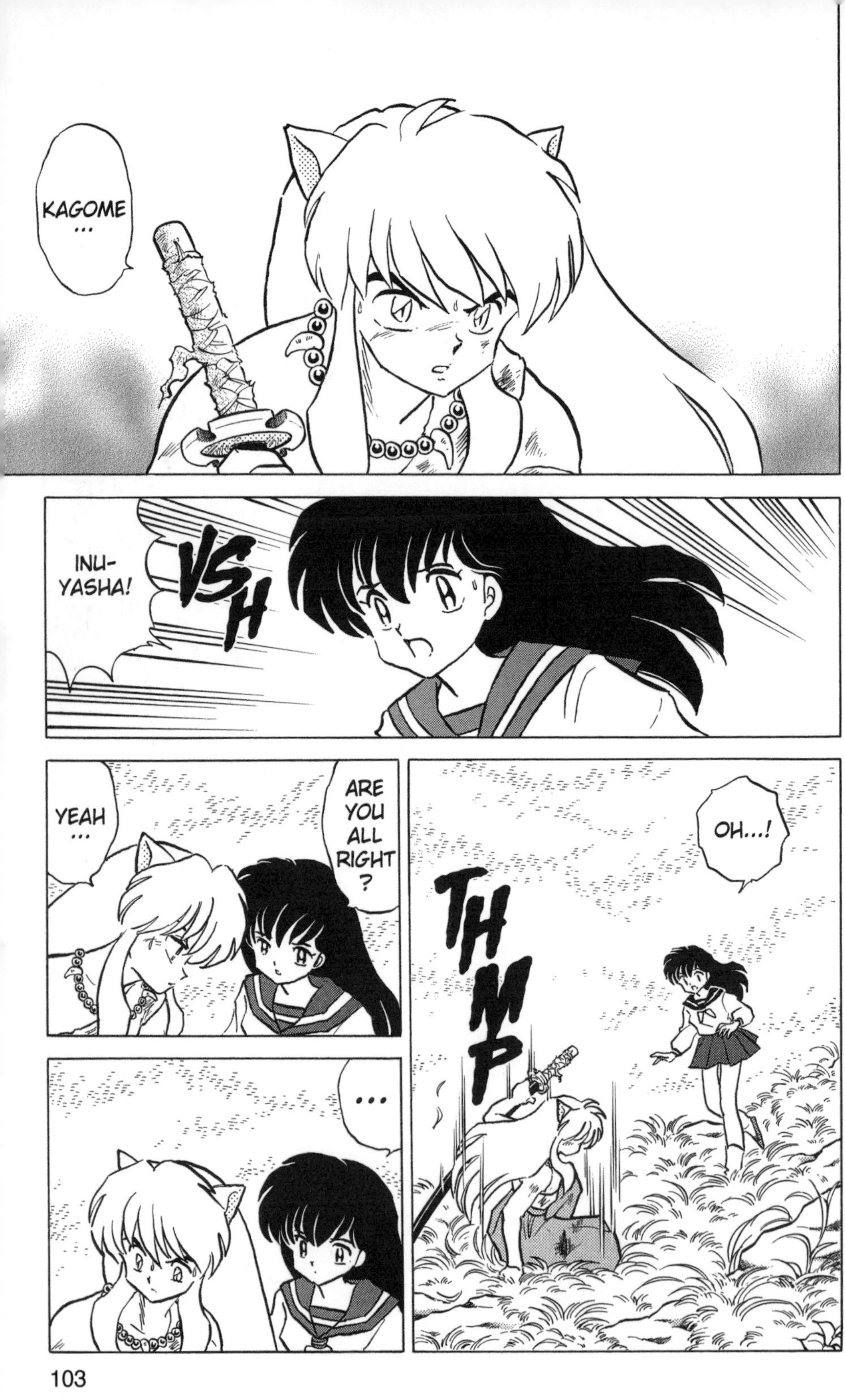
KAGOME ...
INU-YASHA!
VSH
OH...!
THMP
ARE YOU ALL RIGHT ?
YEAH ...
...

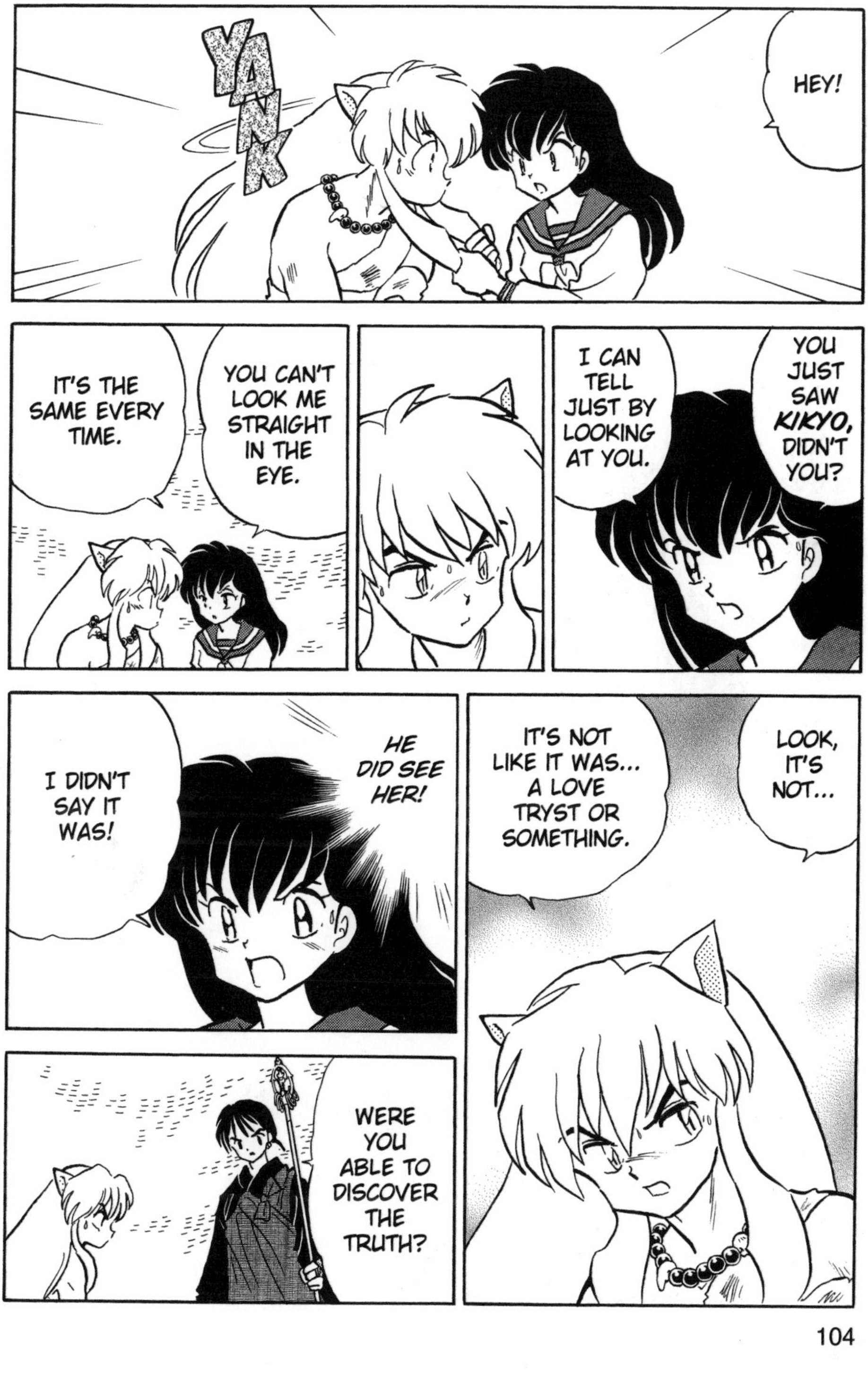
YANK
HEY!
YOU JUST SAW KIKYO, DIDN'T YOU?
I CAN TELL JUST BY LOOKING AT YOU.
YOU CAN'T LOOK ME STRAIGHT IN THE EYE.
IT'S THE SAME EVERY TIME.
LOOK, IT'S NOT...
IT'S NOT LIKE IT WAS... A LOVE TRYST OR SOMETHING.
HE DID SEE HER!
I DIDN'T SAY IT WAS!
WERE YOU ABLE TO DISCOVER THE TRUTH?

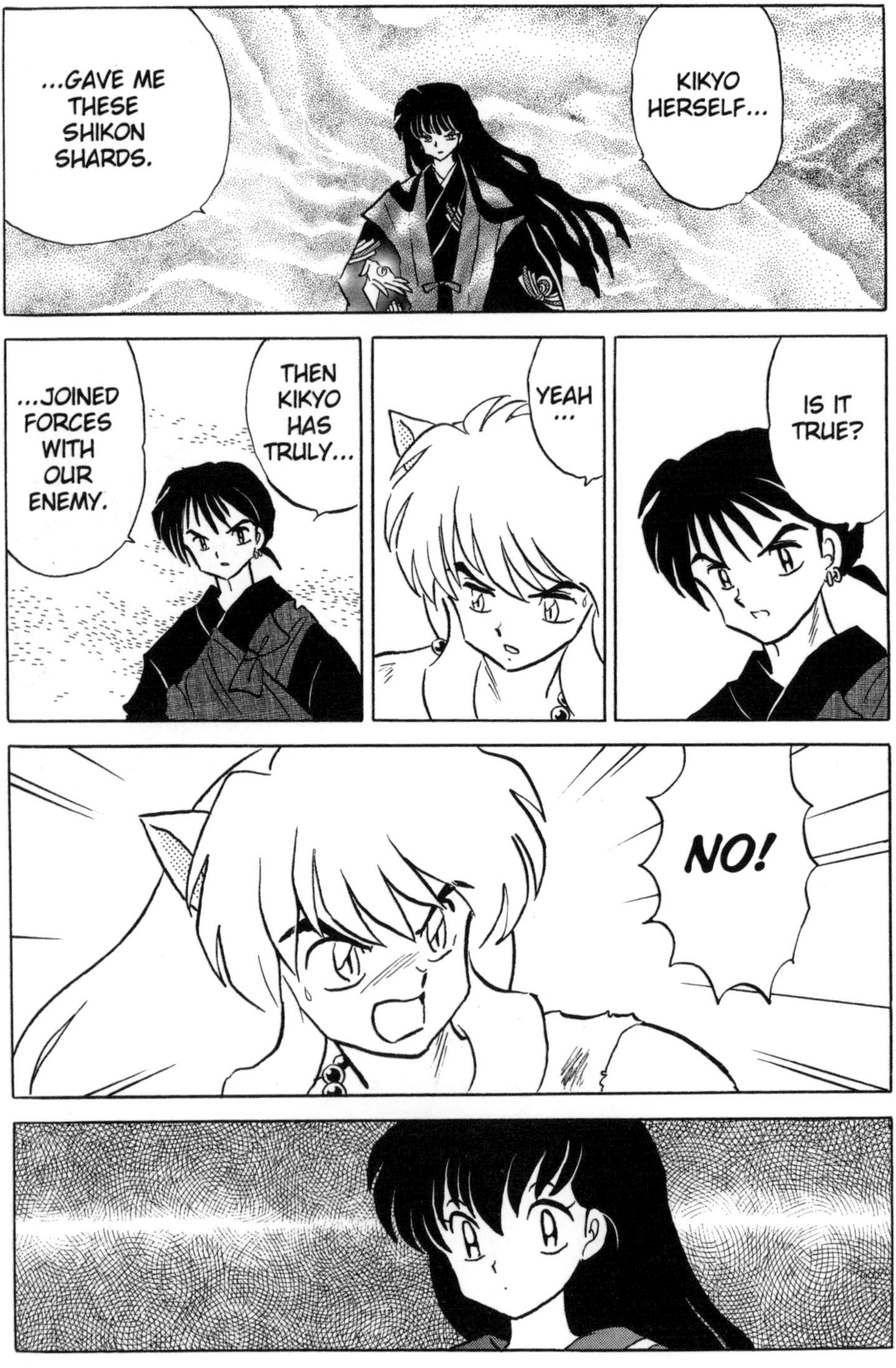

KIKYO HERSELF...
...GAVE ME THESE SHIKON SHARDS.
IS IT TRUE?
YEAH...
THEN KIKYO HAS TRULY...
...JOINED FORCES WITH OUR ENEMY.
NO!

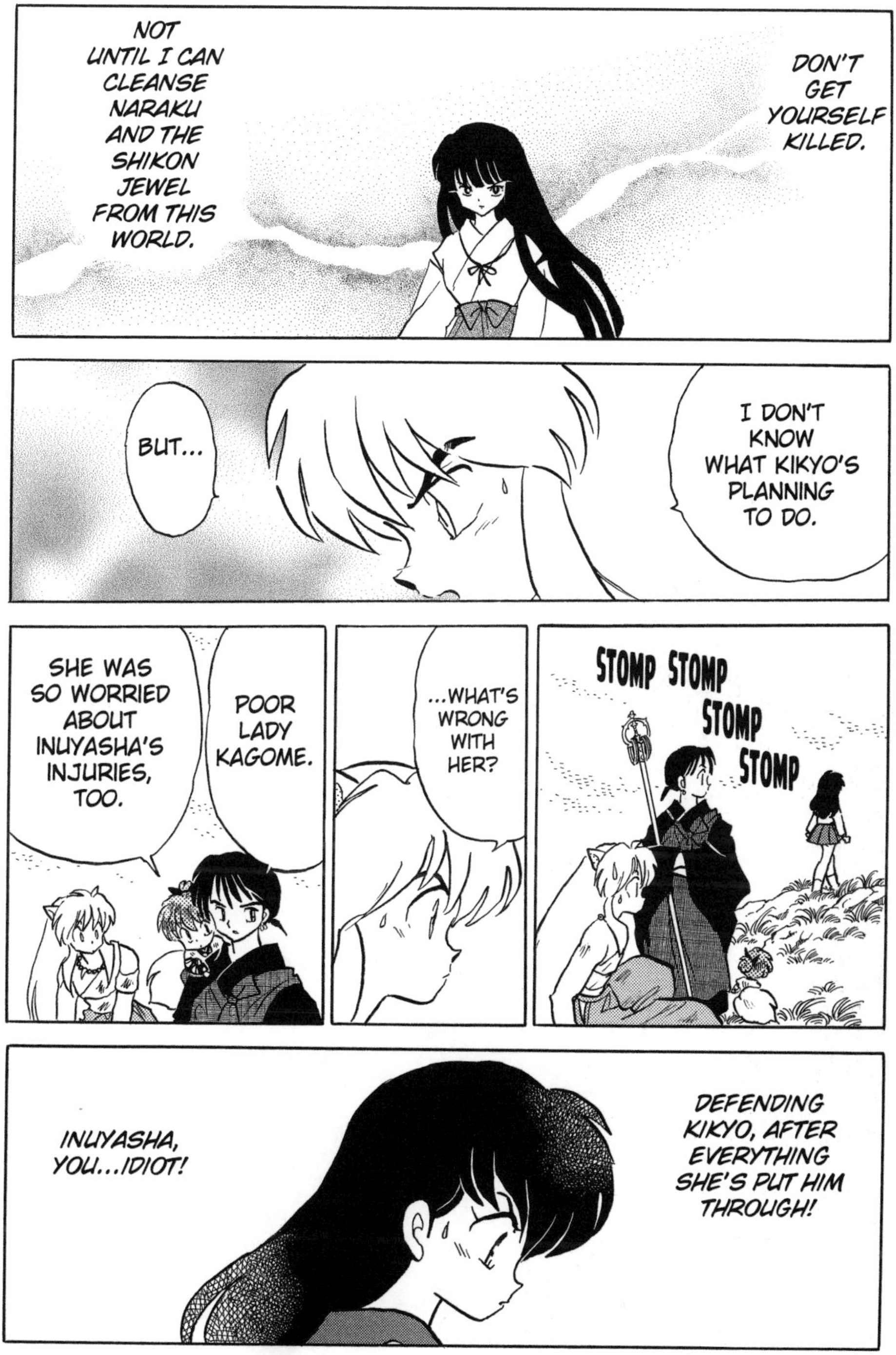
DON'T GET YOURSELF KILLED.
NOT UNTIL I CAN CLEANSE NARAKU AND THE SHIKON JEWEL FROM THIS WORLD.
I DON'T KNOW WHAT KIKYO'S PLANNING TO DO.
BUT...
STOMP STOMP STOMP STOMP
...WHAT'S WRONG WITH HER?
POOR LADY KAGOME.
SHE WAS SO WORRIED ABOUT INUYASHA'S INJURIES, TOO.
DEFENDING KIKYO, AFTER EVERYTHING SHE'S PUT HIM THROUGH!
INUYASHA, YOU...IDIOT!

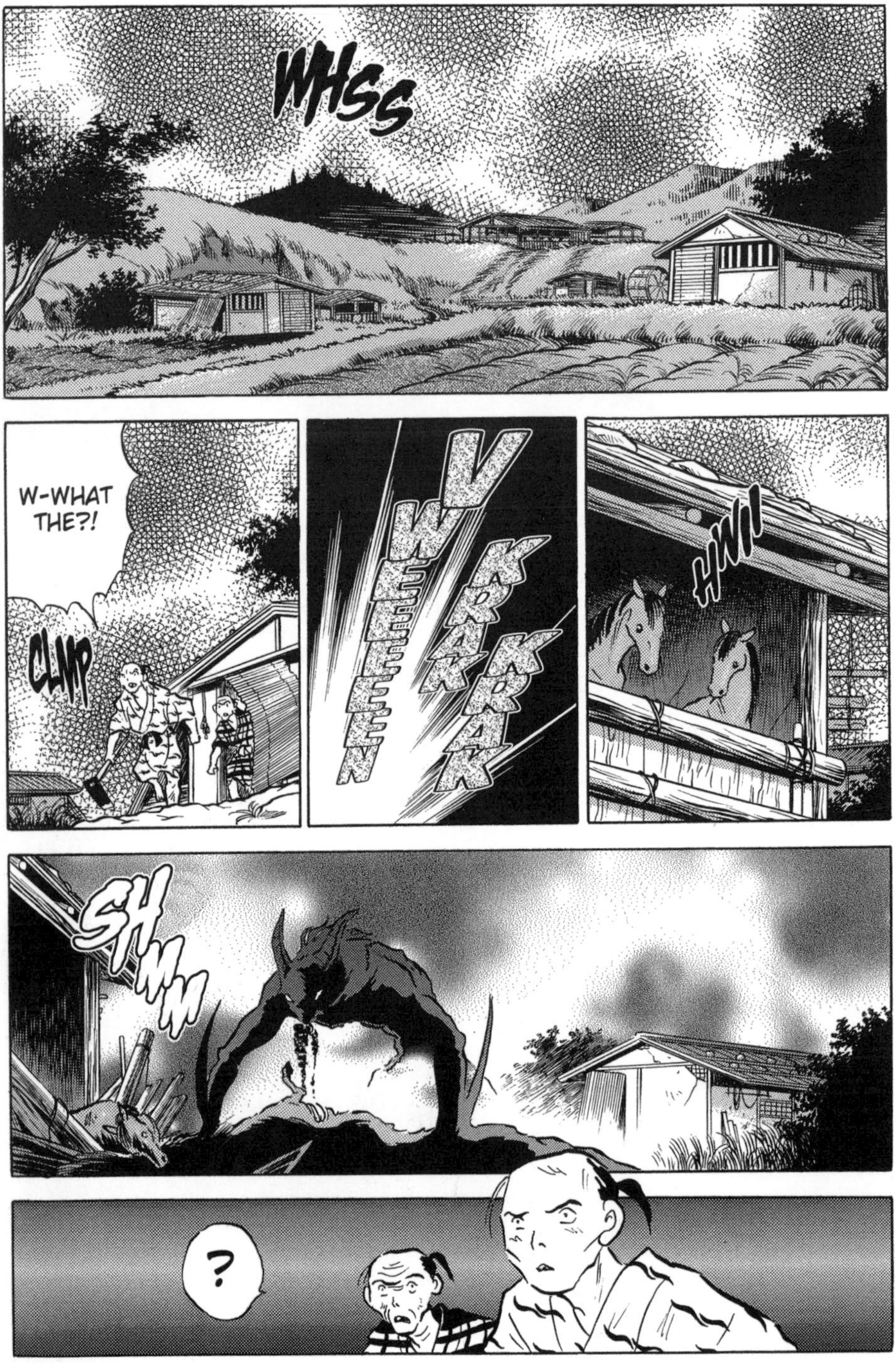
WHSS
HWII
VWEEEEEEN
KRAK
KRAK
W-WHAT THE?!
CLMP
SHMM
?

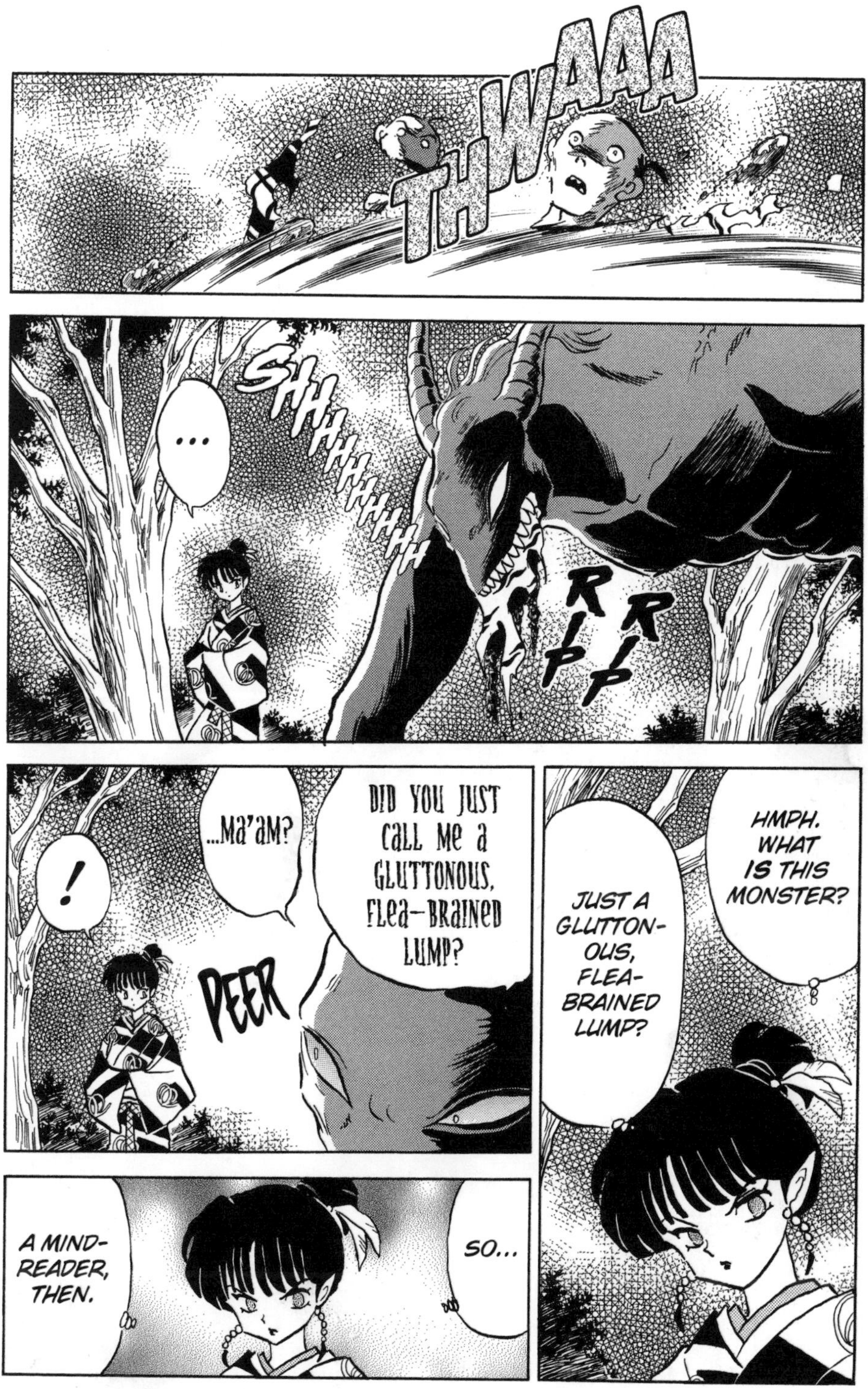
THWAAA
SHHHHHHHHHHH
...
RRIPP RRIPP
HMPH. WHAT IS THIS MONSTER?
JUST A GLUTTONOUS, FLEA-BRAINED LUMP?
DID YOU JUST CALL ME A GLUTTONOUS, FLEA-BRAINED LUMP?
...Ma'aM?
!
PEER
SO...
A MIND-READER, THEN.

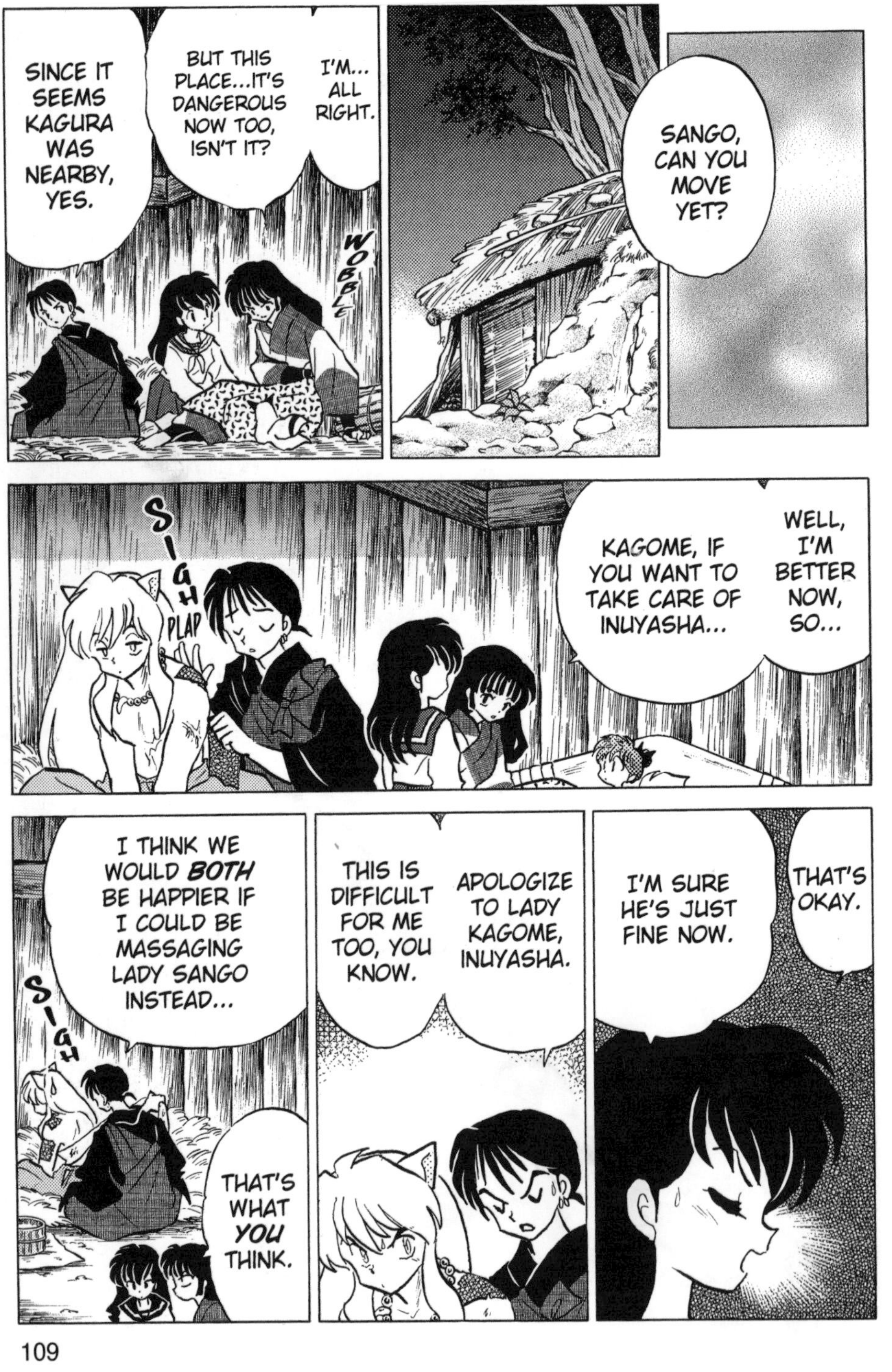
SANGO, CAN YOU MOVE YET?
I'M... ALL RIGHT.
BUT THIS PLACE...IT'S DANGEROUS NOW TOO, ISN'T IT?
SINCE IT SEEMS KAGURA WAS NEARBY, YES.
WOBBLE
WELL, I'M BETTER NOW, SO...
KAGOME, IF YOU WANT TO TAKE CARE OF INUYASHA...
SIGH
PLAP
THAT'S OKAY.
I'M SURE HE'S JUST FINE NOW.
APOLOGIZE TO LADY KAGOME, INUYASHA.
THIS IS DIFFICULT FOR ME TOO, YOU KNOW.
I THINK WE WOULD *BOTH* BE HAPPIER IF I COULD BE MASSAGING LADY SANGO INSTEAD...
SIGH
THAT'S WHAT *YOU* THINK.

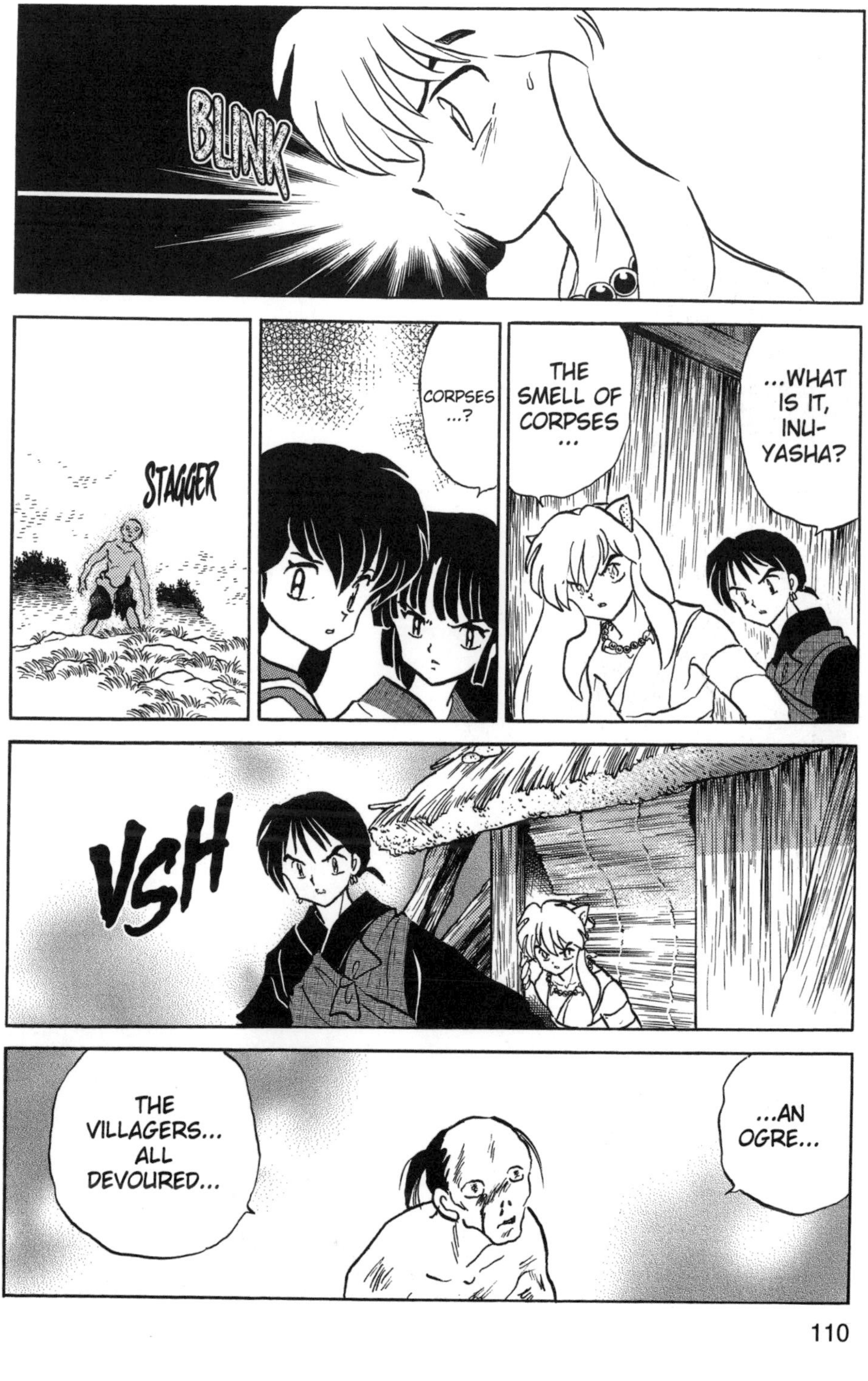
BLINK
...WHAT IS IT, INU-YASHA?
THE SMELL OF CORPSES...
CORPSES...?
STAGGER
VSH
...AN OGRE...
THE VILLAGERS... ALL DEVOURED...

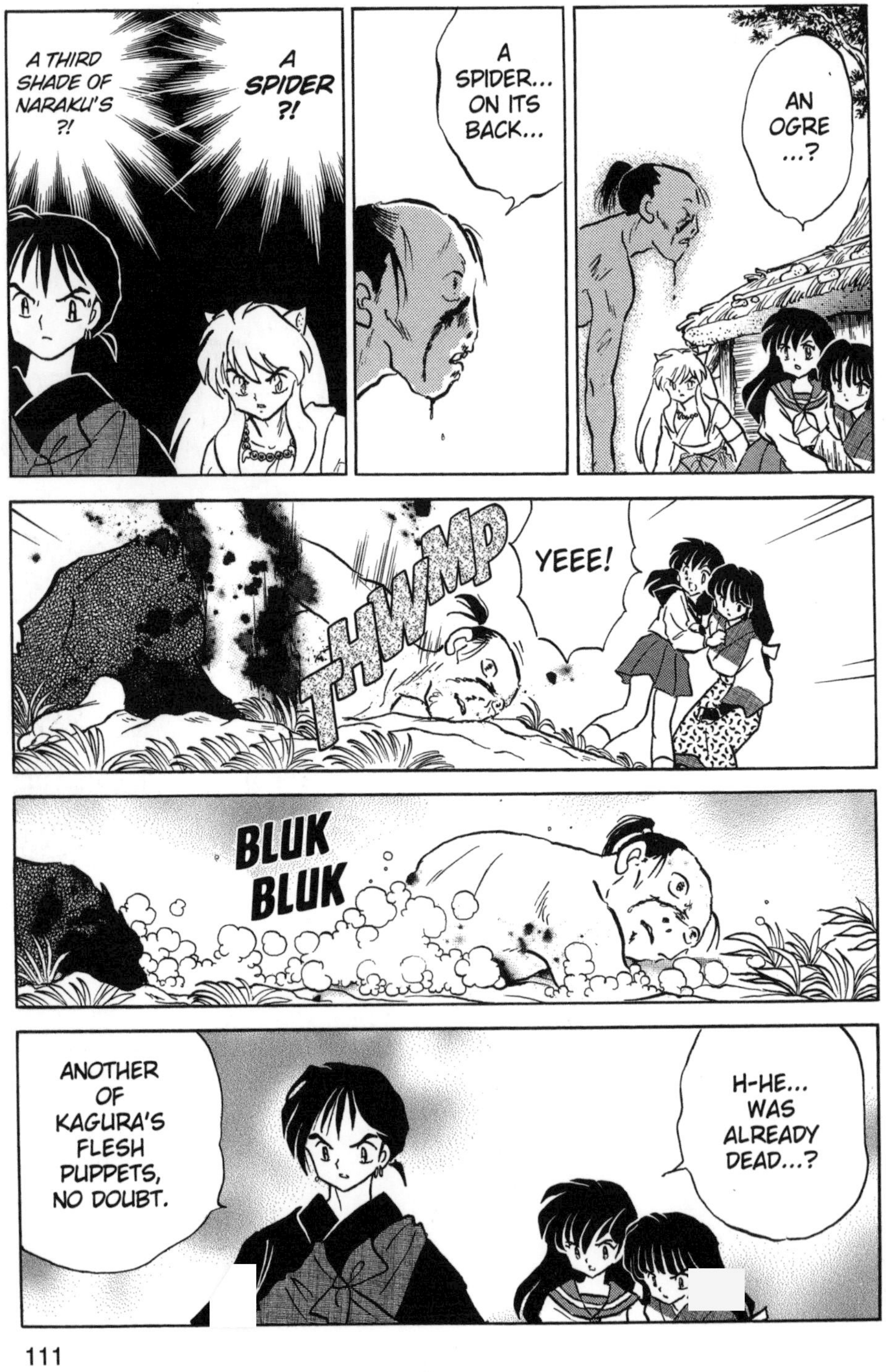

AN OGRE ...?
A SPIDER... ON ITS BACK...
A SPIDER ?!
A THIRD SHADE OF NARAKU'S ?!
YEEE!
THWMP
BLUK BLUK
H-HE... WAS ALREADY DEAD...?
ANOTHER OF KAGURA'S FLESH PUPPETS, NO DOUBT.

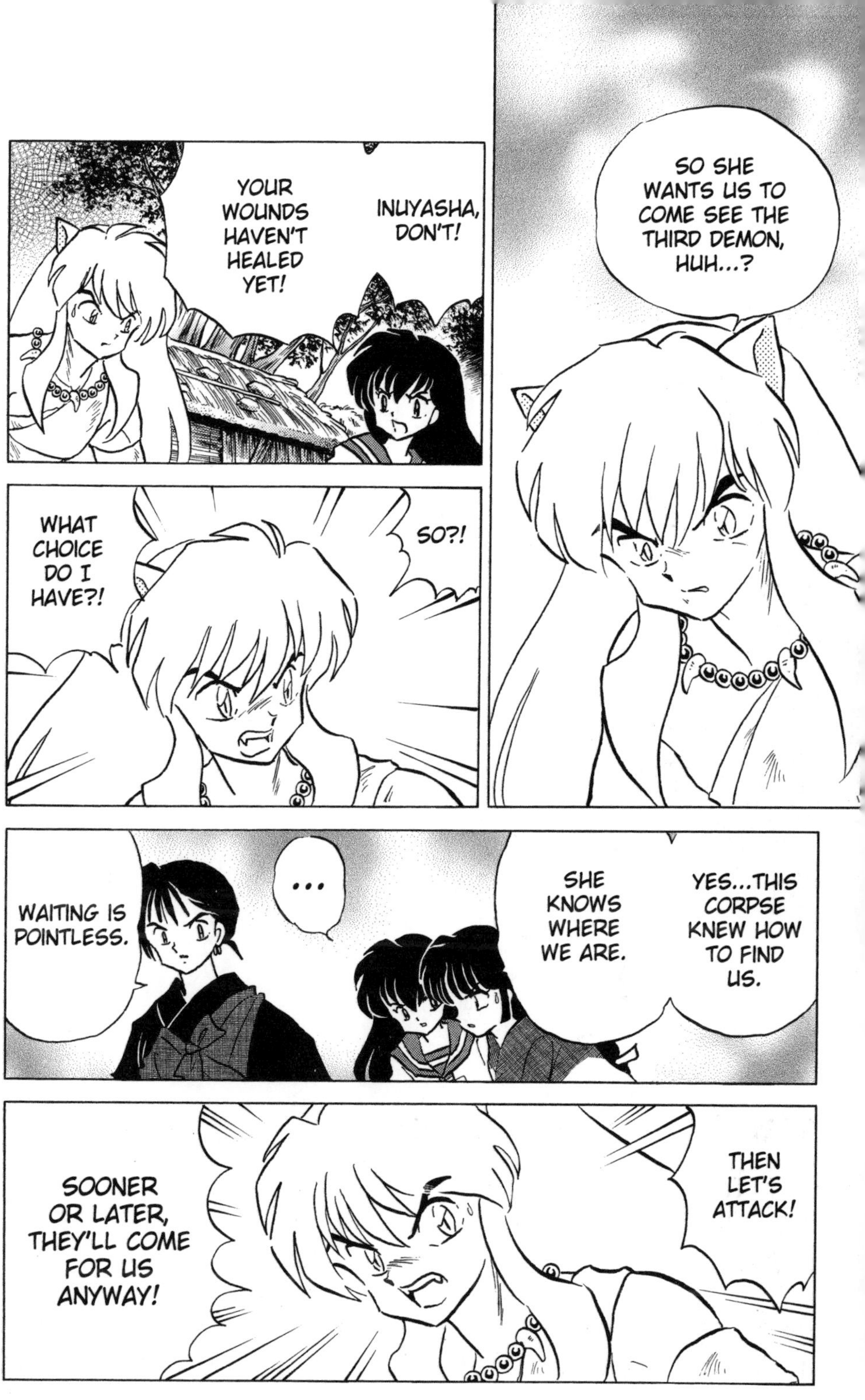
SO SHE WANTS US TO COME SEE THE THIRD DEMON, HUH...?
INUYASHA, DON'T!
YOUR WOUNDS HAVEN'T HEALED YET!
SO?!
WHAT CHOICE DO I HAVE?!
YES...THIS CORPSE KNEW HOW TO FIND US.
SHE KNOWS WHERE WE ARE.
...
WAITING IS POINTLESS.
THEN LET'S ATTACK!
SOONER OR LATER, THEY'LL COME FOR US ANYWAY!

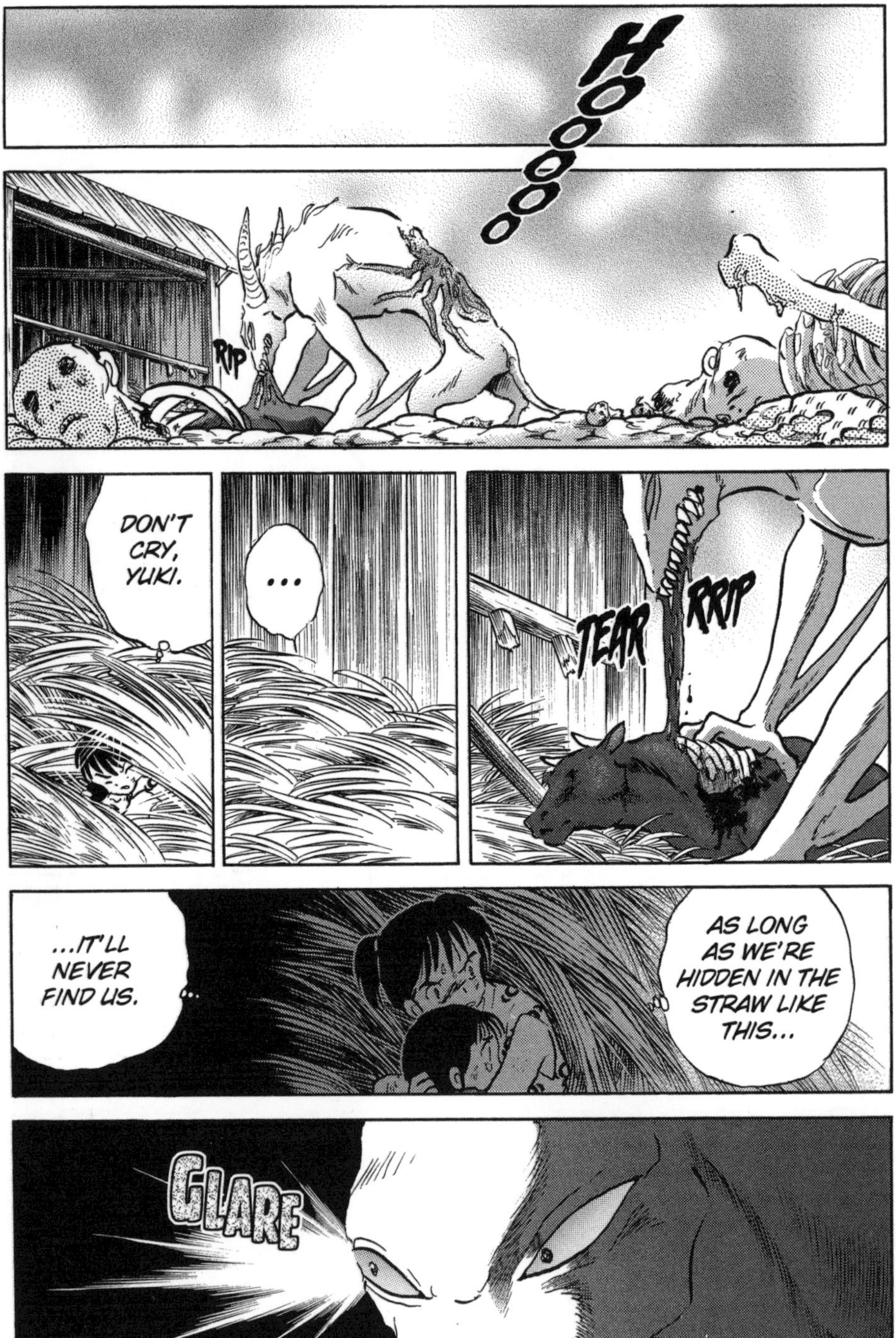

HOOOOOO
RIP
RRIP
TEAR
...
DON'T CRY, YUKI.
AS LONG AS WE'RE HIDDEN IN THE STRAW LIKE THIS...
...IT'LL NEVER FIND US.
GLARE

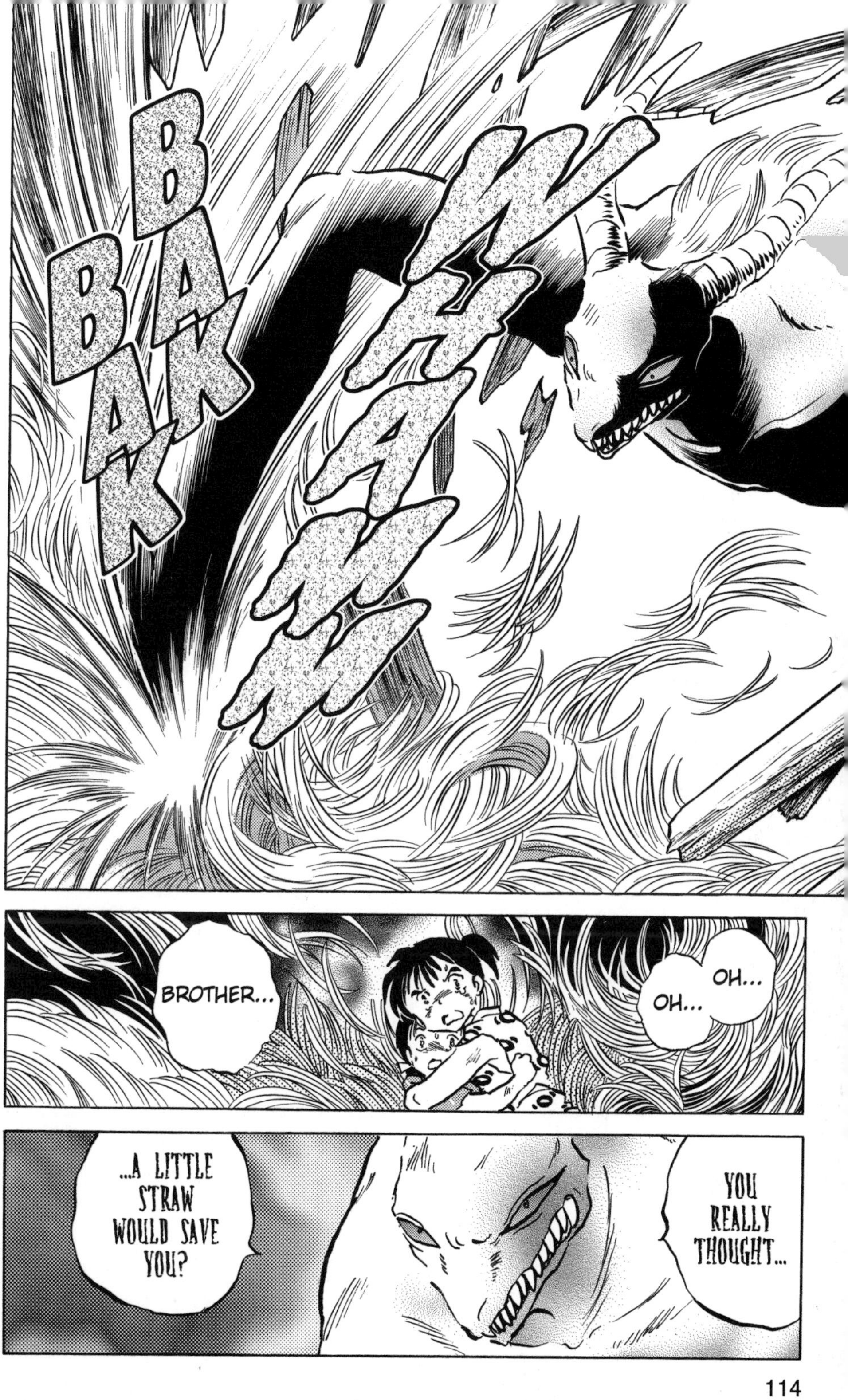
WHAMM
BAK
BAK
OH... OH...
BROTHER...
YOU REALLY THOUGHT...
...A LITTLE STRAW WOULD SAVE YOU?

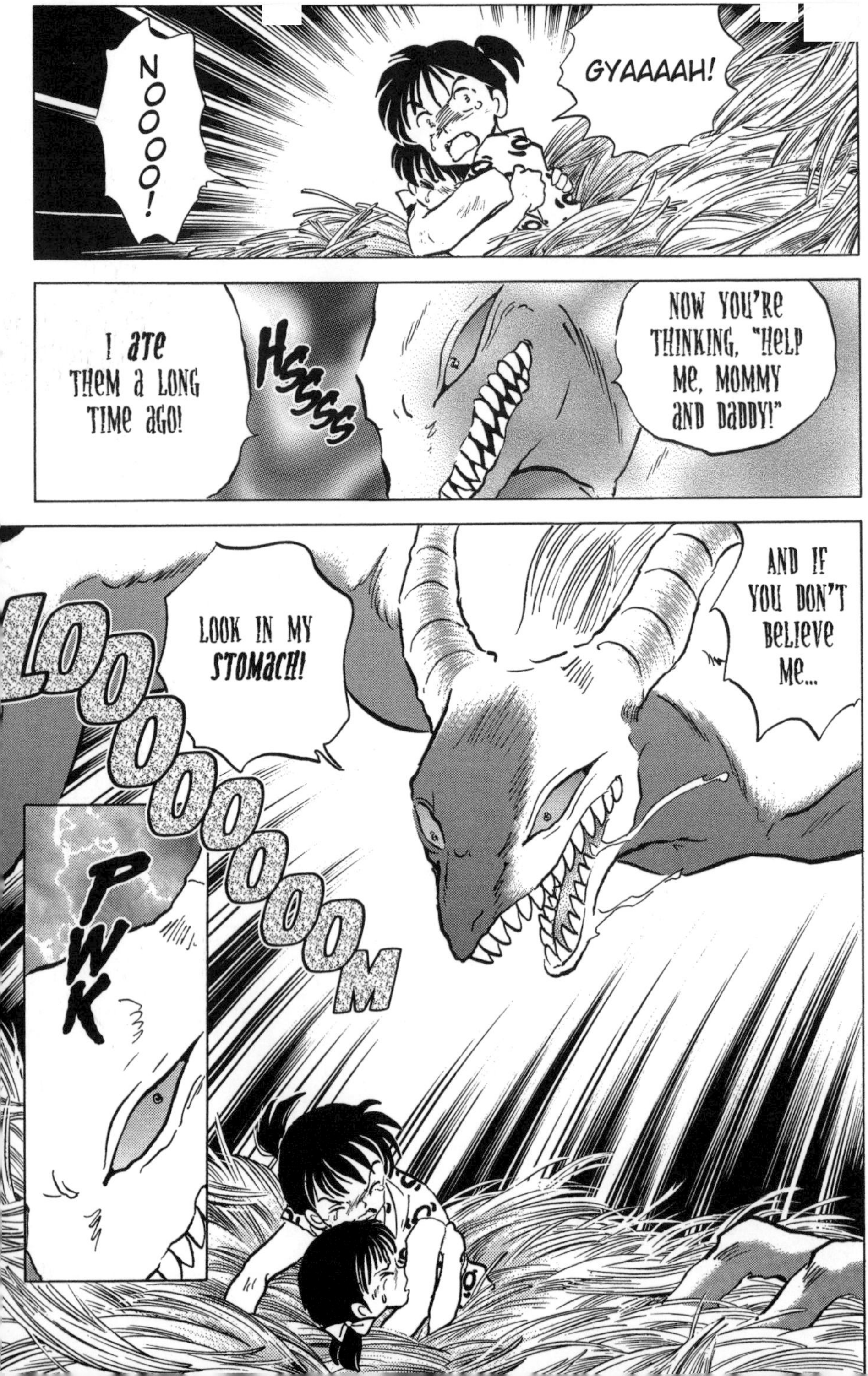
GYAAAAH!
NOOOOO!
NOW YOU'RE THINKING, "HELP ME, MOMMY AND DADDY!"
HSSSSS
I ATE THEM A LONG TIME AGO!
AND IF YOU DON'T BELIEVE ME...
LOOK IN MY STOMACH!
LOOOOOOOOOOOM
PWK

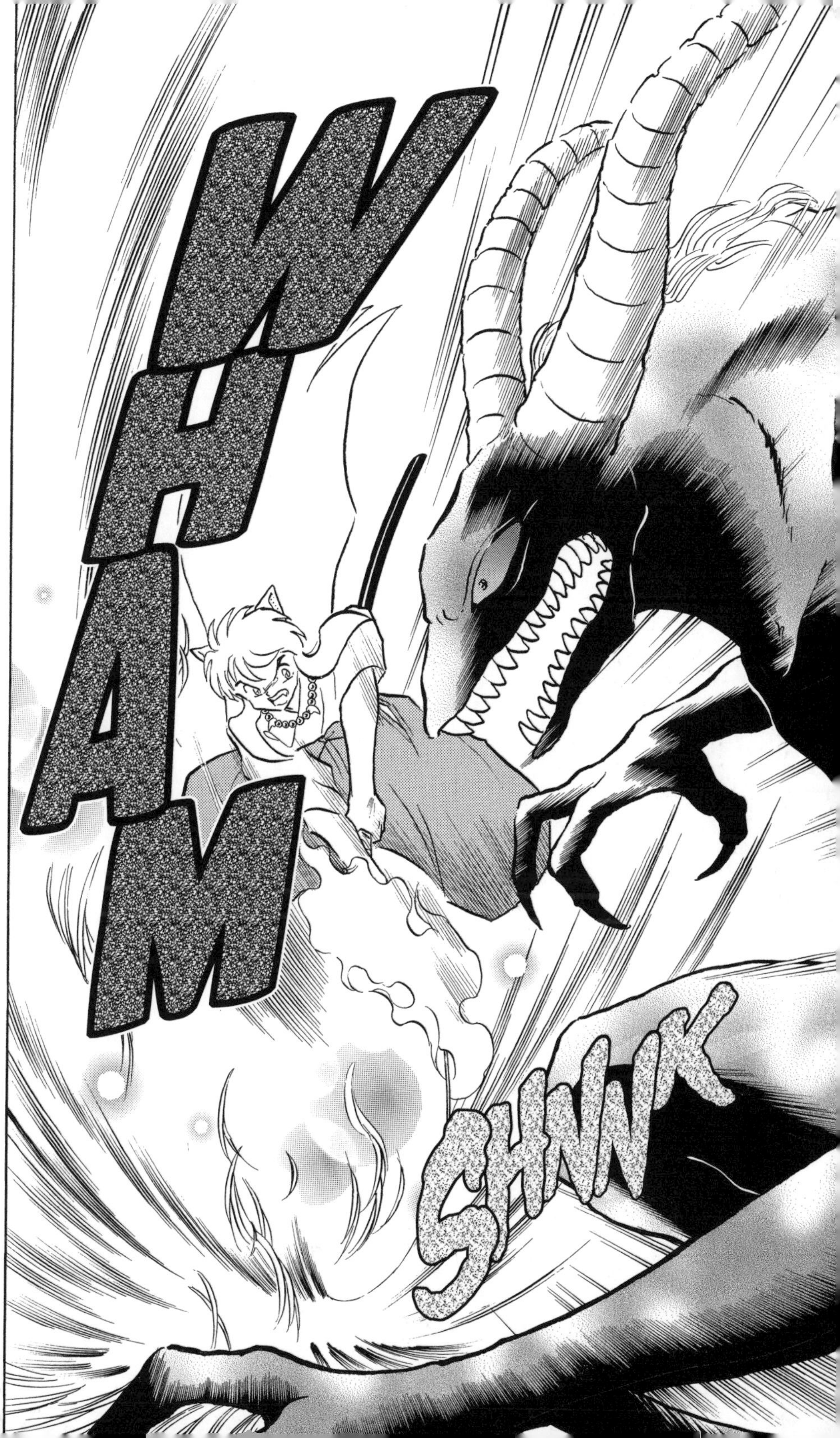
WHAM
SHNNK

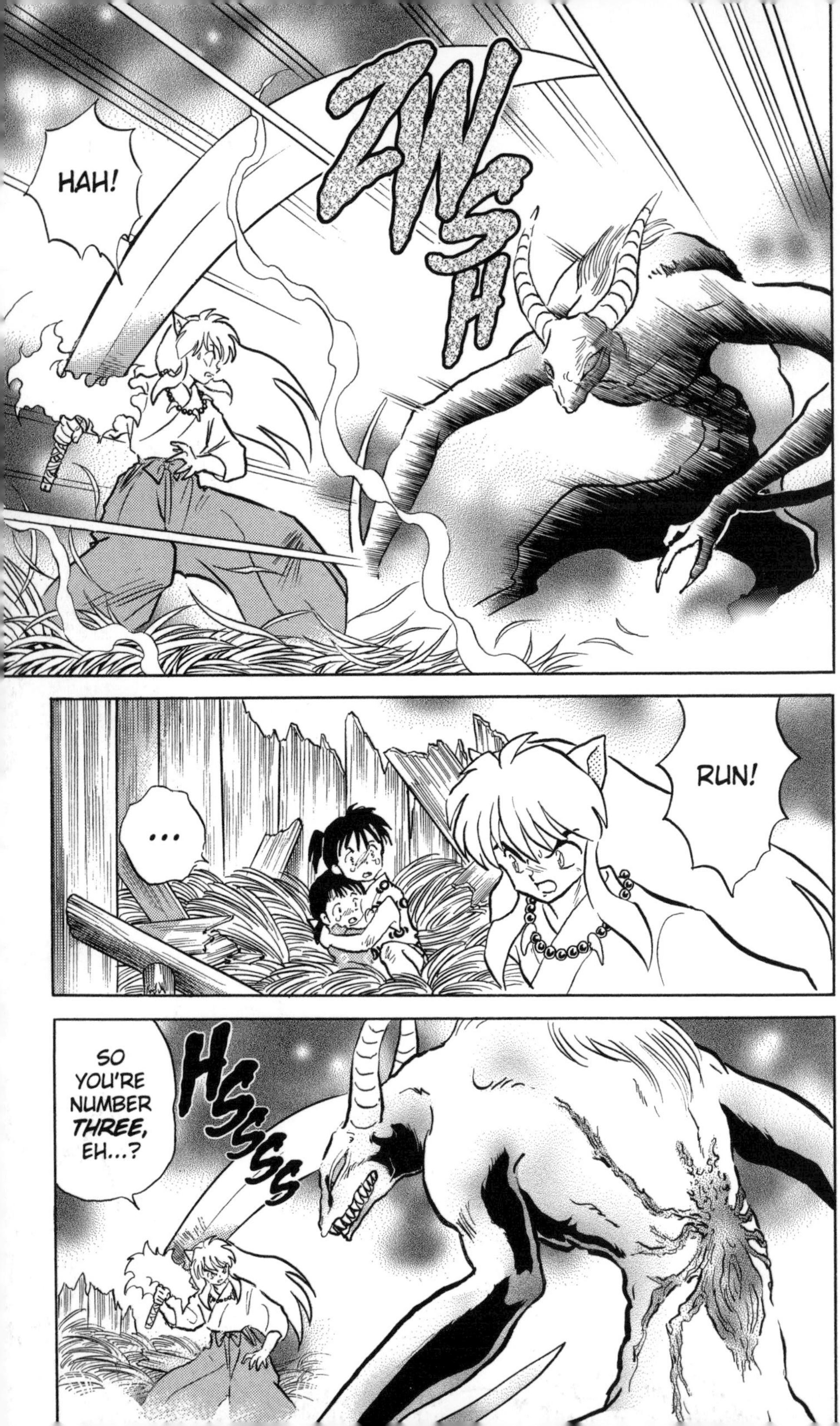
ZWSH
HAH!
RUN!
...
HSSSSS
SO YOU'RE NUMBER *THREE*, EH...?

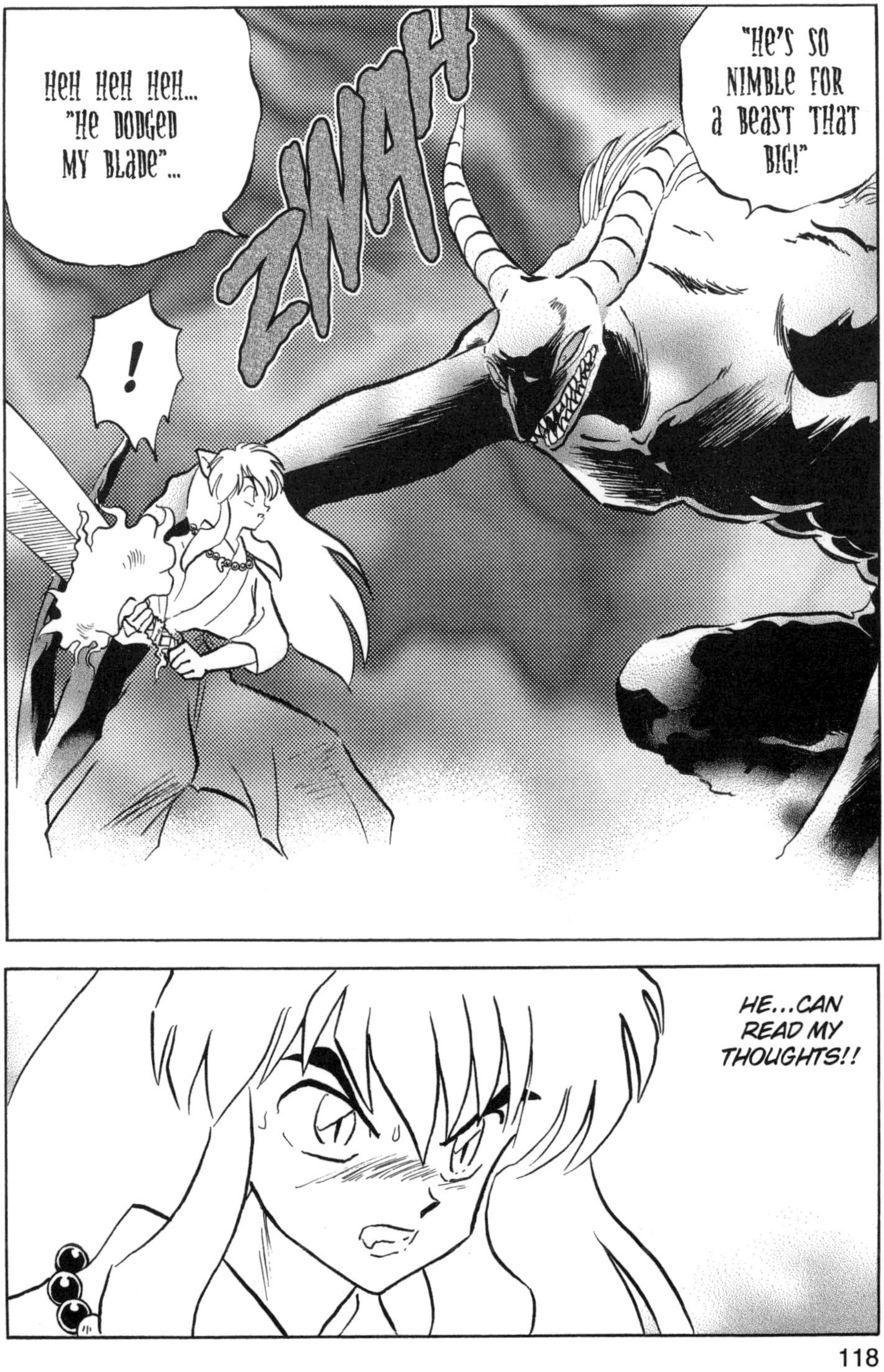
"He's so nimble for a beast that big!"
Heh heh heh... "He dodged my blade"...
ZWAH
!
HE...CAN READ MY THOUGHTS!!

SCROLL SEVEN
GOSHINKI

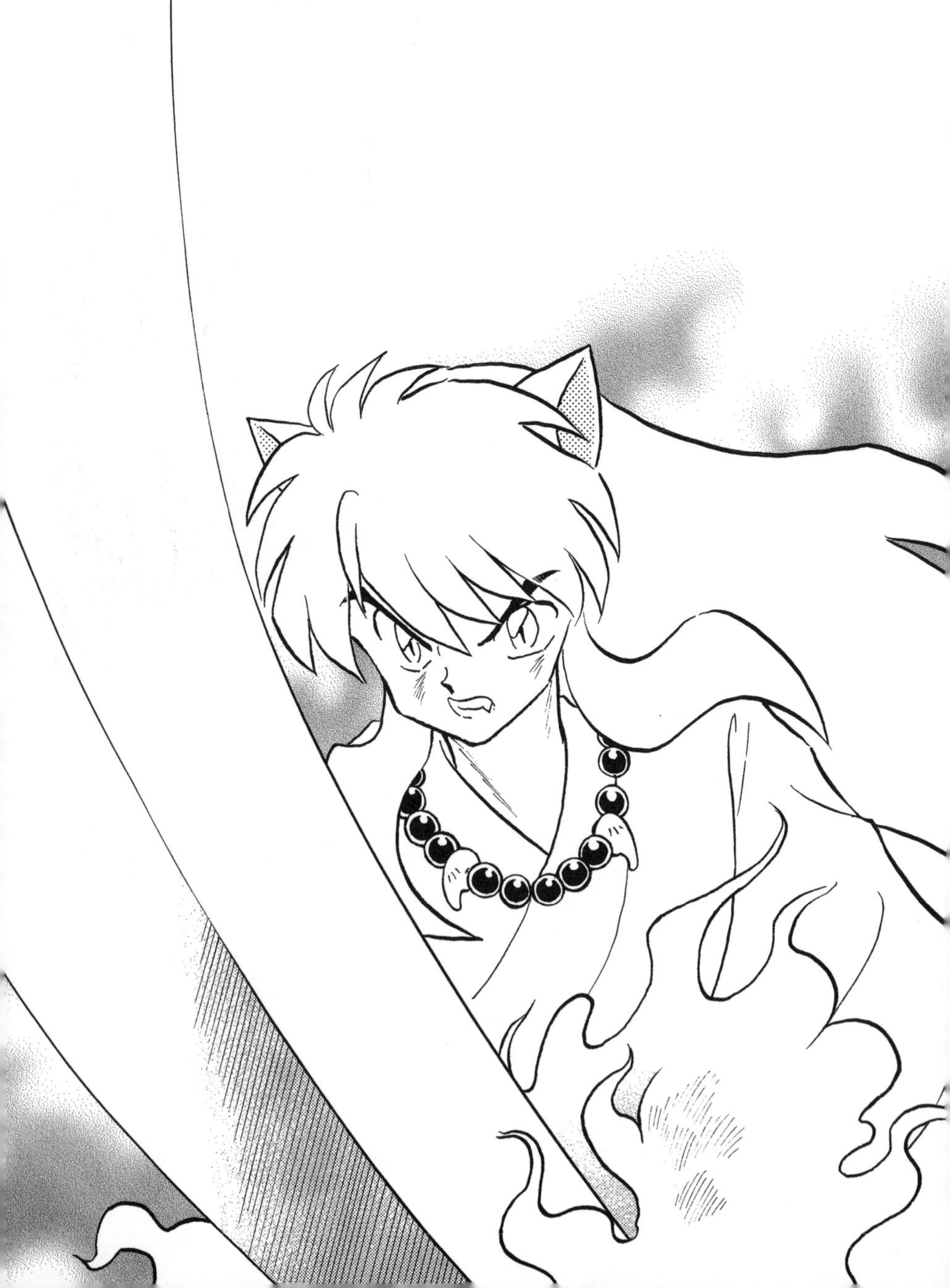

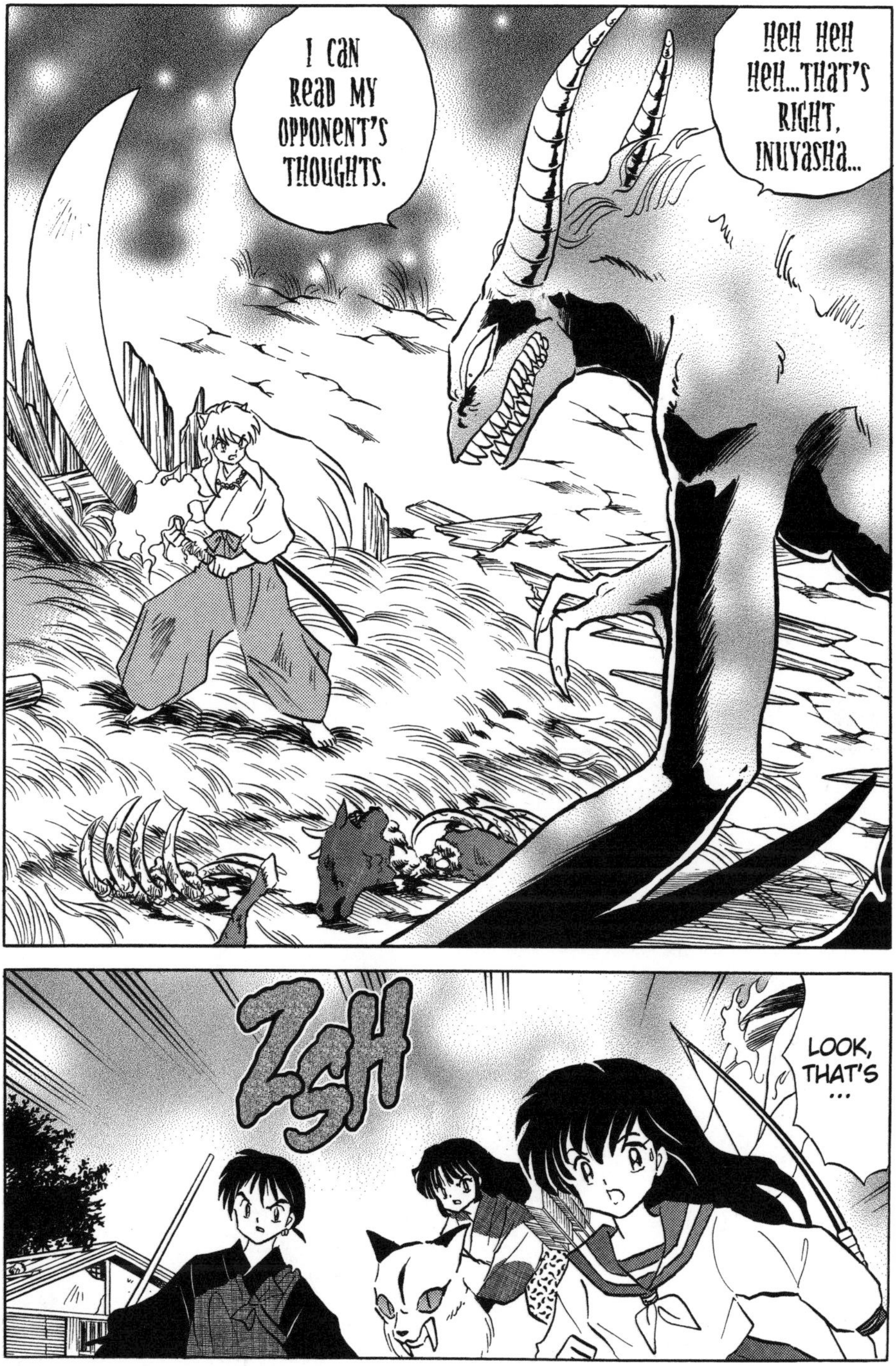
HEH HEH HEH...THAT'S RIGHT, INUYASHA...
I CAN READ MY OPPONENT'S THOUGHTS.
LOOK, THAT'S ...
ZSH

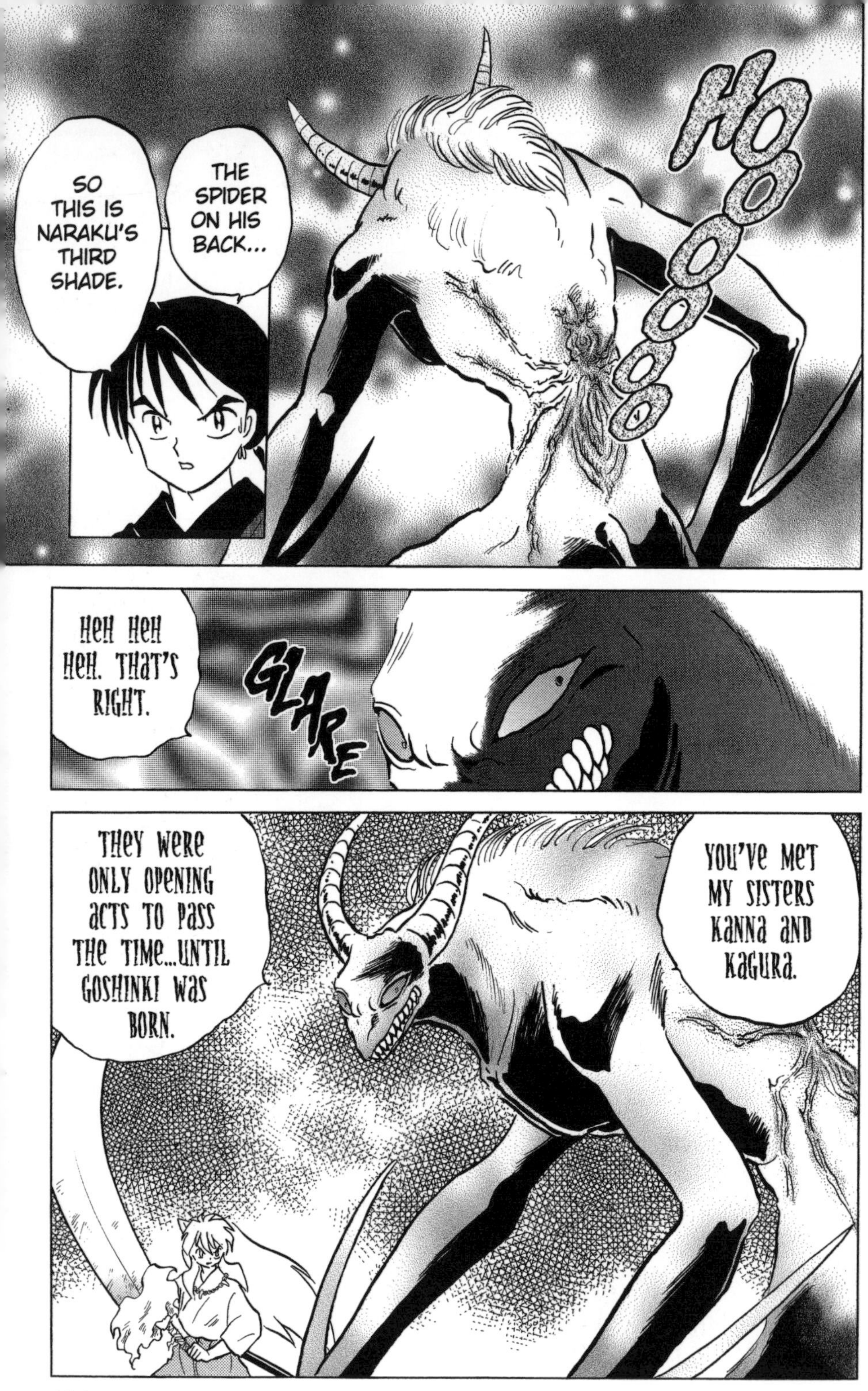

HOOOOOOO
THE SPIDER ON HIS BACK...
SO THIS IS NARAKU'S THIRD SHADE.
GLARE
HEH HEH HEH. THAT'S RIGHT.
YOU'VE MET MY SISTERS KANNA AND KAGURA.
THEY WERE ONLY OPENING ACTS TO PASS THE TIME...UNTIL GOSHINKI WAS BORN.

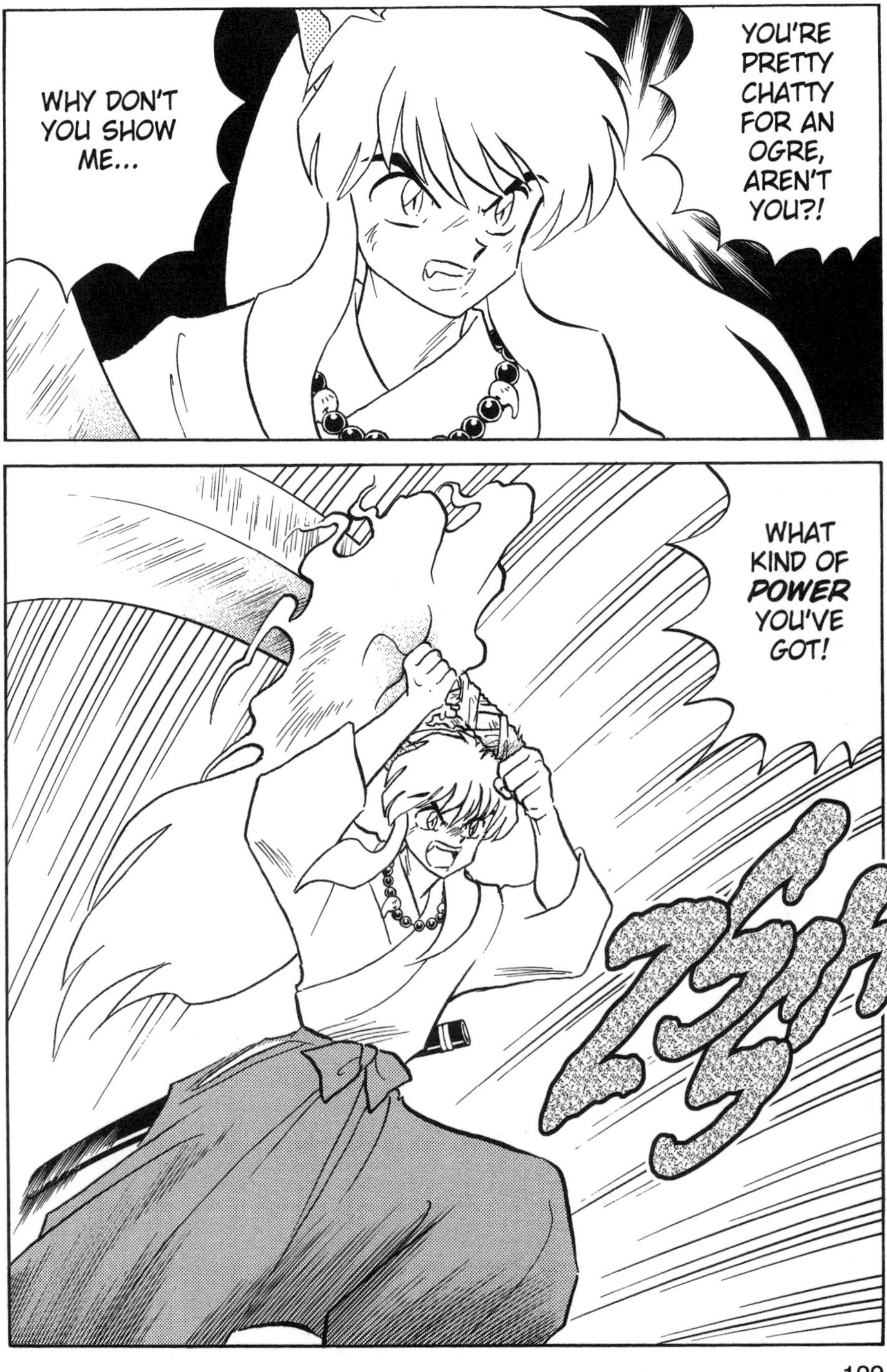
YOU'RE PRETTY CHATTY FOR AN OGRE, AREN'T YOU?!
WHY DON'T YOU SHOW ME...
WHAT KIND OF **POWER** YOU'VE GOT!

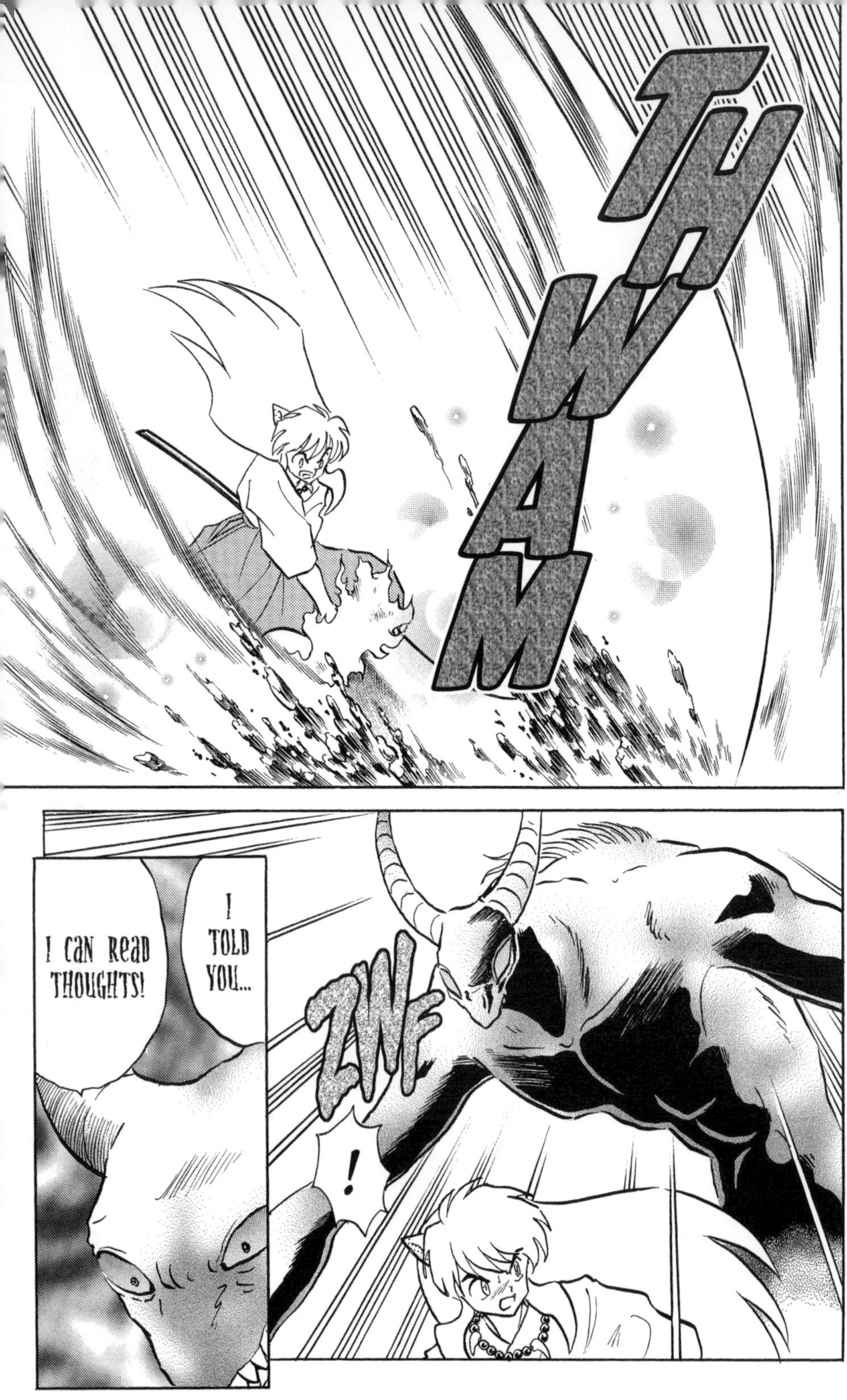
THWAM
ZWF
!
I TOLD YOU...
I CAN READ THOUGHTS!

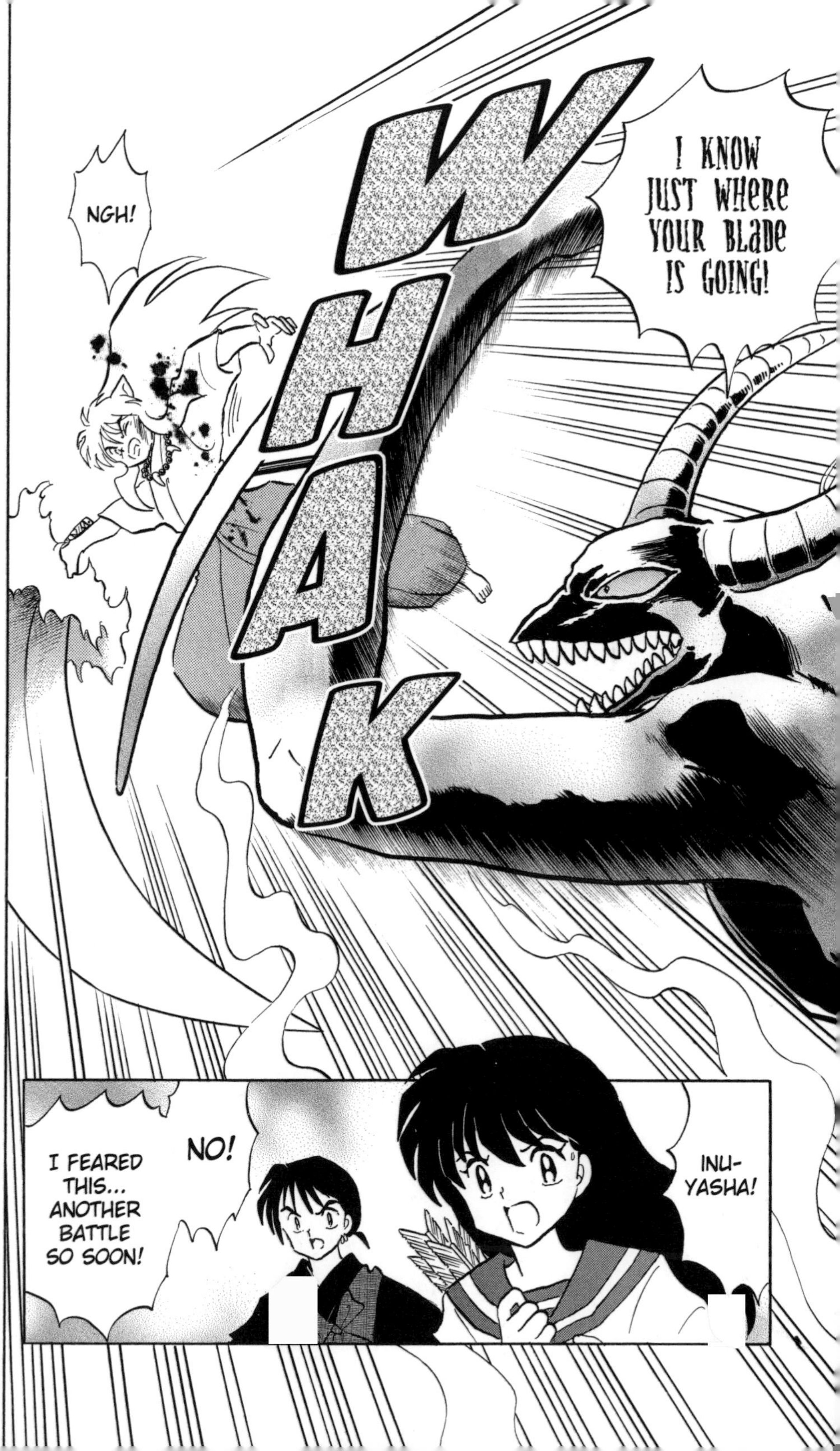
I KNOW JUST WHERE YOUR BLADE IS GOING!
WHAK
NGH!
INU-YASHA!
NO!
I FEARED THIS... ANOTHER BATTLE SO SOON!

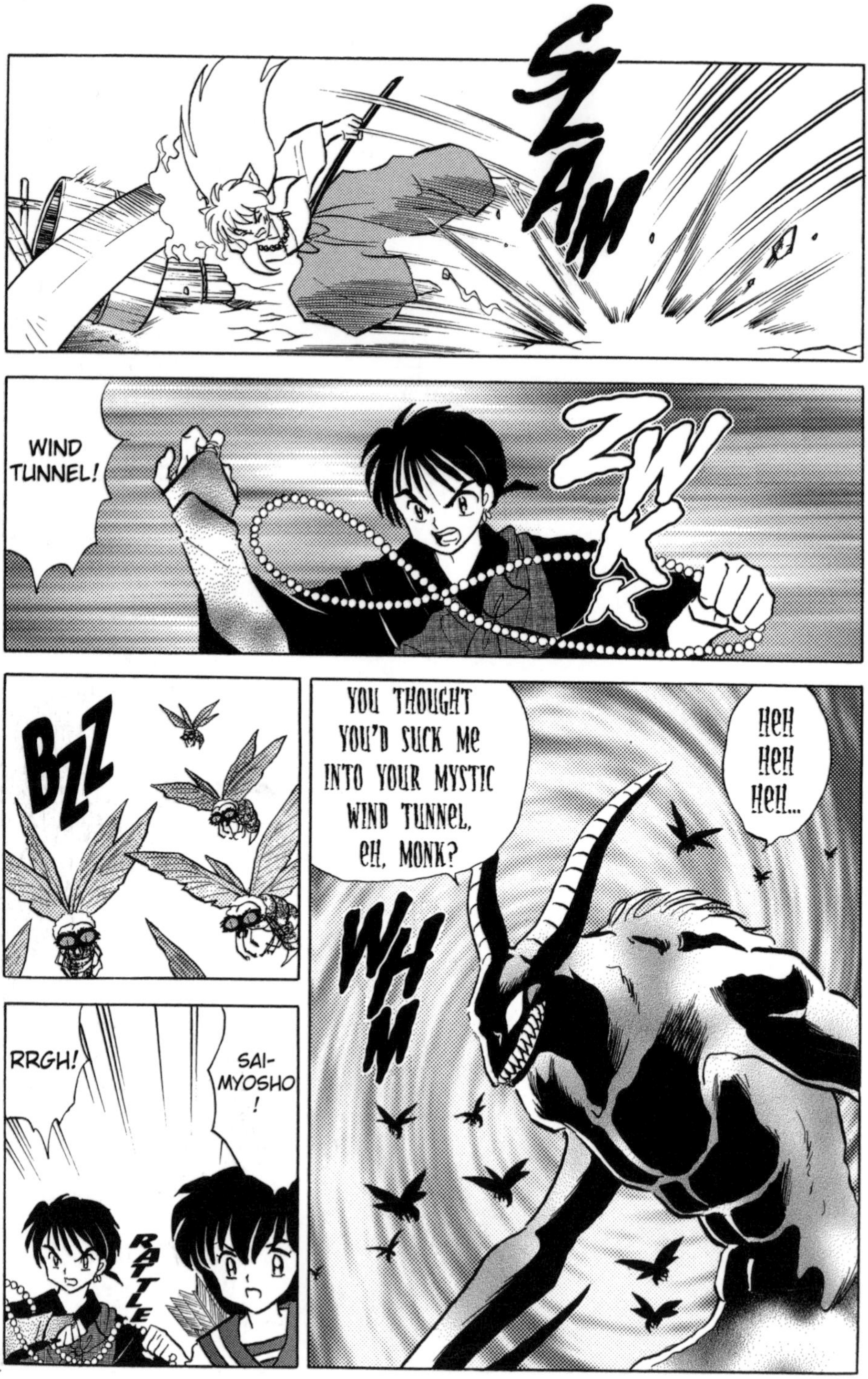
SLAM
ZWKK
WIND TUNNEL!
HEH HEH HEH...
YOU THOUGHT YOU'D SUCK ME INTO YOUR MYSTIC WIND TUNNEL, EH, MONK?
WHMM
BZZ
SAI-MYOSHO!
RRGH!
RATTLE

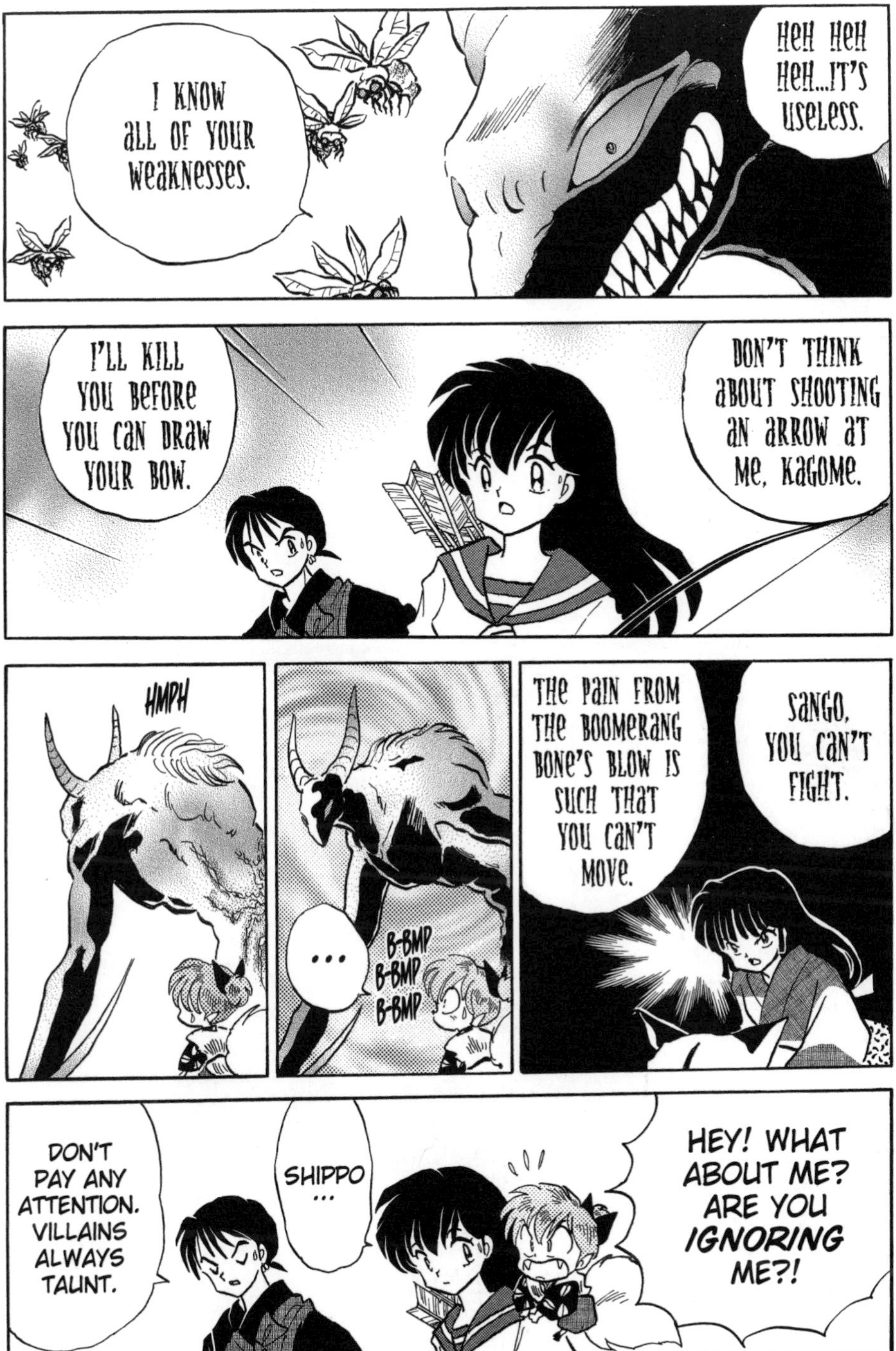
HEH HEH HEH...IT'S USELESS.
I KNOW ALL OF YOUR WEAKNESSES.
DON'T THINK ABOUT SHOOTING AN ARROW AT ME, KAGOME.
I'LL KILL YOU BEFORE YOU CAN DRAW YOUR BOW.
SANGO, YOU CAN'T FIGHT.
THE PAIN FROM THE BOOMERANG BONE'S BLOW IS SUCH THAT YOU CAN'T MOVE.
...
B-BMP B-BMP B-BMP
HMPH
HEY! WHAT ABOUT ME? ARE YOU *IGNORING* ME?!
SHIPPO...
DON'T PAY ANY ATTENTION. VILLAINS ALWAYS TAUNT.

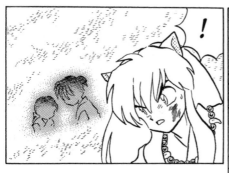

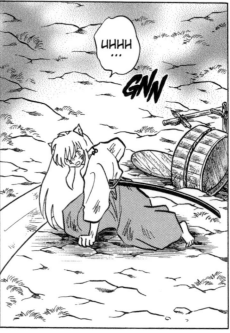

UHHH ...
GNN
!
THOSE BRATS FROM BEFORE...
I TOLD YOU TO RUN AWAY!
WHAT ARE YOU STILL DOING...
!

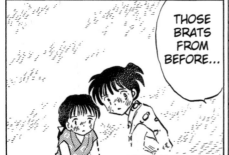

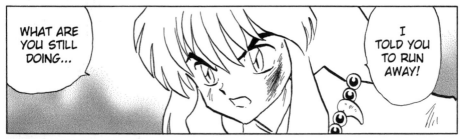

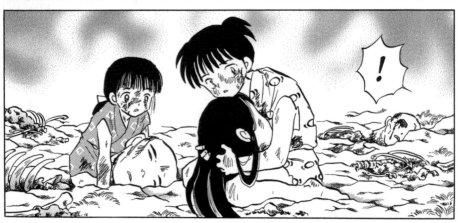

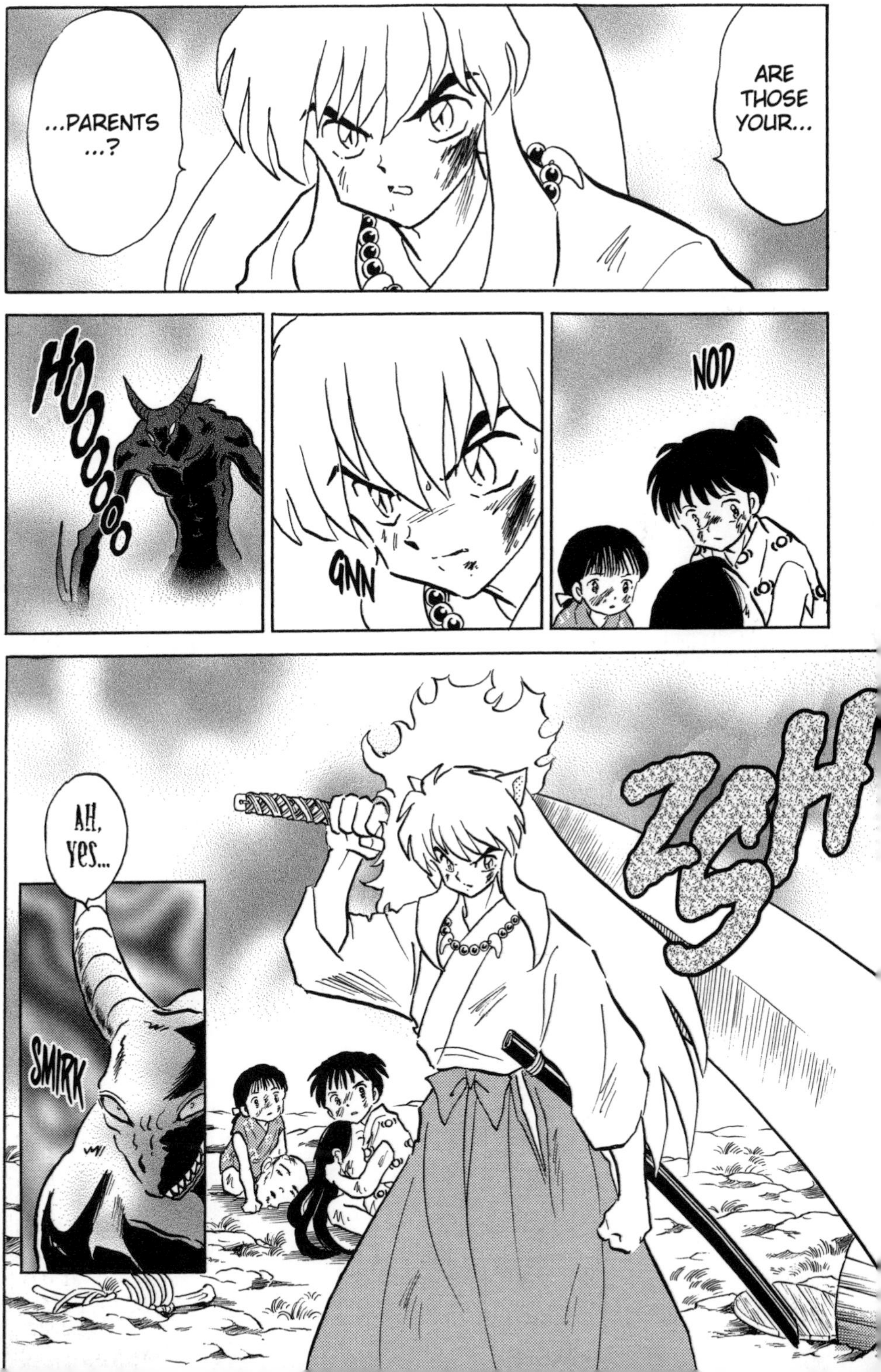
ARE THOSE YOUR...
...PARENTS ...?
NOD
GNN
HOOOOOOO
ZSH
AH, YES...
SMIRK

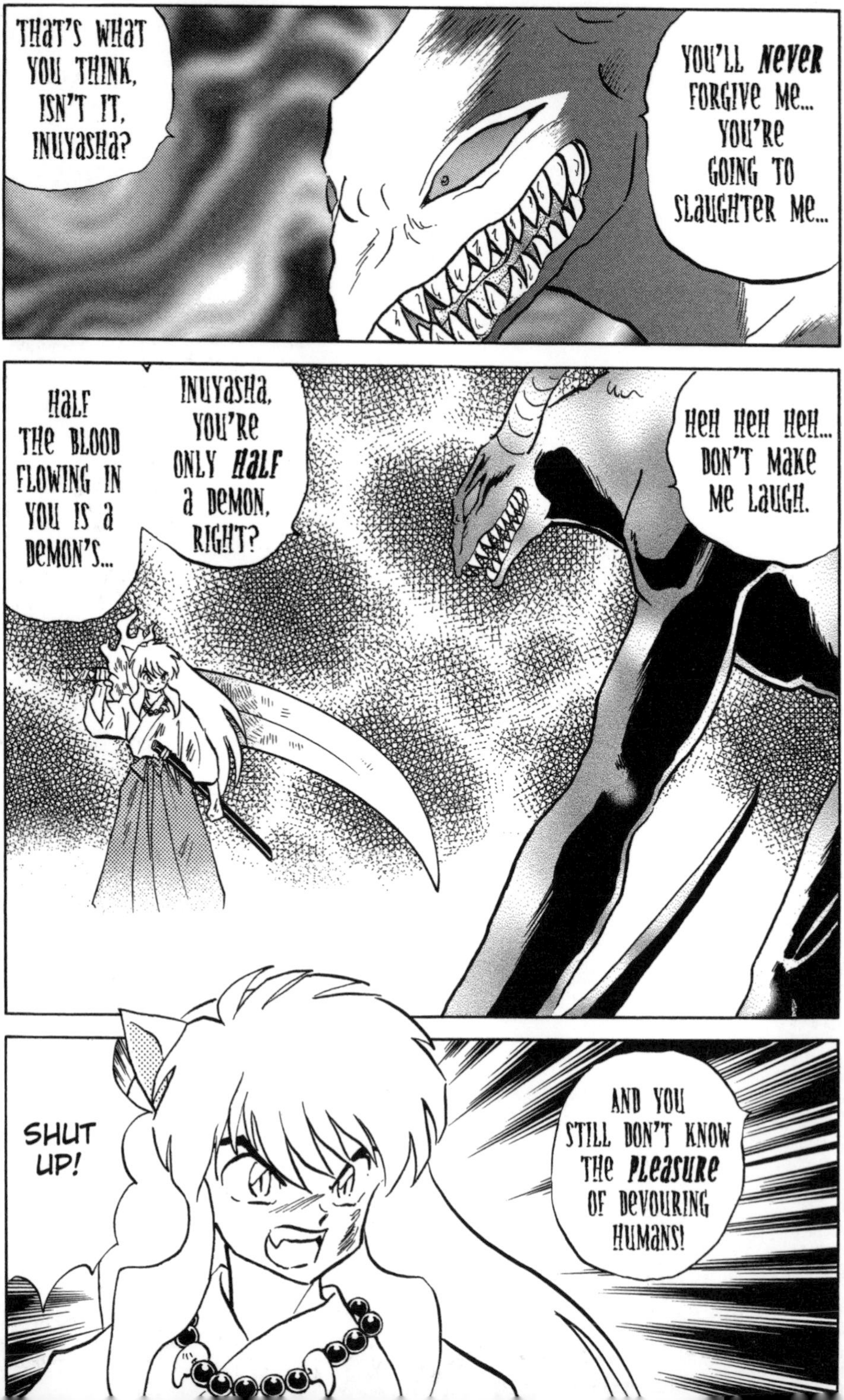
YOU'LL *NEVER* FORGIVE ME... YOU'RE GOING TO SLAUGHTER ME...
THAT'S WHAT YOU THINK, ISN'T IT, INUYASHA?
HEH HEH HEH... DON'T MAKE ME LAUGH.
INUYASHA, YOU'RE ONLY *HALF* A DEMON, RIGHT?
HALF THE BLOOD FLOWING IN YOU IS A DEMON'S...
AND YOU STILL DON'T KNOW THE *PLEASURE* OF DEVOURING HUMANS!
SHUT UP!

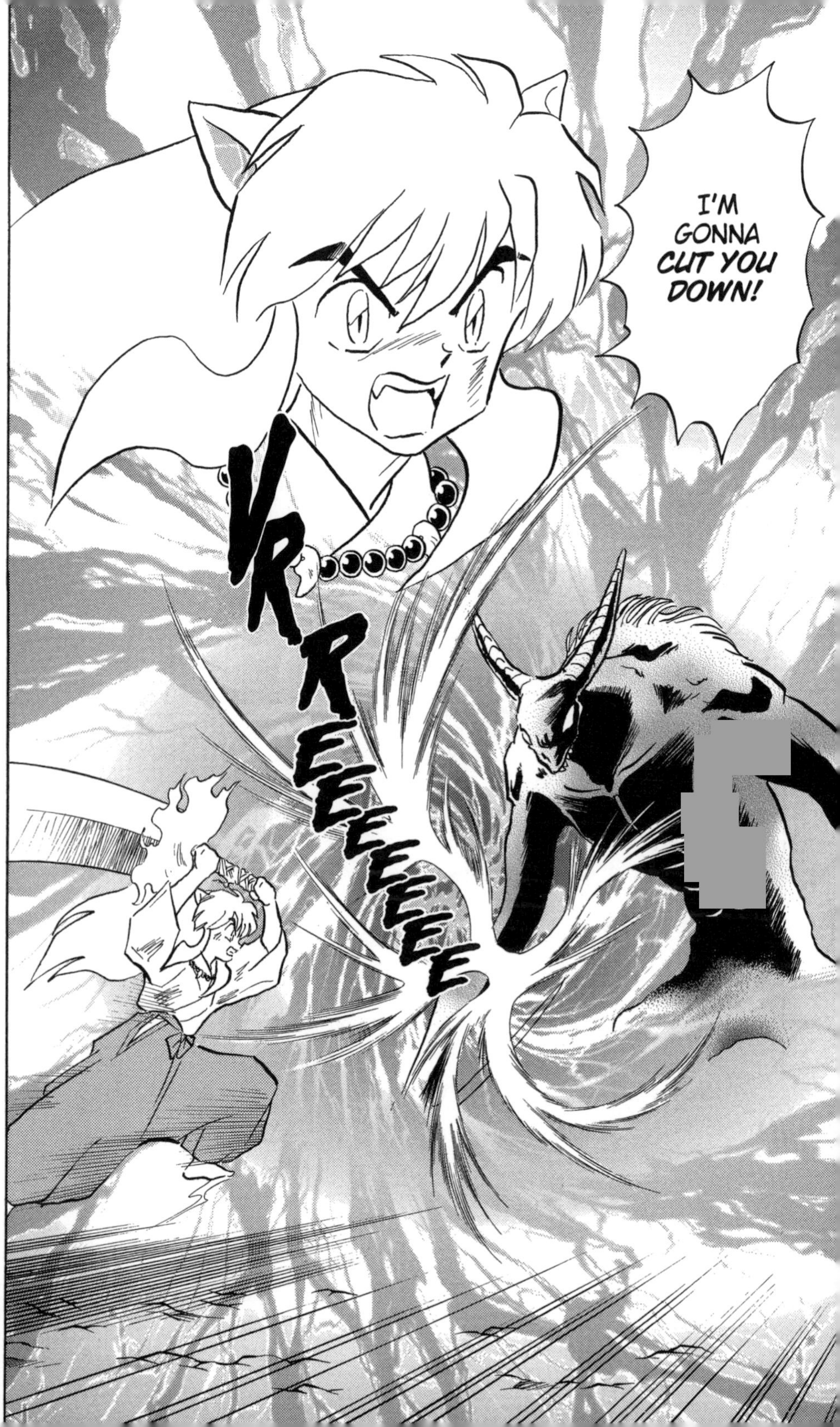
I'M GONNA CUT YOU DOWN!
VRREEEEEEEEE

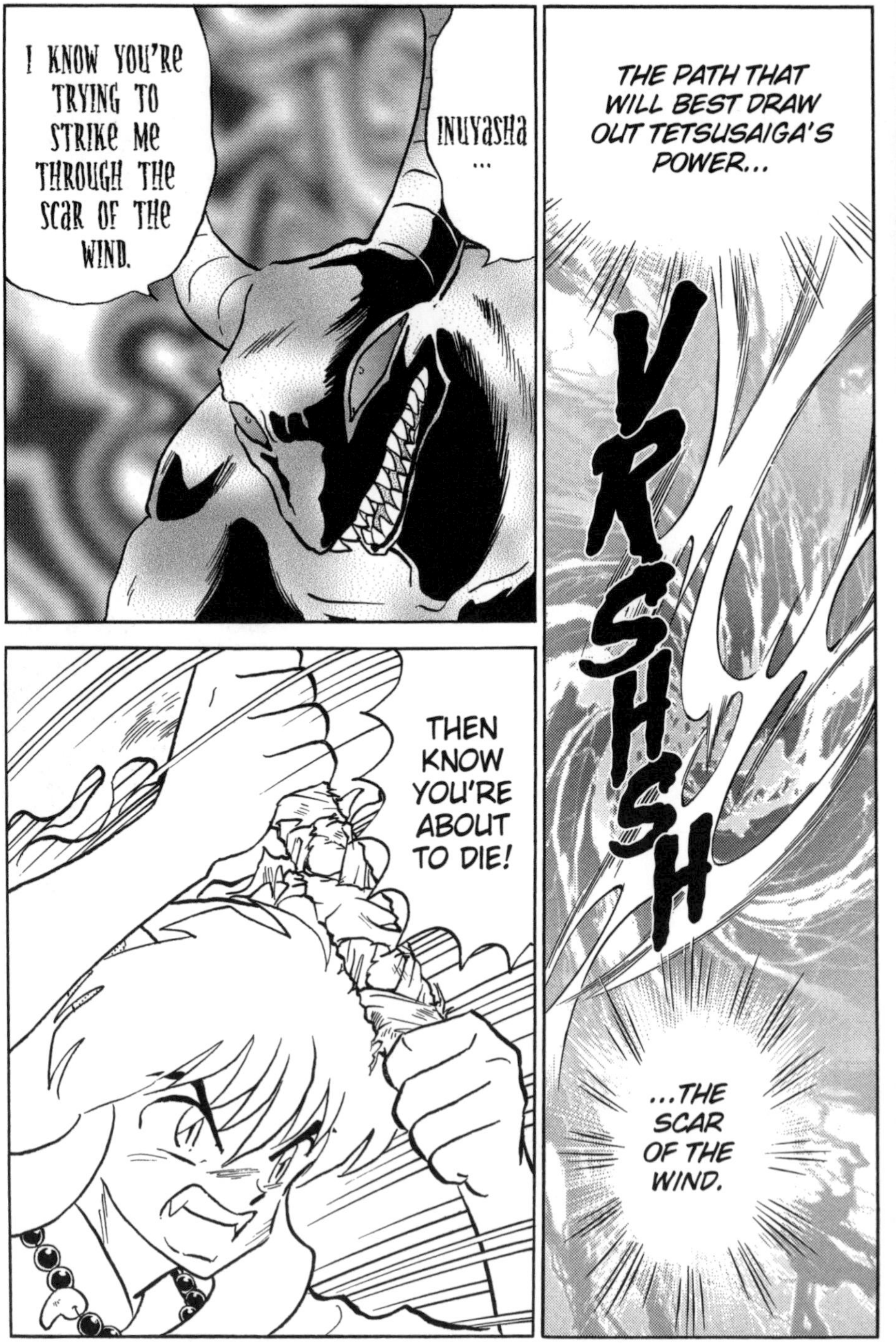
THE PATH THAT WILL BEST DRAW OUT TETSUSAIGA'S POWER...
VRSHSH
...THE SCAR OF THE WIND.
INUYASHA...
I KNOW YOU'RE TRYING TO STRIKE ME THROUGH THE SCAR OF THE WIND.
THEN KNOW YOU'RE ABOUT TO DIE!

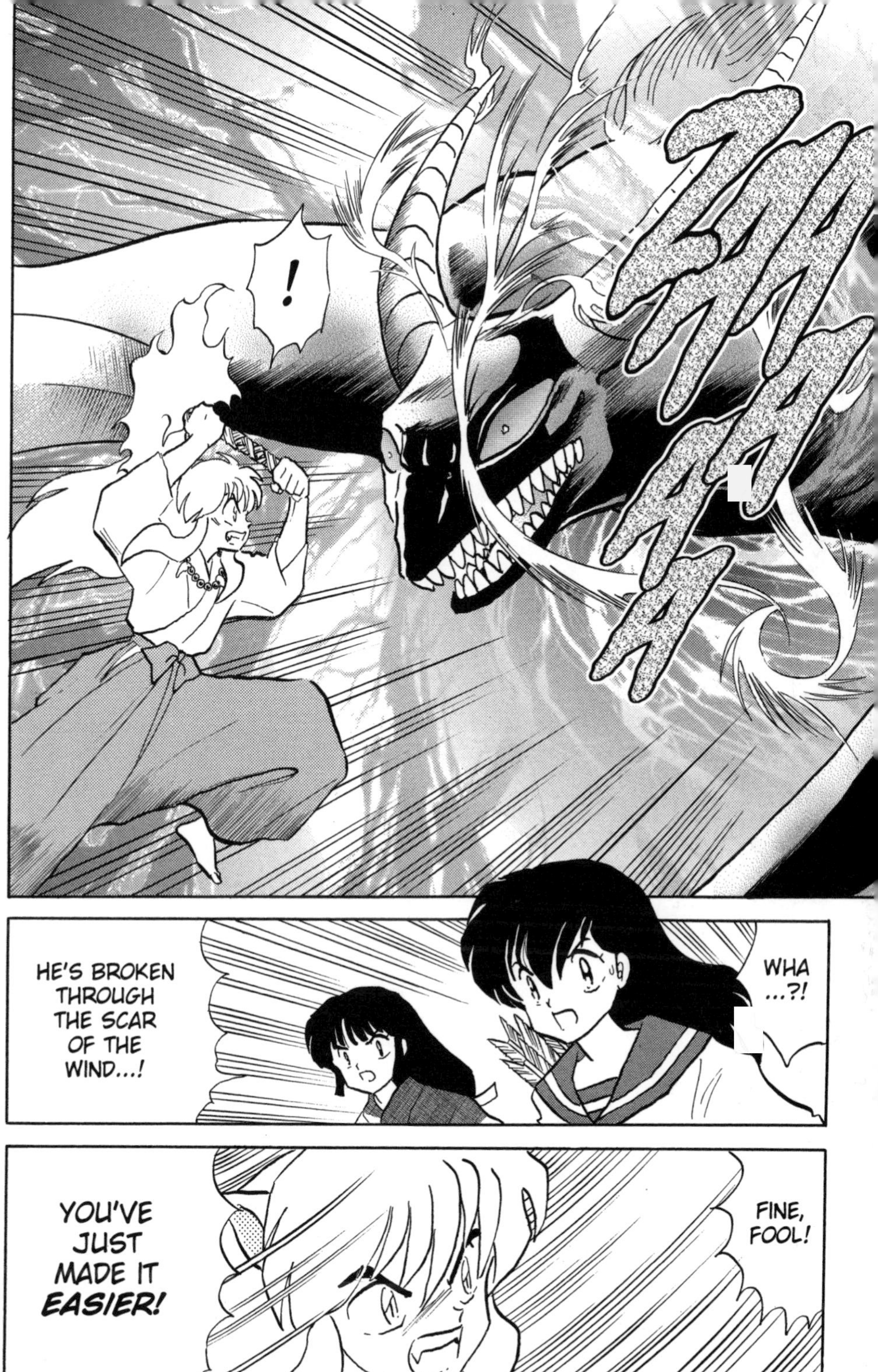
!
WHA ...?!
HE'S BROKEN THROUGH THE SCAR OF THE WIND...!
FINE, FOOL!
YOU'VE JUST MADE IT EASIER!

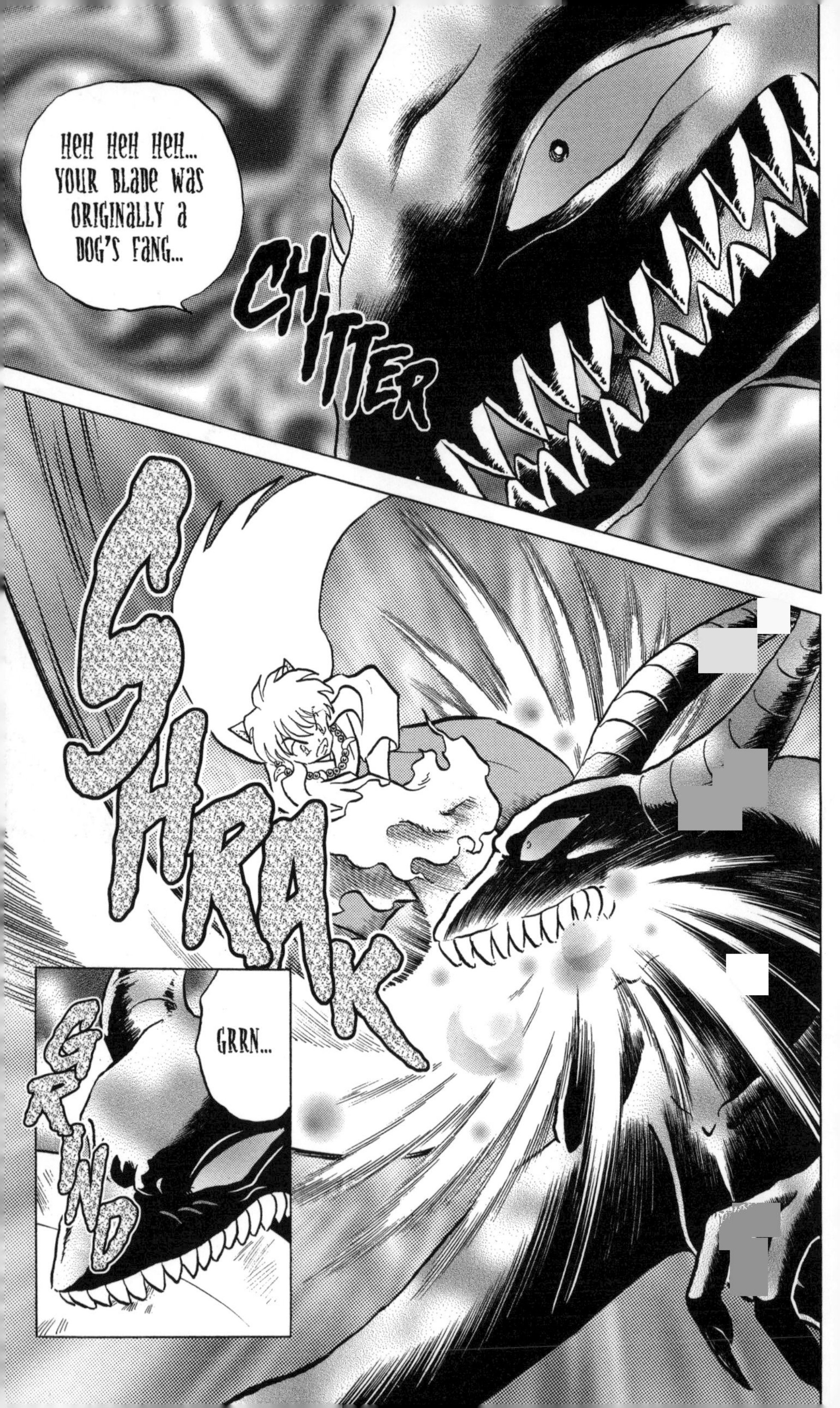
HEH HEH HEH... YOUR BLADE WAS ORIGINALLY A DOG'S FANG...
CHITTER
SHRAK
GRRN...
GRIND

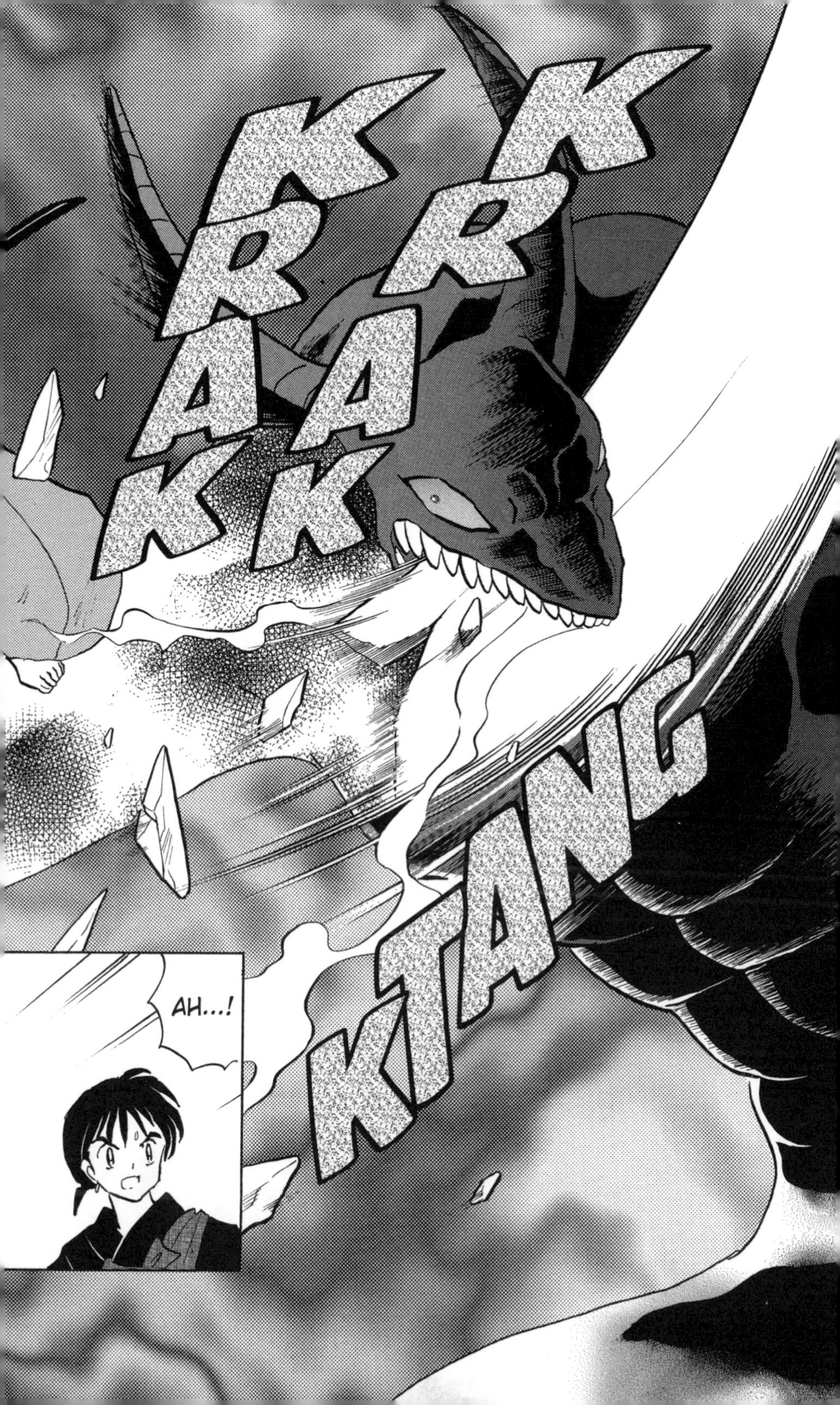
KRAK
KRAK
KTANG
AH...!

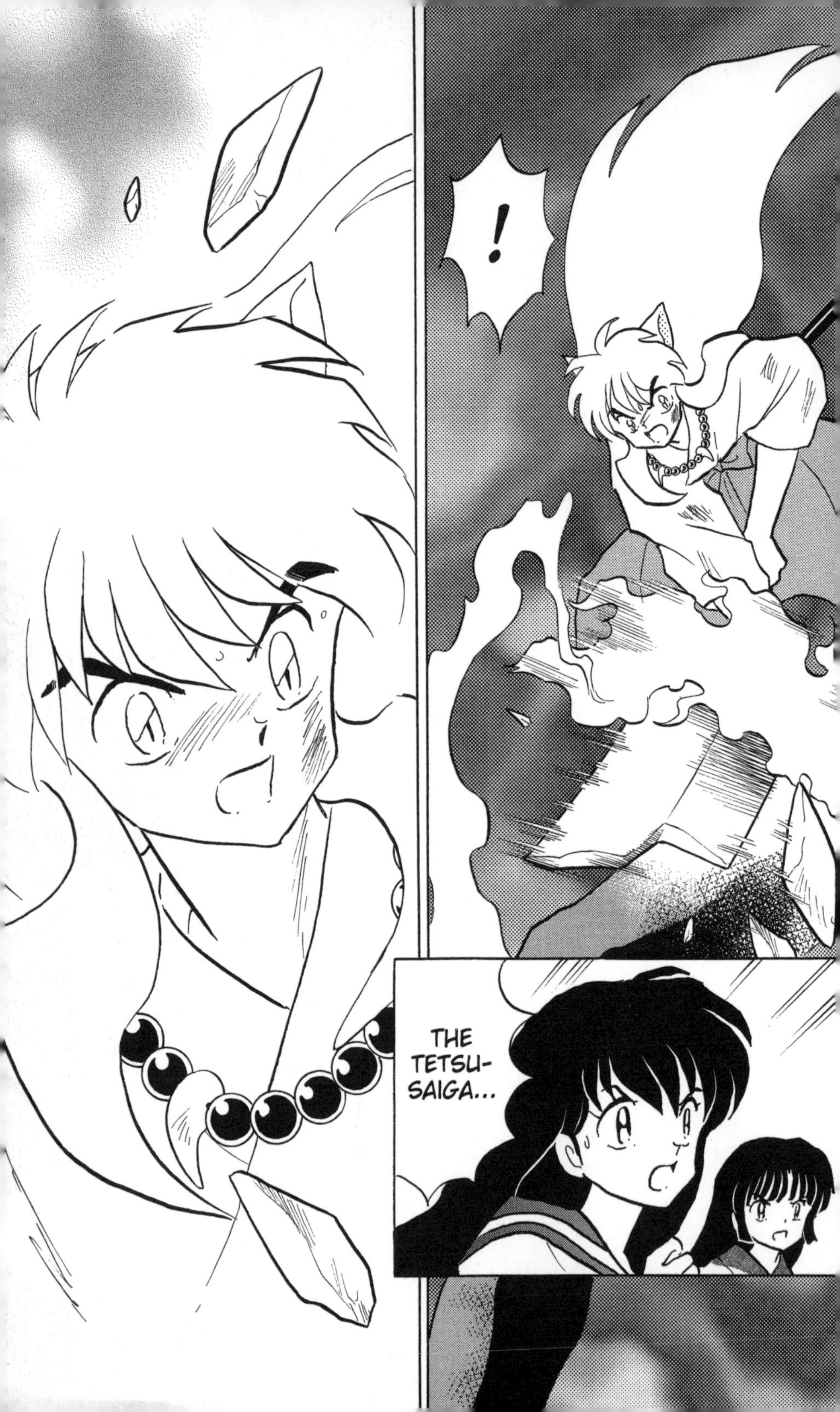
!
THE TETSU-SAIGA...

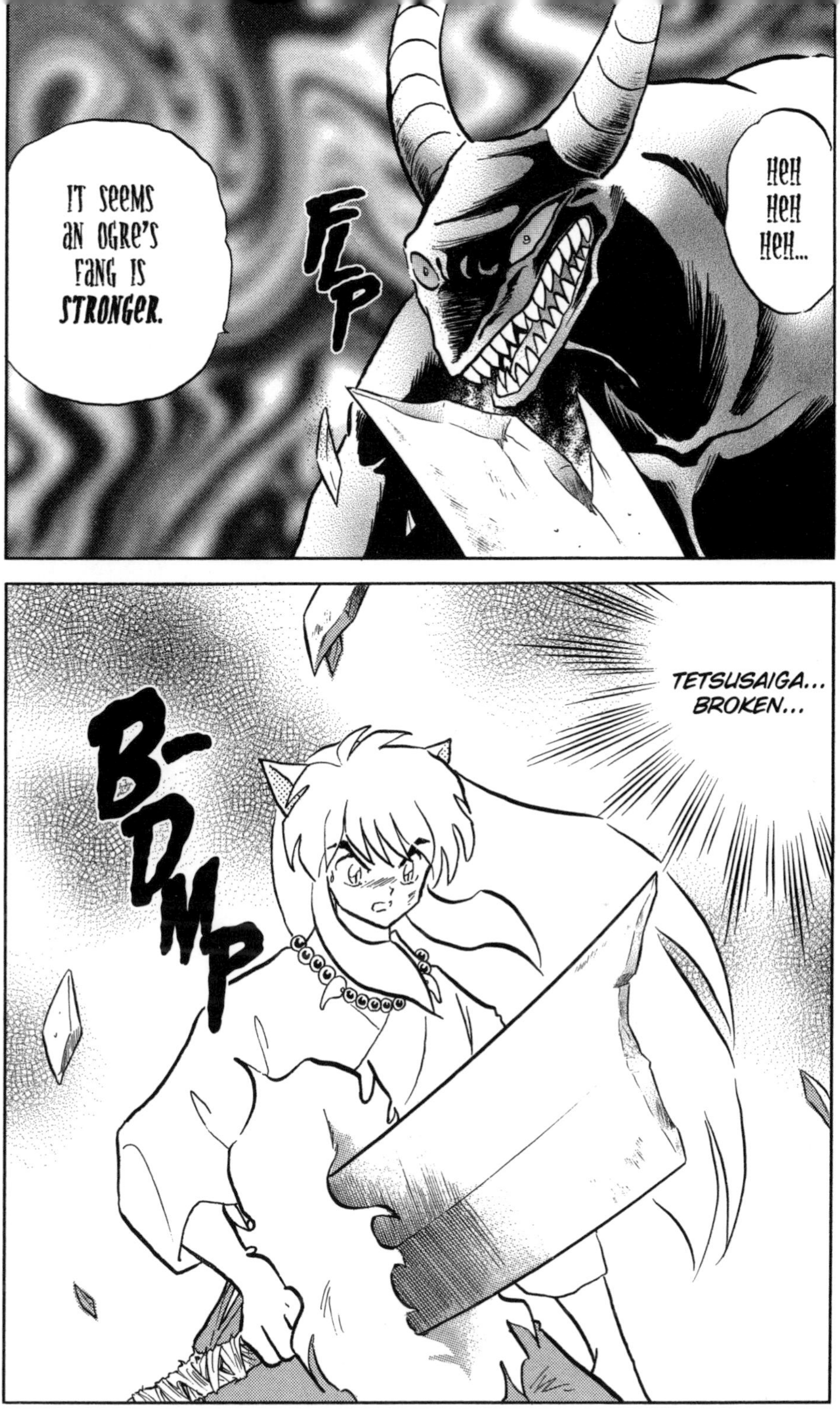
HEH HEH HEH...
FLP
IT SEEMS AN OGRE'S FANG IS STRONGER.
TETSUSAIGA... BROKEN...
B-DUMP

SCROLL EIGHT
DEMON BLOOD

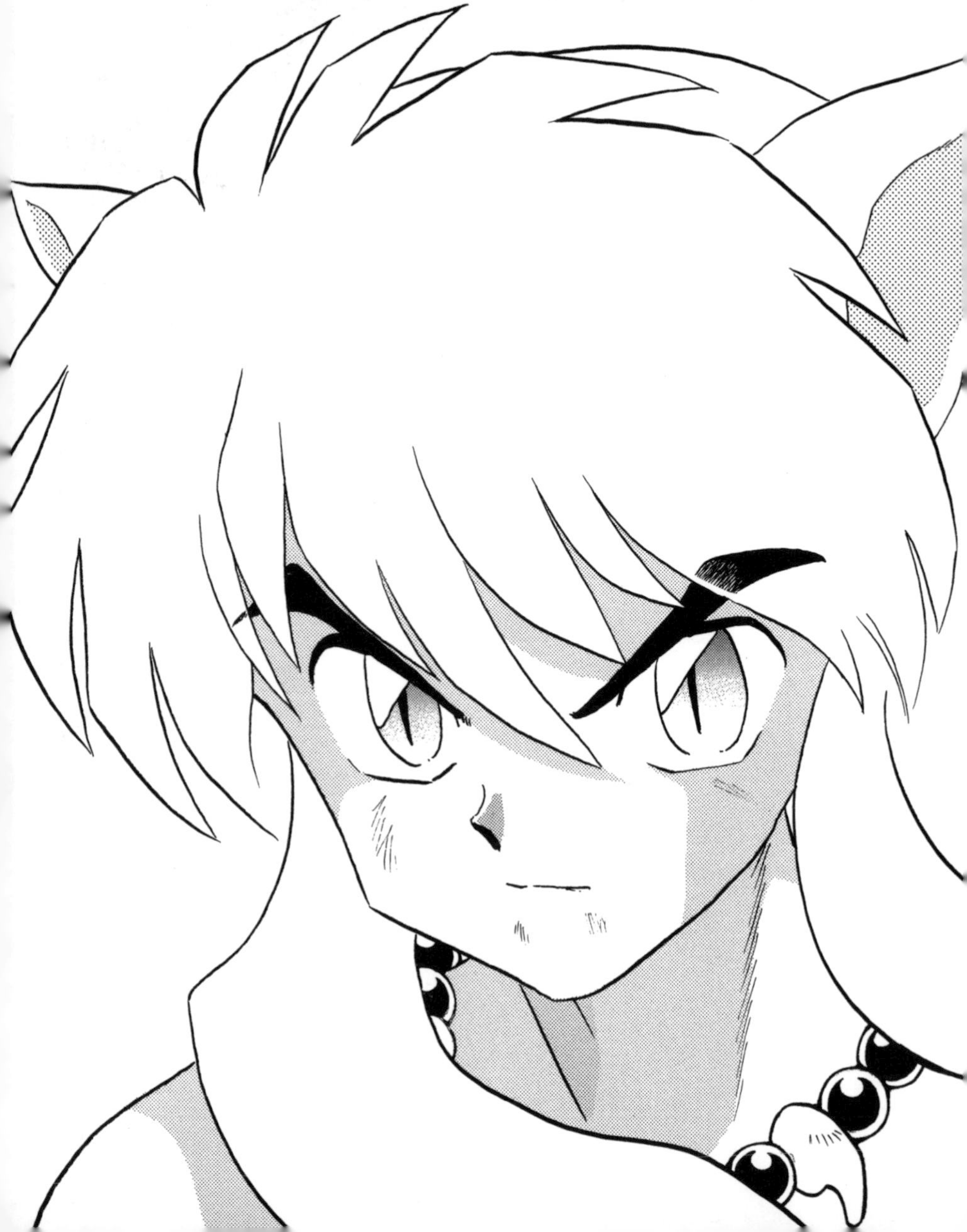

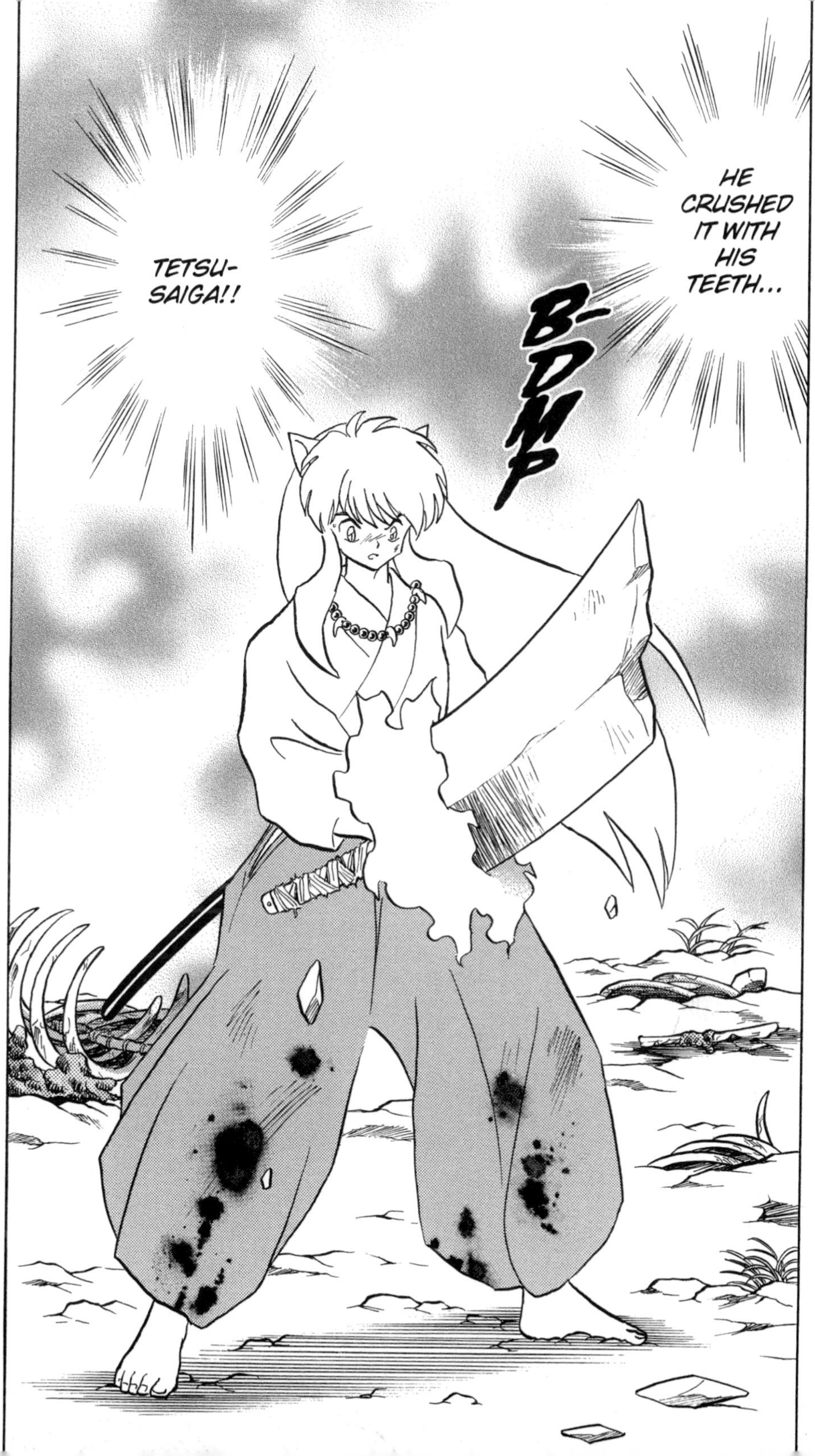
HE CRUSHED IT WITH HIS TEETH...
B-DMP
TETSU-SAIGA!!

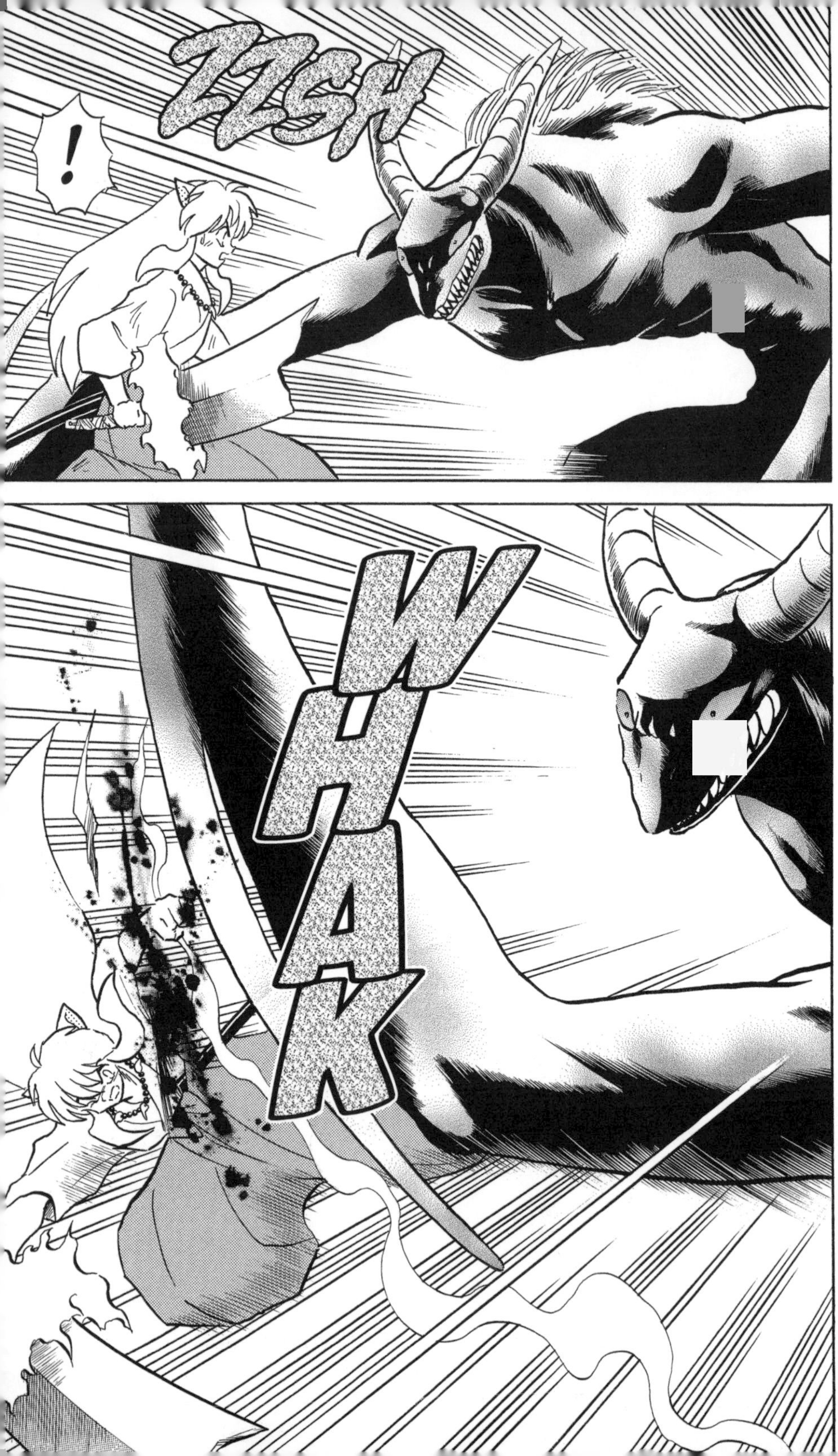
ZZSH
!
WHAK

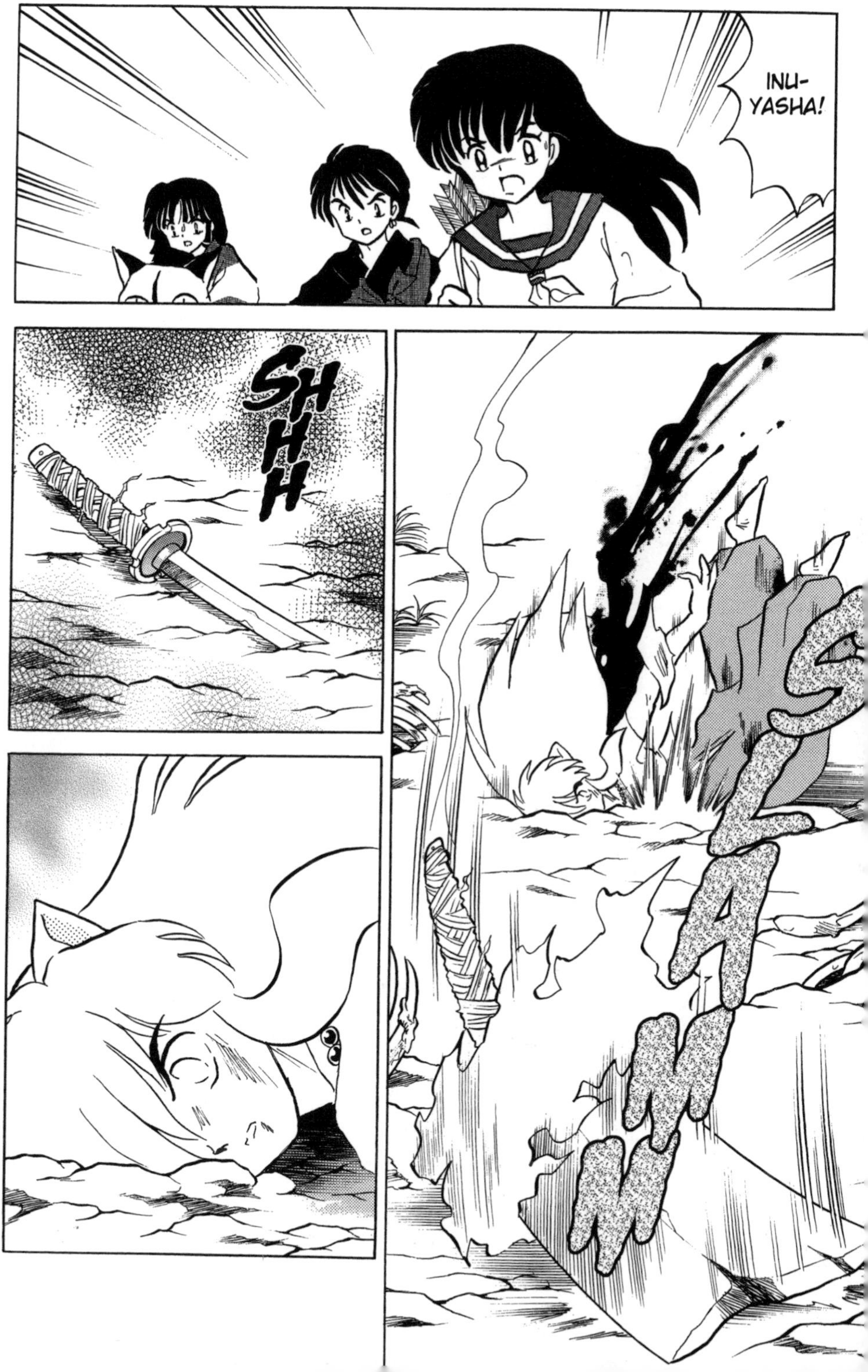
INU-
YASHA!
SLAMM
SHHH

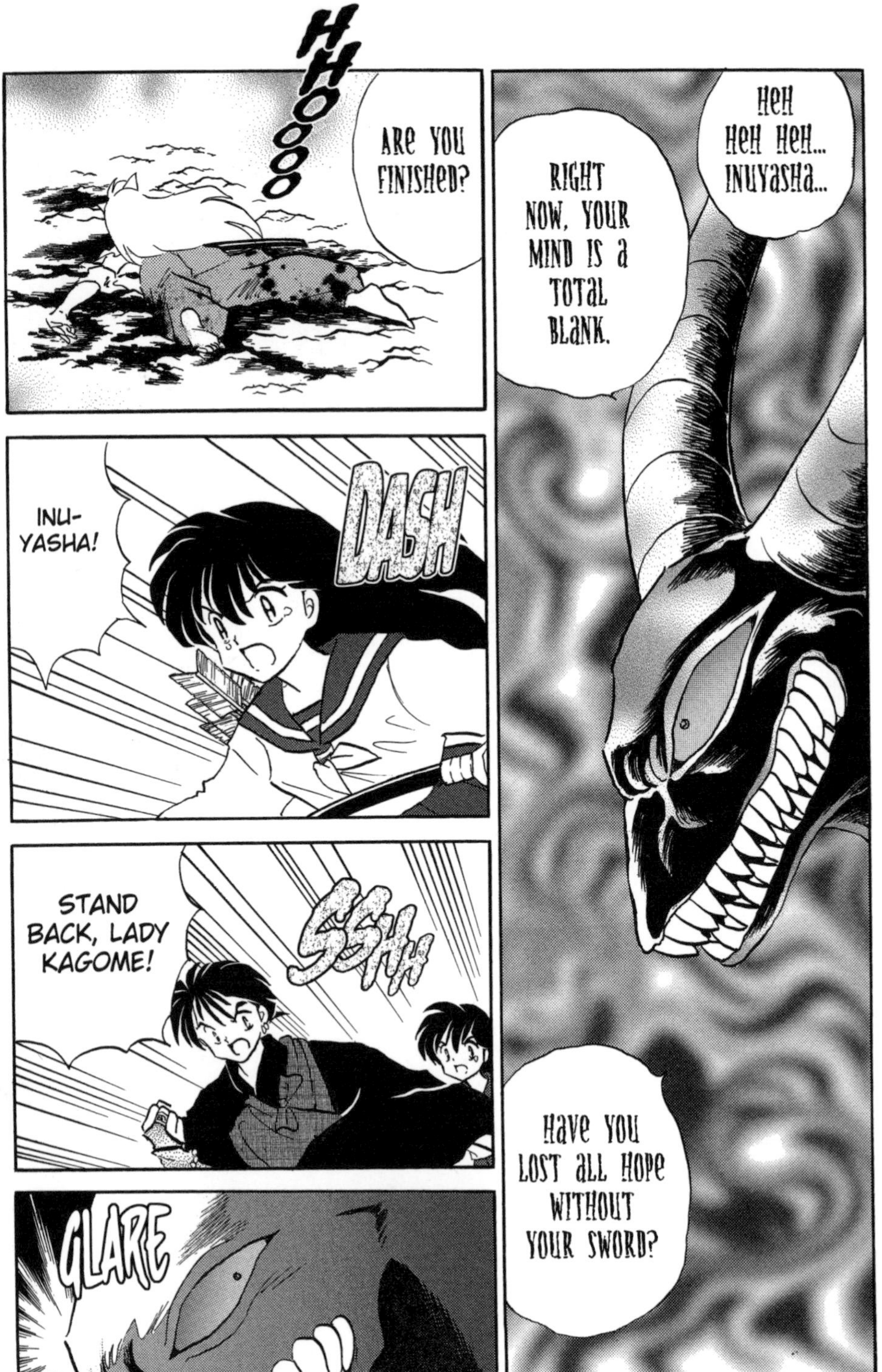
Heh
heh heh... Inuyasha...
Right now, your mind is a total blank.
Have you lost all hope without your sword?
Are you finished?
HHOOOOO
DASH
INU-YASHA!
SSHH
STAND BACK, LADY KAGOME!
GLARE

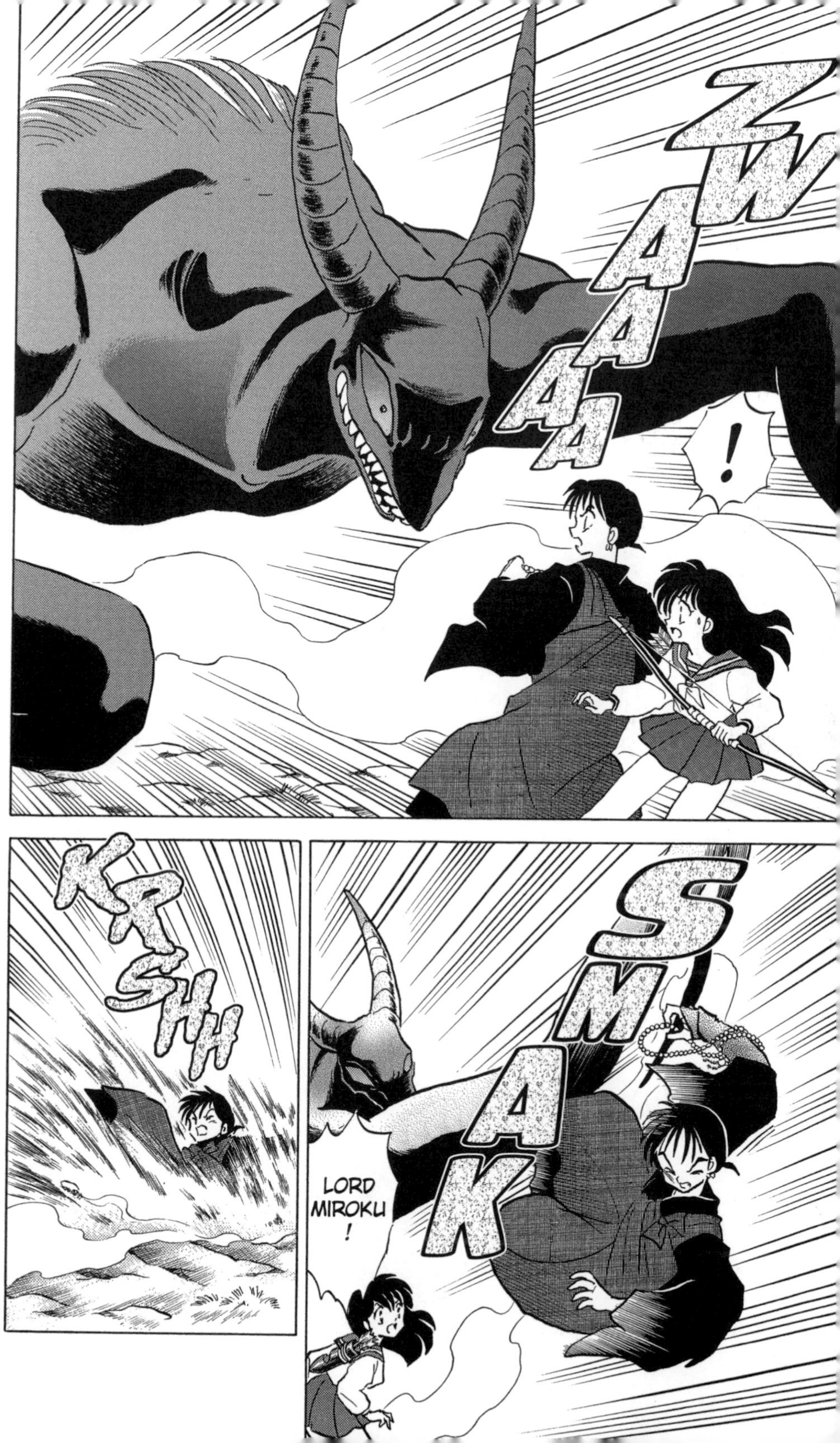
ZWAAAA
!
SMAK
LORD MIROKU!
KRSHH

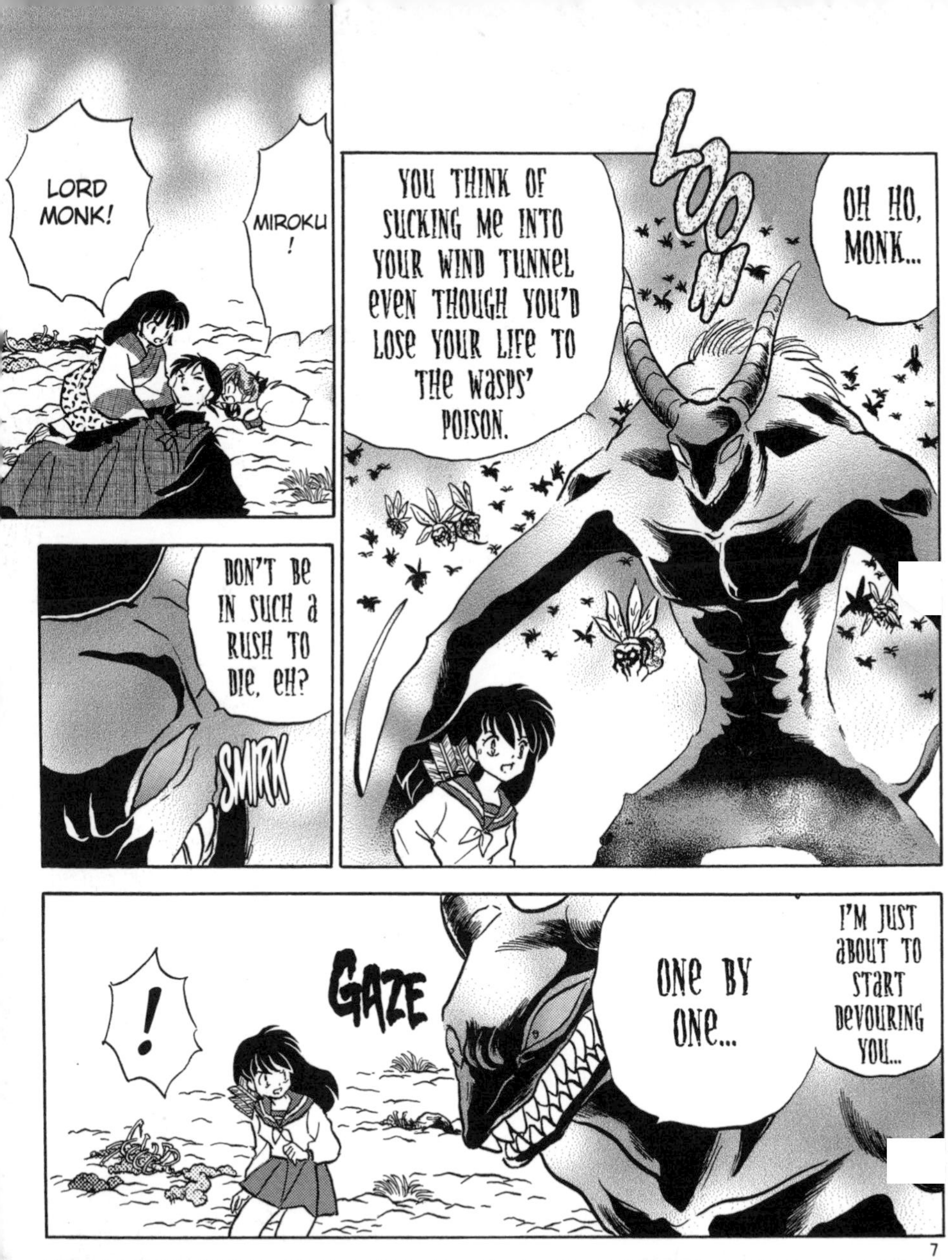

LOOM
OH HO, MONK...
YOU THINK OF SUCKING ME INTO YOUR WIND TUNNEL EVEN THOUGH YOU'D LOSE YOUR LIFE TO THE WASPS' POISON.
MIROKU!
LORD MONK!
DON'T BE IN SUCH A RUSH TO DIE, EH?
SMIRK
I'M JUST ABOUT TO START DEVOURING YOU...
ONE BY ONE...
GAZE
!
SHF

7

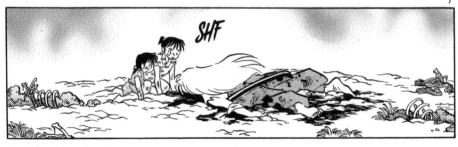

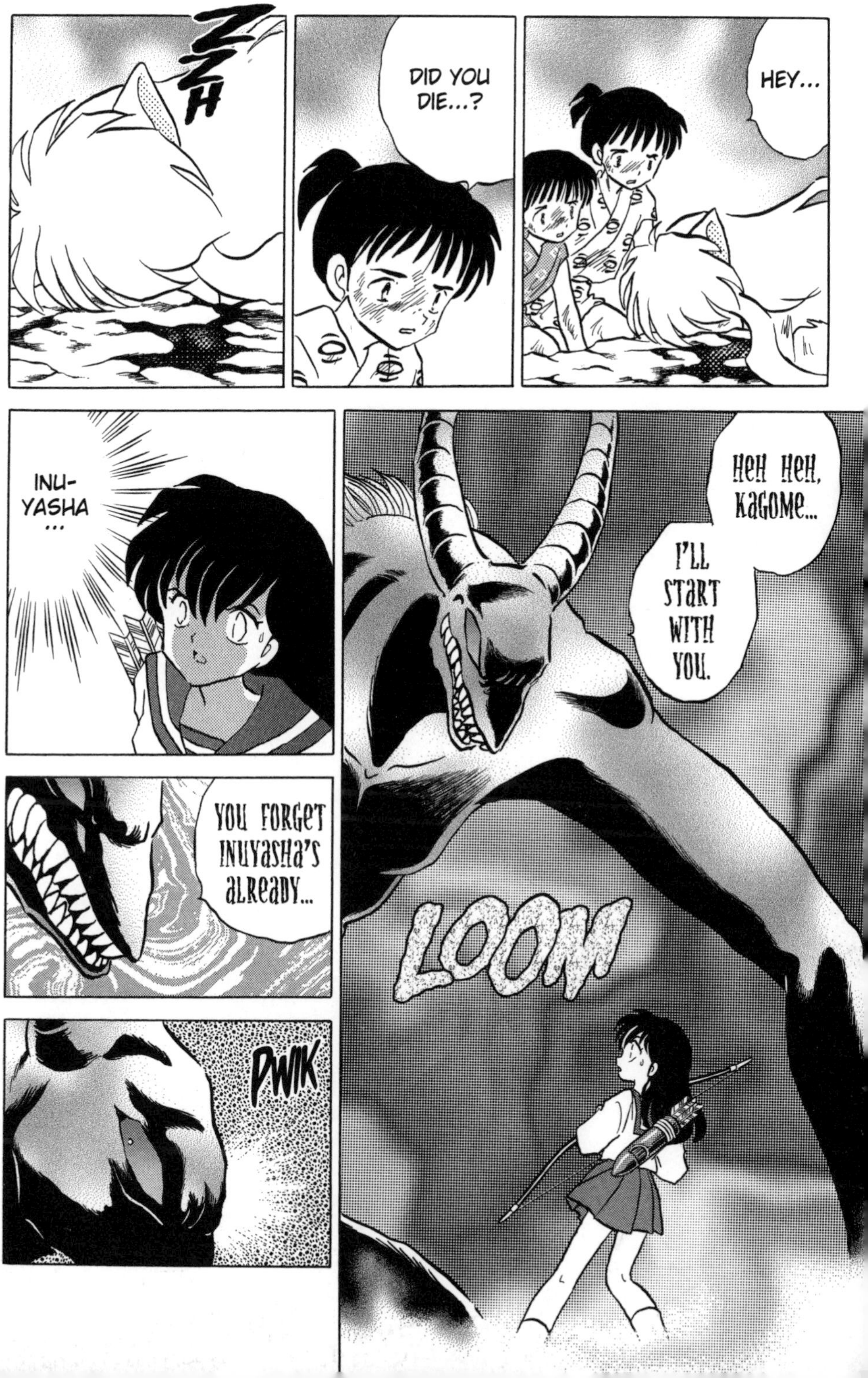
HEY...
DID YOU DIE...?
ZZH
HEH HEH, KAGOME...
I'LL START WITH YOU.
LOOM
INU-YASHA...
YOU FORGET INUYASHA'S ALREADY...
DWIK

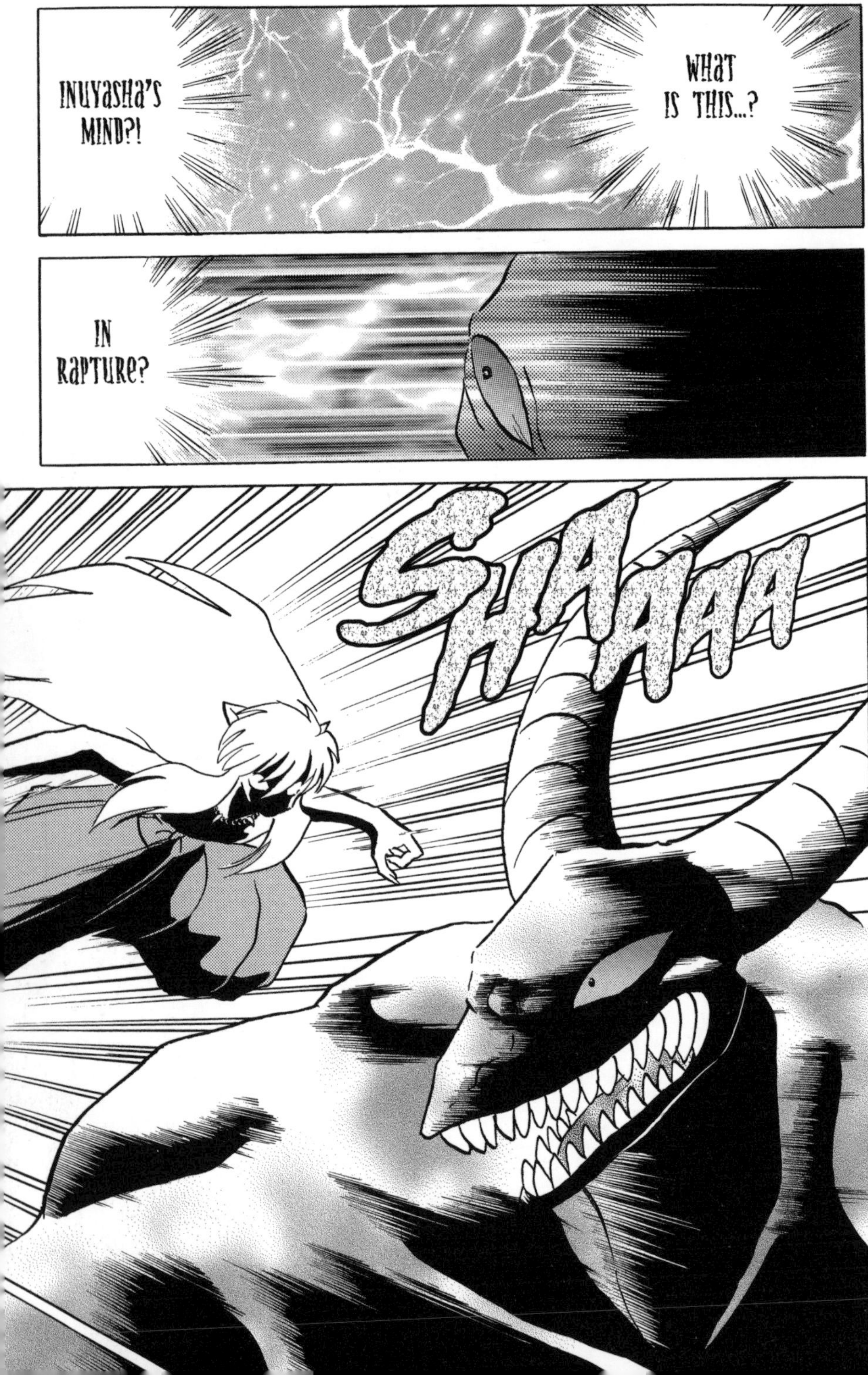
WHAT IS THIS...?
INUYASHA'S MIND?!
IN RAPTURE?
SHAAAAA

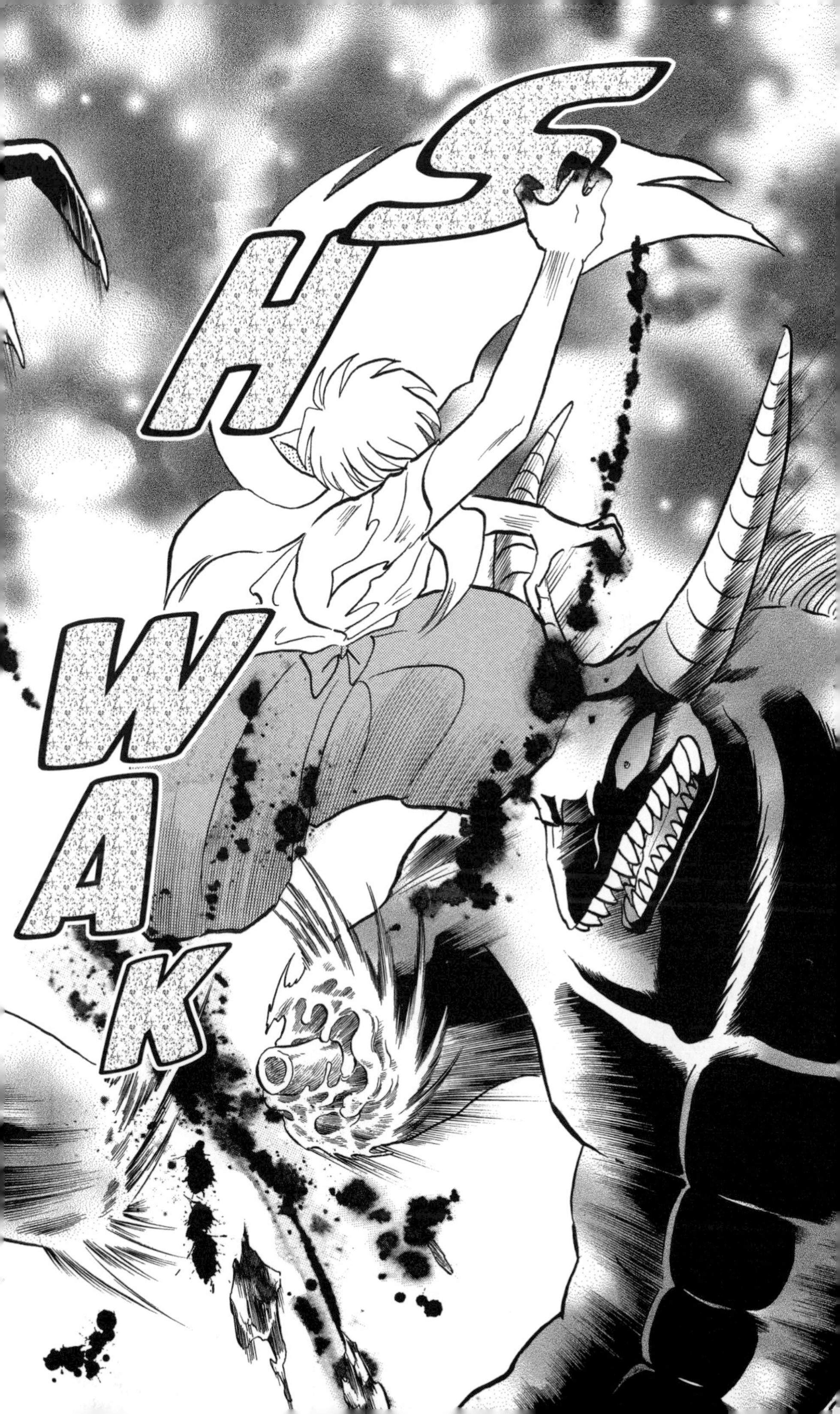
SHWAK

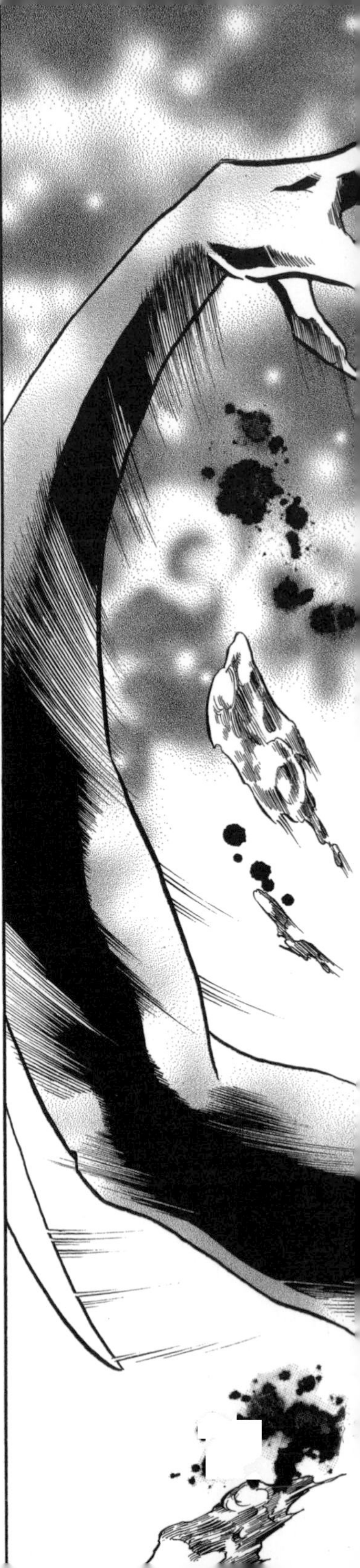

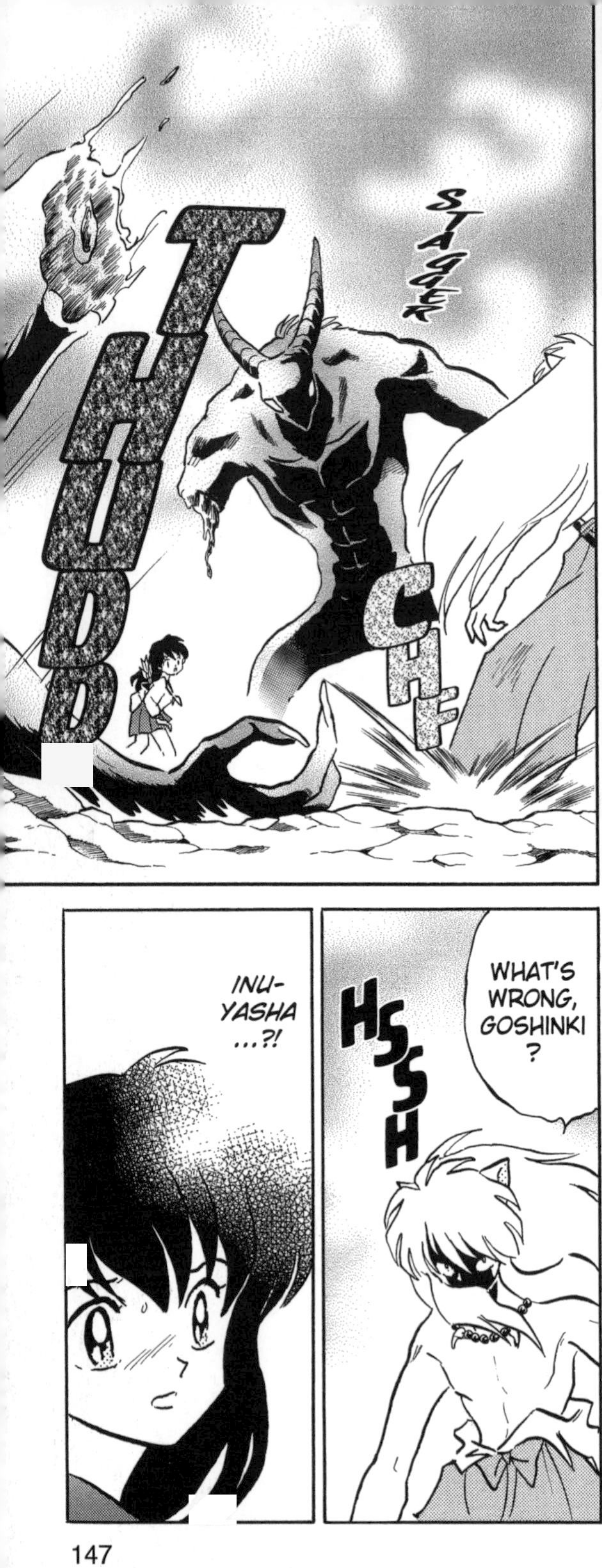
STAGGER
THUDD
CHF
WHAT'S WRONG, GOSHINKI?
HSSH
INU-YASHA...?!

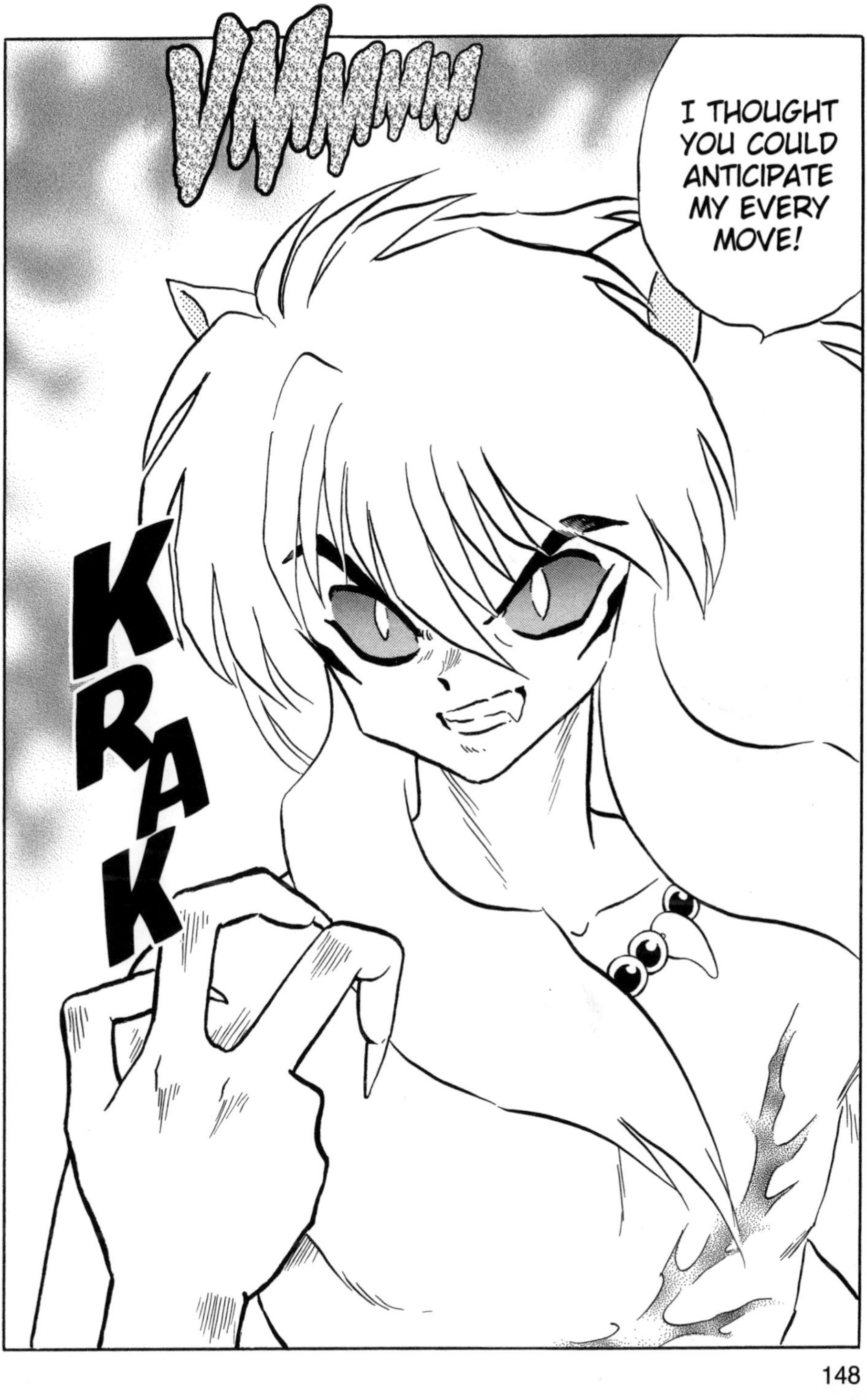
VMMMMM
I THOUGHT YOU COULD ANTICIPATE MY EVERY MOVE!
KRAK

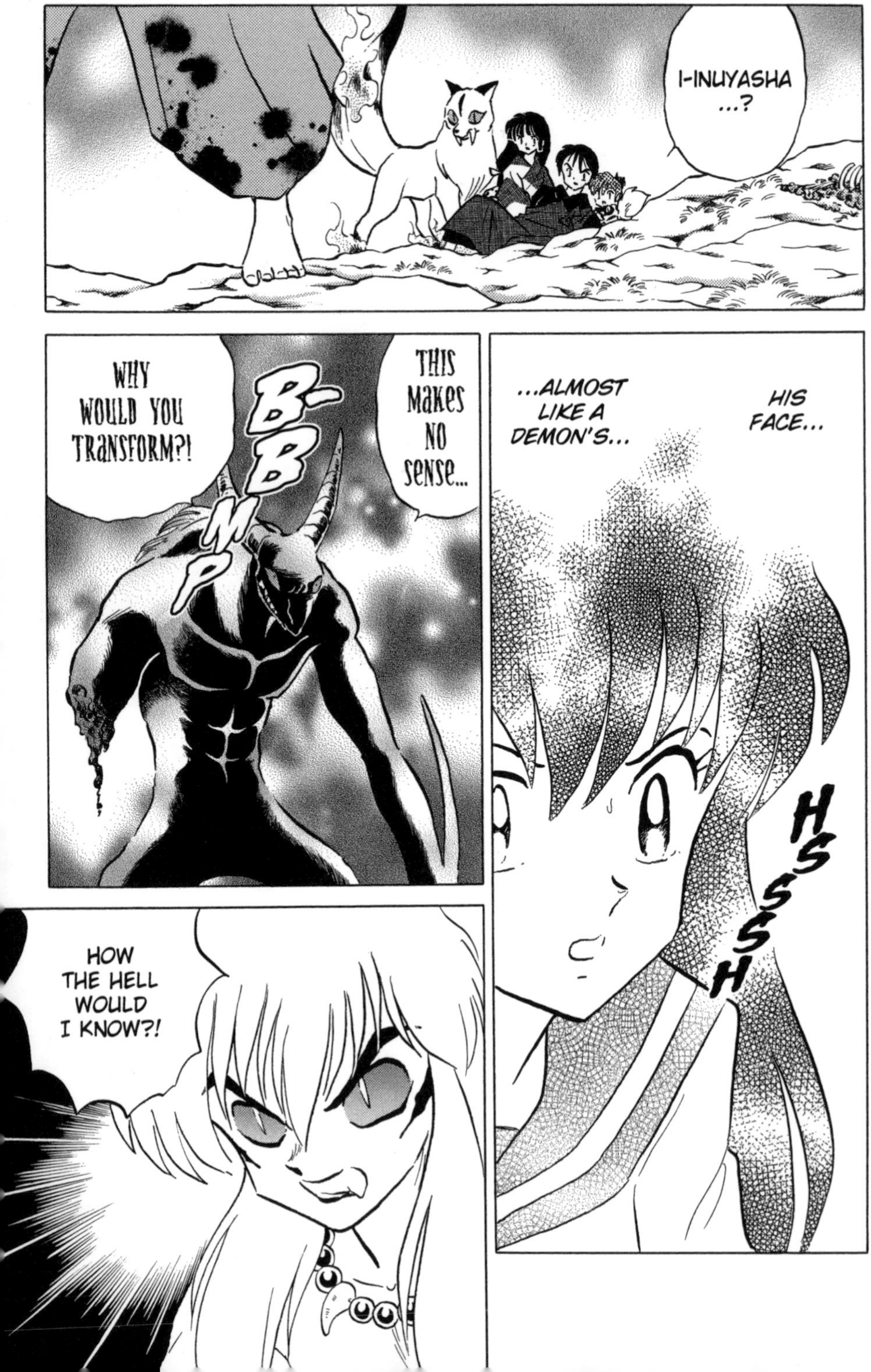
I-INUYASHA ...?
HIS FACE...
...ALMOST LIKE A DEMON'S...
HSSSSH
THIS MAKES NO SENSE...
WHY WOULD YOU TRANSFORM?!
B-BMP
HOW THE HELL WOULD I KNOW?!

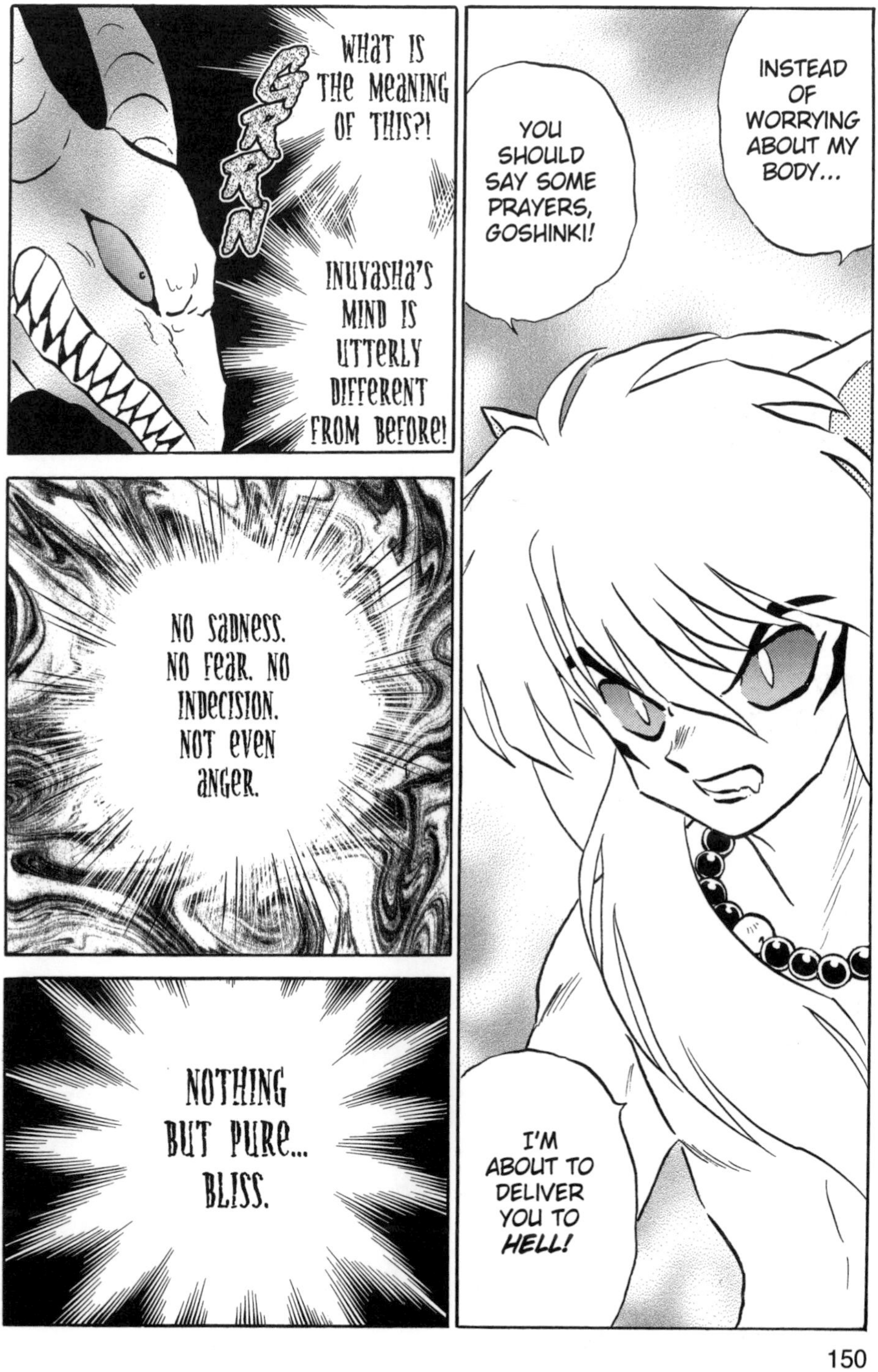
INSTEAD OF WORRYING ABOUT MY BODY...
YOU SHOULD SAY SOME PRAYERS, GOSHINKI!
I'M ABOUT TO DELIVER YOU TO ***HELL!***
WHAT IS THE MEANING OF THIS?!
GRRN
INUYASHA'S MIND IS UTTERLY DIFFERENT FROM BEFORE!
NO SADNESS. NO FEAR. NO INDECISION. NOT EVEN ANGER.
NOTHING BUT PURE... BLISS.

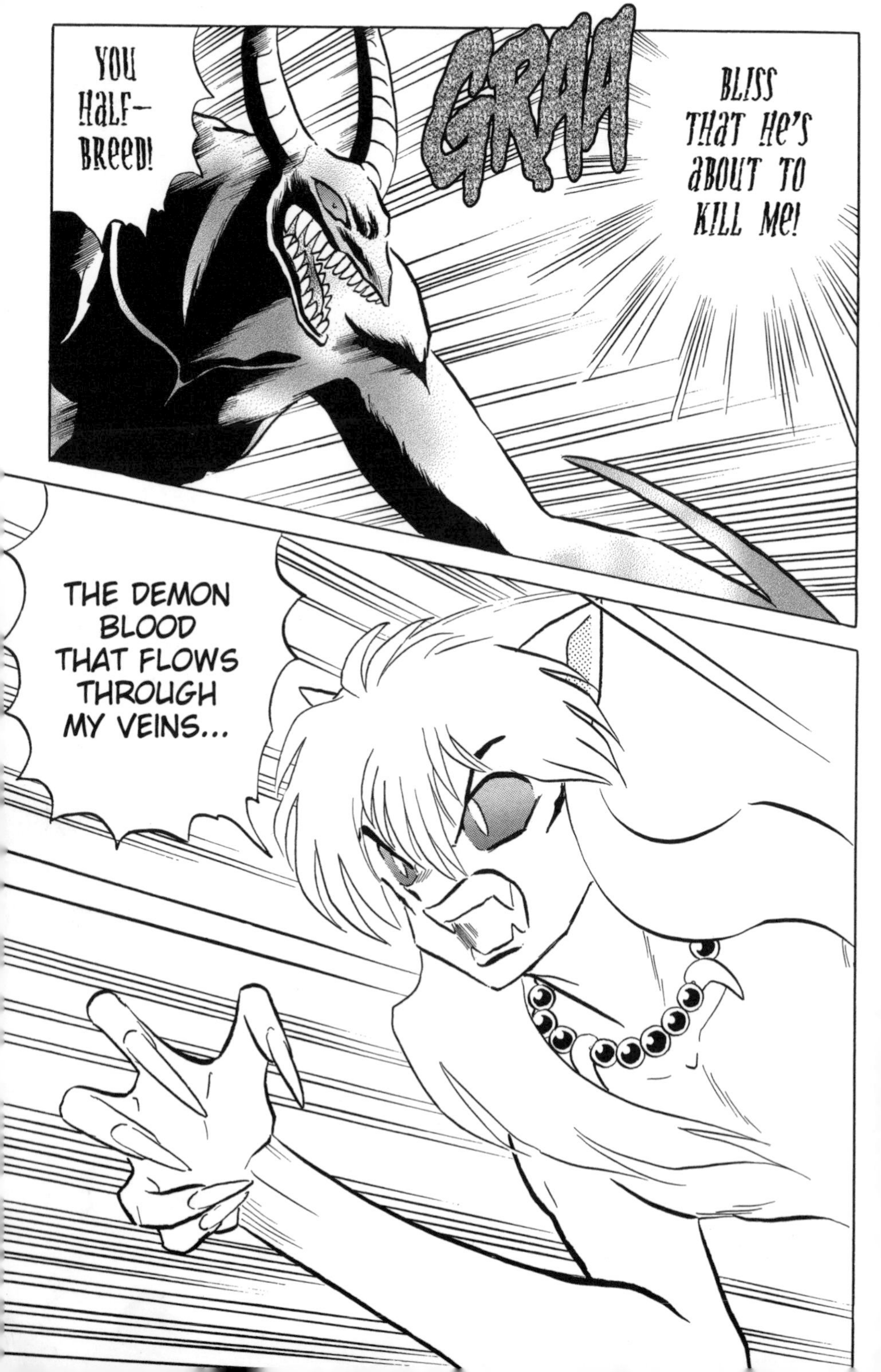
BLISS THAT HE'S ABOUT TO KILL ME!
GRAA
YOU HALF-BREED!
THE DEMON BLOOD THAT FLOWS THROUGH MY VEINS...

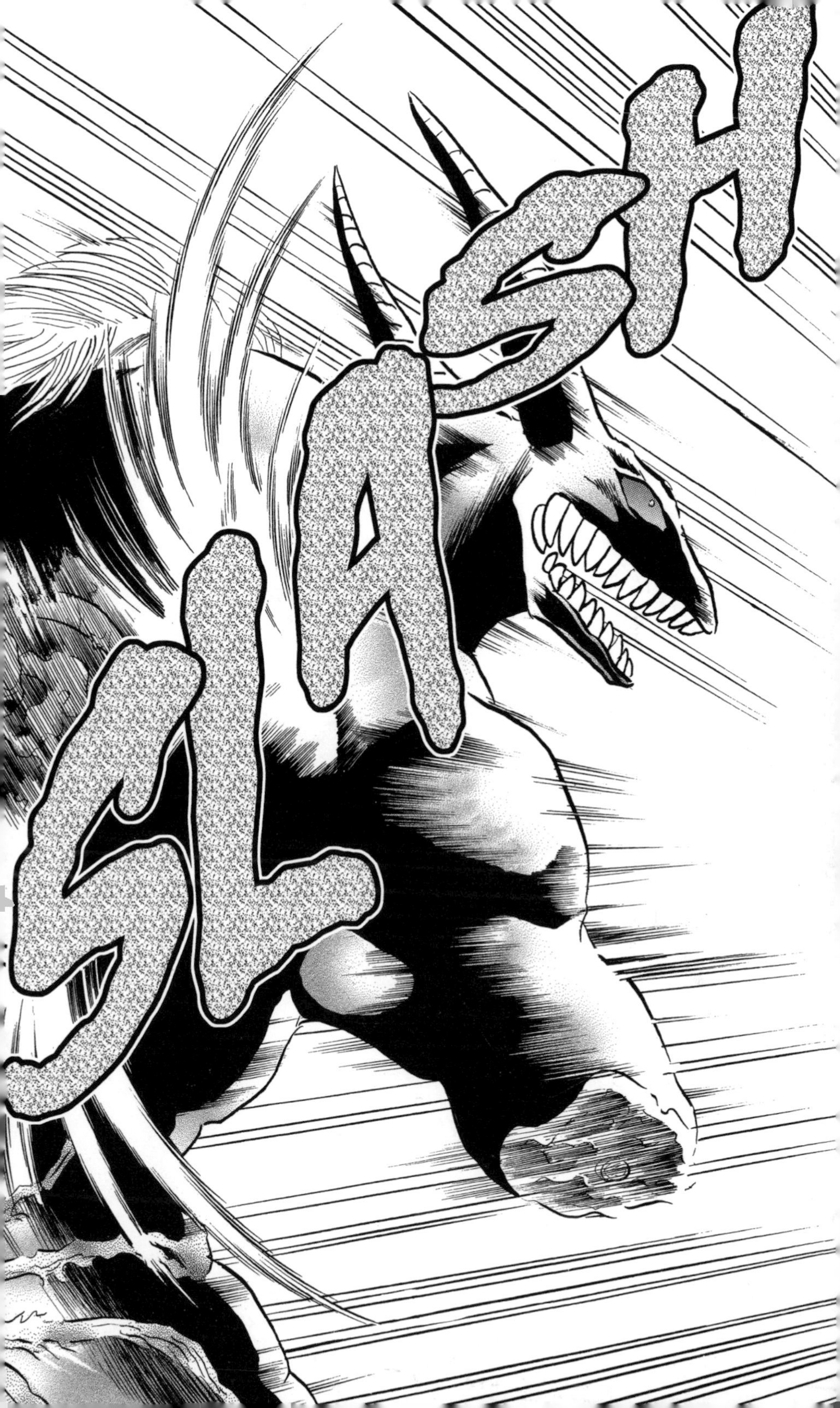
SLASH

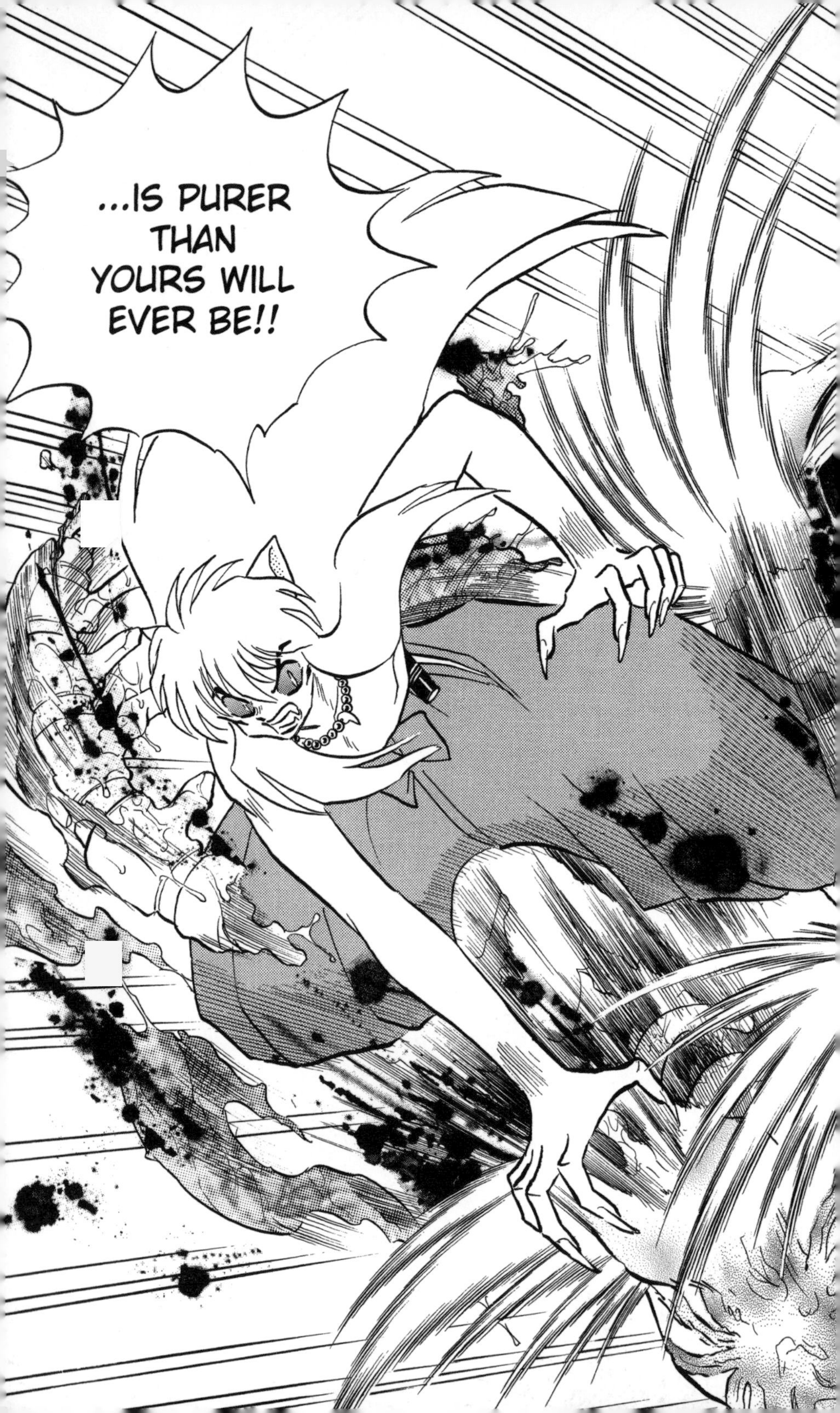
...IS PURER THAN YOURS WILL EVER BE!!

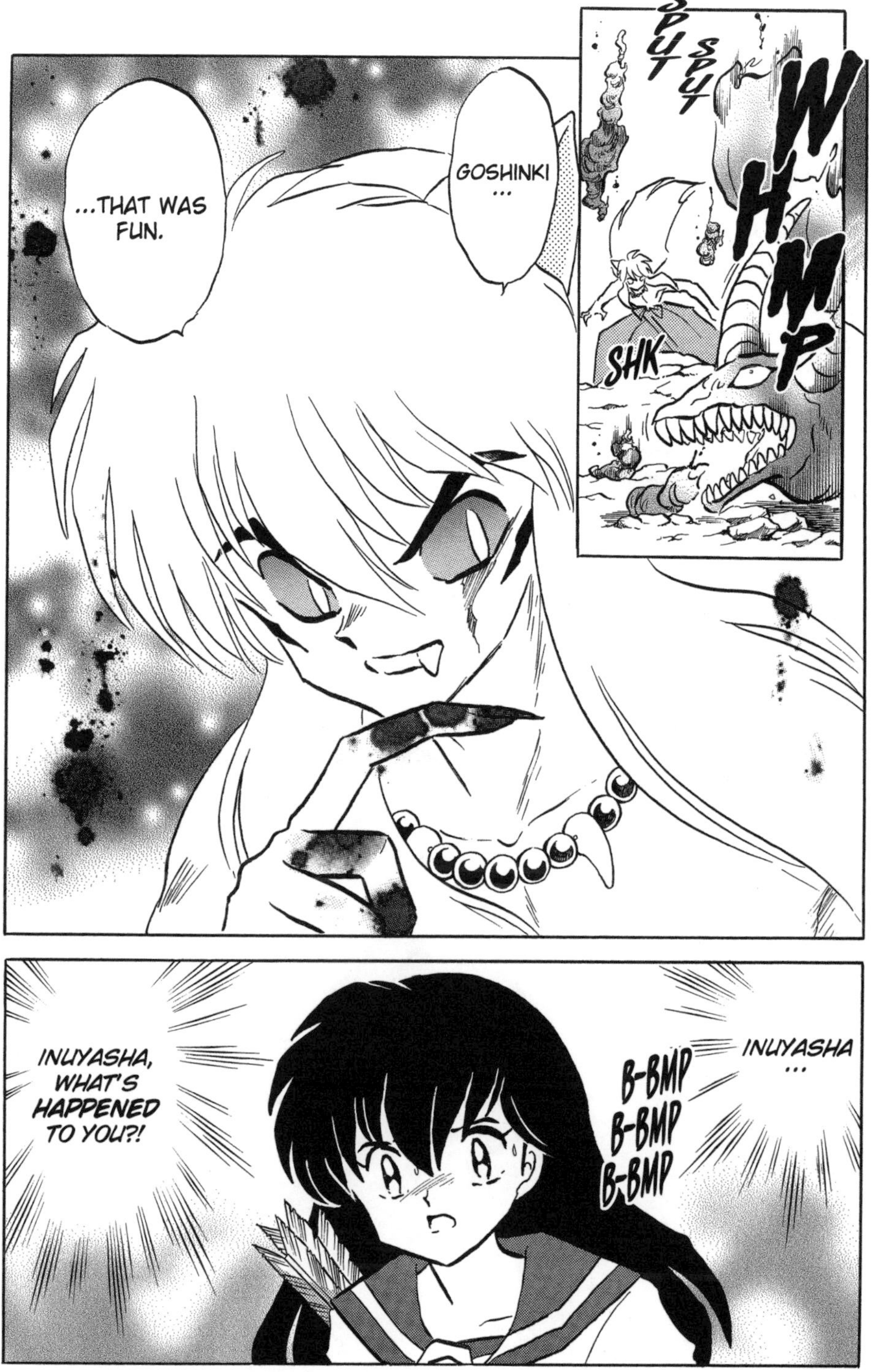
SPUT SPUT
WHMP
SHK
GOSHINKI...
...THAT WAS FUN.
INUYASHA...
B-BMP B-BMP B-BMP
INUYASHA, WHAT'S HAPPENED TO YOU?!

SCROLL NINE
TRUE NATURE

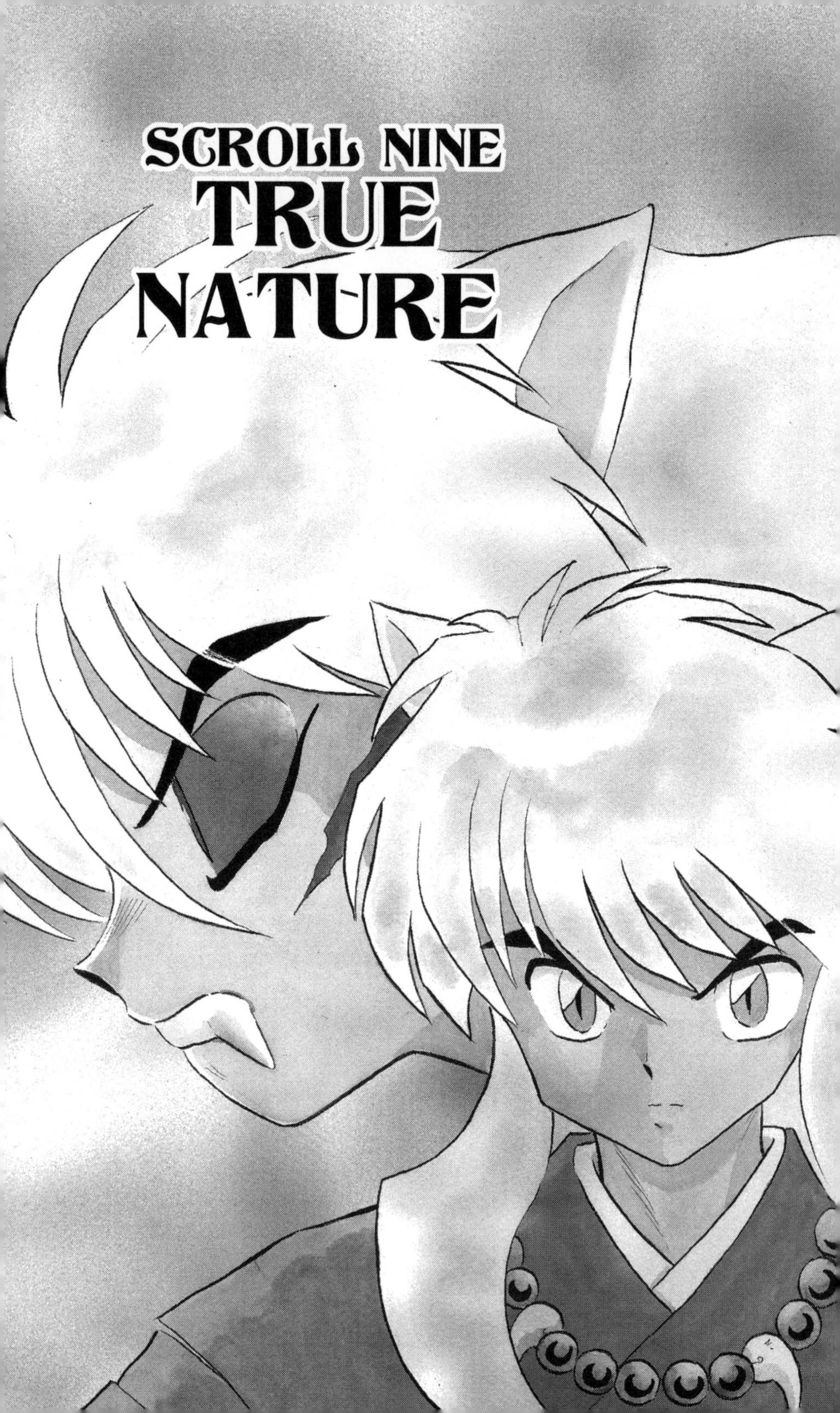

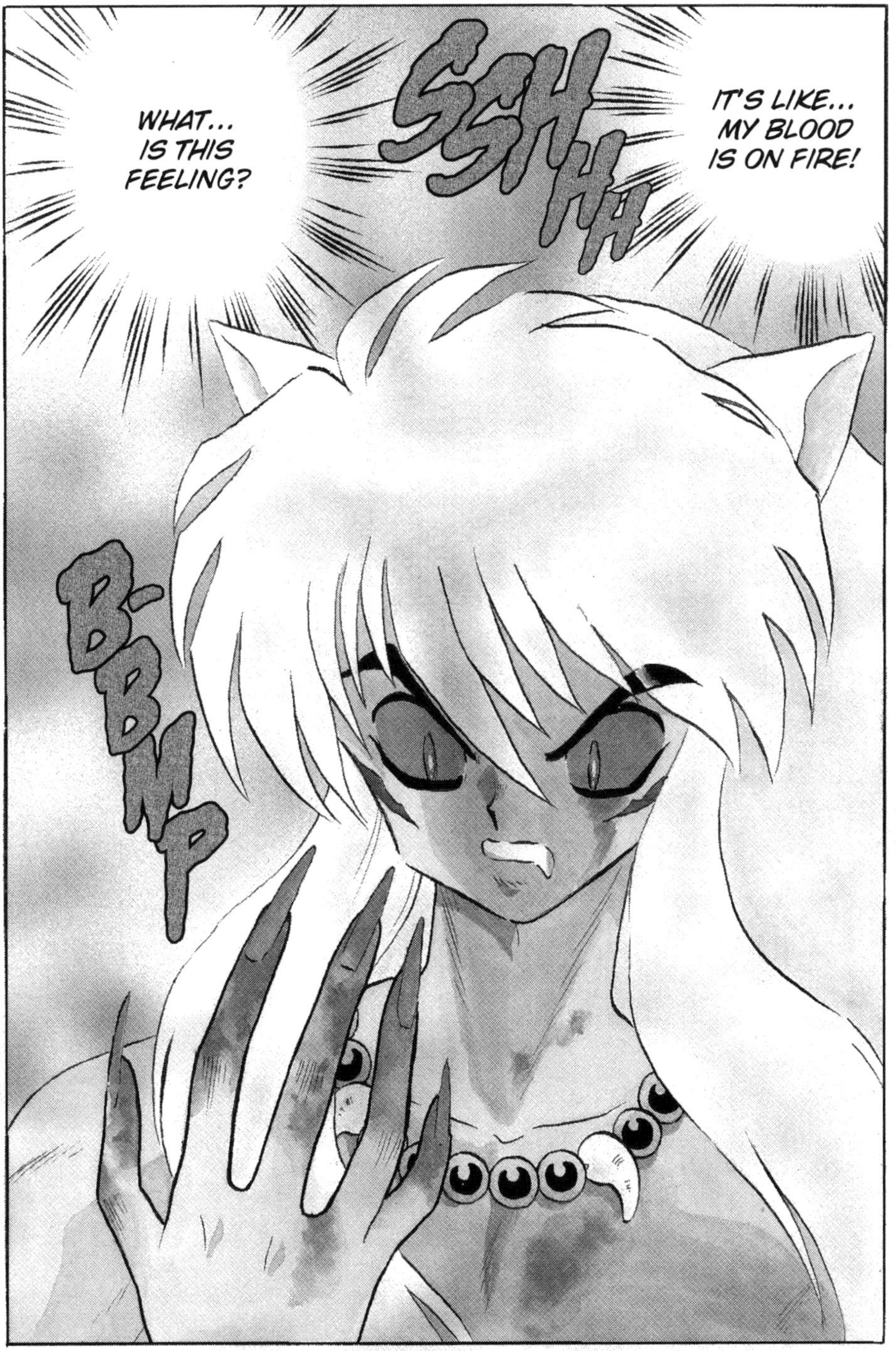
IT'S LIKE... MY BLOOD IS ON FIRE!
SSHHH
WHAT... IS THIS FEELING?
B-BBMP

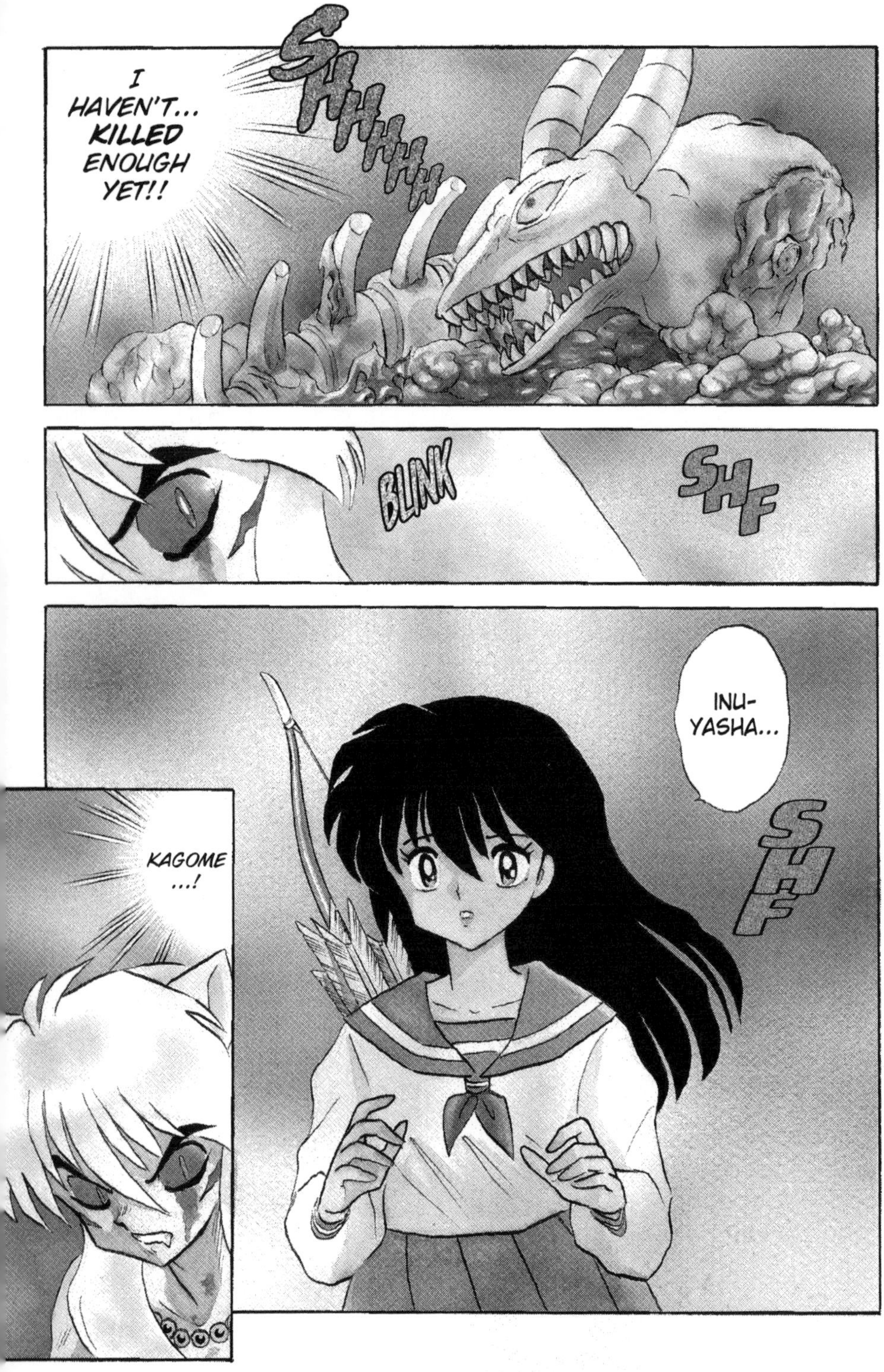
SHHHHHH
I HAVEN'T... KILLED ENOUGH YET!!
SHF
BLINK
INU-YASHA...
SHF
KAGOME ...!

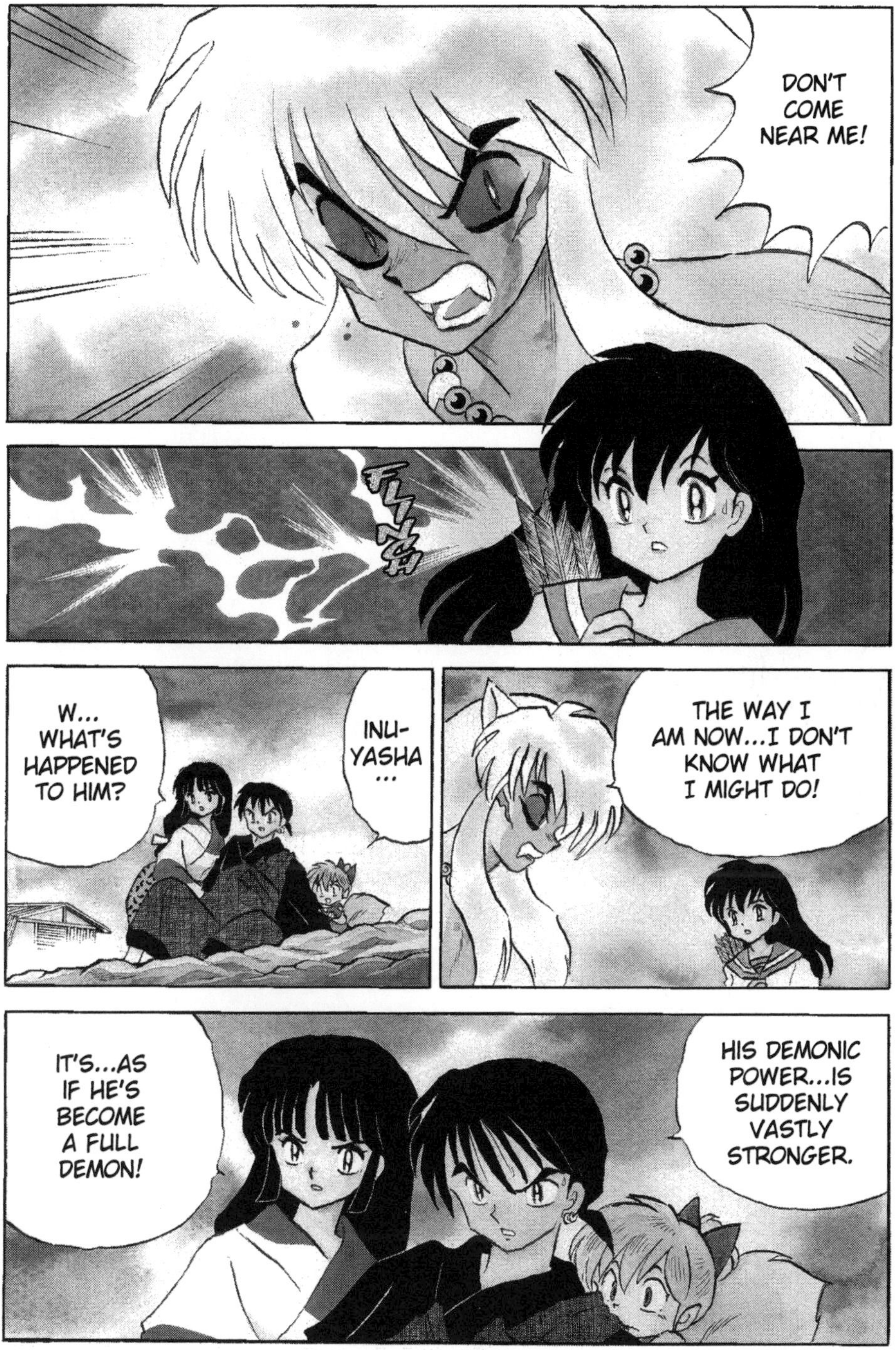
DON'T COME NEAR ME!
INU-YASHA...
W... WHAT'S HAPPENED TO HIM?
THE WAY I AM NOW...I DON'T KNOW WHAT I MIGHT DO!
HIS DEMONIC POWER...IS SUDDENLY VASTLY STRONGER.
IT'S...AS IF HE'S BECOME A FULL DEMON!

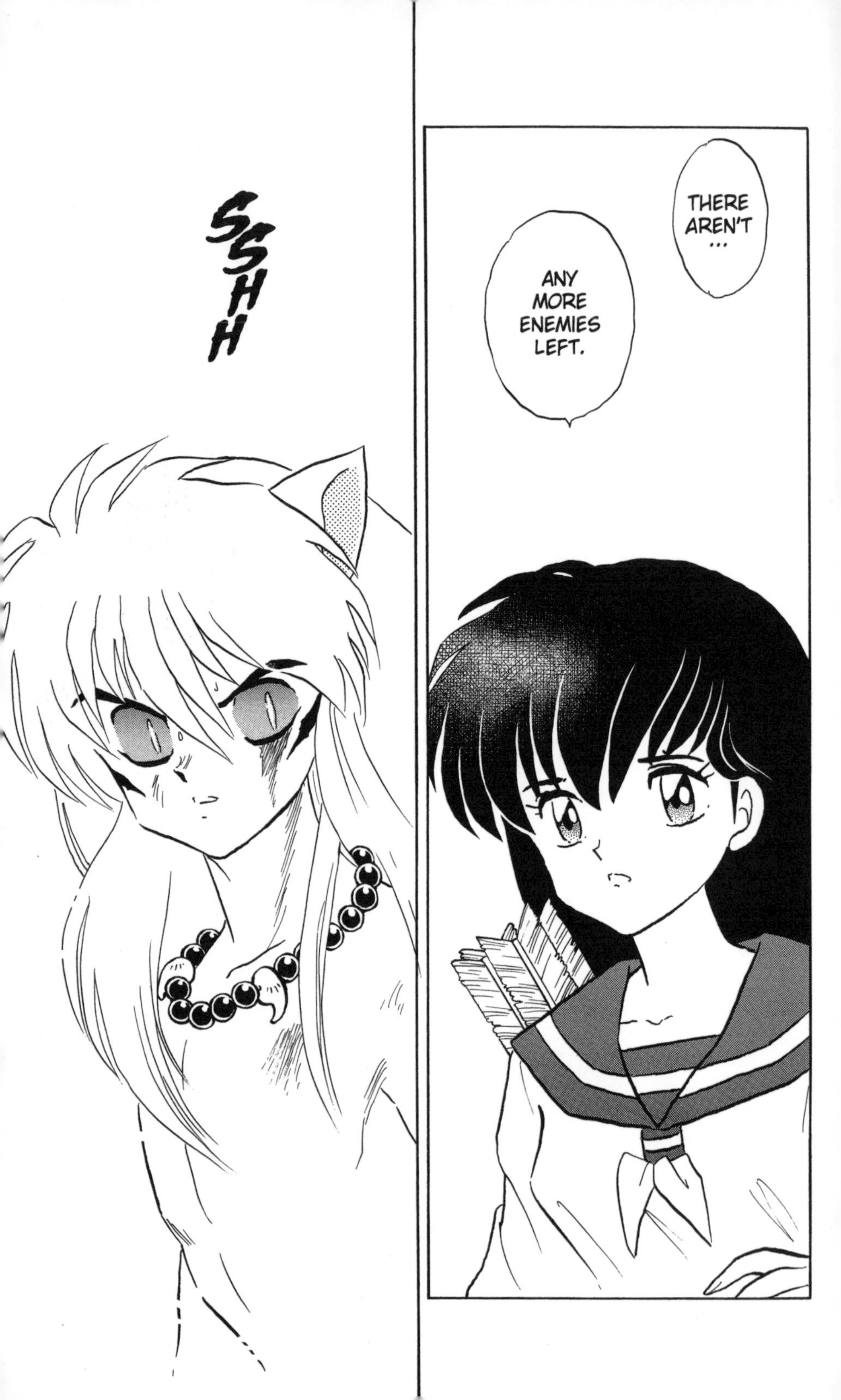
THERE AREN'T ...
ANY MORE ENEMIES LEFT.
SSHH

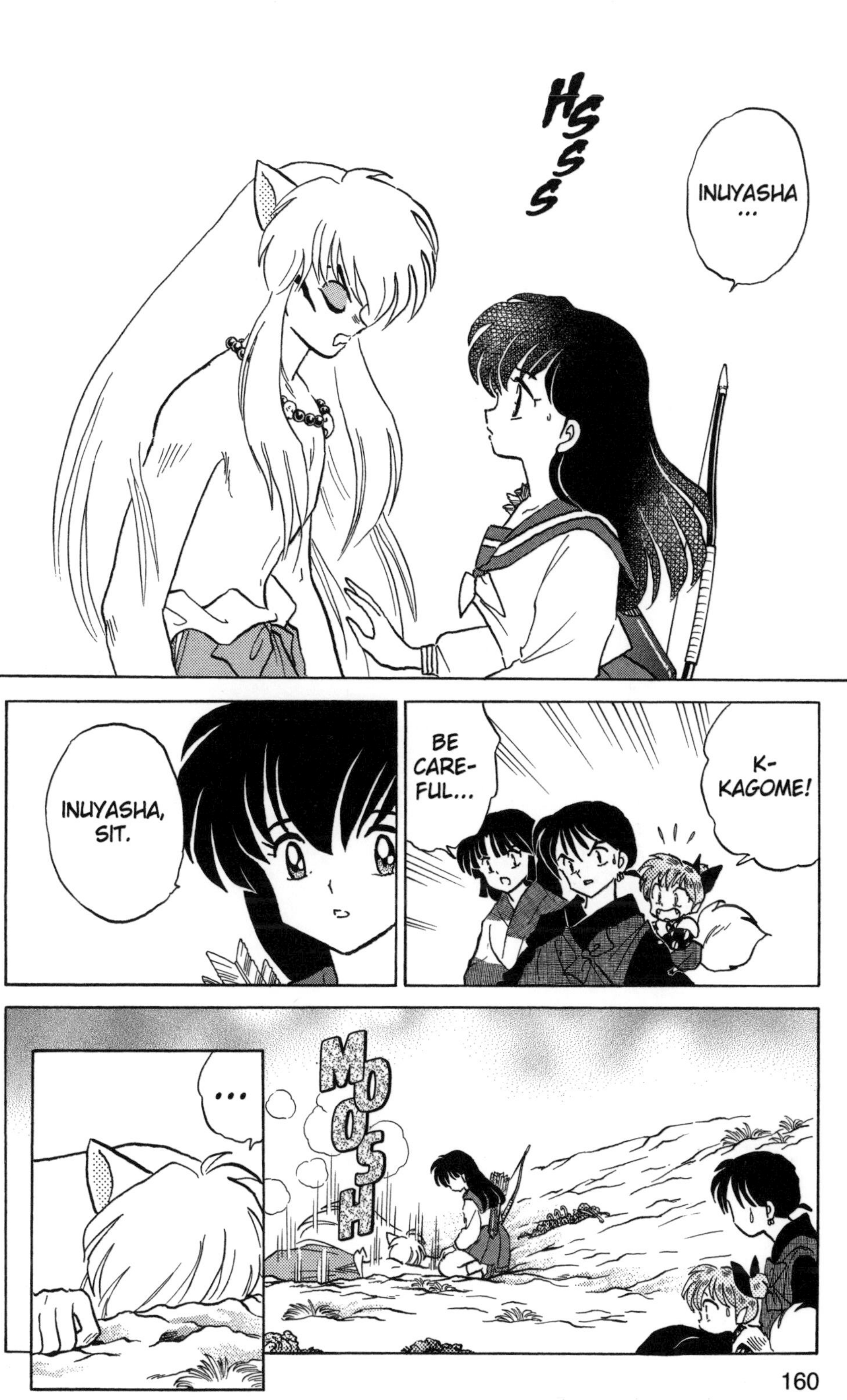
INUYASHA ...
HSSS
K-KAGOME!
BE CARE-FUL...
INUYASHA, SIT.
MOSH
...

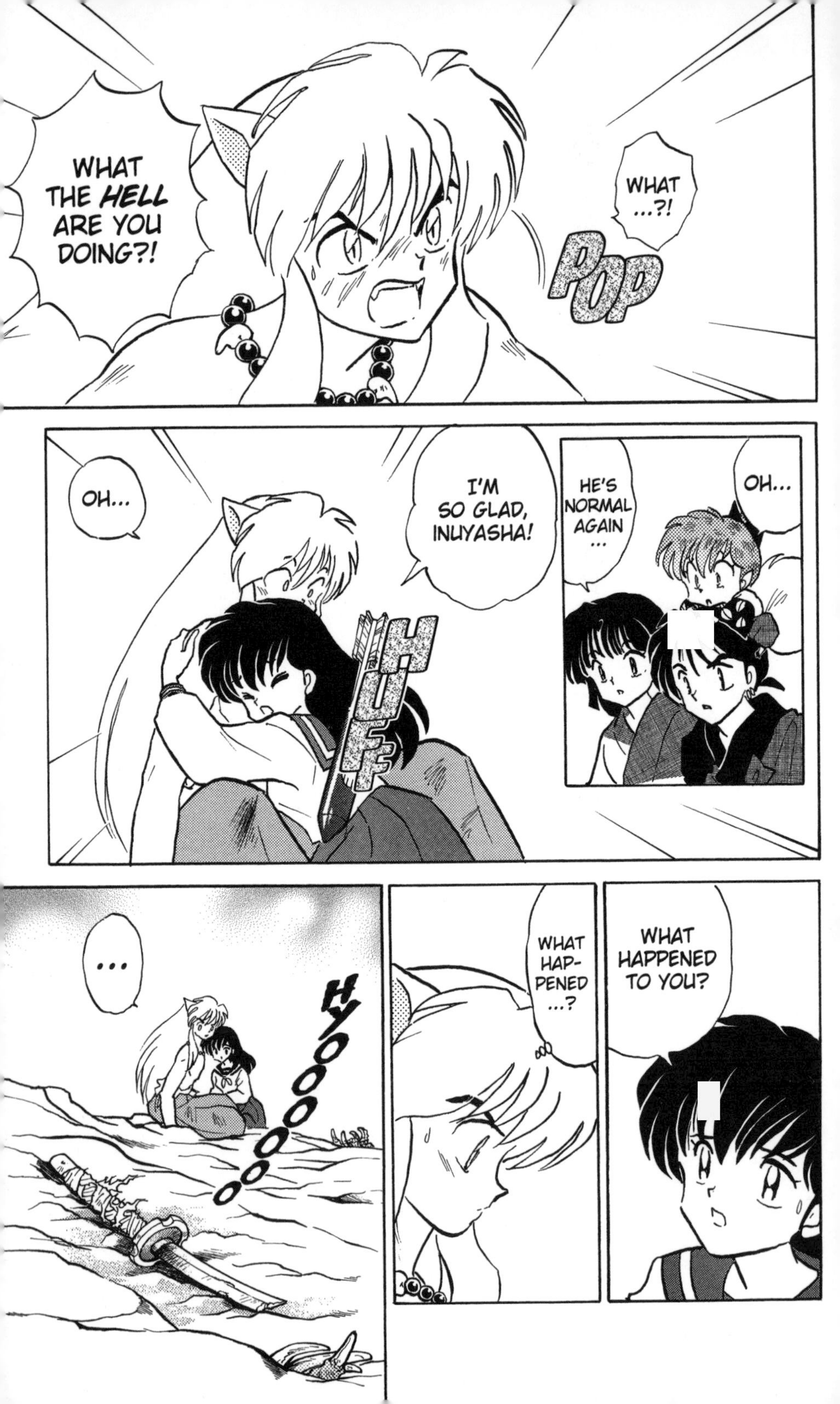
WHAT ...?!
POP
WHAT THE *HELL* ARE YOU DOING?!
OH...
HE'S NORMAL AGAIN ...
I'M SO GLAD, INUYASHA!
HUFF
OH...
WHAT HAPPENED TO YOU?
WHAT HAP-PENED ...?
...
HYOOOOOOOOOO

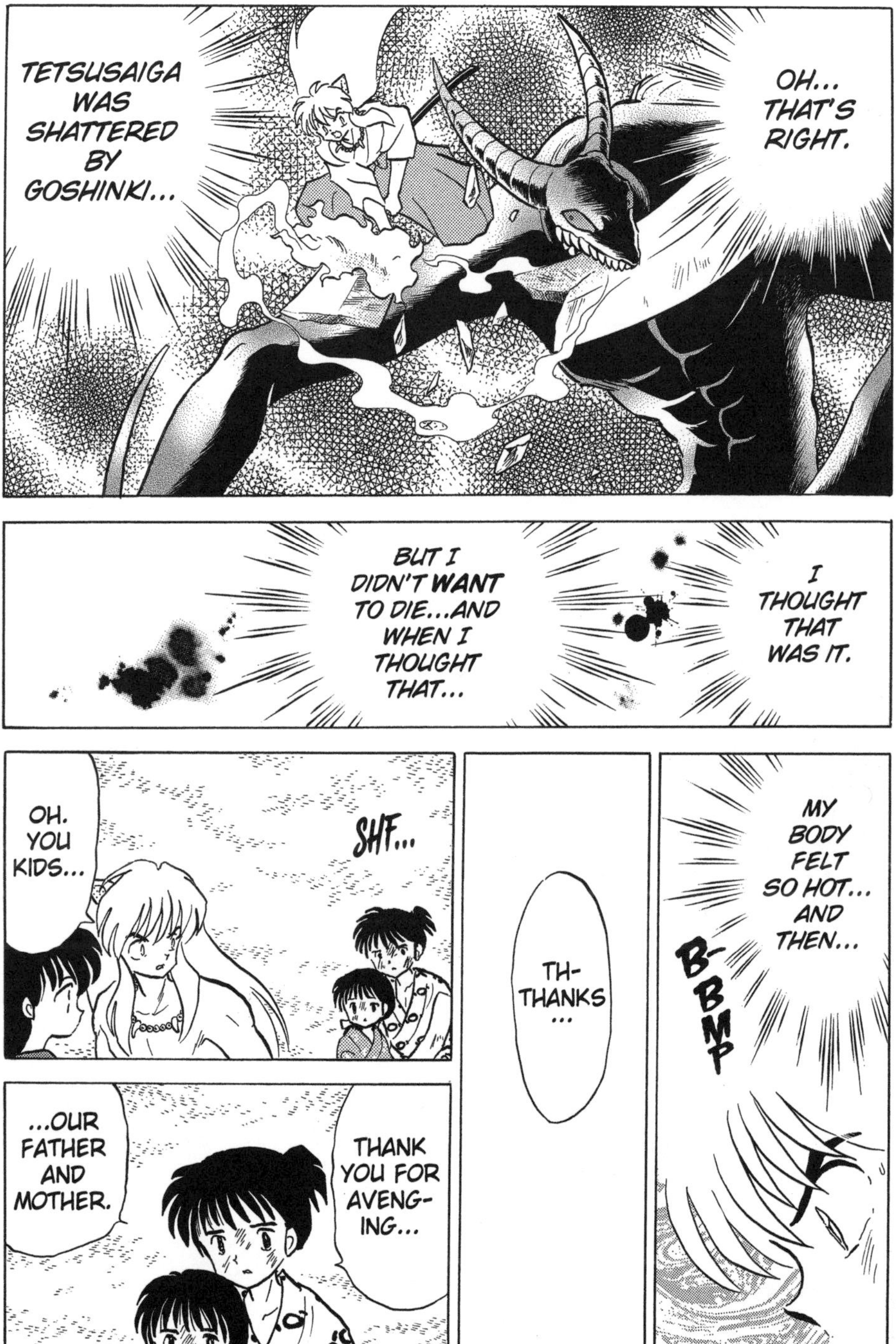
OH... THAT'S RIGHT.
TETSUSAIGA WAS SHATTERED BY GOSHINKI...
I THOUGHT THAT WAS IT.
BUT I DIDN'T WANT TO DIE...AND WHEN I THOUGHT THAT...
MY BODY FELT SO HOT... AND THEN...
B-BMP
TH-THANKS...
SHF...
OH. YOU KIDS...
THANK YOU FOR AVENG-ING...
...OUR FATHER AND MOTHER.

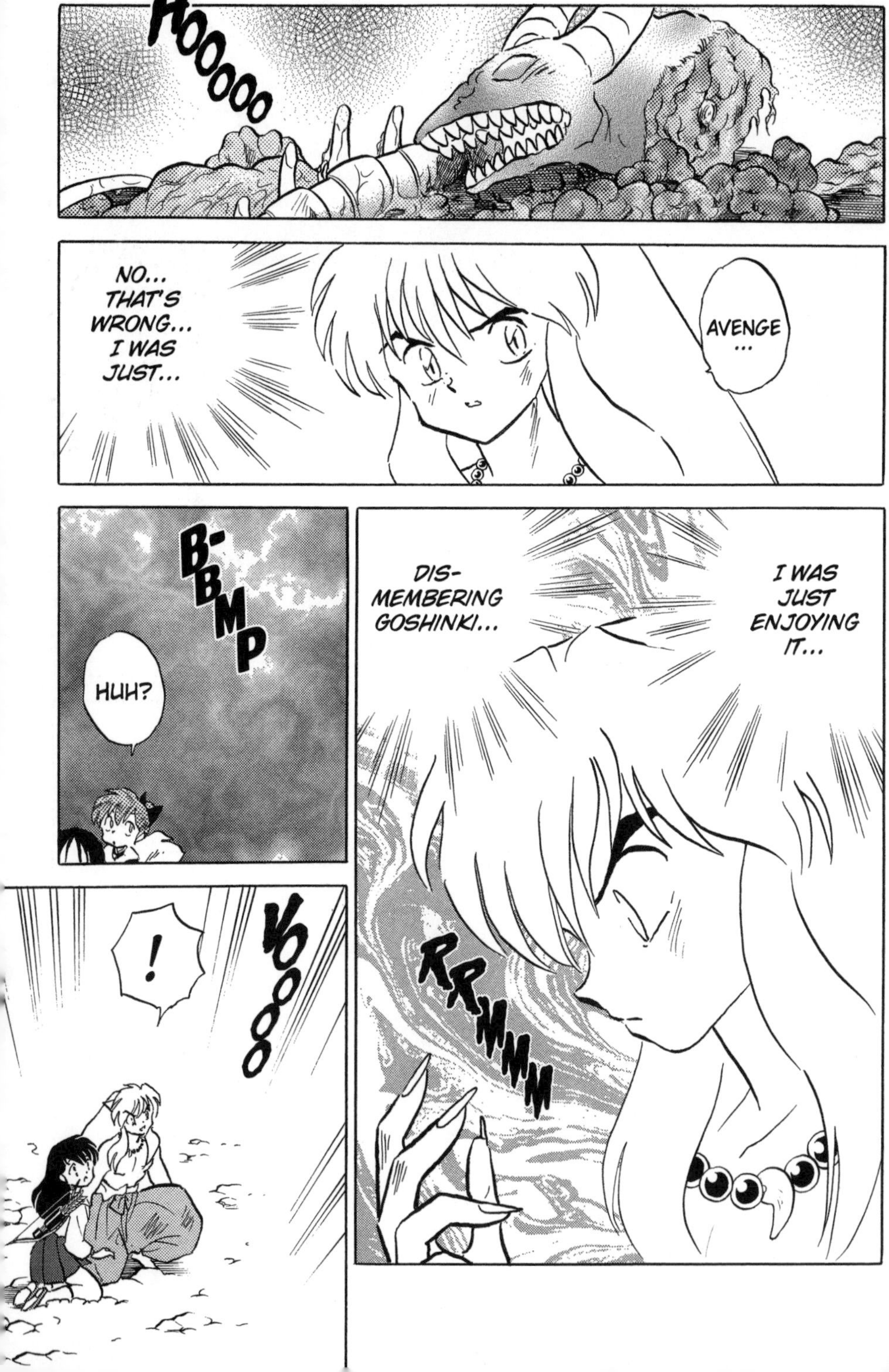
HOOOOO
AVENGE...
NO... THAT'S WRONG... I WAS JUST...
I WAS JUST ENJOYING IT...
DIS-MEMBERING GOSHINKI...
RRRMMMM
B-BMP
HUH?
!
VOOOOO

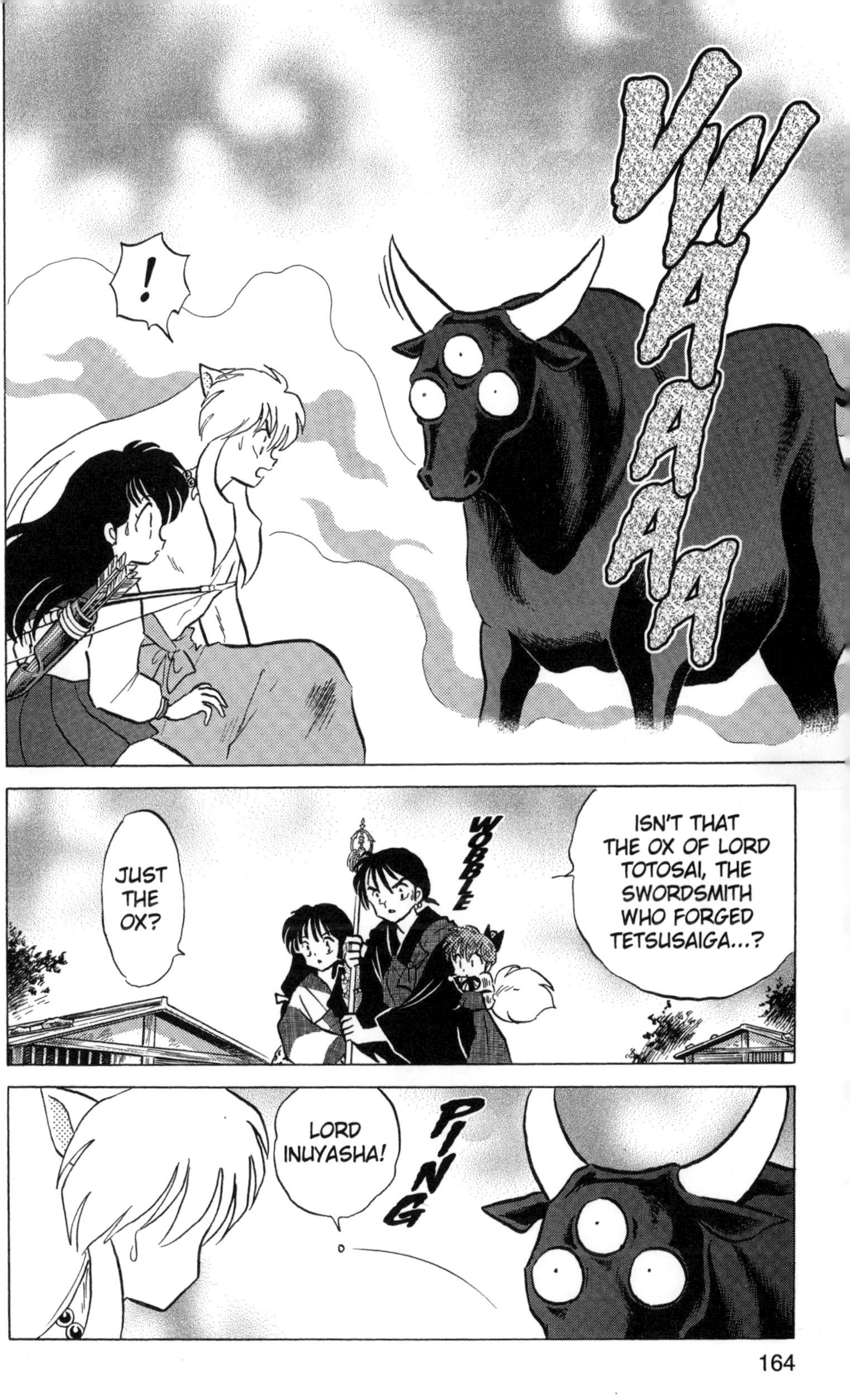
VWAAAA
!
ISN'T THAT THE OX OF LORD TOTOSAI, THE SWORDSMITH WHO FORGED TETSUSAIGA...?
WOBBLE
JUST THE OX?
PING
LORD INUYASHA!

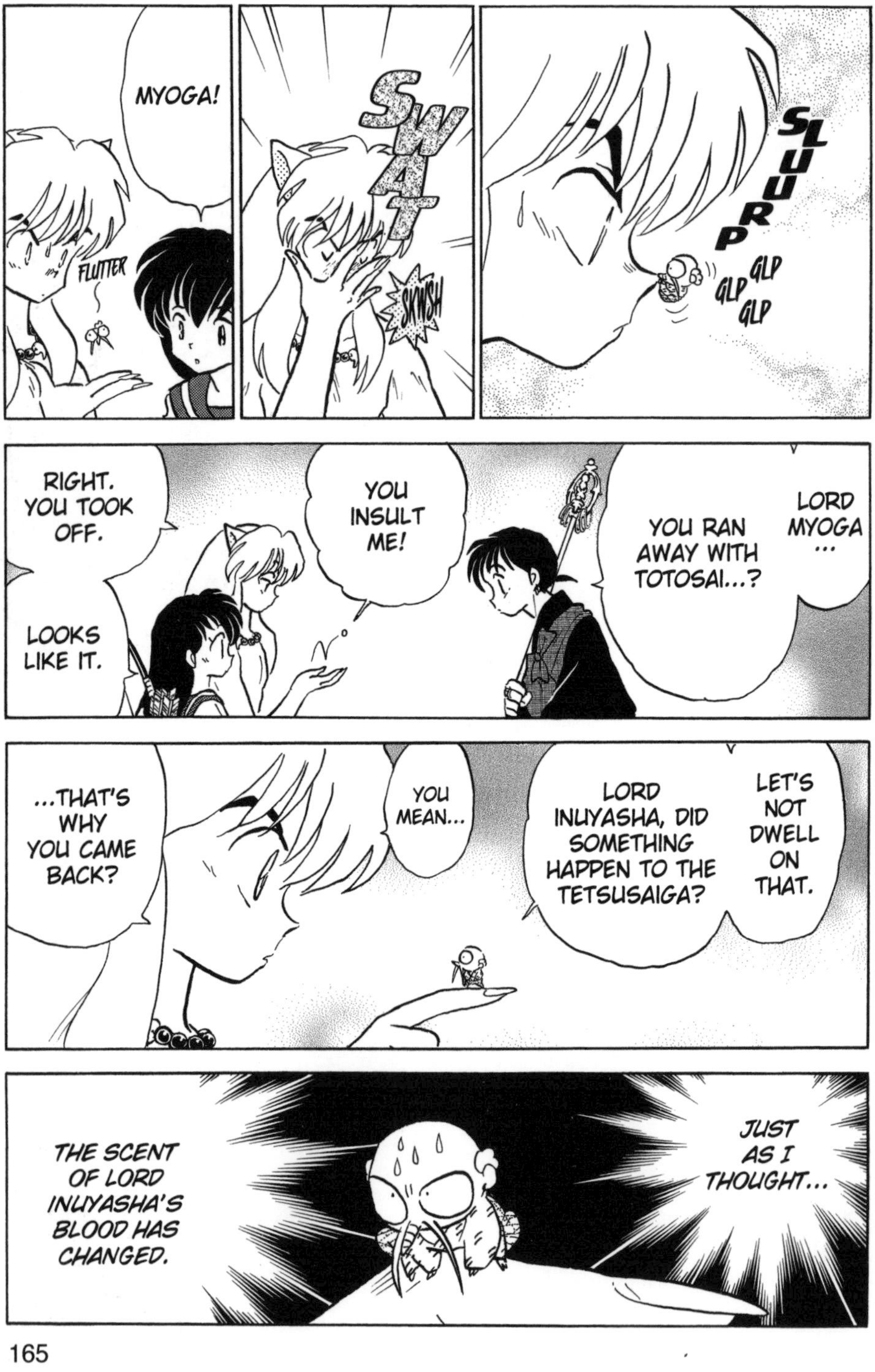
SLUURP
GLP GLP GLP
SWAT
SKWSH
MYOGA!
FLUTTER
LORD MYOGA...
YOU RAN AWAY WITH TOTOSAI...?
YOU INSULT ME!
RIGHT. YOU TOOK OFF.
LOOKS LIKE IT.
LET'S NOT DWELL ON THAT.
LORD INUYASHA, DID SOMETHING HAPPEN TO THE TETSUSAIGA?
YOU MEAN...
...THAT'S WHY YOU CAME BACK?
JUST AS I THOUGHT...
THE SCENT OF LORD INUYASHA'S BLOOD HAS CHANGED.

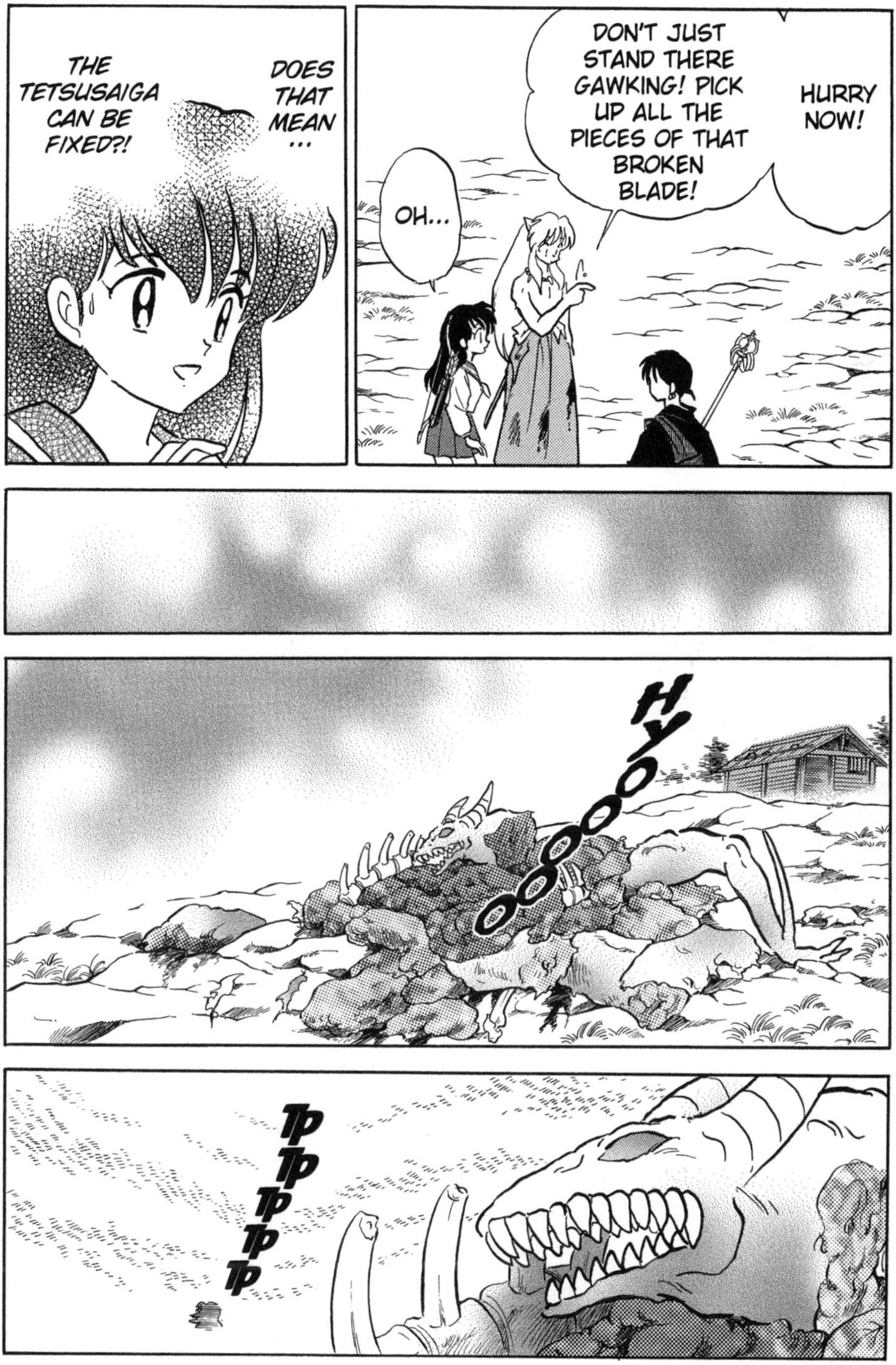
HURRY NOW!
DON'T JUST STAND THERE GAWKING! PICK UP ALL THE PIECES OF THAT BROKEN BLADE!
OH...
DOES THAT MEAN...
THE TETSUSAIGA CAN BE FIXED?!
HYOOOOOOO
TP TP TP TP TP

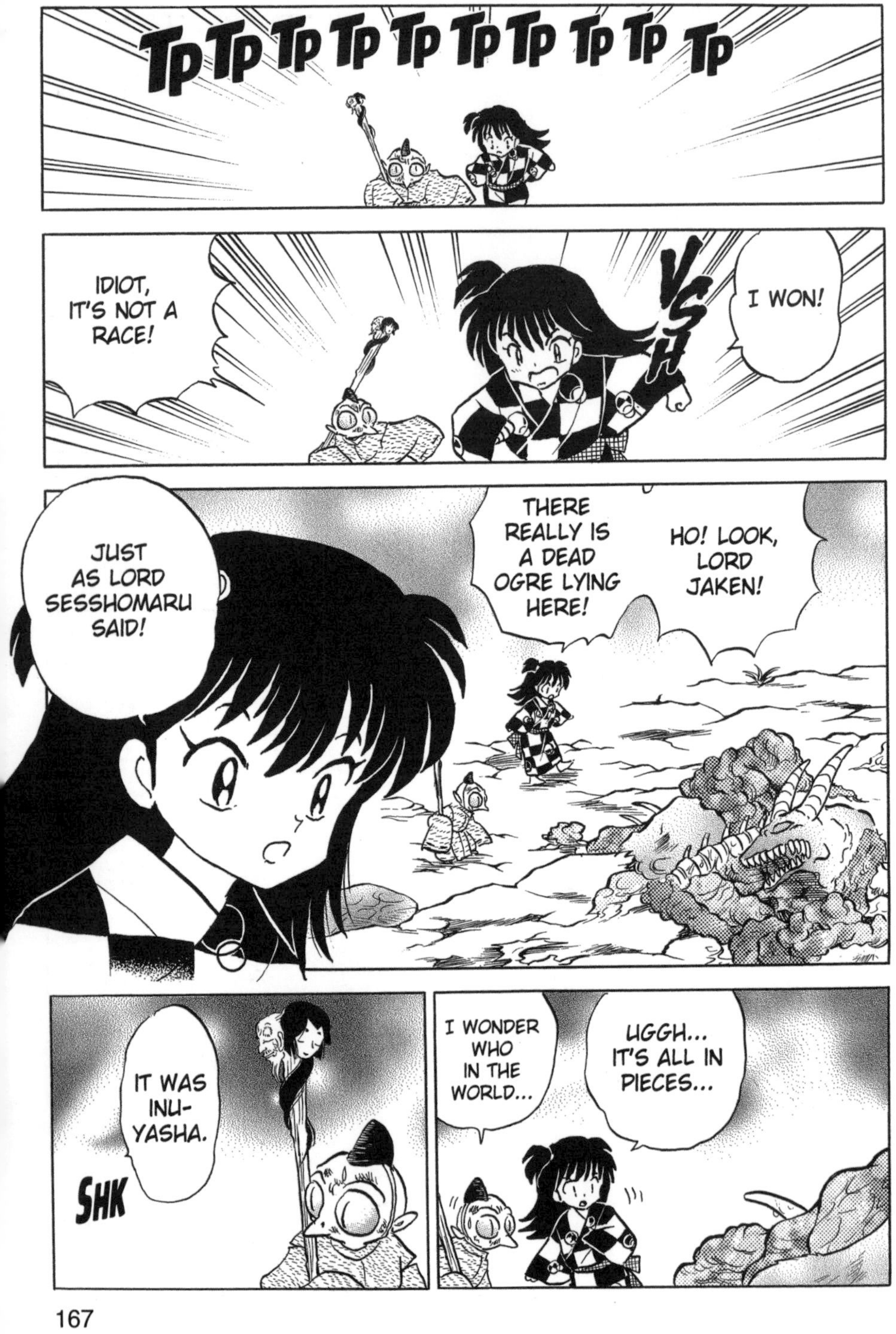
TP TP TP TP TP TP TP TP TP TP
I WON!
VSH
IDIOT, IT'S NOT A RACE!
HO! LOOK, LORD JAKEN!
THERE REALLY IS A DEAD OGRE LYING HERE!
JUST AS LORD SESSHOMARU SAID!
UGGH... IT'S ALL IN PIECES...
I WONDER WHO IN THE WORLD...
IT WAS INU-YASHA.
SHK

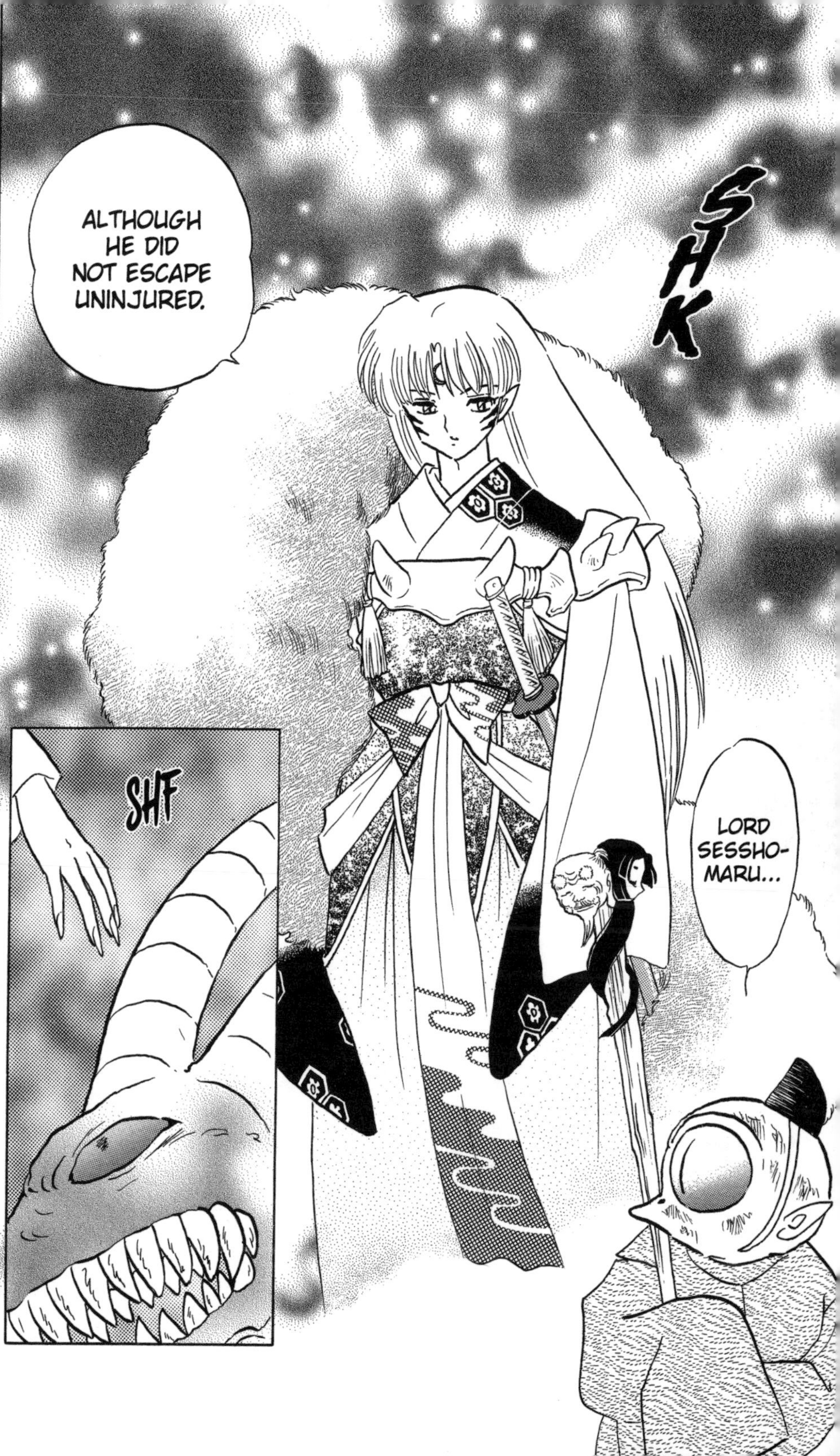
SHK
ALTHOUGH HE DID NOT ESCAPE UNINJURED.
LORD SESSHO-MARU...
SHF

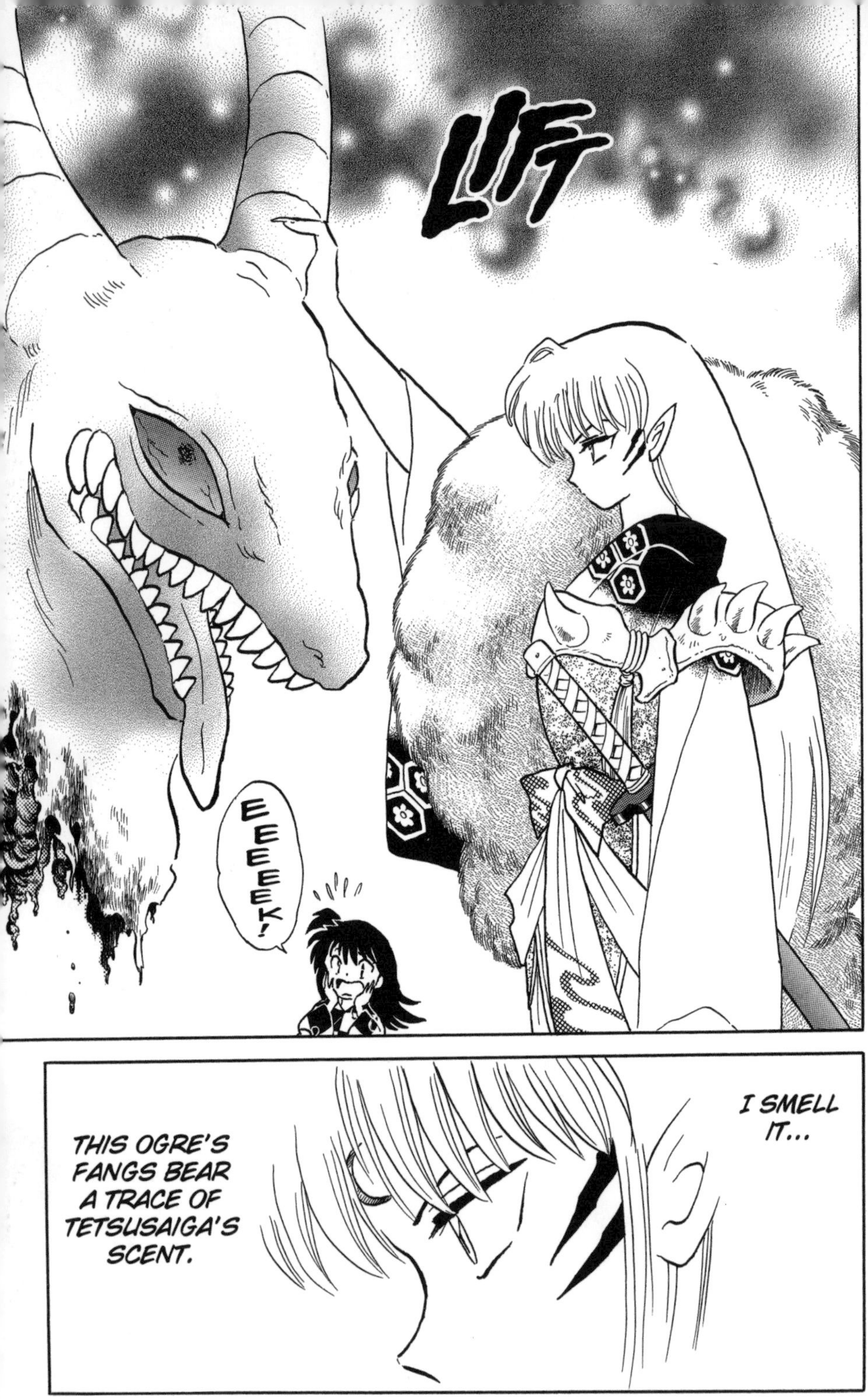
LIFT
EEEEEK!
I SMELL IT...
THIS OGRE'S FANGS BEAR A TRACE OF TETSUSAIGA'S SCENT.

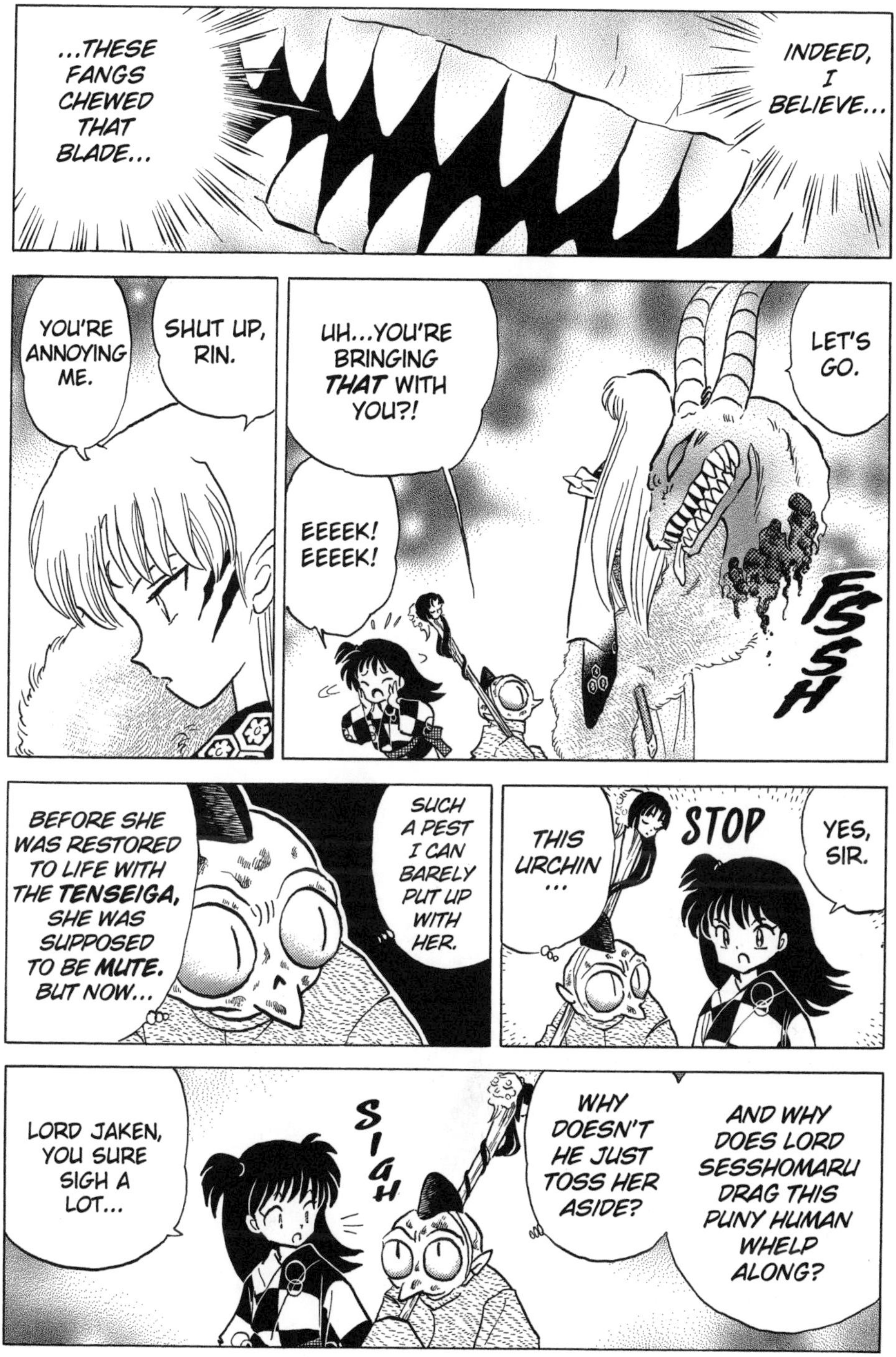
INDEED, I BELIEVE...
...THESE FANGS CHEWED THAT BLADE...
LET'S GO.
UH...YOU'RE BRINGING THAT WITH YOU?!
EEEEK! EEEEK!
FSSH
SHUT UP, RIN.
YOU'RE ANNOYING ME.
YES, SIR.
STOP
THIS URCHIN ...
SUCH A PEST I CAN BARELY PUT UP WITH HER.
BEFORE SHE WAS RESTORED TO LIFE WITH THE TENSEIGA, SHE WAS SUPPOSED TO BE MUTE. BUT NOW...
AND WHY DOES LORD SESSHOMARU DRAG THIS PUNY HUMAN WHELP ALONG?
WHY DOESN'T HE JUST TOSS HER ASIDE?
SIGH
LORD JAKEN, YOU SURE SIGH A LOT...

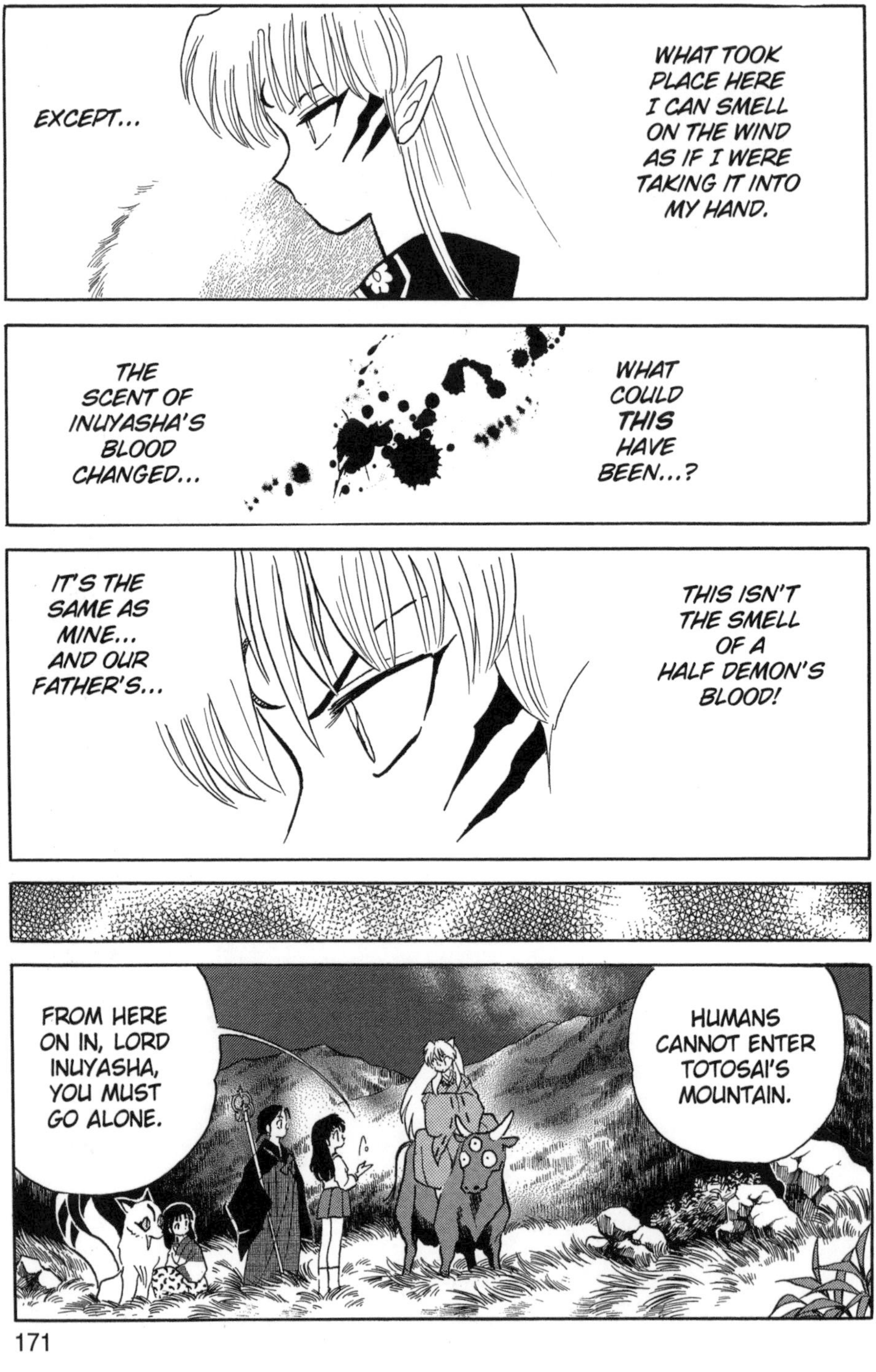
WHAT TOOK PLACE HERE I CAN SMELL ON THE WIND AS IF I WERE TAKING IT INTO MY HAND.
EXCEPT...
WHAT COULD THIS HAVE BEEN...?
THE SCENT OF INUYASHA'S BLOOD CHANGED...
THIS ISN'T THE SMELL OF A HALF DEMON'S BLOOD!
IT'S THE SAME AS MINE... AND OUR FATHER'S...
HUMANS CANNOT ENTER TOTOSAI'S MOUNTAIN.
FROM HERE ON IN, LORD INUYASHA, YOU MUST GO ALONE.

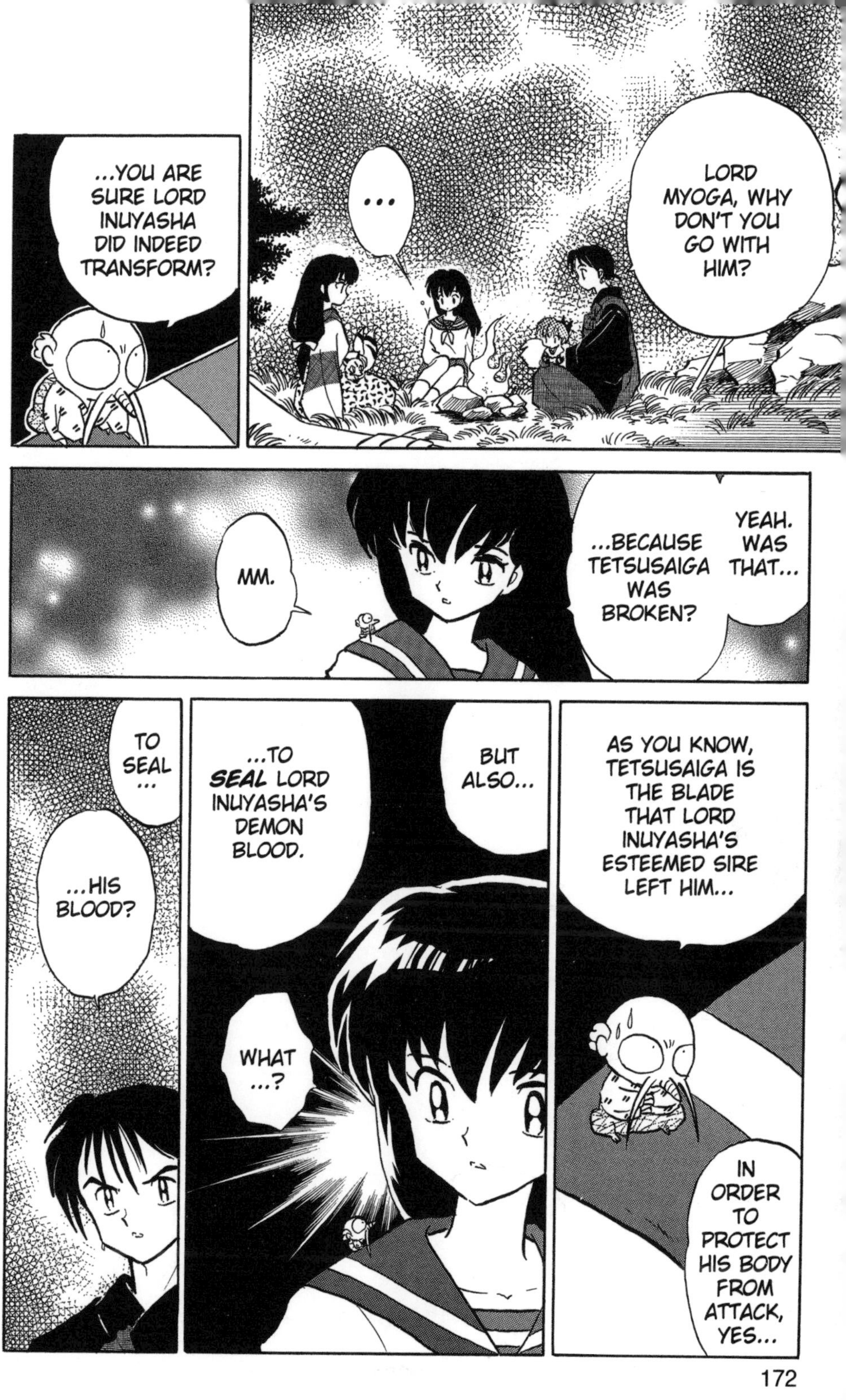
LORD MYOGA, WHY DON'T YOU GO WITH HIM?
...
...YOU ARE SURE LORD INUYASHA DID INDEED TRANSFORM?
YEAH. WAS THAT...
...BECAUSE TETSUSAIGA WAS BROKEN?
MM.
AS YOU KNOW, TETSUSAIGA IS THE BLADE THAT LORD INUYASHA'S ESTEEMED SIRE LEFT HIM...
IN ORDER TO PROTECT HIS BODY FROM ATTACK, YES...
BUT ALSO...
...TO *SEAL* LORD INUYASHA'S DEMON BLOOD.
WHAT ...?
TO SEAL ...
...HIS BLOOD?

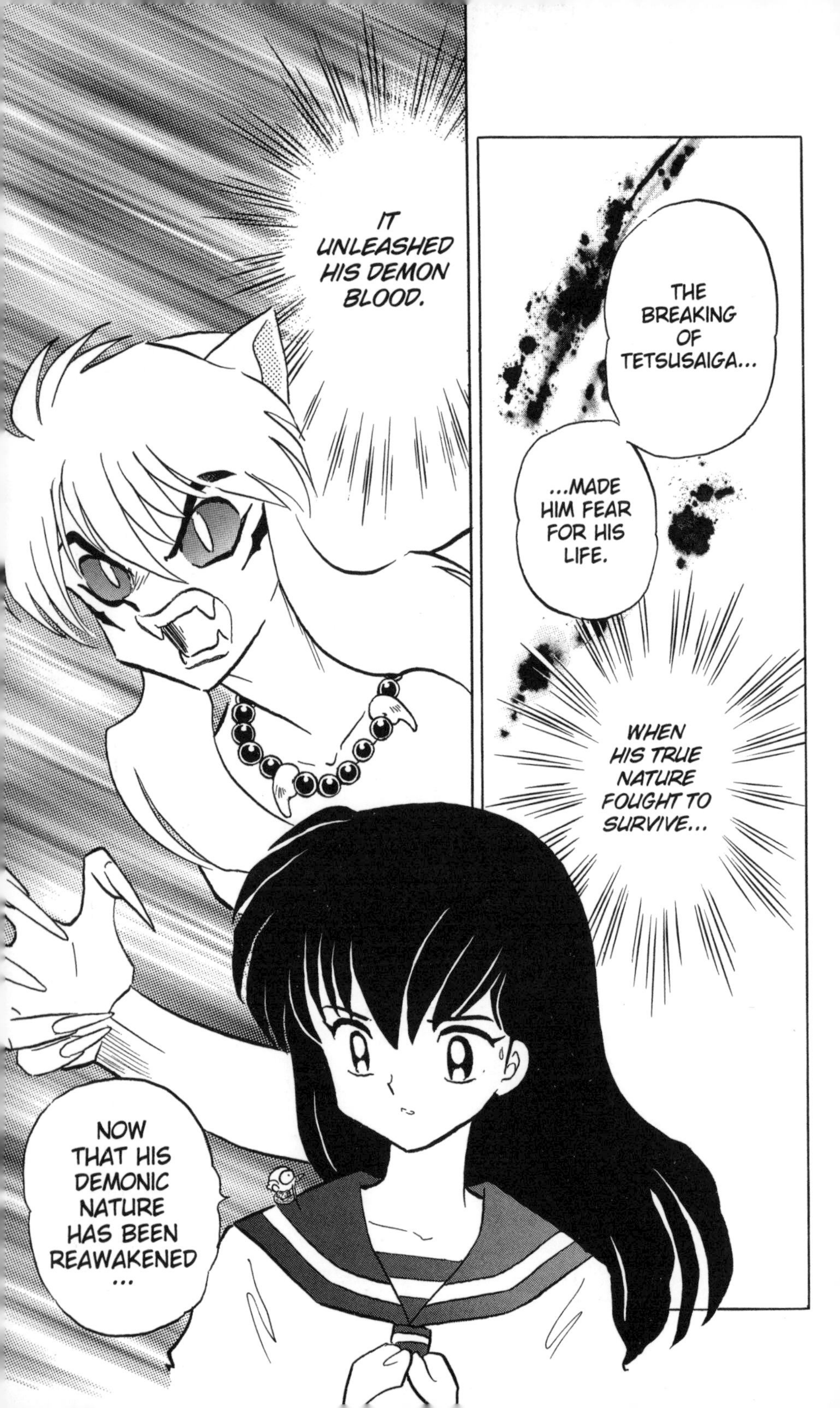
THE BREAKING OF TETSUSAIGA...
...MADE HIM FEAR FOR HIS LIFE.
WHEN HIS TRUE NATURE FOUGHT TO SURVIVE...
IT UNLEASHED HIS DEMON BLOOD.
NOW THAT HIS DEMONIC NATURE HAS BEEN REAWAKENED...

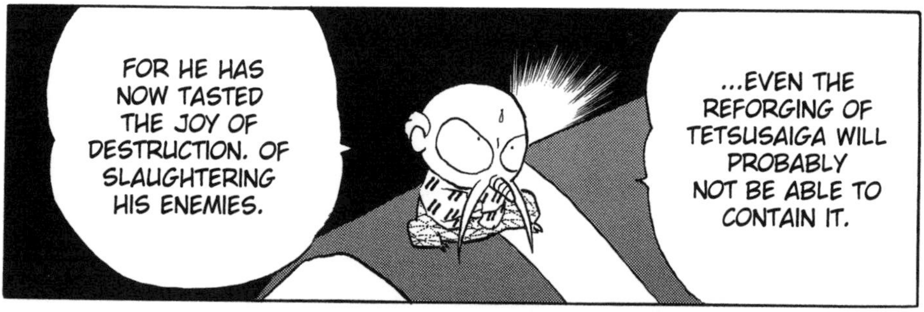
...EVEN THE REFORGING OF TETSUSAIGA WILL PROBABLY NOT BE ABLE TO CONTAIN IT.
FOR HE HAS NOW TASTED THE JOY OF DESTRUCTION. OF SLAUGHTERING HIS ENEMIES.
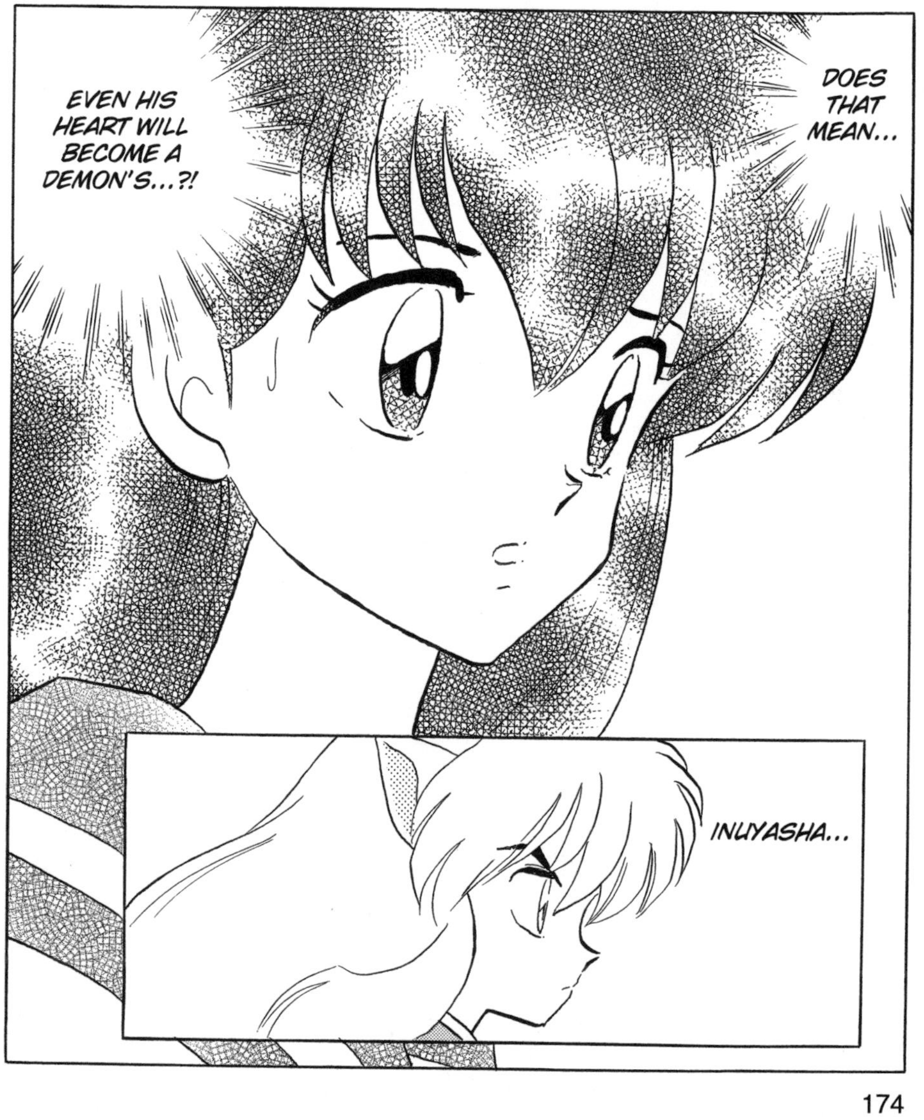
DOES THAT MEAN...
EVEN HIS HEART WILL BECOME A DEMON'S...?!
INUYASHA...

SCROLL TEN

THE OGRE'S SWORD

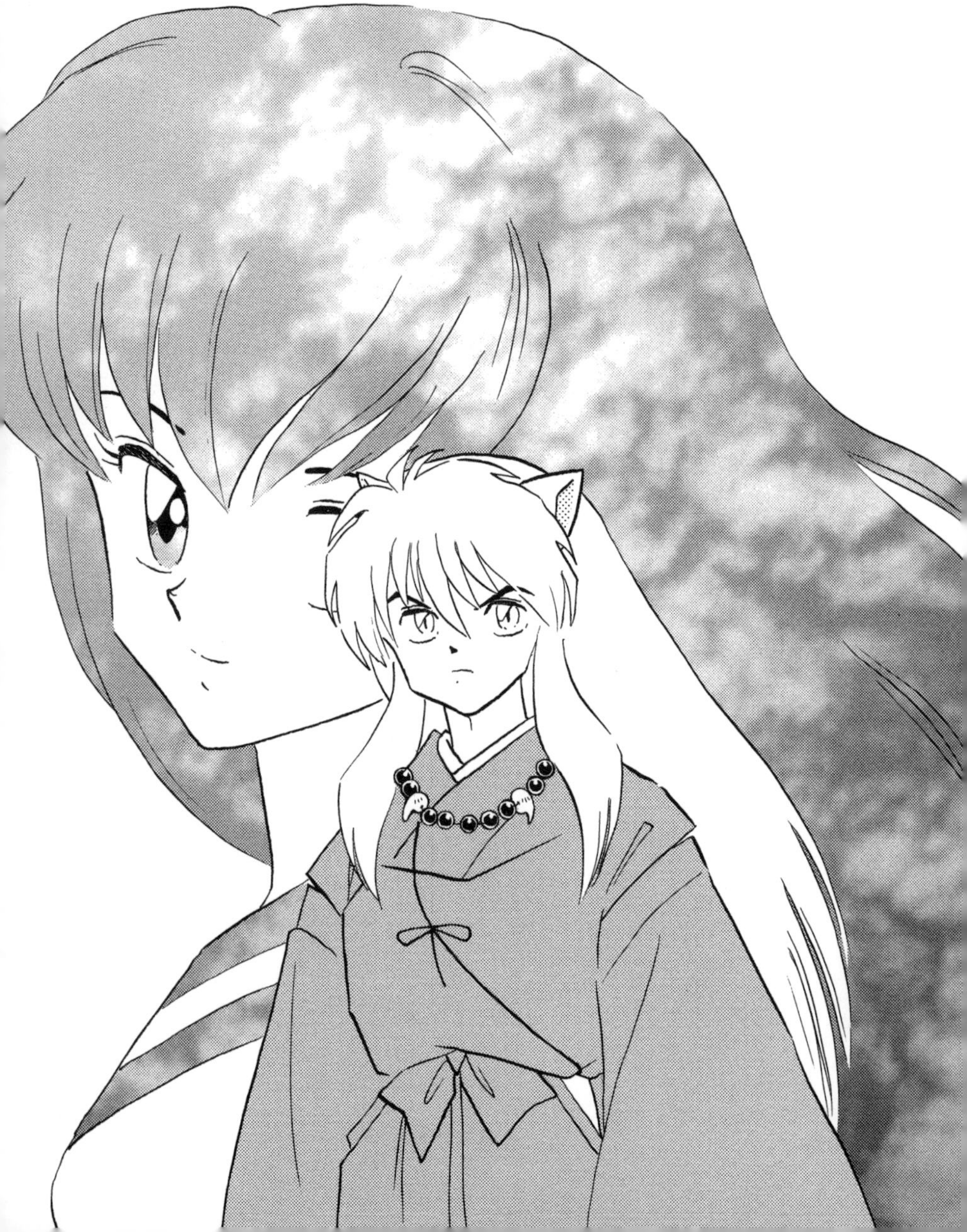

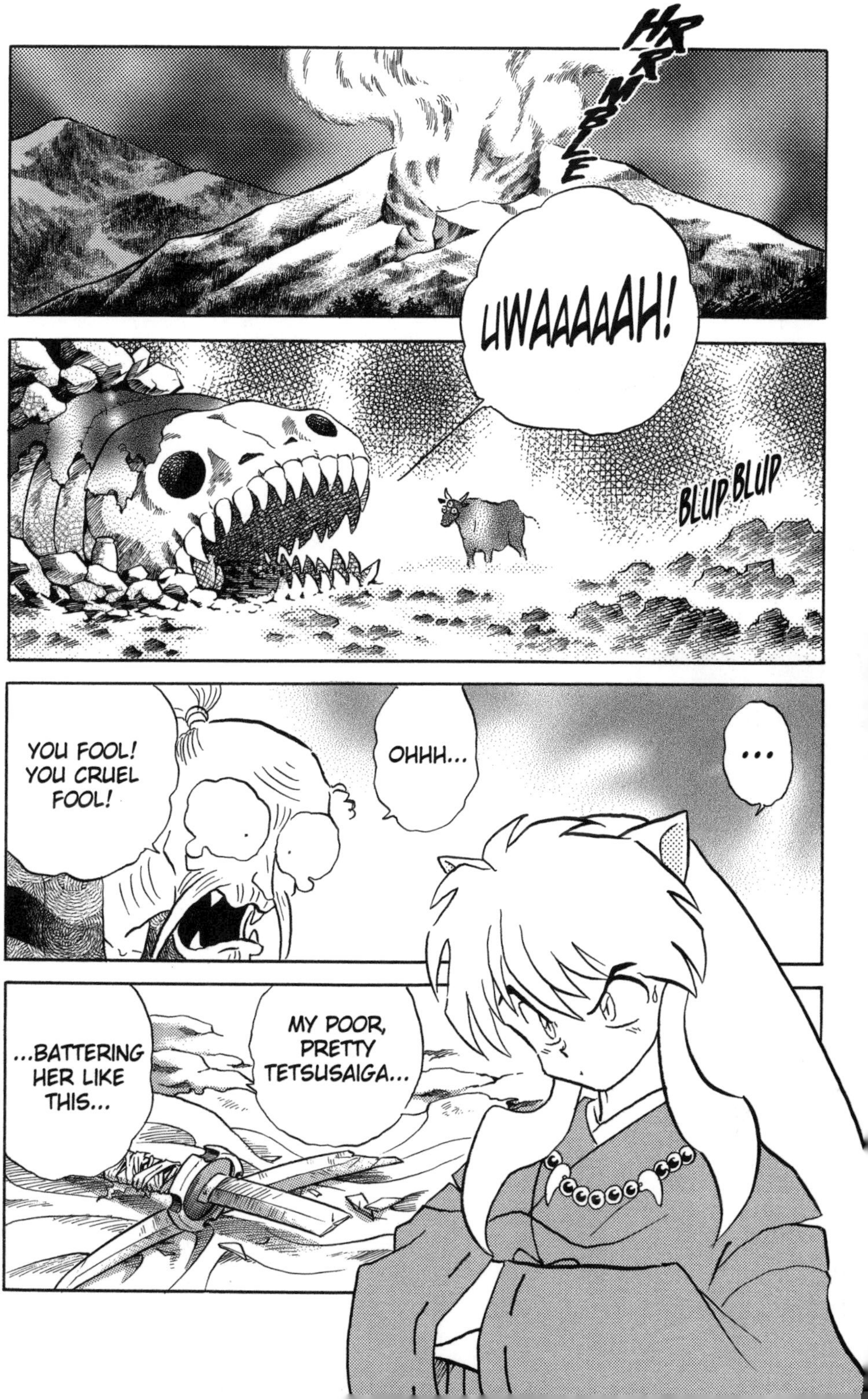
HRRMMBLE
UWAAAAAH!
BLUP BLUP
...
OHHH...
YOU FOOL! YOU CRUEL FOOL!
MY POOR, PRETTY TETSUSAIGA...
...BATTERING HER LIKE THIS...

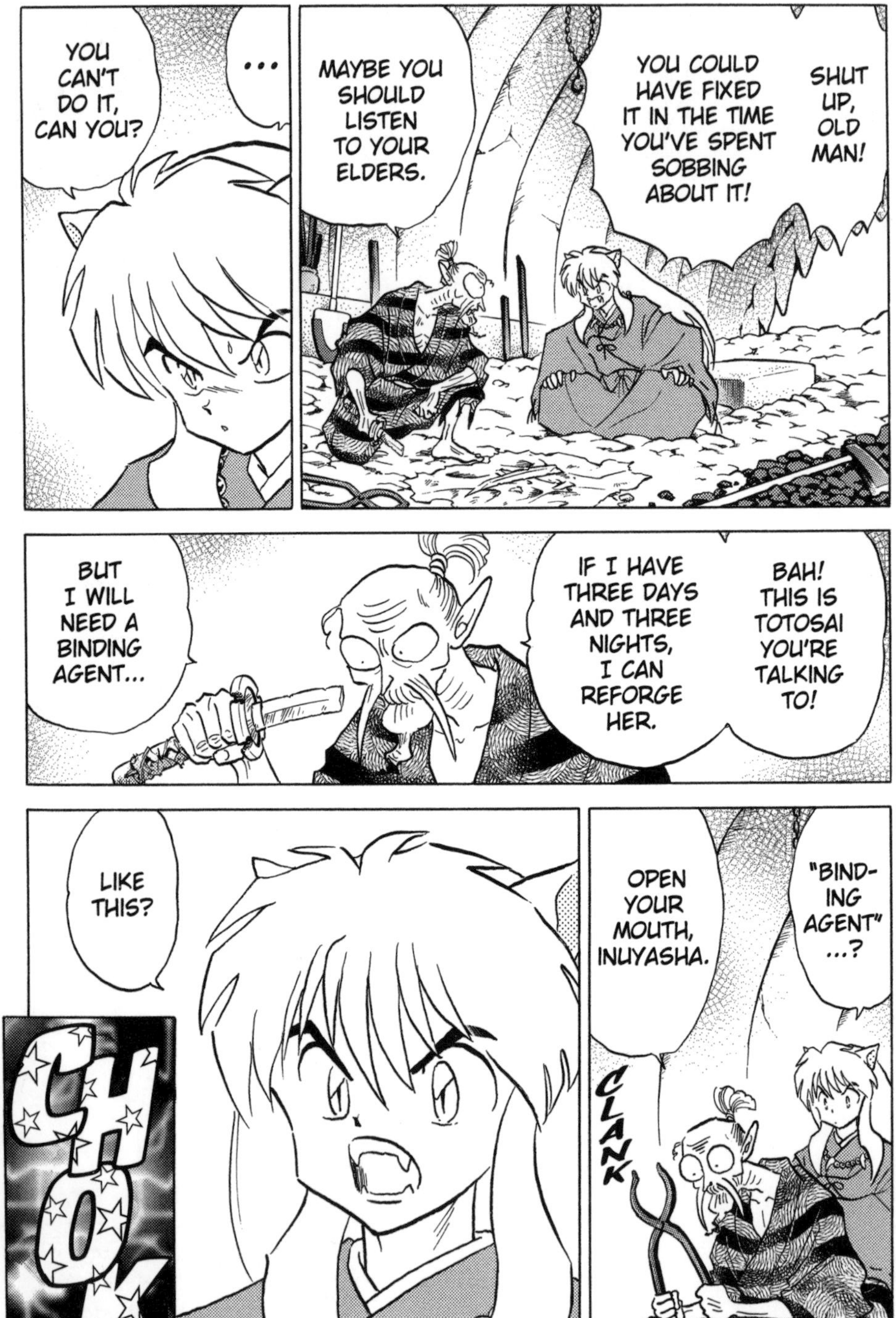
SHUT UP, OLD MAN!
YOU COULD HAVE FIXED IT IN THE TIME YOU'VE SPENT SOBBING ABOUT IT!
MAYBE YOU SHOULD LISTEN TO YOUR ELDERS.
...
YOU CAN'T DO IT, CAN YOU?
BAH! THIS IS TOTOSAI YOU'RE TALKING TO!
IF I HAVE THREE DAYS AND THREE NIGHTS, I CAN REFORGE HER.
BUT I WILL NEED A BINDING AGENT...
"BIND-ING AGENT" ...?
OPEN YOUR MOUTH, INUYASHA.
CLANK
LIKE THIS?
CHOK

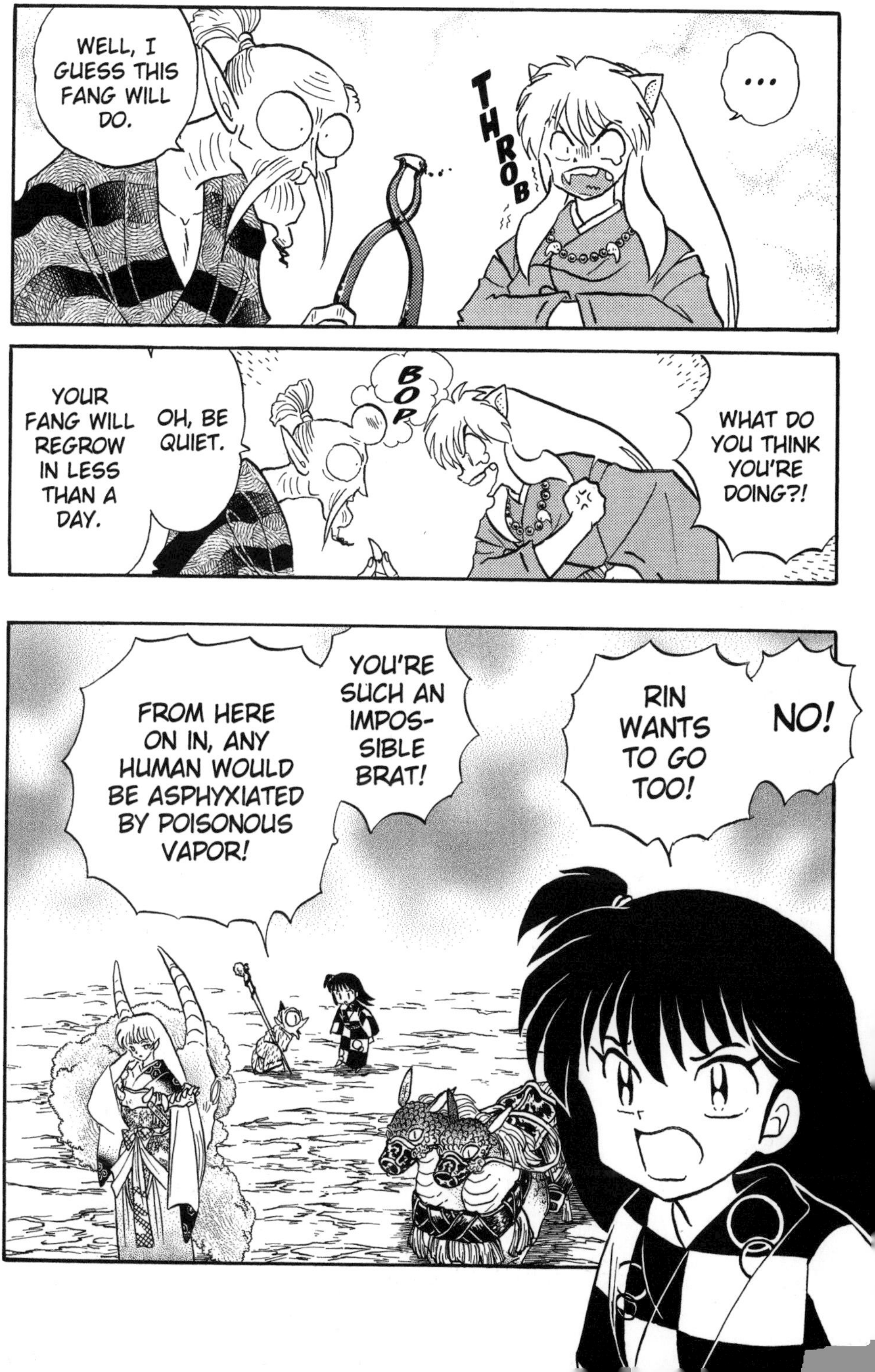
...
THROB
WELL, I GUESS THIS FANG WILL DO.
WHAT DO YOU THINK YOU'RE DOING?!
BOP
OH, BE QUIET.
YOUR FANG WILL REGROW IN LESS THAN A DAY.
NO!
RIN WANTS TO GO TOO!
YOU'RE SUCH AN IMPOS-SIBLE BRAT!
FROM HERE ON IN, ANY HUMAN WOULD BE ASPHYXIATED BY POISONOUS VAPOR!

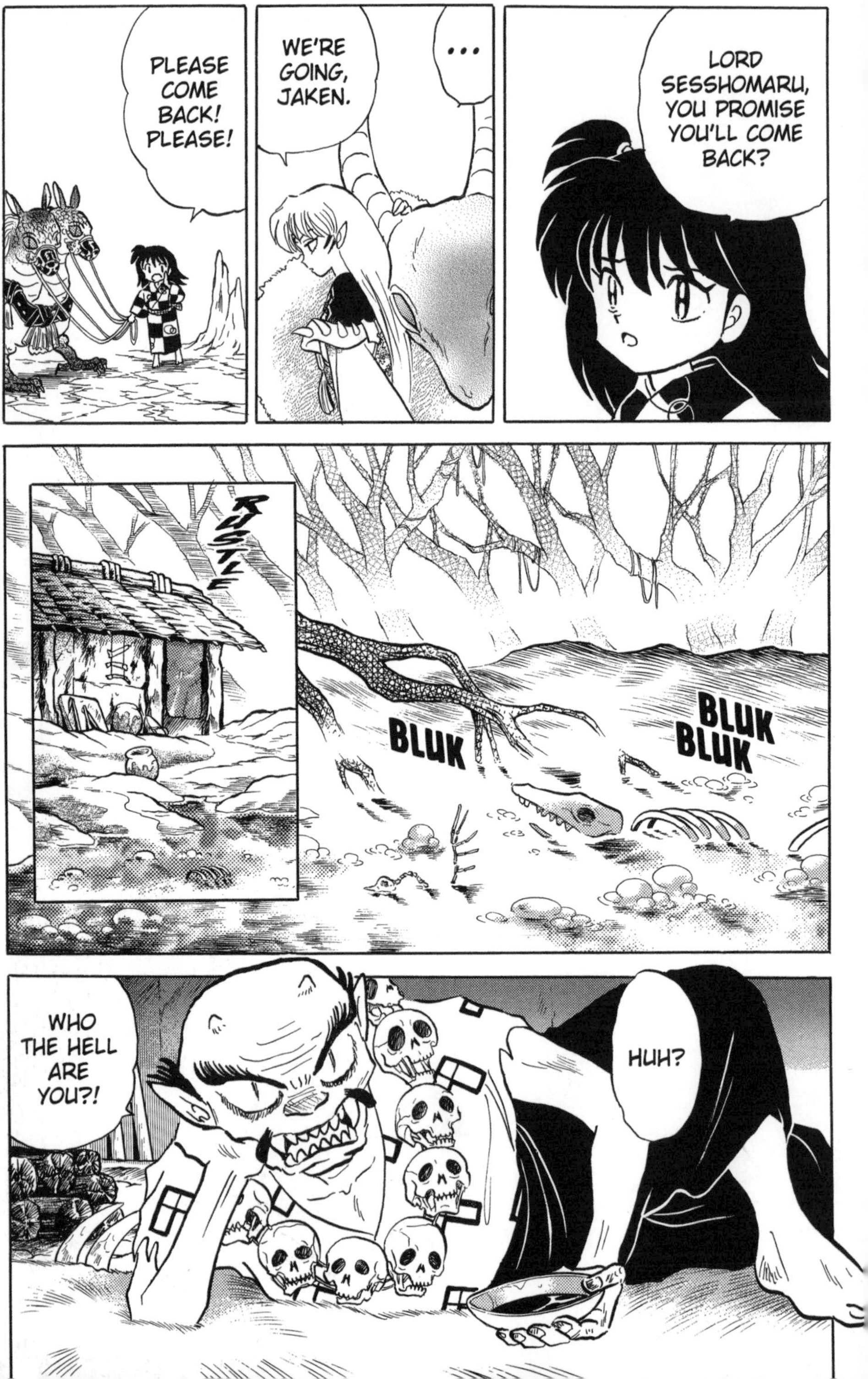
LORD SESSHOMARU, YOU PROMISE YOU'LL COME BACK?
...
WE'RE GOING, JAKEN.
PLEASE COME BACK! PLEASE!
BLUK BLUK
BLUK
RUSTLE
HUH?
WHO THE HELL ARE YOU?!

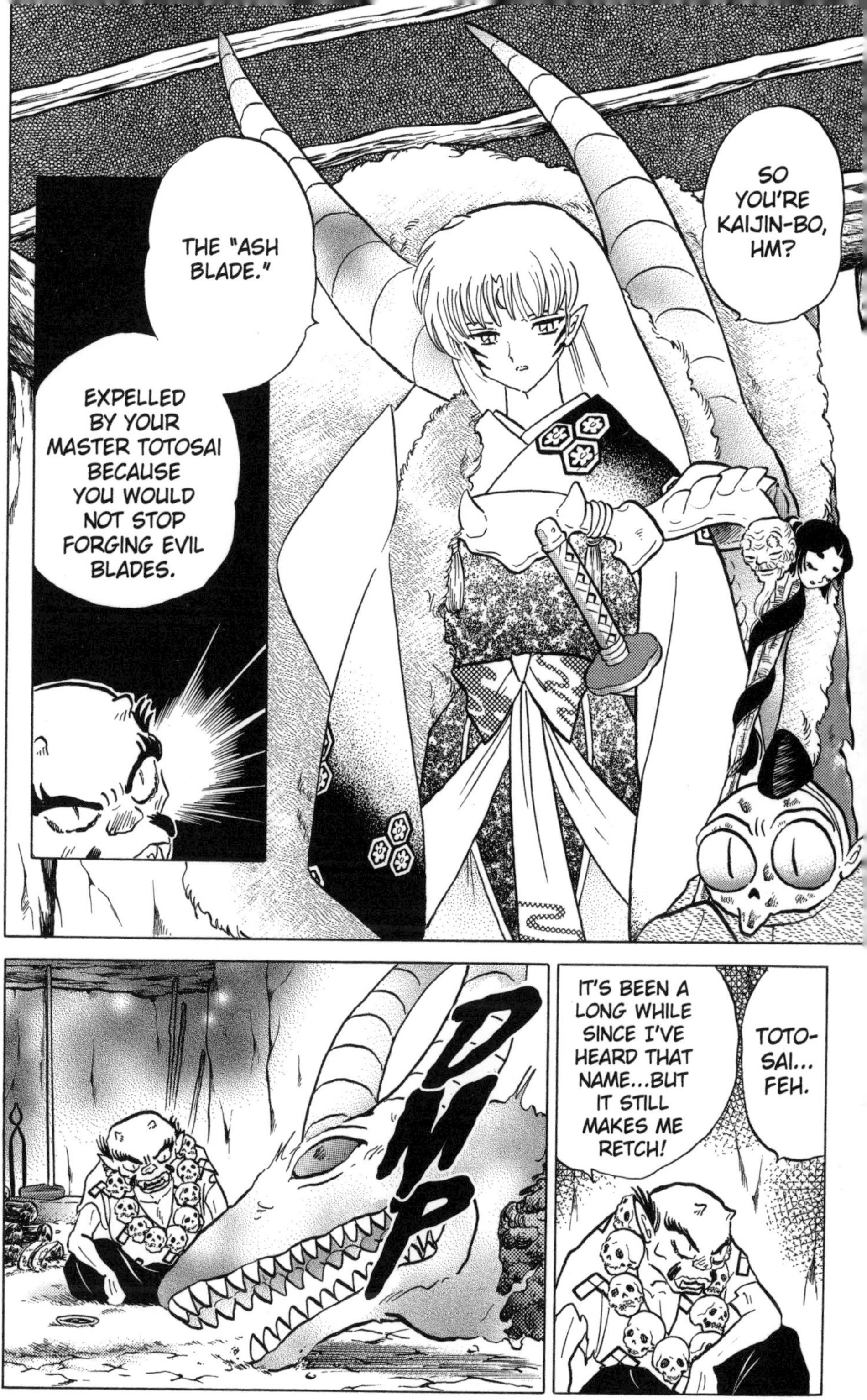
SO YOU'RE KAIJIN-BO, HM?
THE "ASH BLADE."
EXPELLED BY YOUR MASTER TOTOSAI BECAUSE YOU WOULD NOT STOP FORGING EVIL BLADES.
TOTO-SAI... FEH.
IT'S BEEN A LONG WHILE SINCE I'VE HEARD THAT NAME...BUT IT STILL MAKES ME RETCH!
DMP

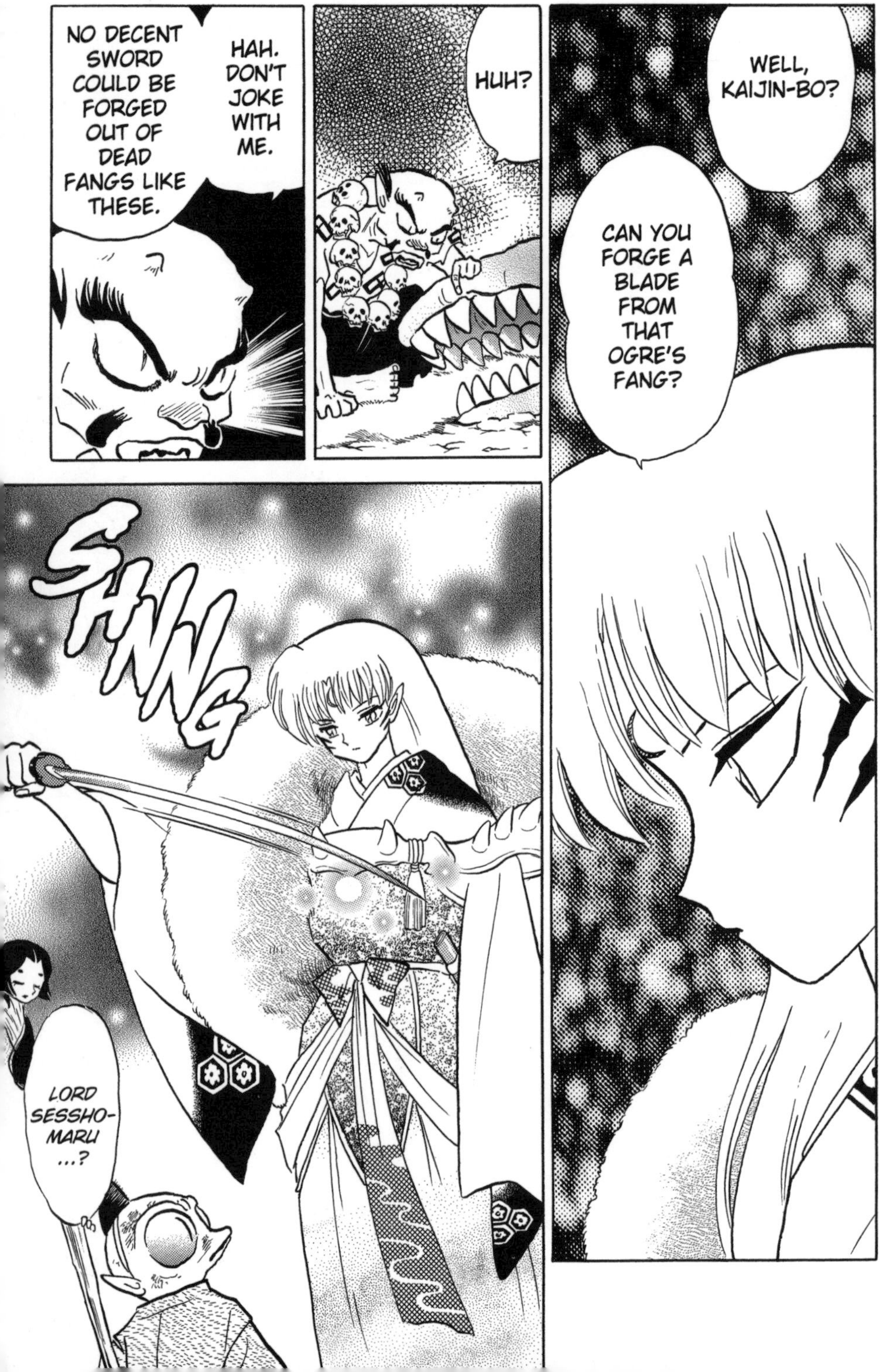
WELL, KAIJIN-BO?
CAN YOU FORGE A BLADE FROM THAT OGRE'S FANG?
HUH?
HAH. DON'T JOKE WITH ME.
NO DECENT SWORD COULD BE FORGED OUT OF DEAD FANGS LIKE THESE.
SHING
LORD SESSHO-MARU ...?

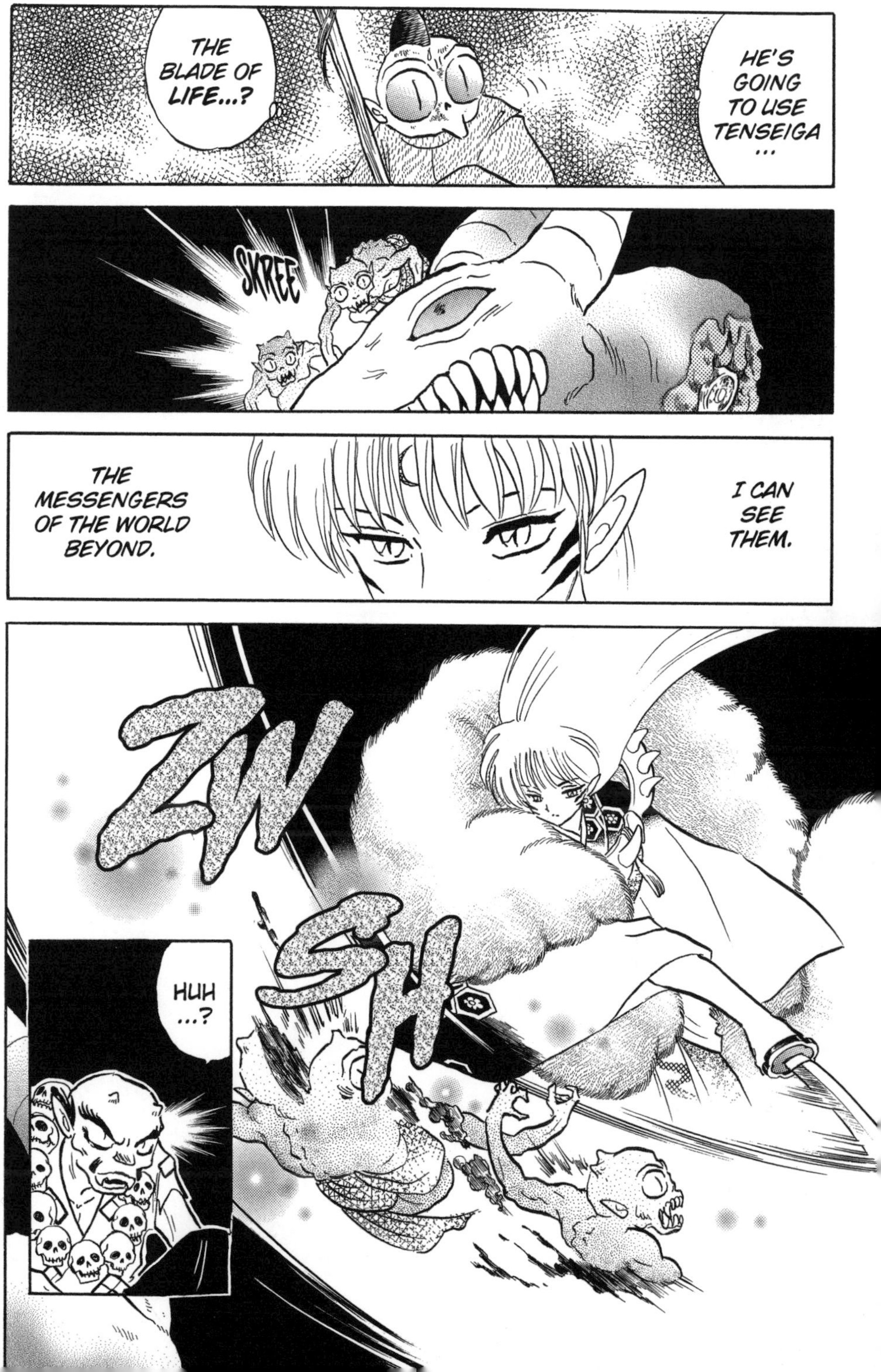
HE'S GOING TO USE TENSEIGA...
THE BLADE OF LIFE...?
SKREE
I CAN SEE THEM.
THE MESSENGERS OF THE WORLD BEYOND.
ZWSH
HUH...?

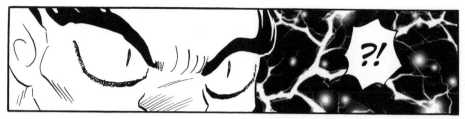

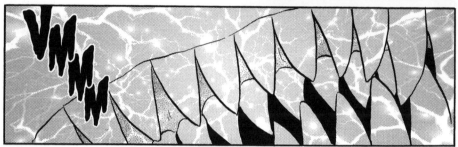

?!
VMMM
THIS IS...
...LIKE A WHOLE DIFFERENT THING...
KAIJIN-BO.
LET ME TELL YOU SOME-THING.
THAT OGRE'S FANGS...
...CHEWED AND SNAPPED THE TETSUSAIGA...
THE BLADE FORGED BY YOUR HATED MASTER, TOTOSAI.
THIS IS... ASTOUND-ING.
WHAT A BLADE I COULD FORGE FROM THIS...

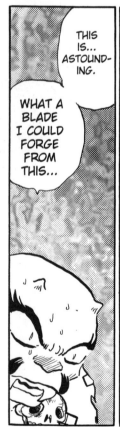

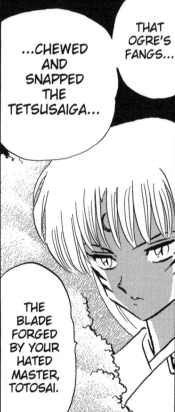

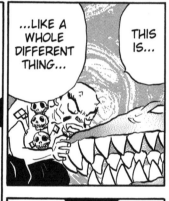

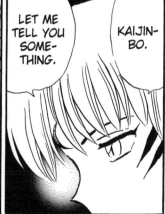

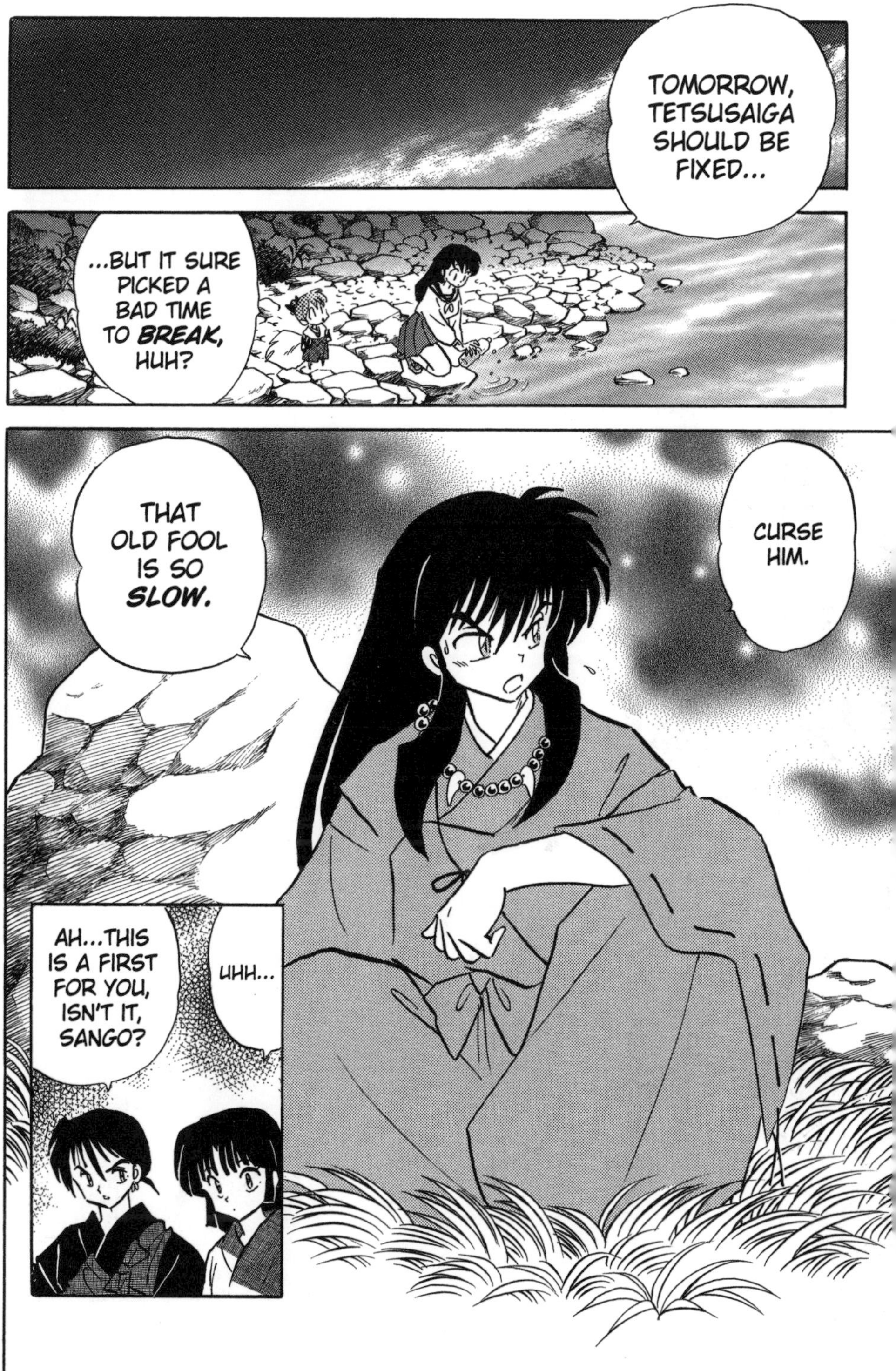
TOMORROW, TETSUSAIGA SHOULD BE FIXED...
...BUT IT SURE PICKED A BAD TIME TO BREAK, HUH?
CURSE HIM.
THAT OLD FOOL IS SO SLOW.
AH...THIS IS A FIRST FOR YOU, ISN'T IT, SANGO?
UHH...

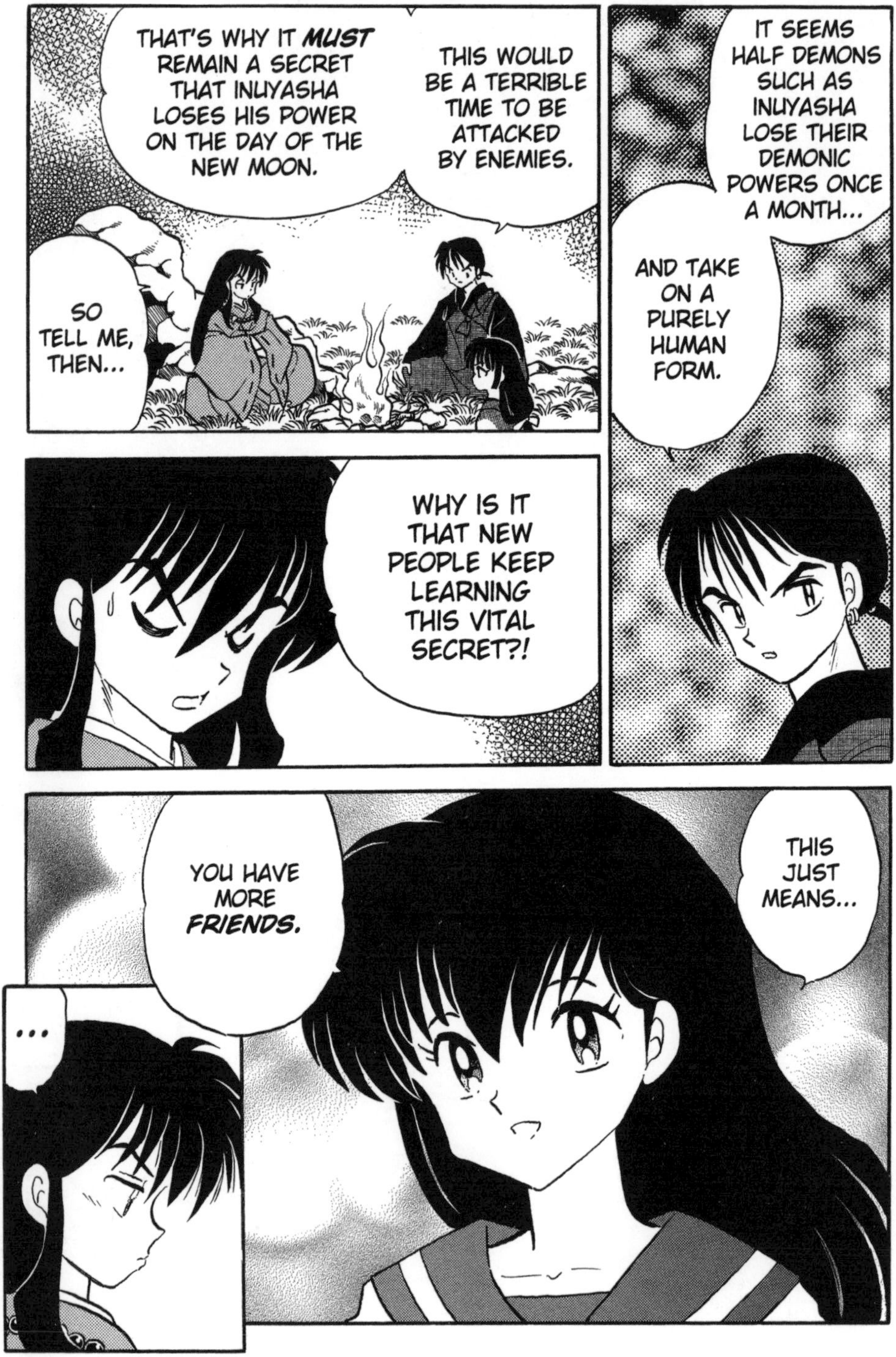
IT SEEMS HALF DEMONS SUCH AS INUYASHA LOSE THEIR DEMONIC POWERS ONCE A MONTH...
AND TAKE ON A PURELY HUMAN FORM.
THIS WOULD BE A TERRIBLE TIME TO BE ATTACKED BY ENEMIES.
THAT'S WHY IT *MUST* REMAIN A SECRET THAT INUYASHA LOSES HIS POWER ON THE DAY OF THE NEW MOON.
SO TELL ME, THEN...
WHY IS IT THAT NEW PEOPLE KEEP LEARNING THIS VITAL SECRET?!
THIS JUST MEANS...
YOU HAVE MORE *FRIENDS.*
...

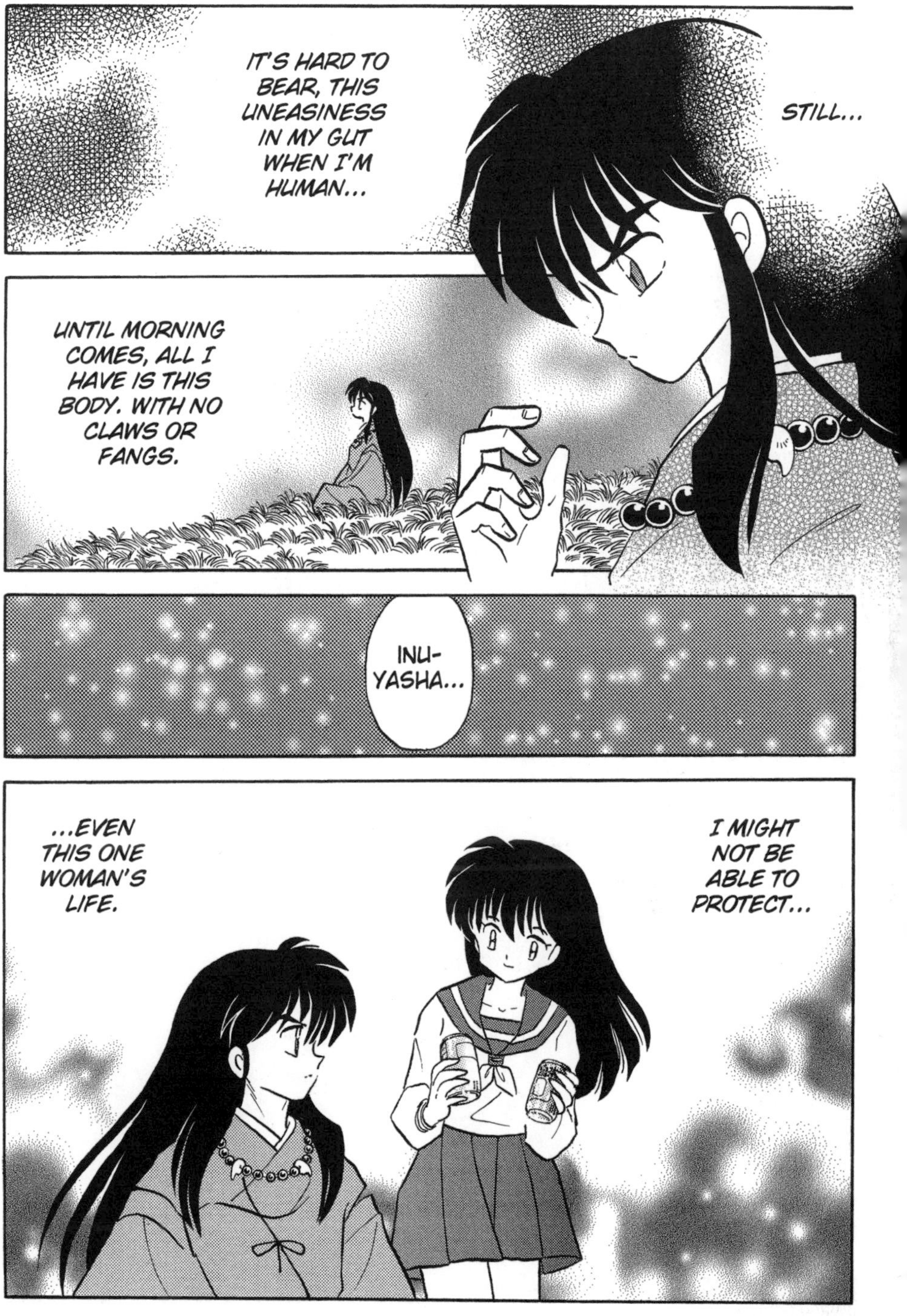
STILL...
IT'S HARD TO BEAR, THIS UNEASINESS IN MY GUT WHEN I'M HUMAN...
UNTIL MORNING COMES, ALL I HAVE IS THIS BODY. WITH NO CLAWS OR FANGS.
INU-YASHA...
I MIGHT NOT BE ABLE TO PROTECT...
...EVEN THIS ONE WOMAN'S LIFE.

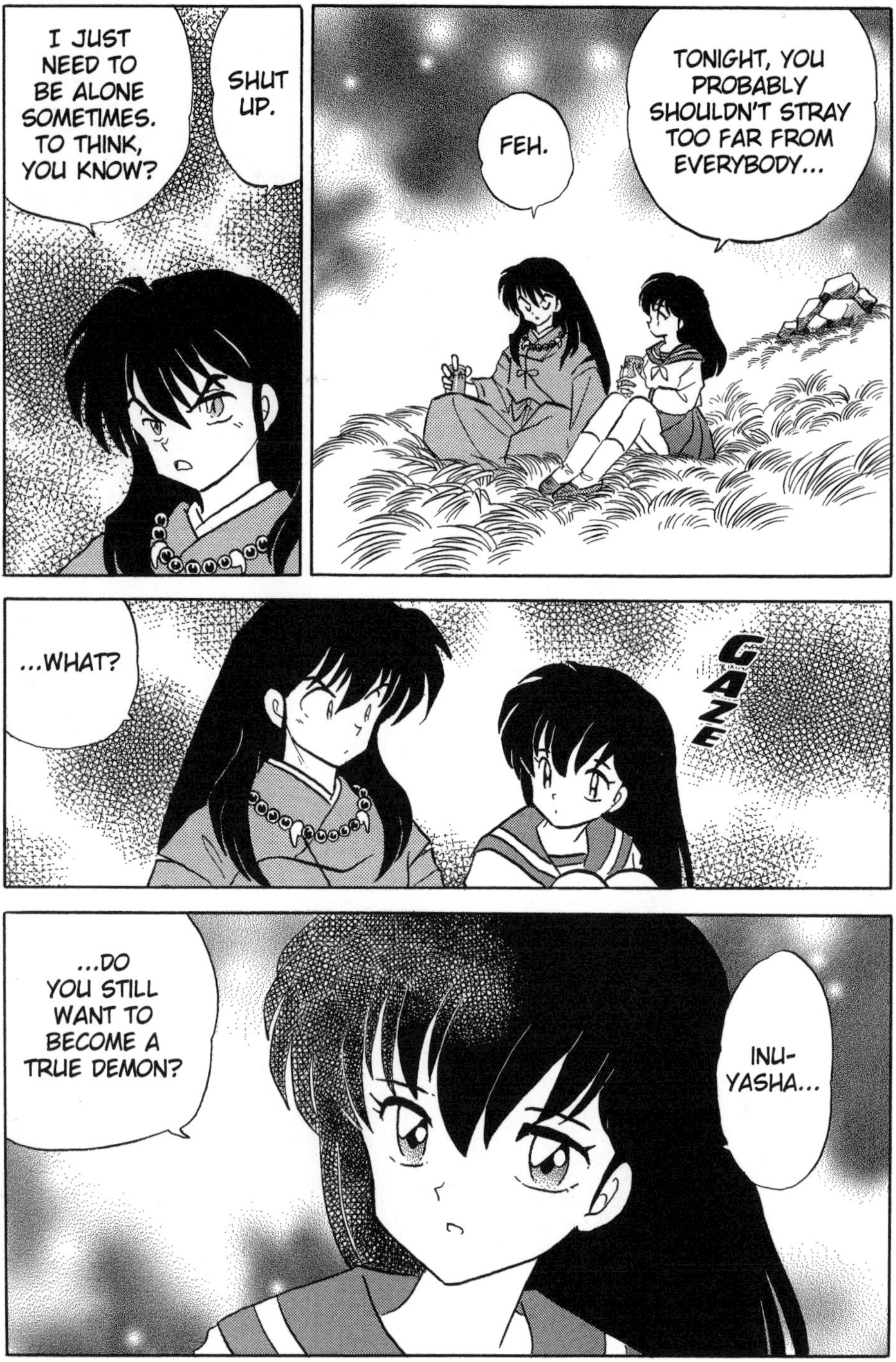
TONIGHT, YOU PROBABLY SHOULDN'T STRAY TOO FAR FROM EVERYBODY...
FEH.
SHUT UP.
I JUST NEED TO BE ALONE SOMETIMES. TO THINK, YOU KNOW?
GAZE
...WHAT?
INU-YASHA...
...DO YOU STILL WANT TO BECOME A TRUE DEMON?

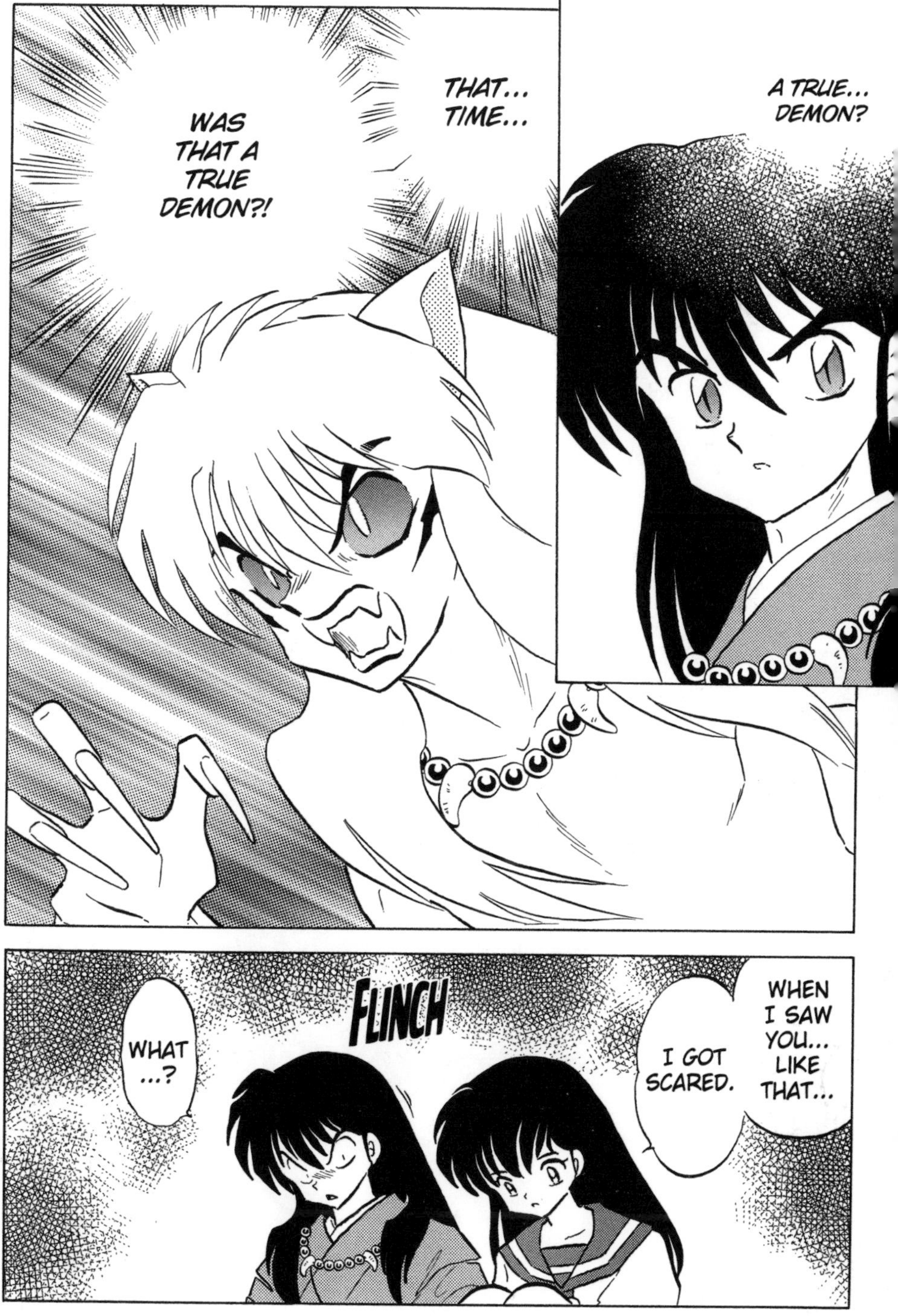
A TRUE... DEMON?
THAT... TIME...
WAS THAT A TRUE DEMON?!
WHEN I SAW YOU... LIKE THAT...
I GOT SCARED.
FLINCH
WHAT ...?

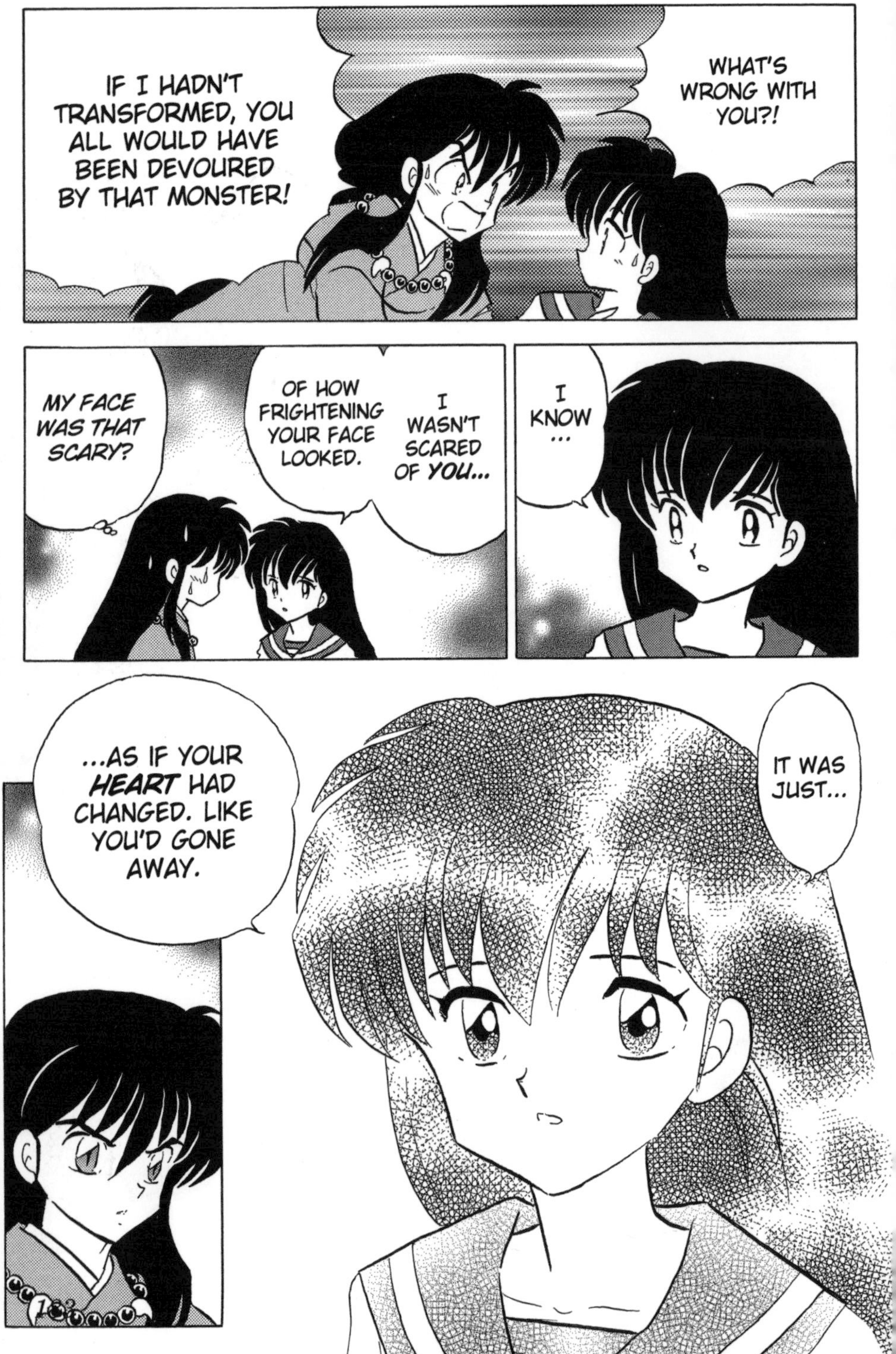
WHAT'S WRONG WITH YOU?!
IF I HADN'T TRANSFORMED, YOU ALL WOULD HAVE BEEN DEVOURED BY THAT MONSTER!
I KNOW...
I WASN'T SCARED OF *YOU*...
OF HOW FRIGHTENING YOUR FACE LOOKED.
MY FACE WAS THAT SCARY?
IT WAS JUST...
...AS IF YOUR ***HEART*** HAD CHANGED. LIKE YOU'D GONE AWAY.

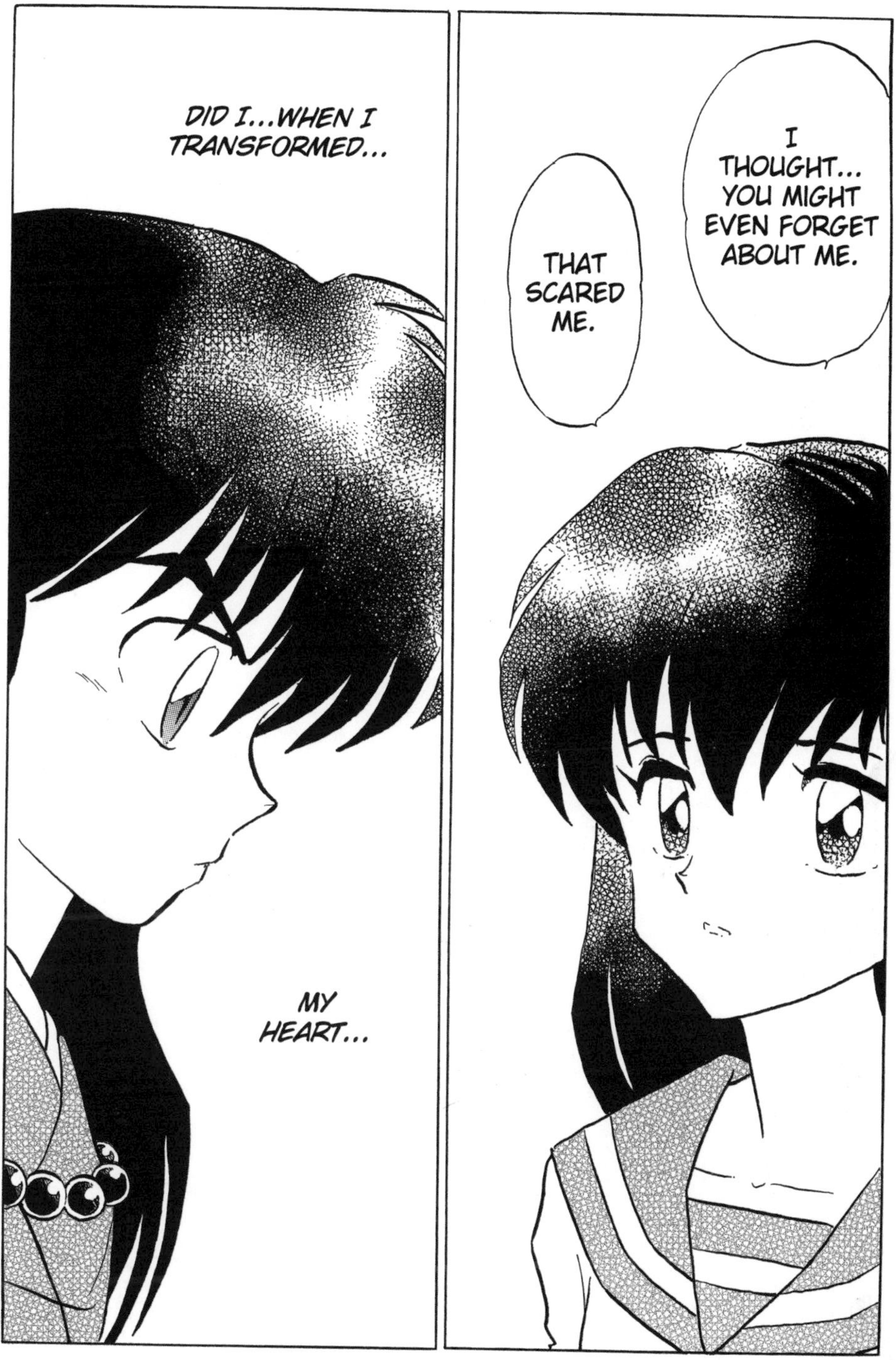
I THOUGHT... YOU MIGHT EVEN FORGET ABOUT ME.
THAT SCARED ME.
DID I...WHEN I TRANSFORMED...
MY HEART...

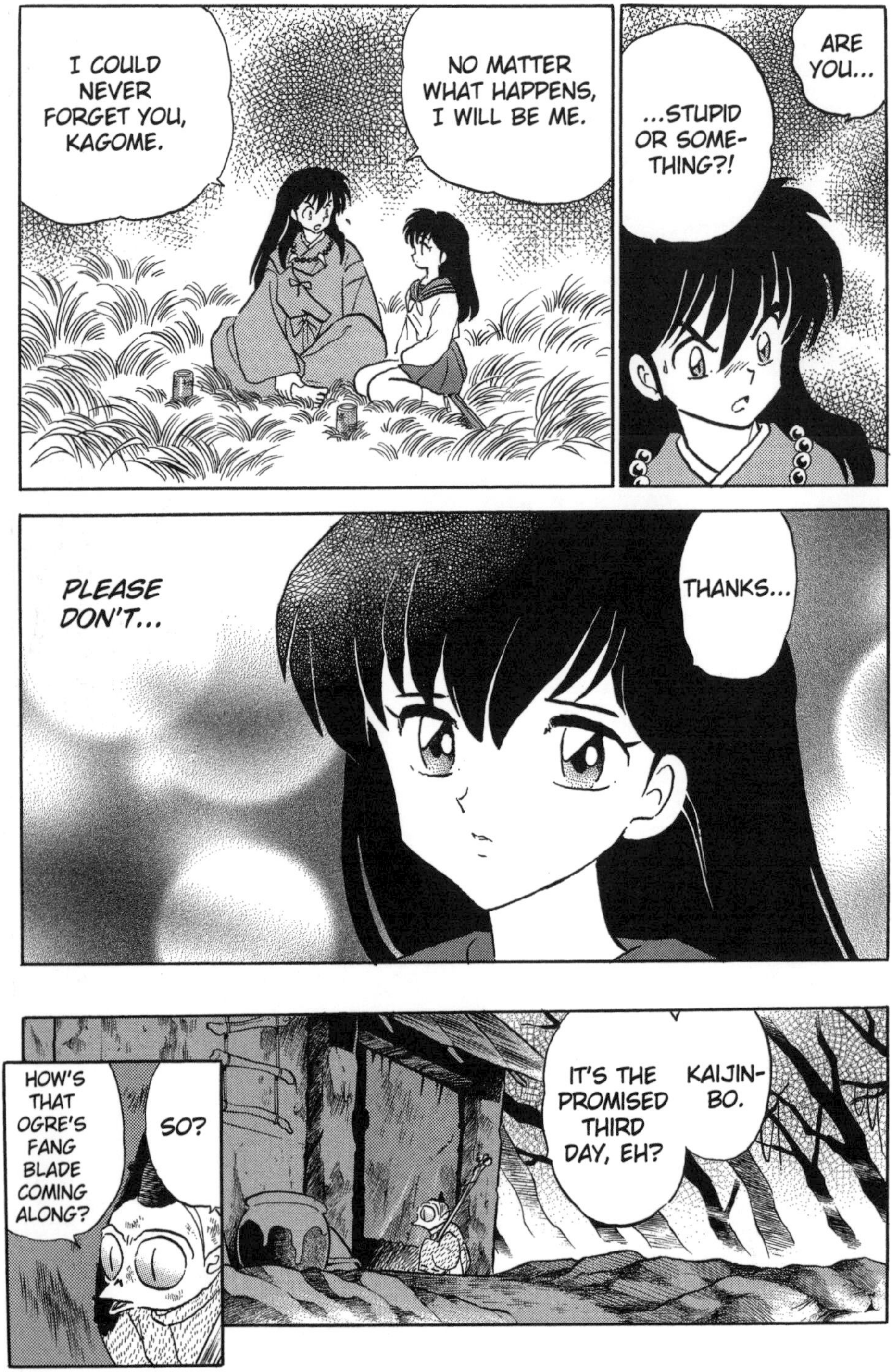
ARE YOU...
...STUPID OR SOME-THING?!
NO MATTER WHAT HAPPENS, I WILL BE ME.
I COULD NEVER FORGET YOU, KAGOME.
THANKS...
PLEASE DON'T...
KAIJIN-BO.
IT'S THE PROMISED THIRD DAY, EH?
SO?
HOW'S THAT OGRE'S FANG BLADE COMING ALONG?

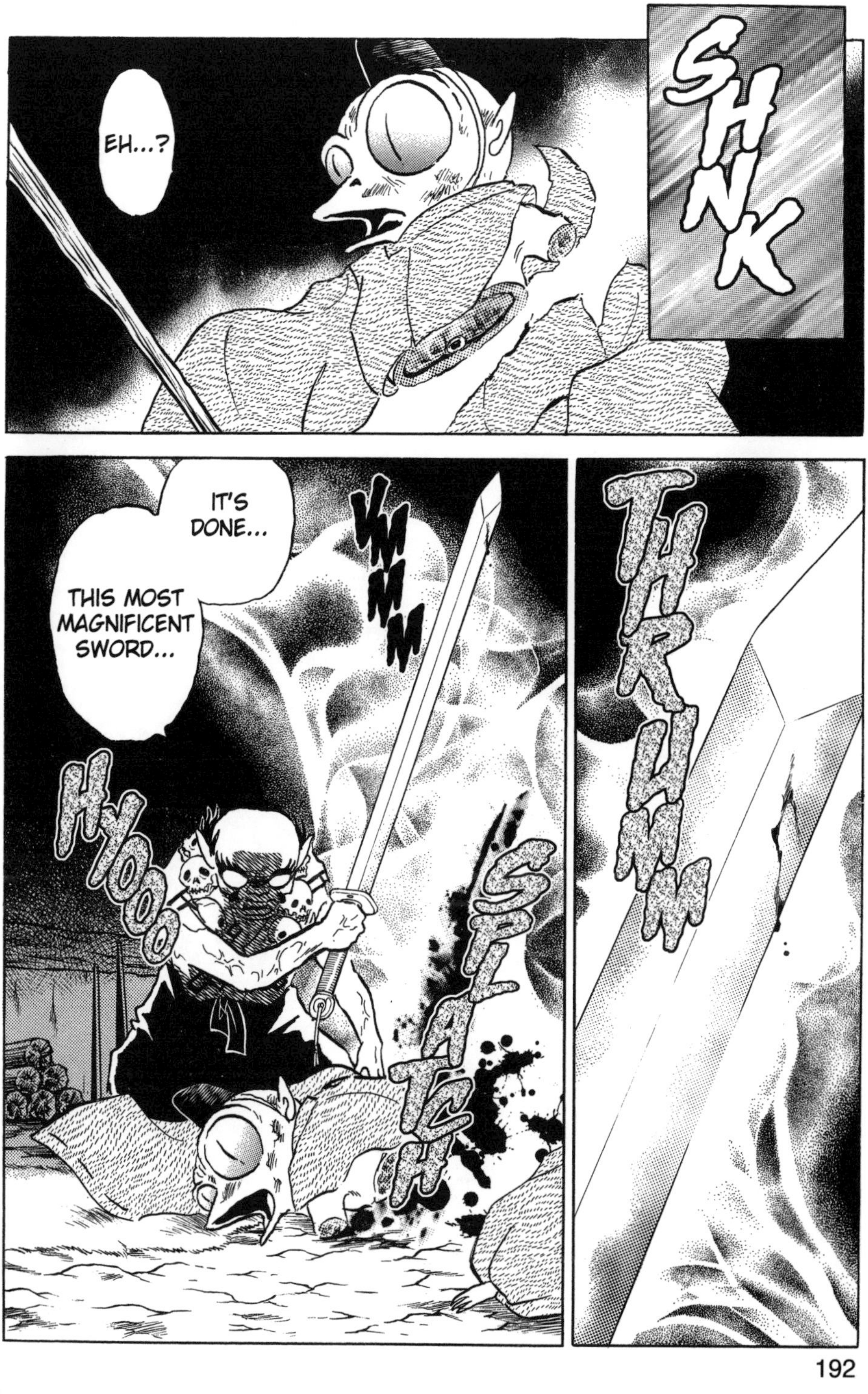
SHNK
EH...?
THRUMMM
IT'S DONE...
THIS MOST MAGNIFICENT SWORD...
VMMMM
HYOOO
SPLATCH

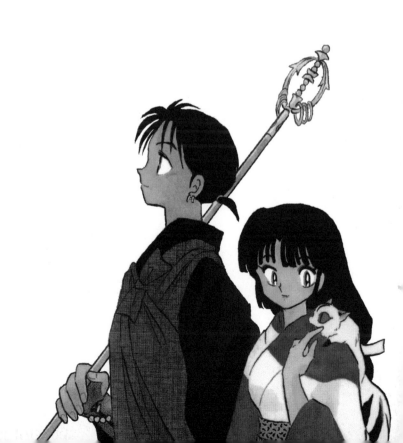

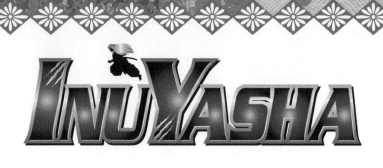

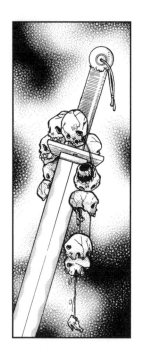

Volume 17
Tetsusaiga Reborn

SCROLL ONE
TOKIJIN

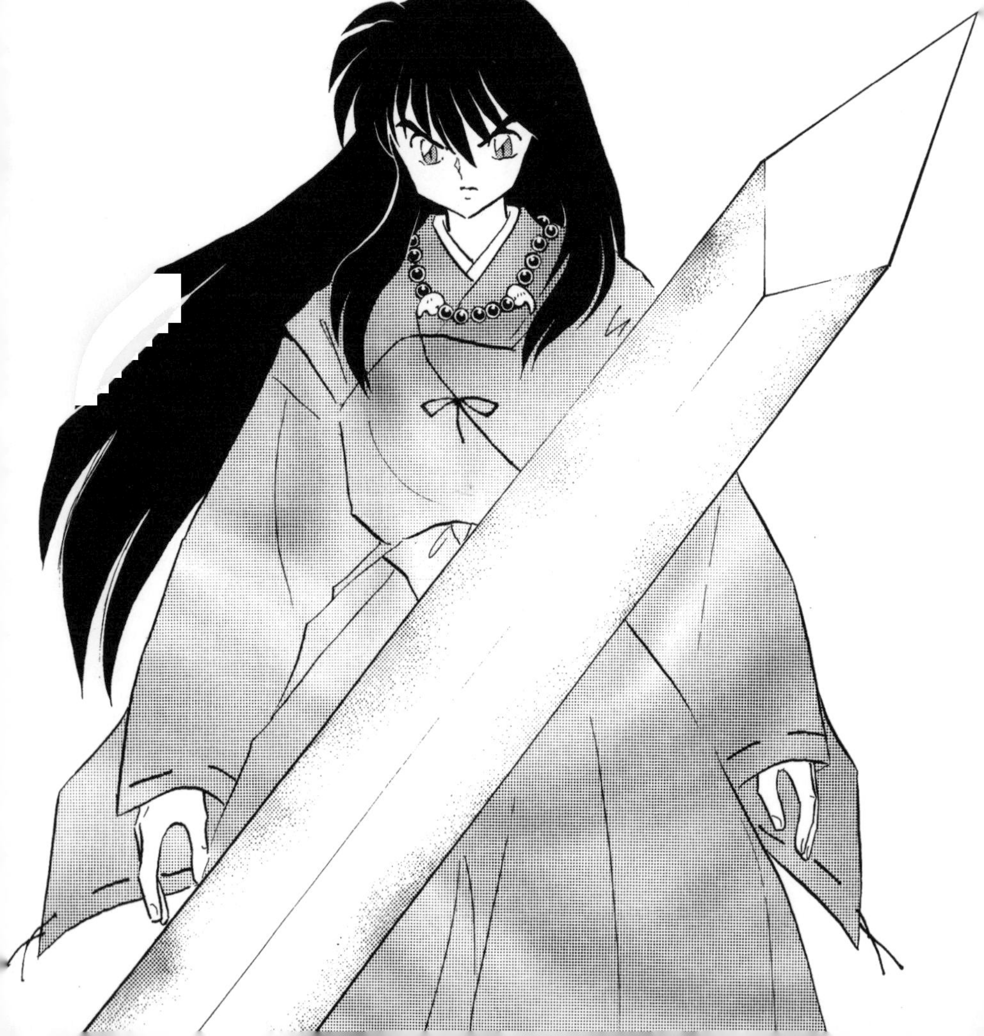

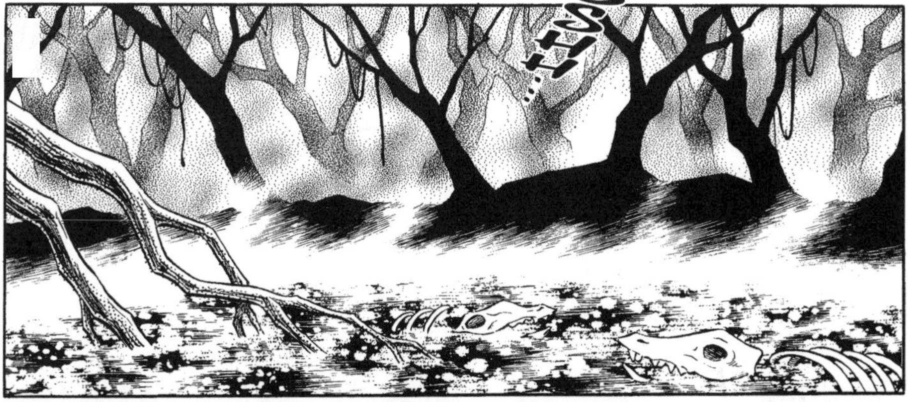
HSSH...

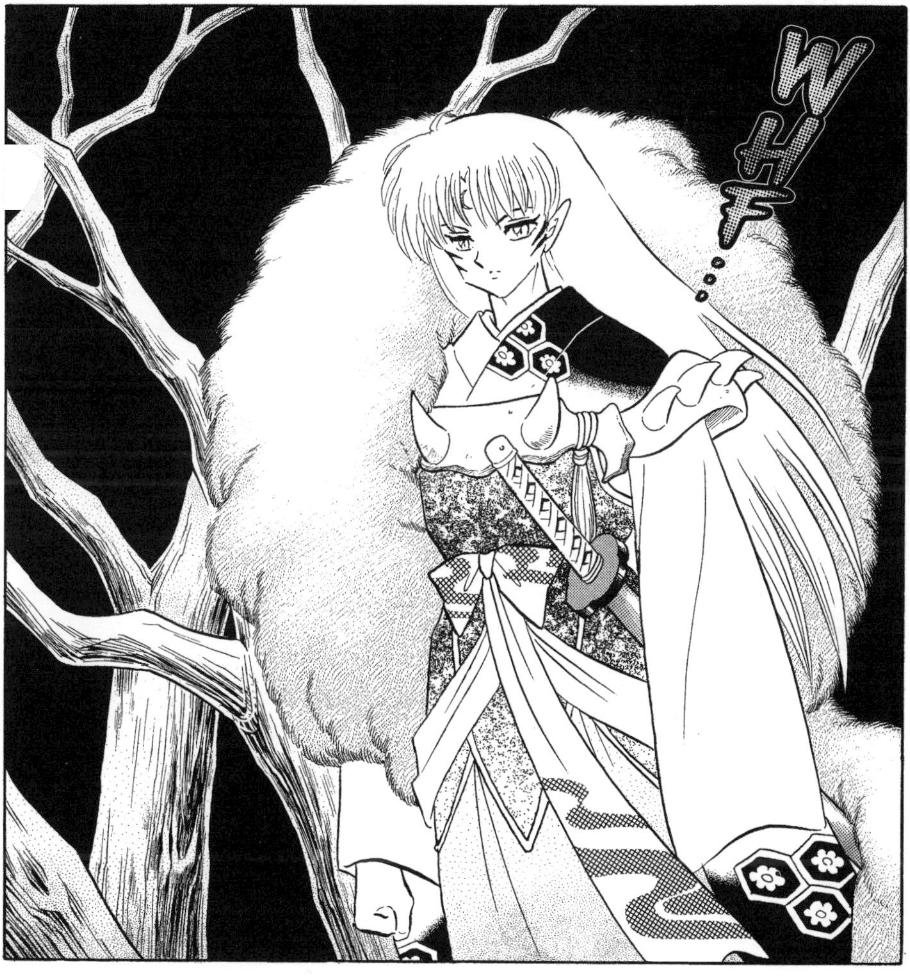
WHF...

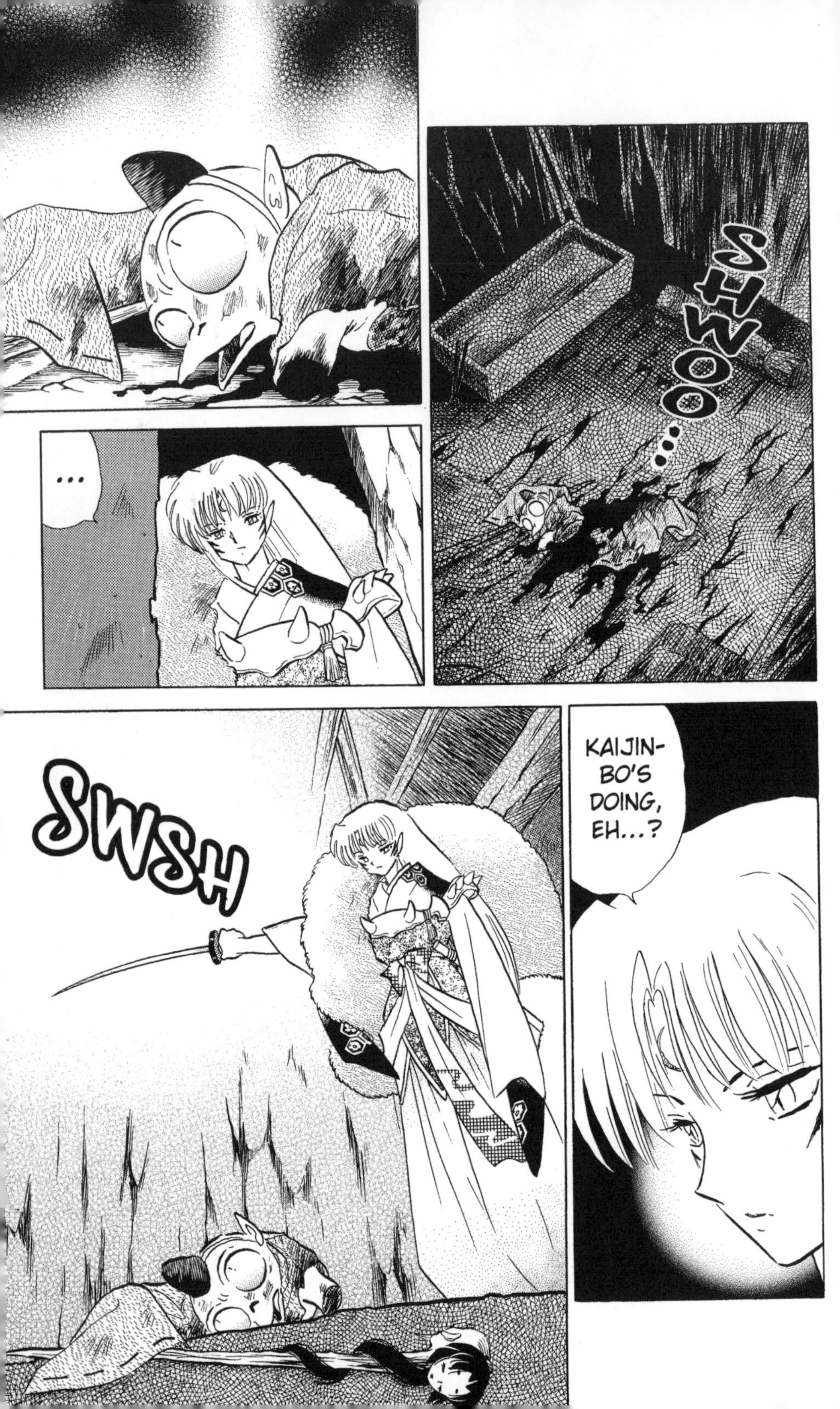
SHWOO...
...
KAIJIN-BO'S DOING, EH...?
SWSH

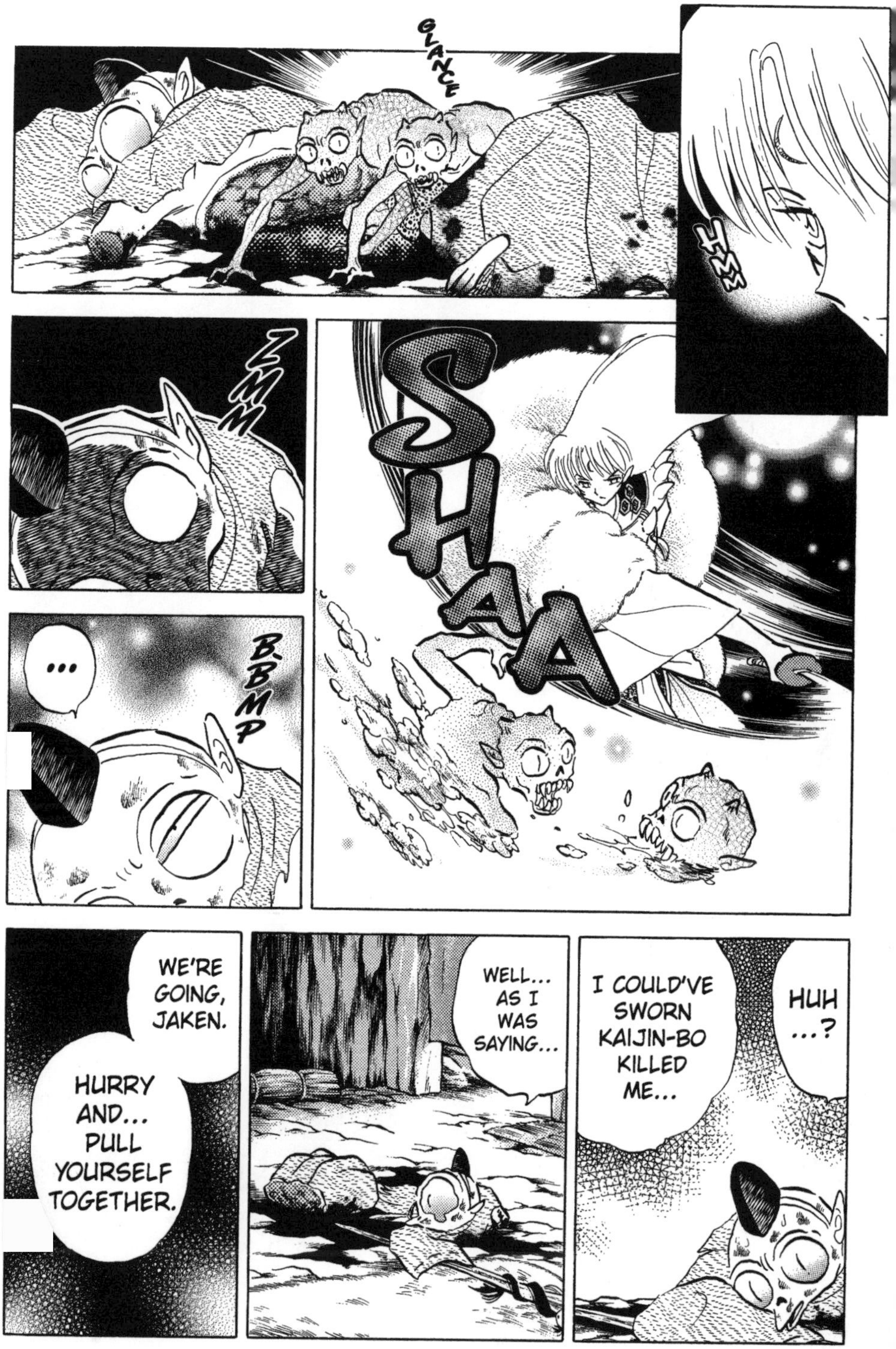
HMM
GLANCE
SHAAA
ZMMM
...
B.BMP
HUH ...?
I COULD'VE SWORN KAIJIN-BO KILLED ME...
WELL... AS I WAS SAYING...
WE'RE GOING, JAKEN.
HURRY AND... PULL YOURSELF TOGETHER.

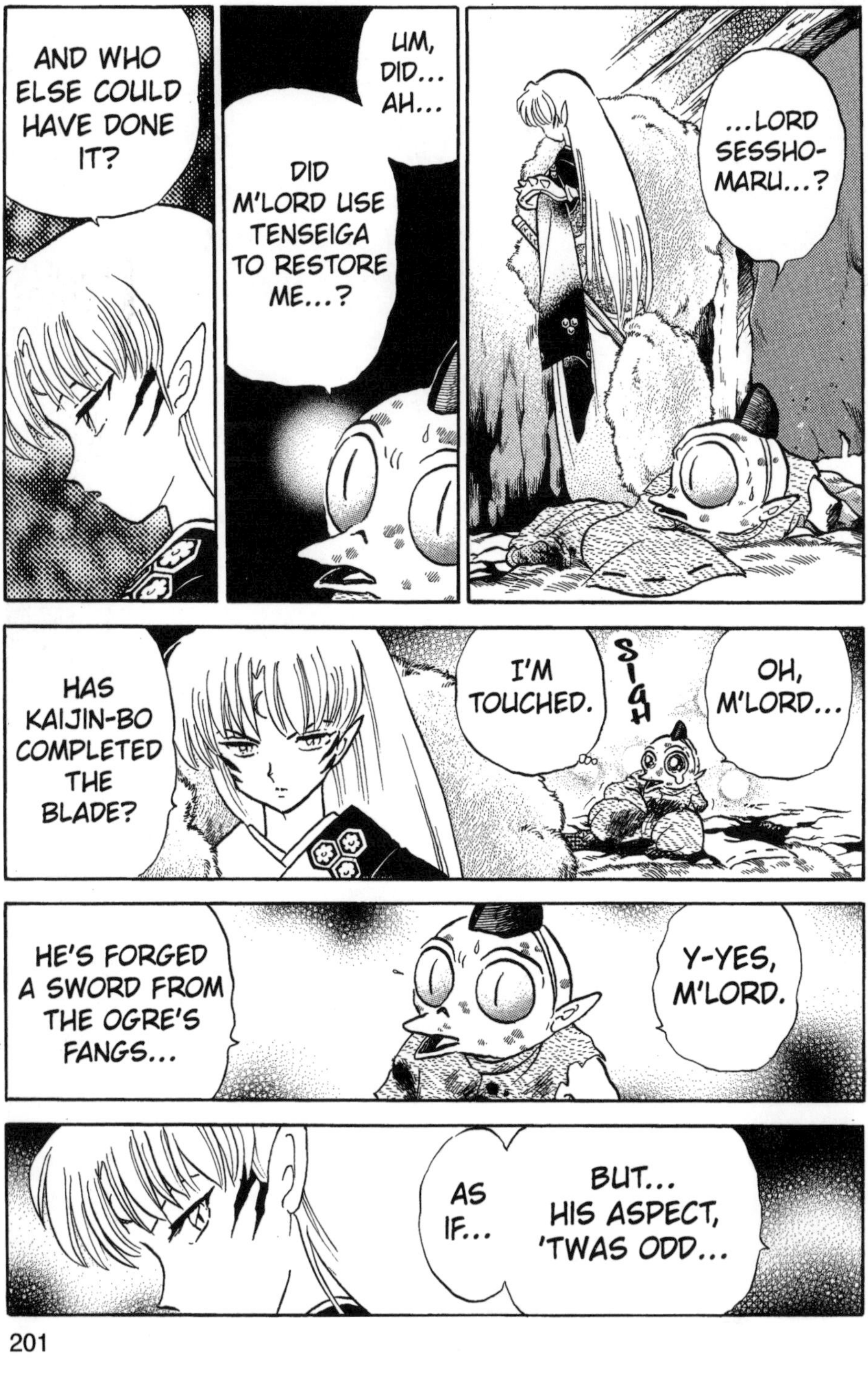
...LORD SESSHO-MARU...?
UM, DID... AH...
DID M'LORD USE TENSEIGA TO RESTORE ME...?
AND WHO ELSE COULD HAVE DONE IT?
OH, M'LORD...
SIGH
I'M TOUCHED.
HAS KAIJIN-BO COMPLETED THE BLADE?
Y-YES, M'LORD.
HE'S FORGED A SWORD FROM THE OGRE'S FANGS...
BUT... HIS ASPECT, 'TWAS ODD...
AS IF...

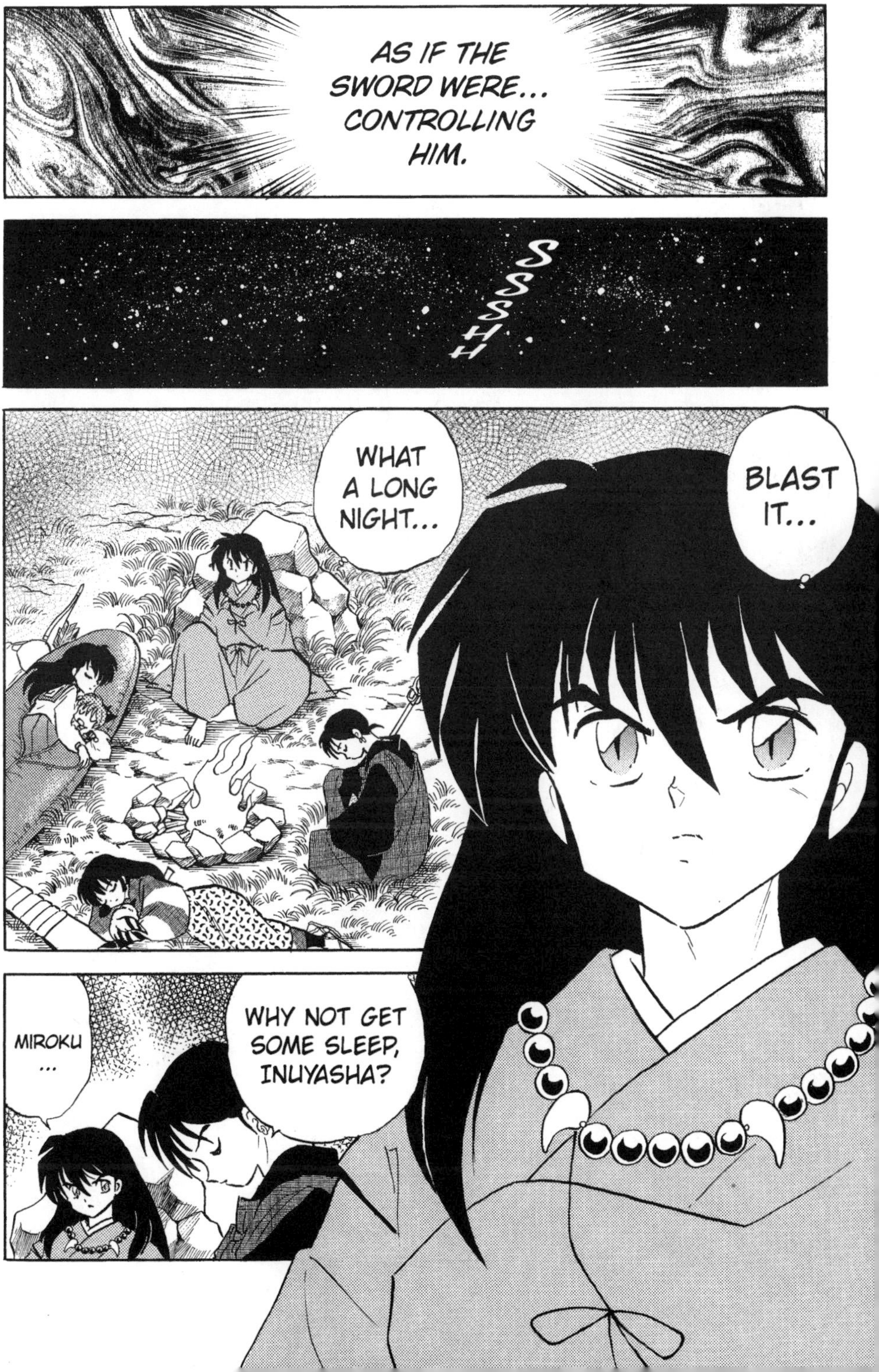
AS IF THE SWORD WERE... CONTROLLING HIM.
SSSHH
BLAST IT...
WHAT A LONG NIGHT...
WHY NOT GET SOME SLEEP, INUYASHA?
MIROKU ...

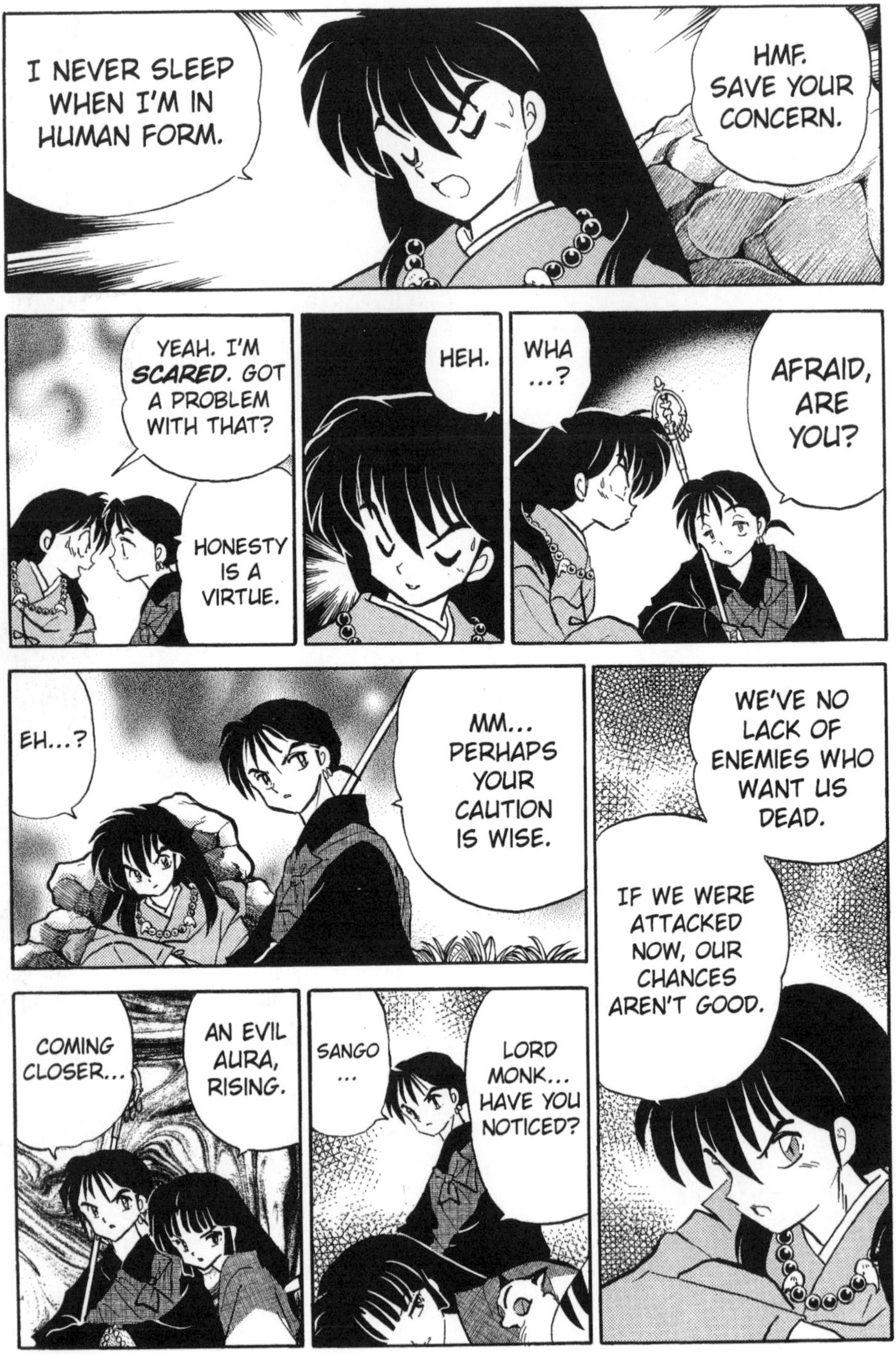
HMF. SAVE YOUR CONCERN.
I NEVER SLEEP WHEN I'M IN HUMAN FORM.
AFRAID, ARE YOU?
WHA ...?
HEH.
YEAH. I'M *SCARED*. GOT A PROBLEM WITH THAT?
HONESTY IS A VIRTUE.
WE'VE NO LACK OF ENEMIES WHO WANT US DEAD.
IF WE WERE ATTACKED NOW, OUR CHANCES AREN'T GOOD.
MM... PERHAPS YOUR CAUTION IS WISE.
EH...?
LORD MONK... HAVE YOU NOTICED?
SANGO ...
AN EVIL AURA, RISING.
COMING CLOSER...

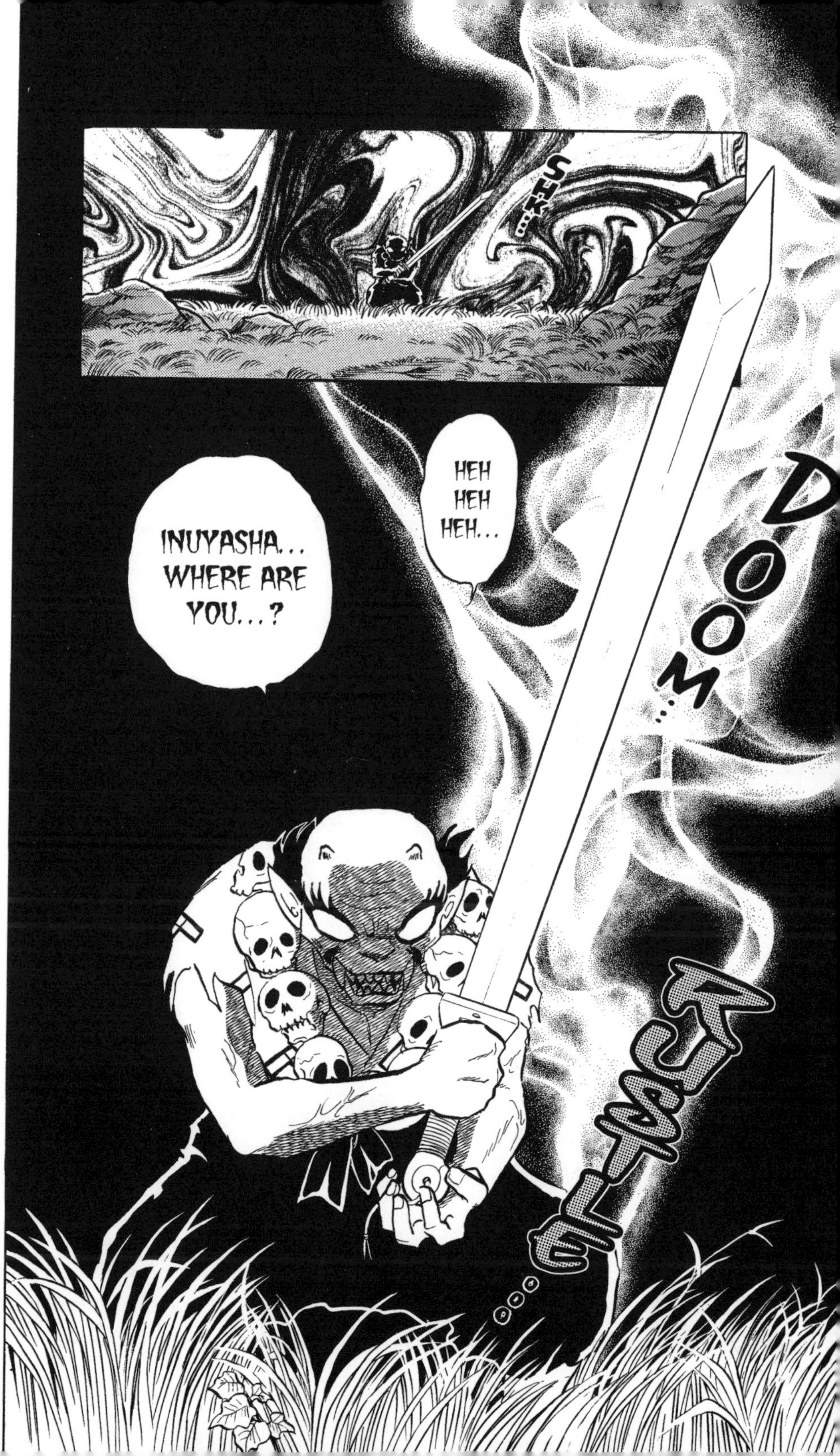
SHK...
DOOOM...
HEH HEH HEH...
INUYASHA... WHERE ARE YOU...?

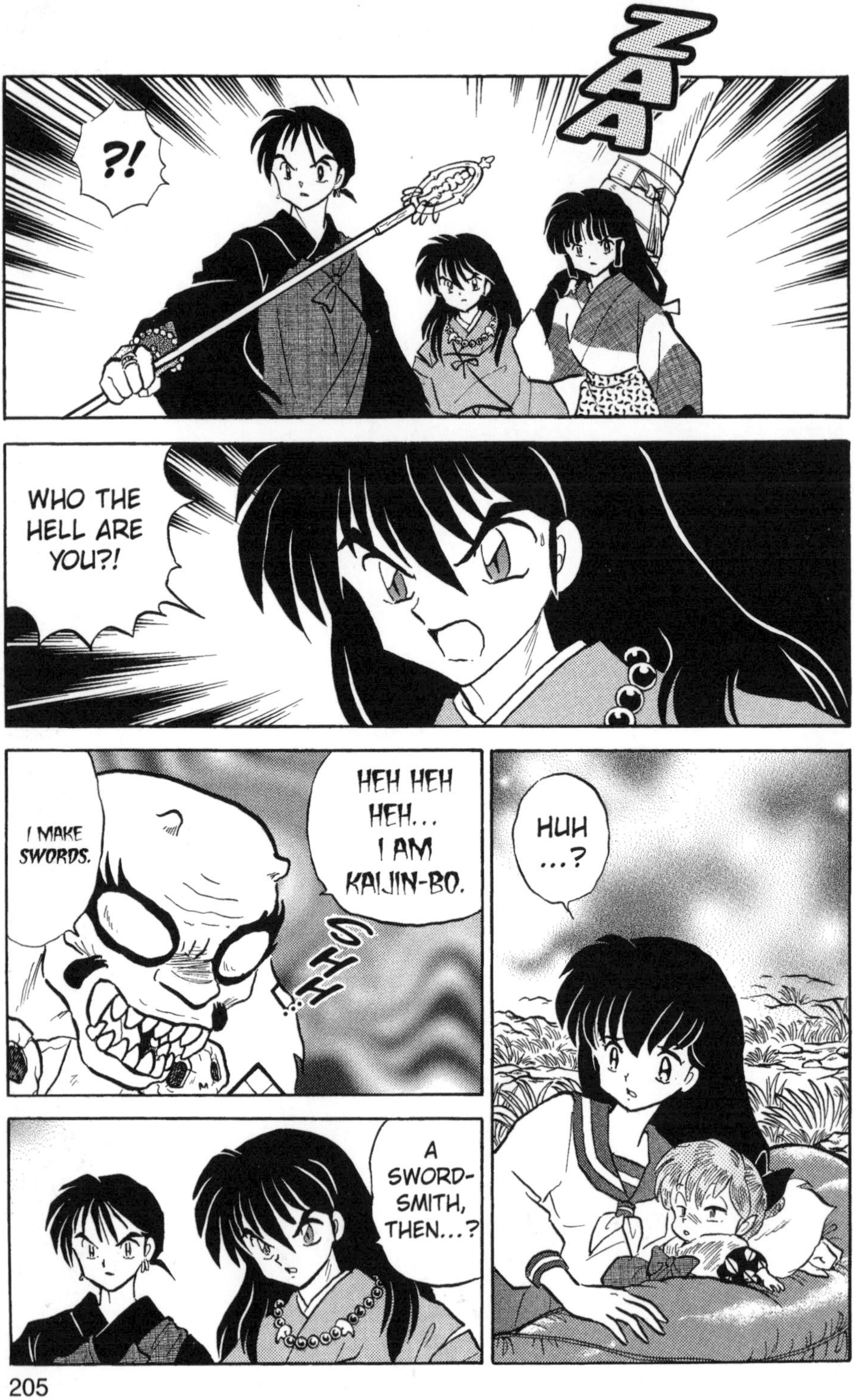
ZAA
?!
WHO THE HELL ARE YOU?!
HUH ...?
HEH HEH HEH... I AM KAIJIN-BO.
SHH
I MAKE SWORDS.
A SWORD-SMITH, THEN...?

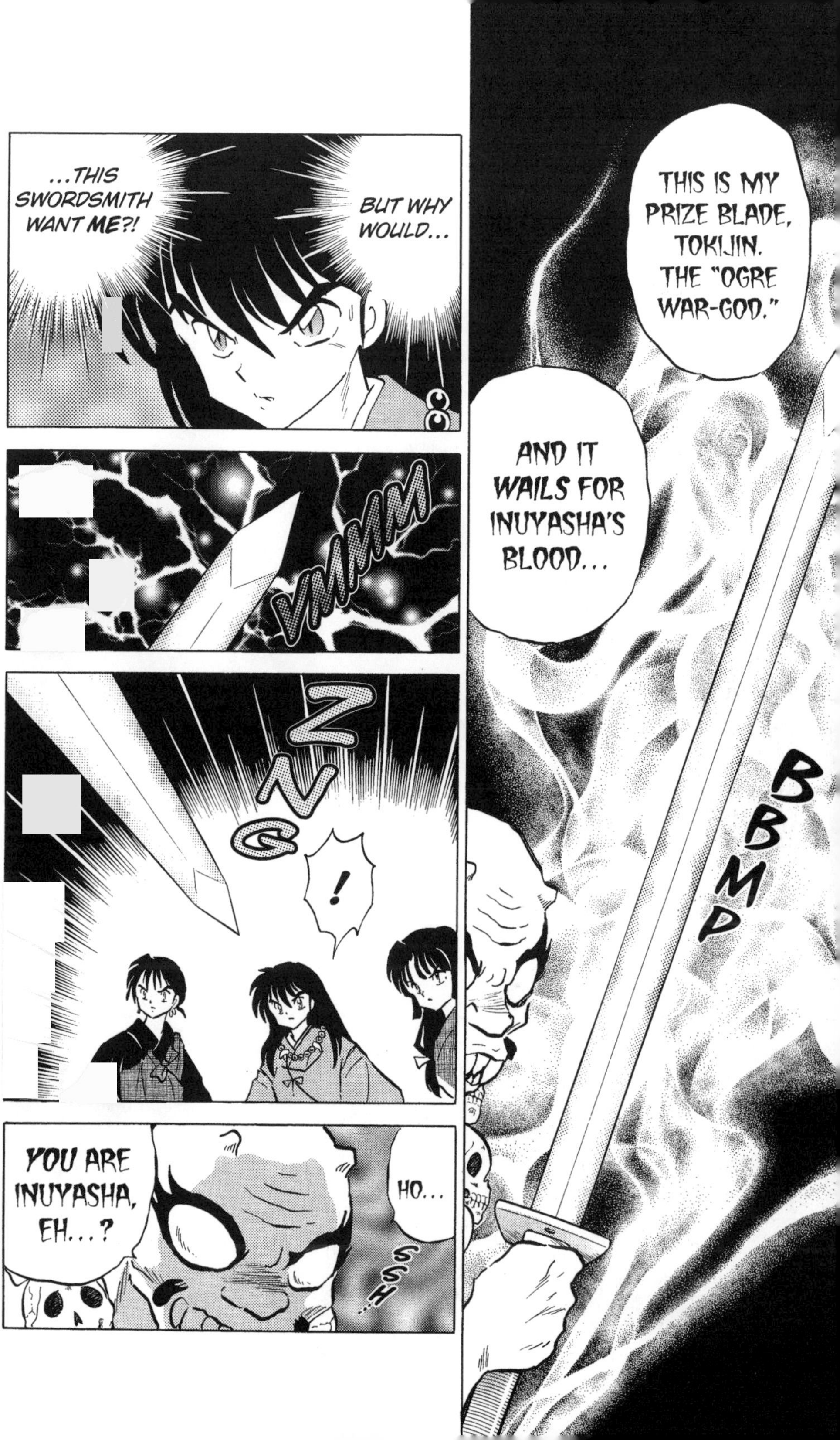
THIS IS MY PRIZE BLADE, TOKIJIN. THE "OGRE WAR-GOD."
AND IT WAILS FOR INUYASHA'S BLOOD...
BBMP
BUT WHY WOULD...
...THIS SWORDSMITH WANT ME?!
VMMM
ZNG
!
HO...
YOU ARE INUYASHA, EH...?
SSH...

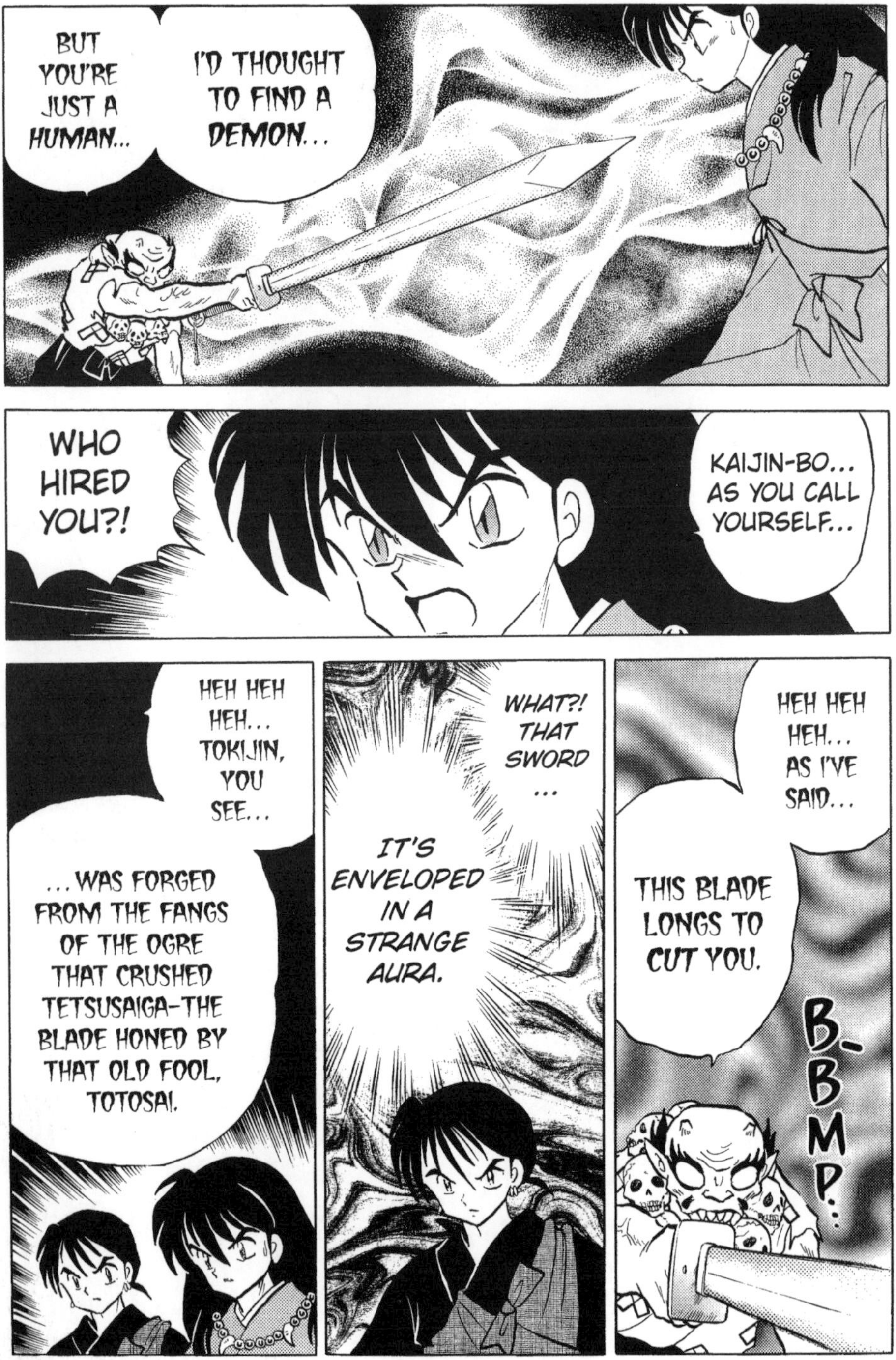
I'D THOUGHT TO FIND A DEMON...
BUT YOU'RE JUST A HUMAN...
KAIJIN-BO... AS YOU CALL YOURSELF...
WHO HIRED YOU?!
HEH HEH HEH... AS I'VE SAID...
THIS BLADE LONGS TO CUT YOU.
B-BMP...
WHAT?! THAT SWORD...
IT'S ENVELOPED IN A STRANGE AURA.
HEH HEH HEH... TOKIJIN, YOU SEE...
...WAS FORGED FROM THE FANGS OF THE OGRE THAT CRUSHED TETSUSAIGA-THE BLADE HONED BY THAT OLD FOOL, TOTOSAI.

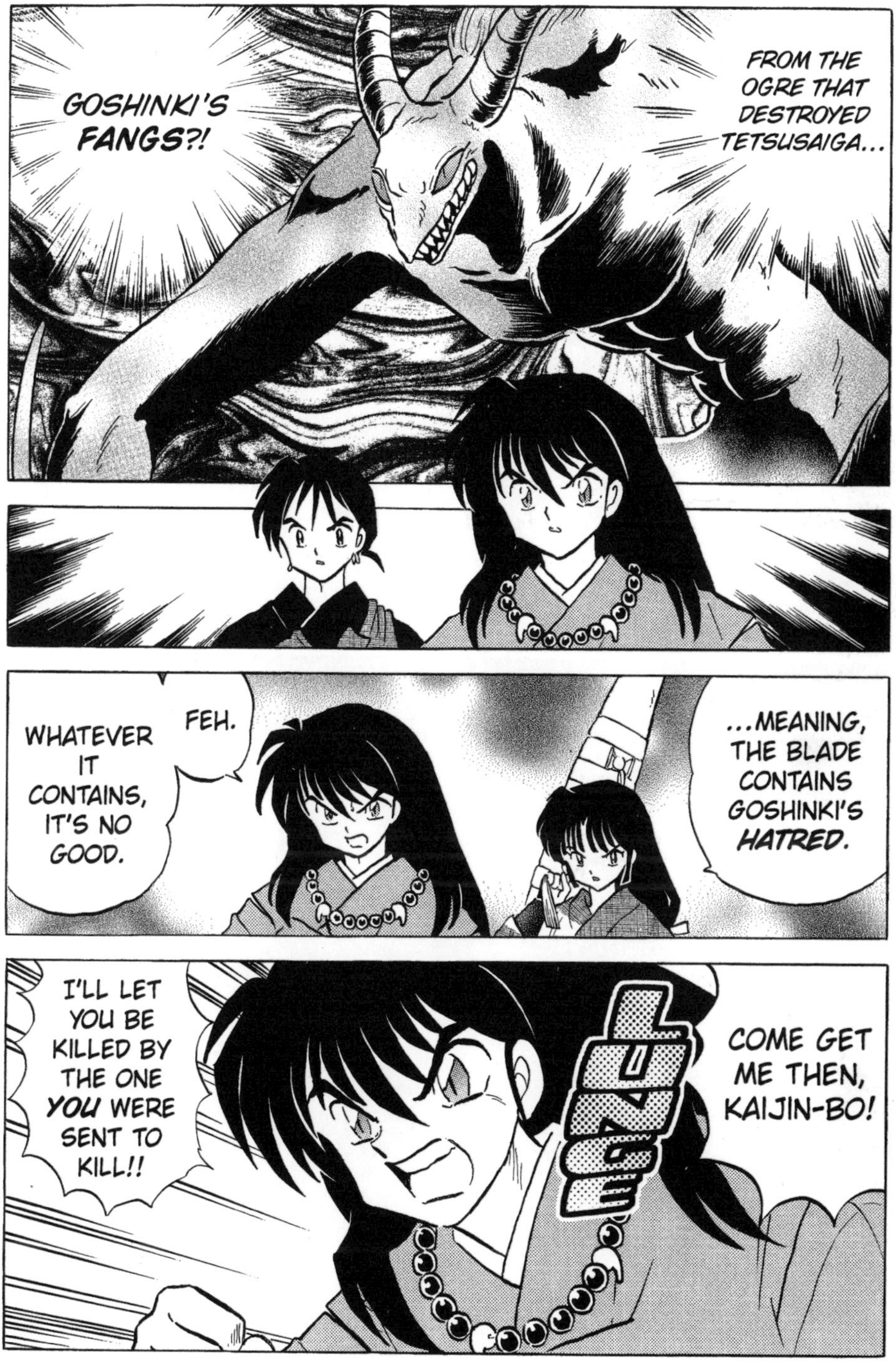
FROM THE OGRE THAT DESTROYED TETSUSAIGA...
GOSHINKI'S **FANGS**?!
...MEANING, THE BLADE CONTAINS GOSHINKI'S **HATRED**.
FEH.
WHATEVER IT CONTAINS, IT'S NO GOOD.
COME GET ME THEN, KAIJIN-BO!
LUNGE
I'LL LET YOU BE KILLED BY THE ONE ***YOU*** WERE SENT TO KILL!!

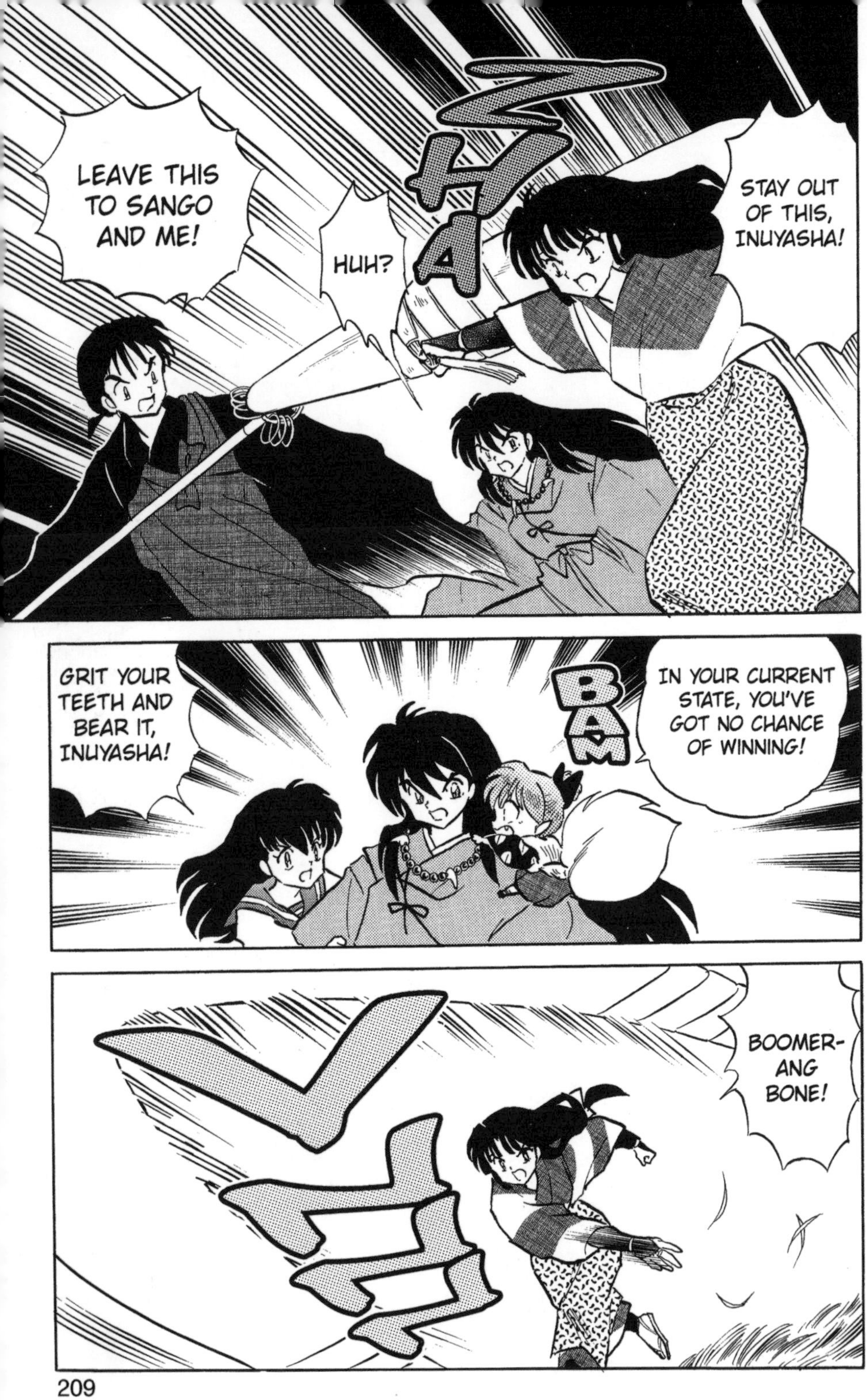
STAY OUT OF THIS, INUYASHA!
HUH?
LEAVE THIS TO SANGO AND ME!
IN YOUR CURRENT STATE, YOU'VE GOT NO CHANCE OF WINNING!
BAM
GRIT YOUR TEETH AND BEAR IT, INUYASHA!
BOOMER-ANG BONE!

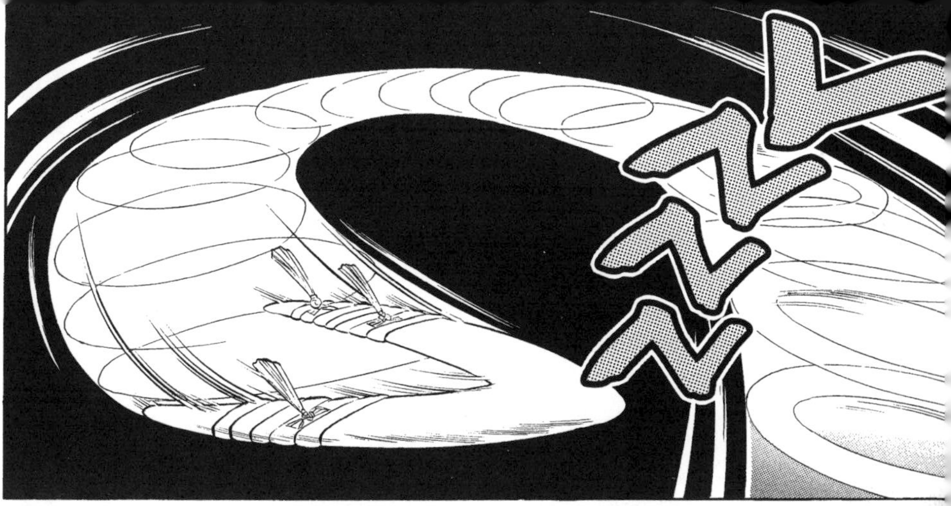

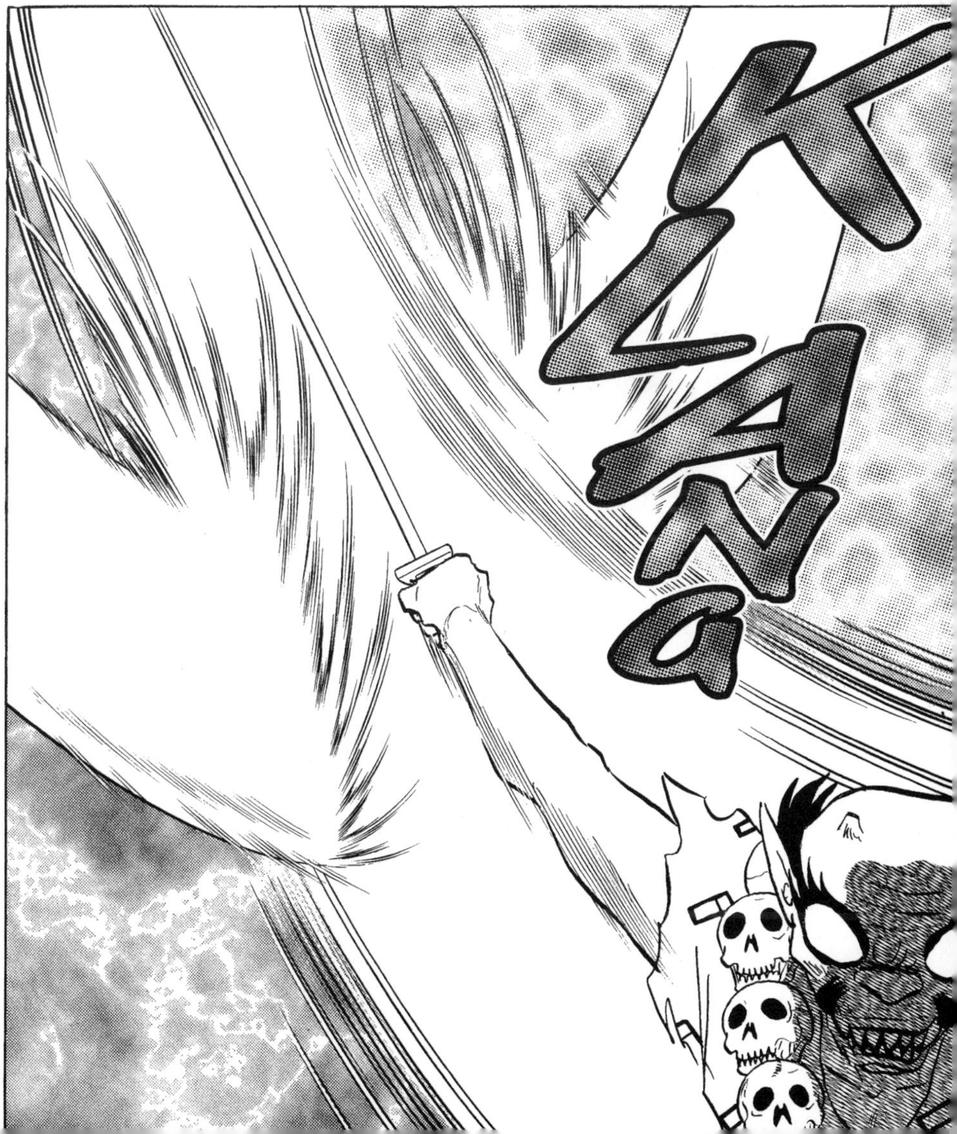
KLANG

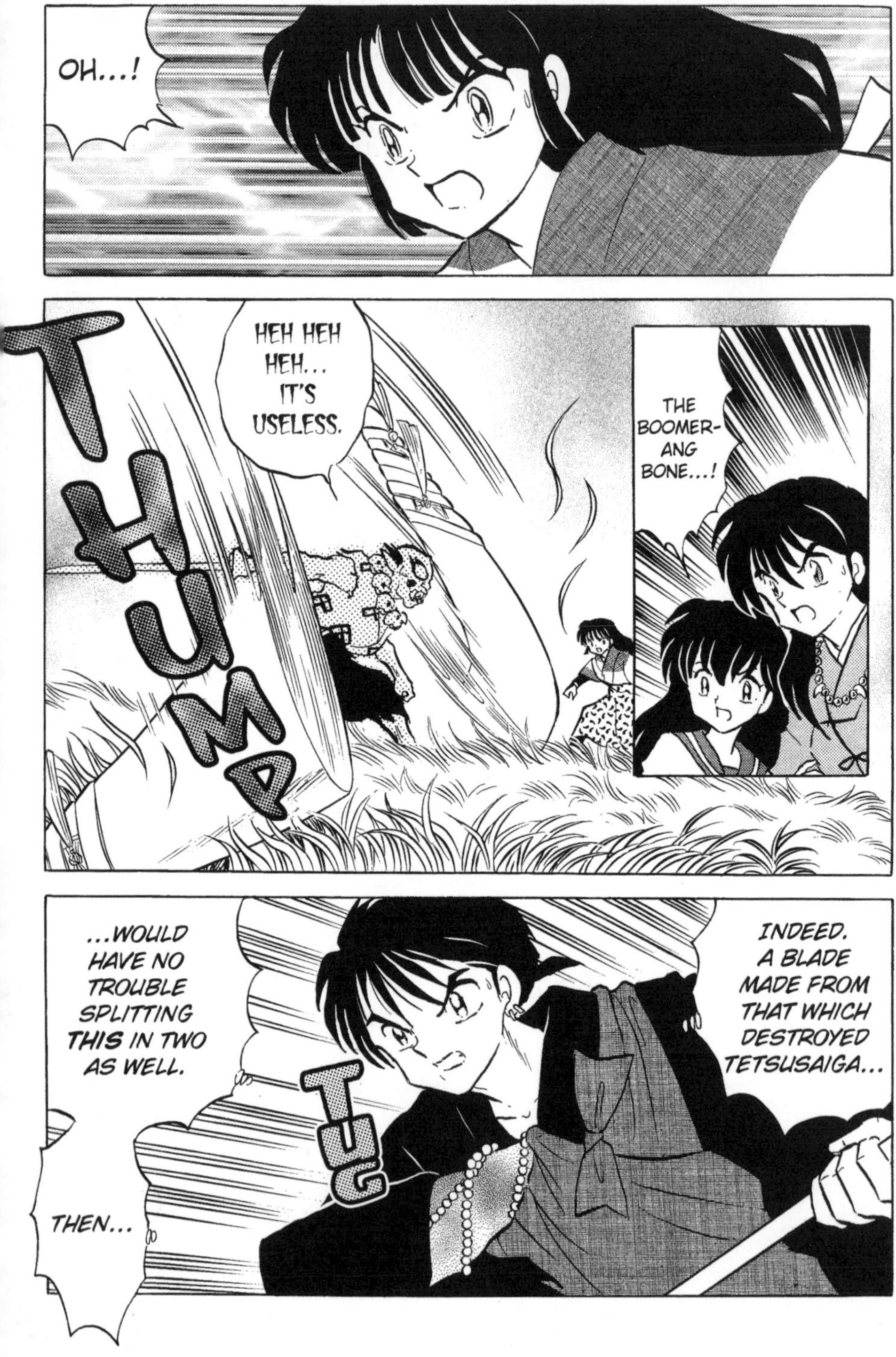
OH...!
THE BOOMER-ANG BONE...!
HEH HEH HEH... IT'S USELESS.
THUMP
INDEED. A BLADE MADE FROM THAT WHICH DESTROYED TETSUSAIGA...
...WOULD HAVE NO TROUBLE SPLITTING **THIS** IN TWO AS WELL.
TUG
THEN...

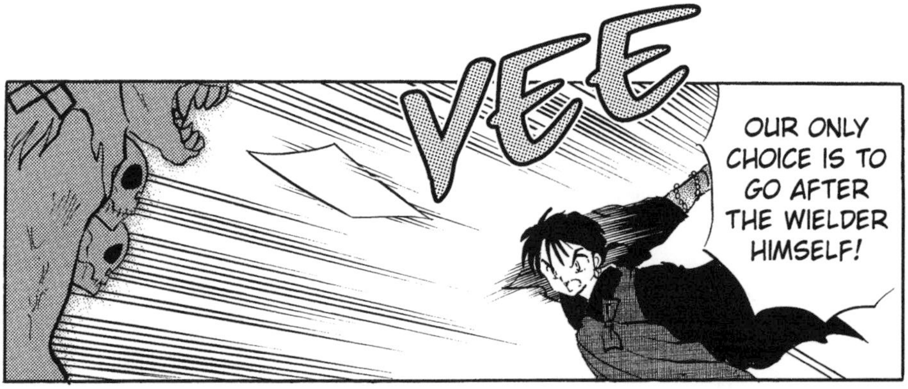
OUR ONLY CHOICE IS TO GO AFTER THE WIELDER HIMSELF!
VEE

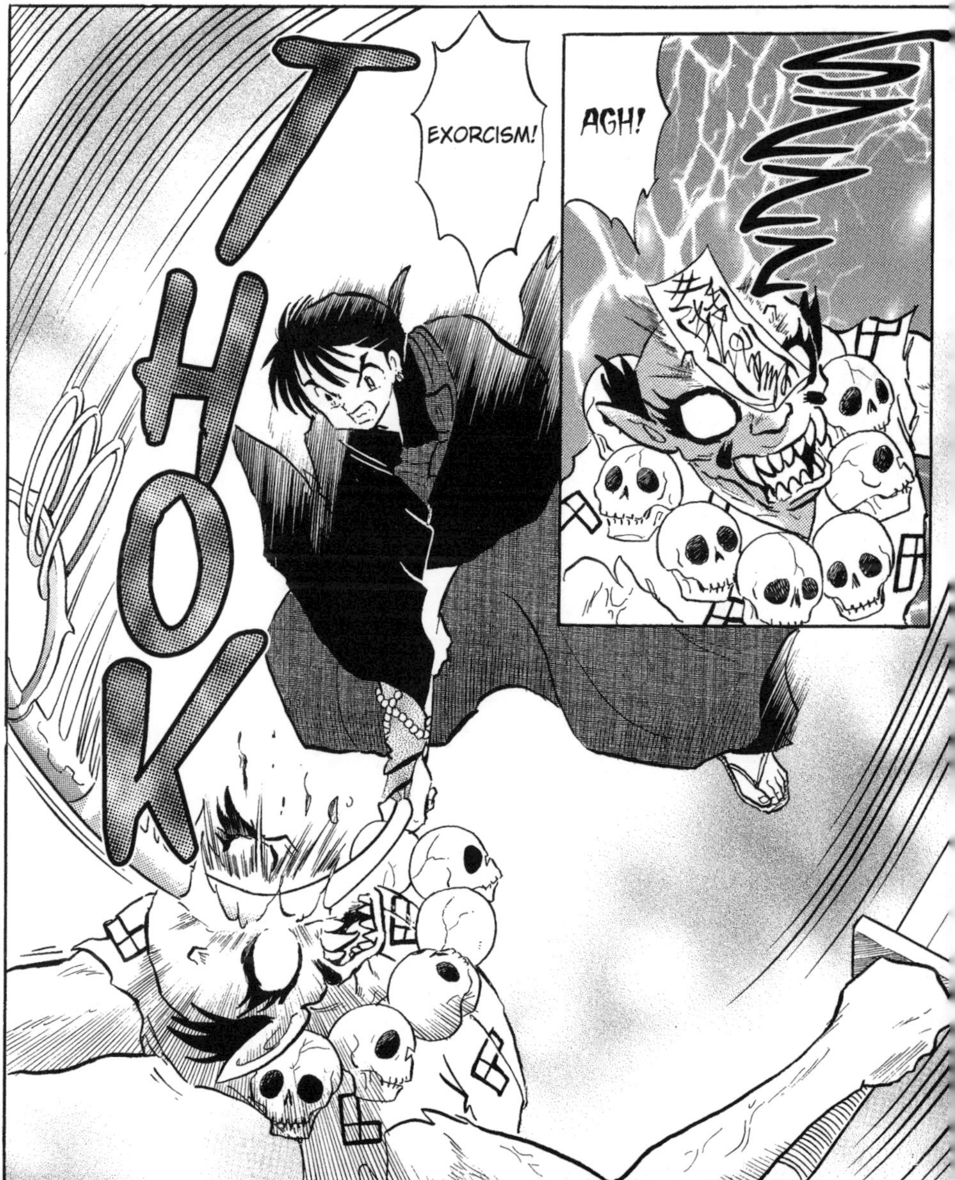
AGH!
EXORCISM!
THOK

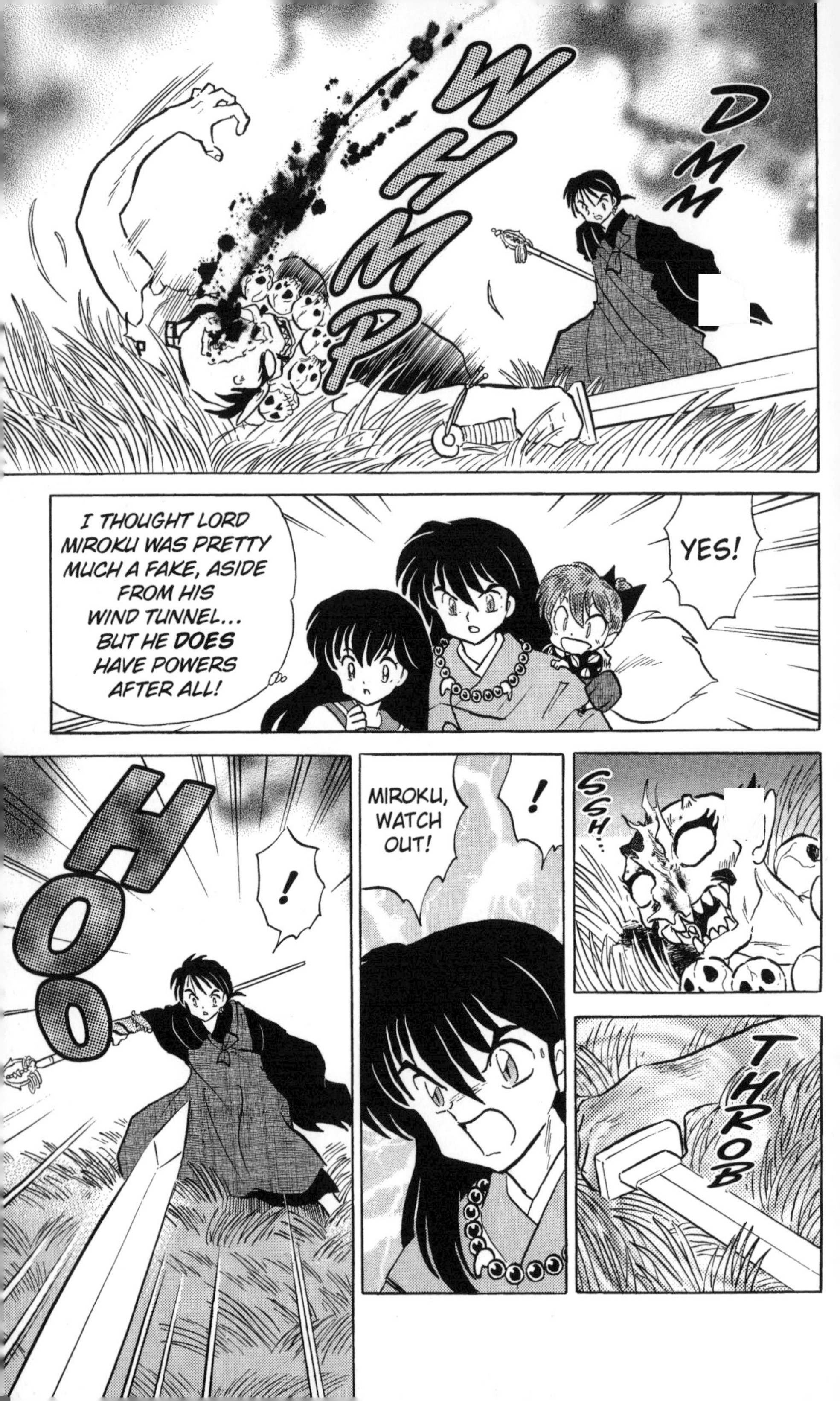

DMMM
WHMP
YES!
I THOUGHT LORD MIROKU WAS PRETTY MUCH A FAKE, ASIDE FROM HIS WIND TUNNEL... BUT HE DOES HAVE POWERS AFTER ALL!
SSH...
THROB
!
MIROKU, WATCH OUT!
HOO
!

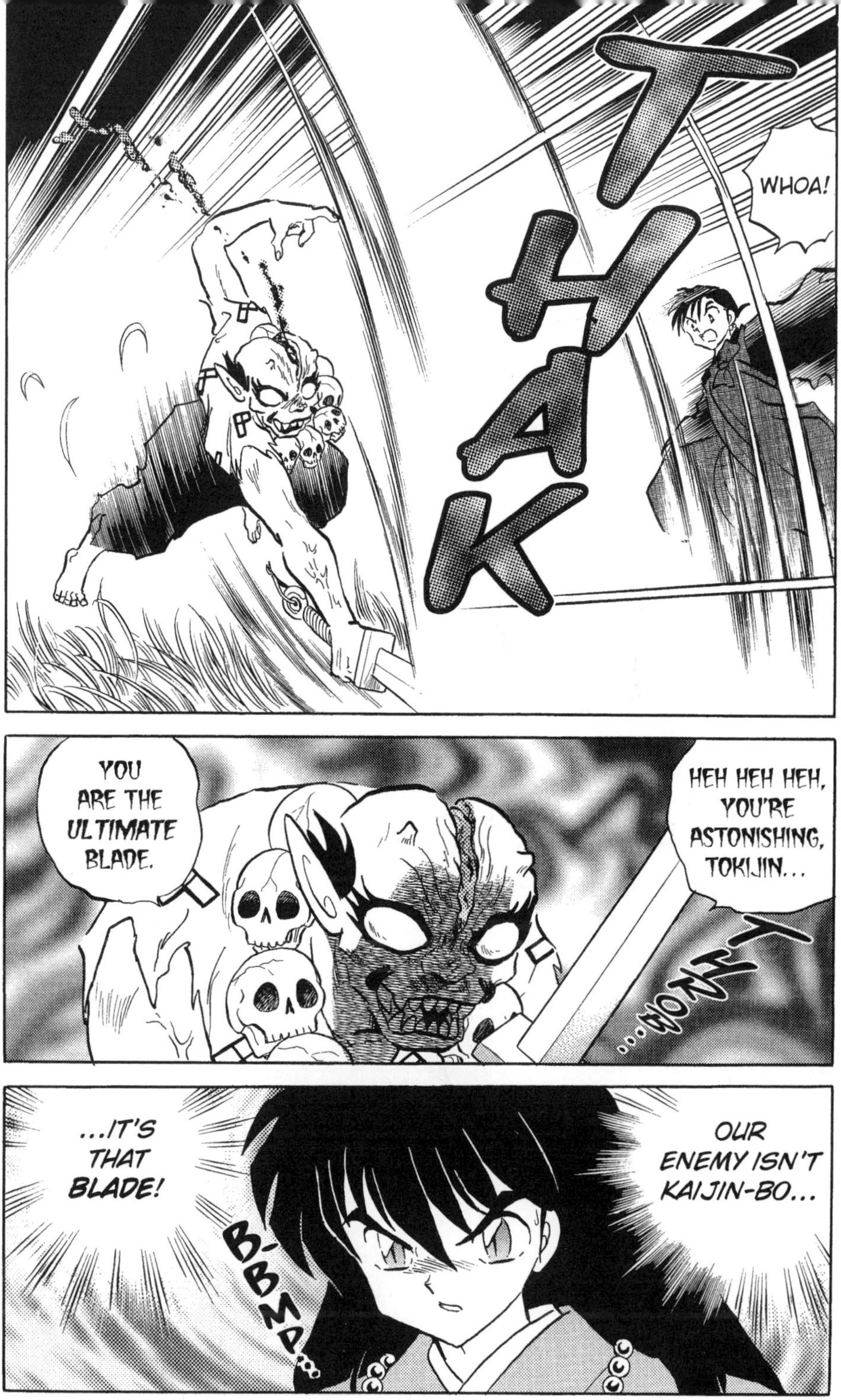
THAK
WHOA!
HEH HEH HEH, YOU'RE ASTONISHING, TOKIJIN...
THROB...
YOU ARE THE ULTIMATE BLADE.
OUR ENEMY ISN'T KAIJIN-BO...
...IT'S THAT BLADE!
B-BMP...

SCROLL TWO
TETSUSAIGA REBORN

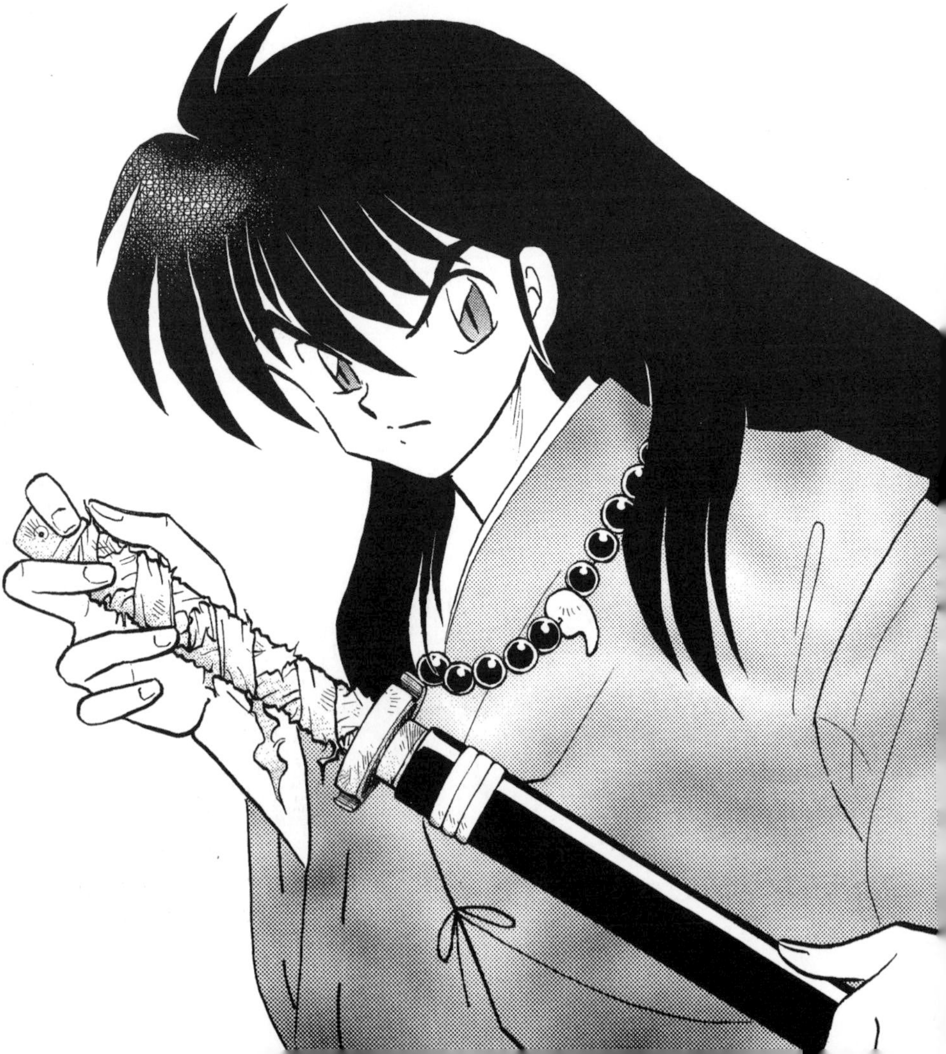

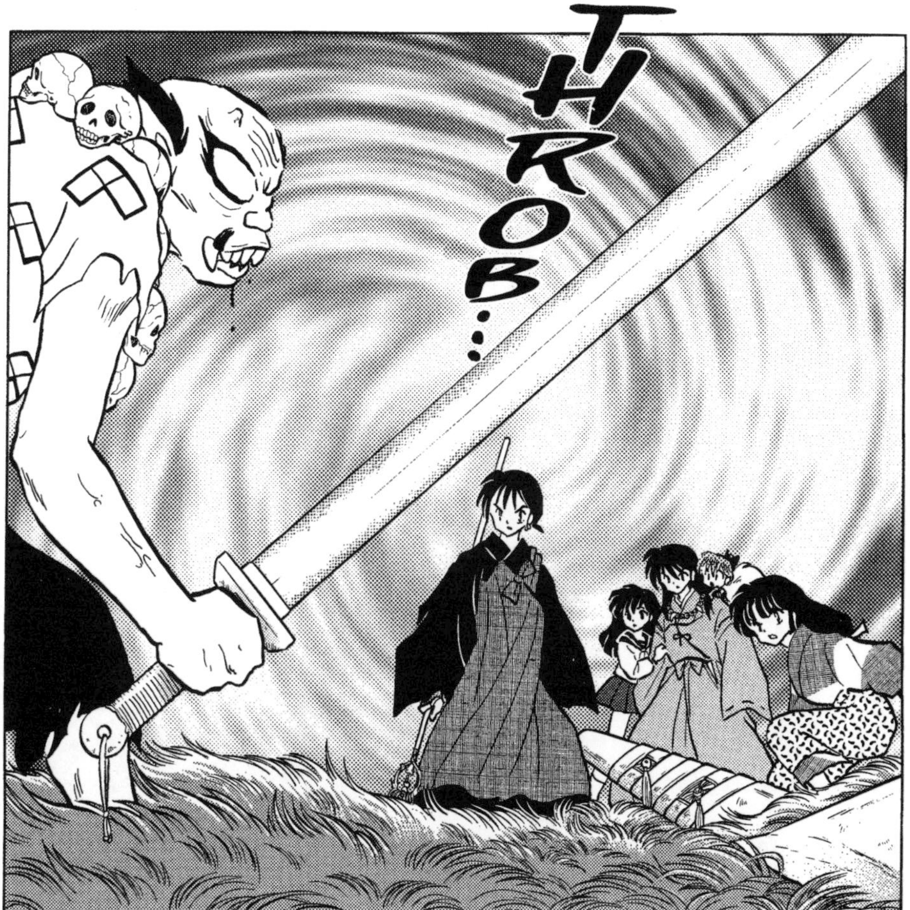
THROB...

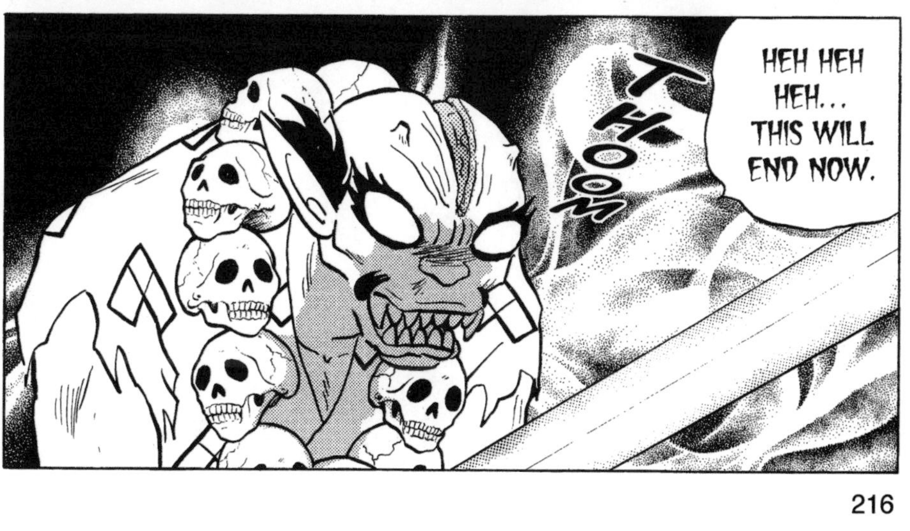
HEH HEH HEH... THIS WILL END NOW.
THOOM

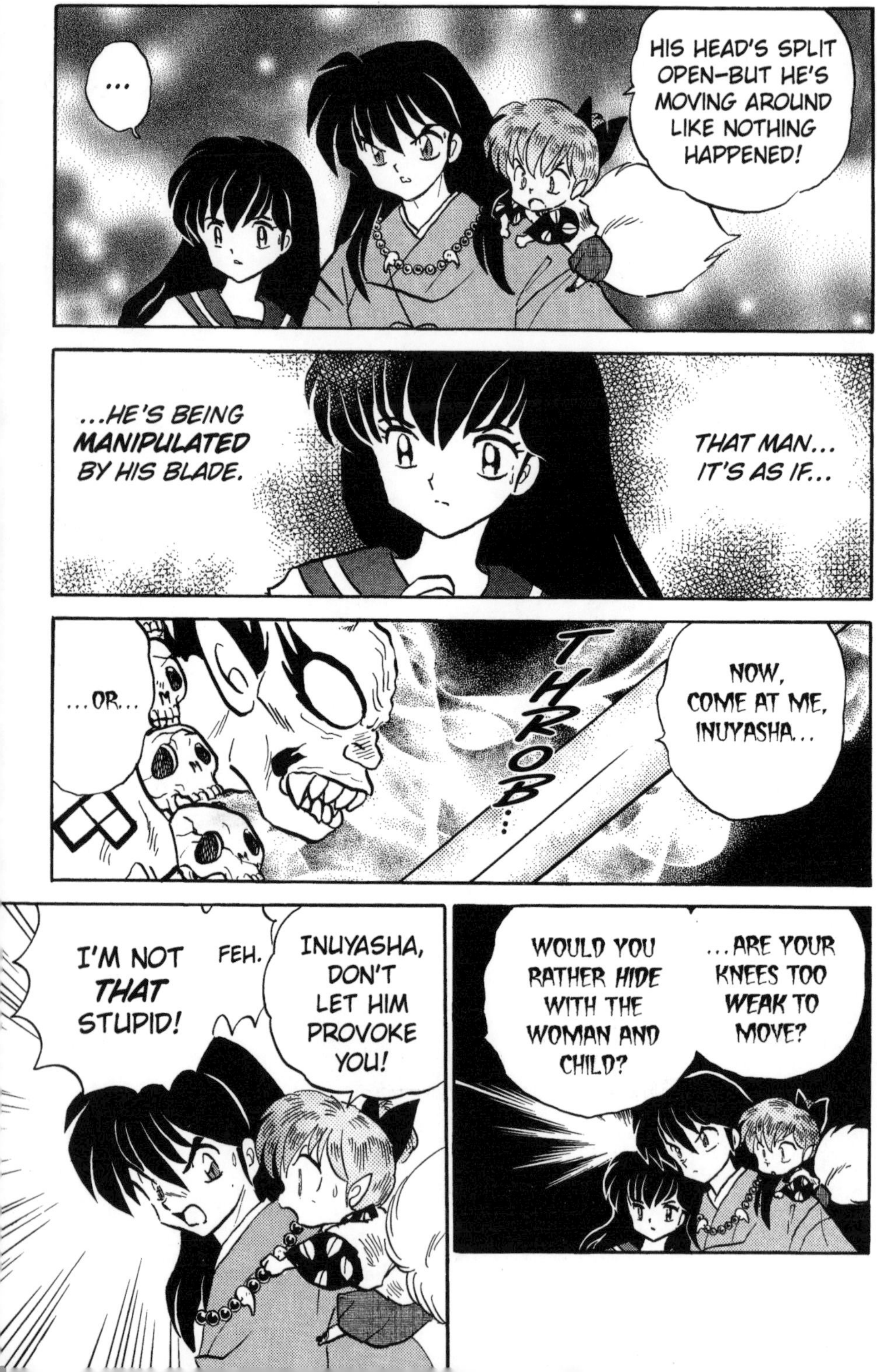

HIS HEAD'S SPLIT OPEN—BUT HE'S MOVING AROUND LIKE NOTHING HAPPENED!
...
THAT MAN... IT'S AS IF...
...HE'S BEING *MANIPULATED* BY HIS BLADE.
NOW, COME AT ME, INUYASHA...
THROB...
...OR...
...ARE YOUR KNEES TOO *WEAK* TO MOVE?
WOULD YOU RATHER *HIDE* WITH THE WOMAN AND CHILD?
INUYASHA, DON'T LET HIM PROVOKE YOU!
FEH.
I'M NOT *THAT* STUPID!

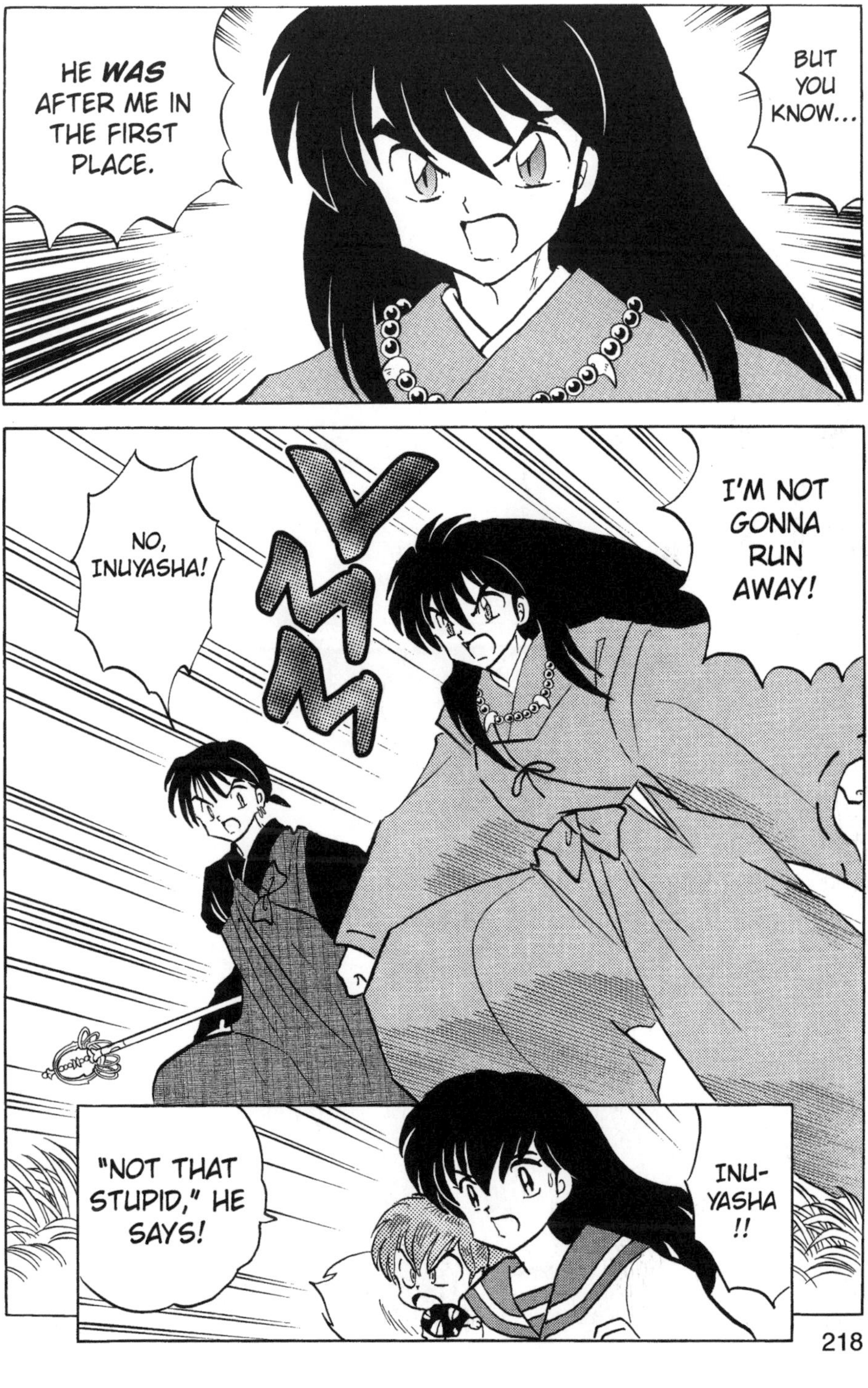
BUT YOU KNOW...
HE *WAS* AFTER ME IN THE FIRST PLACE.
I'M NOT GONNA RUN AWAY!
VMMM
NO, INUYASHA!
INU-YASHA!!
"NOT THAT STUPID," HE SAYS!

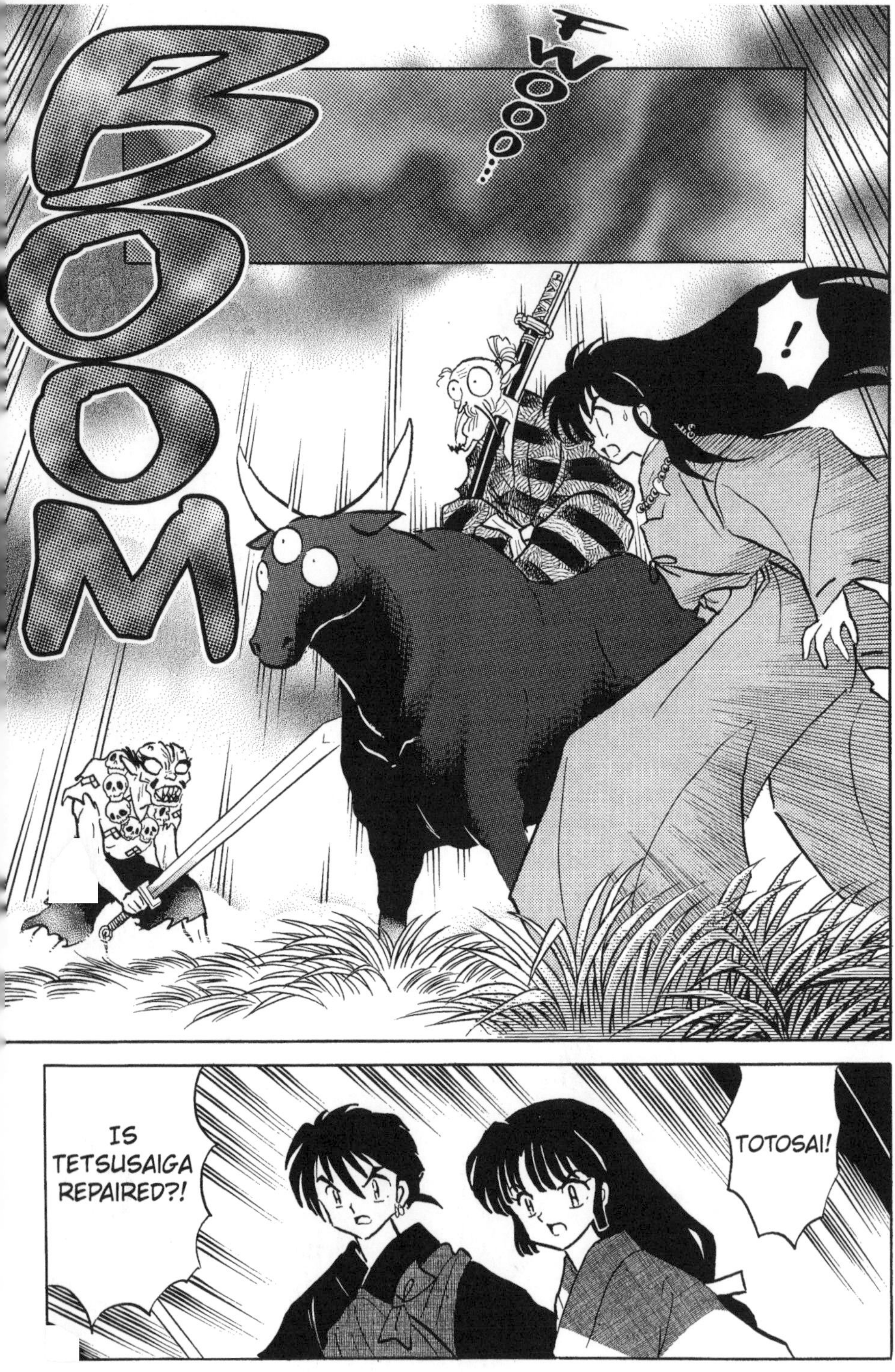
FWOOOOO...
BOOM
!
TOTOSAI!
IS TETSUSAIGA REPAIRED?!

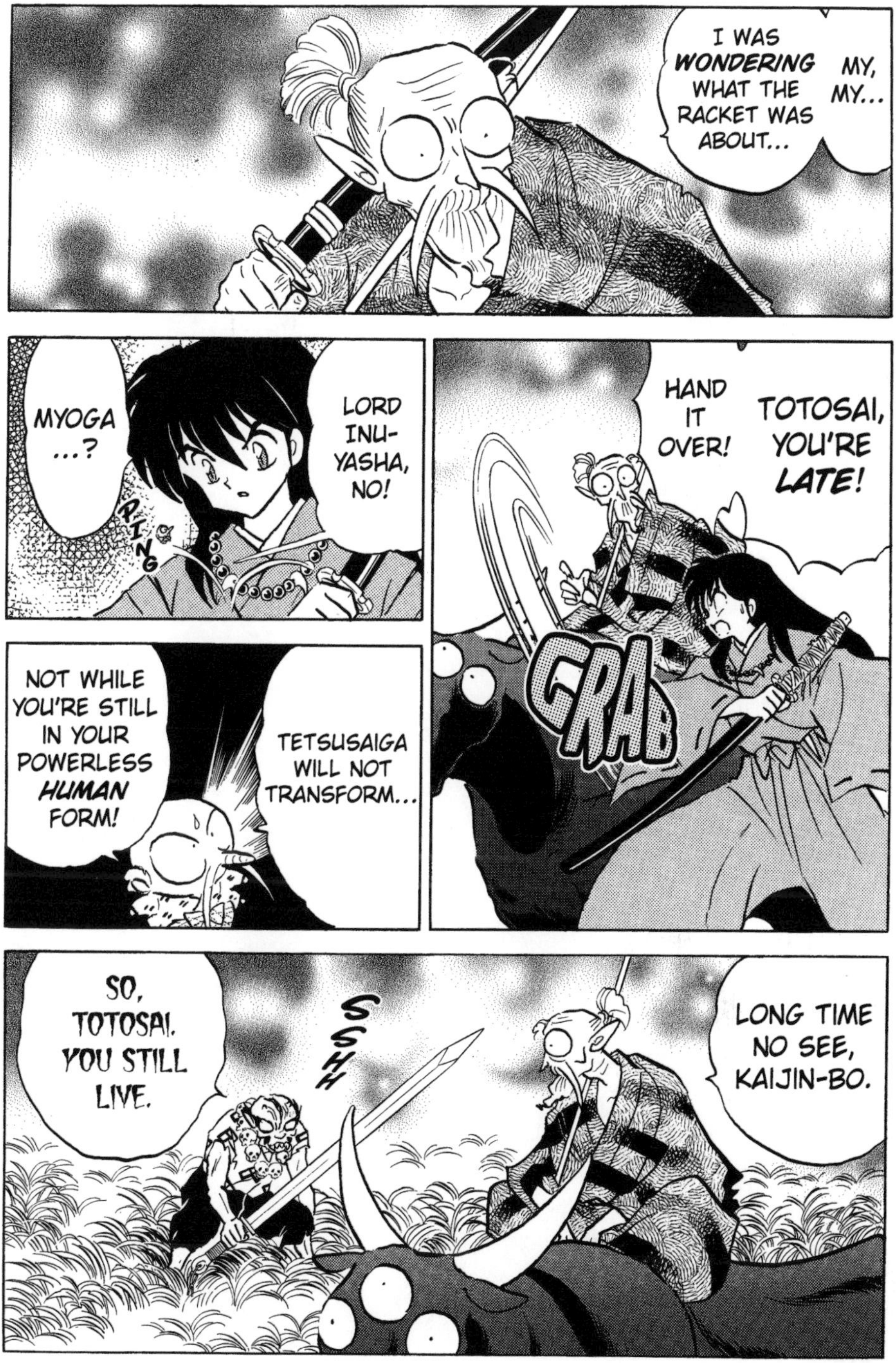
MY, MY...
I WAS WONDERING WHAT THE RACKET WAS ABOUT...
TOTOSAI, YOU'RE LATE!
HAND IT OVER!
GRAB
LORD INU-YASHA, NO!
MYOGA ...?
PING
TETSUSAIGA WILL NOT TRANSFORM...
NOT WHILE YOU'RE STILL IN YOUR POWERLESS HUMAN FORM!
LONG TIME NO SEE, KAIJIN-BO.
SSHH
SO, TOTOSAI. YOU STILL LIVE.

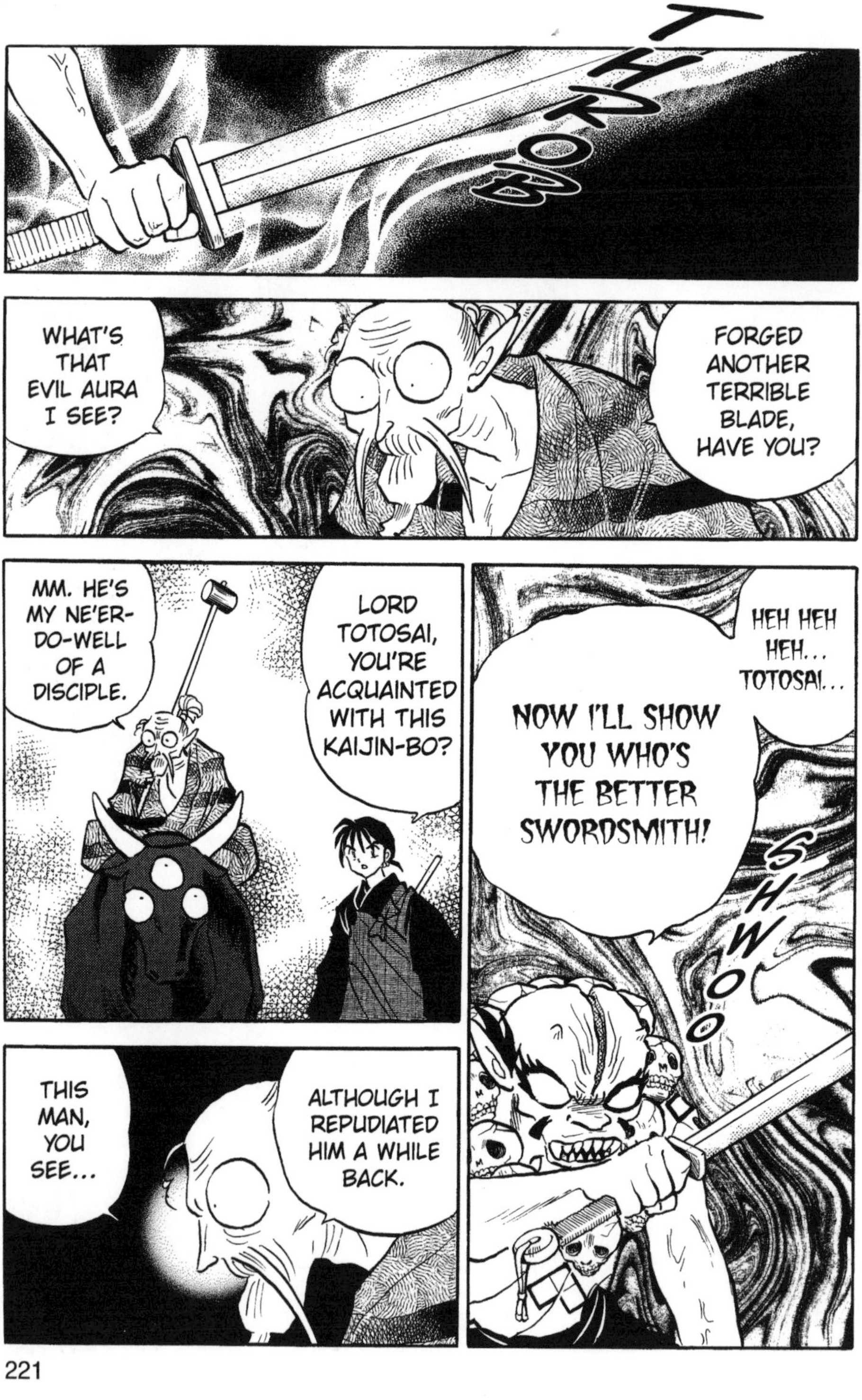
THROB
FORGED ANOTHER TERRIBLE BLADE, HAVE YOU?
WHAT'S THAT EVIL AURA I SEE?
HEH HEH HEH... TOTOSAI...
NOW I'LL SHOW YOU WHO'S THE BETTER SWORDSMITH!
SHWOO
LORD TOTOSAI, YOU'RE ACQUAINTED WITH THIS KAIJIN-BO?
MM. HE'S MY NE'ER-DO-WELL OF A DISCIPLE.
ALTHOUGH I REPUDIATED HIM A WHILE BACK.
THIS MAN, YOU SEE...

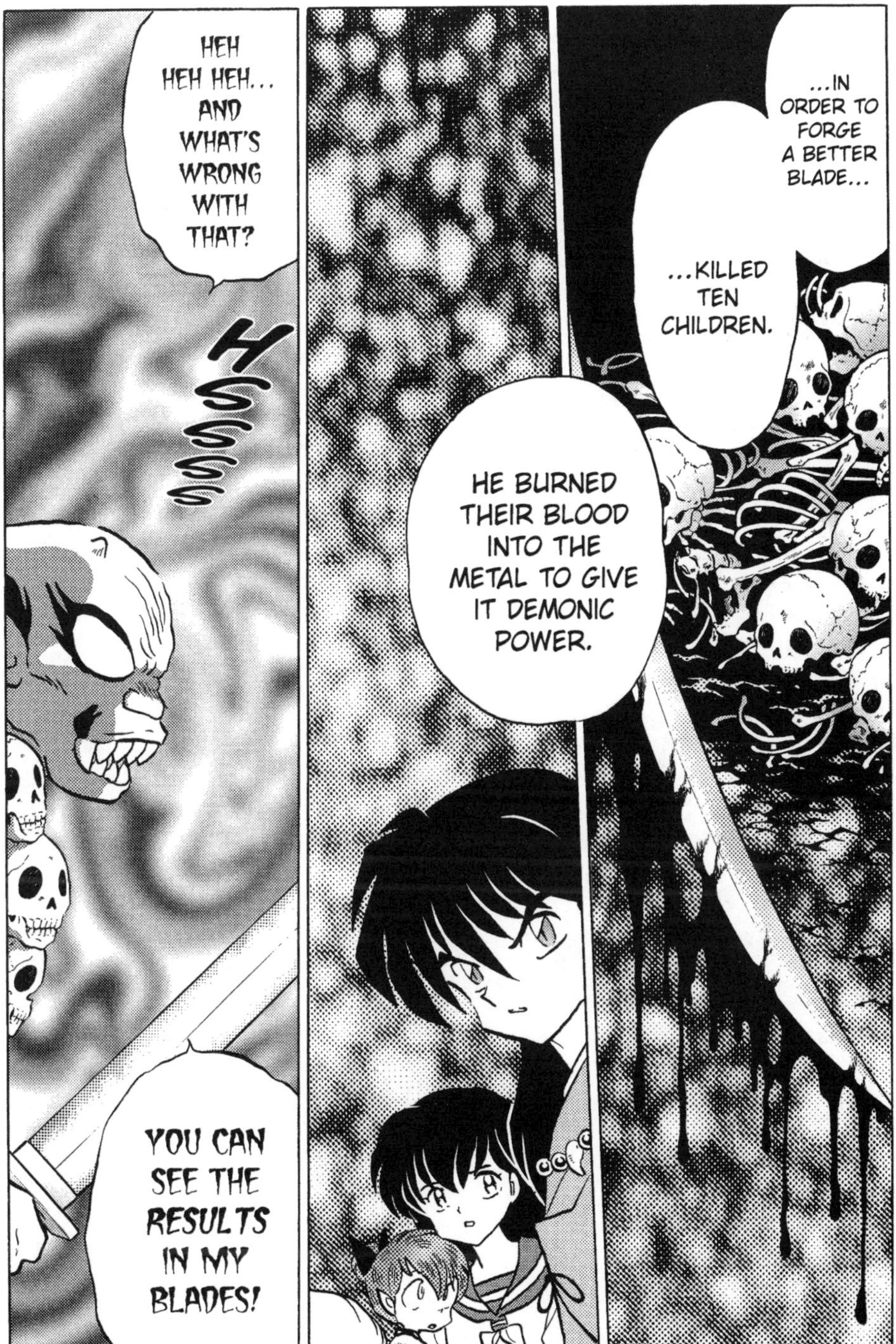
...IN ORDER TO FORGE A BETTER BLADE...
...KILLED TEN CHILDREN.
HE BURNED THEIR BLOOD INTO THE METAL TO GIVE IT DEMONIC POWER.
HEH HEH HEH... AND WHAT'S WRONG WITH THAT?
HSSSSS
YOU CAN SEE THE RESULTS IN MY BLADES!

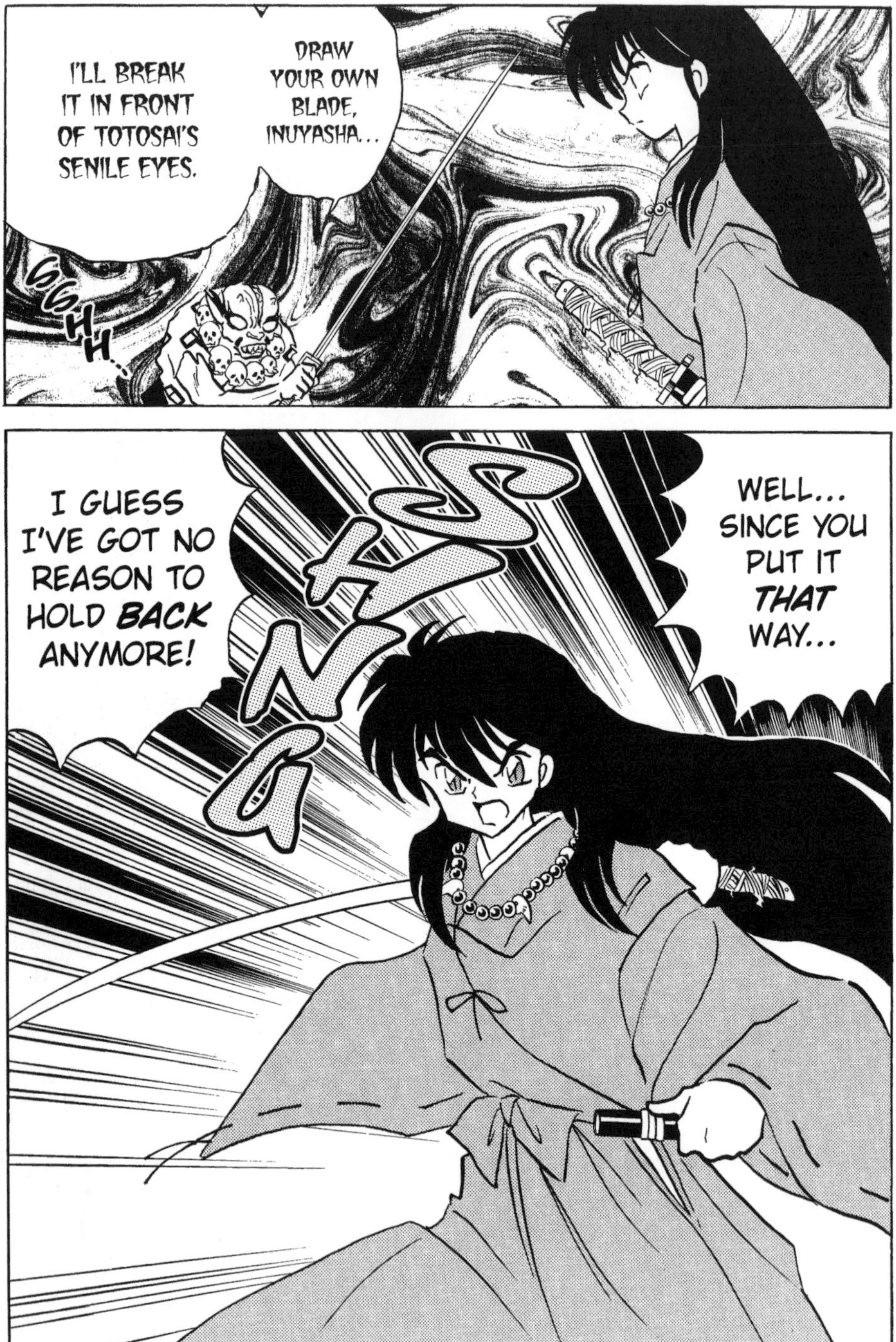
DRAW YOUR OWN BLADE, INUYASHA...
I'LL BREAK IT IN FRONT OF TOTOSAI'S SENILE EYES.
SSHH...
WELL... SINCE YOU PUT IT *THAT* WAY...
SHING
I GUESS I'VE GOT NO REASON TO HOLD *BACK* ANYMORE!

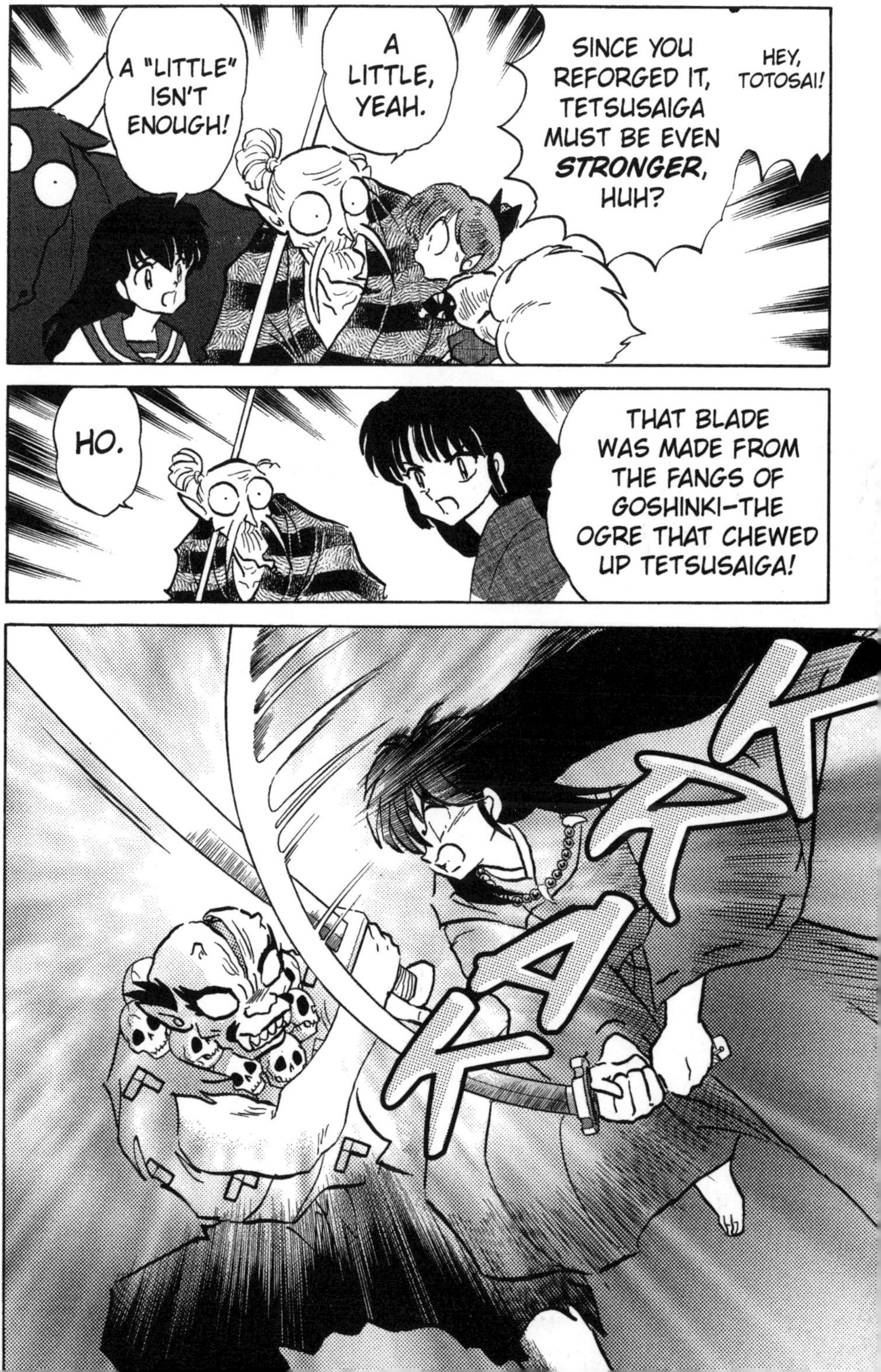
HEY, TOTOSAI!
SINCE YOU REFORGED IT, TETSUSAIGA MUST BE EVEN **STRONGER**, HUH?
A LITTLE, YEAH.
A "LITTLE" ISN'T ENOUGH!
THAT BLADE WAS MADE FROM THE FANGS OF GOSHINKI—THE OGRE THAT CHEWED UP TETSUSAIGA!
HO.
KAKAK

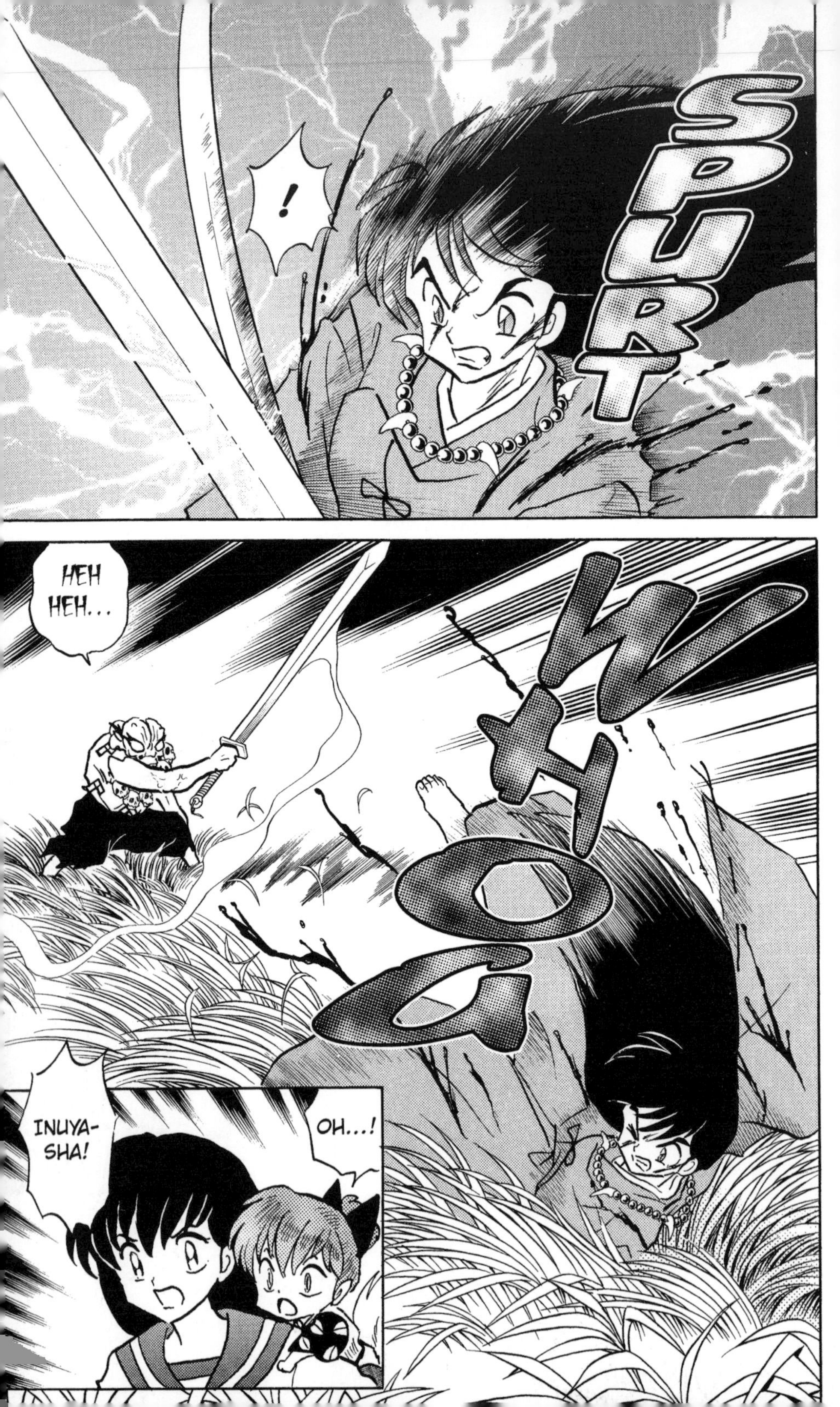

!
SPURT
WHOP
HEH HEH...
OH...!
INUYA-SHA!

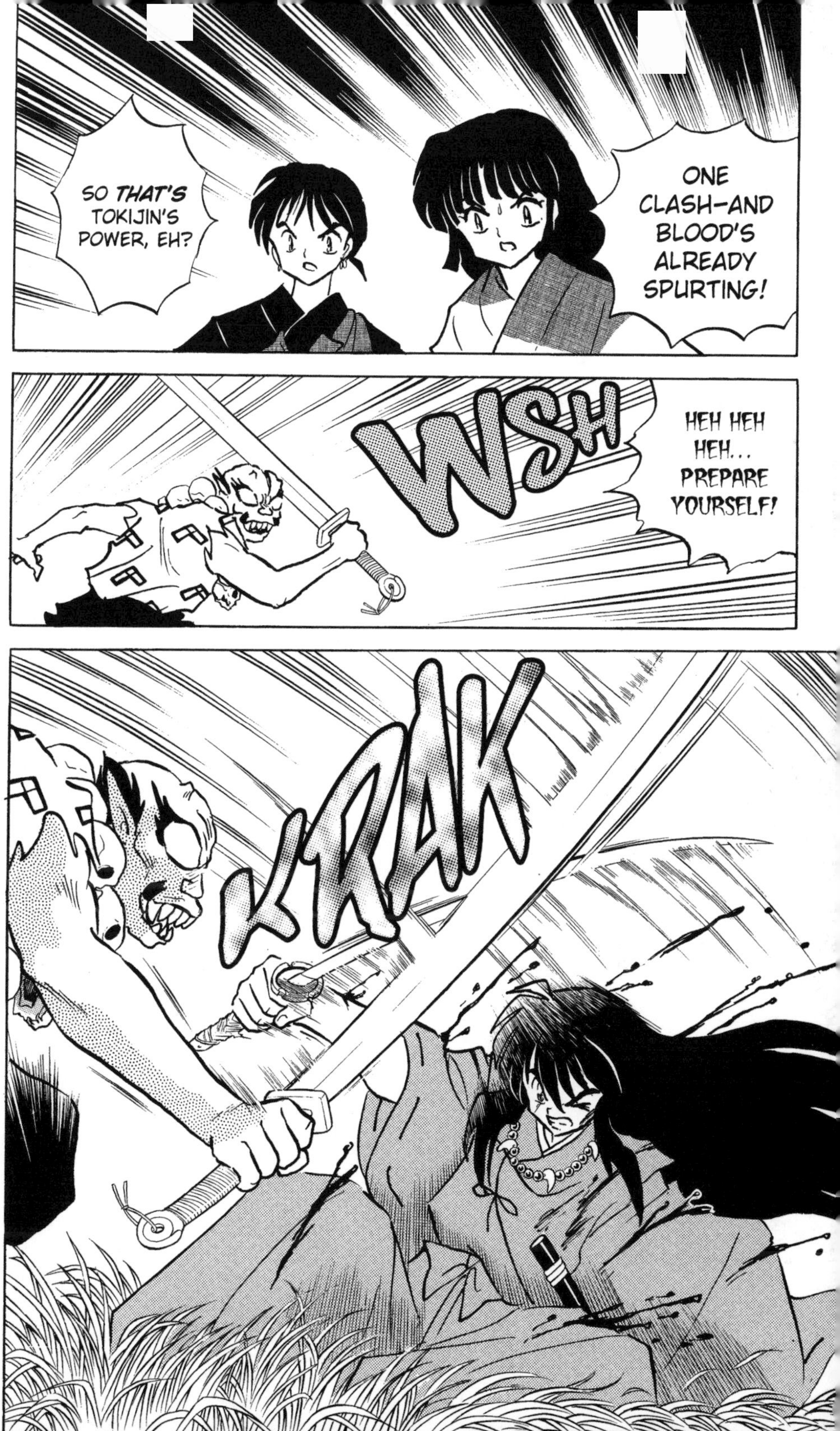

ONE CLASH—AND BLOOD'S ALREADY SPURTING!
SO THAT'S TOKIJIN'S POWER, EH?
HEH HEH HEH... PREPARE YOURSELF!
WSH
KRAK

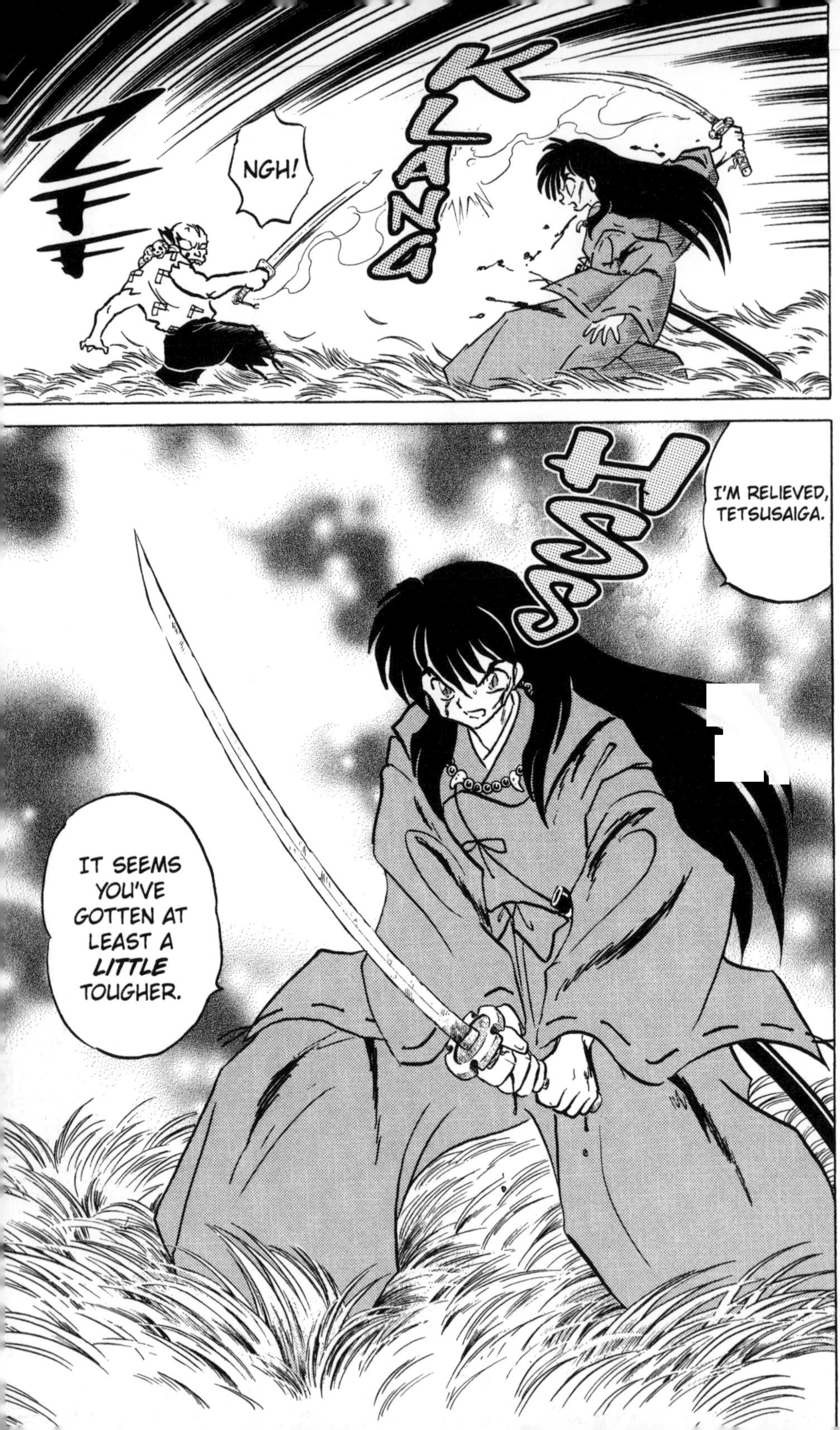
KLANG
NGH!
I'M RELIEVED, TETSUSAIGA.
IT SEEMS YOU'VE GOTTEN AT LEAST A *LITTLE* TOUGHER.

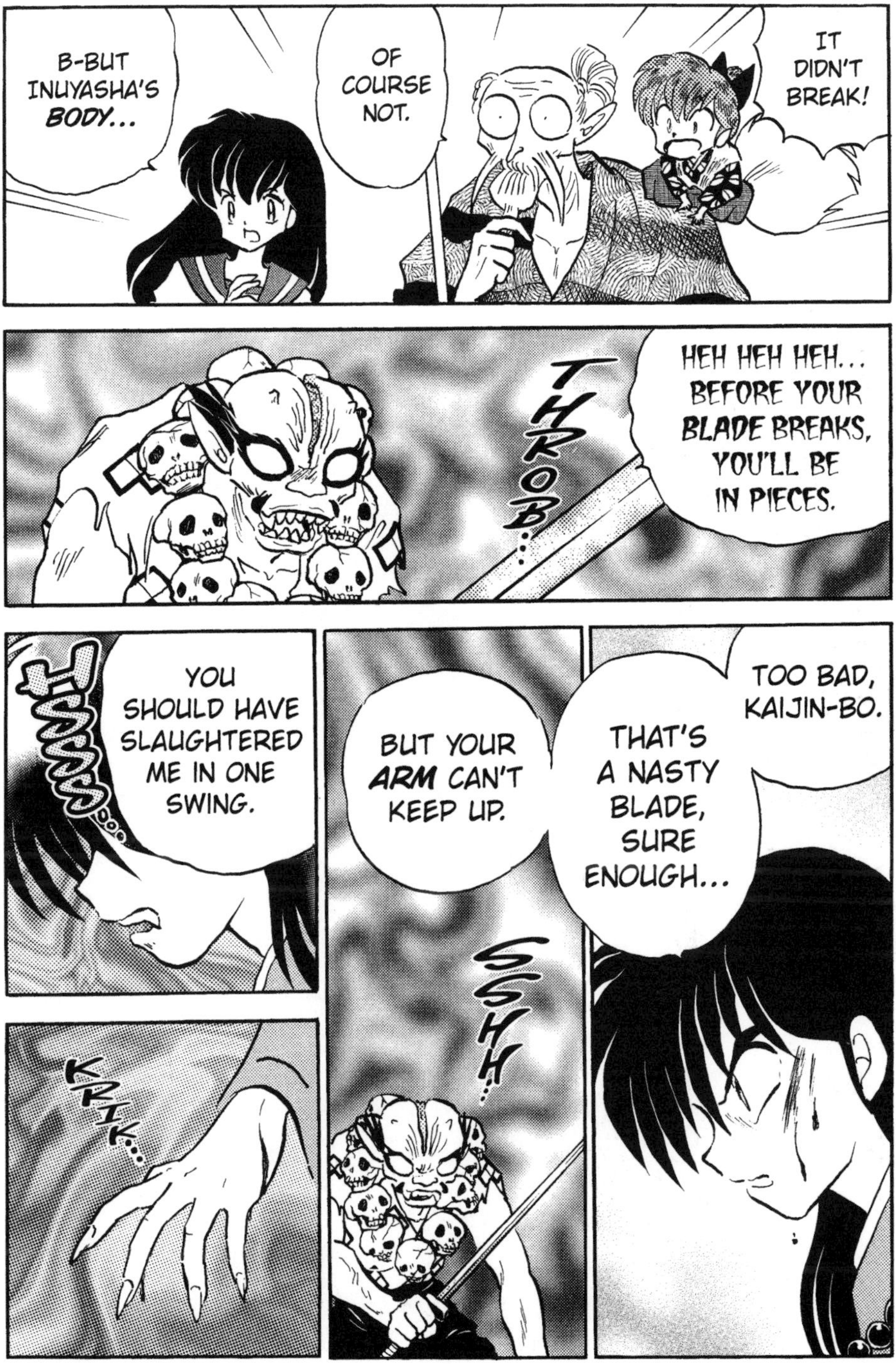
IT DIDN'T BREAK!
OF COURSE NOT.
B-BUT INUYASHA'S *BODY*...
THROB...
HEH HEH HEH... BEFORE YOUR *BLADE* BREAKS, YOU'LL BE IN PIECES.
TOO BAD, KAIJIN-BO.
THAT'S A NASTY BLADE, SURE ENOUGH...
BUT YOUR *ARM* CAN'T KEEP UP.
SSHH...
YOU SHOULD HAVE SLAUGHTERED ME IN ONE SWING.
HSSSS...
KRIK...

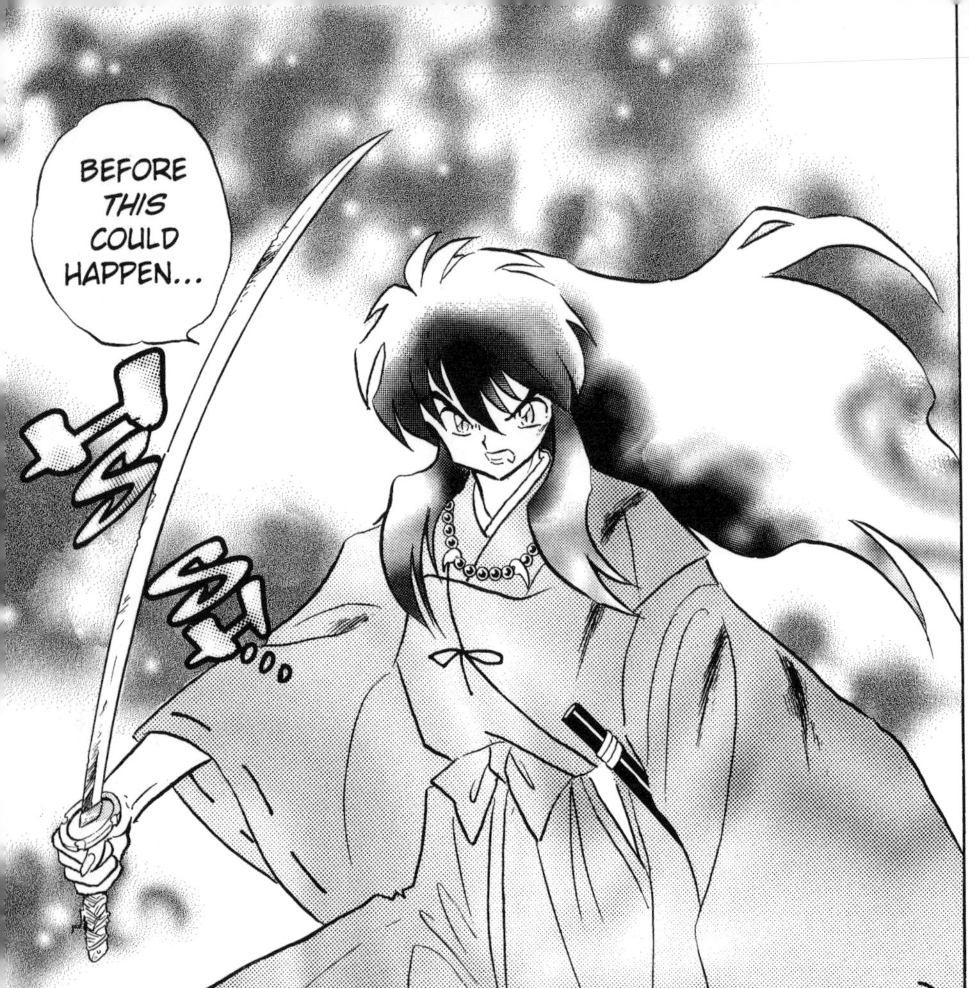
BEFORE THIS COULD HAPPEN...
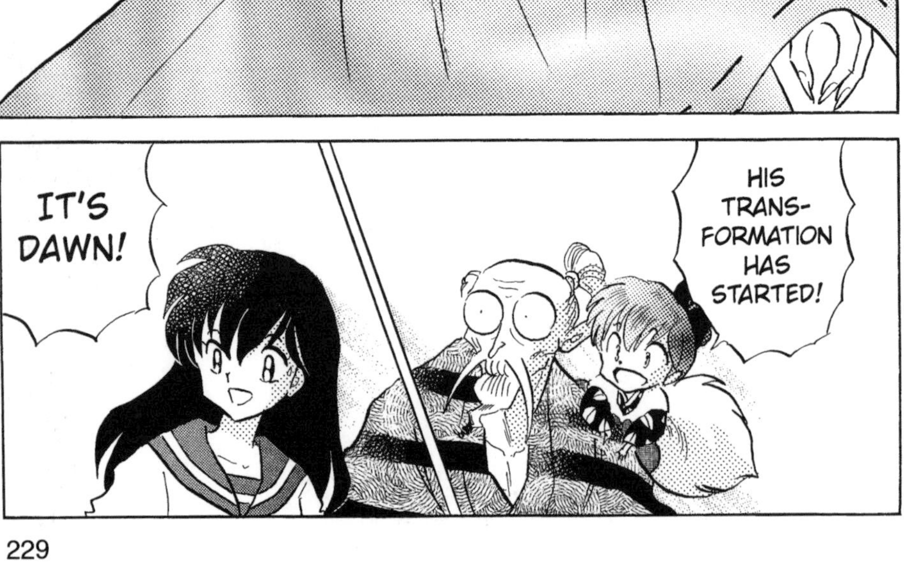
HIS TRANS-FORMATION HAS STARTED!
IT'S DAWN!

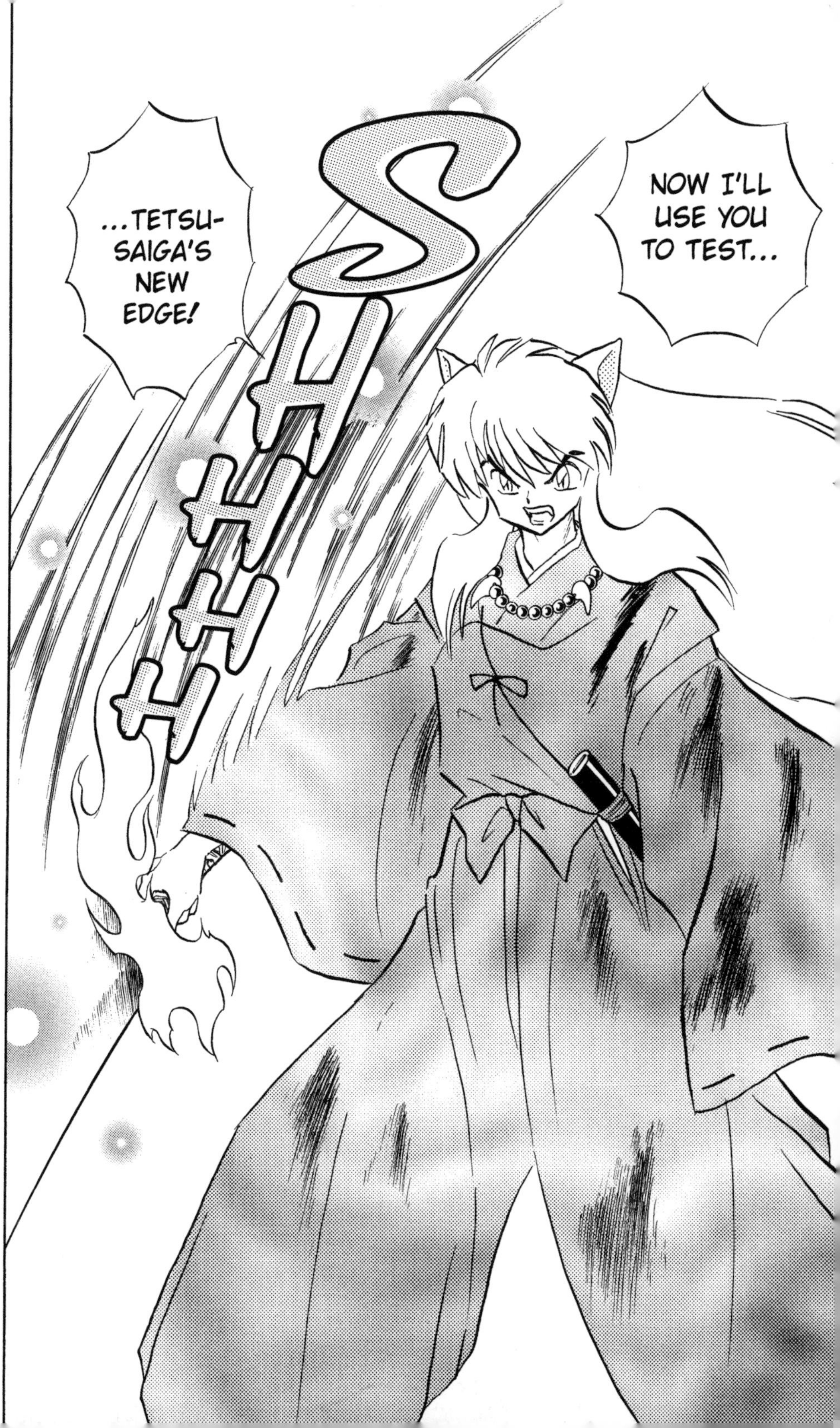
NOW I'LL USE YOU TO TEST...
SHHHH
...TETSU-SAIGA'S NEW EDGE!

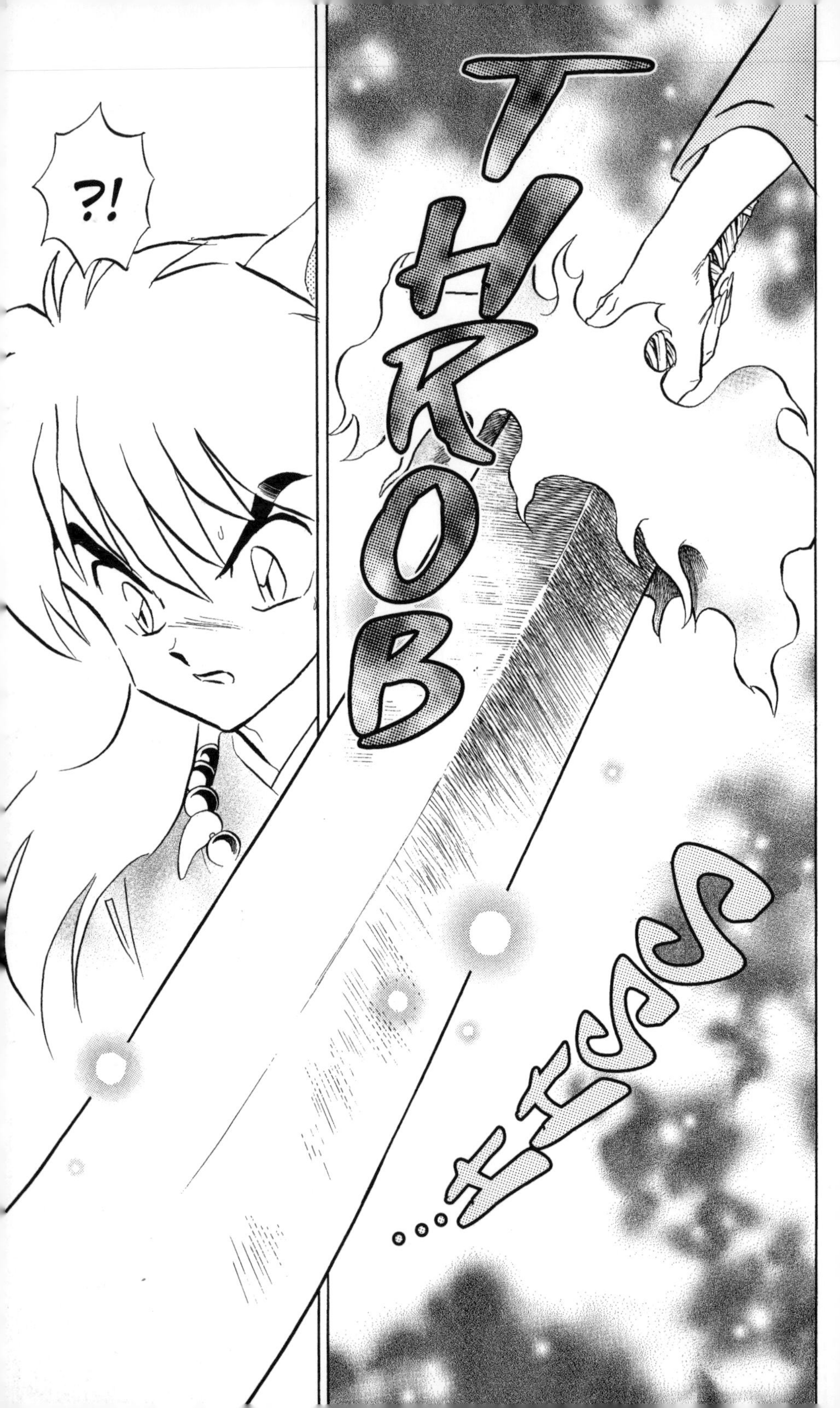
THROB
...HISSSS
?!

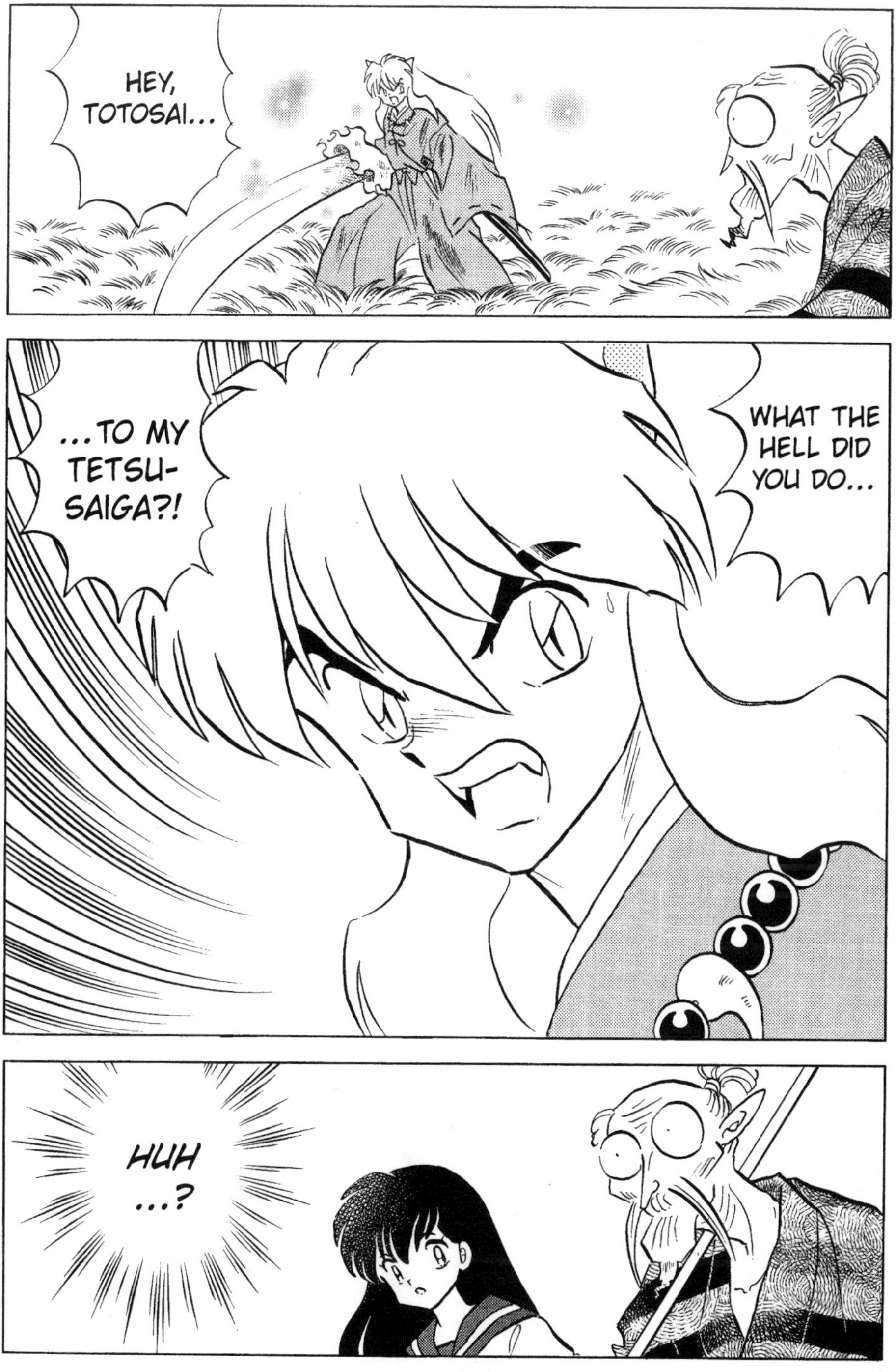
HEY, TOTOSAI...
WHAT THE HELL DID YOU DO...
...TO MY TETSU-SAIGA?!
HUH ...?

SCROLL THREE
TOKIJIN'S CHOICE

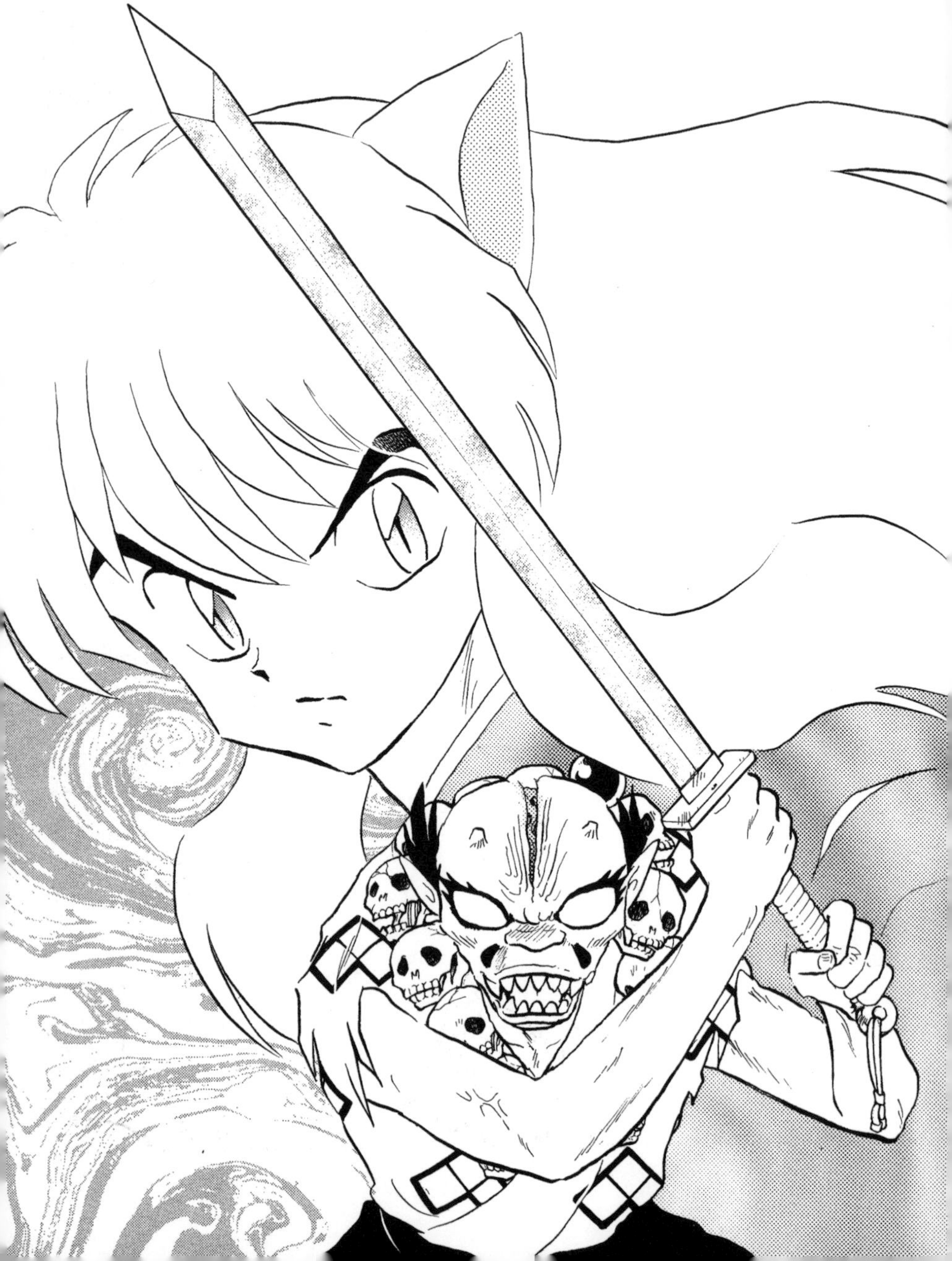

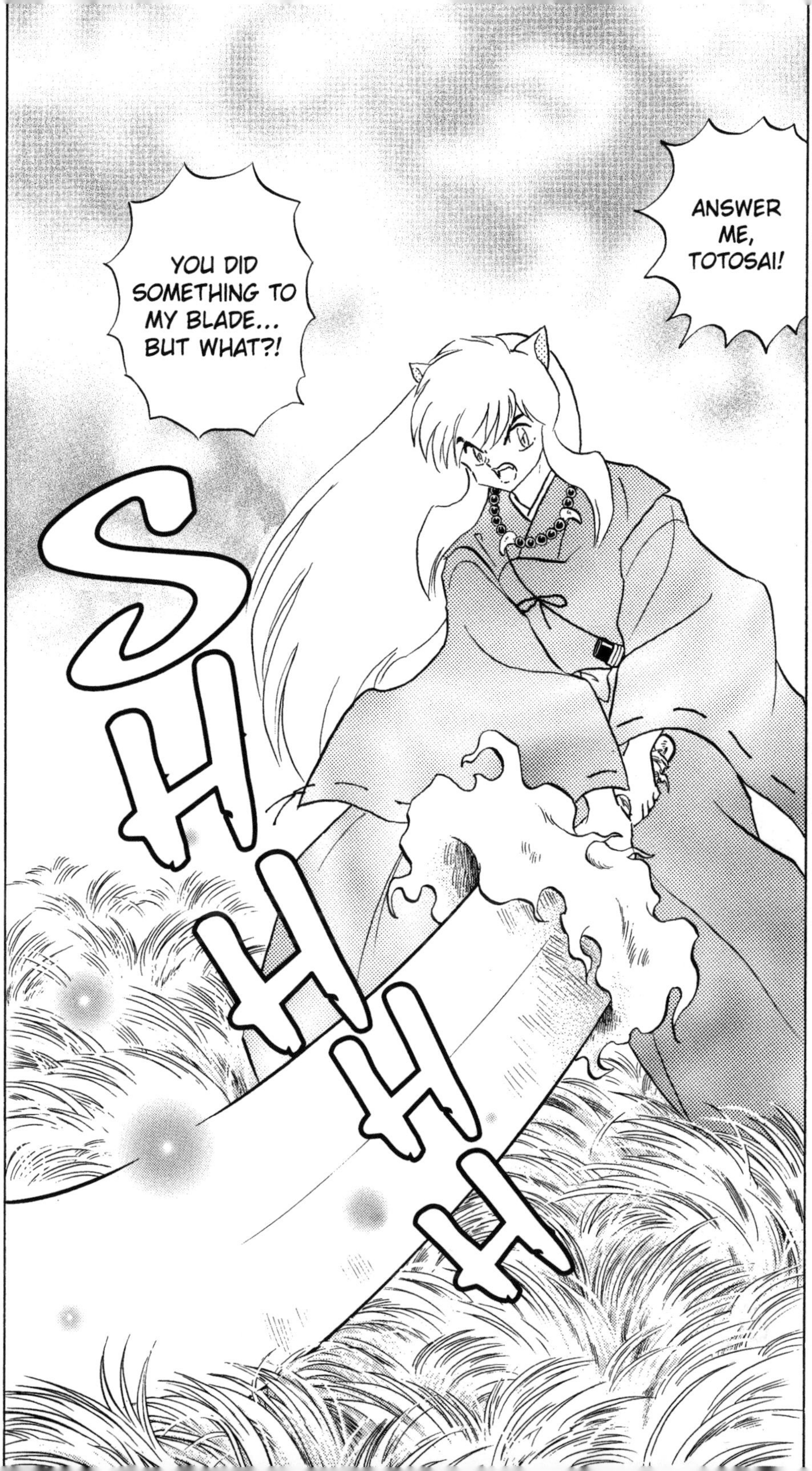
ANSWER ME, TOTOSAI!
YOU DID SOMETHING TO MY BLADE... BUT WHAT?!
SHHHH

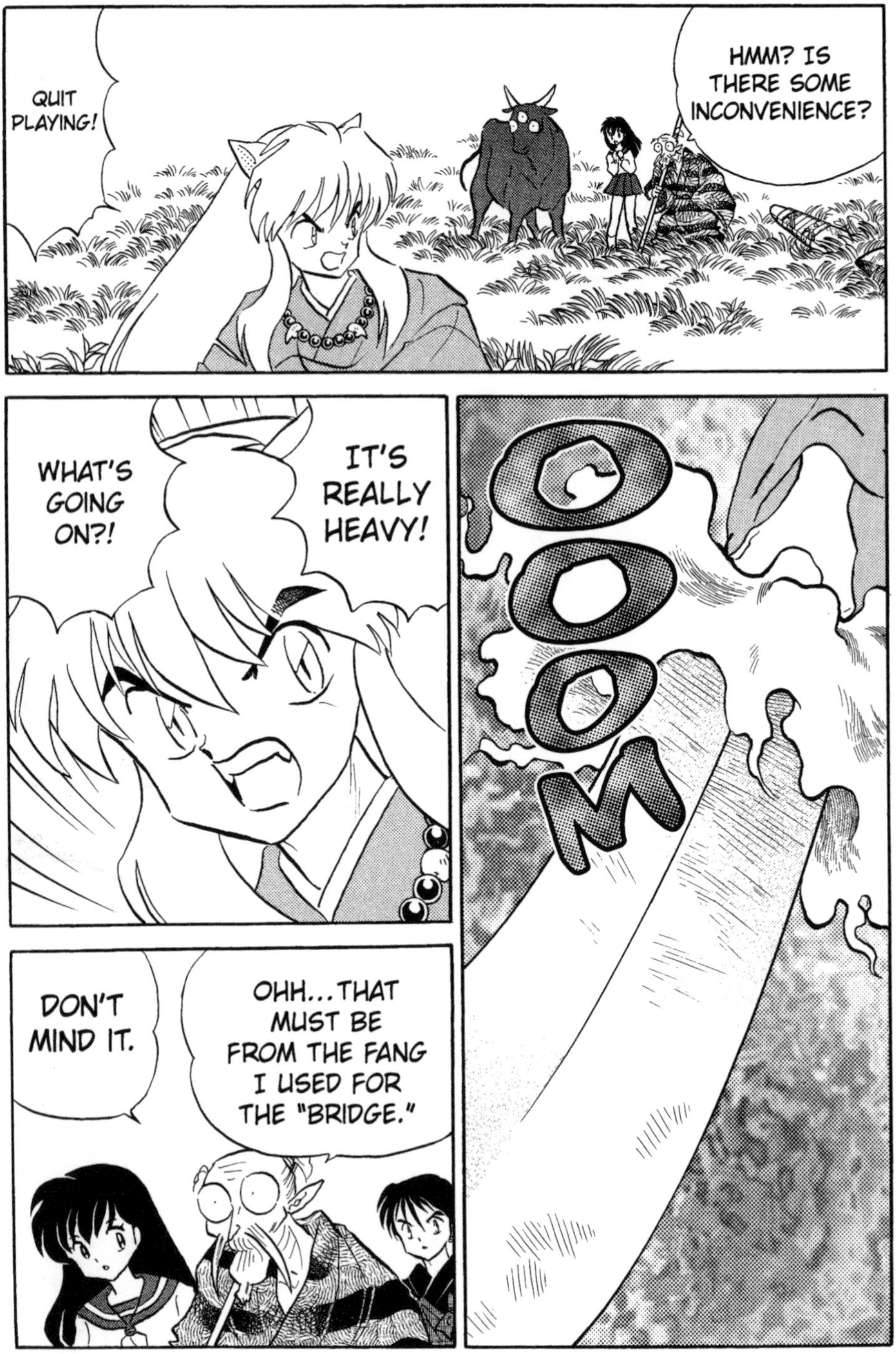
HMM? IS THERE SOME INCONVENIENCE?
QUIT PLAYING!
OOOM
IT'S REALLY HEAVY!
WHAT'S GOING ON?!
OHH...THAT MUST BE FROM THE FANG I USED FOR THE "BRIDGE."
DON'T MIND IT.

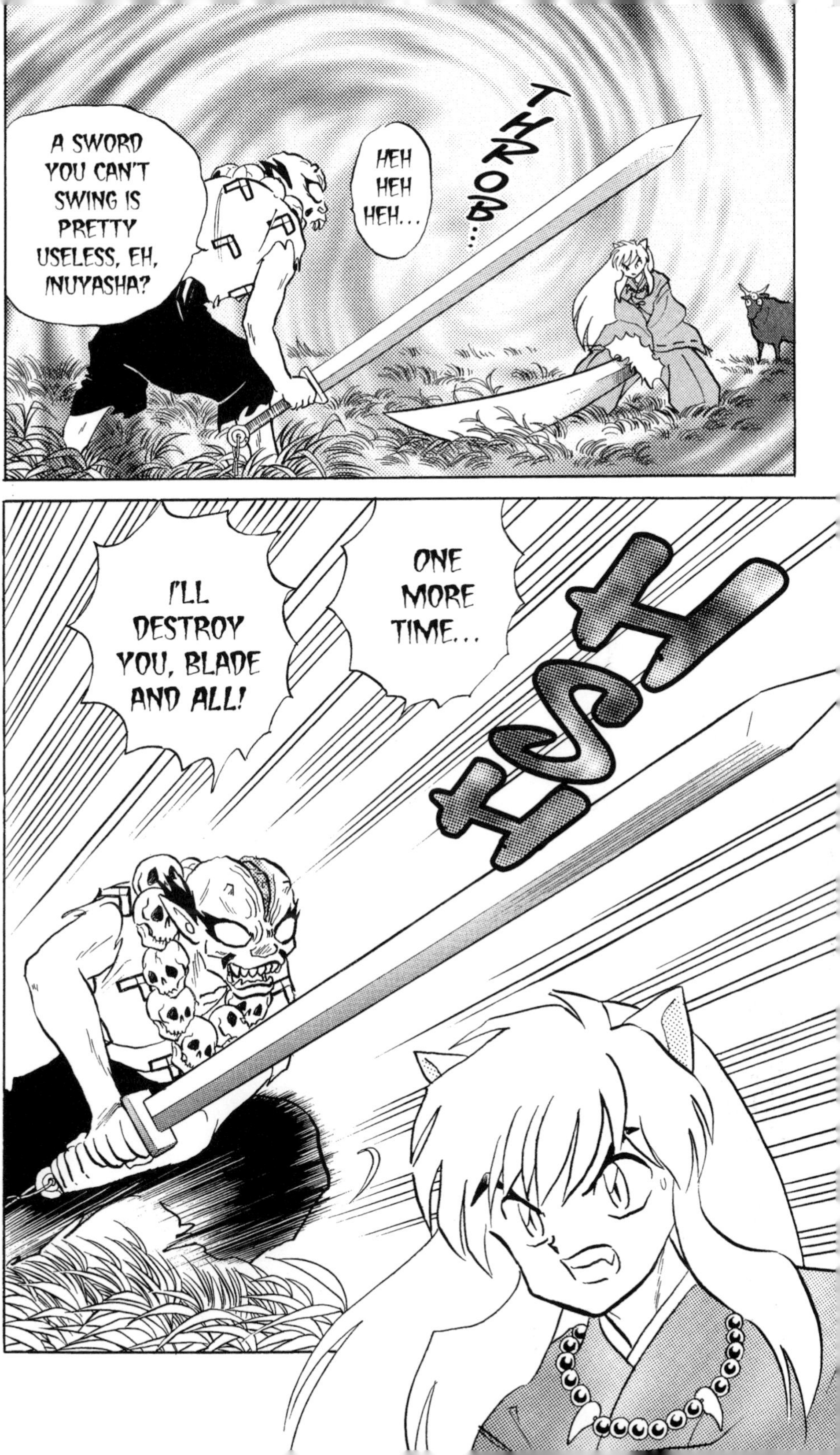
THROB...
HEH HEH HEH...
A SWORD YOU CAN'T SWING IS PRETTY USELESS, EH, INUYASHA?
ONE MORE TIME...
I'LL DESTROY YOU, BLADE AND ALL!
HSSH

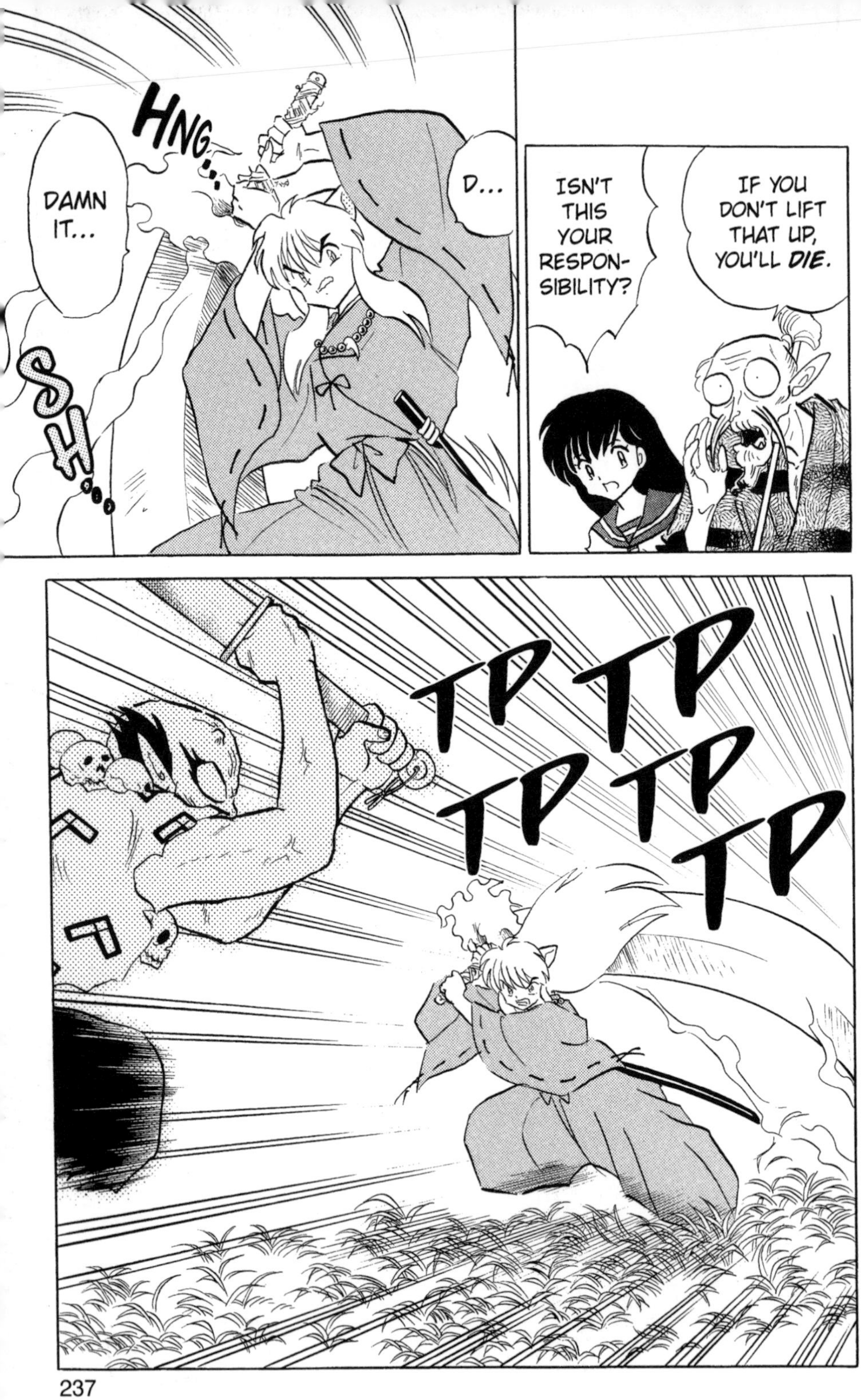
IF YOU DON'T LIFT THAT UP, YOU'LL *DIE*.
ISN'T THIS YOUR RESPON-SIBILITY?
D...
HNG...
DAMN IT...
SH...
TP TP TP TP TP

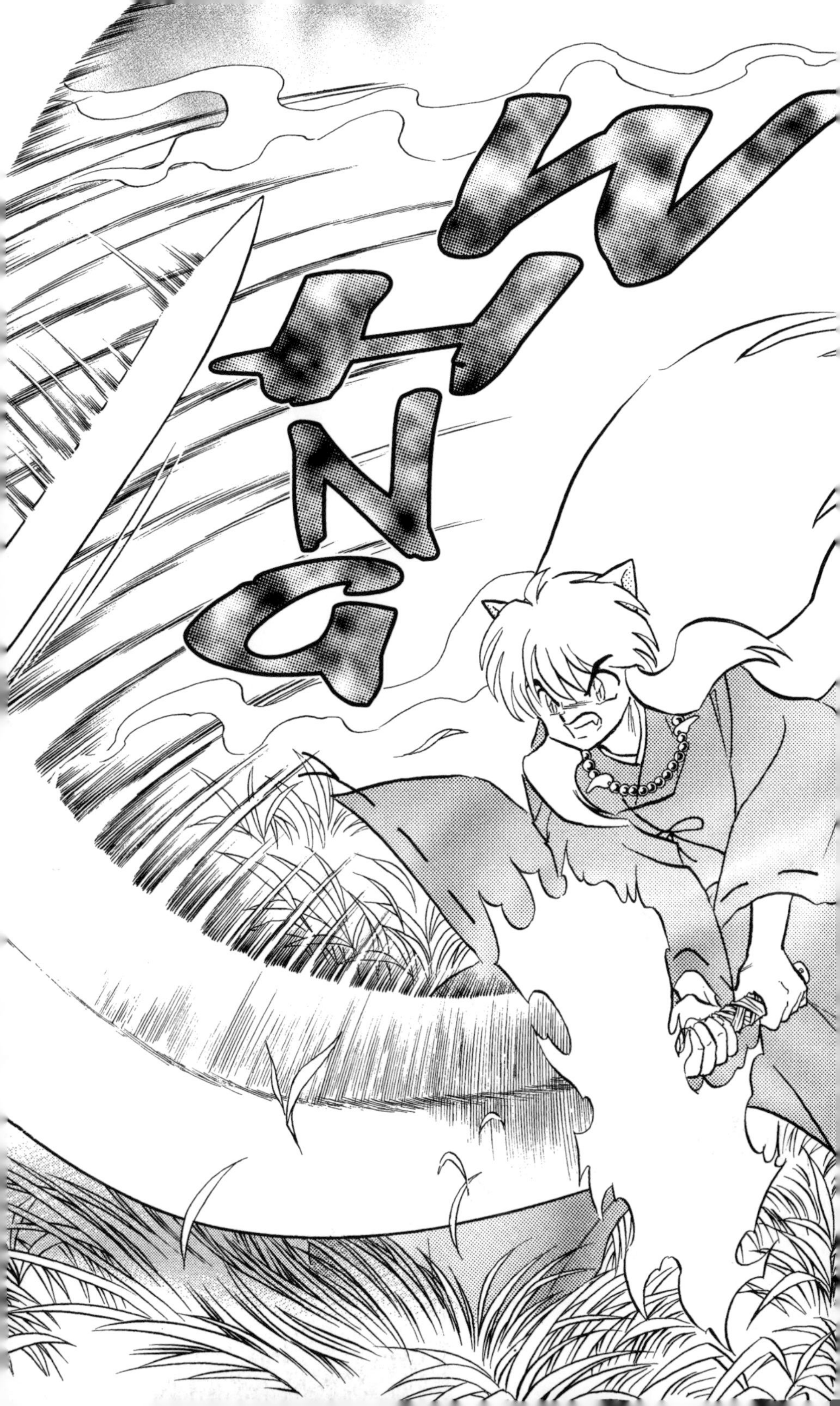
WHNG

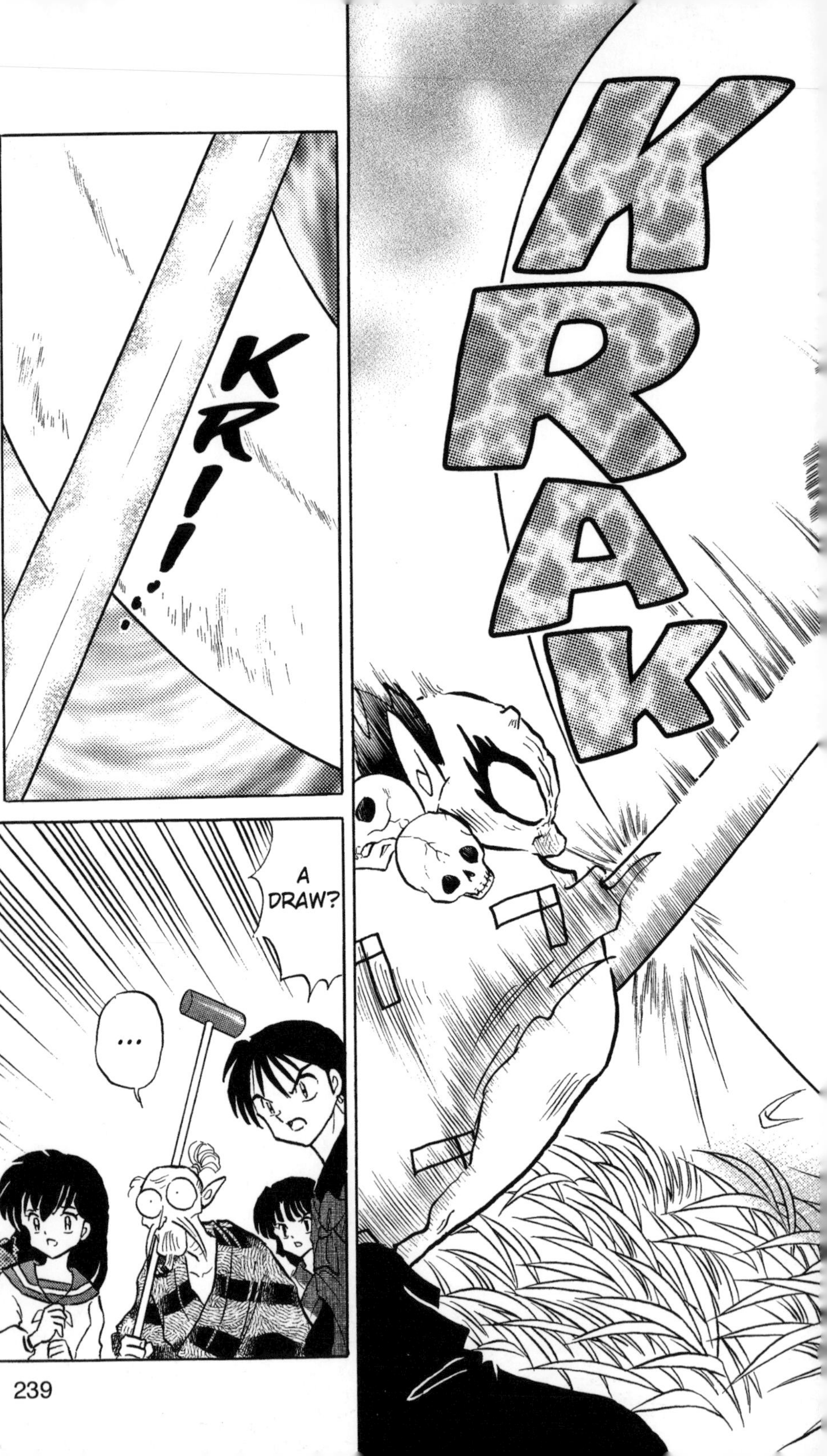
KRAK
KRI!!...
A DRAW?
...

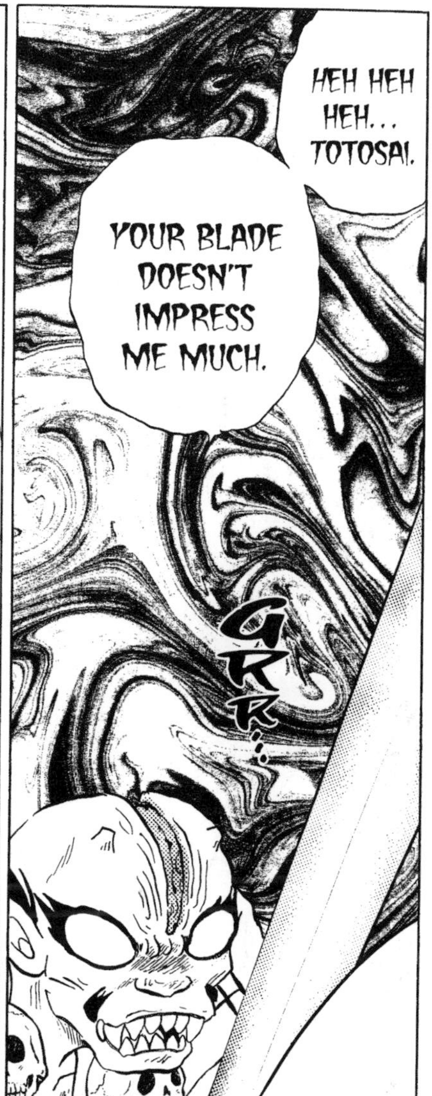
HEH HEH HEH... TOTOSAI.
YOUR BLADE DOESN'T IMPRESS ME MUCH.
GRR...
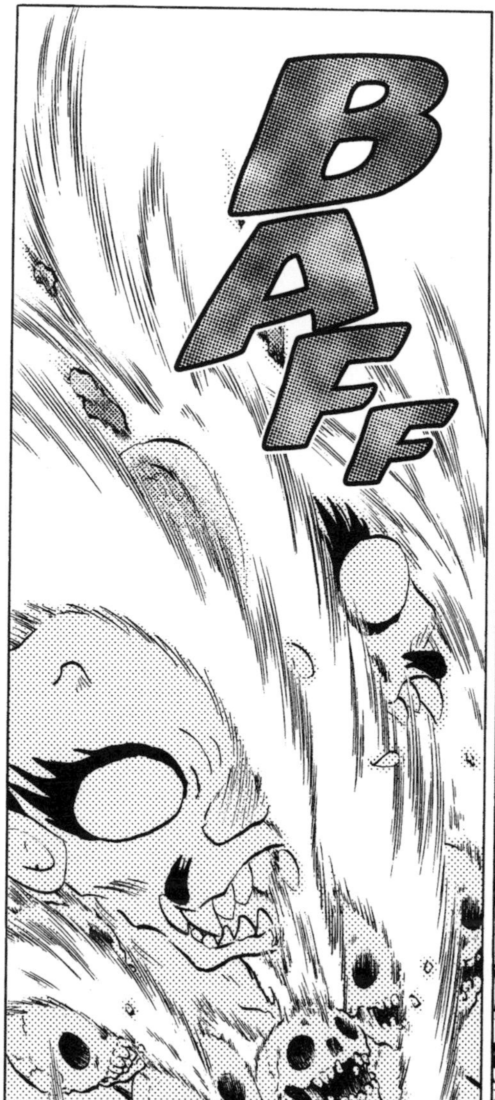
BAFF

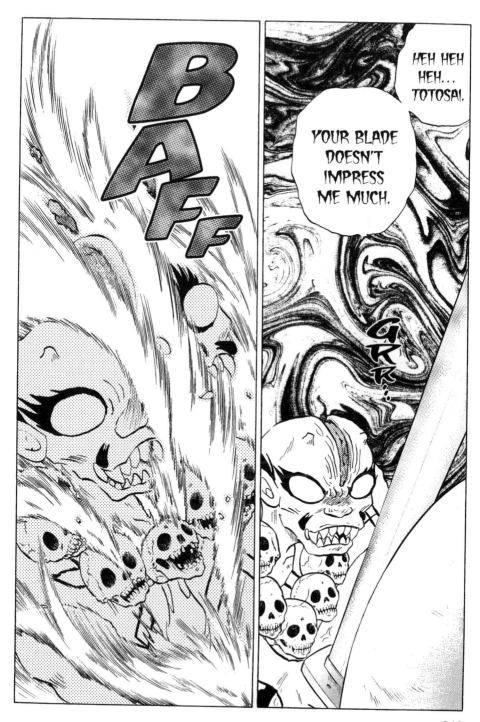

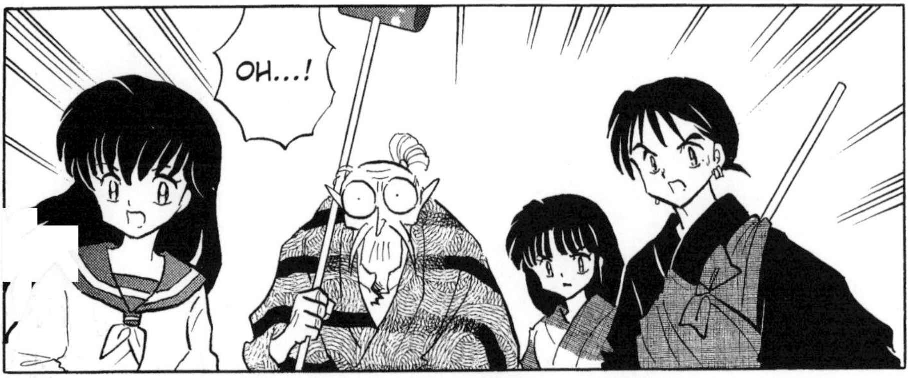
OH...!
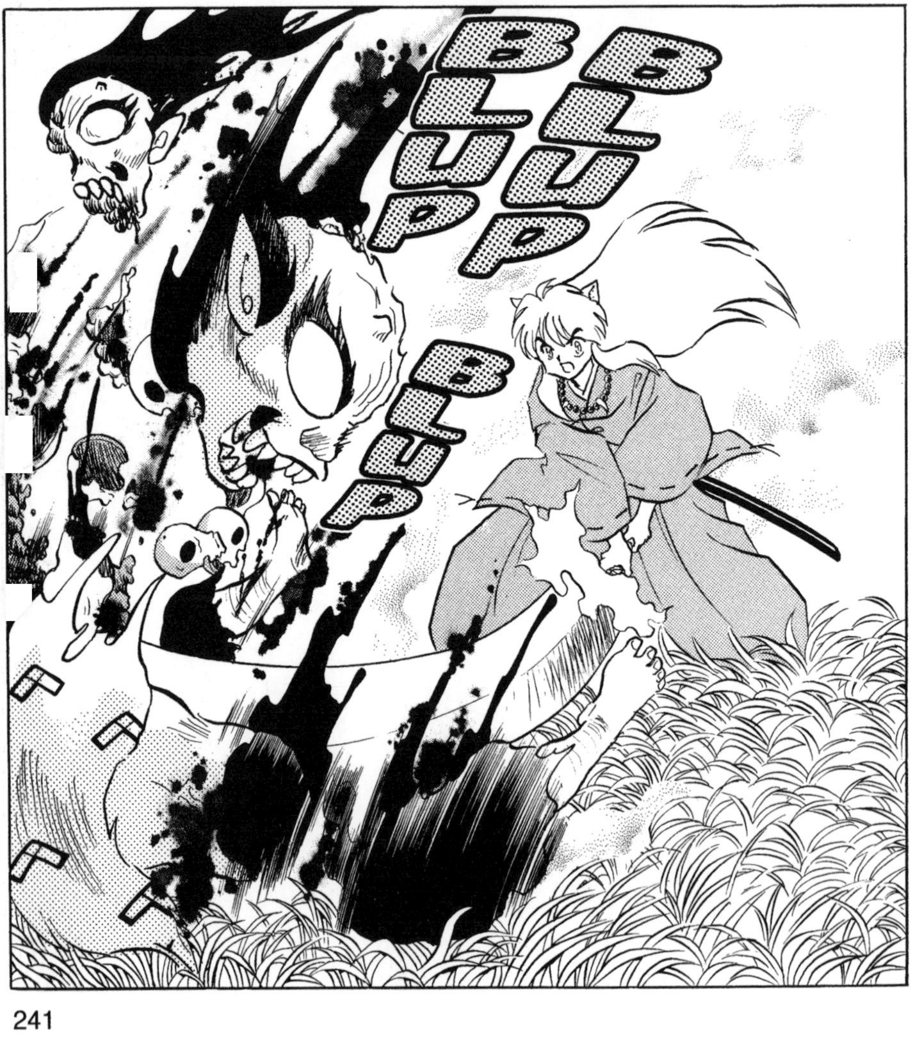
BLUPP
BLUPP
BLUPP

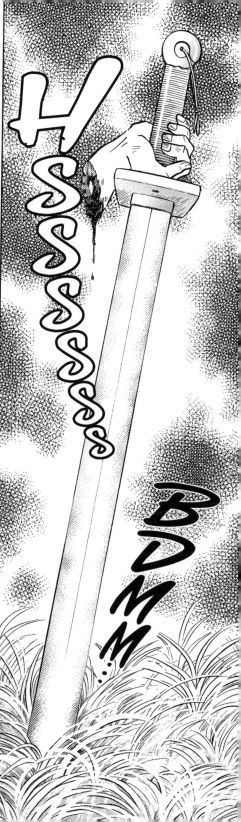

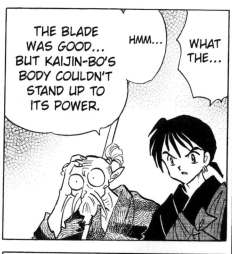

THE BLADE WAS GOOD... BUT KAIJIN-BO'S BODY COULDN'T STAND UP TO ITS POWER.

HMM...

WHAT THE...

POSSESSED BY YOUR OWN SWORD... WHAT AN *AMATEUR.*

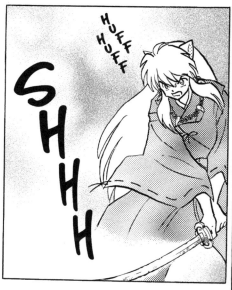

HUFF HUFF

SHHHH

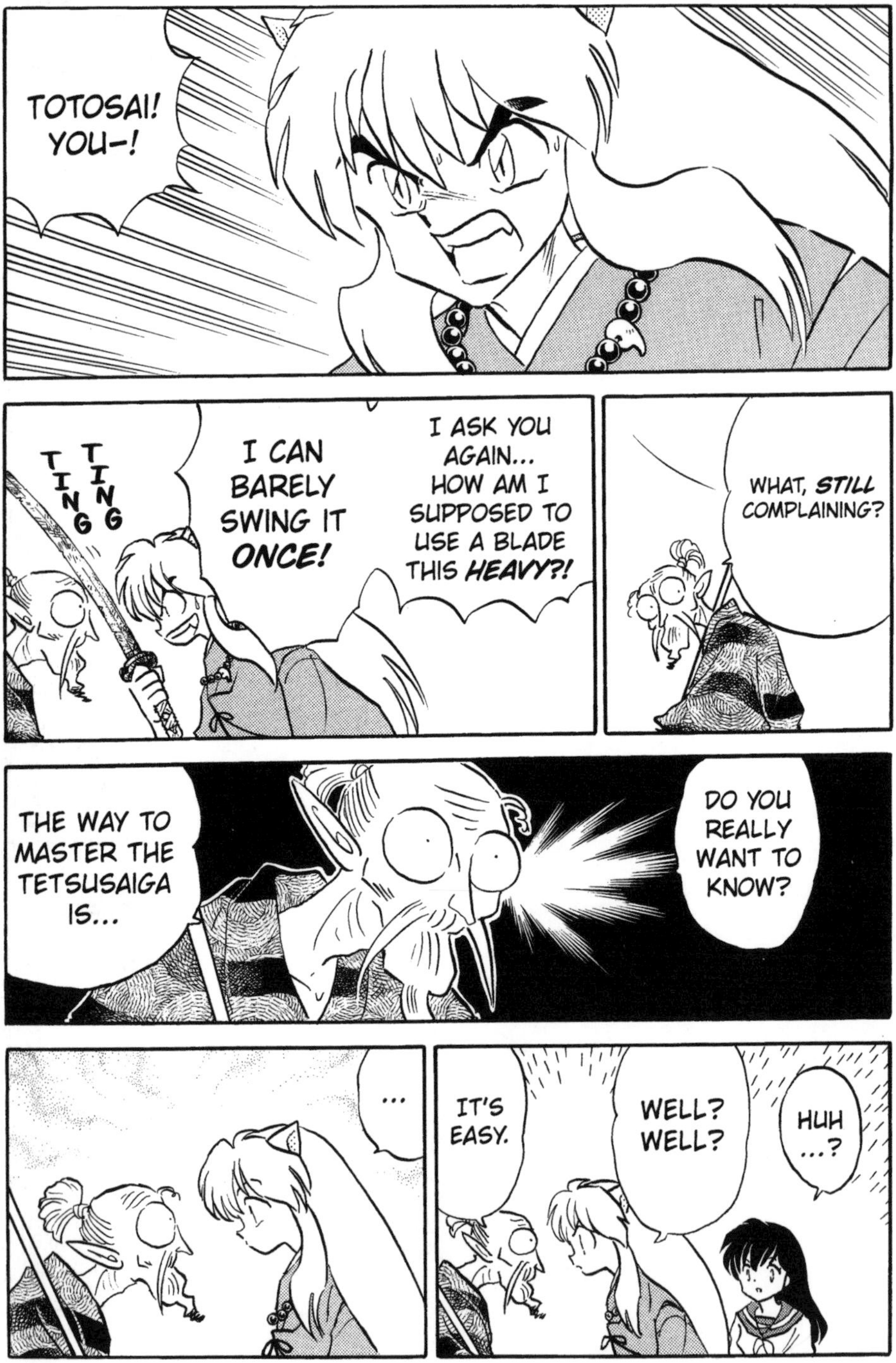
TOTOSAI! YOU-!
WHAT, STILL COMPLAINING?
I ASK YOU AGAIN... HOW AM I SUPPOSED TO USE A BLADE THIS HEAVY?!
I CAN BARELY SWING IT ONCE!
TING TING
DO YOU REALLY WANT TO KNOW?
THE WAY TO MASTER THE TETSUSAIGA IS...
HUH ...?
WELL? WELL?
IT'S EASY.
...

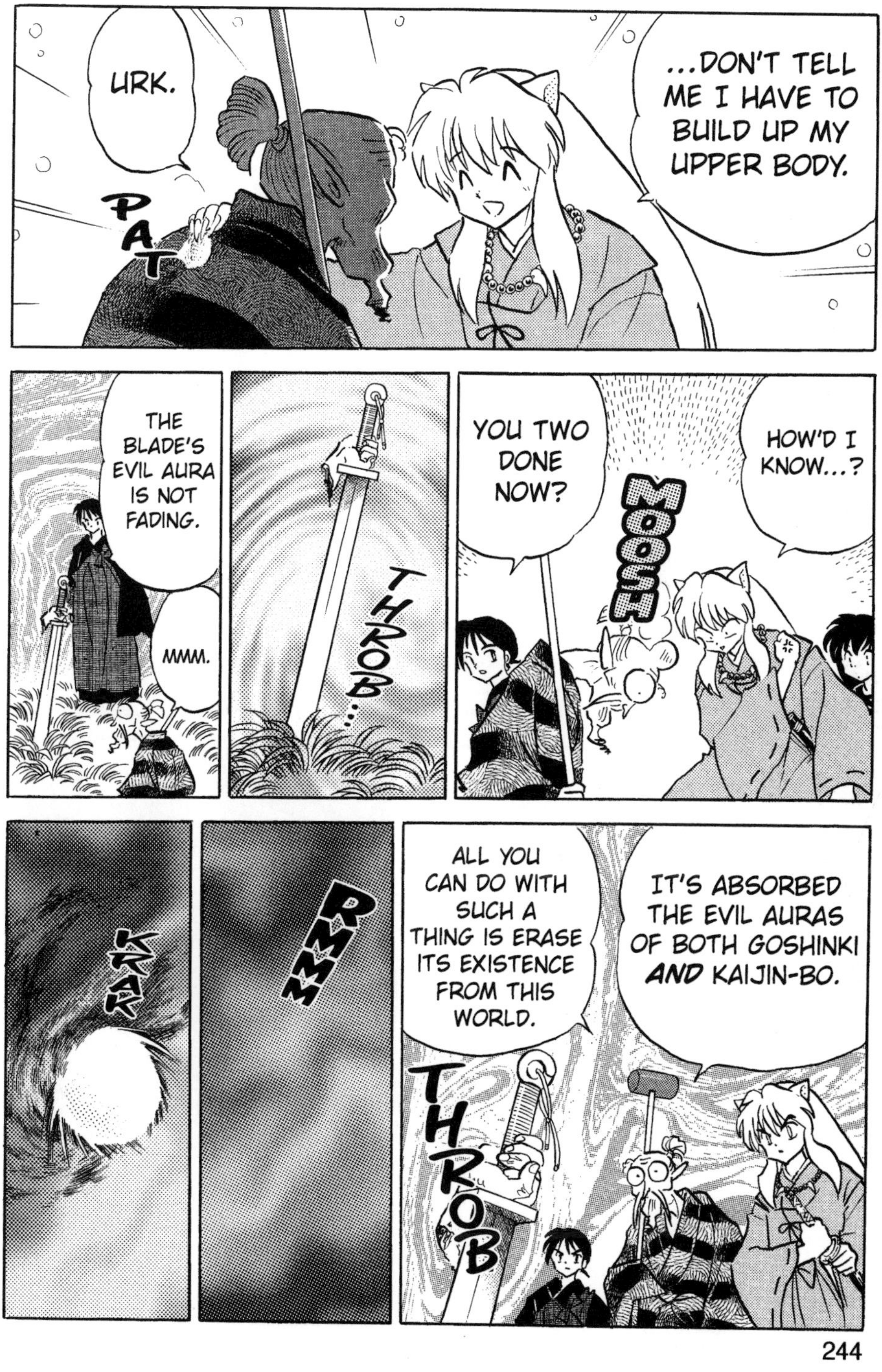
...DON'T TELL ME I HAVE TO BUILD UP MY UPPER BODY.
URK.
PAT
HOW'D I KNOW...?
YOU TWO DONE NOW?
MOOSH
THROB...
THE BLADE'S EVIL AURA IS NOT FADING.
MMM.
IT'S ABSORBED THE EVIL AURAS OF BOTH GOSHINKI AND KAIJIN-BO.
ALL YOU CAN DO WITH SUCH A THING IS ERASE ITS EXISTENCE FROM THIS WORLD.
THROB
RMMM
KRAK

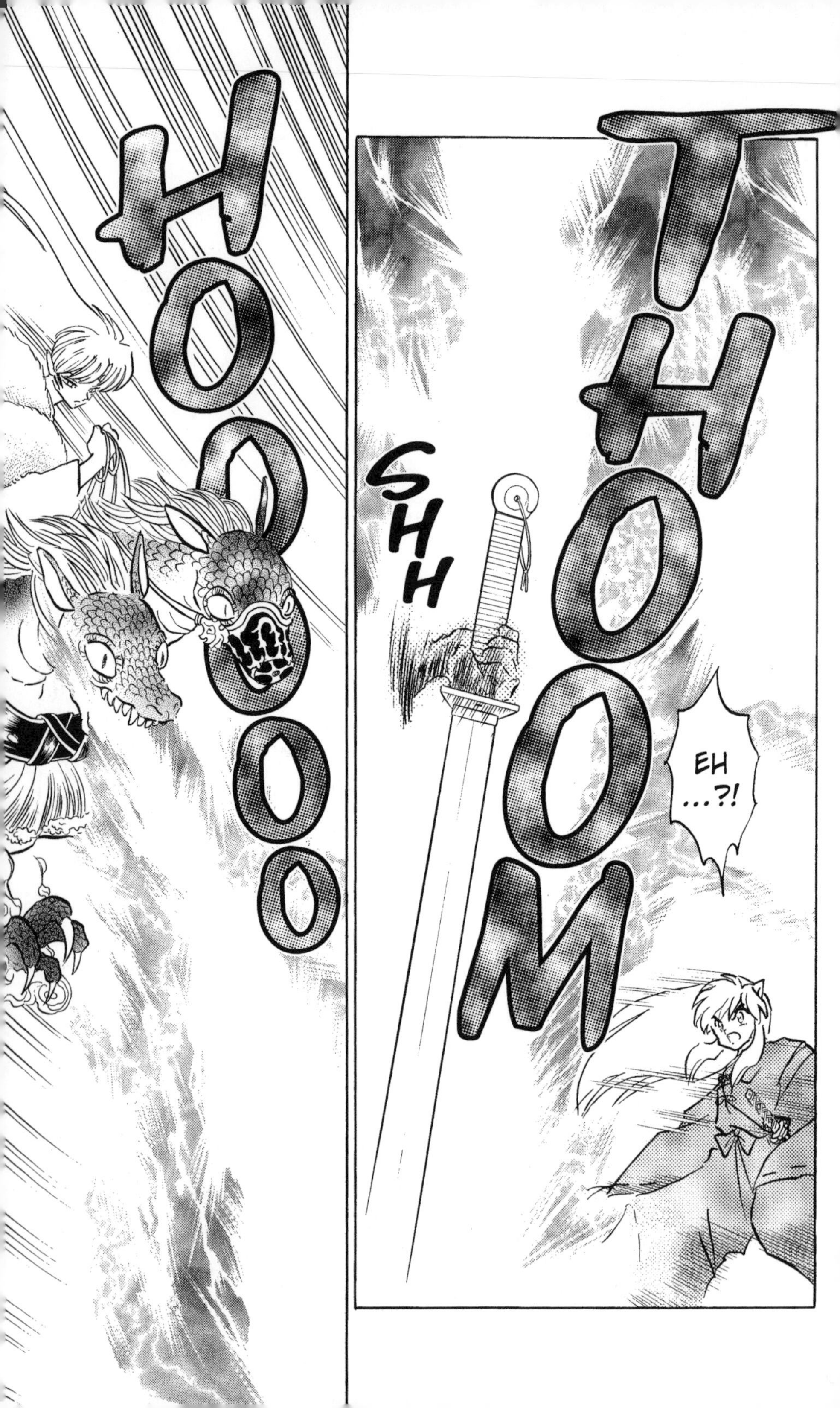
THOOOM
SHH
EH ...?!
HOOOOO

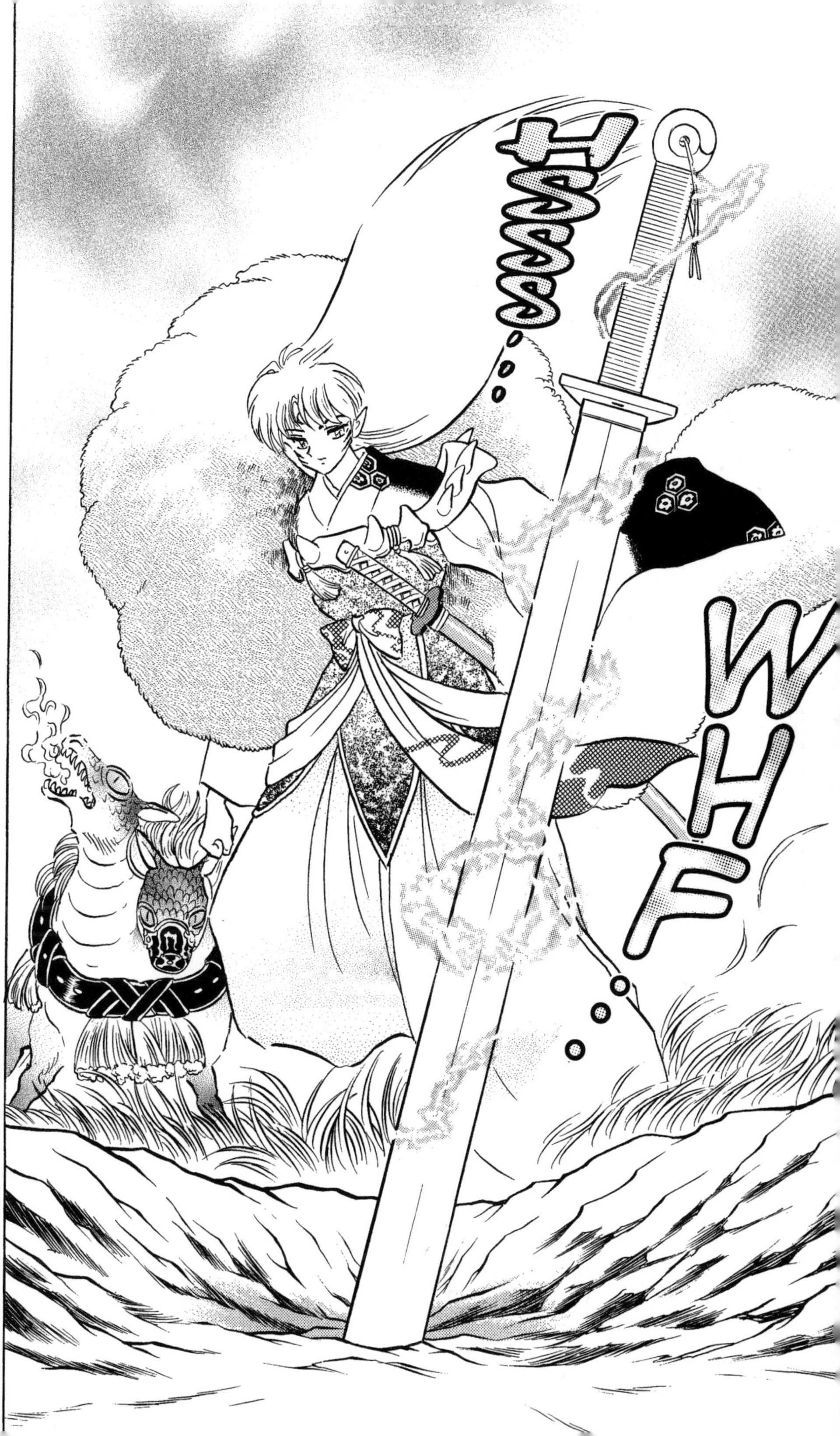
WHF...
HSSSSS...

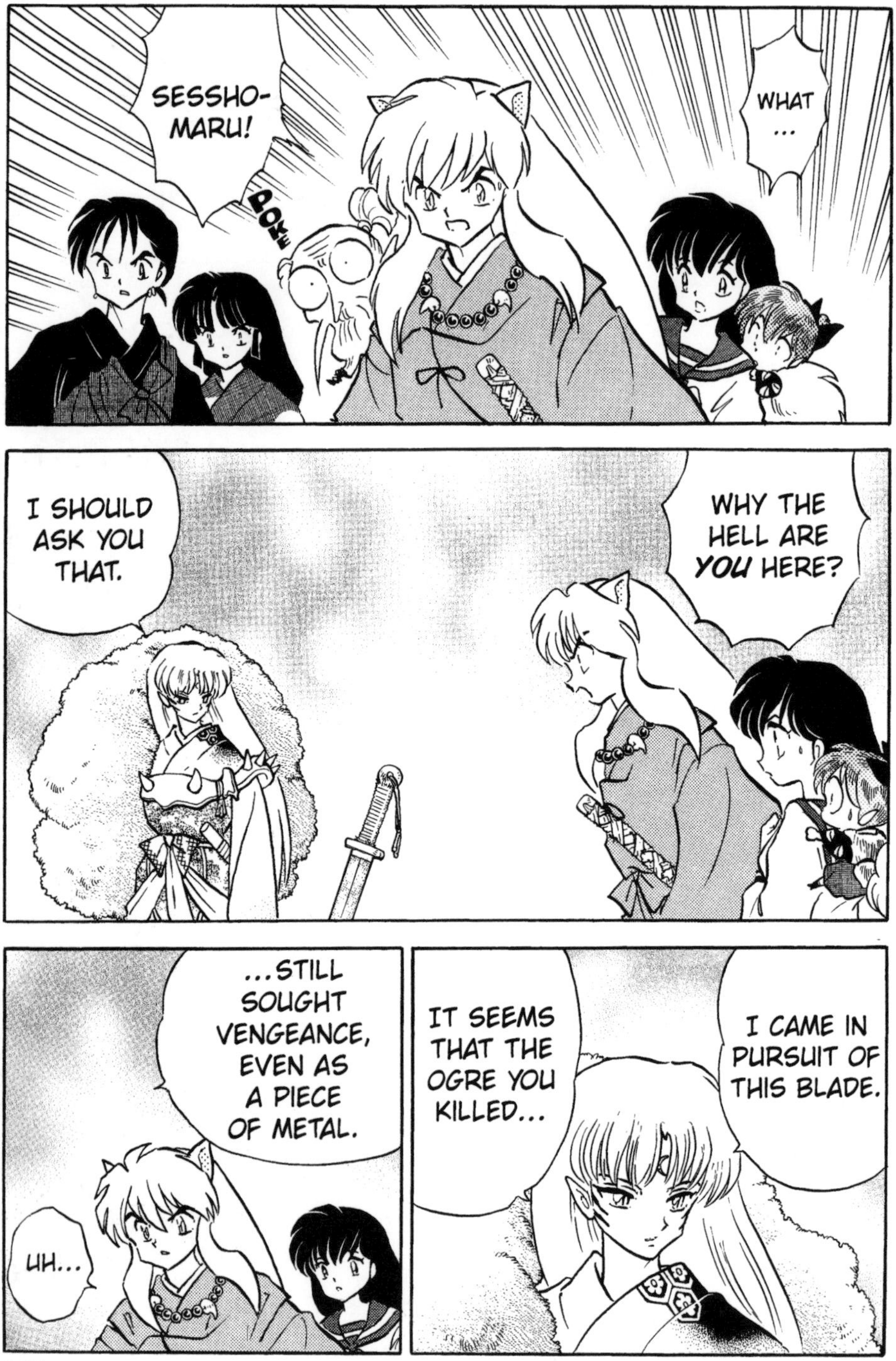
WHAT ...
SESSHO-MARU!
POKE
WHY THE HELL ARE YOU HERE?
I SHOULD ASK YOU THAT.
I CAME IN PURSUIT OF THIS BLADE.
IT SEEMS THAT THE OGRE YOU KILLED...
...STILL SOUGHT VENGEANCE, EVEN AS A PIECE OF METAL.
UH...

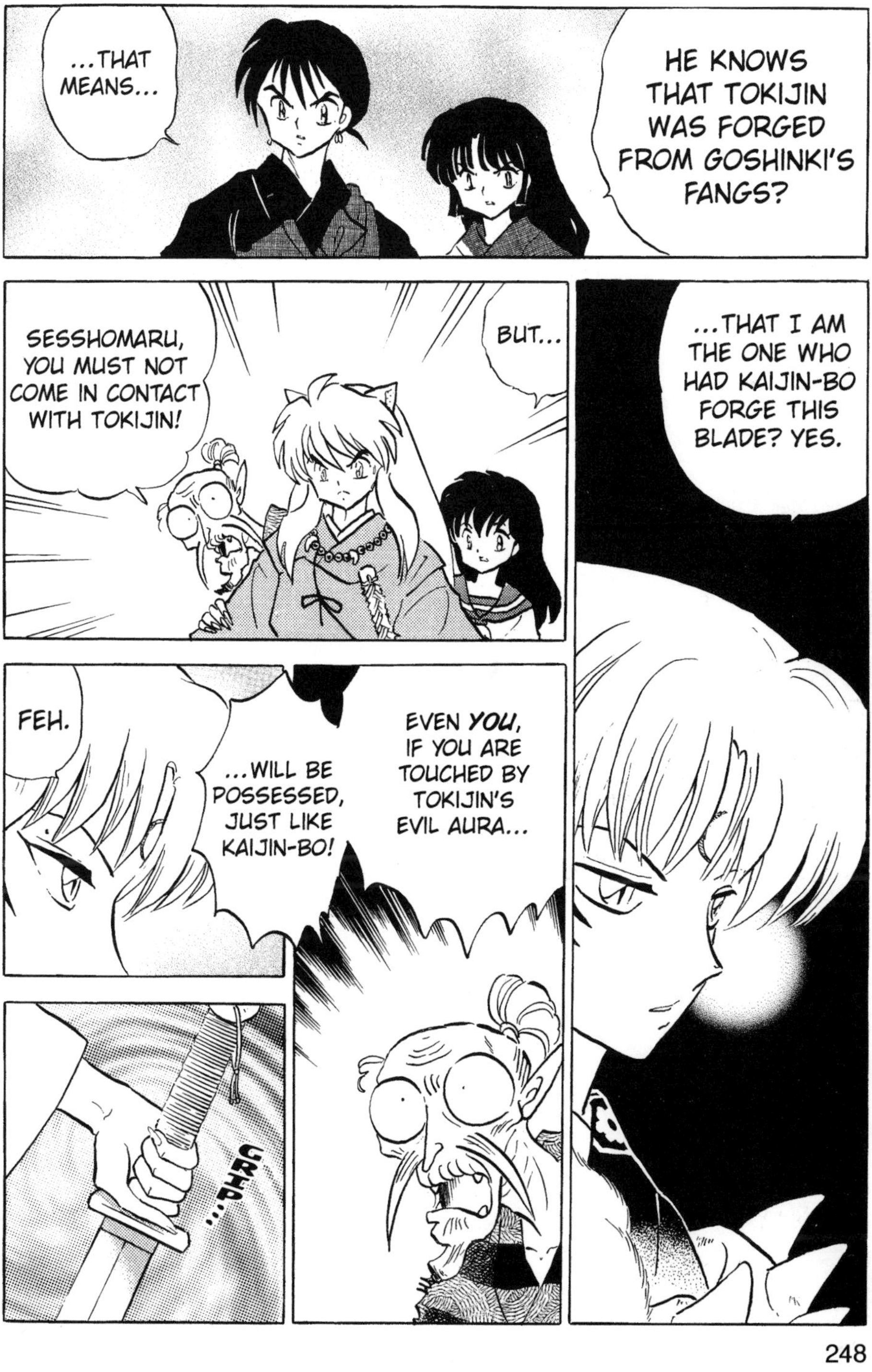
HE KNOWS THAT TOKIJIN WAS FORGED FROM GOSHINKI'S FANGS?
...THAT MEANS...
...THAT I AM THE ONE WHO HAD KAIJIN-BO FORGE THIS BLADE? YES.
BUT...
SESSHOMARU, YOU MUST NOT COME IN CONTACT WITH TOKIJIN!
EVEN *YOU*, IF YOU ARE TOUCHED BY TOKIJIN'S EVIL AURA...
...WILL BE POSSESSED, JUST LIKE KAIJIN-BO!
FEH.
GRIP...

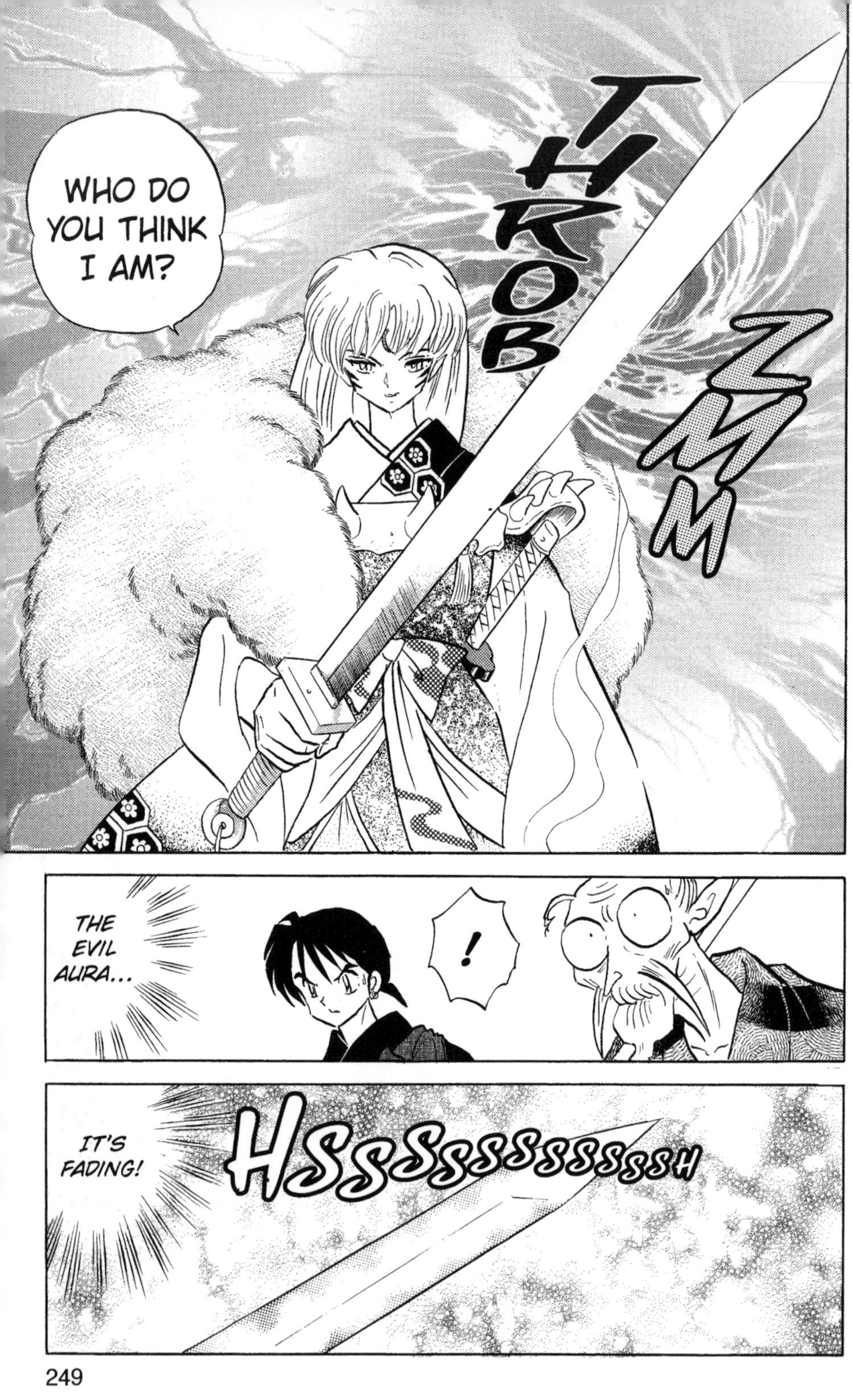
THROB
ZMMM
WHO DO YOU THINK I AM?
!
THE EVIL AURA...
IT'S FADING!
HSSSSSSSSSSSH

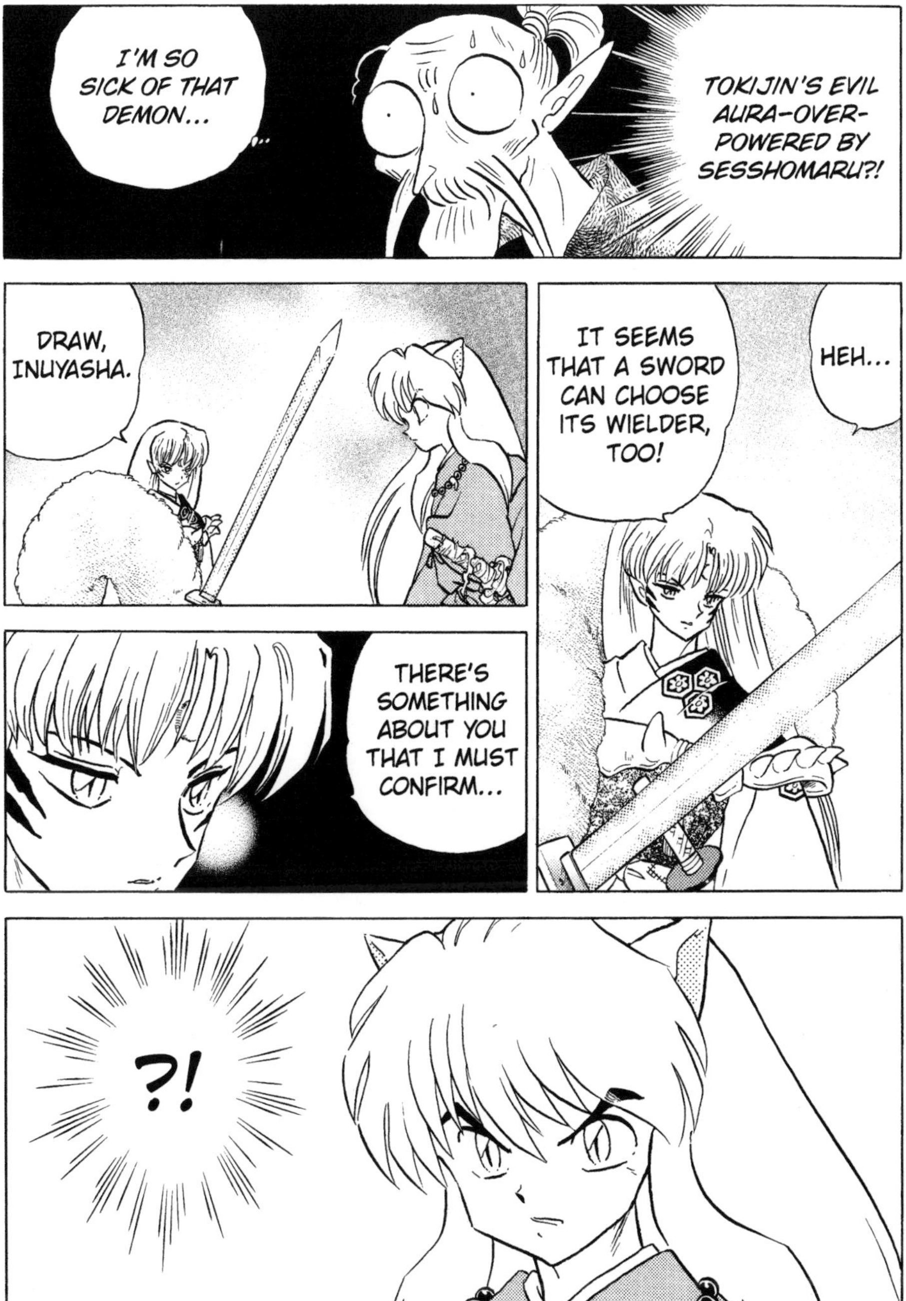
TOKIJIN'S EVIL AURA-OVERPOWERED BY SESSHOMARU?!
I'M SO SICK OF THAT DEMON...
HEH...
IT SEEMS THAT A SWORD CAN CHOOSE ITS WIELDER, TOO!
DRAW, INUYASHA.
THERE'S SOMETHING ABOUT YOU THAT I MUST CONFIRM...
?!

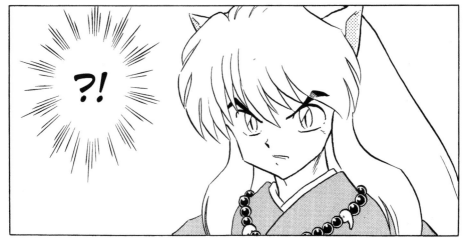

SCROLL FOUR
THE SCENT OF BLOOD

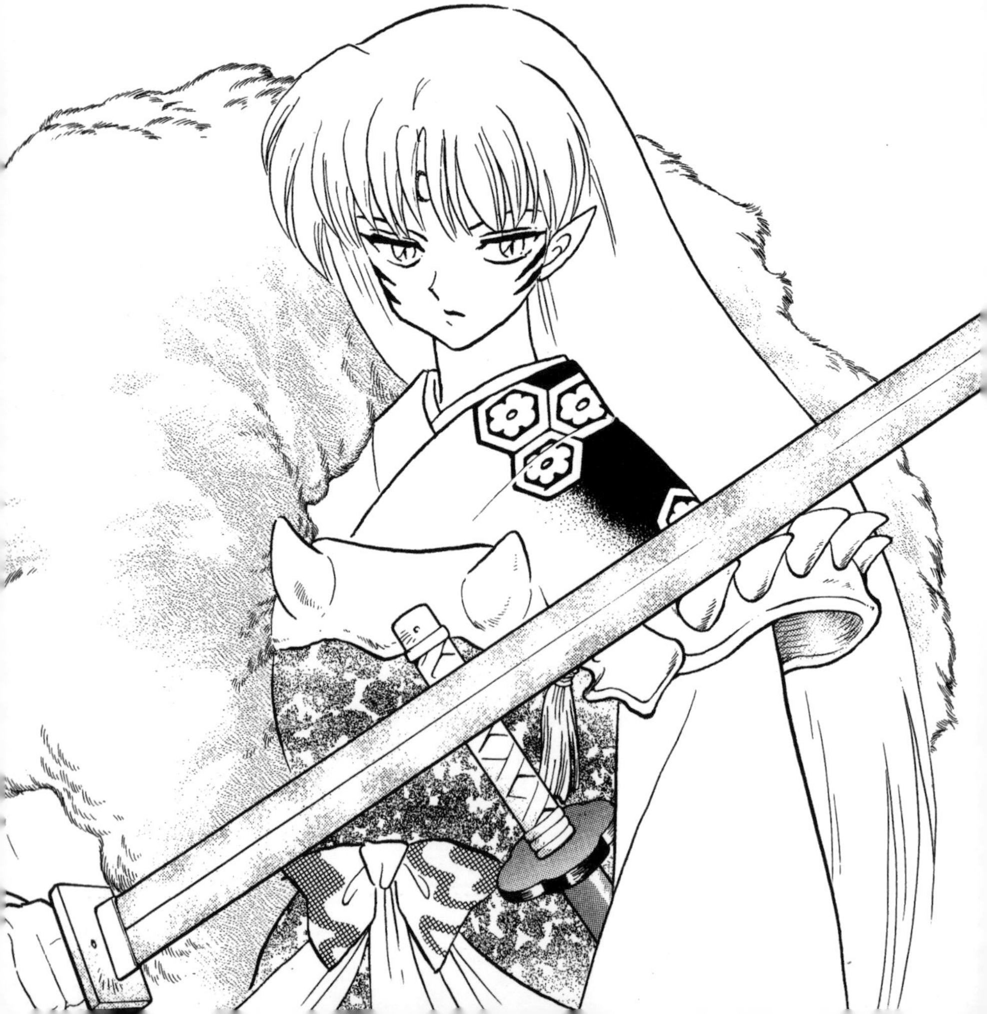

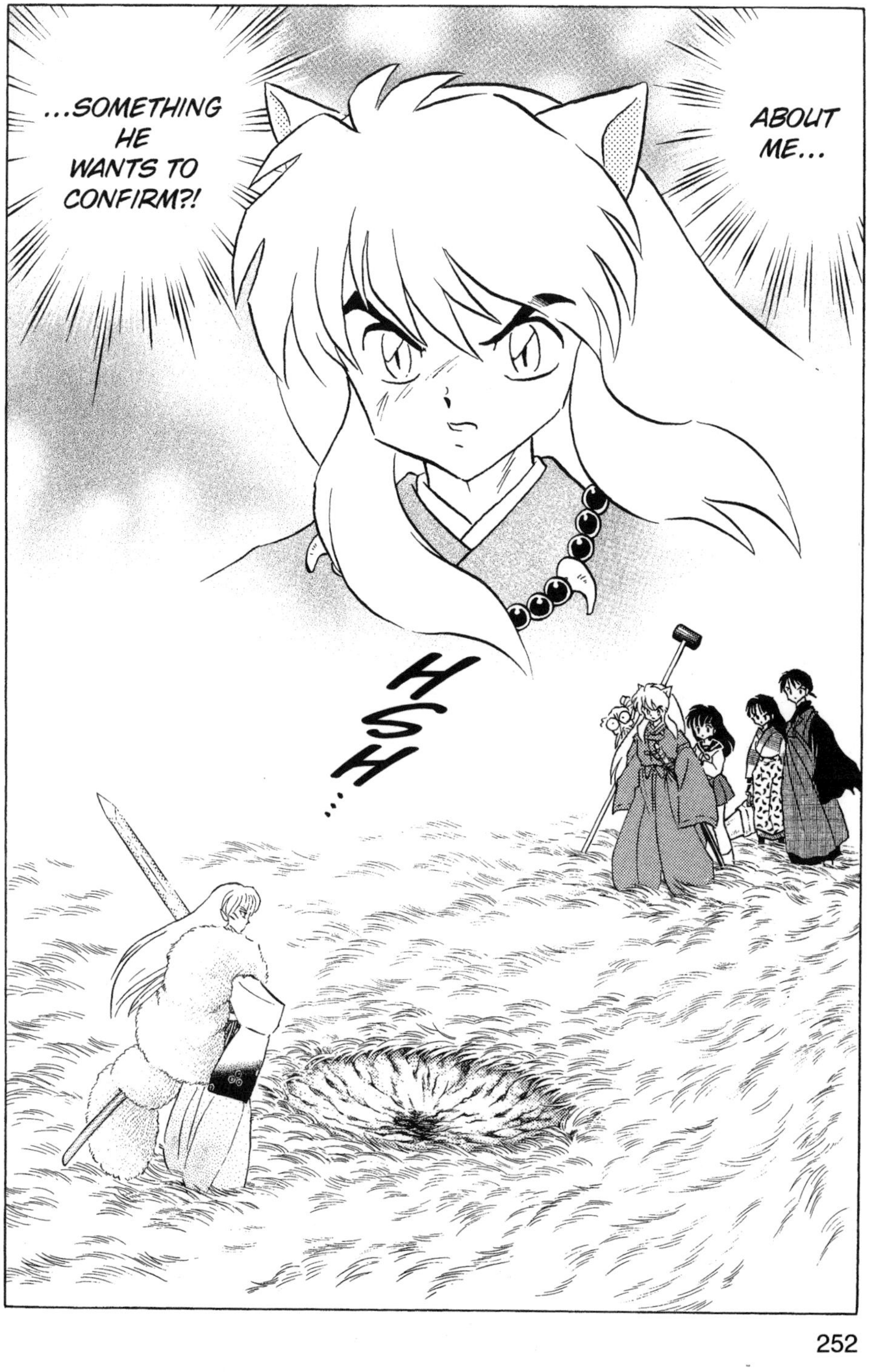
ABOUT ME...
...SOMETHING HE WANTS TO CONFIRM?!
HSH...

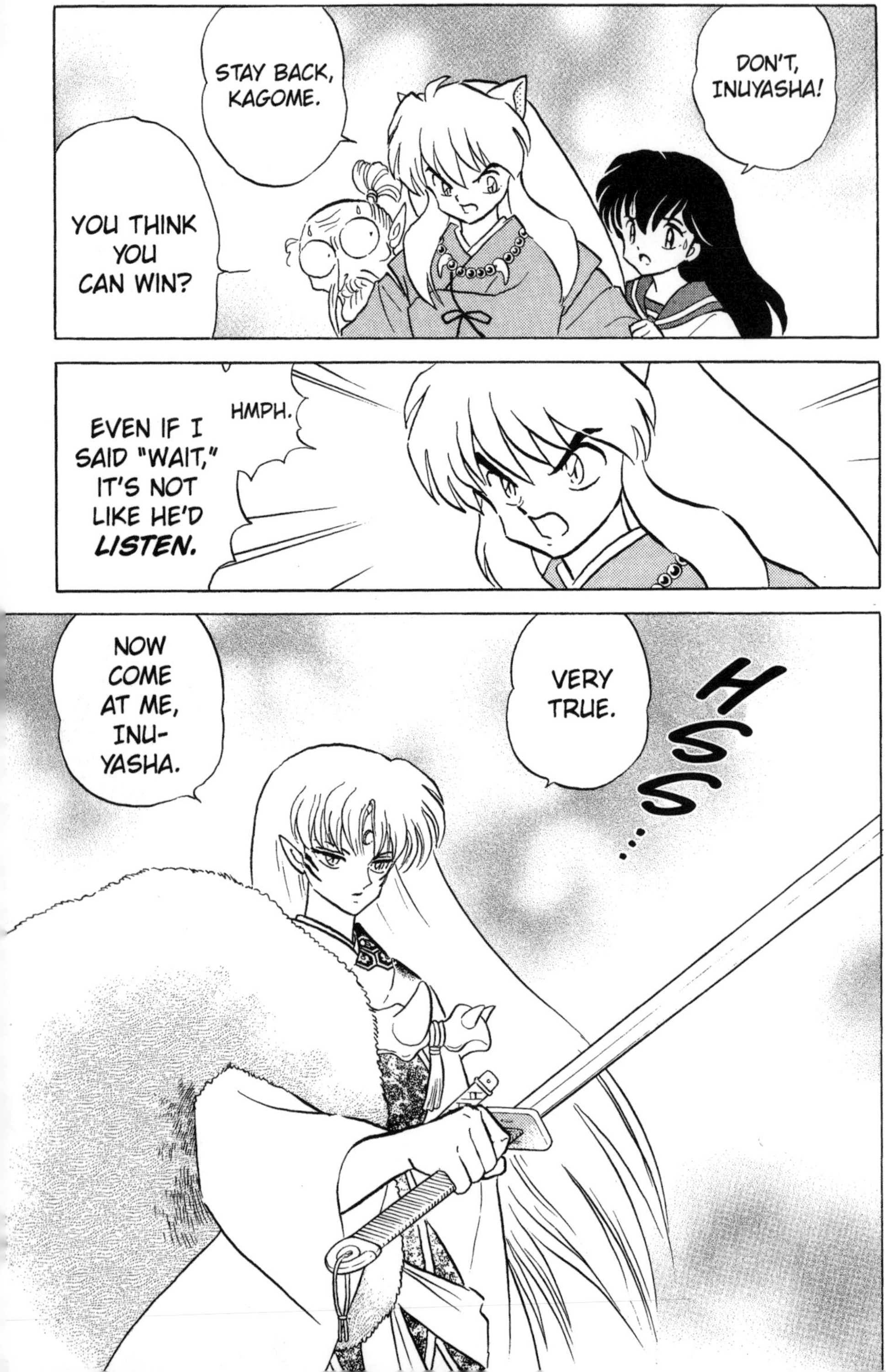
DON'T, INUYASHA!
STAY BACK, KAGOME.
YOU THINK YOU CAN WIN?
HMPH.
EVEN IF I SAID "WAIT," IT'S NOT LIKE HE'D LISTEN.
HSS...
VERY TRUE.
NOW COME AT ME, INU-YASHA.

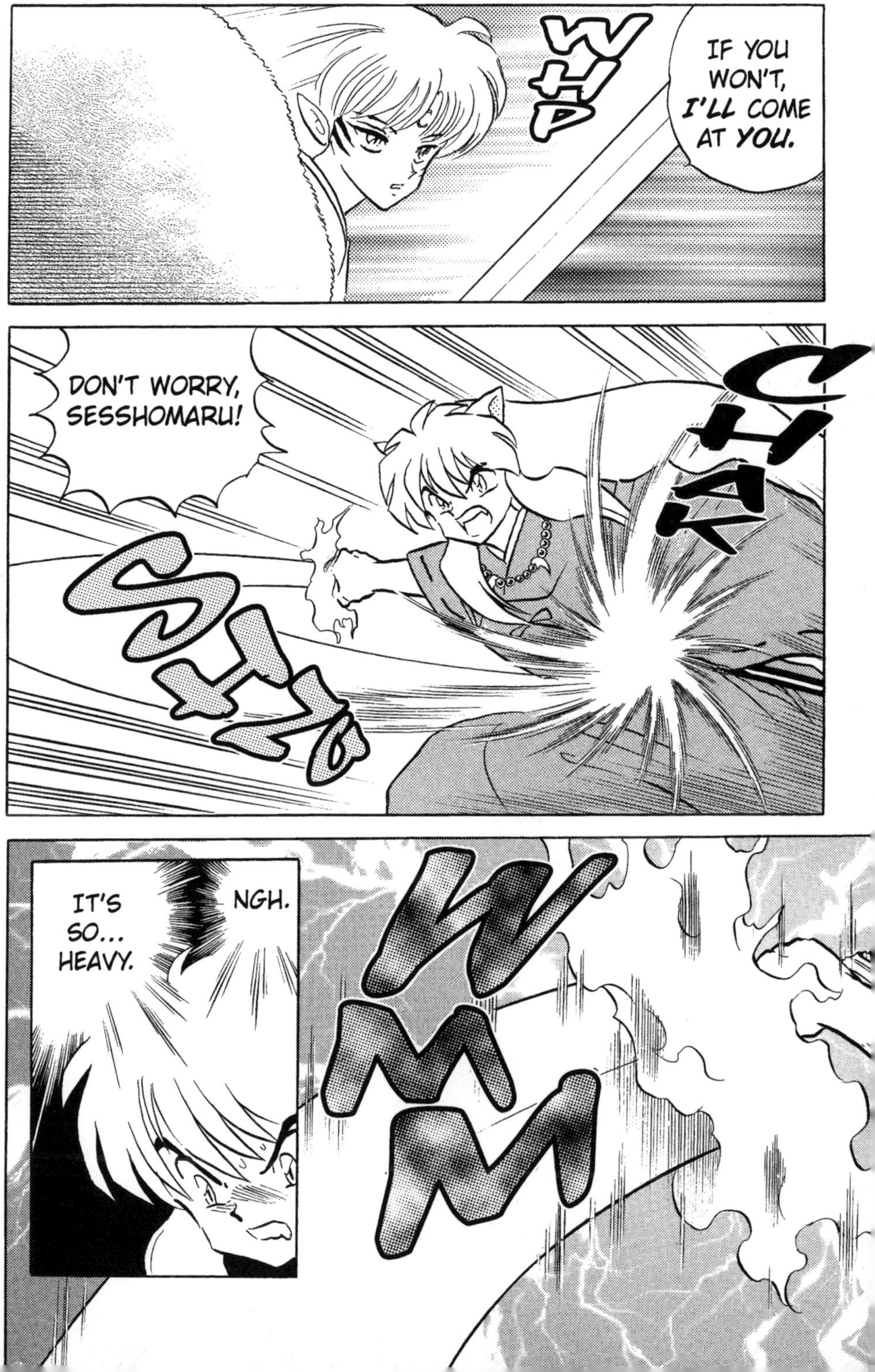
IF YOU WON'T, I'LL COME AT YOU.
WHP
DON'T WORRY, SESSHOMARU!
CHAK
SCHNG
NGH.
IT'S SO... HEAVY.
WMMM

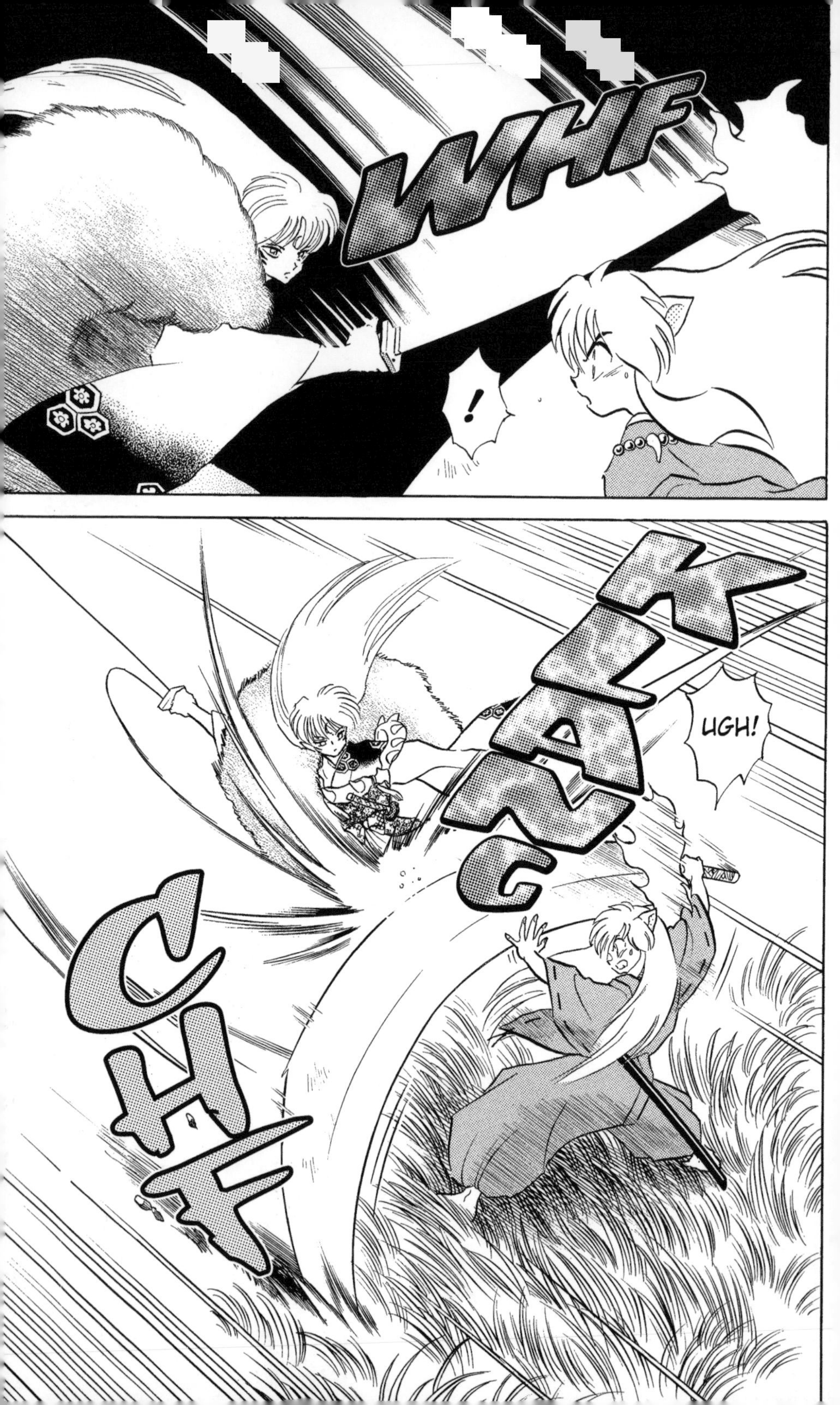
WHF
!
KLANC
UGH!
CHF

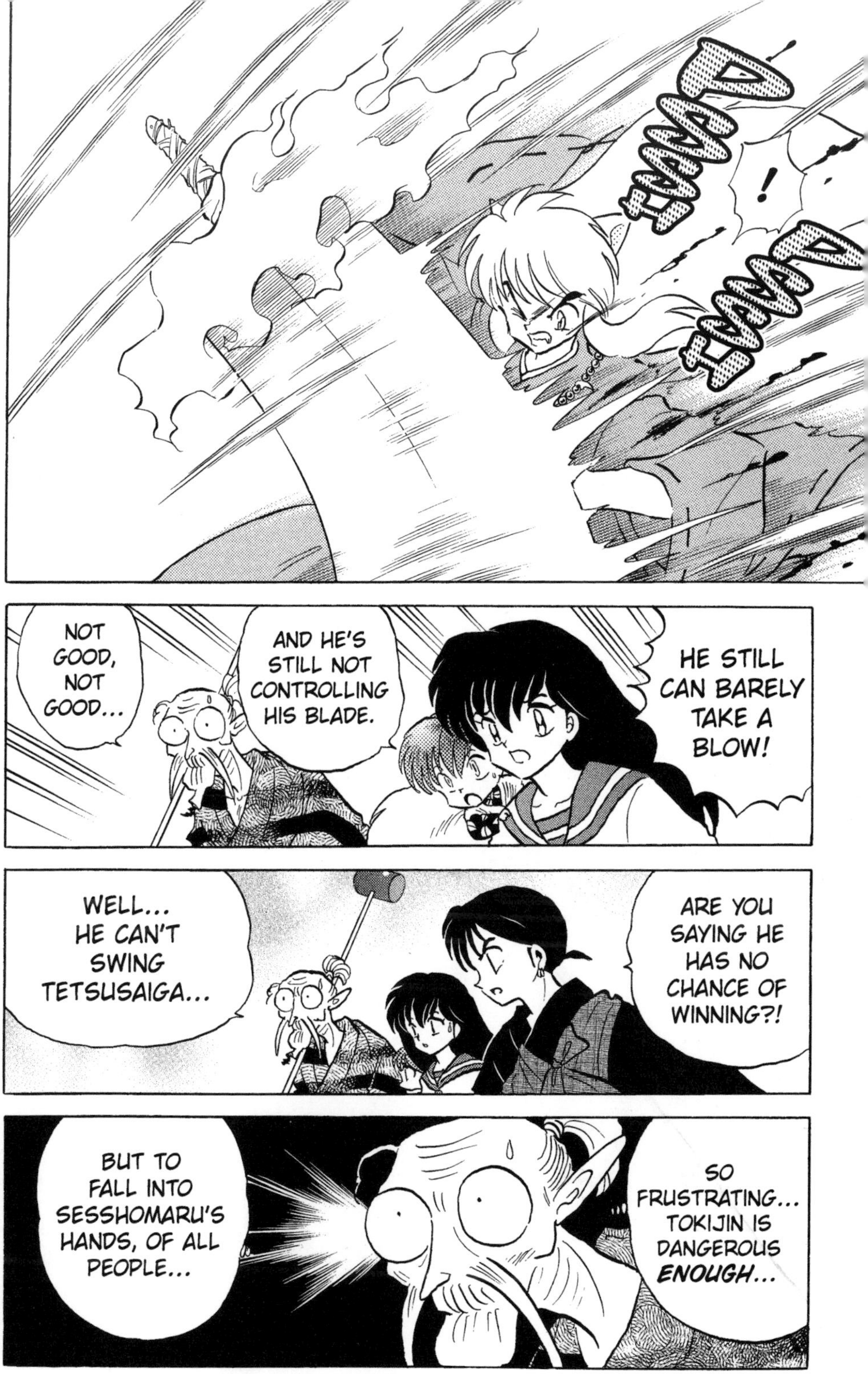
HE STILL CAN BARELY TAKE A BLOW!
AND HE'S STILL NOT CONTROLLING HIS BLADE.
NOT GOOD, NOT GOOD...
ARE YOU SAYING HE HAS NO CHANCE OF WINNING?!
WELL... HE CAN'T SWING TETSUSAIGA...
SO FRUSTRATING... TOKIJIN IS DANGEROUS *ENOUGH*...
BUT TO FALL INTO SESSHOMARU'S HANDS, OF ALL PEOPLE...

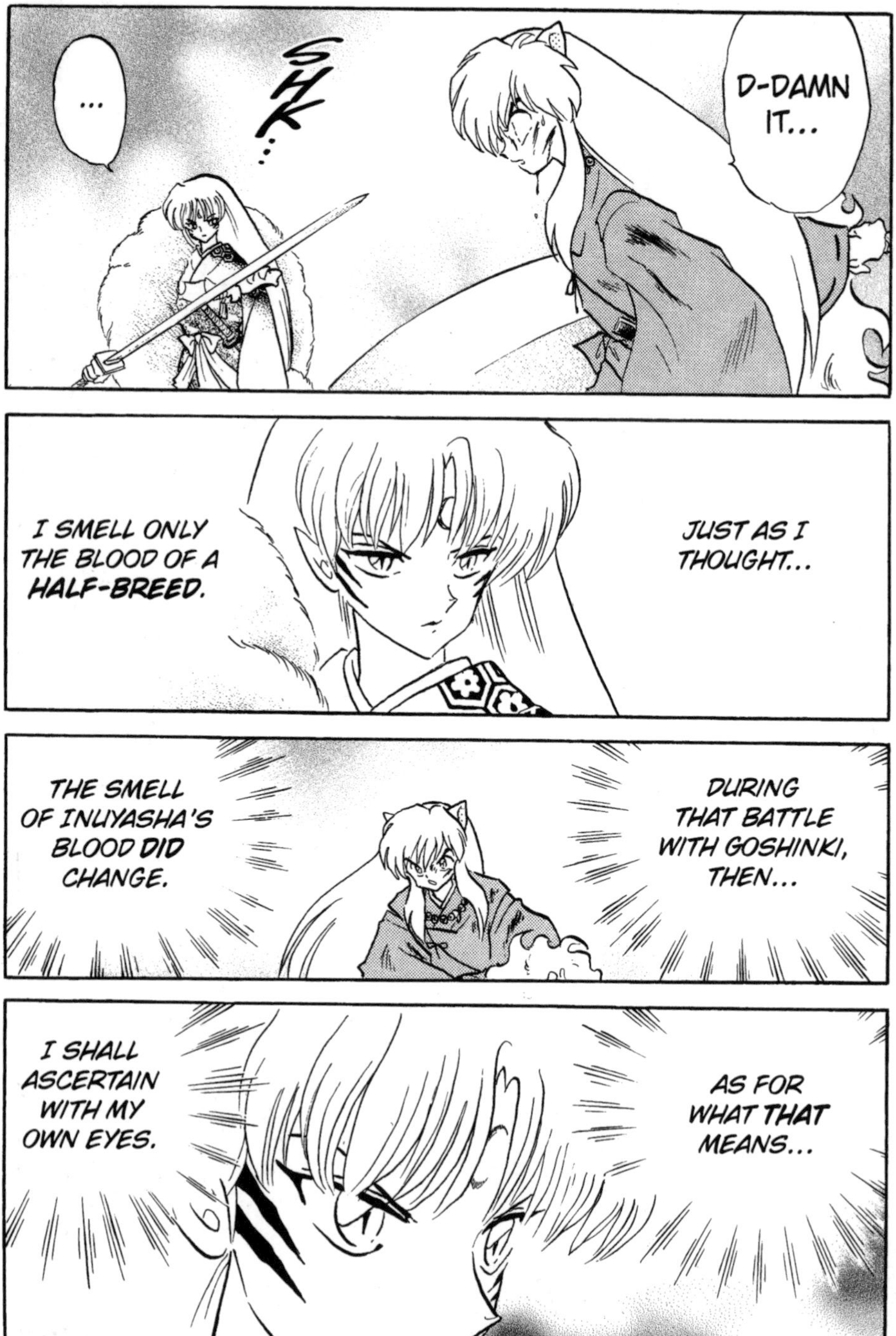
D-DAMN IT...
SHK...
...
JUST AS I THOUGHT...
I SMELL ONLY THE BLOOD OF A HALF-BREED.
DURING THAT BATTLE WITH GOSHINKI, THEN...
THE SMELL OF INUYASHA'S BLOOD DID CHANGE.
AS FOR WHAT THAT MEANS...
I SHALL ASCERTAIN WITH MY OWN EYES.

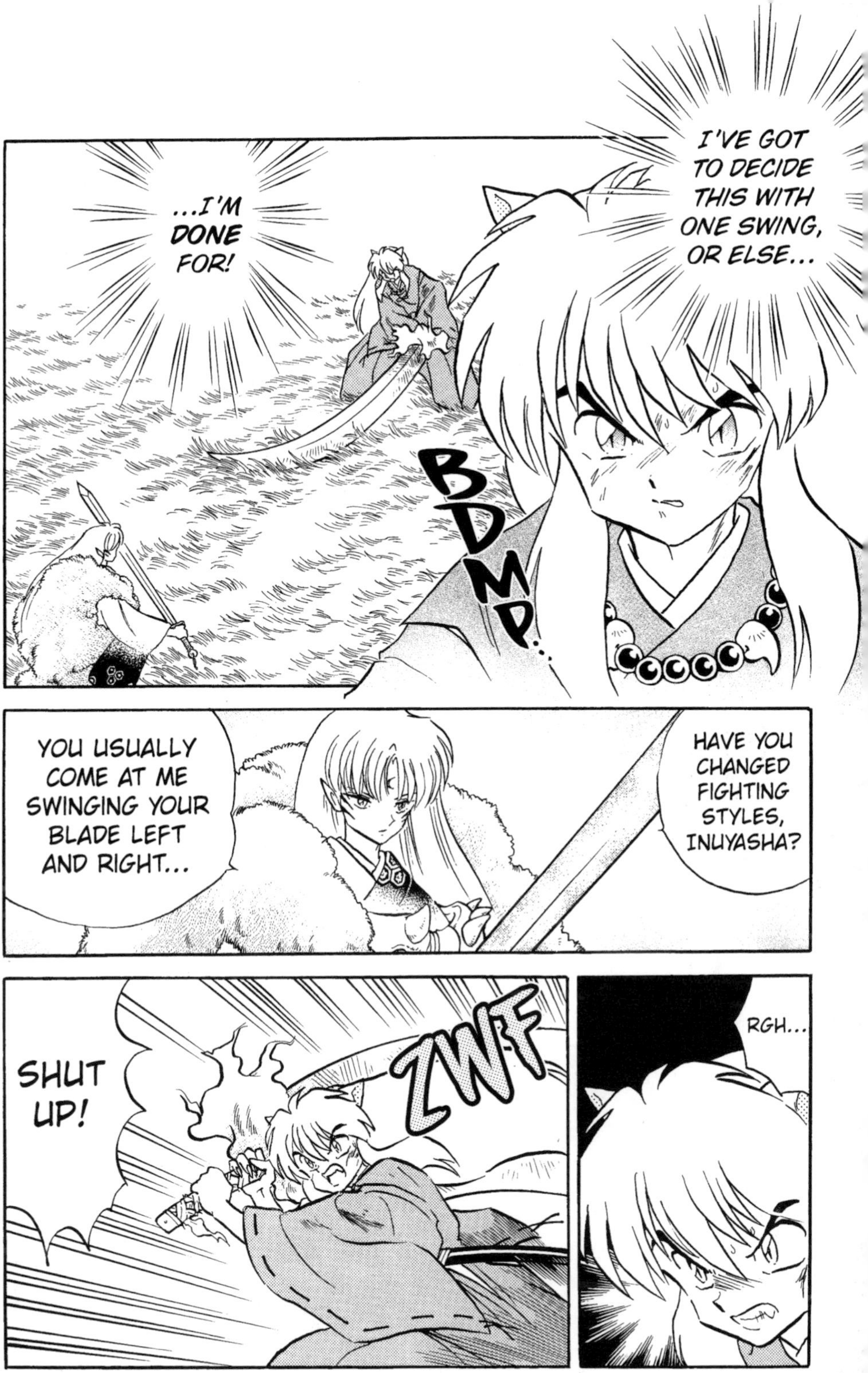
I'VE GOT TO DECIDE THIS WITH ONE SWING, OR ELSE...
...I'M DONE FOR!
BDMP...
HAVE YOU CHANGED FIGHTING STYLES, INUYASHA?
YOU USUALLY COME AT ME SWINGING YOUR BLADE LEFT AND RIGHT...
RGH...
SHUT UP!
ZWF

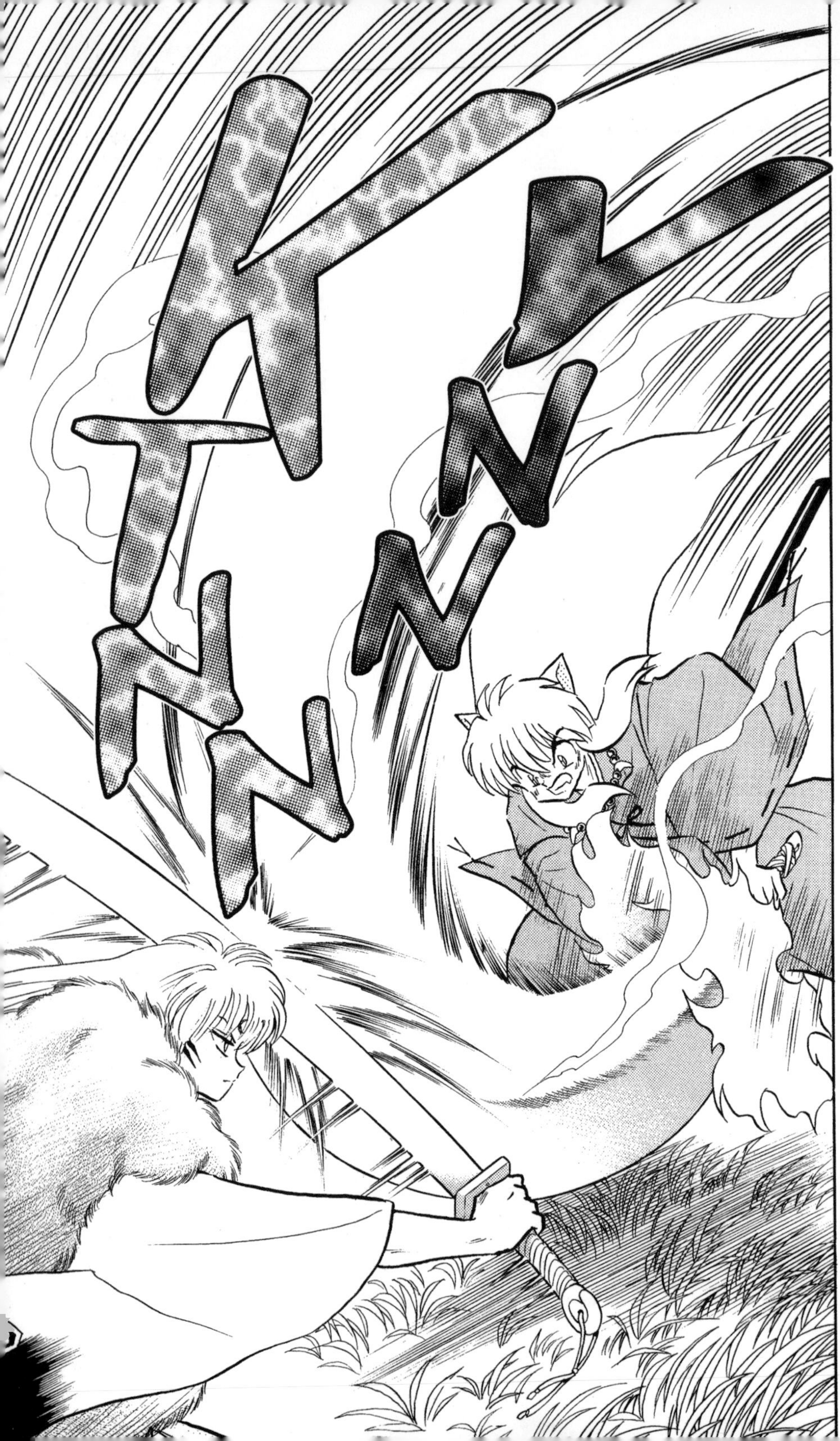
KATINNNNN

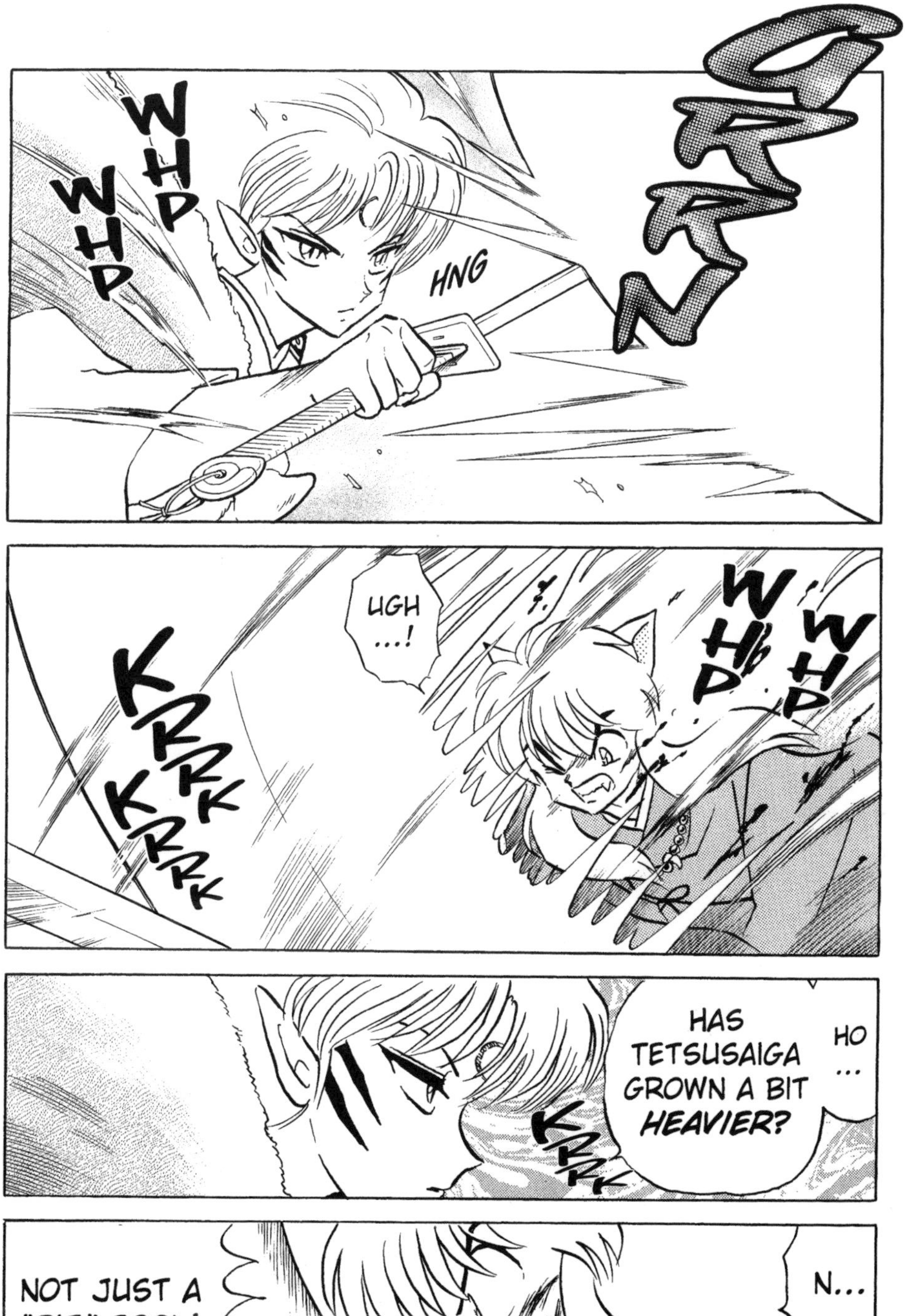
GARAN
HNG
WHP WHP
WHP WHP
UGH ...!
KRRRK KRRRK
HO ...
HAS TETSUSAIGA GROWN A BIT *HEAVIER?*
KRRRK
N...
NOT JUST A "BIT," FOOL!

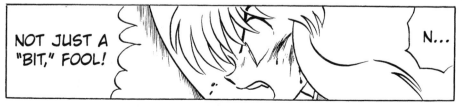

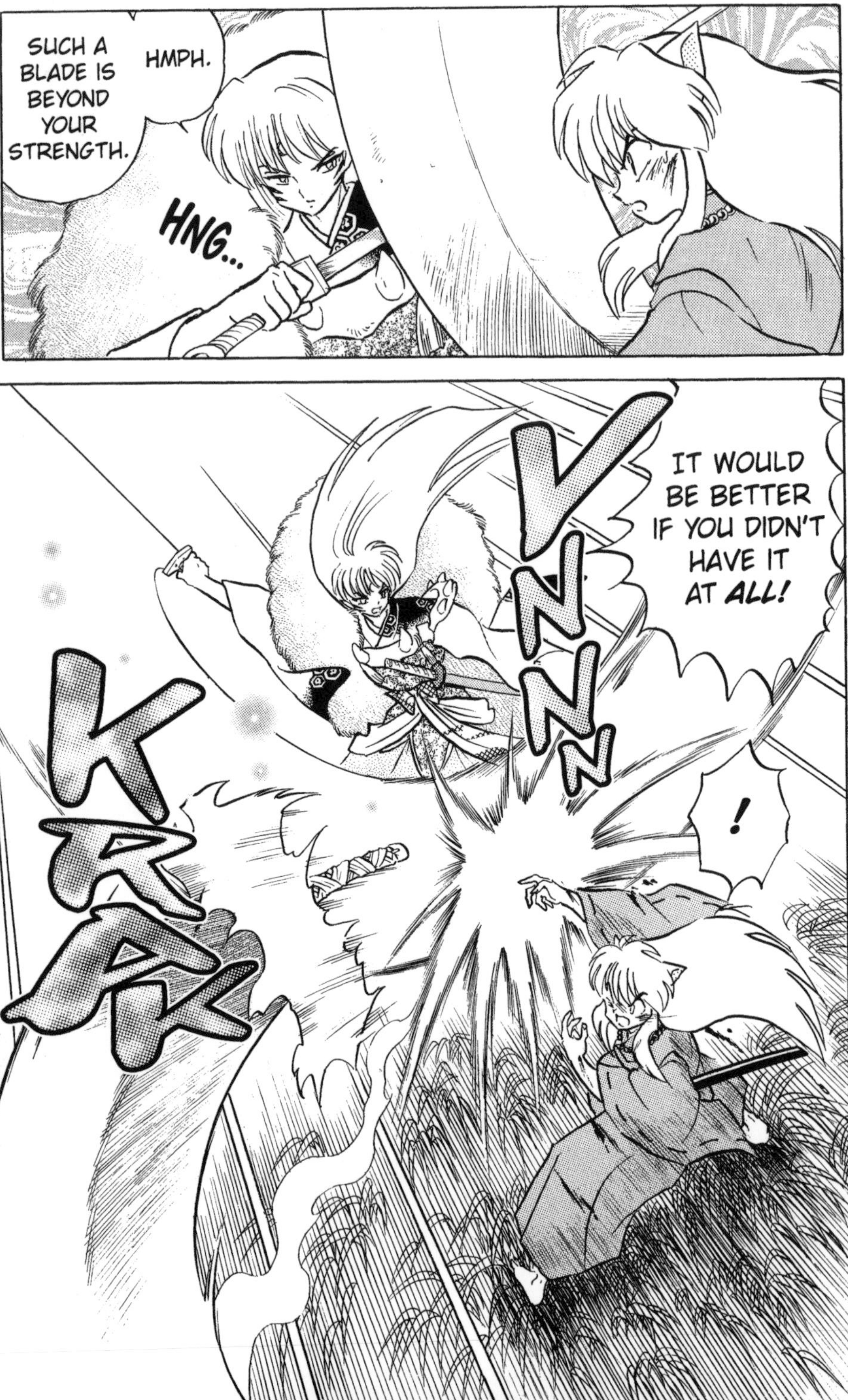
HMPH.
SUCH A BLADE IS BEYOND YOUR STRENGTH.
HNG...
IT WOULD BE BETTER IF YOU DIDN'T HAVE IT AT **ALL!**
VNNNN
!
KRAK

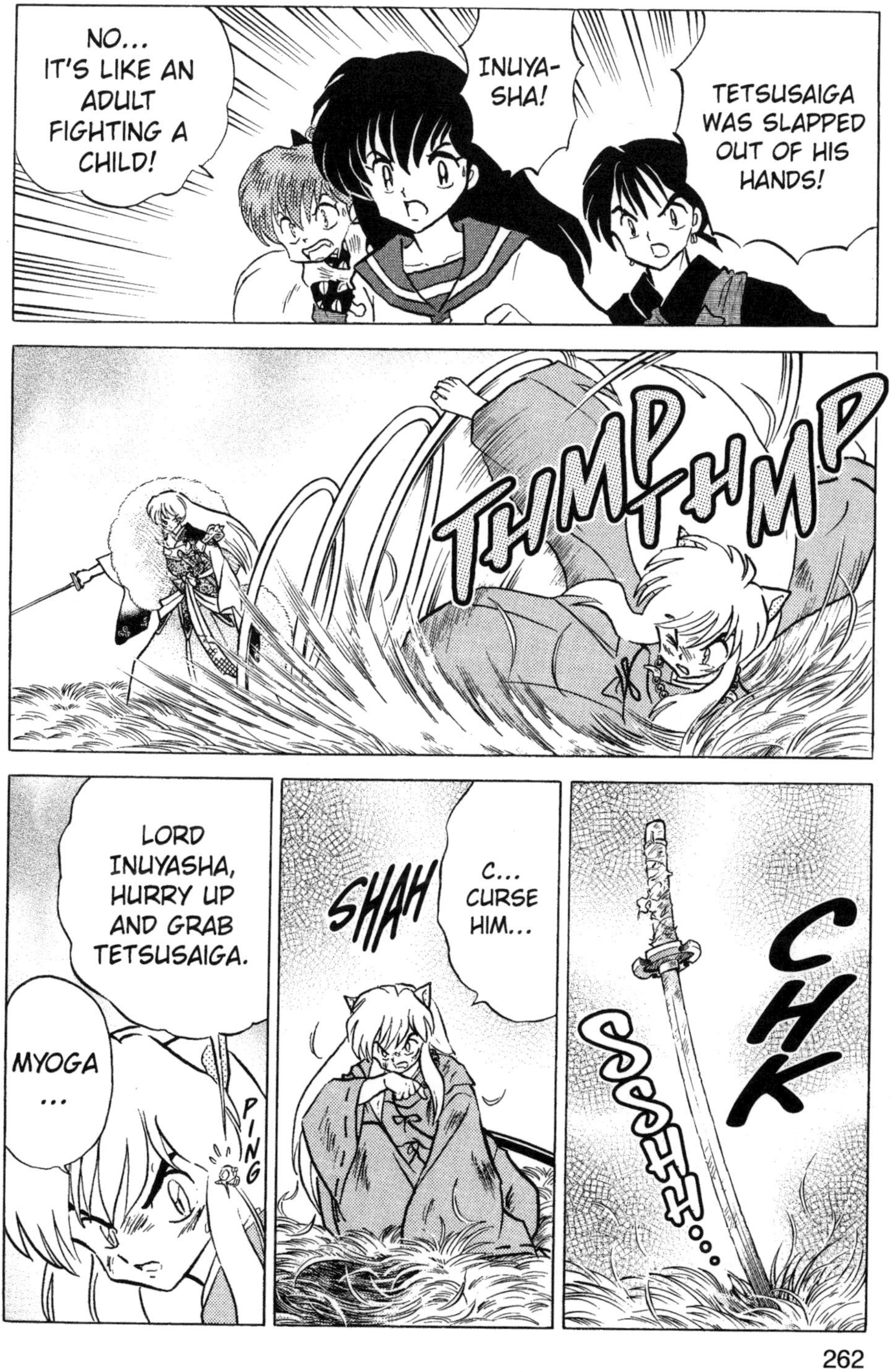
TETSUSAIGA WAS SLAPPED OUT OF HIS HANDS!
INUYA-SHA!
NO... IT'S LIKE AN ADULT FIGHTING A CHILD!
THMP THMP
CHK
SSSHHH...
C... CURSE HIM...
SHAH
LORD INUYASHA, HURRY UP AND GRAB TETSUSAIGA.
PING
MYOGA ...

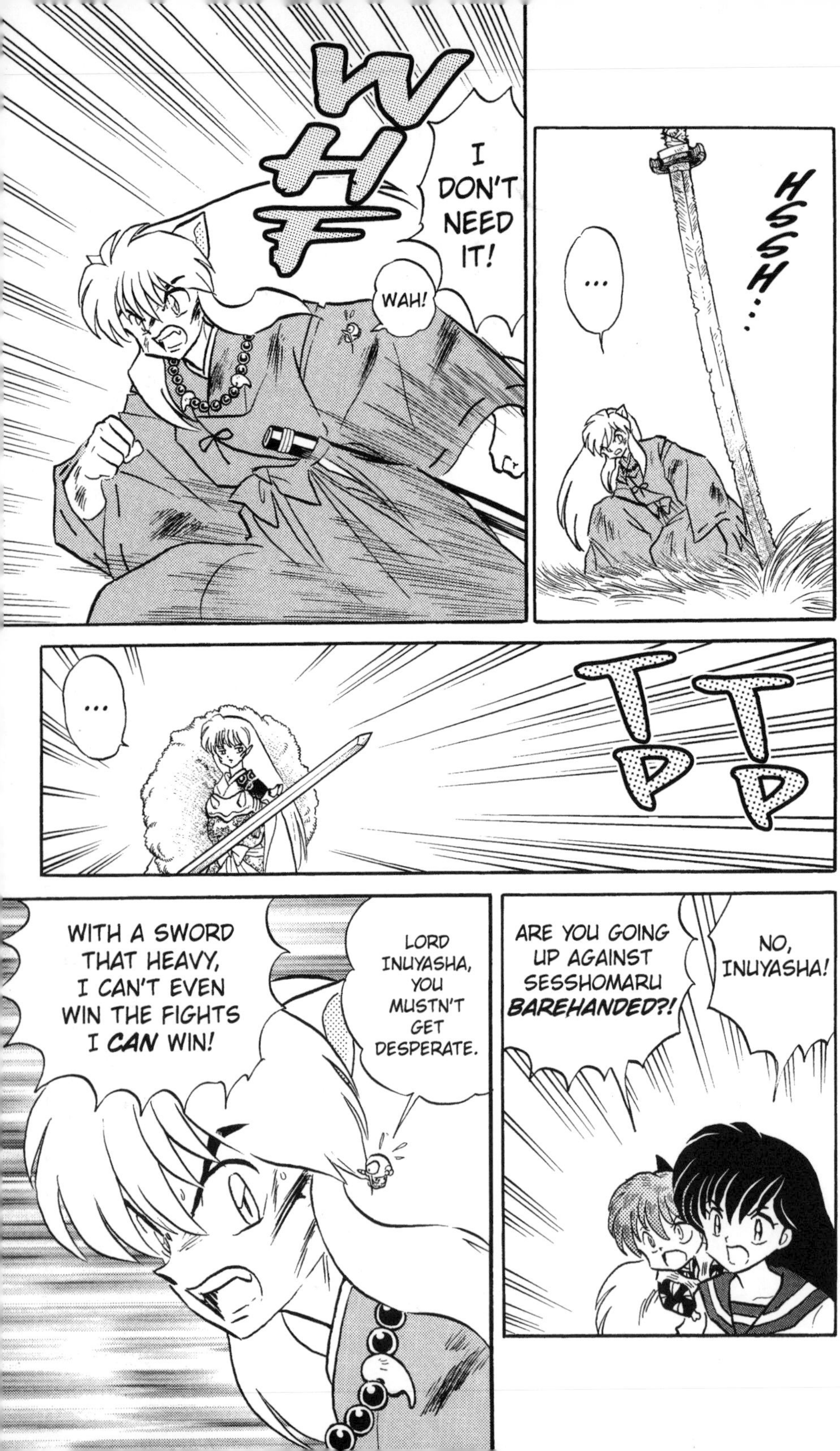
HSSH...
...
I DON'T NEED IT!
WHIF
WAH!
TTP TTP
...
NO, INUYASHA!
ARE YOU GOING UP AGAINST SESSHOMARU **BAREHANDED?!**
LORD INUYASHA, YOU MUSTN'T GET DESPERATE.
WITH A SWORD THAT HEAVY, I CAN'T EVEN WIN THE FIGHTS I **CAN** WIN!

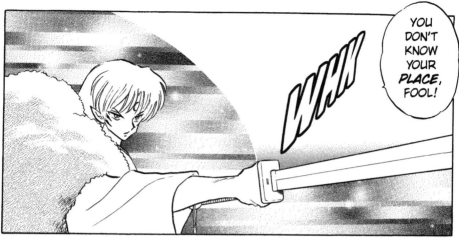

YOU DON'T KNOW YOUR *PLACE*, FOOL!

WHK

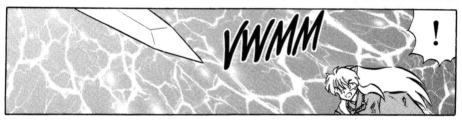

VWMM

!

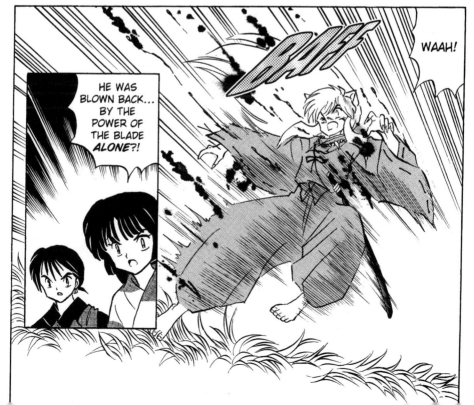

FLL

WAAH!

HE WAS BLOWN BACK... BY THE POWER OF THE BLADE *ALONE*?!

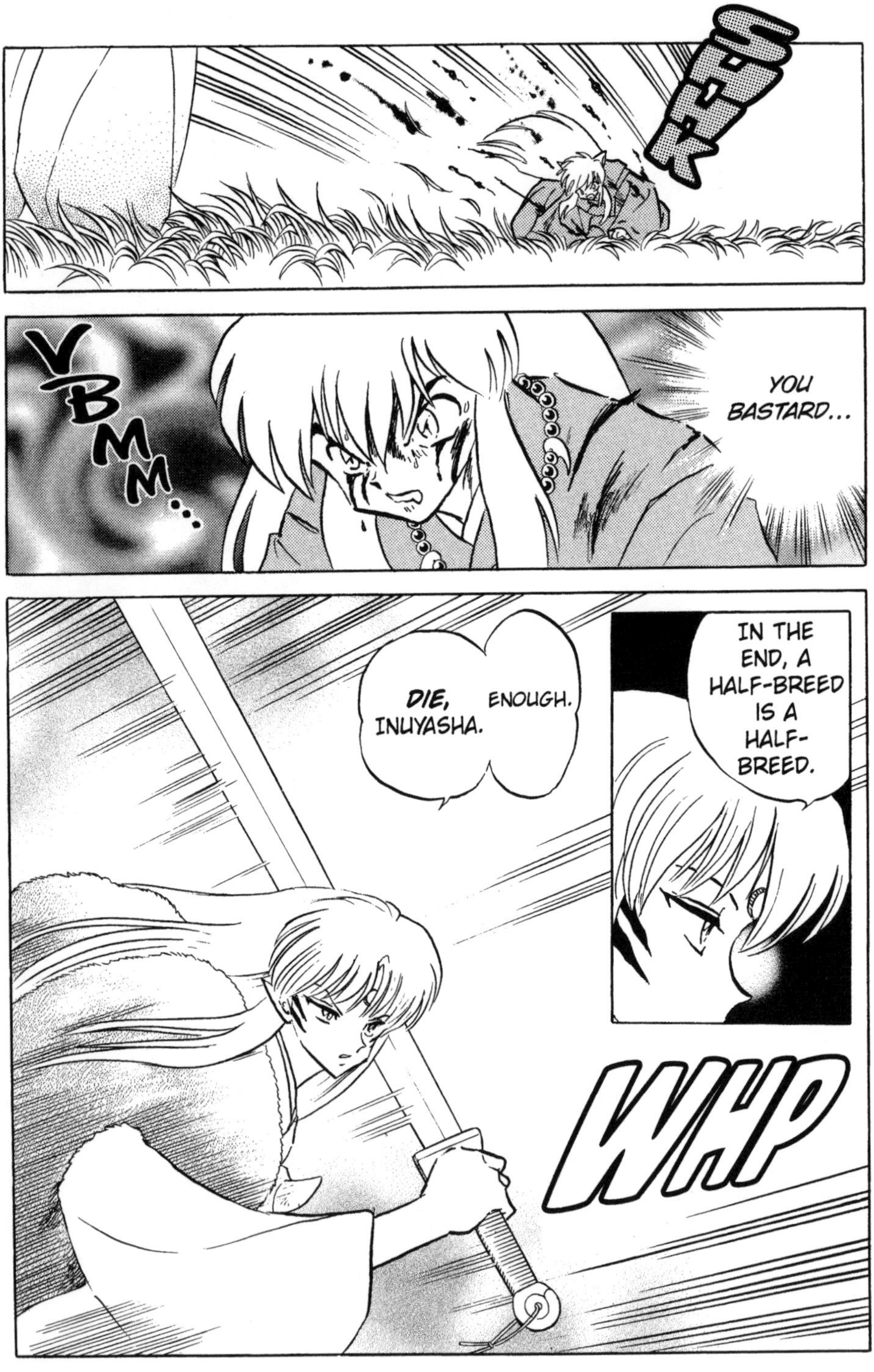
SHK
VBMM...
YOU BASTARD...
IN THE END, A HALF-BREED IS A HALF-BREED.
ENOUGH.
DIE, INUYASHA.
WHP

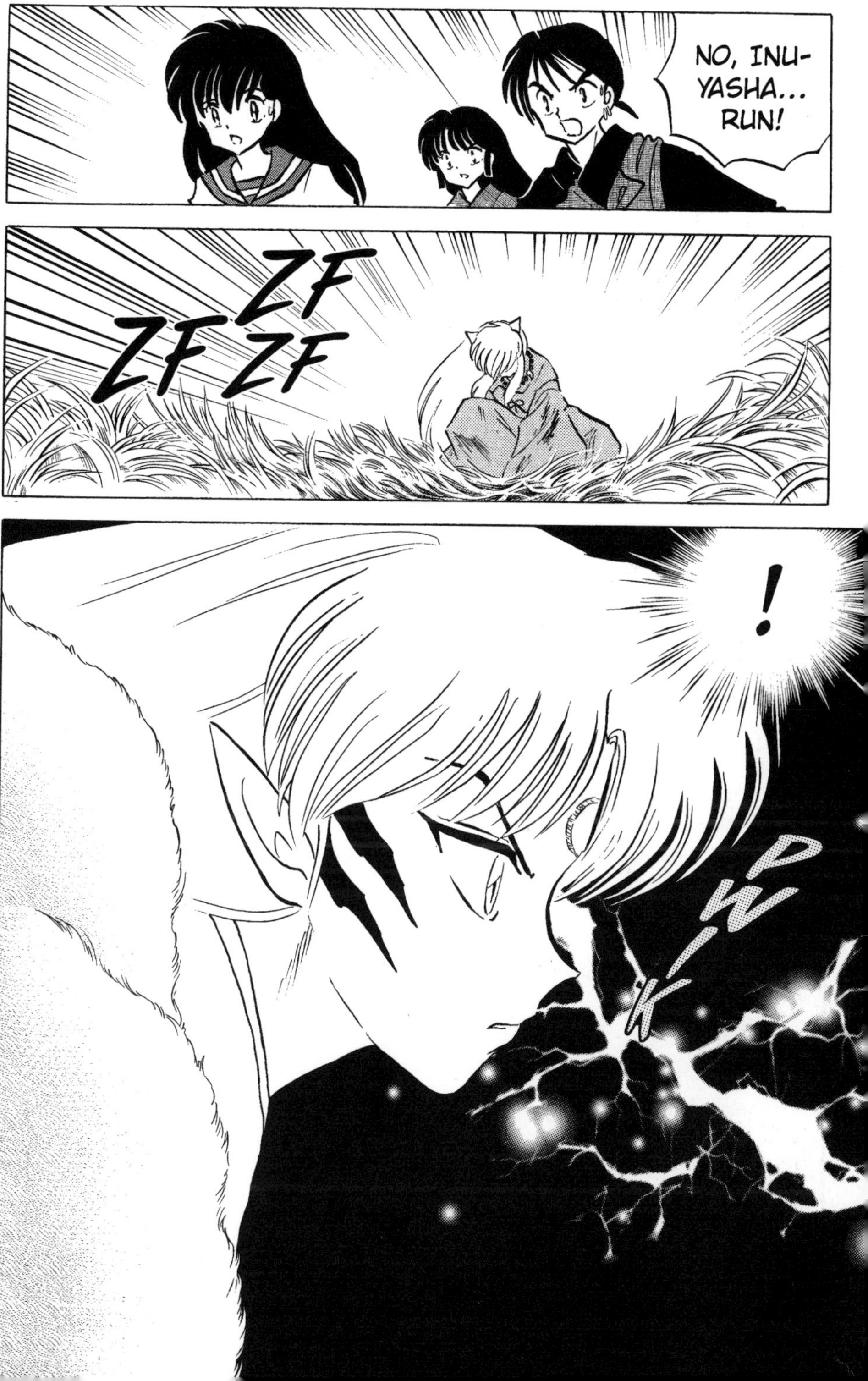
NO, INU-YASHA... RUN!
ZF ZF ZF ZF
!
PWIK

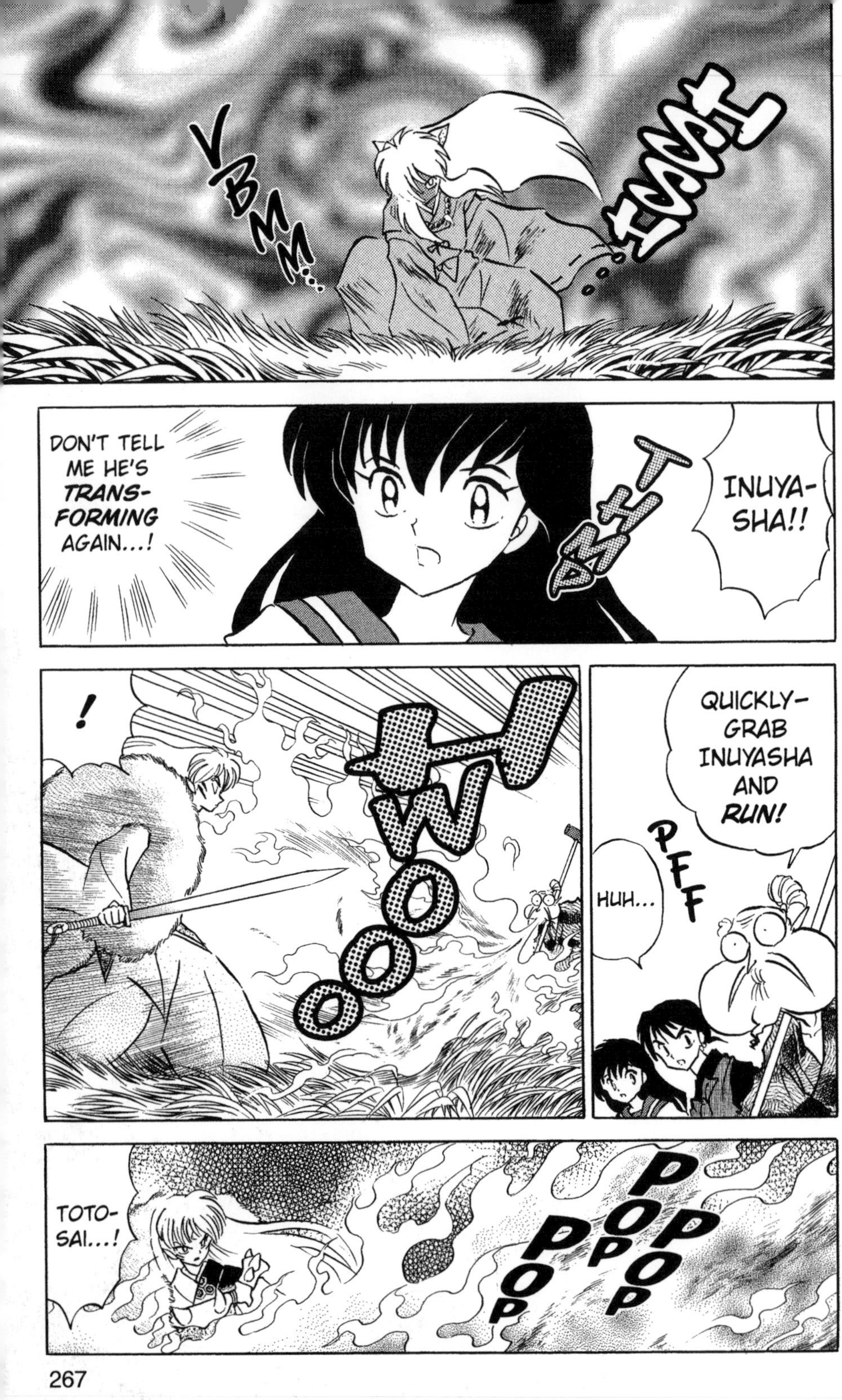
VBMM...
INUYA-SHA!!
THMP
DON'T TELL ME HE'S *TRANS-FORMING* AGAIN...!
QUICKLY-GRAB INUYASHA AND *RUN!*
PFF
HUH...
!
HWOOOOO
POP POP POP POP POP
TOTO-SAI...!

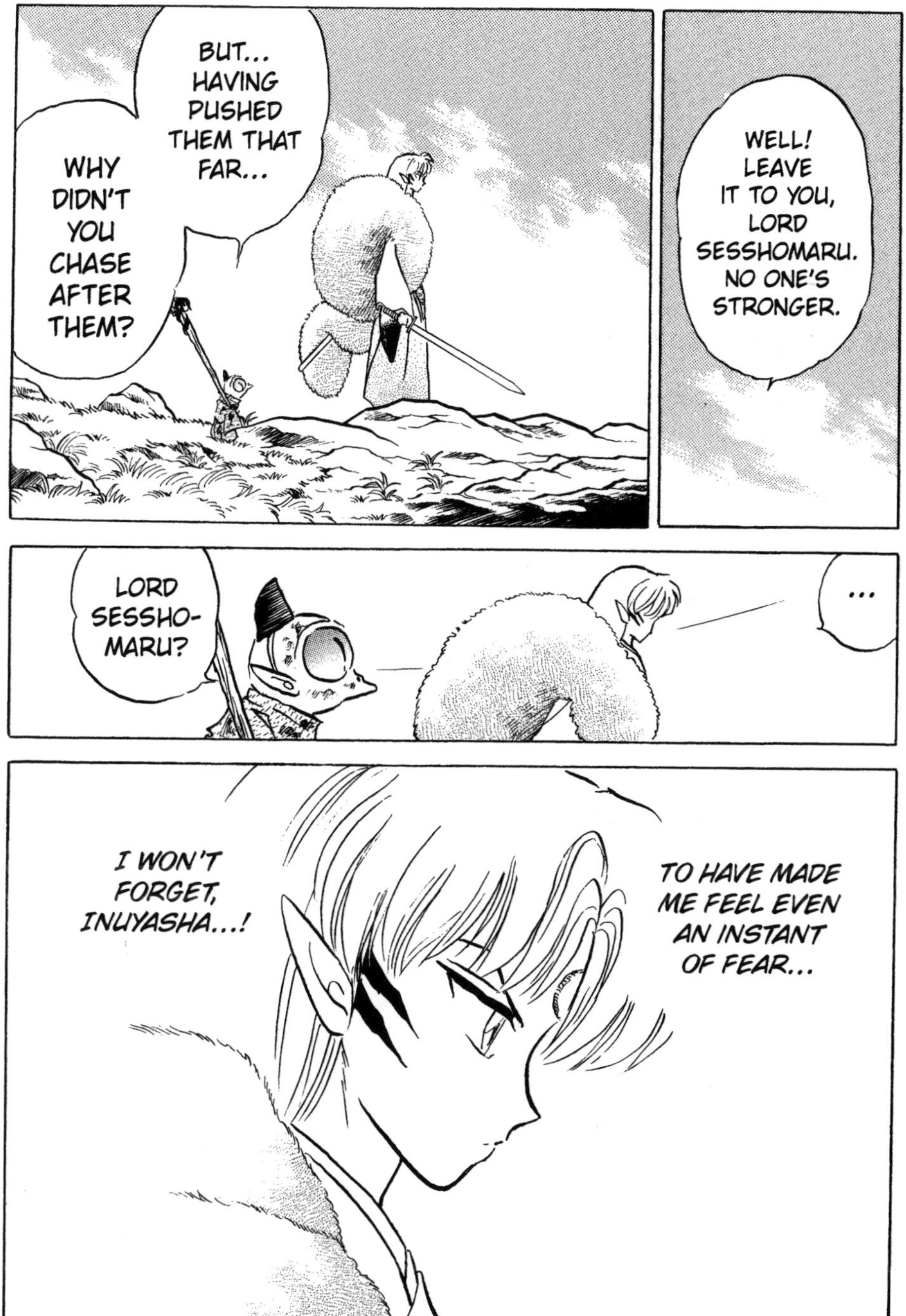
WELL! LEAVE IT TO YOU, LORD SESSHOMARU. NO ONE'S STRONGER.
BUT... HAVING PUSHED THEM THAT FAR...
WHY DIDN'T YOU CHASE AFTER THEM?
...
LORD SESSHO-MARU?
TO HAVE MADE ME FEEL EVEN AN INSTANT OF FEAR...
I WON'T FORGET, INUYASHA...!

SCROLL FIVE
TRUE STRENGTH

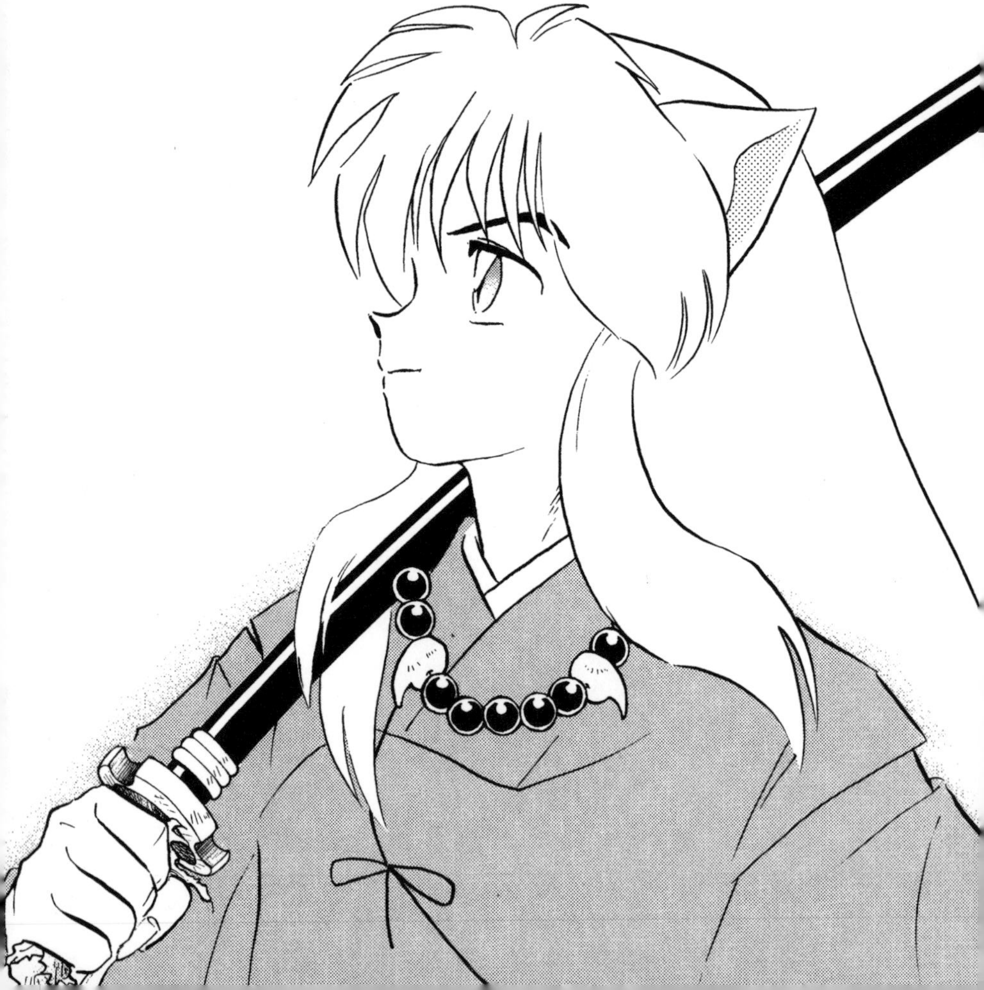

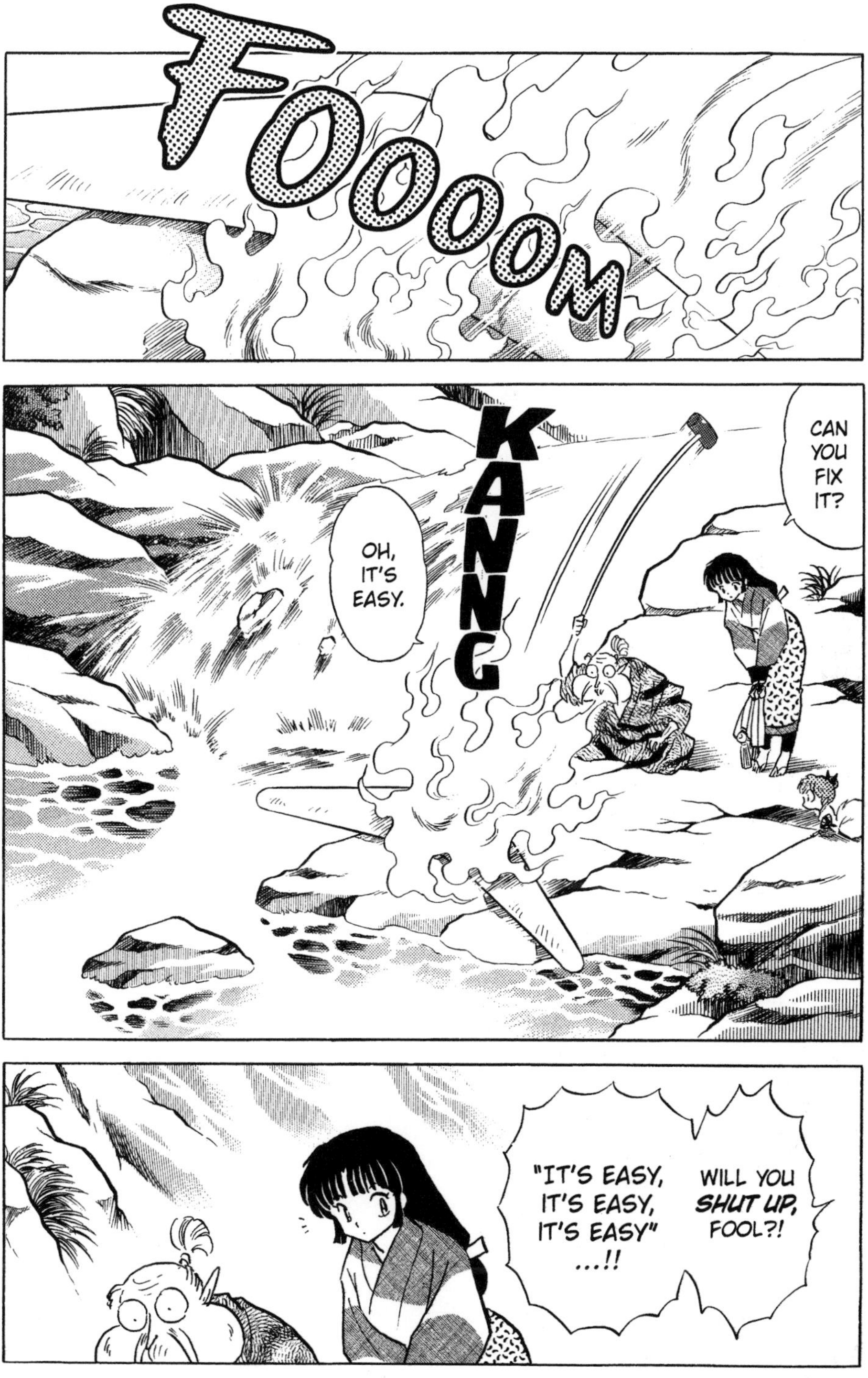
FOOOOOM
CAN YOU FIX IT?
KANNG
OH, IT'S EASY.
"IT'S EASY, IT'S EASY, IT'S EASY" ...!!
WILL YOU **SHUT UP,** FOOL?!

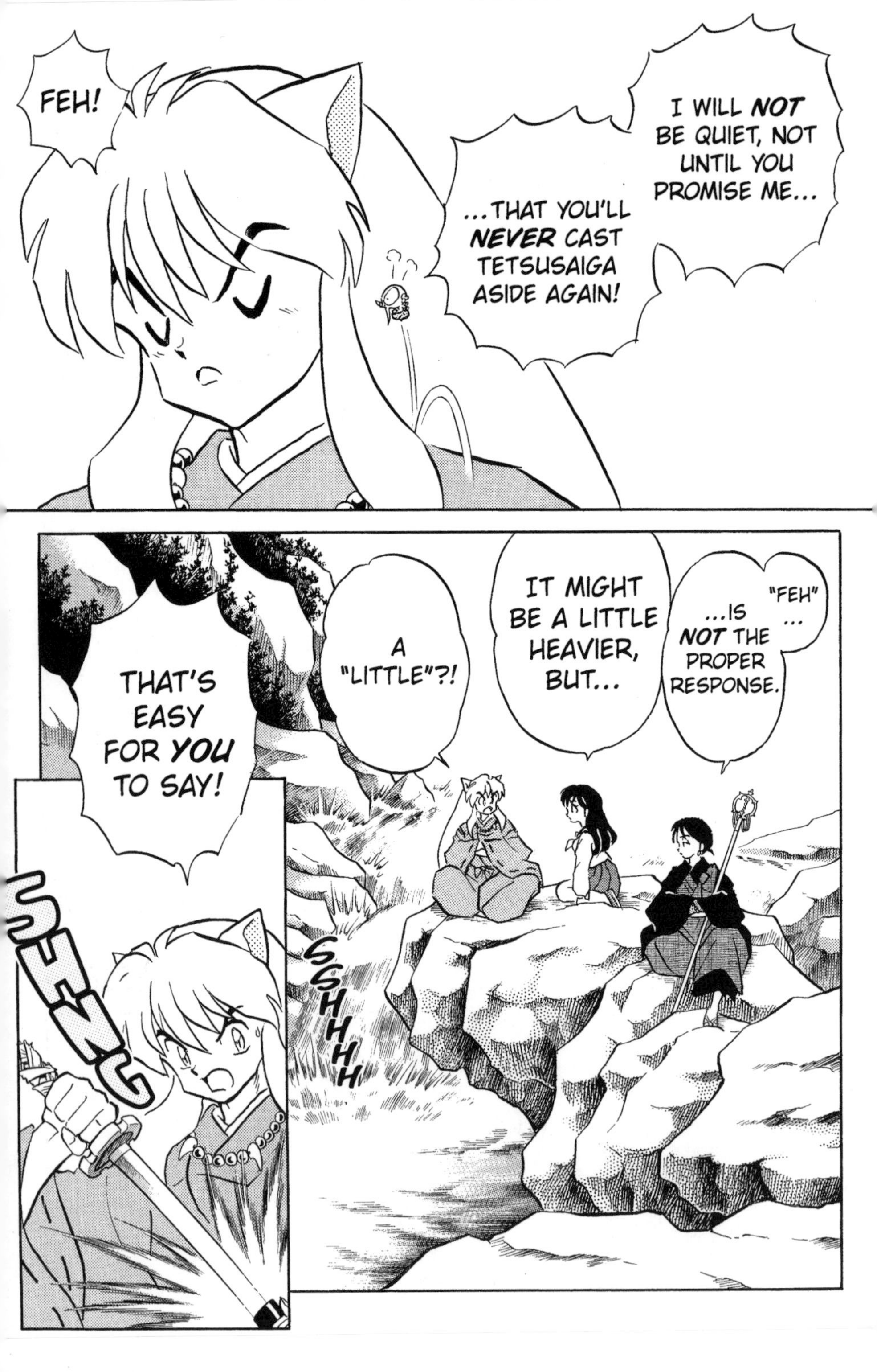
I WILL NOT BE QUIET, NOT UNTIL YOU PROMISE ME...
...THAT YOU'LL NEVER CAST TETSUSAIGA ASIDE AGAIN!
FEH!
"FEH"...
...IS NOT THE PROPER RESPONSE.
IT MIGHT BE A LITTLE HEAVIER, BUT...
A "LITTLE"?!
SSHHHH
THAT'S EASY FOR YOU TO SAY!
SHING

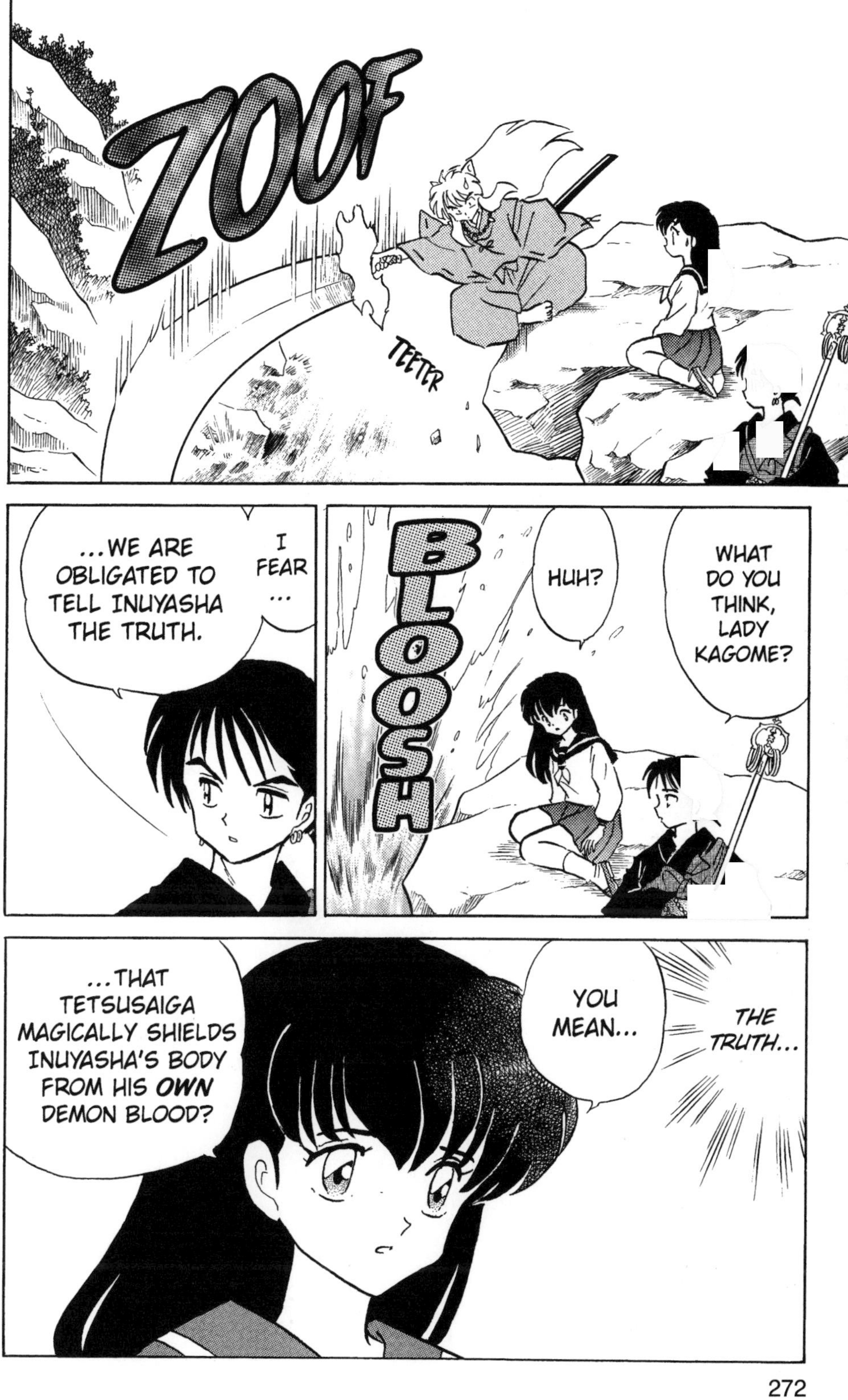
ZOOF
TEETER
WHAT DO YOU THINK, LADY KAGOME?
HUH?
BLOOSH
I FEAR...
...WE ARE OBLIGATED TO TELL INUYASHA THE TRUTH.
THE TRUTH...
YOU MEAN...
...THAT TETSUSAIGA MAGICALLY SHIELDS INUYASHA'S BODY FROM HIS *OWN* DEMON BLOOD?

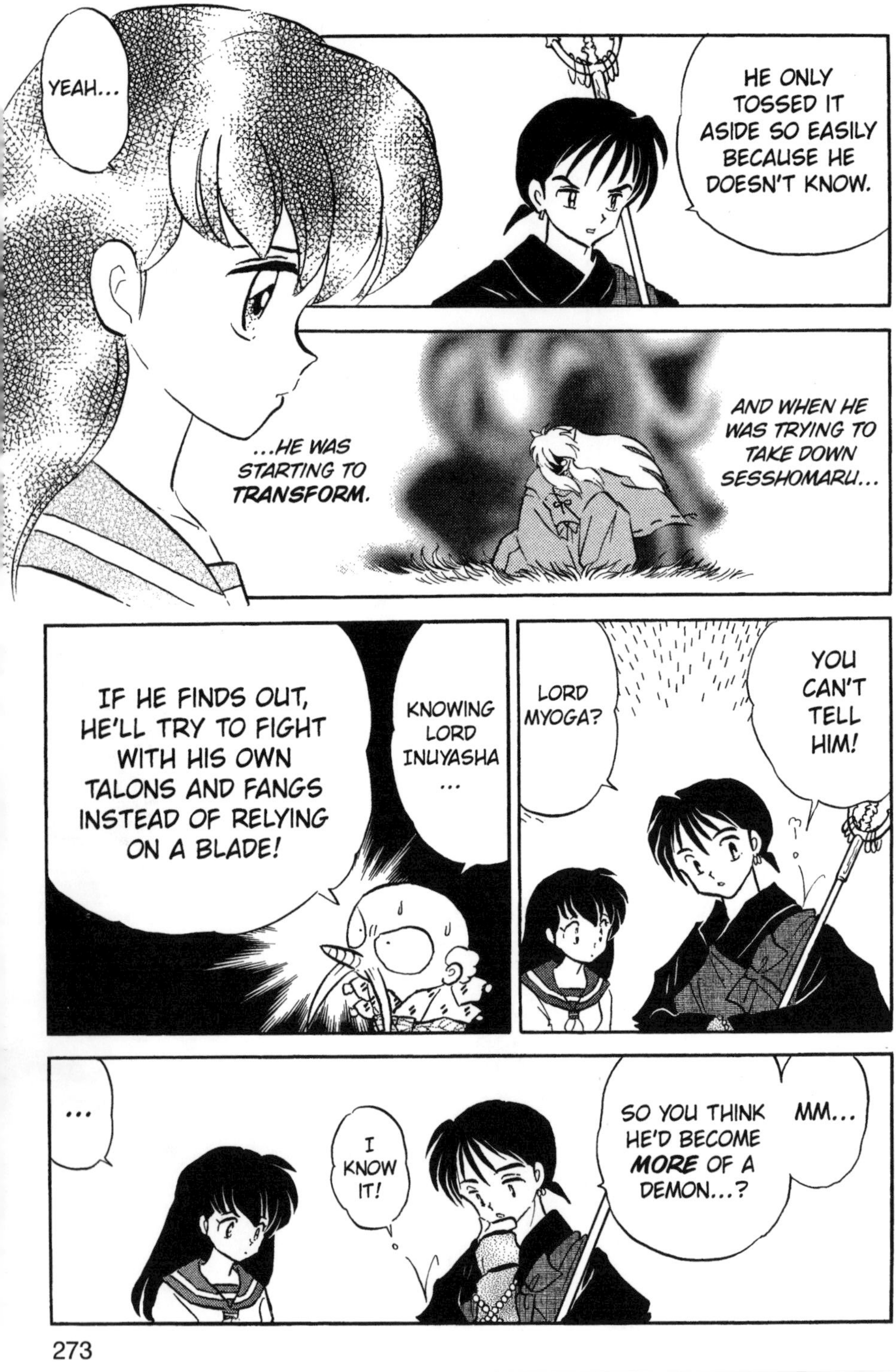
HE ONLY TOSSED IT ASIDE SO EASILY BECAUSE HE DOESN'T KNOW.
AND WHEN HE WAS TRYING TO TAKE DOWN SESSHOMARU...
...HE WAS STARTING TO *TRANSFORM.*
YEAH...
YOU CAN'T TELL HIM!
LORD MYOGA?
KNOWING LORD INUYASHA ...
IF HE FINDS OUT, HE'LL TRY TO FIGHT WITH HIS OWN TALONS AND FANGS INSTEAD OF RELYING ON A BLADE!
MM...
SO YOU THINK HE'D BECOME *MORE* OF A DEMON...?
I KNOW IT!
...

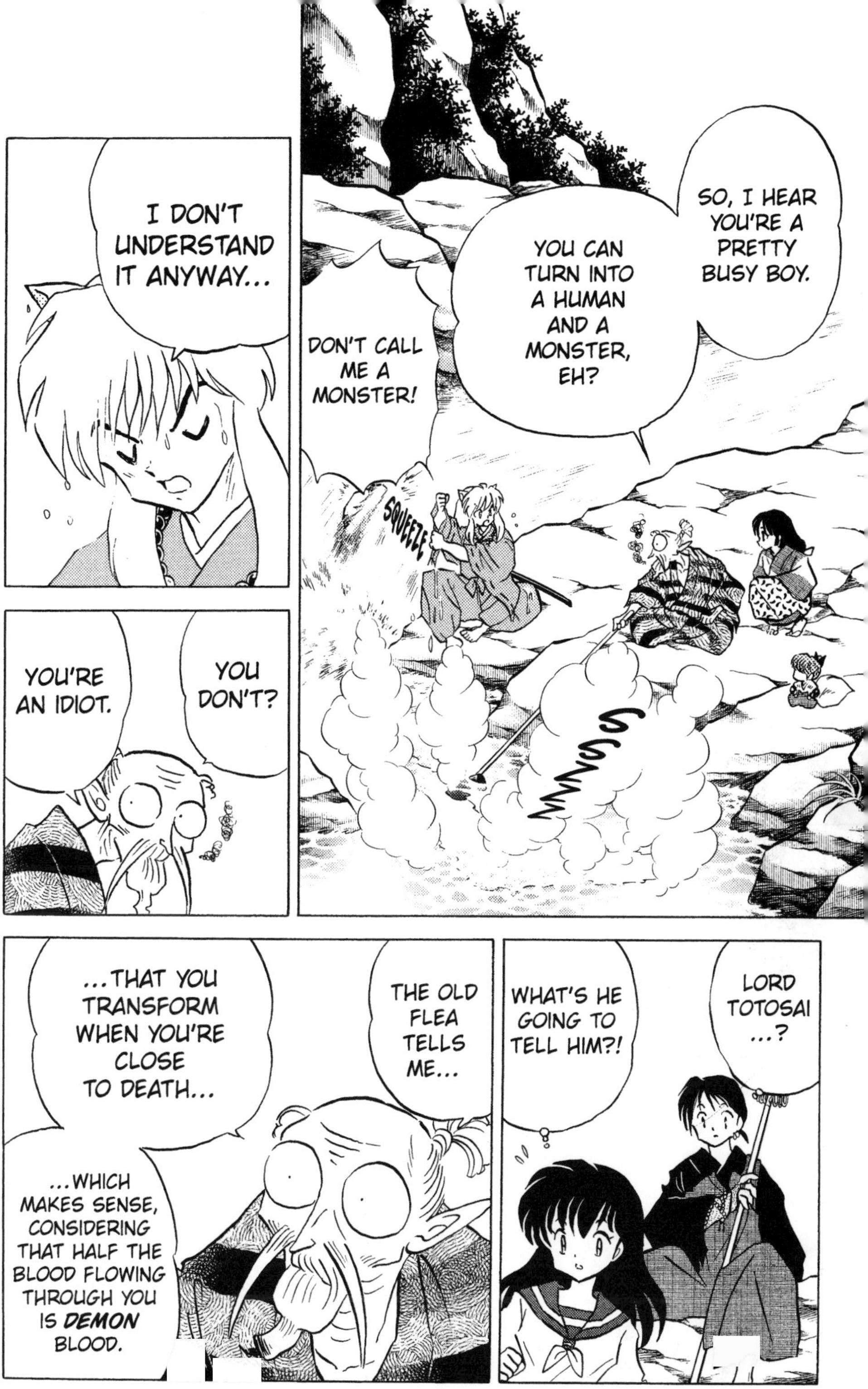
SO, I HEAR YOU'RE A PRETTY BUSY BOY.
YOU CAN TURN INTO A HUMAN AND A MONSTER, EH?
DON'T CALL ME A MONSTER!
SQUEEZE
I DON'T UNDERSTAND IT ANYWAY...
YOU DON'T?
YOU'RE AN IDIOT.
LORD TOTOSAI ...?
WHAT'S HE GOING TO TELL HIM?!
THE OLD FLEA TELLS ME...
...THAT YOU TRANSFORM WHEN YOU'RE CLOSE TO DEATH...
...WHICH MAKES SENSE, CONSIDERING THAT HALF THE BLOOD FLOWING THROUGH YOU IS DEMON BLOOD.

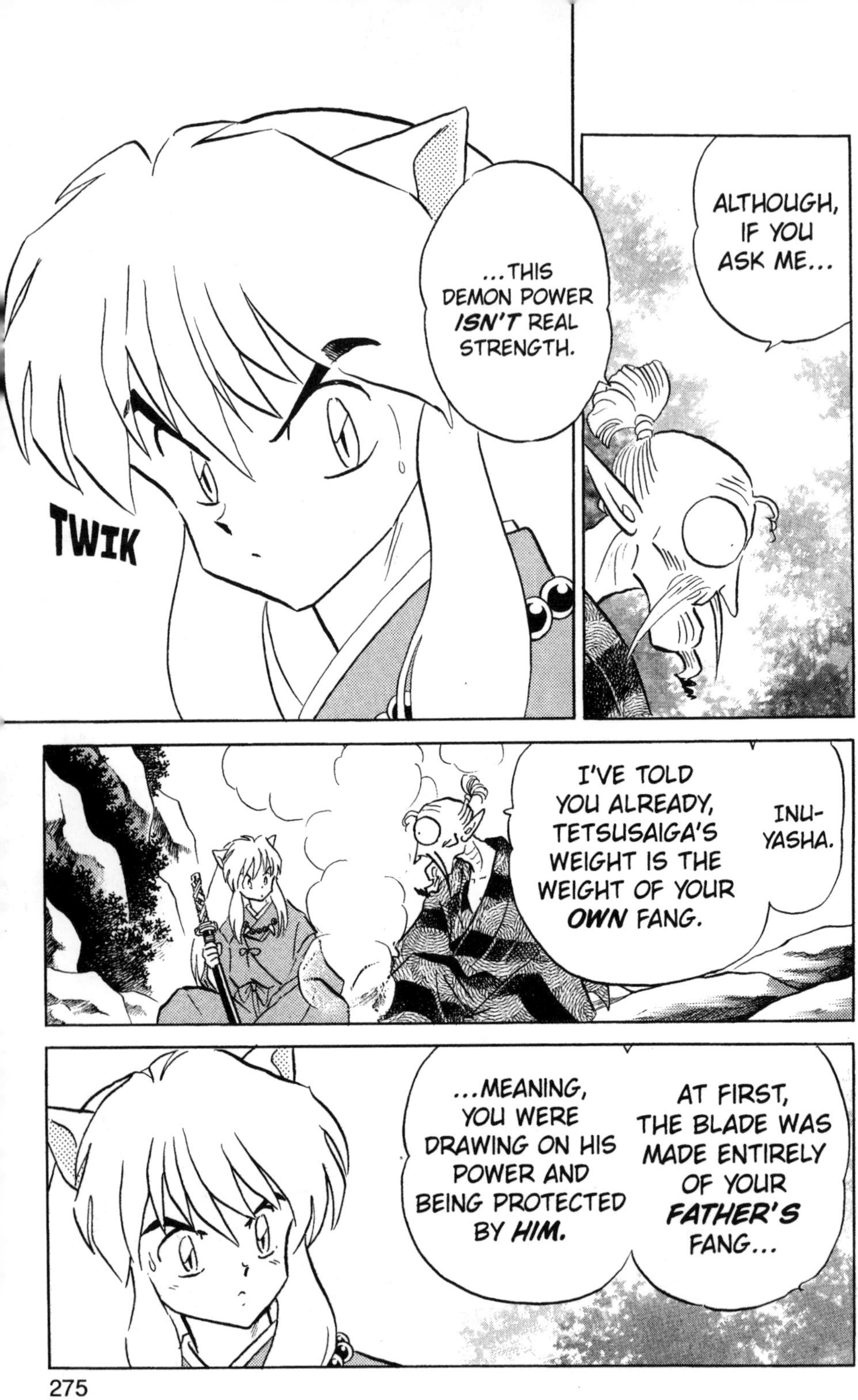
ALTHOUGH, IF YOU ASK ME...
...THIS DEMON POWER *ISN'T* REAL STRENGTH.
TWIK
INU-YASHA.
I'VE TOLD YOU ALREADY, TETSUSAIGA'S WEIGHT IS THE WEIGHT OF YOUR *OWN* FANG.
AT FIRST, THE BLADE WAS MADE ENTIRELY OF YOUR *FATHER'S* FANG...
...MEANING, YOU WERE DRAWING ON HIS POWER AND BEING PROTECTED BY *HIM.*

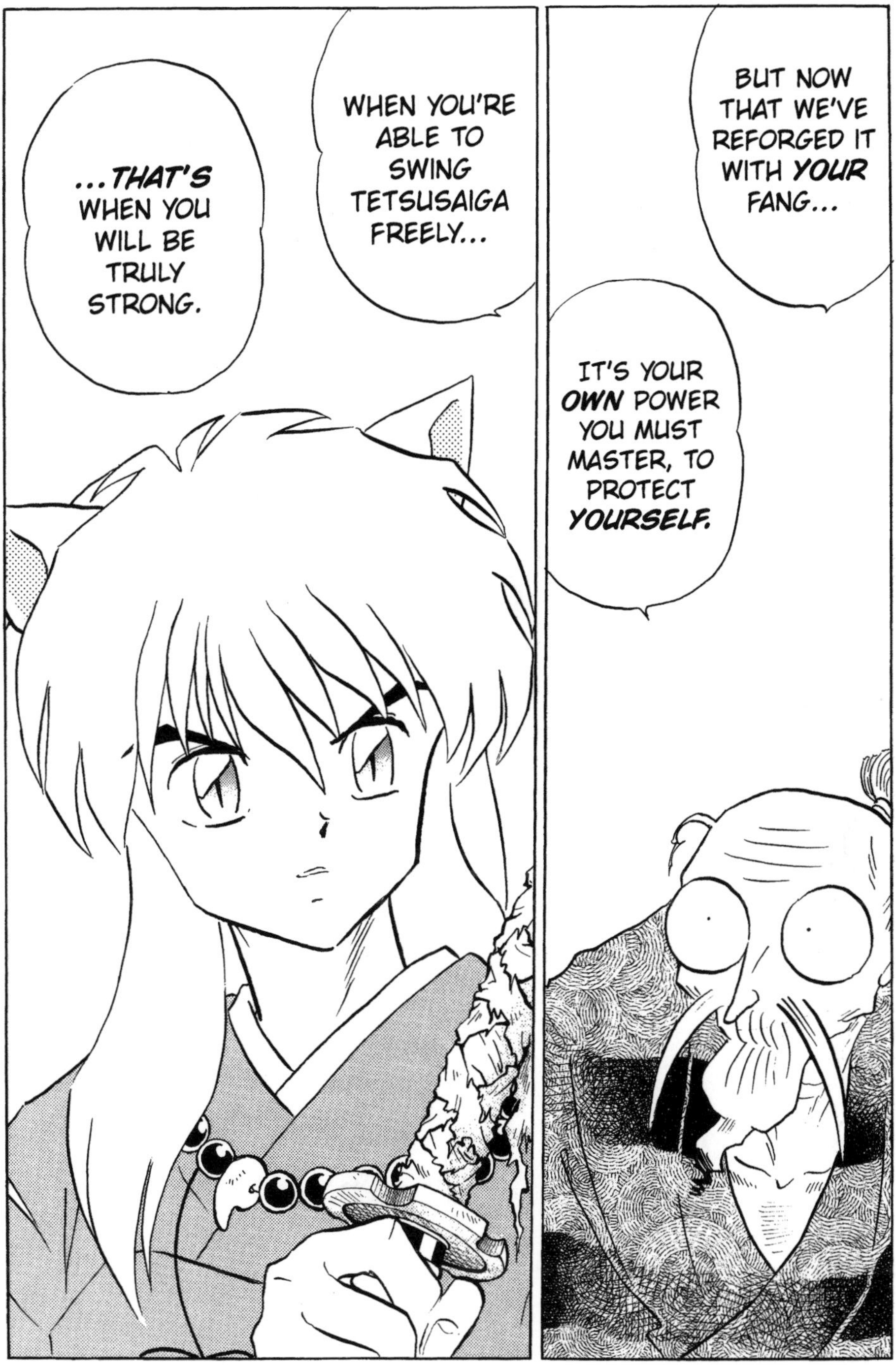
BUT NOW THAT WE'VE REFORGED IT WITH *YOUR* FANG...
IT'S YOUR *OWN* POWER YOU MUST MASTER, TO PROTECT *YOURSELF.*
WHEN YOU'RE ABLE TO SWING TETSUSAIGA FREELY...
...*THAT'S* WHEN YOU WILL BE TRULY STRONG.

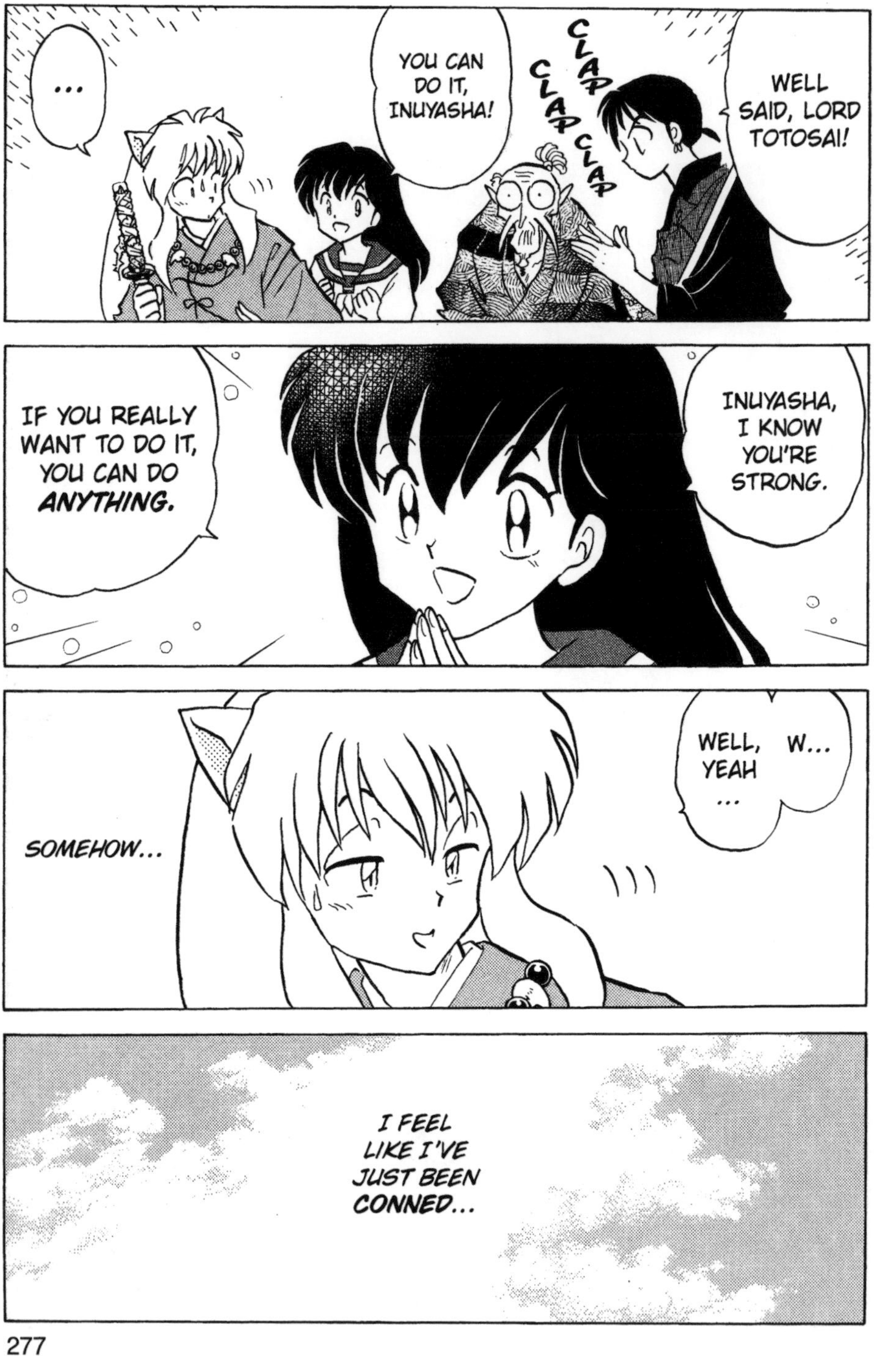
WELL SAID, LORD TOTOSAI!
CLAP CLAP CLAP
YOU CAN DO IT, INUYASHA!
...
INUYASHA, I KNOW YOU'RE STRONG.
IF YOU REALLY WANT TO DO IT, YOU CAN DO ANYTHING.
W...
WELL, YEAH ...
SOMEHOW...
I FEEL LIKE I'VE JUST BEEN CONNED...

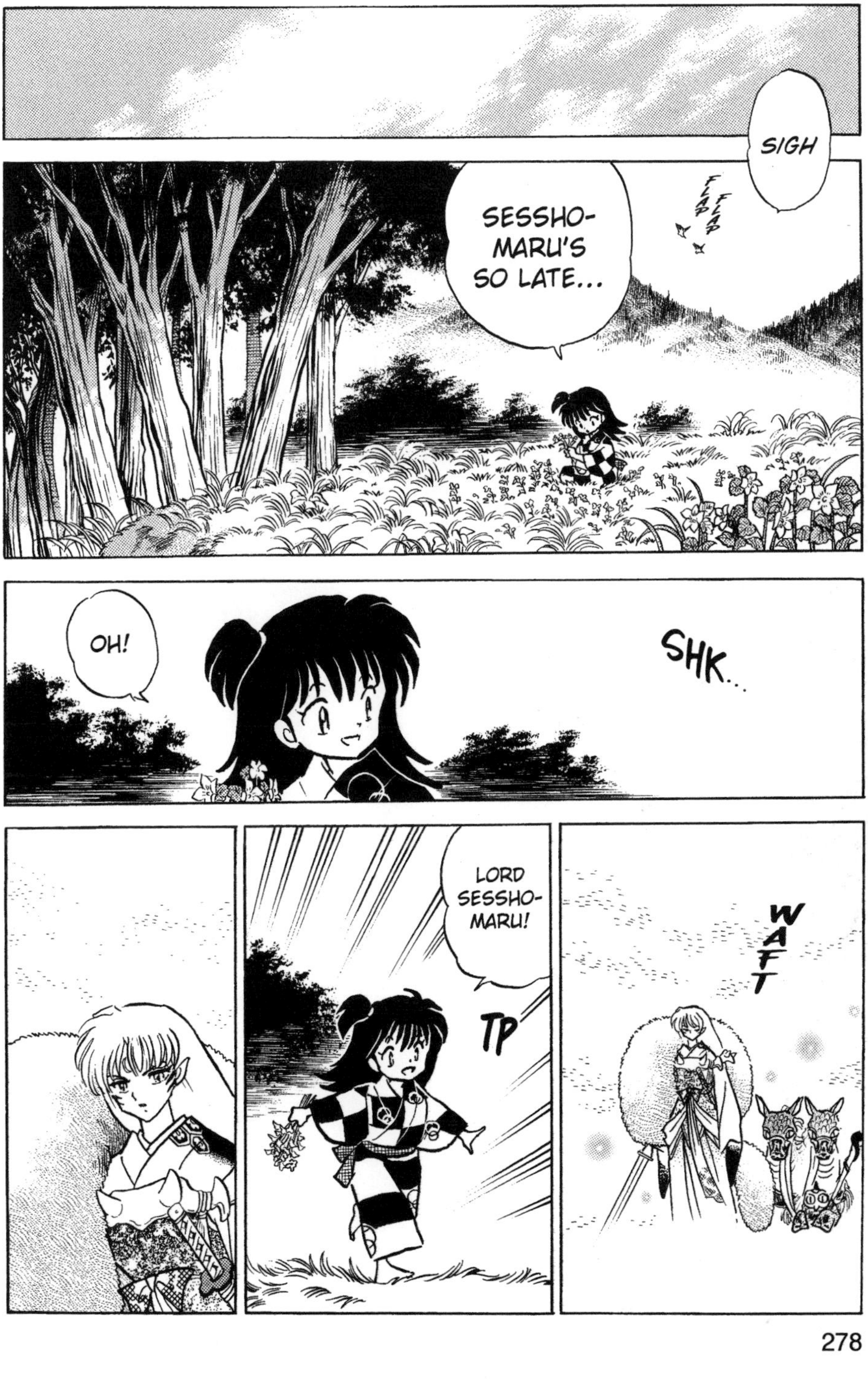
SIGH
FLAP FLAP
SESSHO-MARU'S SO LATE...
SHK...
OH!
WAFT
LORD SESSHO-MARU!
TP

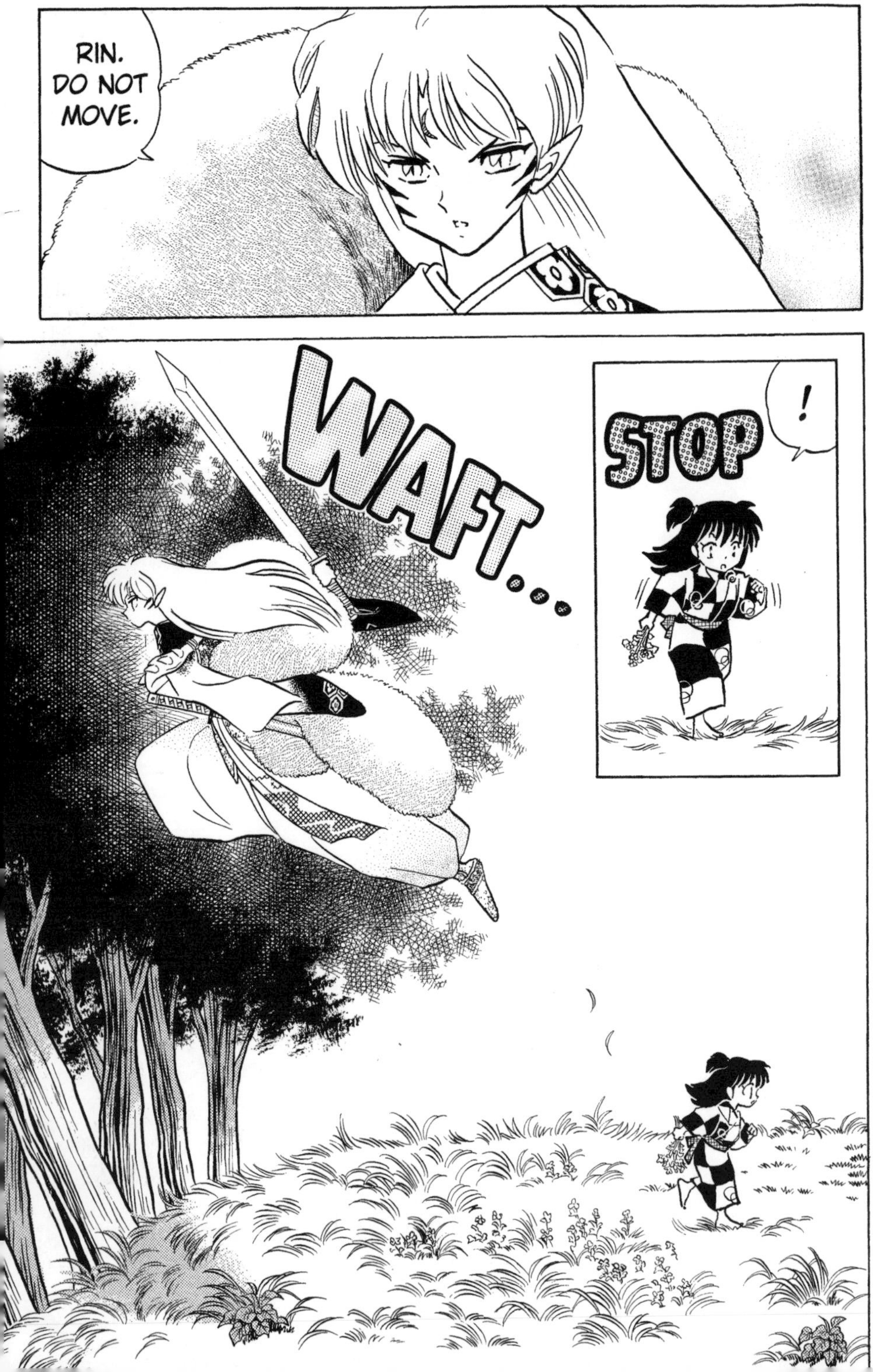
RIN. DO NOT MOVE.
STOP
!
WAFT...

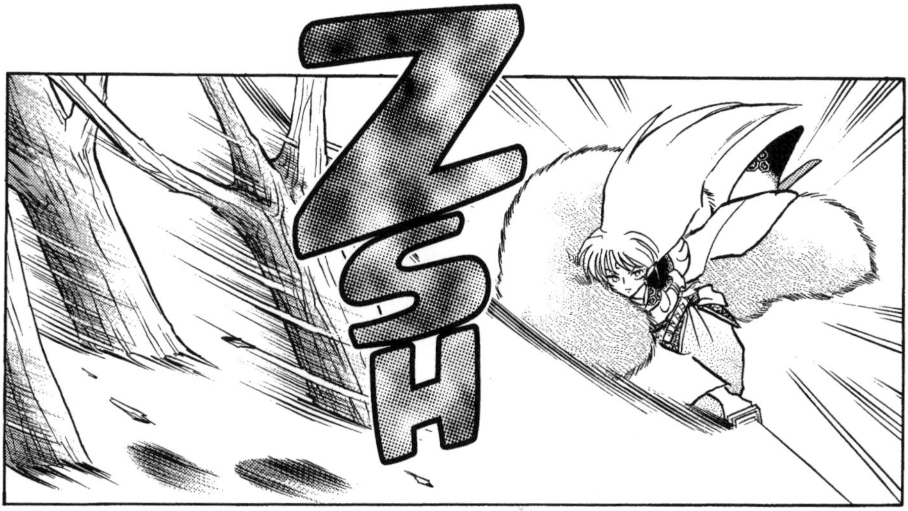
ZSH
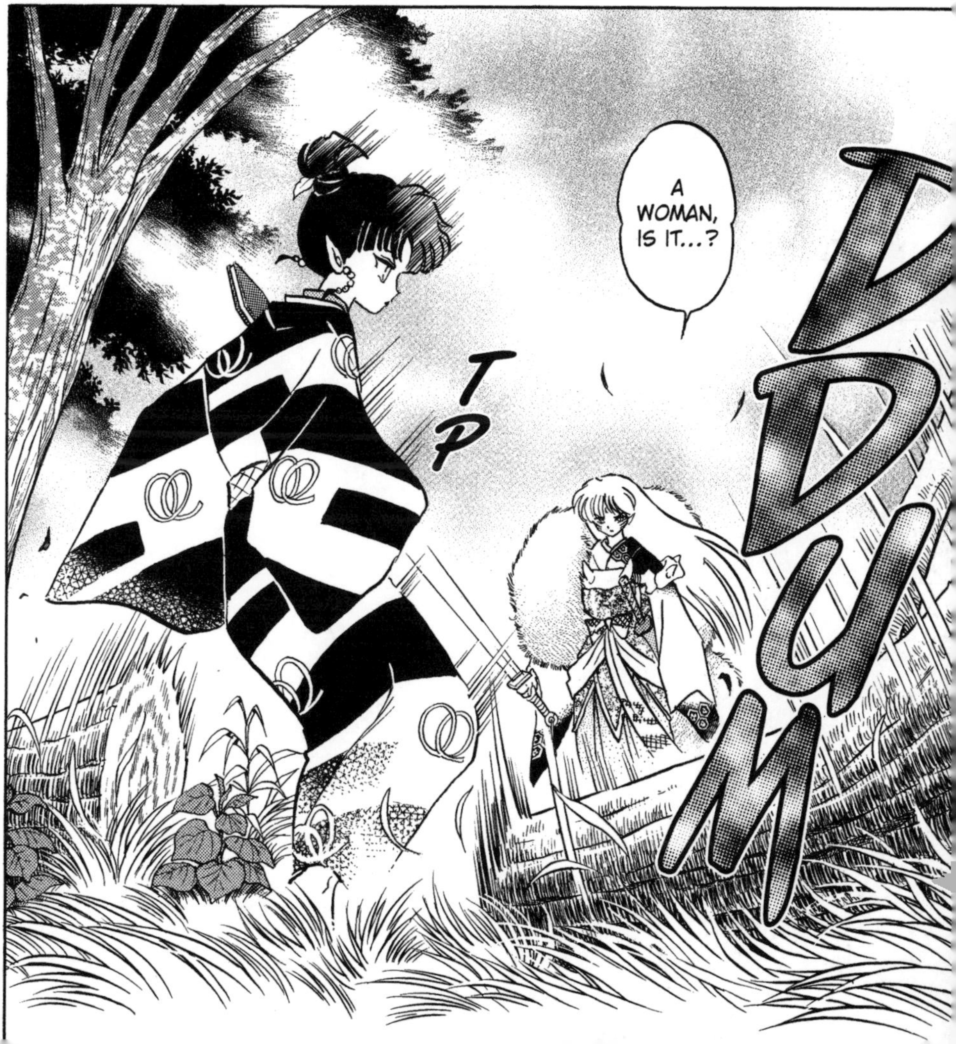
DDUM
A WOMAN, IS IT...?
TP

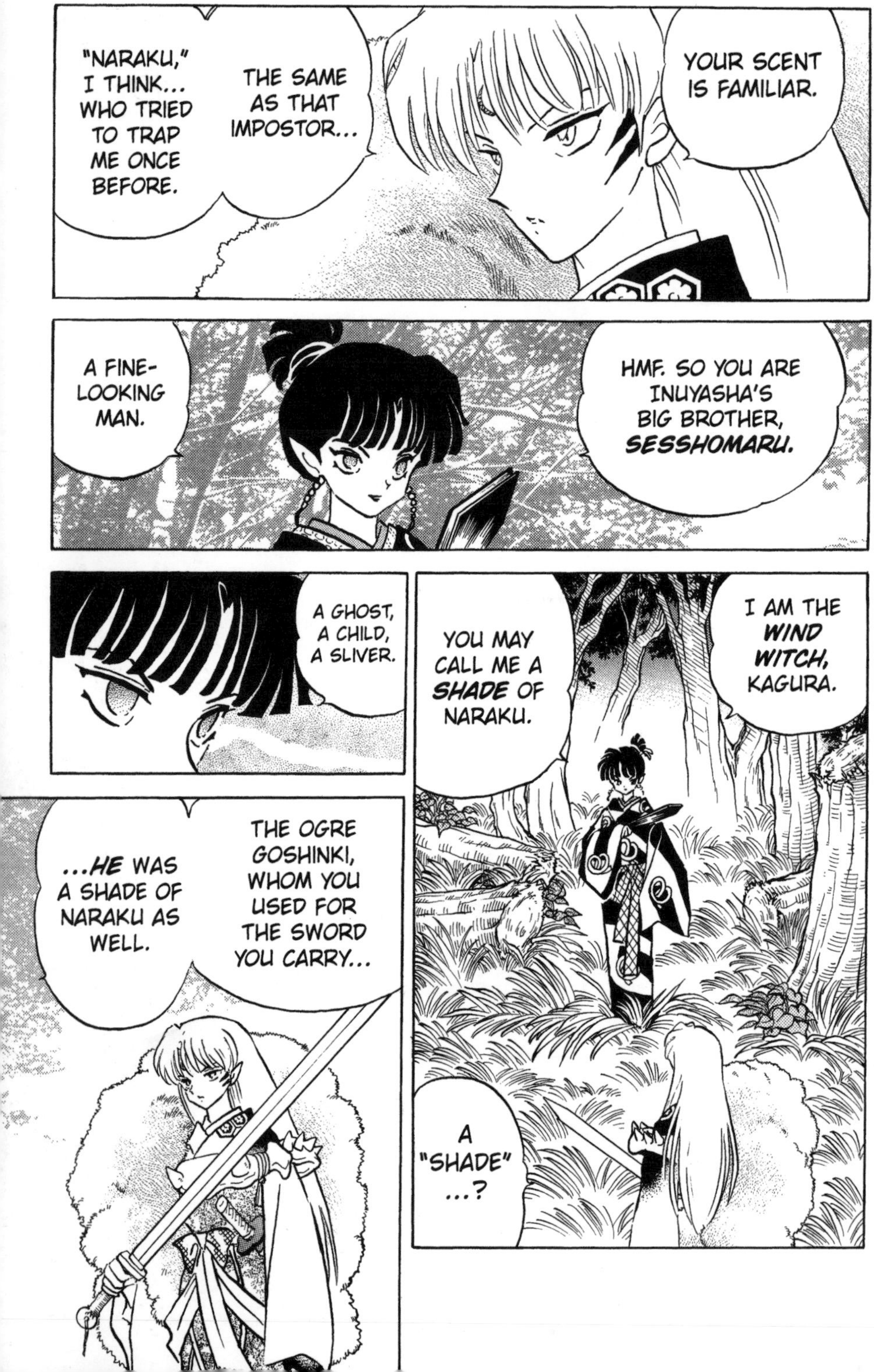
YOUR SCENT IS FAMILIAR.
THE SAME AS THAT IMPOSTOR...
"NARAKU," I THINK... WHO TRIED TO TRAP ME ONCE BEFORE.
HMF. SO YOU ARE INUYASHA'S BIG BROTHER, ***SESSHOMARU.***
A FINE-LOOKING MAN.
I AM THE ***WIND WITCH,*** KAGURA.
YOU MAY CALL ME A ***SHADE*** OF NARAKU.
A "SHADE" ...?
A GHOST, A CHILD, A SLIVER.
THE OGRE GOSHINKI, WHOM YOU USED FOR THE SWORD YOU CARRY...
...***HE*** WAS A SHADE OF NARAKU AS WELL.

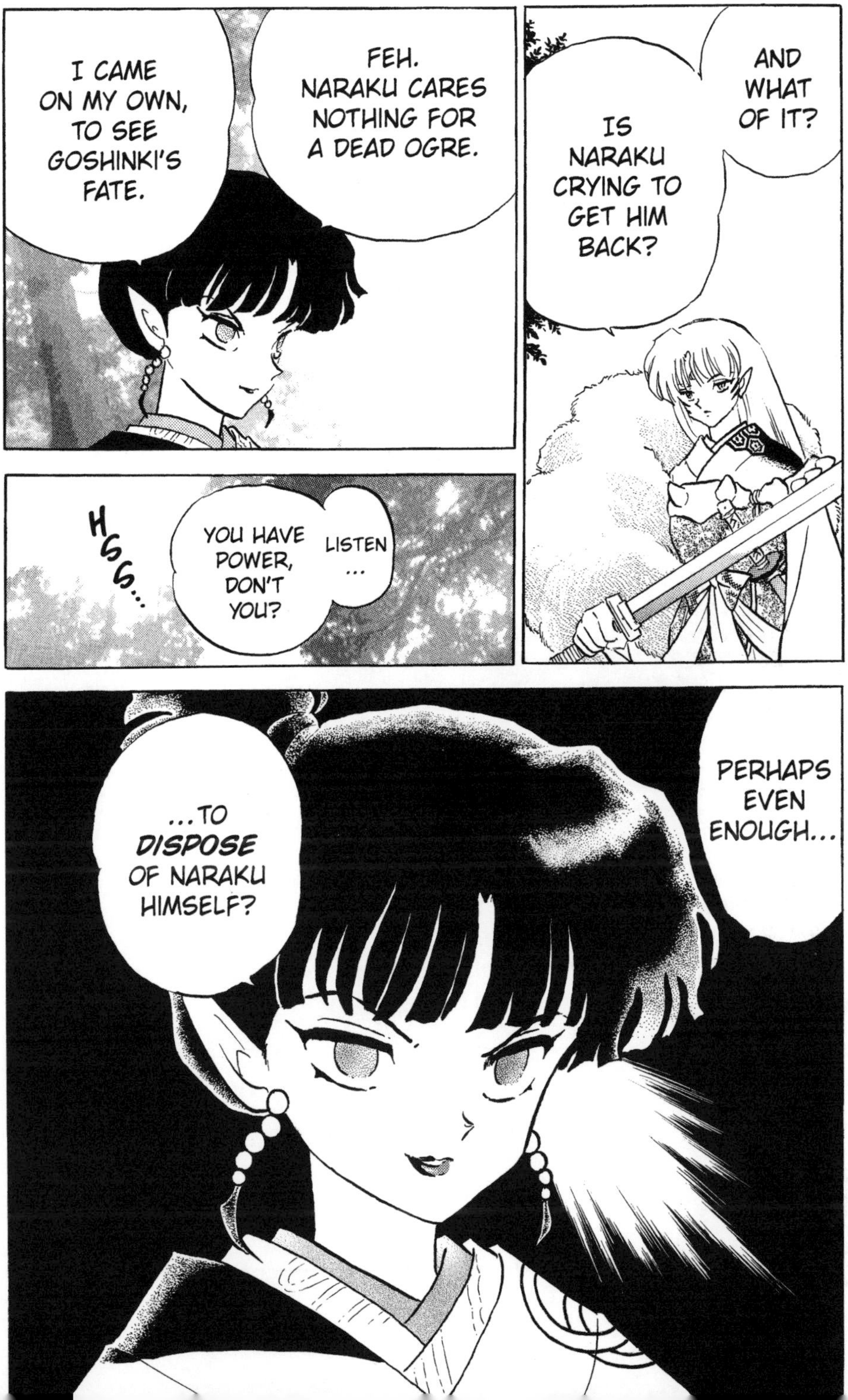
AND WHAT OF IT?
IS NARAKU CRYING TO GET HIM BACK?
FEH. NARAKU CARES NOTHING FOR A DEAD OGRE.
I CAME ON MY OWN, TO SEE GOSHINKI'S FATE.
LISTEN...
YOU HAVE POWER, DON'T YOU?
HSS...
PERHAPS EVEN ENOUGH...
...TO *DISPOSE* OF NARAKU HIMSELF?

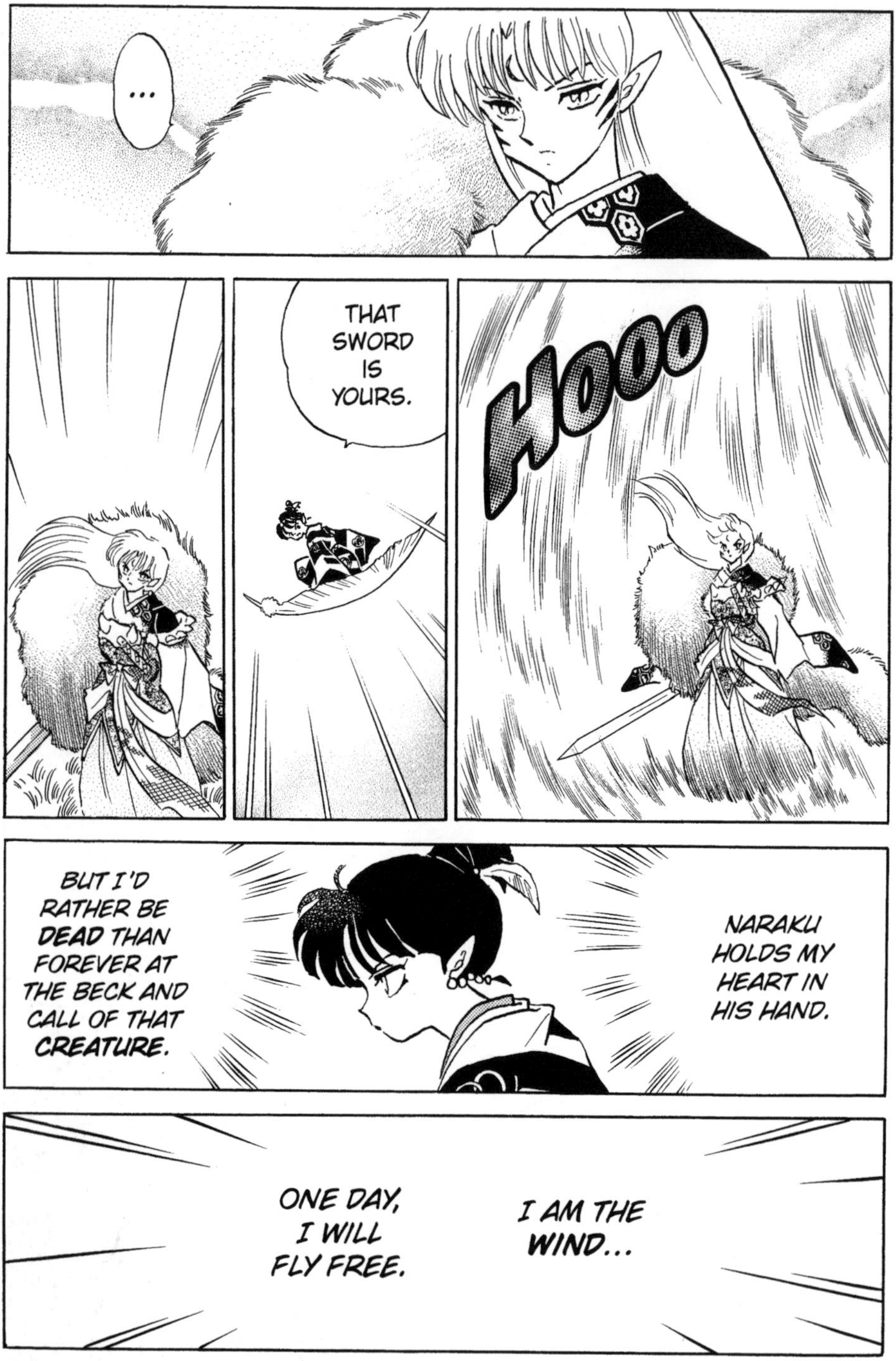
...
HOOO
THAT SWORD IS YOURS.
NARAKU HOLDS MY HEART IN HIS HAND.
BUT I'D RATHER BE DEAD THAN FOREVER AT THE BECK AND CALL OF THAT CREATURE.
I AM THE WIND...
ONE DAY, I WILL FLY FREE.

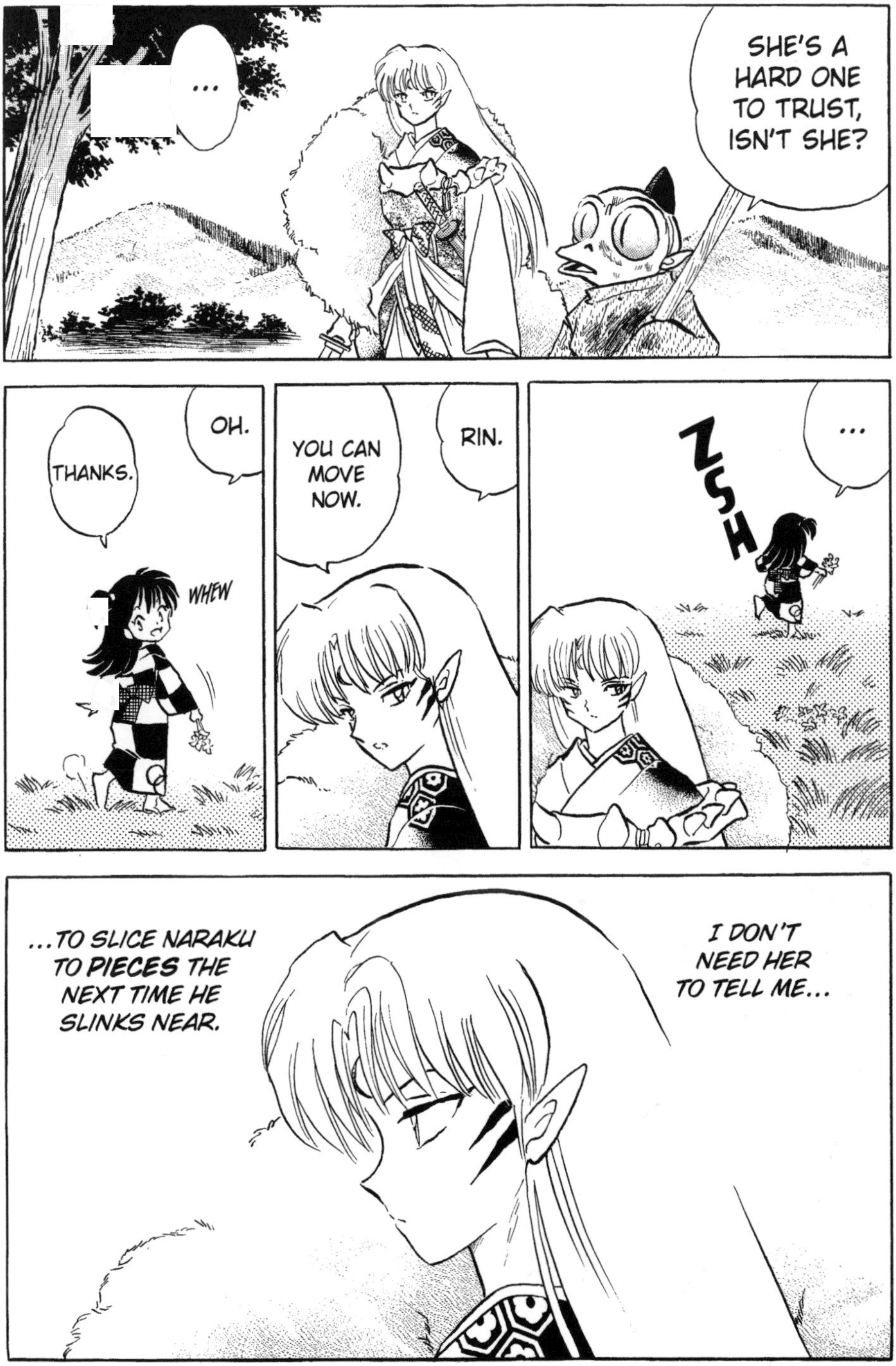
SHE'S A HARD ONE TO TRUST, ISN'T SHE?
...
...
ZSH
RIN.
YOU CAN MOVE NOW.
OH.
THANKS.
WHEW
I DON'T NEED HER TO TELL ME...
...TO SLICE NARAKU TO **PIECES** THE NEXT TIME HE SLINKS NEAR.

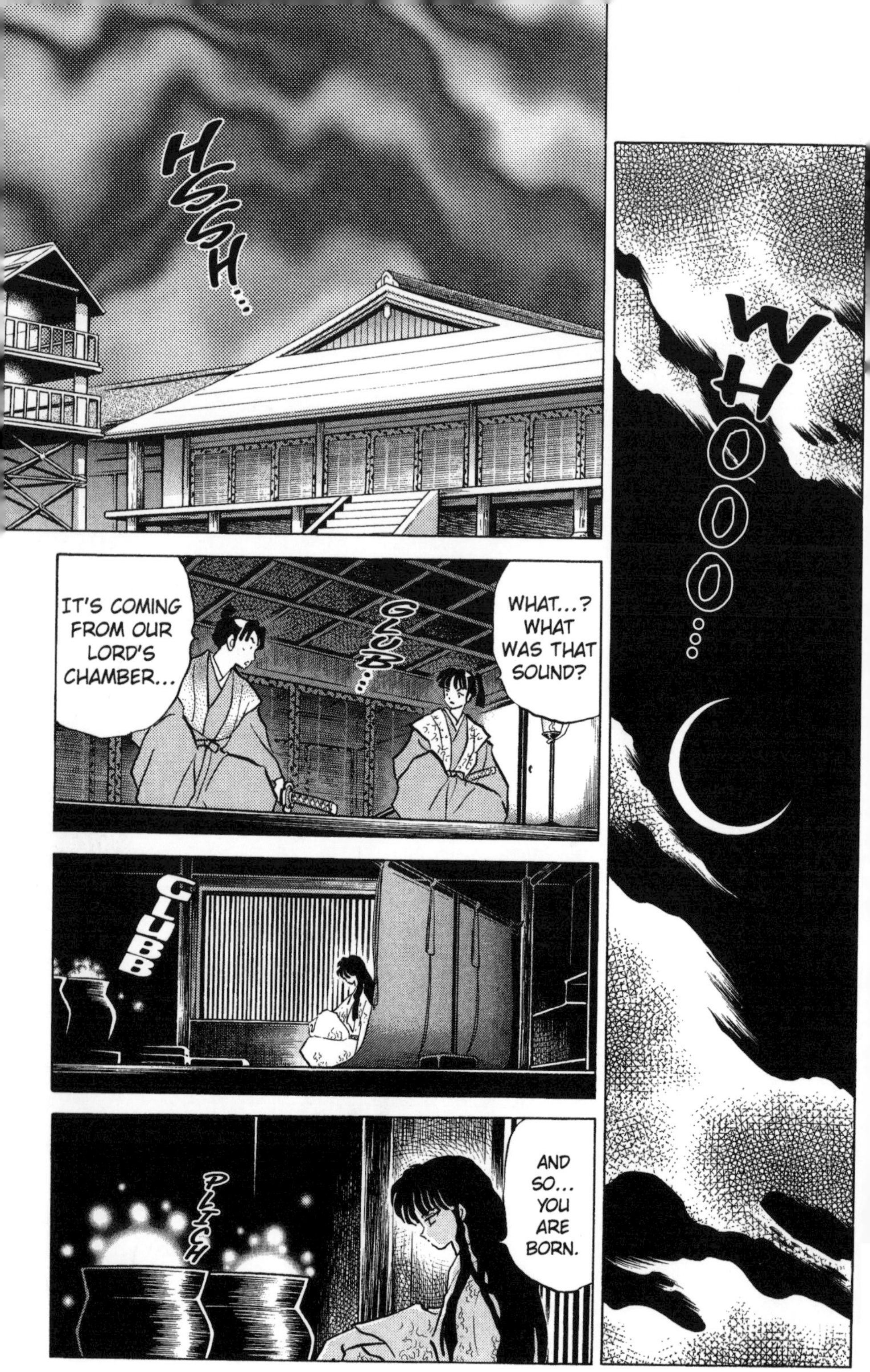
WHOOOO...
HSSGH...
WHAT...? WHAT WAS THAT SOUND?
GLUB...
IT'S COMING FROM OUR LORD'S CHAMBER...
GLUBB
AND SO... YOU ARE BORN.
PLISH

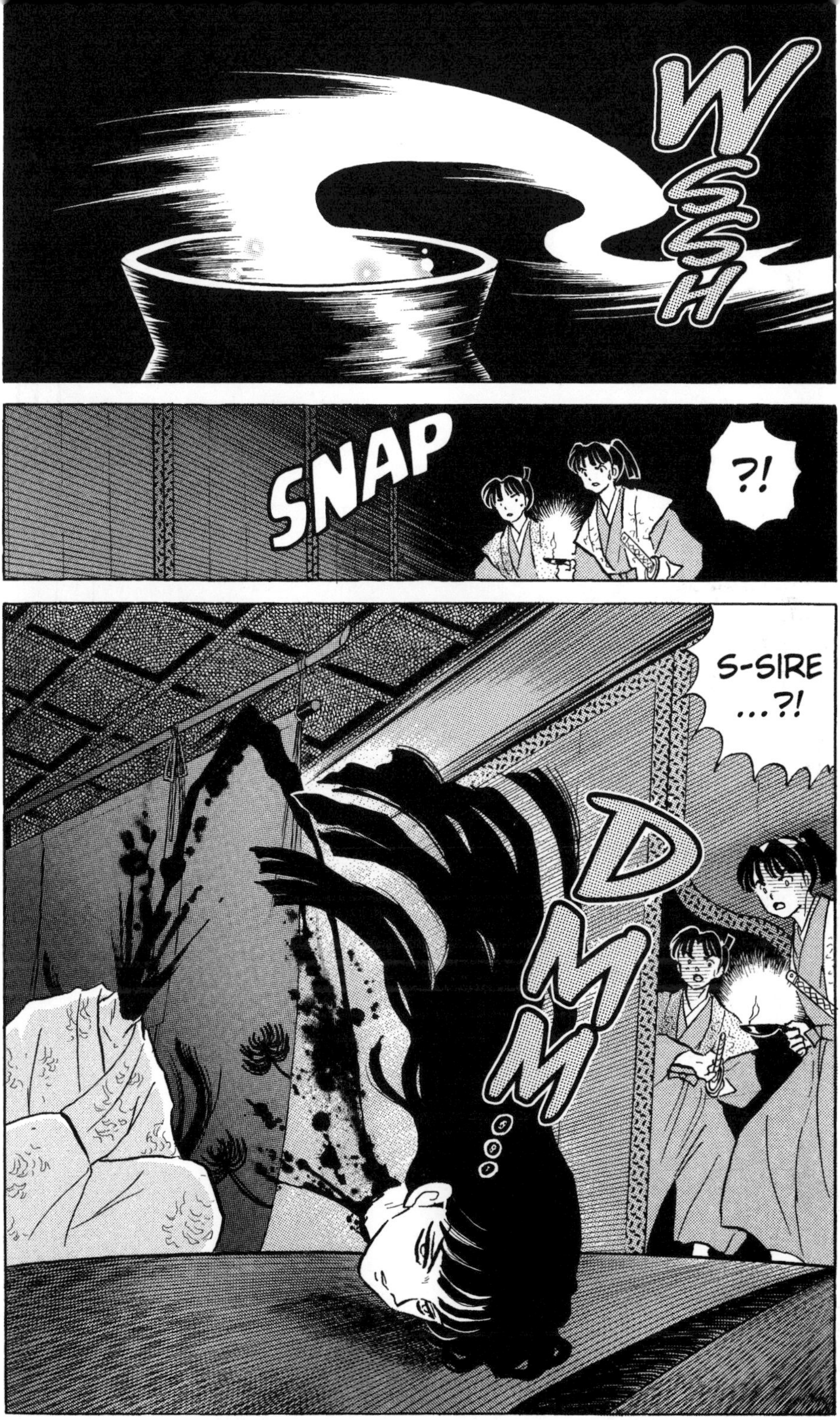
WSSH
?!
SNAP
S-SIRE ...?!
DMMM...

SCROLL SIX
THE FOURTH ONE

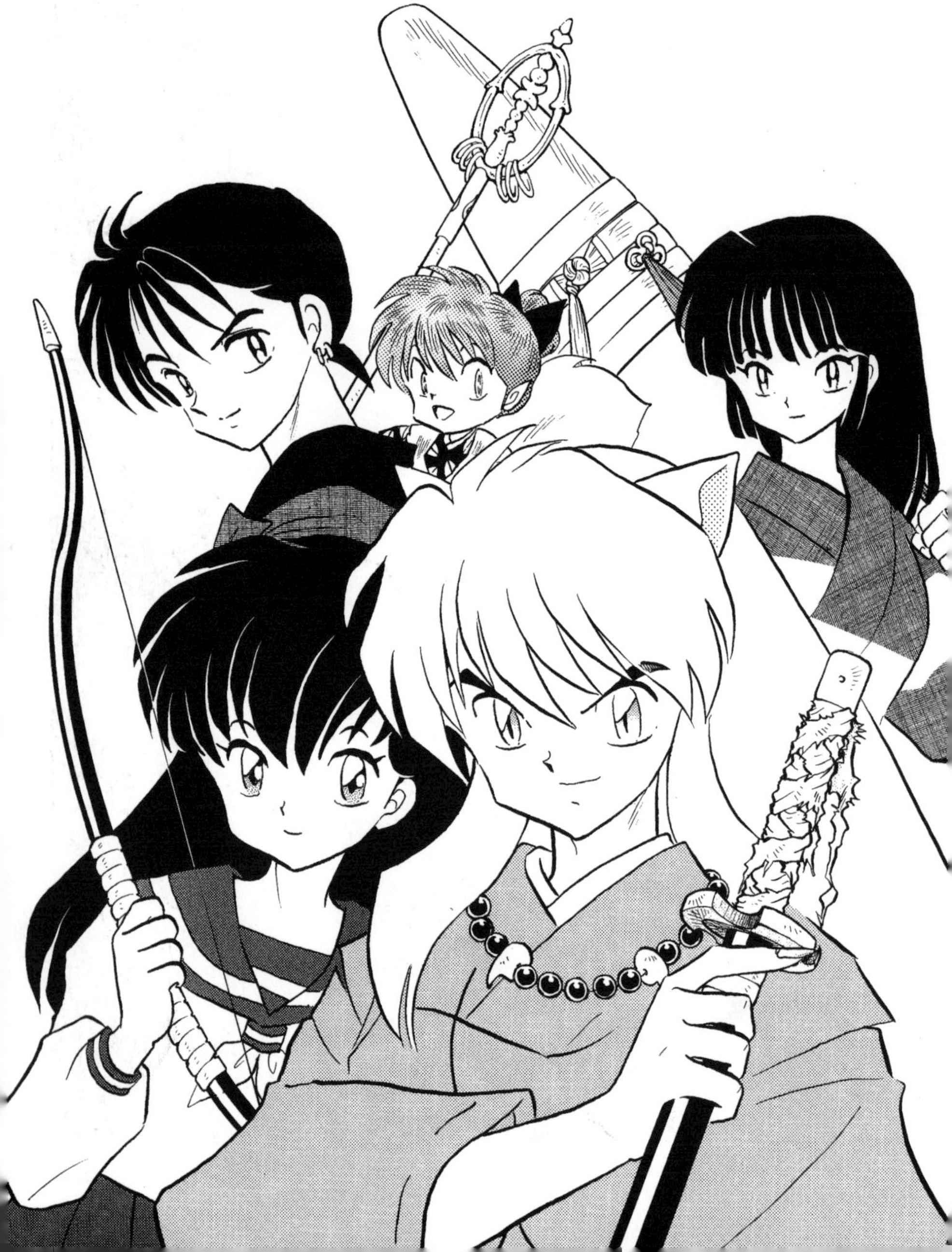

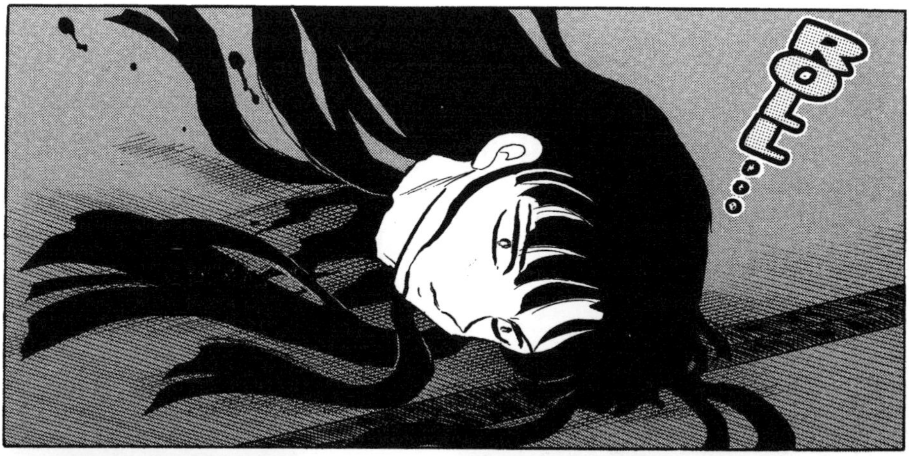
ROLL...

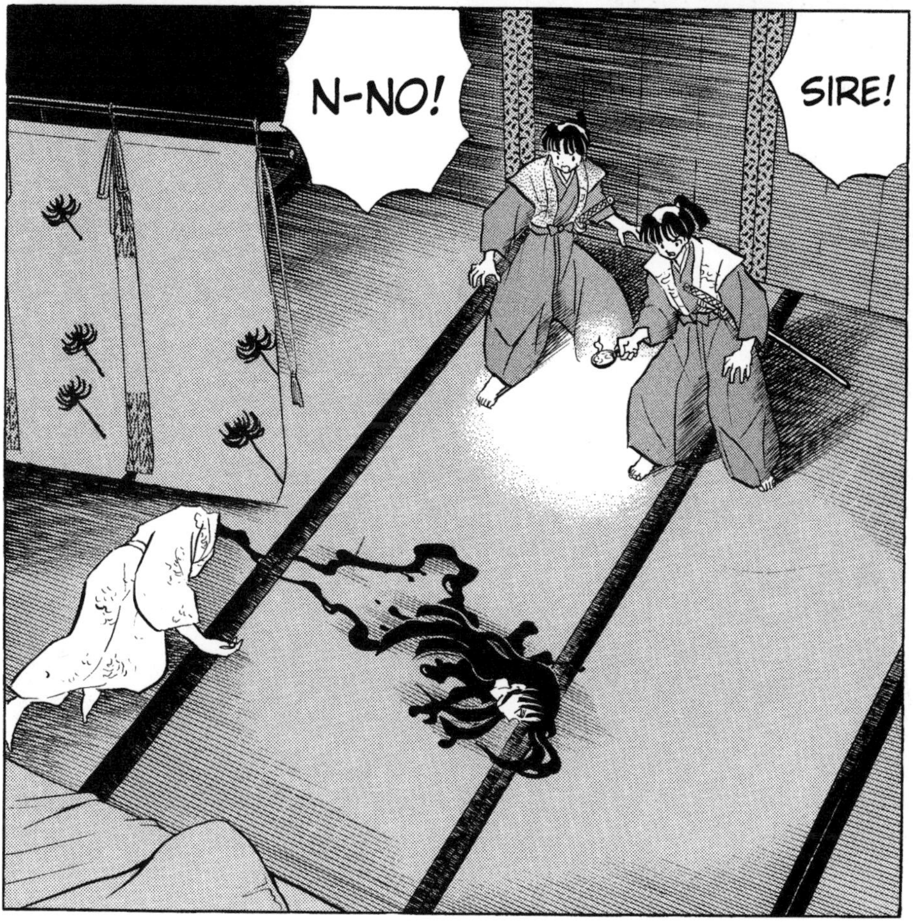
SIRE!
N-NO!

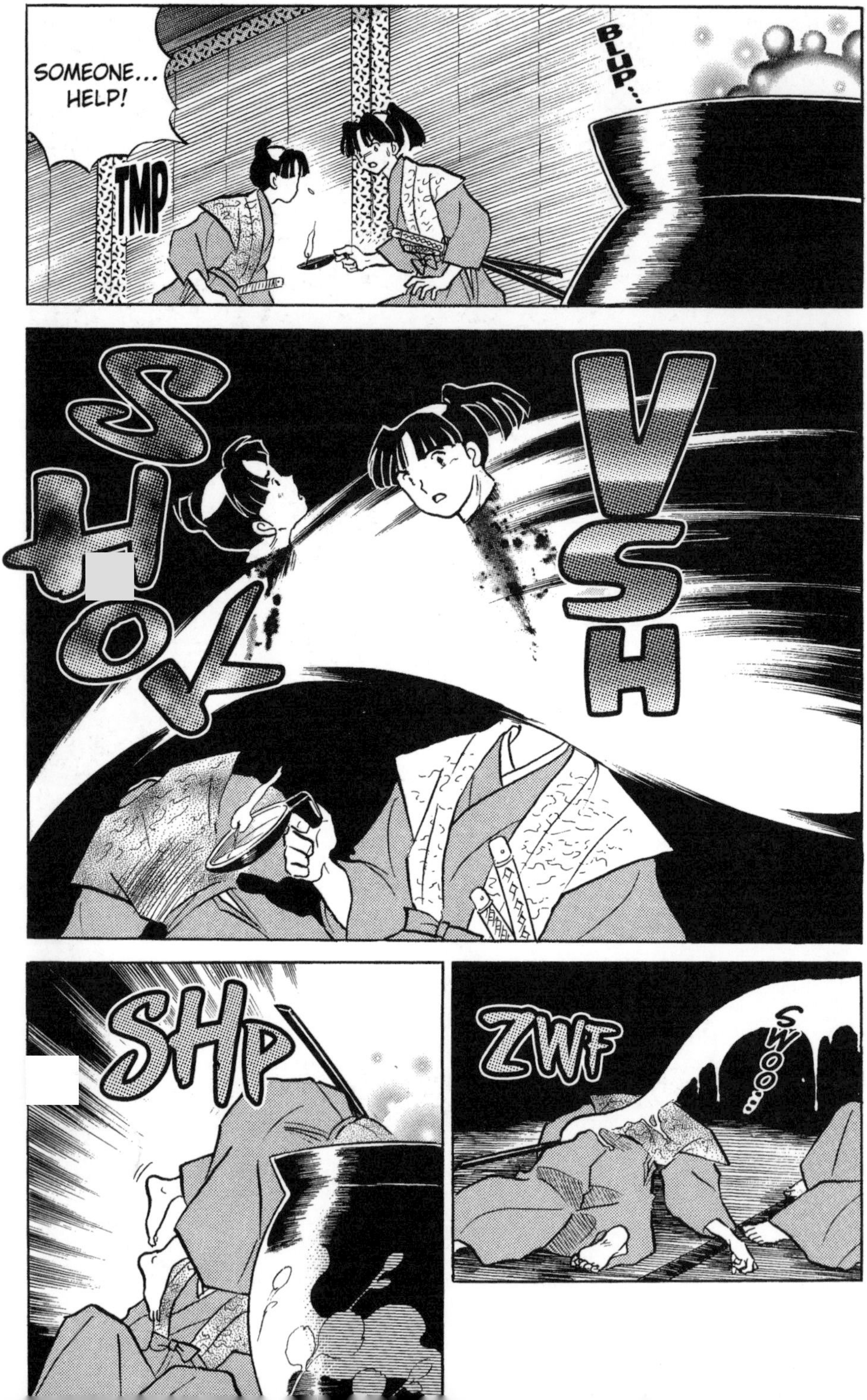
BLUP...
TMP
SOMEONE... HELP!
VSH
SHOK
ZWF
SWOO...
SHP

BRAK...
KRAK KRAK
KRAK KRAK
KRAK
GLUB
THROB
THMP
SKLUCH
GLUB

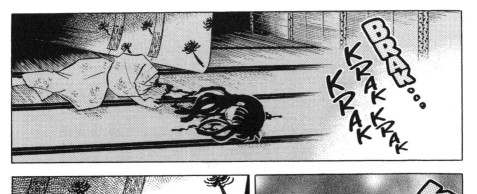

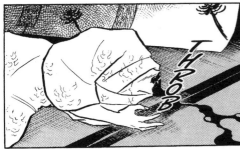

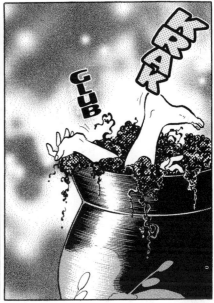

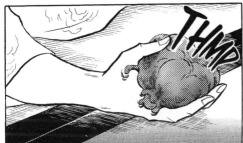

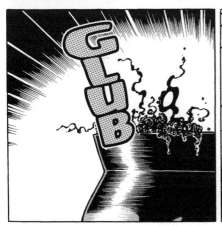

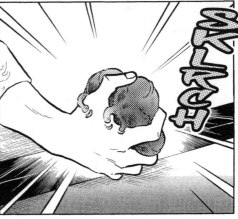

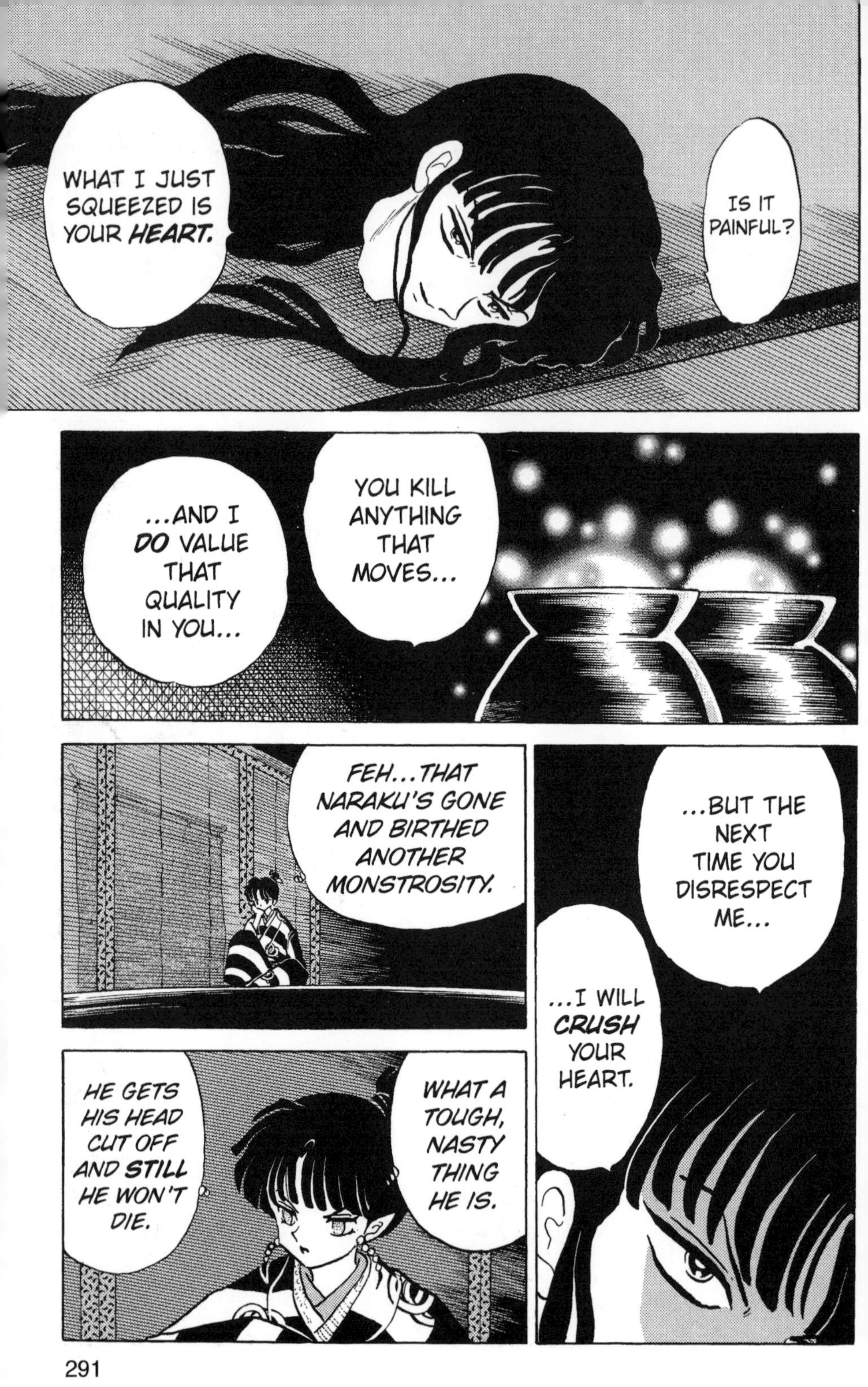

IS IT PAINFUL?
WHAT I JUST SQUEEZED IS YOUR **HEART.**
YOU KILL ANYTHING THAT MOVES...
...AND I ***DO*** VALUE THAT QUALITY IN YOU...
...BUT THE NEXT TIME YOU DISRESPECT ME...
...I WILL ***CRUSH*** YOUR HEART.
FEH...THAT NARAKU'S GONE AND BIRTHED ANOTHER MONSTROSITY.
WHAT A TOUGH, NASTY THING HE IS.
*HE GETS HIS HEAD CUT OFF AND **STILL** HE WON'T DIE.*

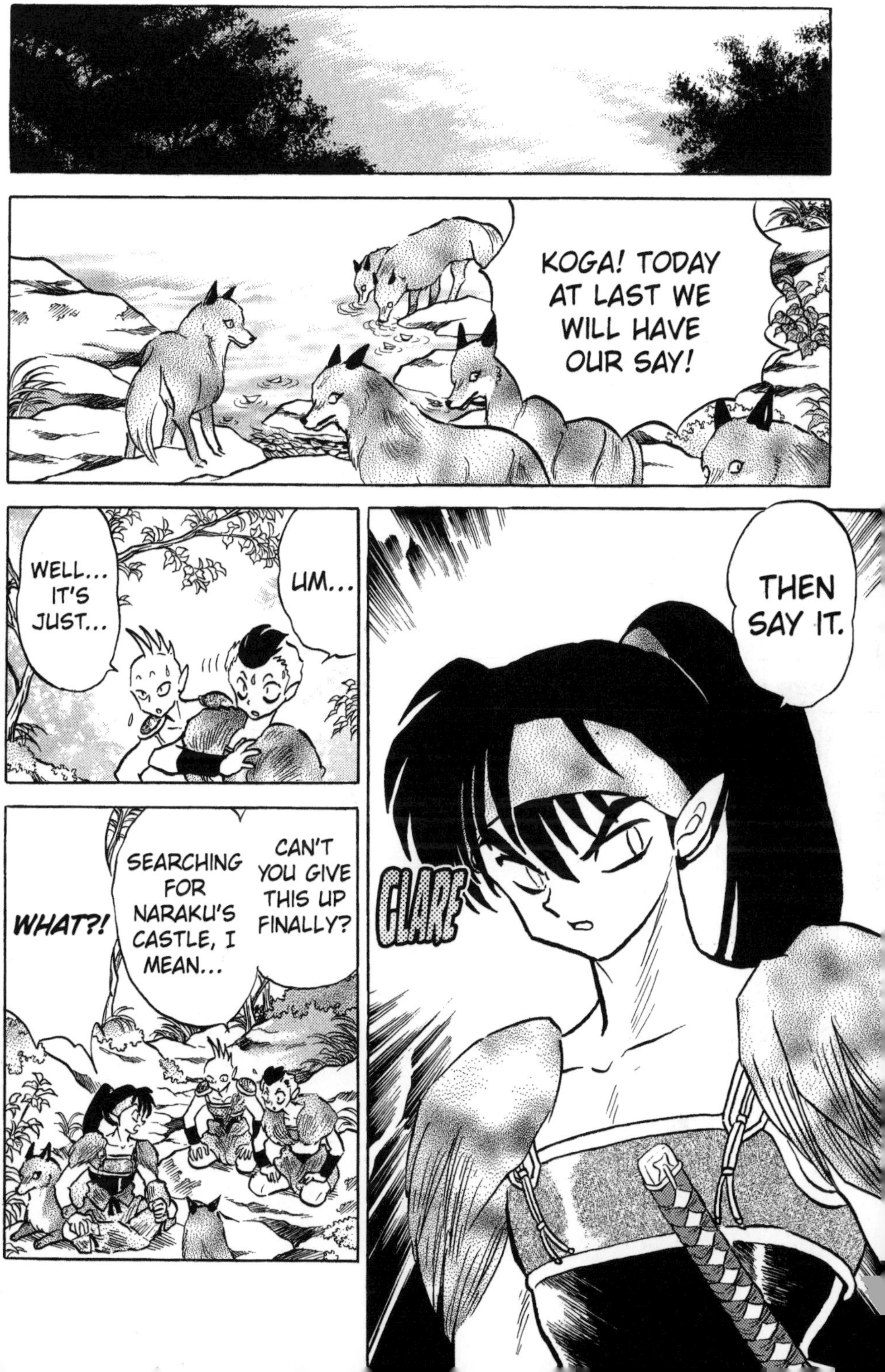
KOGA! TODAY AT LAST WE WILL HAVE OUR SAY!
THEN SAY IT.
GLARE
UM...
WELL... IT'S JUST...
CAN'T YOU GIVE THIS UP FINALLY?
SEARCHING FOR NARAKU'S CASTLE, I MEAN...
WHAT?!

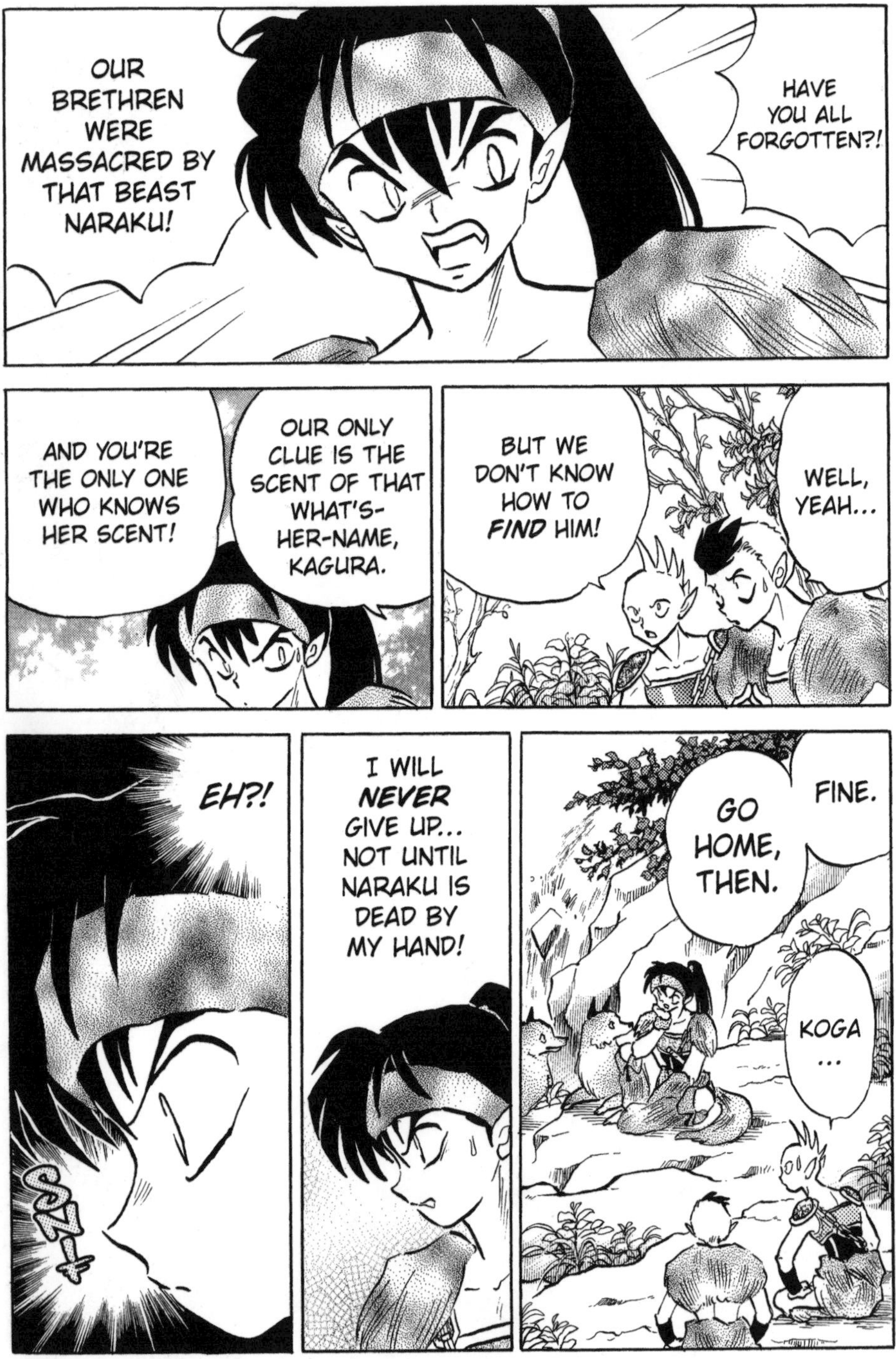
HAVE YOU ALL FORGOTTEN?!
OUR BRETHREN WERE MASSACRED BY THAT BEAST NARAKU!
WELL, YEAH...
BUT WE DON'T KNOW HOW TO FIND HIM!
OUR ONLY CLUE IS THE SCENT OF THAT WHAT'S-HER-NAME, KAGURA.
AND YOU'RE THE ONLY ONE WHO KNOWS HER SCENT!
FINE.
GO HOME, THEN.
KOGA ...
I WILL NEVER GIVE UP... NOT UNTIL NARAKU IS DEAD BY MY HAND!
EH?!
SNIFF

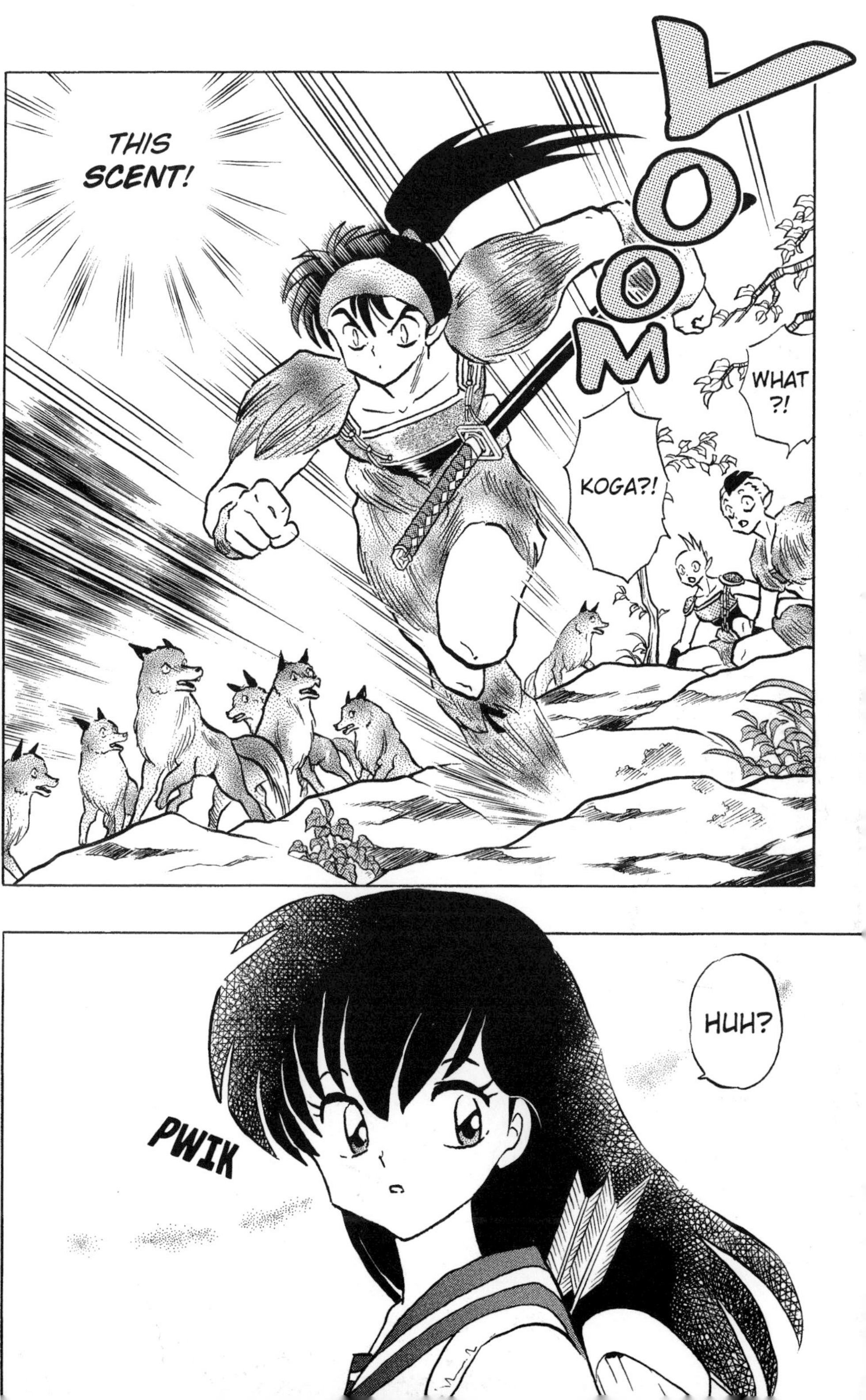
YOOOM
THIS SCENT!
WHAT ?!
KOGA?!
HUH?
PWIK

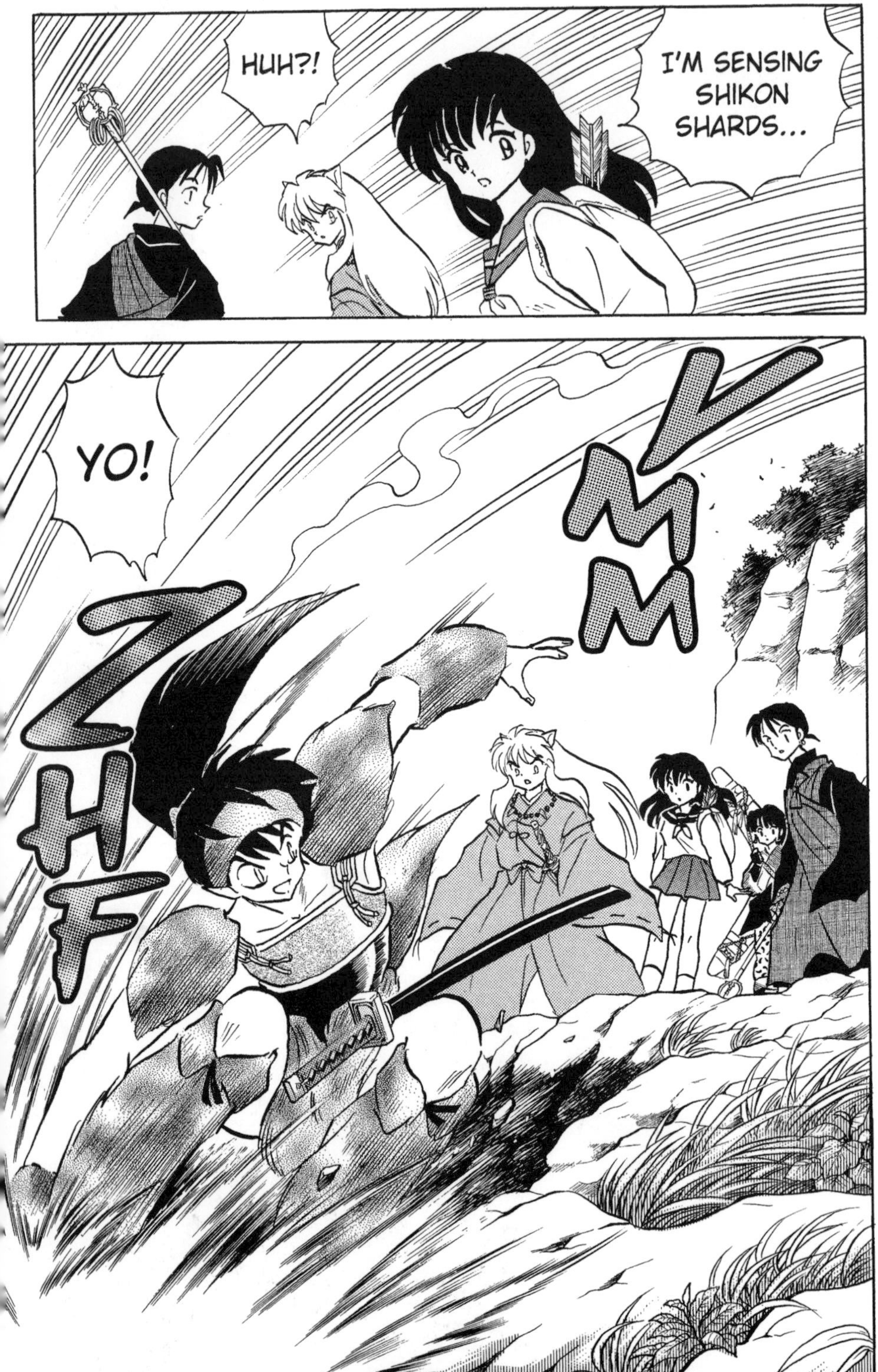
I'M SENSING SHIKON SHARDS...
HUH?!
VMM
YO!
ZHF

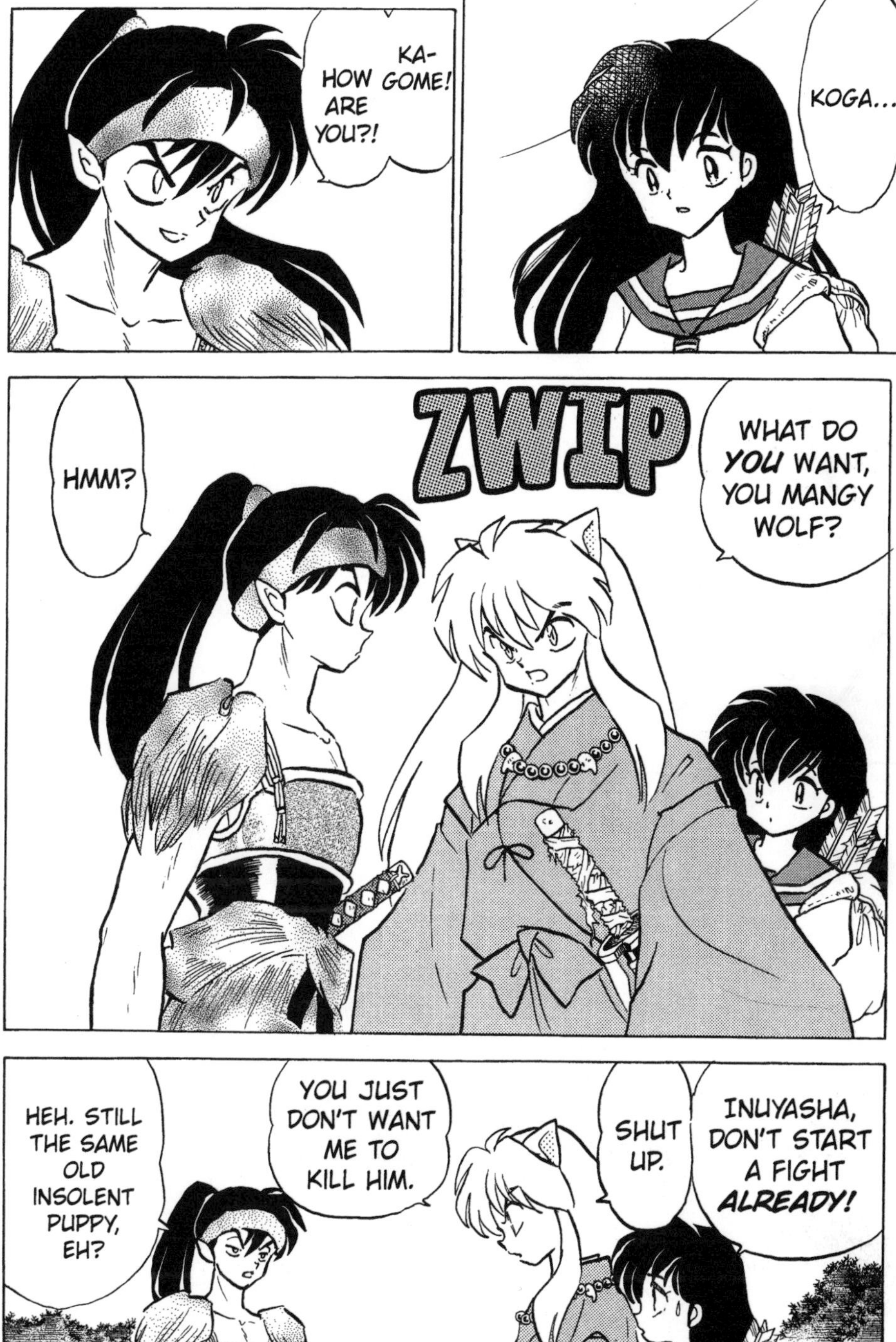
KOGA...
KA-GOME! HOW ARE YOU?!
WHAT DO *YOU* WANT, YOU MANGY WOLF?
ZWIP
HMM?
INUYASHA, DON'T START A FIGHT *ALREADY!*
SHUT UP.
YOU JUST DON'T WANT ME TO KILL HIM.
HEH. STILL THE SAME OLD INSOLENT PUPPY, EH?

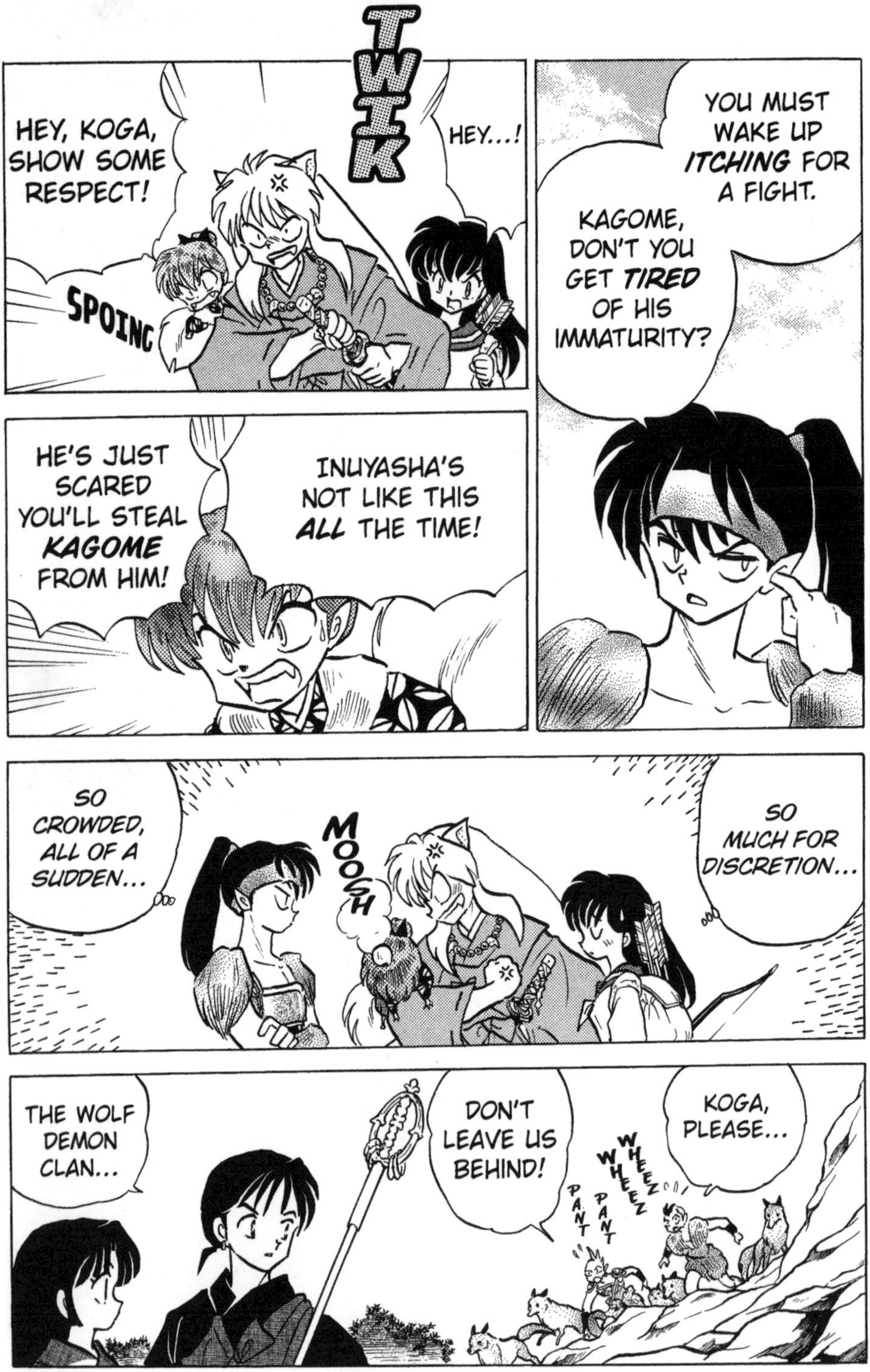
YOU MUST WAKE UP *ITCHING* FOR A FIGHT.
KAGOME, DON'T YOU GET *TIRED* OF HIS IMMATURITY?
TWIK
HEY...!
HEY, KOGA, SHOW SOME RESPECT!
SPOING
INUYASHA'S NOT LIKE THIS *ALL* THE TIME!
HE'S JUST SCARED YOU'LL STEAL *KAGOME* FROM HIM!
SO MUCH FOR DISCRETION...
MOOSH
SO CROWDED, ALL OF A SUDDEN...
KOGA, PLEASE...
WHEEZ WHEEZ
PANT PANT
DON'T LEAVE US BEHIND!
THE WOLF DEMON CLAN...

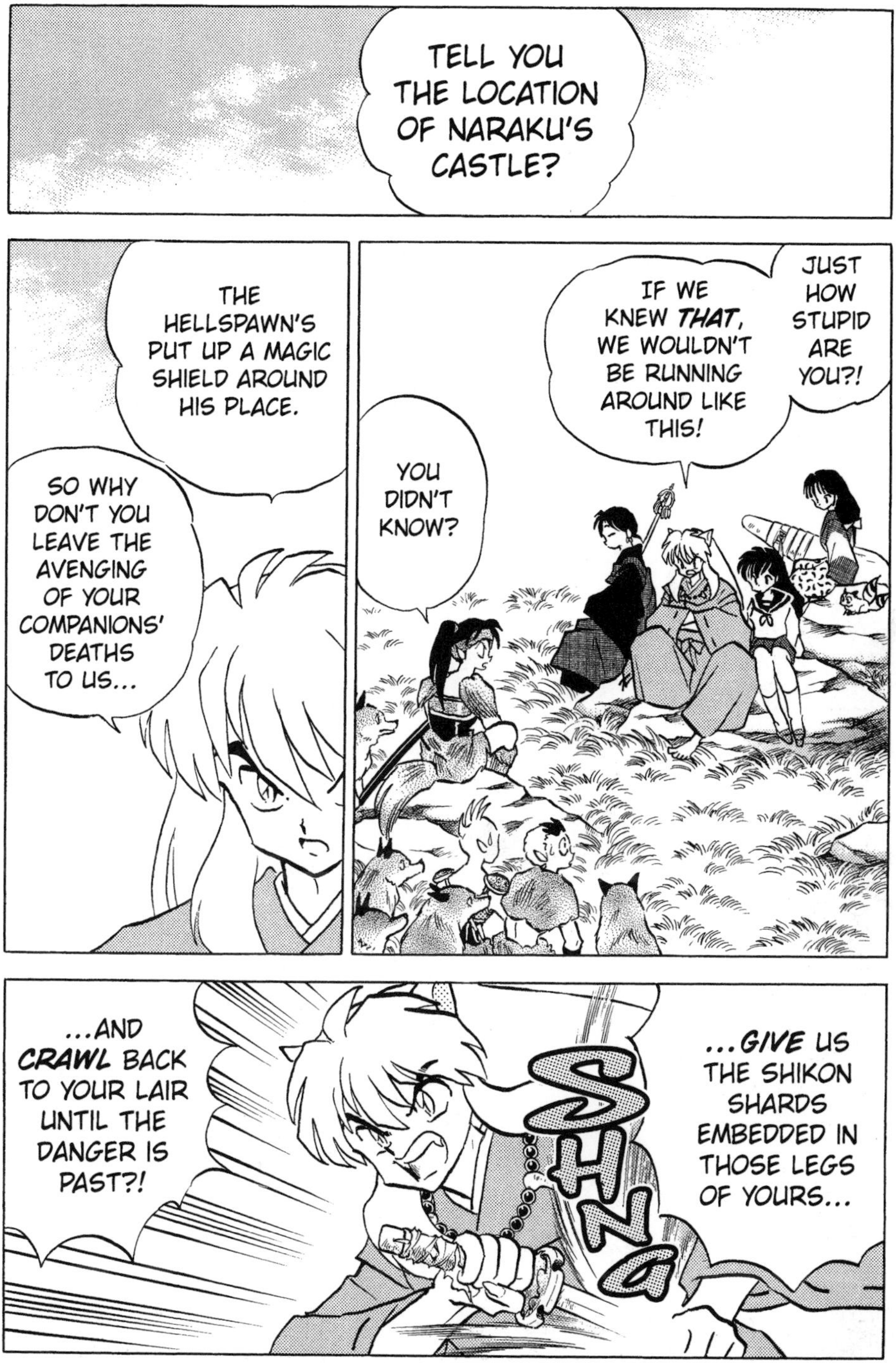
TELL YOU THE LOCATION OF NARAKU'S CASTLE?
JUST HOW STUPID ARE YOU?!
IF WE KNEW *THAT*, WE WOULDN'T BE RUNNING AROUND LIKE THIS!
YOU DIDN'T KNOW?
THE HELLSPAWN'S PUT UP A MAGIC SHIELD AROUND HIS PLACE.
SO WHY DON'T YOU LEAVE THE AVENGING OF YOUR COMPANIONS' DEATHS TO US...
...*GIVE* US THE SHIKON SHARDS EMBEDDED IN THOSE LEGS OF YOURS...
SHING
...AND *CRAWL* BACK TO YOUR LAIR UNTIL THE DANGER IS PAST?!

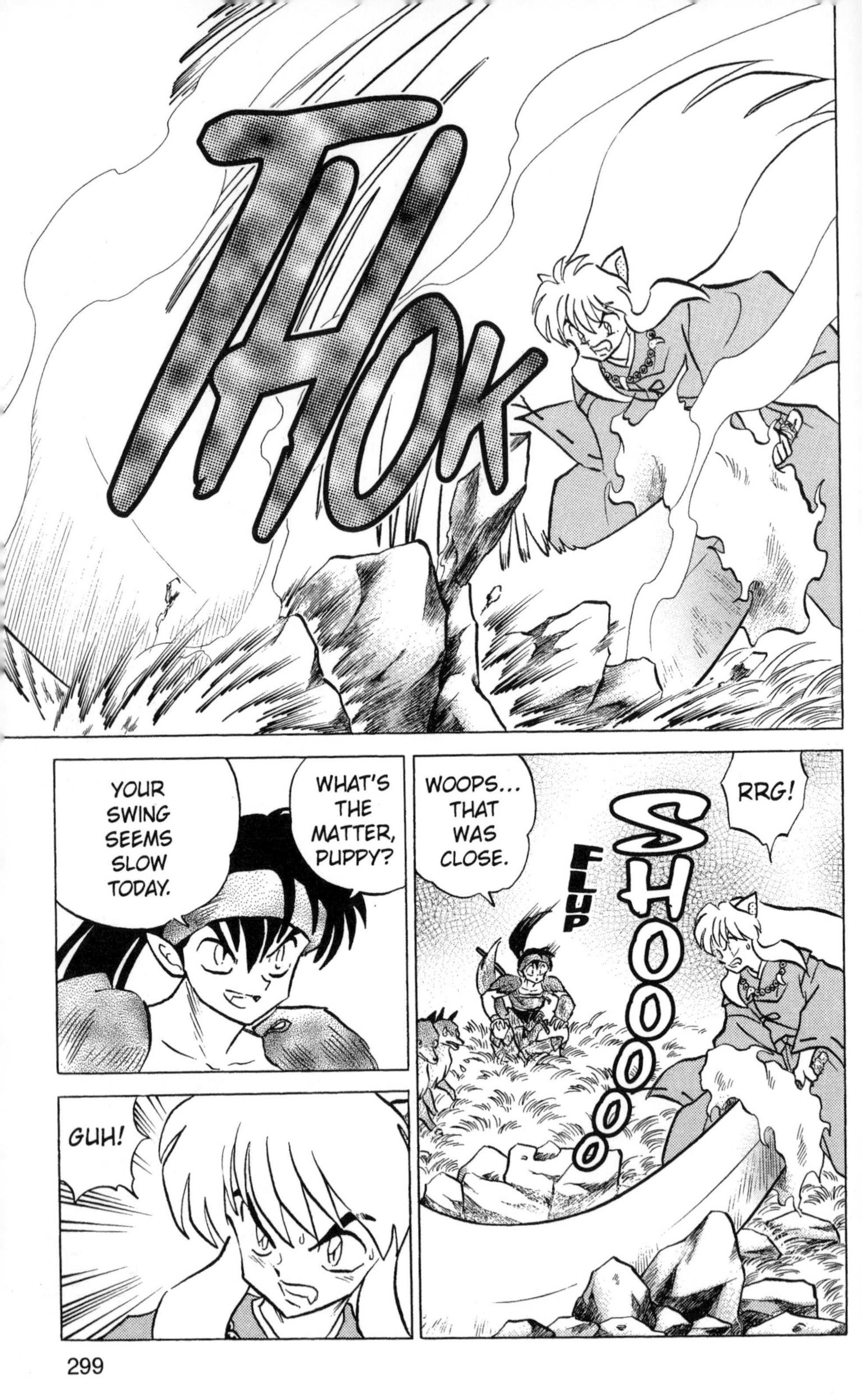
THOK
RRG!
SHOOOOOO
FLUP
WOOPS... THAT WAS CLOSE.
WHAT'S THE MATTER, PUPPY?
YOUR SWING SEEMS SLOW TODAY.
GUH!

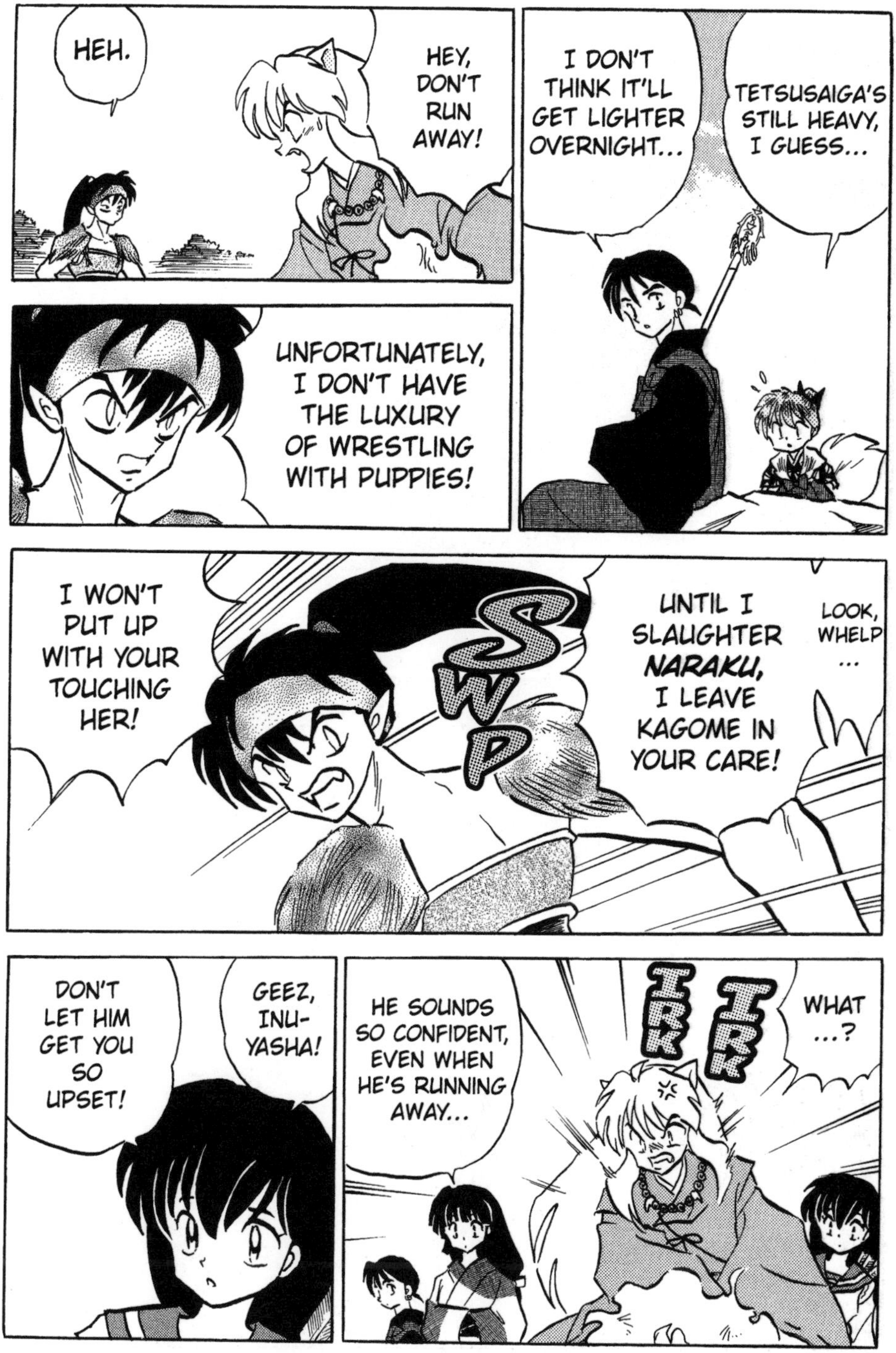
TETSUSAIGA'S STILL HEAVY, I GUESS...
I DON'T THINK IT'LL GET LIGHTER OVERNIGHT...
HEY, DON'T RUN AWAY!
HEH.
UNFORTUNATELY, I DON'T HAVE THE LUXURY OF WRESTLING WITH PUPPIES!
LOOK, WHELP...
UNTIL I SLAUGHTER *NARAKU,* I LEAVE KAGOME IN YOUR CARE!
SWP
I WON'T PUT UP WITH YOUR TOUCHING HER!
WHAT...?
IRK
IRK
HE SOUNDS SO CONFIDENT, EVEN WHEN HE'S RUNNING AWAY...
GEEZ, INU-YASHA!
DON'T LET HIM GET YOU SO UPSET!

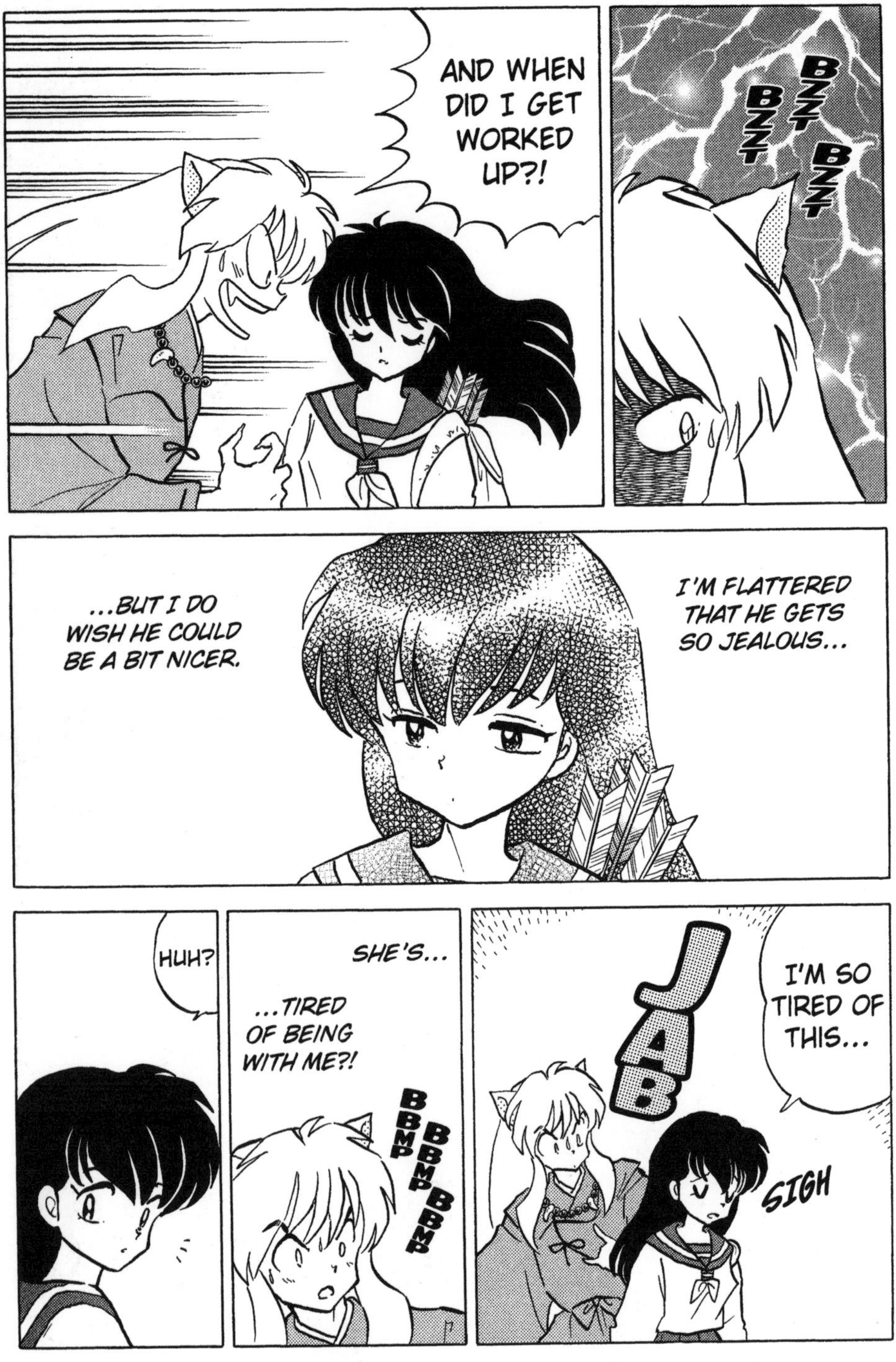
BZZT
BZZT
BZZT
AND WHEN DID I GET WORKED UP?!
I'M FLATTERED THAT HE GETS SO JEALOUS...
...BUT I DO WISH HE COULD BE A BIT NICER.
I'M SO TIRED OF THIS...
JAB
SIGH
SHE'S...
...TIRED OF BEING WITH ME?!
BBMP
BBMP
BBMP
HUH?

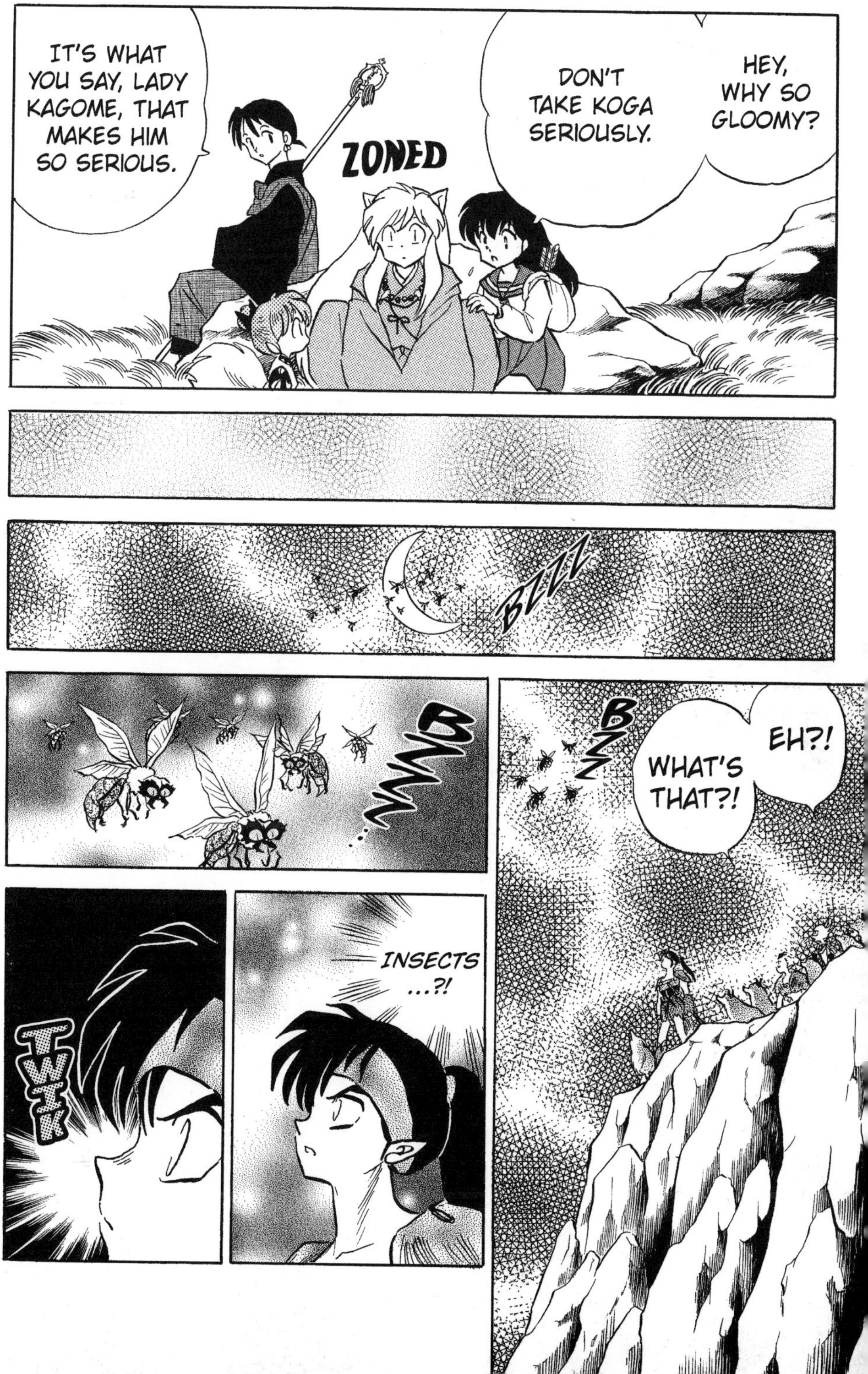
HEY, WHY SO GLOOMY?
DON'T TAKE KOGA SERIOUSLY.
ZONED
IT'S WHAT YOU SAY, LADY KAGOME, THAT MAKES HIM SO SERIOUS.
BZZZ
BZZ
EH?!
WHAT'S THAT?!
BZZZ...
INSECTS ...?!
TWIK

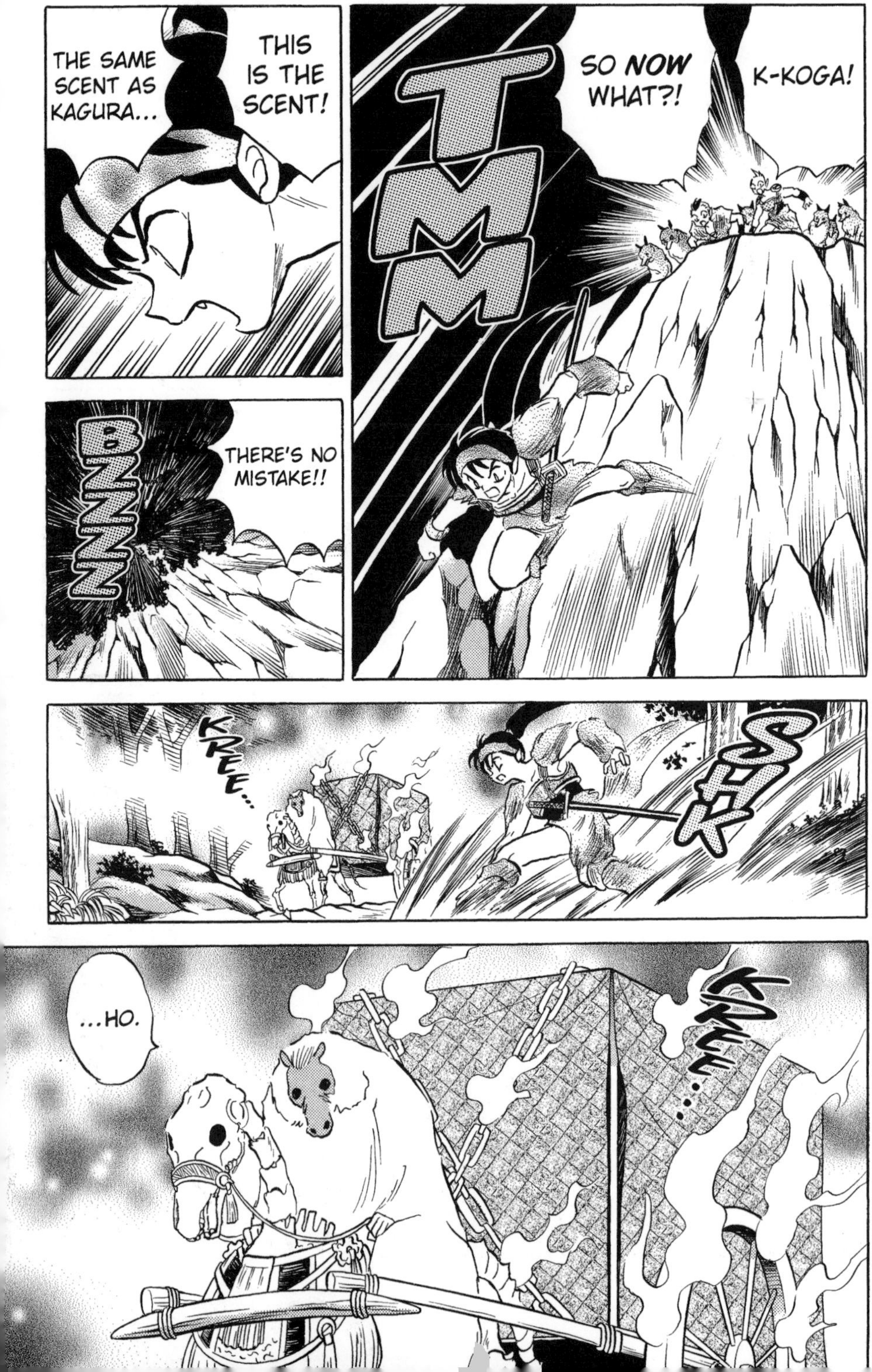

K-KOGA!
SO NOW WHAT?!
TMMM
THIS IS THE SCENT!
THE SAME SCENT AS KAGURA...
THERE'S NO MISTAKE!!
BZZZZ
SHK
KREE...
KREE...
...HO.

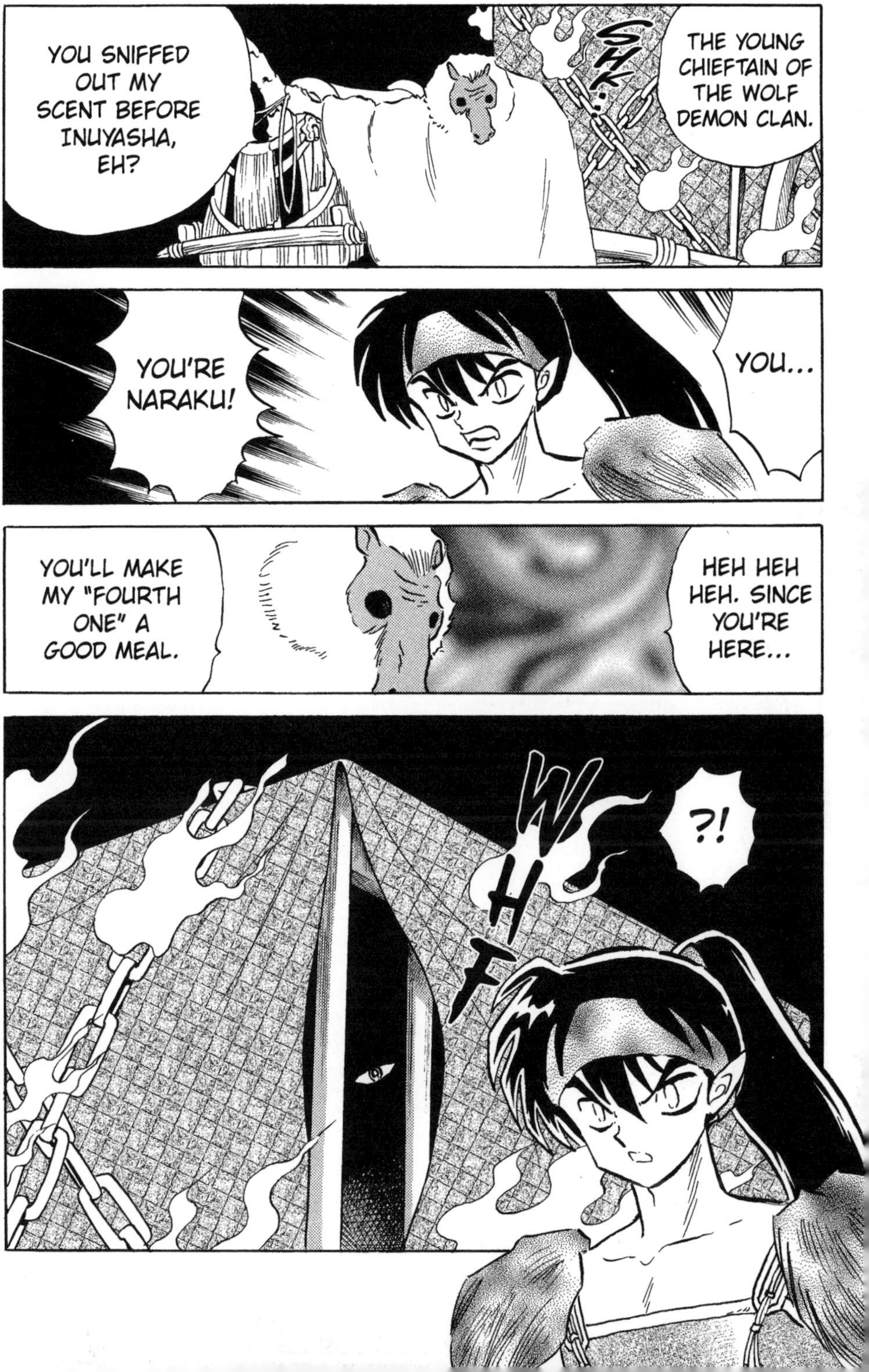
THE YOUNG CHIEFTAIN OF THE WOLF DEMON CLAN.
SHK
YOU SNIFFED OUT MY SCENT BEFORE INUYASHA, EH?
YOU...
YOU'RE NARAKU!
HEH HEH HEH. SINCE YOU'RE HERE...
YOU'LL MAKE MY "FOURTH ONE" A GOOD MEAL.
?!
WHF

SCROLL SEVEN
JUROMARU

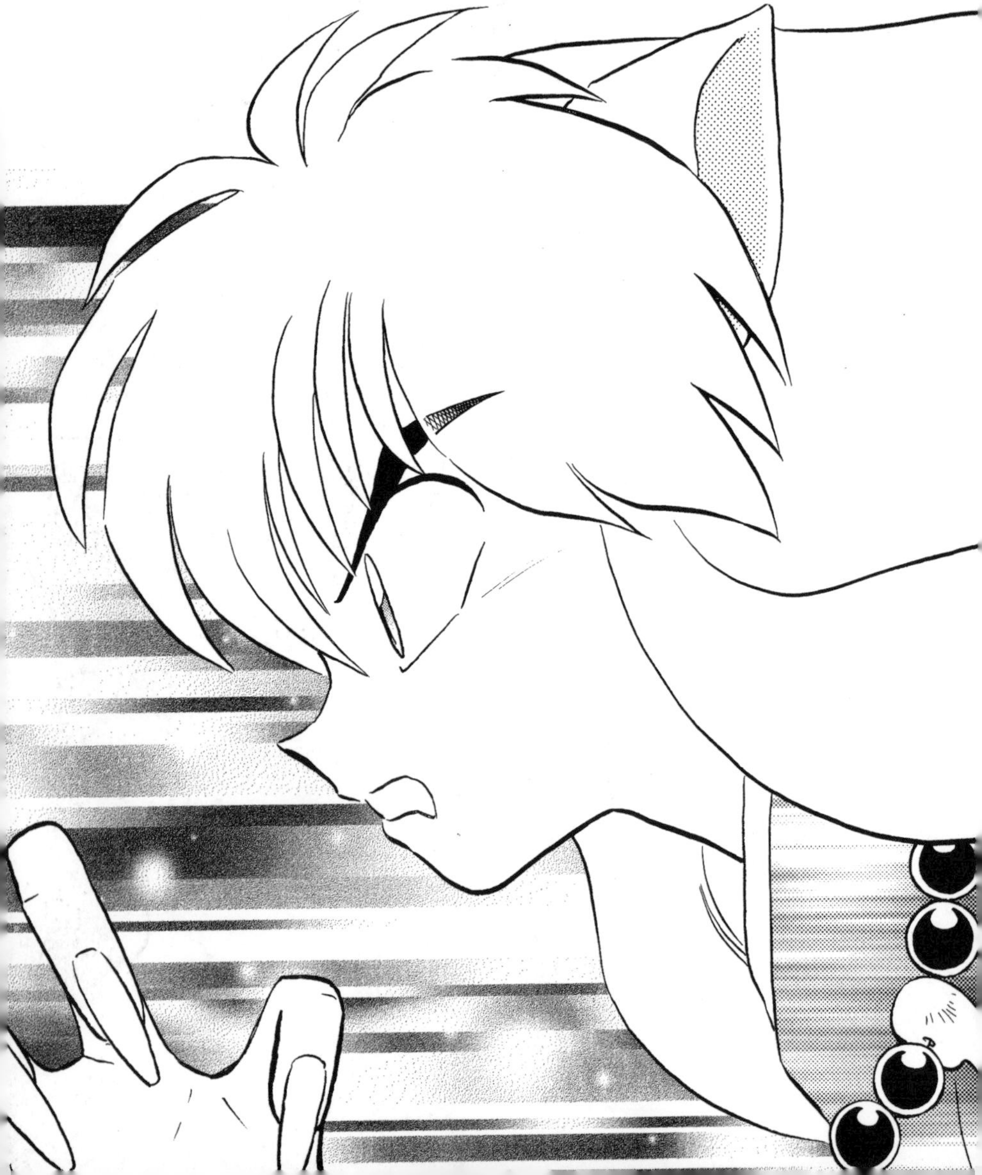

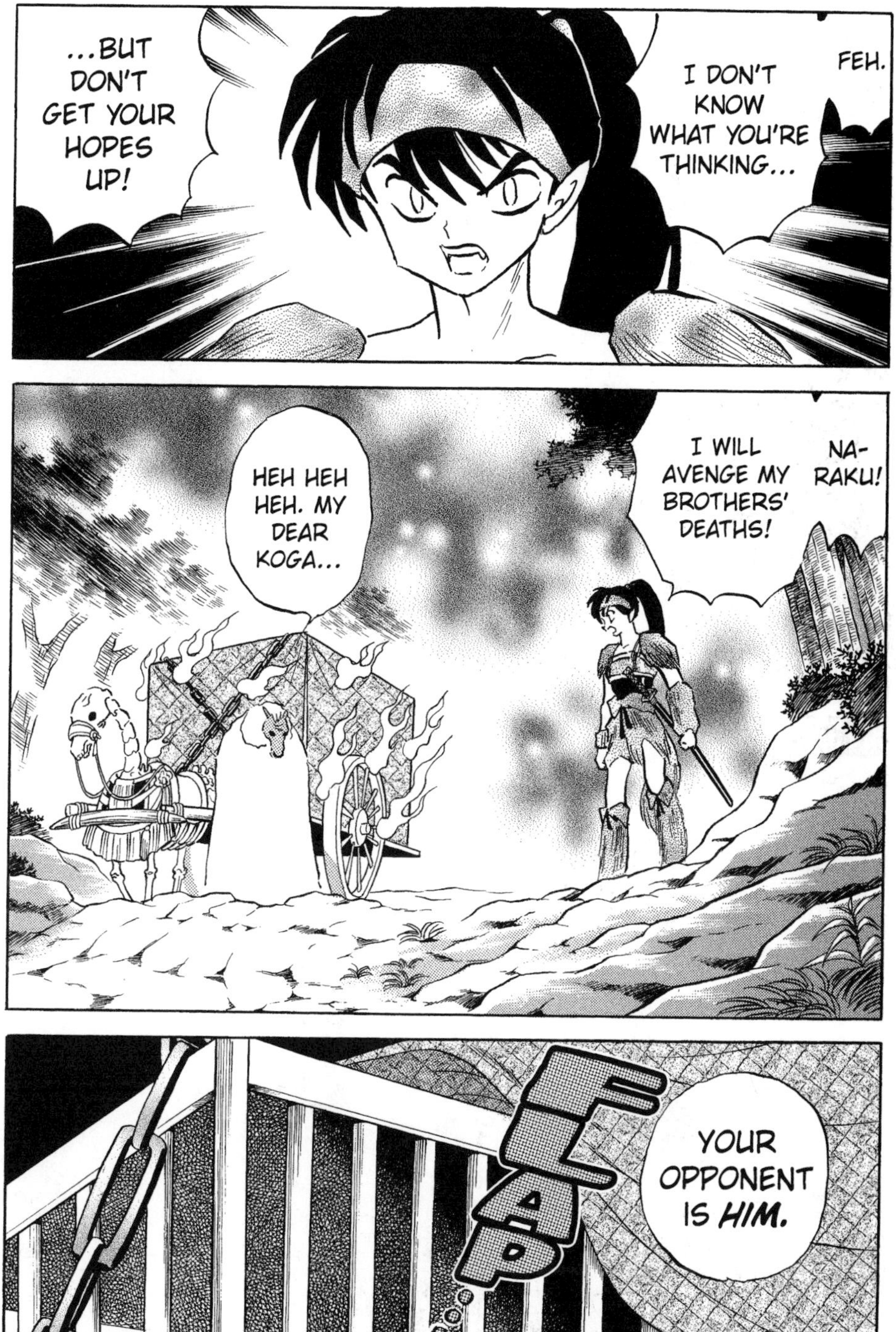
FEH.
I DON'T KNOW WHAT YOU'RE THINKING...
...BUT DON'T GET YOUR HOPES UP!
NA-RAKU!
I WILL AVENGE MY BROTHERS' DEATHS!
HEH HEH HEH. MY DEAR KOGA...
YOUR OPPONENT IS *HIM.*
FLAP

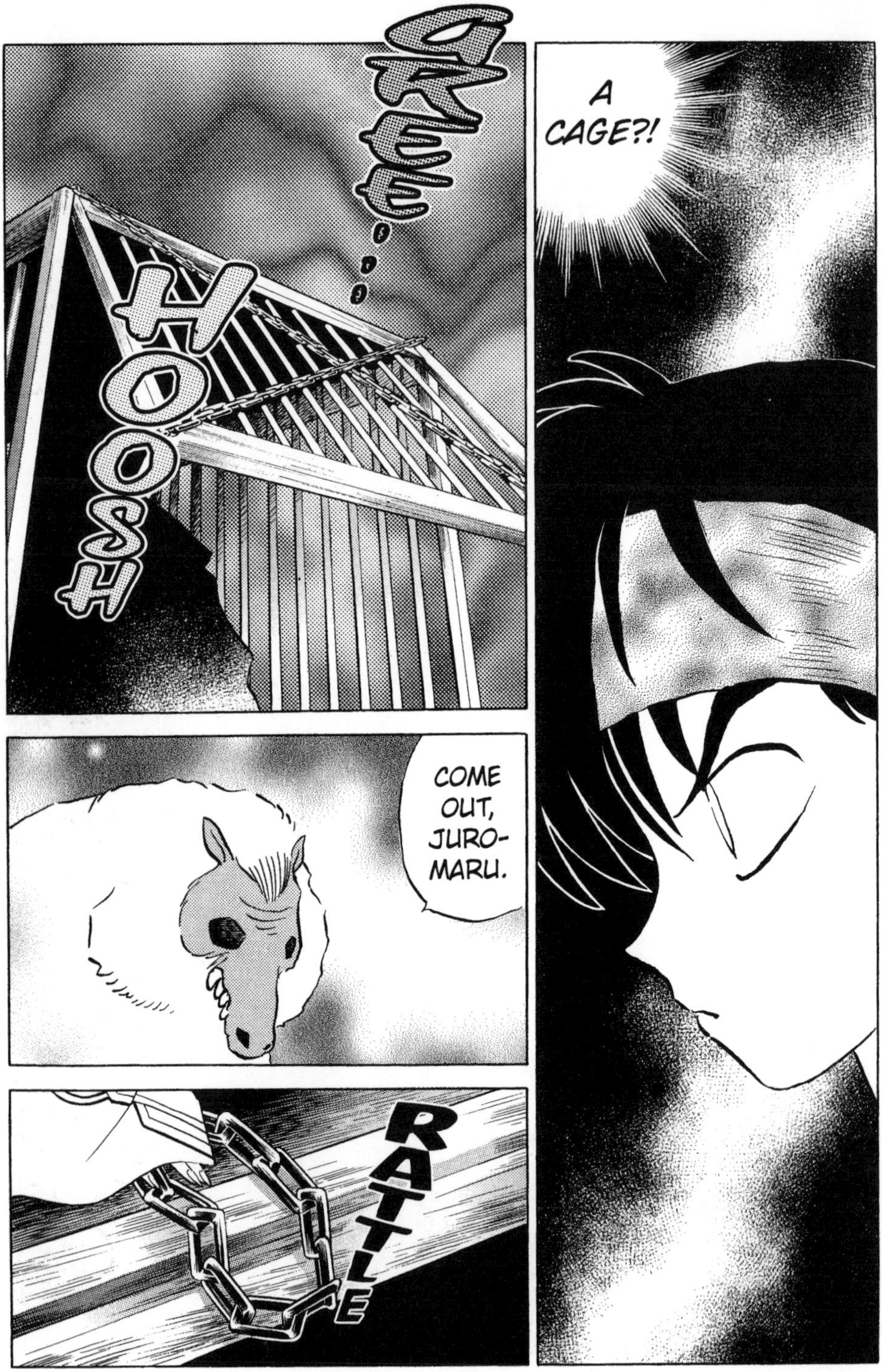
A CAGE?!
CREEE...
WHOOSH
COME OUT, JURO-MARU.
RATTLE

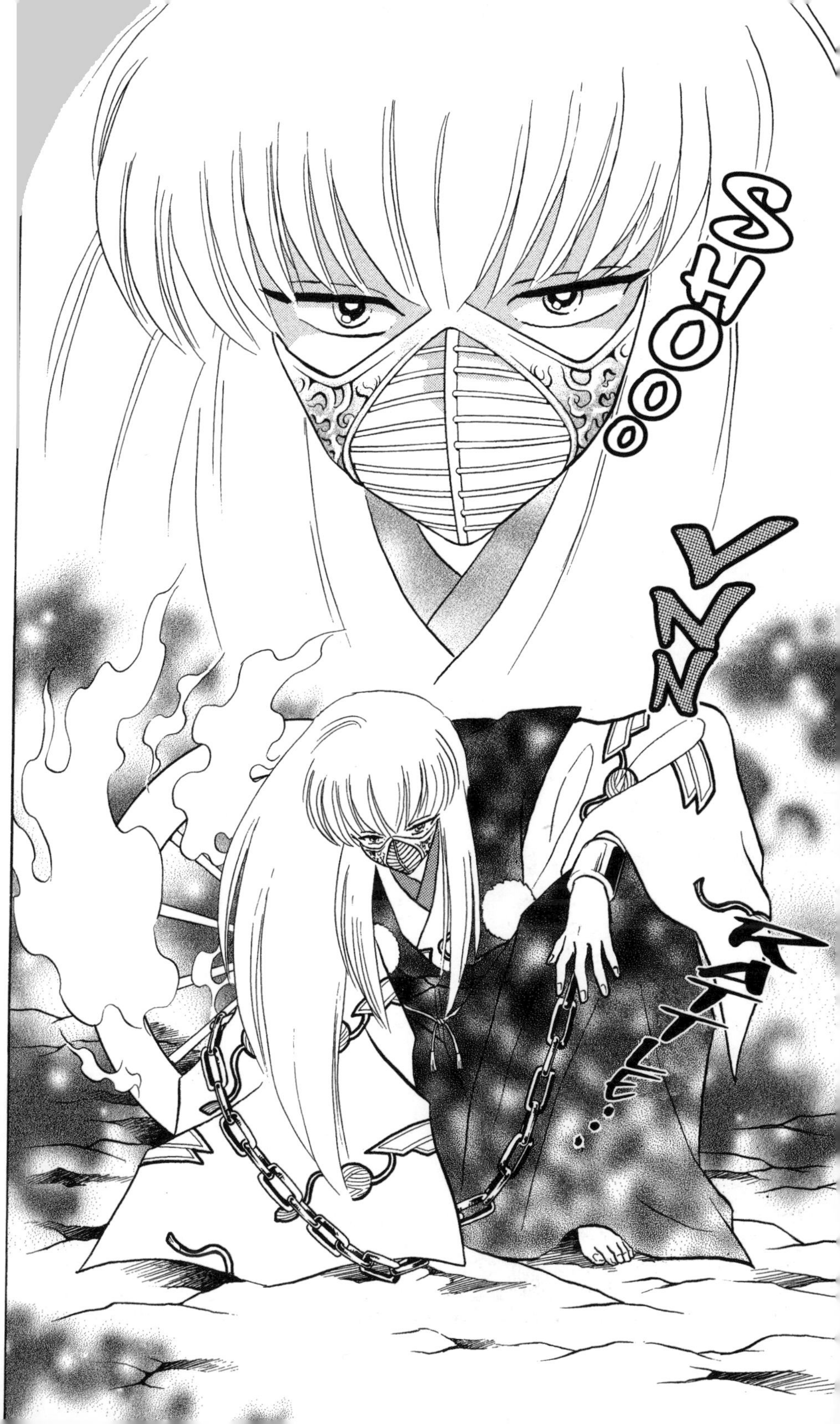
SHOOO...
VNNN
RATTLE...

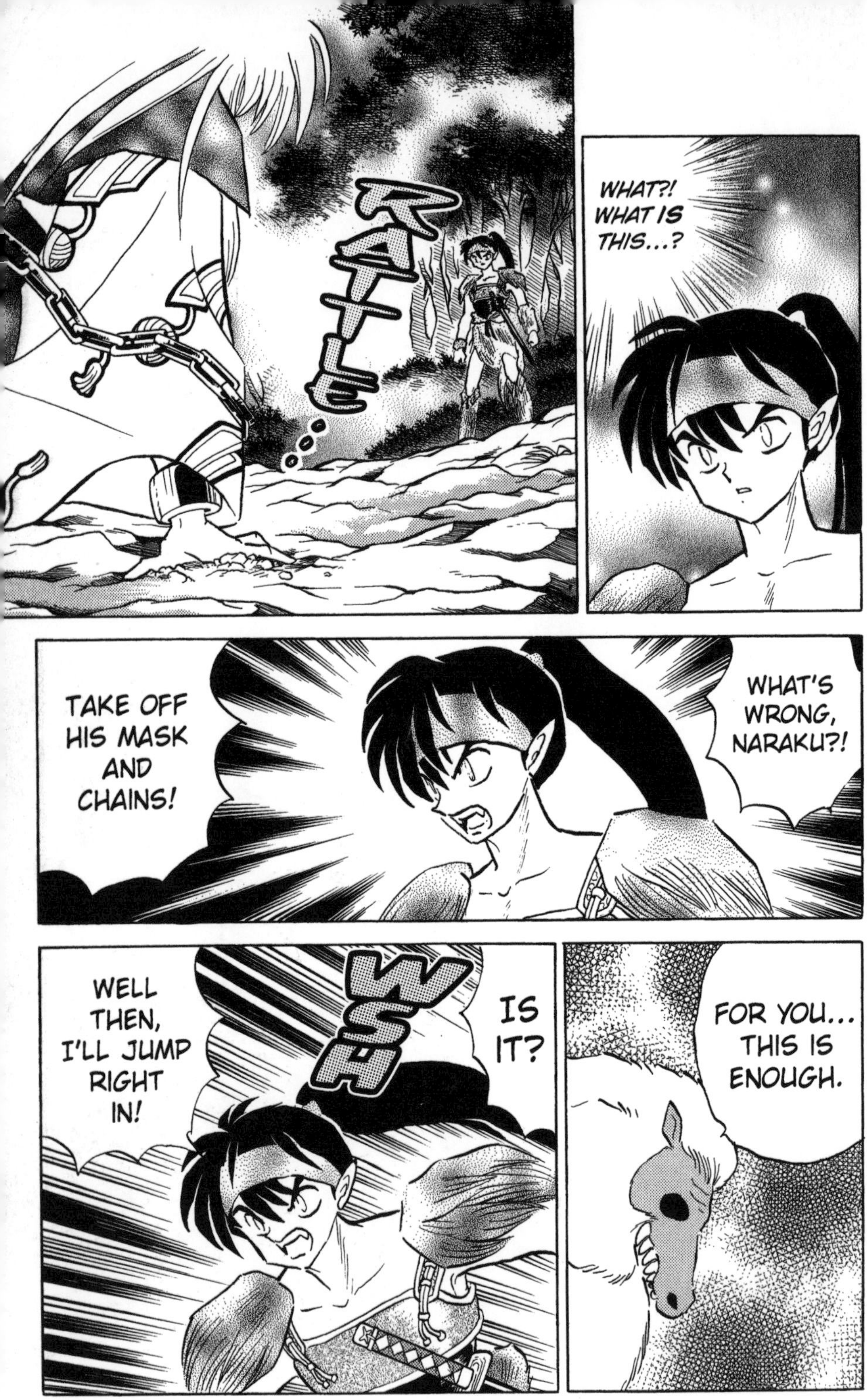
WHAT?! WHAT IS THIS...?
RATTLE...
WHAT'S WRONG, NARAKU?!
TAKE OFF HIS MASK AND CHAINS!
FOR YOU... THIS IS ENOUGH.
IS IT?
WSH
WELL THEN, I'LL JUMP RIGHT IN!

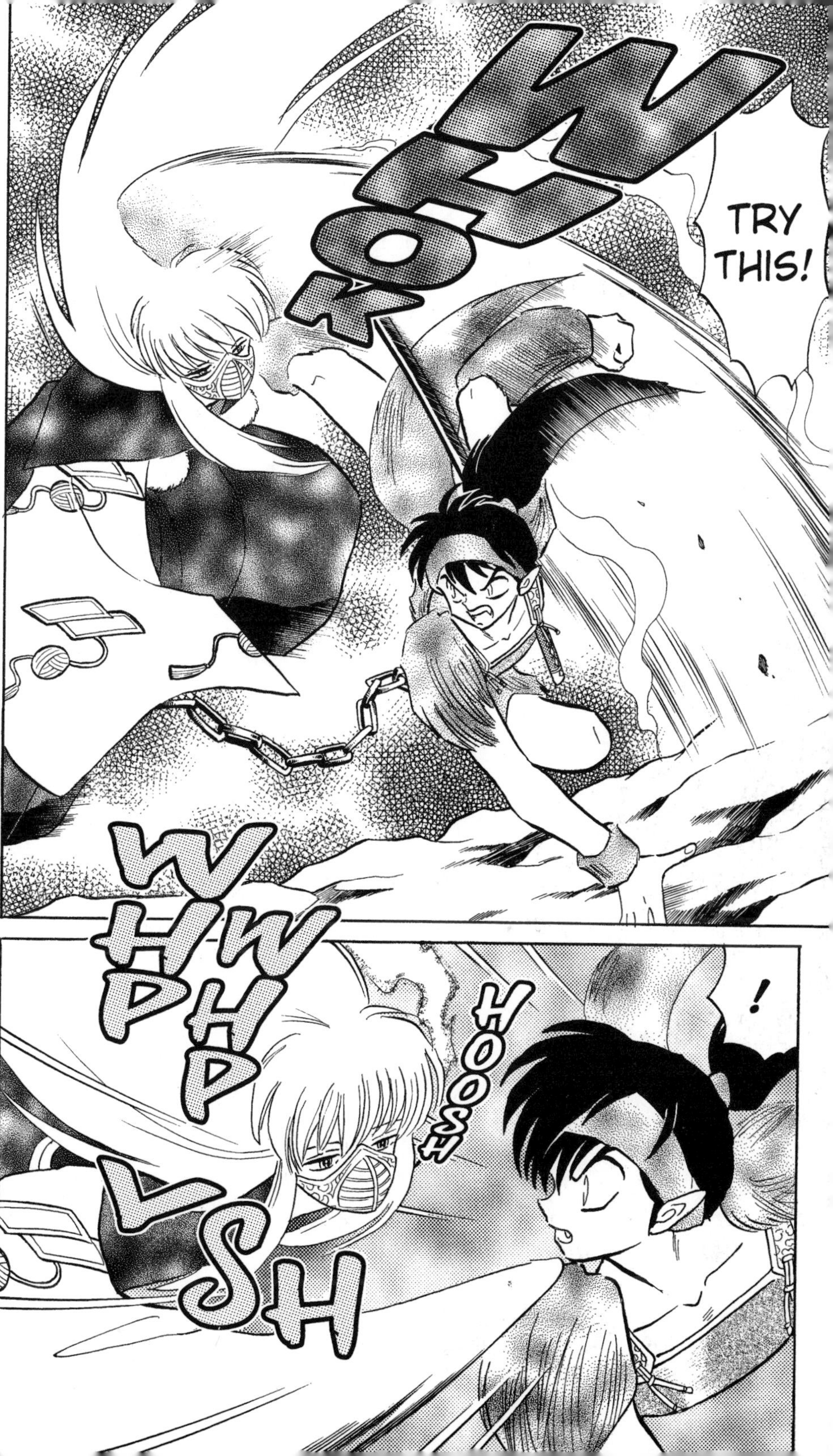
WHOK
TRY THIS!
WHP
WHP
HOOOSH
VSH
!

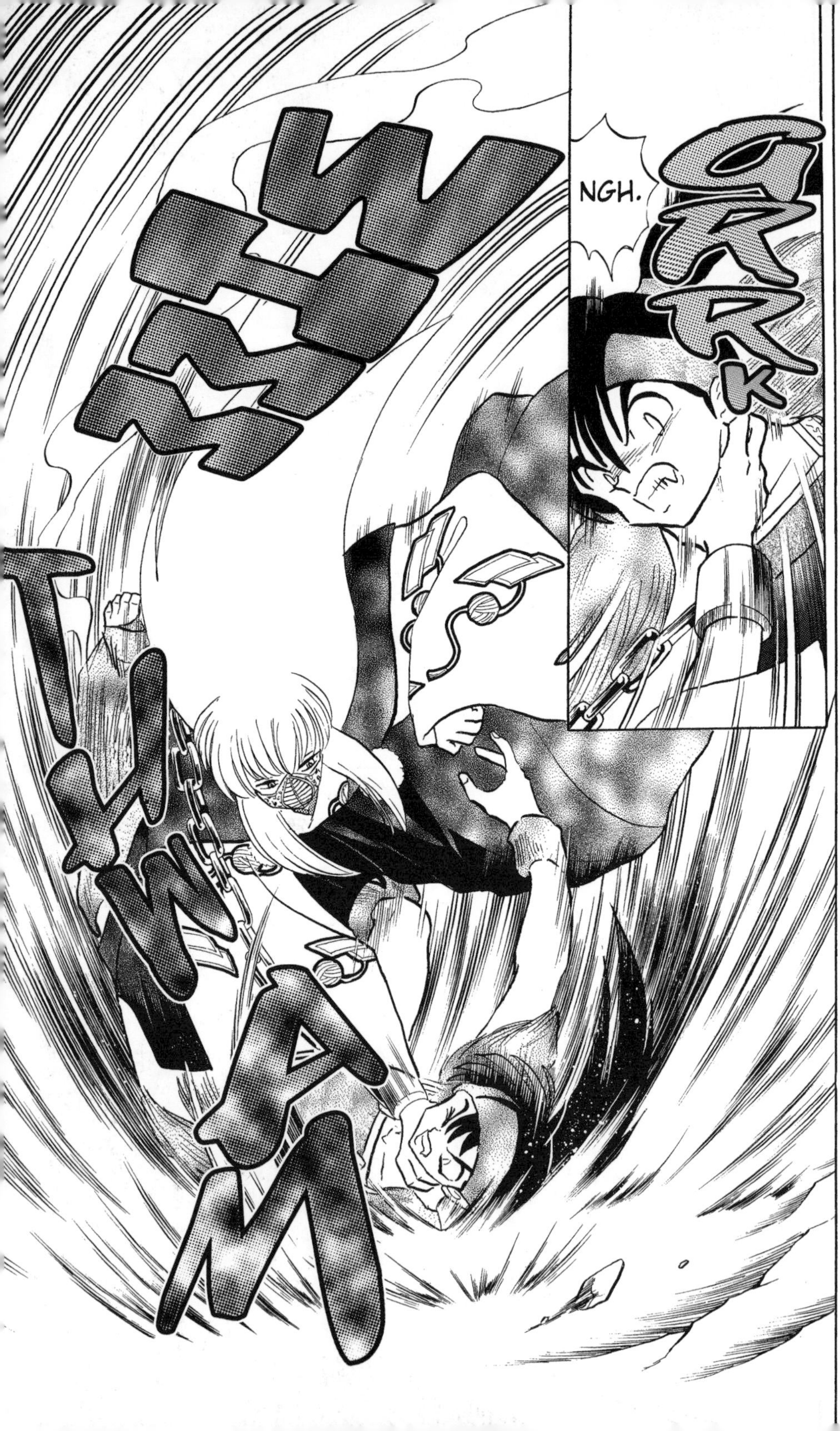
GRRk
NGH.
WHMM
THWAM

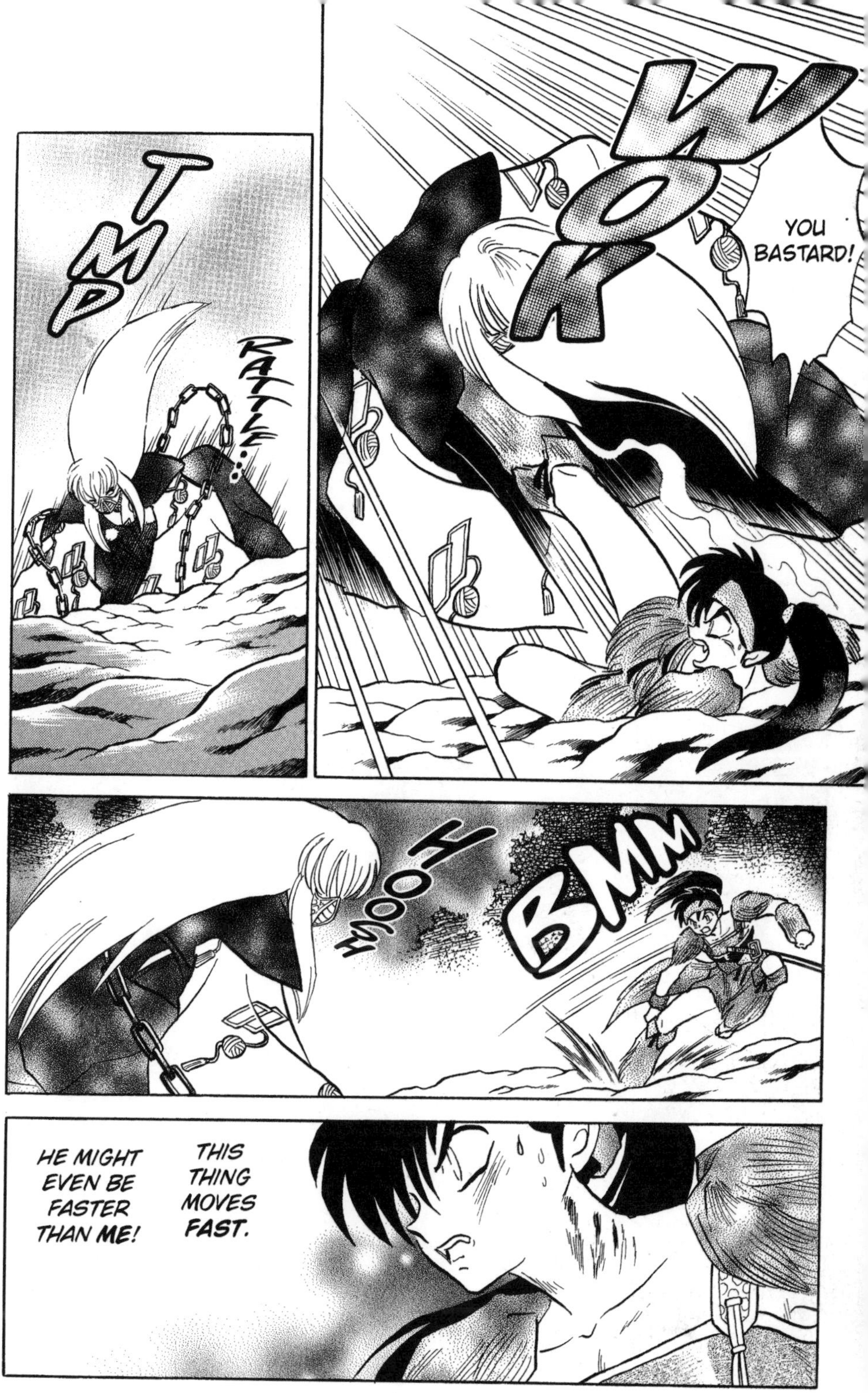
WOK
YOU BASTARD!
TMP
RATTLE...
BMM
HOOSH
THIS THING MOVES FAST.
HE MIGHT EVEN BE FASTER THAN ME!

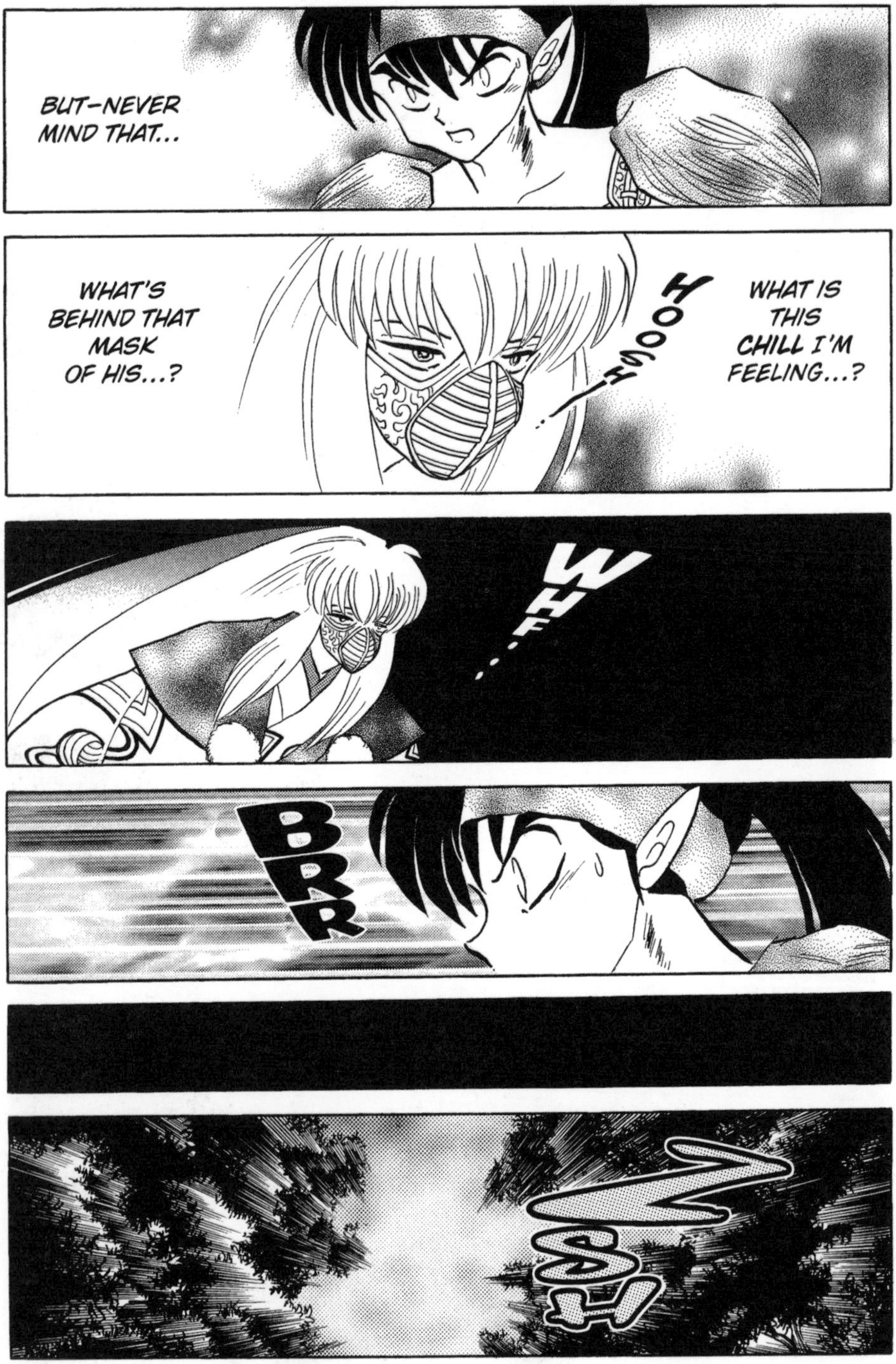
BUT—NEVER MIND THAT...
WHAT IS THIS CHILL I'M FEELING...?
HOOSH...
WHAT'S BEHIND THAT MASK OF HIS...?
WHF...
BRR
ZSSH!

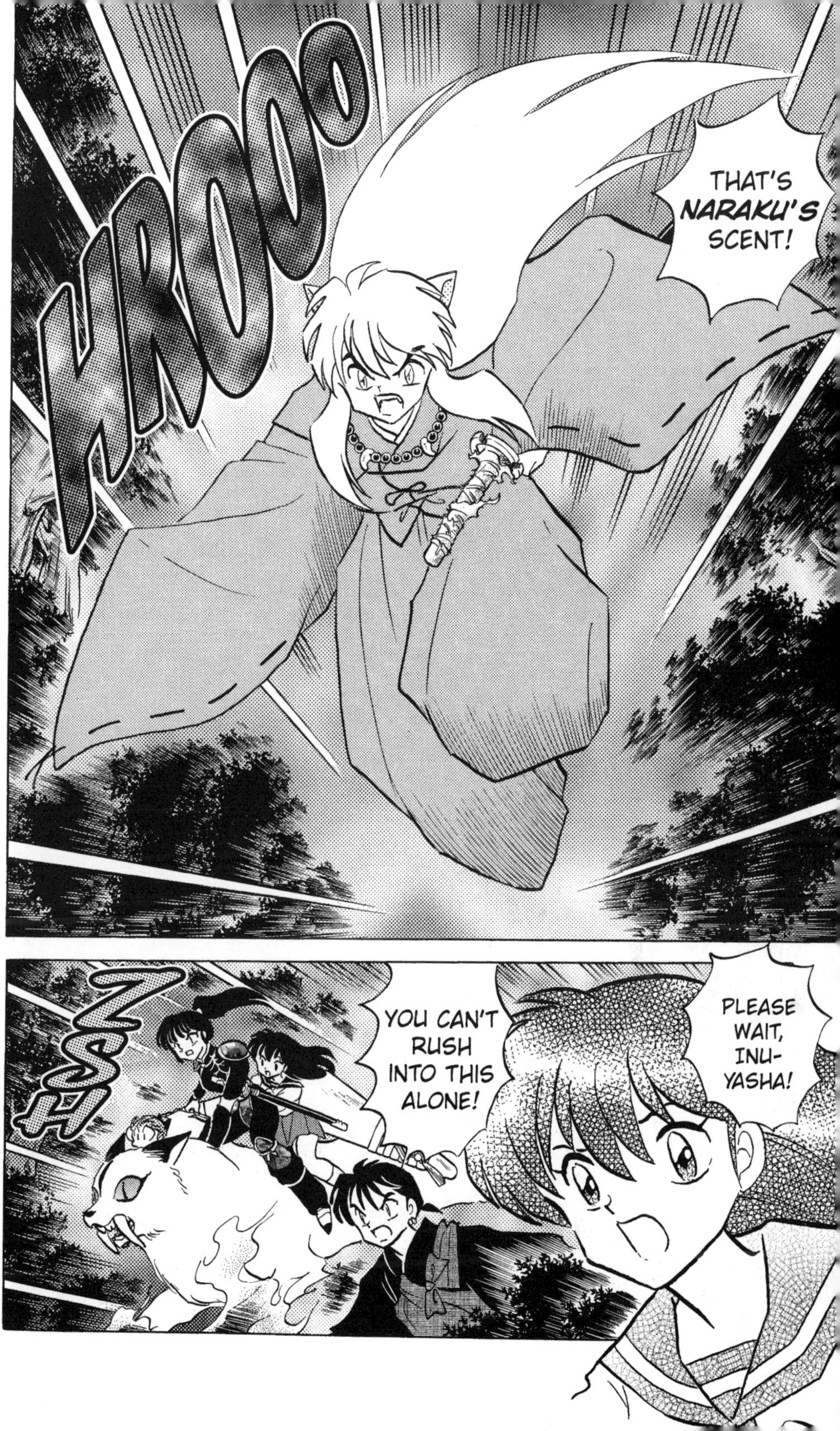
KROOOO
THAT'S **NARAKU'S** SCENT!
PLEASE WAIT, INU-YASHA!
YOU CAN'T RUSH INTO THIS ALONE!
ZSH

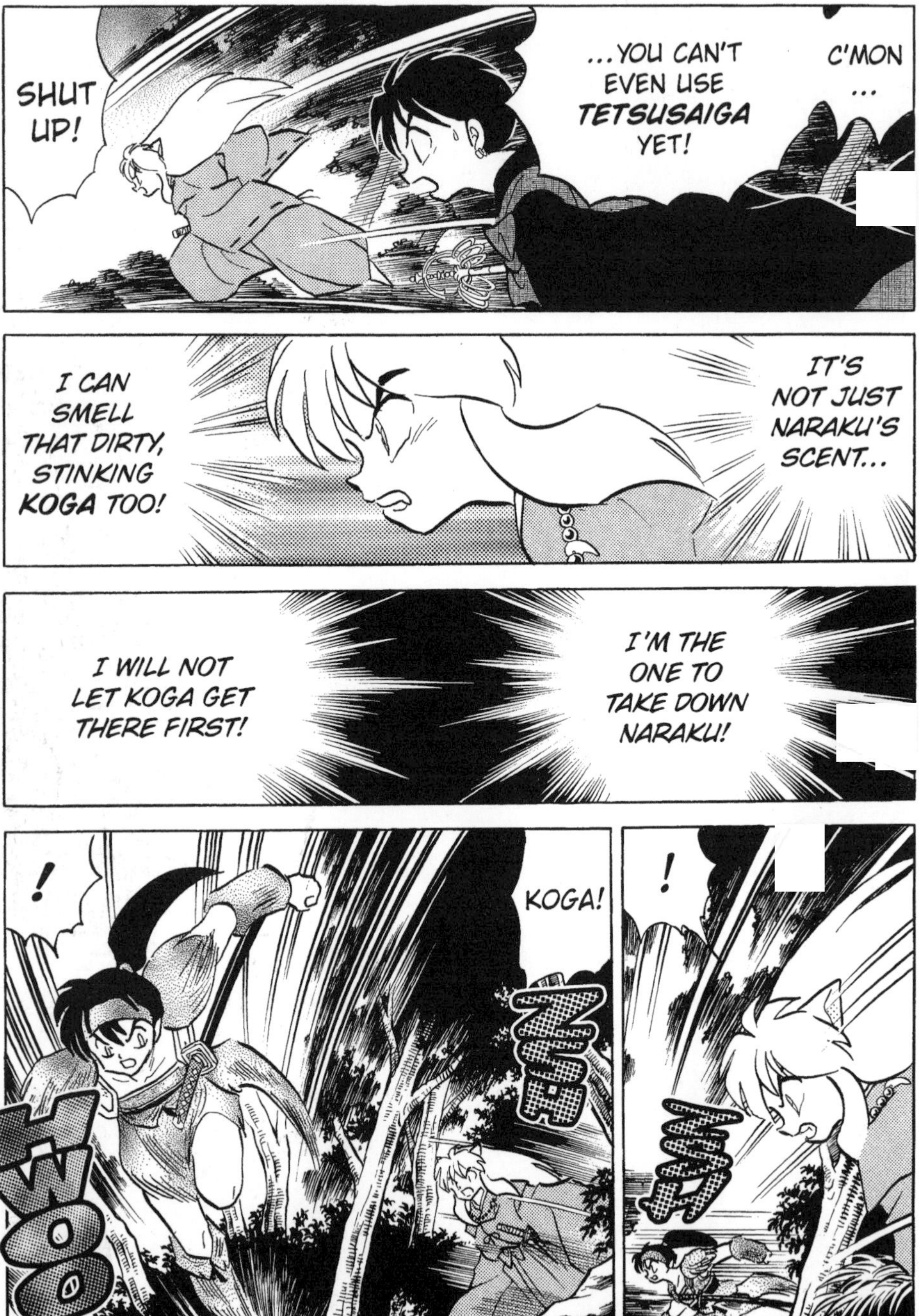
C'MON ...
...YOU CAN'T EVEN USE TETSUSAIGA YET!
SHUT UP!
IT'S NOT JUST NARAKU'S SCENT...
I CAN SMELL THAT DIRTY, STINKING KOGA TOO!
I'M THE ONE TO TAKE DOWN NARAKU!
I WILL NOT LET KOGA GET THERE FIRST!
!
KOGA!
!

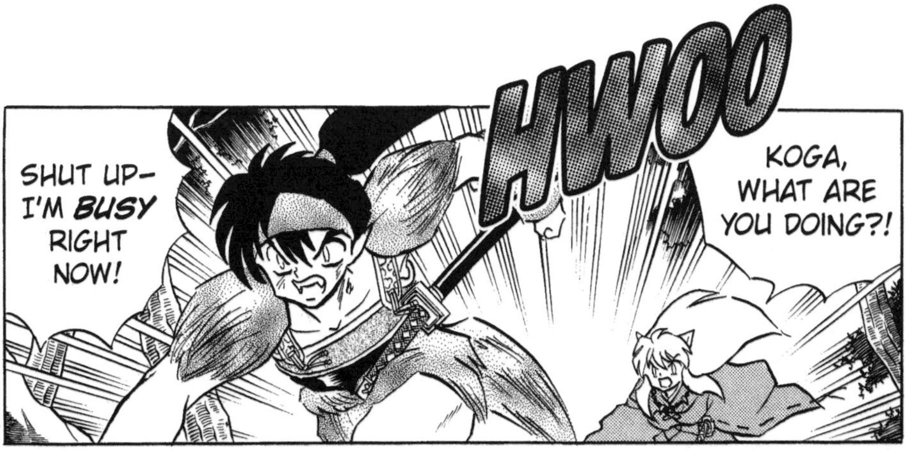
HWOO
KOGA, WHAT ARE YOU DOING?!
SHUT UP– I'M **BUSY** RIGHT NOW!

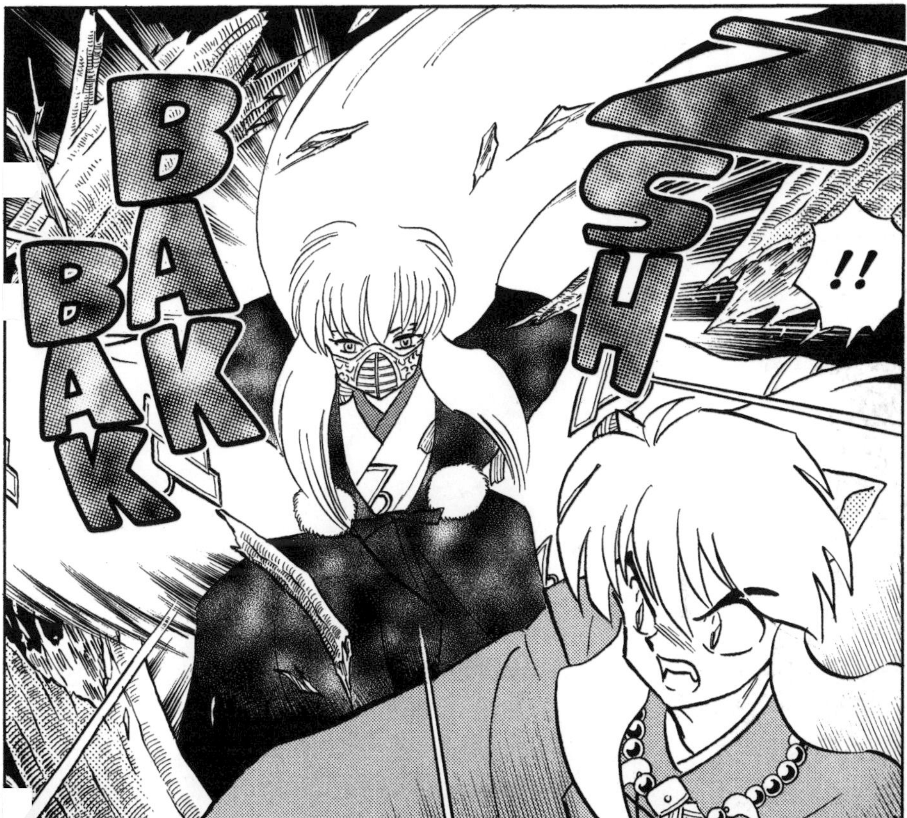
ZSHH
!!
BAK BAK

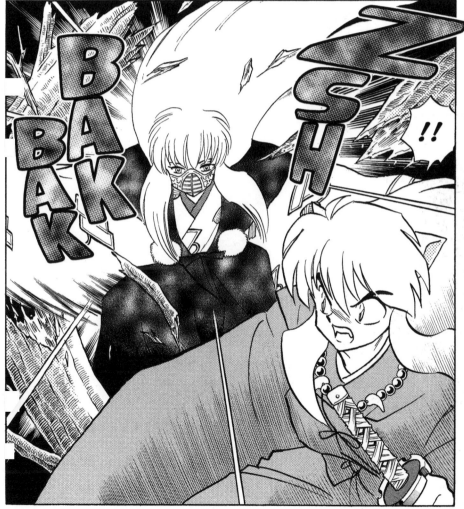

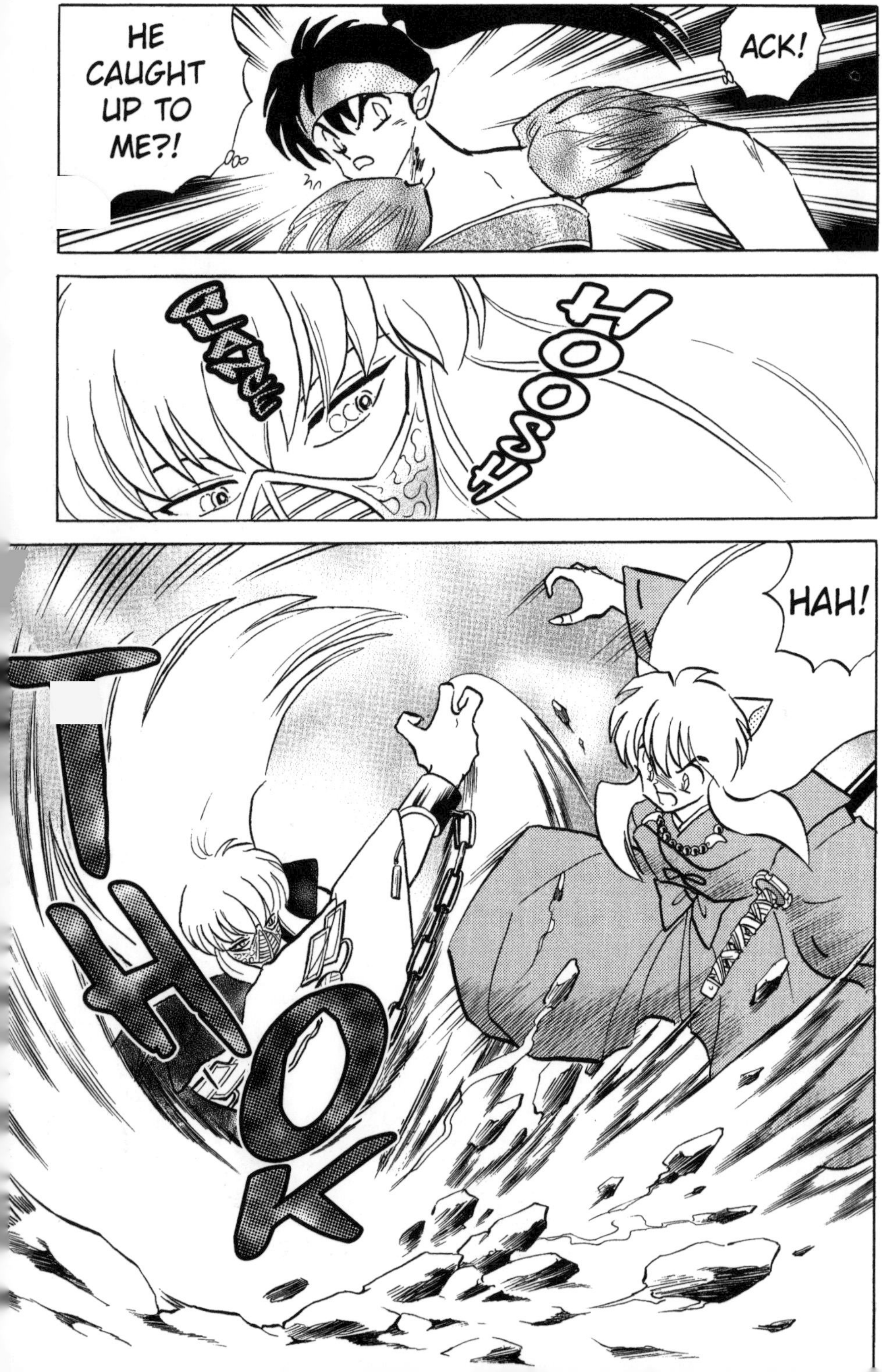
ACK!
HE CAUGHT UP TO ME?!
WHOOSH
GLARE
HAH!
THOK

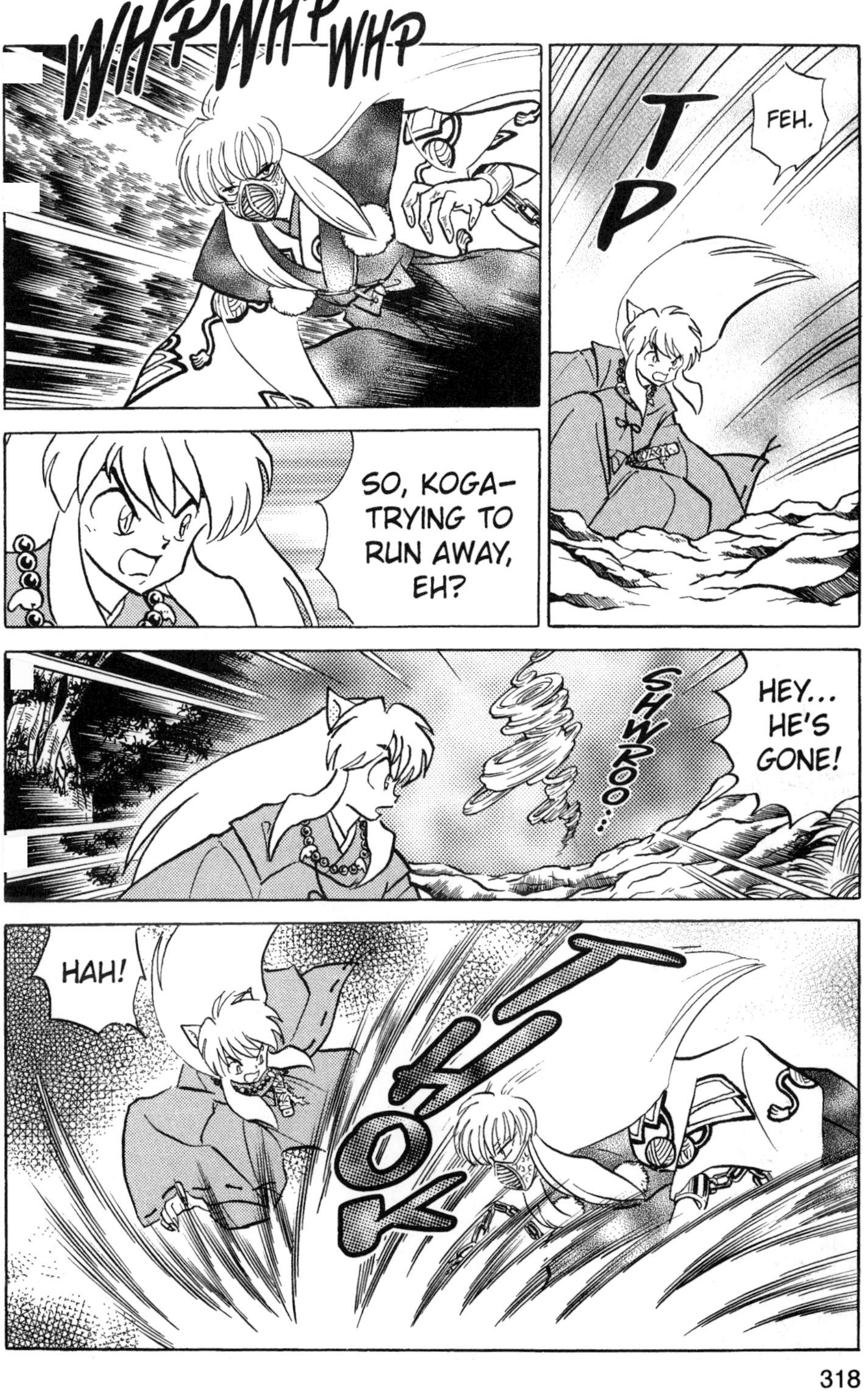

TP
FEH.
WHP WHP WHP
SO, KOGA-TRYING TO RUN AWAY, EH?
HEY... HE'S GONE!
SHWROOO...
THOK
HAH!

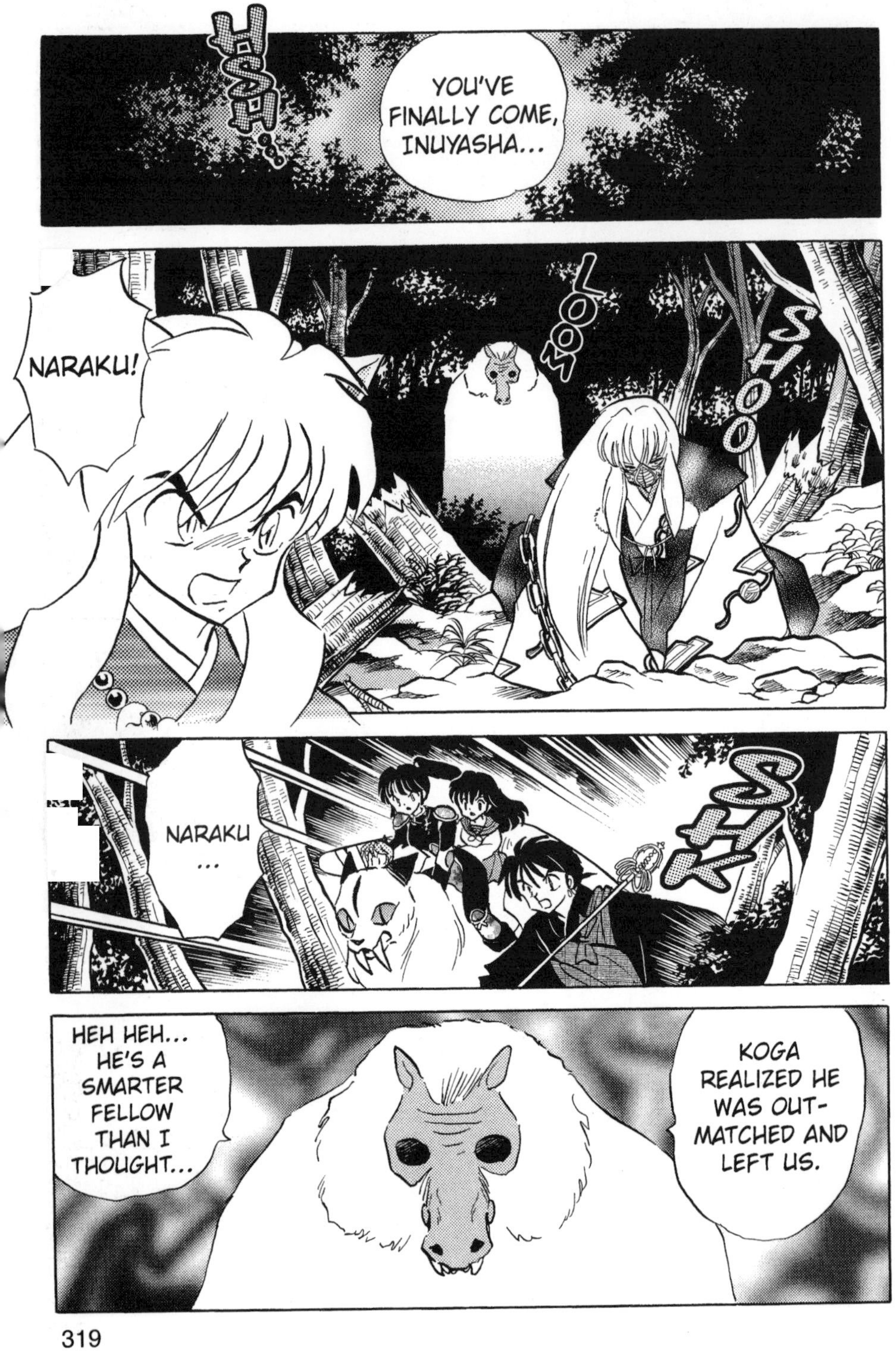
HSSH...
YOU'VE FINALLY COME, INUYASHA...
SHOOO
LOOOM
NARAKU!
SHK
NARAKU ...
KOGA REALIZED HE WAS OUT-MATCHED AND LEFT US.
HEH HEH... HE'S A SMARTER FELLOW THAN I THOUGHT...

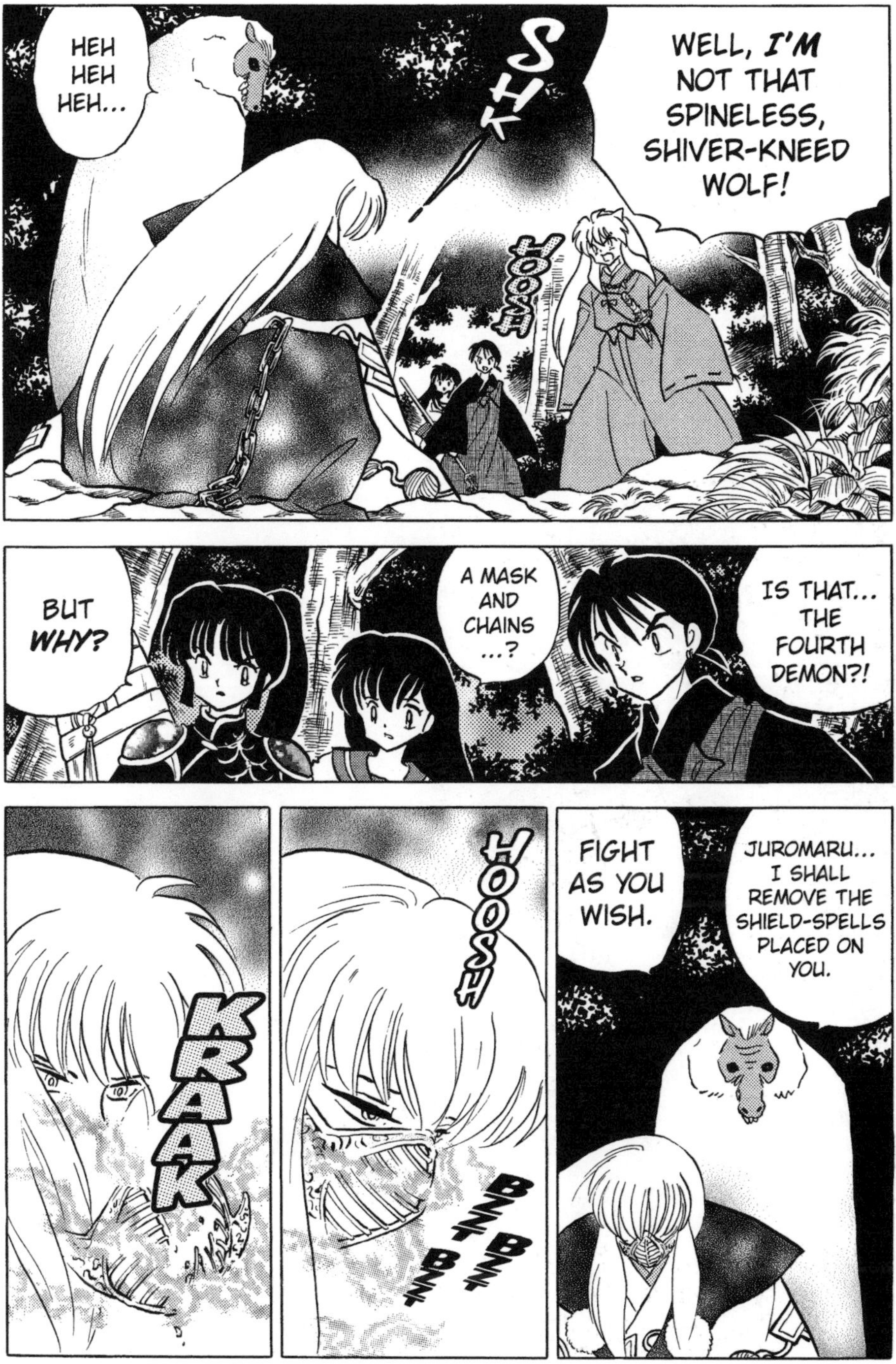
WELL, *I'M* NOT THAT SPINELESS, SHIVER-KNEED WOLF!
SHK
HEH HEH HEH...
WHOOSH
IS THAT... THE FOURTH DEMON?!
A MASK AND CHAINS ...?
BUT *WHY?*
JUROMARU... I SHALL REMOVE THE SHIELD-SPELLS PLACED ON YOU.
FIGHT AS YOU WISH.
WHOOSH
BZZT BZZT
KRAAK

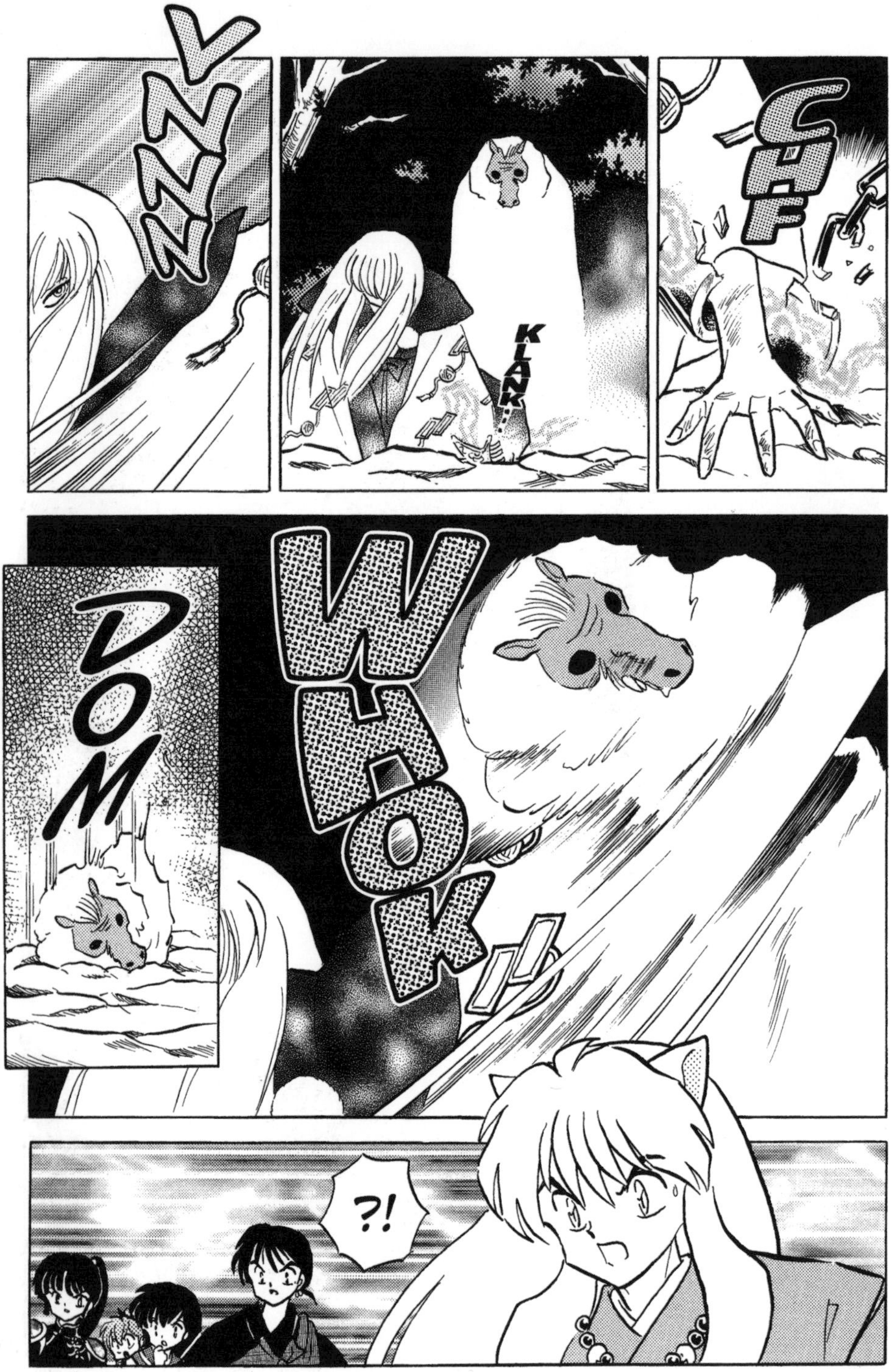
CHF
KLANK...
VNNNN
WHOK
DOM
?!

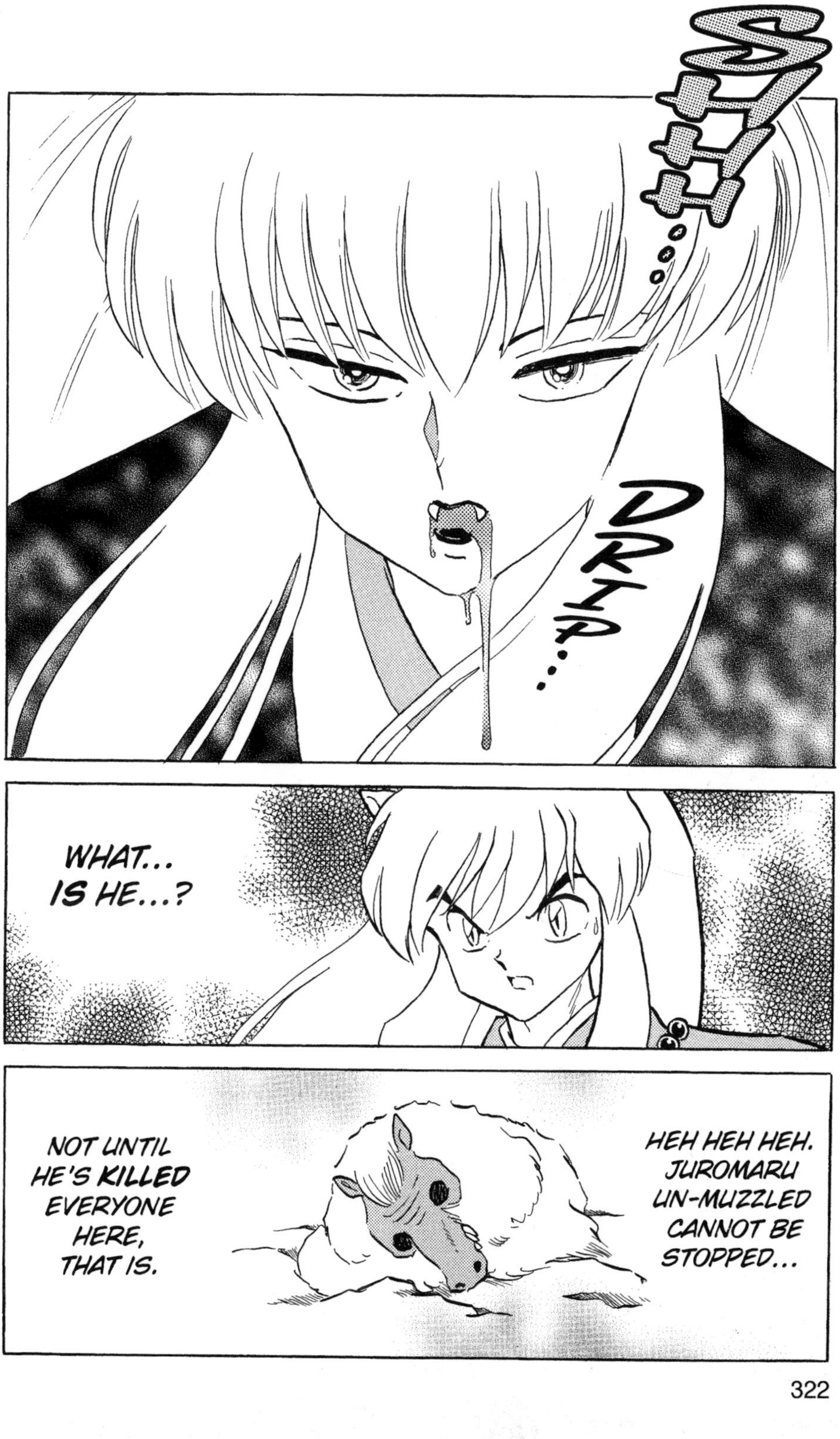
SHHH...
DRIP...
WHAT... IS HE...?
HEH HEH HEH. JUROMARU UN-MUZZLED CANNOT BE STOPPED...
NOT UNTIL HE'S **KILLED** EVERYONE HERE, THAT IS.

SCROLL EIGHT
WITHOUT SHIELDS

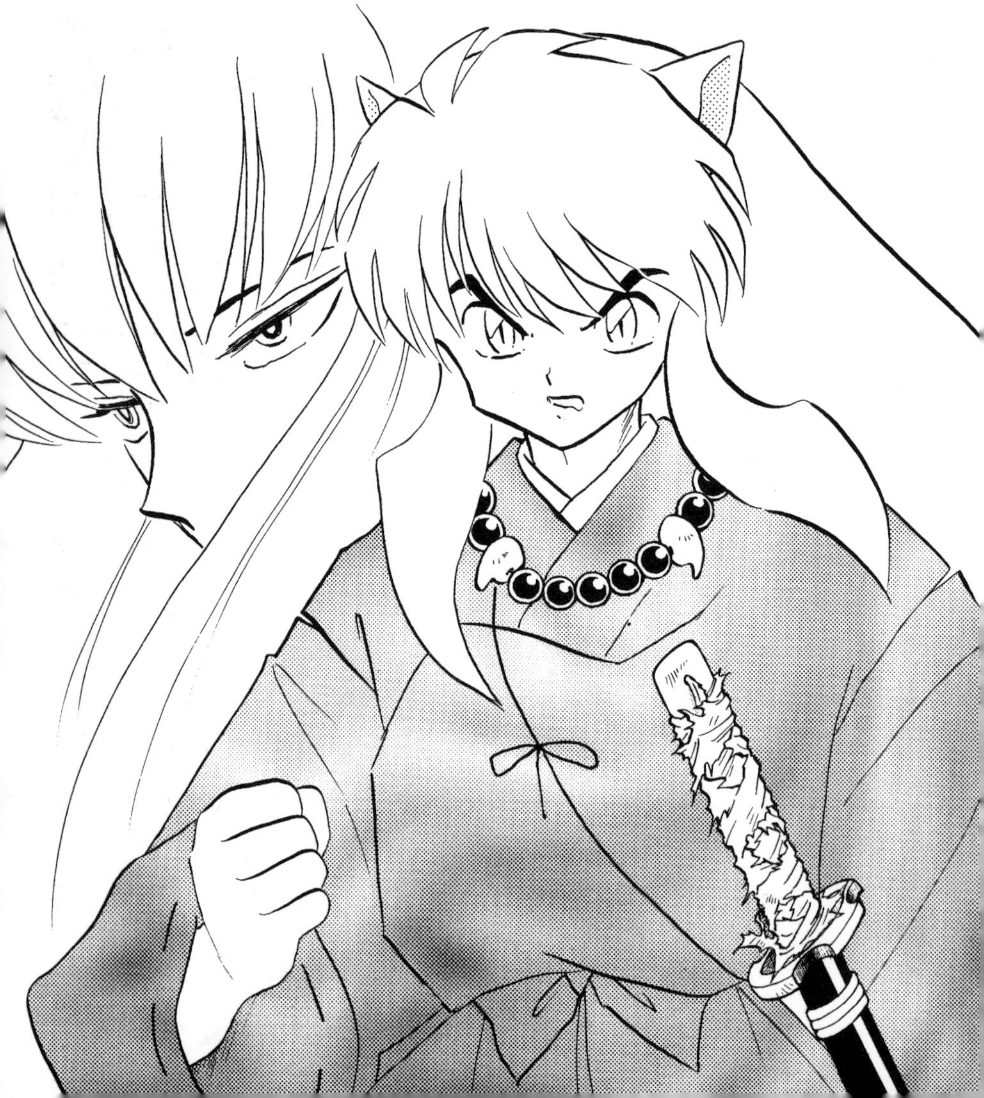

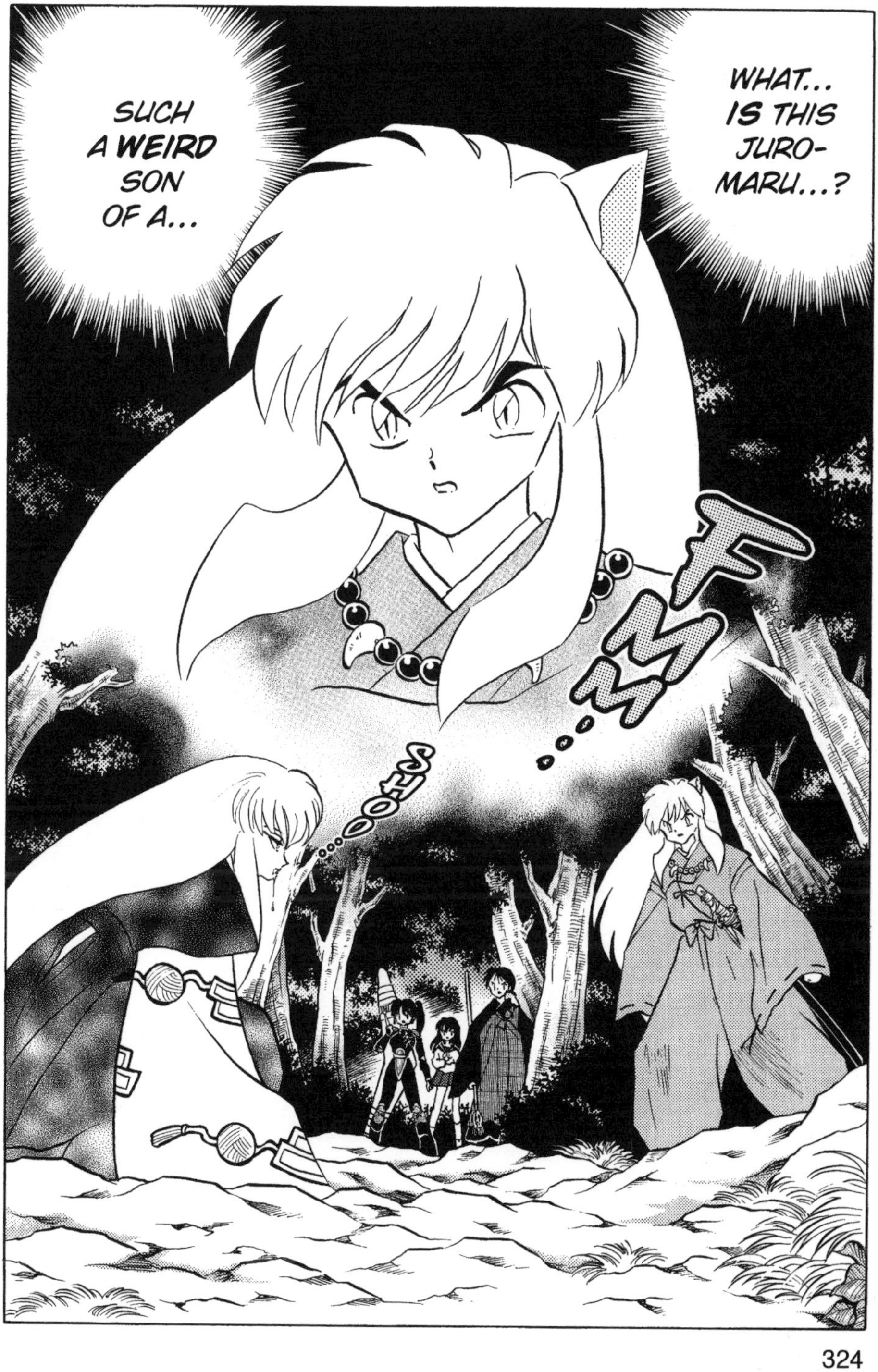
WHAT... IS THIS JURO-MARU...?
SUCH A WEIRD SON OF A...
FMM...
SHOO...

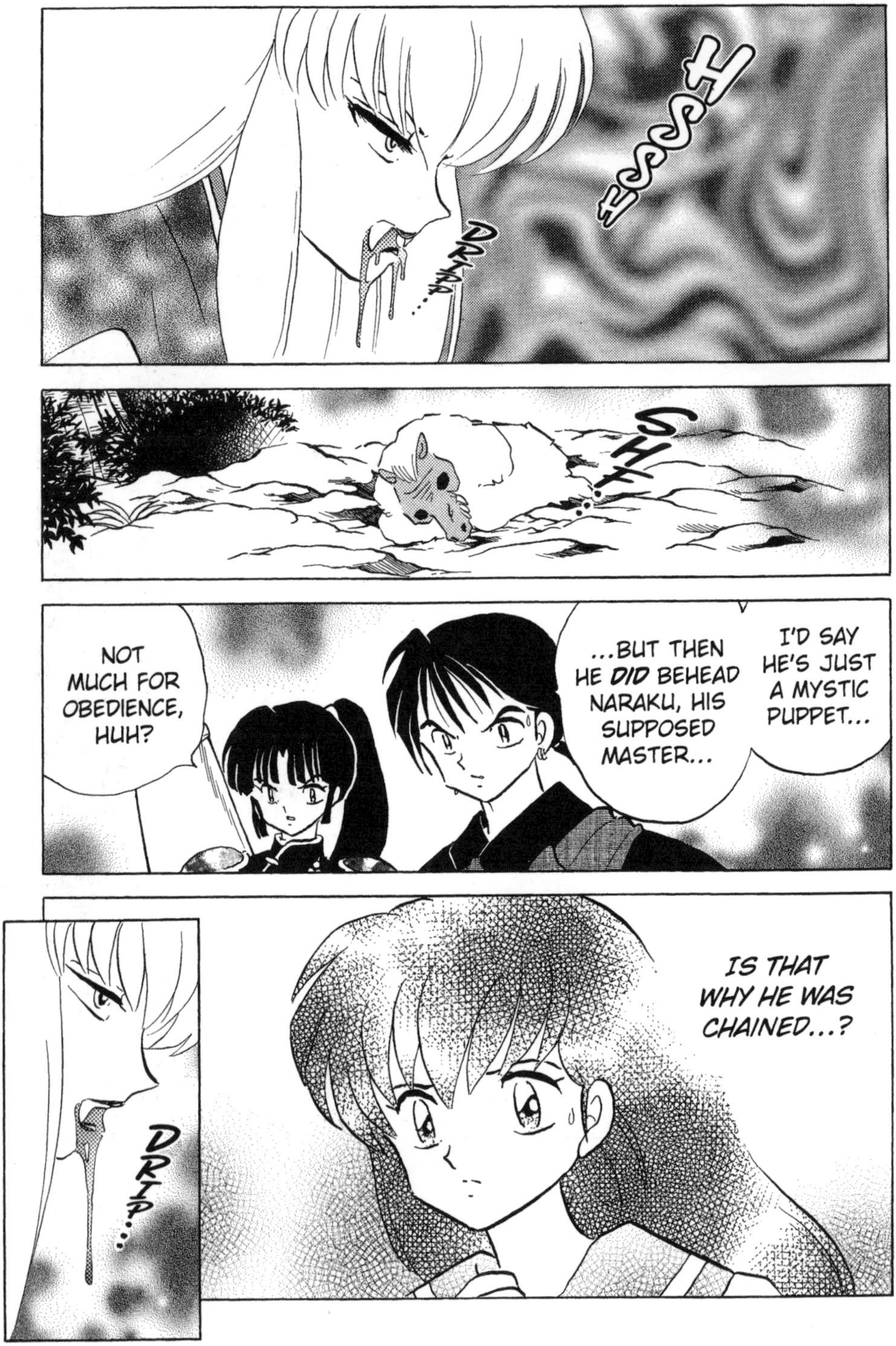
HSSSH
DRIP...
SHF!!
I'D SAY HE'S JUST A MYSTIC PUPPET...
...BUT THEN HE *DID* BEHEAD NARAKU, HIS SUPPOSED MASTER...
NOT MUCH FOR OBEDIENCE, HUH?
IS THAT WHY HE WAS CHAINED...?
DRIP...

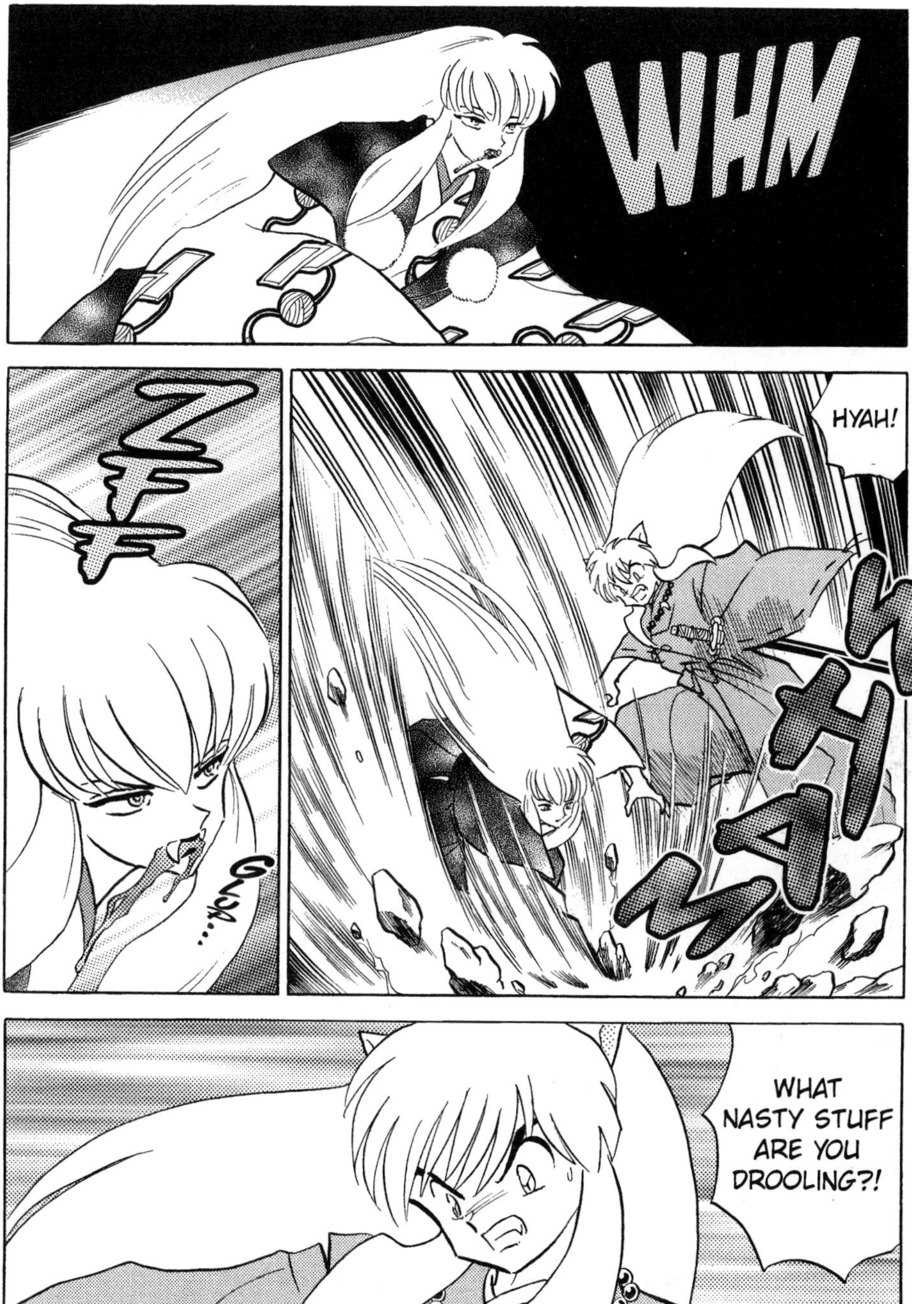
WHM
HYAH!
WHAM
ZFF
GUCK...
WHAT NASTY STUFF ARE YOU DROOLING?!

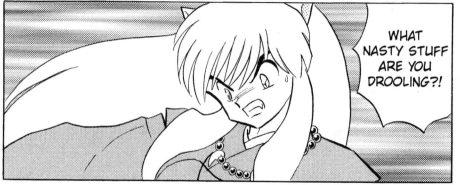

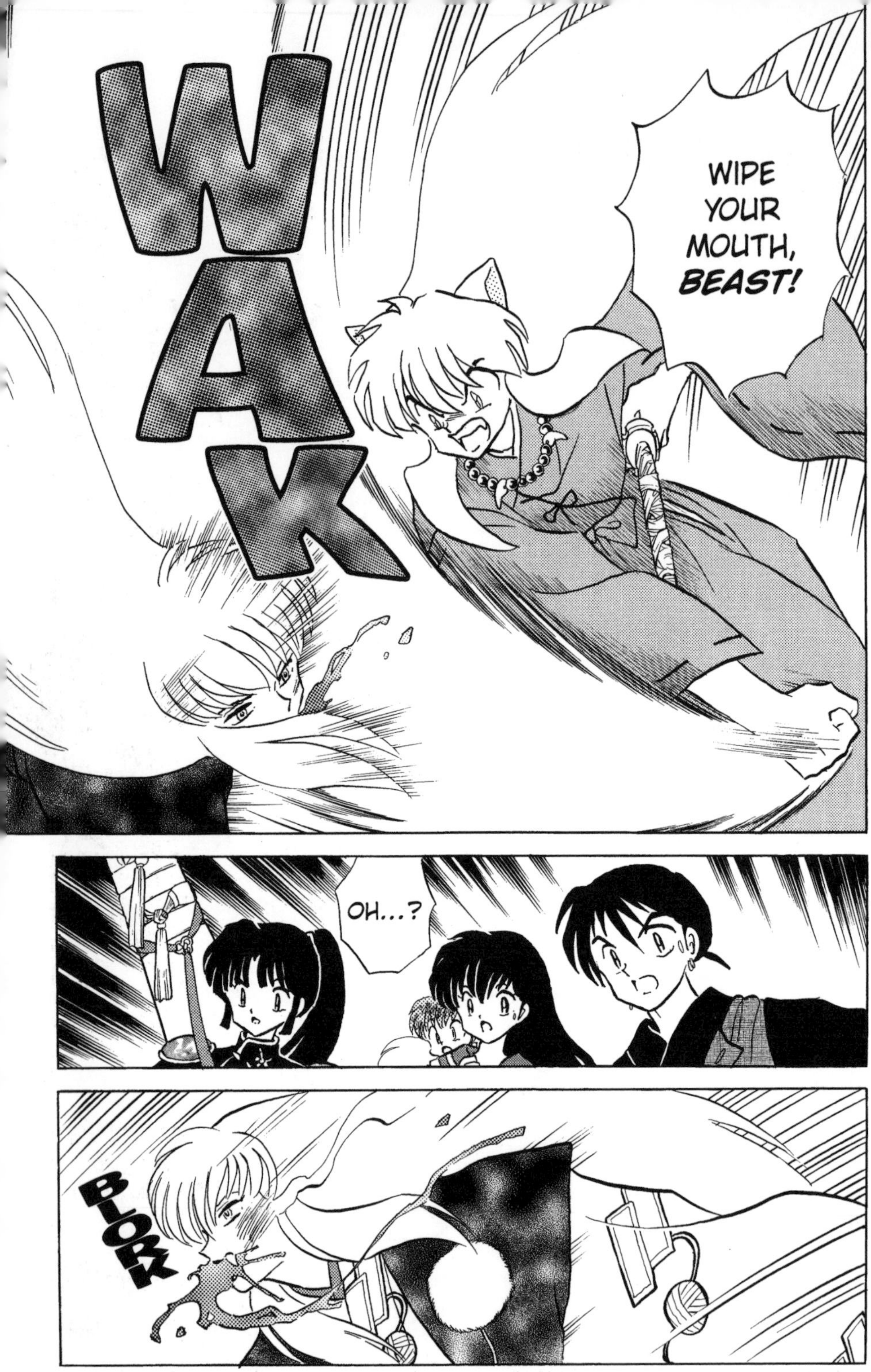
WAK
WIPE YOUR MOUTH, BEAST!
OH...?
BLORK

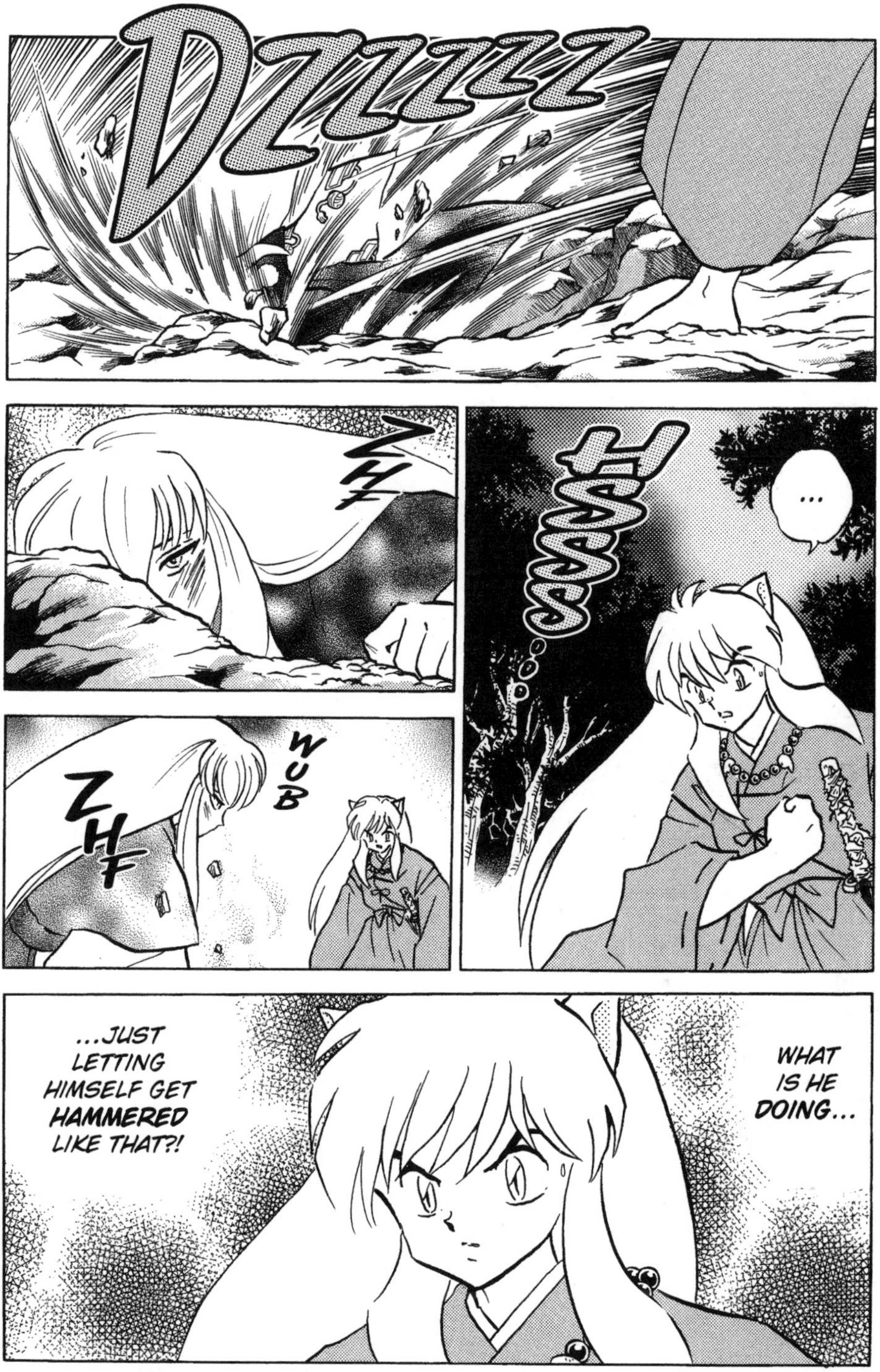
DZZZZZ
SSSSSH!
...
ZHF
ZHF
WUB
WHAT IS HE DOING...
...JUST LETTING HIMSELF GET **HAMMERED** LIKE THAT?!

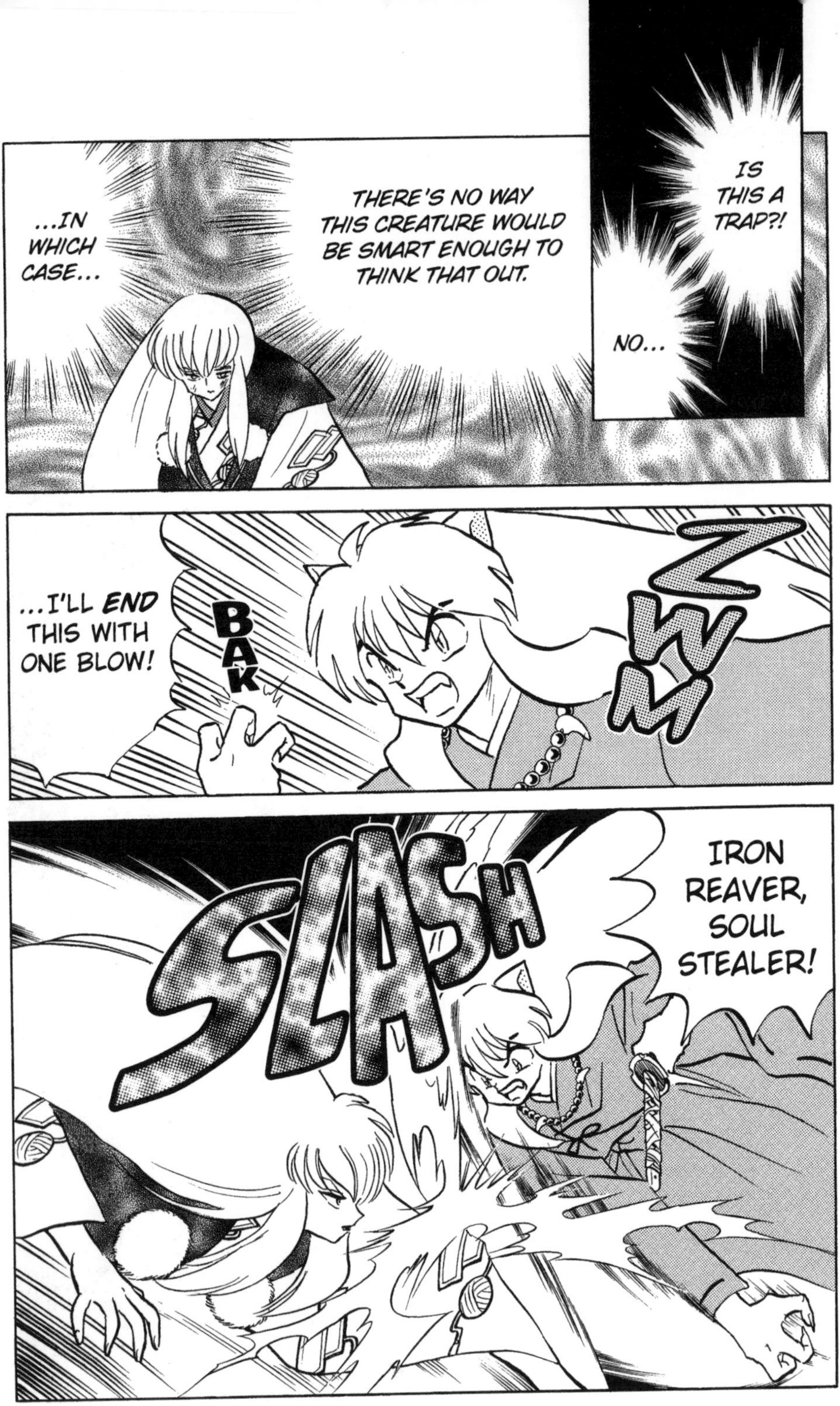
IS THIS A TRAP?!
NO...
THERE'S NO WAY THIS CREATURE WOULD BE SMART ENOUGH TO THINK THAT OUT.
...IN WHICH CASE...
ZWM
BAK
...I'LL END THIS WITH ONE BLOW!
IRON REAVER, SOUL STEALER!
SLASH

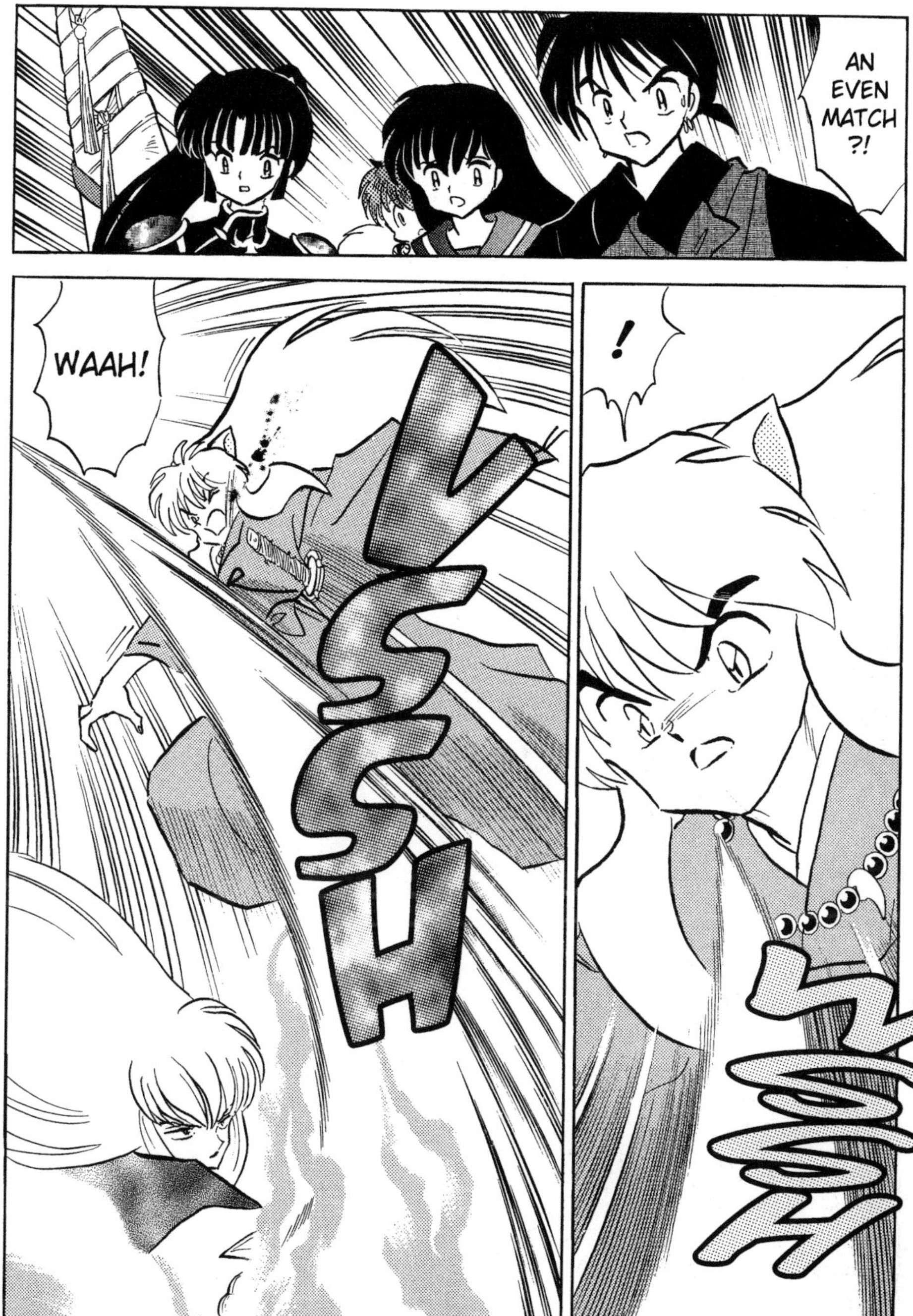
AN EVEN MATCH ?!
!
WAAH!
VSSH

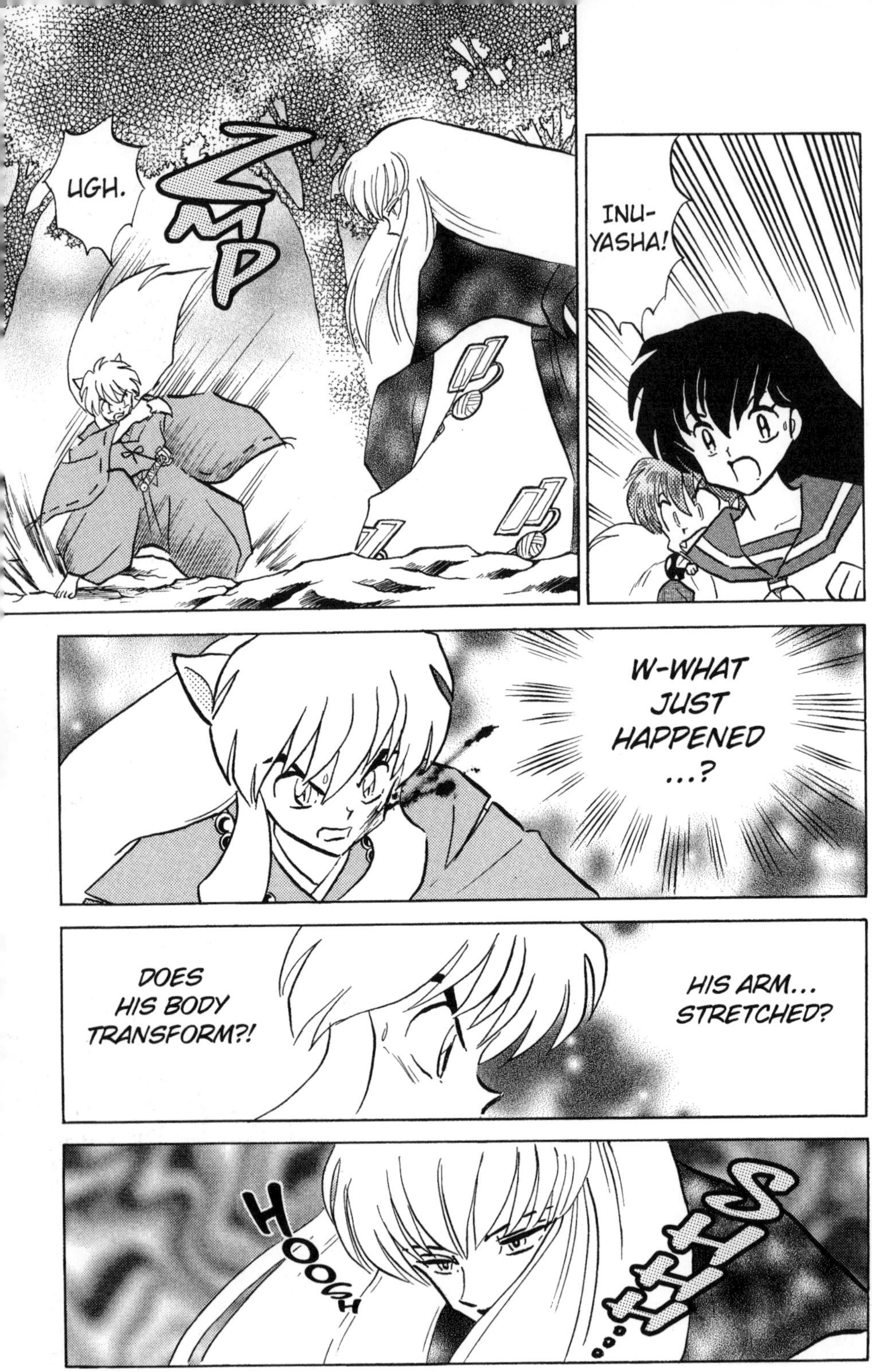
INU-YASHA!
UGH.
ZMP
W-WHAT JUST HAPPENED ...?
HIS ARM... STRETCHED?
DOES HIS BODY TRANSFORM?!
SHHH...
HOOGH

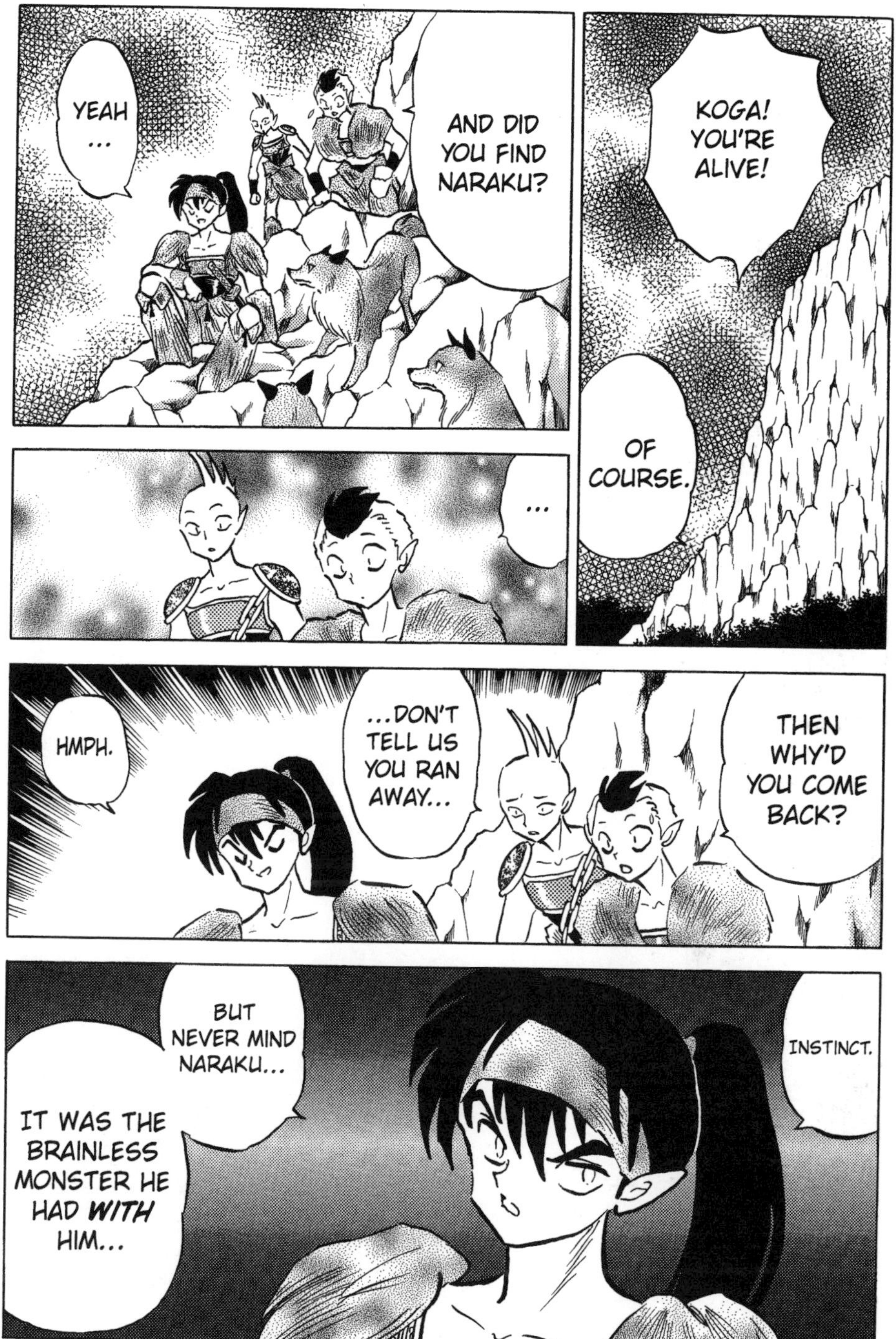
KOGA! YOU'RE ALIVE!
OF COURSE.
AND DID YOU FIND NARAKU?
YEAH ...
...
THEN WHY'D YOU COME BACK?
...DON'T TELL US YOU RAN AWAY...
HMPH.
INSTINCT.
BUT NEVER MIND NARAKU...
IT WAS THE BRAINLESS MONSTER HE HAD *WITH* HIM...

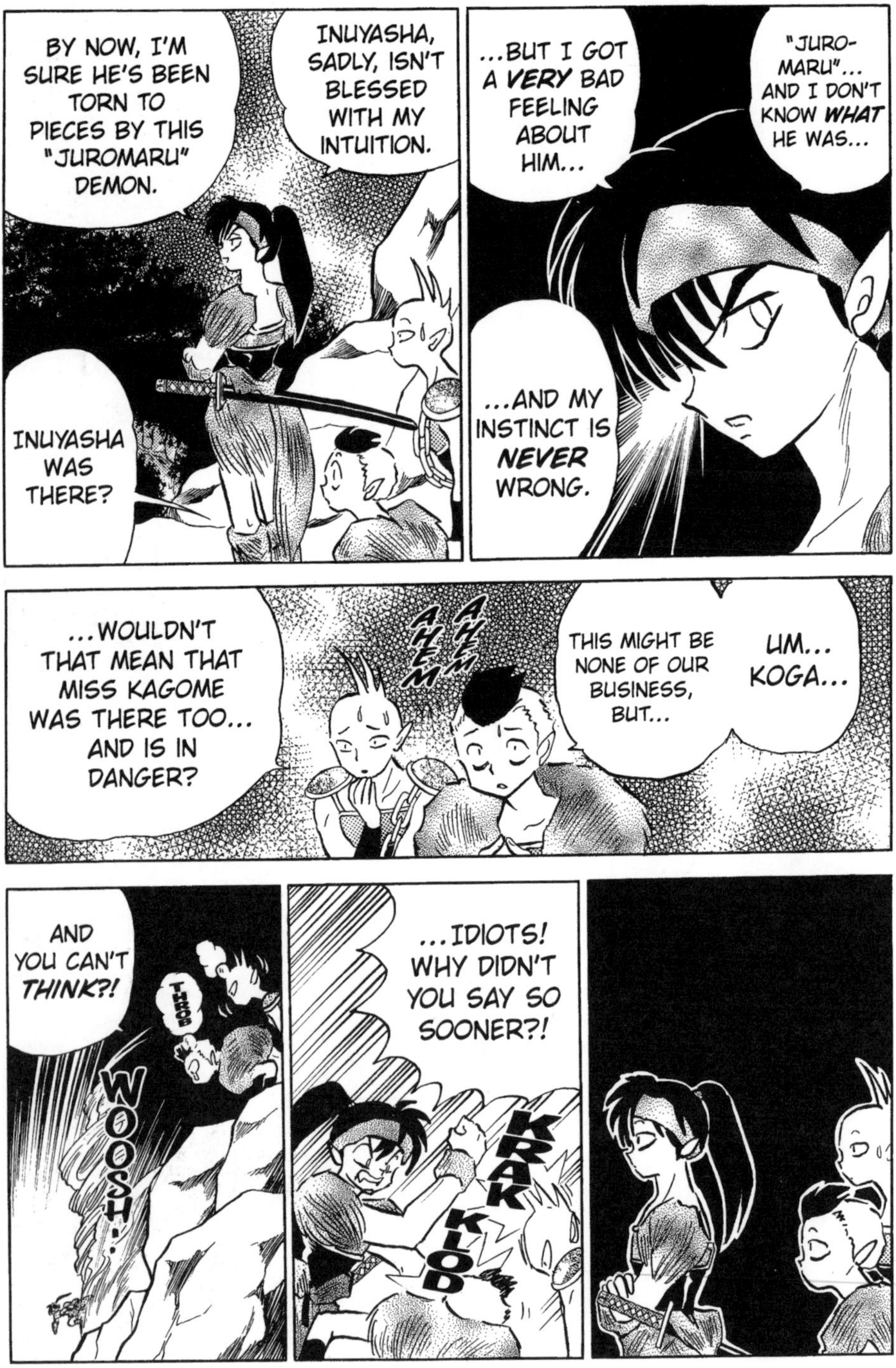
"JURO-MARU"... AND I DON'T KNOW *WHAT* HE WAS...
...BUT I GOT A *VERY* BAD FEELING ABOUT HIM...
...AND MY INSTINCT IS *NEVER* WRONG.
INUYASHA, SADLY, ISN'T BLESSED WITH MY INTUITION.
BY NOW, I'M SURE HE'S BEEN TORN TO PIECES BY THIS "JUROMARU" DEMON.
INUYASHA WAS THERE?
UM... KOGA...
THIS MIGHT BE NONE OF OUR BUSINESS, BUT...
AHEM
AHEM
...WOULDN'T THAT MEAN THAT MISS KAGOME WAS THERE TOO... AND IS IN DANGER?
...IDIOTS! WHY DIDN'T YOU SAY SO SOONER?!
KRAK
KLOD
AND YOU CAN'T *THINK*?!
THROB
WOOSH!!

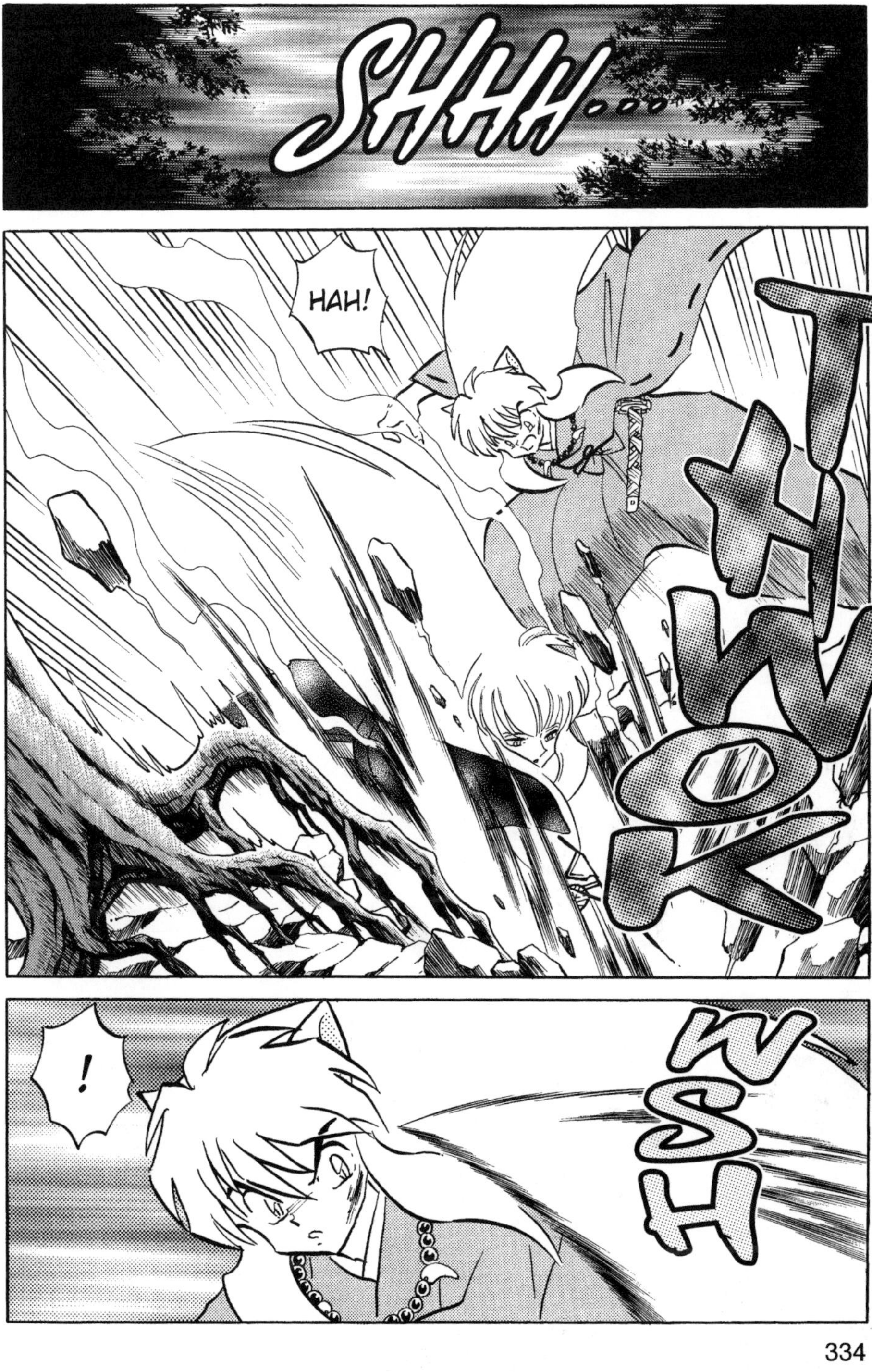
SHHH...
HAH!
THWOK
!
WSH

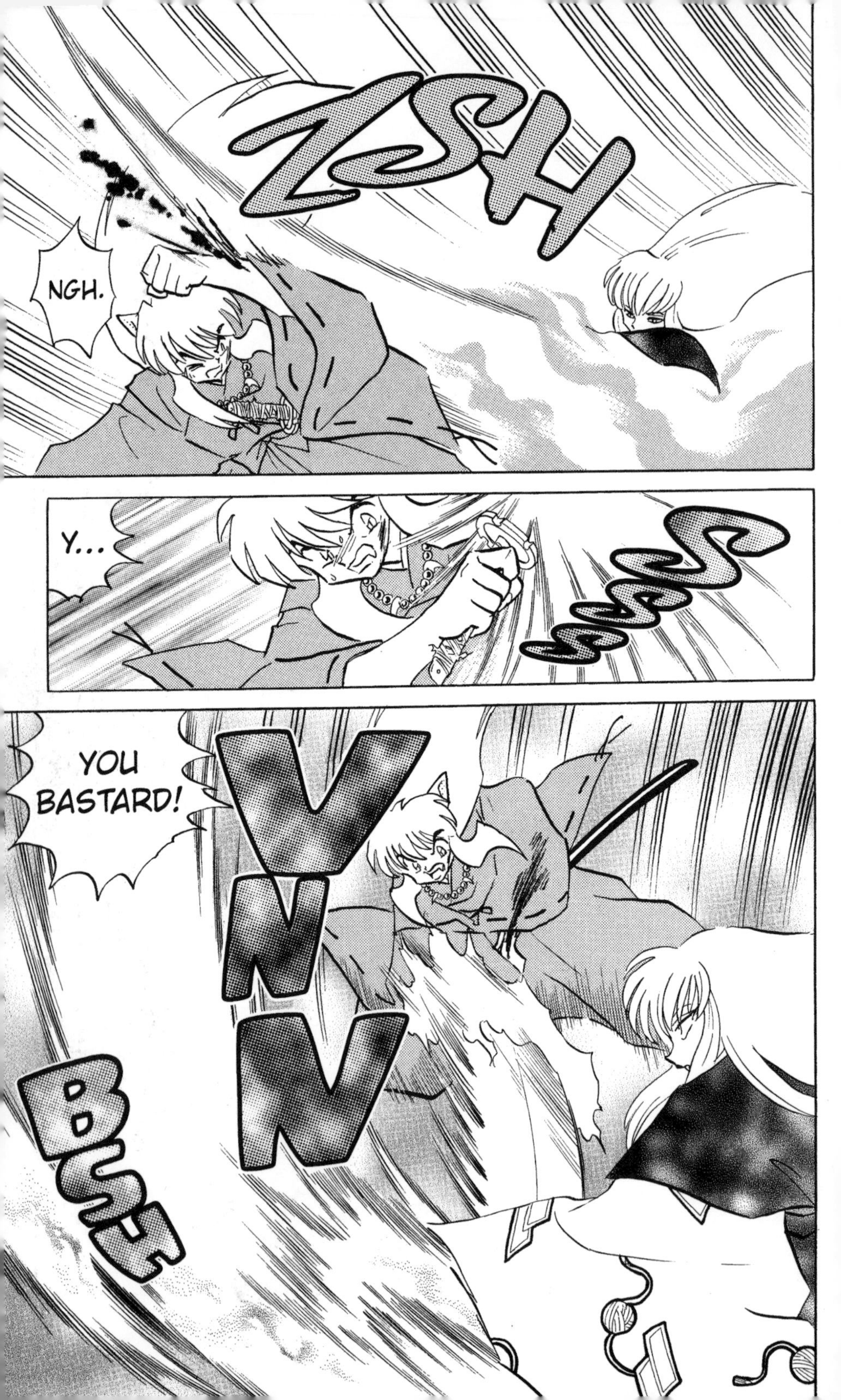

TSH
NGH.
SSSS
Y...
VNN
YOU BASTARD!
BUSH

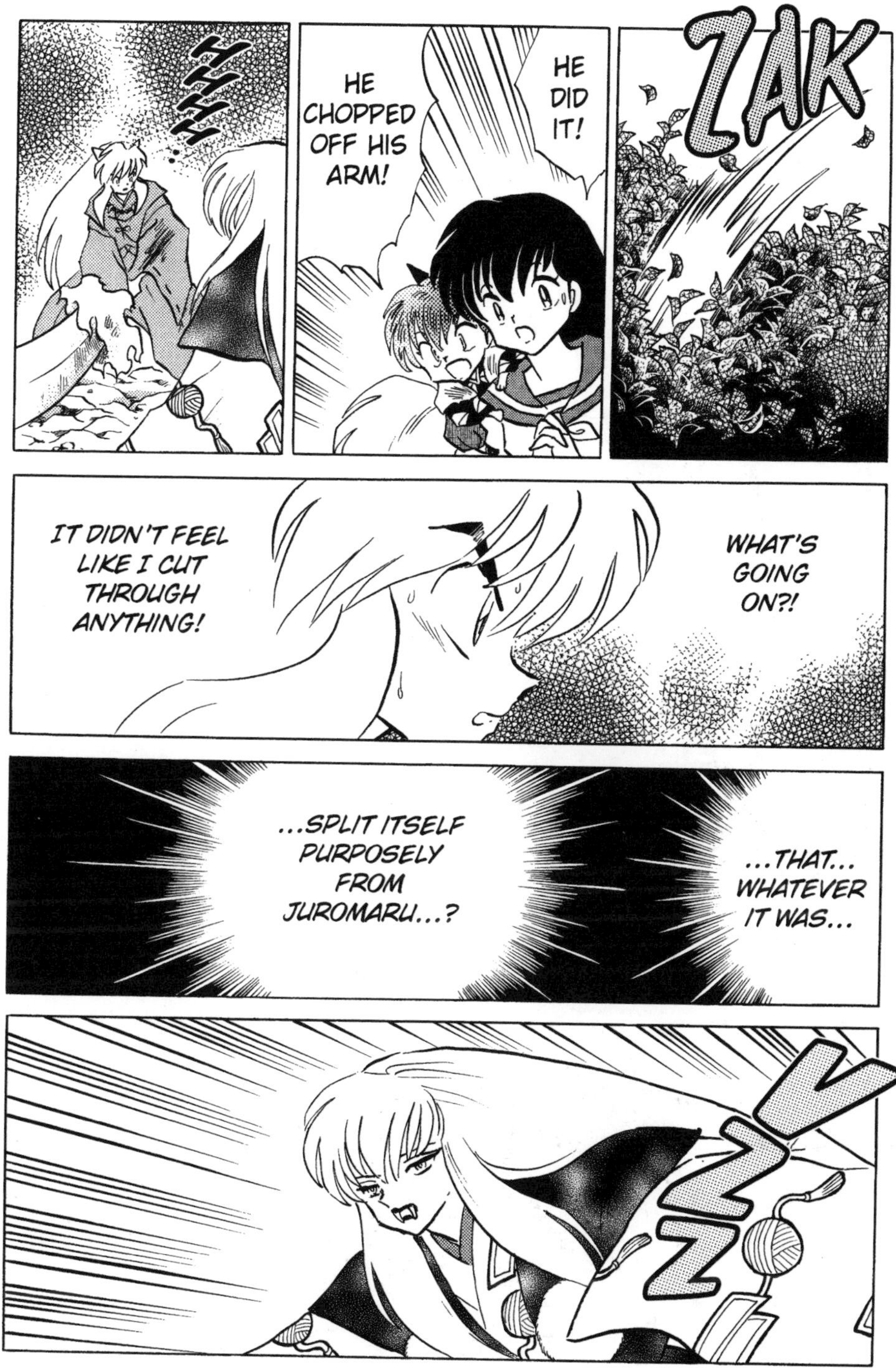
ZAK
HE DID IT!
HE CHOPPED OFF HIS ARM!
HHHH
WHAT'S GOING ON?!
IT DIDN'T FEEL LIKE I CUT THROUGH ANYTHING!
...THAT... WHATEVER IT WAS...
...SPLIT ITSELF PURPOSELY FROM JUROMARU...?
VZZZ

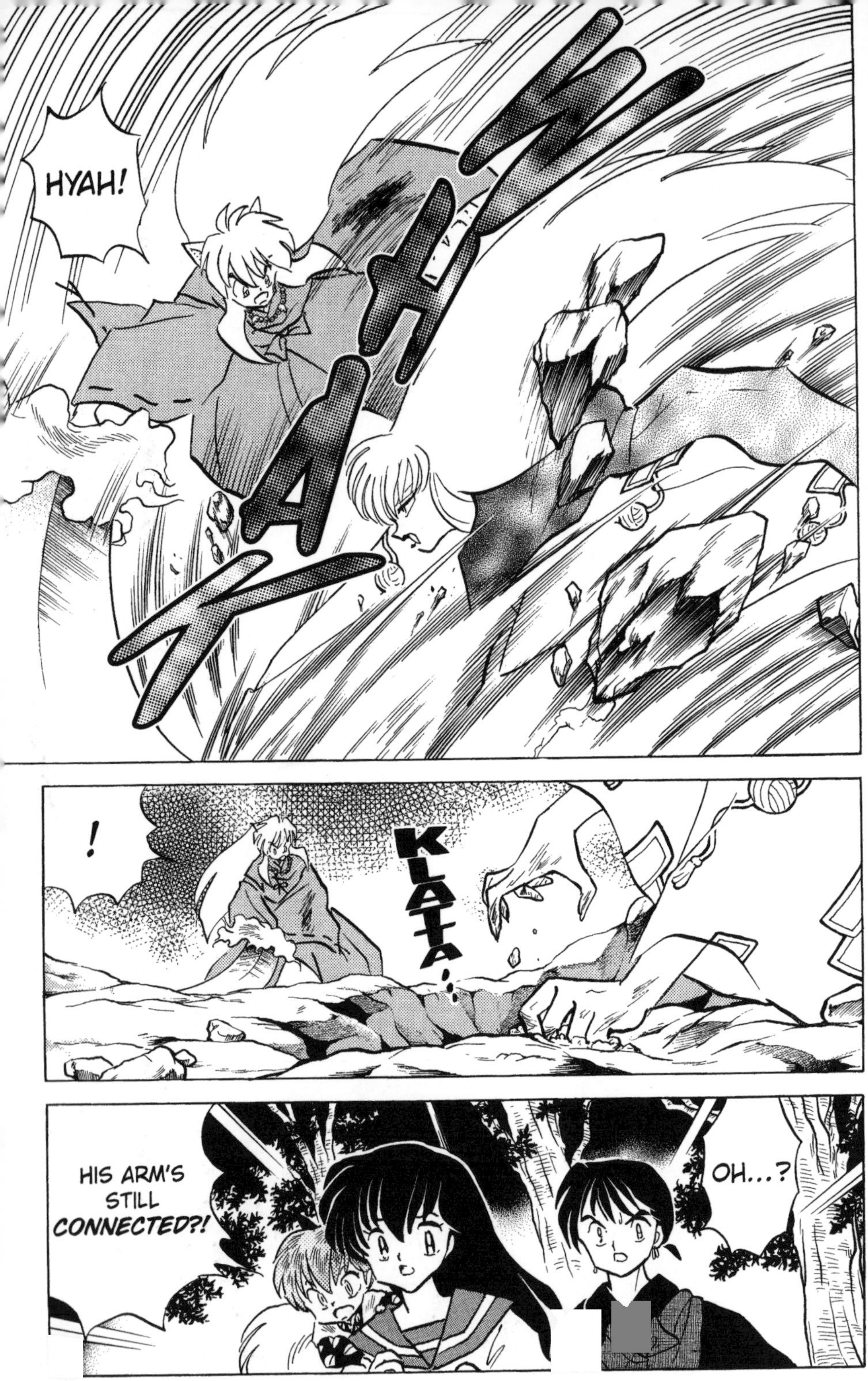
WHAK
HYAH!
KLATTA...
!
OH...?
HIS ARM'S STILL CONNECTED?!

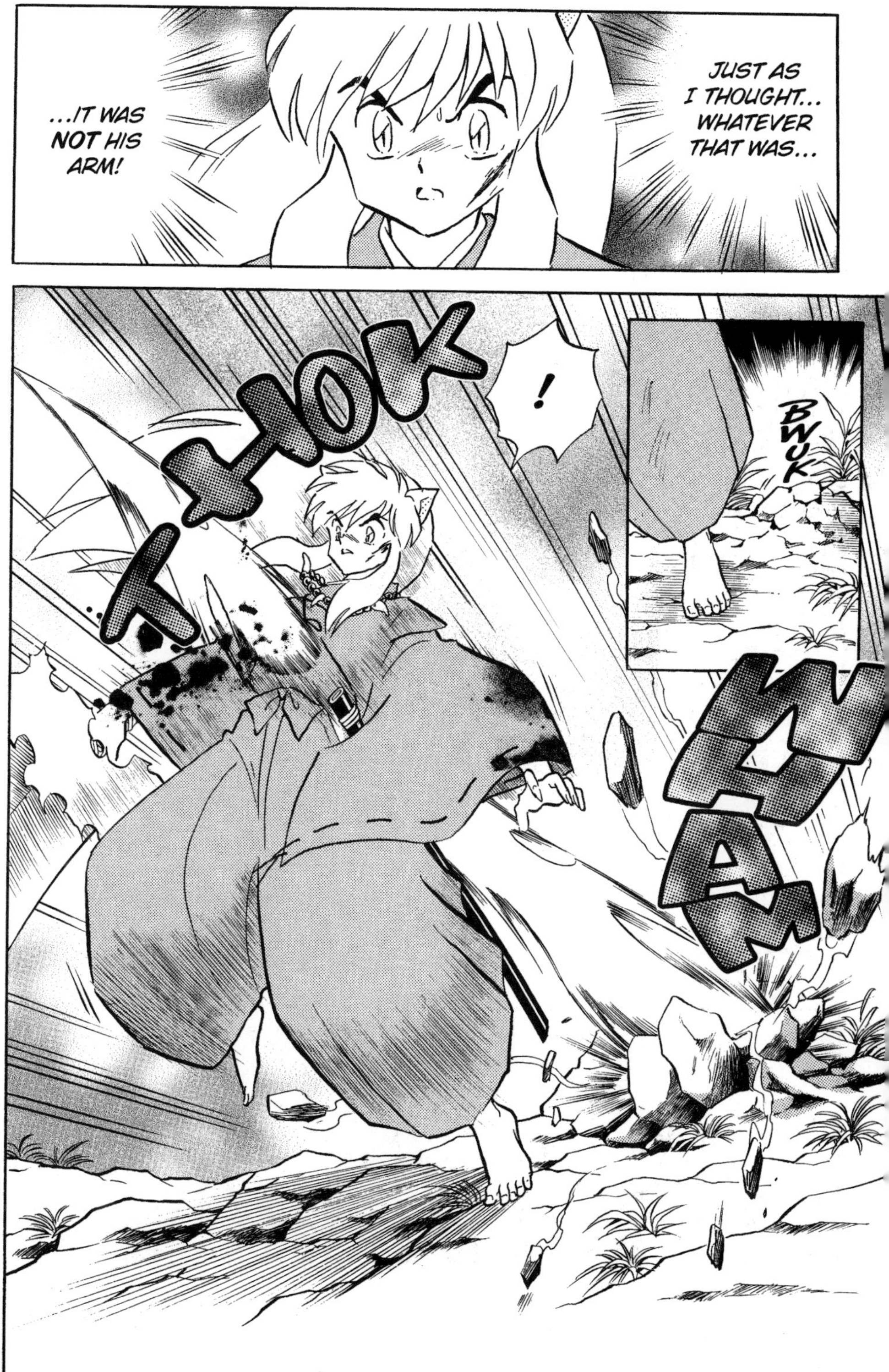
JUST AS I THOUGHT... WHATEVER THAT WAS...
...IT WAS **NOT** HIS ARM!
BWUK
WHAM
!
THOOK

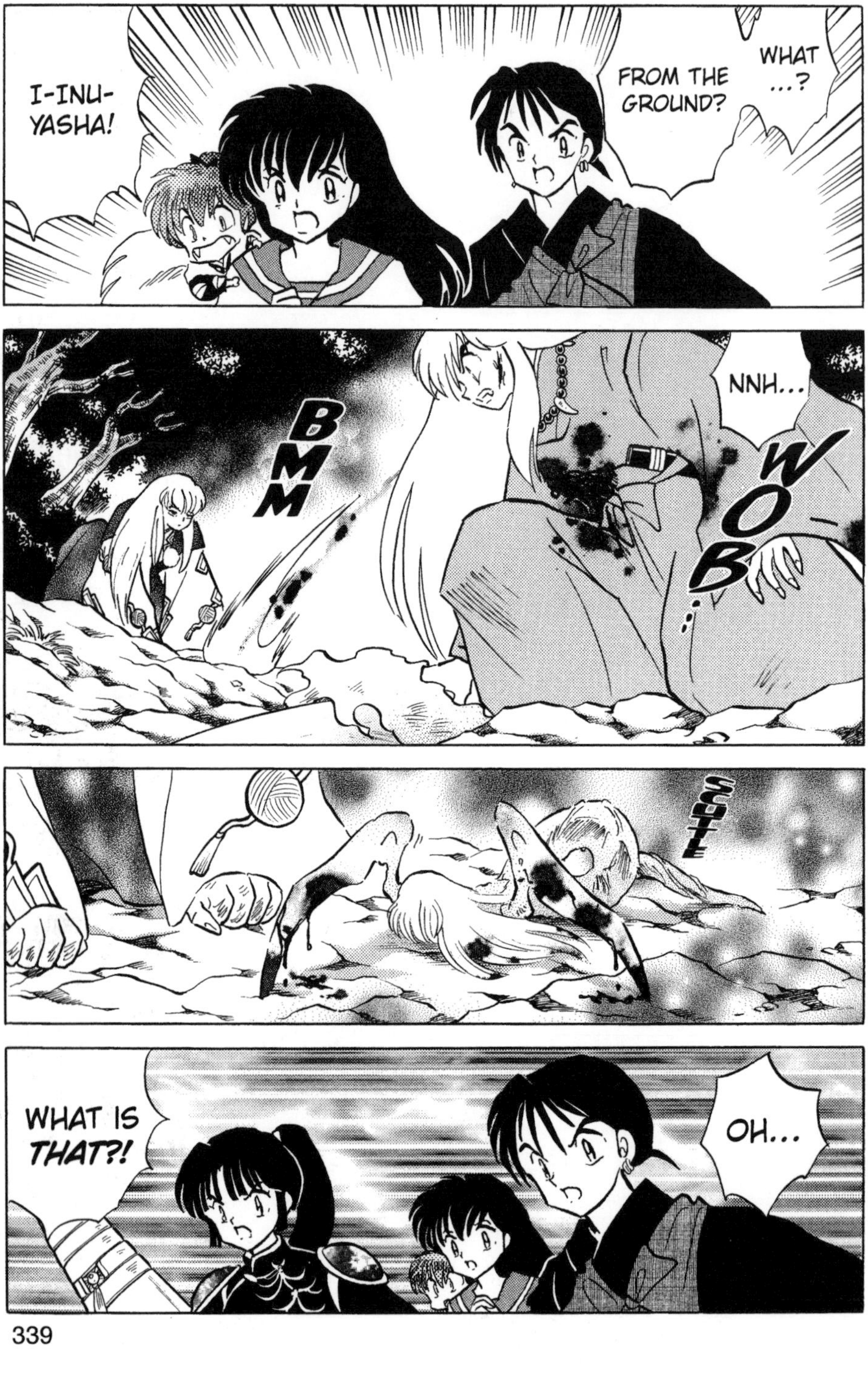

WHAT ...?
FROM THE GROUND?
I-INU-YASHA!
NNH...
WOB
BMM
SCUTTLE
OH...
WHAT IS *THAT?!*

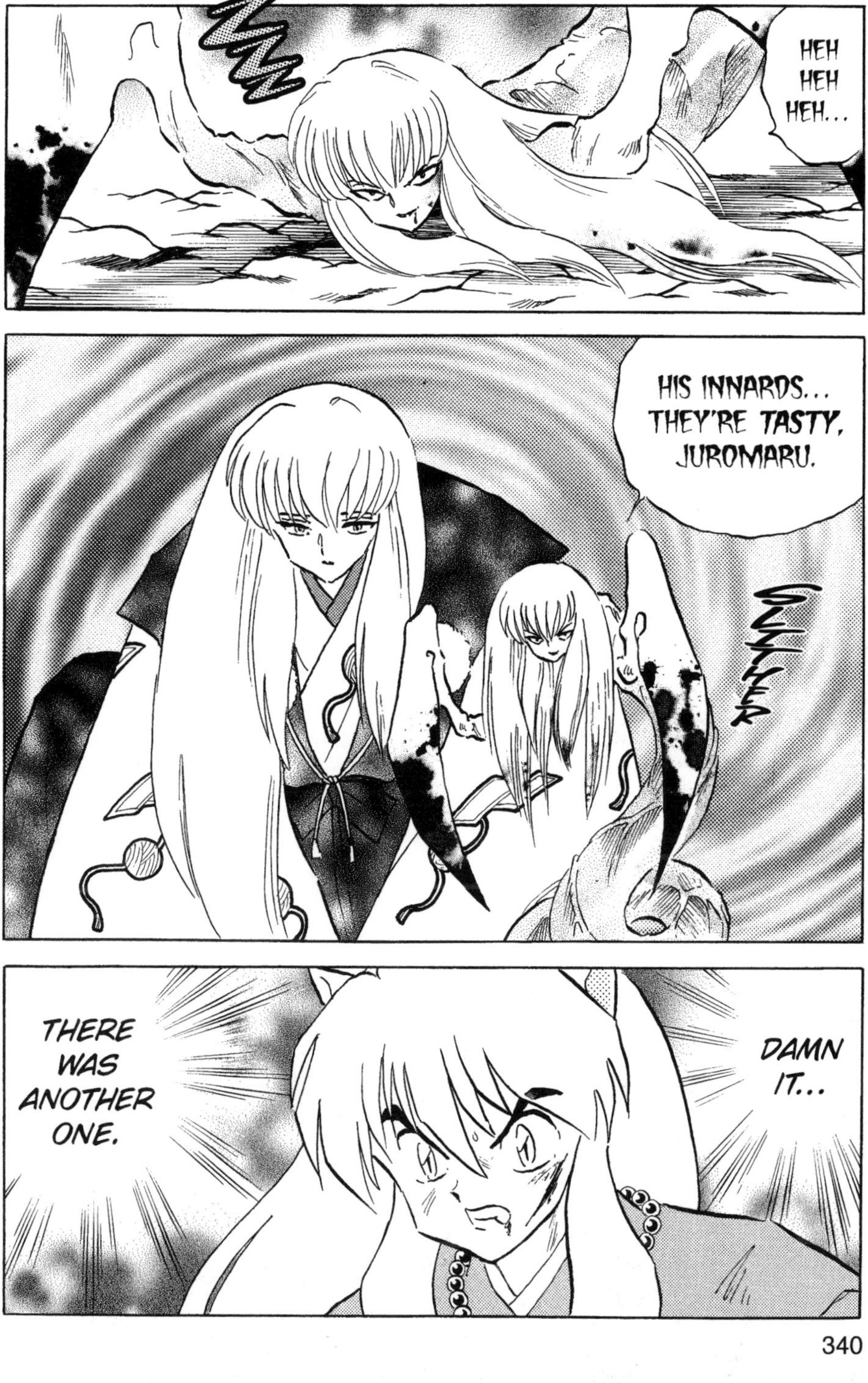
HEH HEH HEH...
HIS INNARDS... THEY'RE TASTY, JUROMARU.
SLITHER
DAMN IT...
THERE WAS ANOTHER ONE.

SCROLL NINE
KAGEROMARU

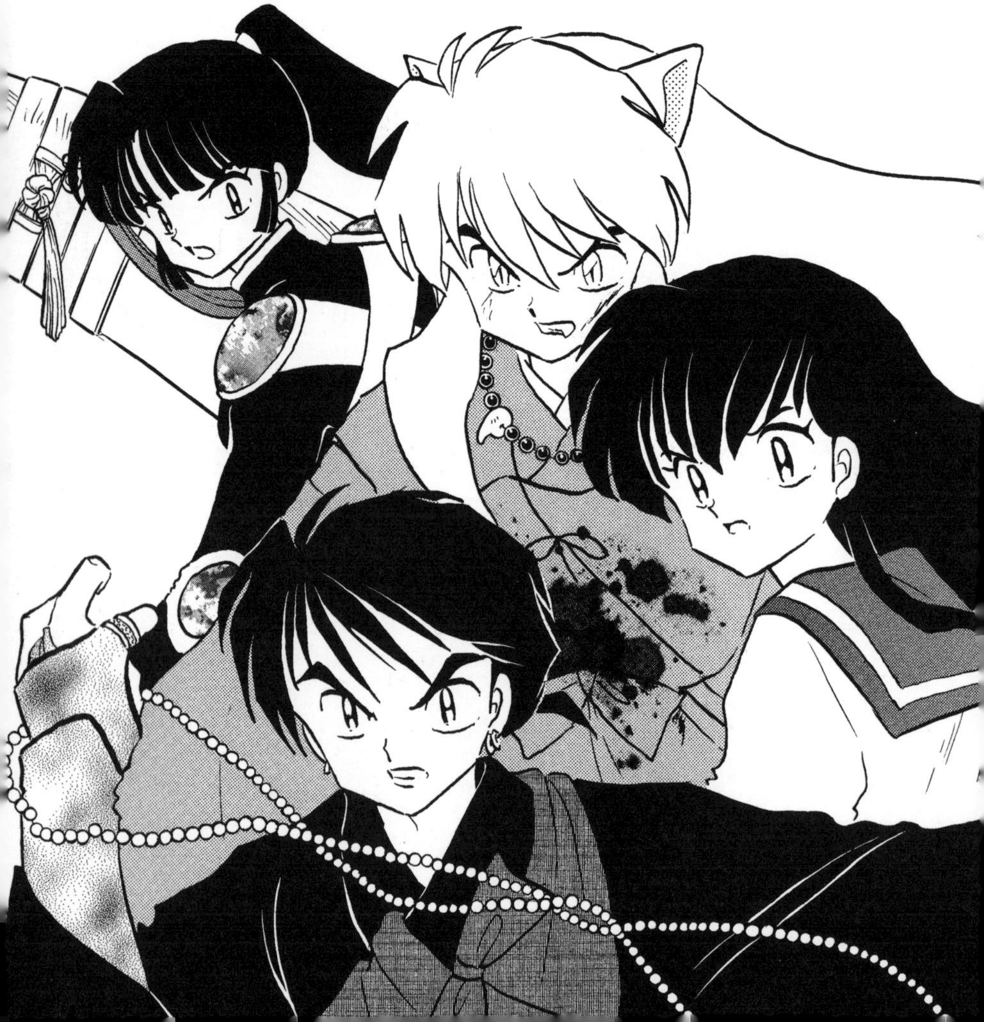

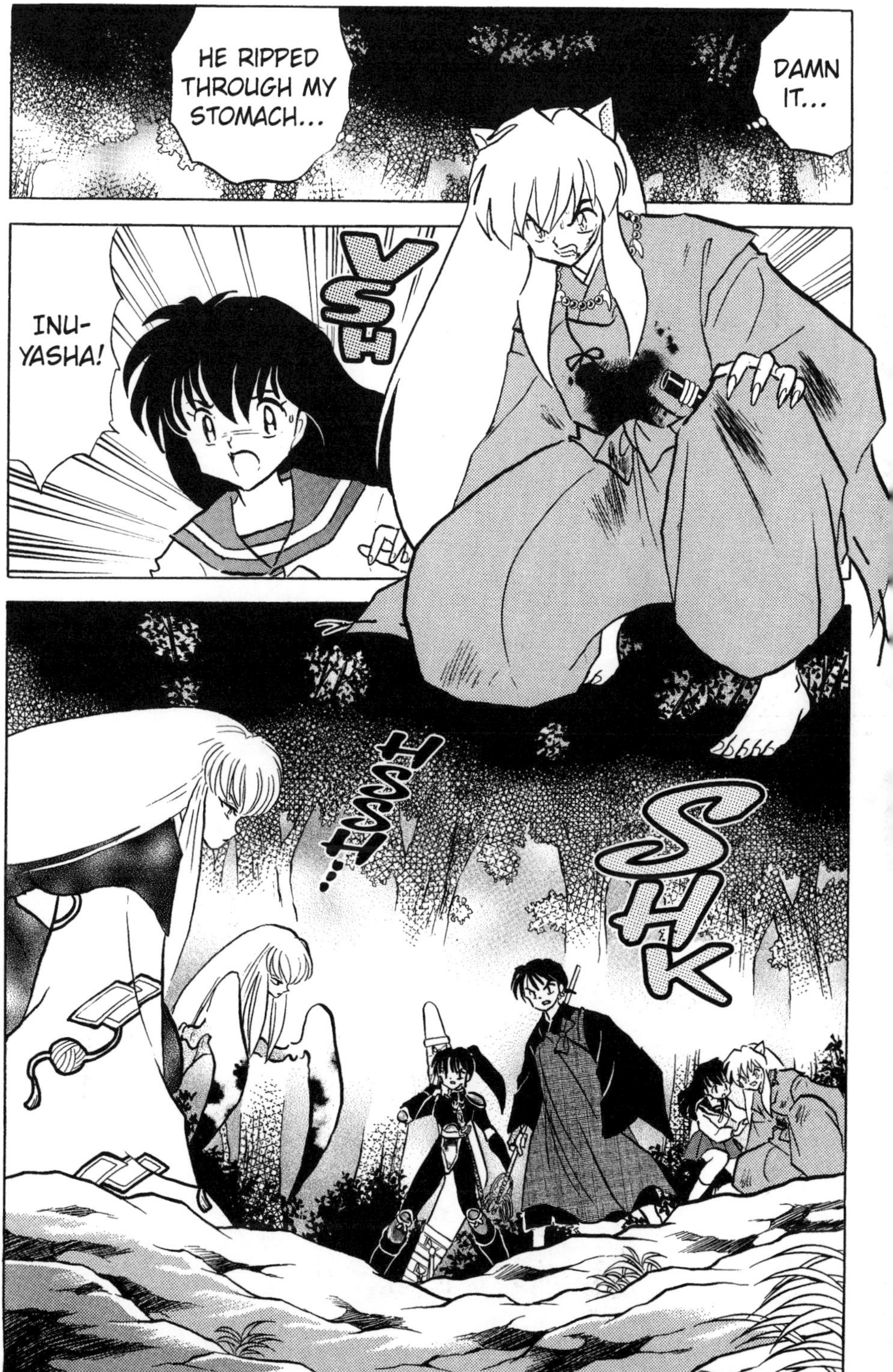

DAMN IT...
HE RIPPED THROUGH MY STOMACH...
YSH
INU-YASHA!
SHK
HSSH...

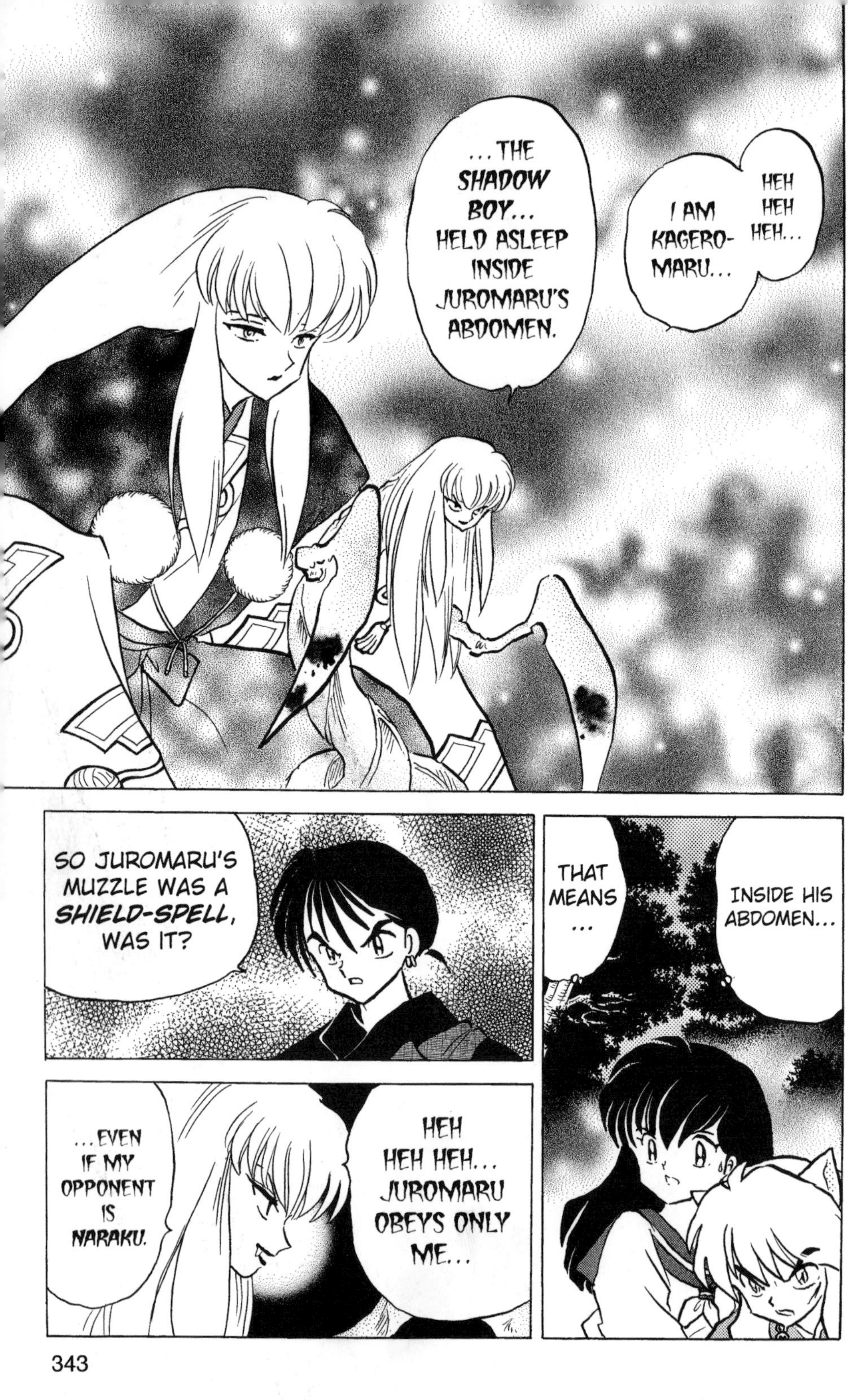
HEH HEH HEH...
I AM KAGERO-MARU...
...THE SHADOW BOY... HELD ASLEEP INSIDE JUROMARU'S ABDOMEN.
INSIDE HIS ABDOMEN...
THAT MEANS ...
SO JUROMARU'S MUZZLE WAS A SHIELD-SPELL, WAS IT?
HEH HEH HEH... JUROMARU OBEYS ONLY ME...
...EVEN IF MY OPPONENT IS NARAKU.

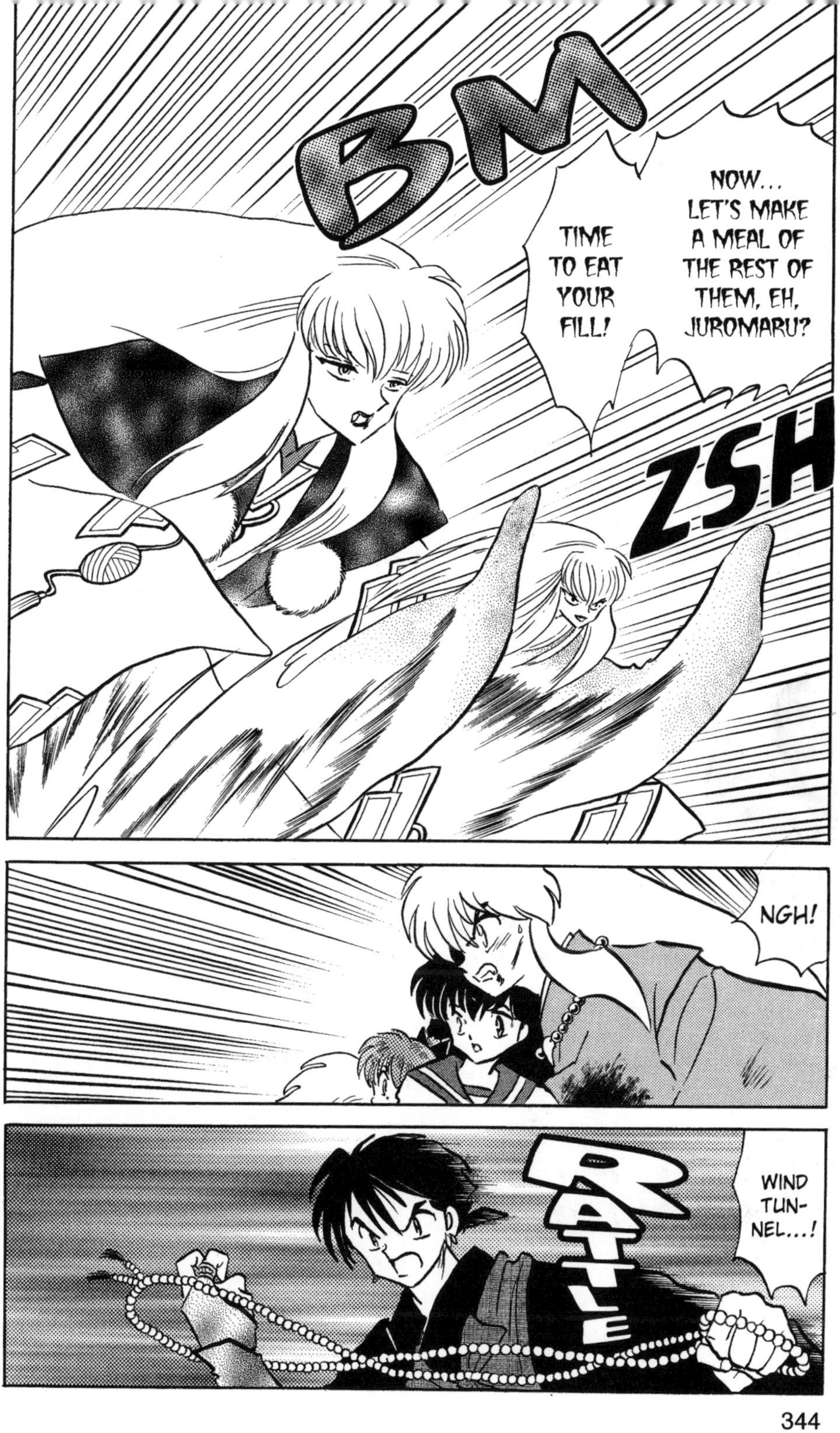
BM
NOW... LET'S MAKE A MEAL OF THE REST OF THEM, EH, JUROMARU?
TIME TO EAT YOUR FILL!
ZSH
NGH!
WIND TUN-NEL...!
RATTLE

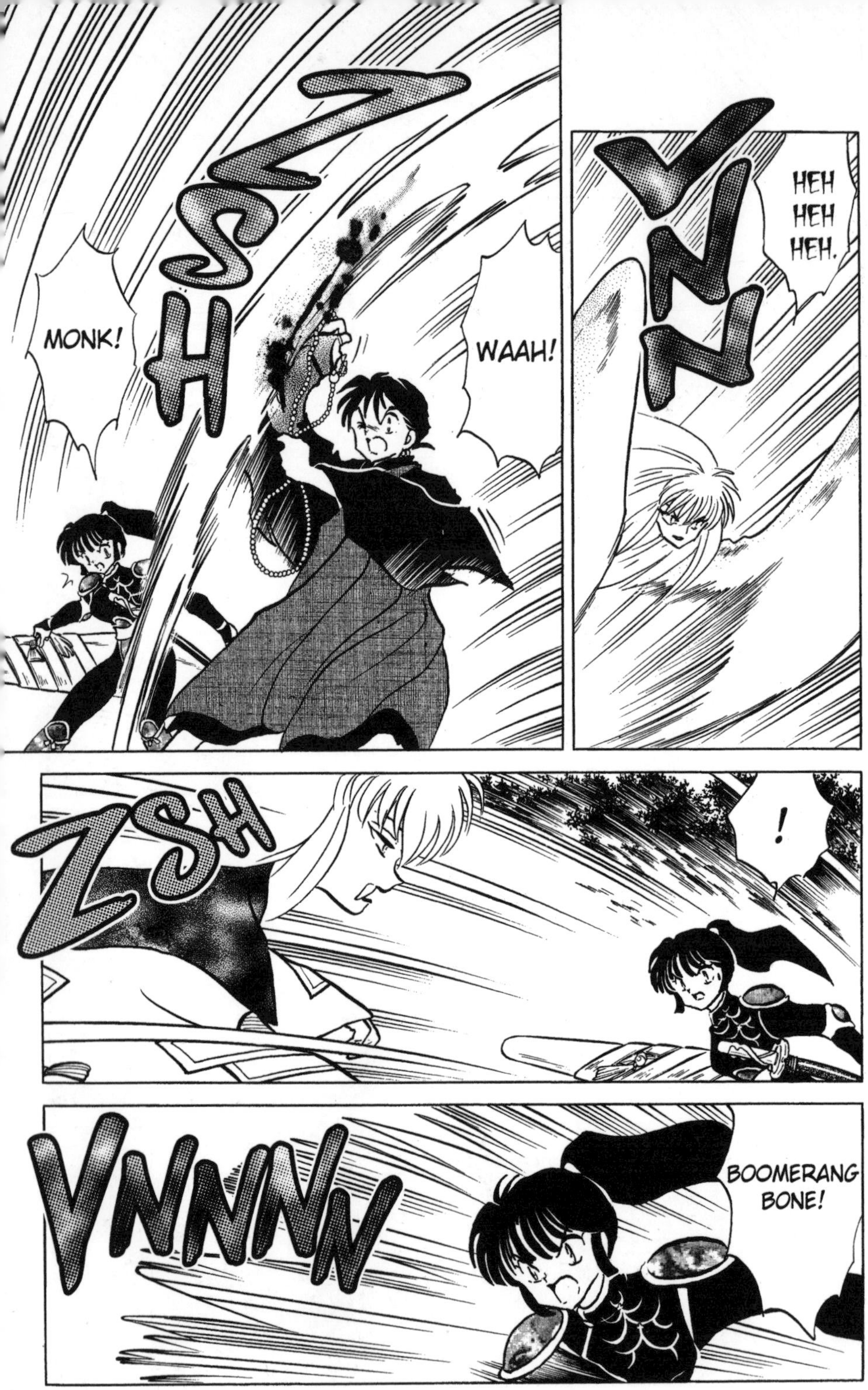
HEH HEH HEH.
VNN
WAAH!
ZSH
MONK!
!
ZSH
BOOMERANG BONE!
VNNNNN

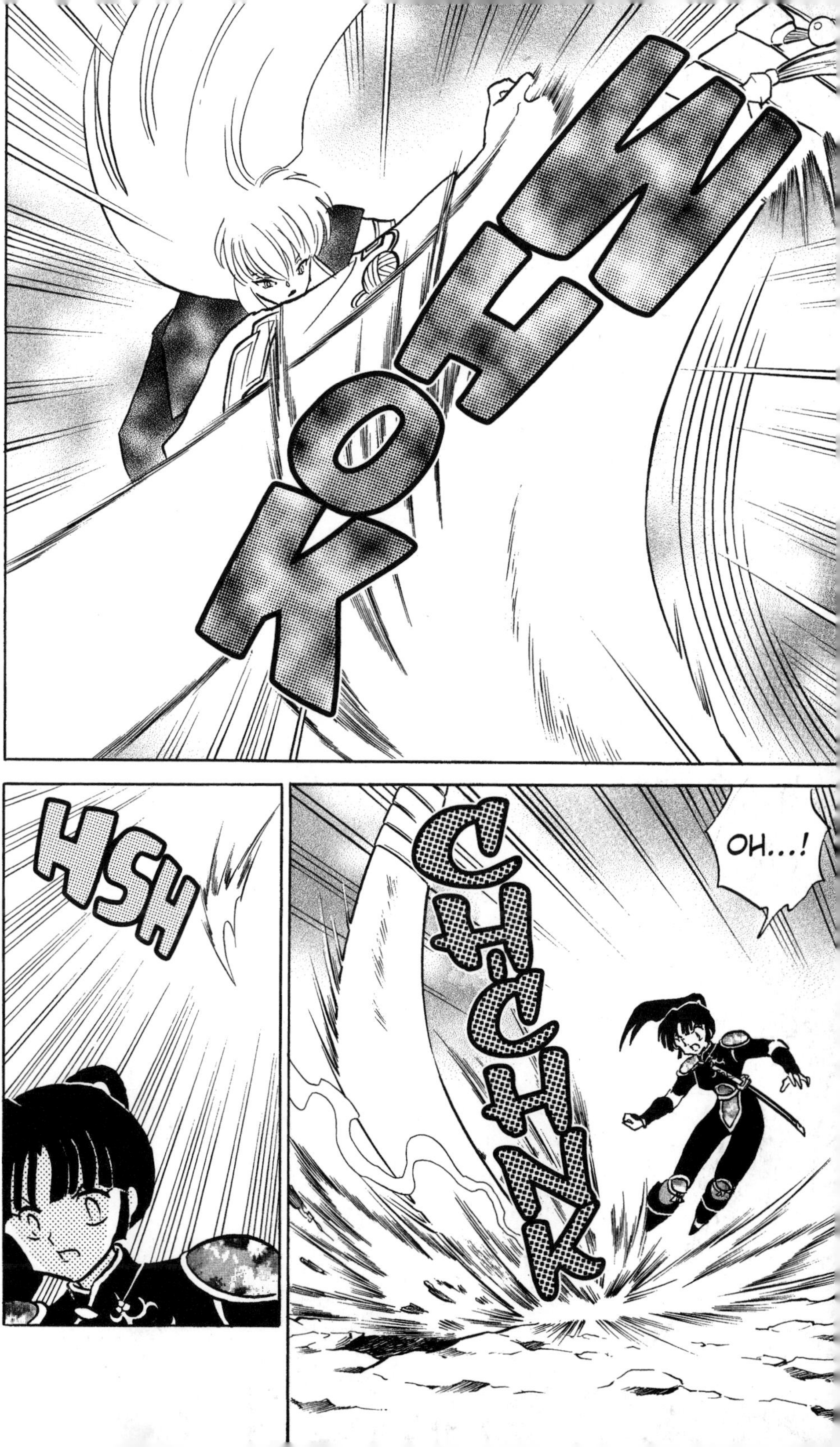
WHOK
CHCHINK
OH...!
HSH

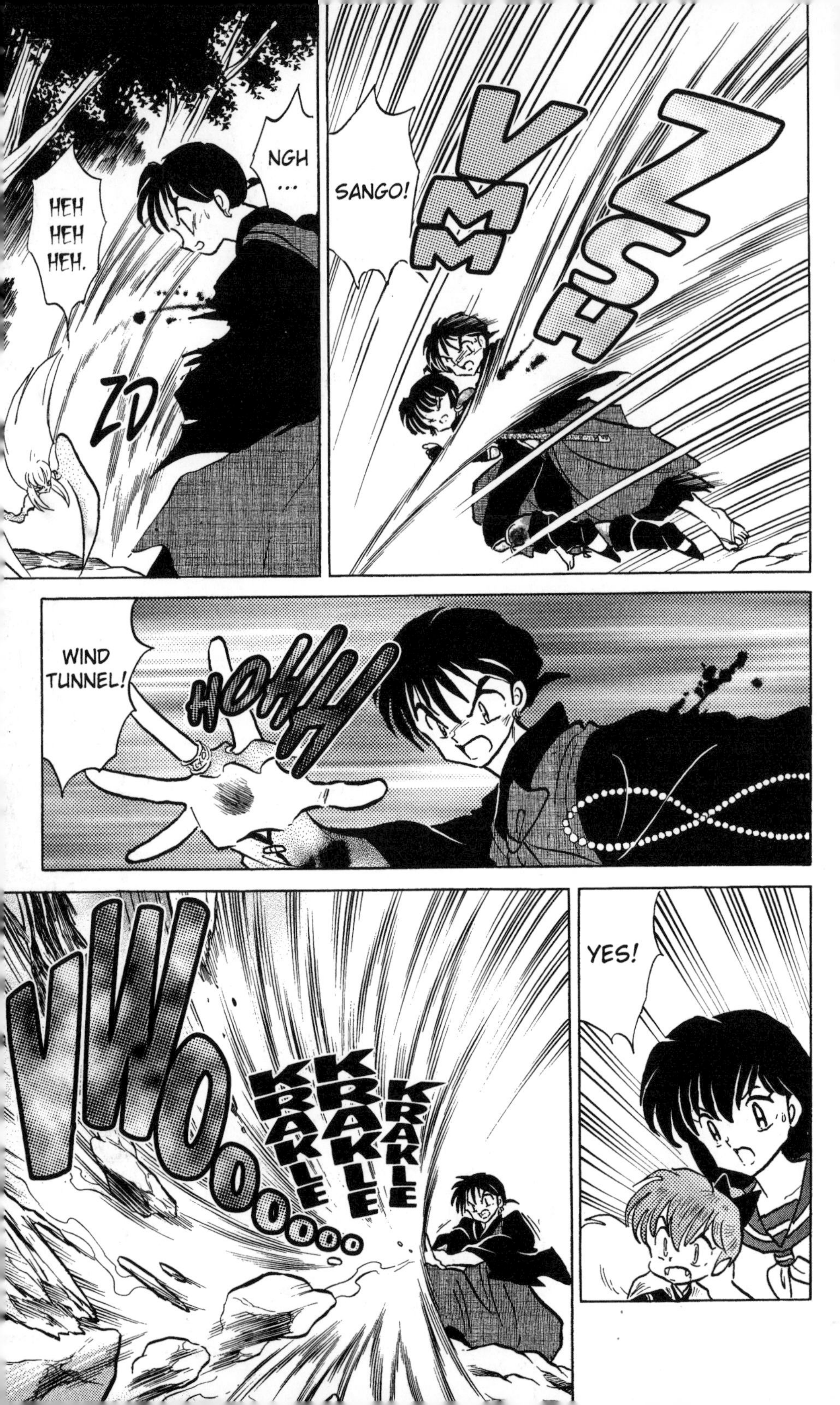
SANGO!
VMM
ZISH
NGH...
HEH HEH HEH.
ZD
WIND TUNNEL!
YES!
VWOOOOOO
KRAKLE
KRAKLE
KRAKLE

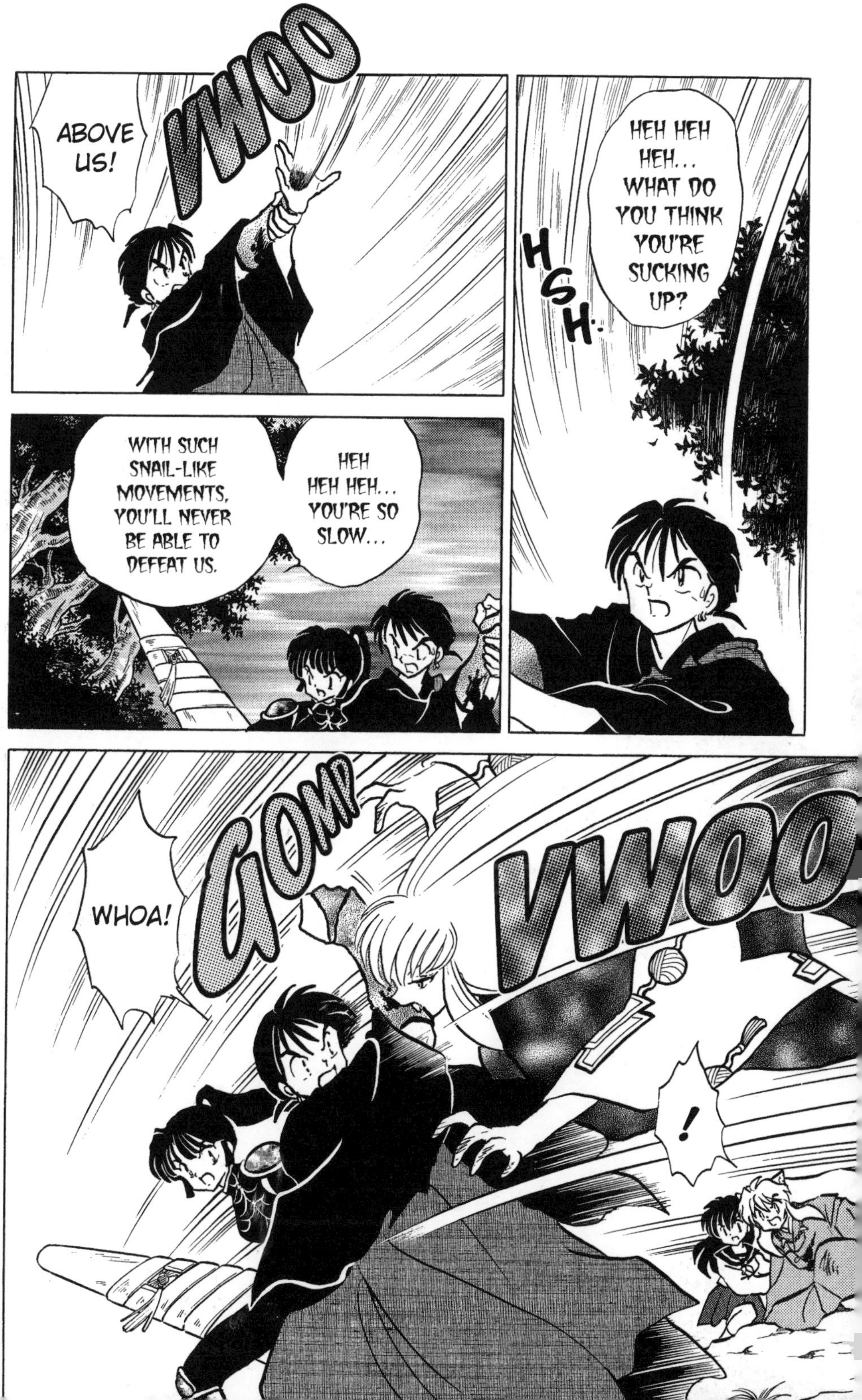
HEH HEH HEH... WHAT DO YOU THINK YOU'RE SUCKING UP?
HSH
ABOVE US!
VWOO
HEH HEH HEH... YOU'RE SO SLOW...
WITH SUCH SNAIL-LIKE MOVEMENTS, YOU'LL NEVER BE ABLE TO DEFEAT US.
VWOO
GOMP
WHOA!
!

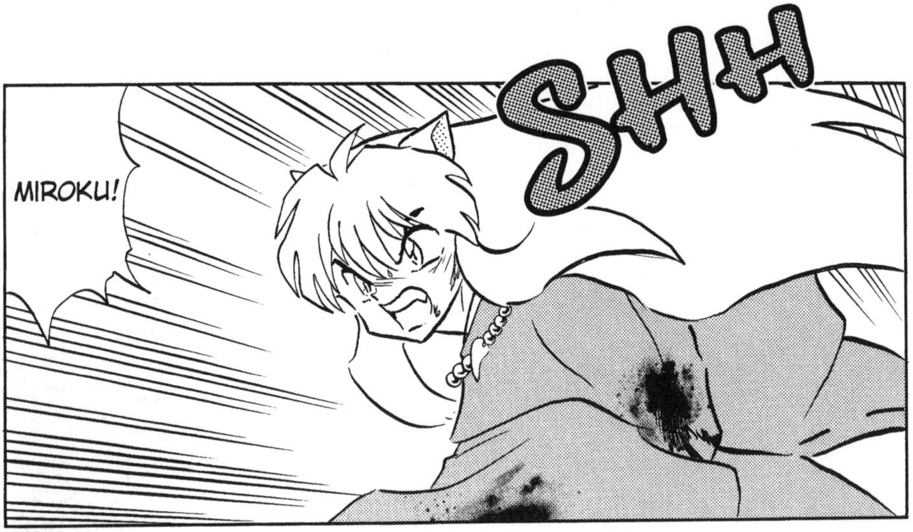
SHH
MIROKU!
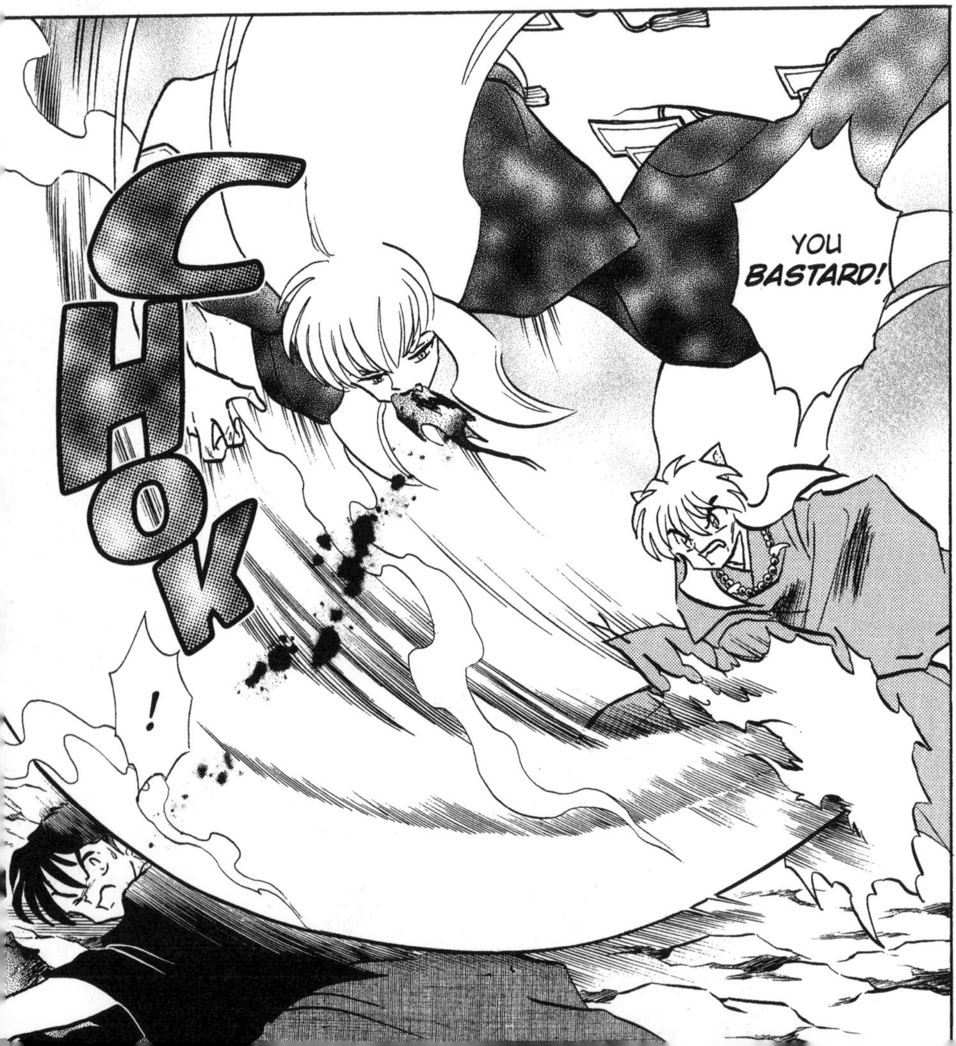
YOU BASTARD!
CHOK
!

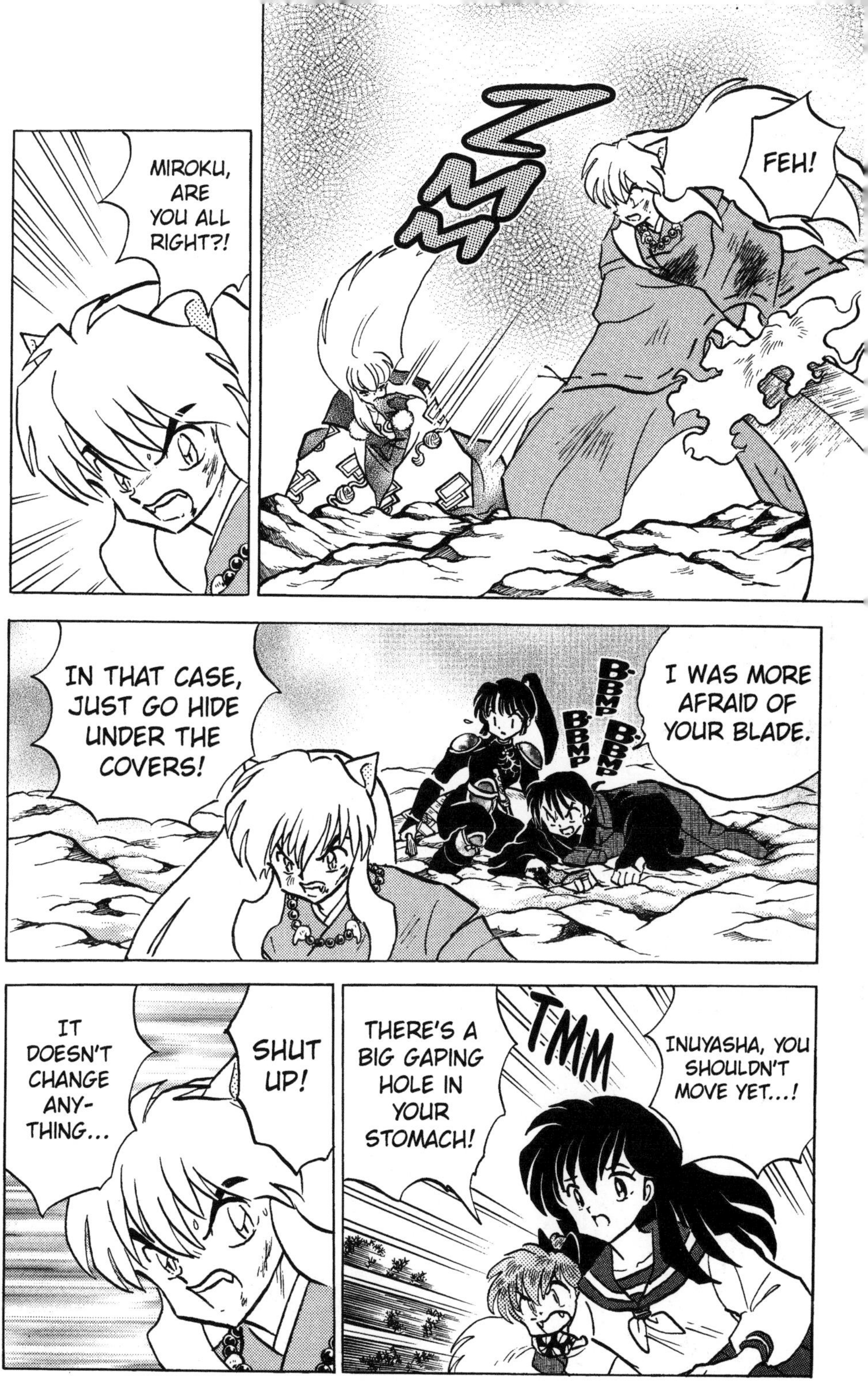

FEH!
ZMM
MIROKU, ARE YOU ALL RIGHT?!
I WAS MORE AFRAID OF YOUR BLADE.
B-BBMP
B-BBMP
B-BBMP
IN THAT CASE, JUST GO HIDE UNDER THE COVERS!
INUYASHA, YOU SHOULDN'T MOVE YET...!
TMM
THERE'S A BIG GAPING HOLE IN YOUR STOMACH!
SHUT UP!
IT DOESN'T CHANGE ANY-THING...

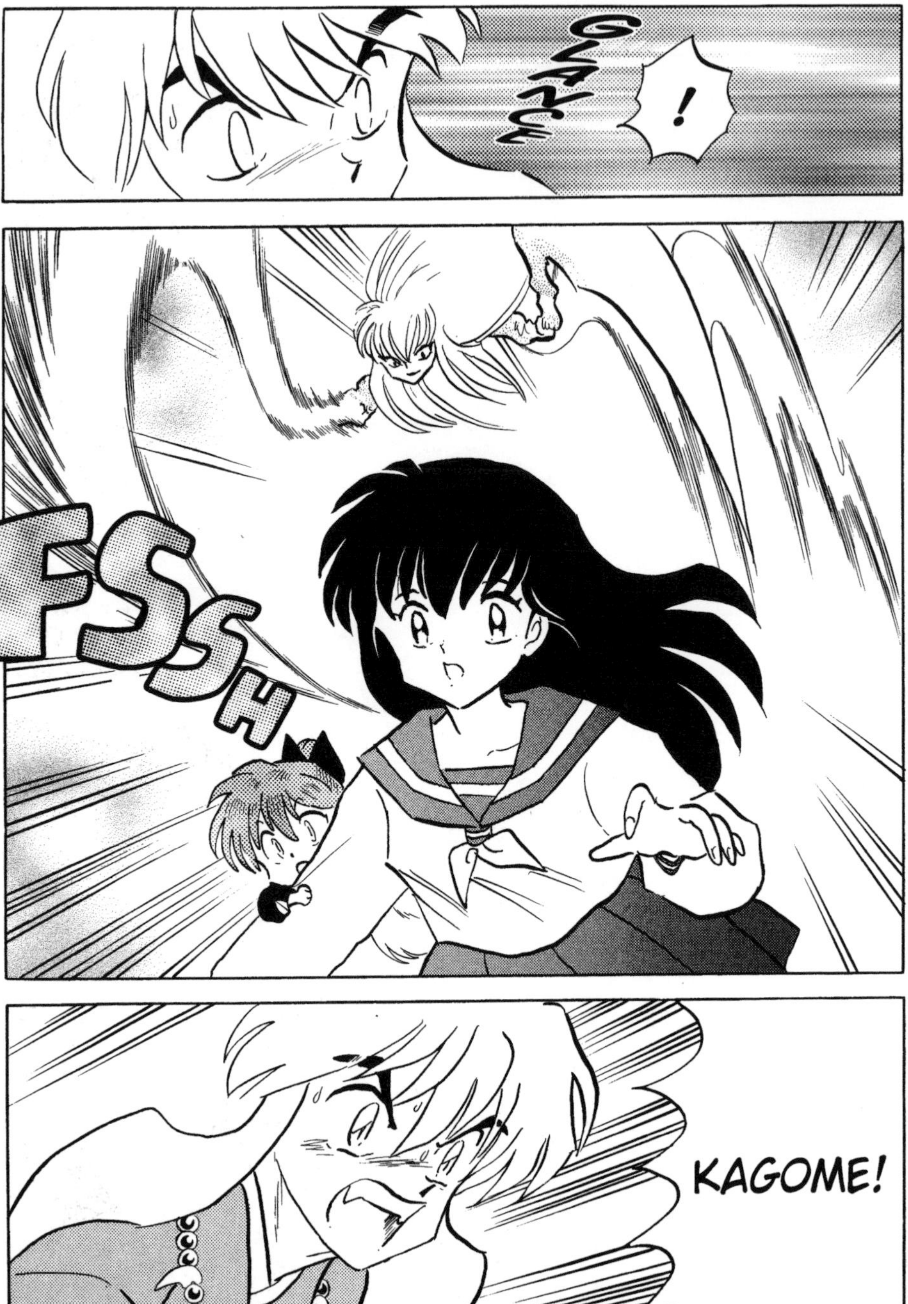
GLANCE
!
FSSH
KAGOME!

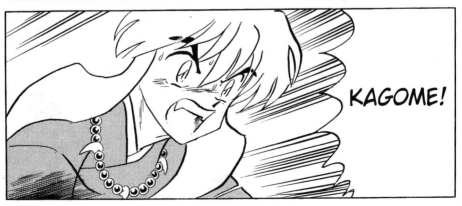

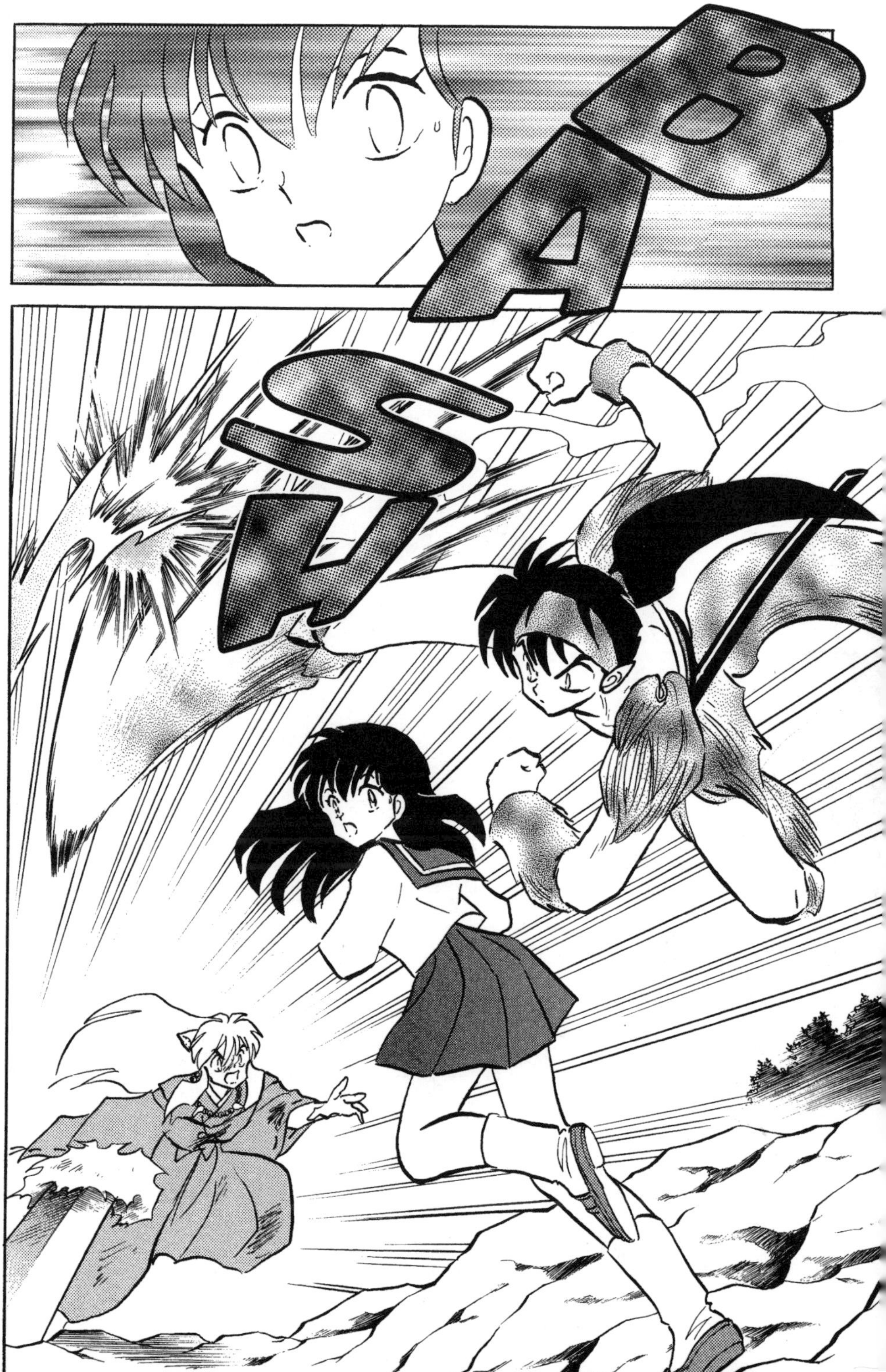
BASH

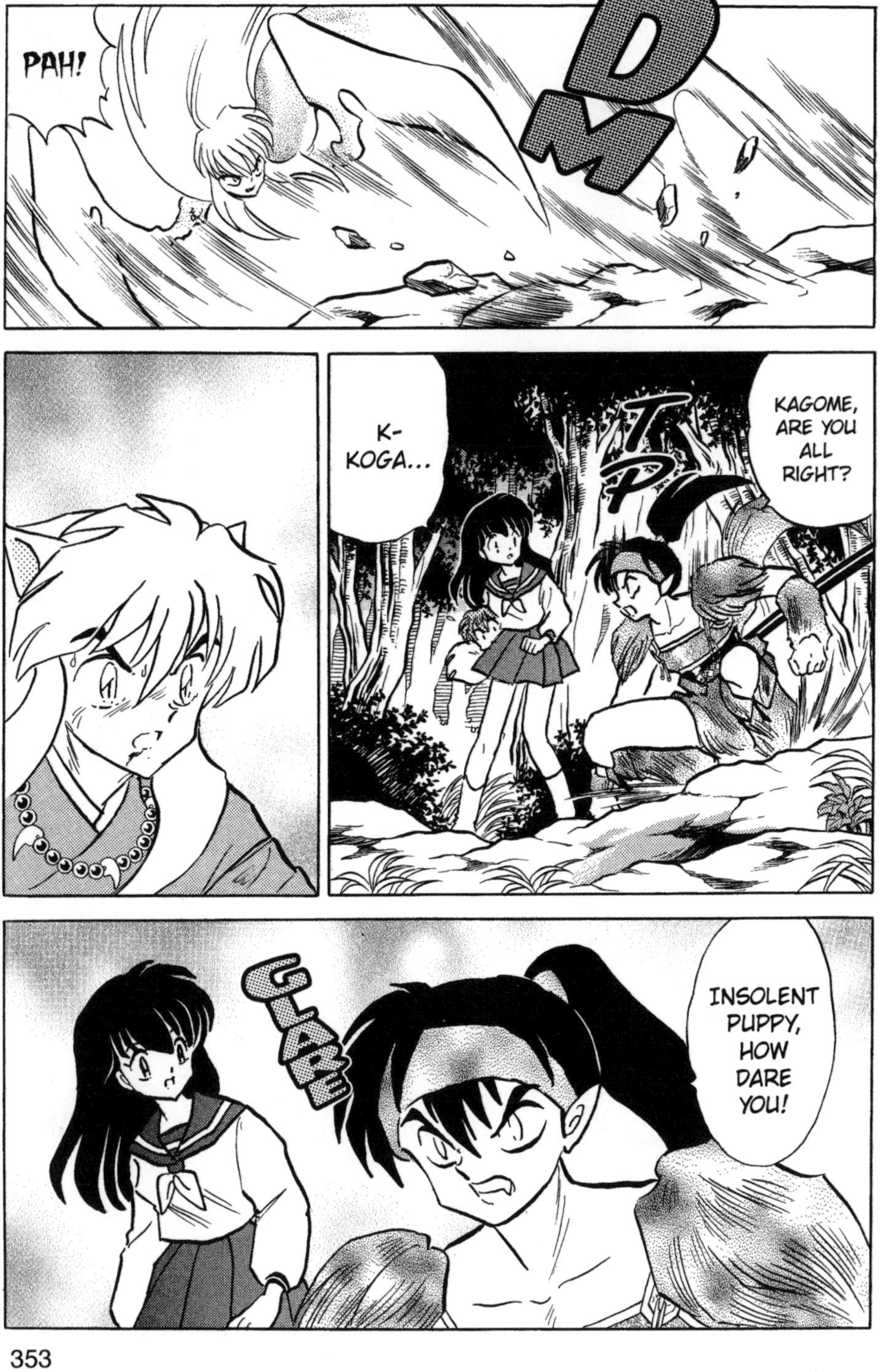
DM
PAH!
KAGOME, ARE YOU ALL RIGHT?
TP
K-KOGA...
INSOLENT PUPPY, HOW DARE YOU!
GLARE

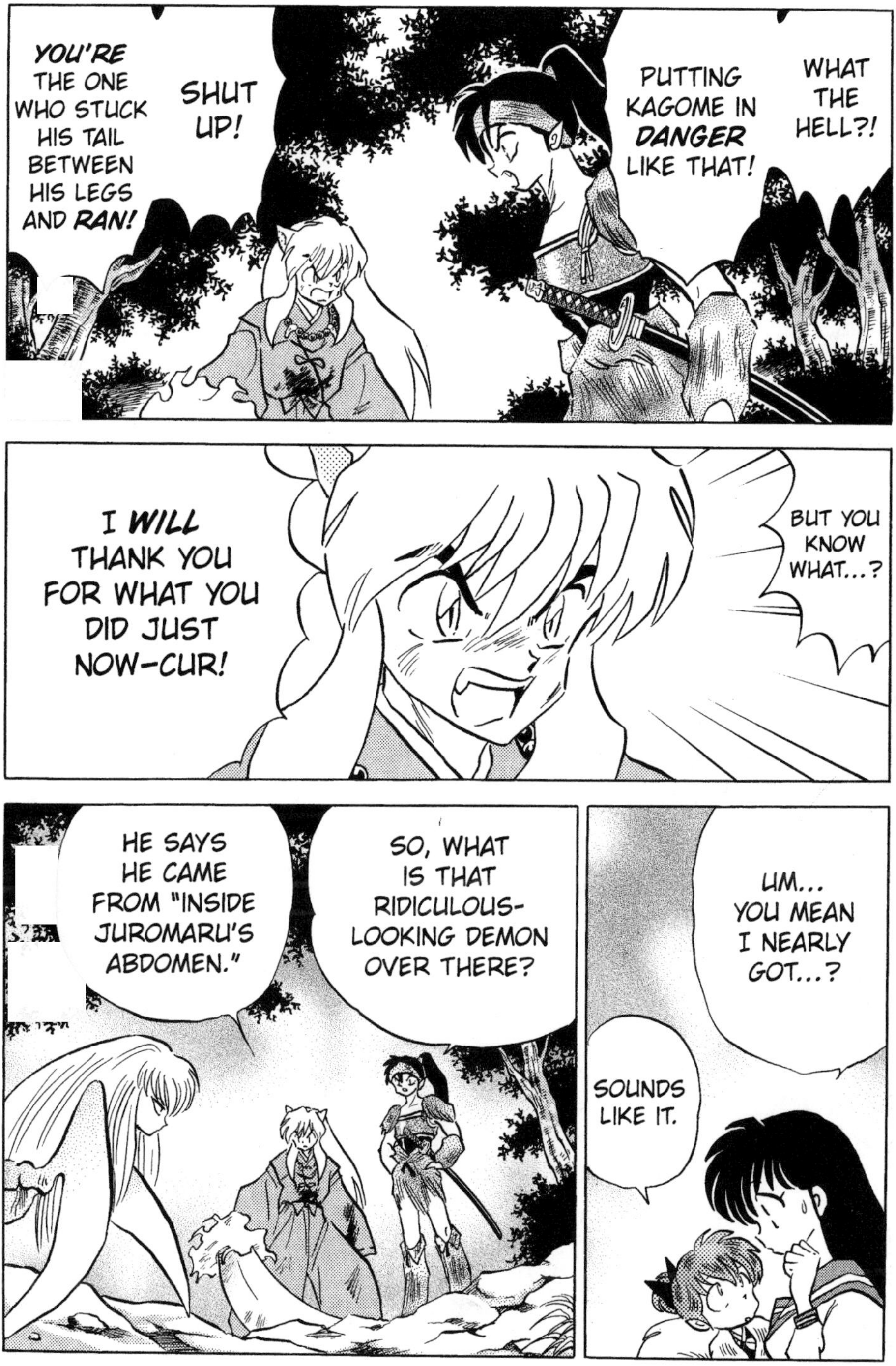
WHAT THE HELL?!
PUTTING KAGOME IN DANGER LIKE THAT!
SHUT UP!
YOU'RE THE ONE WHO STUCK HIS TAIL BETWEEN HIS LEGS AND RAN!
BUT YOU KNOW WHAT...?
I WILL THANK YOU FOR WHAT YOU DID JUST NOW—CUR!
UM... YOU MEAN I NEARLY GOT...?
SOUNDS LIKE IT.
SO, WHAT IS THAT RIDICULOUS-LOOKING DEMON OVER THERE?
HE SAYS HE CAME FROM "INSIDE JUROMARU'S ABDOMEN."

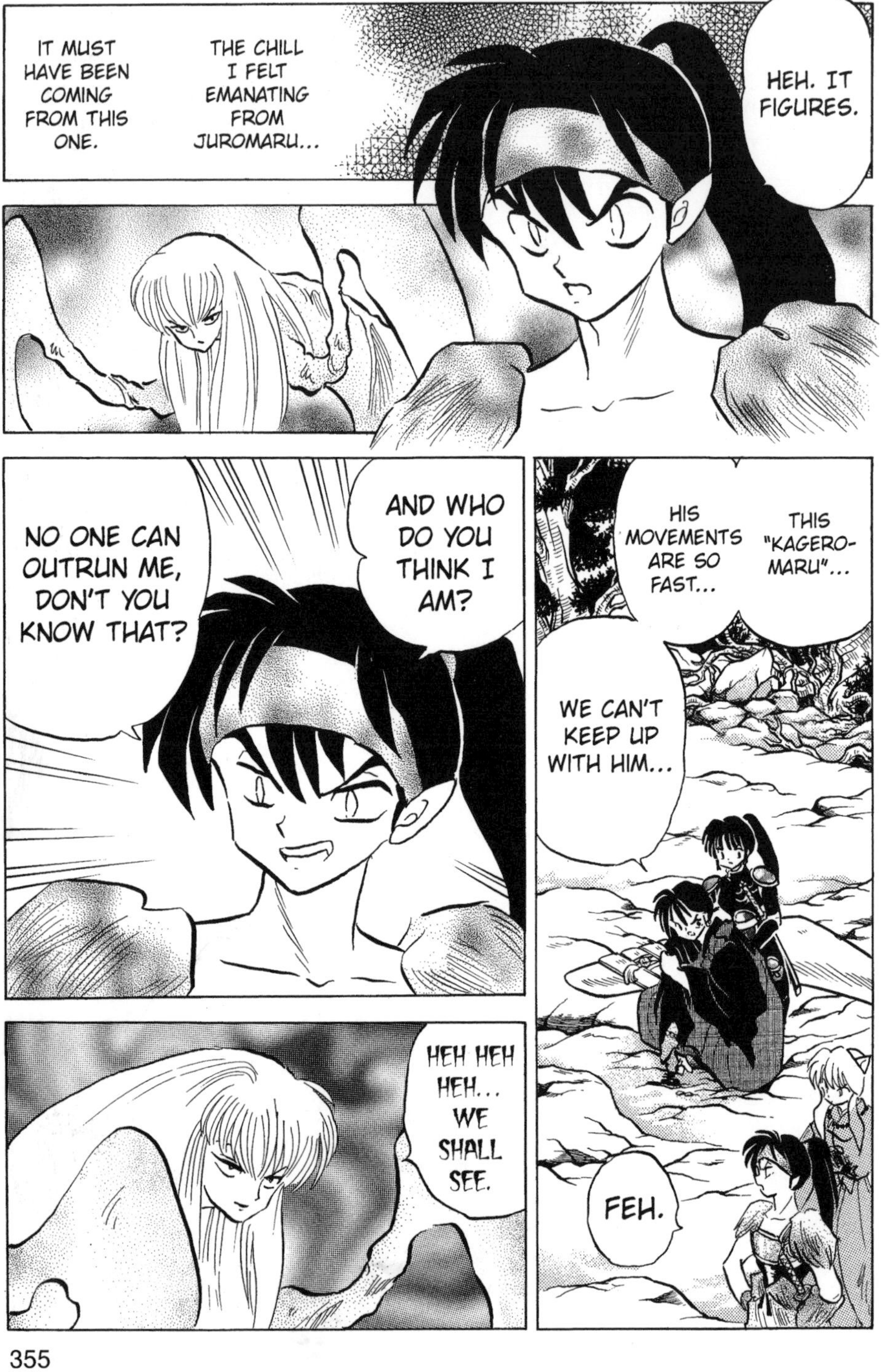
HEH. IT FIGURES.
THE CHILL I FELT EMANATING FROM JUROMARU...
IT MUST HAVE BEEN COMING FROM THIS ONE.
THIS "KAGERO-MARU"...
HIS MOVEMENTS ARE SO FAST...
WE CAN'T KEEP UP WITH HIM...
FEH.
AND WHO DO YOU THINK I AM?
NO ONE CAN OUTRUN ME, DON'T YOU KNOW THAT?
HEH HEH HEH... WE SHALL SEE.

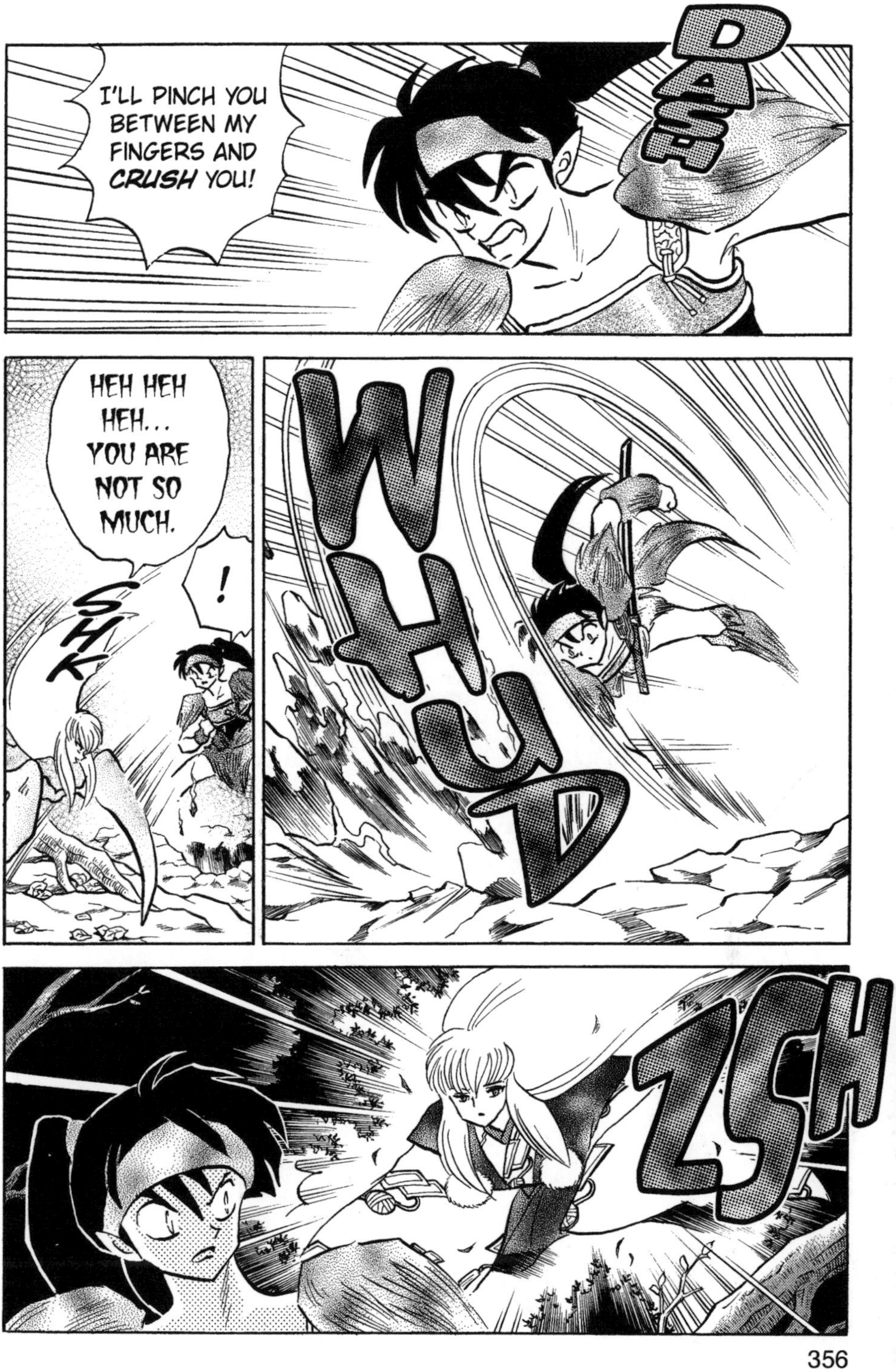
DASH
I'LL PINCH YOU BETWEEN MY FINGERS AND *CRUSH* YOU!
WHUD
HEH HEH HEH... YOU ARE NOT SO MUCH.
!
SHK
ZSCH

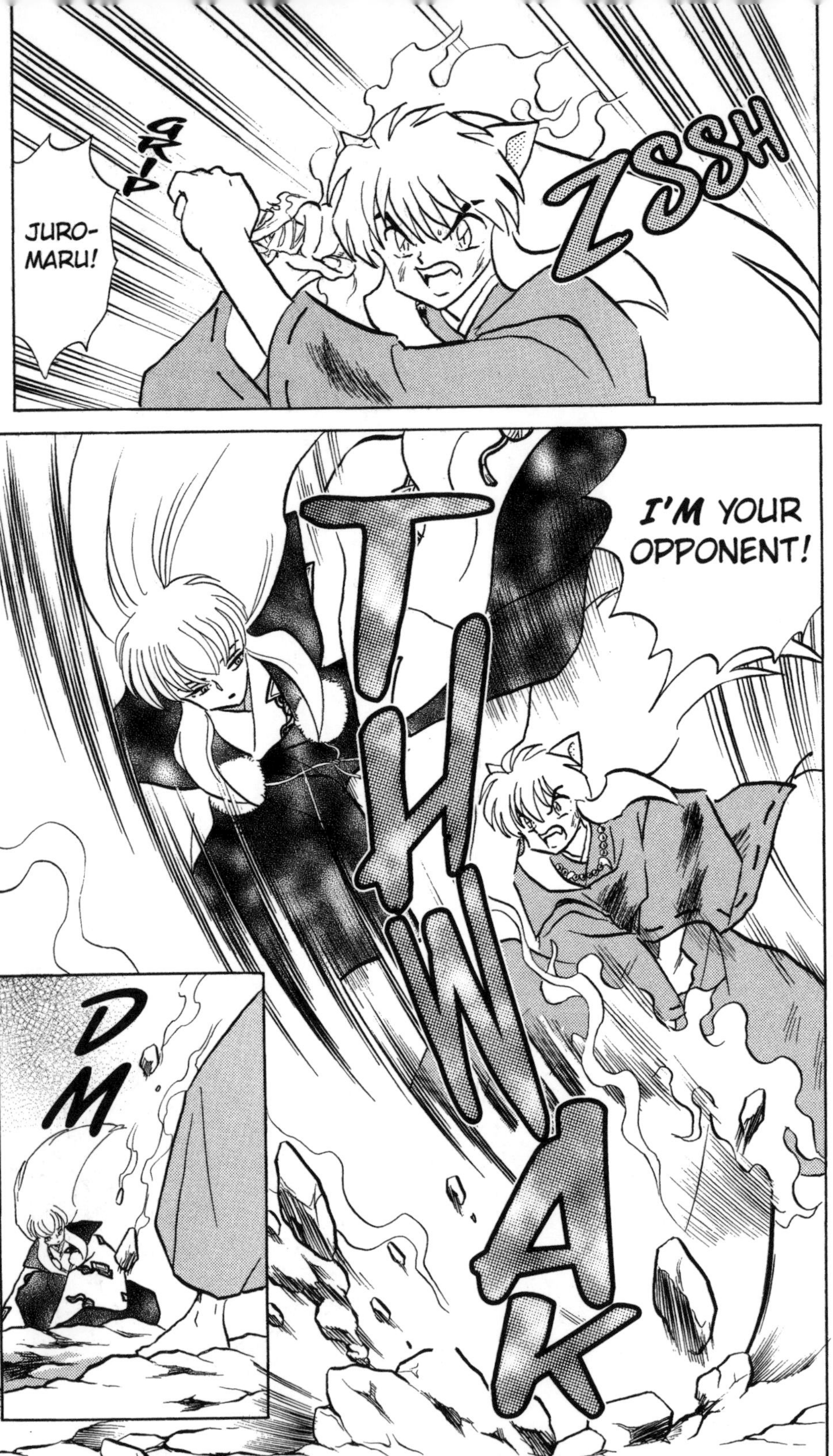
ZSSH
GRIP
JURO-MARU!
I'M YOUR OPPONENT!
THWAK
DM

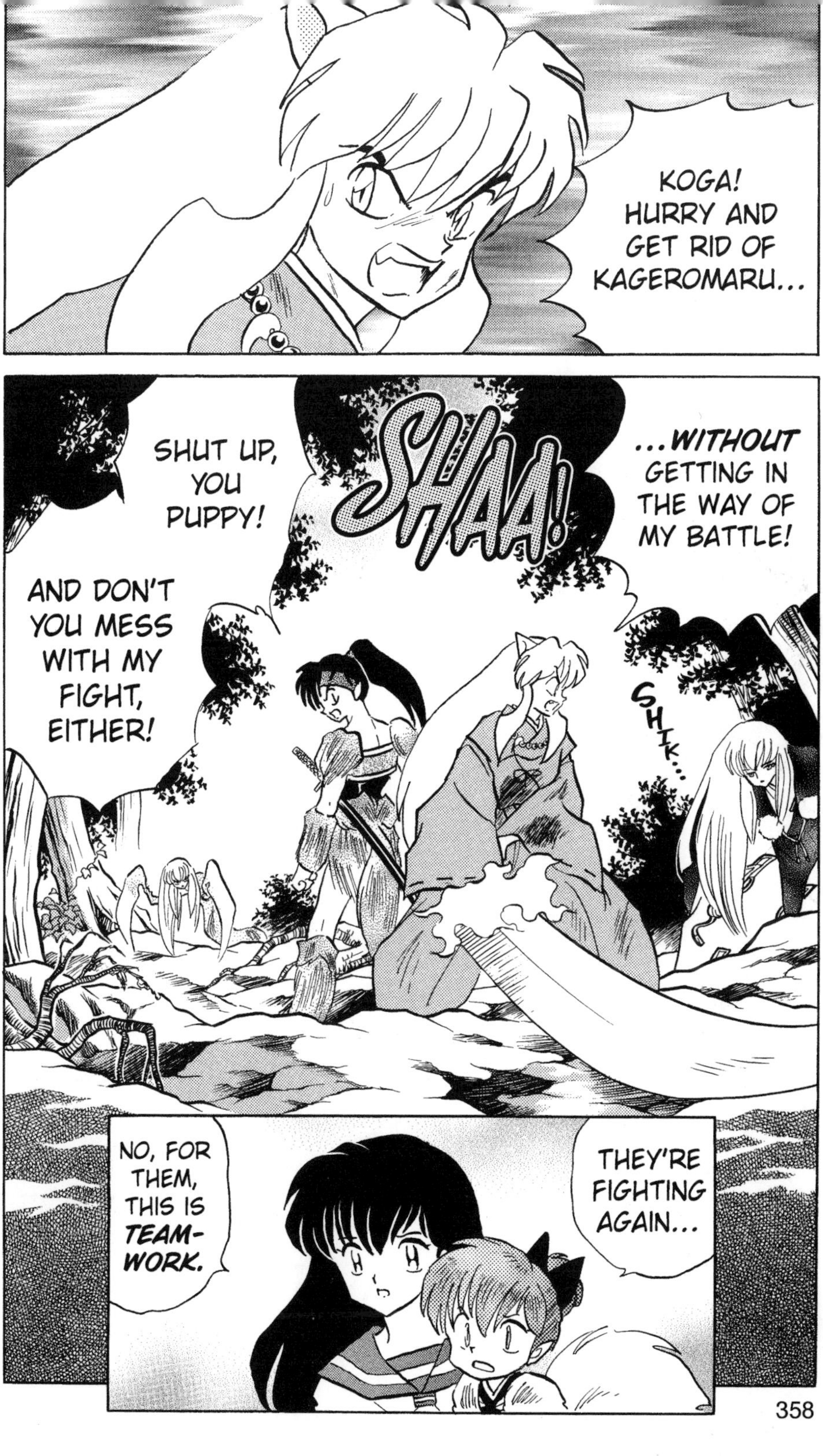
KOGA! HURRY AND GET RID OF KAGEROMARU...
...*WITHOUT* GETTING IN THE WAY OF MY BATTLE!
SHAA!
SHUT UP, YOU PUPPY!
AND DON'T YOU MESS WITH MY FIGHT, EITHER!
SHIK...
THEY'RE FIGHTING AGAIN...
NO, FOR THEM, THIS IS *TEAM-WORK.*

SCROLL TEN
TWO AGAINST TWO

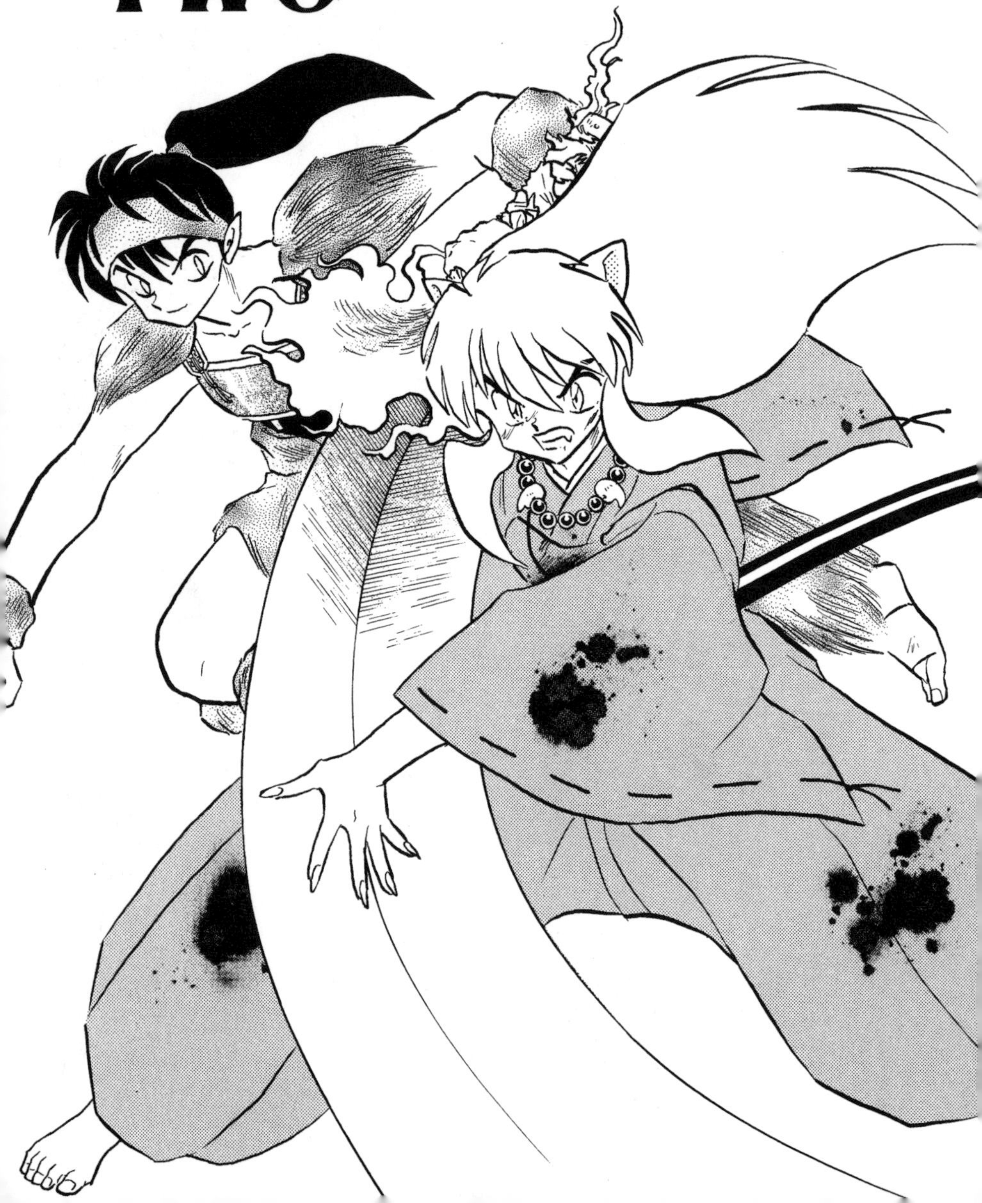

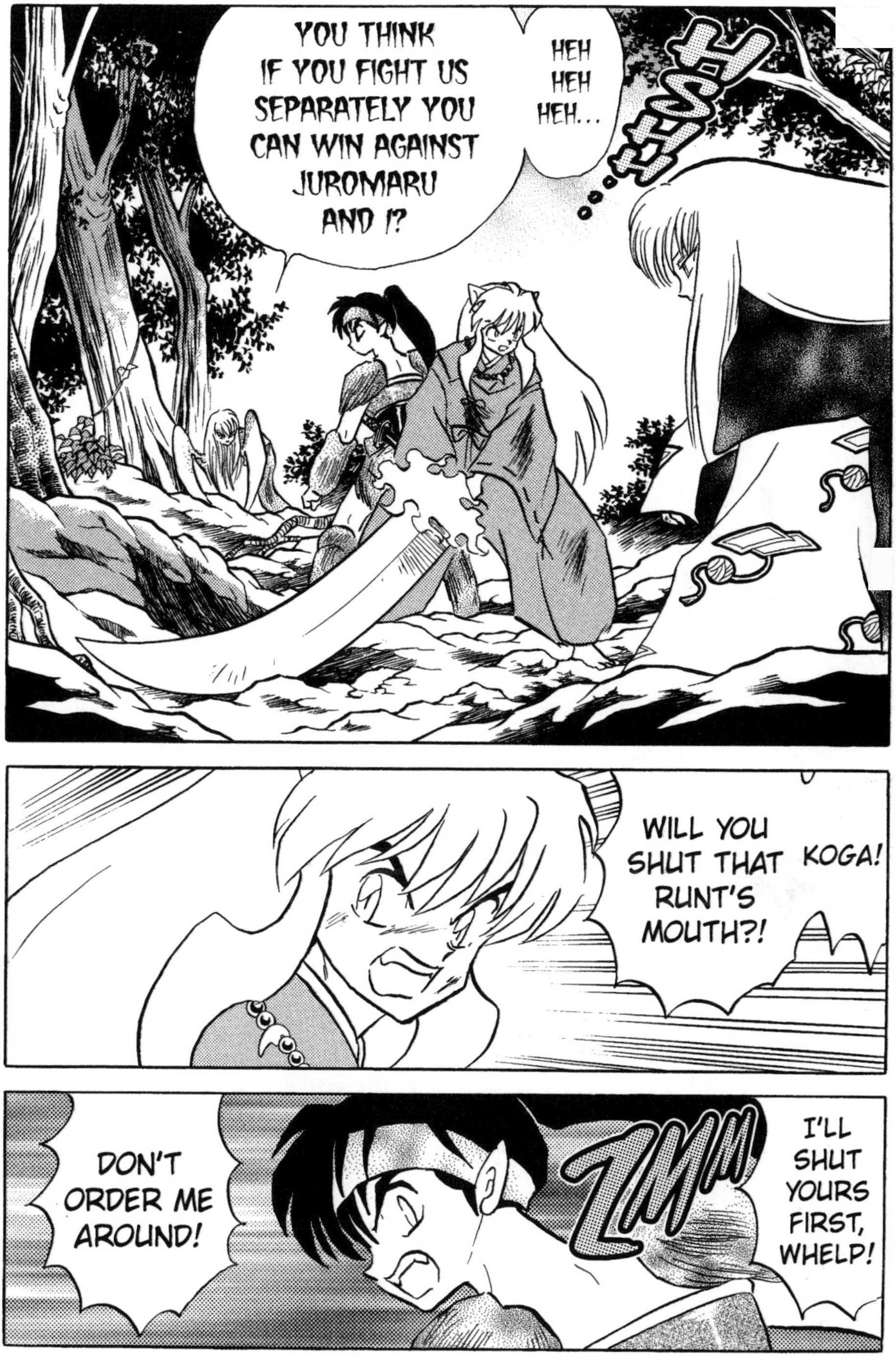
HEH HEH HEH...
HSSH...
YOU THINK IF YOU FIGHT US SEPARATELY YOU CAN WIN AGAINST JUROMARU AND I!?
KOGA!
WILL YOU SHUT THAT RUNT'S MOUTH?!
I'LL SHUT YOURS FIRST, WHELP!
ZM
DON'T ORDER ME AROUND!

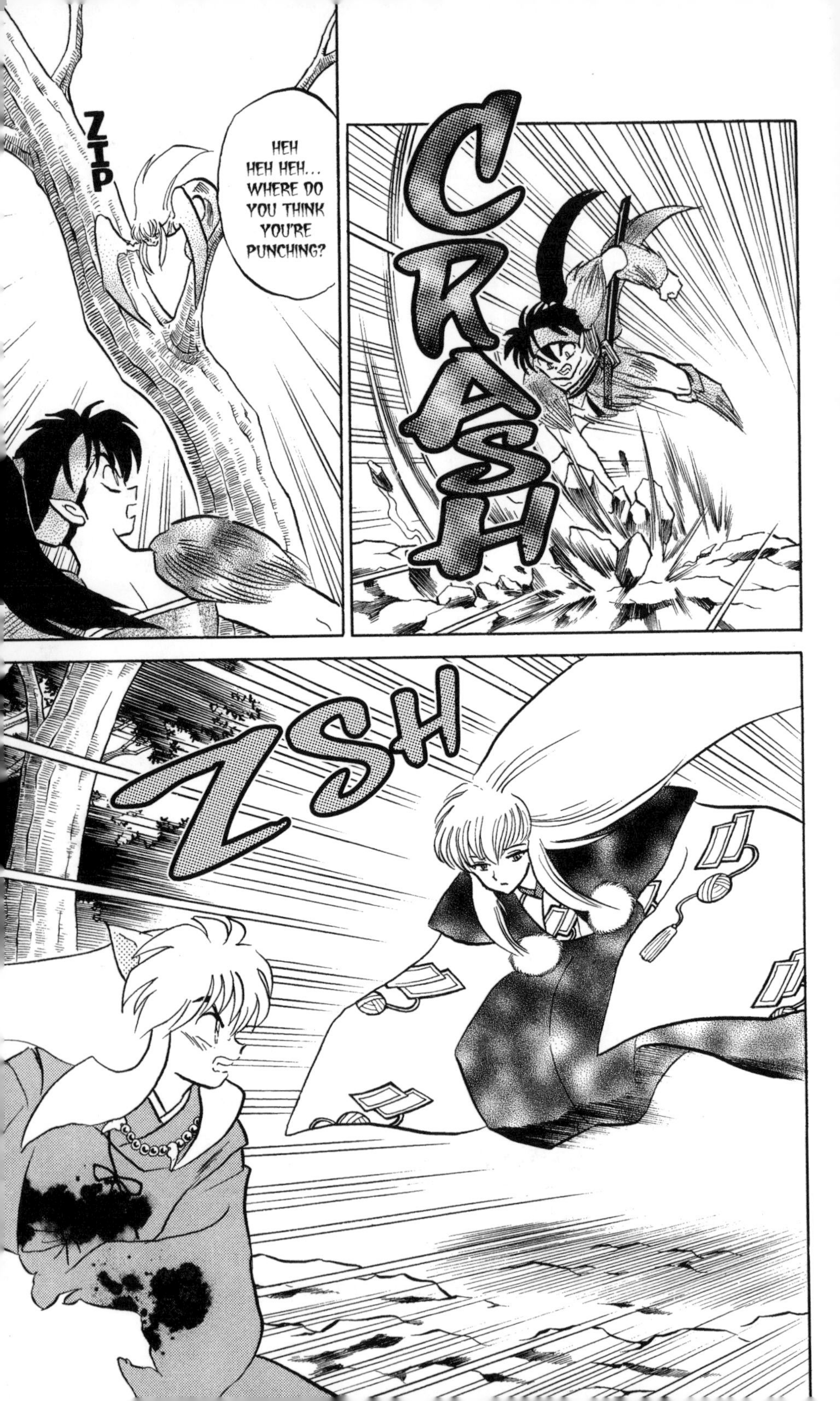
CRASH
ZIP
HEH HEH HEH... WHERE DO YOU THINK YOU'RE PUNCHING?
ZSH

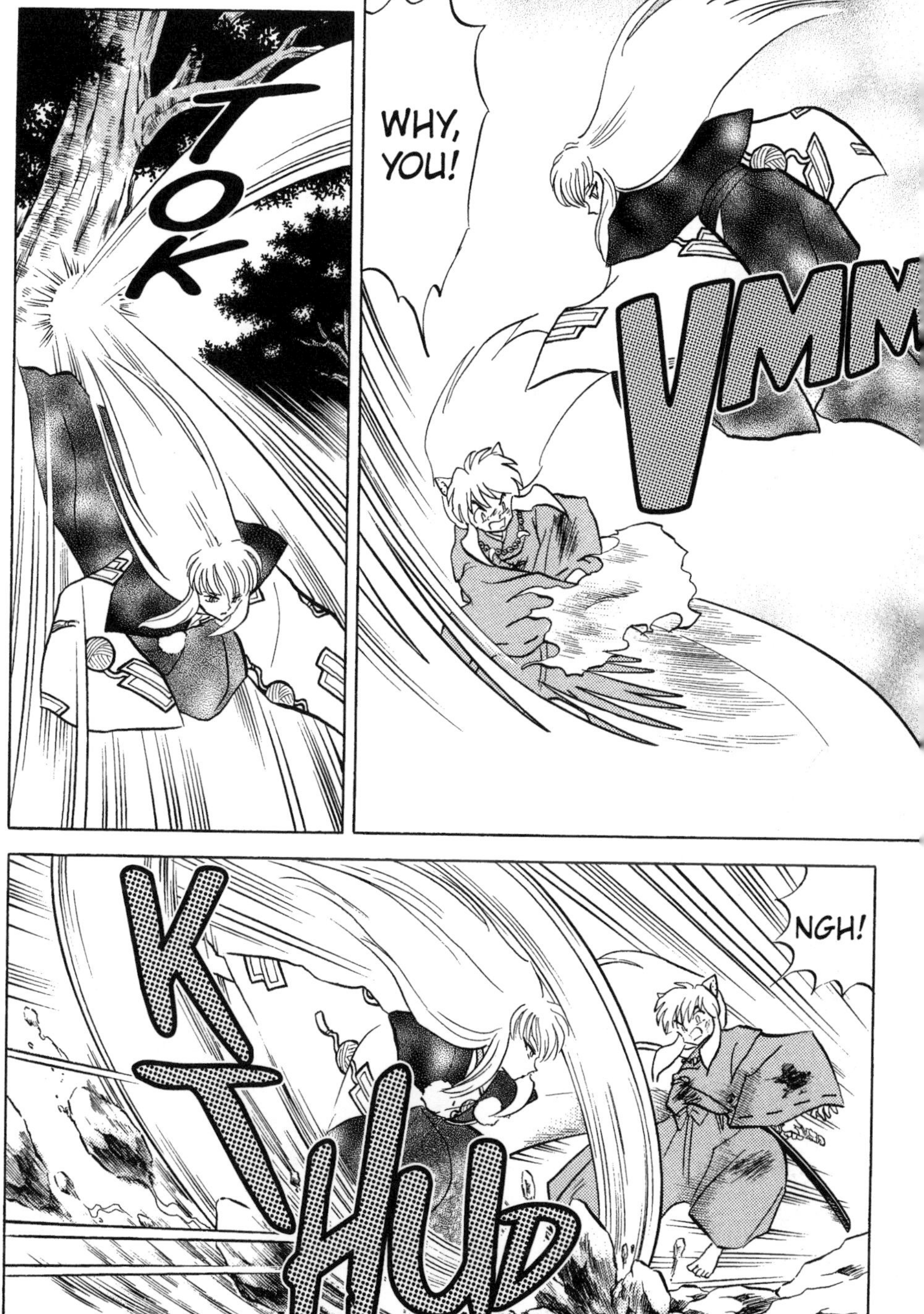
WHY, YOU!
VMMM
TOK
NGH!
K-THUD

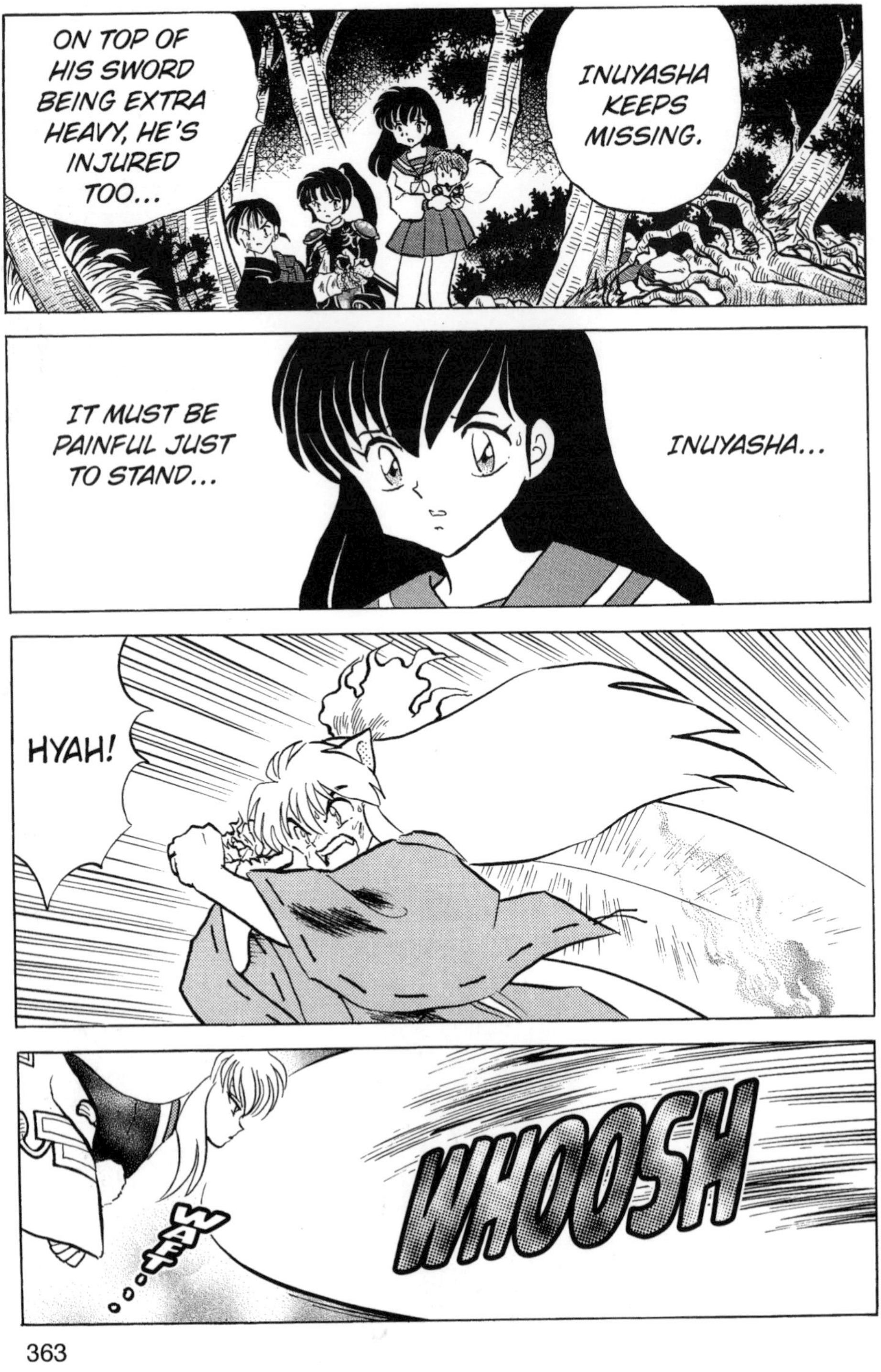
INUYASHA KEEPS MISSING.
ON TOP OF HIS SWORD BEING EXTRA HEAVY, HE'S INJURED TOO...
INUYASHA...
IT MUST BE PAINFUL JUST TO STAND...
HYAH!
WHOOSH
WAFT...

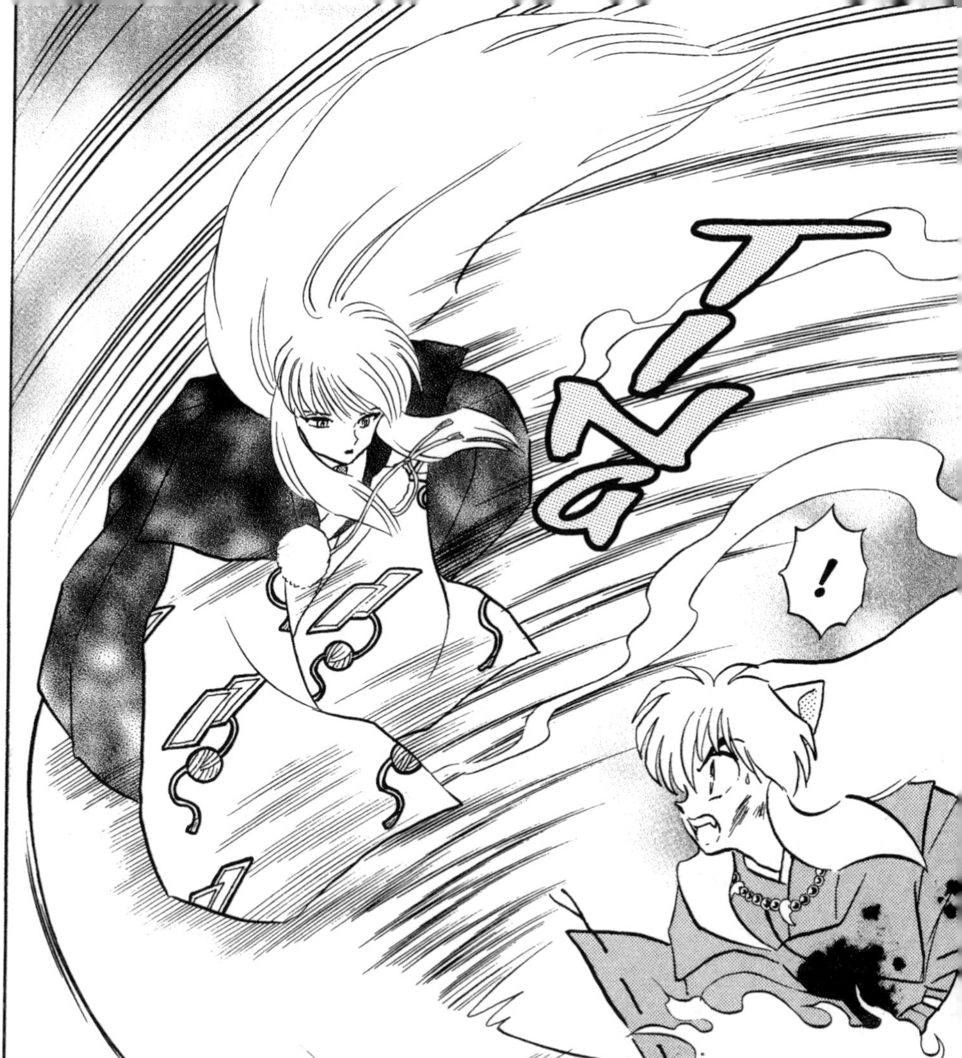
!

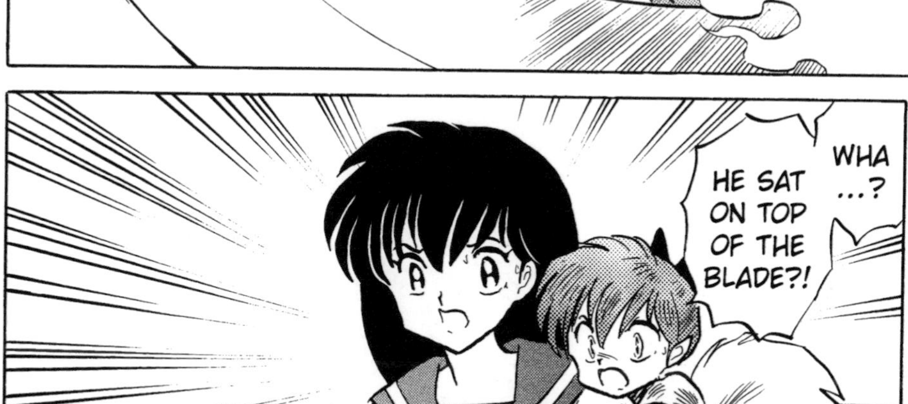
WHA ...?
HE SAT ON TOP OF THE BLADE?!

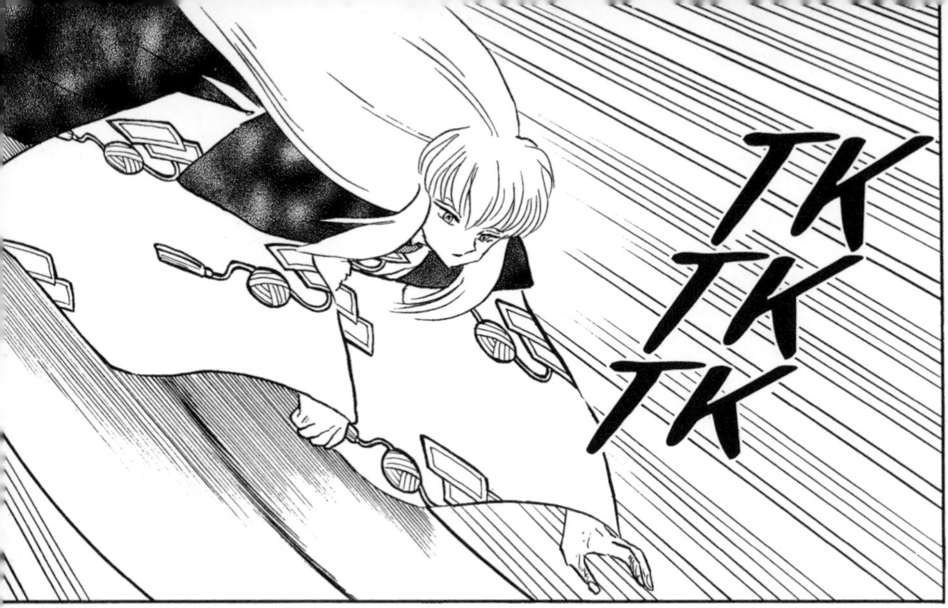
TK
TK
TK
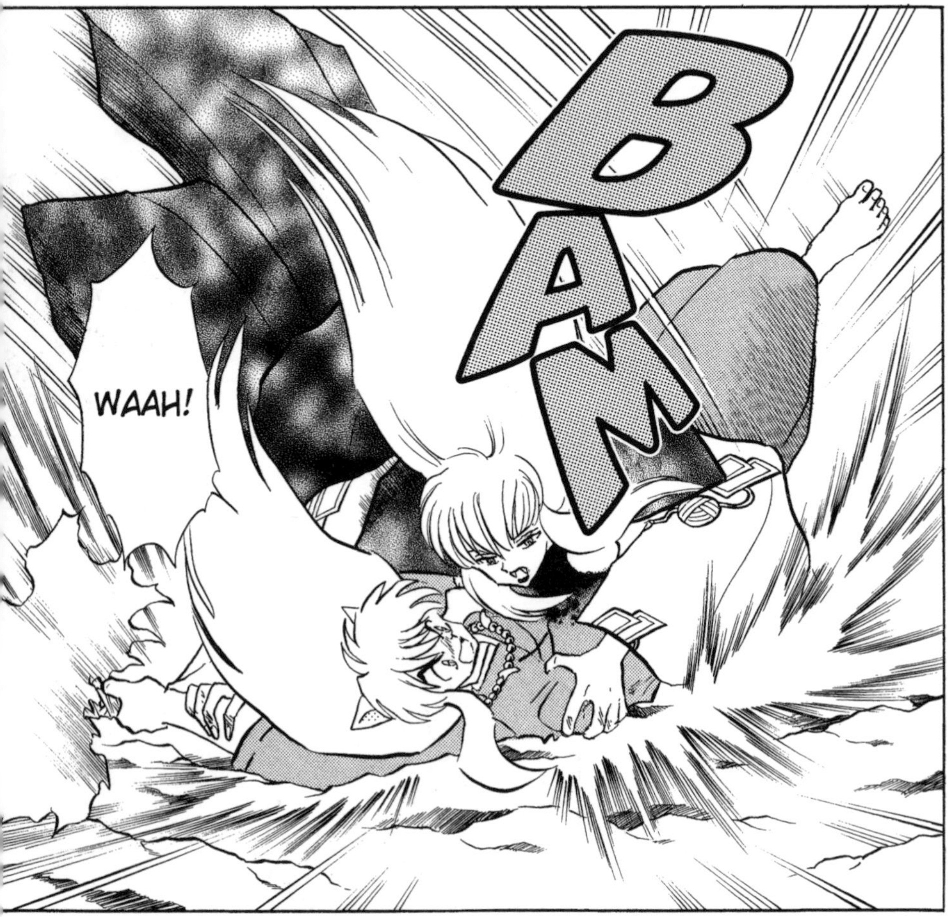
BAM
WAAH!

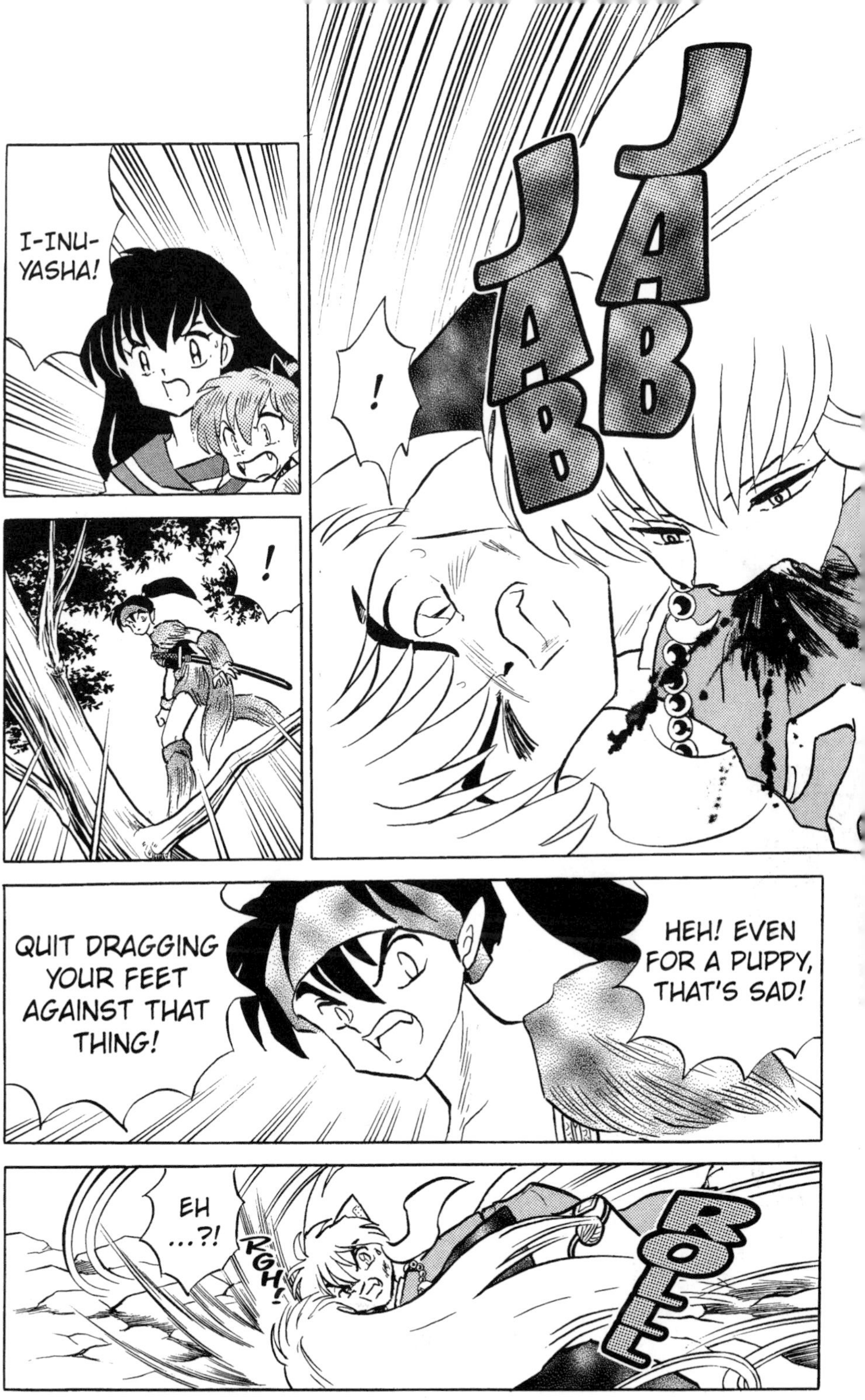
JAB
JAB
!
I-INU-YASHA!
!
HEH! EVEN FOR A PUPPY, THAT'S SAD!
QUIT DRAGGING YOUR FEET AGAINST THAT THING!
ROLL
RGH!
EH ...?!

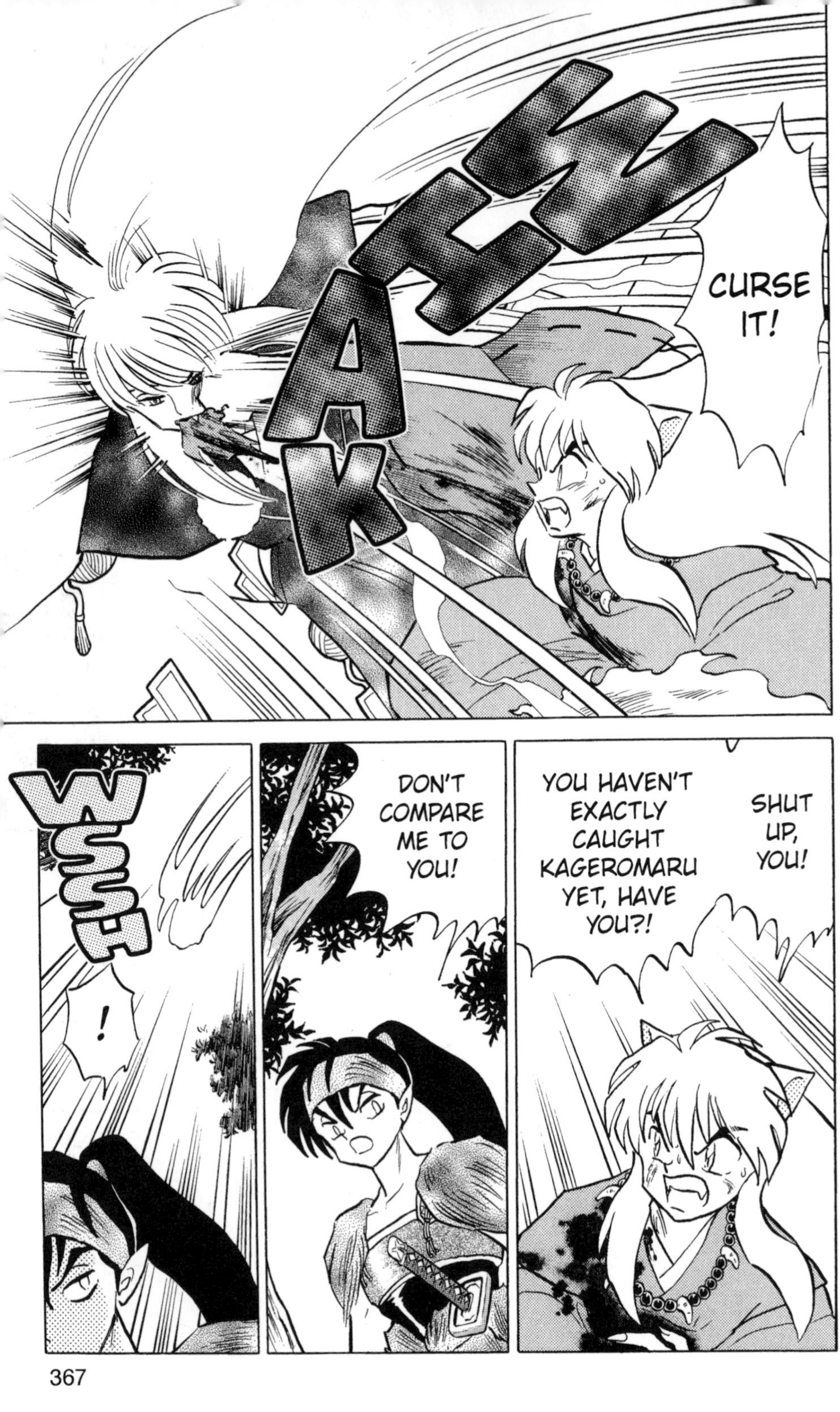
CURSE IT!
WHACK
SHUT UP, YOU!
YOU HAVEN'T EXACTLY CAUGHT KAGEROMARU YET, HAVE YOU?!
DON'T COMPARE ME TO YOU!
WSSH
!

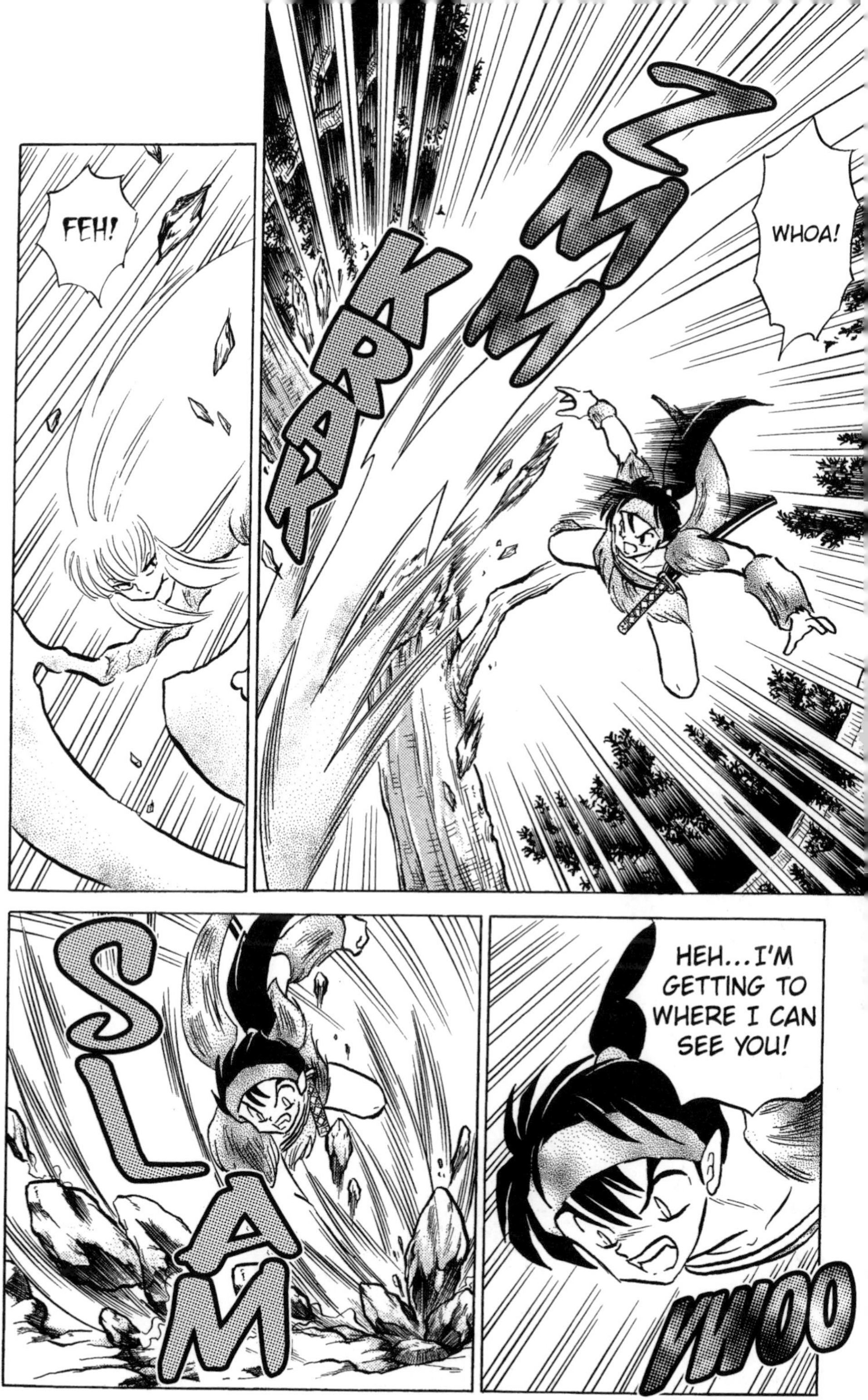
WHOA!
KRAK
FEH!
HEH...I'M GETTING TO WHERE I CAN SEE YOU!
WHOO
SLAM

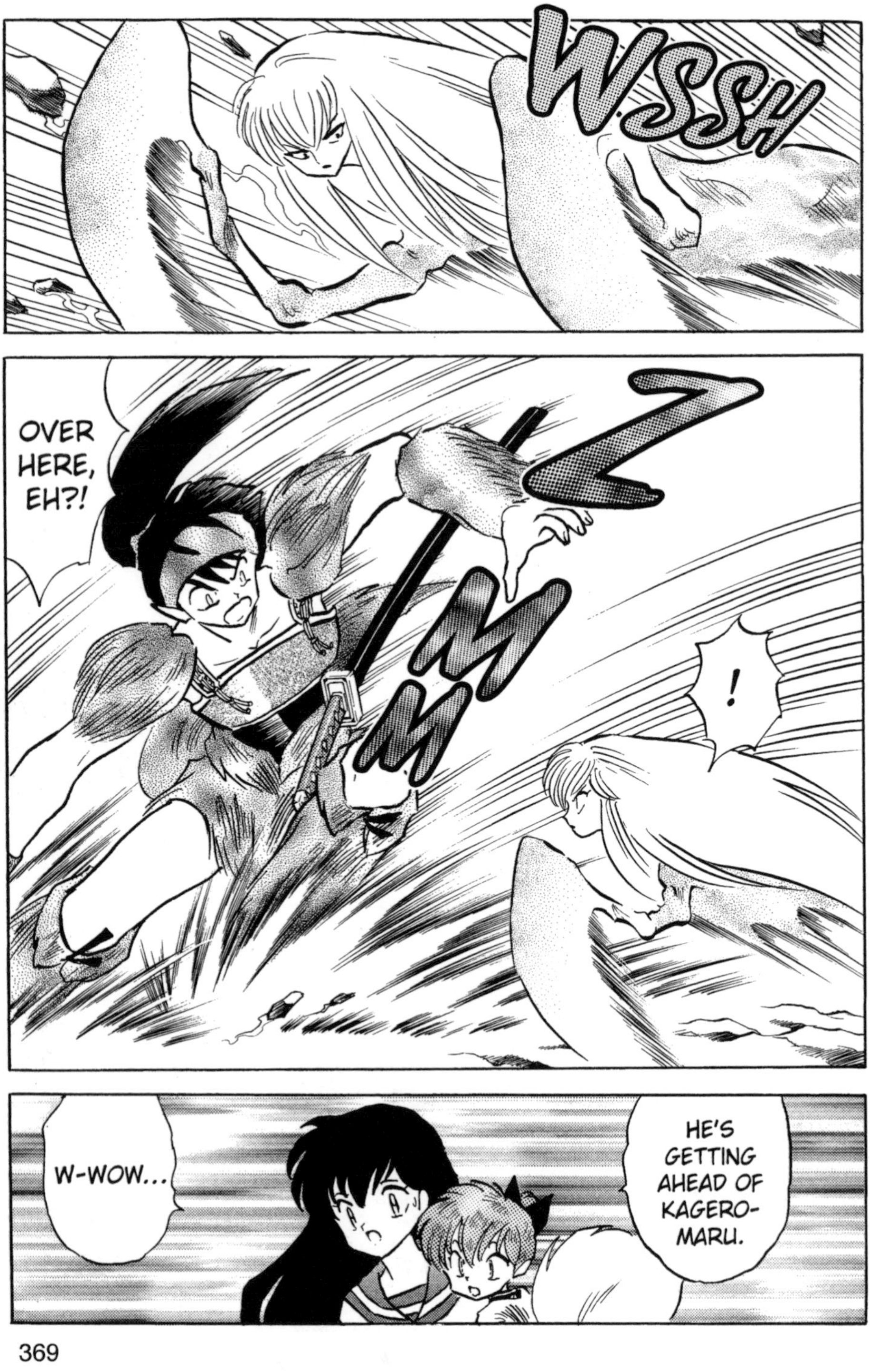
WSSH
ZMMM
!
OVER HERE, EH?!
HE'S GETTING AHEAD OF KAGERO-MARU.
W-WOW...

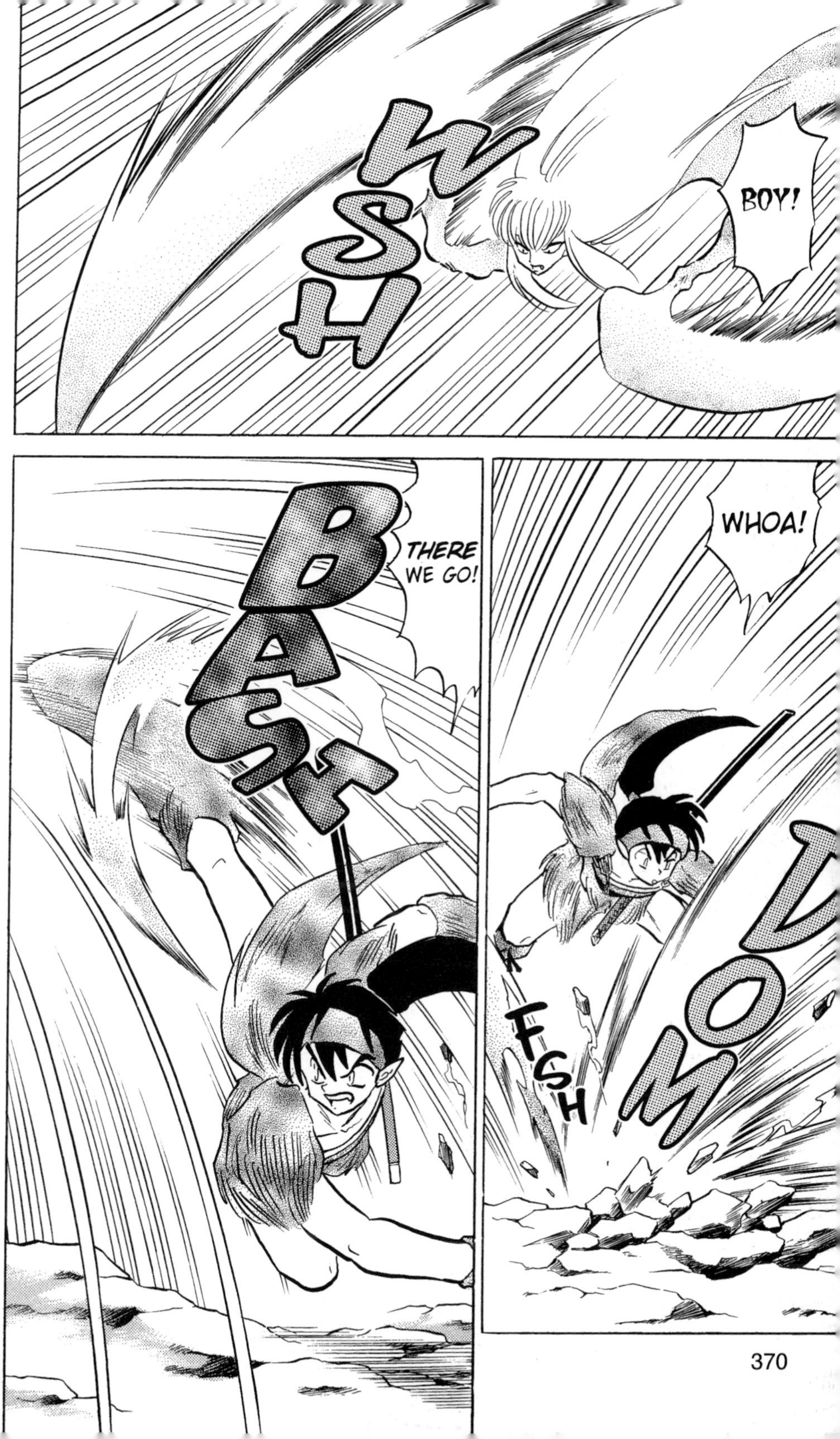
BOY!
WSH
WHOA!
DOOM
FSH
BASH
THERE WE GO!

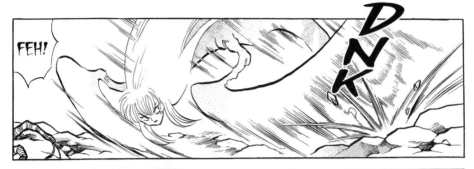

FEH!

DNK

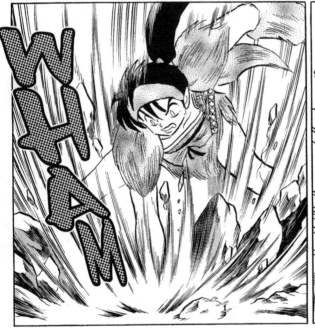

WHAM

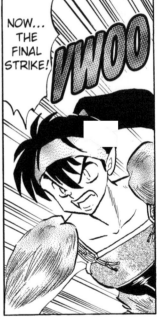

NOW...
THE
FINAL
STRIKE!

VWOO

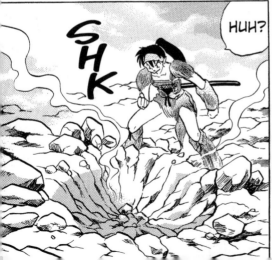

SHK

HUH?

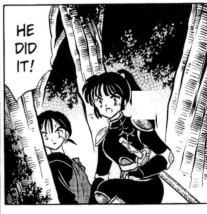

HE
DID
IT!

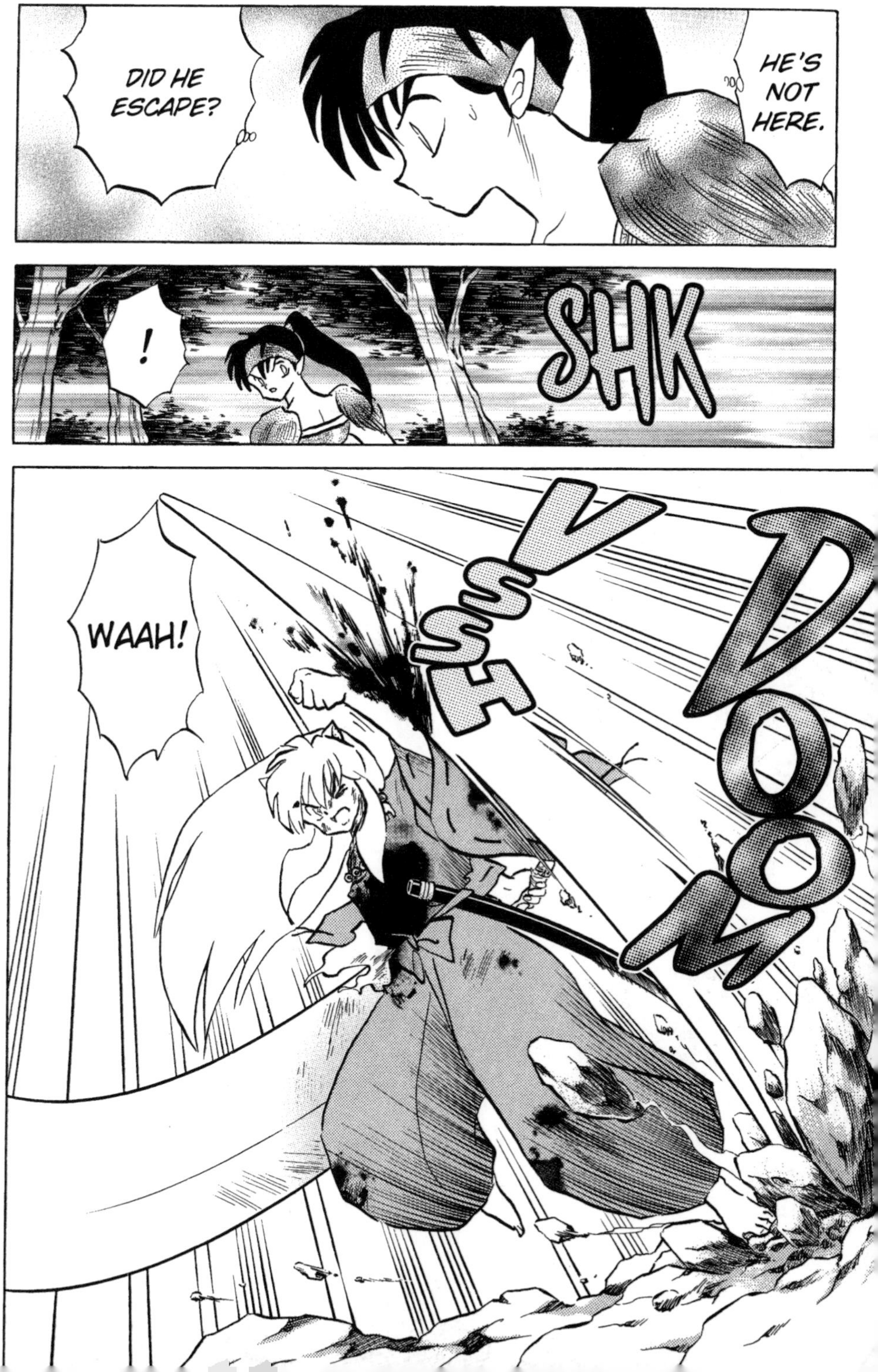
HE'S NOT HERE.
DID HE ESCAPE?
SHK
!
DOOM
VSSH
WAAH!

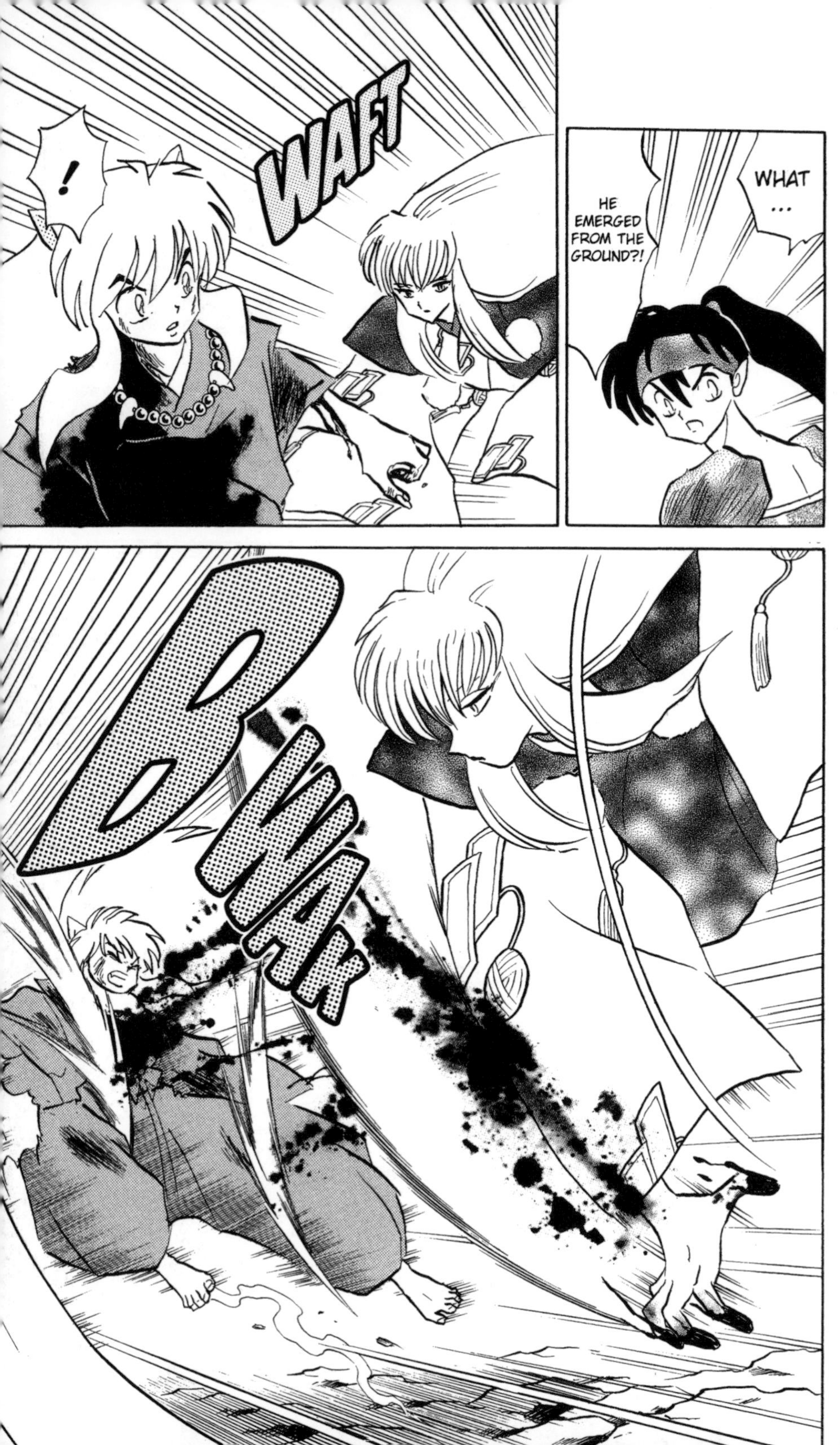
WHAT ...
HE EMERGED FROM THE GROUND?!
WAFT
!
BWAK

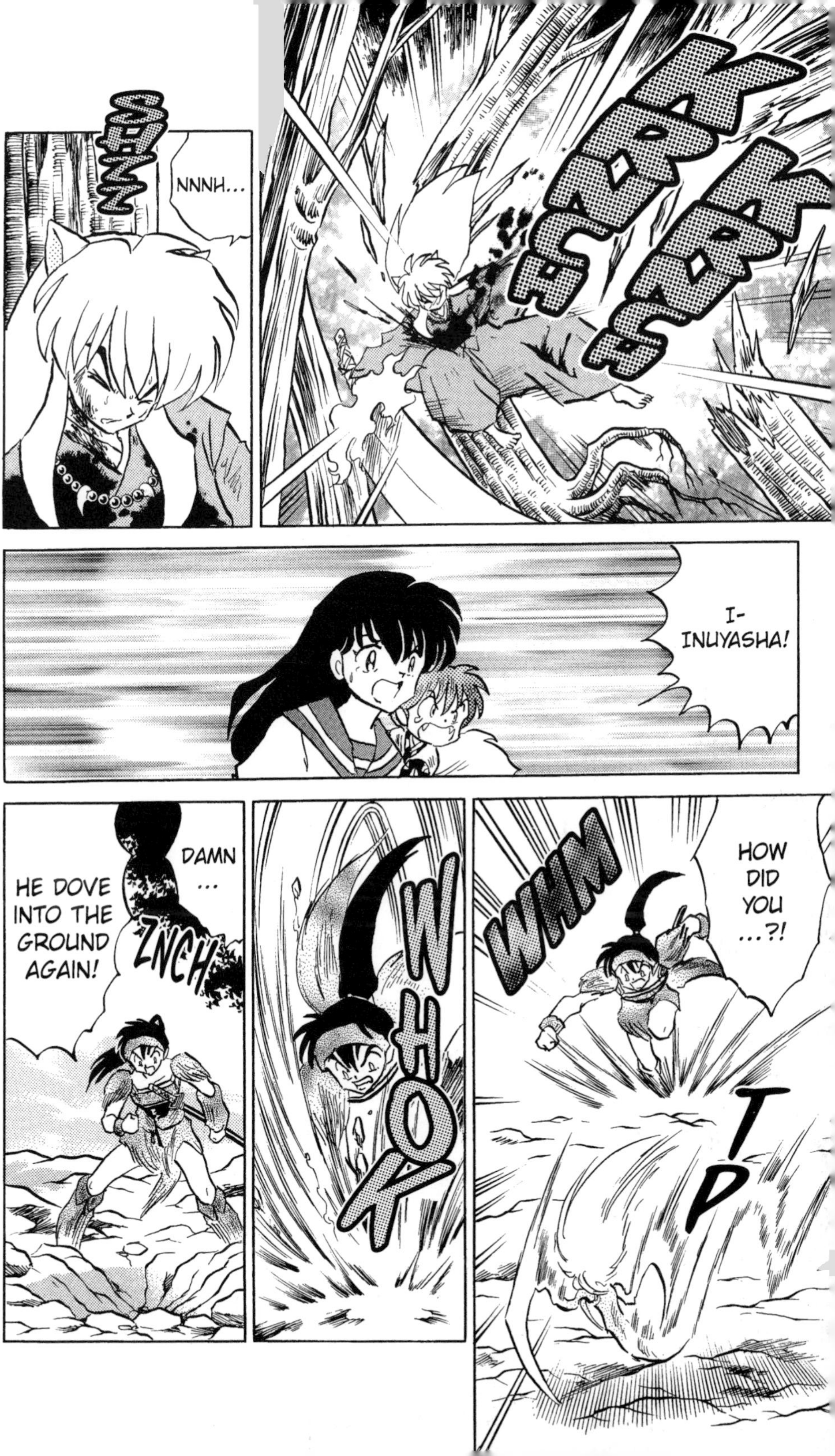
KRAKSH
KRAKSH
NNNH...
SHNN
I- INUYASHA!
HOW DID YOU ...?!
WHM
TD
WHOK
DAMN ...
ZNCH
HE DOVE INTO THE GROUND AGAIN!

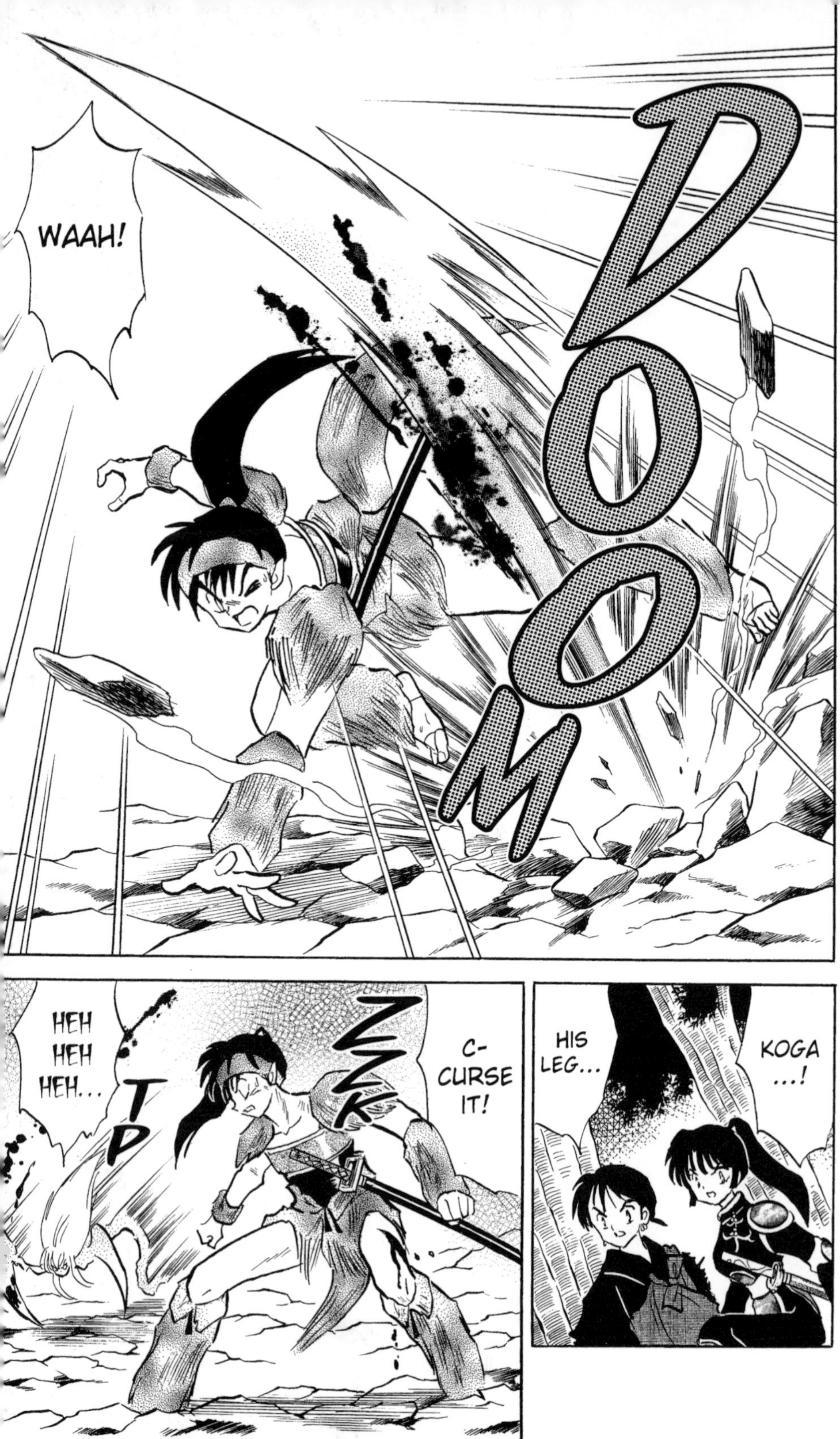
DOOM
WAAH!
KOGA ...!
HIS LEG...
C-CURSE IT!
ZZK
HEH HEH HEH...
TP

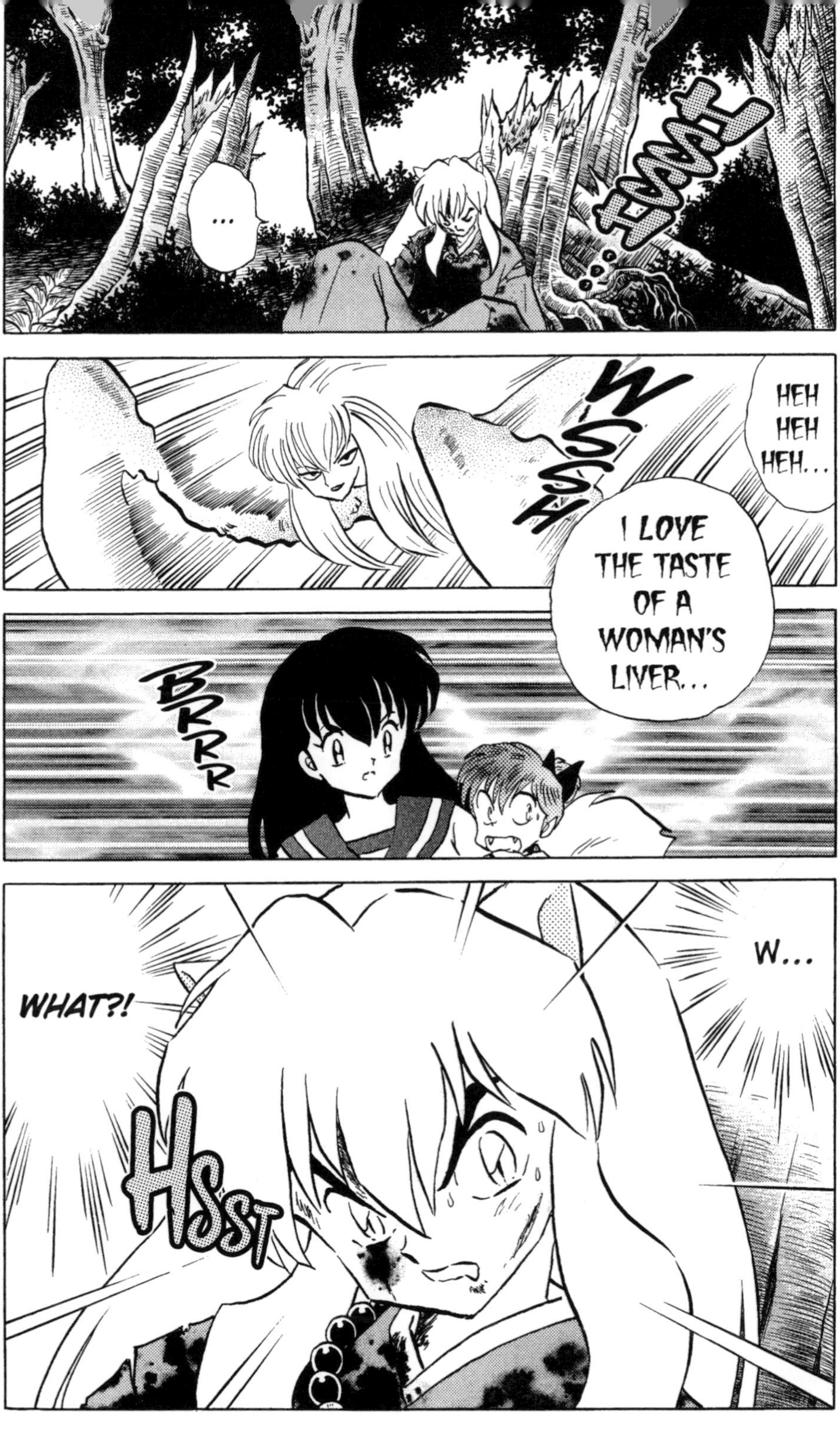
...
HEH HEH HEH...
WSSH
I LOVE THE TASTE OF A WOMAN'S LIVER...
BRRRR
W...
WHAT?!
HSST

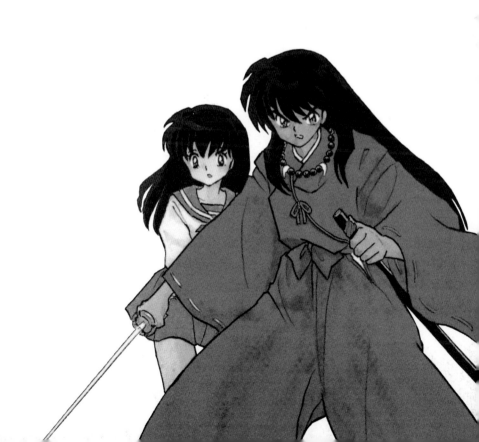

InuYasha

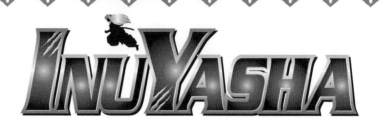

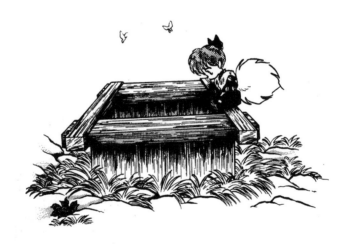

Volume 18

Onigumo's Heart

SCROLL ONE
THE ENEMY IN THE EARTH

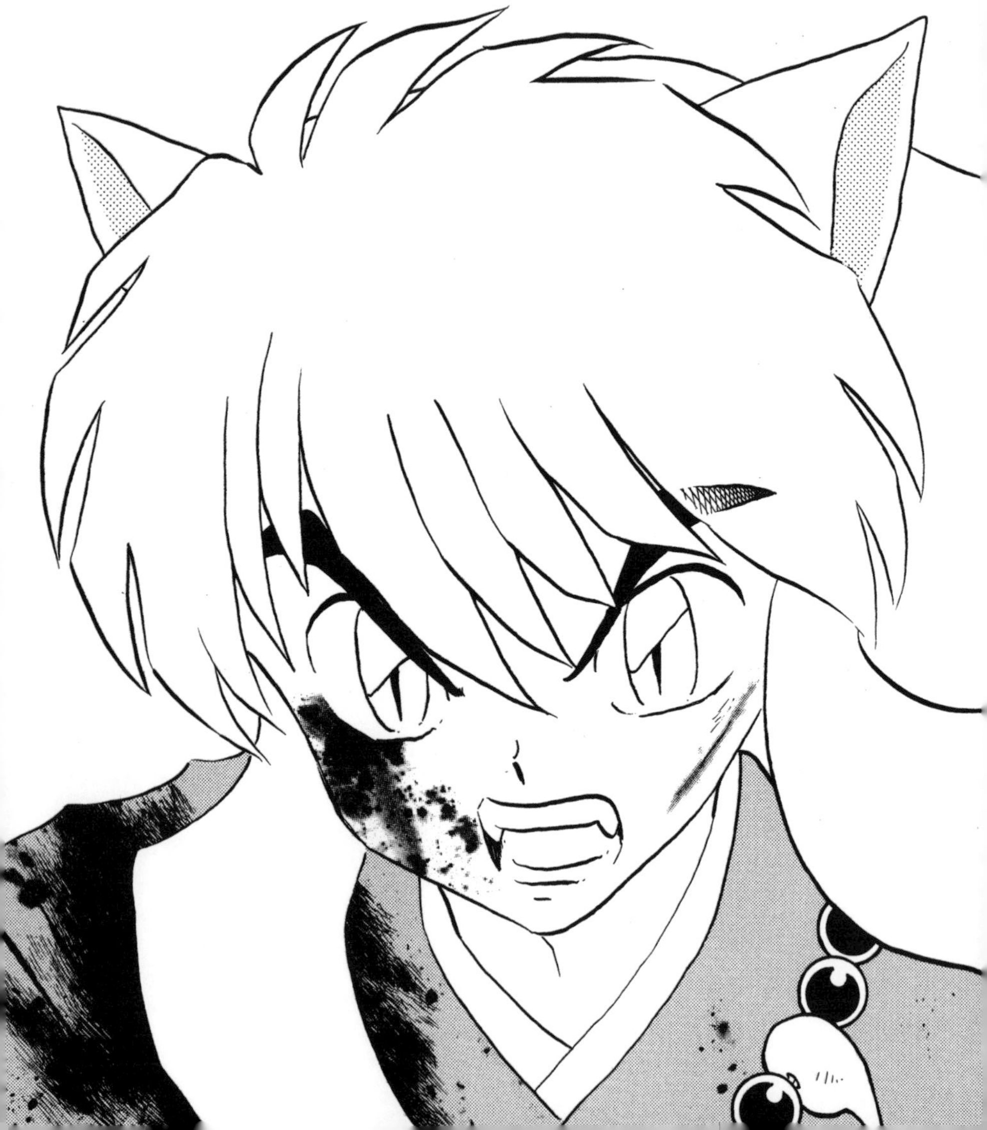

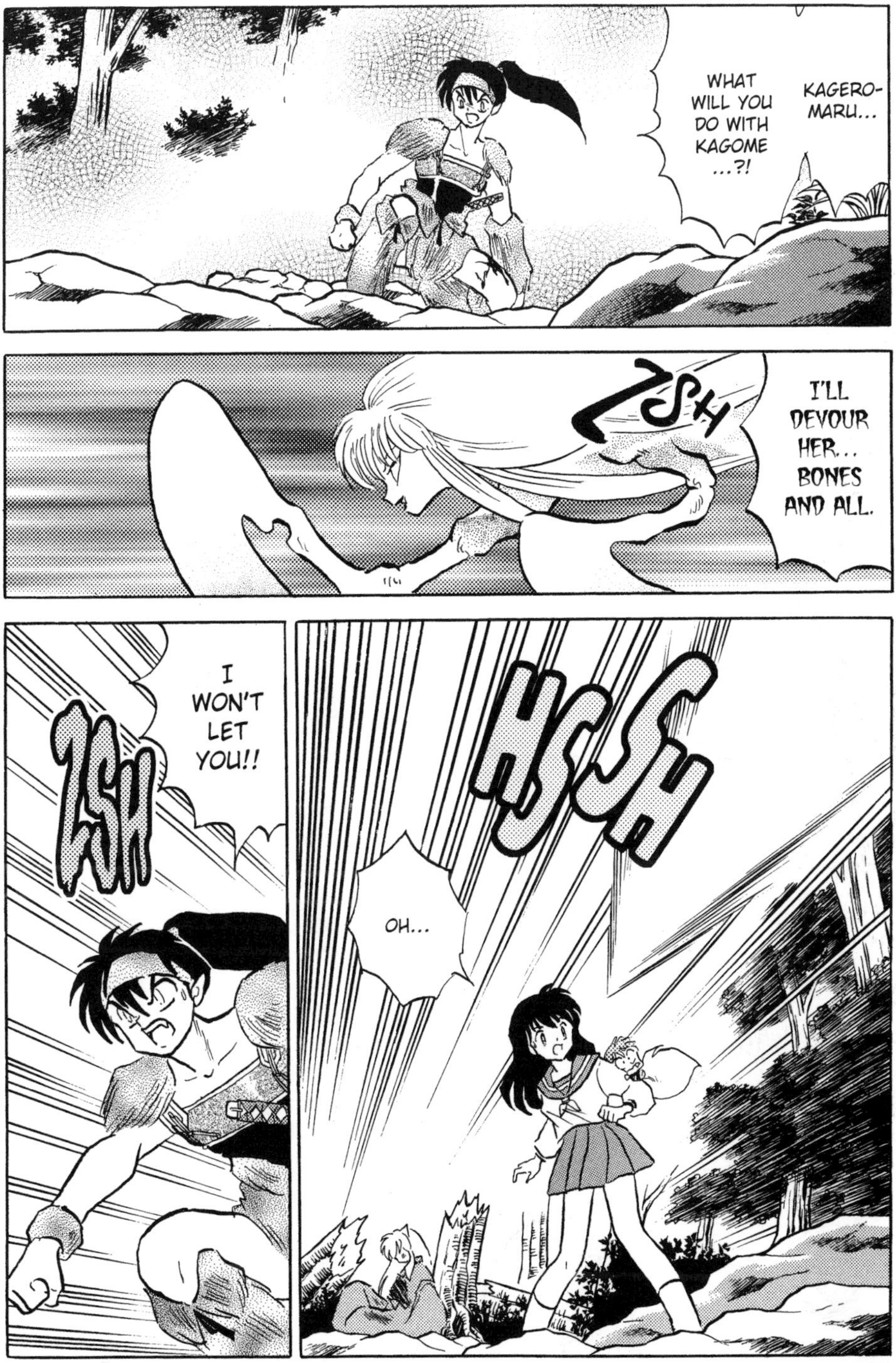
KAGERO-MARU...
WHAT WILL YOU DO WITH KAGOME ...?!
ZSH
I'LL DEVOUR HER... BONES AND ALL.
OH...
I WON'T LET YOU!!
ZSH

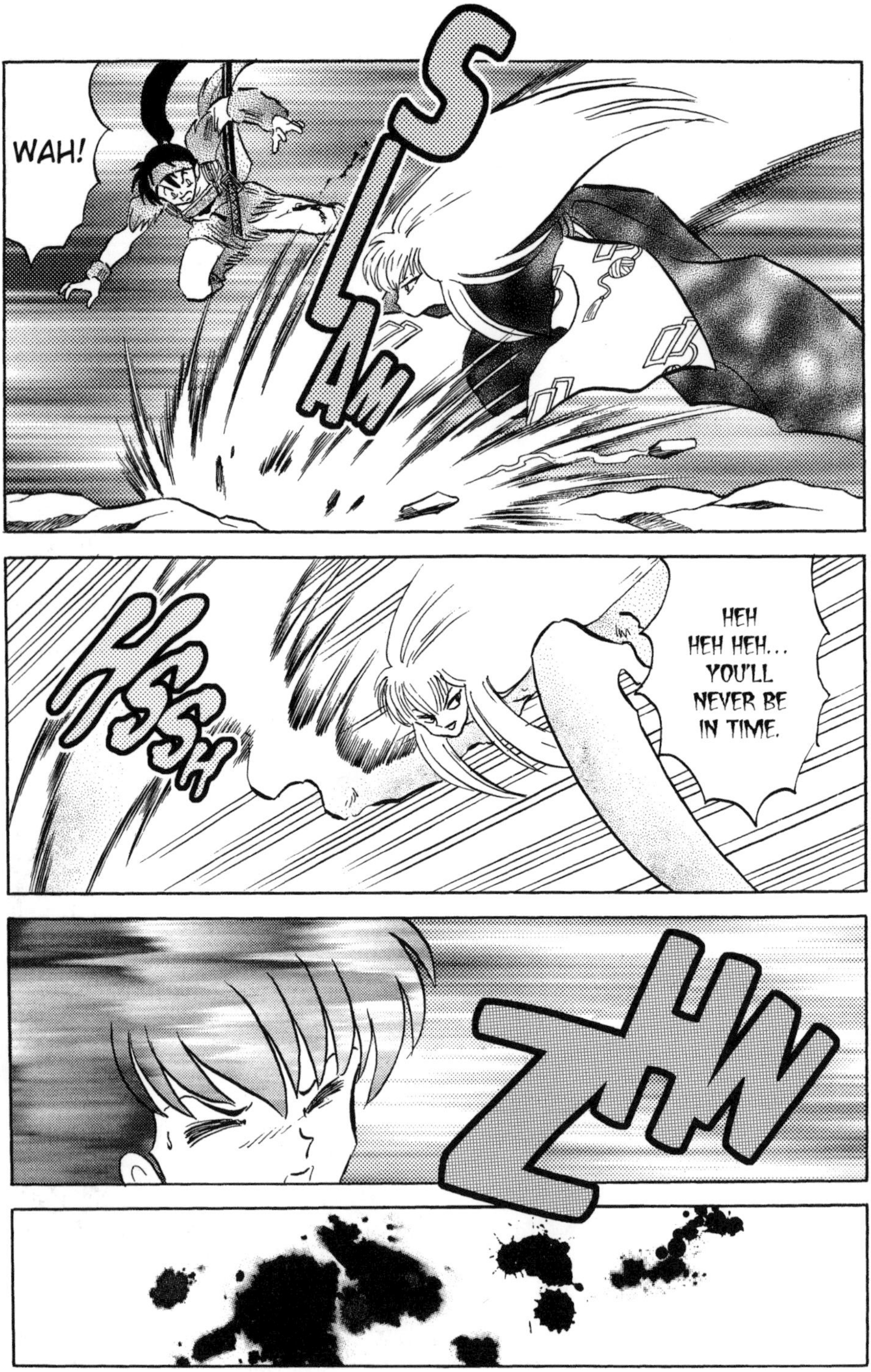
SLAM
WAH!
HEH HEH HEH... YOU'LL NEVER BE IN TIME.
HSSH
ZHN

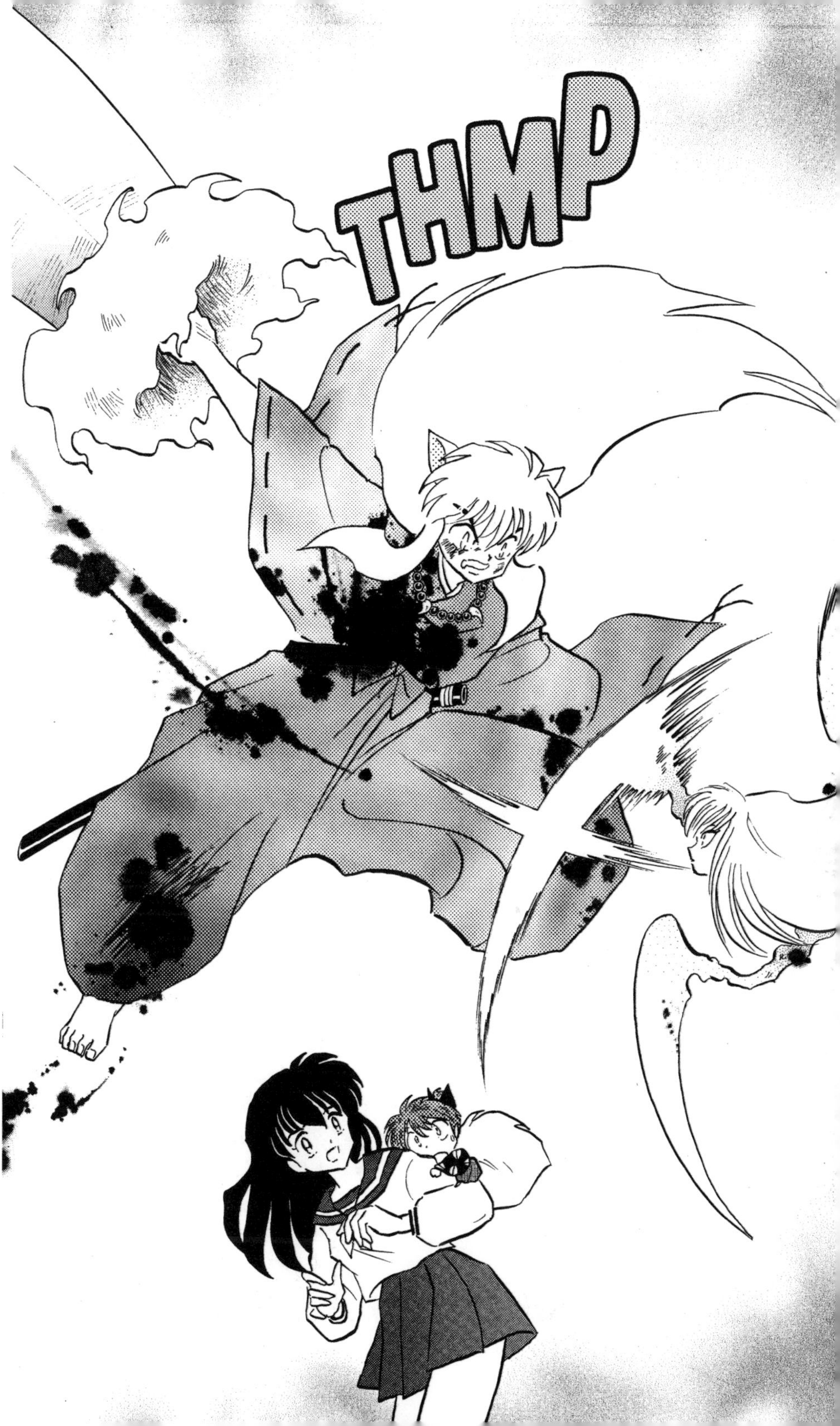
THMP

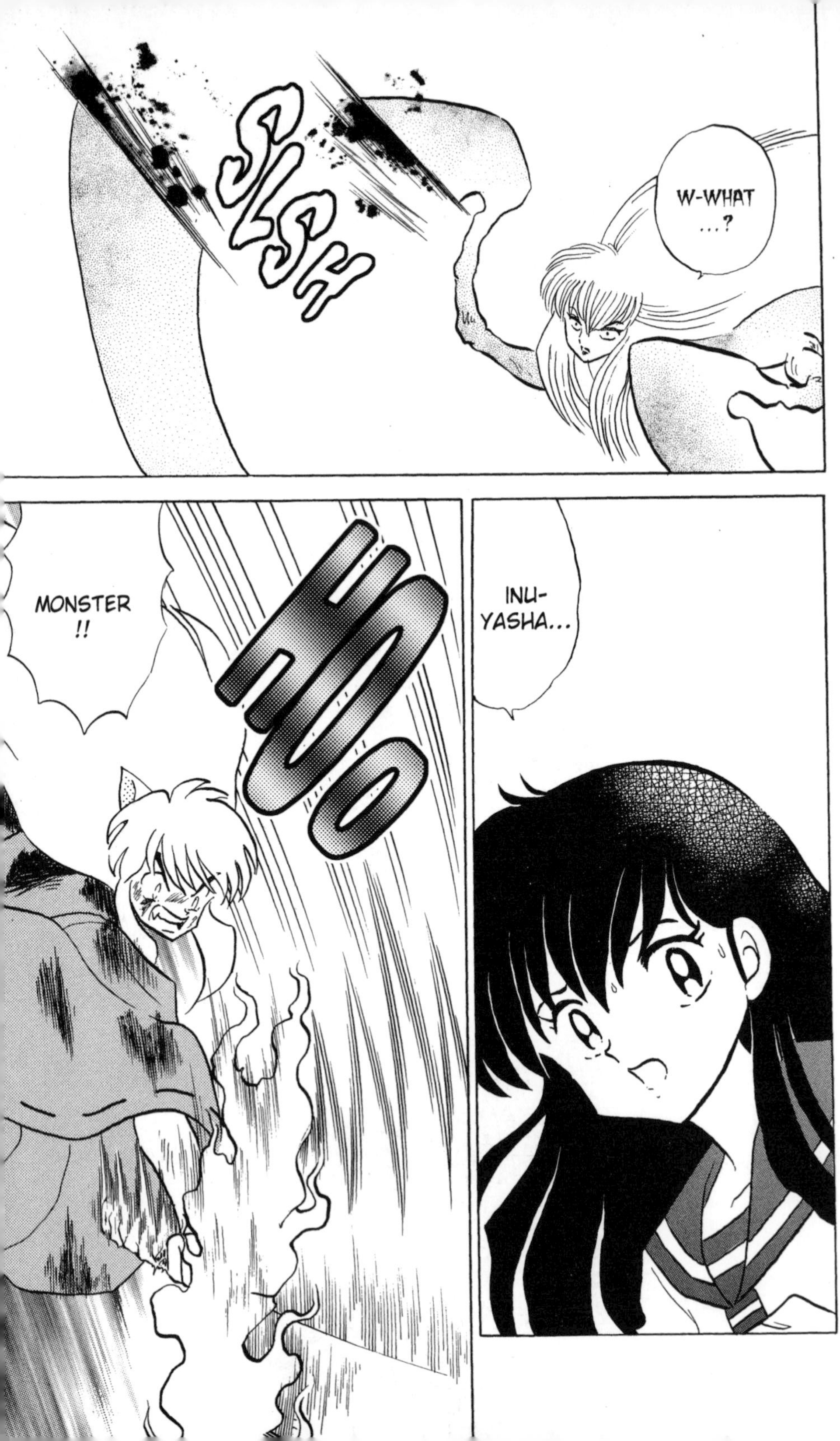
W-WHAT ...?
SLISH
INU-YASHA...
MONSTER !!

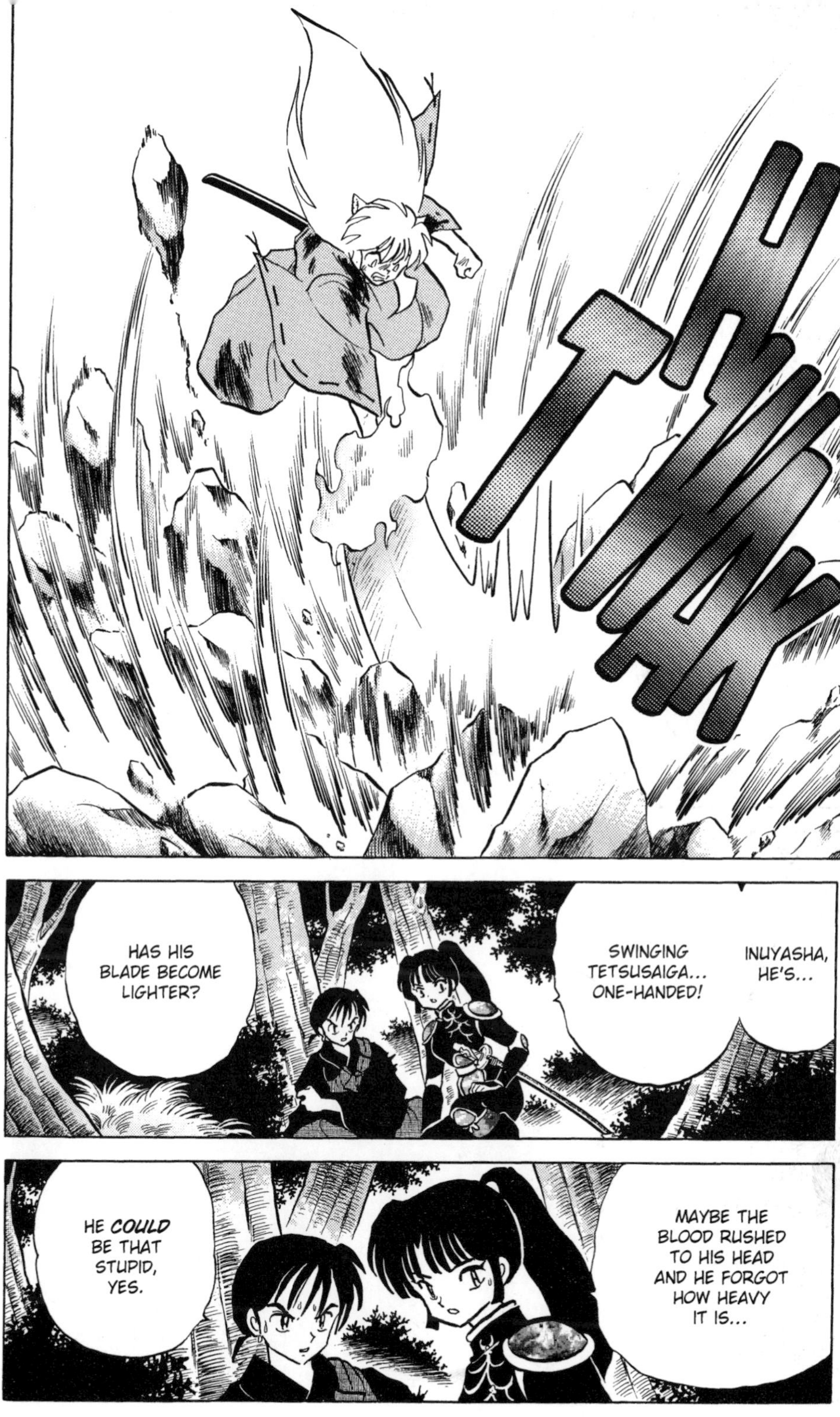
THWAK
INUYASHA, HE'S...
SWINGING TETSUSAIGA... ONE-HANDED!
HAS HIS BLADE BECOME LIGHTER?
MAYBE THE BLOOD RUSHED TO HIS HEAD AND HE FORGOT HOW HEAVY IT IS...
HE *COULD* BE THAT STUPID, YES.

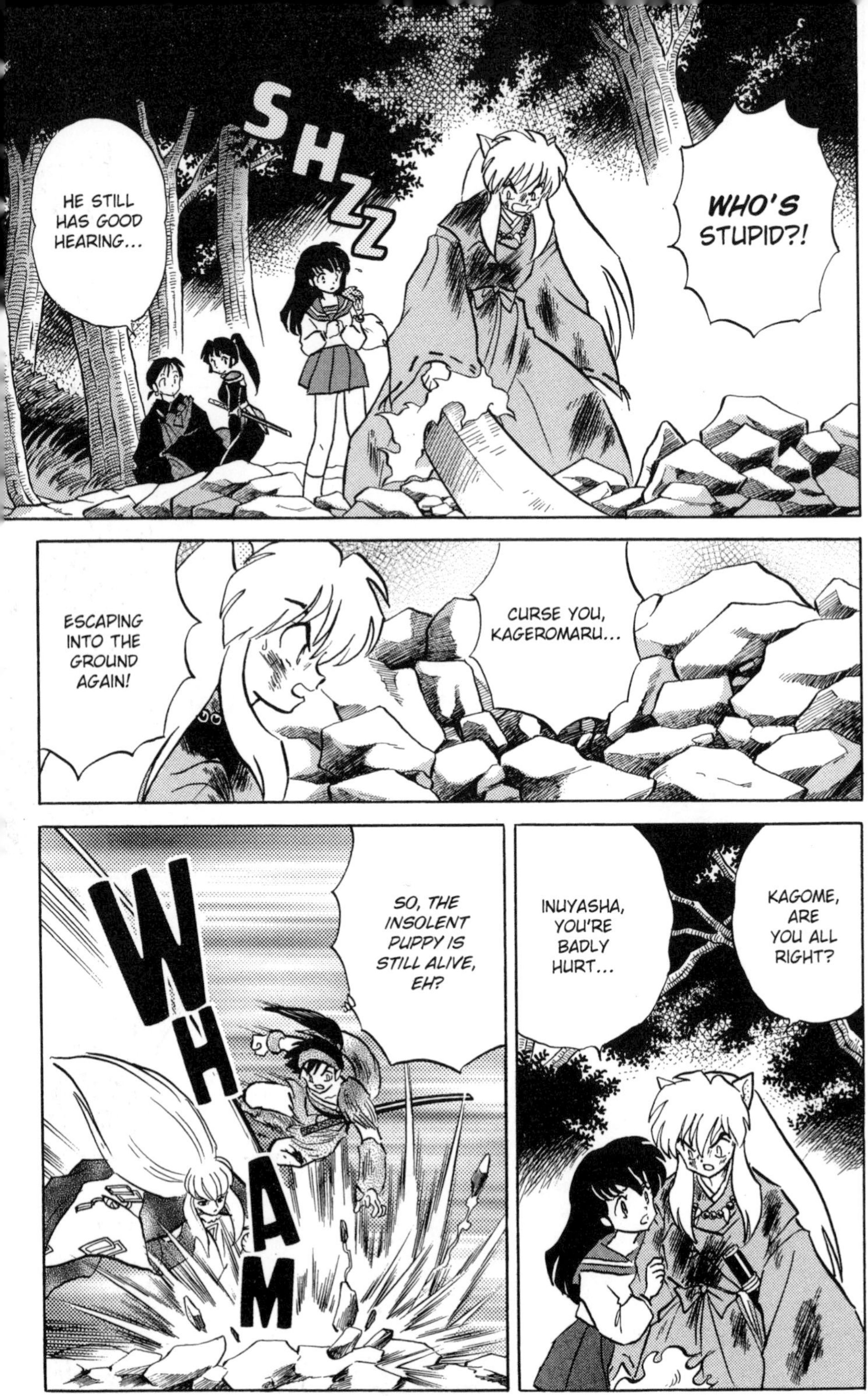

WHO'S STUPID?!
SHZZ
HE STILL HAS GOOD HEARING...
CURSE YOU, KAGEROMARU...
ESCAPING INTO THE GROUND AGAIN!
KAGOME, ARE YOU ALL RIGHT?
INUYASHA, YOU'RE BADLY HURT...
SO, THE INSOLENT PUPPY IS STILL ALIVE, EH?
WHHAM

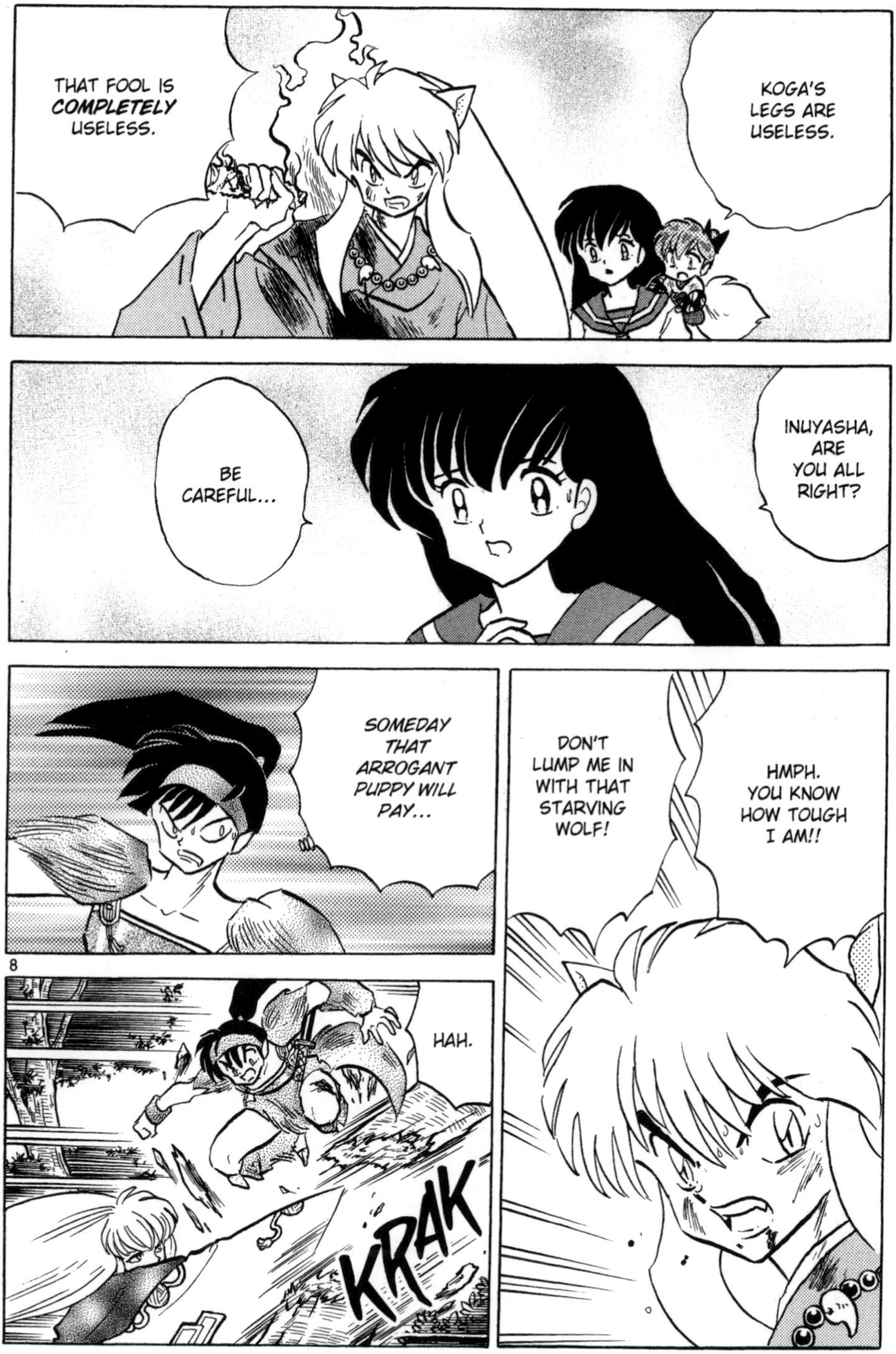
KOGA'S LEGS ARE USELESS.
THAT FOOL IS **COMPLETELY** USELESS.
INUYASHA, ARE YOU ALL RIGHT?
BE CAREFUL...
HMPH. YOU KNOW HOW TOUGH I AM!!
DON'T LUMP ME IN WITH THAT STARVING WOLF!
SOMEDAY THAT ARROGANT PUPPY WILL PAY...
HAH.
KRAK

8

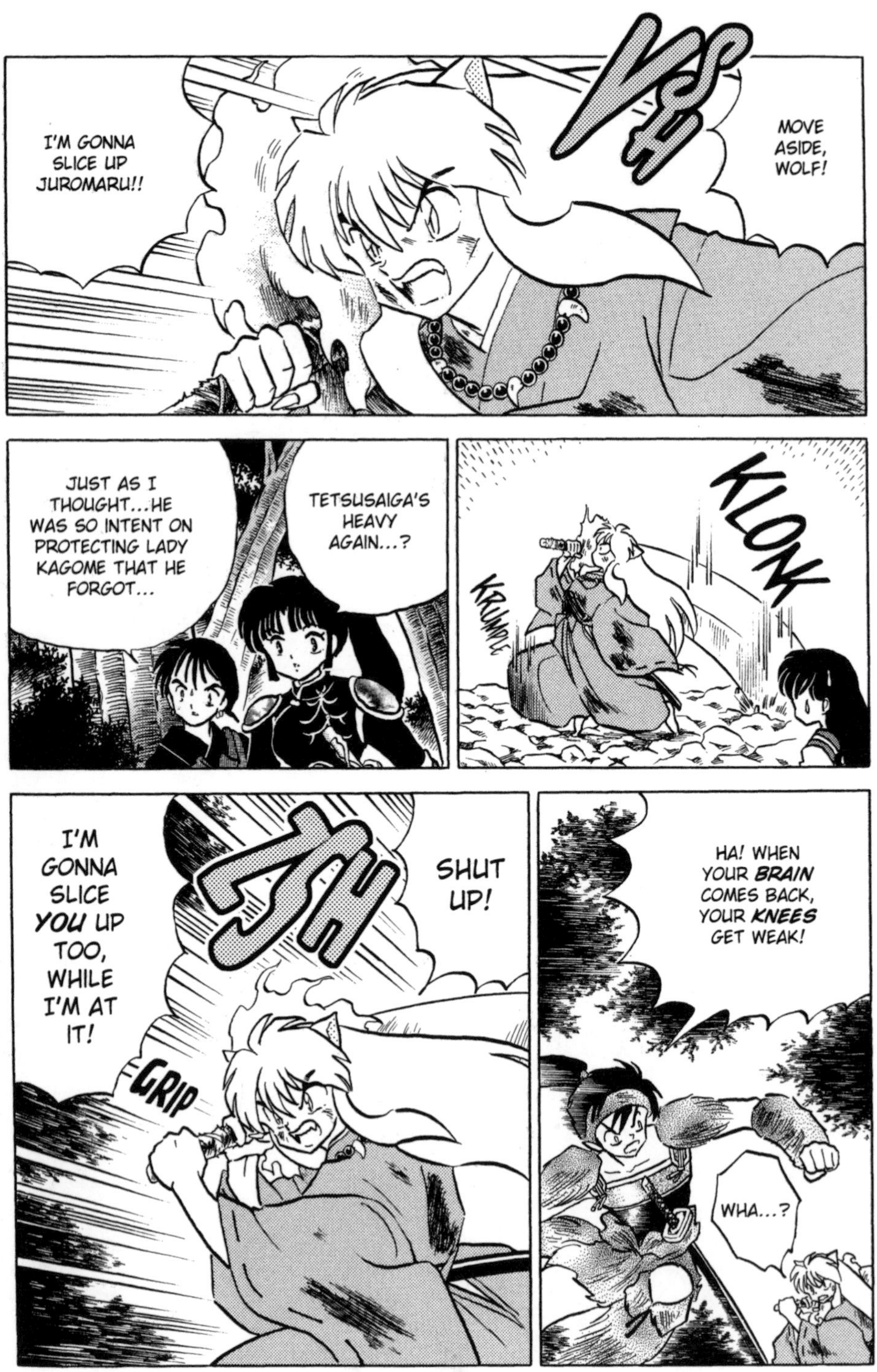

MOVE ASIDE, WOLF!
VSH
I'M GONNA SLICE UP JUROMARU!!
KLONK
KRUMPLE
TETSUSAIGA'S HEAVY AGAIN...?
JUST AS I THOUGHT...HE WAS SO INTENT ON PROTECTING LADY KAGOME THAT HE FORGOT...
HA! WHEN YOUR BRAIN COMES BACK, YOUR KNEES GET WEAK!
WHA...?
SHUT UP!
TSH
I'M GONNA SLICE YOU UP TOO, WHILE I'M AT IT!
GRIP

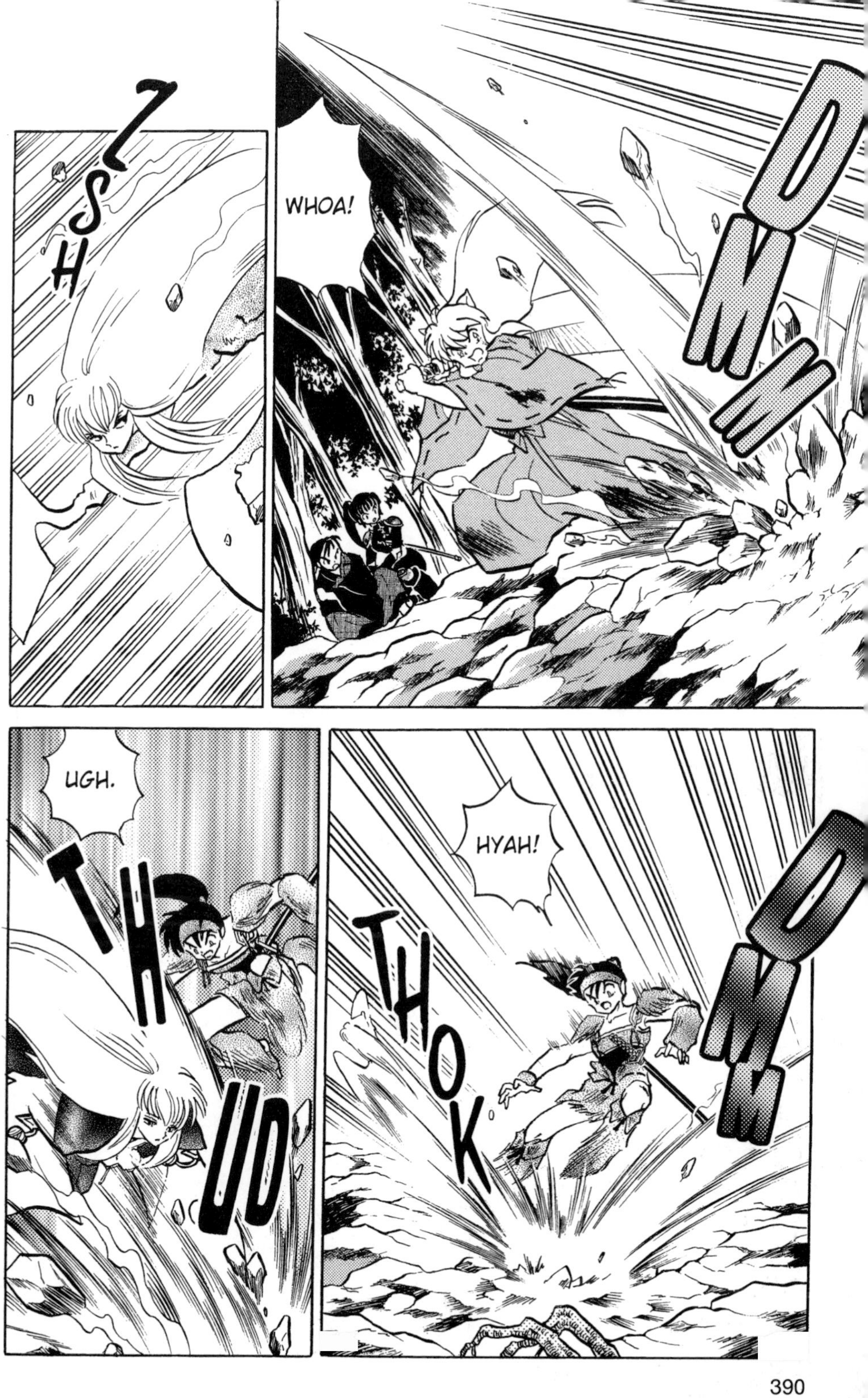
WHOA!
DOMMM
ZSH
HYAH!
DOMMM
THOK
UGH.
THUD

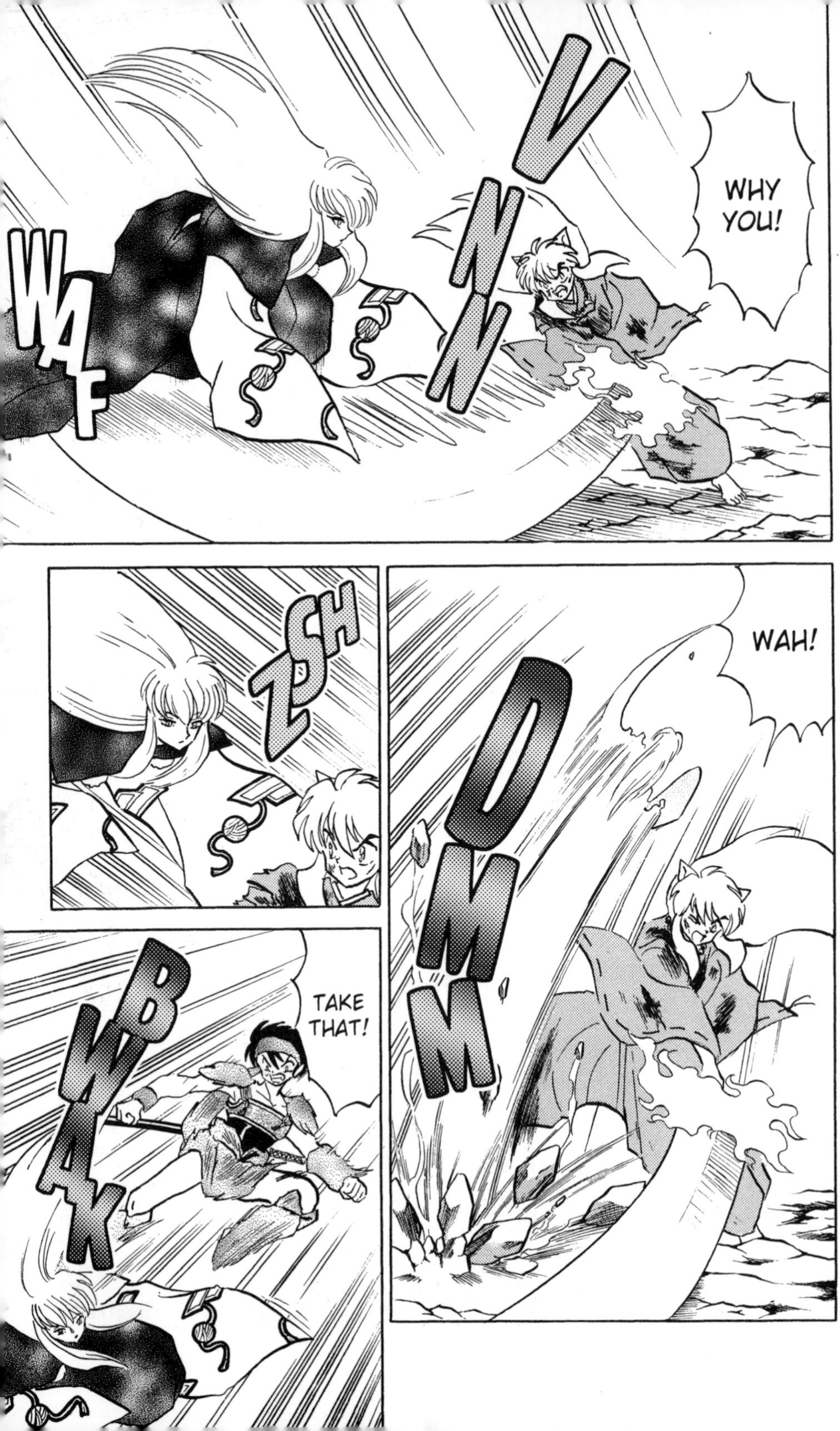
WHY YOU!
VNNN
WAF
WAH!
DMMM
ZSH
TAKE THAT!
BWAK

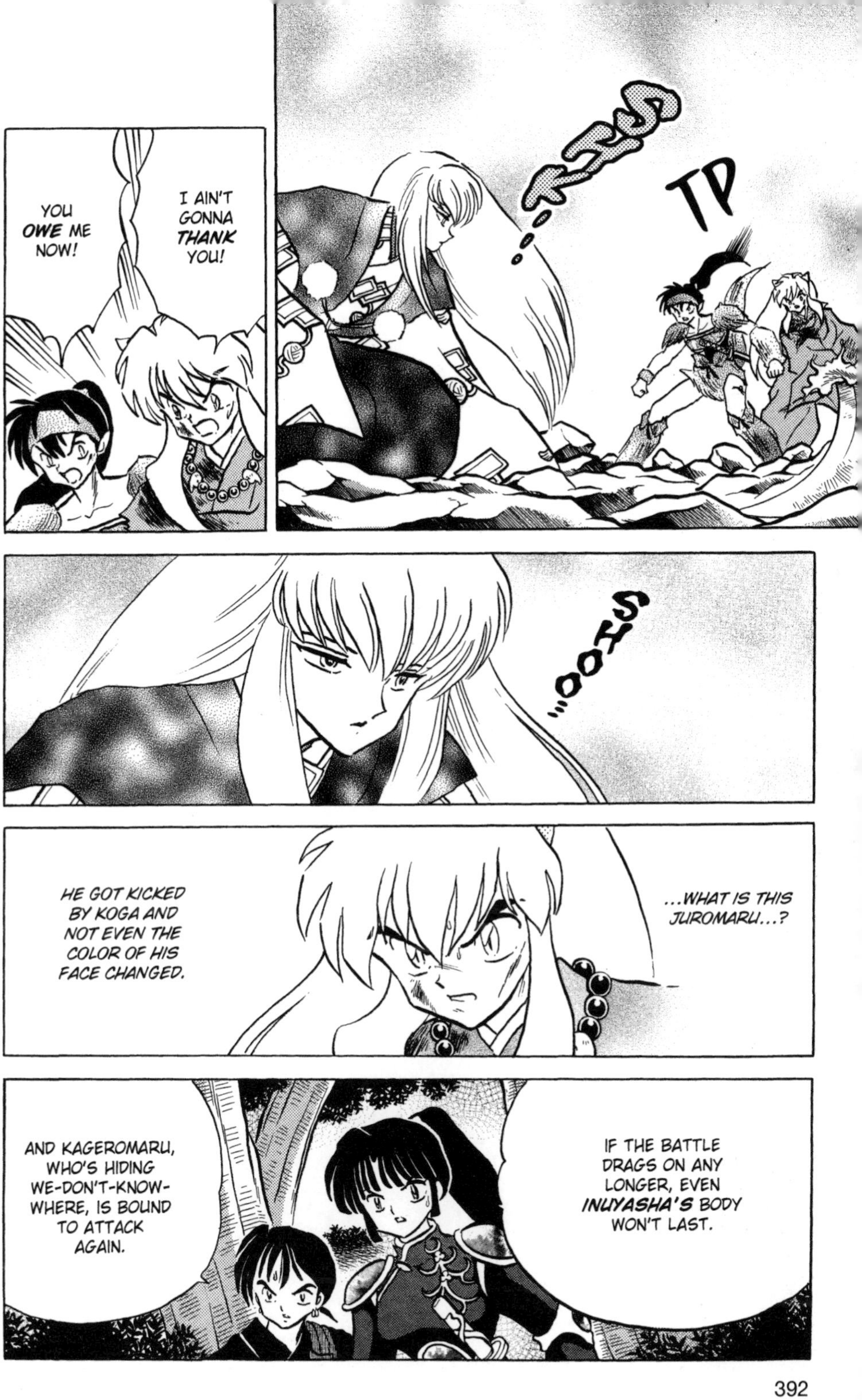
TP
I AIN'T GONNA THANK YOU!
YOU OWE ME NOW!
SHOO...
...WHAT IS THIS JUROMARU...?
HE GOT KICKED BY KOGA AND NOT EVEN THE COLOR OF HIS FACE CHANGED.
IF THE BATTLE DRAGS ON ANY LONGER, EVEN INUYASHA'S BODY WON'T LAST.
AND KAGEROMARU, WHO'S HIDING WE-DON'T-KNOW-WHERE, IS BOUND TO ATTACK AGAIN.

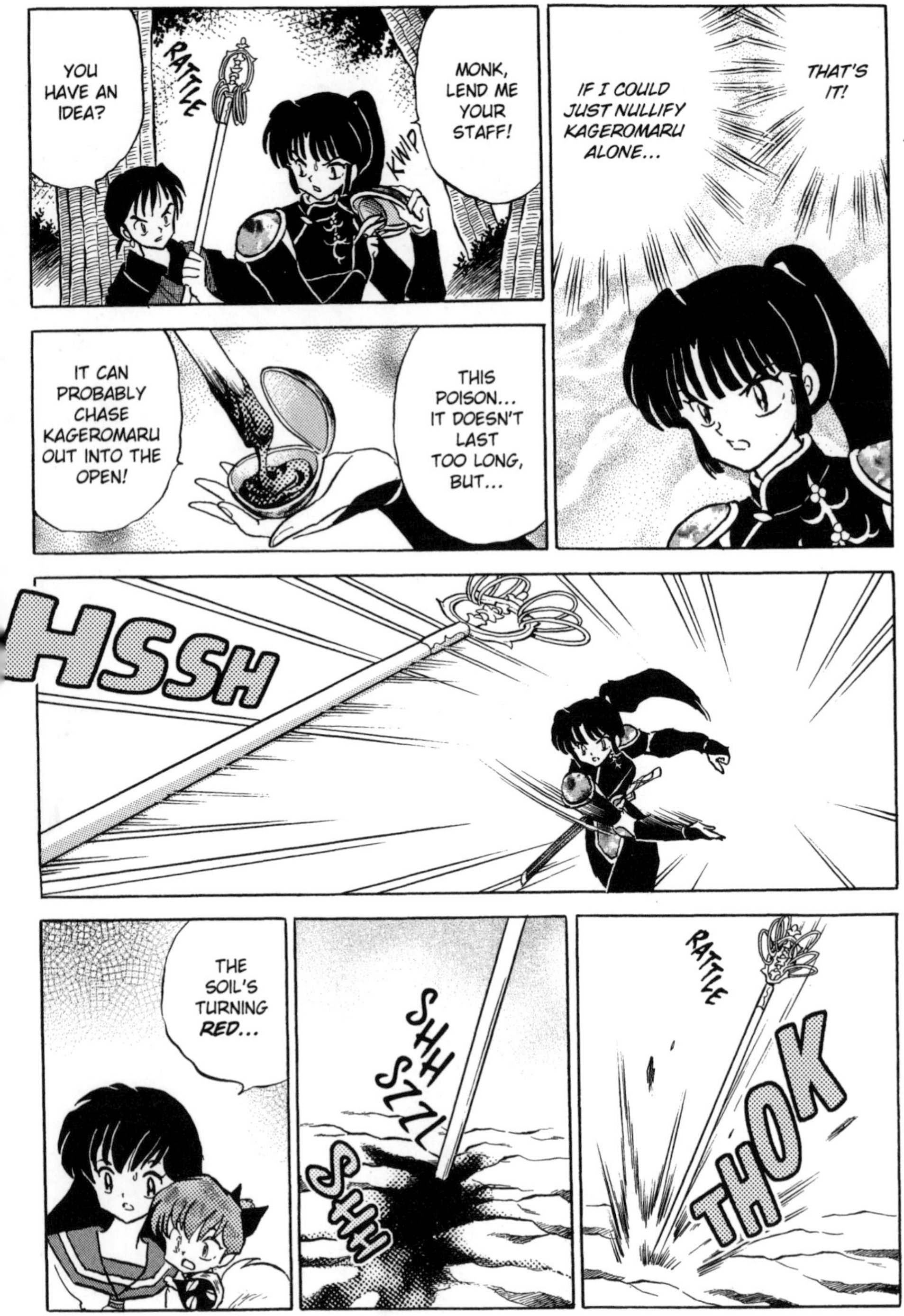
THAT'S IT!
IF I COULD JUST NULLIFY KAGEROMARU ALONE...
MONK, LEND ME YOUR STAFF!
KWIP
RATTLE
YOU HAVE AN IDEA?
THIS POISON... IT DOESN'T LAST TOO LONG, BUT...
IT CAN PROBABLY CHASE KAGEROMARU OUT INTO THE OPEN!
HSSH
RATTLE
THOK
SHH SZZZ
SHH
THE SOIL'S TURNING RED...

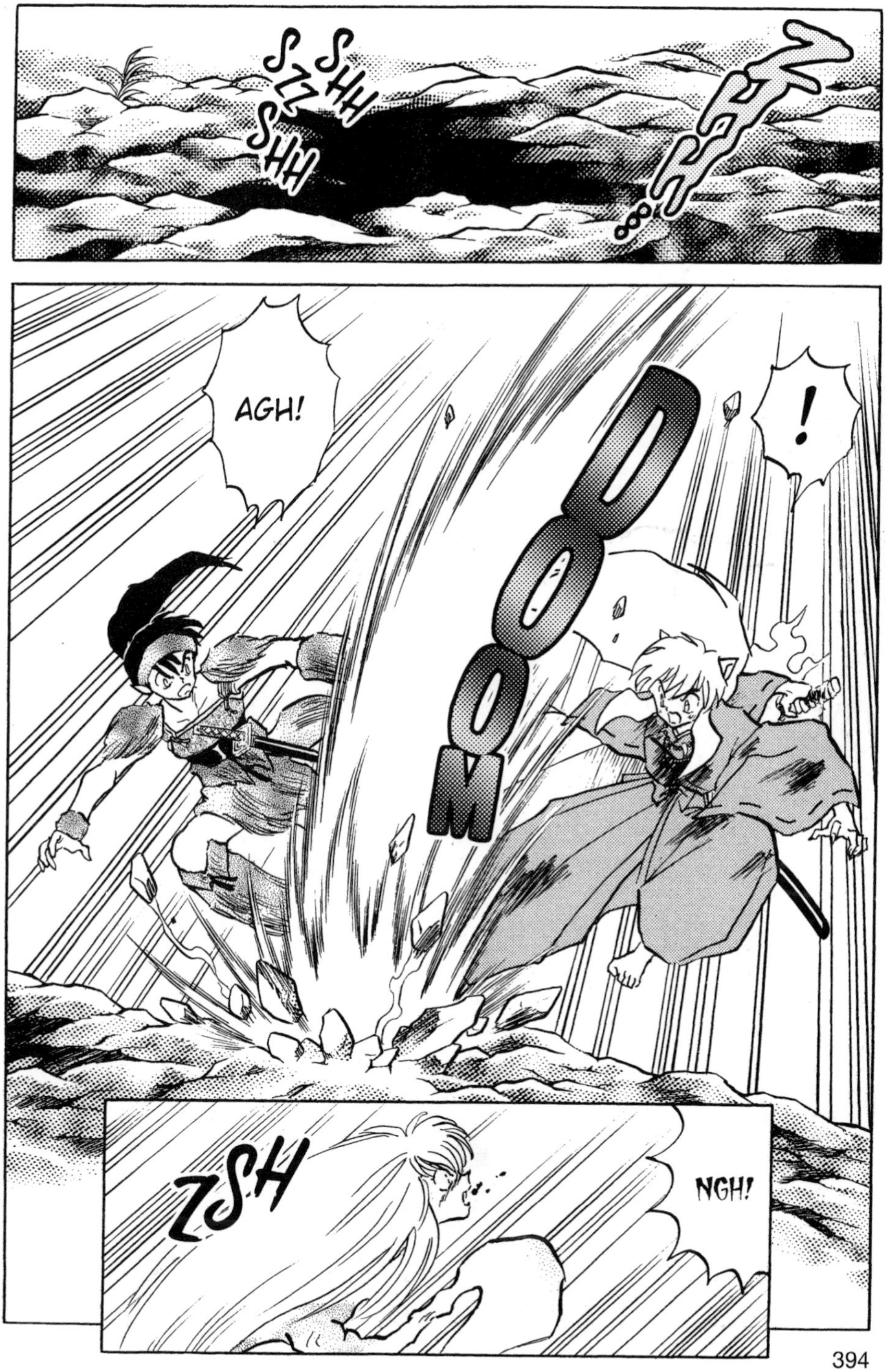
SHH
SZZ
SHH
!
DOOOOM
AGH!
NGH!
ZSH

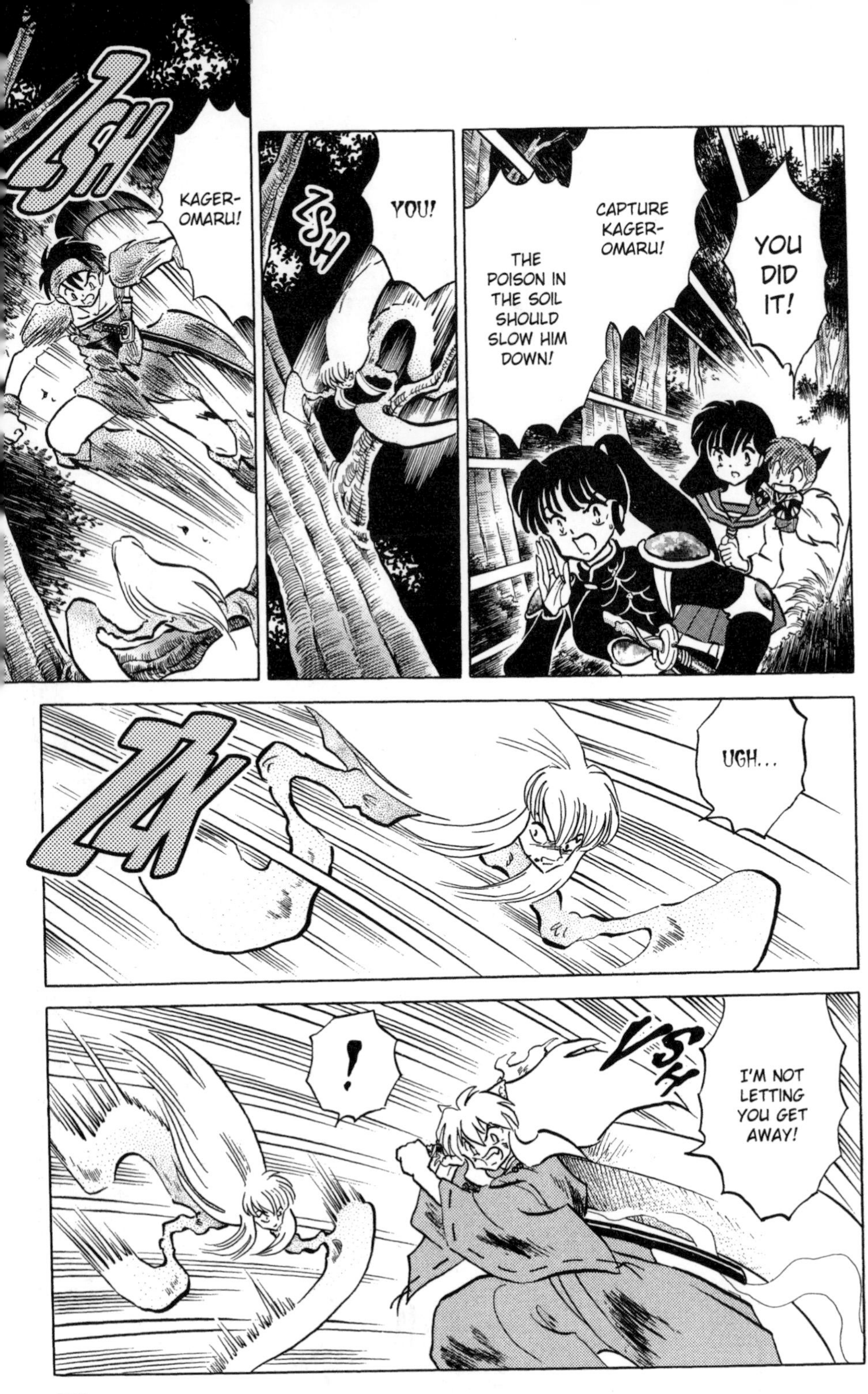
YOU DID IT!
CAPTURE KAGER-OMARU!
THE POISON IN THE SOIL SHOULD SLOW HIM DOWN!
YOU!
ZSH
KAGER-OMARU!
ZSH
UGH...
ZAK
I'M NOT LETTING YOU GET AWAY!
VSH
!

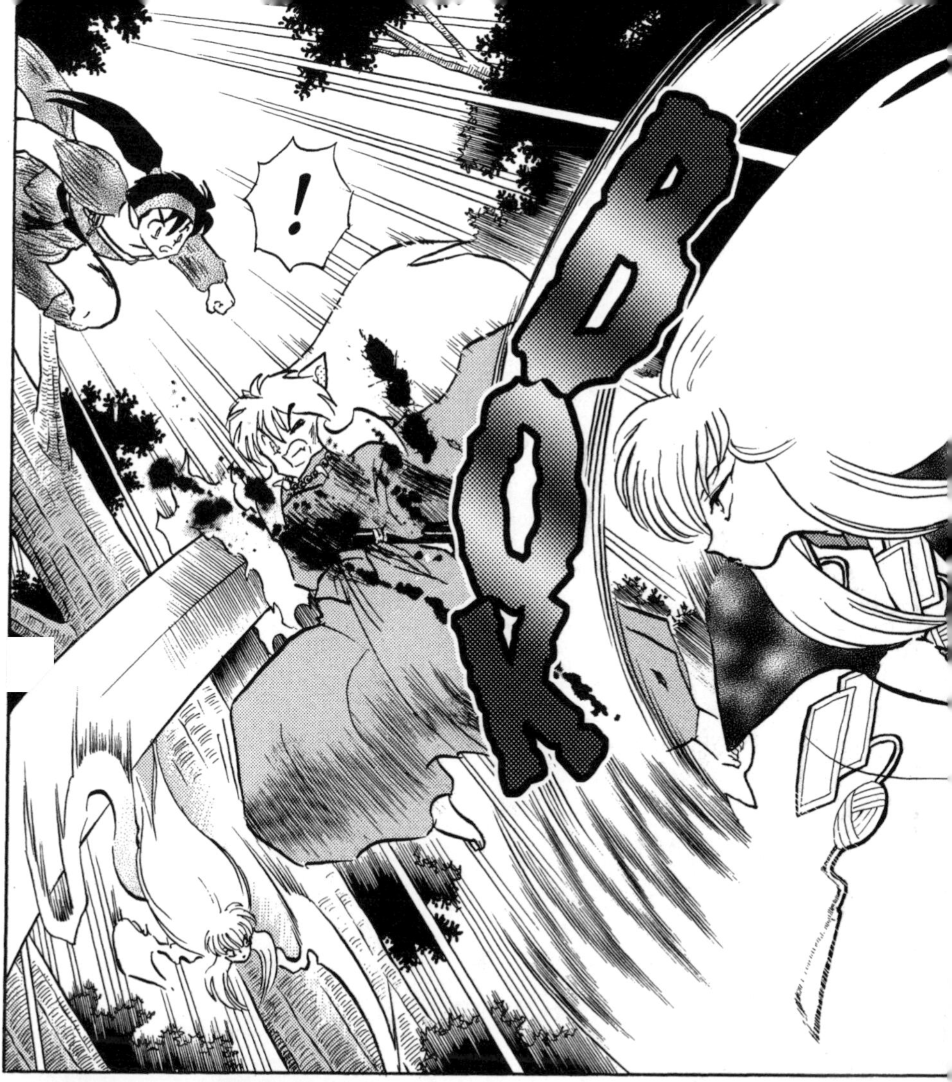
!
BOK
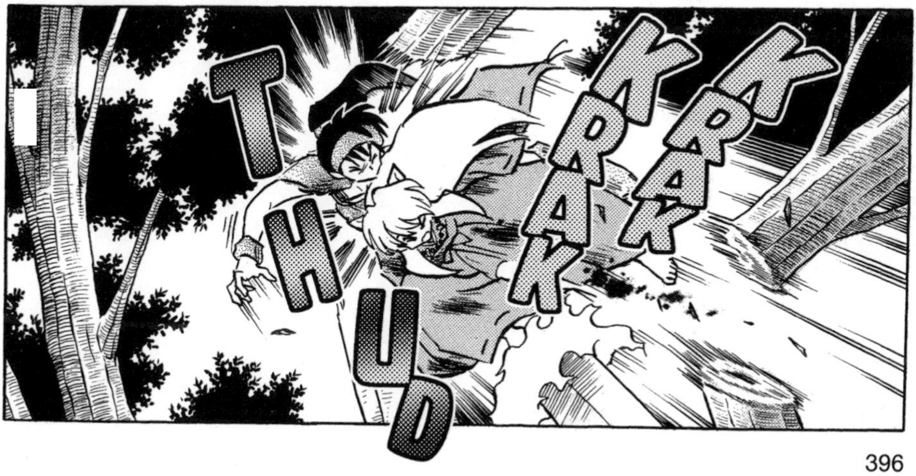
KRAK
KRAK
THUD

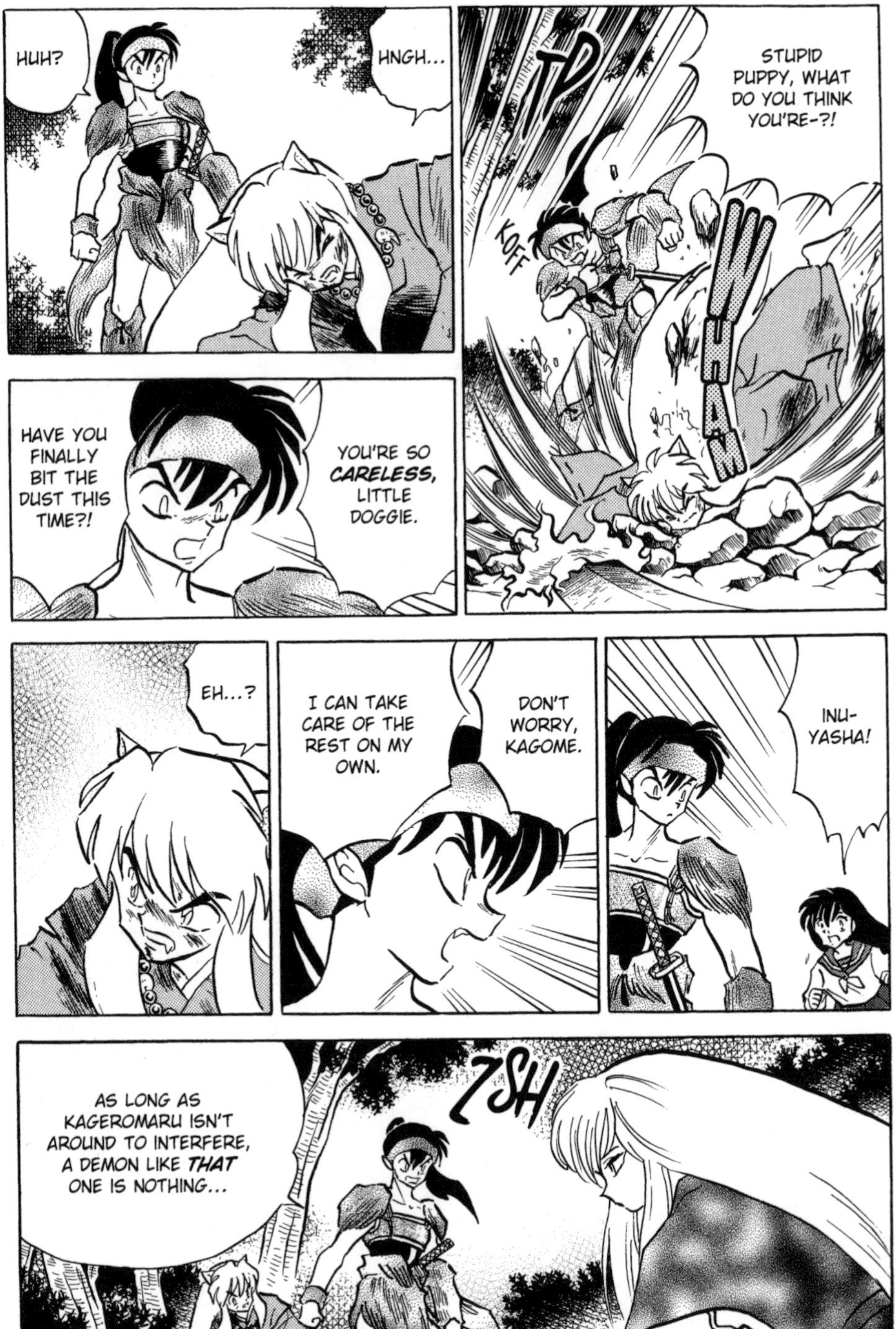

STUPID PUPPY, WHAT DO YOU THINK YOU'RE-?!
TP
KOFF
WHAM
HNGH...
HUH?
YOU'RE SO CARELESS, LITTLE DOGGIE.
HAVE YOU FINALLY BIT THE DUST THIS TIME?!
INU-YASHA!
DON'T WORRY, KAGOME.
I CAN TAKE CARE OF THE REST ON MY OWN.
EH...?
ZSH
AS LONG AS KAGEROMARU ISN'T AROUND TO INTERFERE, A DEMON LIKE *THAT* ONE IS NOTHING...

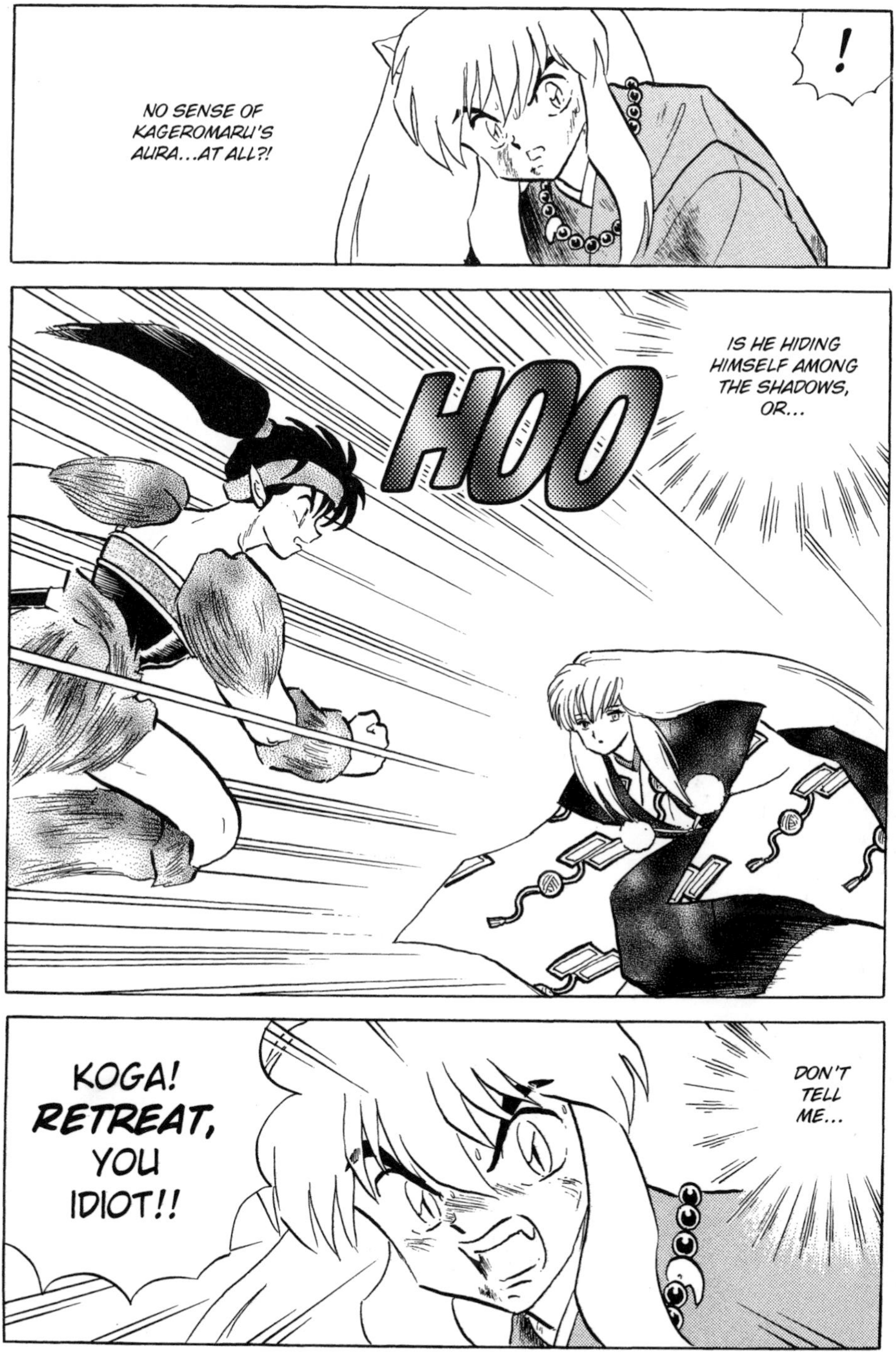
!
NO SENSE OF KAGEROMARU'S AURA...AT ALL?!
IS HE HIDING HIMSELF AMONG THE SHADOWS, OR...
HOO
DON'T TELL ME...
KOGA! **RETREAT,** YOU IDIOT!!

SCROLL TWO
PULVERIZED

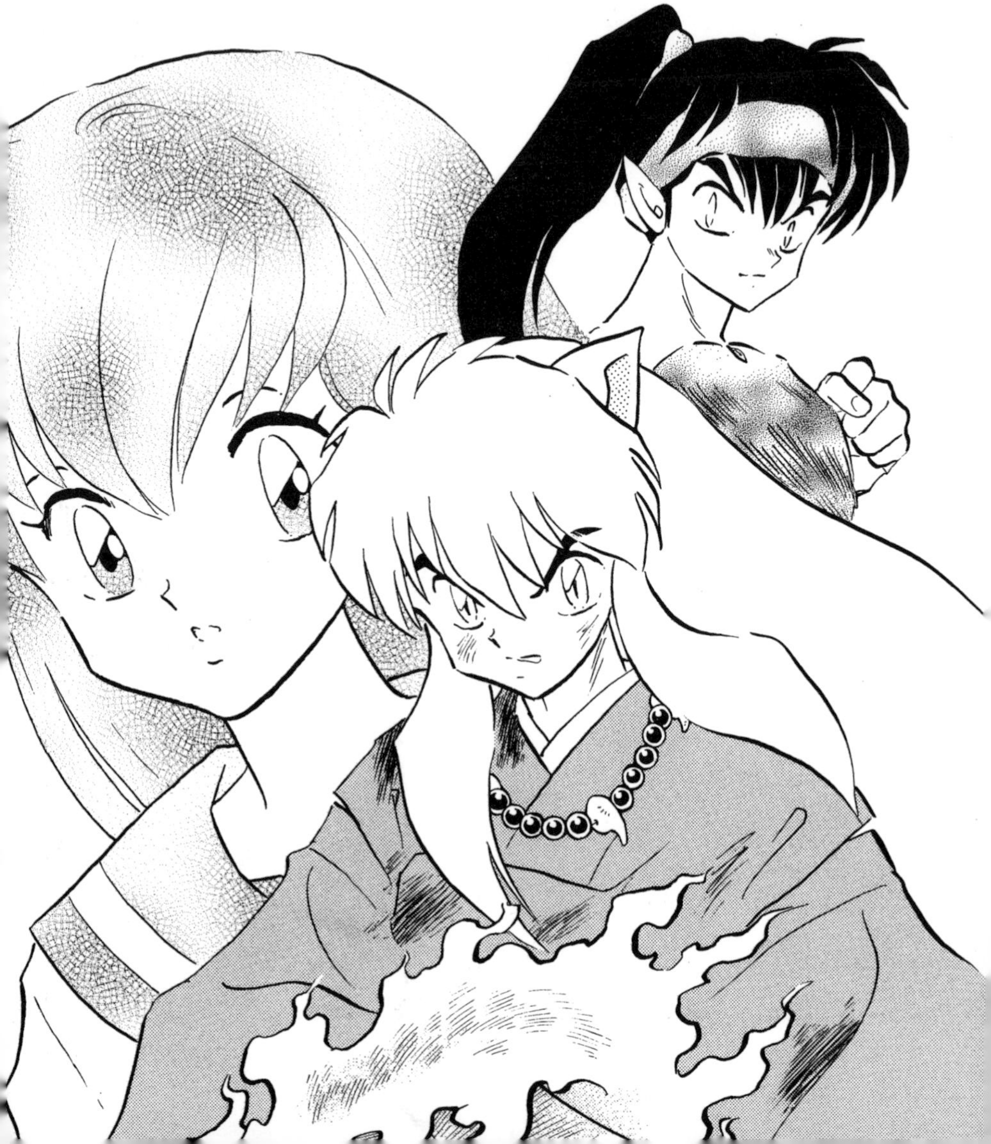

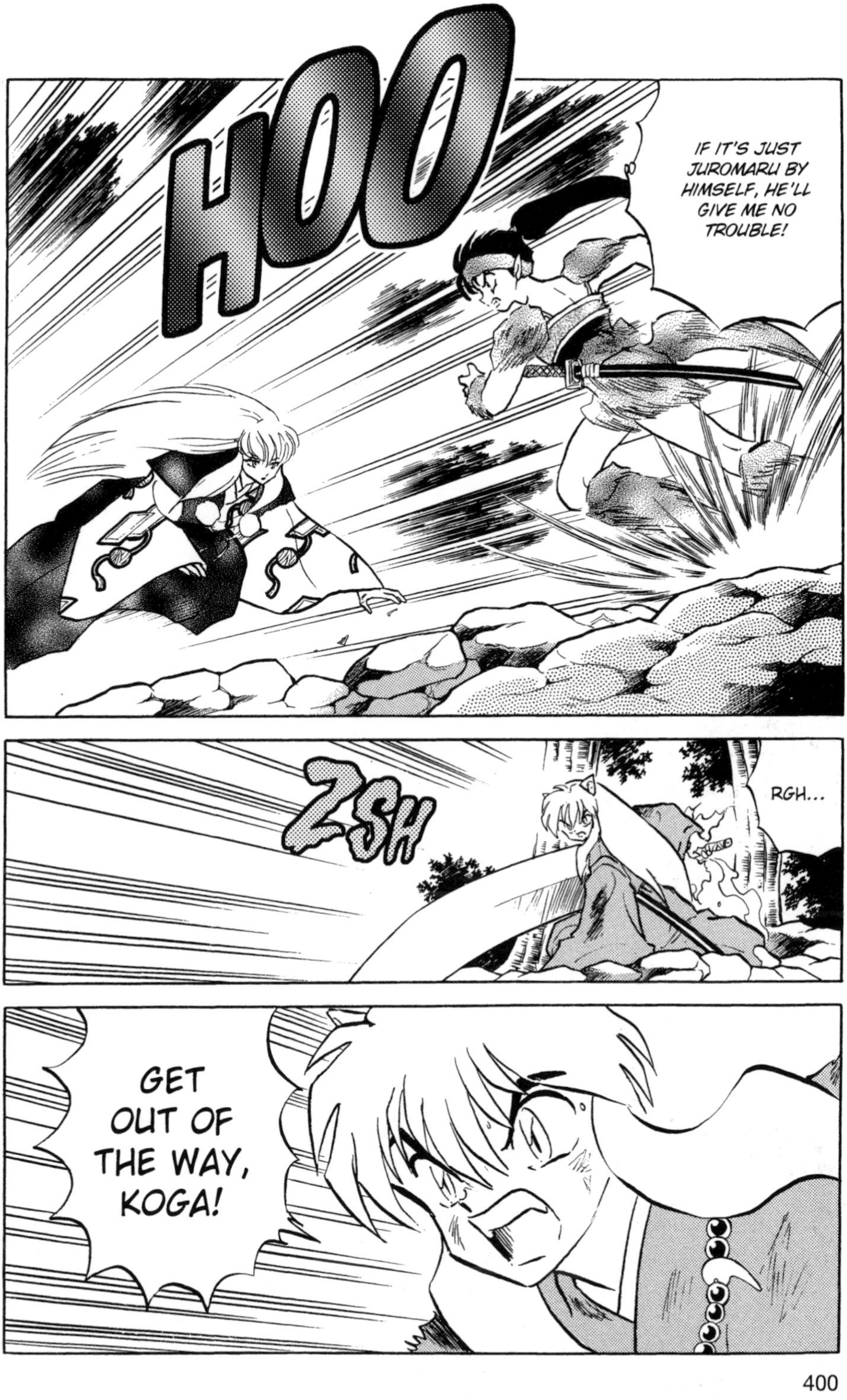
HOO
IF IT'S JUST JUROMARU BY HIMSELF, HE'LL GIVE ME NO TROUBLE!
RGH...
ZSH
GET OUT OF THE WAY, KOGA!

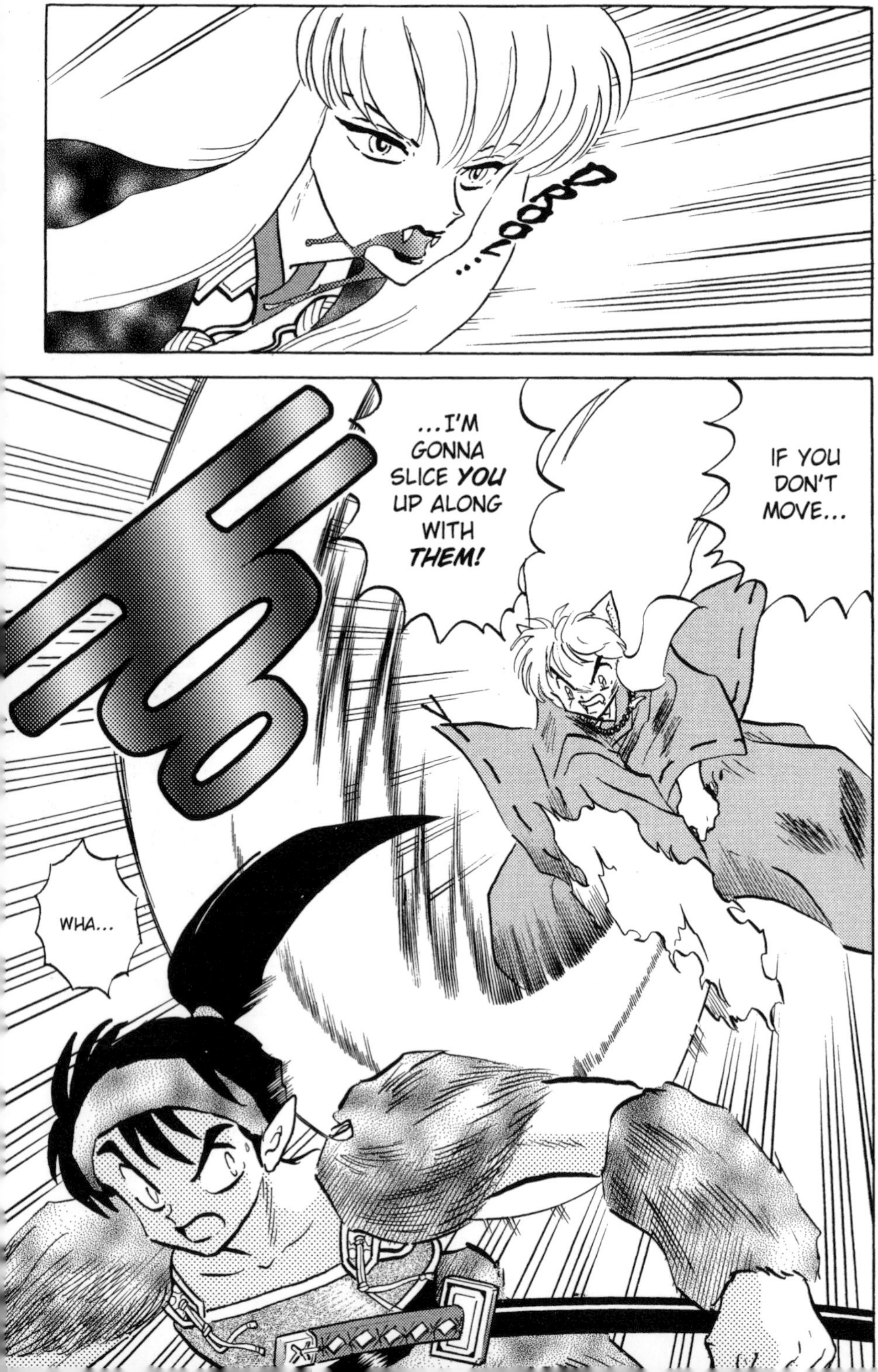
DROOL...
IF YOU DON'T MOVE...
...I'M GONNA SLICE **YOU** UP ALONG WITH **THEM!**
WHA...

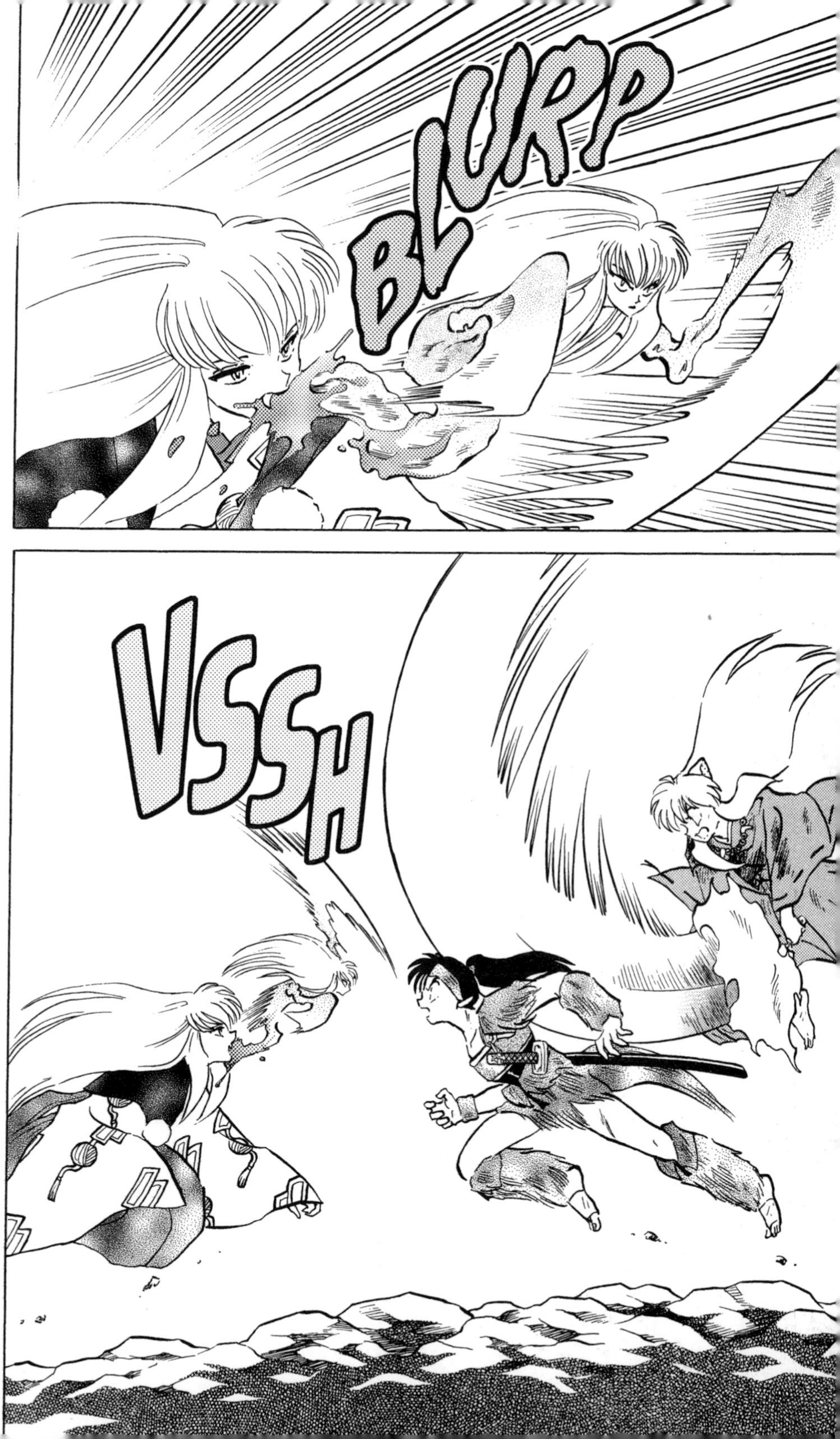
BLURP
VSSH

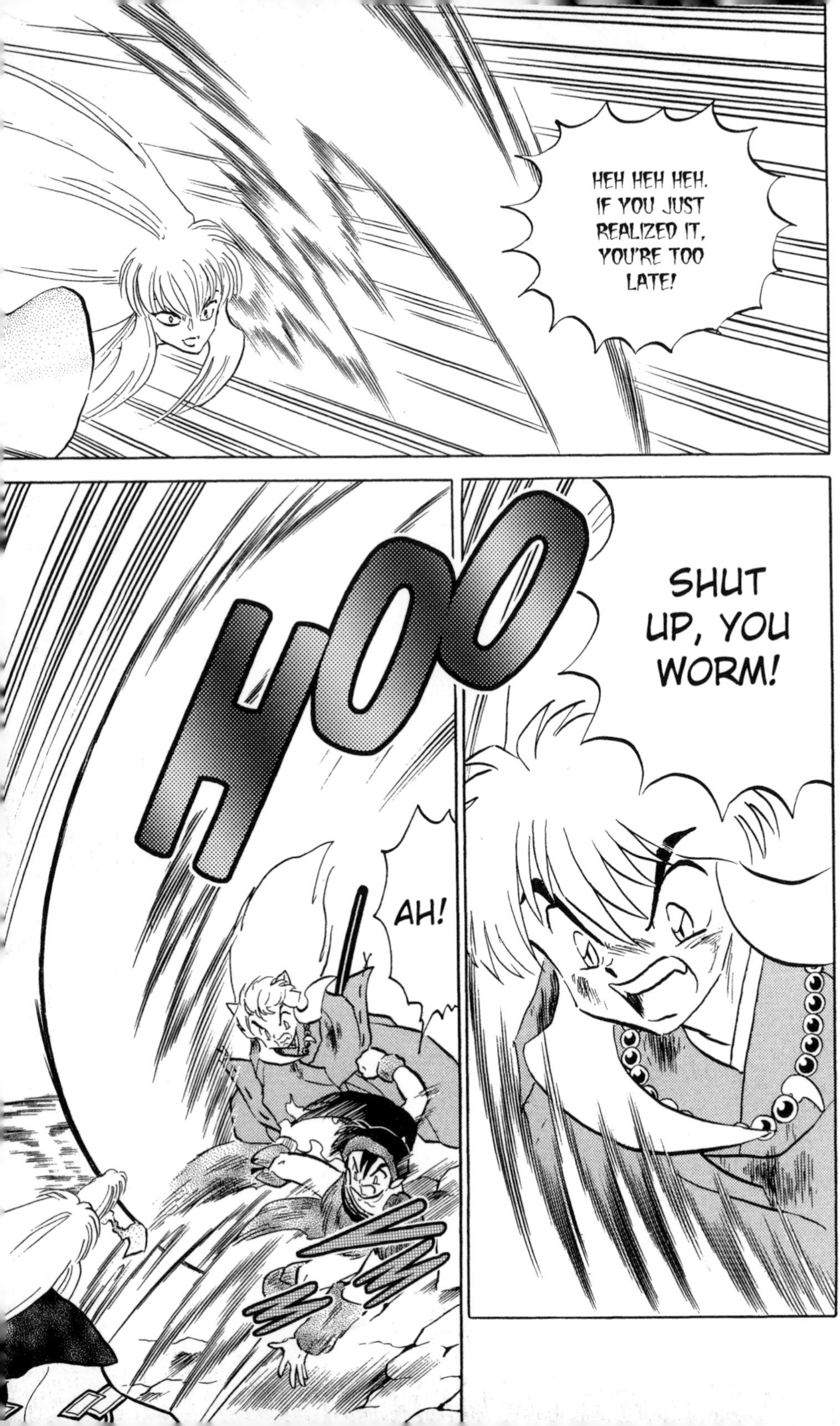
HEH HEH HEH. IF YOU JUST REALIZED IT, YOU'RE TOO LATE!
SHUT UP, YOU WORM!
HOO
AH!

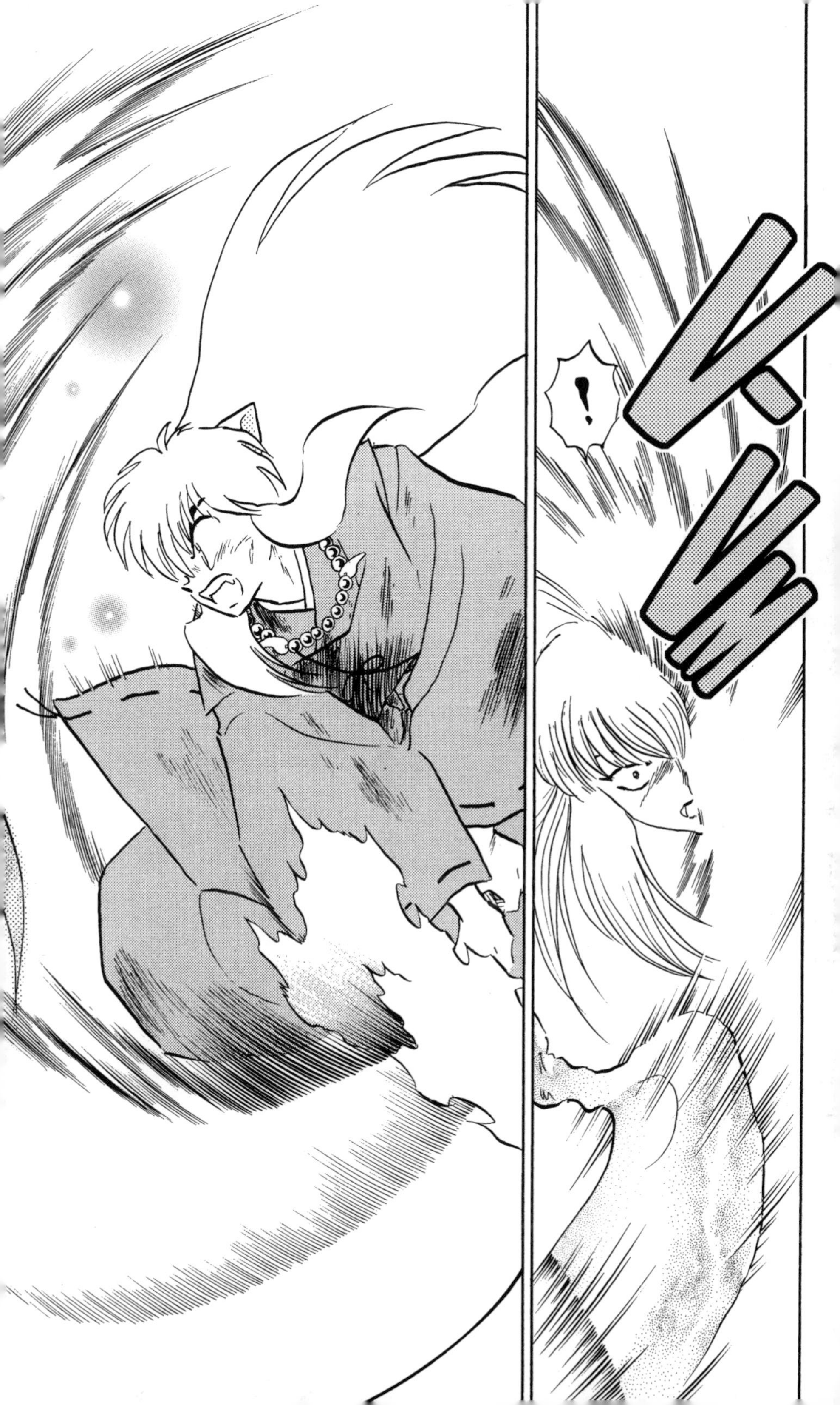
!

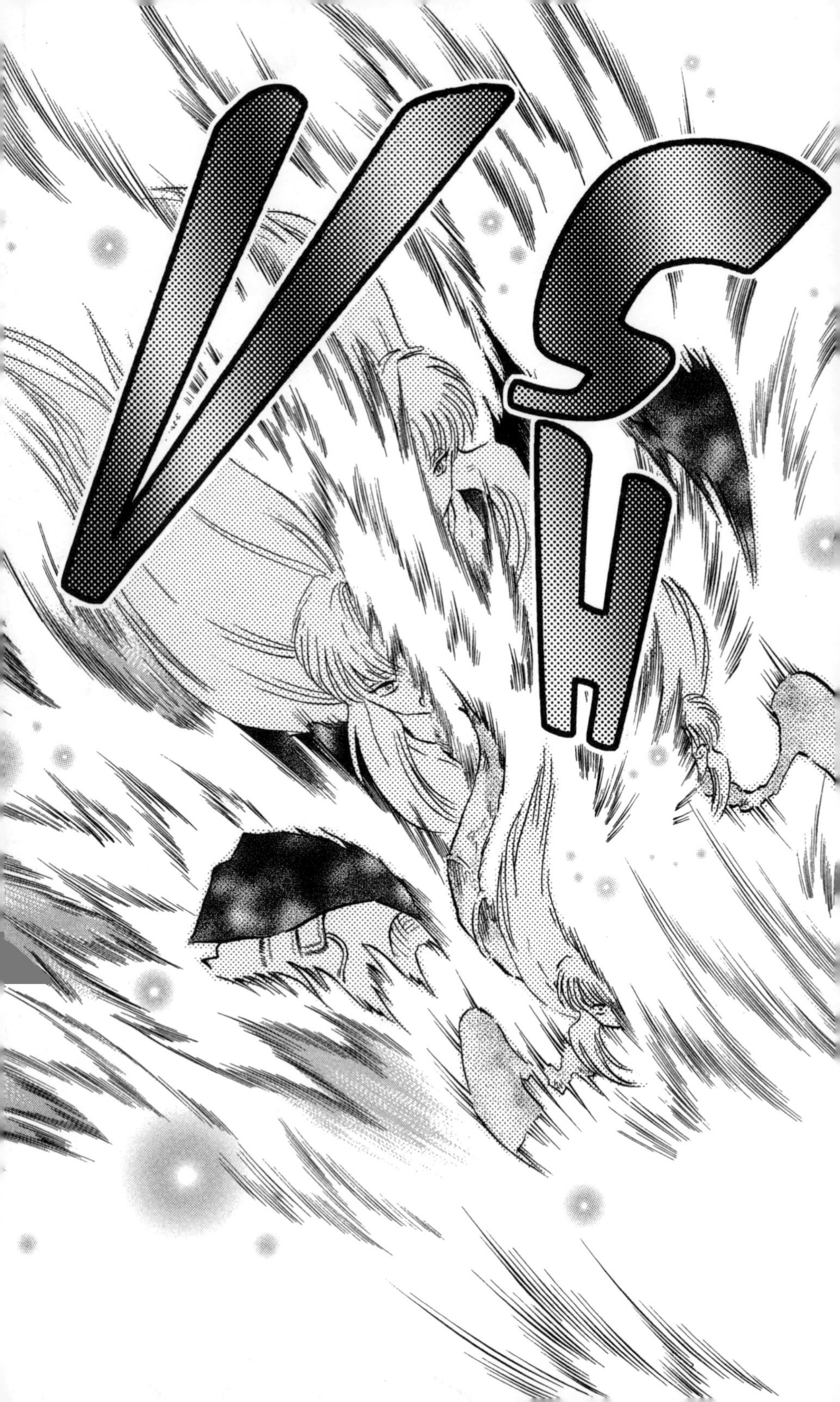
VSHH

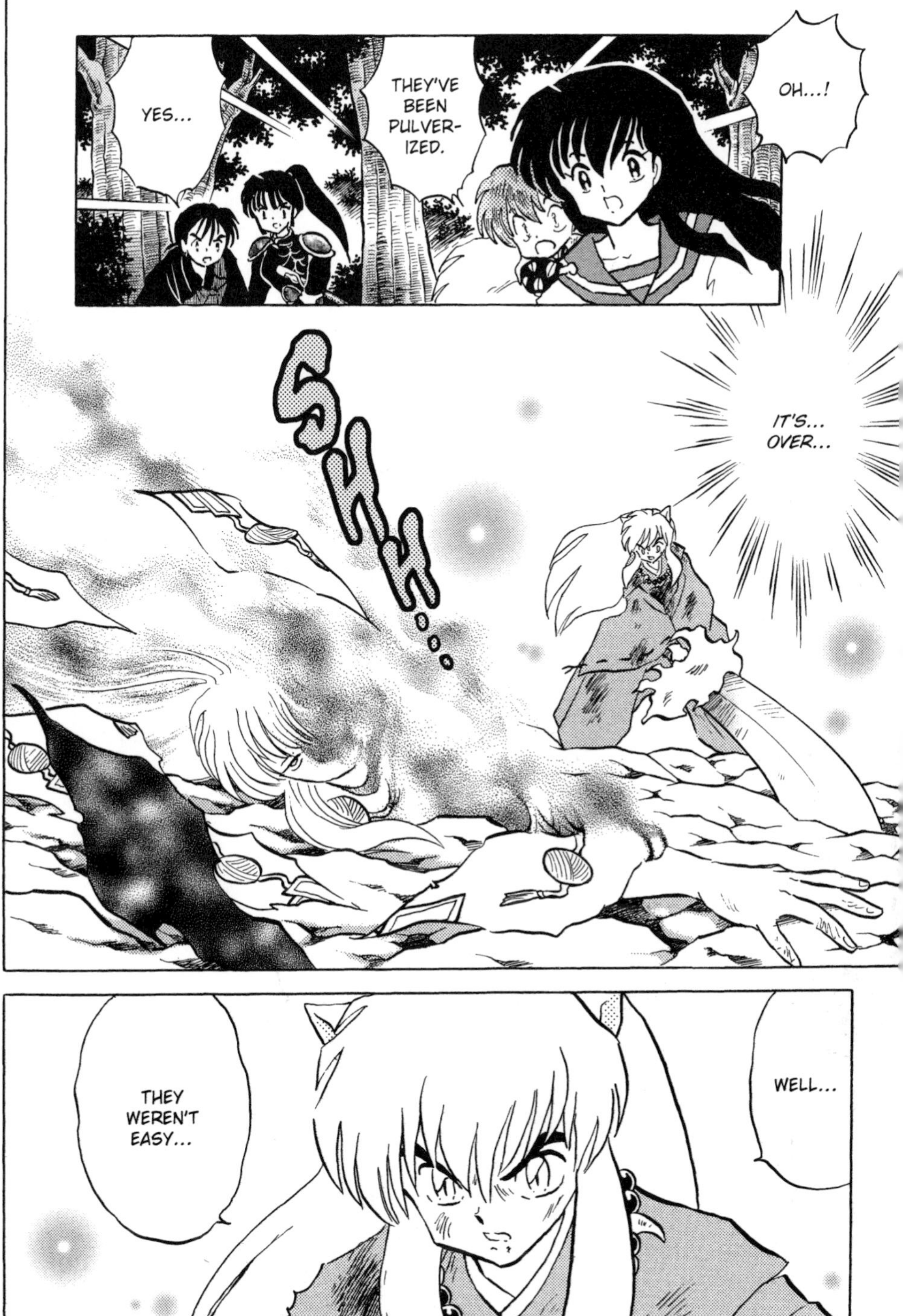
OH...!
THEY'VE BEEN PULVER-IZED.
YES...
IT'S... OVER...
SHHH...
WELL...
THEY WEREN'T EASY...

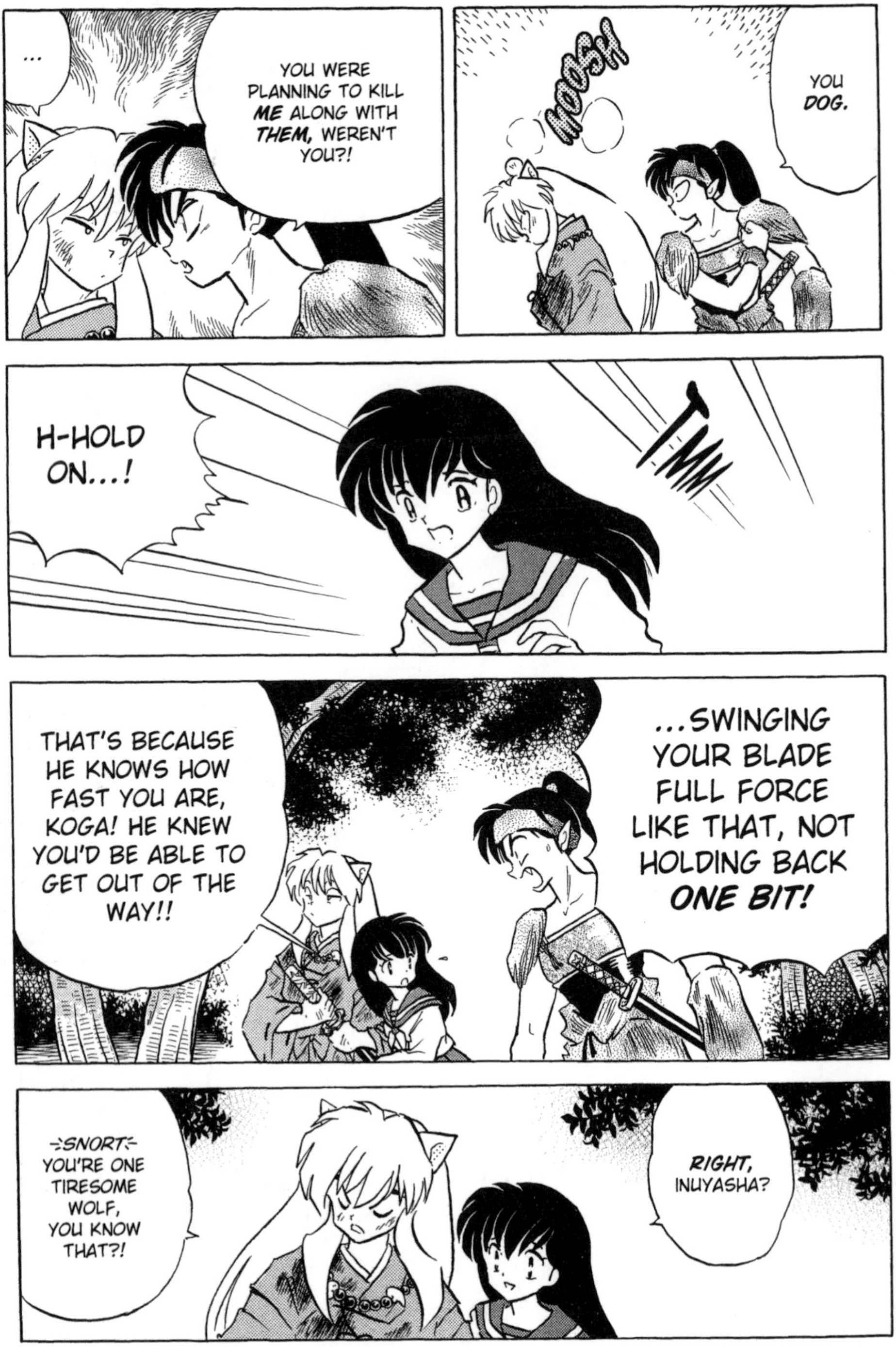
WOOSH
YOU DOG.
YOU WERE PLANNING TO KILL ME ALONG WITH THEM, WEREN'T YOU?!
...
TMM
H-HOLD ON...!
...SWINGING YOUR BLADE FULL FORCE LIKE THAT, NOT HOLDING BACK ONE BIT!
THAT'S BECAUSE HE KNOWS HOW FAST YOU ARE, KOGA! HE KNEW YOU'D BE ABLE TO GET OUT OF THE WAY!!
RIGHT, INUYASHA?
SNORT
YOU'RE ONE TIRESOME WOLF, YOU KNOW THAT?!

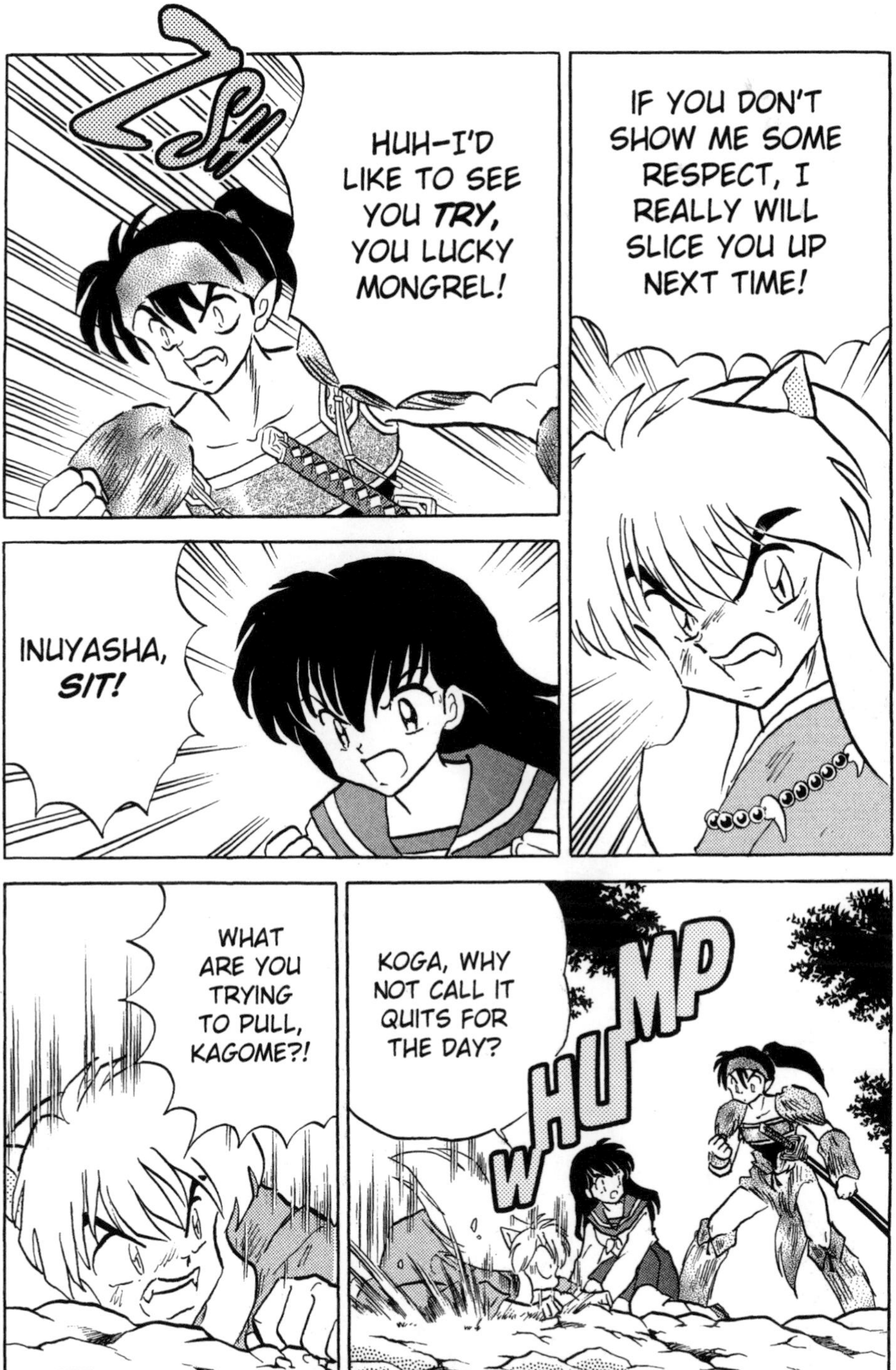
IF YOU DON'T SHOW ME SOME RESPECT, I REALLY WILL SLICE YOU UP NEXT TIME!
ZSH
HUH–I'D LIKE TO SEE YOU *TRY,* YOU LUCKY MONGREL!
INUYASHA, *SIT!*
WHUMP
KOGA, WHY NOT CALL IT QUITS FOR THE DAY?
WHAT ARE YOU TRYING TO PULL, KAGOME?!

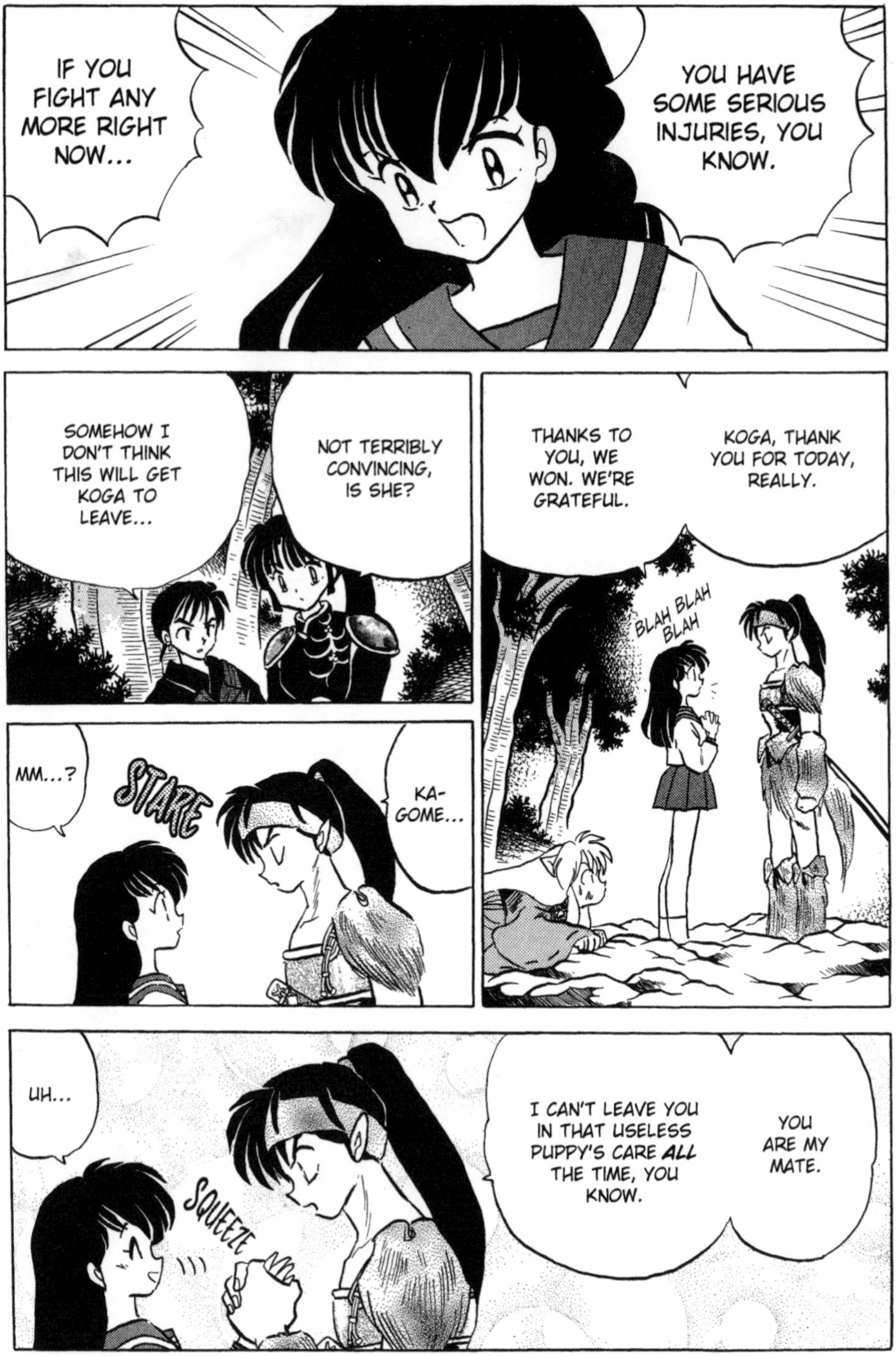
YOU HAVE SOME SERIOUS INJURIES, YOU KNOW.
IF YOU FIGHT ANY MORE RIGHT NOW...
KOGA, THANK YOU FOR TODAY, REALLY.
THANKS TO YOU, WE WON. WE'RE GRATEFUL.
BLAH BLAH BLAH
NOT TERRIBLY CONVINCING, IS SHE?
SOMEHOW I DON'T THINK THIS WILL GET KOGA TO LEAVE...
KA-GOME...
STARE
MM...?
YOU ARE MY MATE.
I CAN'T LEAVE YOU IN THAT USELESS PUPPY'S CARE ***ALL*** THE TIME, YOU KNOW.
SQUEEZE
UH...

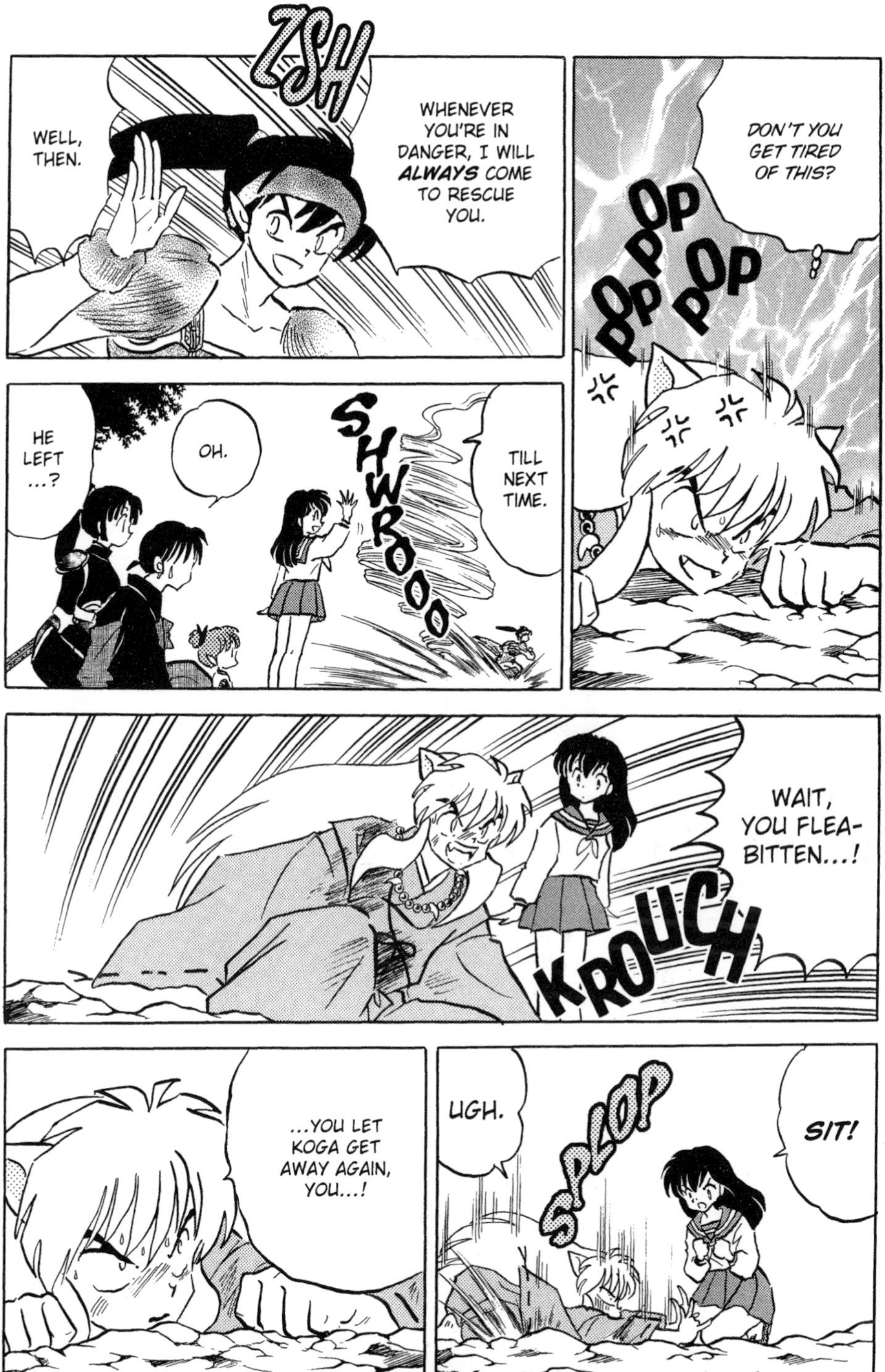
DON'T YOU GET TIRED OF THIS?
POP POP POP
ZSH
WHENEVER YOU'RE IN DANGER, I WILL ALWAYS COME TO RESCUE YOU.
WELL, THEN.
TILL NEXT TIME.
SHWROOOO
OH.
HE LEFT ...?
WAIT, YOU FLEA-BITTEN...!
KROUCH
SIT!
SPLOP
UGH.
...YOU LET KOGA GET AWAY AGAIN, YOU...!

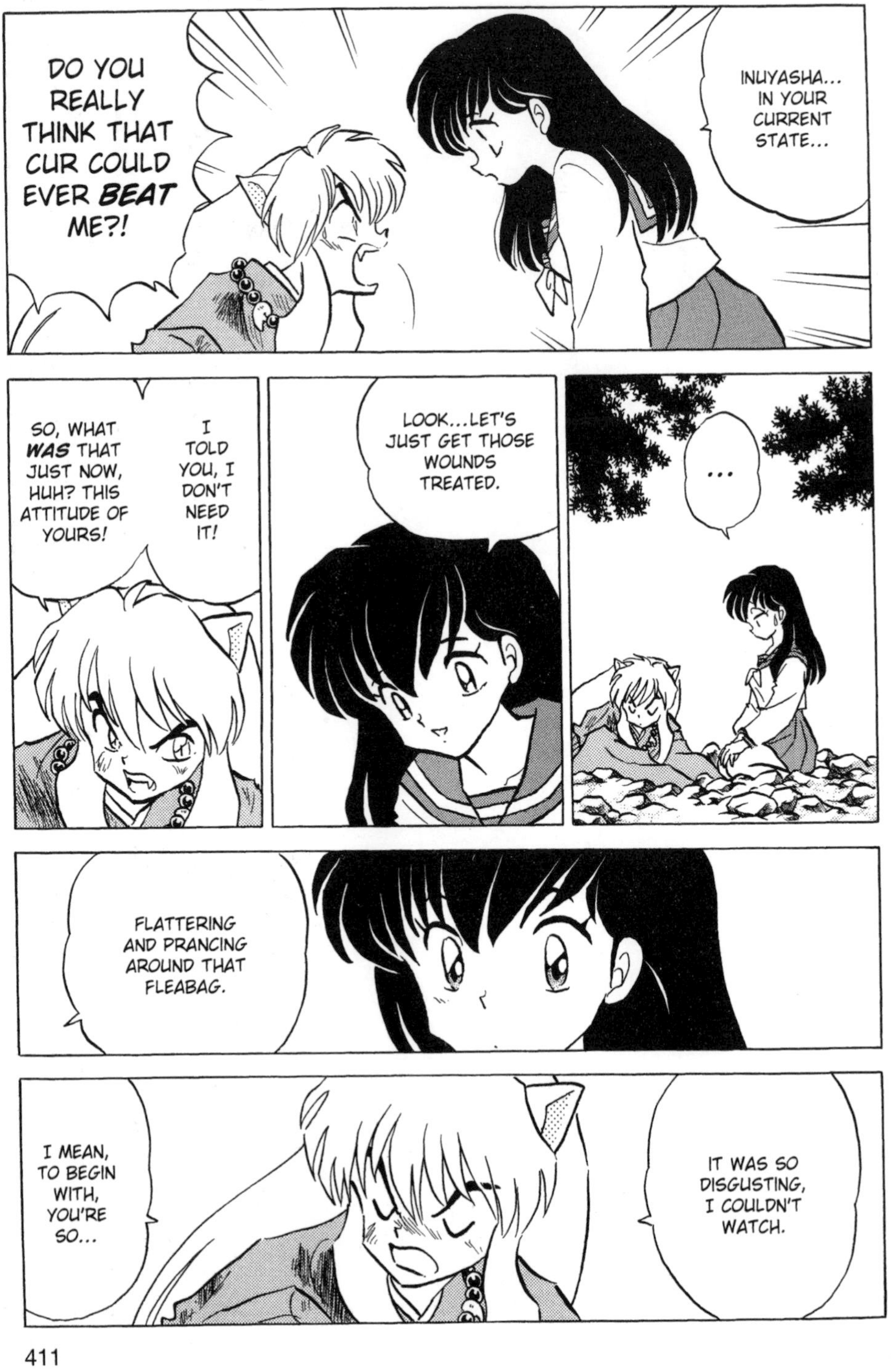
INUYASHA... IN YOUR CURRENT STATE...
DO YOU REALLY THINK THAT CUR COULD EVER *BEAT* ME?!
...
LOOK...LET'S JUST GET THOSE WOUNDS TREATED.
I TOLD YOU, I DON'T NEED IT!
SO, WHAT *WAS* THAT JUST NOW, HUH? THIS ATTITUDE OF YOURS!
FLATTERING AND PRANCING AROUND THAT FLEABAG.
IT WAS SO DISGUSTING, I COULDN'T WATCH.
I MEAN, TO BEGIN WITH, YOU'RE SO...

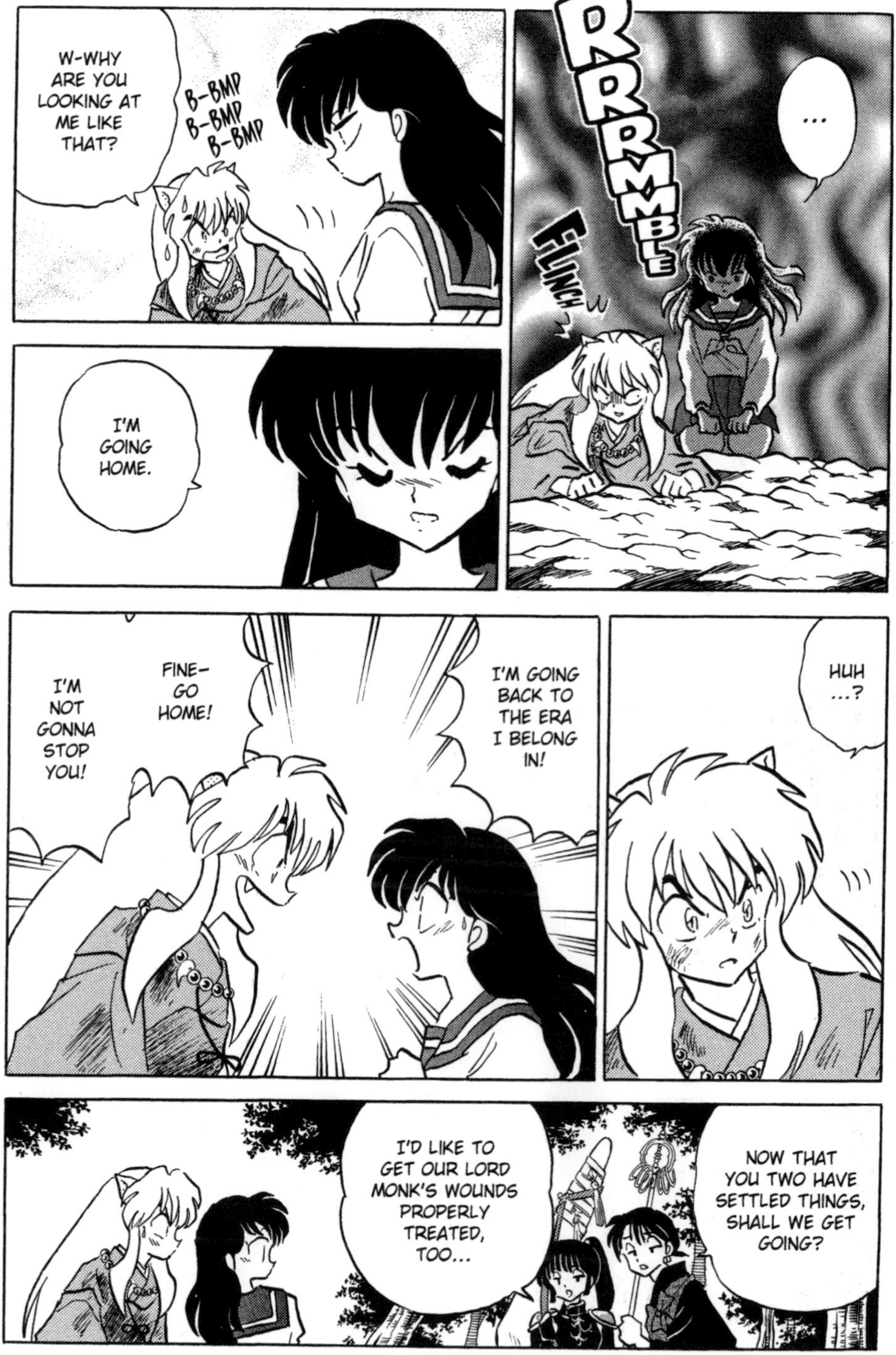
RRRMMBLE
...
FLINCH
W-WHY ARE YOU LOOKING AT ME LIKE THAT?
B-BMP B-BMP B-BMP
I'M GOING HOME.
HUH ...?
I'M GOING BACK TO THE ERA I BELONG IN!
FINE- GO HOME!
I'M NOT GONNA STOP YOU!
NOW THAT YOU TWO HAVE SETTLED THINGS, SHALL WE GET GOING?
I'D LIKE TO GET OUR LORD MONK'S WOUNDS PROPERLY TREATED, TOO...

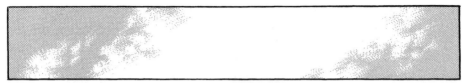

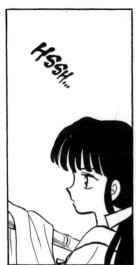

HSSH...

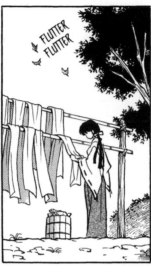

FLUTTER
FLUTTER

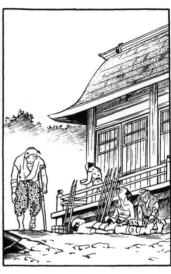

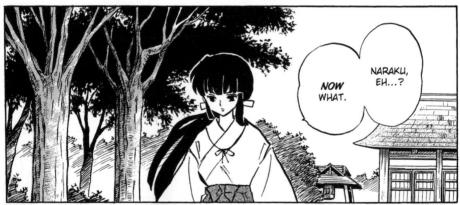

NARAKU, EH...?

NOW WHAT.

YOUR INSTINCTS ARE RAZOR-SHARP AS USUAL, KIKYO.

HSSH

...HO.

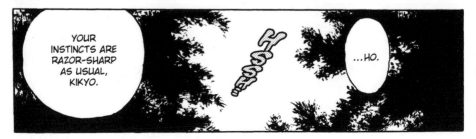

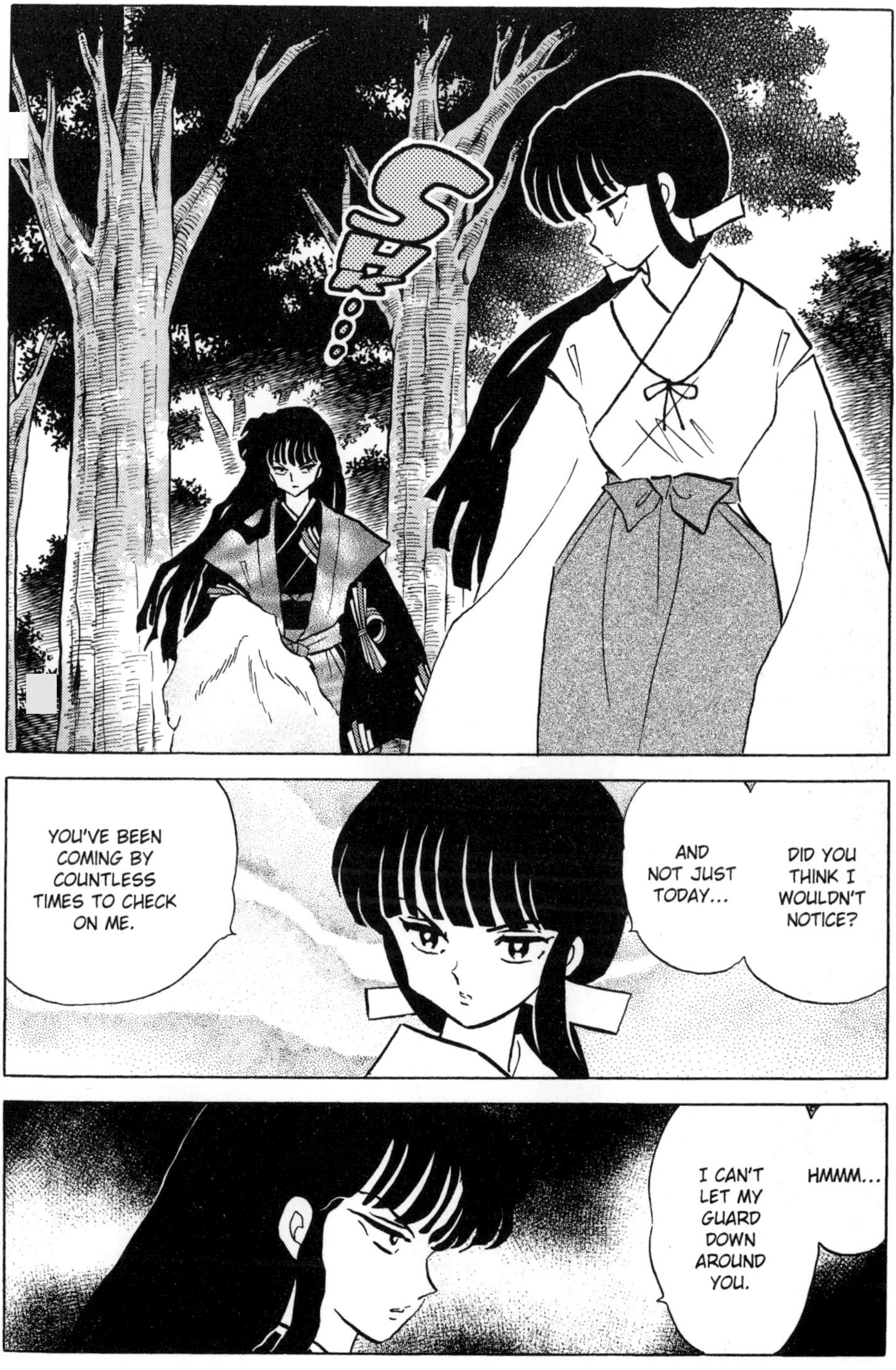
SA...
DID YOU THINK I WOULDN'T NOTICE?
AND NOT JUST TODAY...
YOU'VE BEEN COMING BY COUNTLESS TIMES TO CHECK ON ME.
HMMM...
I CAN'T LET MY GUARD DOWN AROUND YOU.

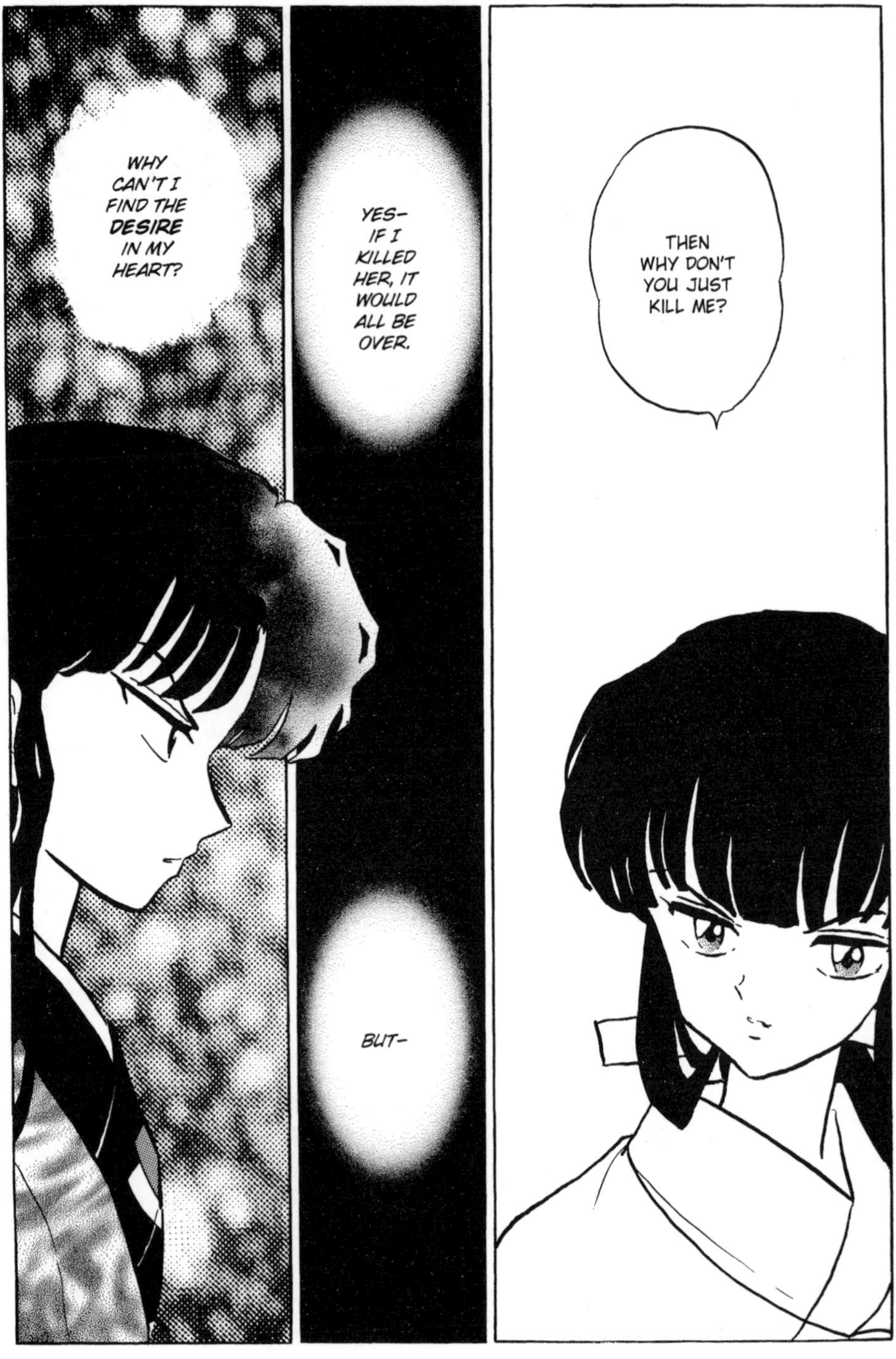
THEN WHY DON'T YOU JUST KILL ME?
YES- IF I KILLED HER, IT WOULD ALL BE OVER.
BUT-
WHY CAN'T I FIND THE **DESIRE** IN MY HEART?

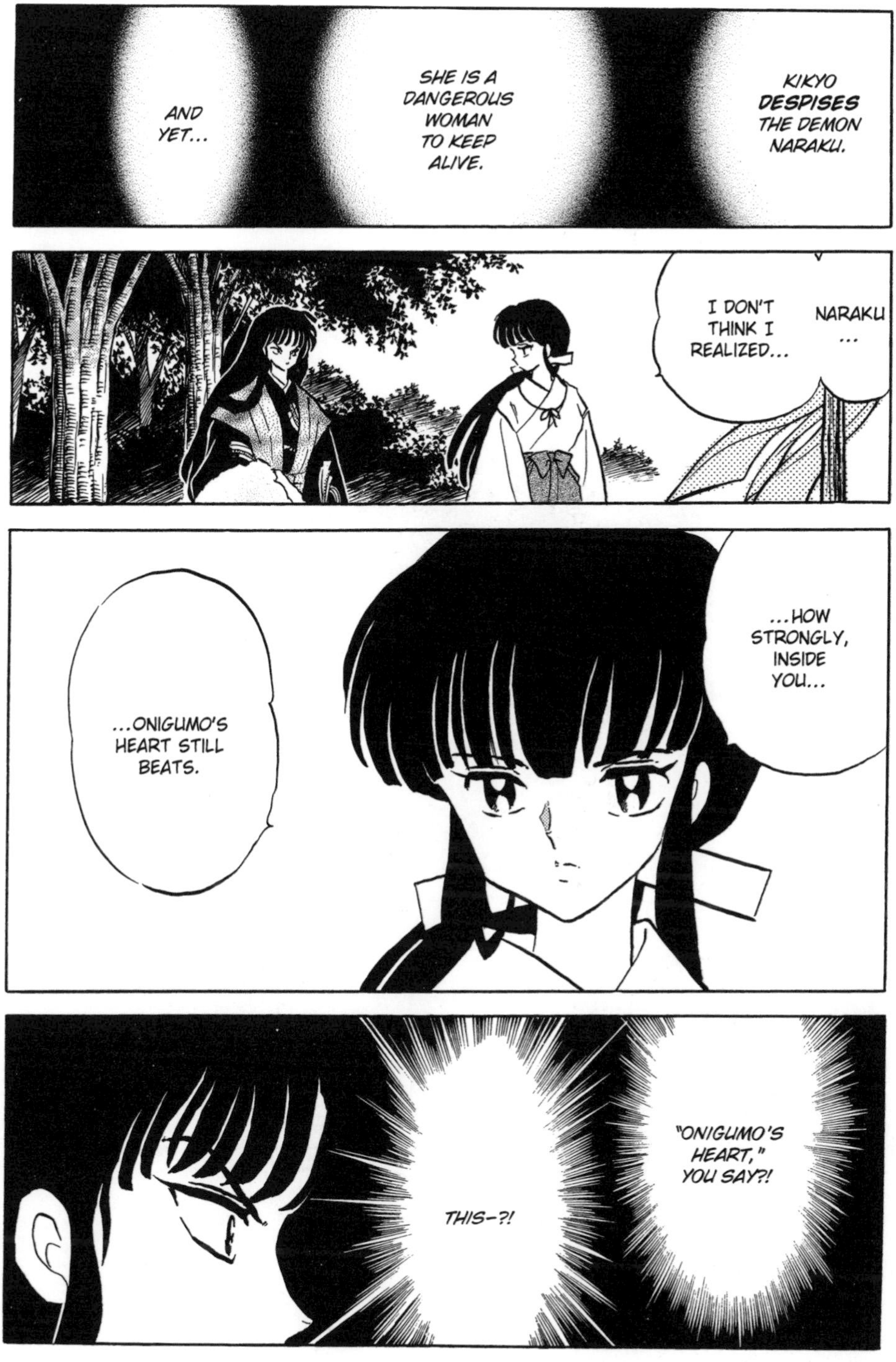
KIKYO DESPISES THE DEMON NARAKU.
SHE IS A DANGEROUS WOMAN TO KEEP ALIVE.
AND YET...
NARAKU...
I DON'T THINK I REALIZED...
...HOW STRONGLY, INSIDE YOU...
...ONIGUMO'S HEART STILL BEATS.
"ONIGUMO'S HEART," YOU SAY?!
THIS-?!

SCROLL THREE
KIKYO'S CRISIS

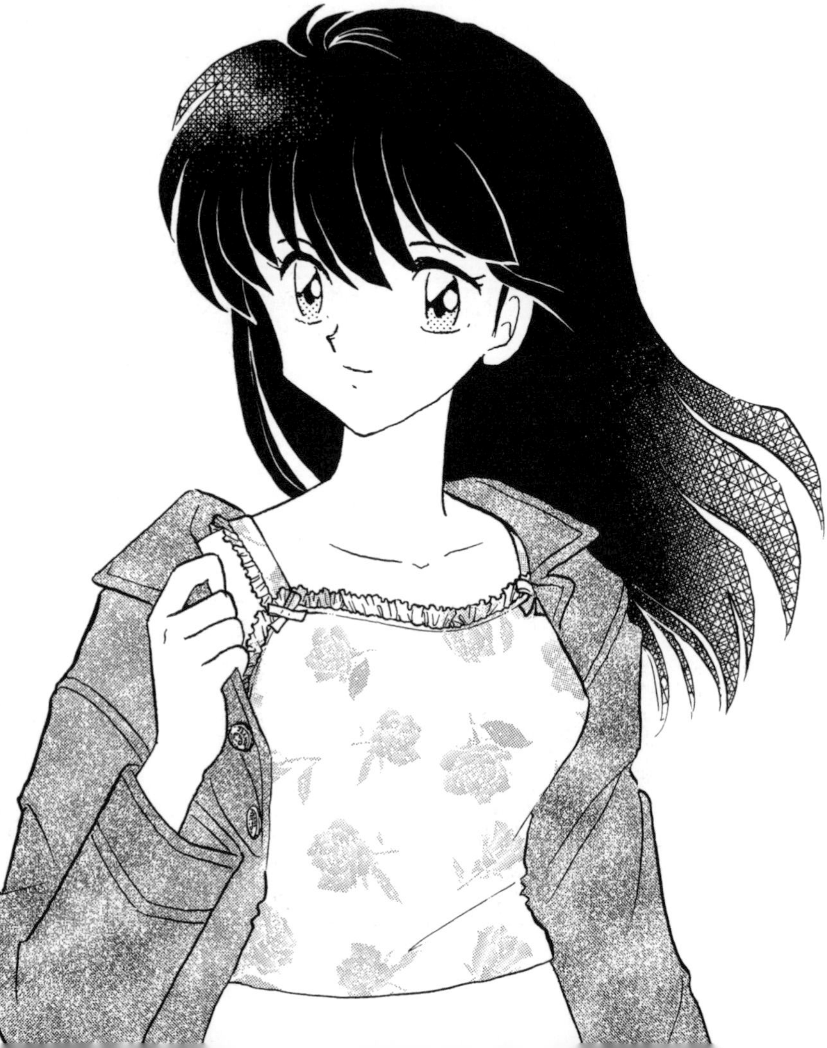

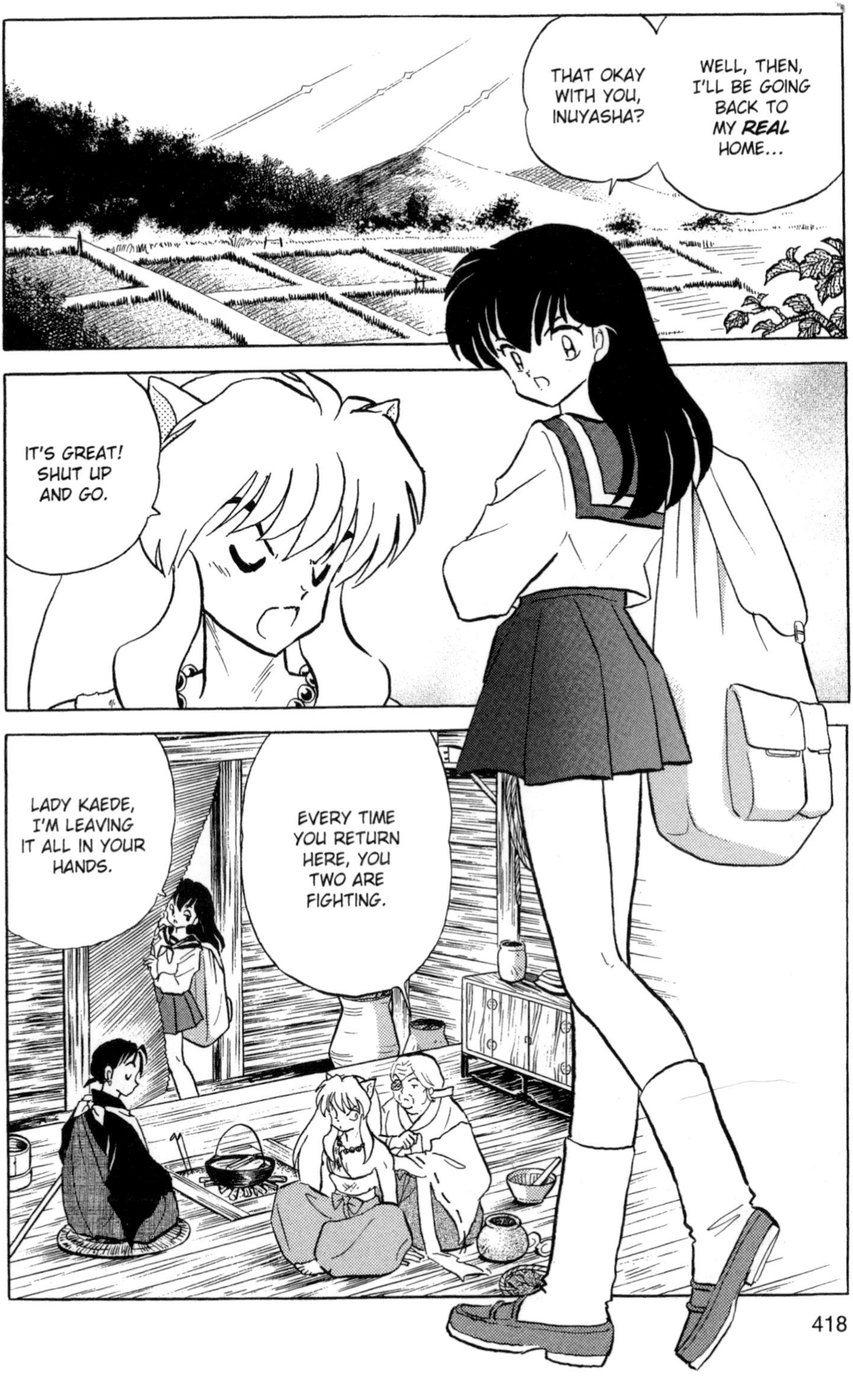
WELL, THEN, I'LL BE GOING BACK TO MY **REAL** HOME...
THAT OKAY WITH YOU, INUYASHA?
IT'S GREAT! SHUT UP AND GO.
EVERY TIME YOU RETURN HERE, YOU TWO ARE FIGHTING.
LADY KAEDE, I'M LEAVING IT ALL IN YOUR HANDS.

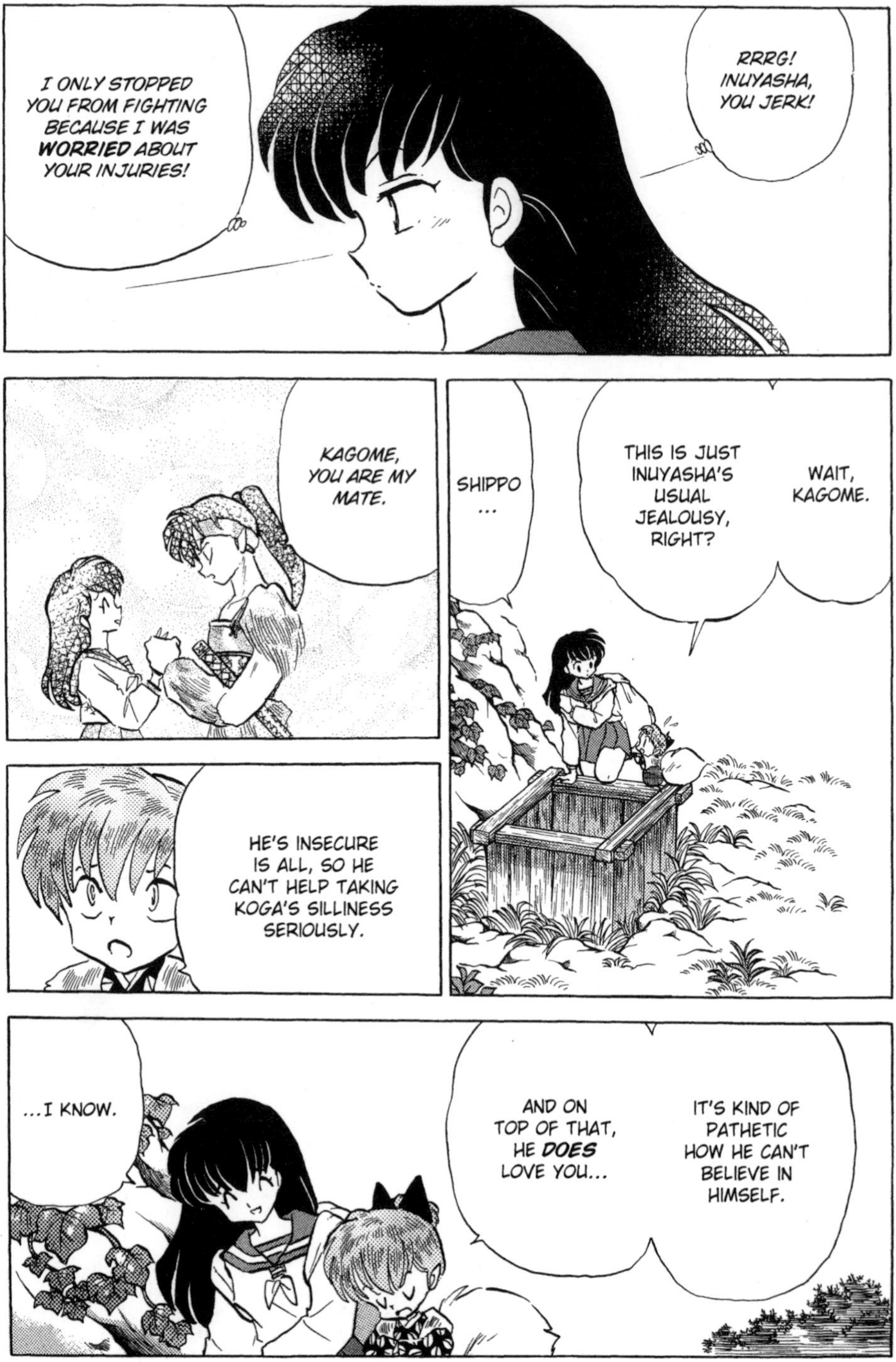
RRRG! INUYASHA, YOU JERK!
I ONLY STOPPED YOU FROM FIGHTING BECAUSE I WAS **WORRIED** ABOUT YOUR INJURIES!
WAIT, KAGOME.
THIS IS JUST INUYASHA'S USUAL JEALOUSY, RIGHT?
SHIPPO ...
KAGOME, YOU ARE MY MATE.
HE'S INSECURE IS ALL, SO HE CAN'T HELP TAKING KOGA'S SILLINESS SERIOUSLY.
IT'S KIND OF PATHETIC HOW HE CAN'T BELIEVE IN HIMSELF.
AND ON TOP OF THAT, HE **DOES** LOVE YOU...
...I KNOW.

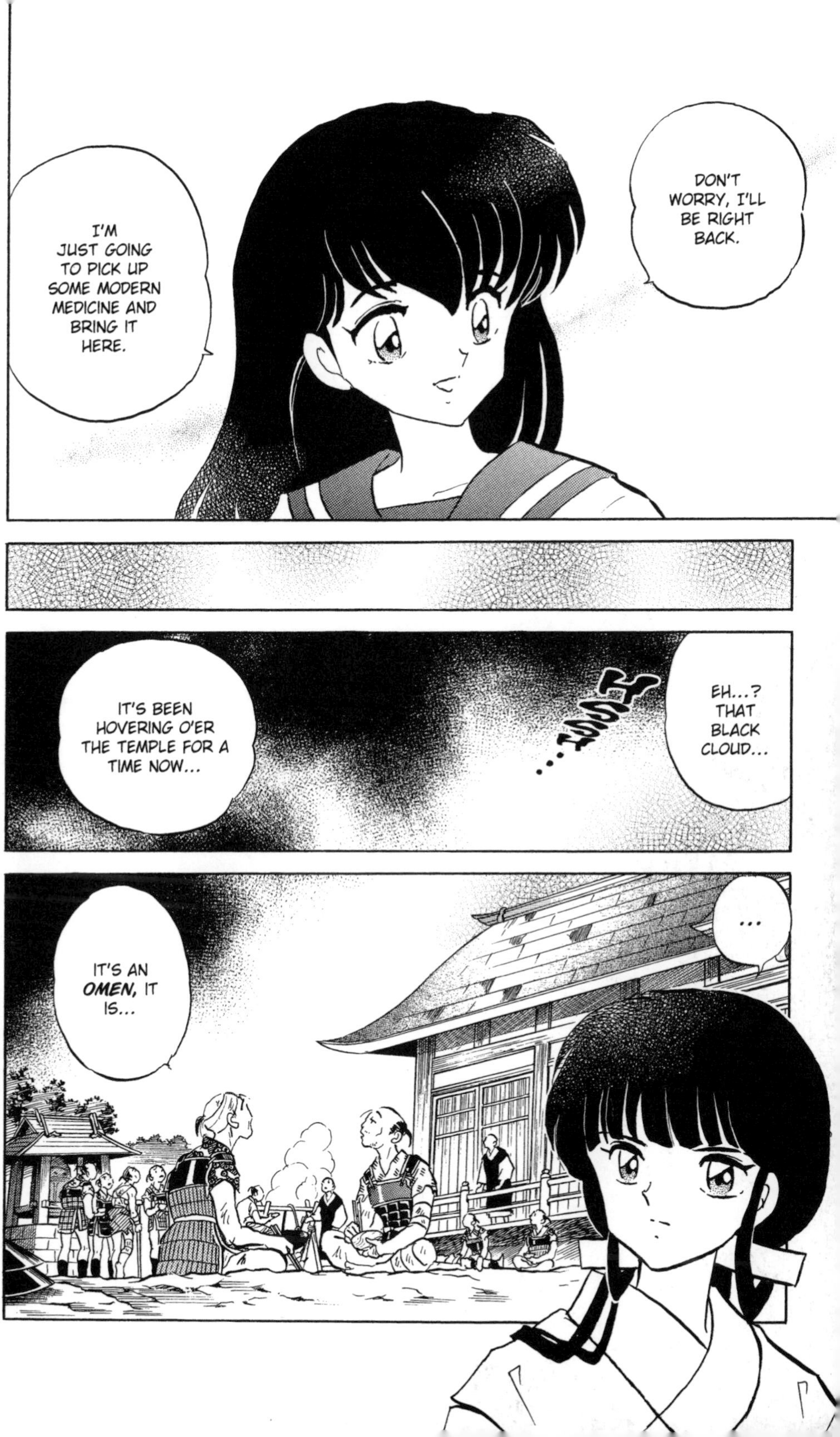
DON'T WORRY, I'LL BE RIGHT BACK.
I'M JUST GOING TO PICK UP SOME MODERN MEDICINE AND BRING IT HERE.
EH...? THAT BLACK CLOUD...
IT'S BEEN HOVERING O'ER THE TEMPLE FOR A TIME NOW...
...
IT'S AN **OMEN,** IT IS...

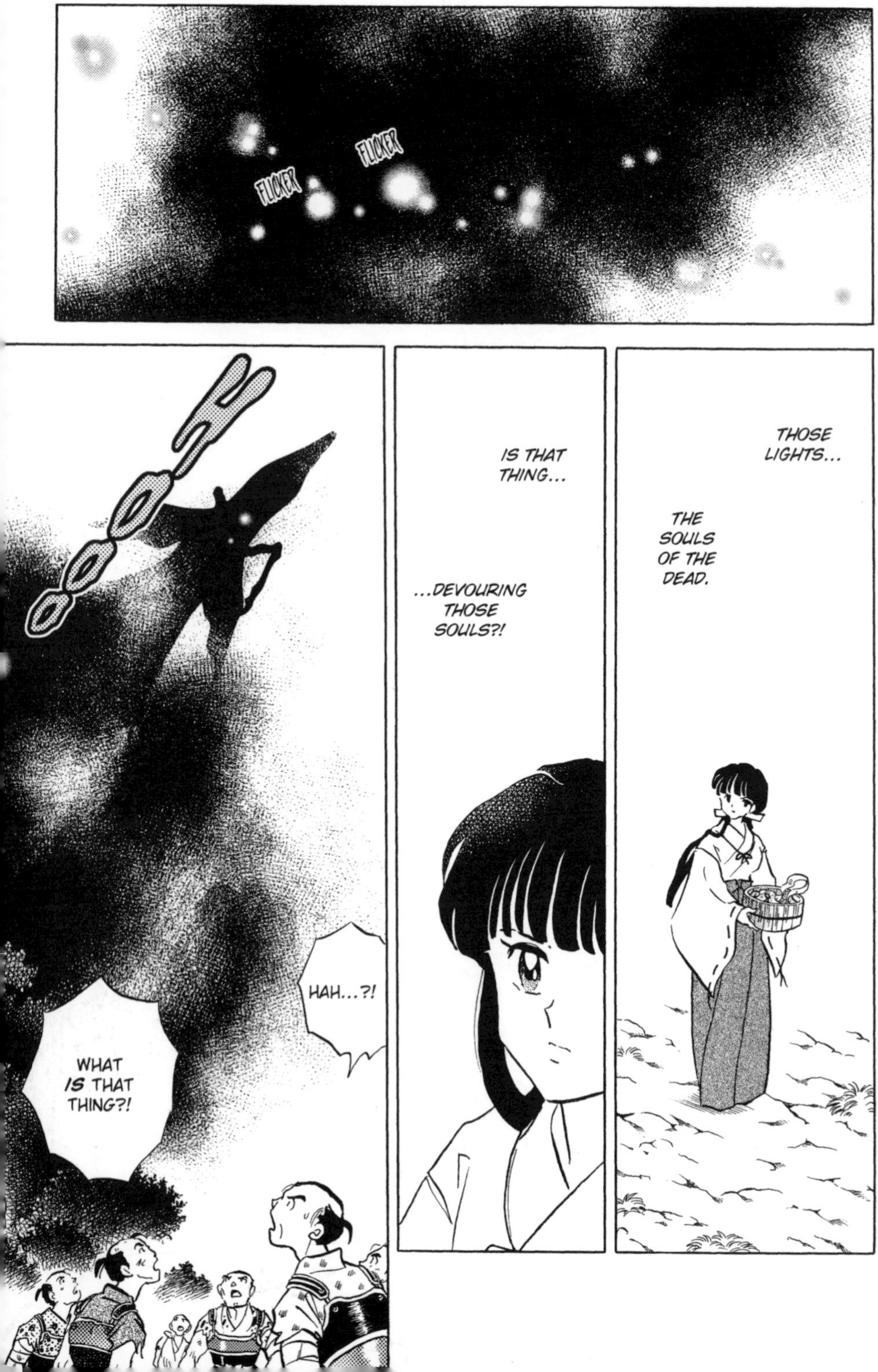
FLICKER
FLICKER
THOSE LIGHTS...
THE SOULS OF THE DEAD.
IS THAT THING...
...DEVOURING THOSE SOULS?!
HAH...?!
WHAT *IS* THAT THING?!

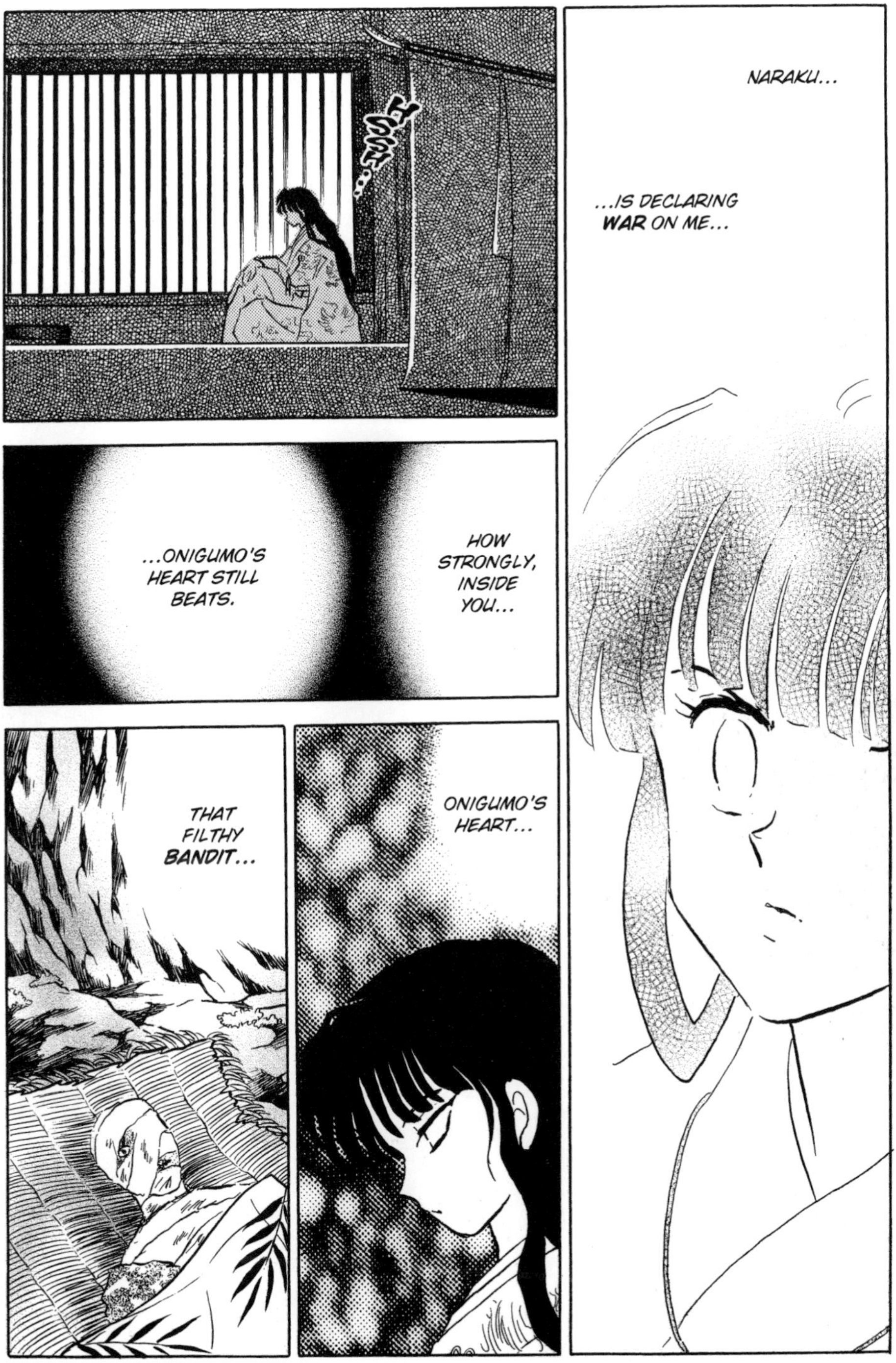
NARAKU...
...IS DECLARING WAR ON ME...
HOW STRONGLY, INSIDE YOU...
...ONIGUMO'S HEART STILL BEATS.
ONIGUMO'S HEART...
THAT FILTHY BANDIT...

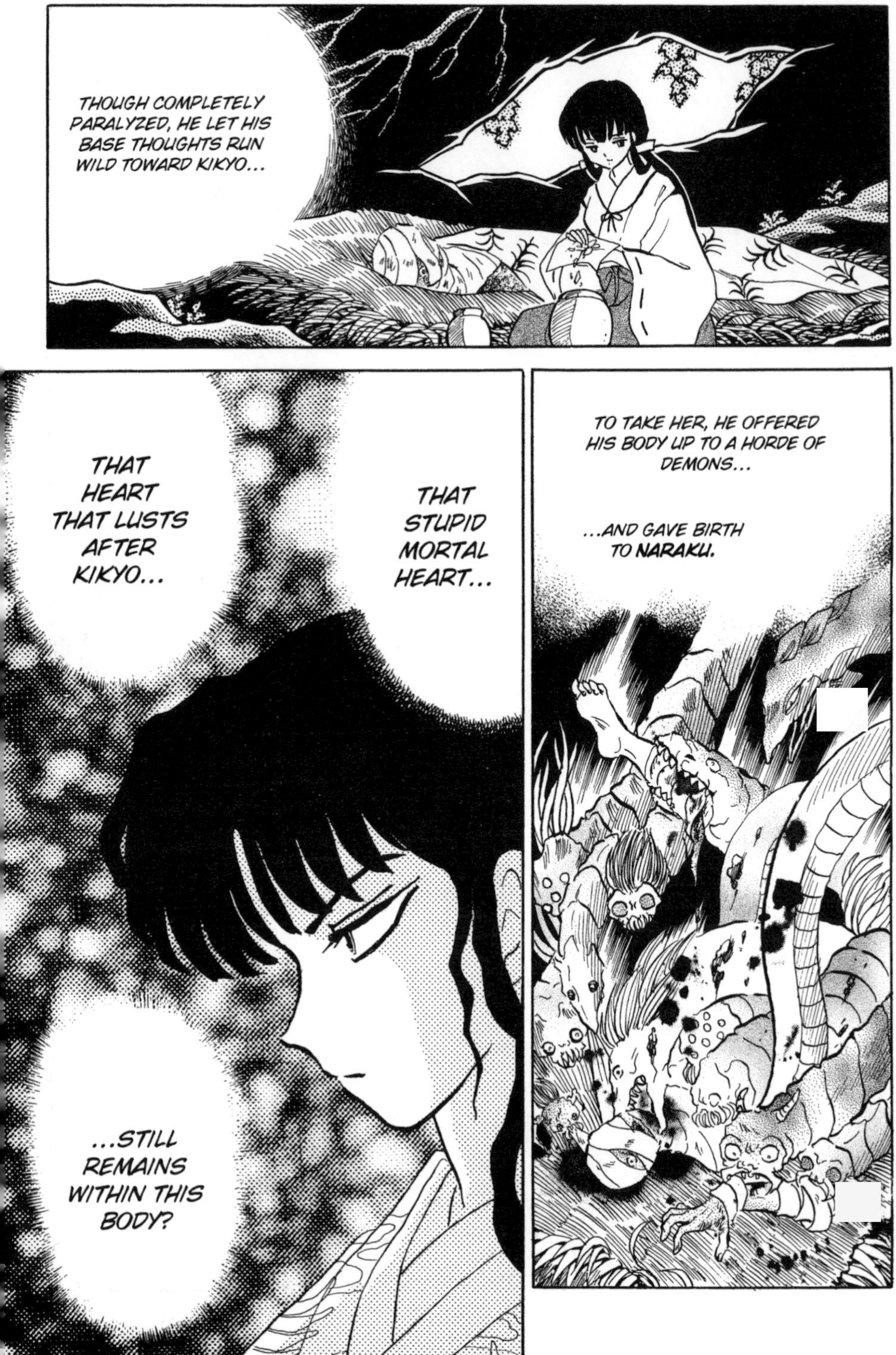
THOUGH COMPLETELY PARALYZED, HE LET HIS BASE THOUGHTS RUN WILD TOWARD KIKYO...
TO TAKE HER, HE OFFERED HIS BODY UP TO A HORDE OF DEMONS...
...AND GAVE BIRTH TO NARAKU.
THAT STUPID MORTAL HEART...
THAT HEART THAT LUSTS AFTER KIKYO...
...STILL REMAINS WITHIN THIS BODY?

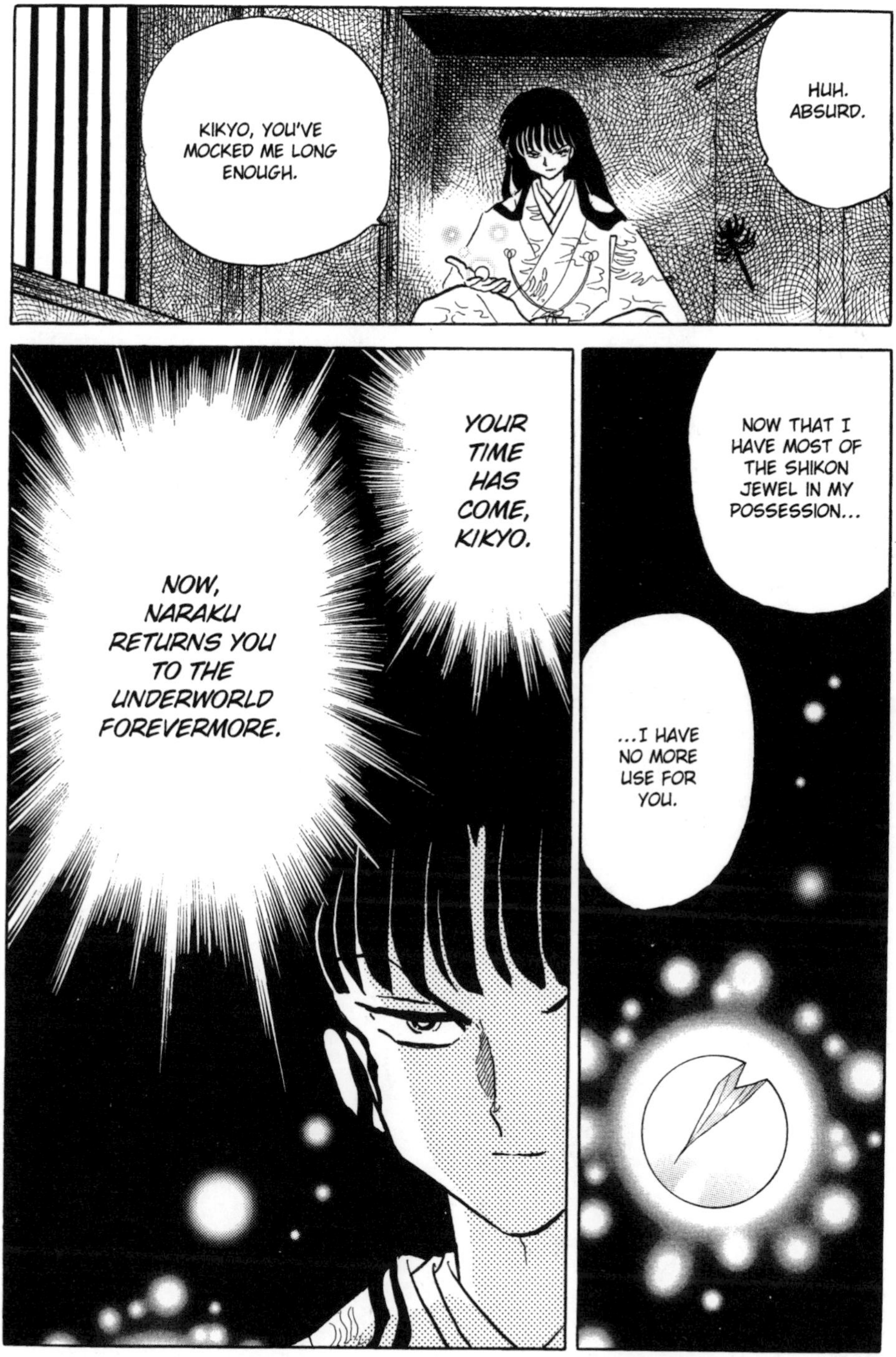
HUH. ABSURD.
KIKYO, YOU'VE MOCKED ME LONG ENOUGH.
NOW THAT I HAVE MOST OF THE SHIKON JEWEL IN MY POSSESSION...
...I HAVE NO MORE USE FOR YOU.
YOUR TIME HAS COME, KIKYO.
NOW, NARAKU RETURNS YOU TO THE UNDERWORLD FOREVERMORE.

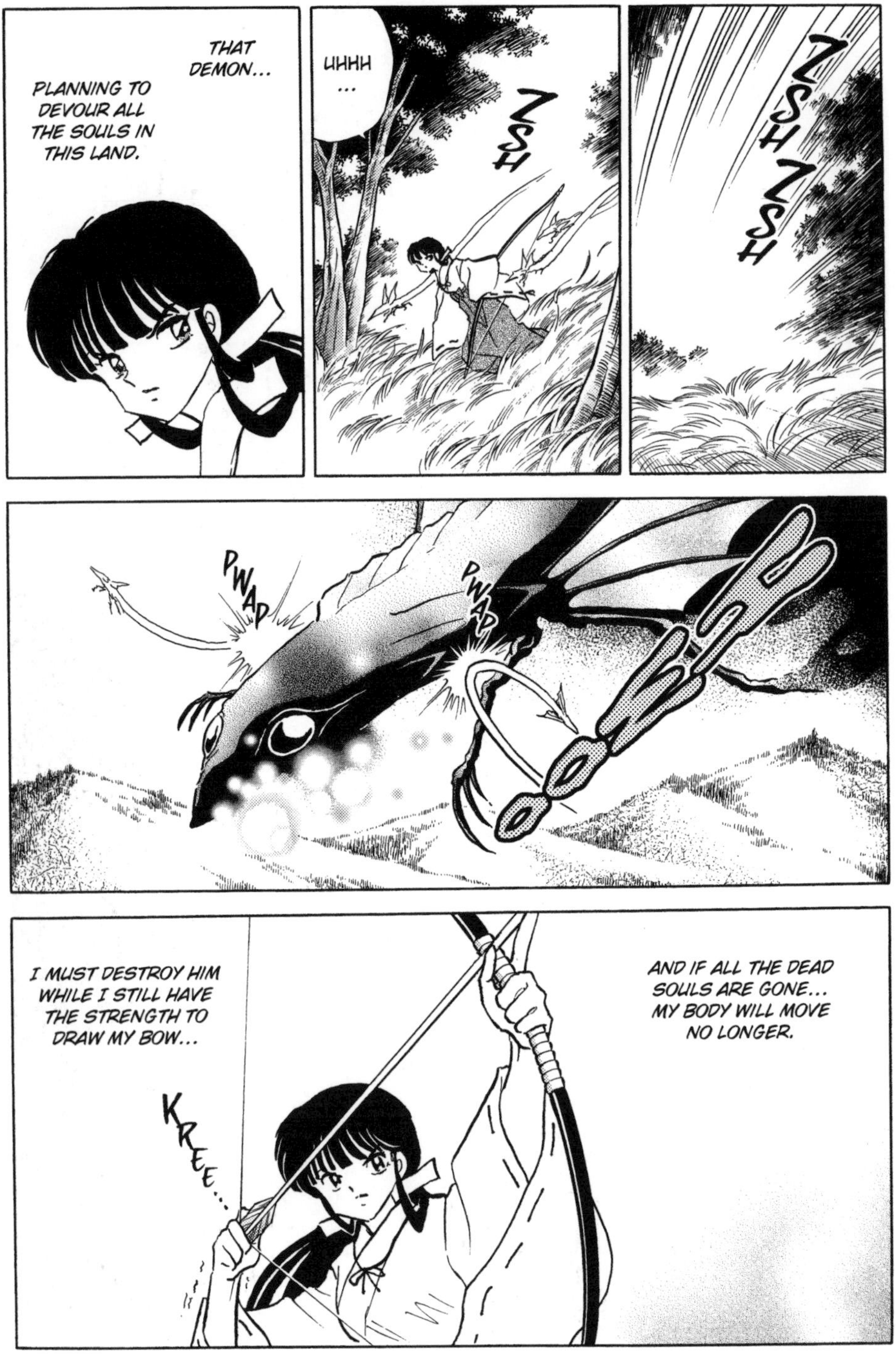
ZSH ZSH
UHHH ...
ZSH
THAT DEMON...
PLANNING TO DEVOUR ALL THE SOULS IN THIS LAND.
PWAP
PWAP
AND IF ALL THE DEAD SOULS ARE GONE... MY BODY WILL MOVE NO LONGER.
I MUST DESTROY HIM WHILE I STILL HAVE THE STRENGTH TO DRAW MY BOW...
KREEE...

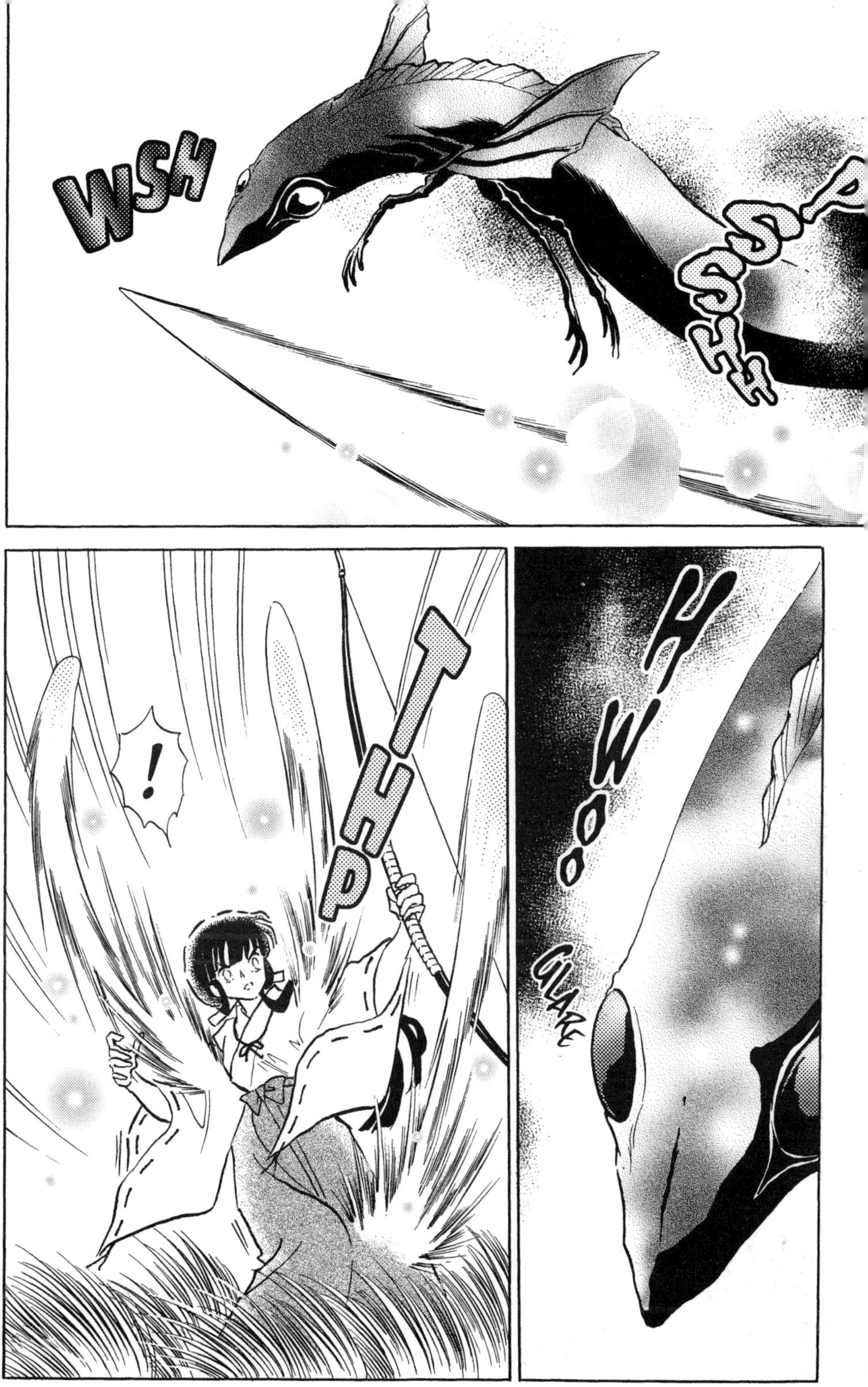
PSSHH
WSH
HWOO...
GLARE
THHP
!

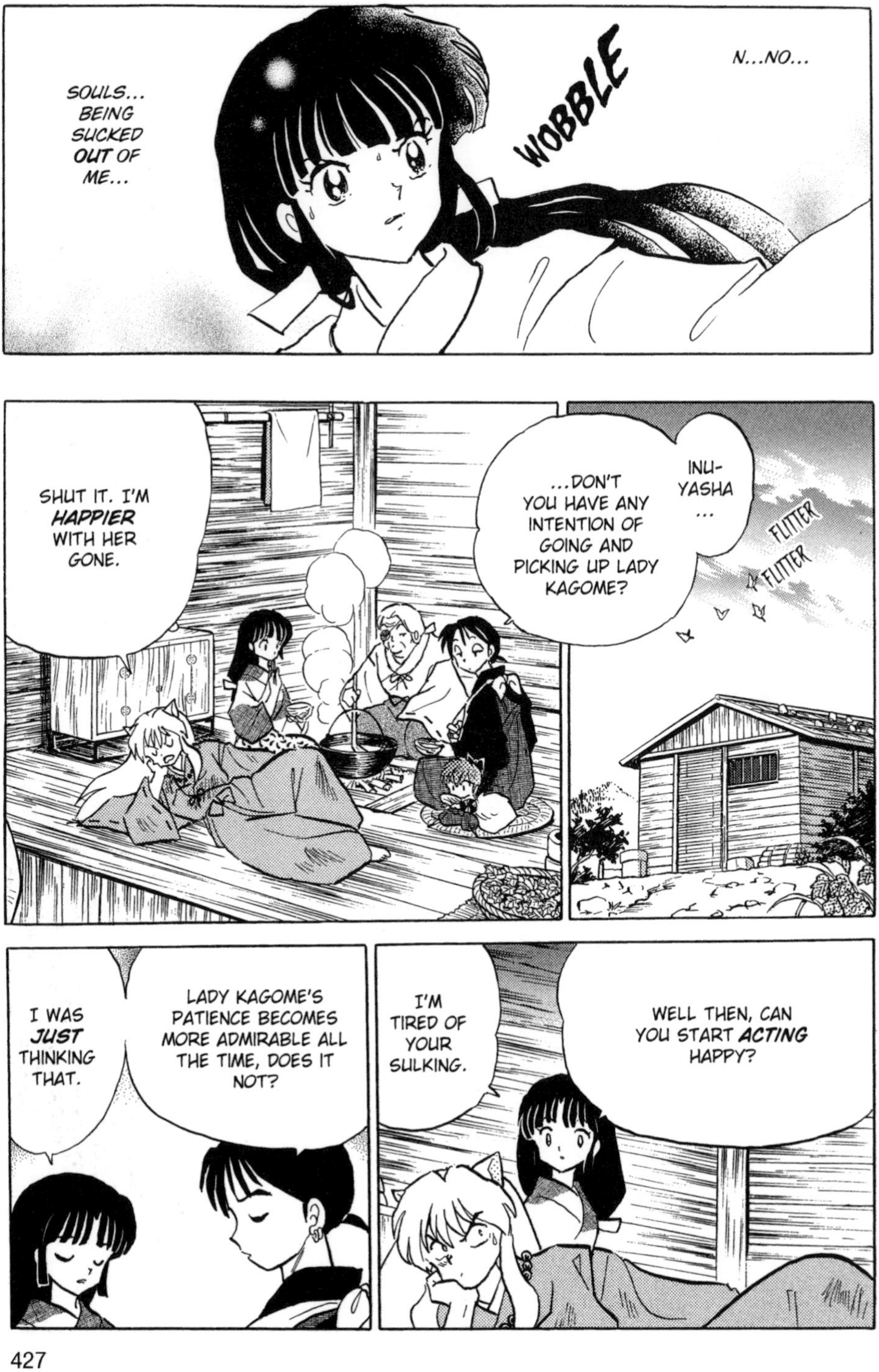
N...NO...
WOBBLE
SOULS... BEING SUCKED OUT OF ME...
FLITTER FLITTER
INU-YASHA...
...DON'T YOU HAVE ANY INTENTION OF GOING AND PICKING UP LADY KAGOME?
SHUT IT. I'M HAPPIER WITH HER GONE.
WELL THEN, CAN YOU START ACTING HAPPY?
I'M TIRED OF YOUR SULKING.
LADY KAGOME'S PATIENCE BECOMES MORE ADMIRABLE ALL THE TIME, DOES IT NOT?
I WAS JUST THINKING THAT.

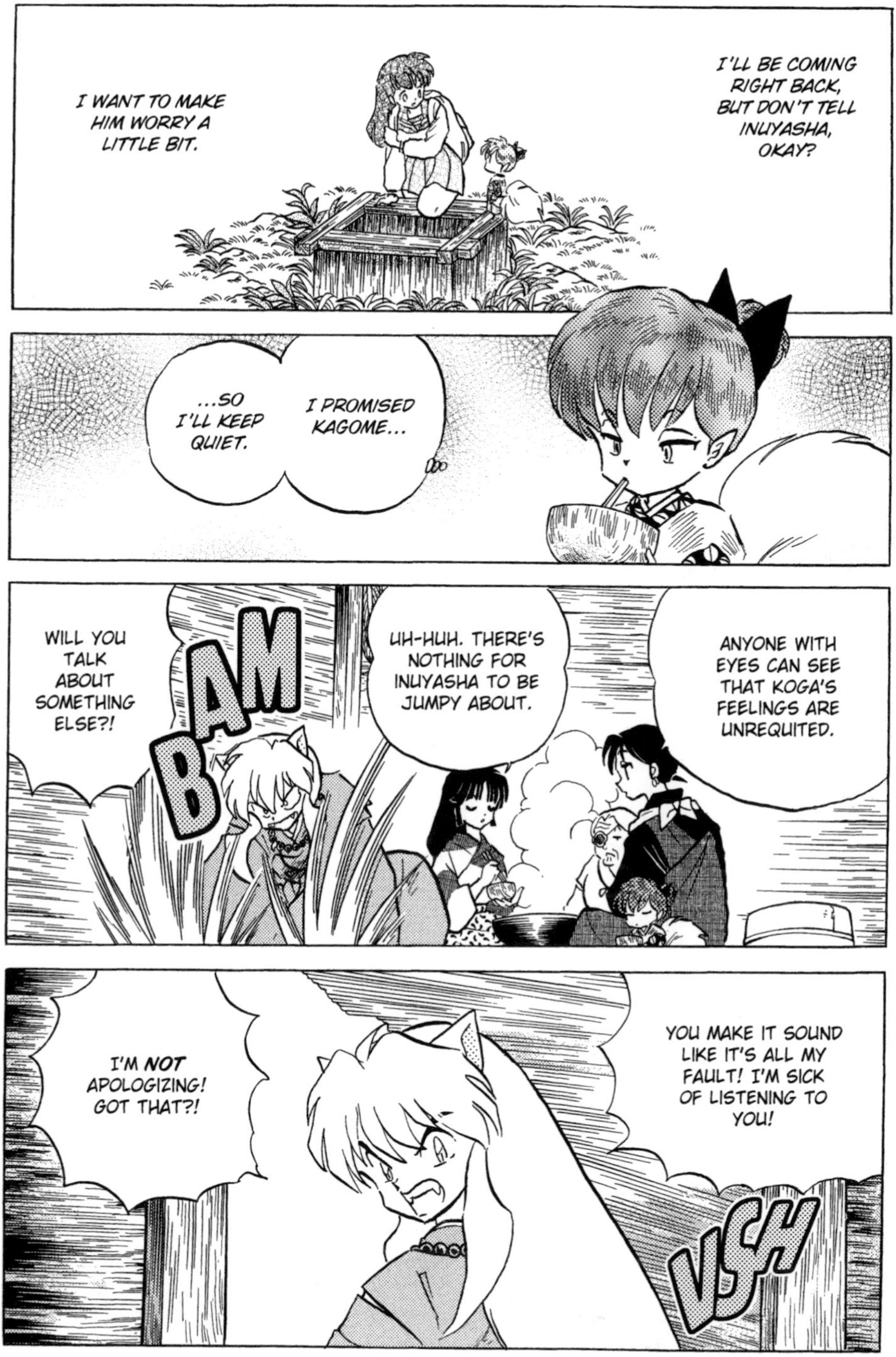
I'LL BE COMING RIGHT BACK, BUT DON'T TELL INUYASHA, OKAY?
I WANT TO MAKE HIM WORRY A LITTLE BIT.
I PROMISED KAGOME...
...SO I'LL KEEP QUIET.
ANYONE WITH EYES CAN SEE THAT KOGA'S FEELINGS ARE UNREQUITED.
UH-HUH. THERE'S NOTHING FOR INUYASHA TO BE JUMPY ABOUT.
BAM
WILL YOU TALK ABOUT SOMETHING ELSE?!
YOU MAKE IT SOUND LIKE IT'S ALL MY FAULT! I'M SICK OF LISTENING TO YOU!
VSH
I'M NOT APOLOGIZING! GOT THAT?!

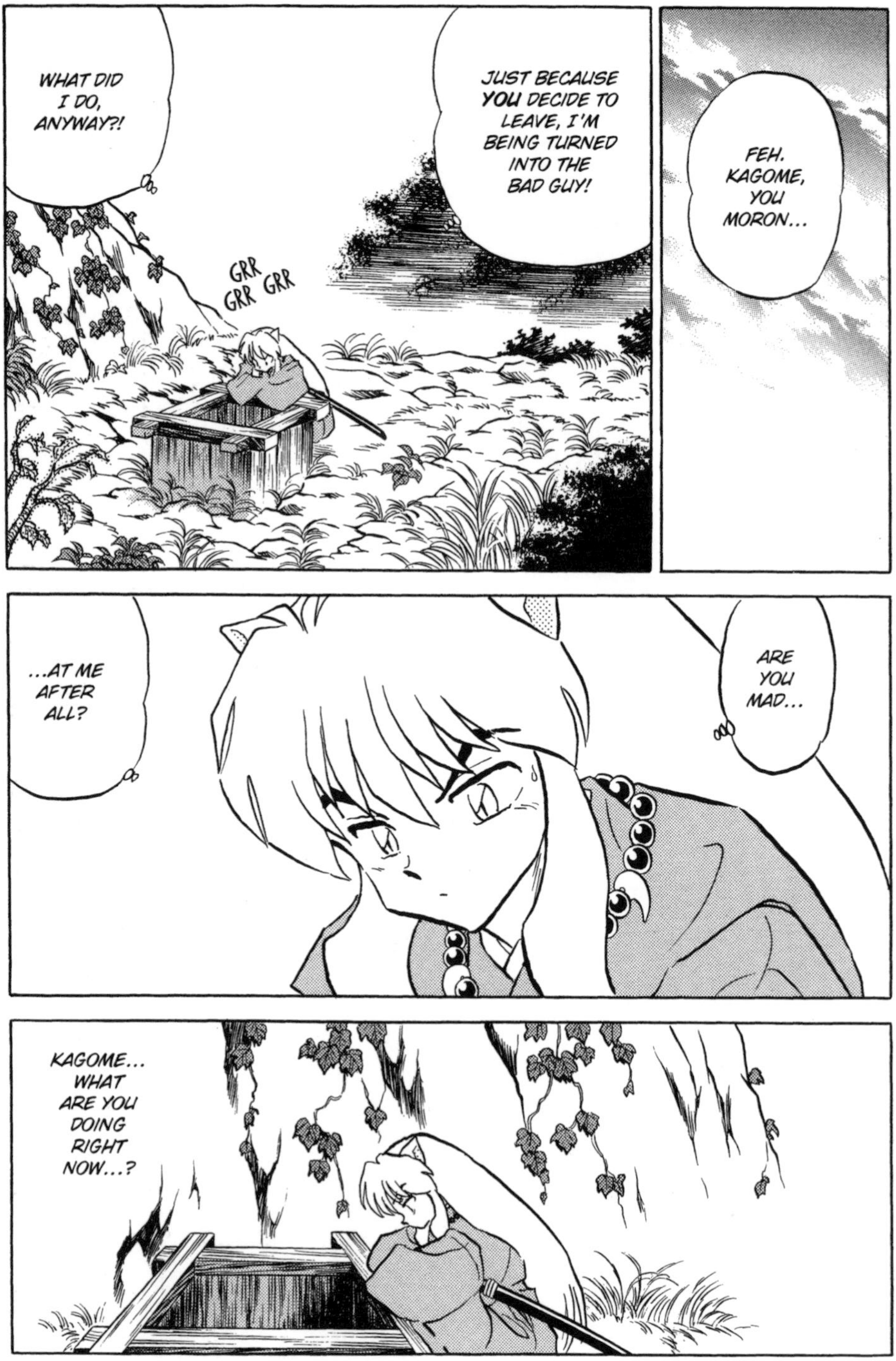
FEH. KAGOME, YOU MORON...
JUST BECAUSE **YOU** DECIDE TO LEAVE, I'M BEING TURNED INTO THE BAD GUY!
GRR GRR GRR
WHAT DID I DO, ANYWAY?!
ARE YOU MAD...
...AT ME AFTER ALL?
KAGOME... WHAT ARE YOU DOING RIGHT NOW...?

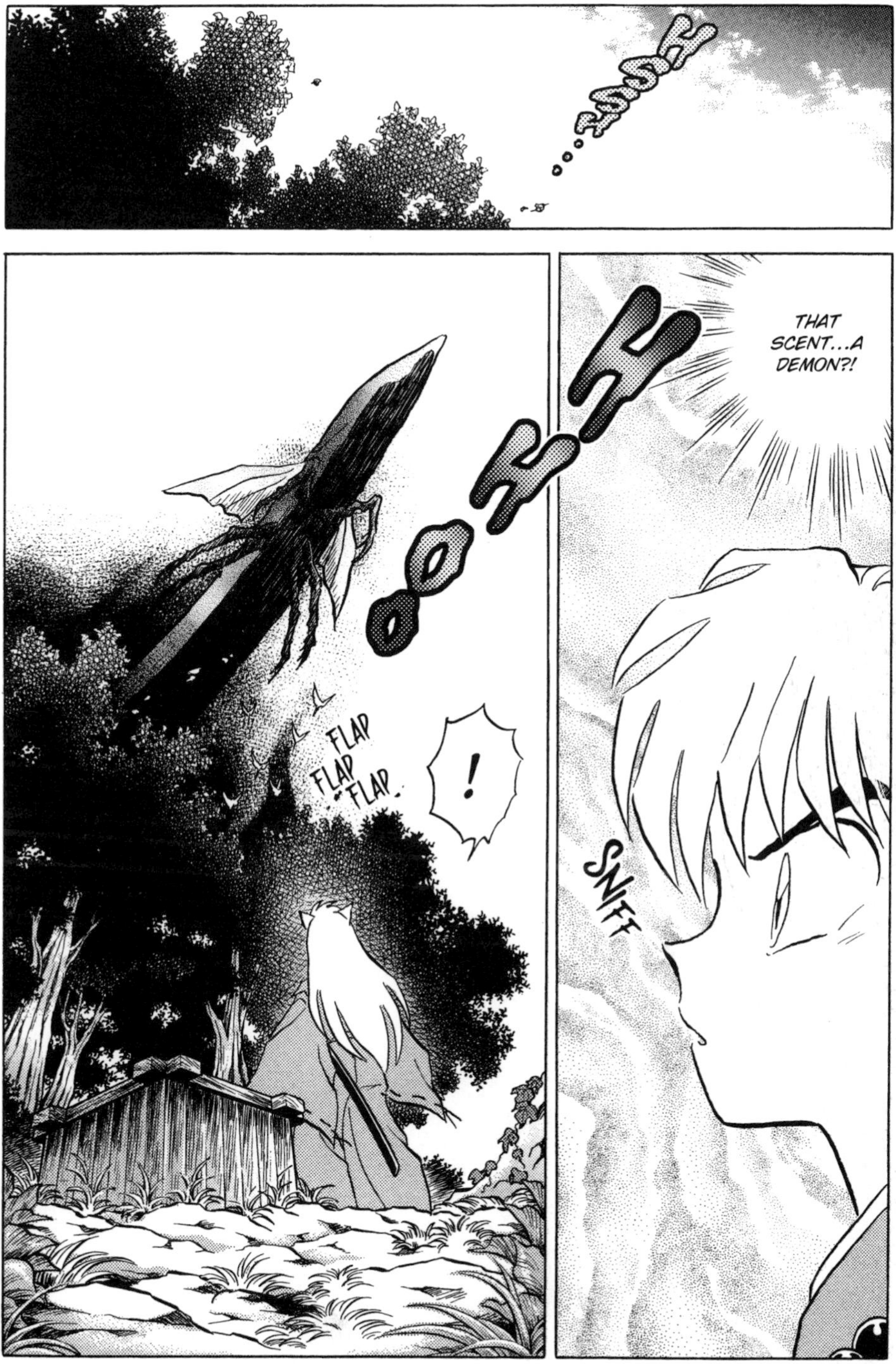
THAT SCENT...A DEMON?!
SNIFF
FLAP FLAP FLAP
!

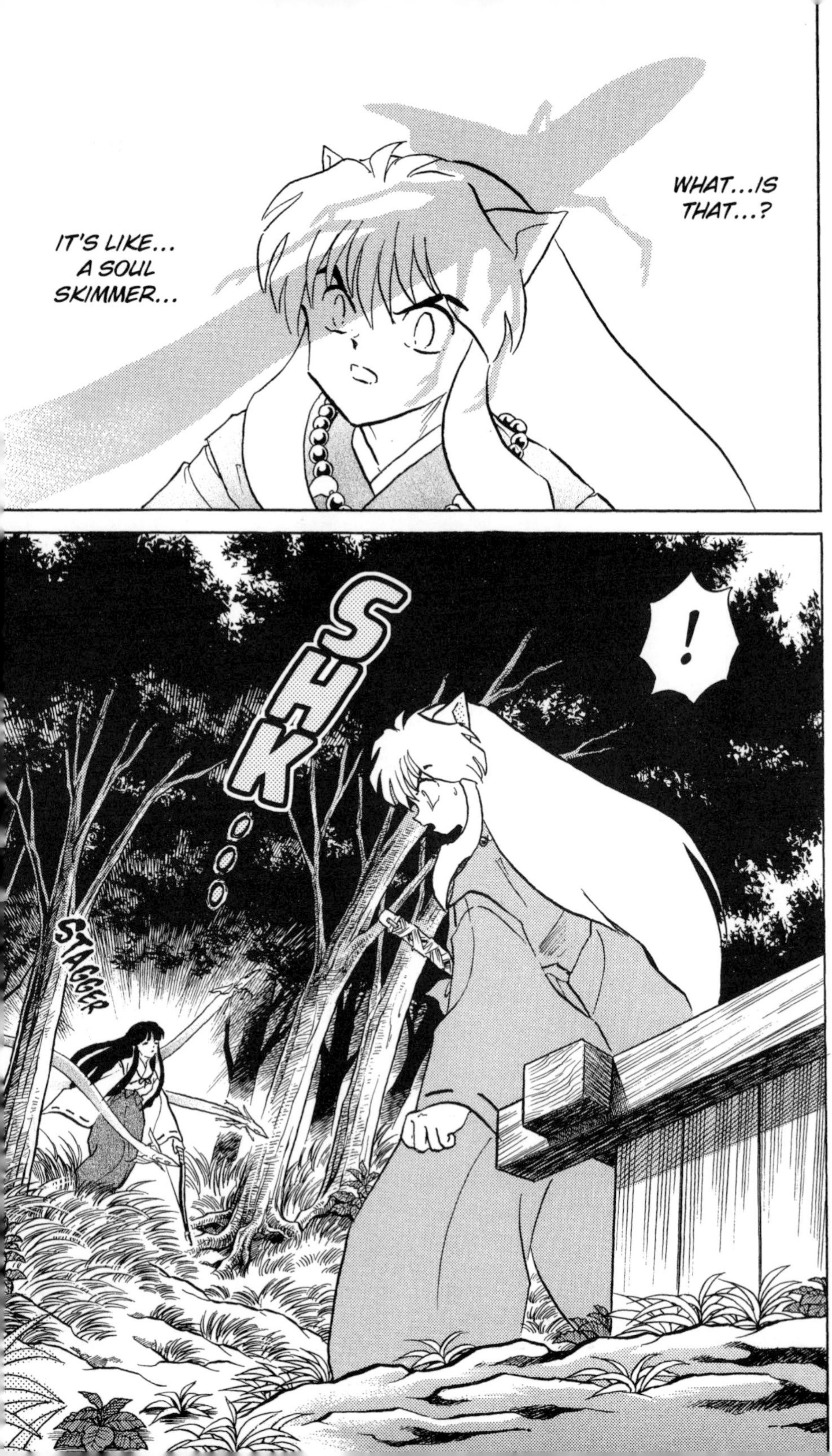
WHAT...IS THAT...?
IT'S LIKE... A SOUL SKIMMER...
!
SHK
STAGGER

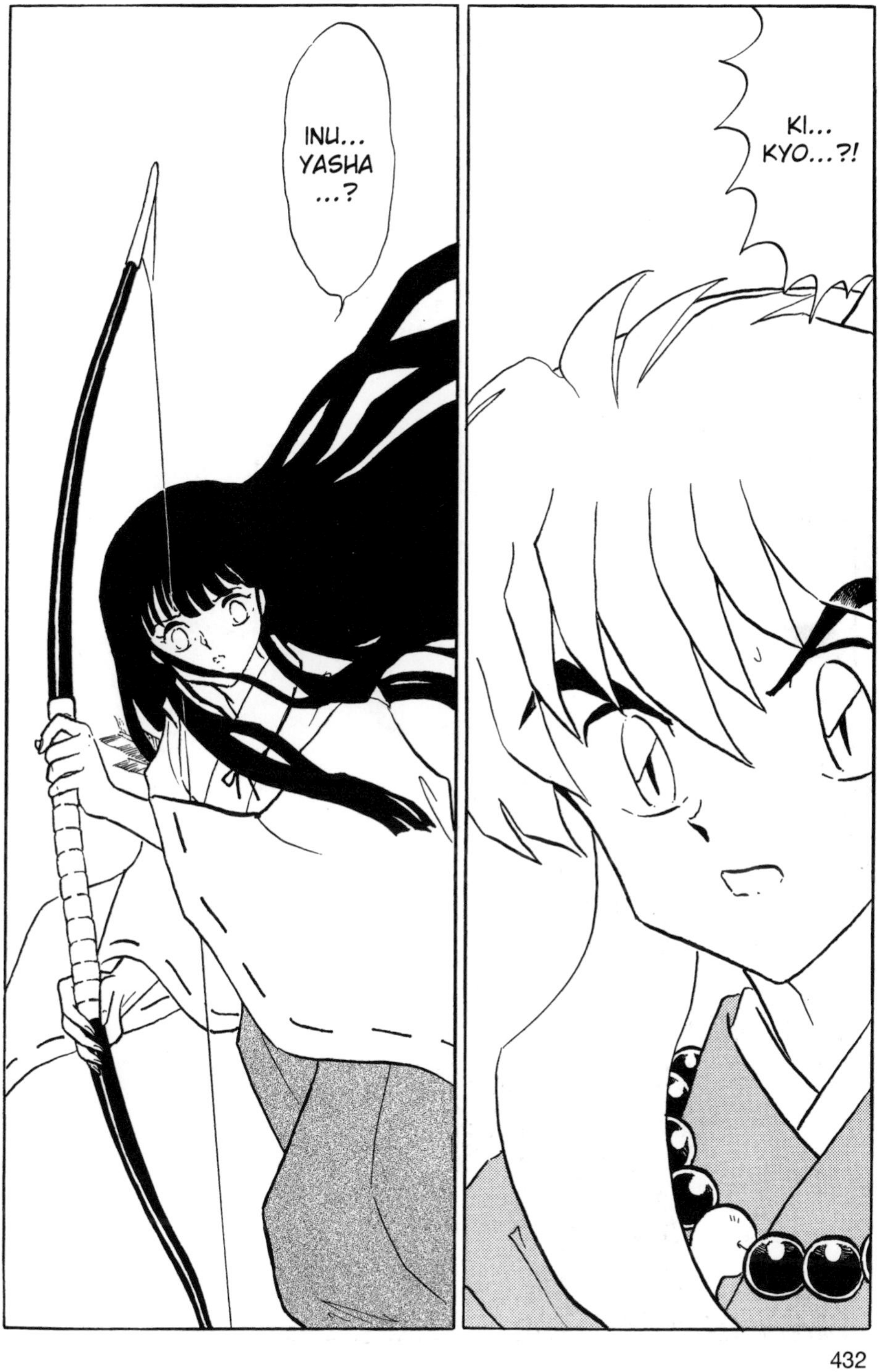
KI... KYO...?!
INU... YASHA ...?

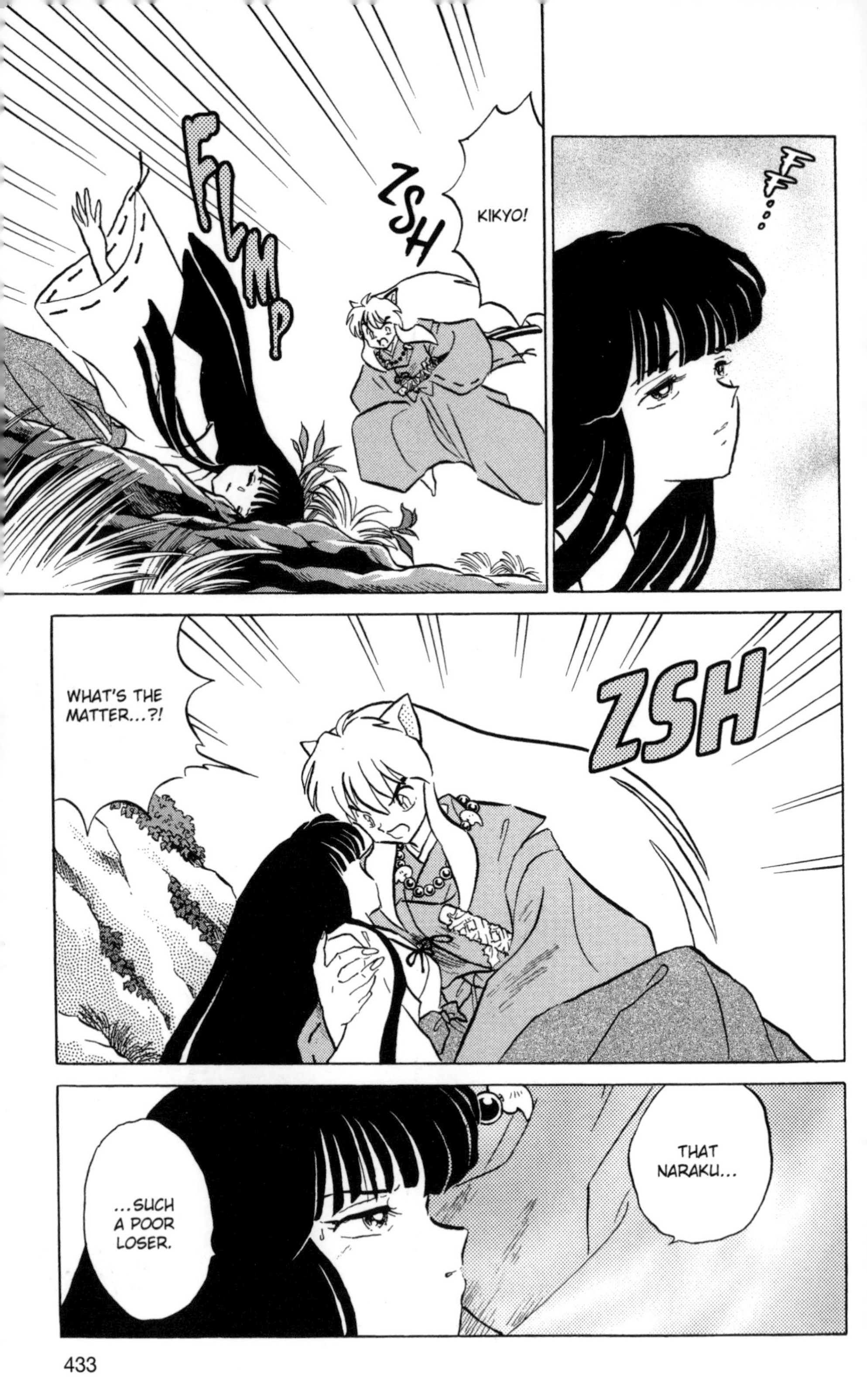
KIKYO!
ZSH
FLMP
ZSH
WHAT'S THE MATTER...?!
THAT NARAKU...
...SUCH A POOR LOSER.

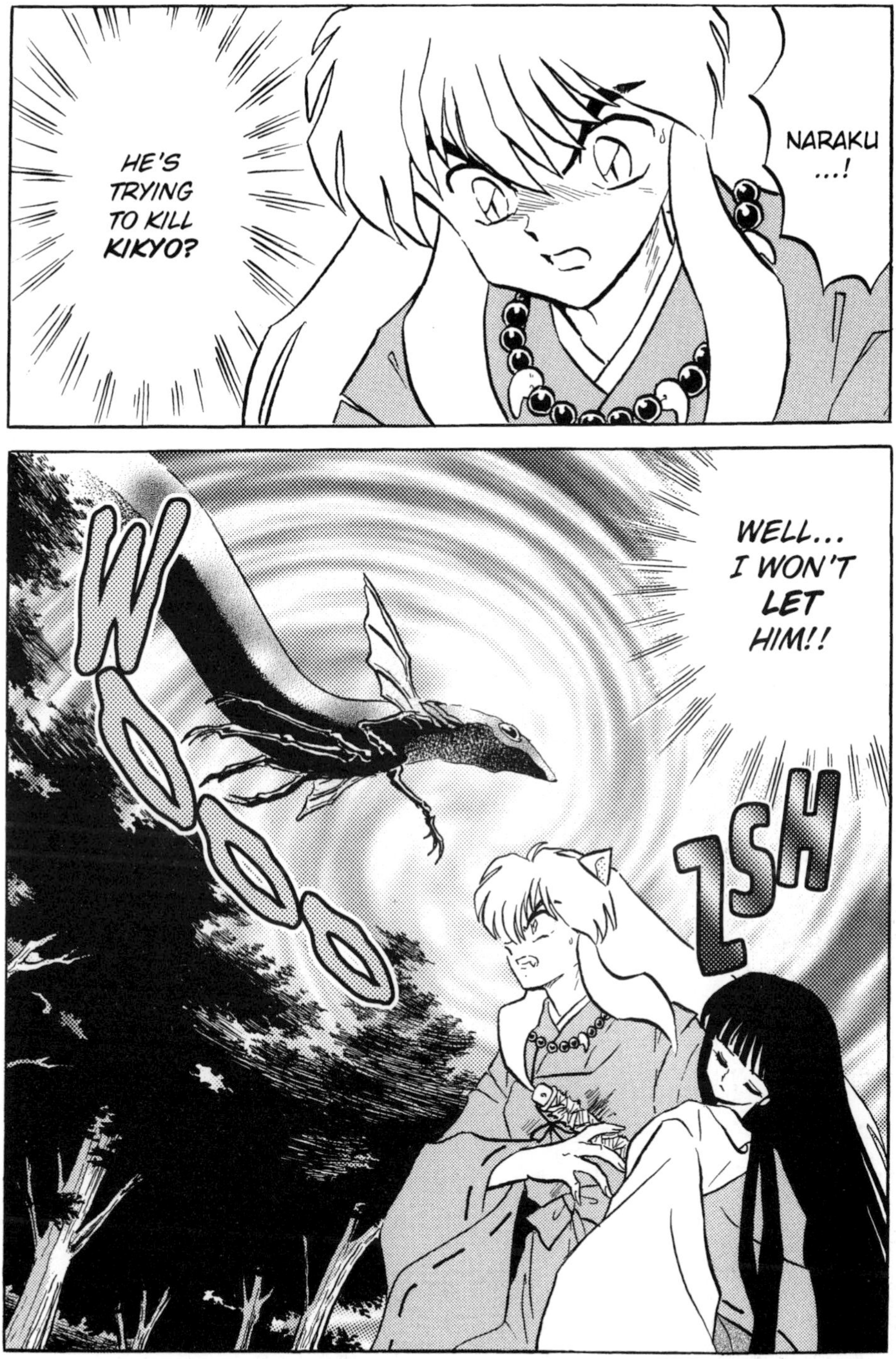
NARAKU ...!
HE'S TRYING TO KILL KIKYO?
WELL... I WON'T LET HIM!!
ZSH
WOOO

SCROLL FOUR
ONIGUMO'S HEART

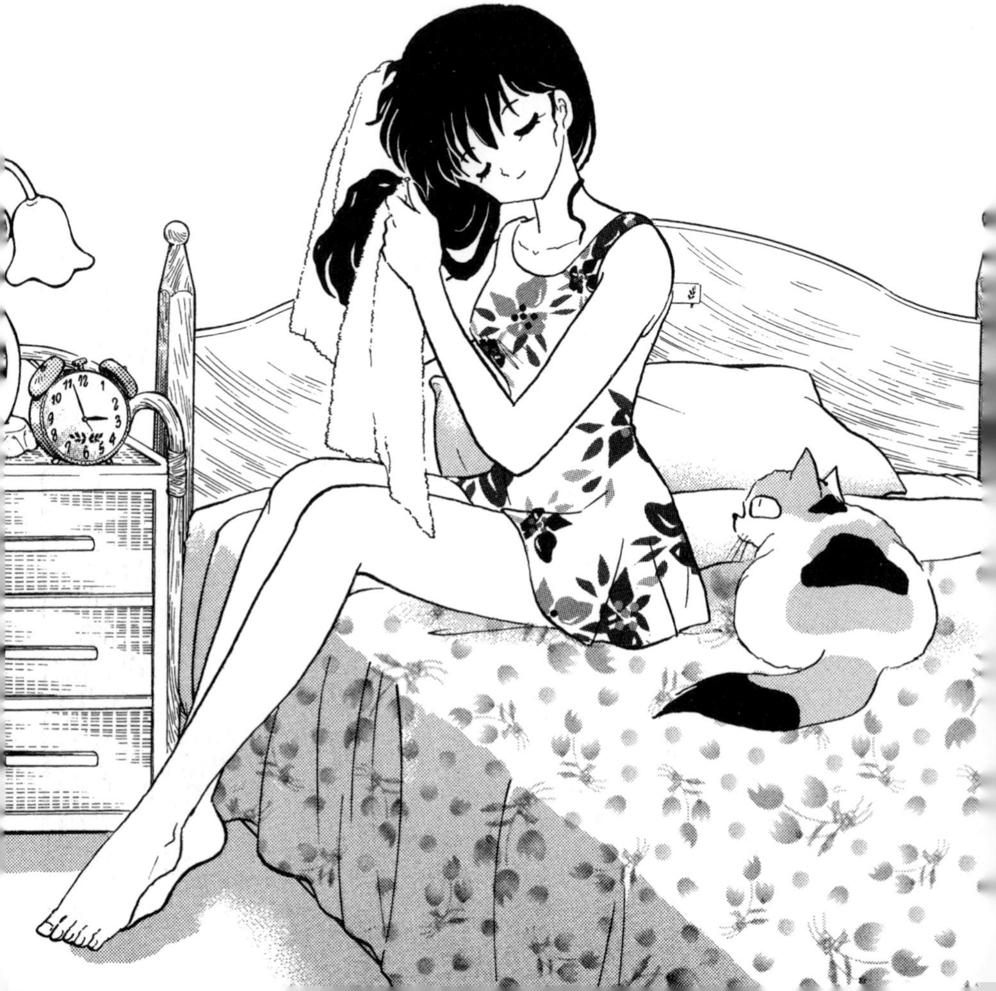

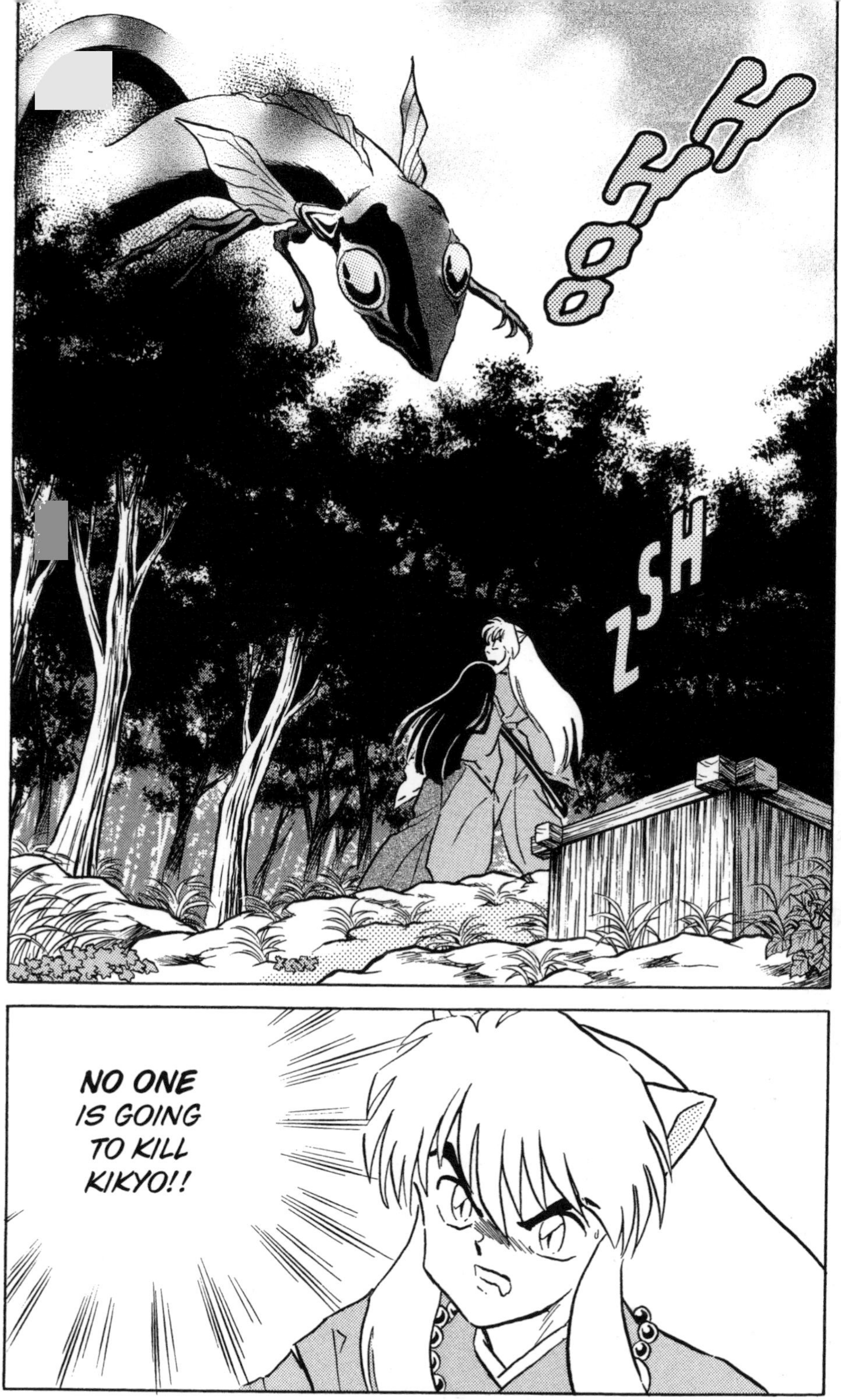
ZSH
NO ONE IS GOING TO KILL KIKYO!!

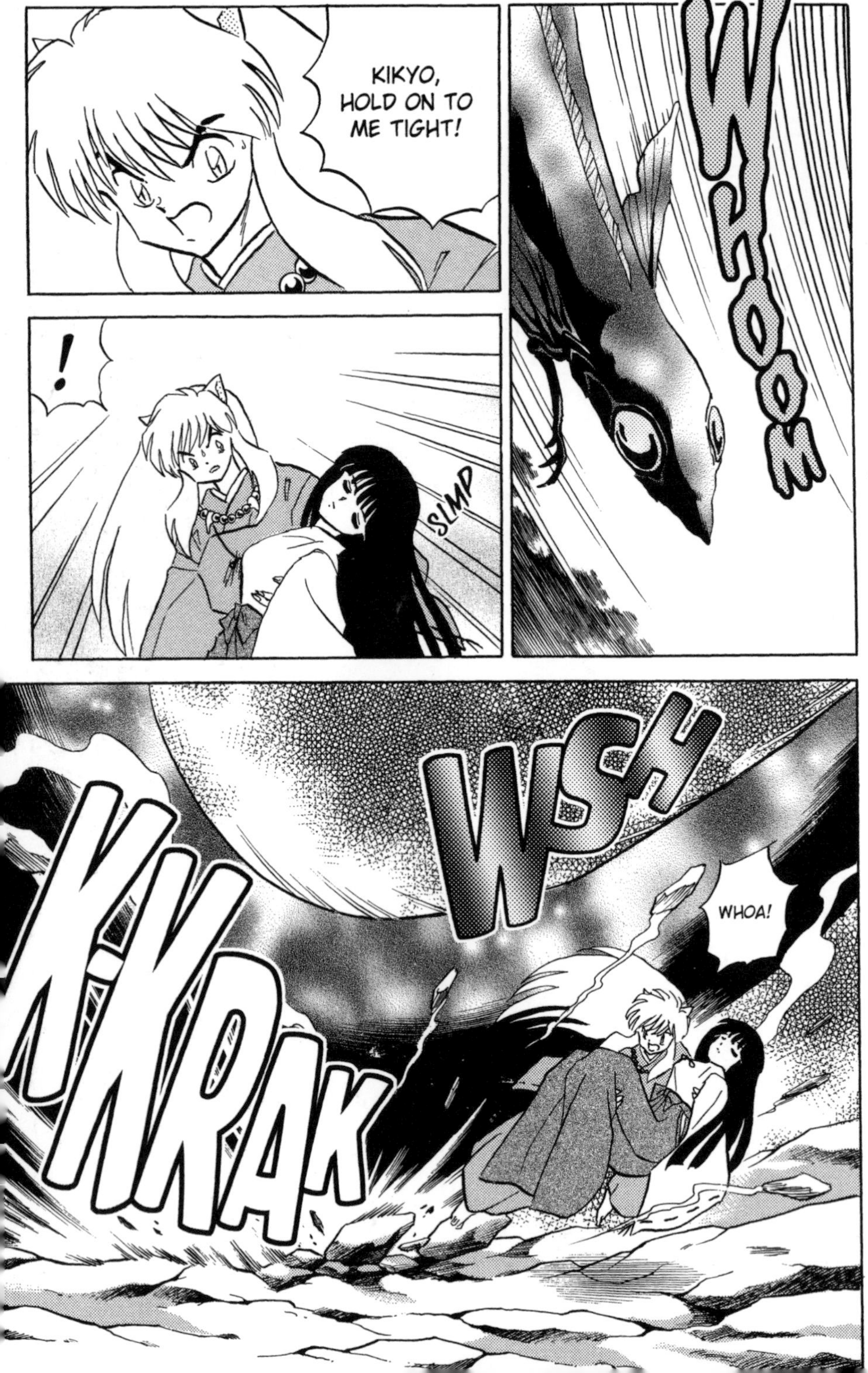
WHOOM
KIKYO, HOLD ON TO ME TIGHT!
!
SLMP
WSH
WHOA!
KKRAK

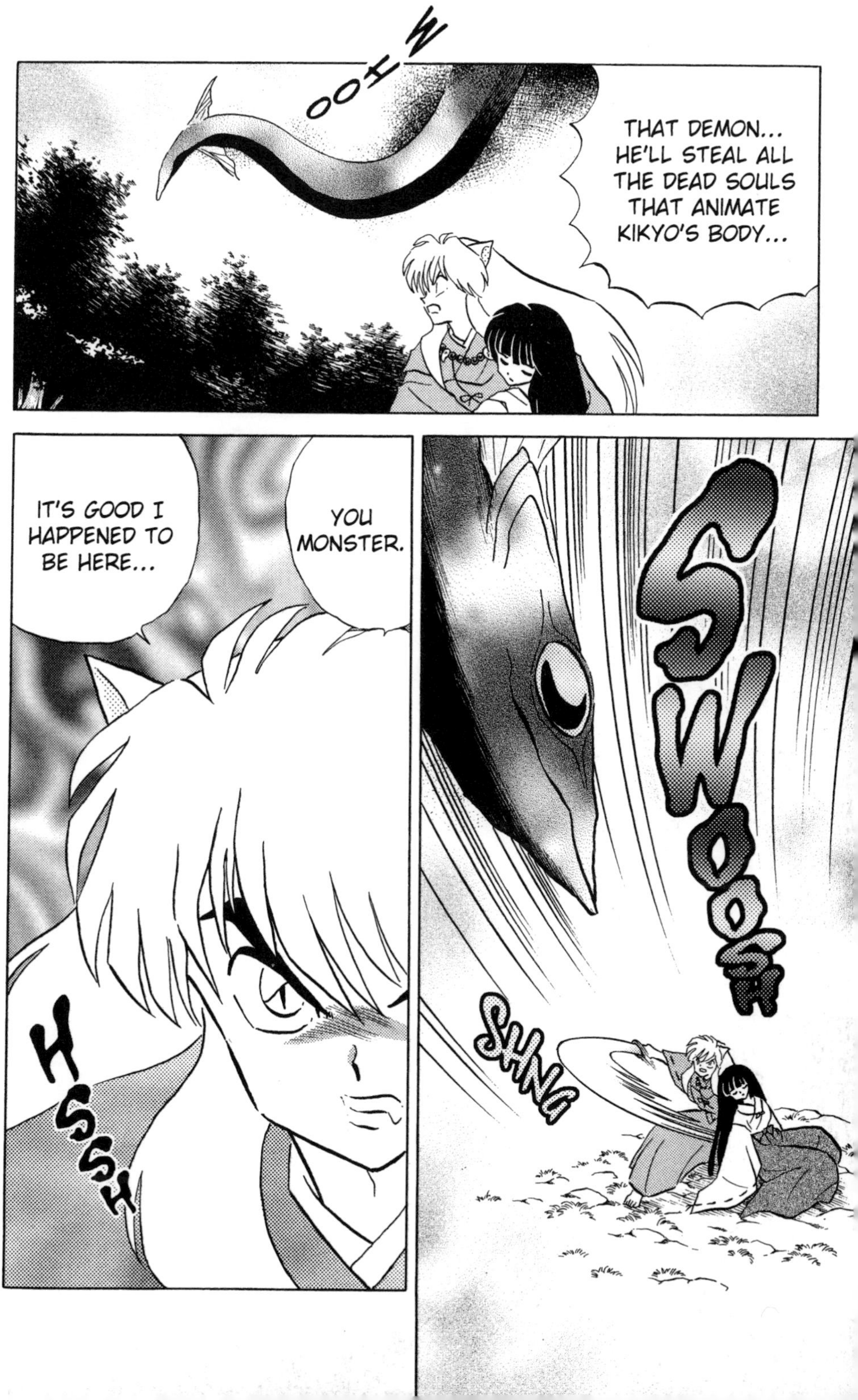
WHOO
THAT DEMON... HE'LL STEAL ALL THE DEAD SOULS THAT ANIMATE KIKYO'S BODY...
SWOOSH
SHNG
YOU MONSTER.
IT'S GOOD I HAPPENED TO BE HERE...
HSSSH

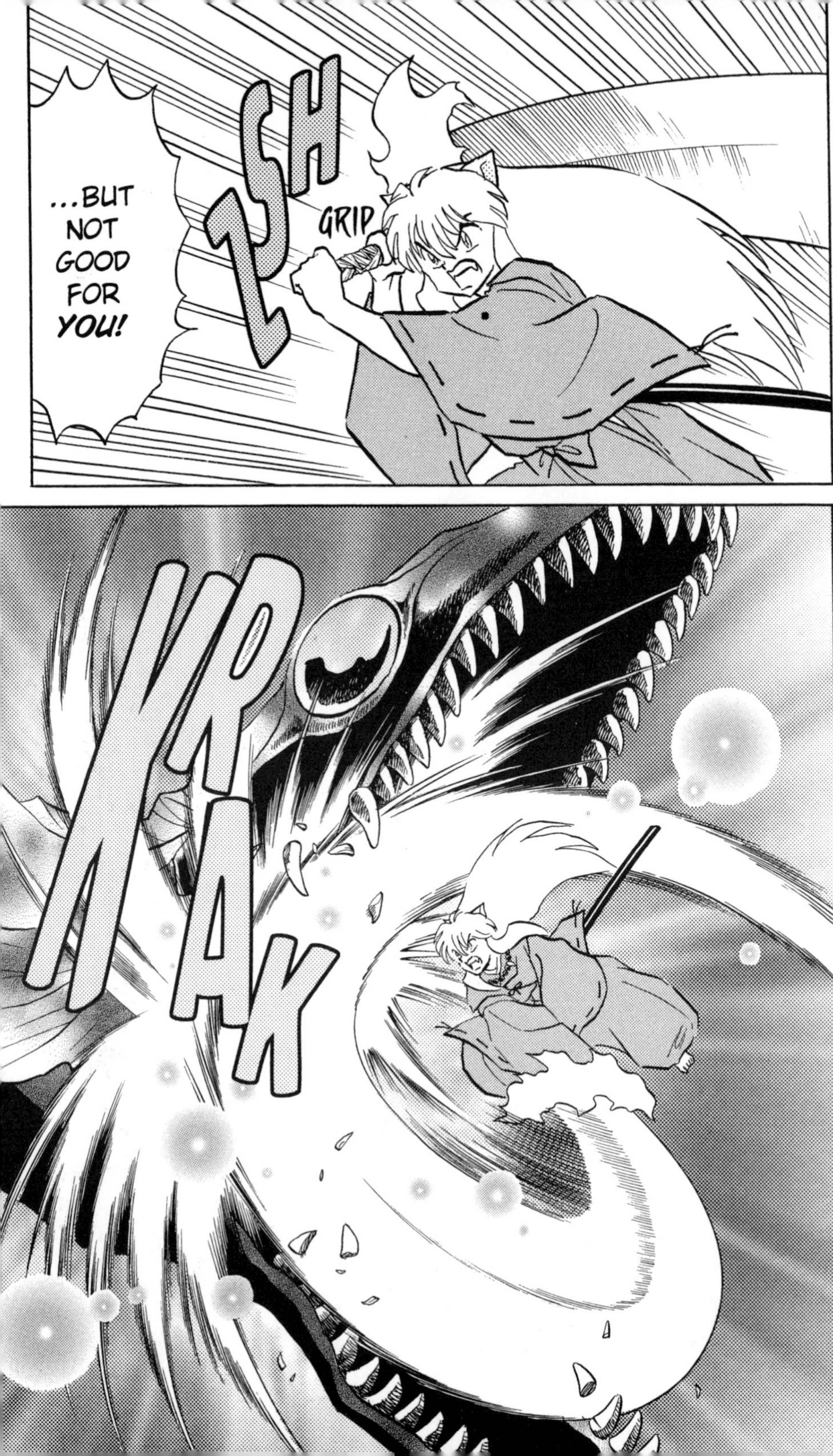
ZSH
GRIP
...BUT NOT GOOD FOR YOU!
KRAK

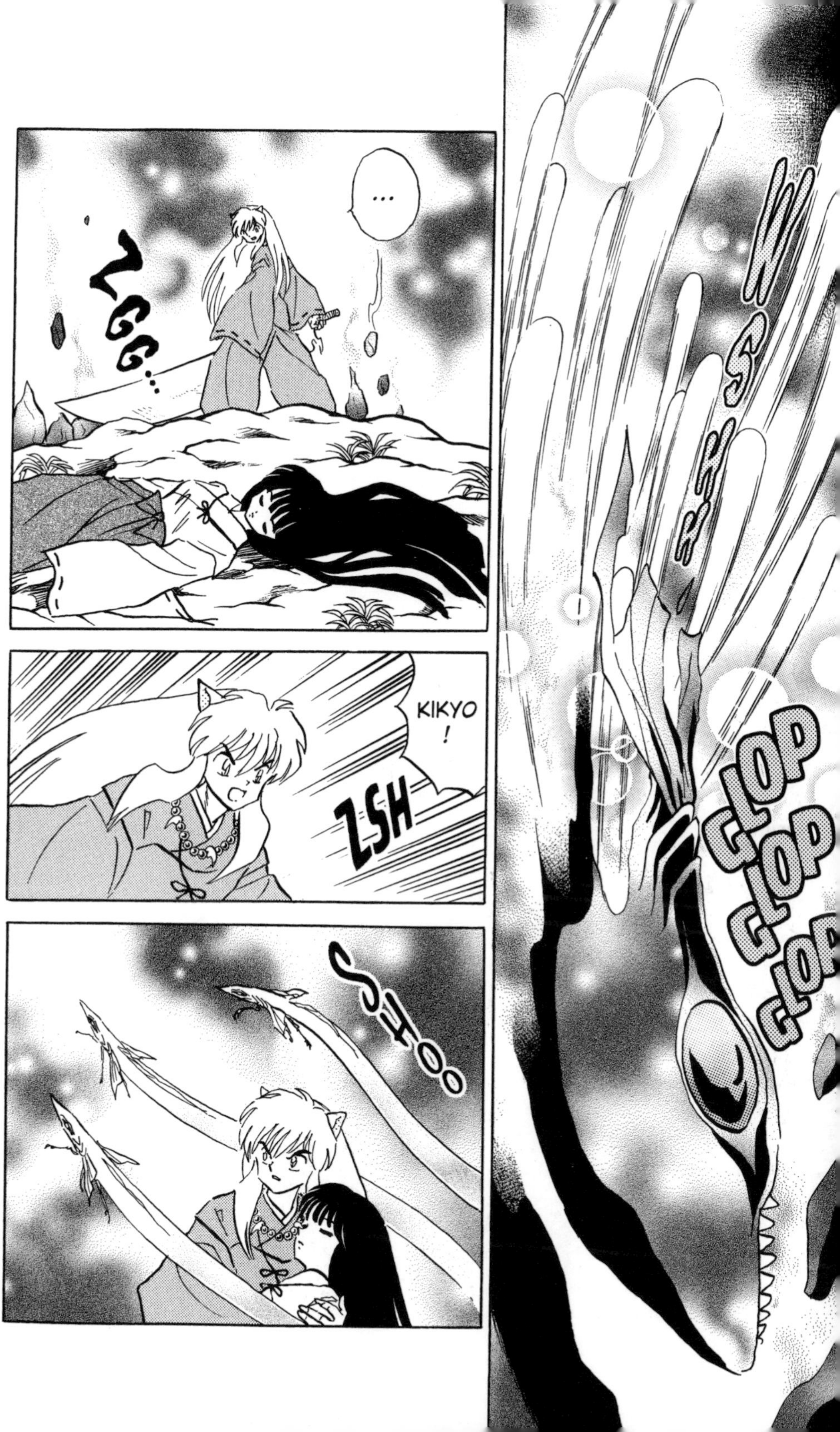
WSHH
GLOP GLOP GLOP
...
ZGG...
KIKYO!
ZSH
SHOO

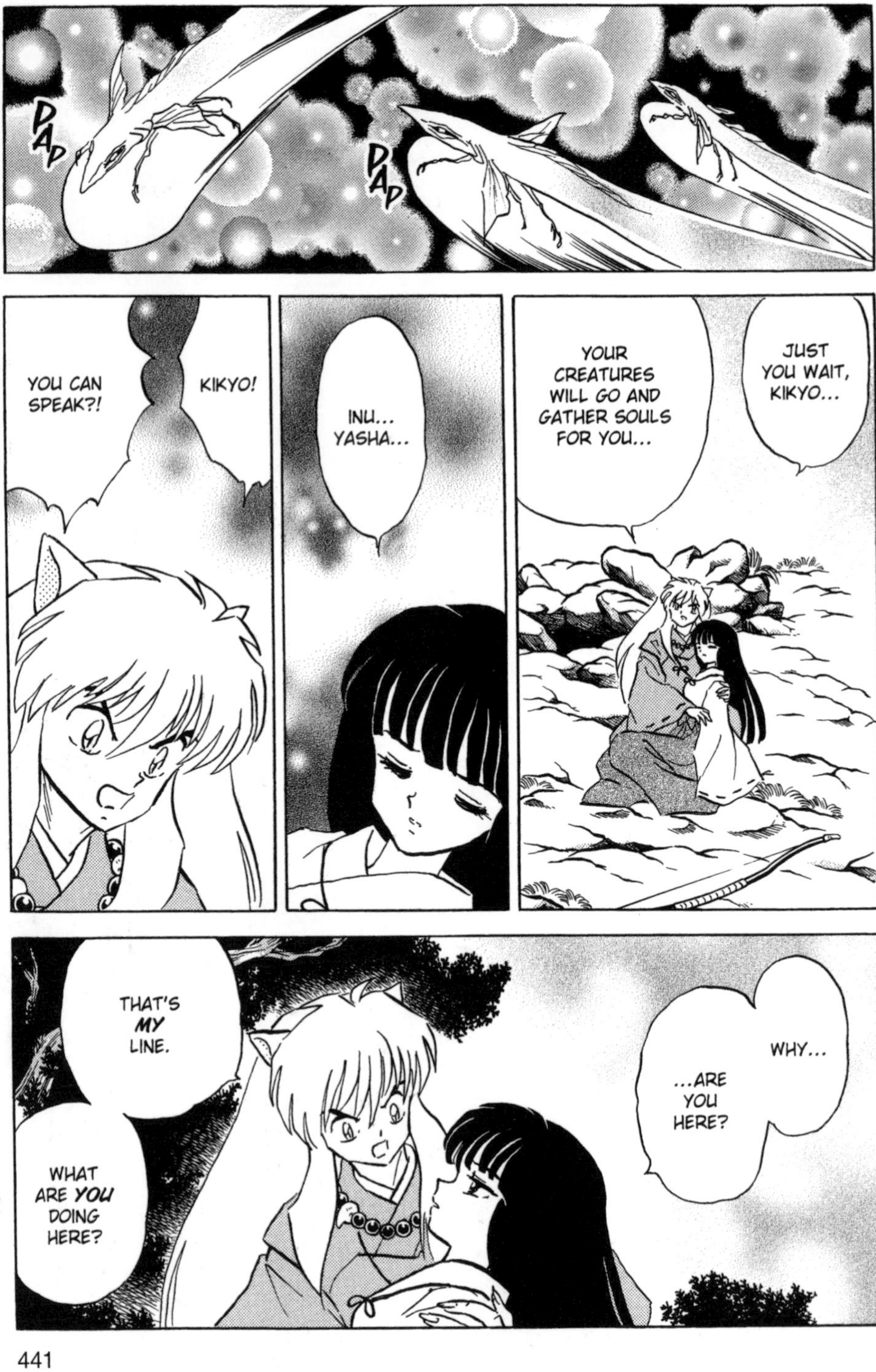
DAP
DAP
JUST YOU WAIT, KIKYO...
YOUR CREATURES WILL GO AND GATHER SOULS FOR YOU...
INU... YASHA...
KIKYO!
YOU CAN SPEAK?!
WHY...
...ARE YOU HERE?
THAT'S **MY** LINE.
WHAT ARE **YOU** DOING HERE?

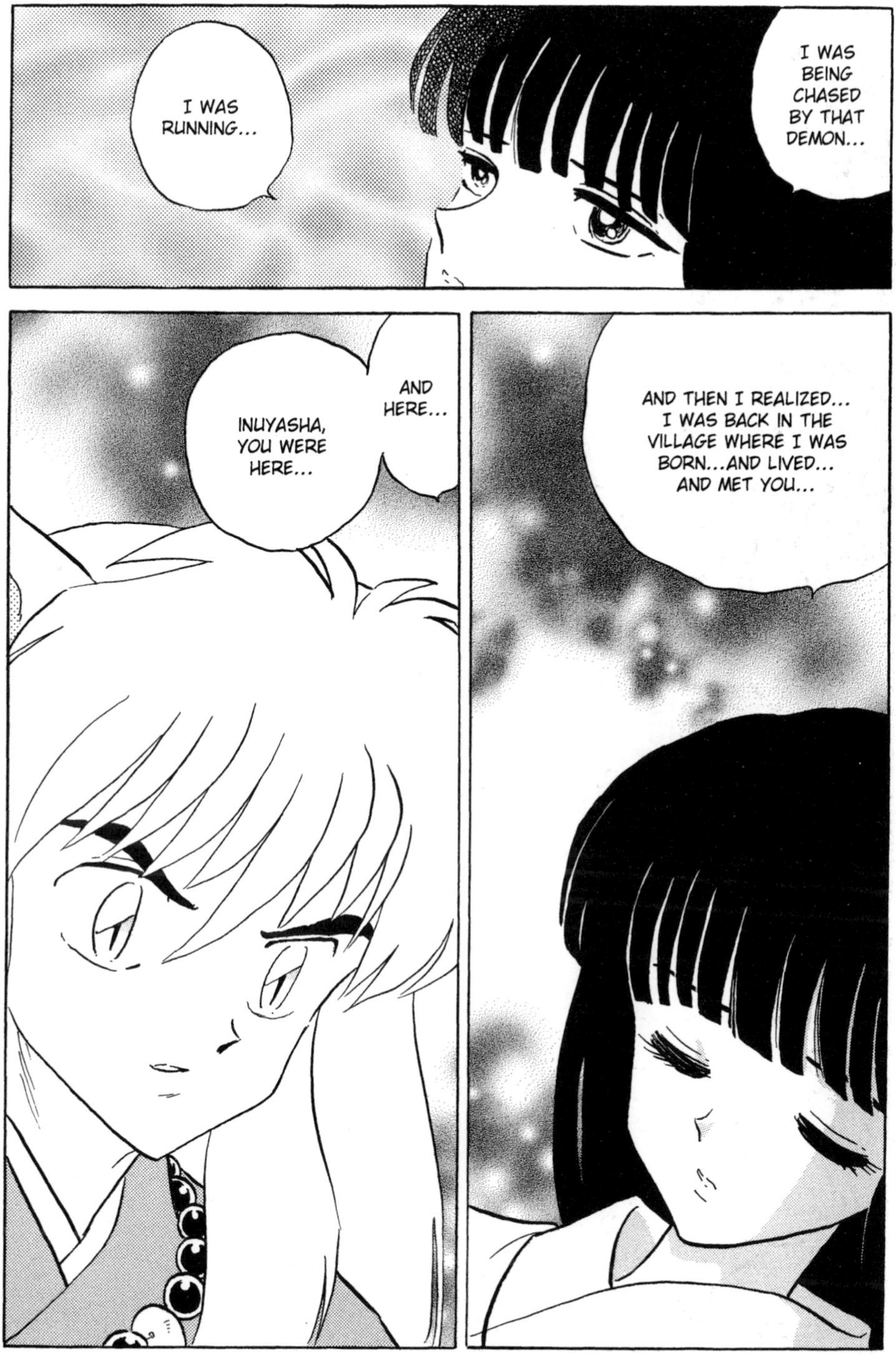
I WAS BEING CHASED BY THAT DEMON...
I WAS RUNNING...
AND THEN I REALIZED... I WAS BACK IN THE VILLAGE WHERE I WAS BORN...AND LIVED... AND MET YOU...
INUYASHA, YOU WERE HERE...
AND HERE...

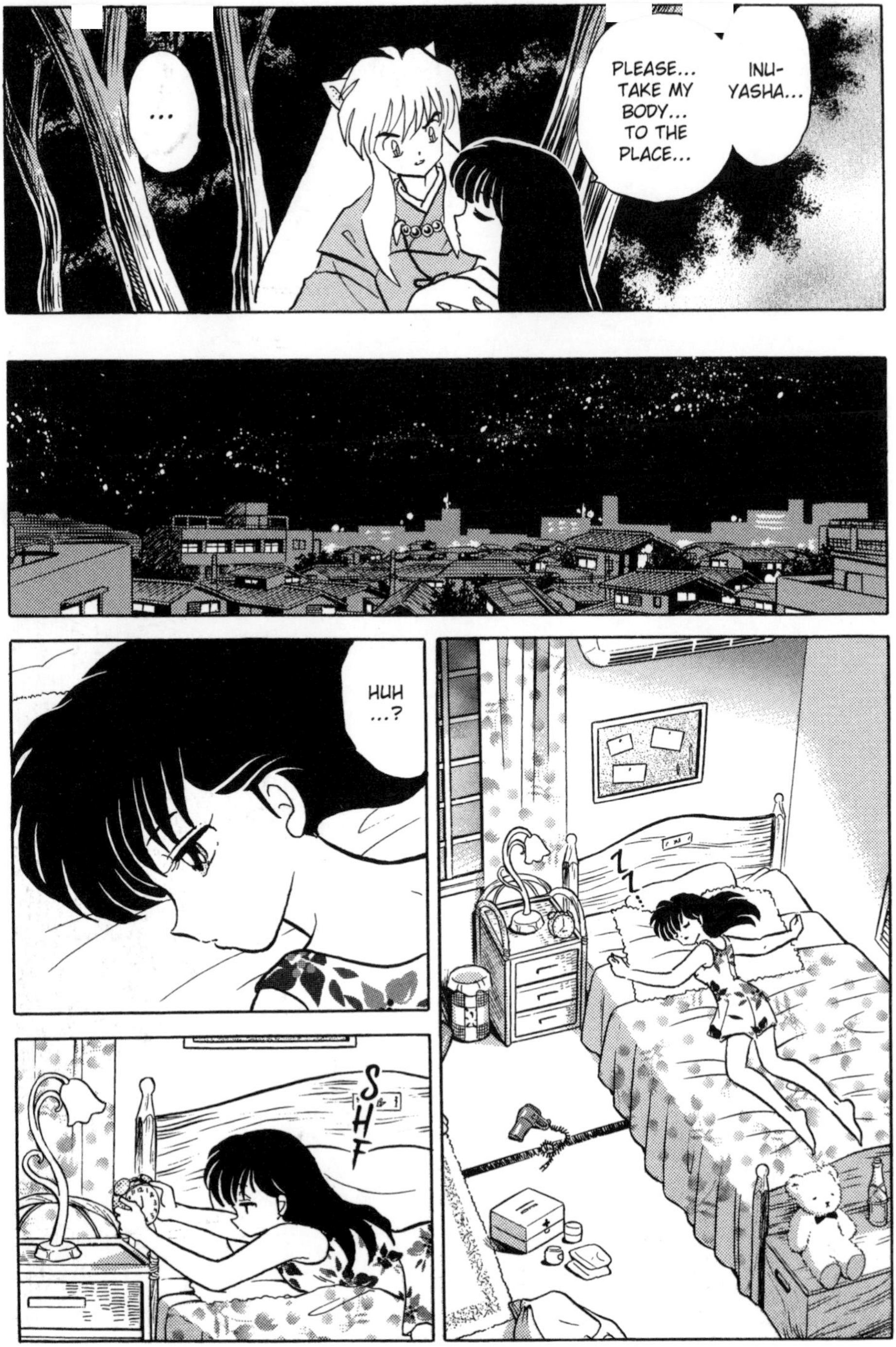
INU-YASHA...
PLEASE... TAKE MY BODY... TO THE PLACE...
...
HUH ...?
SHF

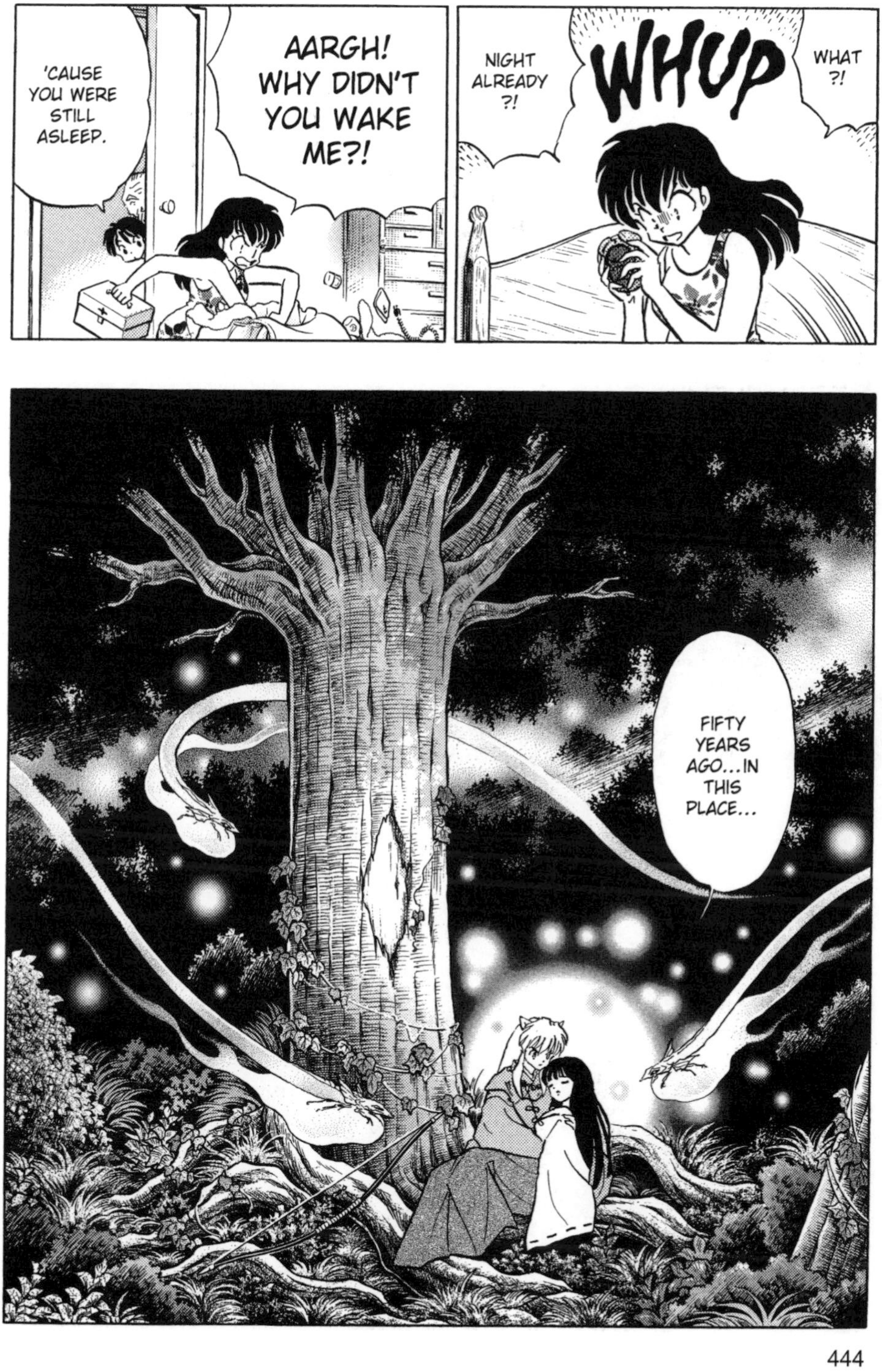
WHAT ?!
WHUP
NIGHT ALREADY ?!
AARGH! WHY DIDN'T YOU WAKE ME?!
'CAUSE YOU WERE STILL ASLEEP.
FIFTY YEARS AGO...IN THIS PLACE...

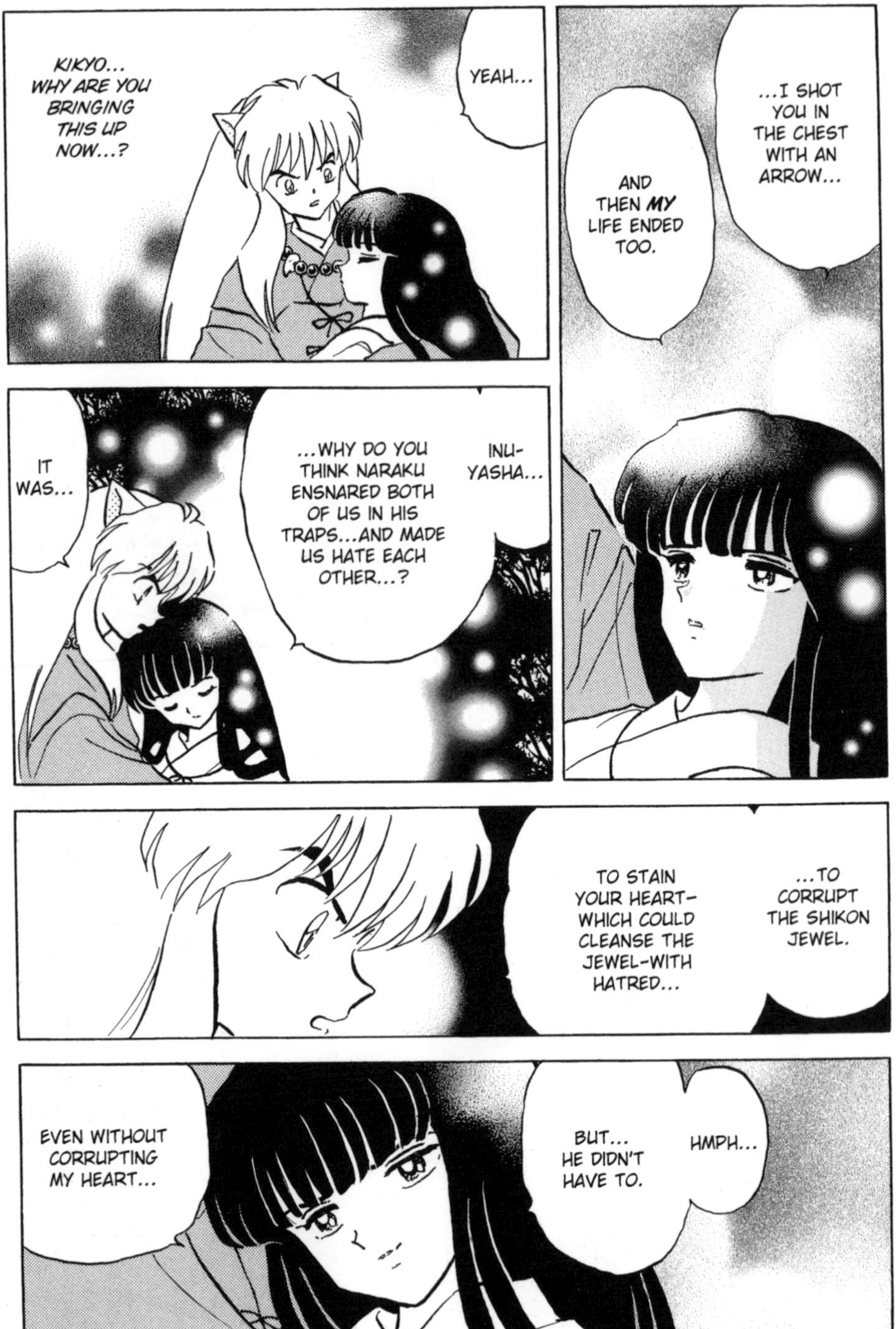
...I SHOT YOU IN THE CHEST WITH AN ARROW...
AND THEN *MY* LIFE ENDED TOO.
YEAH...
KIKYO... WHY ARE YOU BRINGING THIS UP NOW...?
INU-YASHA...
...WHY DO YOU THINK NARAKU ENSNARED BOTH OF US IN HIS TRAPS...AND MADE US HATE EACH OTHER...?
IT WAS...
...TO CORRUPT THE SHIKON JEWEL.
TO STAIN YOUR HEART—WHICH COULD CLEANSE THE JEWEL—WITH HATRED...
HMPH...
BUT... HE DIDN'T HAVE TO.
EVEN WITHOUT CORRUPTING MY HEART...

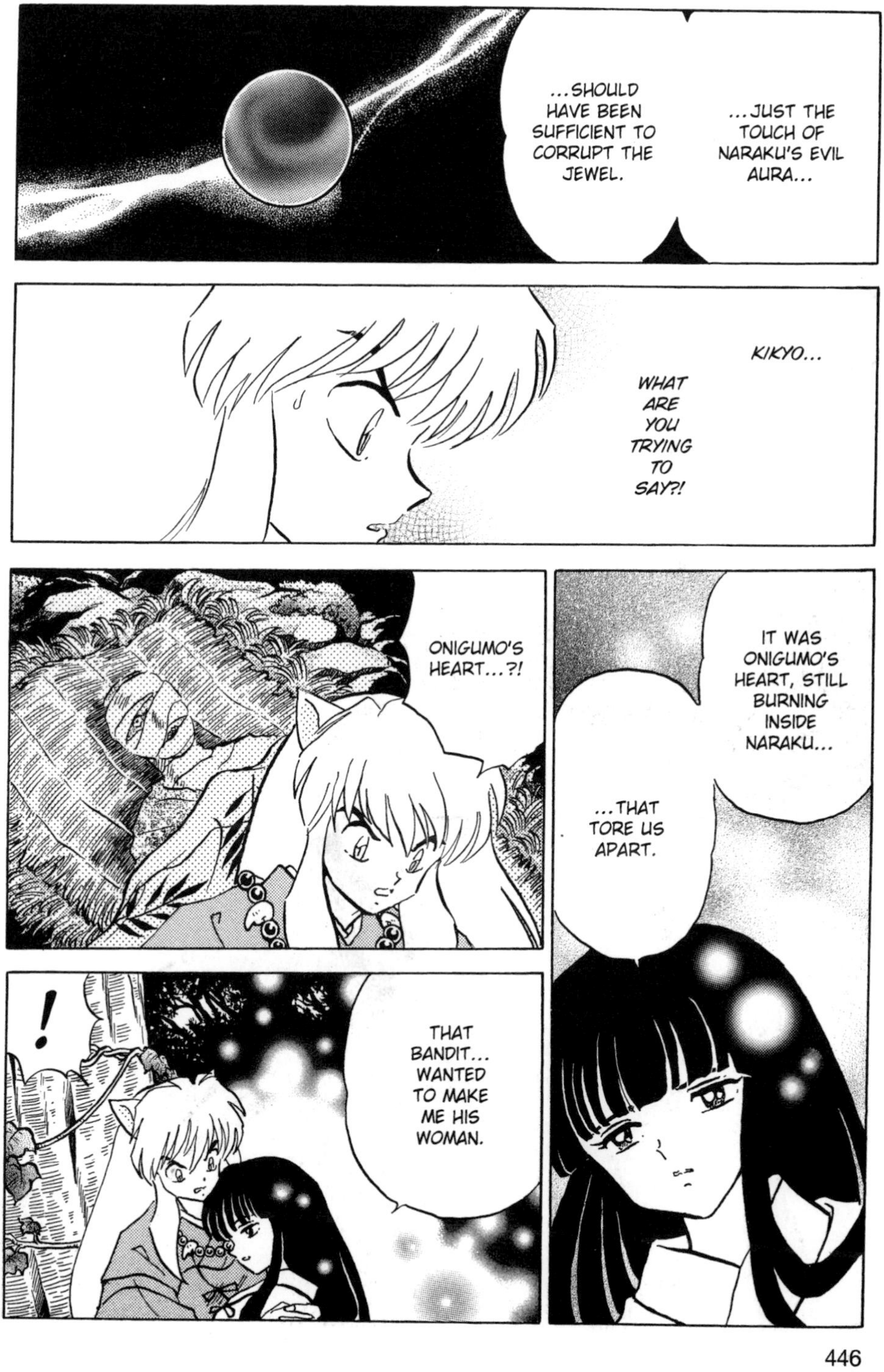
...JUST THE TOUCH OF NARAKU'S EVIL AURA...
...SHOULD HAVE BEEN SUFFICIENT TO CORRUPT THE JEWEL.
KIKYO...
WHAT ARE YOU TRYING TO SAY?!
IT WAS ONIGUMO'S HEART, STILL BURNING INSIDE NARAKU...
...THAT TORE US APART.
ONIGUMO'S HEART...?!
THAT BANDIT... WANTED TO MAKE ME HIS WOMAN.
!

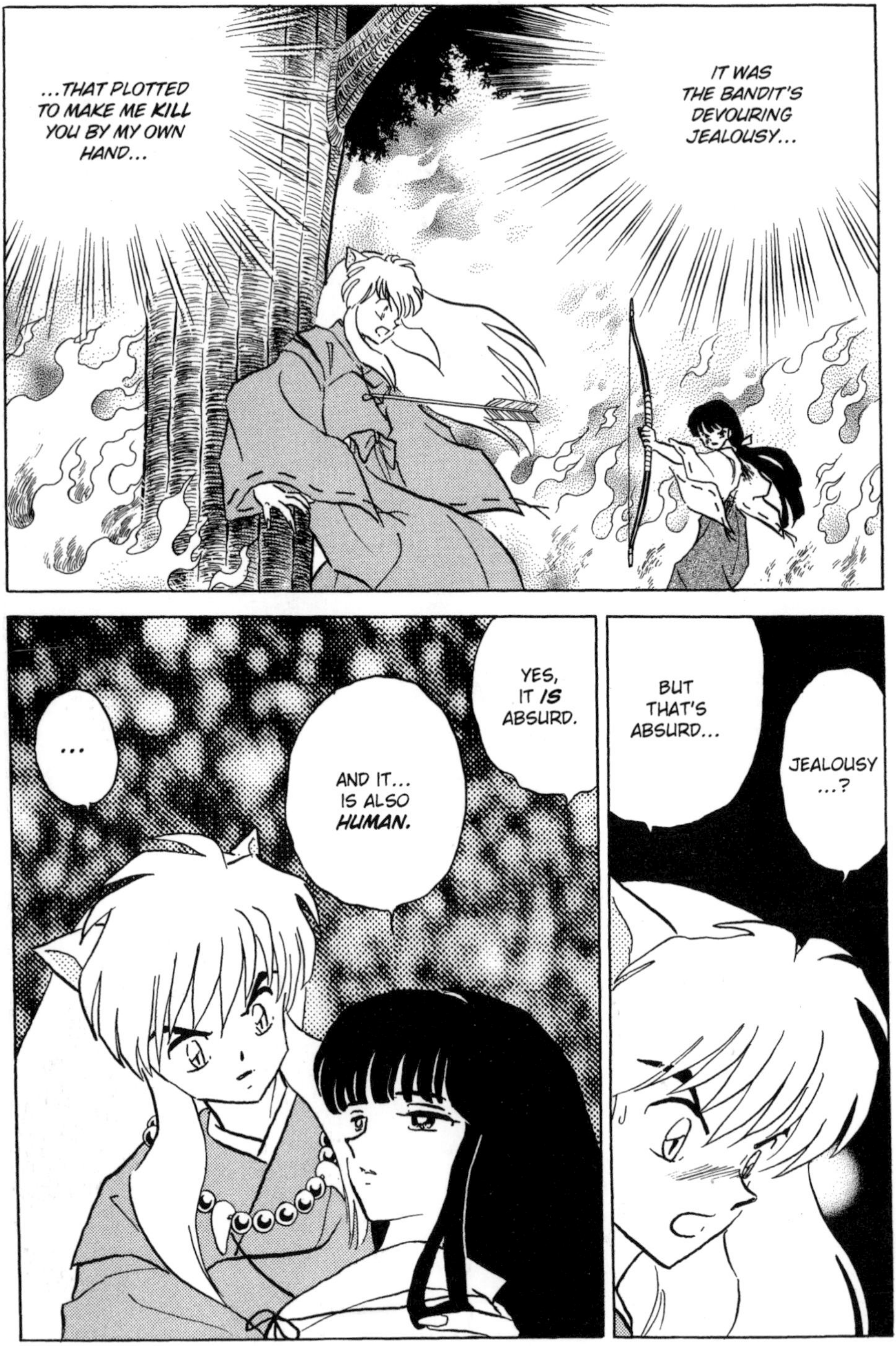
IT WAS THE BANDIT'S DEVOURING JEALOUSY...
...THAT PLOTTED TO MAKE ME KILL YOU BY MY OWN HAND...
JEALOUSY ...?
BUT THAT'S ABSURD...
YES, IT IS ABSURD.
AND IT... IS ALSO HUMAN.
...

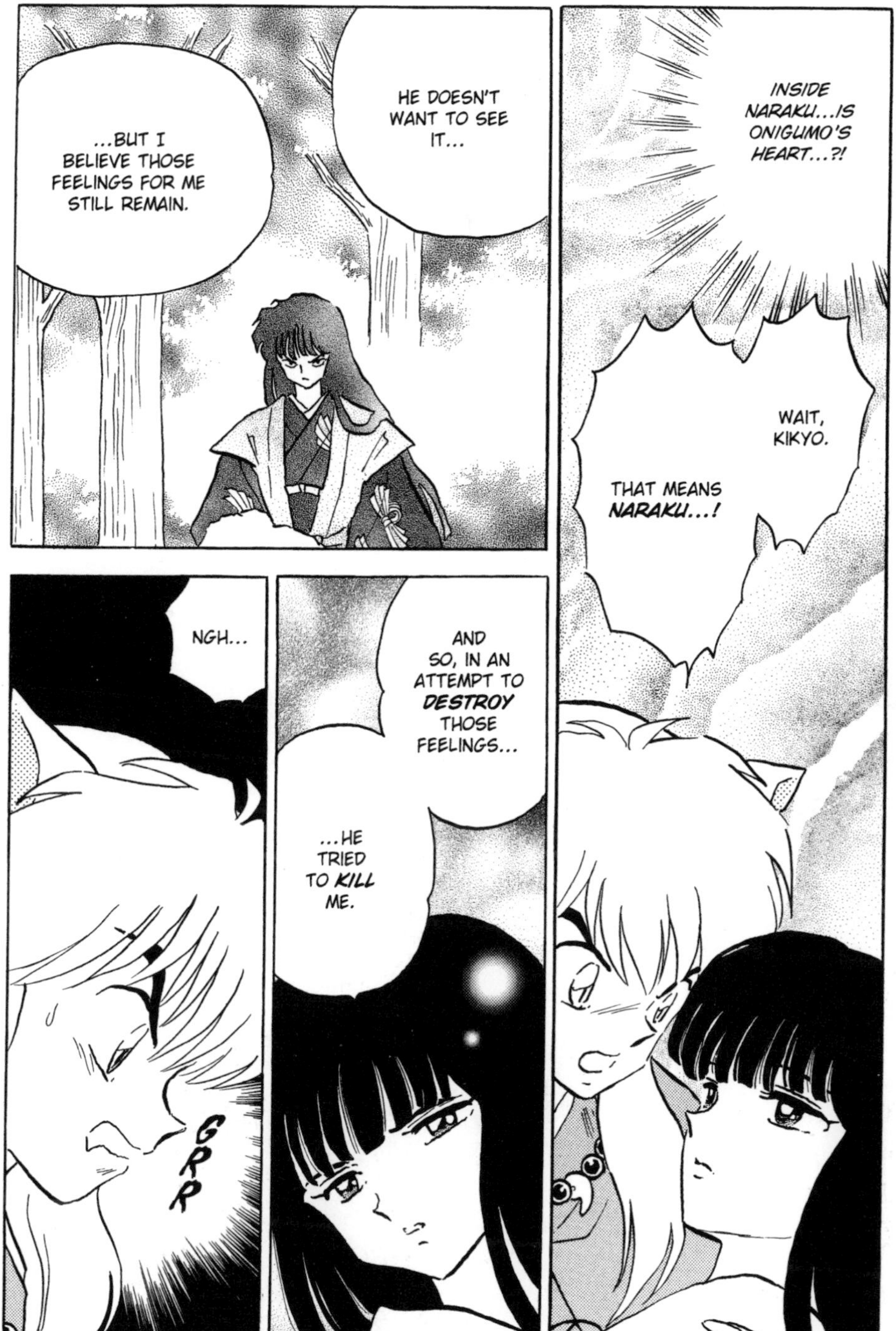

INSIDE NARAKU...IS ONIGUMO'S HEART...?!
WAIT, KIKYO.
THAT MEANS **NARAKU...!**
HE DOESN'T WANT TO SEE IT...
...BUT I BELIEVE THOSE FEELINGS FOR ME STILL REMAIN.
AND SO, IN AN ATTEMPT TO **DESTROY** THOSE FEELINGS...
...HE TRIED TO **KILL** ME.
NGH...
GRR

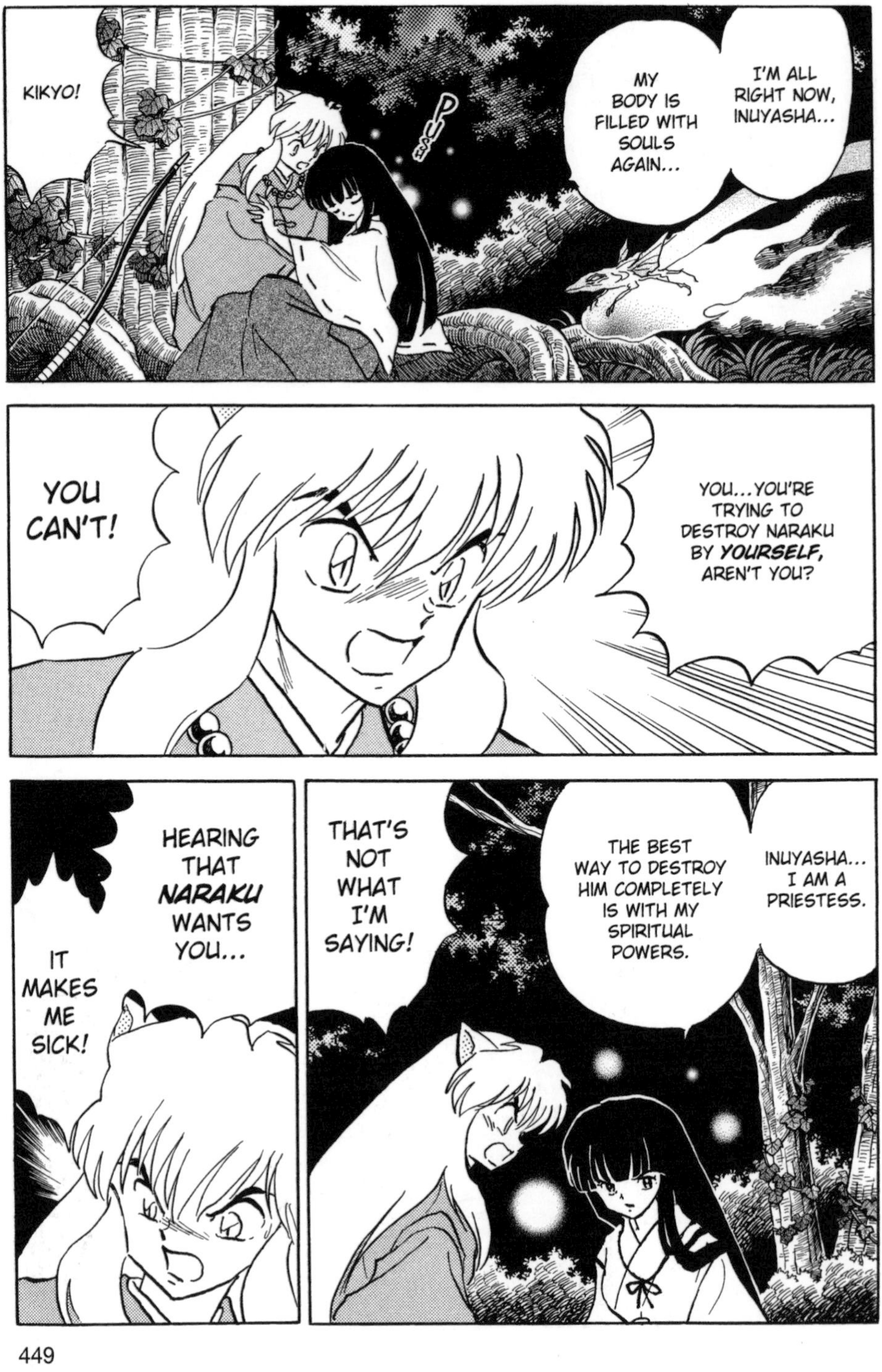
I'M ALL RIGHT NOW, INUYASHA...
MY BODY IS FILLED WITH SOULS AGAIN...
PUSH
KIKYO!
YOU...YOU'RE TRYING TO DESTROY NARAKU BY YOURSELF, AREN'T YOU?
YOU CAN'T!
INUYASHA... I AM A PRIESTESS.
THE BEST WAY TO DESTROY HIM COMPLETELY IS WITH MY SPIRITUAL POWERS.
THAT'S NOT WHAT I'M SAYING!
HEARING THAT NARAKU WANTS YOU...
IT MAKES ME SICK!

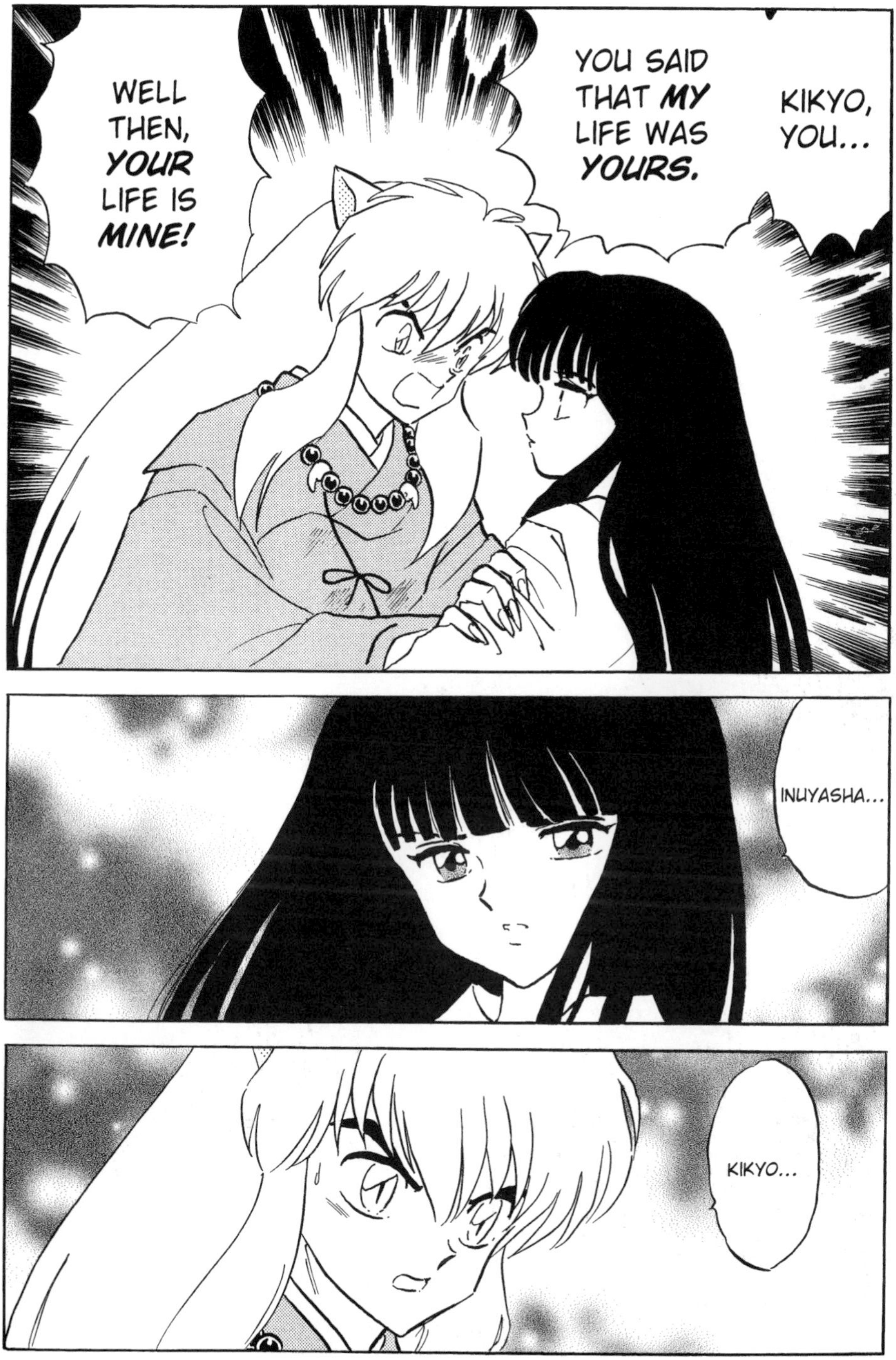
KIKYO, YOU...
YOU SAID THAT MY LIFE WAS YOURS.
WELL THEN, YOUR LIFE IS MINE!
INUYASHA...
KIKYO...

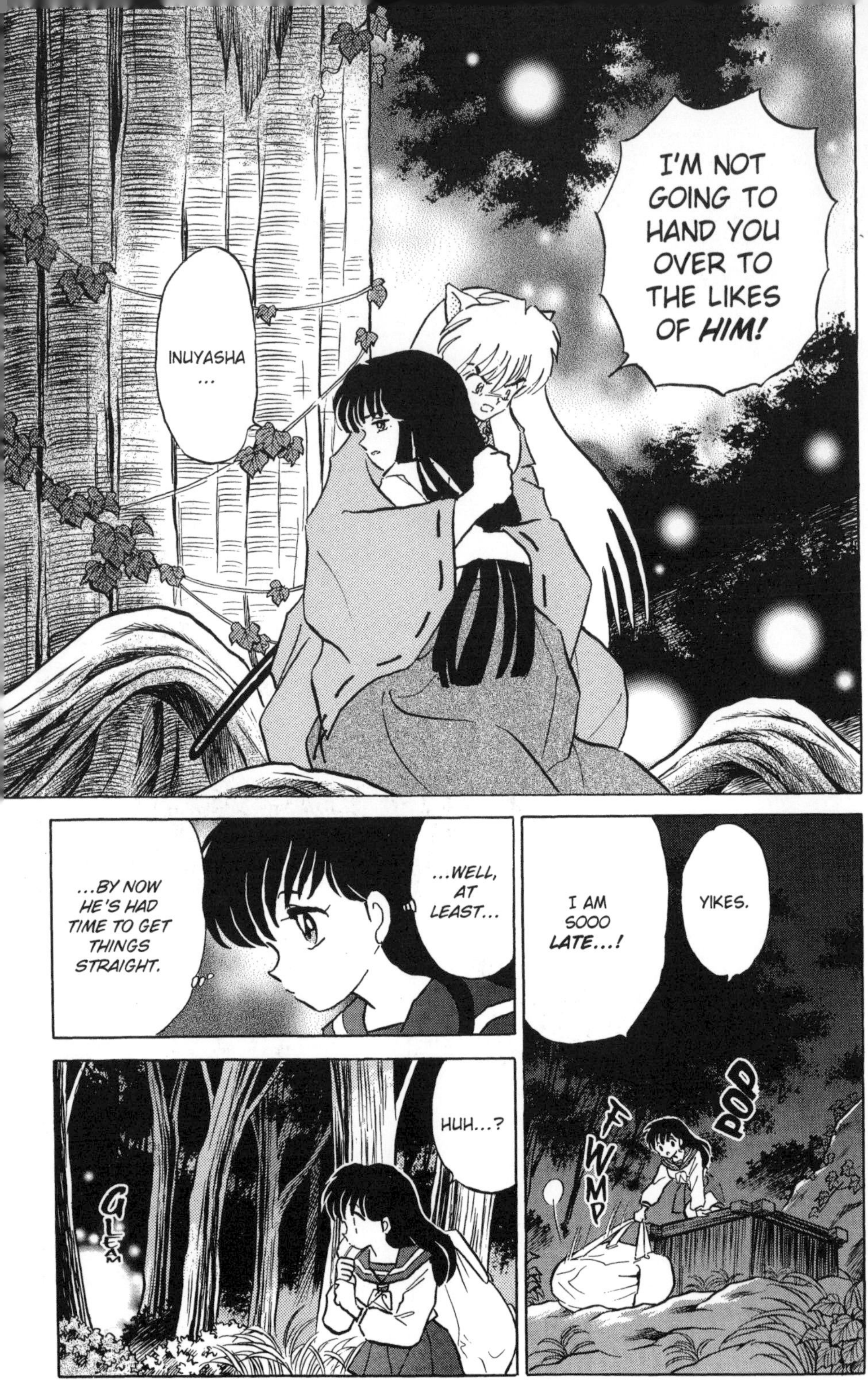

I'M NOT GOING TO HAND YOU OVER TO THE LIKES OF *HIM!*
INUYASHA ...
YIKES.
I AM SOOO *LATE...!*
POP
FWMP
...WELL, AT LEAST...
...BY NOW HE'S HAD TIME TO GET THINGS STRAIGHT.
HUH...?
GLEAM

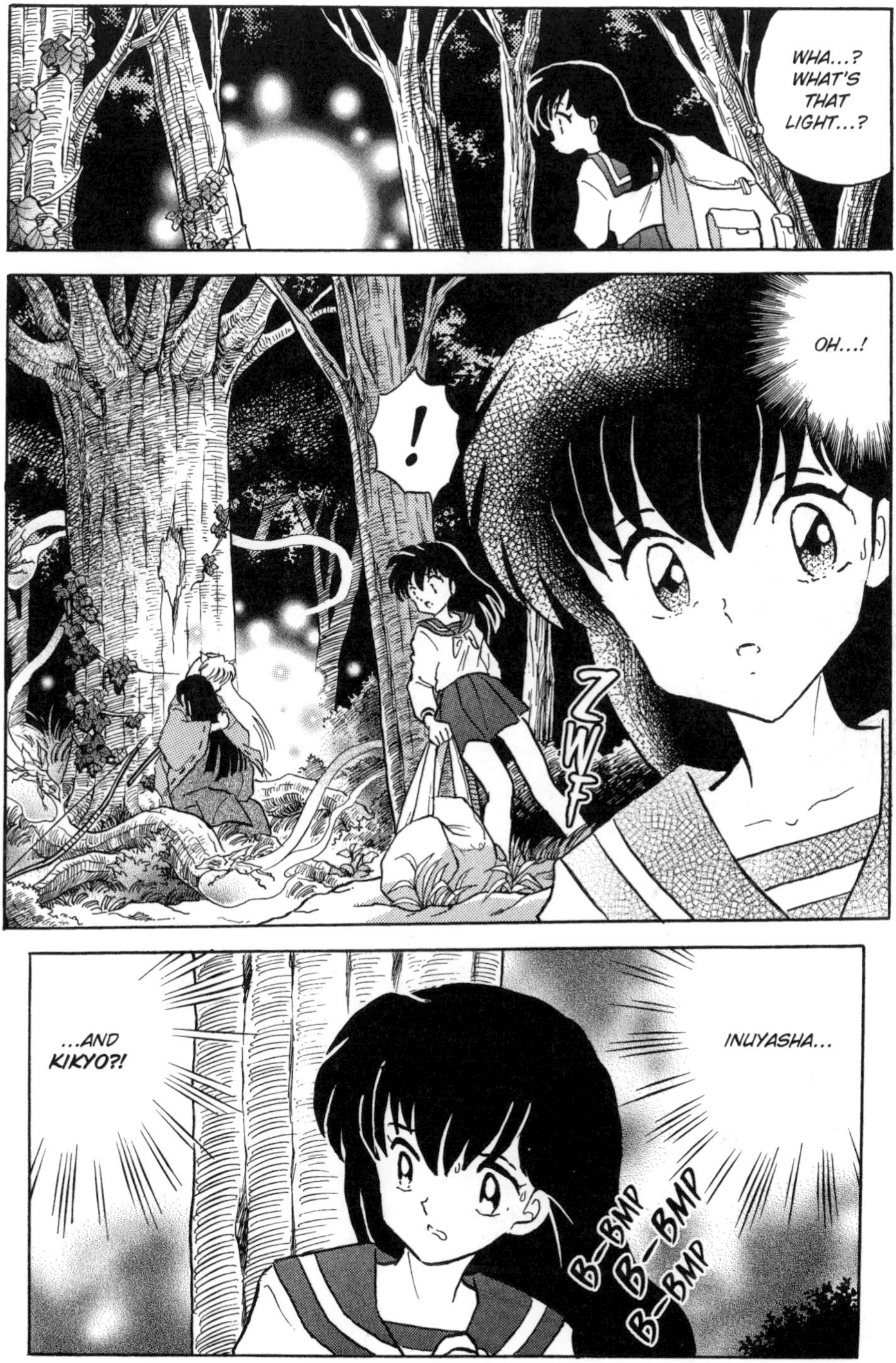
WHA...? WHAT'S THAT LIGHT...?
OH...!
!
ZWF
INUYASHA...
...AND KIKYO?!
B-BMP B-BMP B-BMP

SCROLL FIVE
JEALOUSY

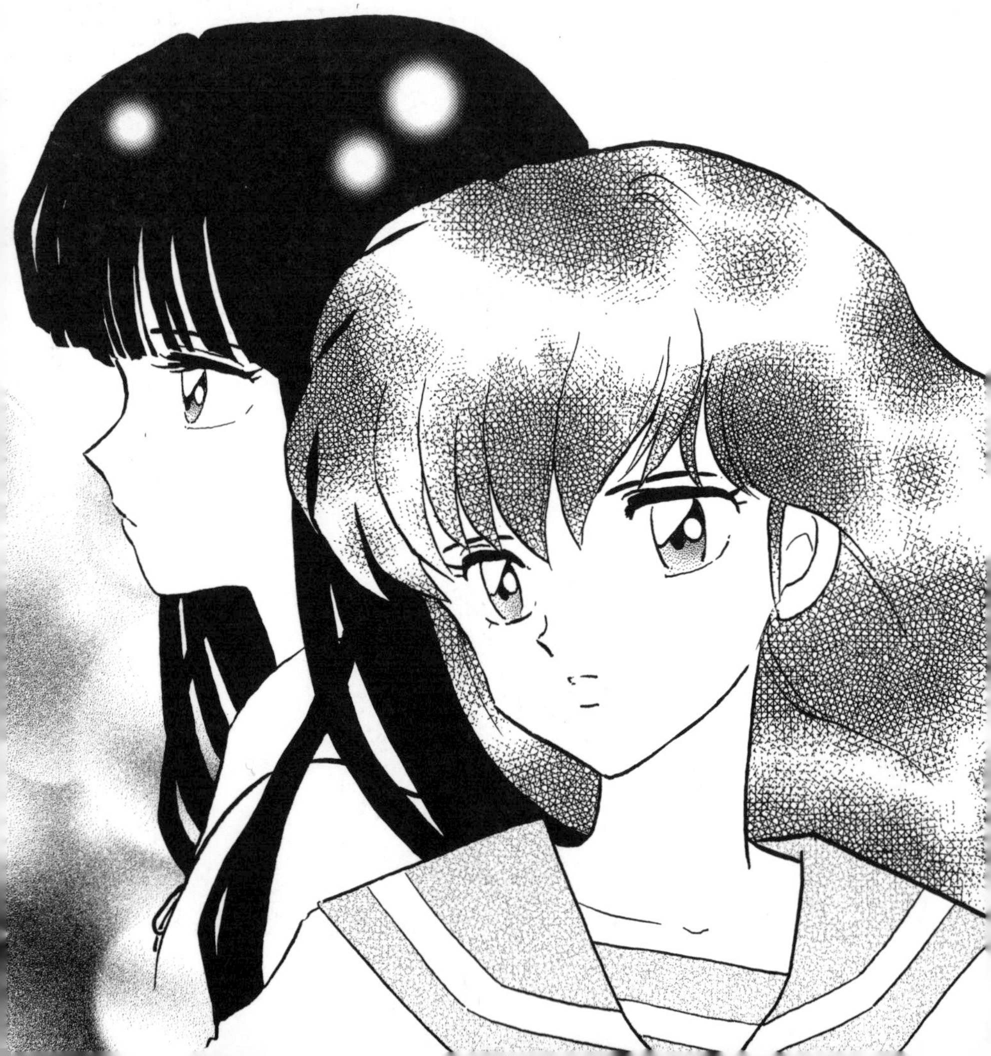

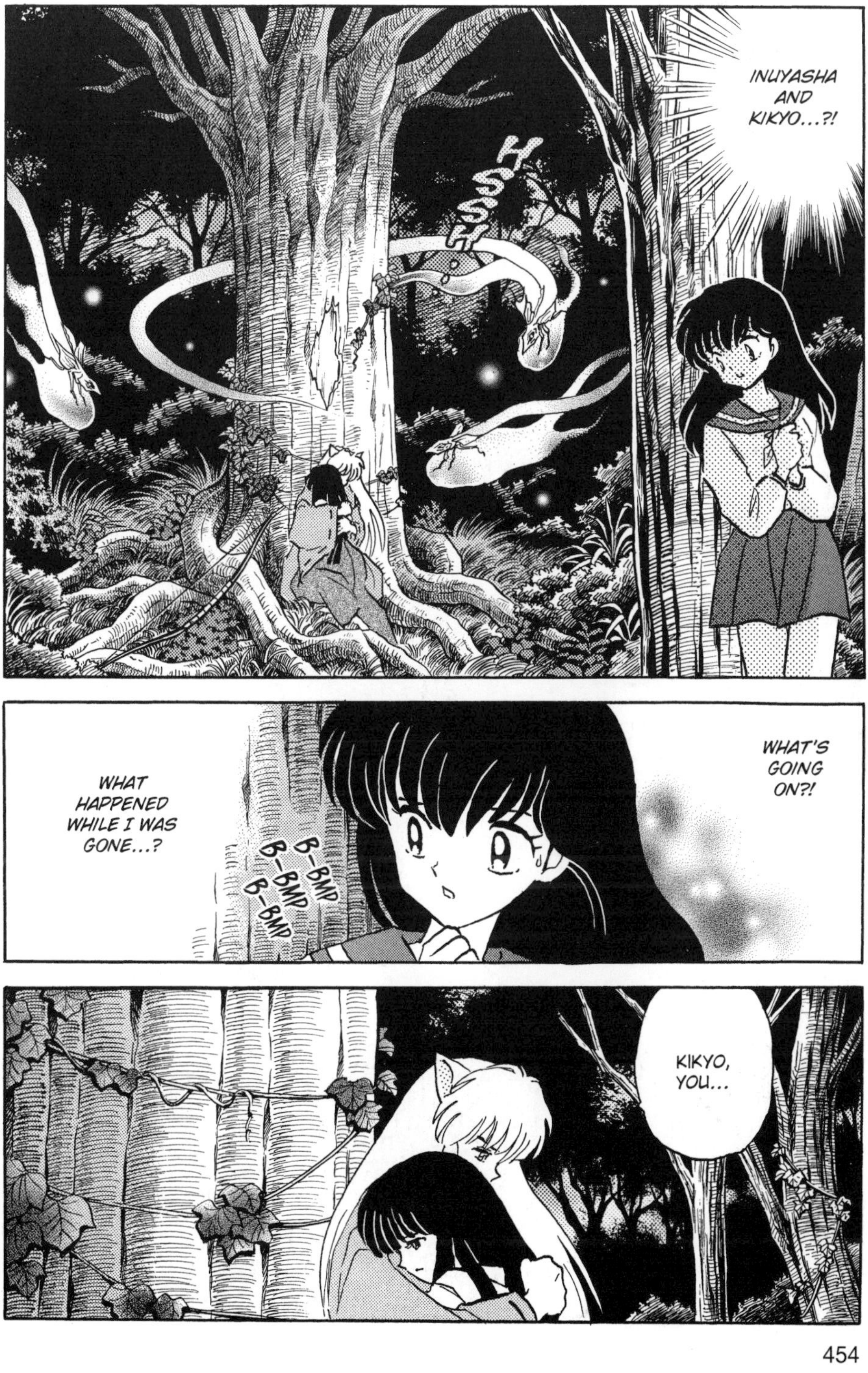
HSSSH
INUYASHA AND KIKYO...?!
WHAT'S GOING ON?!
WHAT HAPPENED WHILE I WAS GONE...?
B-BMP B-BMP B-BMP
KIKYO, YOU...

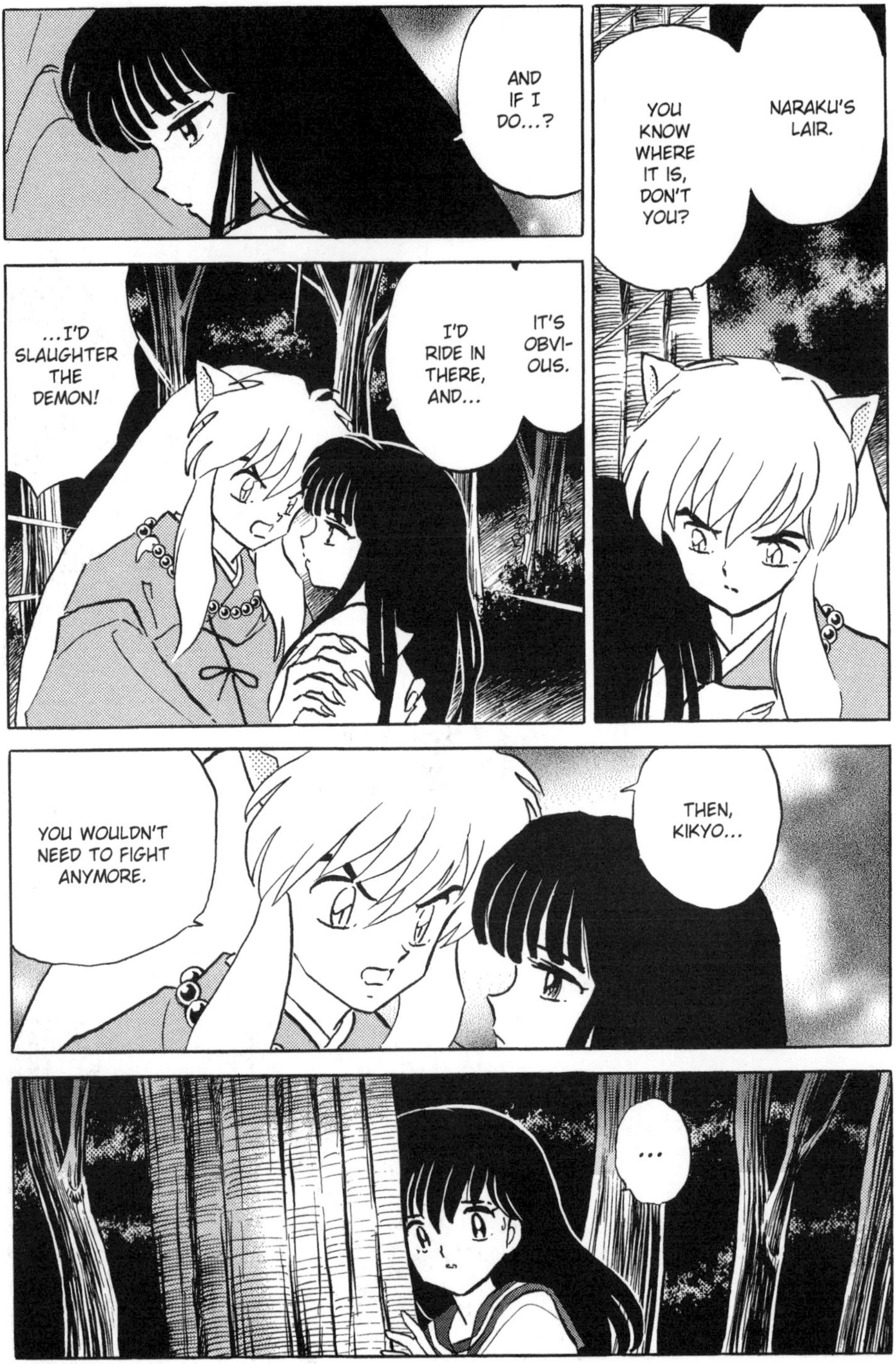
NARAKU'S LAIR.
YOU KNOW WHERE IT IS, DON'T YOU?
AND IF I DO...?
IT'S OBVIOUS.
I'D RIDE IN THERE, AND...
...I'D SLAUGHTER THE DEMON!
THEN, KIKYO...
YOU WOULDN'T NEED TO FIGHT ANYMORE.
...

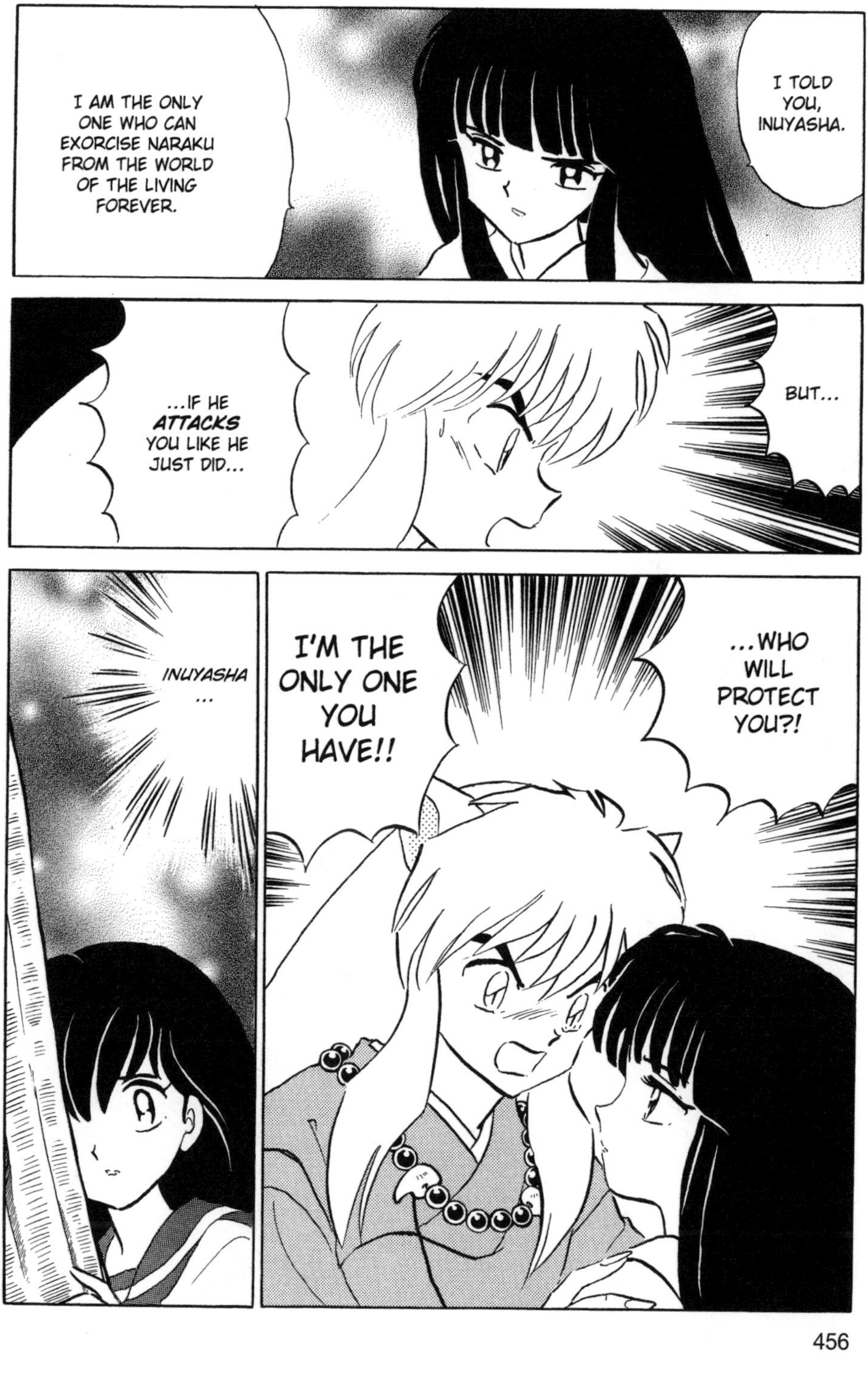
I TOLD YOU, INUYASHA.
I AM THE ONLY ONE WHO CAN EXORCISE NARAKU FROM THE WORLD OF THE LIVING FOREVER.
BUT...
...IF HE **ATTACKS** YOU LIKE HE JUST DID...
...WHO WILL PROTECT YOU?!
I'M THE ONLY ONE YOU HAVE!!
INUYASHA ...

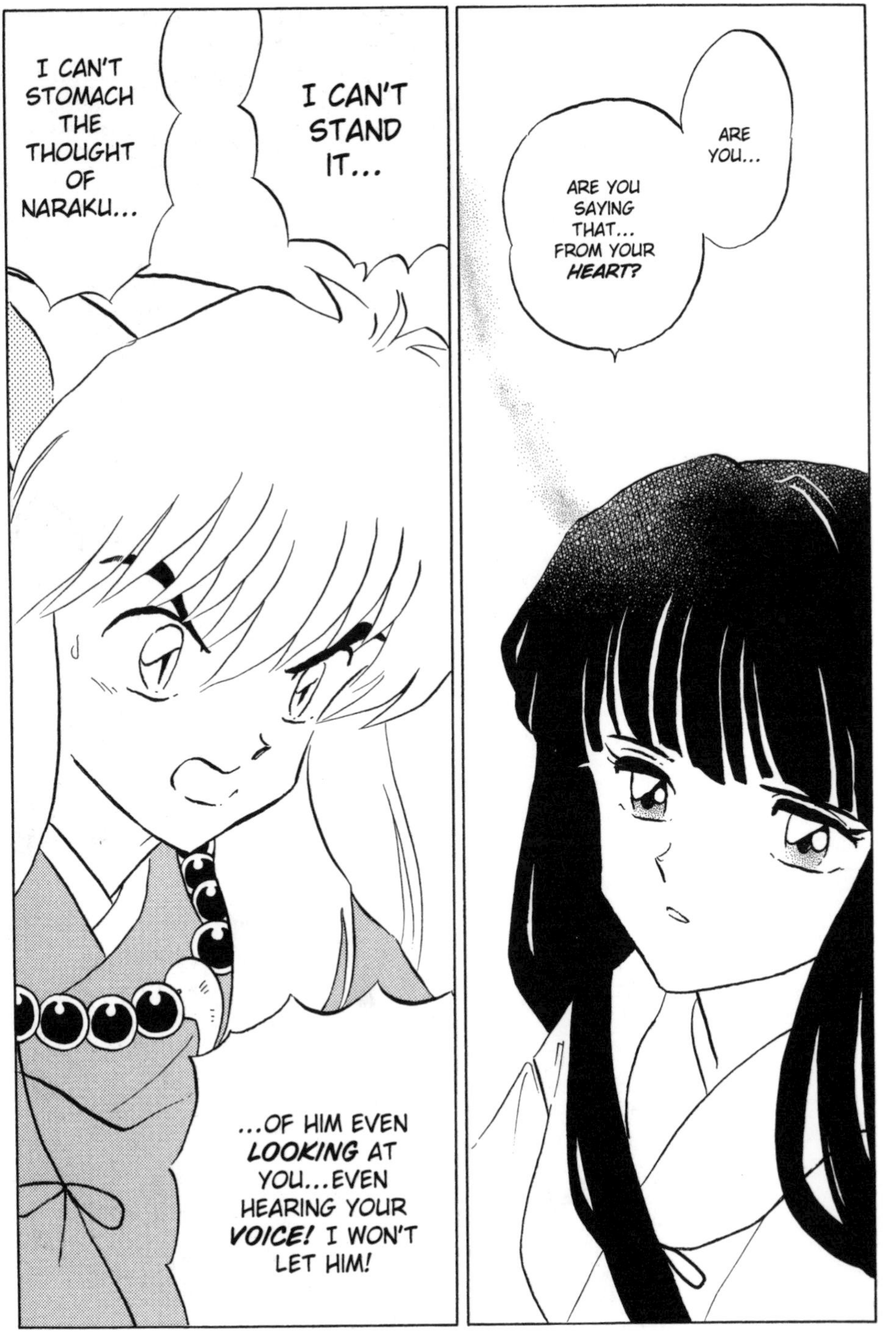
ARE YOU...
ARE YOU SAYING THAT... FROM YOUR *HEART?*
I CAN'T STAND IT...
I CAN'T STOMACH THE THOUGHT OF NARAKU...
...OF HIM EVEN *LOOKING* AT YOU...EVEN HEARING YOUR *VOICE!* I WON'T LET HIM!

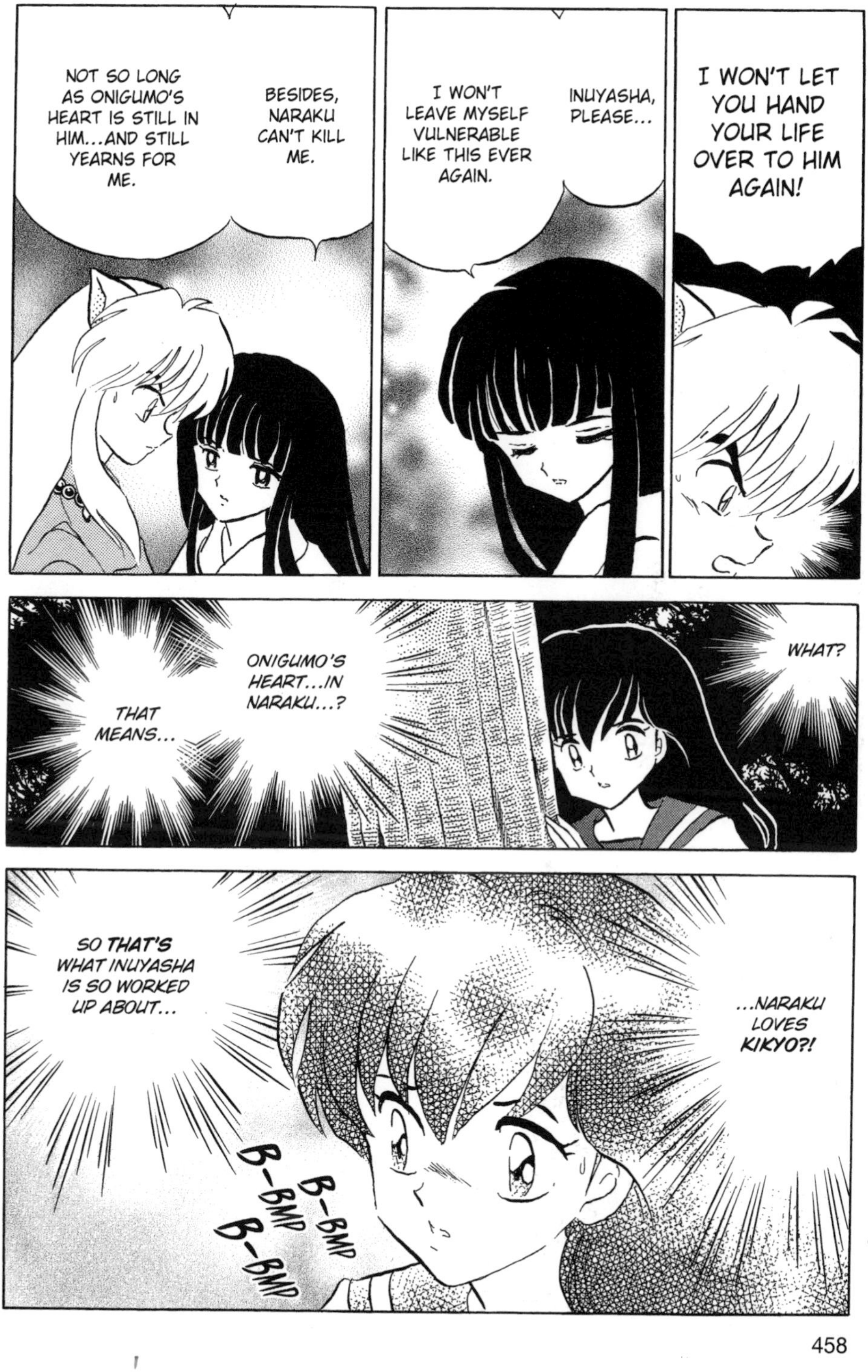
I WON'T LET YOU HAND YOUR LIFE OVER TO HIM AGAIN!
INUYASHA, PLEASE...
I WON'T LEAVE MYSELF VULNERABLE LIKE THIS EVER AGAIN.
BESIDES, NARAKU CAN'T KILL ME.
NOT SO LONG AS ONIGUMO'S HEART IS STILL IN HIM...AND STILL YEARNS FOR ME.
WHAT?
ONIGUMO'S HEART...IN NARAKU...?
THAT MEANS...
...NARAKU LOVES KIKYO?!
SO THAT'S WHAT INUYASHA IS SO WORKED UP ABOUT...
B-BMP
B-BMP
B-BMP

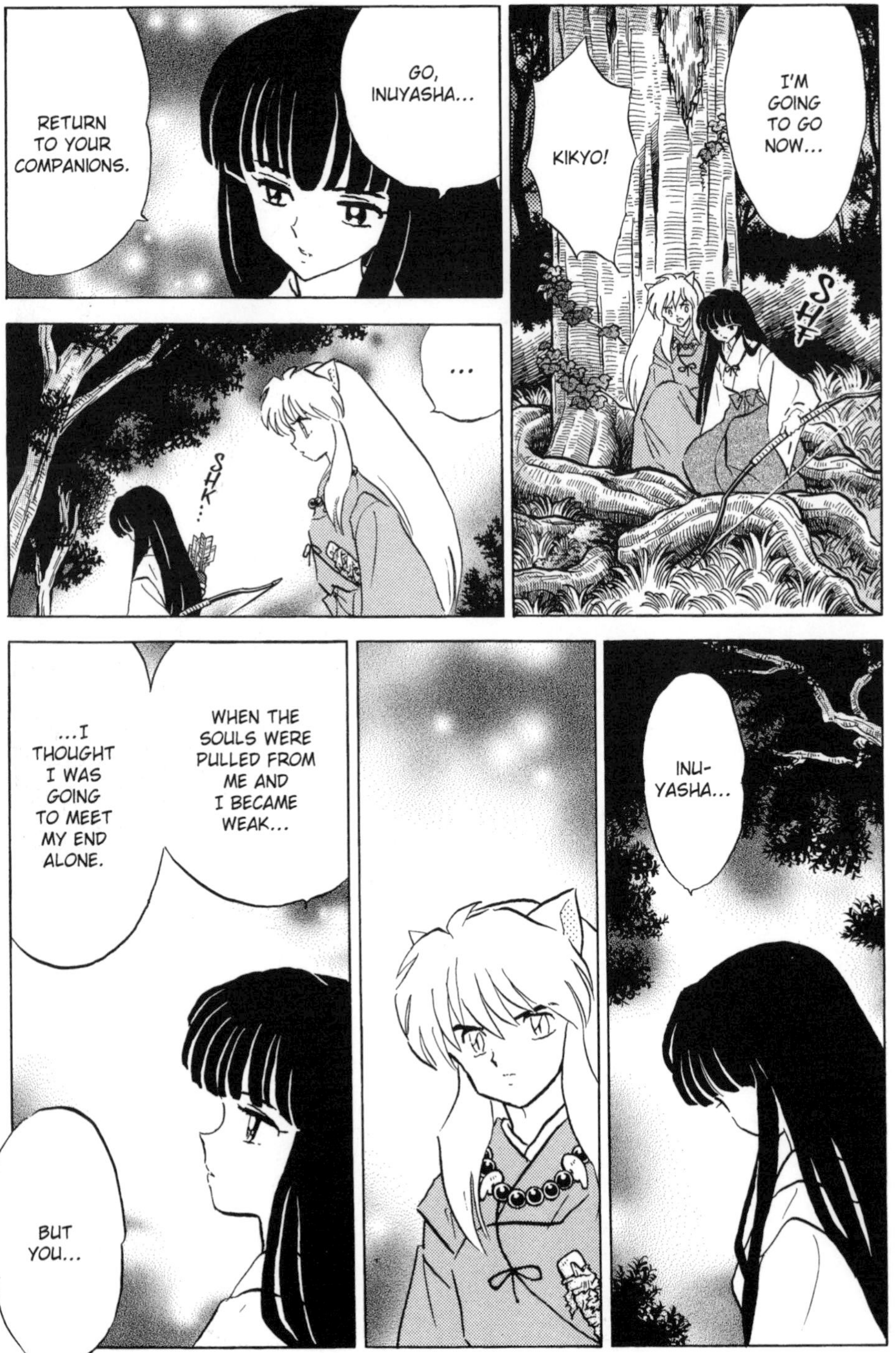
I'M GOING TO GO NOW...
KIKYO!
SHK
GO, INUYASHA...
RETURN TO YOUR COMPANIONS.
...
SHK...
INU-YASHA...
WHEN THE SOULS WERE PULLED FROM ME AND I BECAME WEAK...
...I THOUGHT I WAS GOING TO MEET MY END ALONE.
BUT YOU...

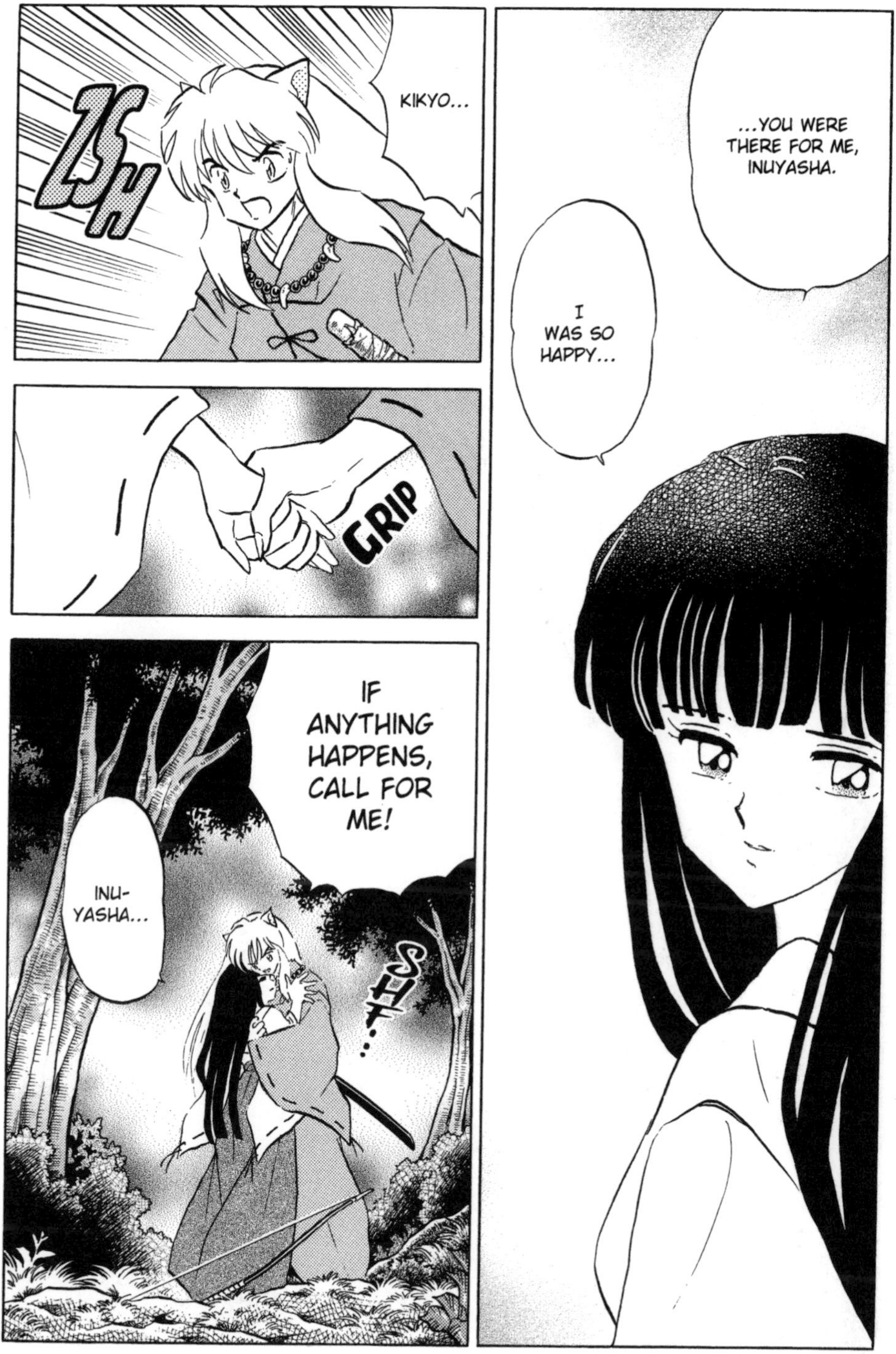
...YOU WERE THERE FOR ME, INUYASHA.
I WAS SO HAPPY...
KIKYO...
ZSH
GRIP
IF ANYTHING HAPPENS, CALL FOR ME!
SHF...
INU-YASHA...

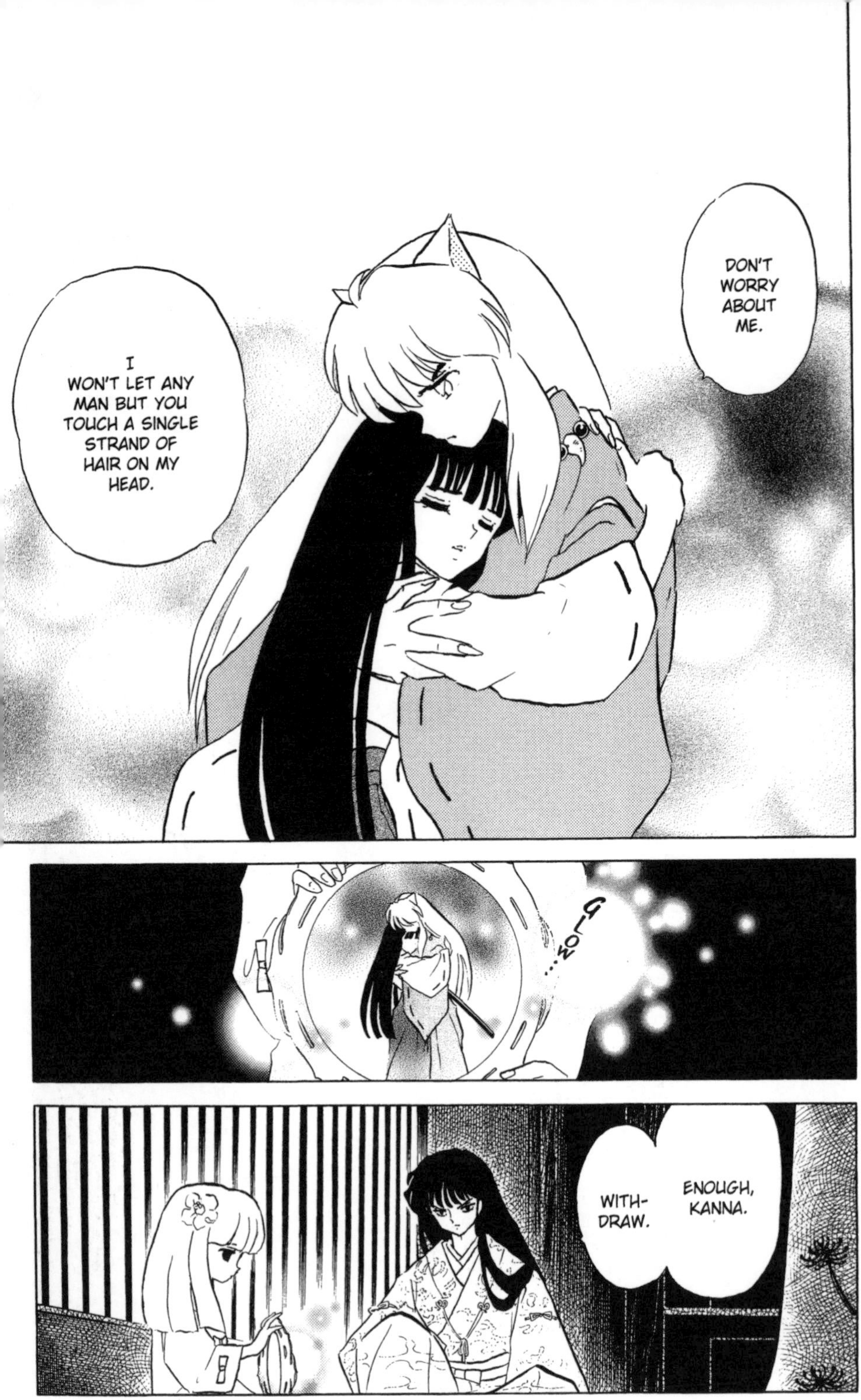
DON'T WORRY ABOUT ME.
I WON'T LET ANY MAN BUT YOU TOUCH A SINGLE STRAND OF HAIR ON MY HEAD.
GLOW...
ENOUGH, KANNA.
WITH-DRAW.

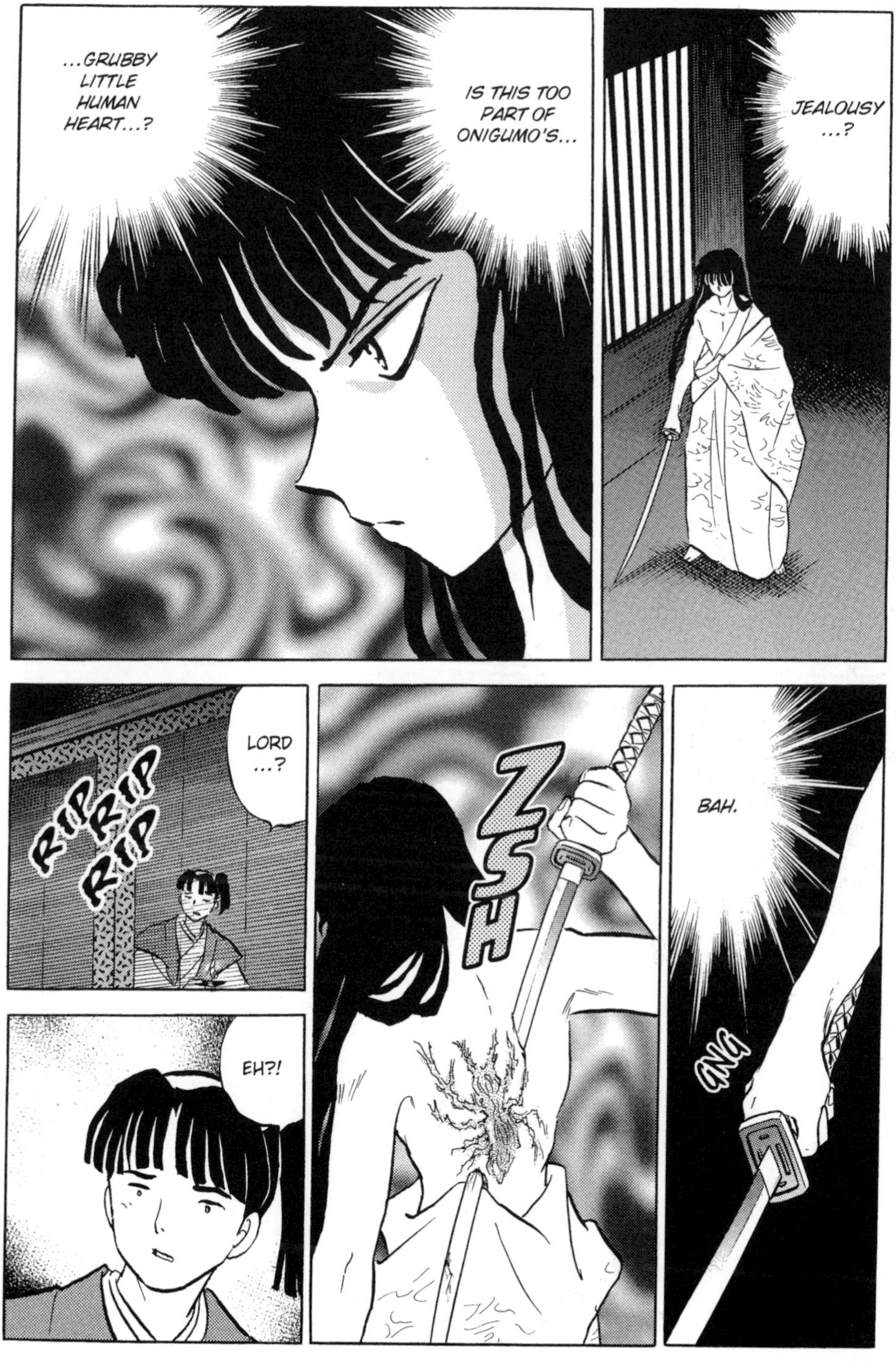
JEALOUSY ...?
IS THIS TOO PART OF ONIGUMO'S...
...GRUBBY LITTLE HUMAN HEART...?
BAH.
GNG
ZSH
LORD ...?
RIP RIP RIP
EH?!

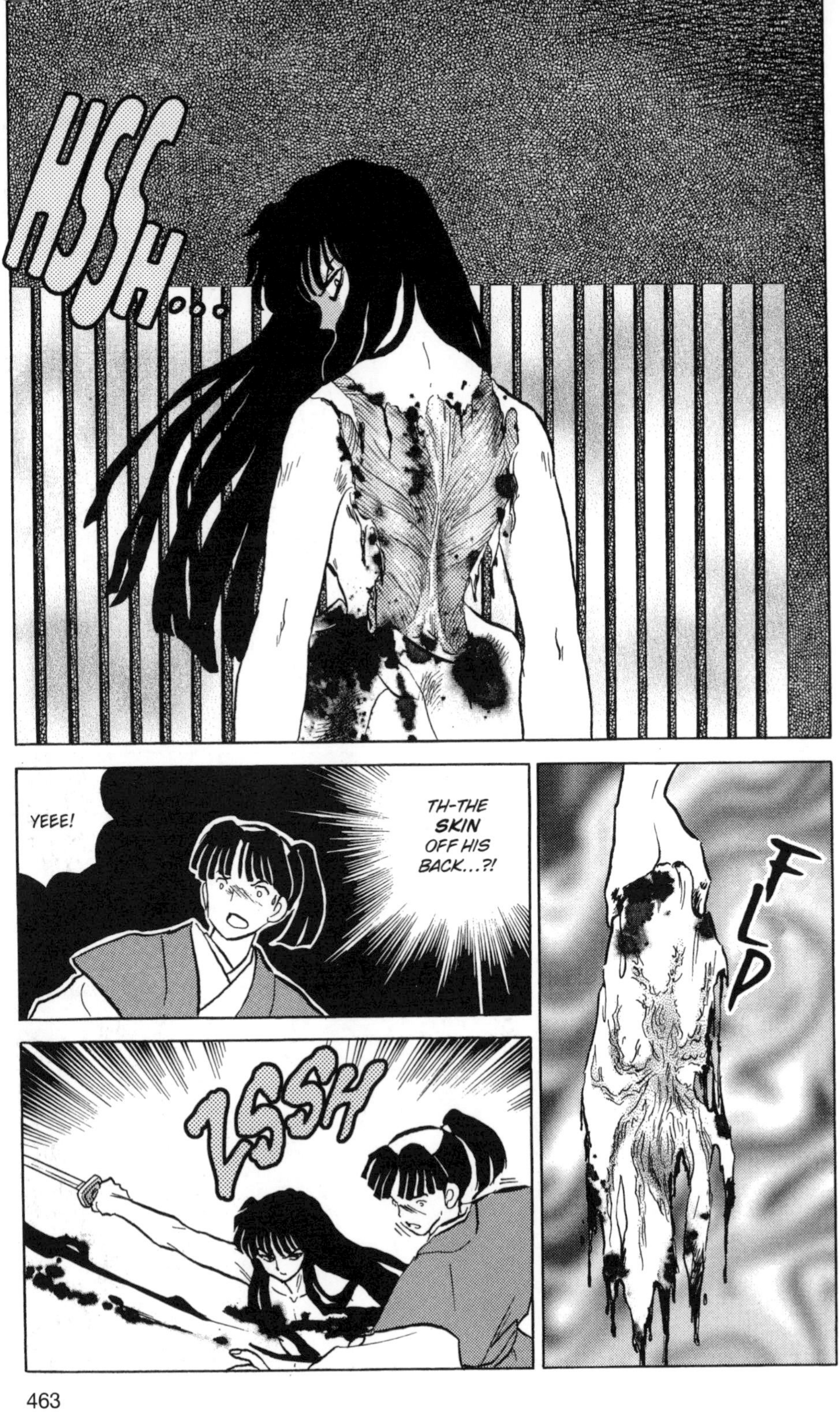
HSSH...
FLP
TH-THE **SKIN** OFF HIS BACK...?!
YEEE!
ZSSH

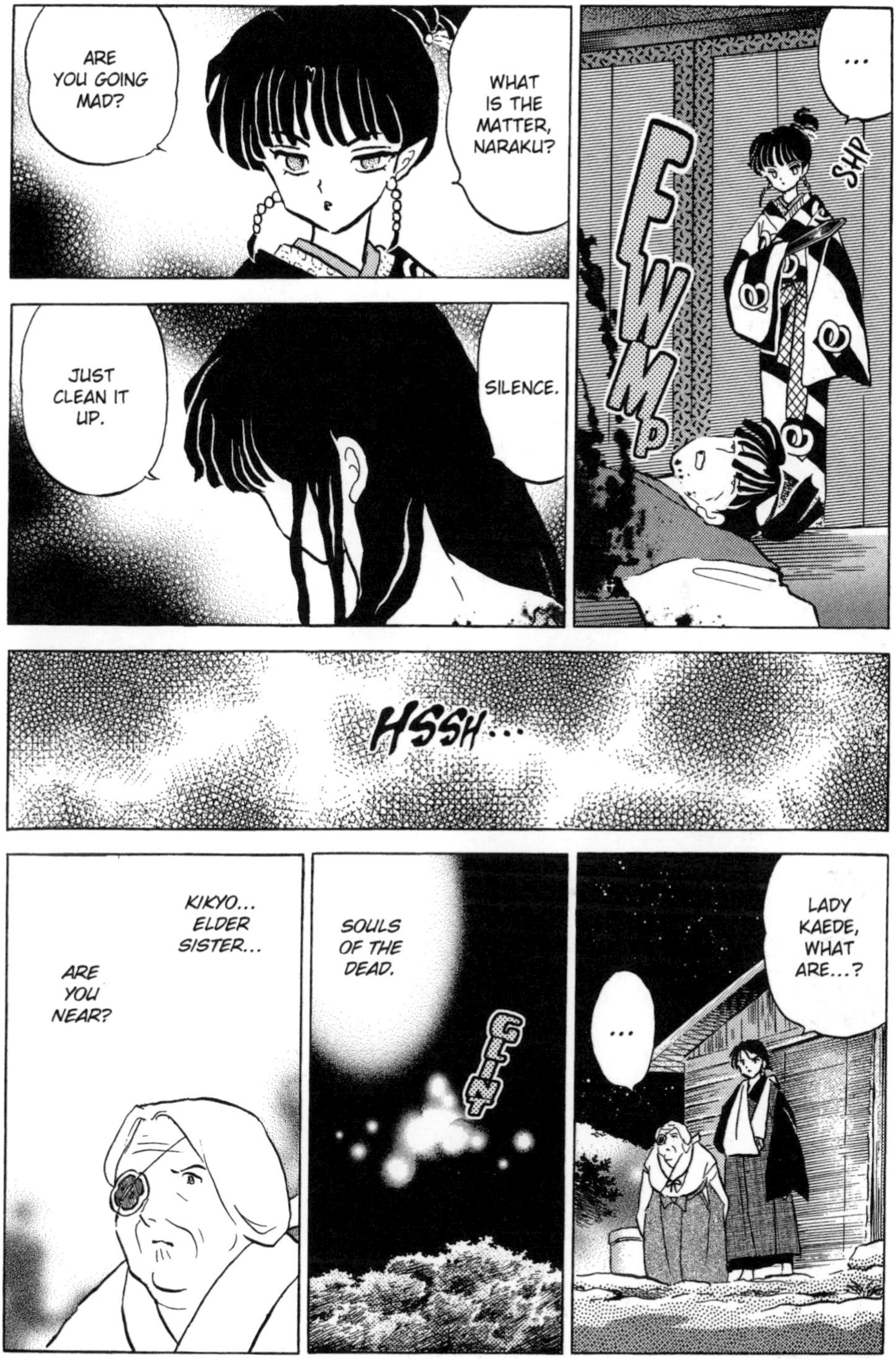
...
FWMP
SHP
WHAT IS THE MATTER, NARAKU?
ARE YOU GOING MAD?
SILENCE.
JUST CLEAN IT UP.
HSSH...
LADY KAEDE, WHAT ARE...?
...
SOULS OF THE DEAD.
GLINT
KIKYO... ELDER SISTER...
ARE YOU NEAR?

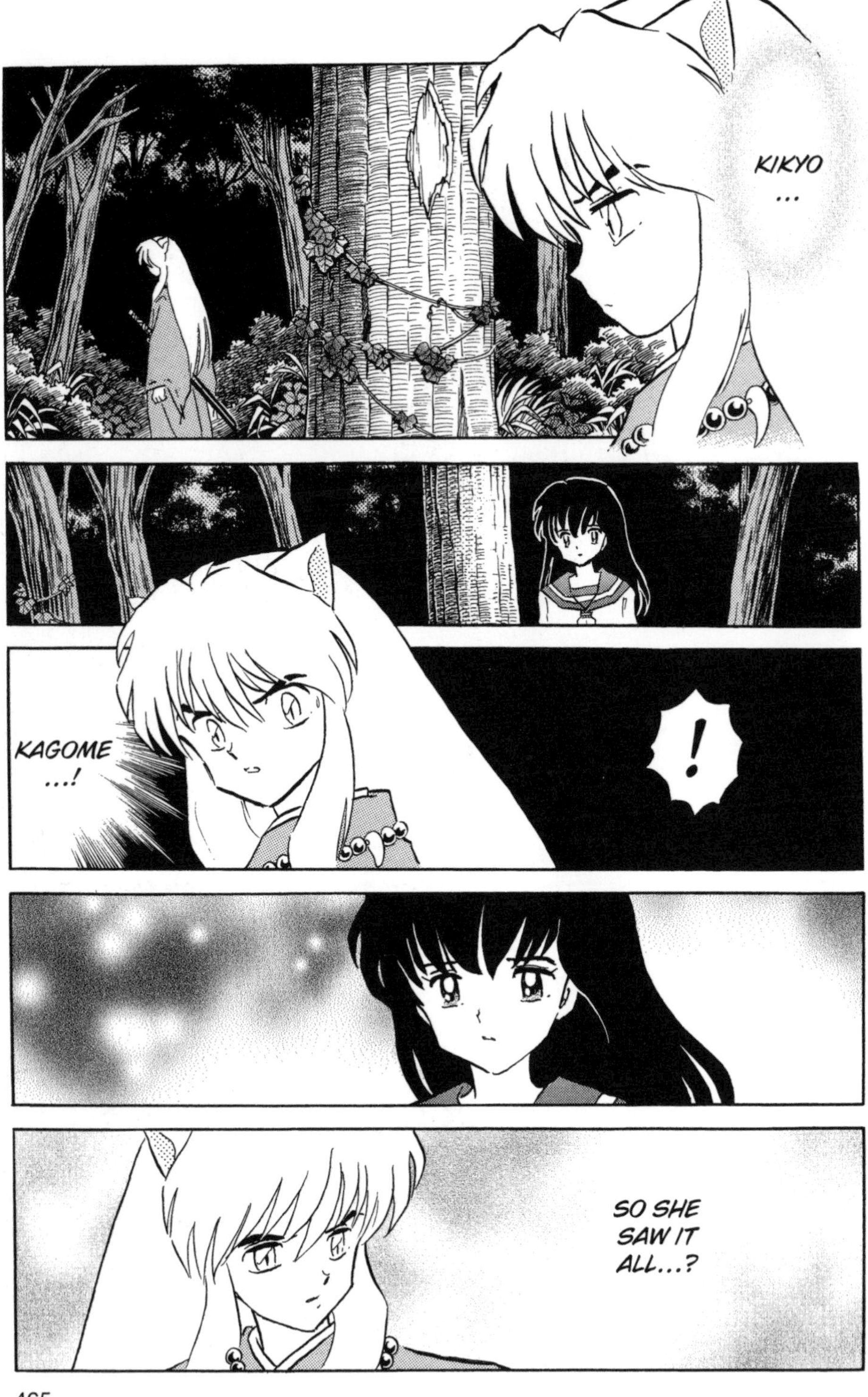
KIKYO
...
!
KAGOME
...!
SO SHE
SAW IT
ALL...?

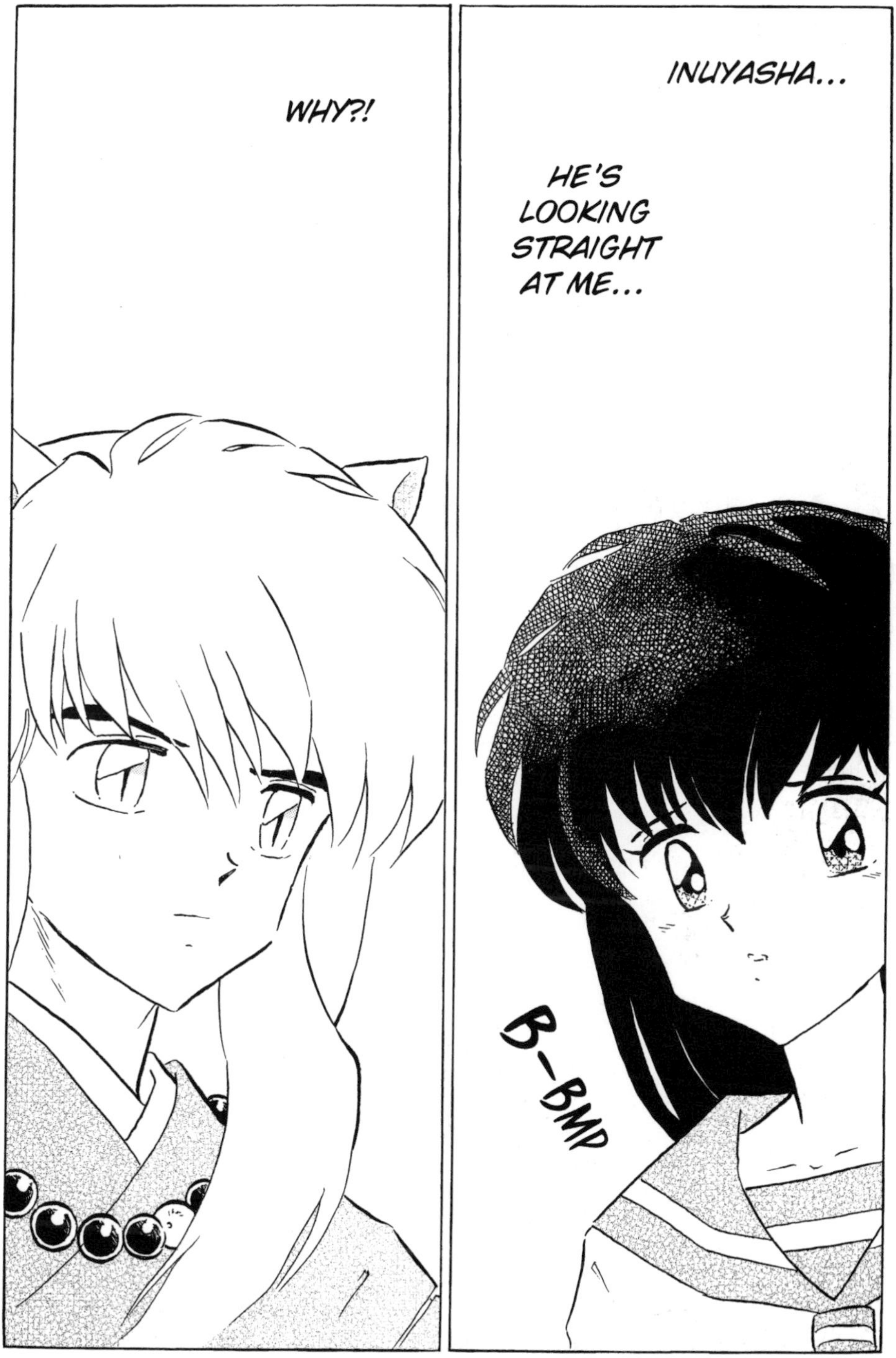
INUYASHA...
HE'S LOOKING STRAIGHT AT ME...
B-BMP
WHY?!

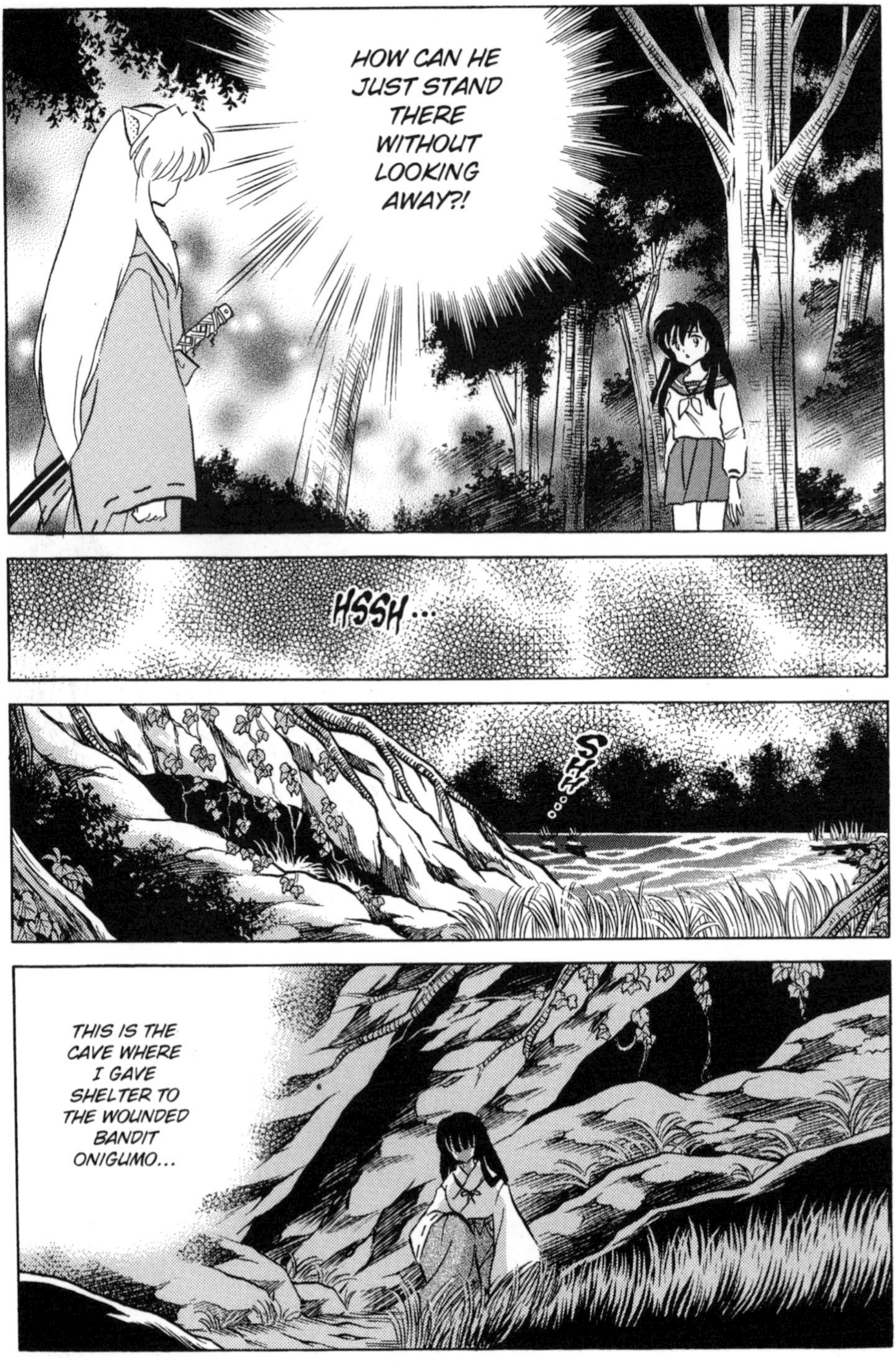
HOW CAN HE JUST STAND THERE WITHOUT LOOKING AWAY?!
HSSH...
SHH...
THIS IS THE CAVE WHERE I GAVE SHELTER TO THE WOUNDED BANDIT ONIGUMO...

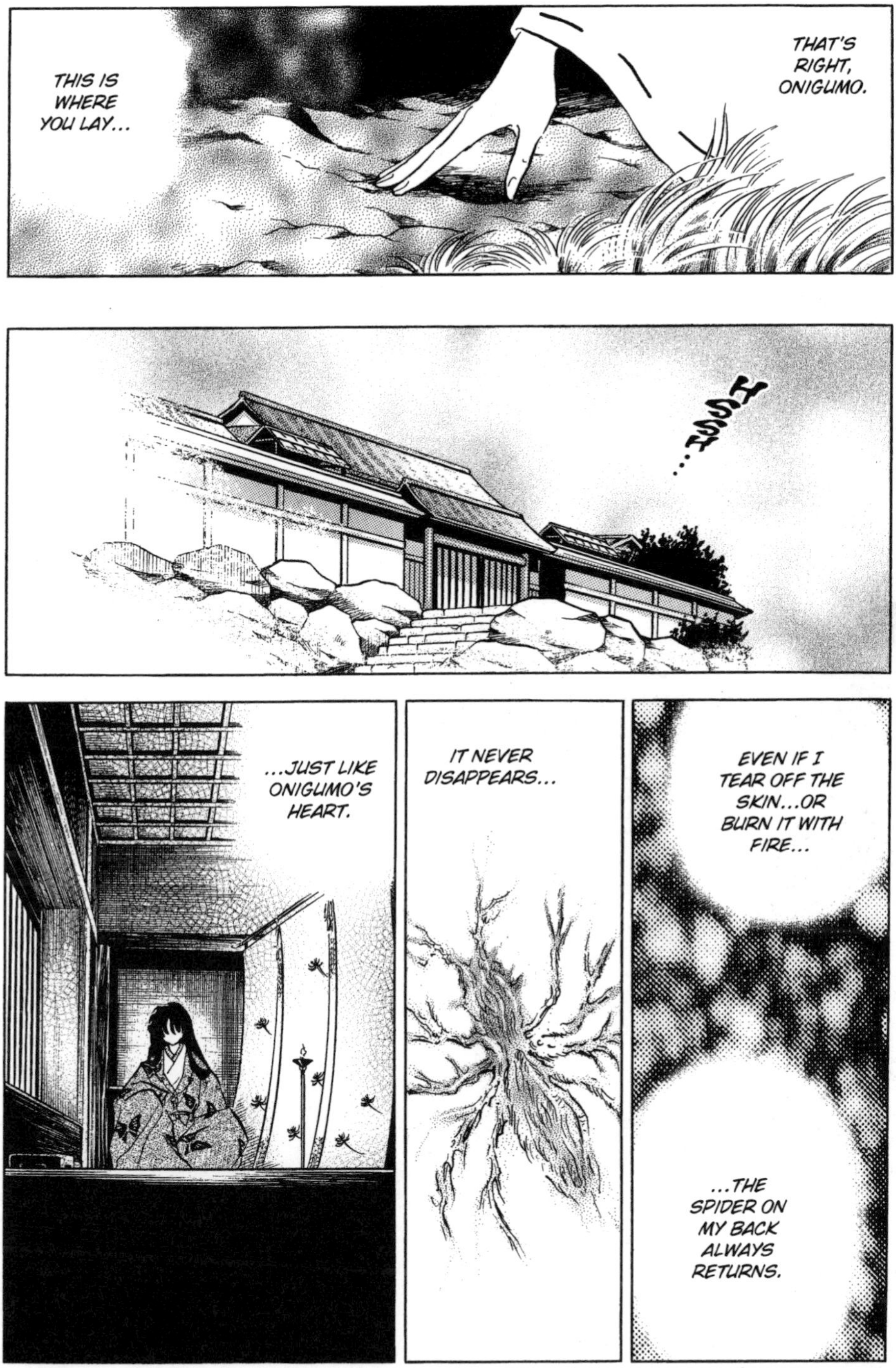
THAT'S RIGHT, ONIGUMO.
THIS IS WHERE YOU LAY...
HSSH...
EVEN IF I TEAR OFF THE SKIN...OR BURN IT WITH FIRE...
...THE SPIDER ON MY BACK ALWAYS RETURNS.
IT NEVER DISAPPEARS...
...JUST LIKE ONIGUMO'S HEART.

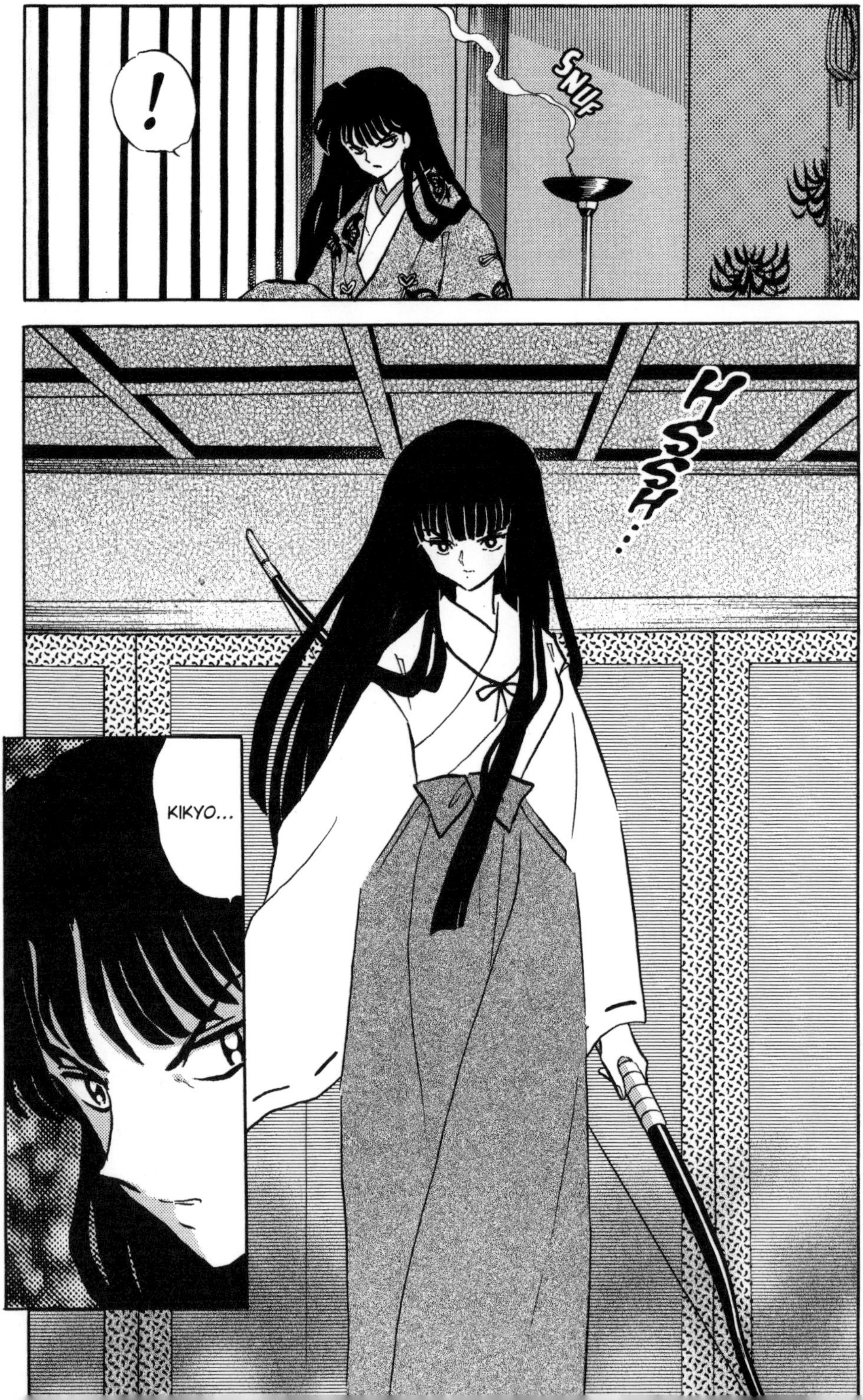

SNUF
!
HISSH...
KIKYO...

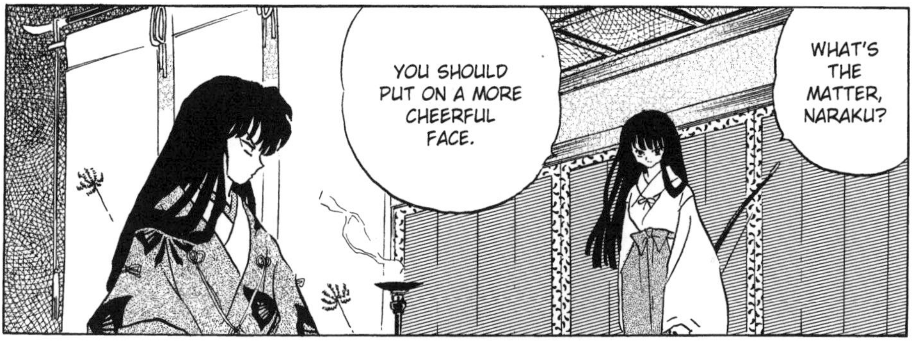
WHAT'S THE MATTER, NARAKU?
YOU SHOULD PUT ON A MORE CHEERFUL FACE.
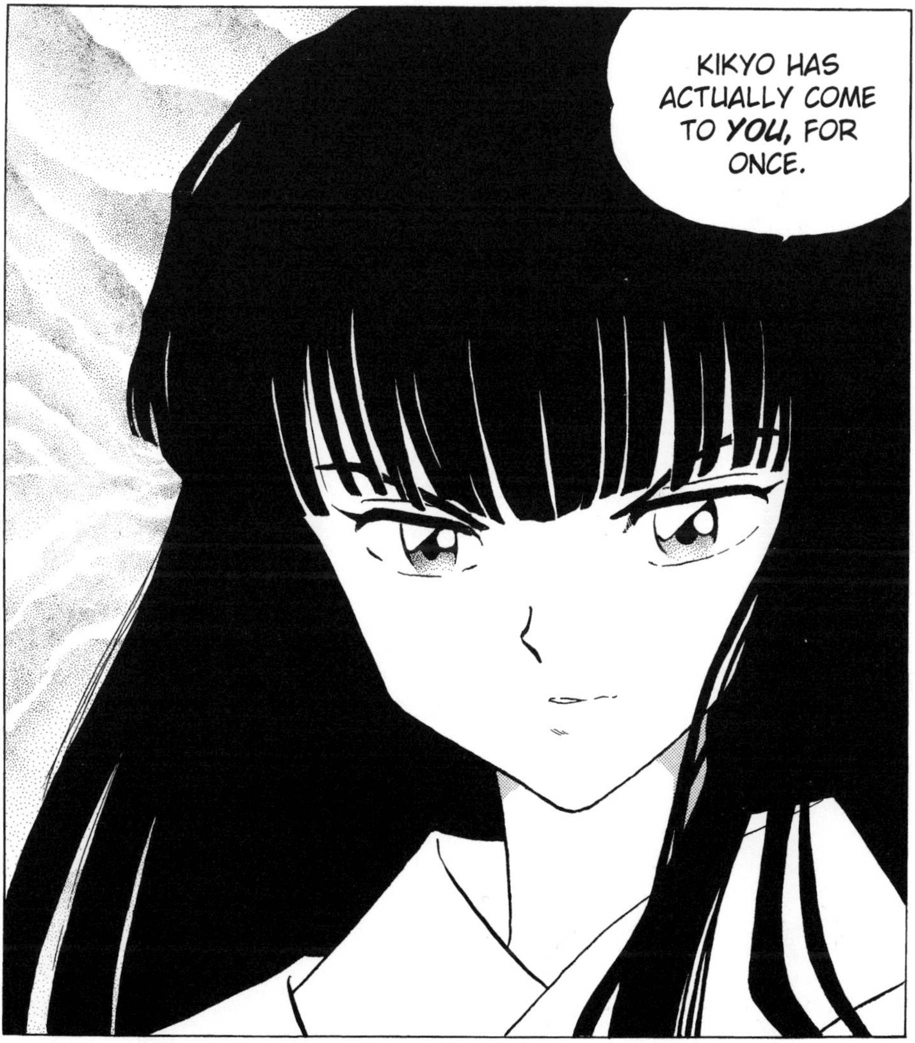
KIKYO HAS ACTUALLY COME TO *YOU,* FOR ONCE.

SCROLL SIX
THE SOIL SHIELD

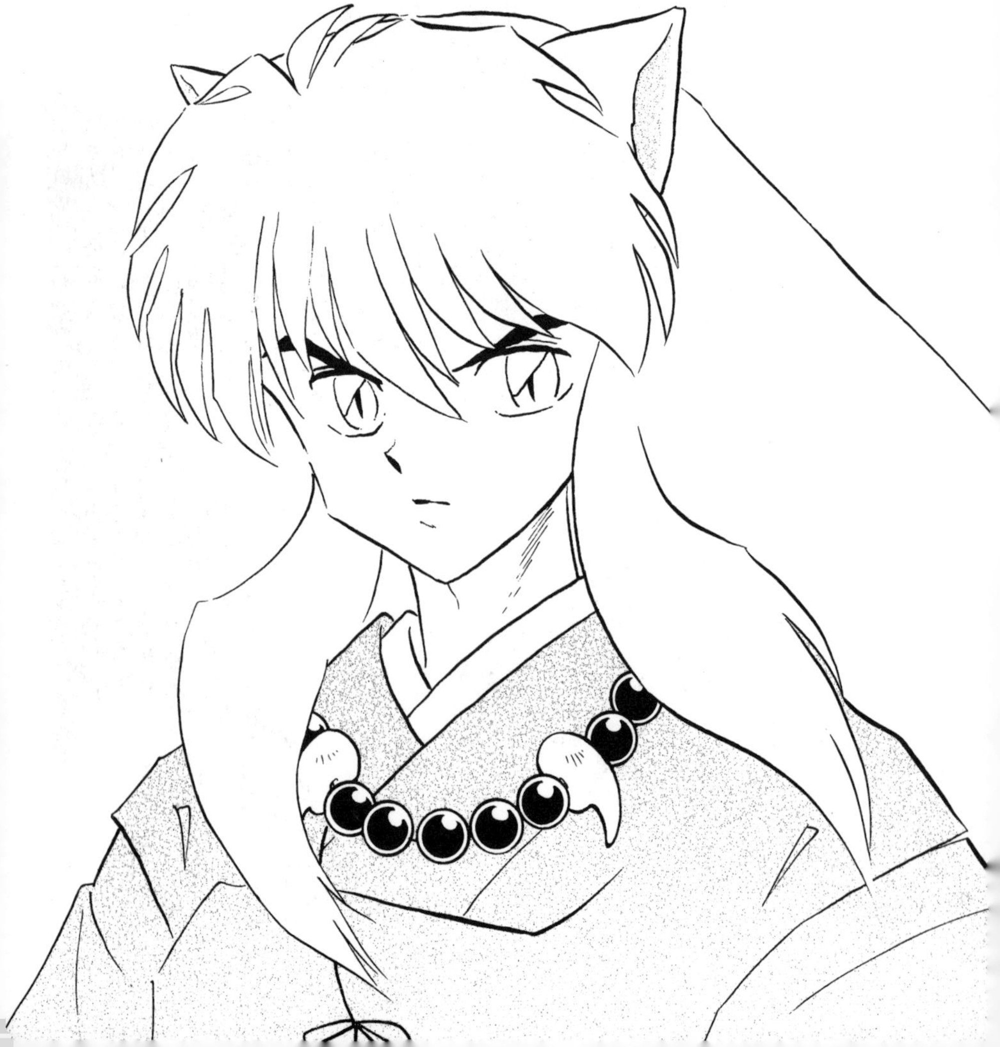

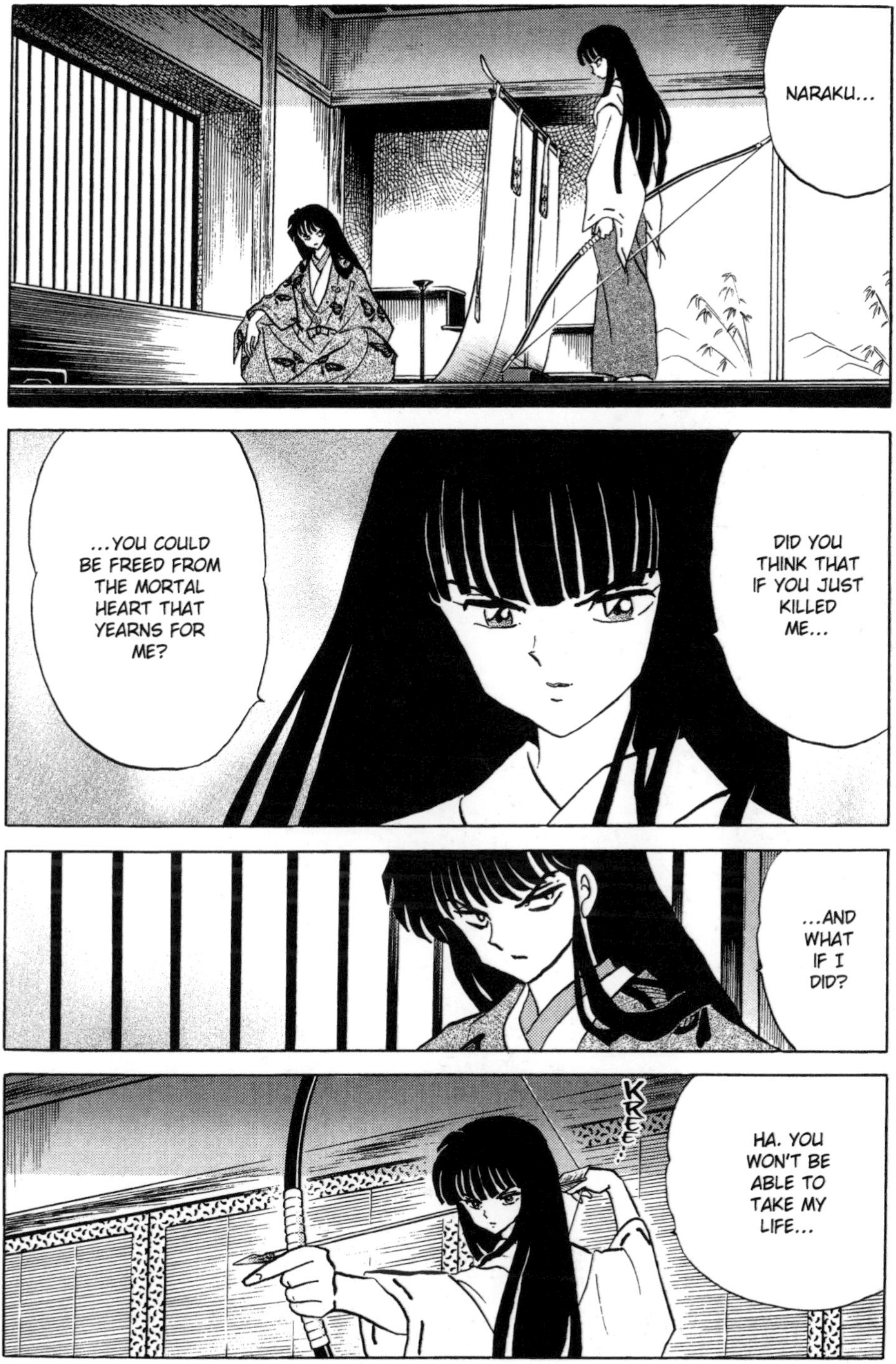
NARAKU...
DID YOU THINK THAT IF YOU JUST KILLED ME...
...YOU COULD BE FREED FROM THE MORTAL HEART THAT YEARNS FOR ME?
...AND WHAT IF I DID?
HA. YOU WON'T BE ABLE TO TAKE MY LIFE...
KREE...

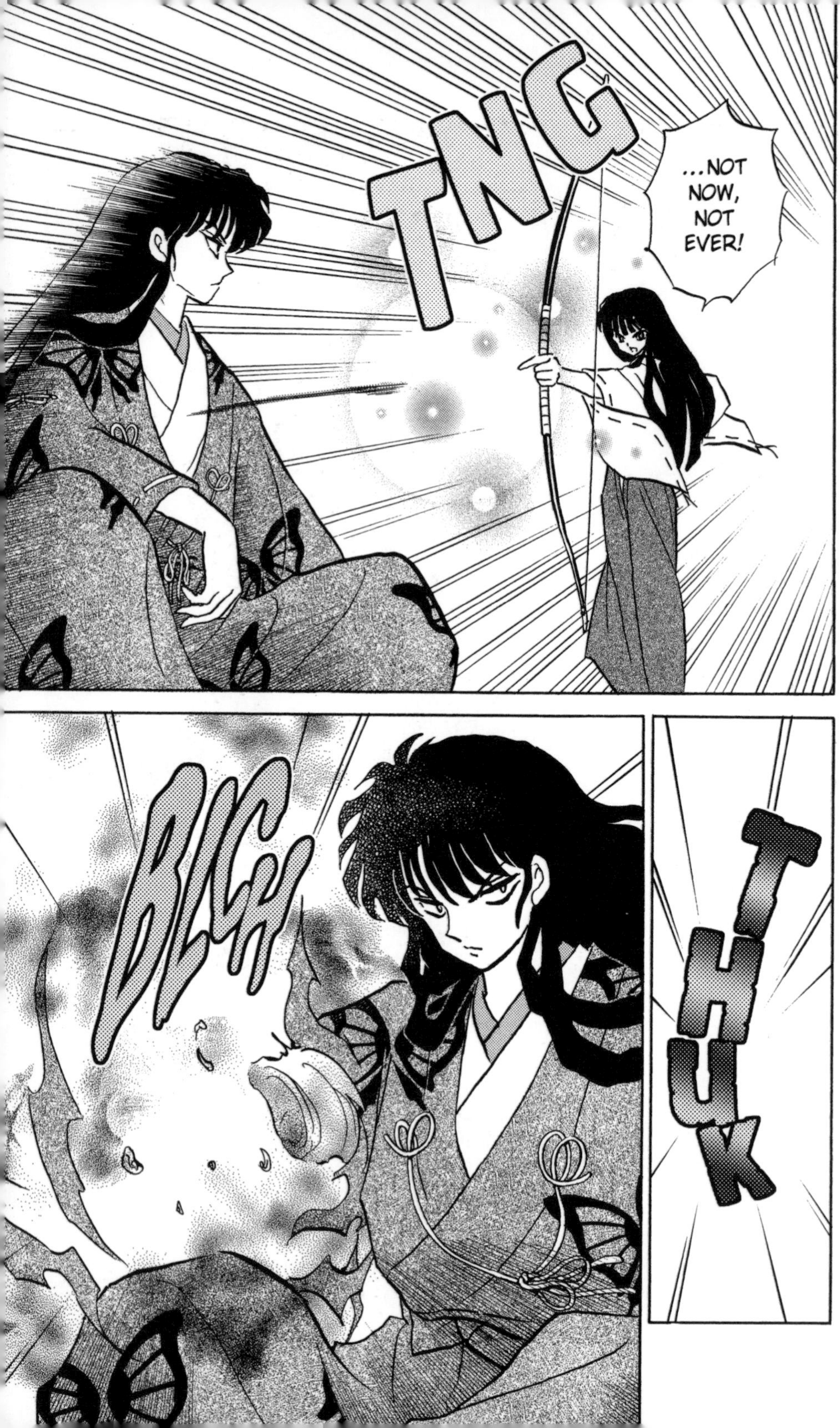
...NOT NOW, NOT EVER!
TNG
THUK
BLCH

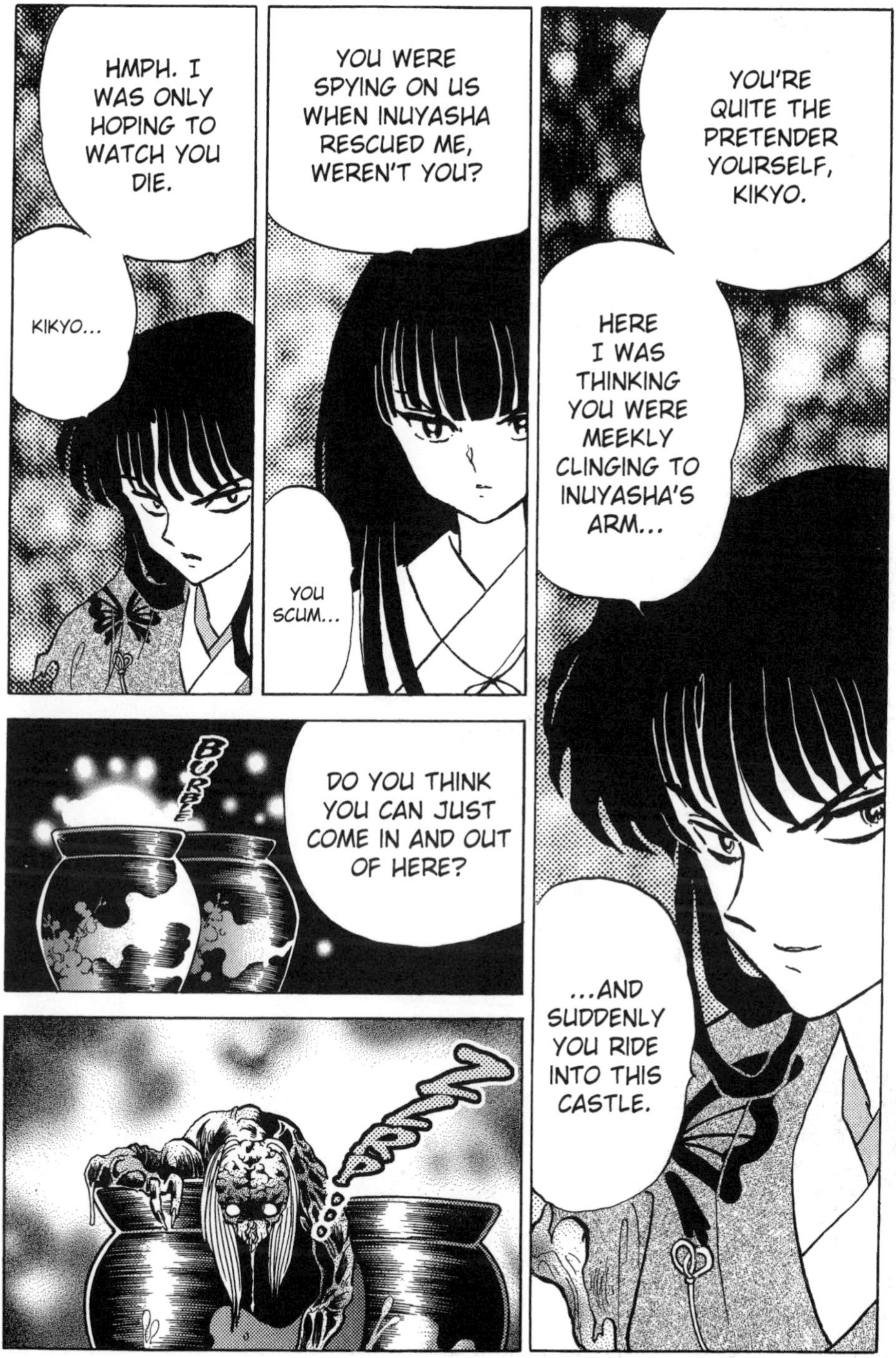
YOU'RE QUITE THE PRETENDER YOURSELF, KIKYO.
HERE I WAS THINKING YOU WERE MEEKLY CLINGING TO INUYASHA'S ARM...
...AND SUDDENLY YOU RIDE INTO THIS CASTLE.
YOU WERE SPYING ON US WHEN INUYASHA RESCUED ME, WEREN'T YOU?
YOU SCUM...
HMPH. I WAS ONLY HOPING TO WATCH YOU DIE.
KIKYO...
DO YOU THINK YOU CAN JUST COME IN AND OUT OF HERE?
BURBLE

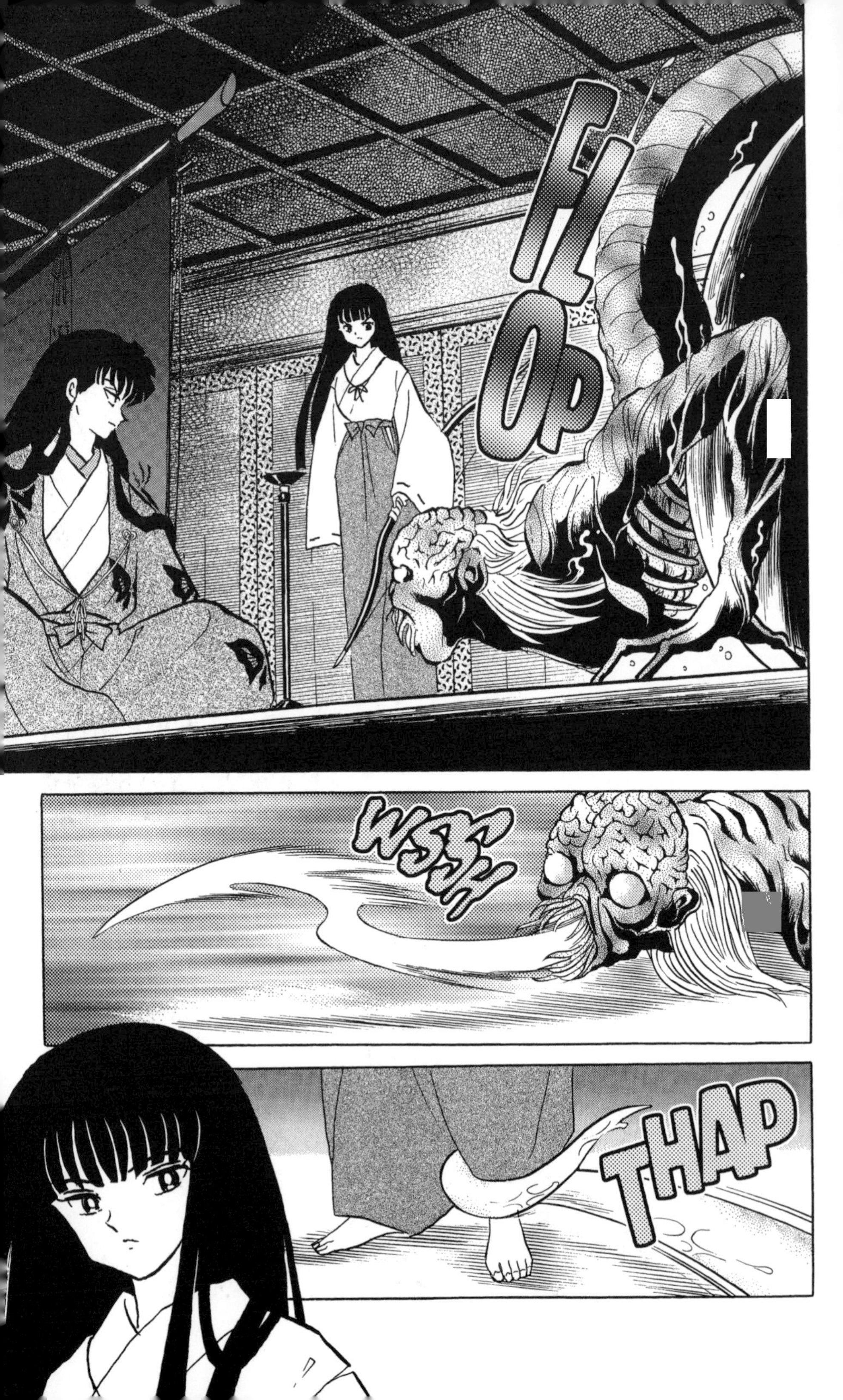
FLOP
WSSH
THAP

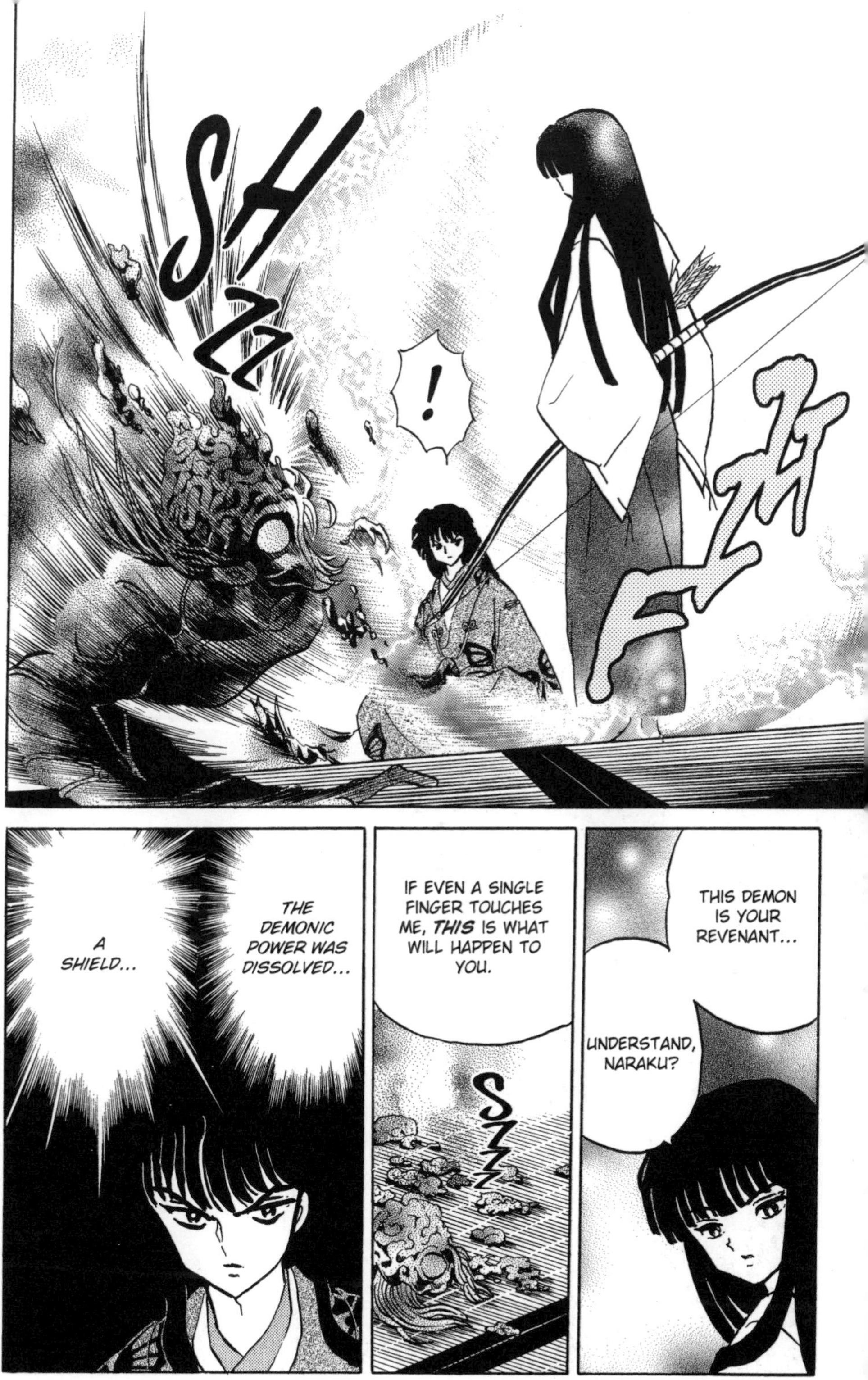
FZZT
!
SHZZ
THIS DEMON IS YOUR REVENANT...
UNDERSTAND, NARAKU?
IF EVEN A SINGLE FINGER TOUCHES ME, *THIS* IS WHAT WILL HAPPEN TO YOU.
SZZZ
THE DEMONIC POWER WAS DISSOLVED...
A SHIELD...

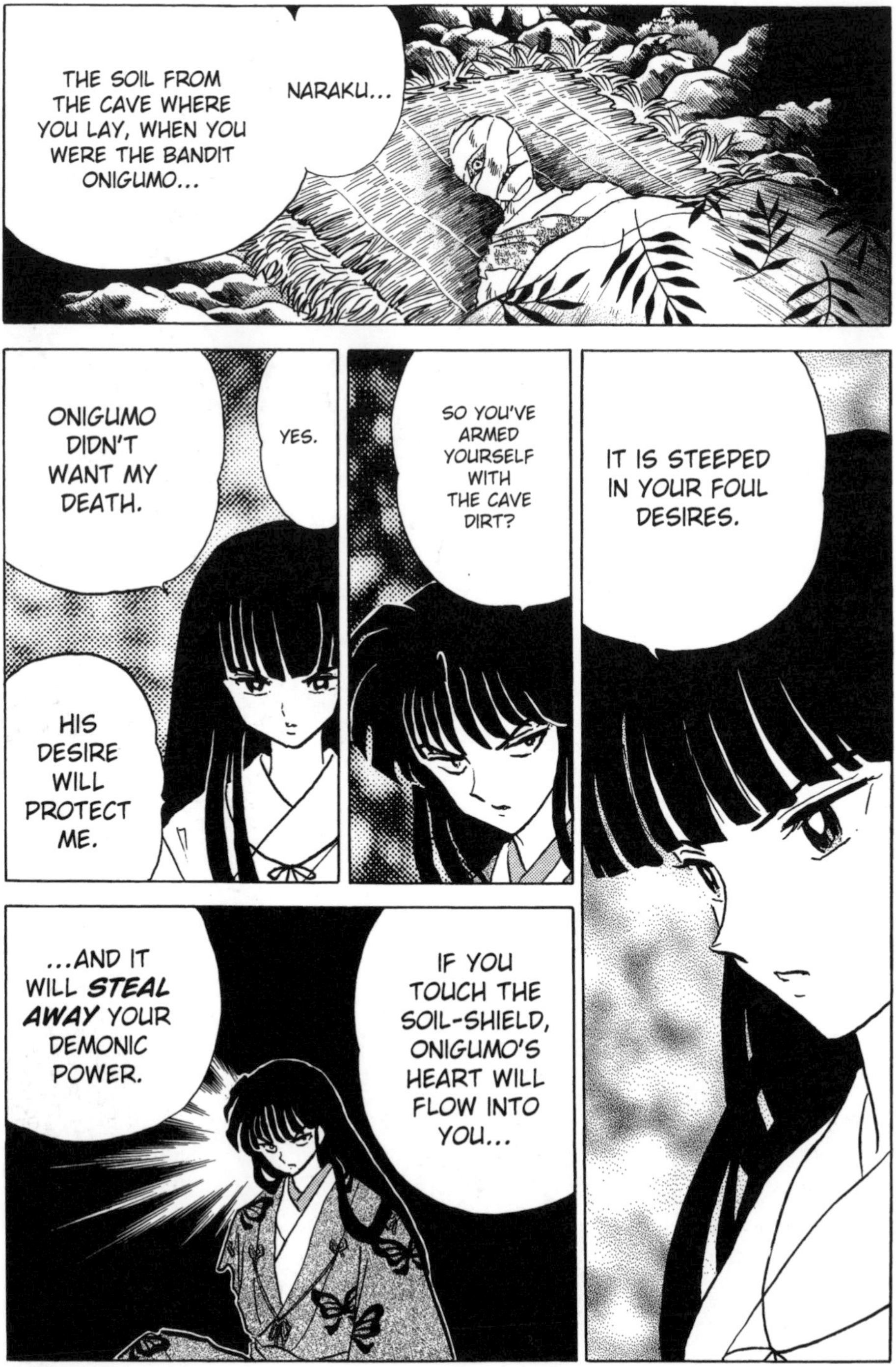
NARAKU...
THE SOIL FROM THE CAVE WHERE YOU LAY, WHEN YOU WERE THE BANDIT ONIGUMO...
IT IS STEEPED IN YOUR FOUL DESIRES.
SO YOU'VE ARMED YOURSELF WITH THE CAVE DIRT?
YES.
ONIGUMO DIDN'T WANT MY DEATH.
HIS DESIRE WILL PROTECT ME.
IF YOU TOUCH THE SOIL-SHIELD, ONIGUMO'S HEART WILL FLOW INTO YOU...
...AND IT WILL **STEAL AWAY** YOUR DEMONIC POWER.

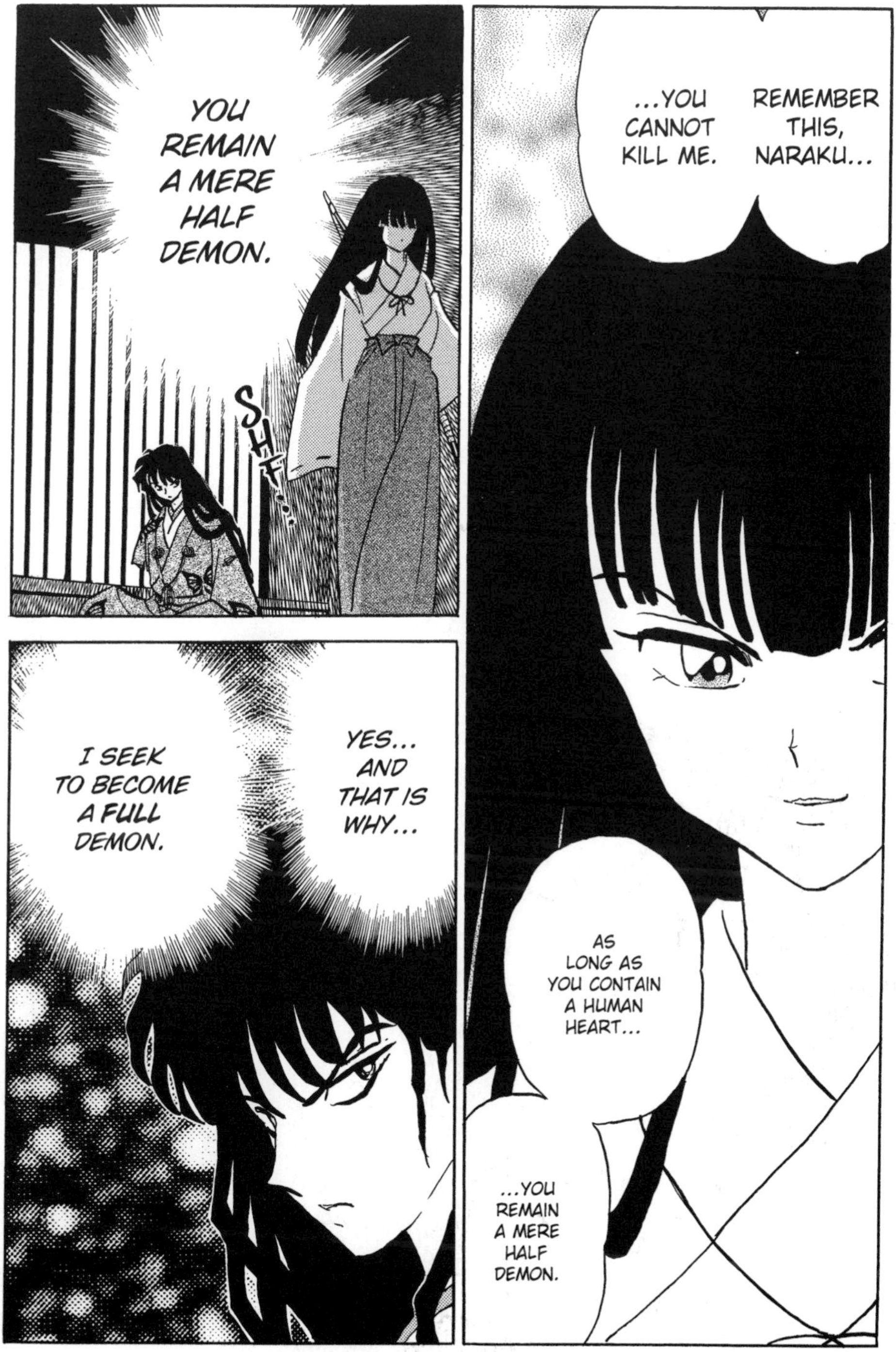

REMEMBER THIS, NARAKU...
...YOU CANNOT KILL ME.
AS LONG AS YOU CONTAIN A HUMAN HEART...
...YOU REMAIN A MERE HALF DEMON.
YOU REMAIN A MERE HALF DEMON.
SHF...
YES... AND THAT IS WHY...
I SEEK TO BECOME A **FULL** DEMON.

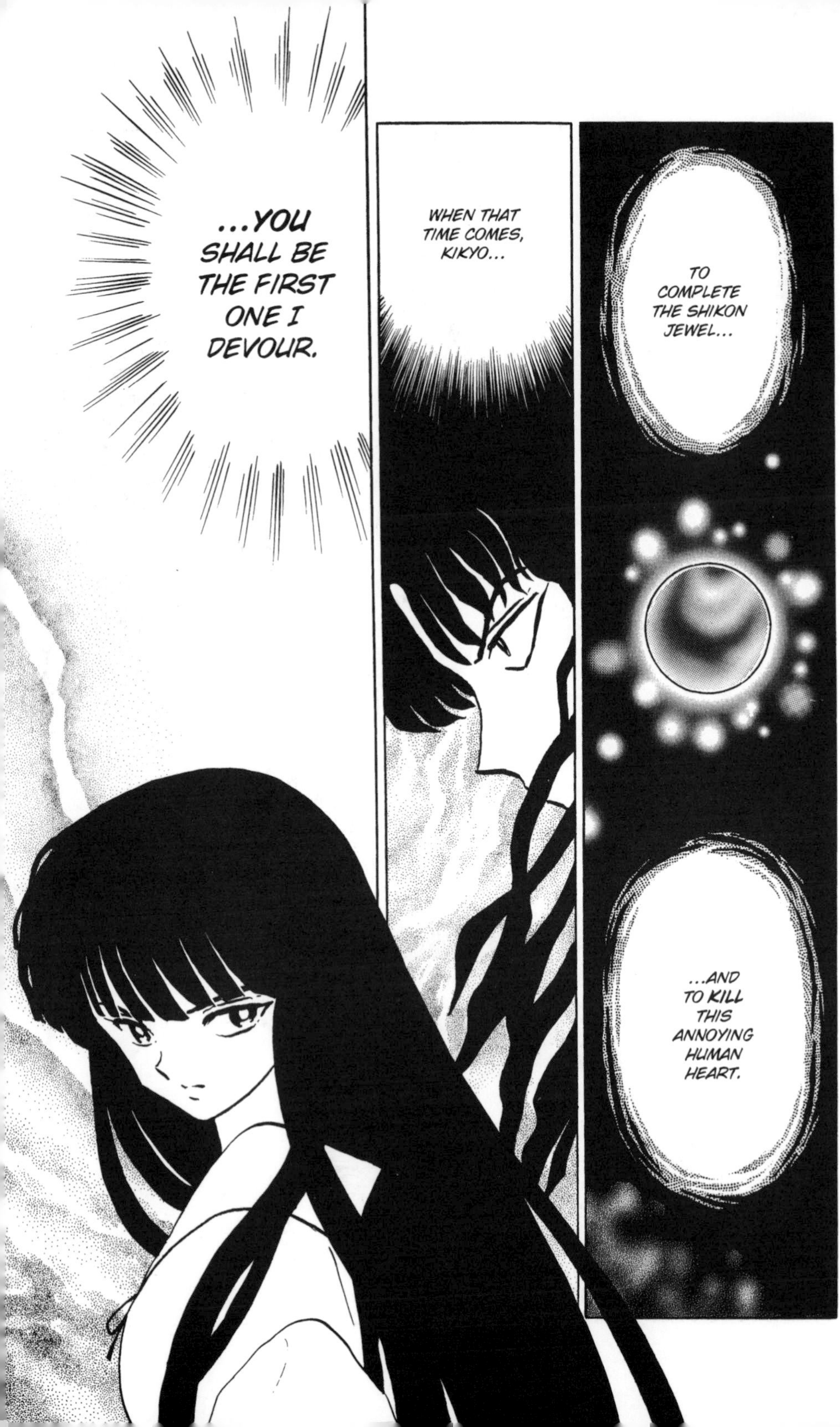
TO COMPLETE THE SHIKON JEWEL...
...AND TO KILL THIS ANNOYING HUMAN HEART.
WHEN THAT TIME COMES, KIKYO...
...YOU SHALL BE THE FIRST ONE I DEVOUR.

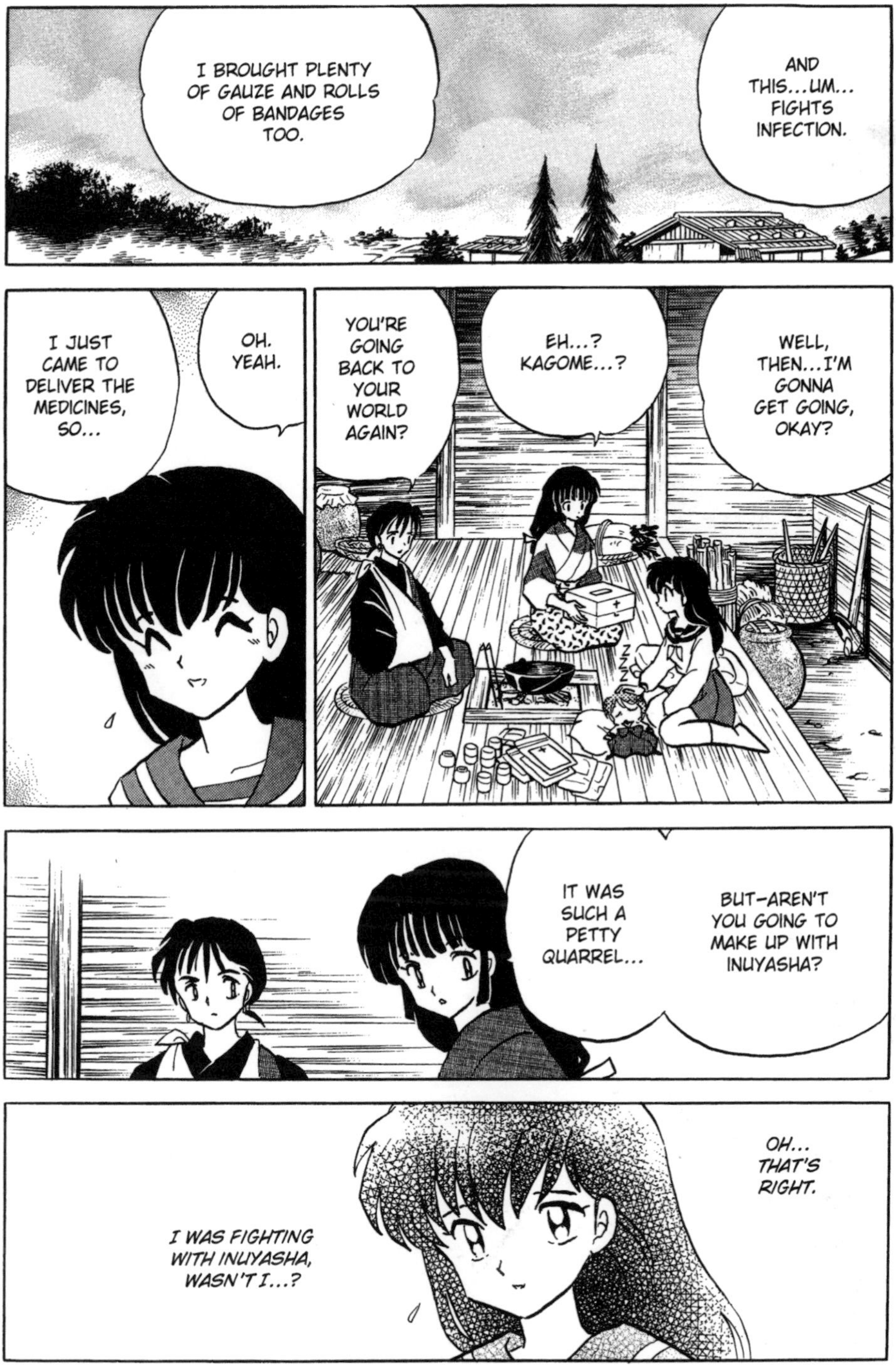
AND THIS...UM... FIGHTS INFECTION.
I BROUGHT PLENTY OF GAUZE AND ROLLS OF BANDAGES TOO.
WELL, THEN...I'M GONNA GET GOING, OKAY?
EH...? KAGOME...?
YOU'RE GOING BACK TO YOUR WORLD AGAIN?
OH. YEAH.
I JUST CAME TO DELIVER THE MEDICINES, SO...
ZZZ
BUT—AREN'T YOU GOING TO MAKE UP WITH INUYASHA?
IT WAS SUCH A PETTY QUARREL...
OH... THAT'S RIGHT.
I WAS FIGHTING WITH INUYASHA, WASN'T I...?

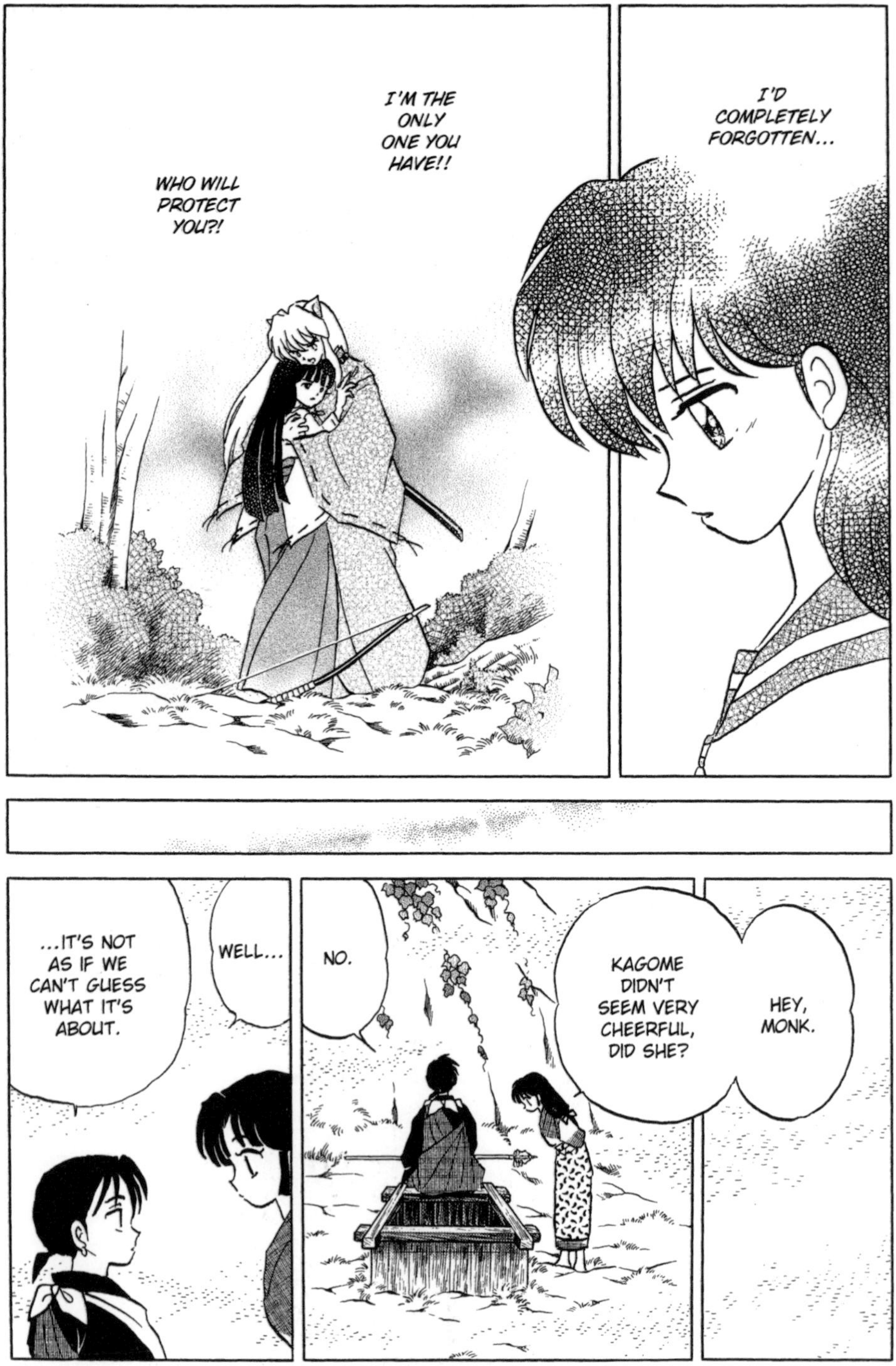
I'D COMPLETELY FORGOTTEN...
I'M THE ONLY ONE YOU HAVE!!
WHO WILL PROTECT YOU?!
HEY, MONK.
KAGOME DIDN'T SEEM VERY CHEERFUL, DID SHE?
NO.
WELL...
...IT'S NOT AS IF WE CAN'T GUESS WHAT IT'S ABOUT.

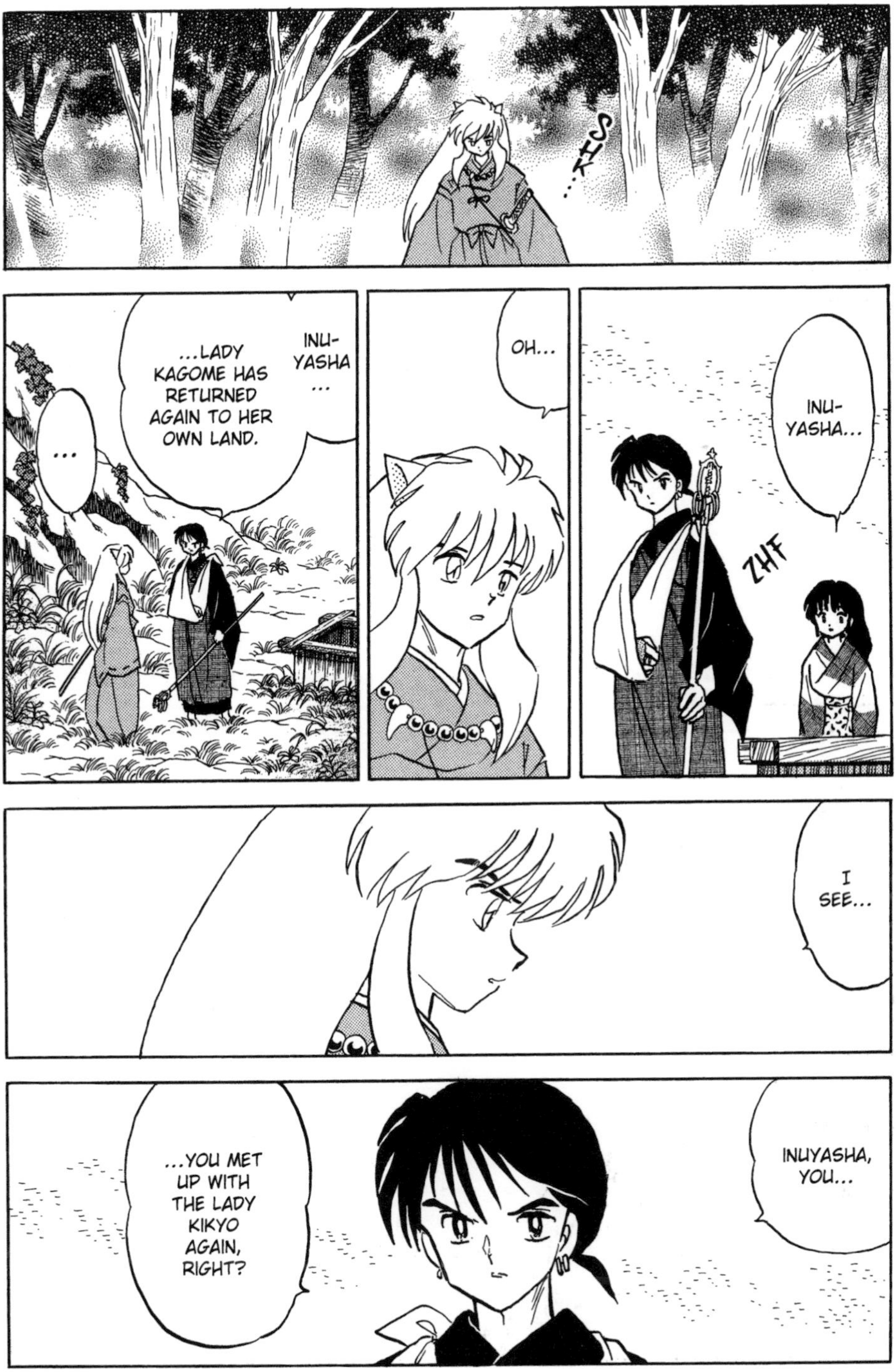
SHK...
INU-YASHA...
ZHF
OH...
INU-YASHA...
...LADY KAGOME HAS RETURNED AGAIN TO HER OWN LAND.
...
I SEE...
INUYASHA, YOU...
...YOU MET UP WITH THE LADY KIKYO AGAIN, RIGHT?

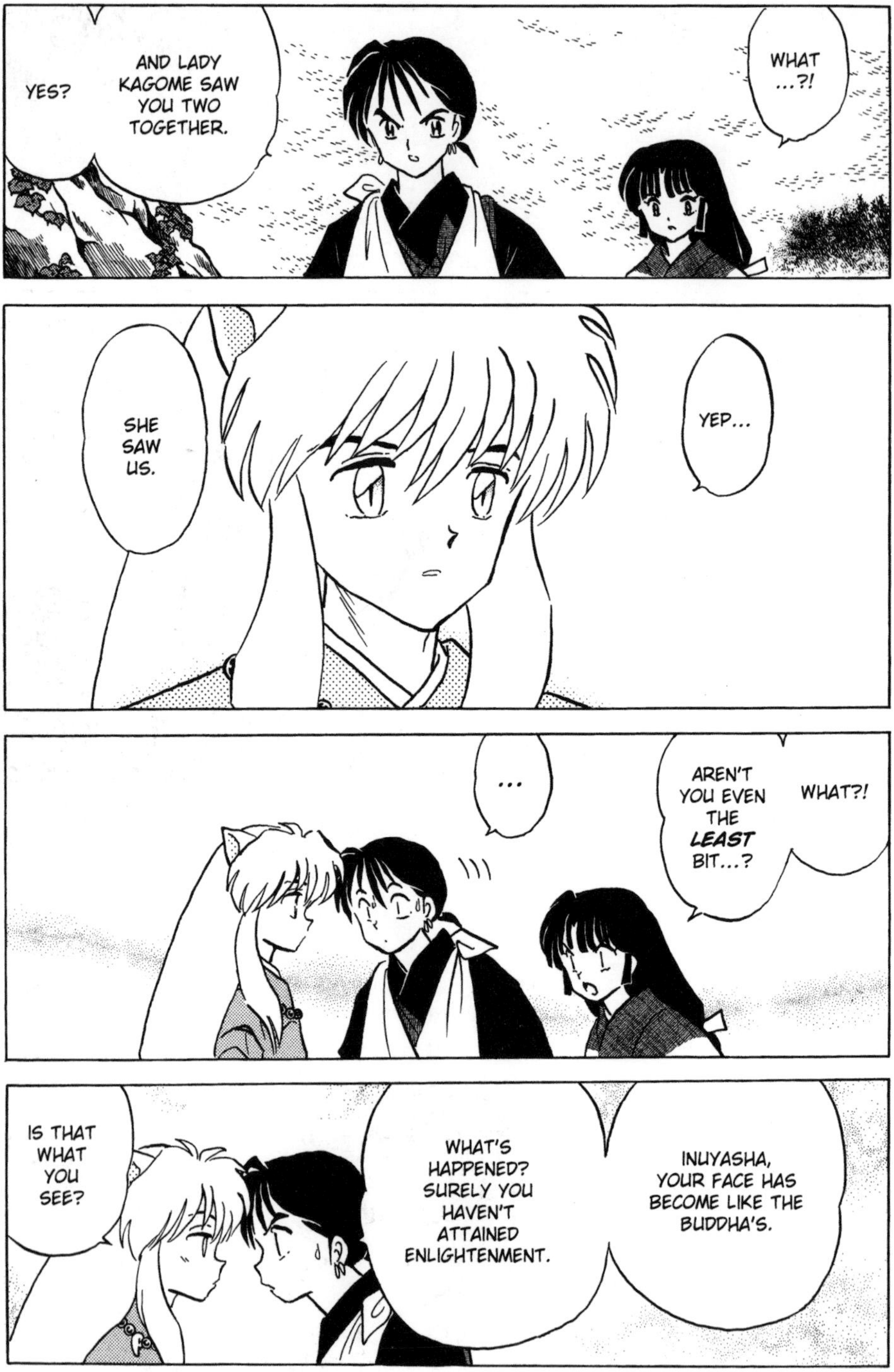
WHAT ...?!
AND LADY KAGOME SAW YOU TWO TOGETHER.
YES?
YEP...
SHE SAW US.
WHAT?!
AREN'T YOU EVEN THE **LEAST** BIT...?
...
INUYASHA, YOUR FACE HAS BECOME LIKE THE BUDDHA'S.
WHAT'S HAPPENED? SURELY YOU HAVEN'T ATTAINED ENLIGHTENMENT.
IS THAT WHAT YOU SEE?

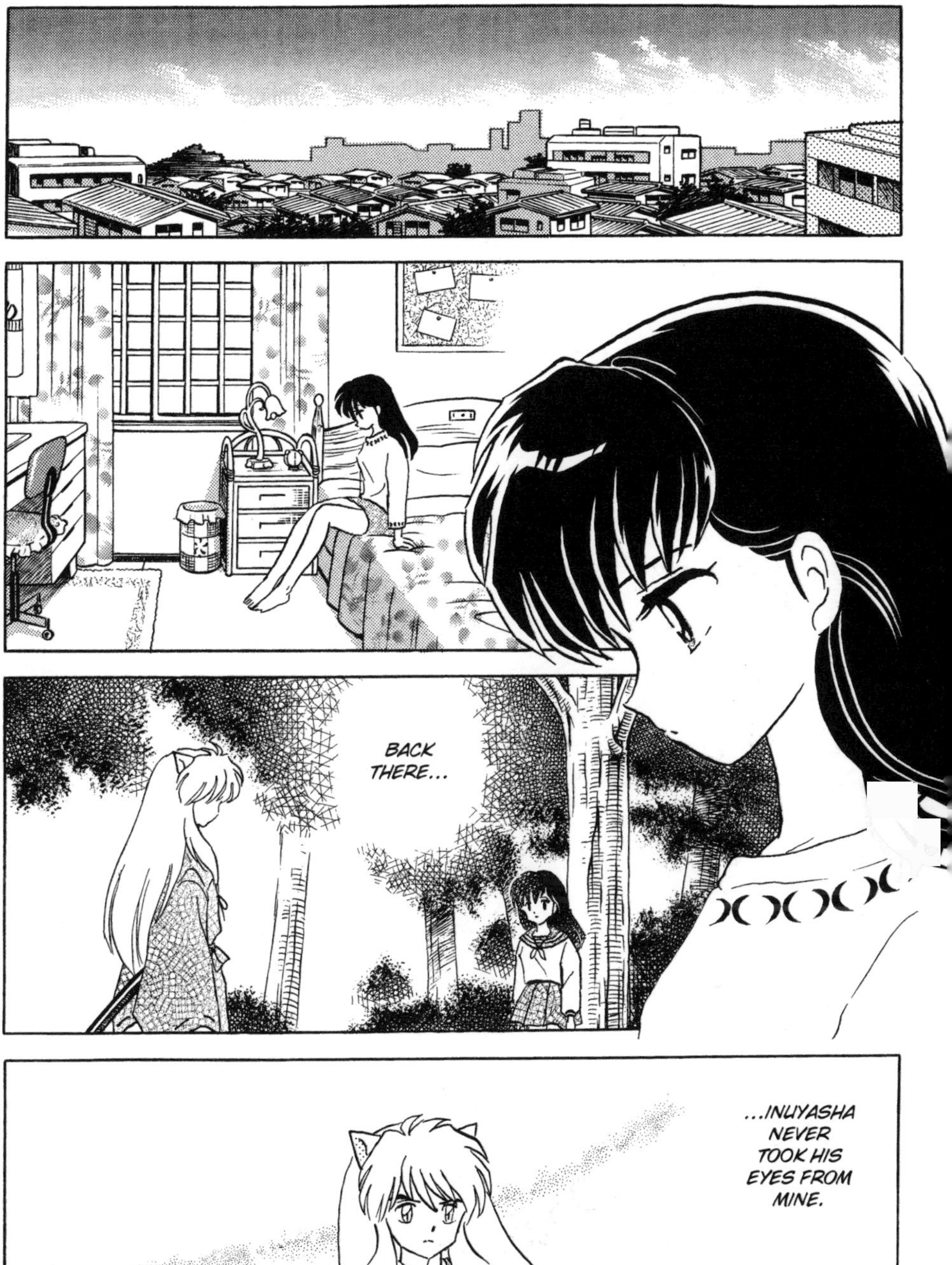
BACK THERE...
...INUYASHA NEVER TOOK HIS EYES FROM MINE.

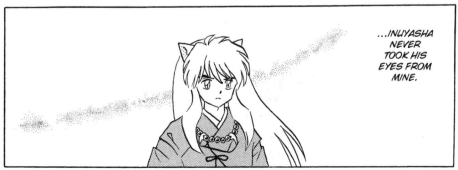

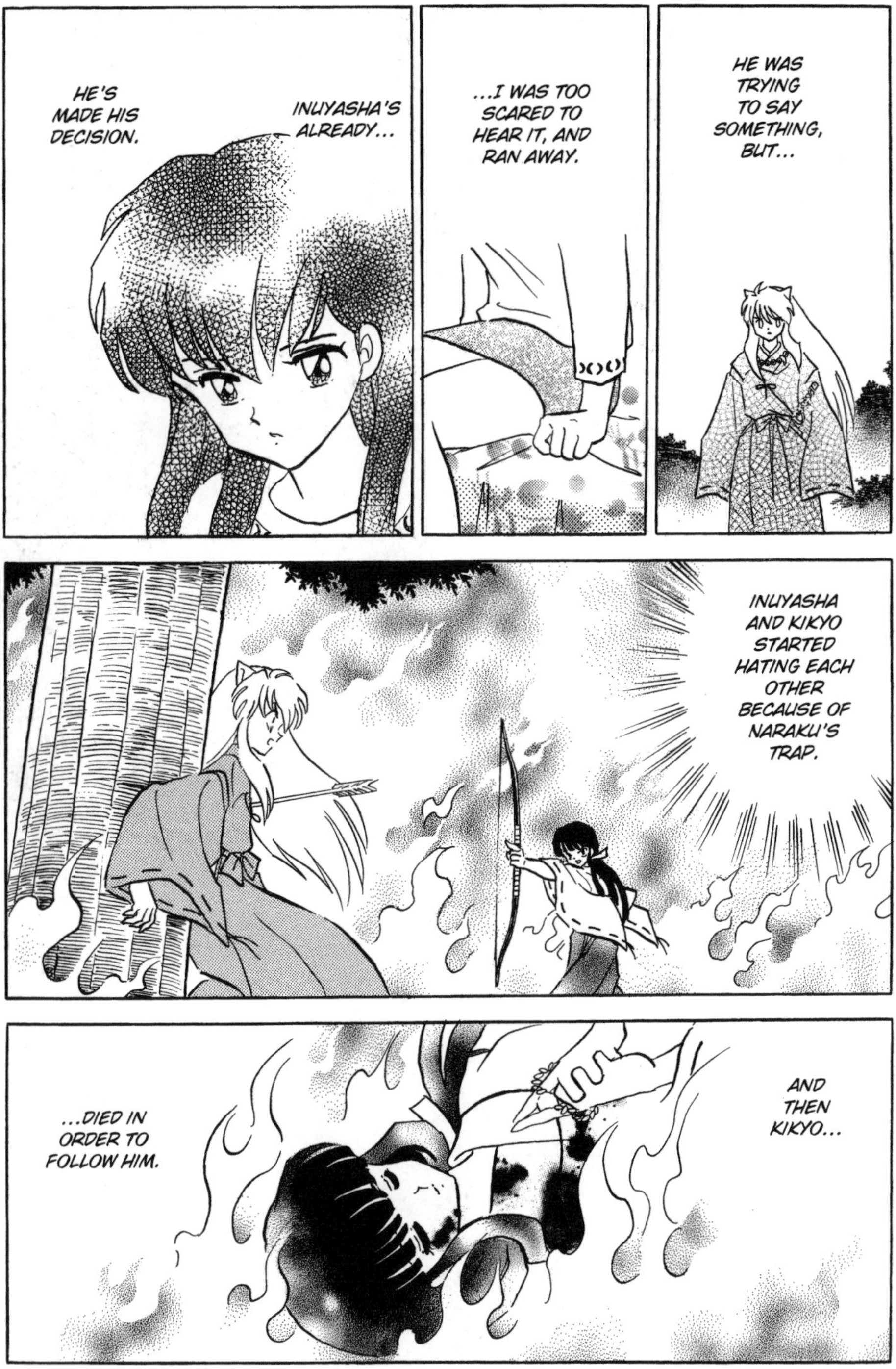
HE WAS TRYING TO SAY SOMETHING, BUT…
…I WAS TOO SCARED TO HEAR IT, AND RAN AWAY.
INUYASHA'S ALREADY…
HE'S MADE HIS DECISION.
INUYASHA AND KIKYO STARTED HATING EACH OTHER BECAUSE OF NARAKU'S TRAP.
AND THEN KIKYO…
…DIED IN ORDER TO FOLLOW HIM.

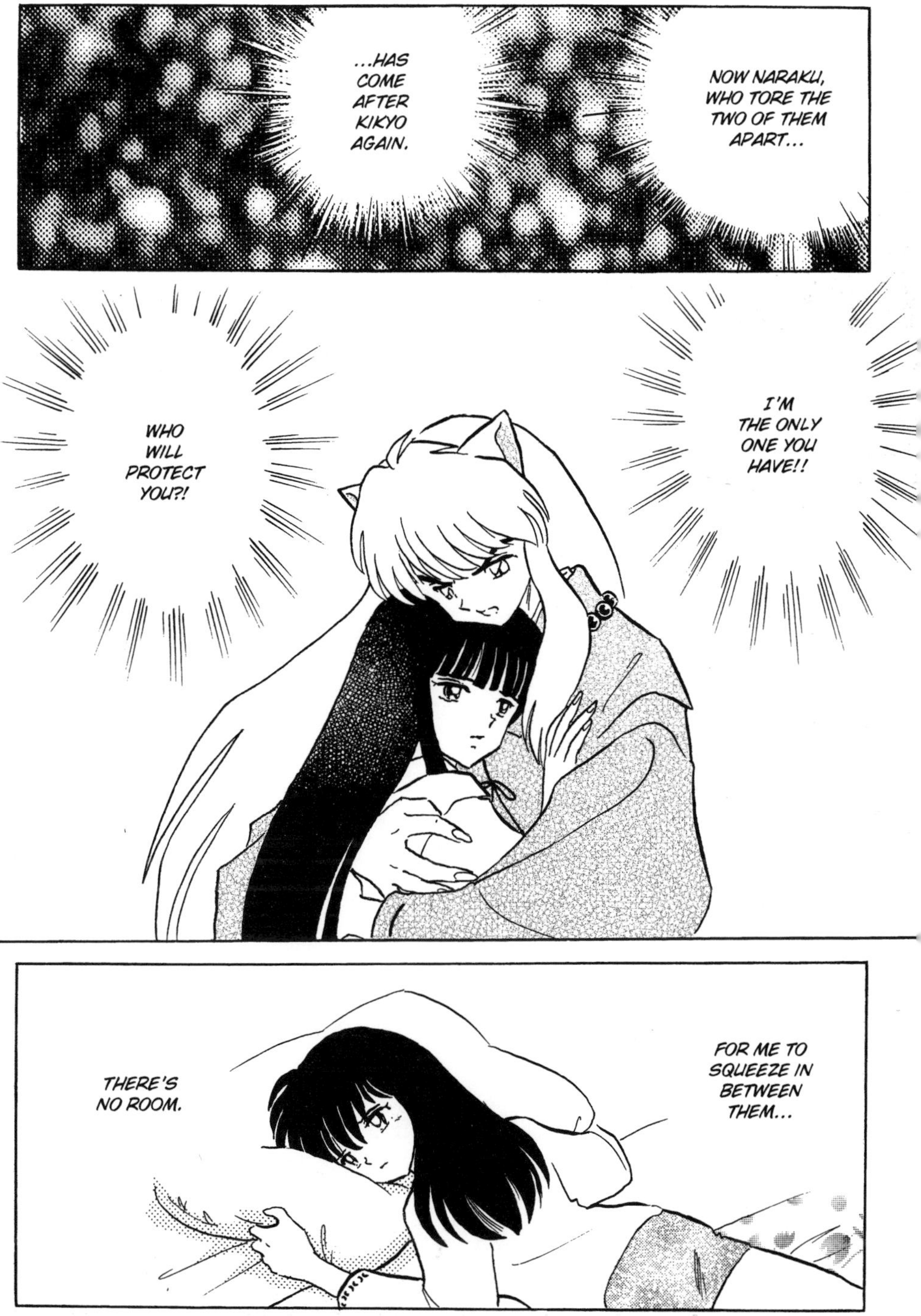
NOW NARAKU, WHO TORE THE TWO OF THEM APART...
...HAS COME AFTER KIKYO AGAIN.
I'M THE ONLY ONE YOU HAVE!!
WHO WILL PROTECT YOU?!
FOR ME TO SQUEEZE IN BETWEEN THEM...
THERE'S NO ROOM.

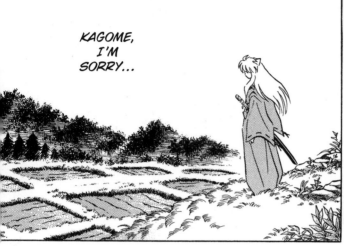

KAGOME, I'M SORRY...

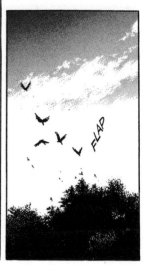

FLAP

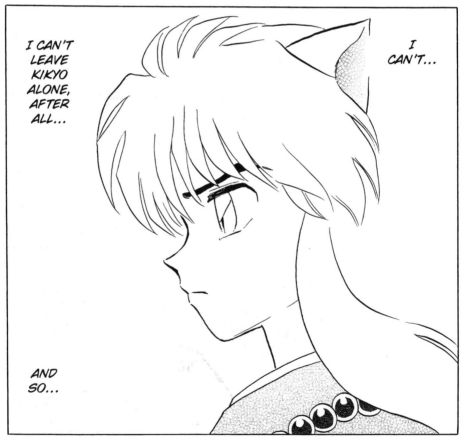

I CAN'T LEAVE KIKYO ALONE, AFTER ALL...

I CAN'T...

AND SO...

487

KAGOME,
I CAN'T
SEE YOU
ANYMORE.

I MUSTN'T
SEE YOU
ANYMORE.

I CAN'T
COMPETE
AGAINST
THAT.

KIKYO SACRIFICED
HER LIFE FOR
INUYASHA'S SAKE.

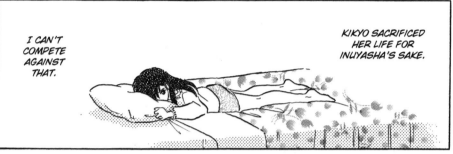

I CAN'T GO
BACK TO
INUYASHA'S
SIDE EVER
AGAIN.

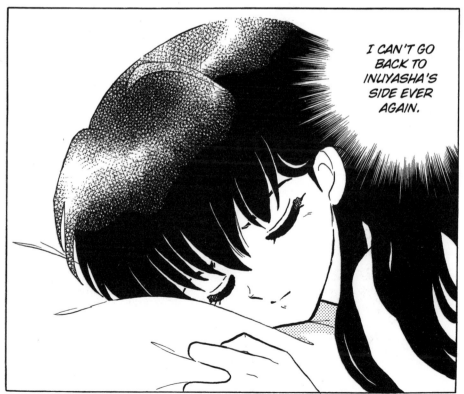

SCROLL SEVEN
WHERE THEY FIRST MET

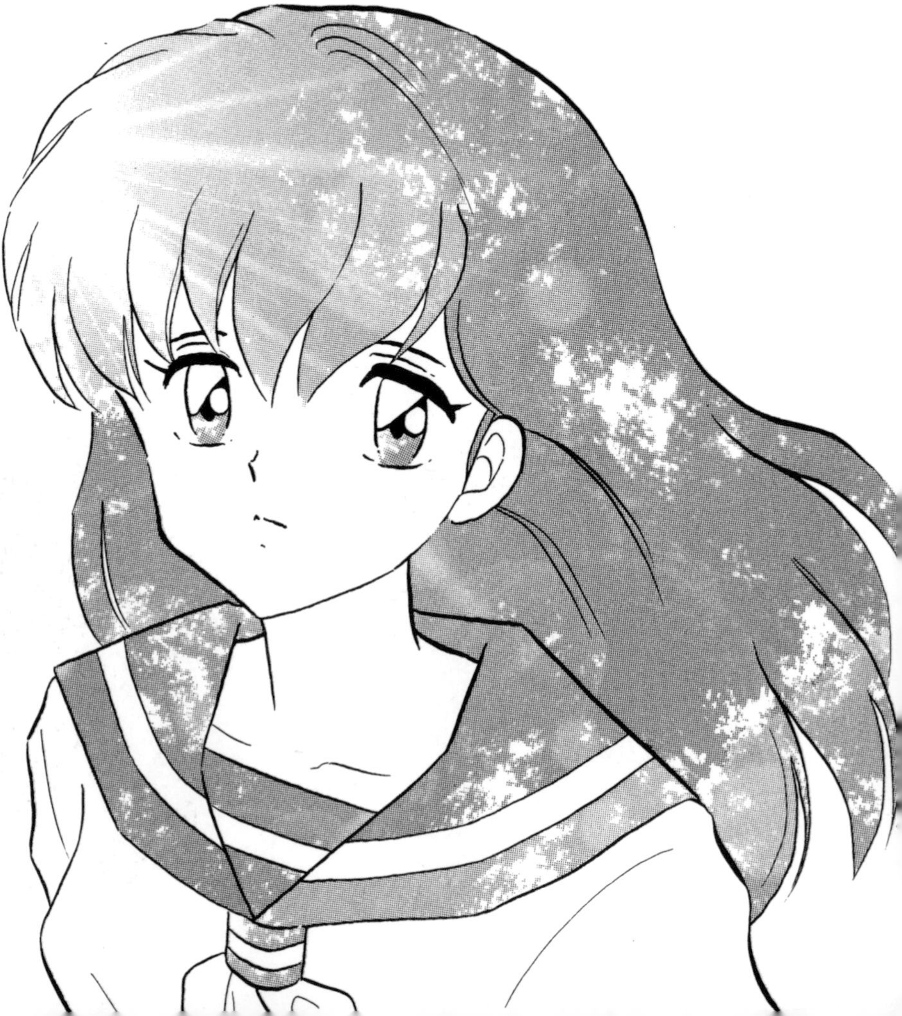

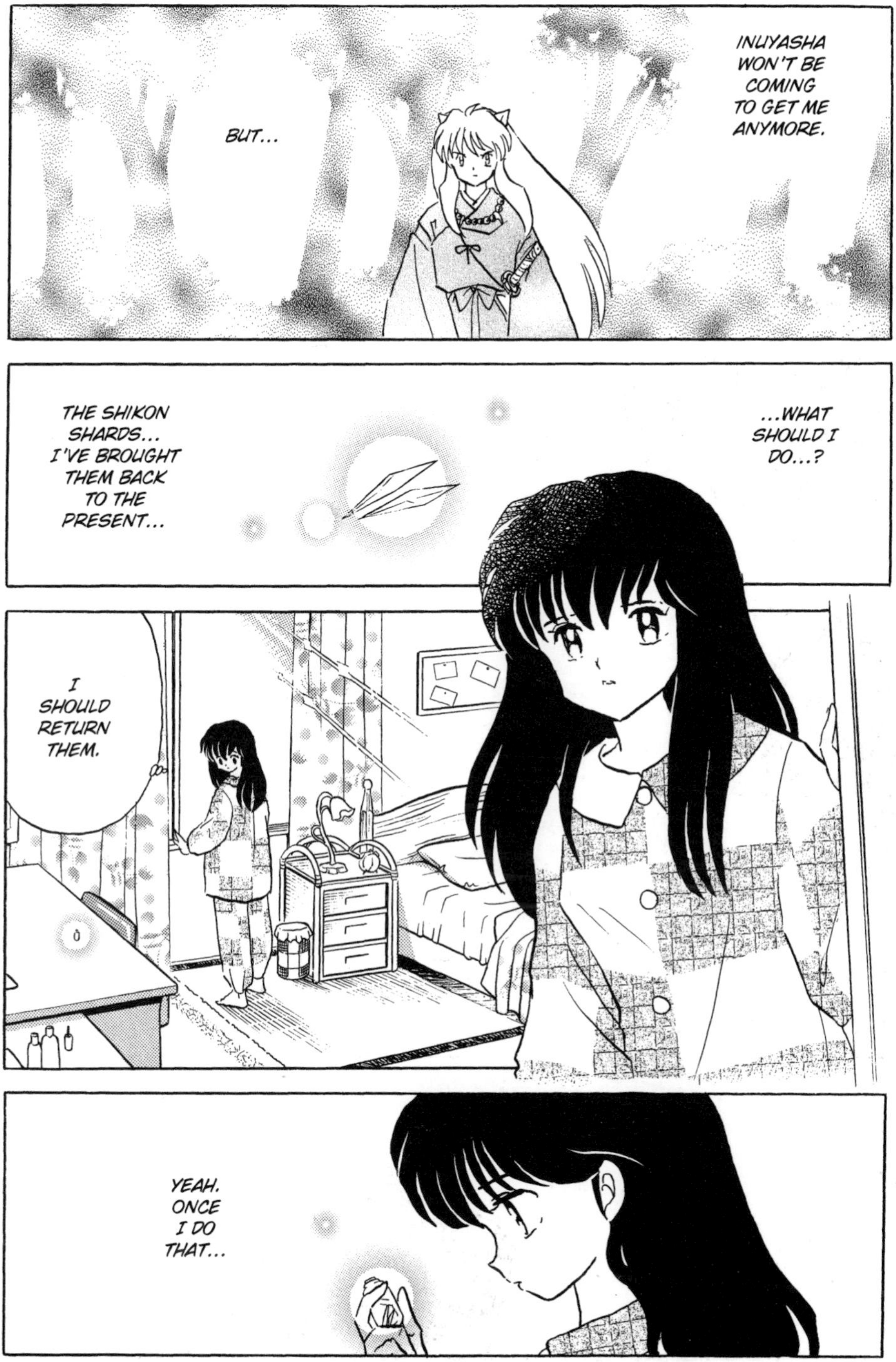
INUYASHA WON'T BE COMING TO GET ME ANYMORE.
BUT...
...WHAT SHOULD I DO...?
THE SHIKON SHARDS... I'VE BROUGHT THEM BACK TO THE PRESENT...
I SHOULD RETURN THEM.
YEAH. ONCE I DO THAT...

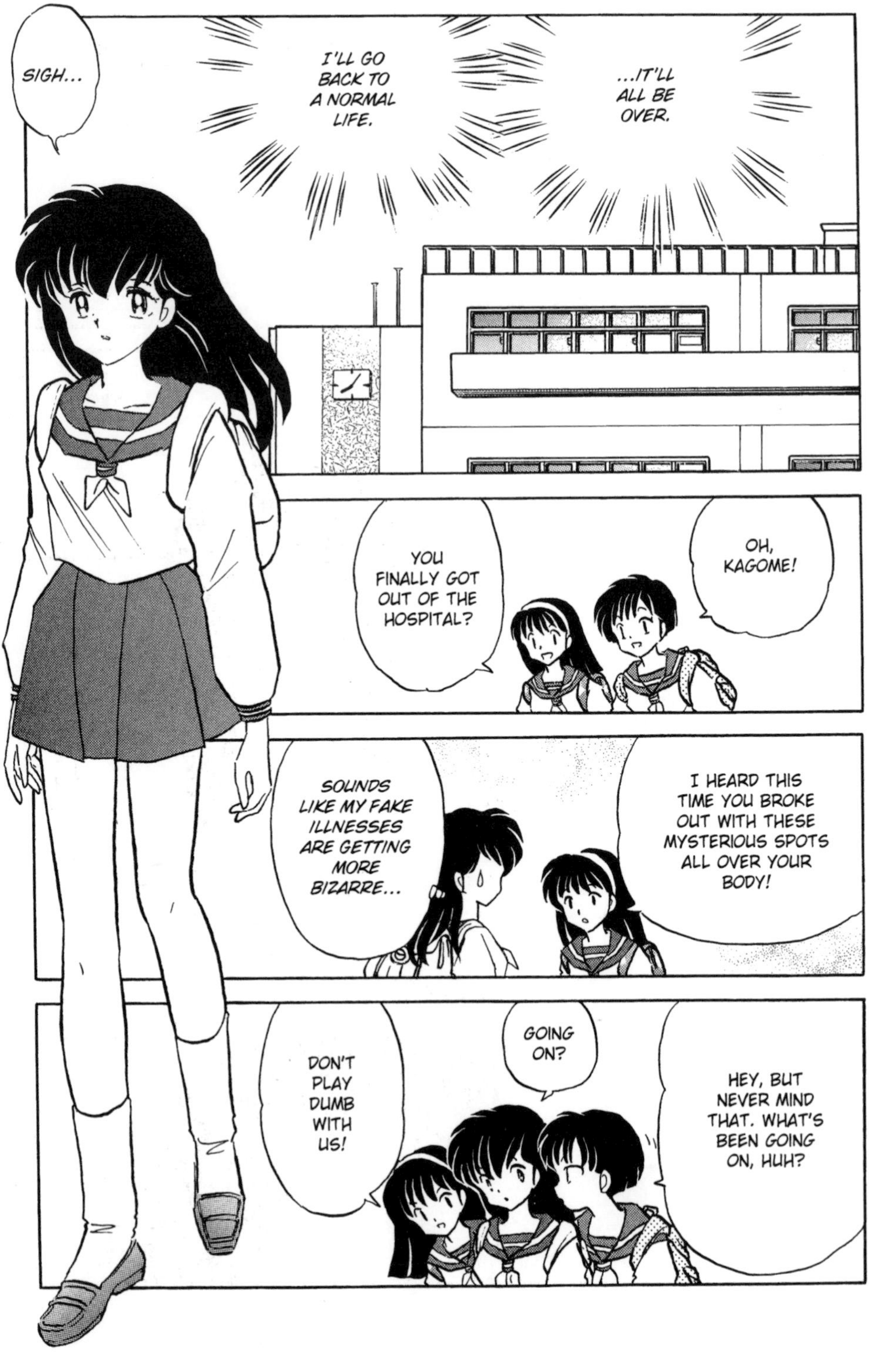
...IT'LL ALL BE OVER.
I'LL GO BACK TO A NORMAL LIFE.
SIGH...
OH, KAGOME!
YOU FINALLY GOT OUT OF THE HOSPITAL?
I HEARD THIS TIME YOU BROKE OUT WITH THESE MYSTERIOUS SPOTS ALL OVER YOUR BODY!
SOUNDS LIKE MY FAKE ILLNESSES ARE GETTING MORE BIZARRE...
HEY, BUT NEVER MIND THAT. WHAT'S BEEN GOING ON, HUH?
GOING ON?
DON'T PLAY DUMB WITH US!

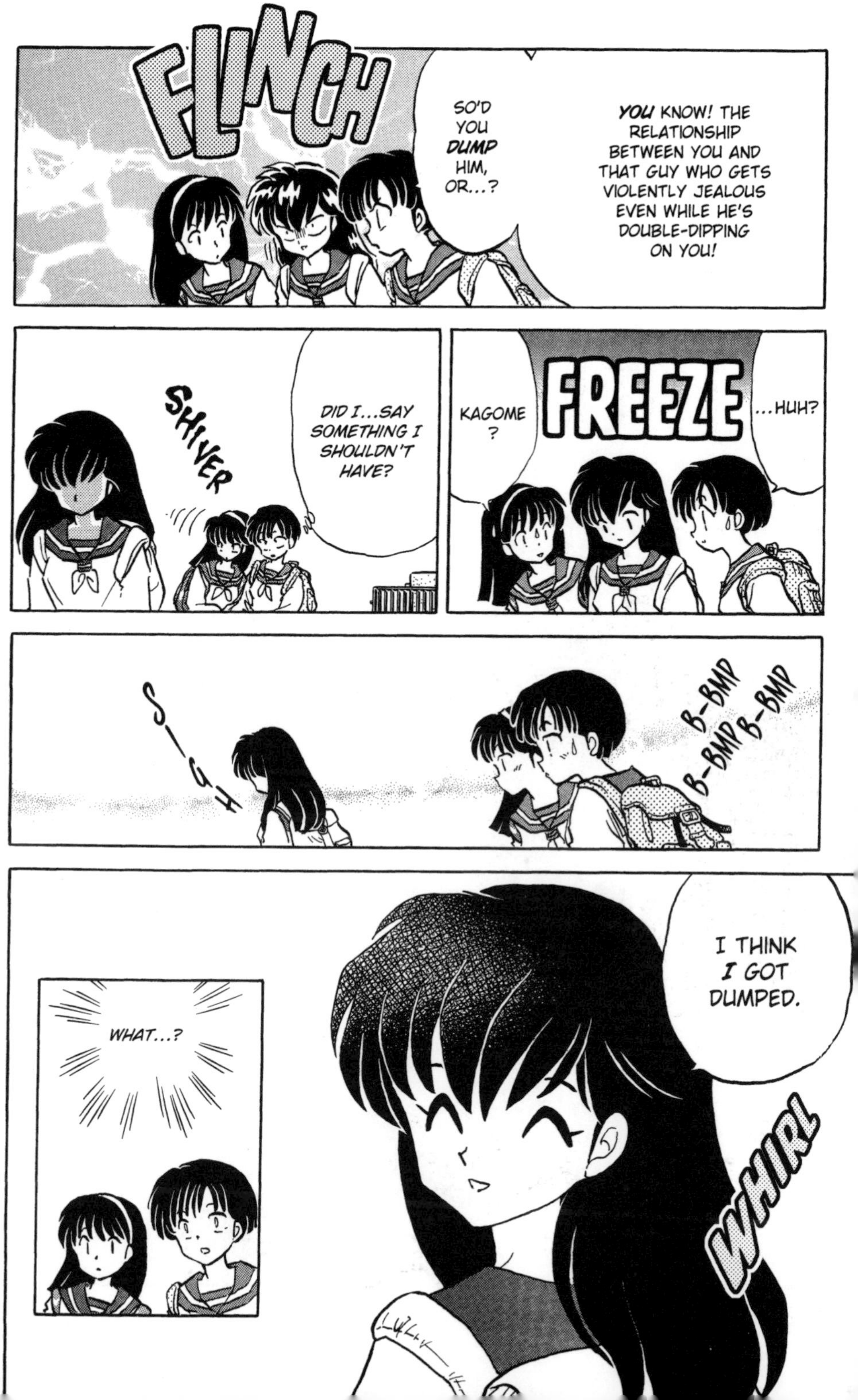
YOU KNOW! THE RELATIONSHIP BETWEEN YOU AND THAT GUY WHO GETS VIOLENTLY JEALOUS EVEN WHILE HE'S DOUBLE-DIPPING ON YOU!
SO'D YOU DUMP HIM, OR...?
FLINCH
...HUH?
FREEZE
KAGOME?
DID I...SAY SOMETHING I SHOULDN'T HAVE?
SHIVER
B-BMP B-BMP B-BMP
S-I-G-H
I THINK I GOT DUMPED.
WHIRL
WHAT...?

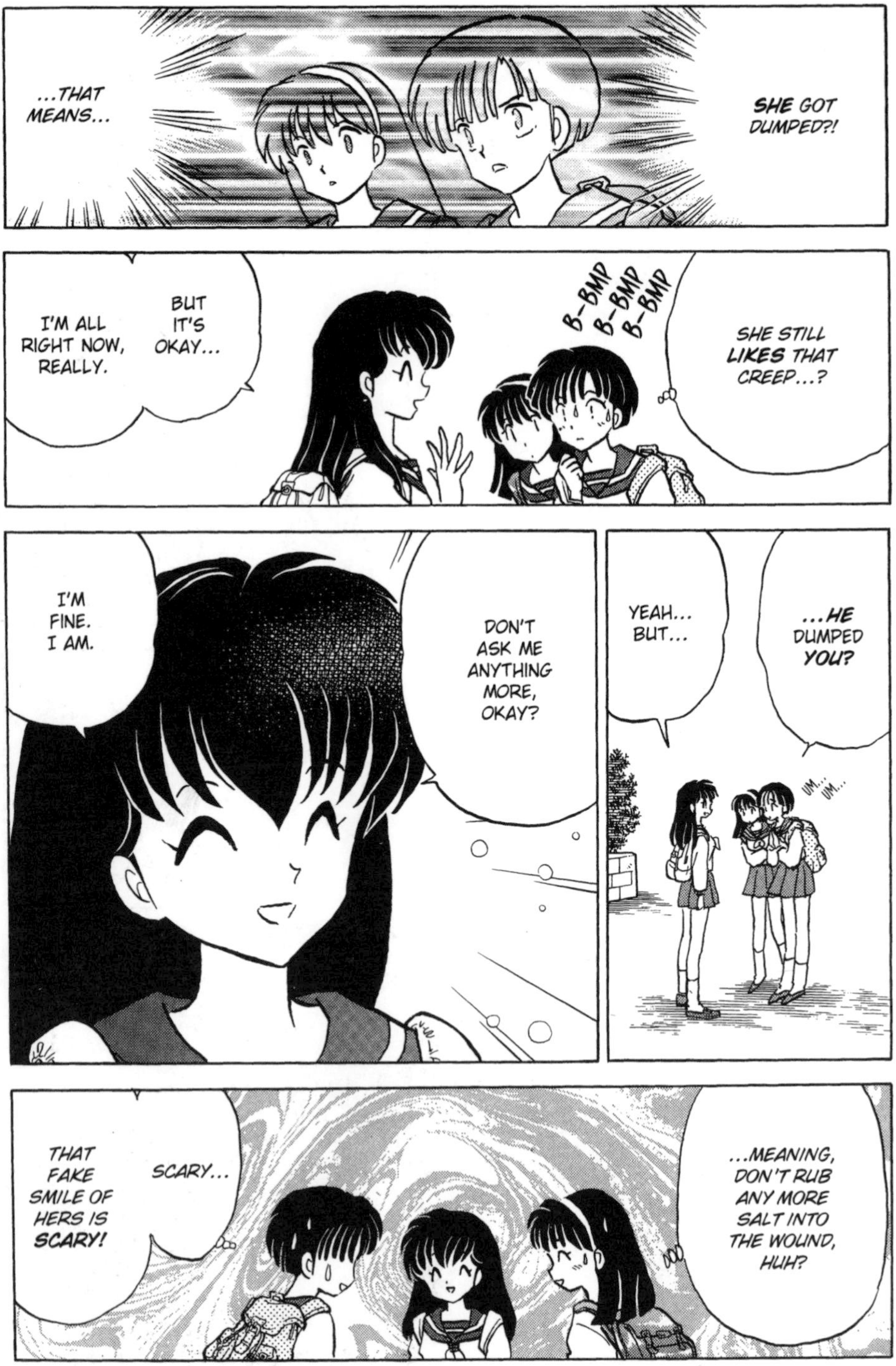

...THAT MEANS...
SHE GOT DUMPED?!
SHE STILL **LIKES** THAT CREEP...?
B-BMP B-BMP B-BMP
BUT IT'S OKAY...
I'M ALL RIGHT NOW, REALLY.
...**HE** DUMPED **YOU?**
YEAH... BUT...
UM... UM...
DON'T ASK ME ANYTHING MORE, OKAY?
I'M FINE. I AM.
...MEANING, DON'T RUB ANY MORE SALT INTO THE WOUND, HUH?
SCARY...
THAT FAKE SMILE OF HERS IS **SCARY!**

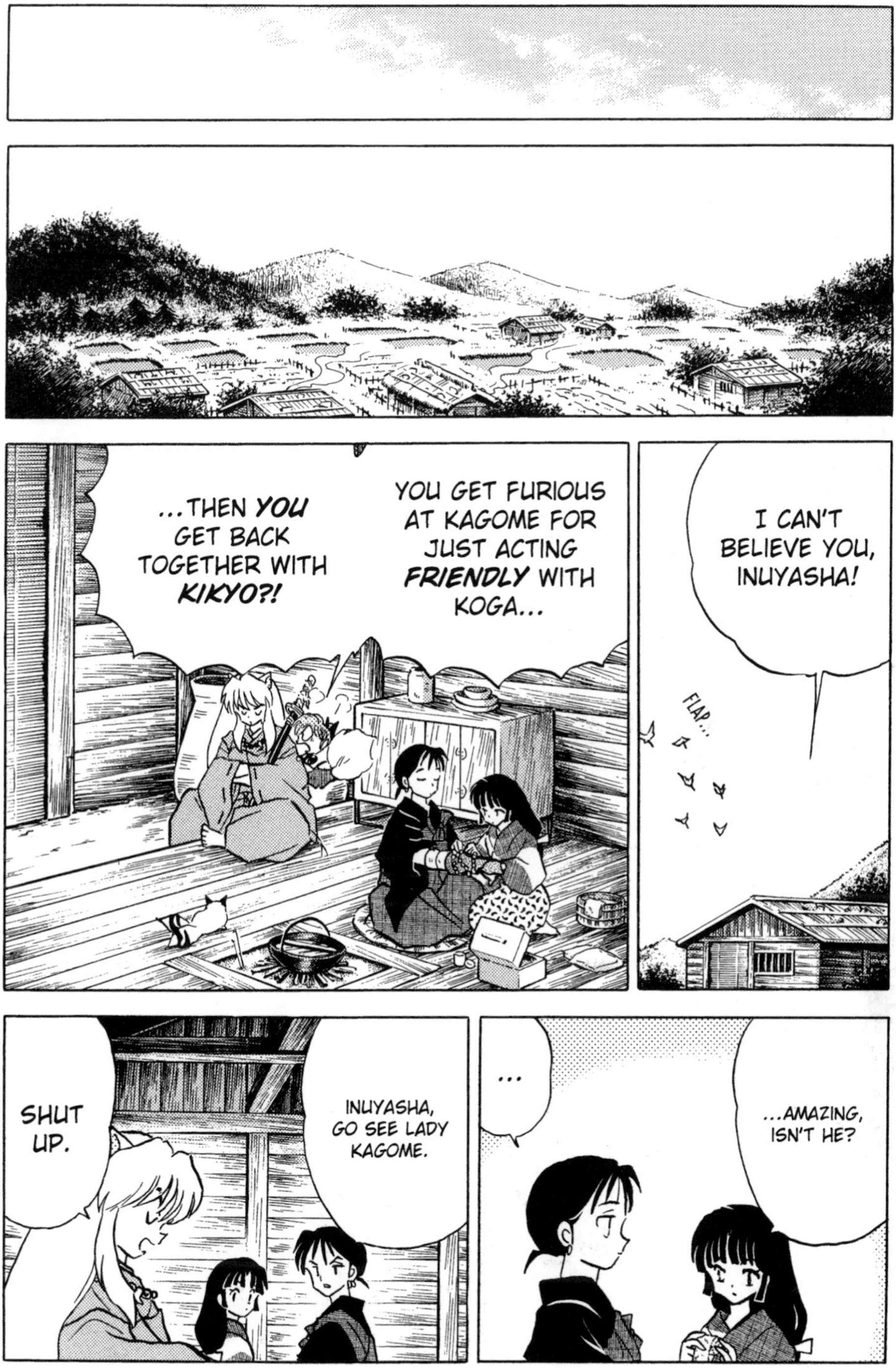
I CAN'T BELIEVE YOU, INUYASHA!
FLAP...
YOU GET FURIOUS AT KAGOME FOR JUST ACTING FRIENDLY WITH KOGA...
...THEN YOU GET BACK TOGETHER WITH KIKYO?!
...AMAZING, ISN'T HE?
...
INUYASHA, GO SEE LADY KAGOME.
SHUT UP.

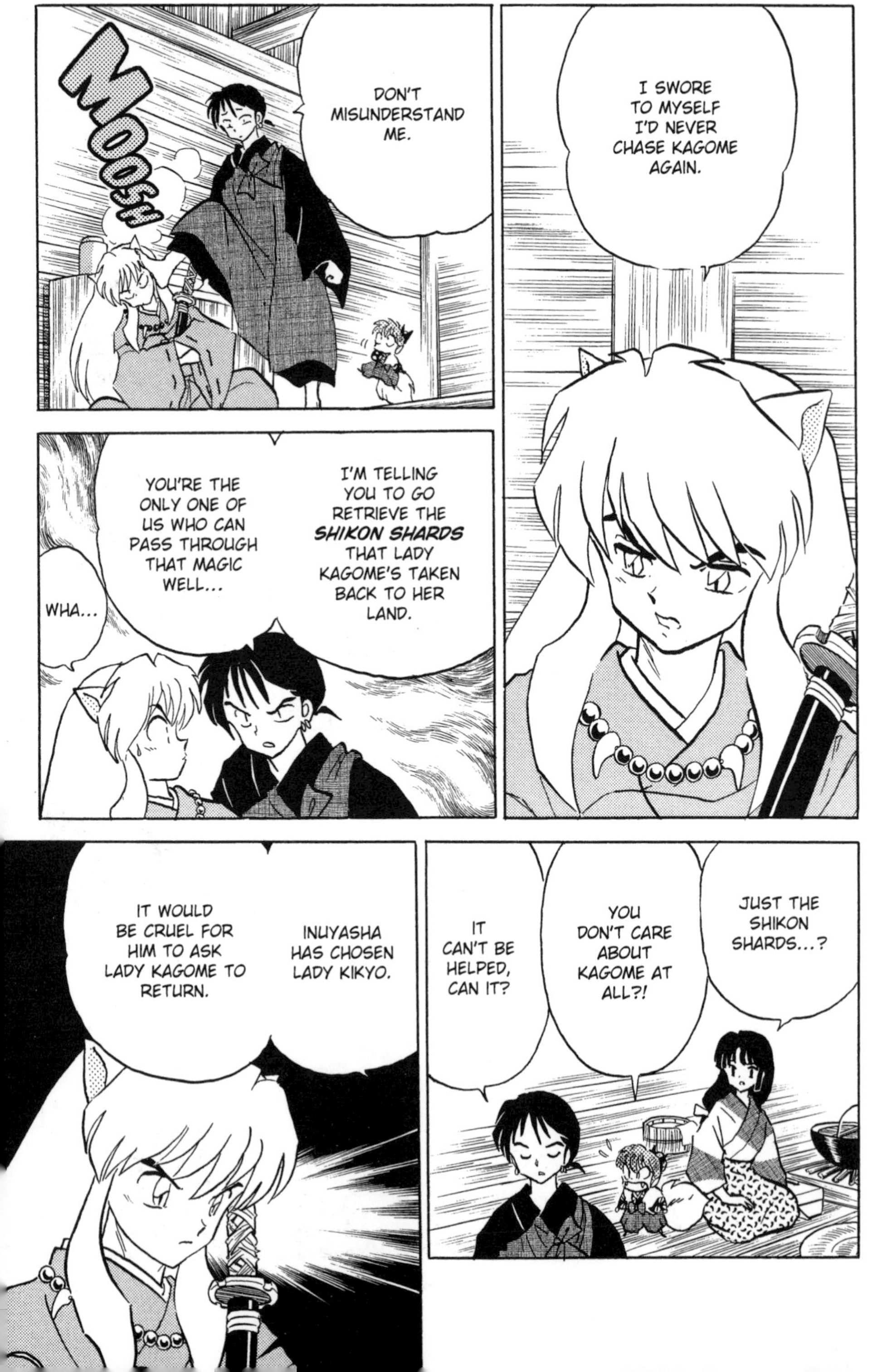
I SWORE TO MYSELF I'D NEVER CHASE KAGOME AGAIN.
DON'T MISUNDERSTAND ME.
MOOSH
I'M TELLING YOU TO GO RETRIEVE THE *SHIKON SHARDS* THAT LADY KAGOME'S TAKEN BACK TO HER LAND.
YOU'RE THE ONLY ONE OF US WHO CAN PASS THROUGH THAT MAGIC WELL...
WHA...
JUST THE SHIKON SHARDS...?
YOU DON'T CARE ABOUT KAGOME AT ALL?!
IT CAN'T BE HELPED, CAN IT?
INUYASHA HAS CHOSEN LADY KIKYO.
IT WOULD BE CRUEL FOR HIM TO ASK LADY KAGOME TO RETURN.

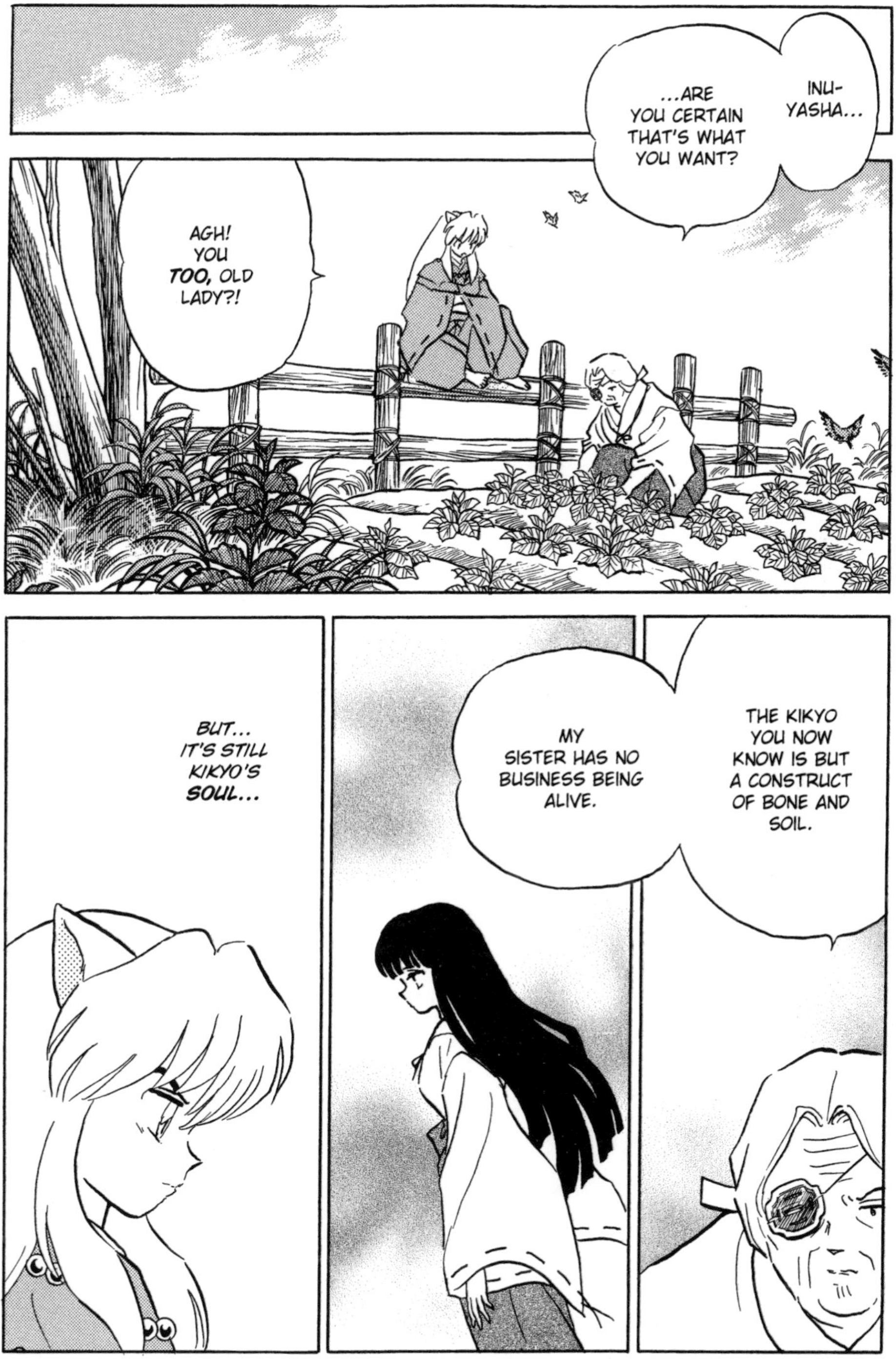
INU-YASHA... ...ARE YOU CERTAIN THAT'S WHAT YOU WANT?
AGH! YOU TOO, OLD LADY?!
THE KIKYO YOU NOW KNOW IS BUT A CONSTRUCT OF BONE AND SOIL.
MY SISTER HAS NO BUSINESS BEING ALIVE.
BUT... IT'S STILL KIKYO'S SOUL...

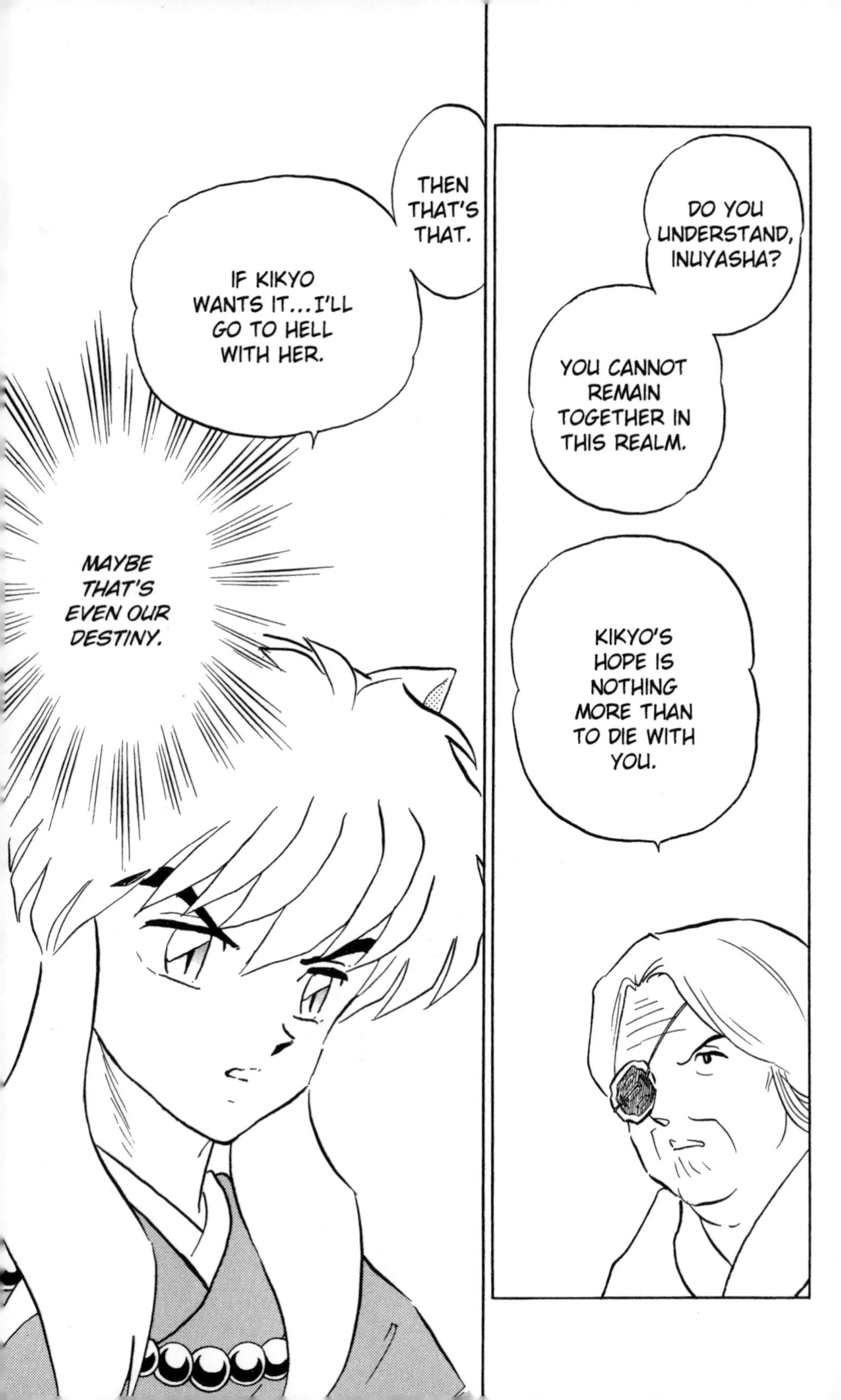
DO YOU UNDERSTAND, INUYASHA?
YOU CANNOT REMAIN TOGETHER IN THIS REALM.
KIKYO'S HOPE IS NOTHING MORE THAN TO DIE WITH YOU.
THEN THAT'S THAT.
IF KIKYO WANTS IT...I'LL GO TO HELL WITH HER.
MAYBE THAT'S EVEN OUR DESTINY.

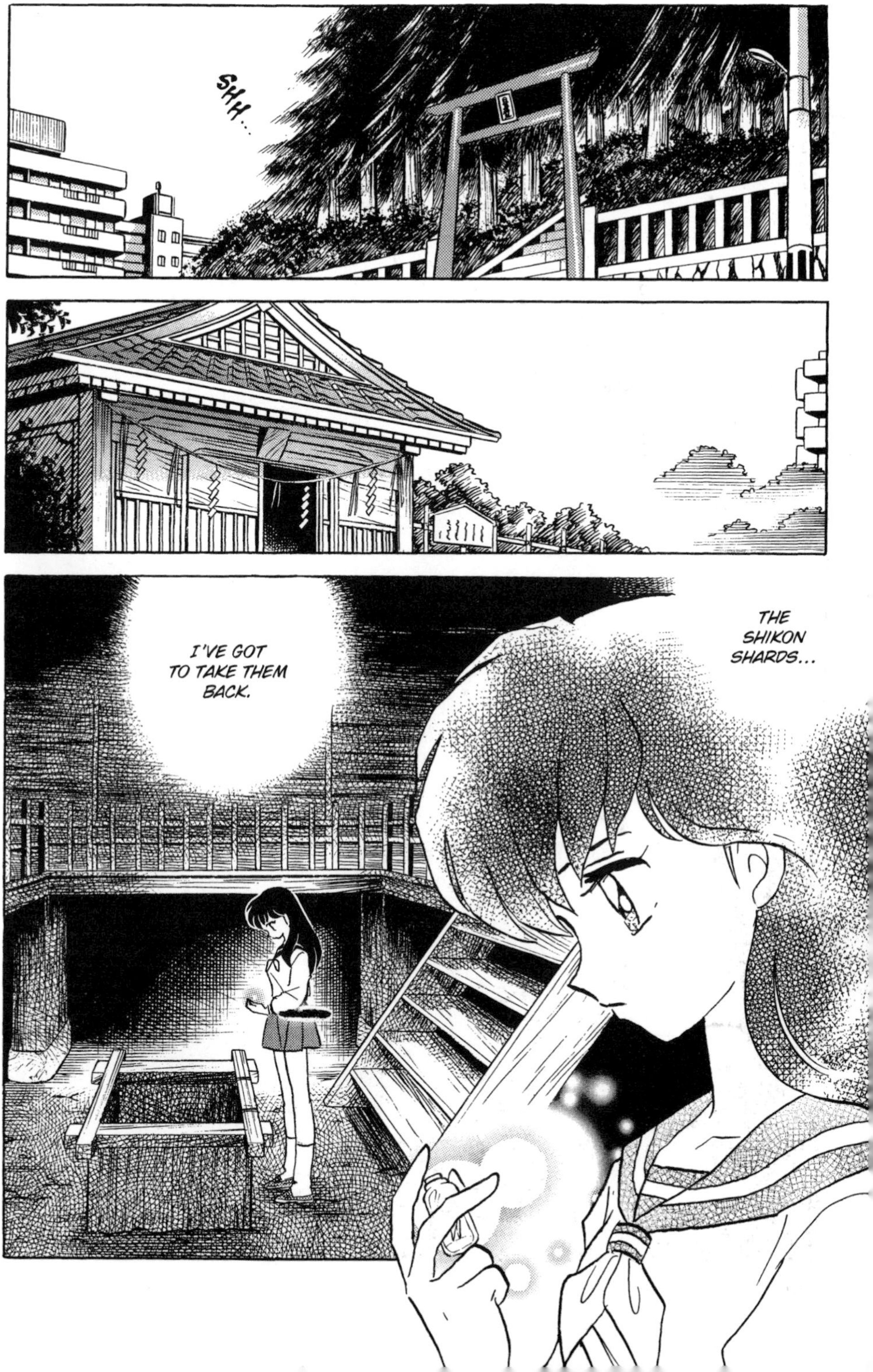
SHH...
THE SHIKON SHARDS...
I'VE GOT TO TAKE THEM BACK.

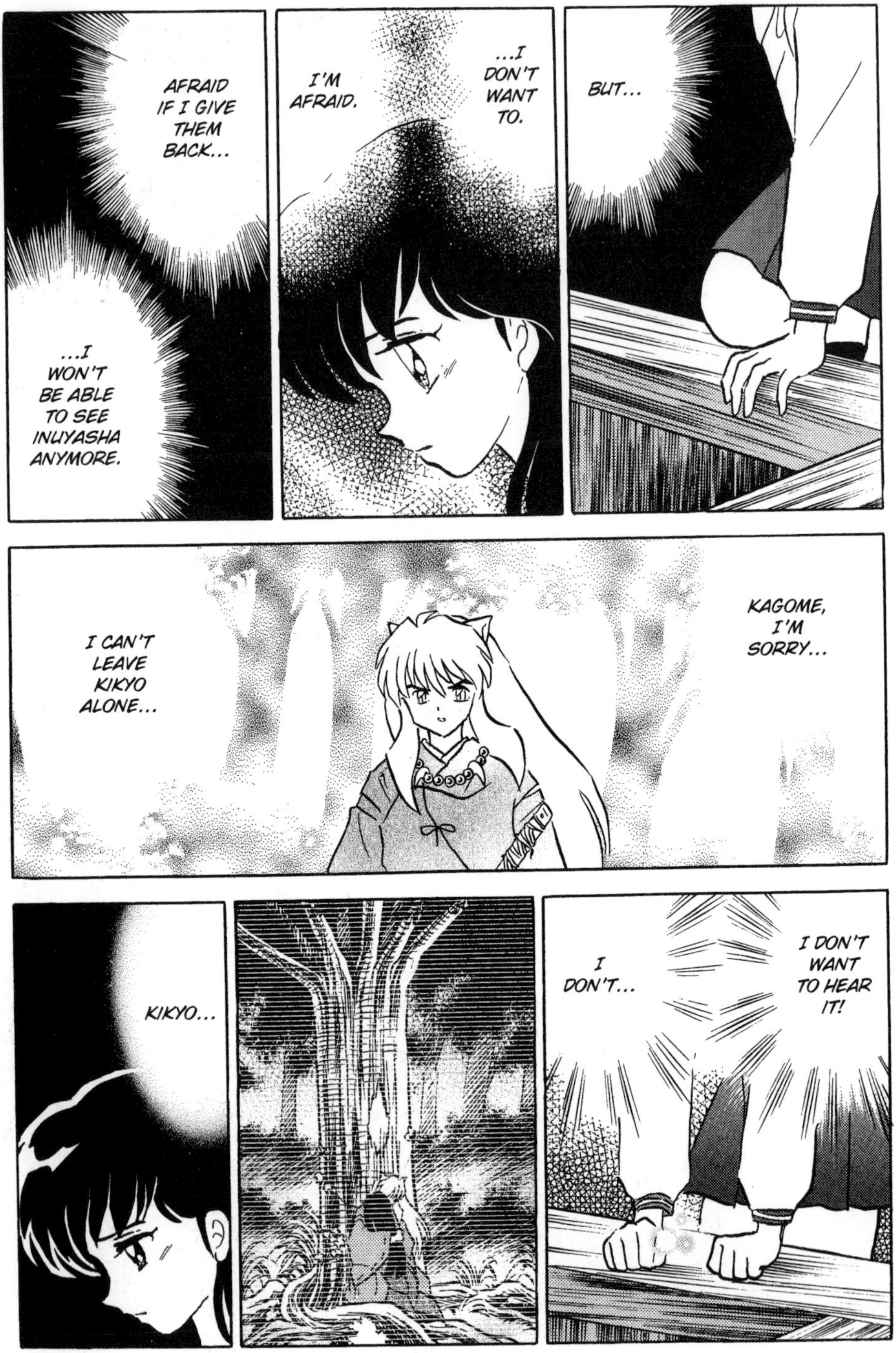
BUT...
...I DON'T WANT TO.
I'M AFRAID.
AFRAID IF I GIVE THEM BACK...
...I WON'T BE ABLE TO SEE INUYASHA ANYMORE.
KAGOME, I'M SORRY...
I CAN'T LEAVE KIKYO ALONE...
I DON'T WANT TO HEAR IT!
I DON'T...
KIKYO...

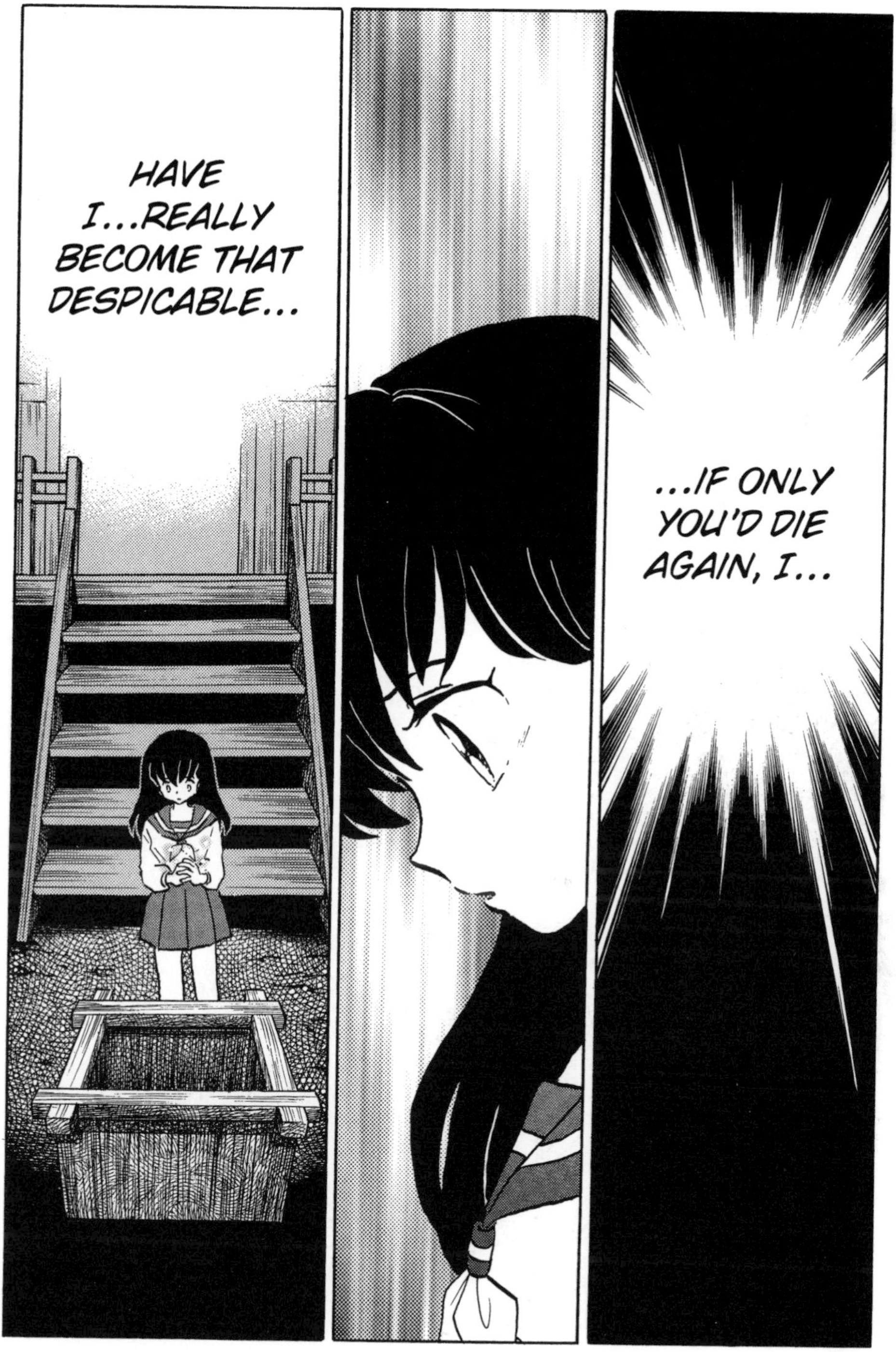
...IF ONLY YOU'D DIE AGAIN, I...
HAVE I...REALLY BECOME THAT DESPICABLE...

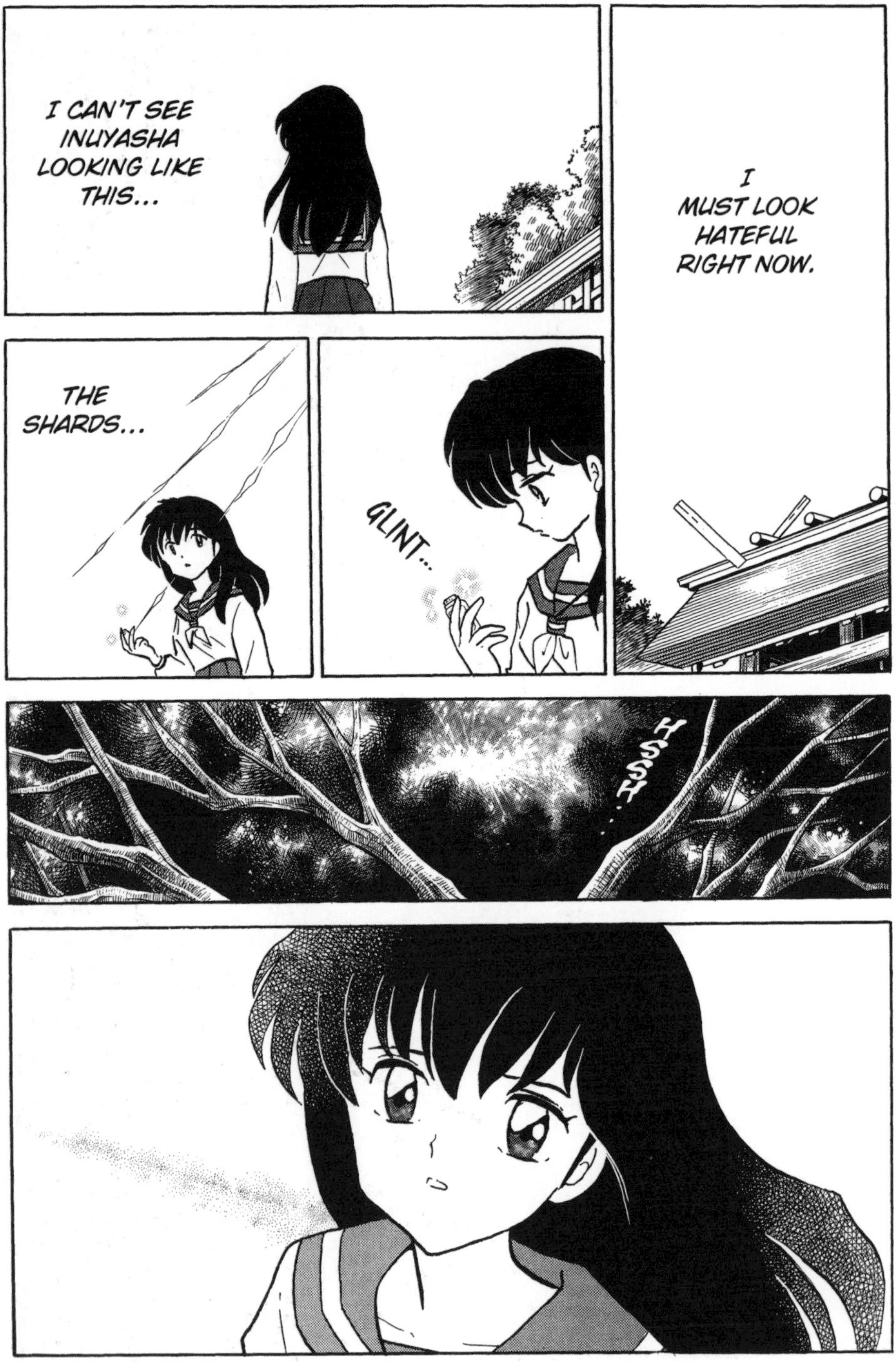
I CAN'T SEE INUYASHA LOOKING LIKE THIS...
THE SHARDS...
GLINT...
I MUST LOOK HATEFUL RIGHT NOW.
HSSSH...

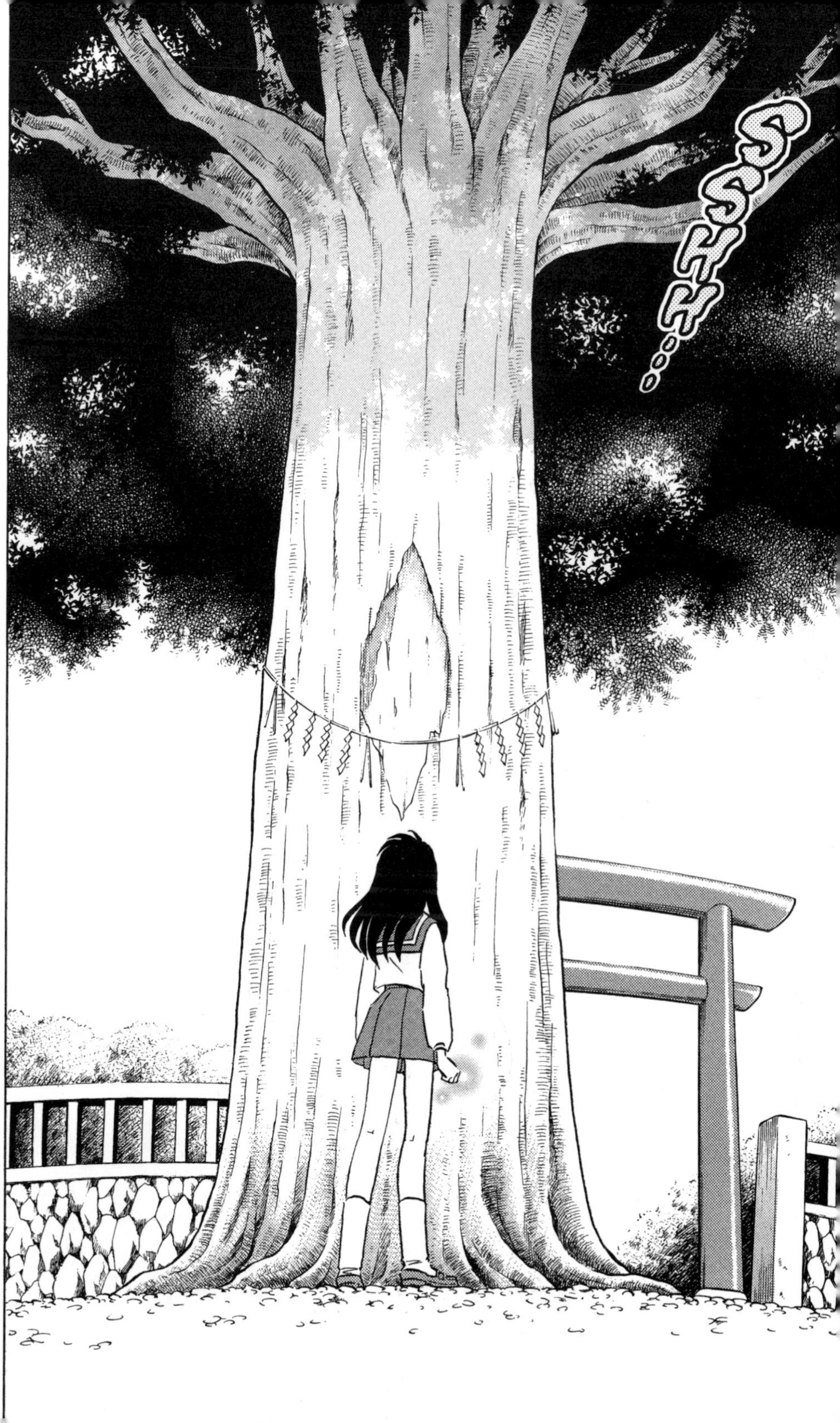
SSHHH...

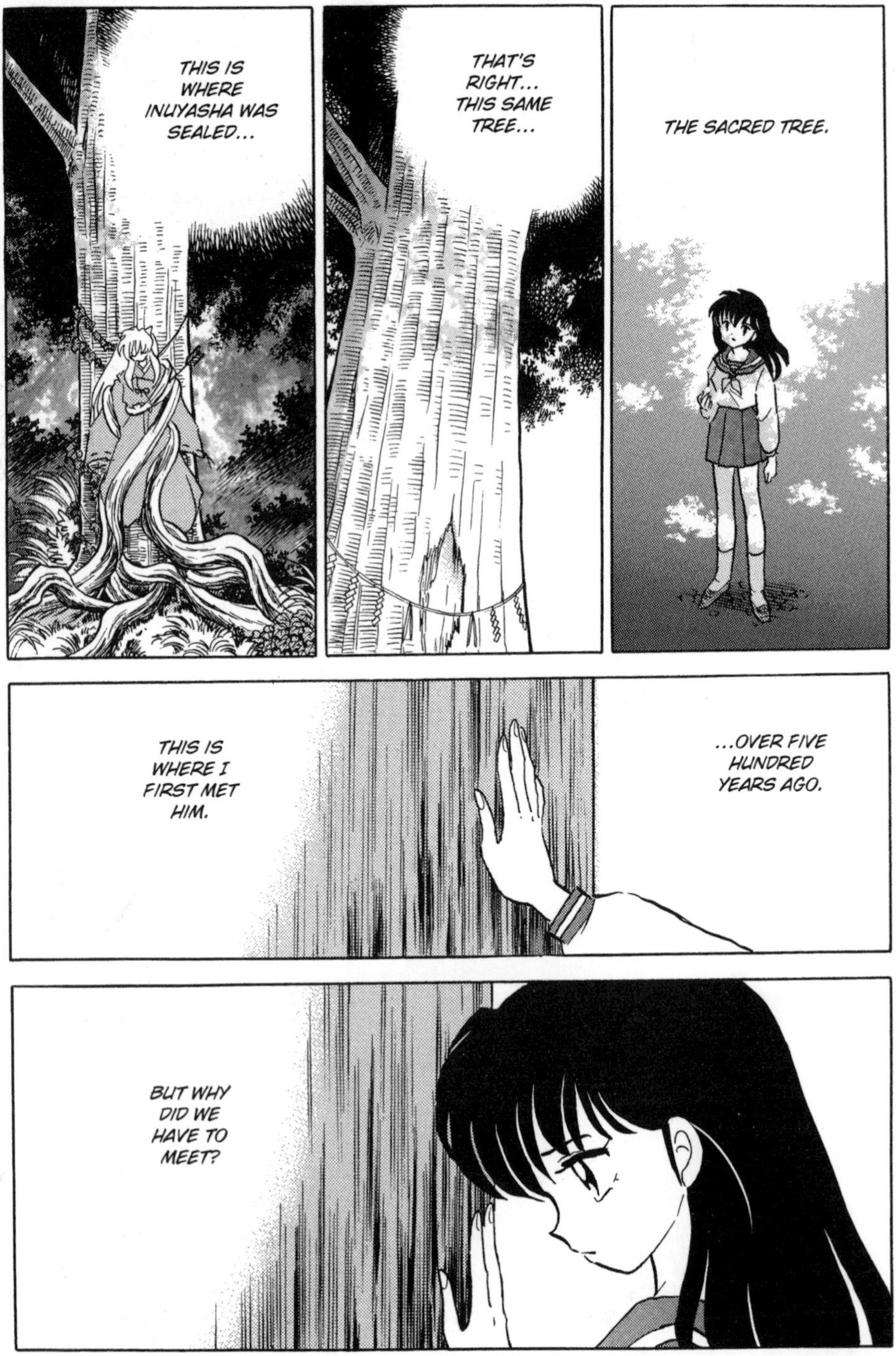
THE SACRED TREE.
THAT'S RIGHT... THIS SAME TREE...
THIS IS WHERE INUYASHA WAS SEALED...
THIS IS WHERE I FIRST MET HIM.
...OVER FIVE HUNDRED YEARS AGO.
BUT WHY DID WE HAVE TO MEET?

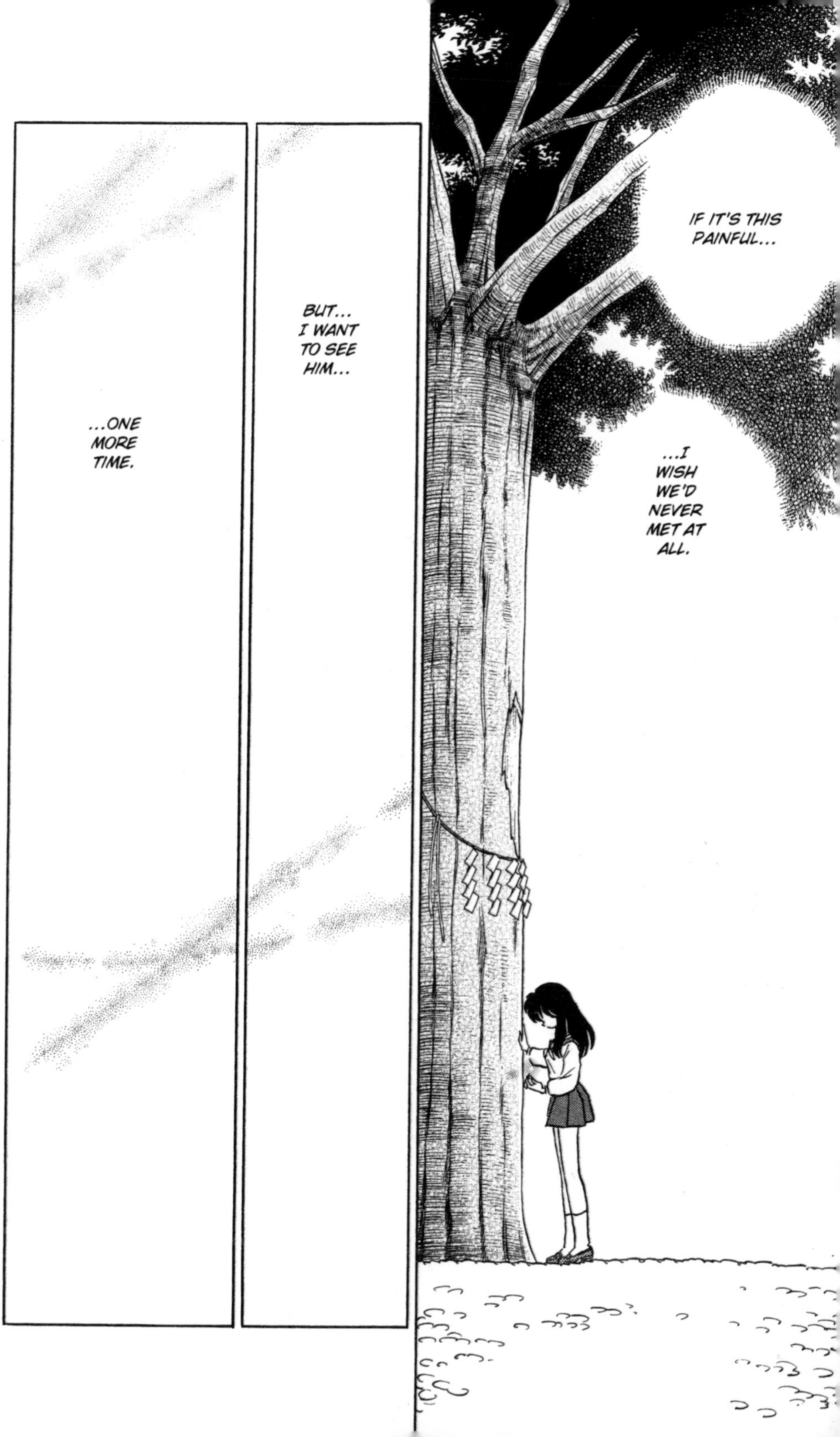
IF IT'S THIS PAINFUL...
...I WISH WE'D NEVER MET AT ALL.
BUT... I WANT TO SEE HIM...
...ONE MORE TIME.

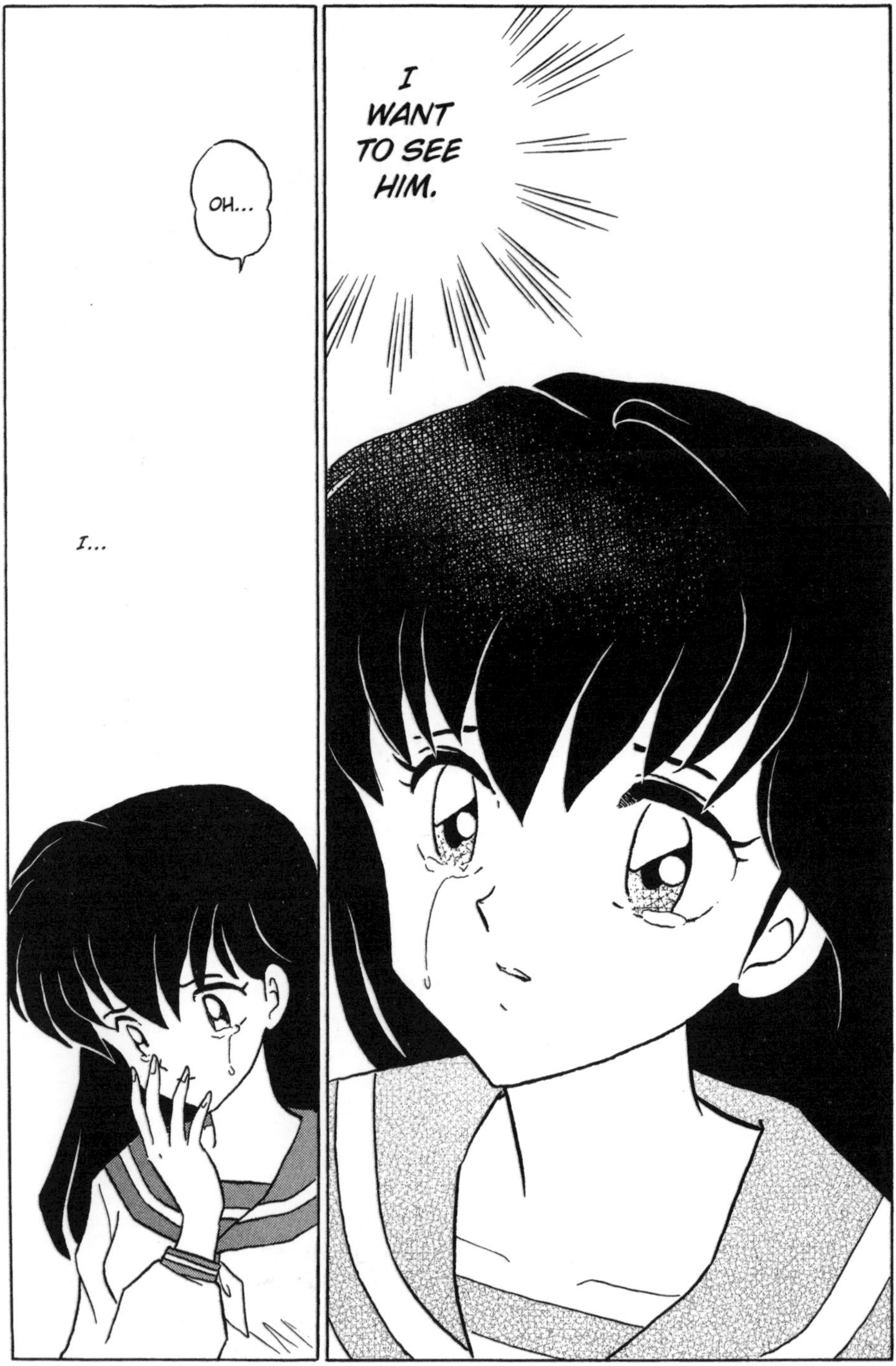
I WANT TO SEE HIM.
OH...
I...

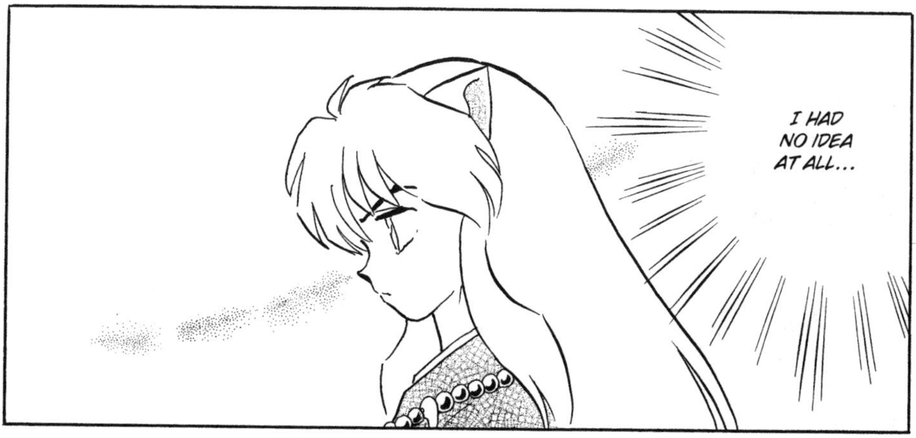
I HAD NO IDEA AT ALL...

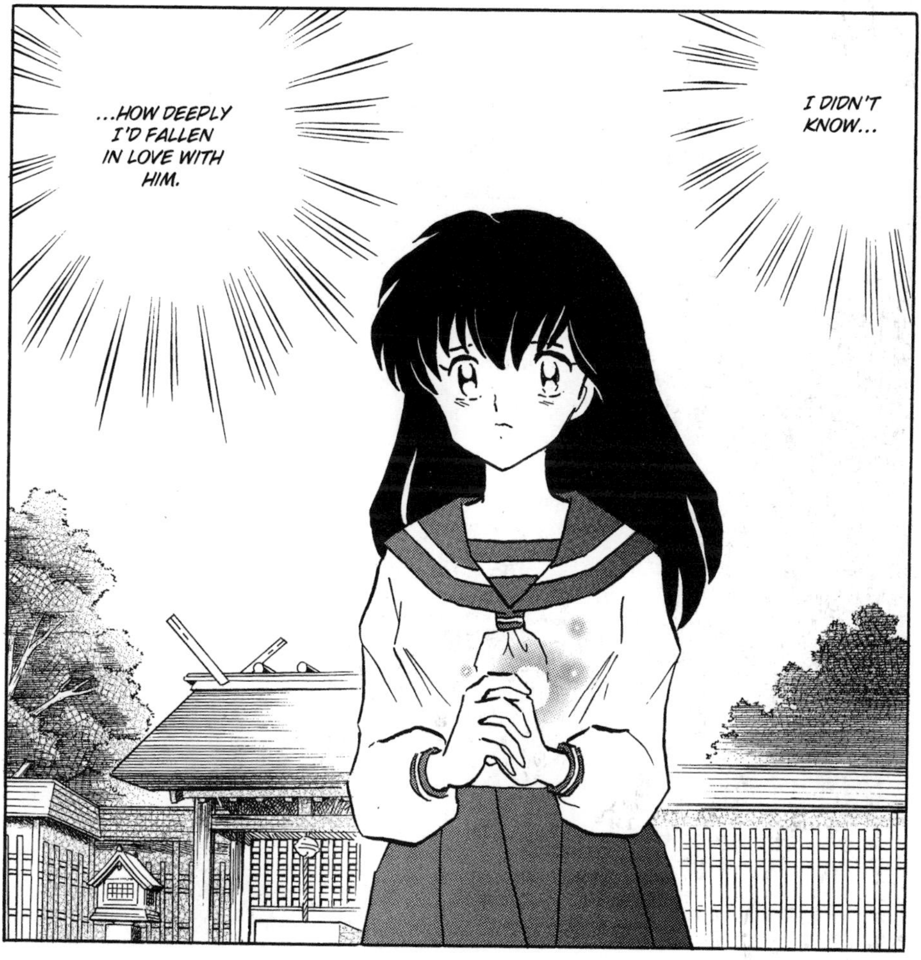
I DIDN'T KNOW...
...HOW DEEPLY I'D FALLEN IN LOVE WITH HIM.

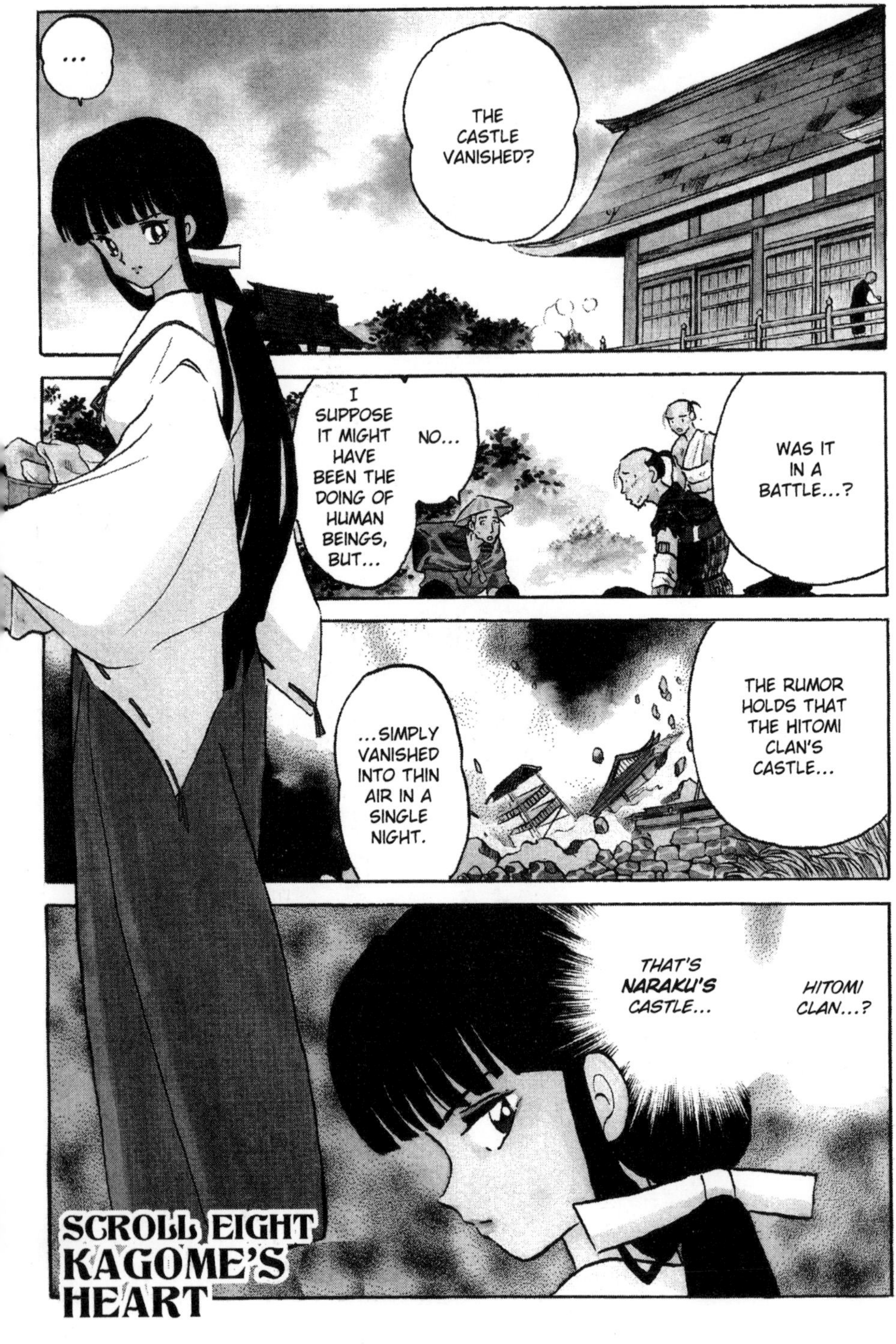
THE CASTLE VANISHED?
...
WAS IT IN A BATTLE...?
NO...
I SUPPOSE IT MIGHT HAVE BEEN THE DOING OF HUMAN BEINGS, BUT...
THE RUMOR HOLDS THAT THE HITOMI CLAN'S CASTLE...
...SIMPLY VANISHED INTO THIN AIR IN A SINGLE NIGHT.
HITOMI CLAN...?
THAT'S **NARAKU'S** CASTLE...
SCROLL EIGHT
KAGOME'S HEART

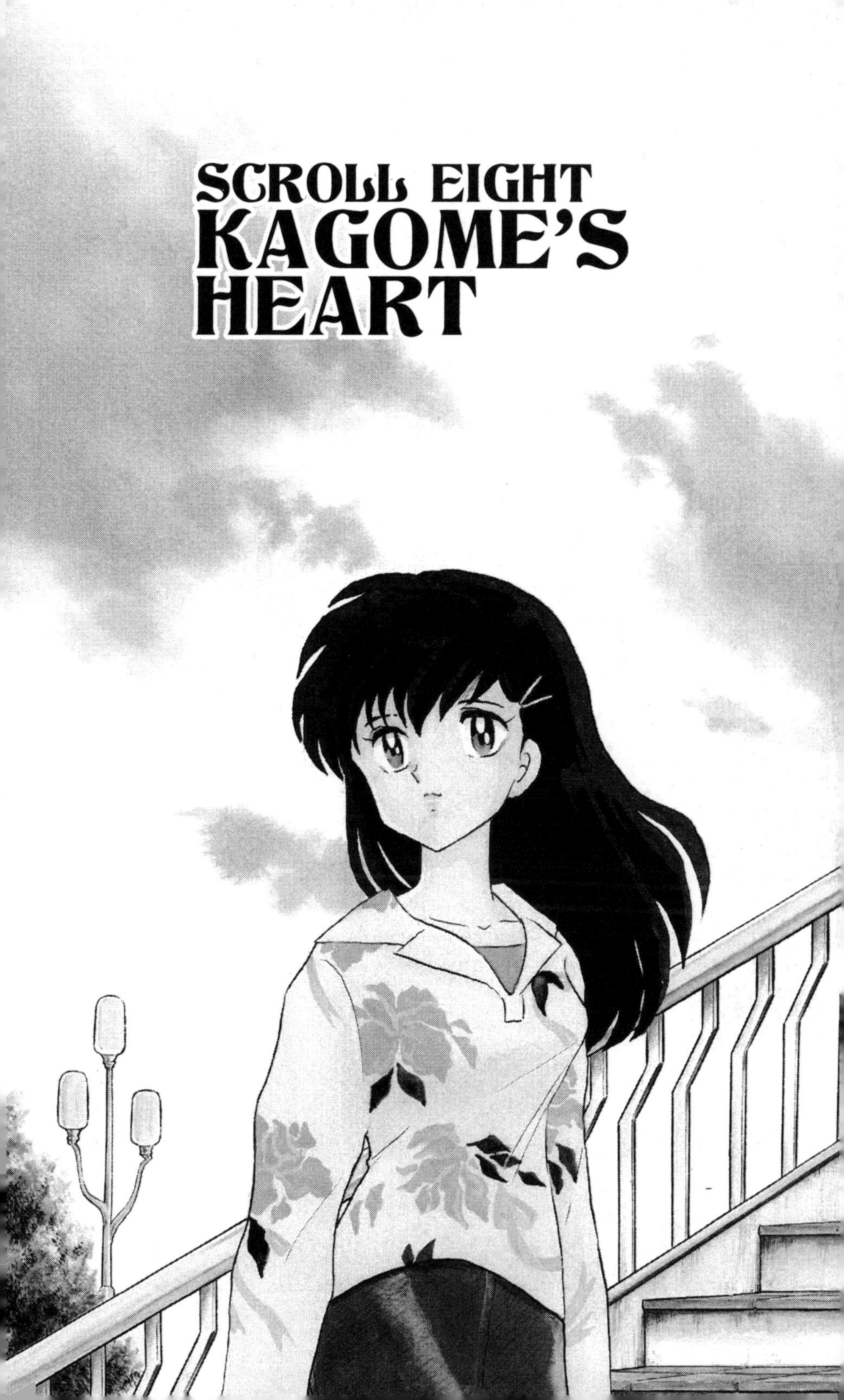
SCROLL EIGHT
KAGOME'S
HEART

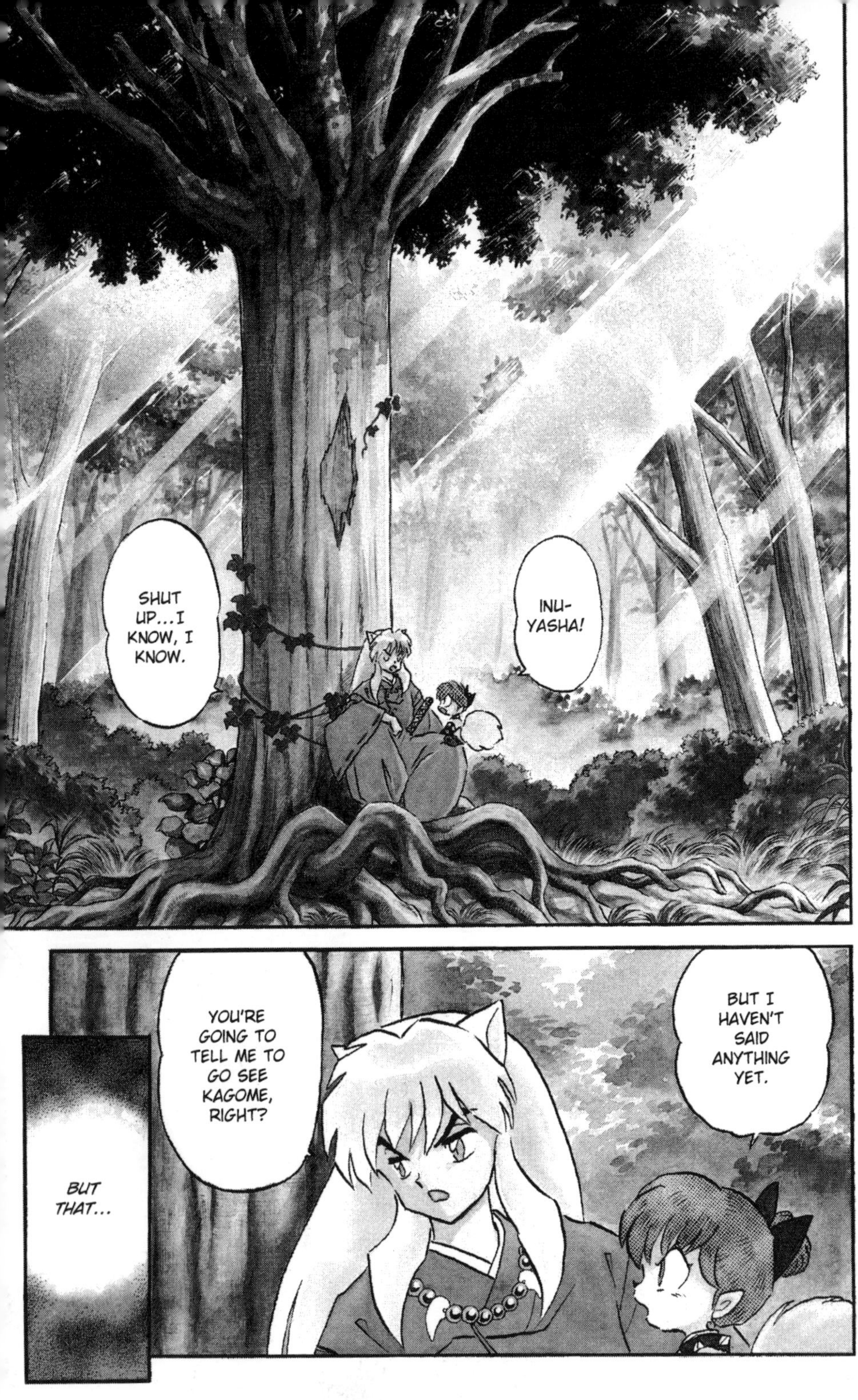
INU-YASHA!
SHUT UP...I KNOW, I KNOW.
YOU'RE GOING TO TELL ME TO GO SEE KAGOME, RIGHT?
BUT I HAVEN'T SAID ANYTHING YET.
BUT THAT...

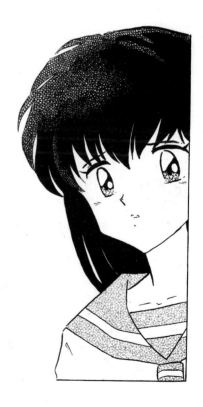

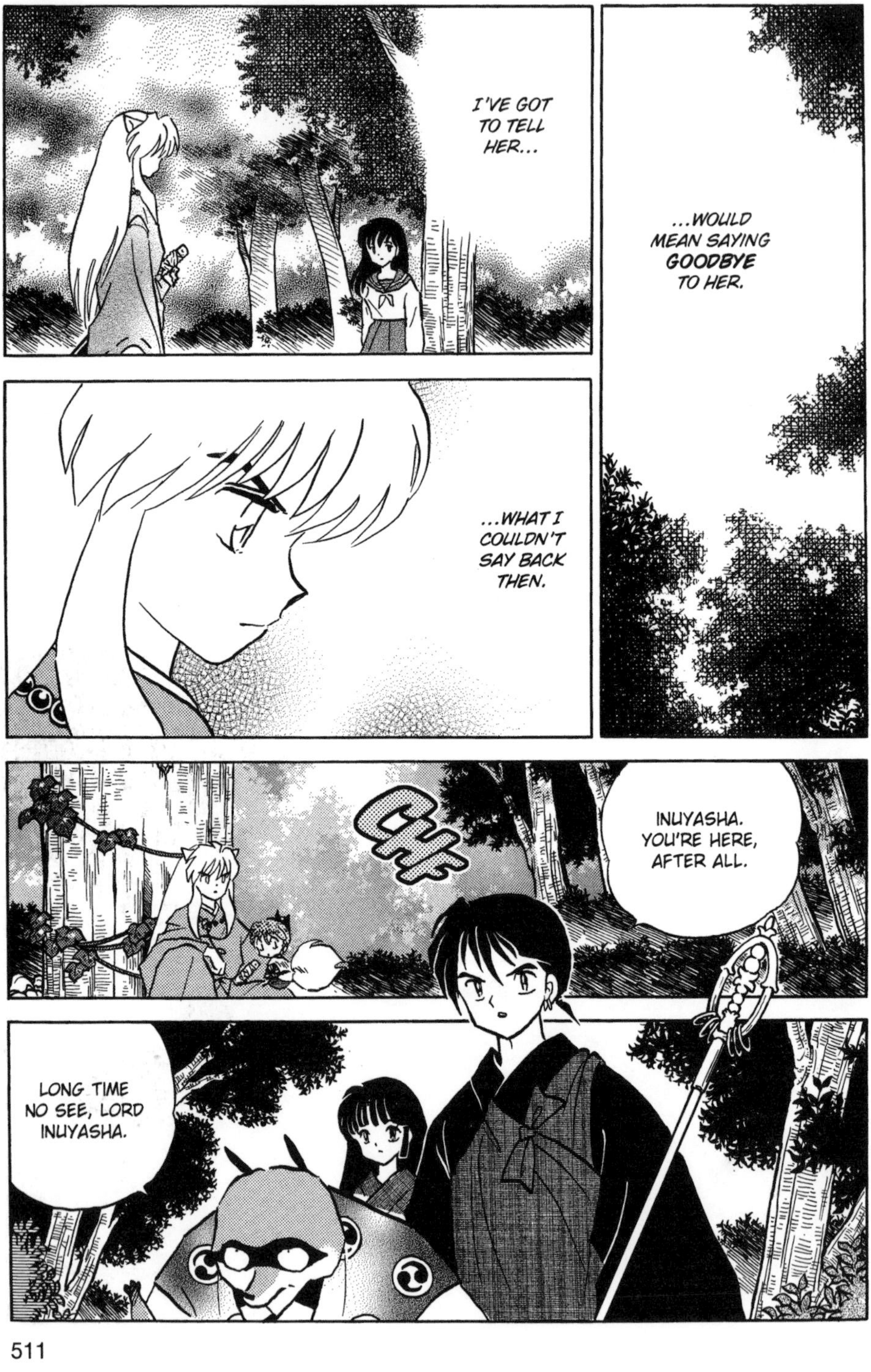
...WOULD MEAN SAYING GOODBYE TO HER.
I'VE GOT TO TELL HER...
...WHAT I COULDN'T SAY BACK THEN.
INUYASHA. YOU'RE HERE, AFTER ALL.
CHF
LONG TIME NO SEE, LORD INUYASHA.

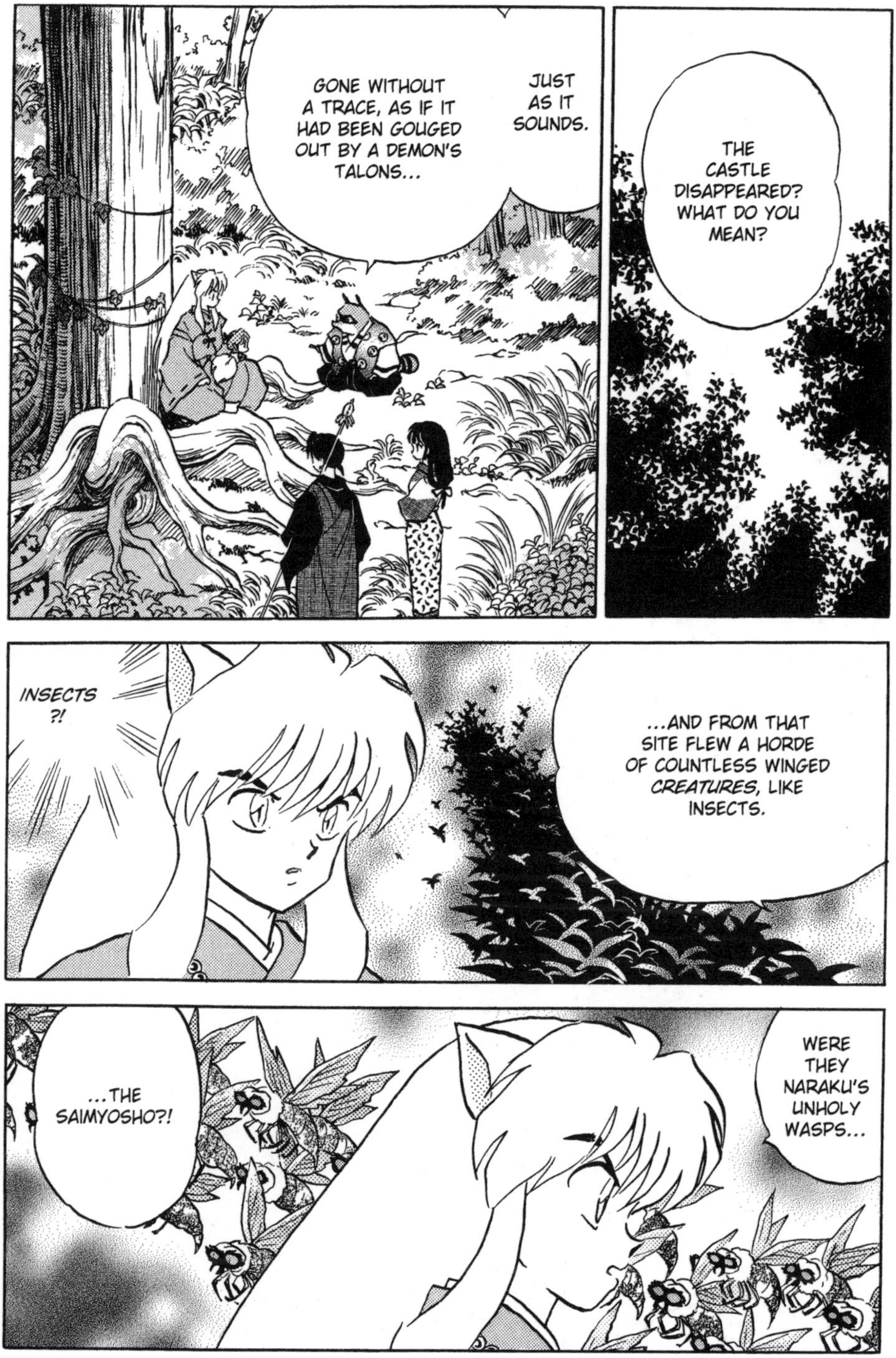
THE CASTLE DISAPPEARED? WHAT DO YOU MEAN?
JUST AS IT SOUNDS.
GONE WITHOUT A TRACE, AS IF IT HAD BEEN GOUGED OUT BY A DEMON'S TALONS...
...AND FROM THAT SITE FLEW A HORDE OF COUNTLESS WINGED *CREATURES*, LIKE INSECTS.
INSECTS ?!
WERE THEY NARAKU'S UNHOLY WASPS...
...THE SAIMYOSHO?!

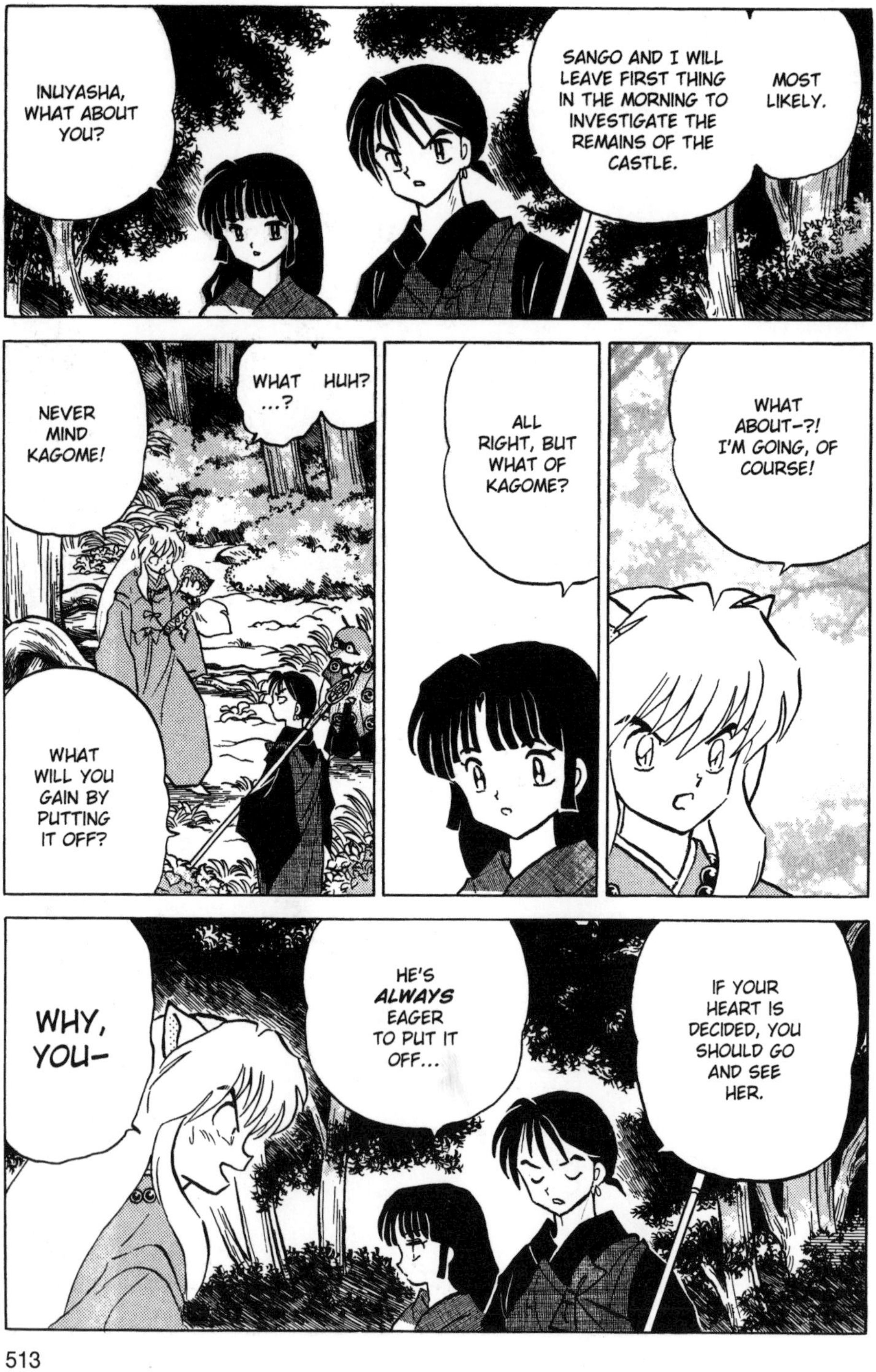
MOST LIKELY.
SANGO AND I WILL LEAVE FIRST THING IN THE MORNING TO INVESTIGATE THE REMAINS OF THE CASTLE.
INUYASHA, WHAT ABOUT YOU?
WHAT ABOUT-?! I'M GOING, OF COURSE!
ALL RIGHT, BUT WHAT OF KAGOME?
HUH?
WHAT ...?
NEVER MIND KAGOME!
WHAT WILL YOU GAIN BY PUTTING IT OFF?
IF YOUR HEART IS DECIDED, YOU SHOULD GO AND SEE HER.
HE'S *ALWAYS* EAGER TO PUT IT OFF...
WHY, YOU-

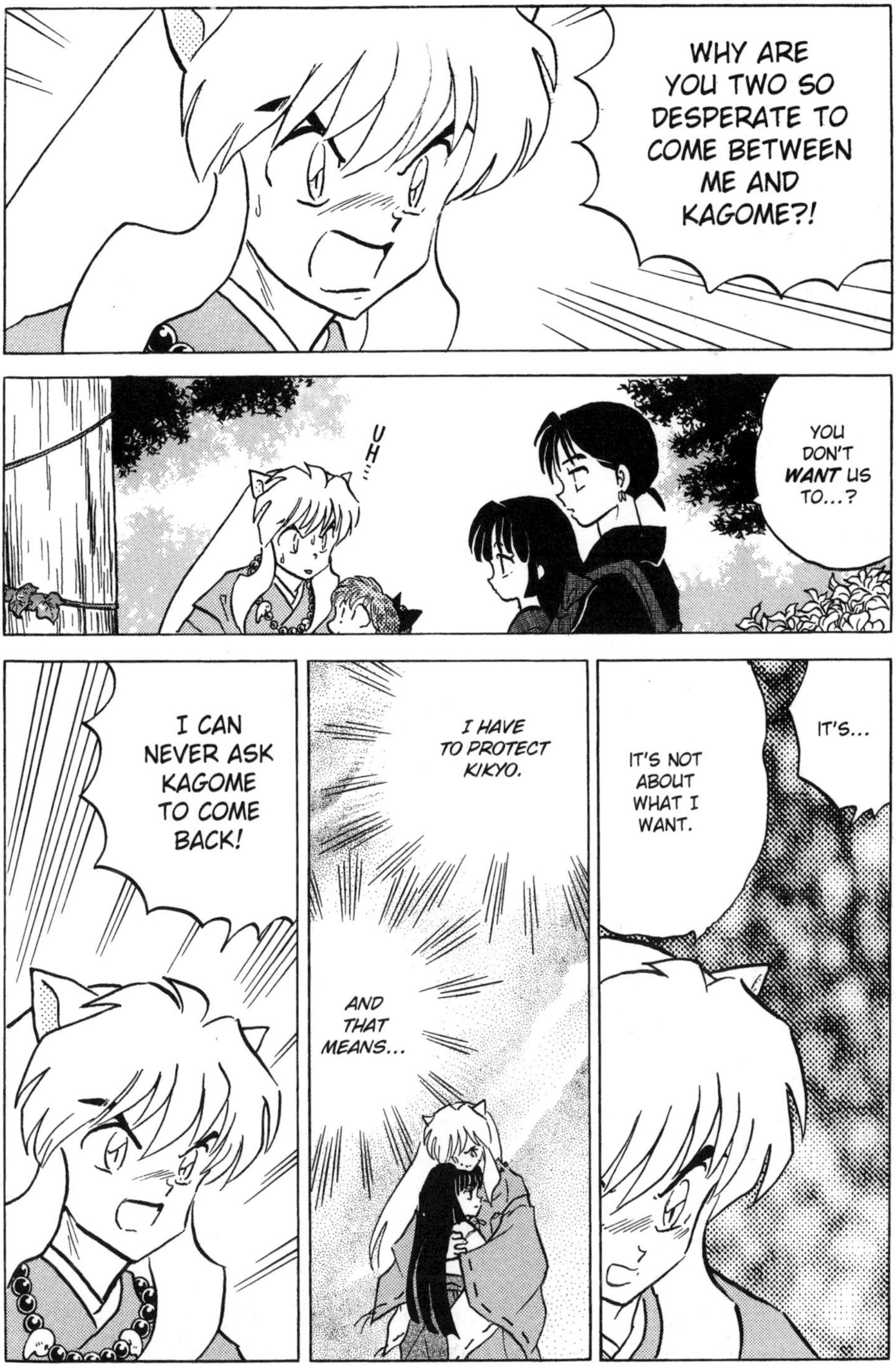
WHY ARE YOU TWO SO DESPERATE TO COME BETWEEN ME AND KAGOME?!
YOU DON'T *WANT* US TO...?
UH..!
IT'S...
IT'S NOT ABOUT WHAT I WANT.
I HAVE TO PROTECT KIKYO.
AND THAT MEANS...
I CAN NEVER ASK KAGOME TO COME BACK!

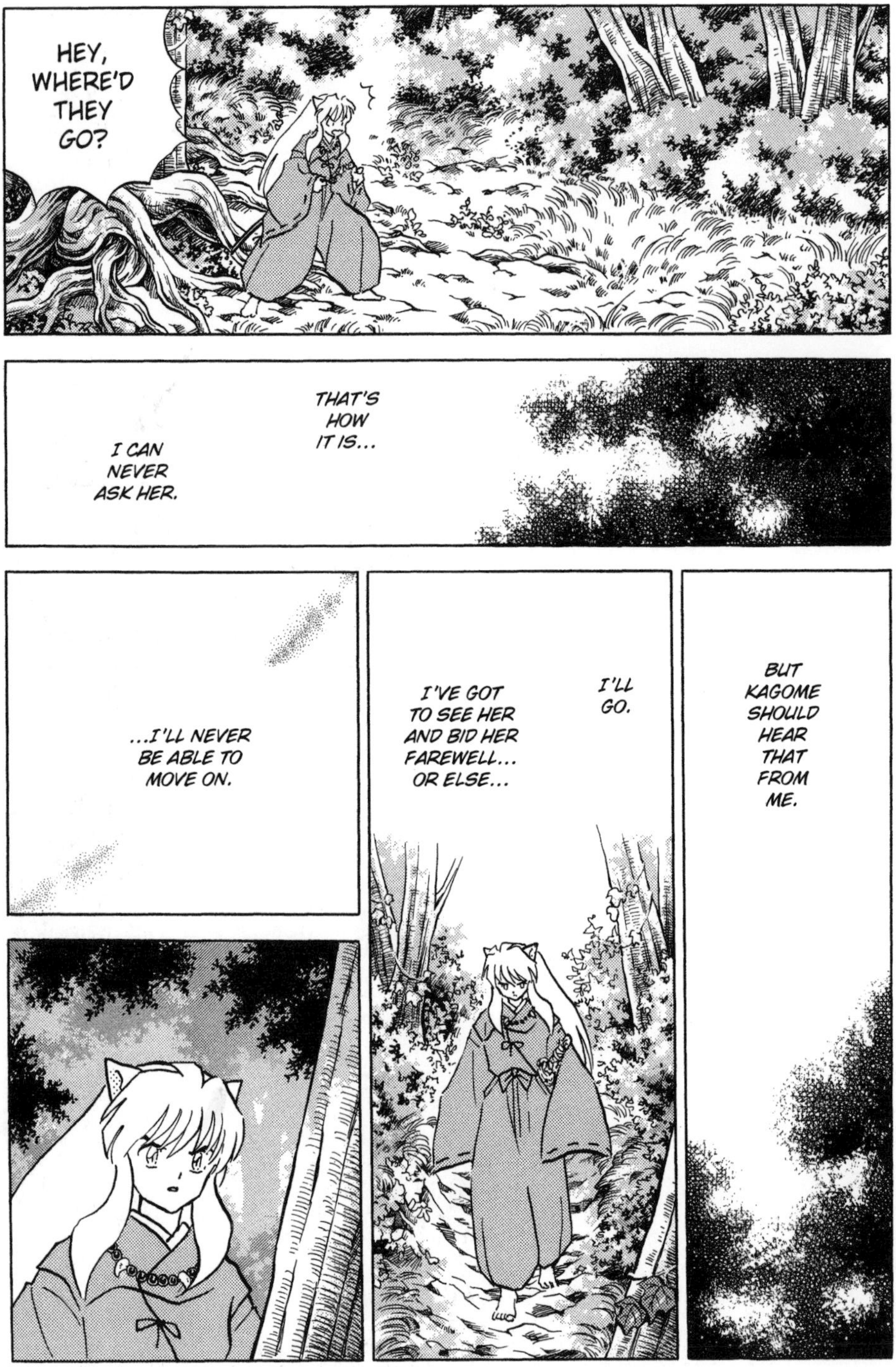
HEY, WHERE'D THEY GO?
THAT'S HOW IT IS...
I CAN NEVER ASK HER.
BUT KAGOME SHOULD HEAR THAT FROM ME.
I'LL GO.
I'VE GOT TO SEE HER AND BID HER FAREWELL... OR ELSE...
...I'LL NEVER BE ABLE TO MOVE ON.

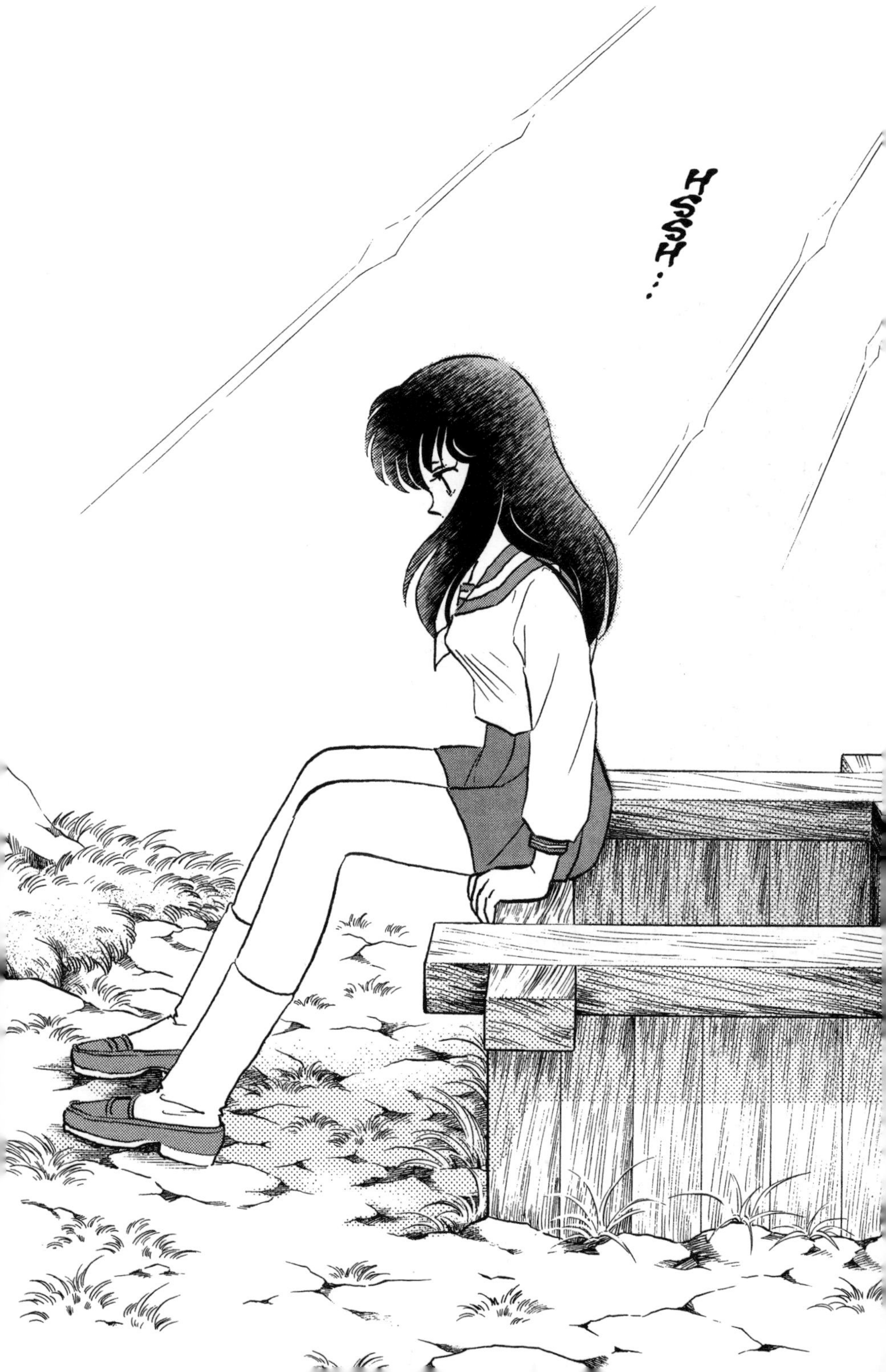
HSSSH...

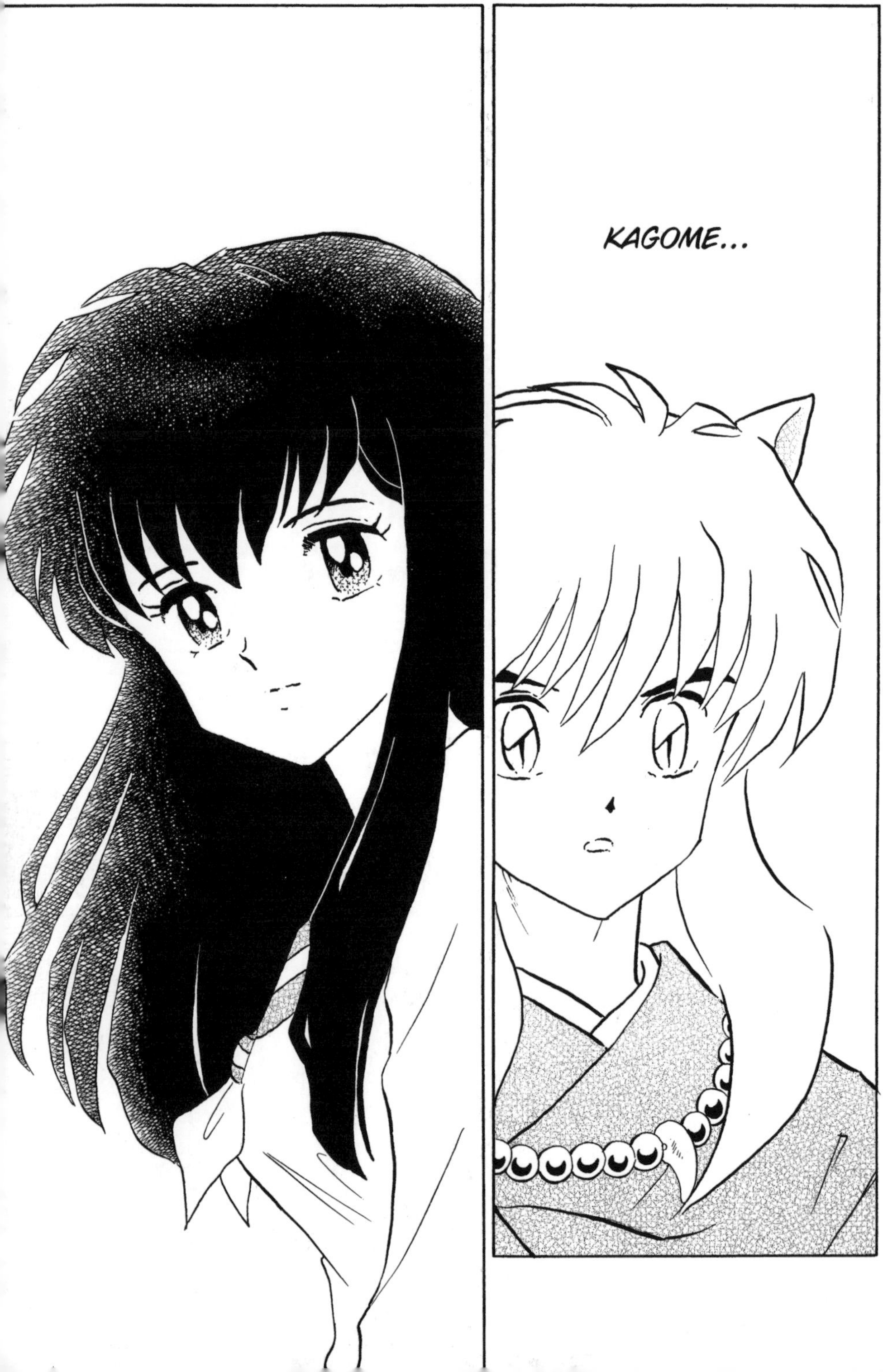
KAGOME...

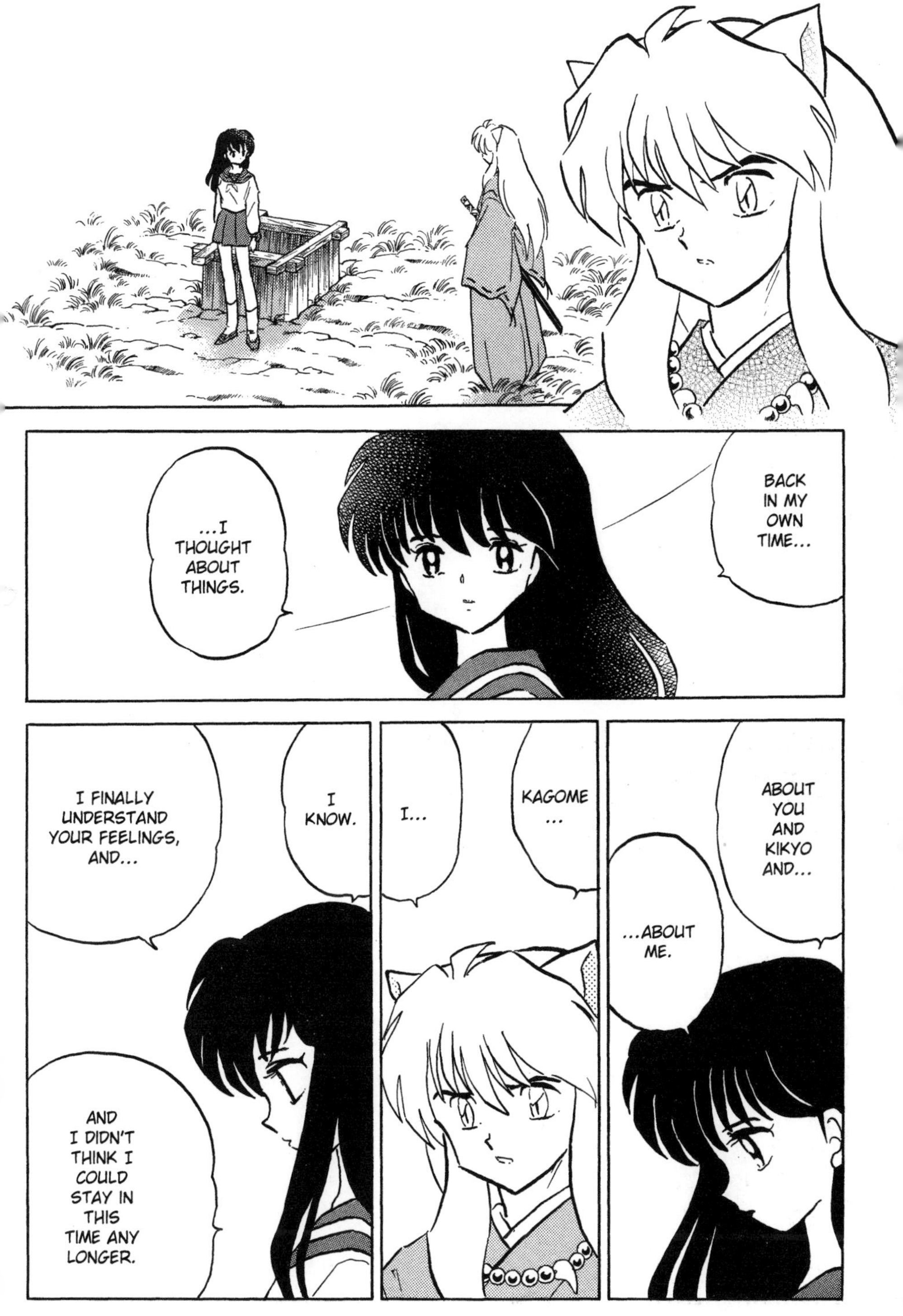
BACK IN MY OWN TIME...
...I THOUGHT ABOUT THINGS.
ABOUT YOU AND KIKYO AND...
...ABOUT ME.
KAGOME...
I...
I KNOW.
I FINALLY UNDERSTAND YOUR FEELINGS, AND...
AND I DIDN'T THINK I COULD STAY IN THIS TIME ANY LONGER.

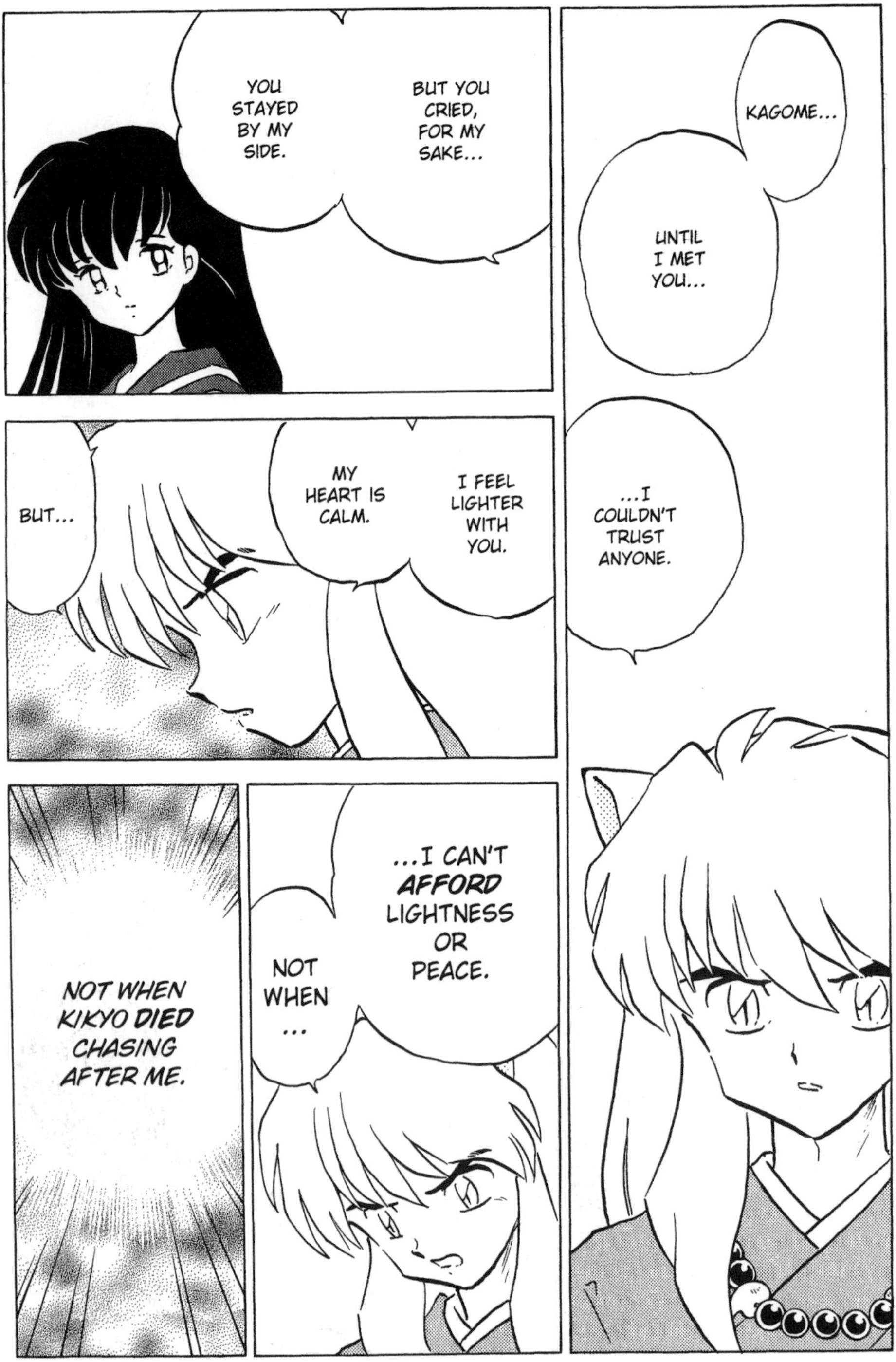
KAGOME...
UNTIL I MET YOU...
...I COULDN'T TRUST ANYONE.
BUT YOU CRIED, FOR MY SAKE...
YOU STAYED BY MY SIDE.
I FEEL LIGHTER WITH YOU.
MY HEART IS CALM.
BUT...
...I CAN'T **AFFORD** LIGHTNESS OR PEACE.
NOT WHEN ...
*NOT WHEN KIKYO **DIED** CHASING AFTER ME.*

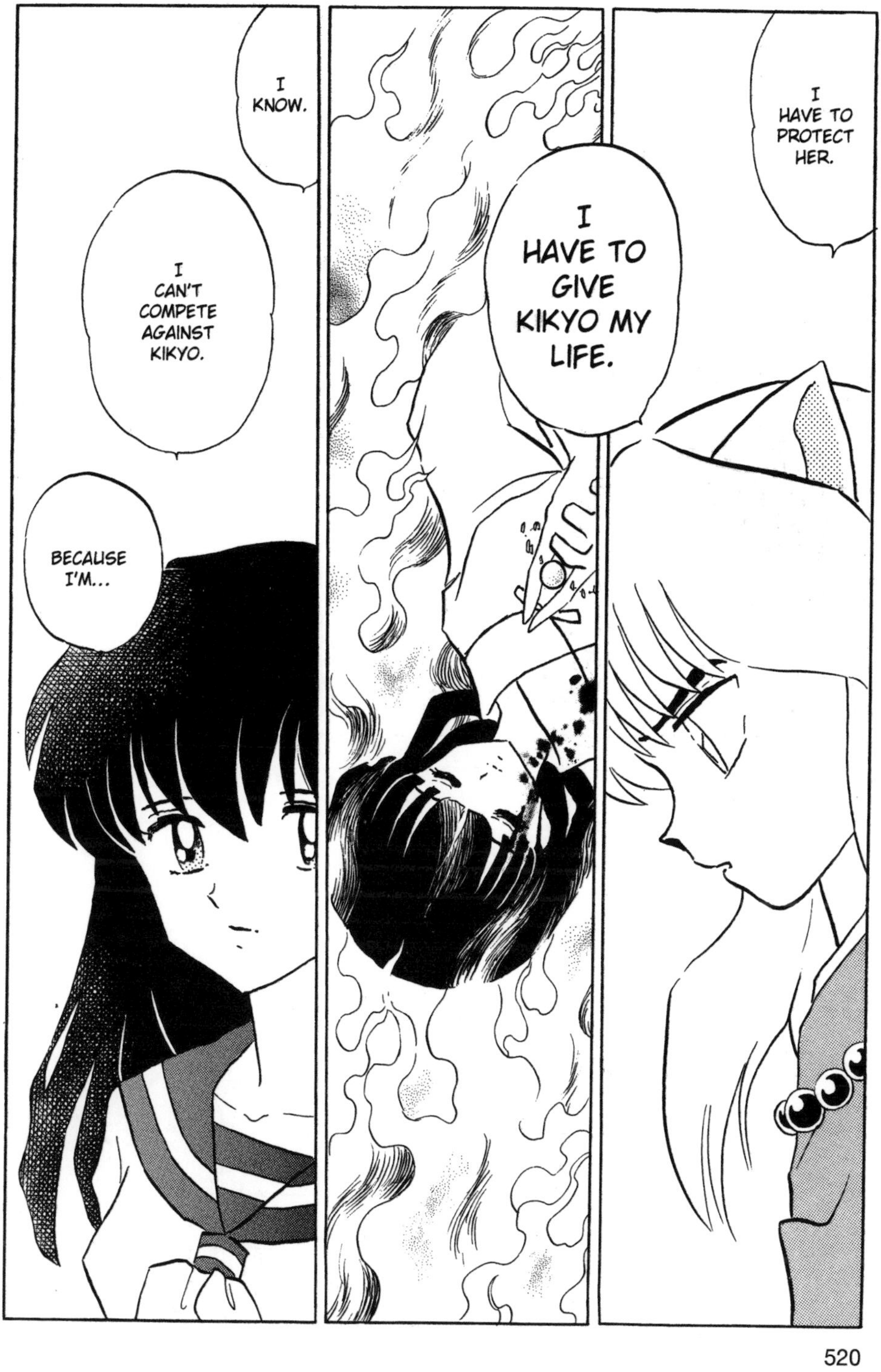
I HAVE TO PROTECT HER.
I HAVE TO GIVE KIKYO MY LIFE.
I KNOW.
I CAN'T COMPETE AGAINST KIKYO.
BECAUSE I'M...

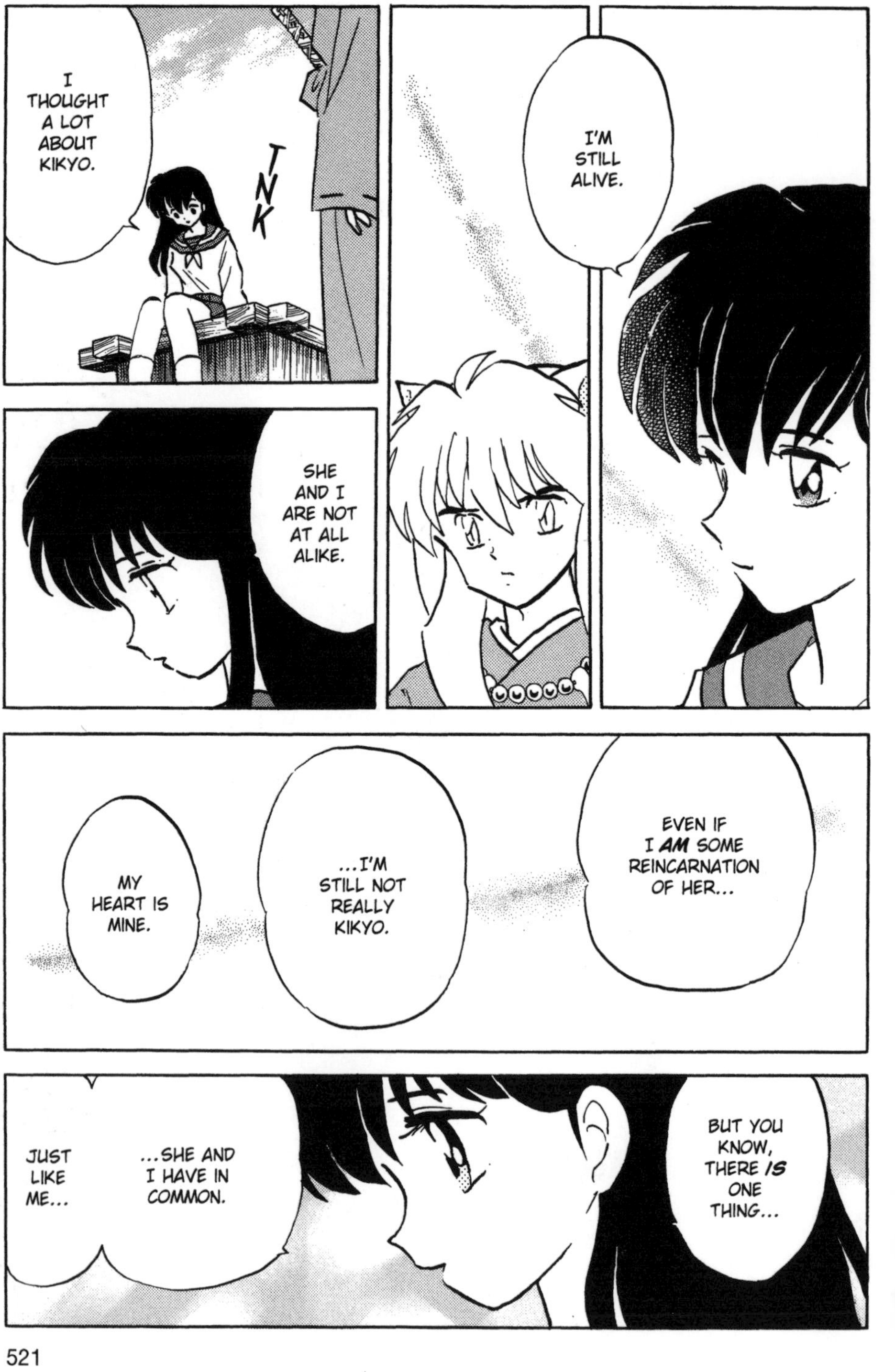
I'M STILL ALIVE.
I THOUGHT A LOT ABOUT KIKYO.
TNK
SHE AND I ARE NOT AT ALL ALIKE.
EVEN IF I *AM* SOME REINCARNATION OF HER...
...I'M STILL NOT REALLY KIKYO.
MY HEART IS MINE.
BUT YOU KNOW, THERE *IS* ONE THING...
...SHE AND I HAVE IN COMMON.
JUST LIKE ME...

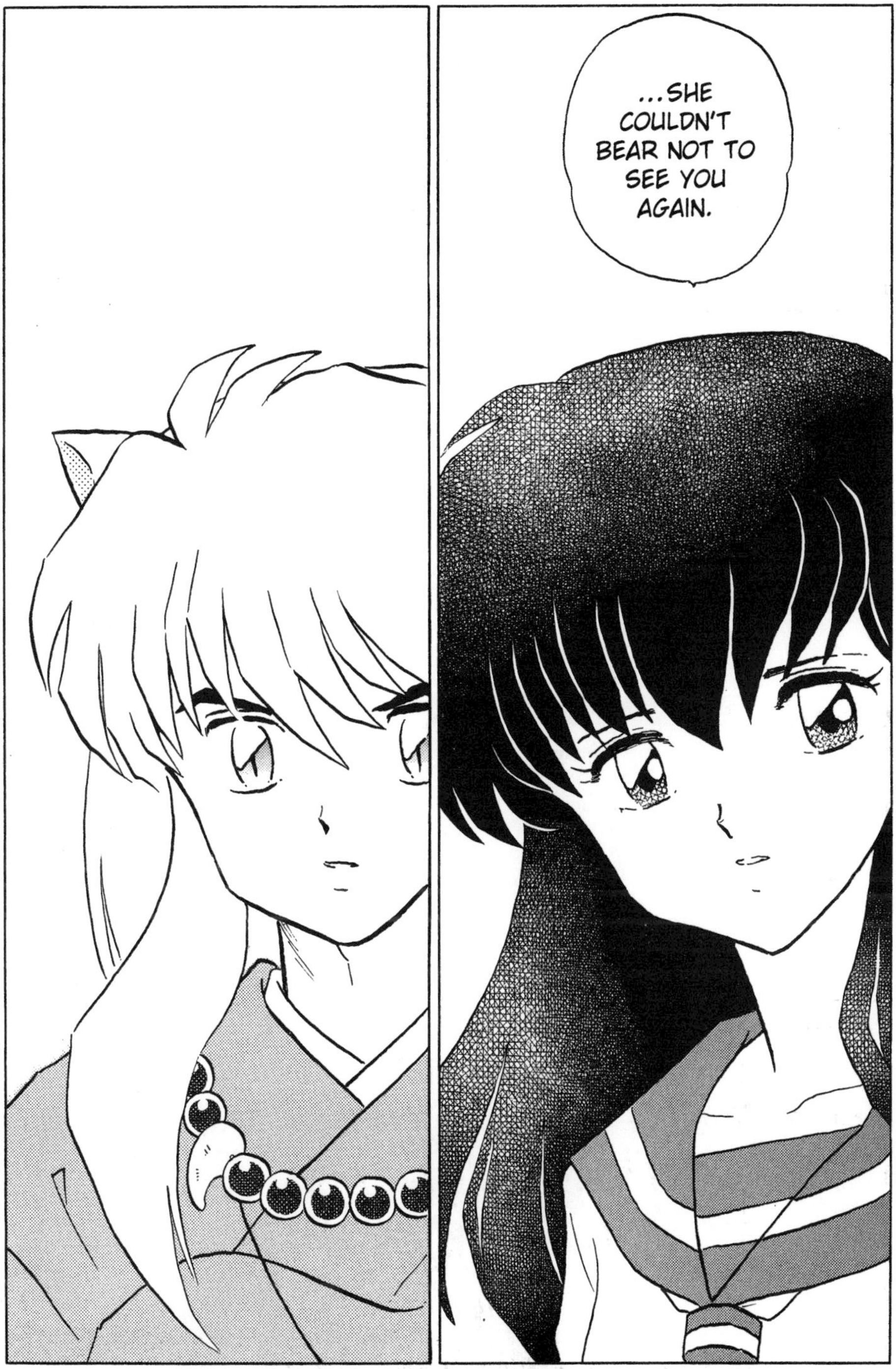
...SHE COULDN'T BEAR NOT TO SEE YOU AGAIN.

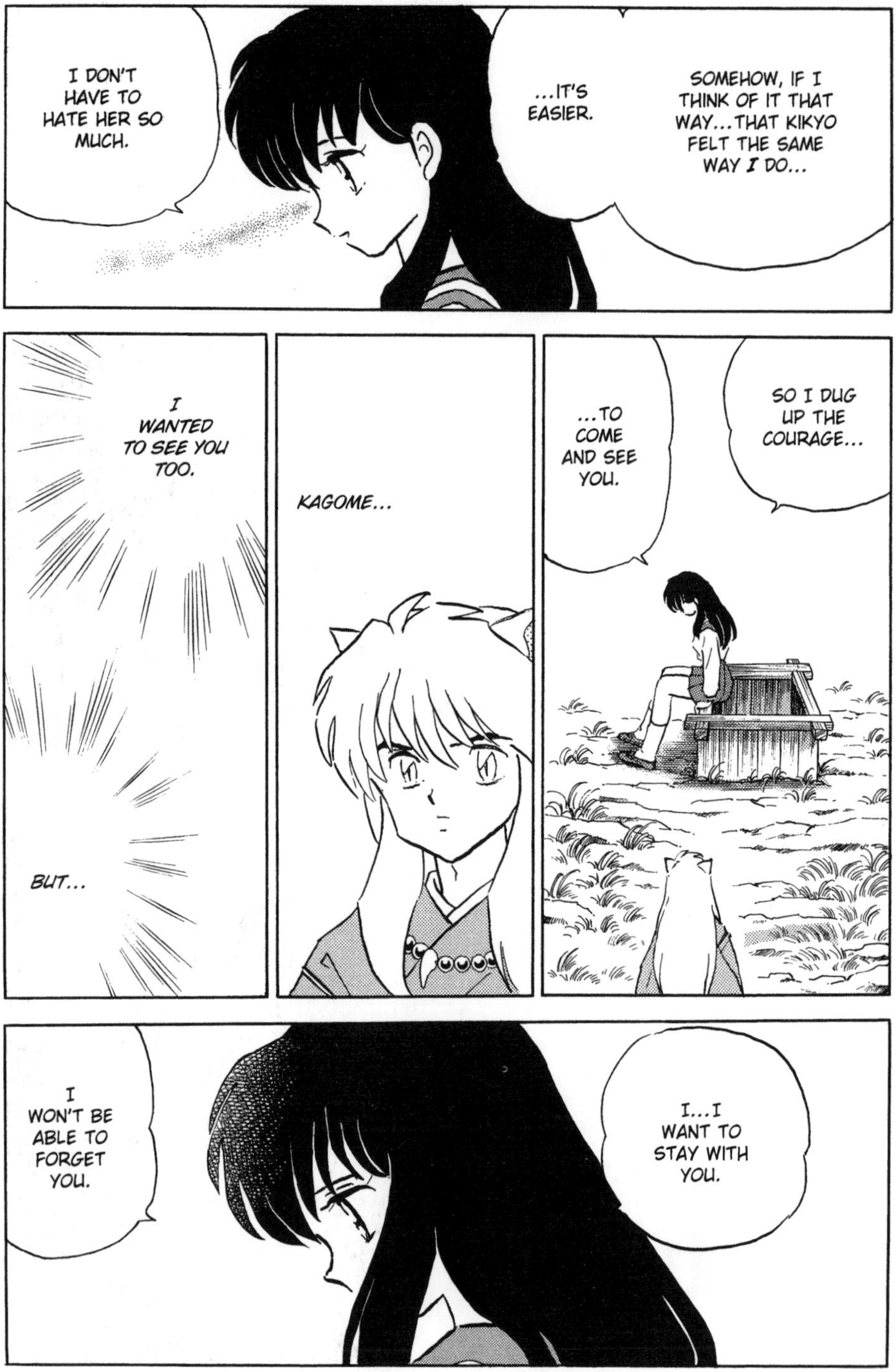
SOMEHOW, IF I THINK OF IT THAT WAY...THAT KIKYO FELT THE SAME WAY *I* DO...
...IT'S EASIER.
I DON'T HAVE TO HATE HER SO MUCH.
SO I DUG UP THE COURAGE...
...TO COME AND SEE YOU.
KAGOME...
I WANTED TO SEE YOU TOO.
BUT...
I...I WANT TO STAY WITH YOU.
I WON'T BE ABLE TO FORGET YOU.

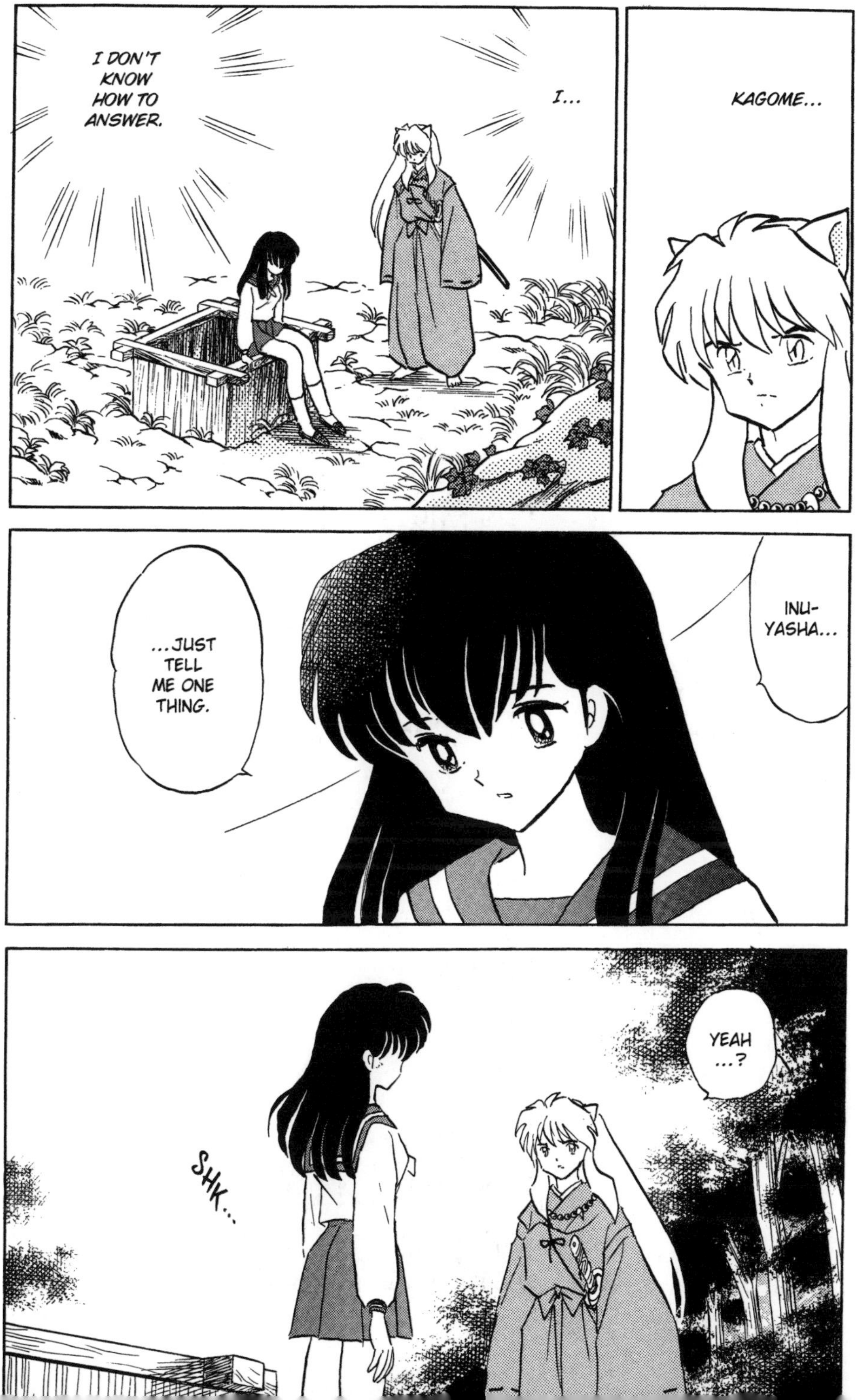
KAGOME...
I...
I DON'T KNOW HOW TO ANSWER.
INU-YASHA...
...JUST TELL ME ONE THING.
YEAH ...?
SHK...

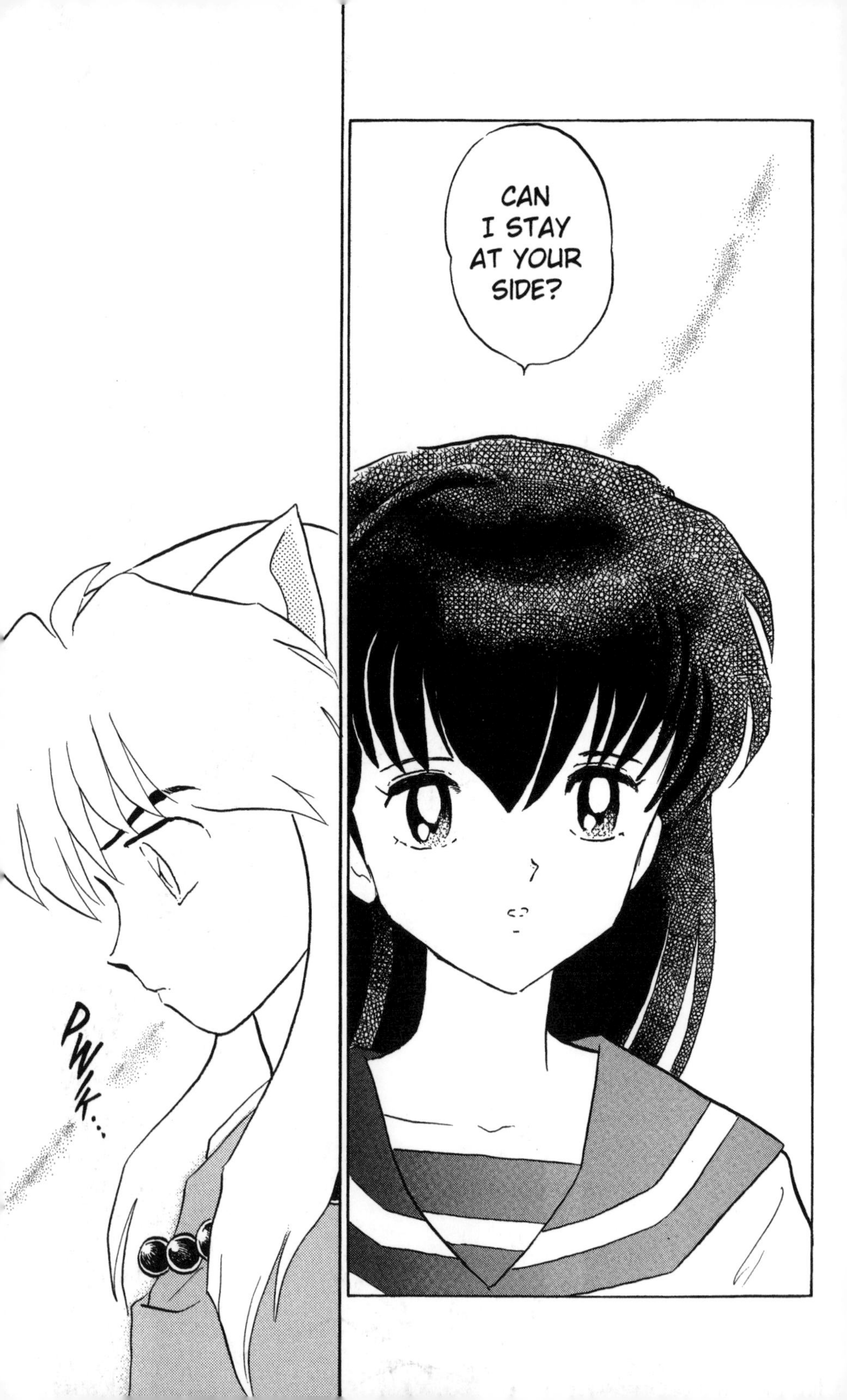
CAN I STAY AT YOUR SIDE?
PWIK...

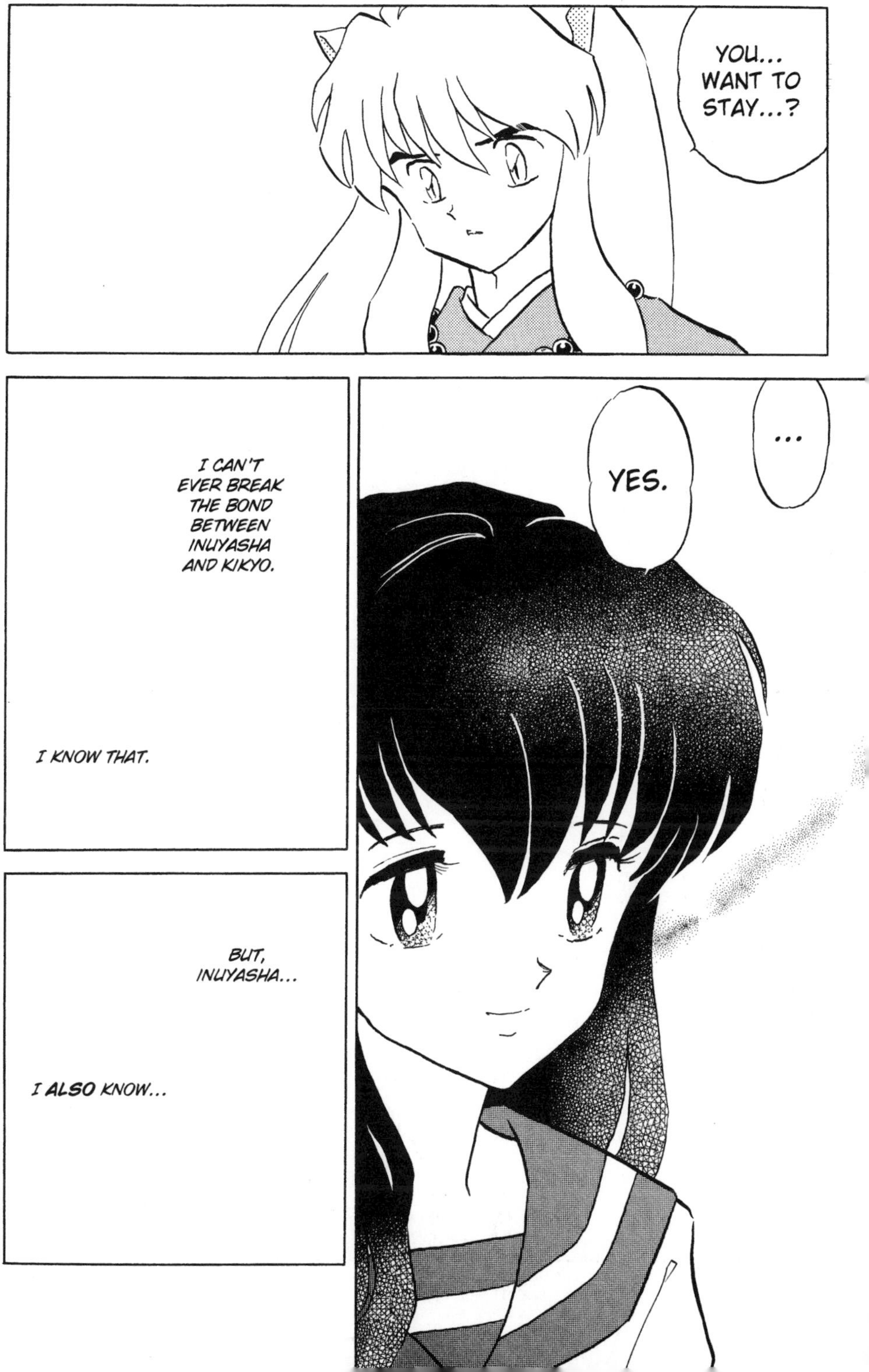
YOU... WANT TO STAY...?
...
YES.
I CAN'T EVER BREAK THE BOND BETWEEN INUYASHA AND KIKYO.
I KNOW THAT.
BUT, INUYASHA...
I ALSO KNOW...

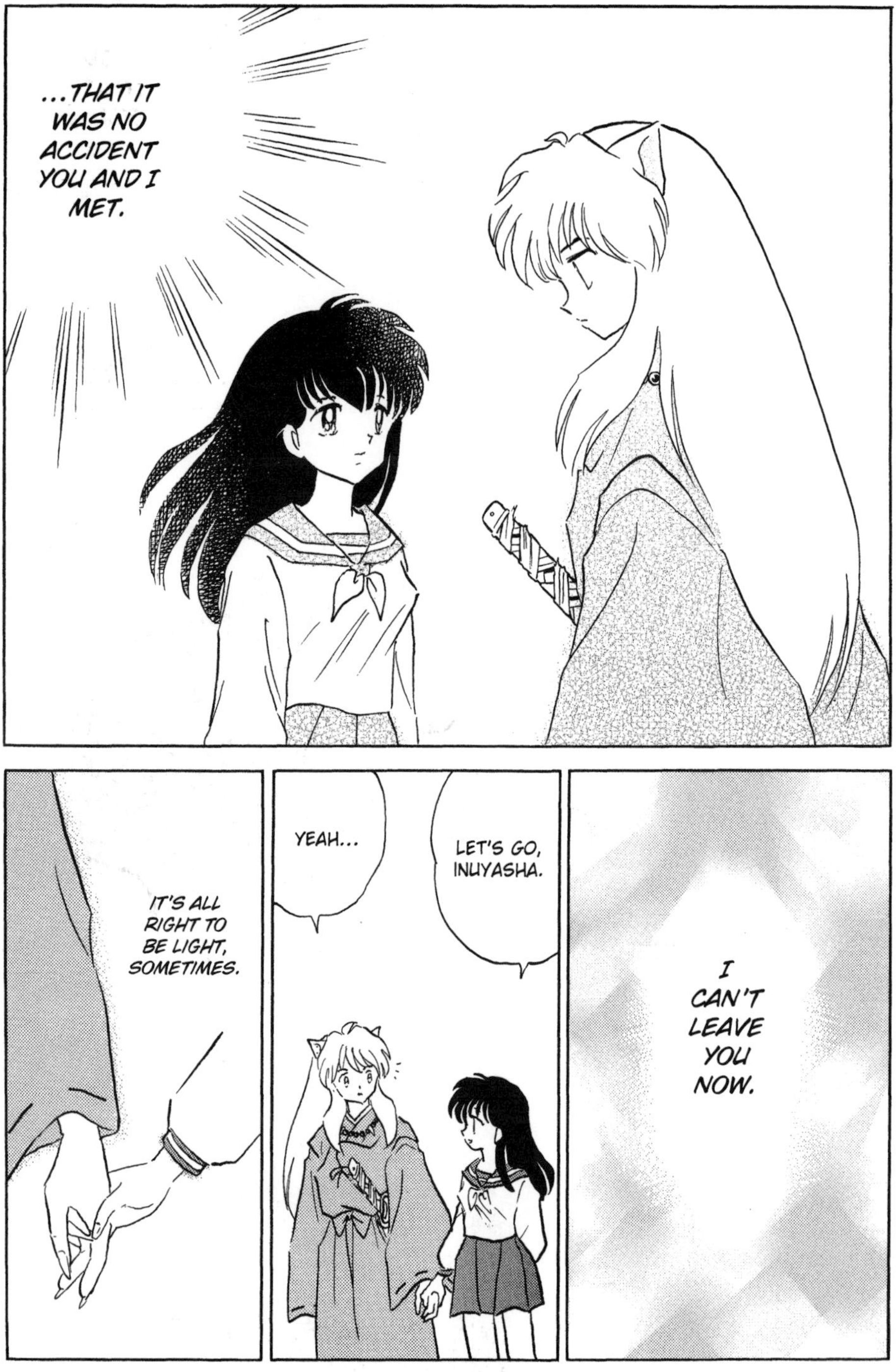
...THAT IT WAS NO ACCIDENT YOU AND I MET.
I CAN'T LEAVE YOU NOW.
LET'S GO, INUYASHA.
YEAH...
IT'S ALL RIGHT TO BE LIGHT, SOMETIMES.

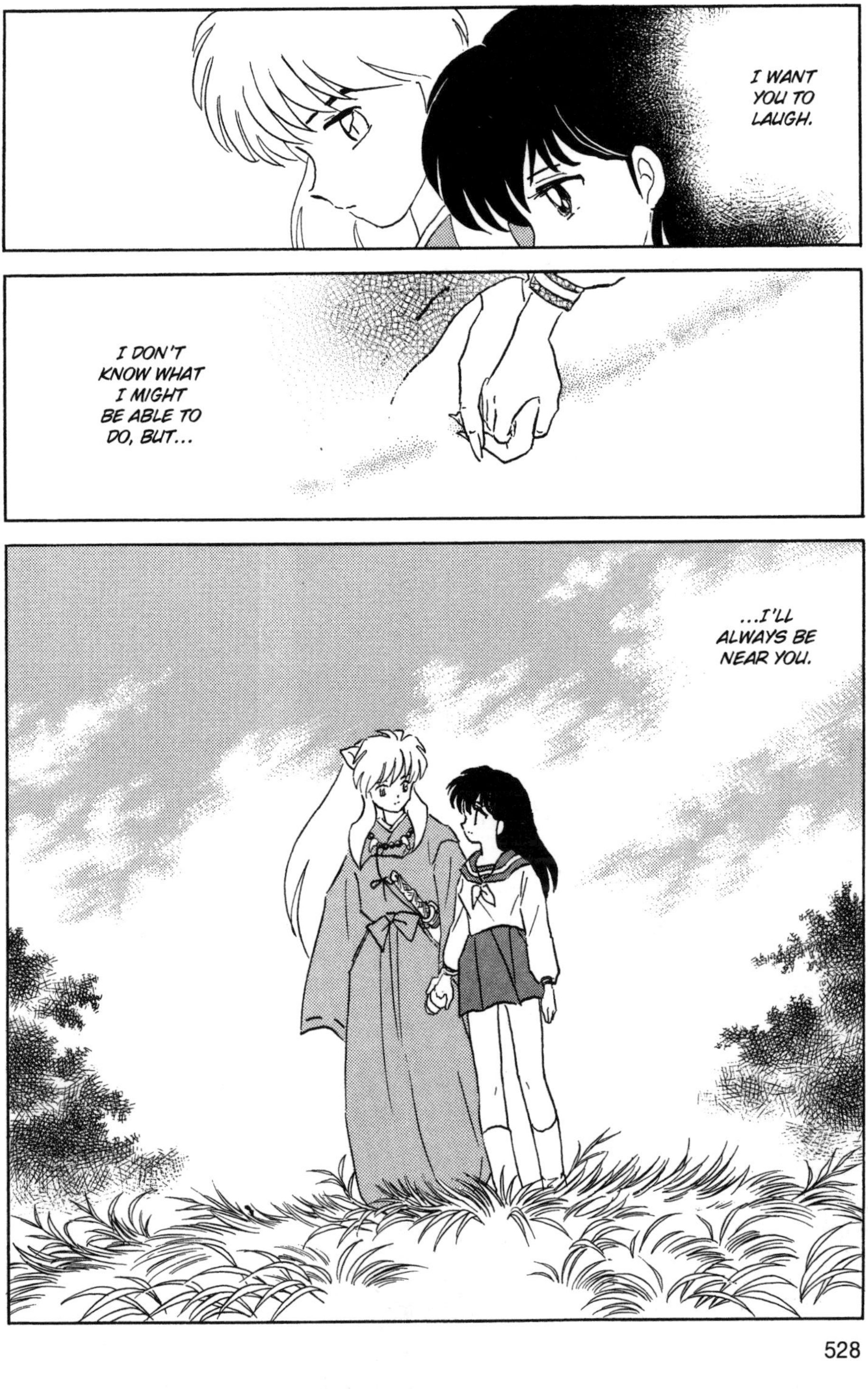
I WANT YOU TO LAUGH.
I DON'T KNOW WHAT I MIGHT BE ABLE TO DO, BUT...
...I'LL ALWAYS BE NEAR YOU.

SCROLL NINE
THE CASTLE GHOST

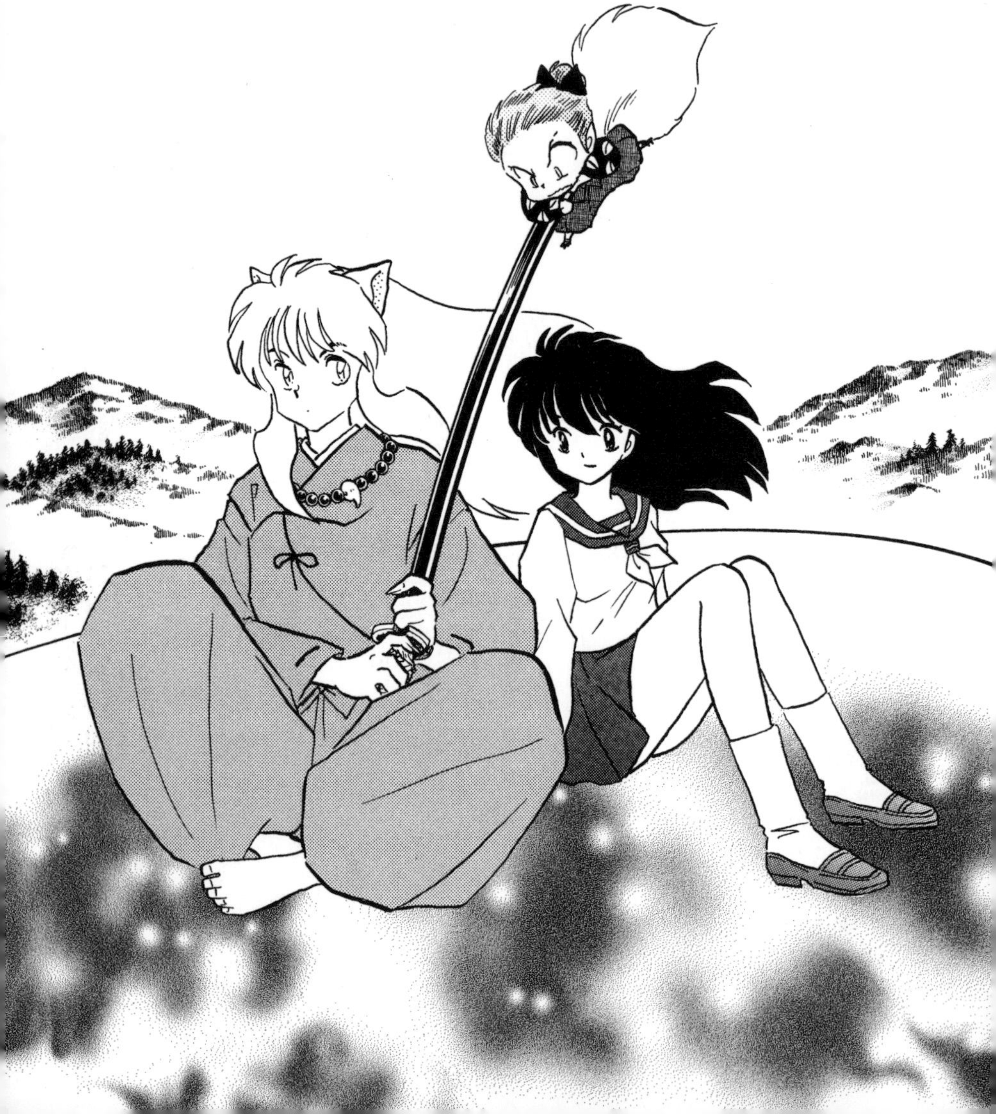

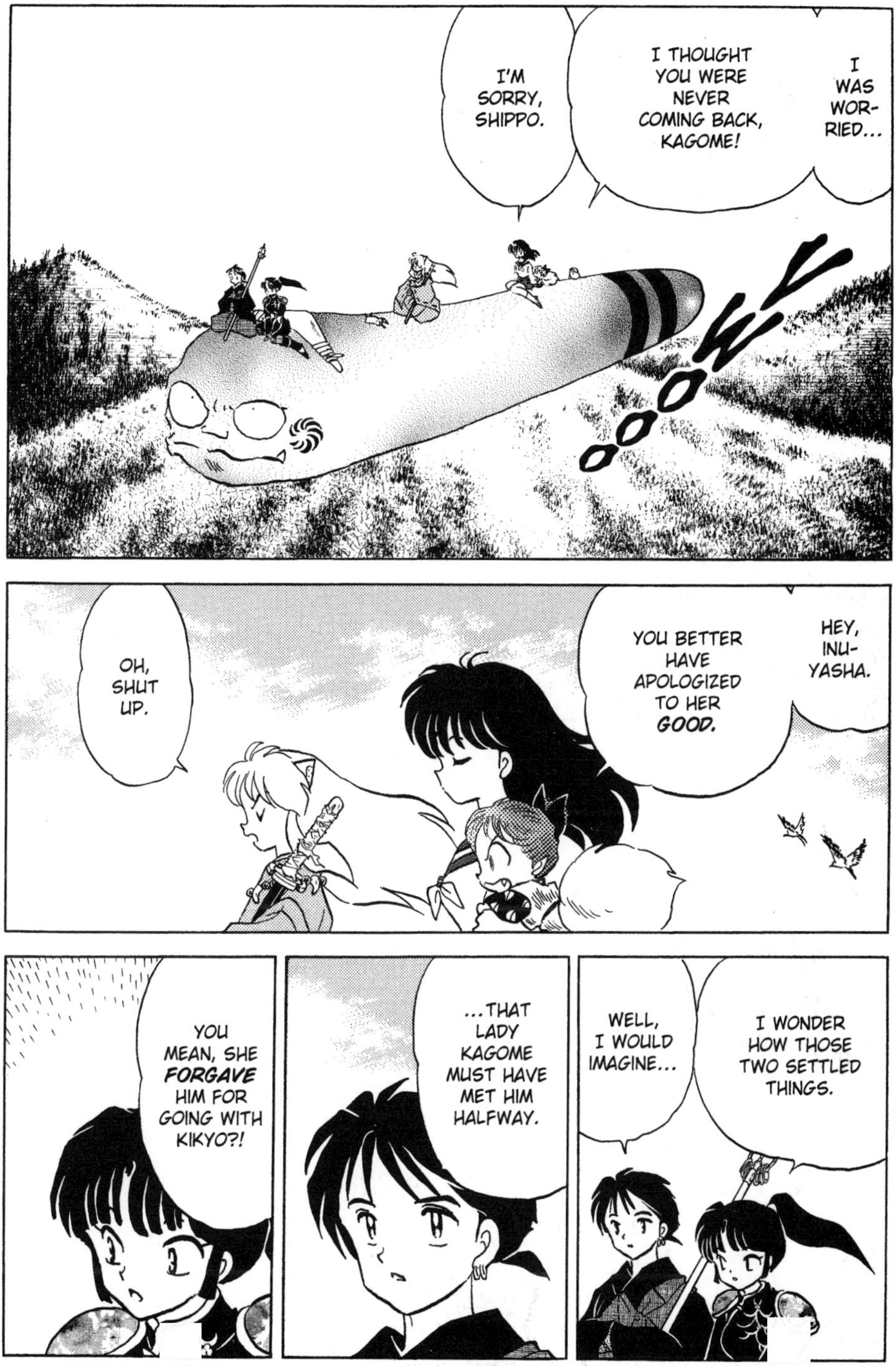
I WAS WORRIED...
I THOUGHT YOU WERE NEVER COMING BACK, KAGOME!
I'M SORRY, SHIPPO.
VWOOOO
HEY, INU-YASHA.
YOU BETTER HAVE APOLOGIZED TO HER GOOD.
OH, SHUT UP.
I WONDER HOW THOSE TWO SETTLED THINGS.
WELL, I WOULD IMAGINE...
...THAT LADY KAGOME MUST HAVE MET HIM HALFWAY.
YOU MEAN, SHE FORGAVE HIM FOR GOING WITH KIKYO?!

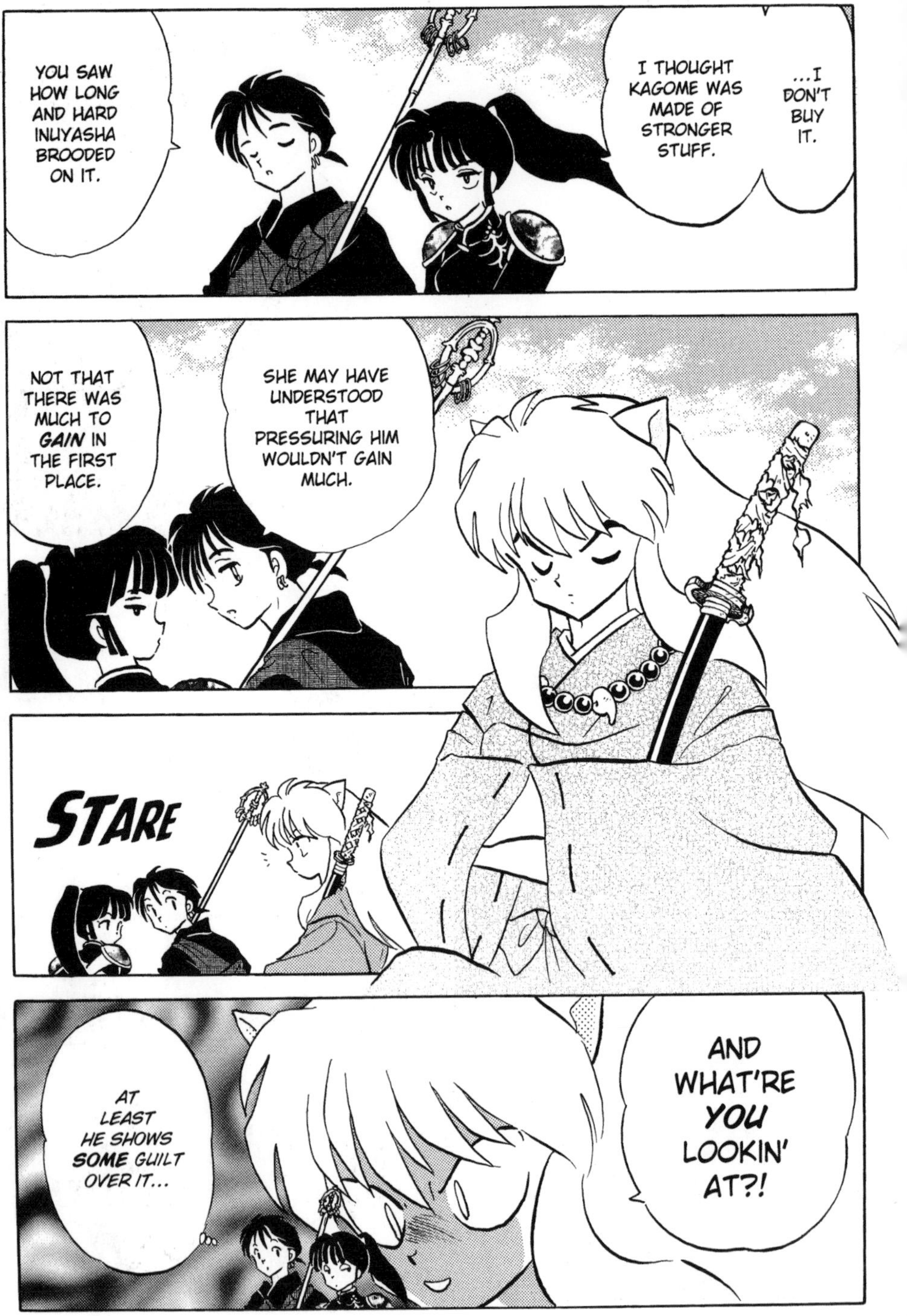
I THOUGHT KAGOME WAS MADE OF STRONGER STUFF.
...I DON'T BUY IT.
YOU SAW HOW LONG AND HARD INUYASHA BROODED ON IT.
SHE MAY HAVE UNDERSTOOD THAT PRESSURING HIM WOULDN'T GAIN MUCH.
NOT THAT THERE WAS MUCH TO *GAIN* IN THE FIRST PLACE.
STARE
AND WHAT'RE *YOU* LOOKIN' AT?!
AT LEAST HE SHOWS **SOME** GUILT OVER IT...

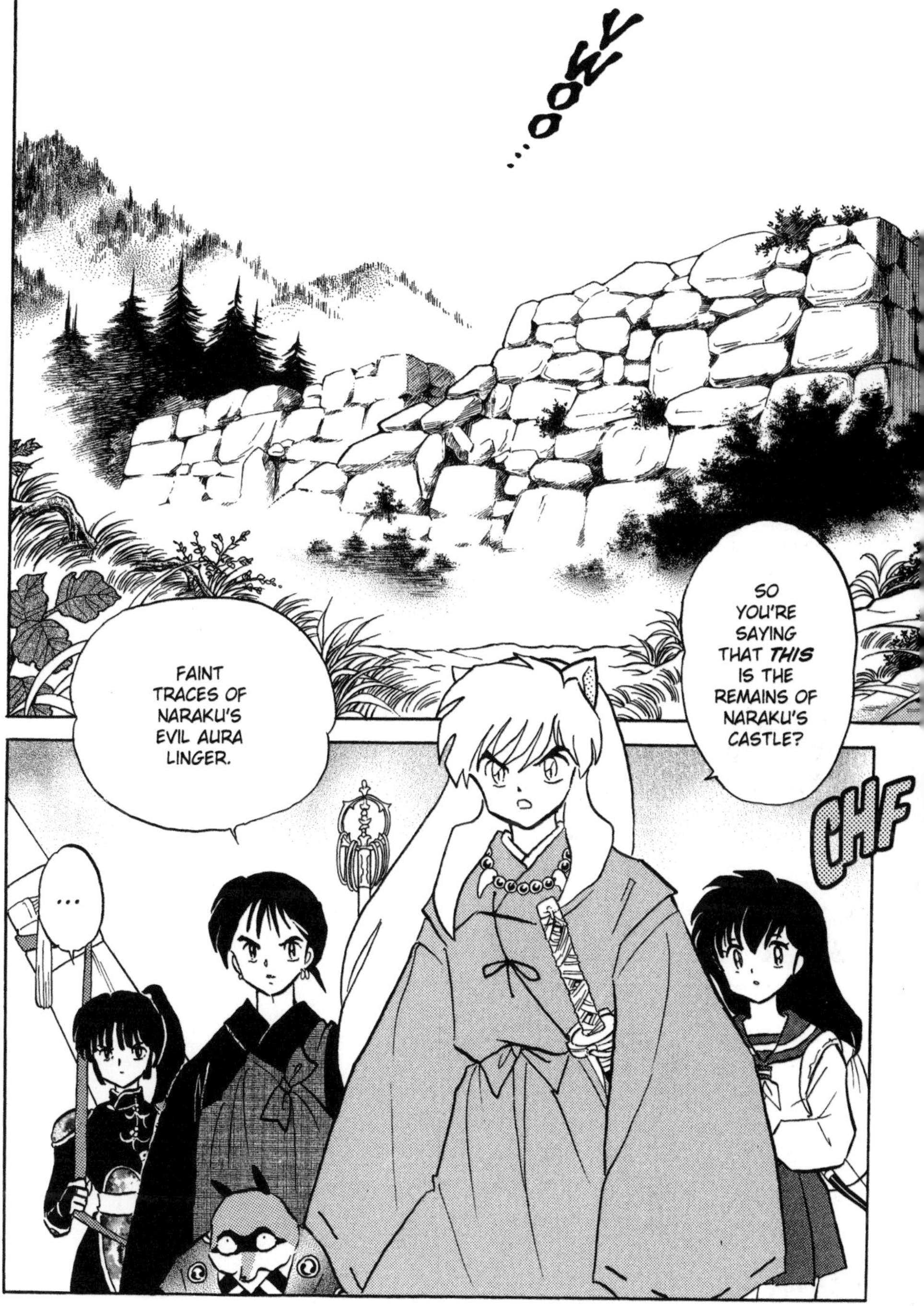
VWOO...
SO YOU'RE SAYING THAT *THIS* IS THE REMAINS OF NARAKU'S CASTLE?
FAINT TRACES OF NARAKU'S EVIL AURA LINGER.
CHF
...

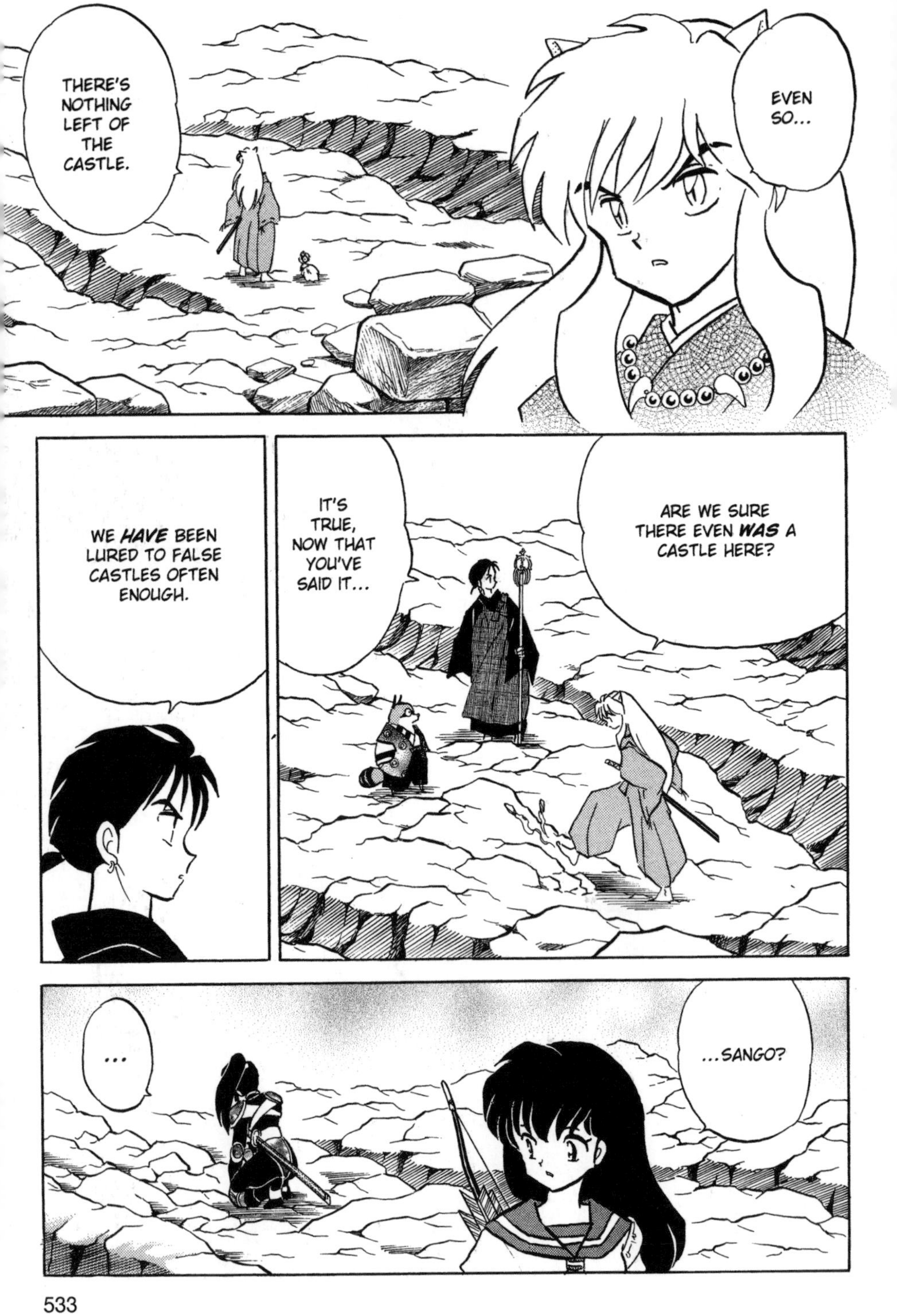
EVEN SO...
THERE'S NOTHING LEFT OF THE CASTLE.
ARE WE SURE THERE EVEN *WAS* A CASTLE HERE?
IT'S TRUE, NOW THAT YOU'VE SAID IT...
WE *HAVE* BEEN LURED TO FALSE CASTLES OFTEN ENOUGH.
...SANGO?
...

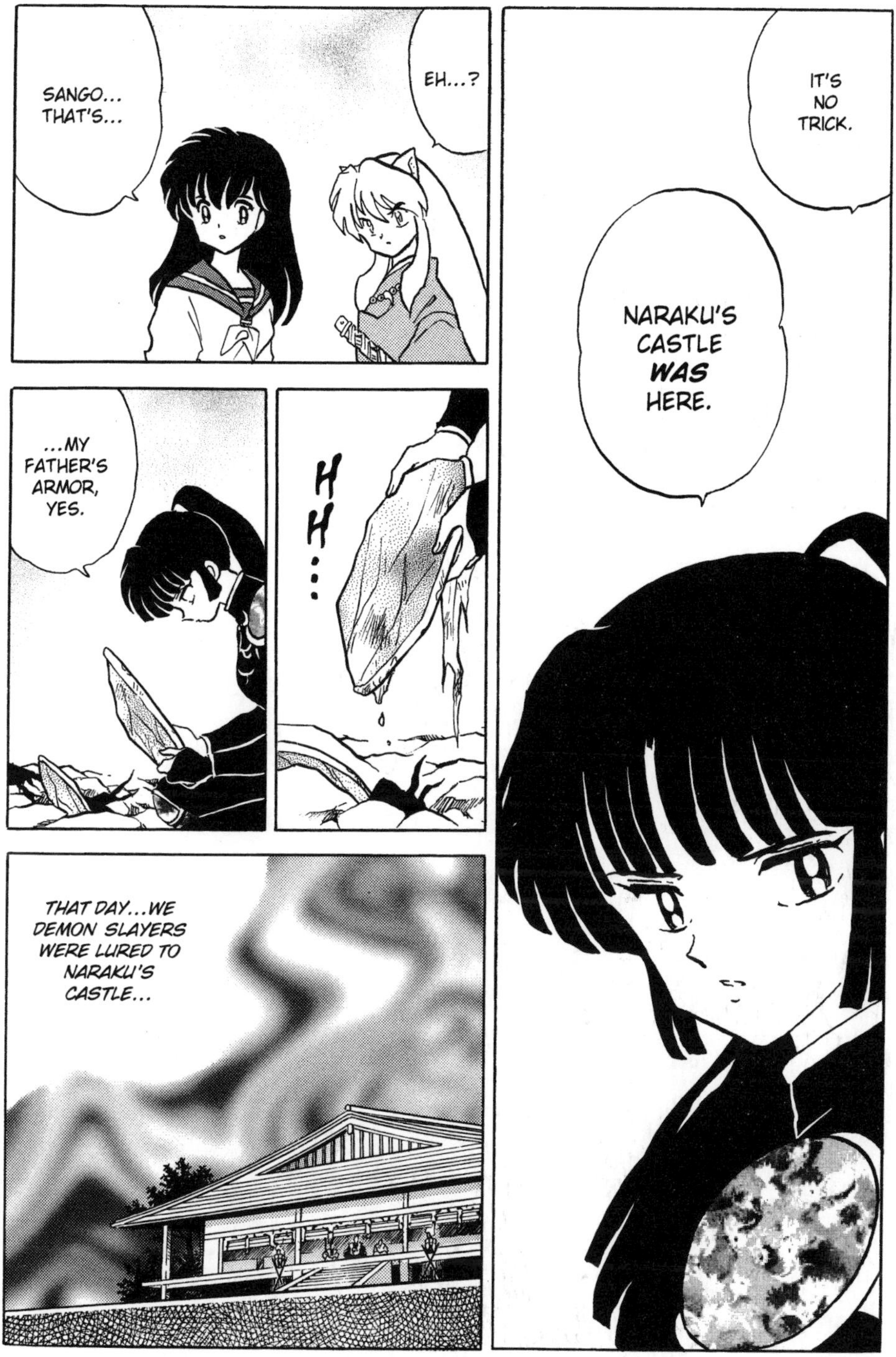
IT'S NO TRICK.
NARAKU'S CASTLE **WAS** HERE.
EH...?
SANGO... THAT'S...
HH...
...MY FATHER'S ARMOR, YES.
THAT DAY...WE DEMON SLAYERS WERE LURED TO NARAKU'S CASTLE...

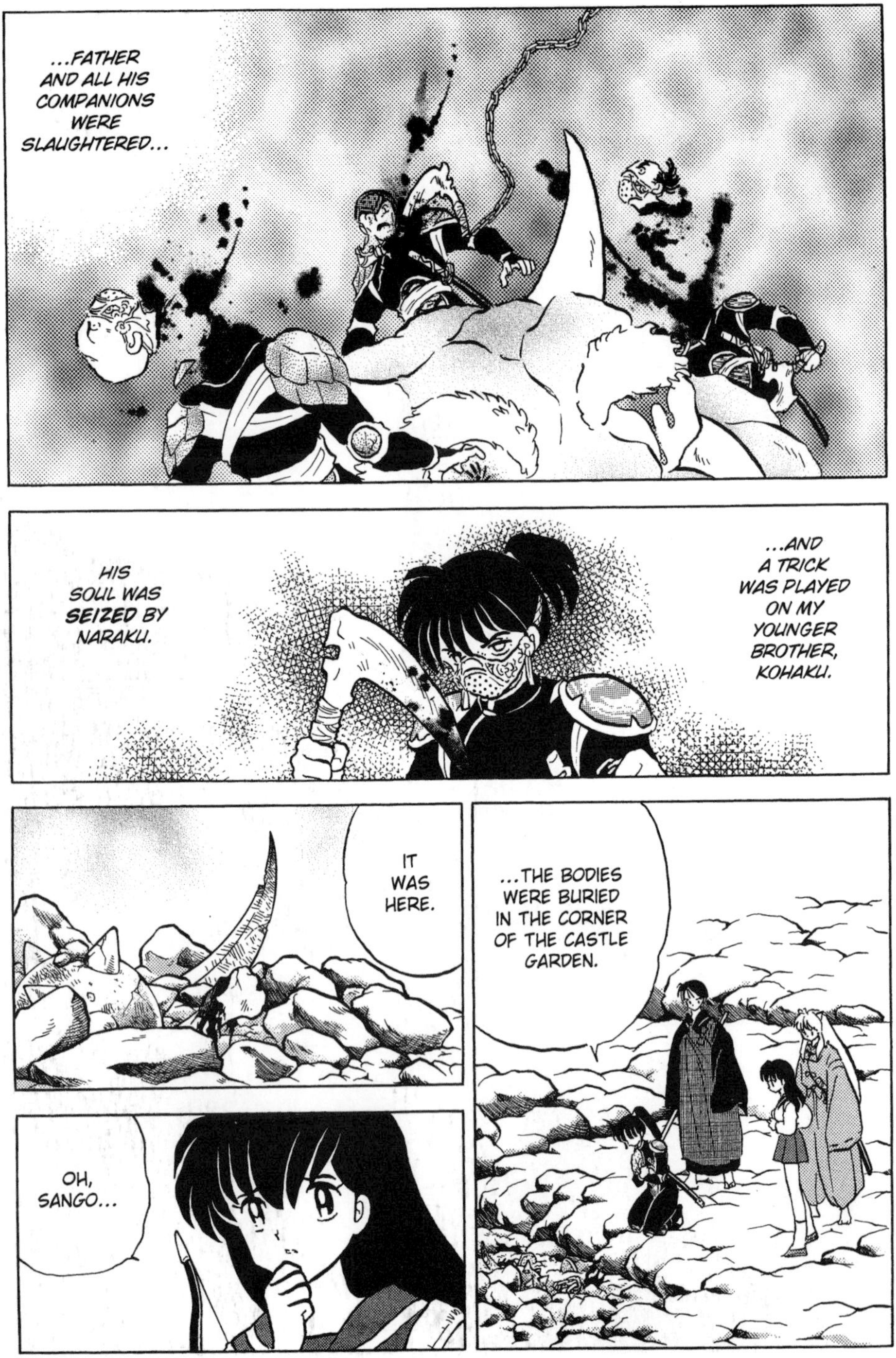
...FATHER AND ALL HIS COMPANIONS WERE SLAUGHTERED...
...AND A TRICK WAS PLAYED ON MY YOUNGER BROTHER, KOHAKU.
HIS SOUL WAS SEIZED BY NARAKU.
...THE BODIES WERE BURIED IN THE CORNER OF THE CASTLE GARDEN.
IT WAS HERE.
OH, SANGO...

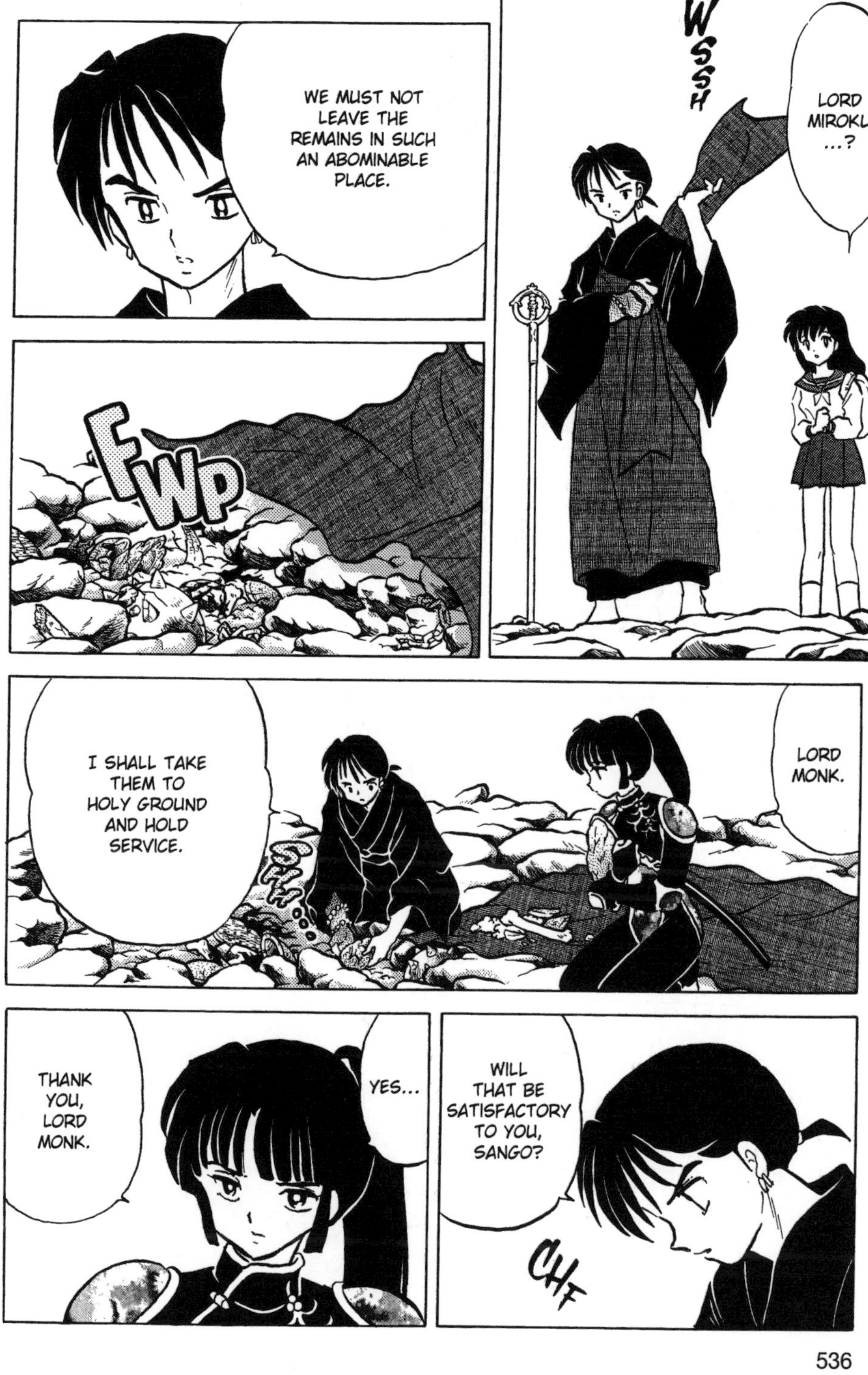
WSSH
LORD MIROKU ...?
WE MUST NOT LEAVE THE REMAINS IN SUCH AN ABOMINABLE PLACE.
FWP
LORD MONK.
I SHALL TAKE THEM TO HOLY GROUND AND HOLD SERVICE.
SHH...
WILL THAT BE SATISFACTORY TO YOU, SANGO?
CHF
YES...
THANK YOU, LORD MONK.

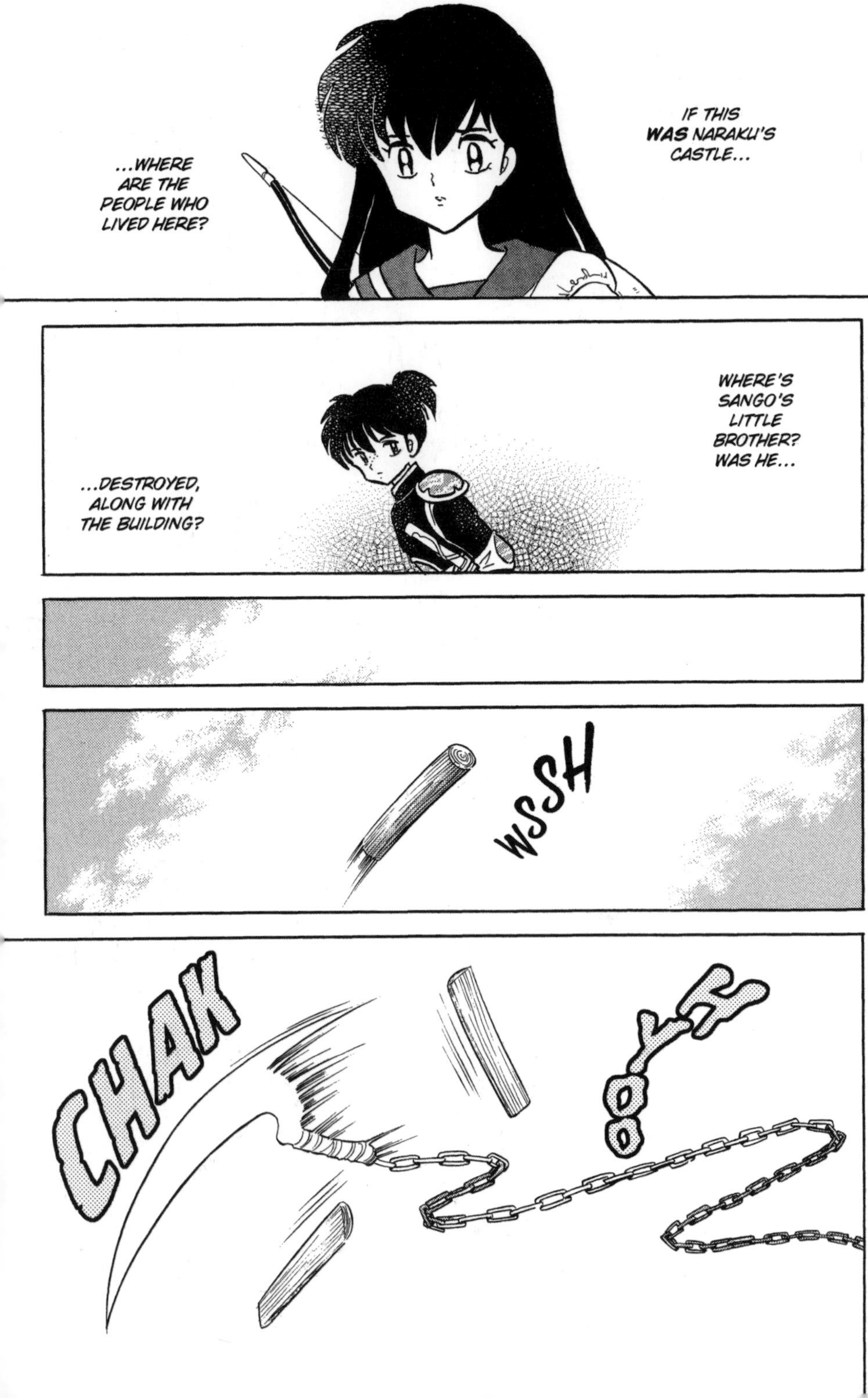
IF THIS WAS NARAKU'S CASTLE...
...WHERE ARE THE PEOPLE WHO LIVED HERE?
WHERE'S SANGO'S LITTLE BROTHER? WAS HE...
...DESTROYED, ALONG WITH THE BUILDING?
WSSH
CHAK

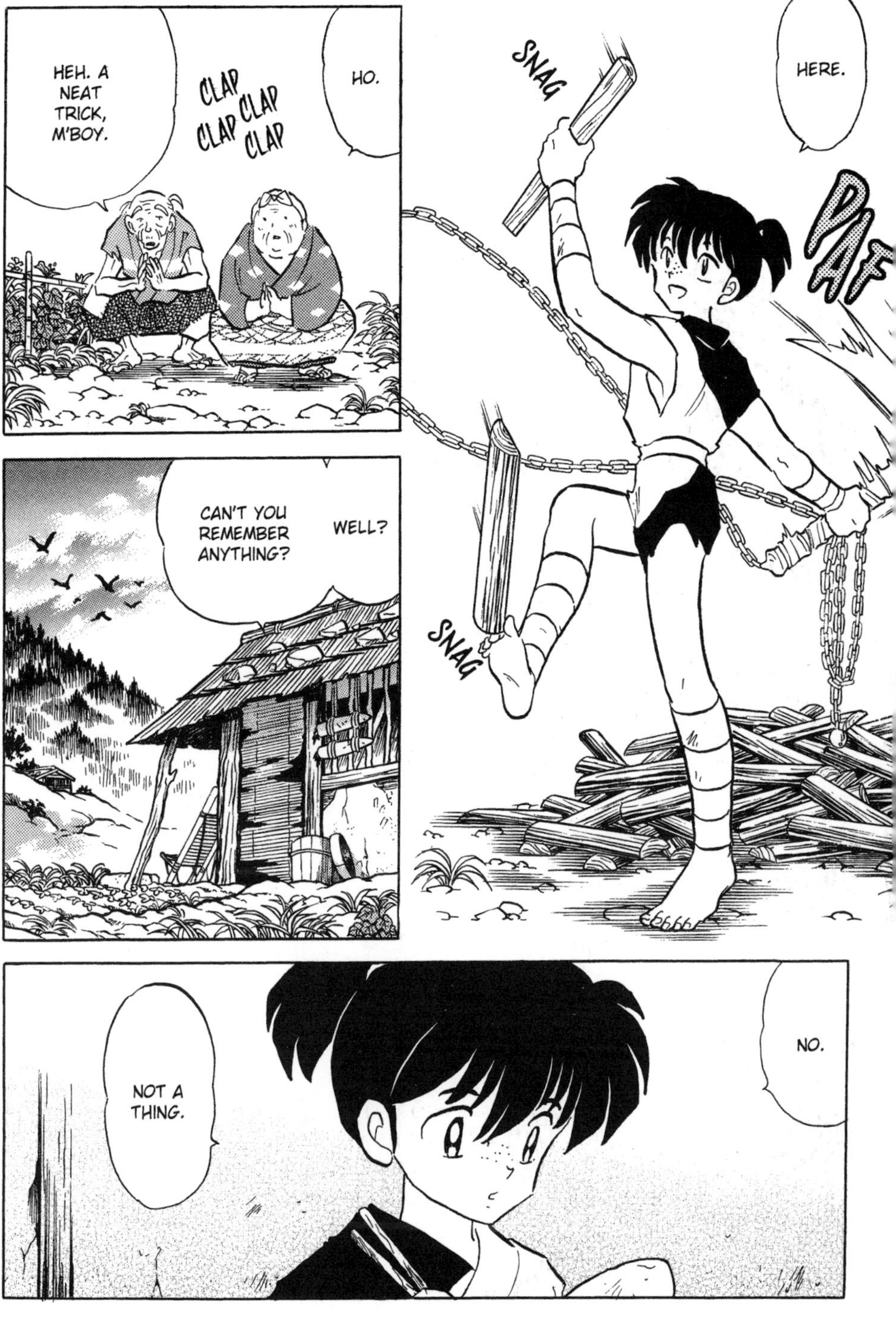
HERE.
PAF
SNAG
SNAG
HO.
CLAP CLAP CLAP CLAP
HEH. A NEAT TRICK, M'BOY.
WELL?
CAN'T YOU REMEMBER ANYTHING?
NO.
NOT A THING.

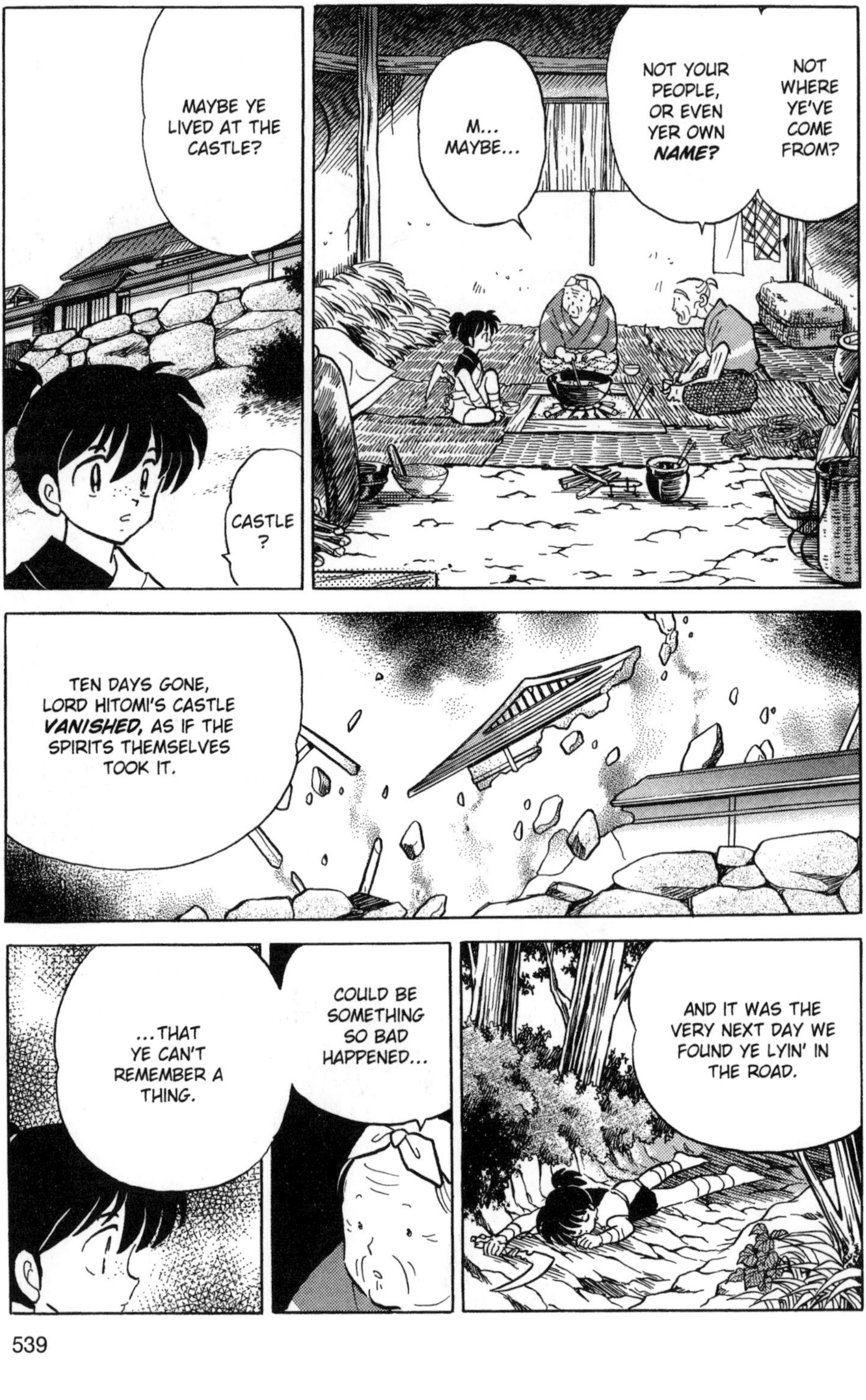
NOT WHERE YE'VE COME FROM?
NOT YOUR PEOPLE, OR EVEN YER OWN ***NAME?***
M... MAYBE...
MAYBE YE LIVED AT THE CASTLE?
CASTLE?
TEN DAYS GONE, LORD HITOMI'S CASTLE ***VANISHED,*** AS IF THE SPIRITS THEMSELVES TOOK IT.
AND IT WAS THE VERY NEXT DAY WE FOUND YE LYIN' IN THE ROAD.
COULD BE SOMETHING SO BAD HAPPENED...
...THAT YE CAN'T REMEMBER A THING.

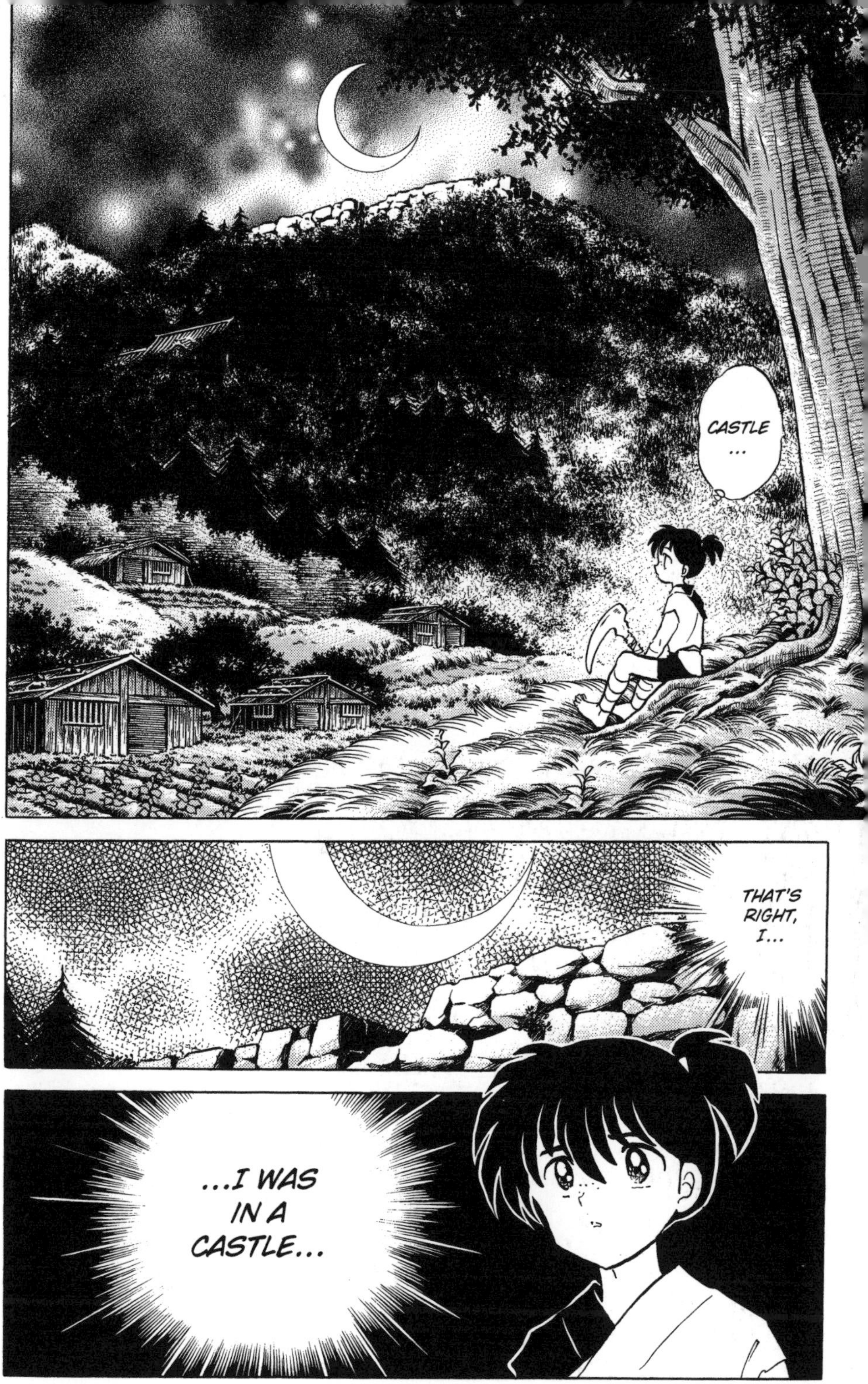
CASTLE ...
THAT'S RIGHT, I...
...I WAS IN A CASTLE...

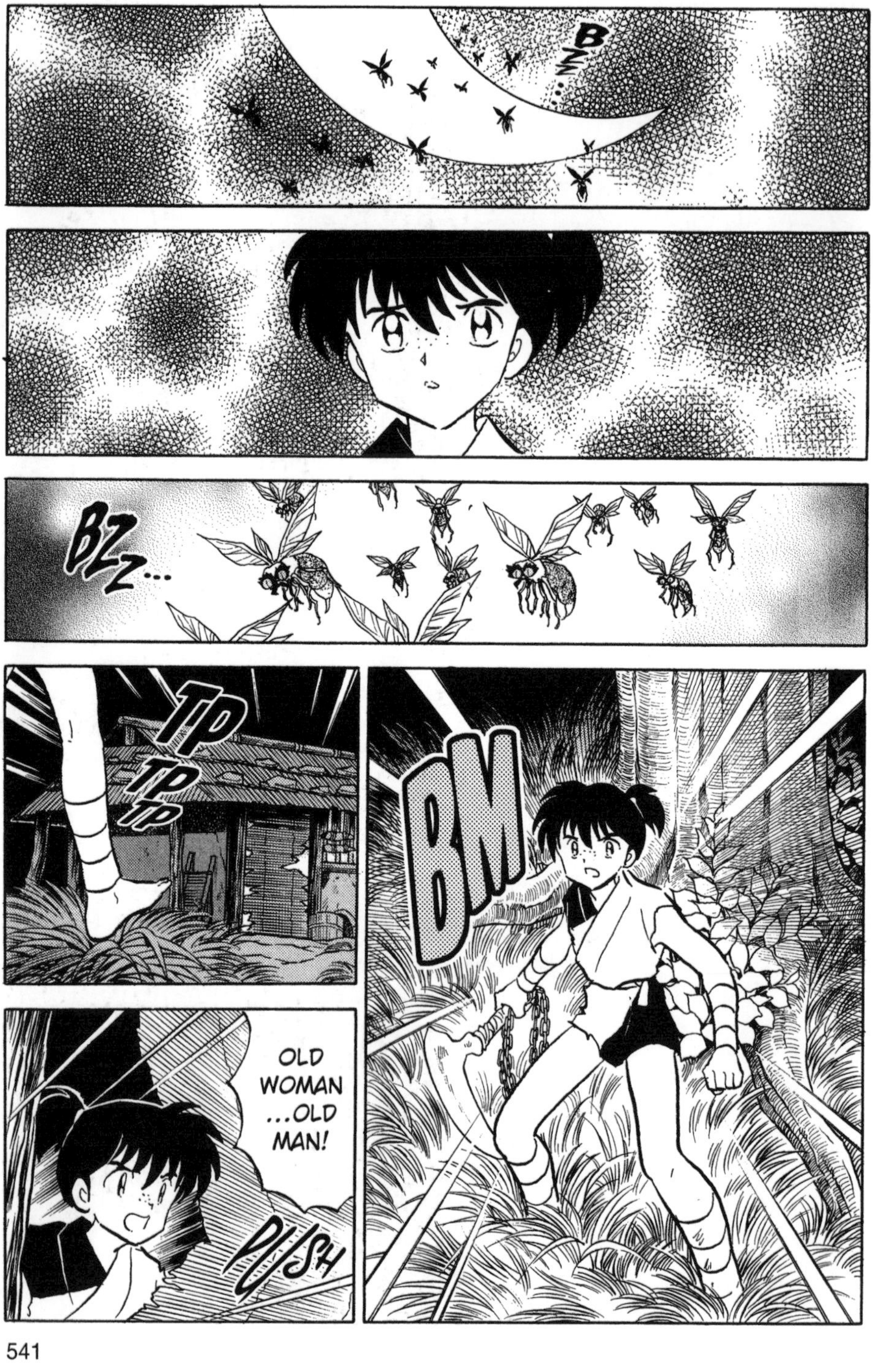
BZZ...
BZZ...
BM
TP
TP
TP
OLD WOMAN ...OLD MAN!
PUSH

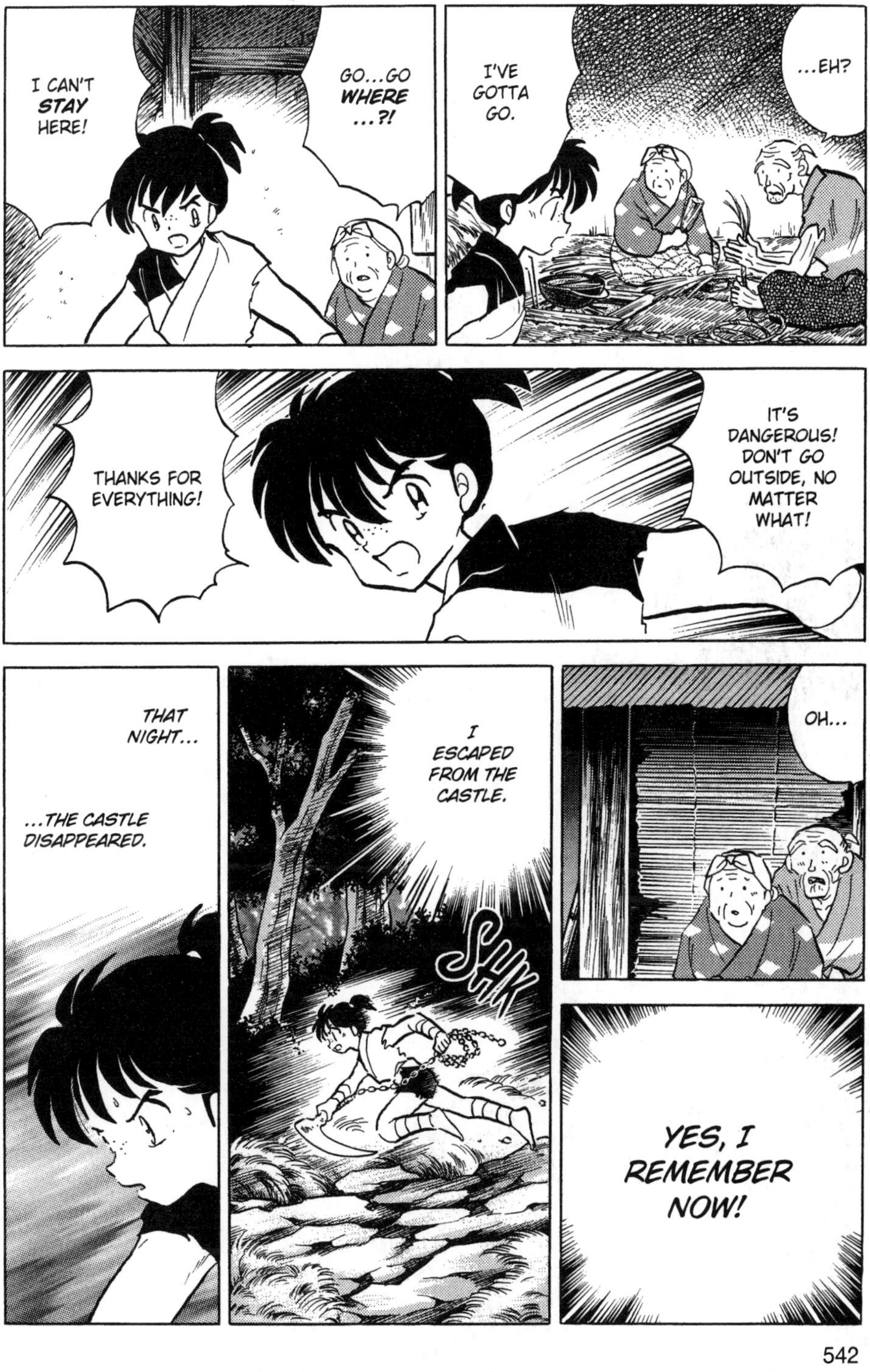
...EH?
I'VE GOTTA GO.
GO...GO WHERE...?!
I CAN'T STAY HERE!
IT'S DANGEROUS! DON'T GO OUTSIDE, NO MATTER WHAT!
THANKS FOR EVERYTHING!
OH...
YES, I REMEMBER NOW!
I ESCAPED FROM THE CASTLE.
SHK
THAT NIGHT...
...THE CASTLE DISAPPEARED.

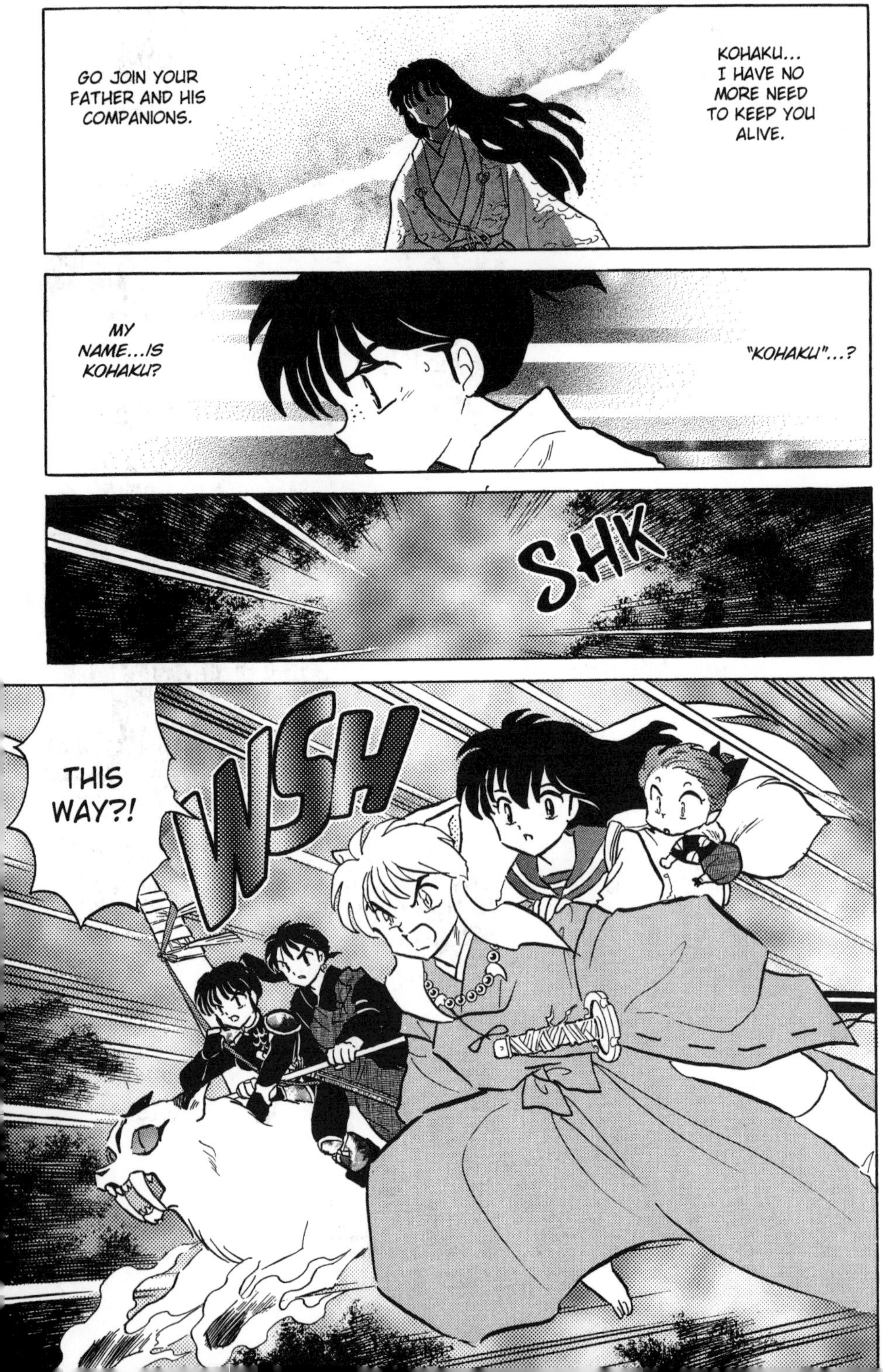
KOHAKU... I HAVE NO MORE NEED TO KEEP YOU ALIVE.
GO JOIN YOUR FATHER AND HIS COMPANIONS.
"KOHAKU"...?
MY NAME...IS KOHAKU?
SHK
WSH
THIS WAY?!

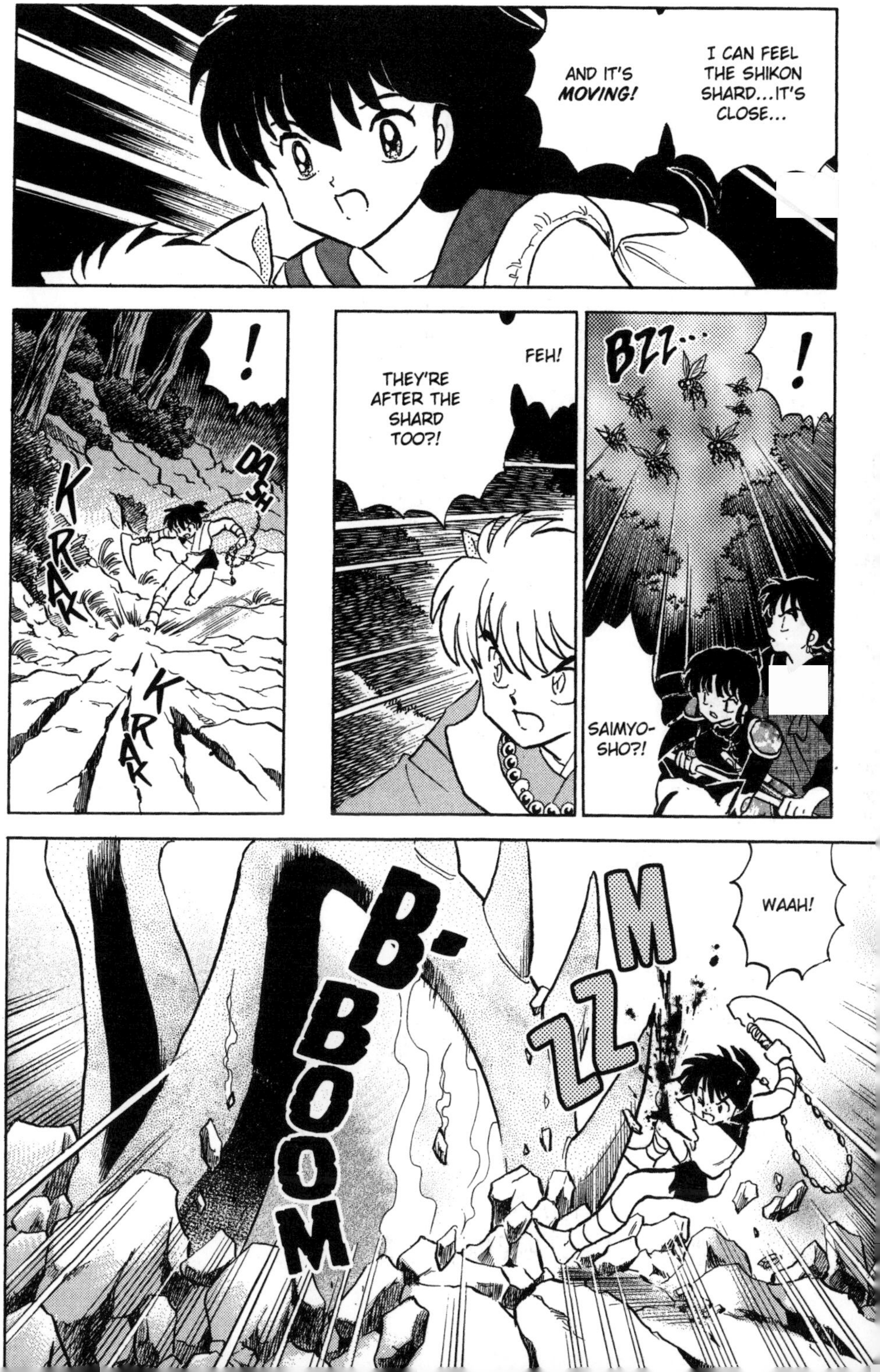
I CAN FEEL THE SHIKON SHARD...IT'S CLOSE...
AND IT'S *MOVING!*
BZZ...
!
SAIMYO-SHO?!
FEH!
THEY'RE AFTER THE SHARD TOO?!
!
DASH
KRAK
KRAK
WAAH!
ZZM
B-BOOM

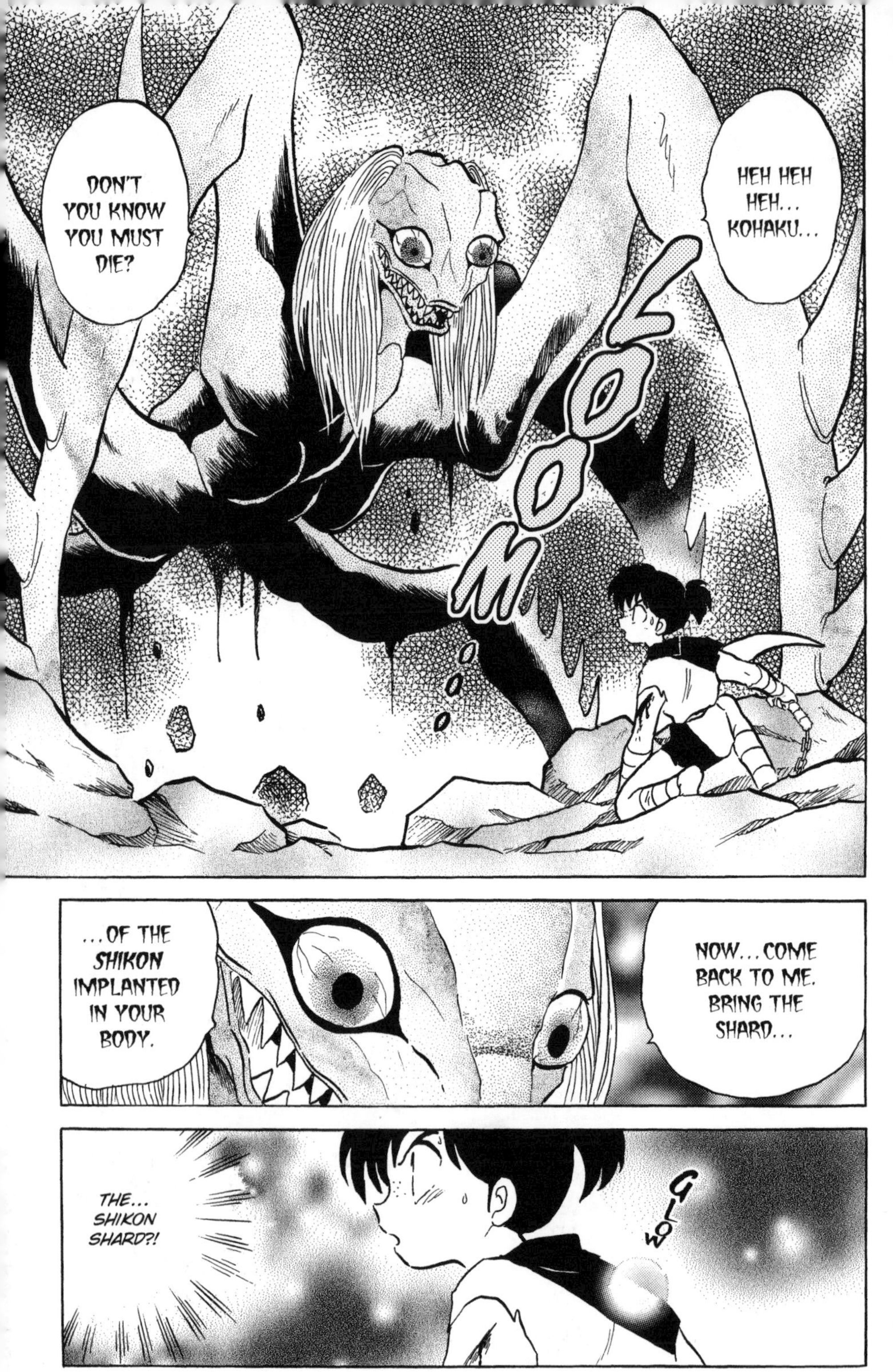
HEH HEH HEH... KOHAKU...
VOOOM
DON'T YOU KNOW YOU MUST DIE?
NOW...COME BACK TO ME. BRING THE SHARD...
...OF THE SHIKON IMPLANTED IN YOUR BODY.
GLOW
THE... SHIKON SHARD?!

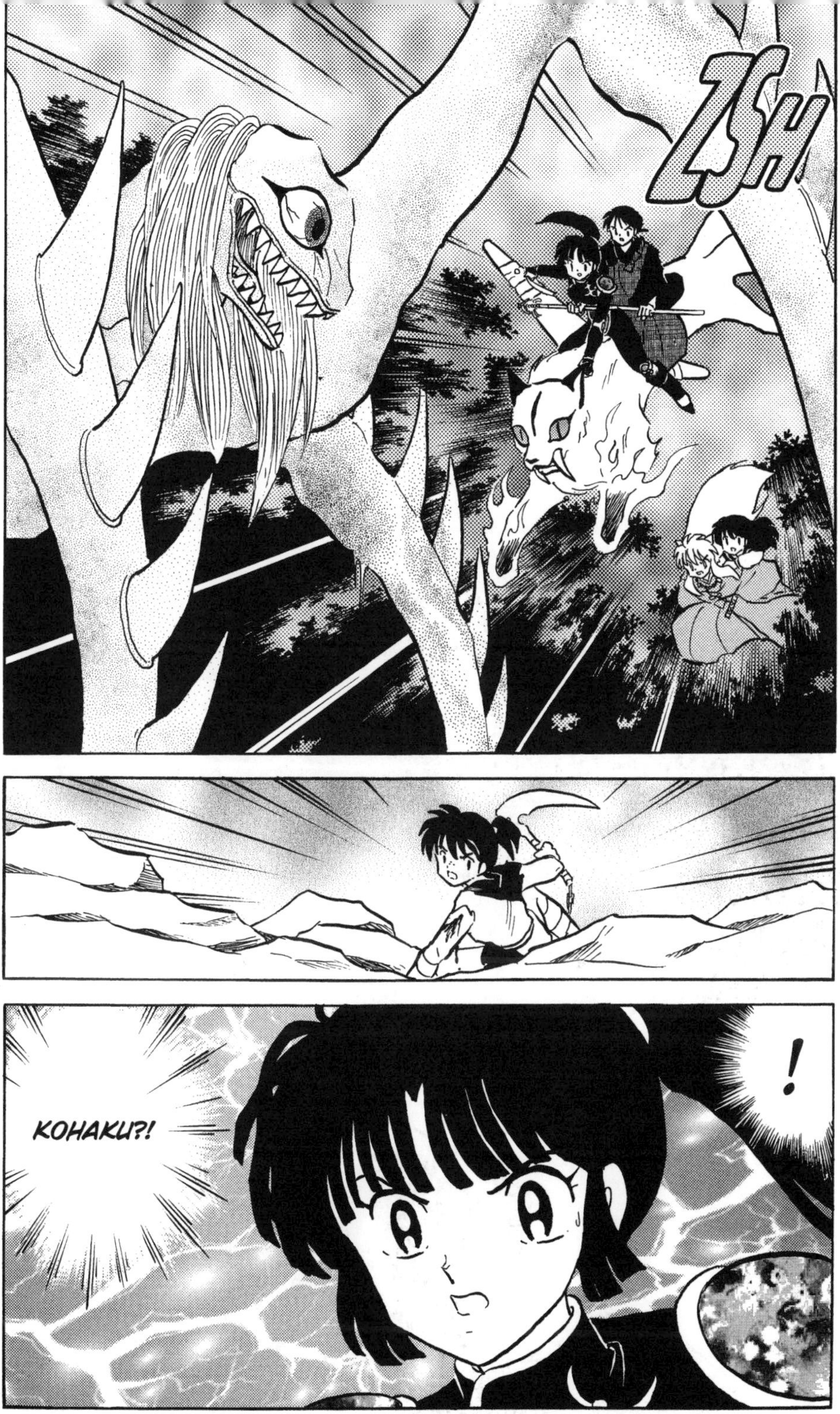
ZSH
!
KOHAKU?!

SCROLL TEN
KOHAKU'S MEMORY

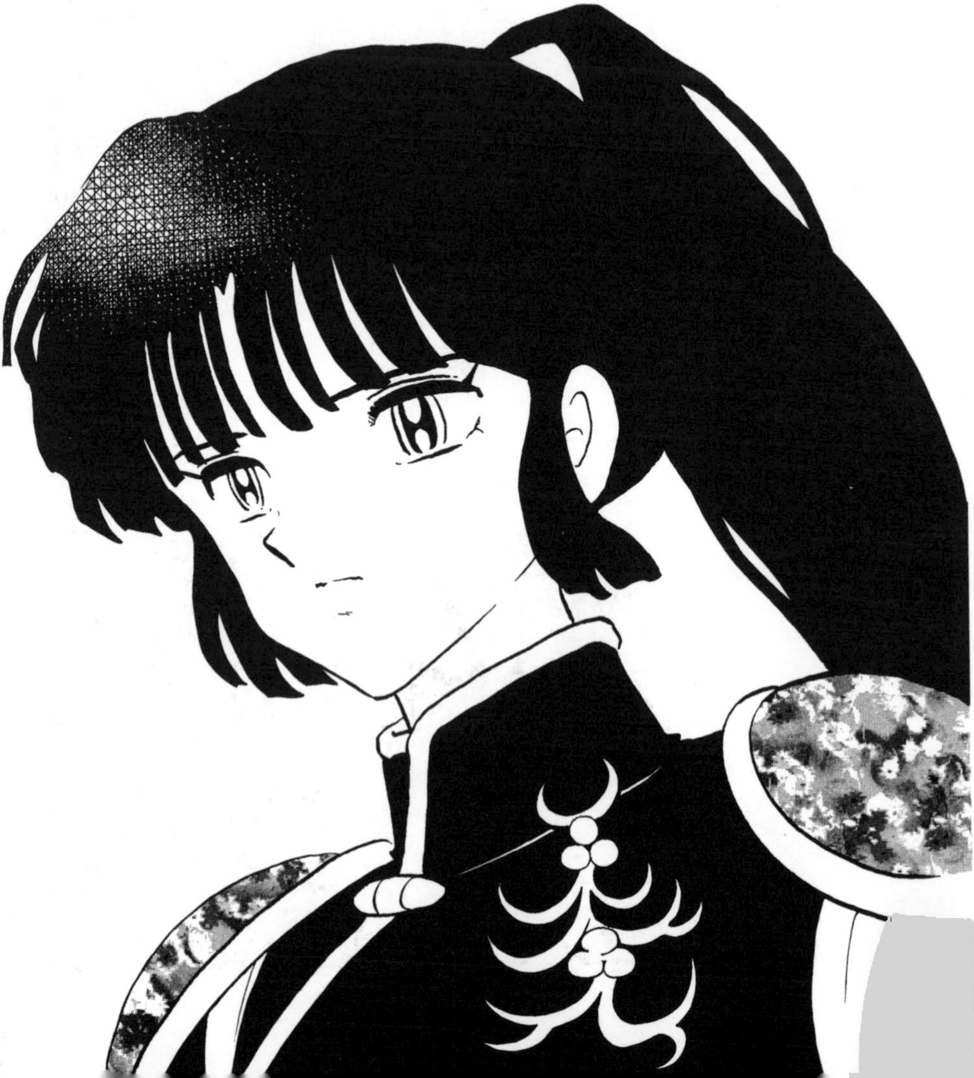

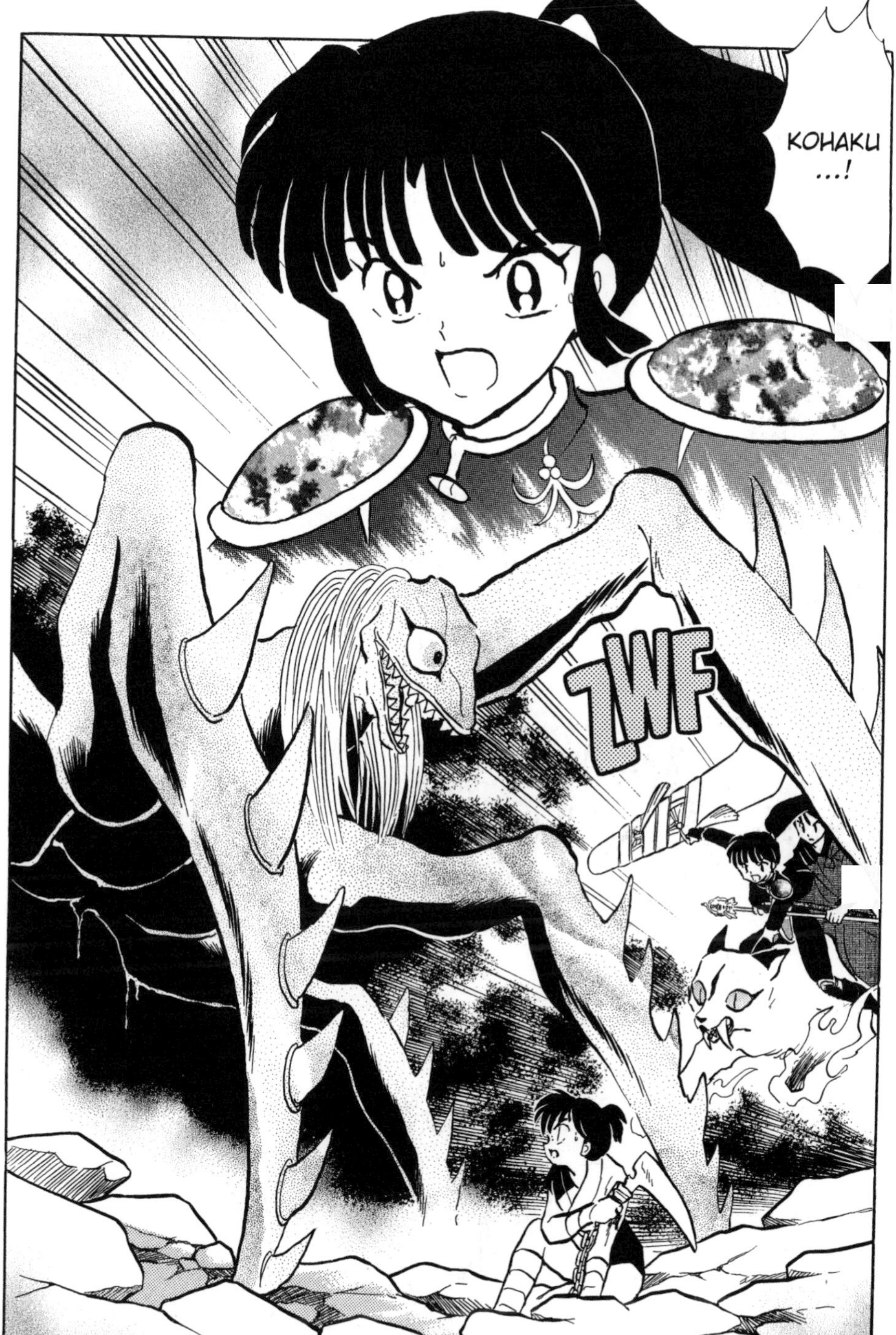
KOHAKU ...!
ZWF

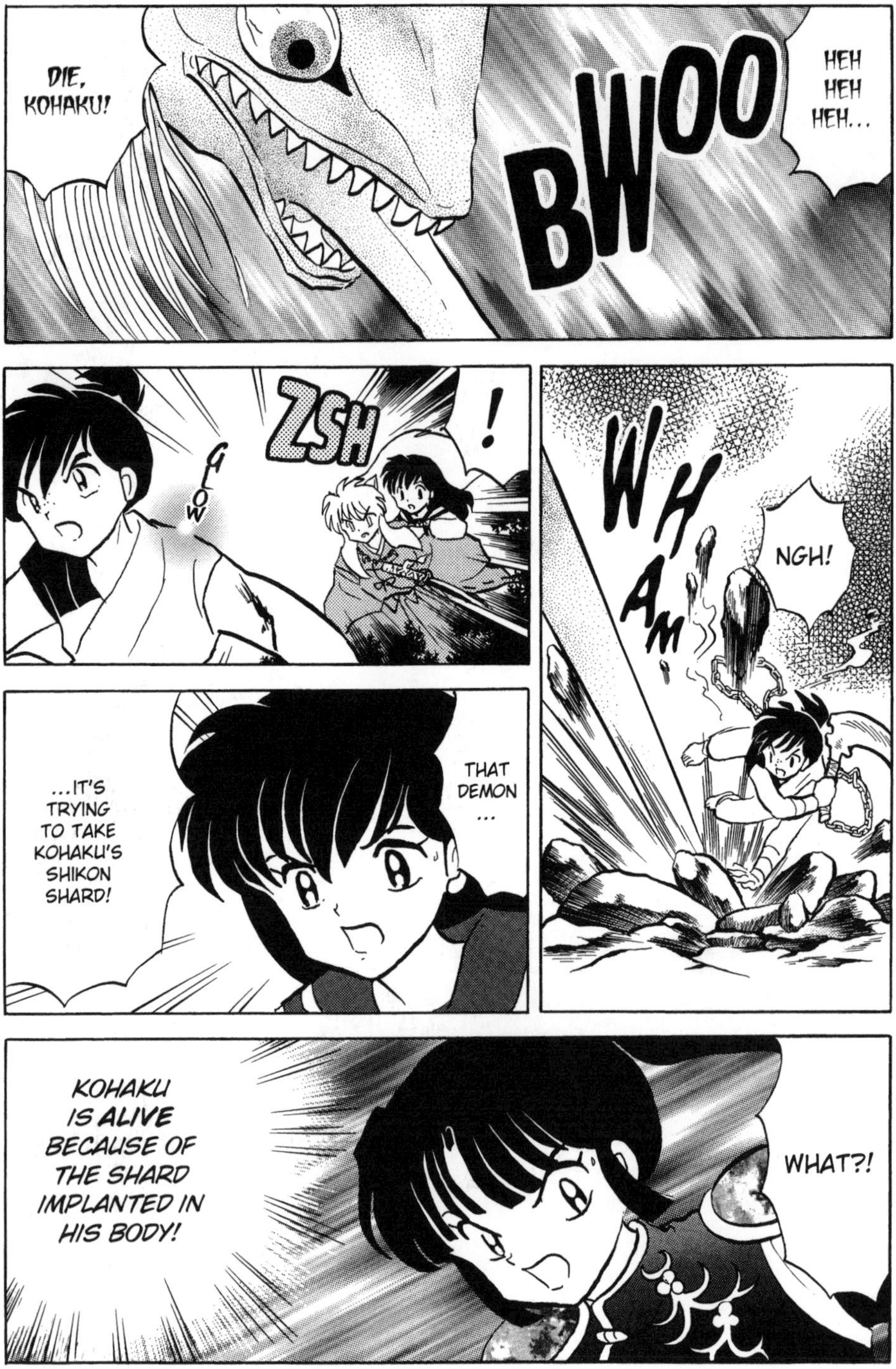
HEH HEH HEH...
BWOO
DIE, KOHAKU!
WHAM
NGH!
ZSH
!
GLOW
THAT DEMON...
...IT'S TRYING TO TAKE KOHAKU'S SHIKON SHARD!
WHAT?!
KOHAKU IS **ALIVE** BECAUSE OF THE SHARD IMPLANTED IN HIS BODY!

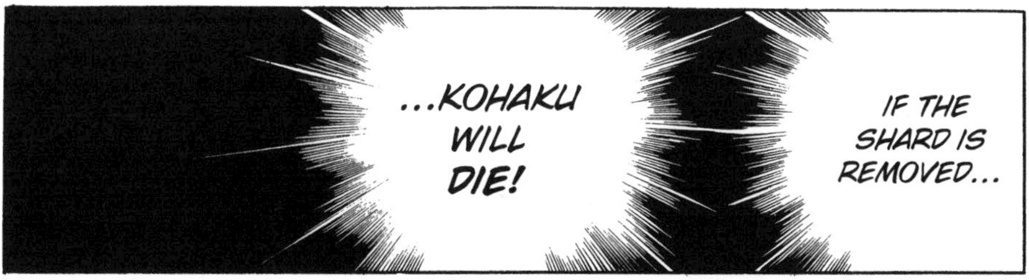
IF THE SHARD IS REMOVED...
...KOHAKU WILL DIE!
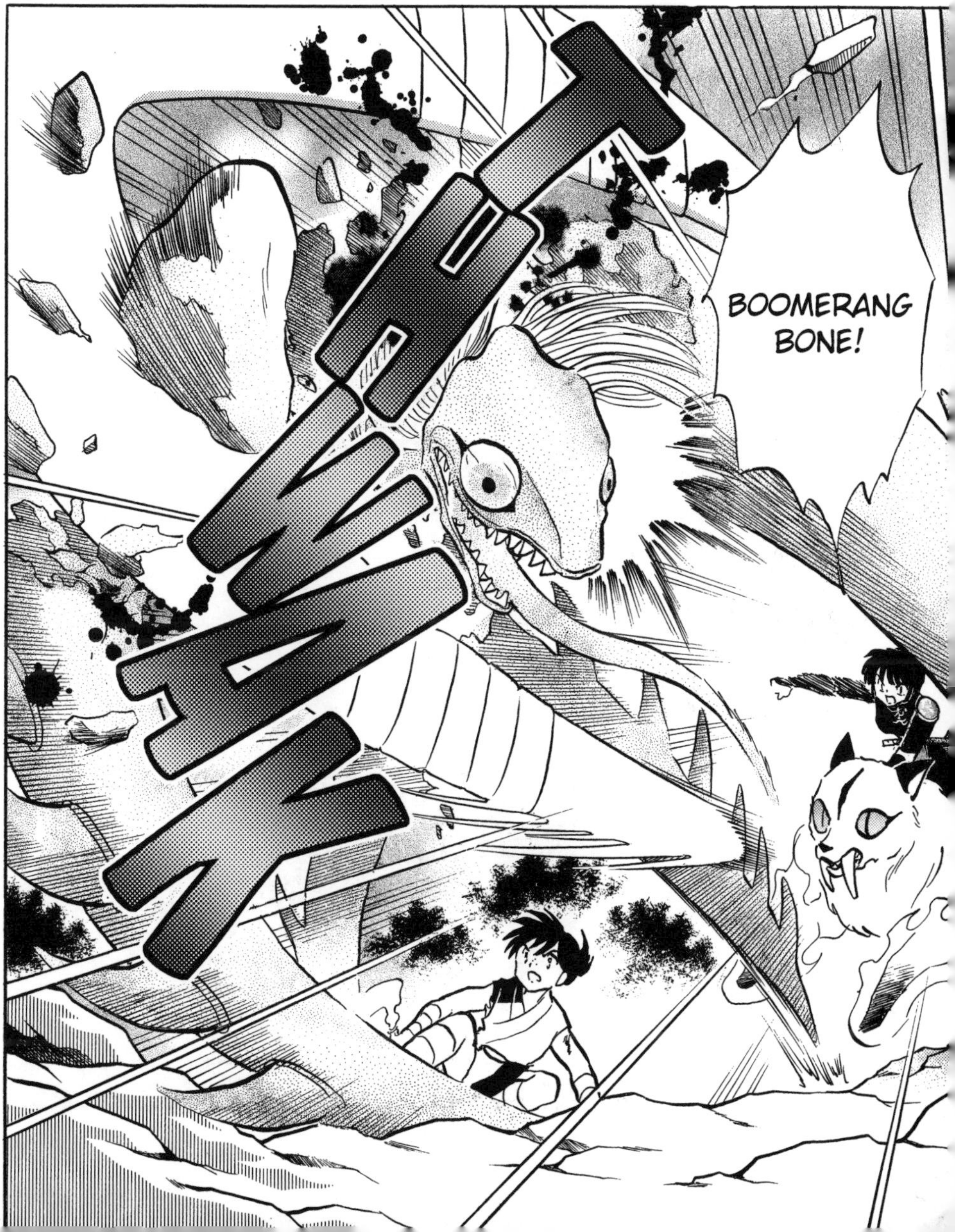
BOOMERANG BONE!
THWAK

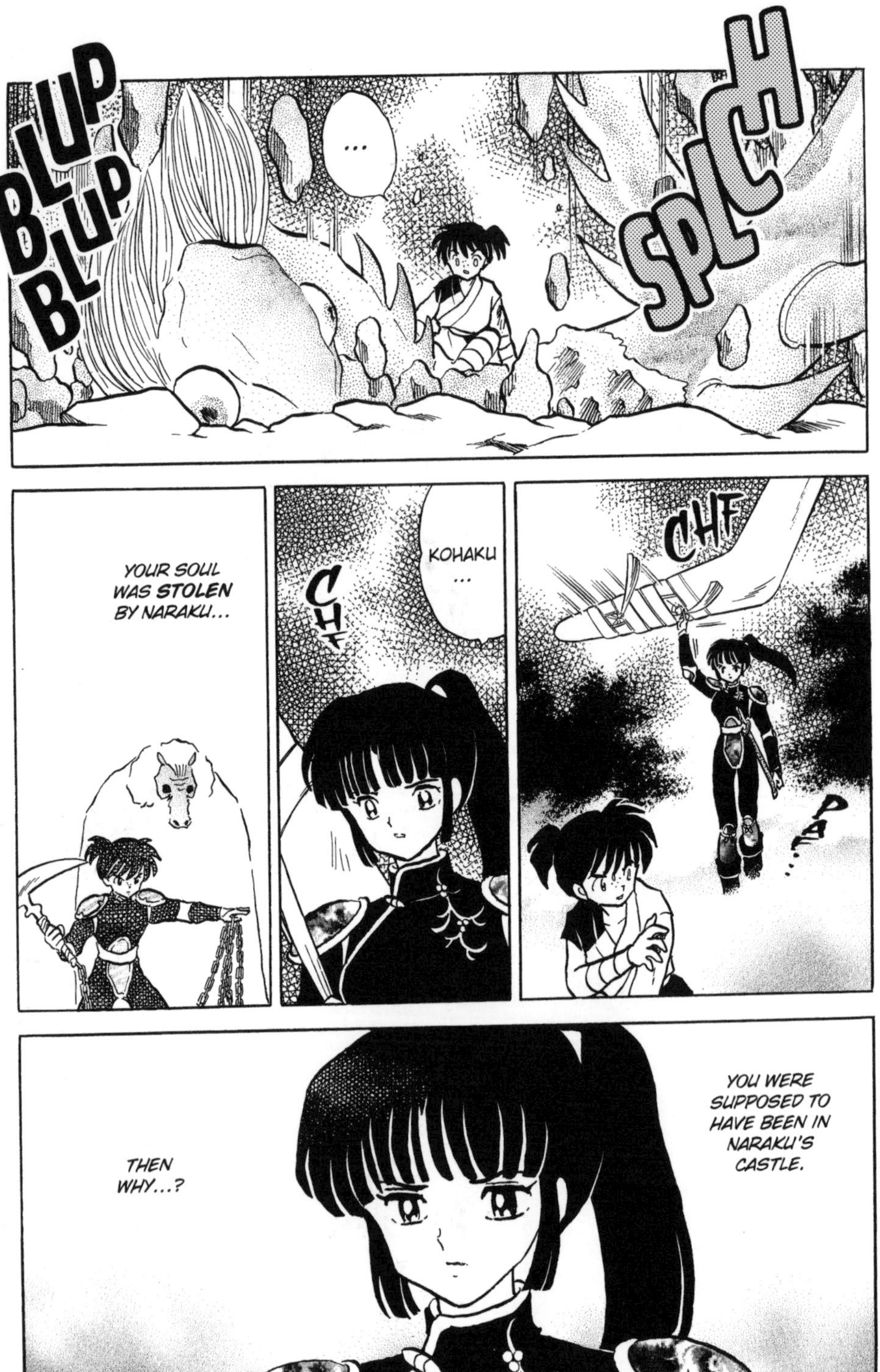
SPLCH
...
BLUP BLUP
CHF
PAF...
KOHAKU...
CHF
YOUR SOUL WAS STOLEN BY NARAKU...
YOU WERE SUPPOSED TO HAVE BEEN IN NARAKU'S CASTLE.
THEN WHY...?

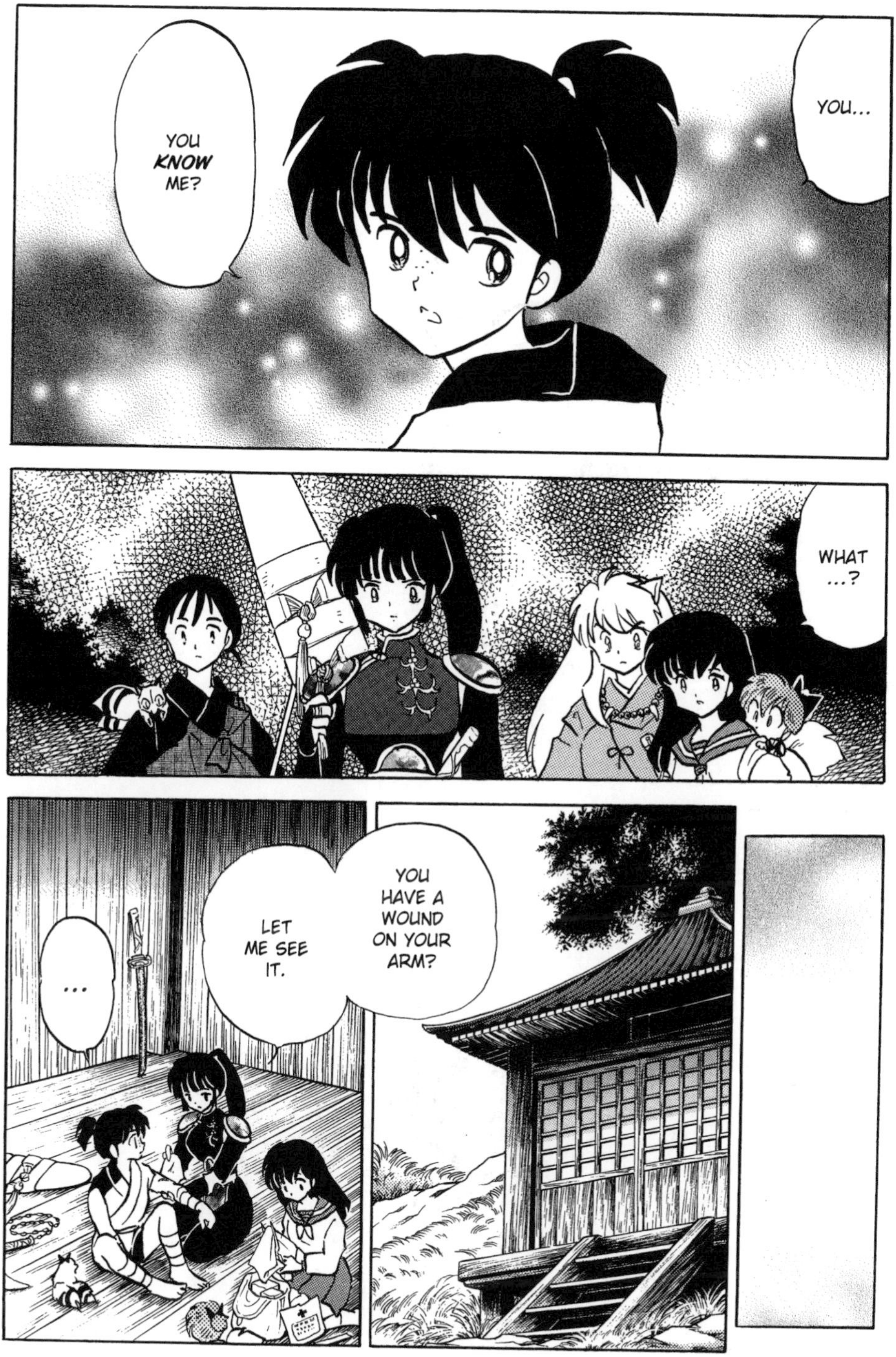
YOU...
YOU KNOW ME?
WHAT ...?
YOU HAVE A WOUND ON YOUR ARM?
LET ME SEE IT.
...

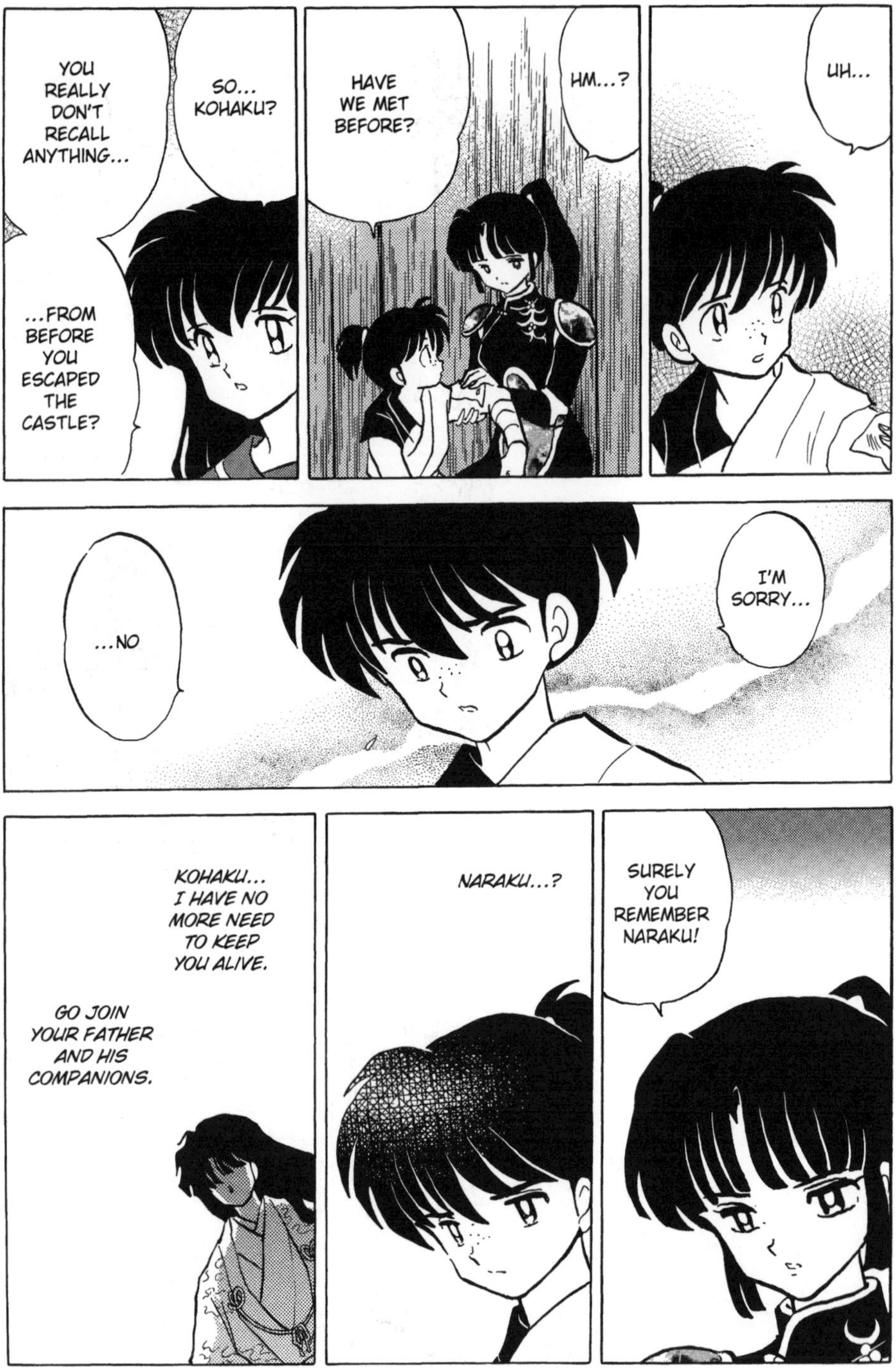
UH...
HM...?
HAVE WE MET BEFORE?
SO... KOHAKU?
YOU REALLY DON'T RECALL ANYTHING...
...FROM BEFORE YOU ESCAPED THE CASTLE?
I'M SORRY...
...NO
SURELY YOU REMEMBER NARAKU!
NARAKU...?
KOHAKU... I HAVE NO MORE NEED TO KEEP YOU ALIVE.
GO JOIN YOUR FATHER AND HIS COMPANIONS.

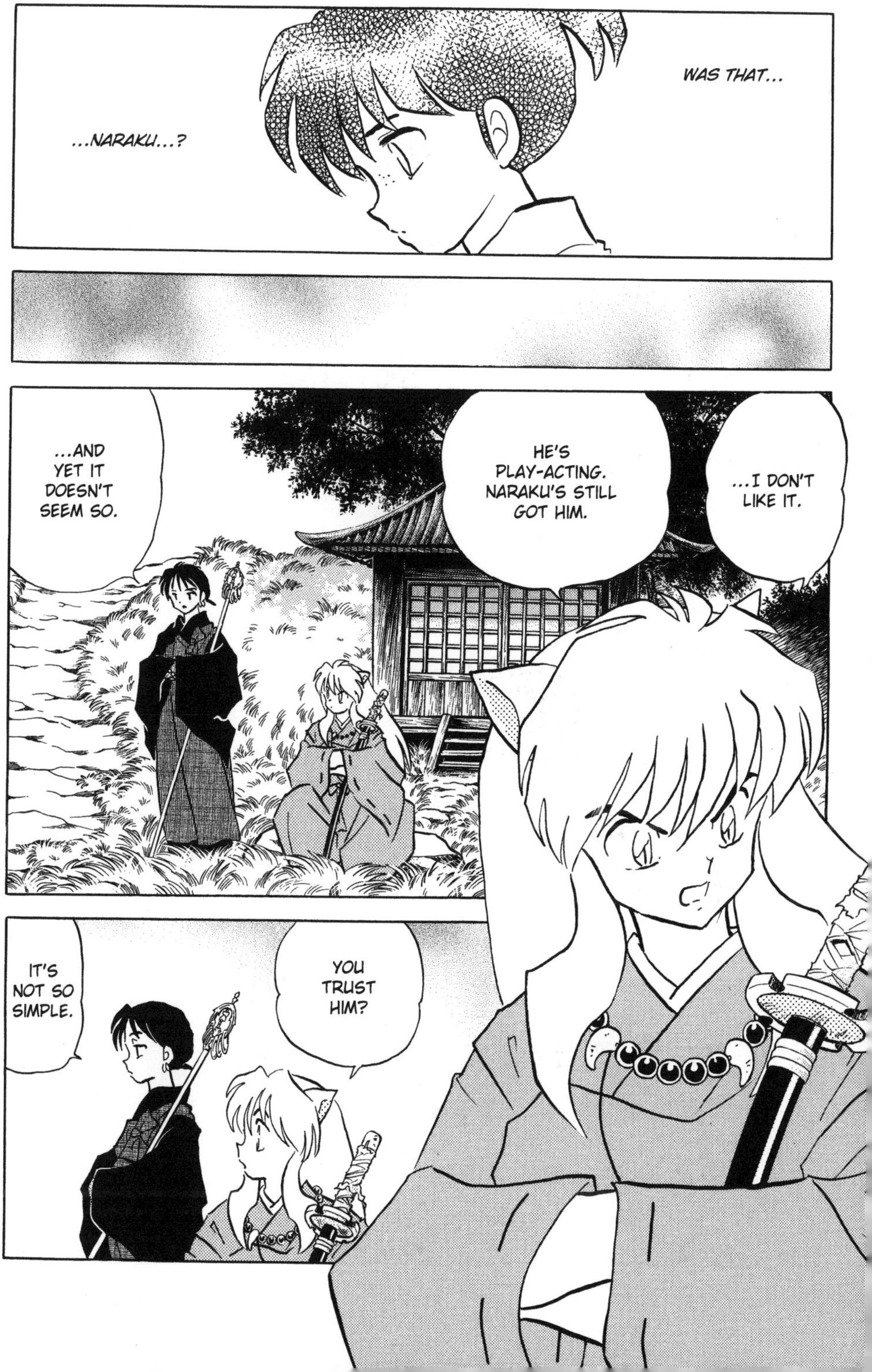
WAS THAT...
...NARAKU...?
...I DON'T LIKE IT.
HE'S PLAY-ACTING. NARAKU'S STILL GOT HIM.
...AND YET IT DOESN'T SEEM SO.
YOU TRUST HIM?
IT'S NOT SO SIMPLE.

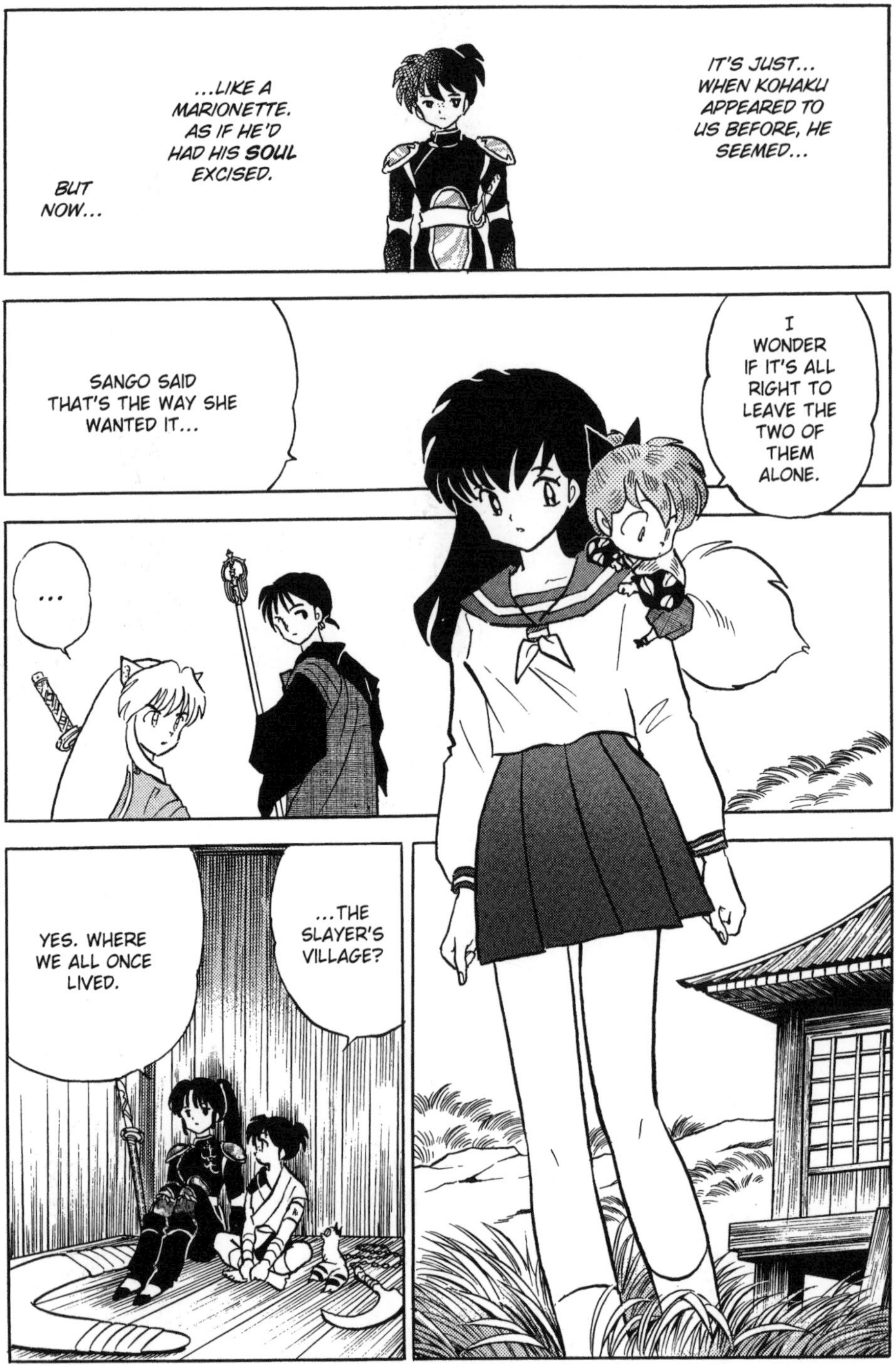
IT'S JUST... WHEN KOHAKU APPEARED TO US BEFORE, HE SEEMED...
...LIKE A MARIONETTE. AS IF HE'D HAD HIS **SOUL** EXCISED.
BUT NOW...
I WONDER IF IT'S ALL RIGHT TO LEAVE THE TWO OF THEM ALONE.
SANGO SAID THAT'S THE WAY SHE WANTED IT...
...
...THE SLAYER'S VILLAGE?
YES. WHERE WE ALL ONCE LIVED.

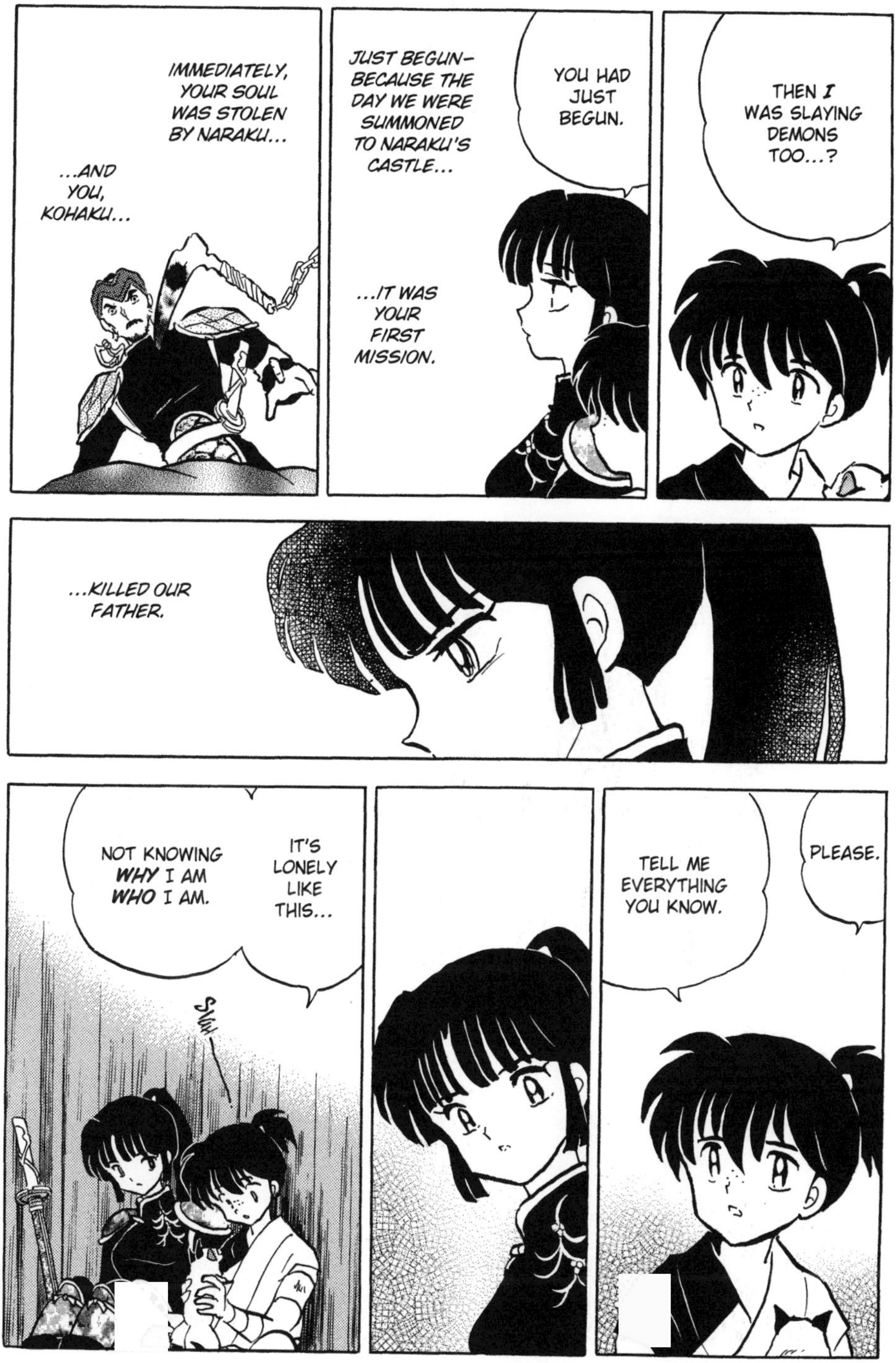
THEN *I* WAS SLAYING DEMONS TOO...?
YOU HAD JUST BEGUN.
JUST BEGUN— BECAUSE THE DAY WE WERE SUMMONED TO NARAKU'S CASTLE...
...IT WAS YOUR FIRST MISSION.
IMMEDIATELY, YOUR SOUL WAS STOLEN BY NARAKU...
...AND YOU, KOHAKU...
...KILLED OUR FATHER.
PLEASE.
TELL ME EVERYTHING YOU KNOW.
IT'S LONELY LIKE THIS...
NOT KNOWING ***WHY*** I AM ***WHO*** I AM.
SLUM—

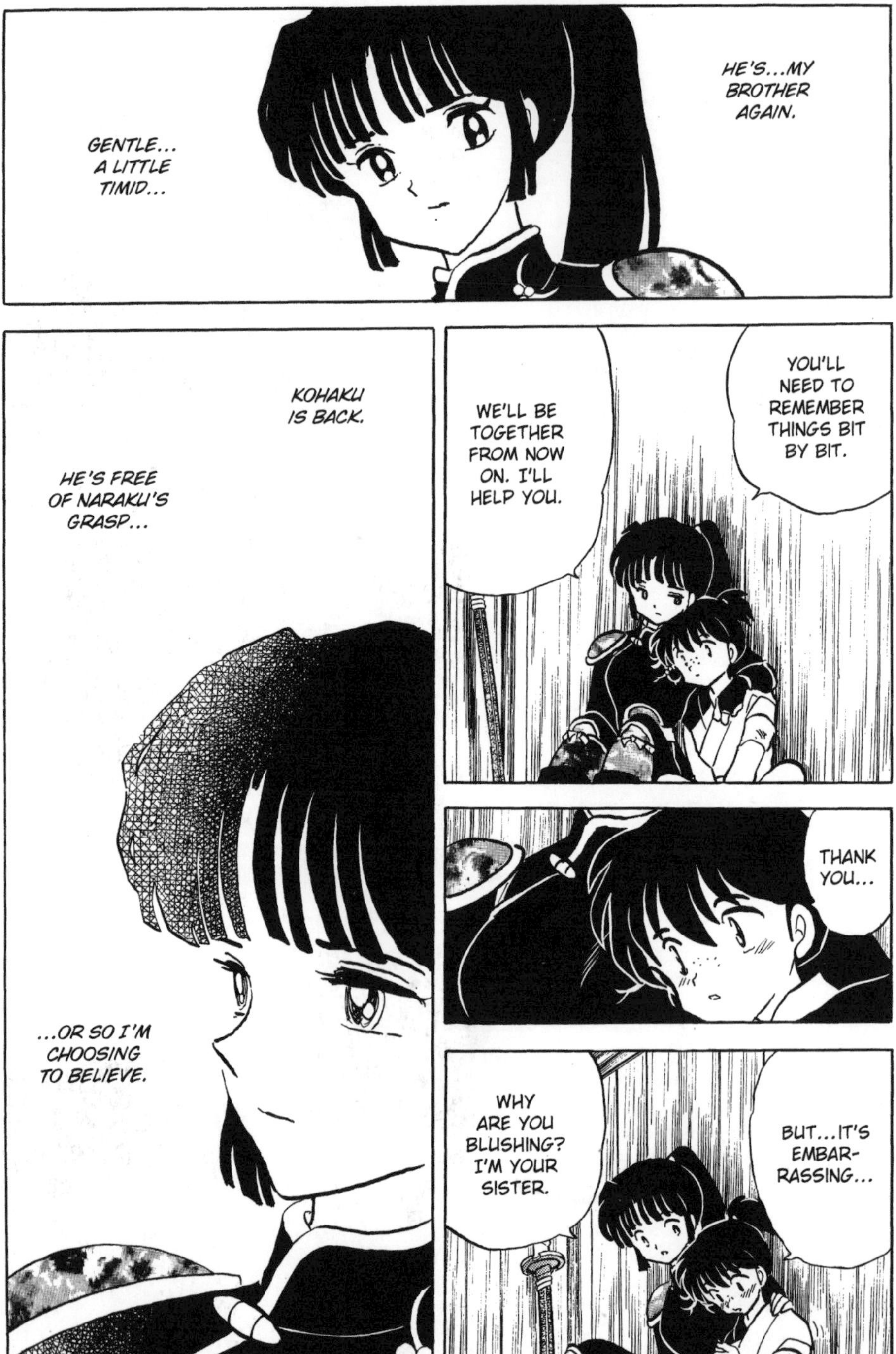
HE'S...MY BROTHER AGAIN.
GENTLE... A LITTLE TIMID...
YOU'LL NEED TO REMEMBER THINGS BIT BY BIT.
WE'LL BE TOGETHER FROM NOW ON. I'LL HELP YOU.
THANK YOU...
WHY ARE YOU BLUSHING? I'M YOUR SISTER.
BUT...IT'S EMBARRASSING...
KOHAKU IS BACK.
HE'S FREE OF NARAKU'S GRASP...
...OR SO I'M CHOOSING TO BELIEVE.

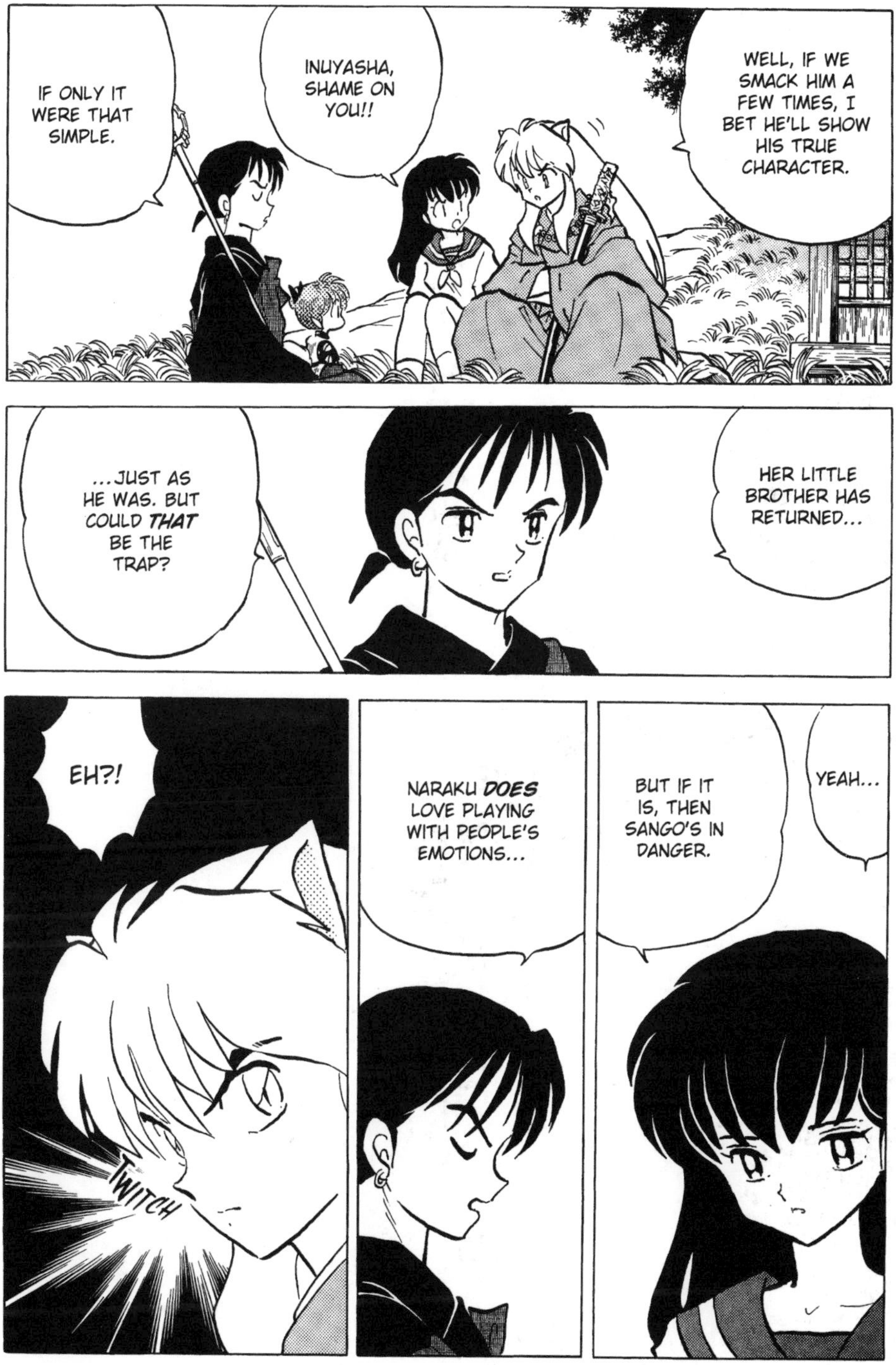
WELL, IF WE SMACK HIM A FEW TIMES, I BET HE'LL SHOW HIS TRUE CHARACTER.
INUYASHA, SHAME ON YOU!!
IF ONLY IT WERE THAT SIMPLE.
HER LITTLE BROTHER HAS RETURNED...
...JUST AS HE WAS. BUT COULD *THAT* BE THE TRAP?
YEAH...
BUT IF IT IS, THEN SANGO'S IN DANGER.
NARAKU *DOES* LOVE PLAYING WITH PEOPLE'S EMOTIONS...
EH?!
TWITCH

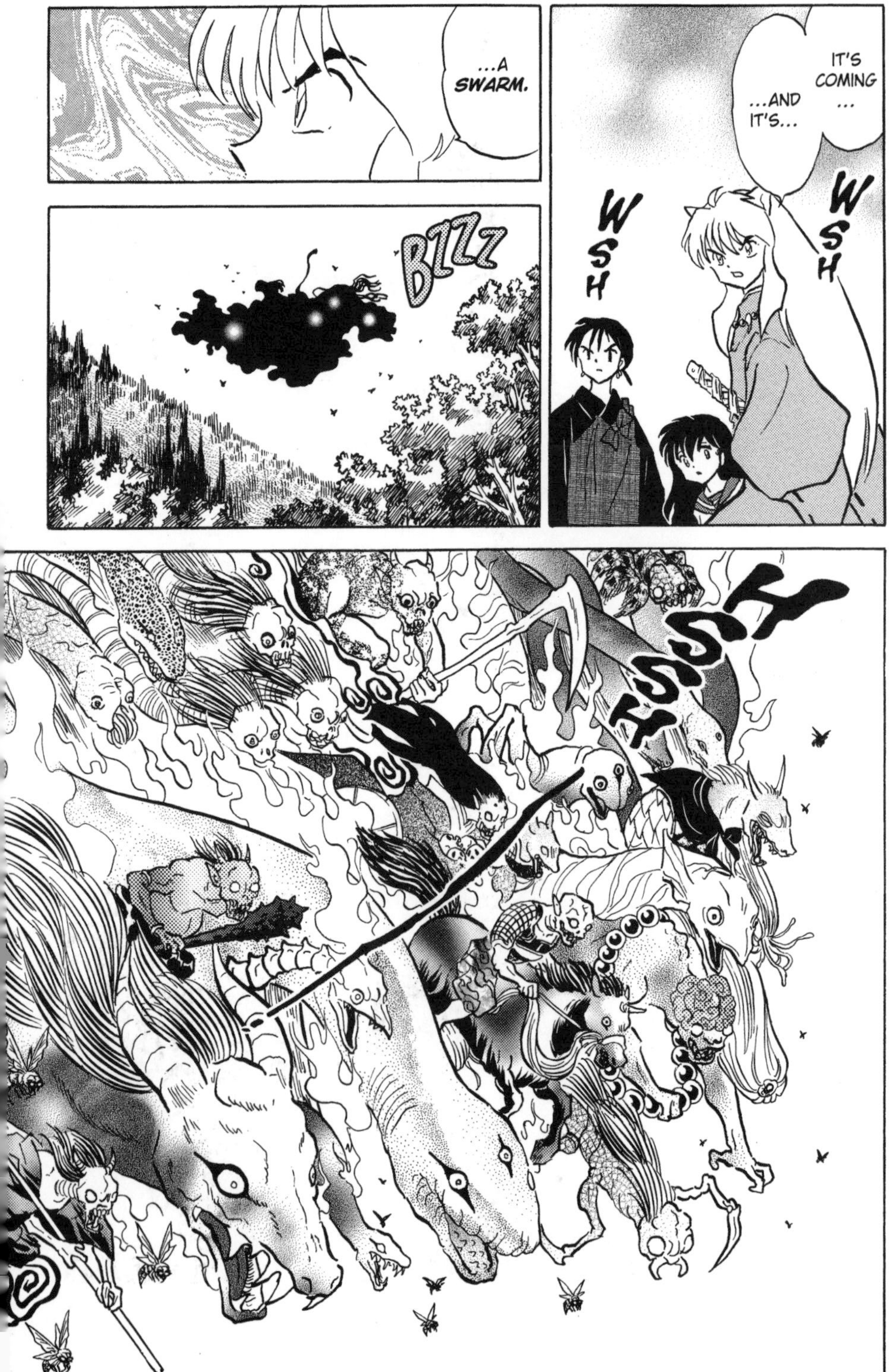
IT'S COMING...
...AND IT'S...
WSH
WSH
...A SWARM.
BZZZ
HUSSH

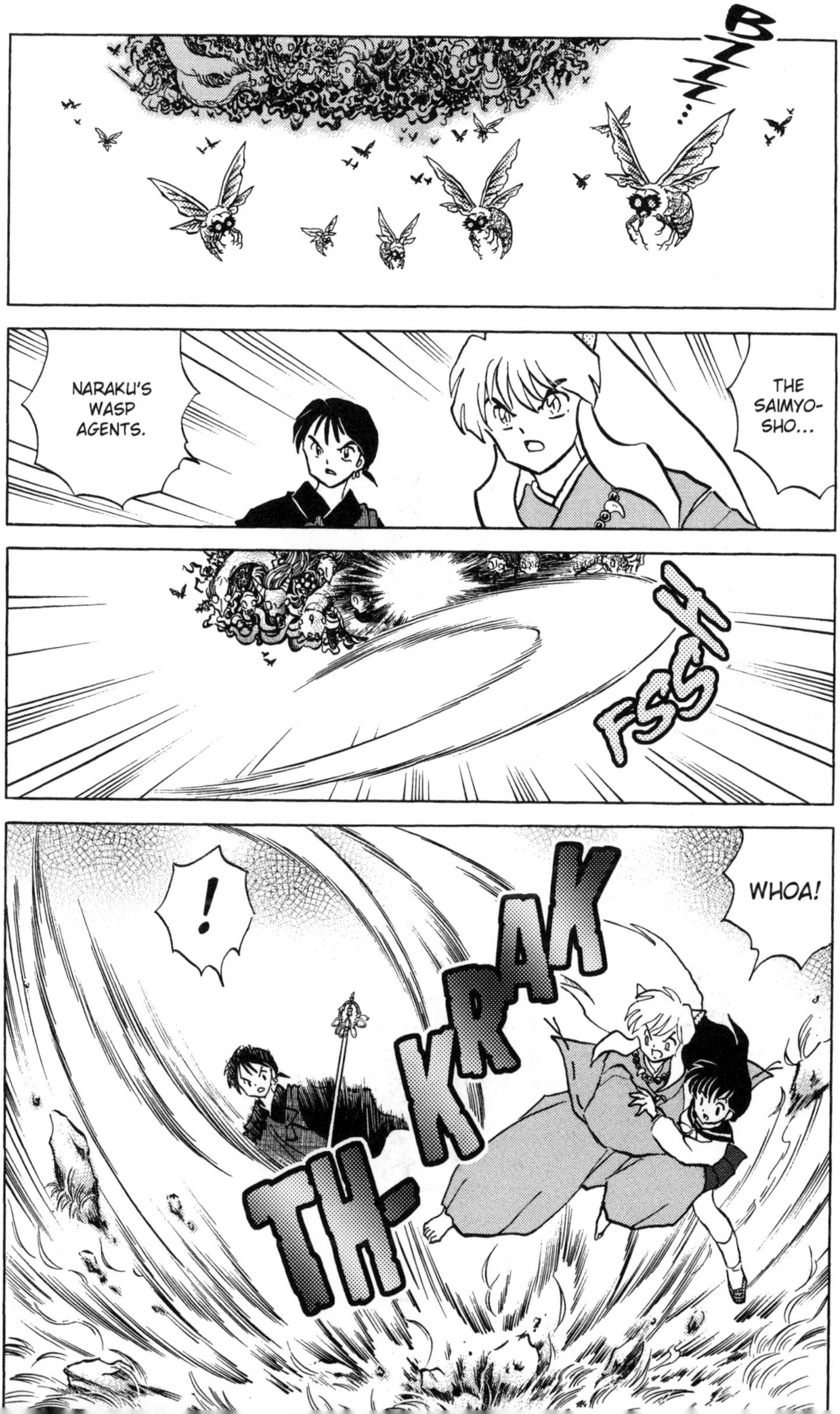
BZZZ...
THE SAIMYO-SHO...
NARAKU'S WASP AGENTS.
FSSSH
WHOA!
TH-KRAK
!

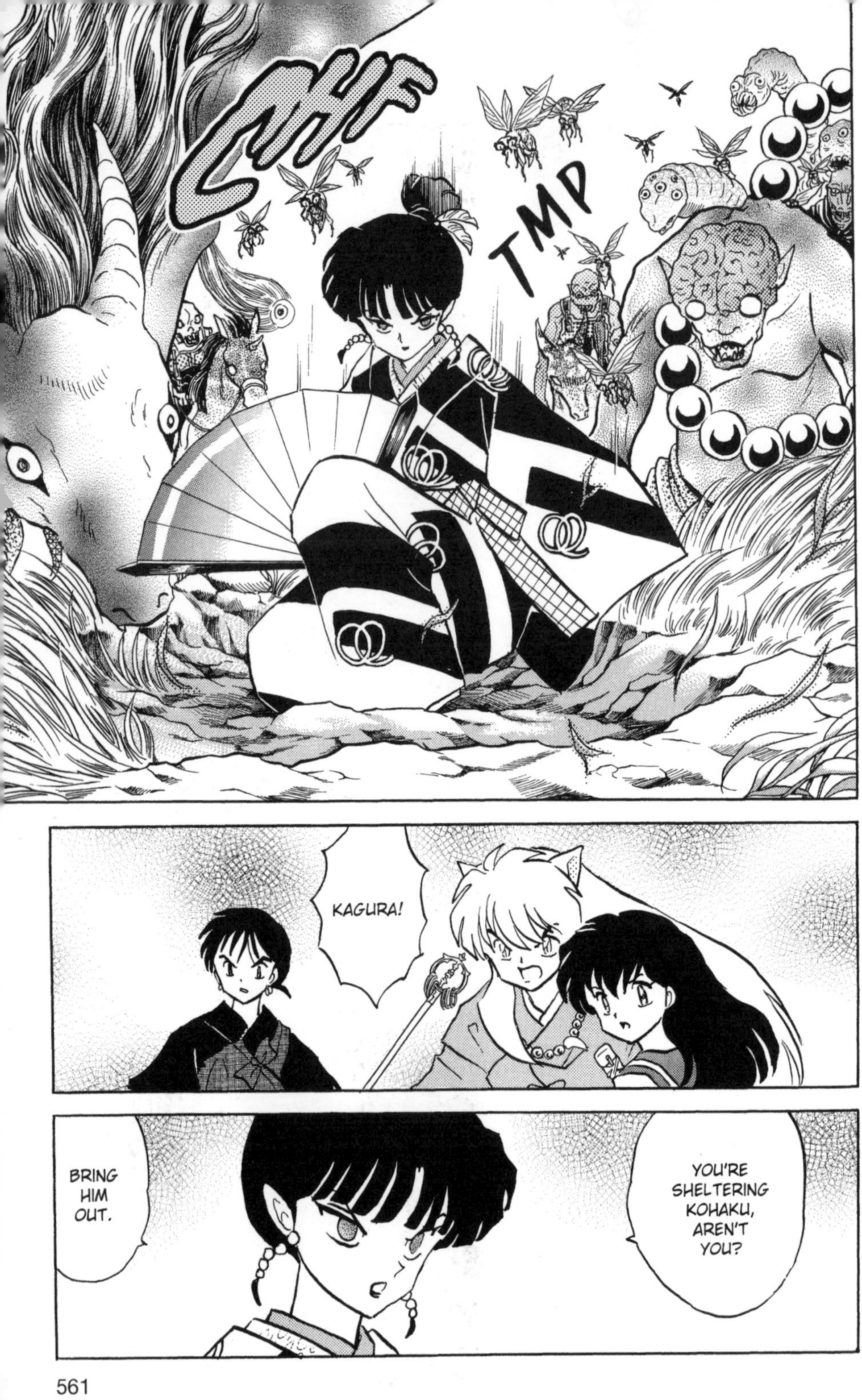
TMP
KAGURA!
YOU'RE SHELTERING KOHAKU, AREN'T YOU?
BRING HIM OUT.

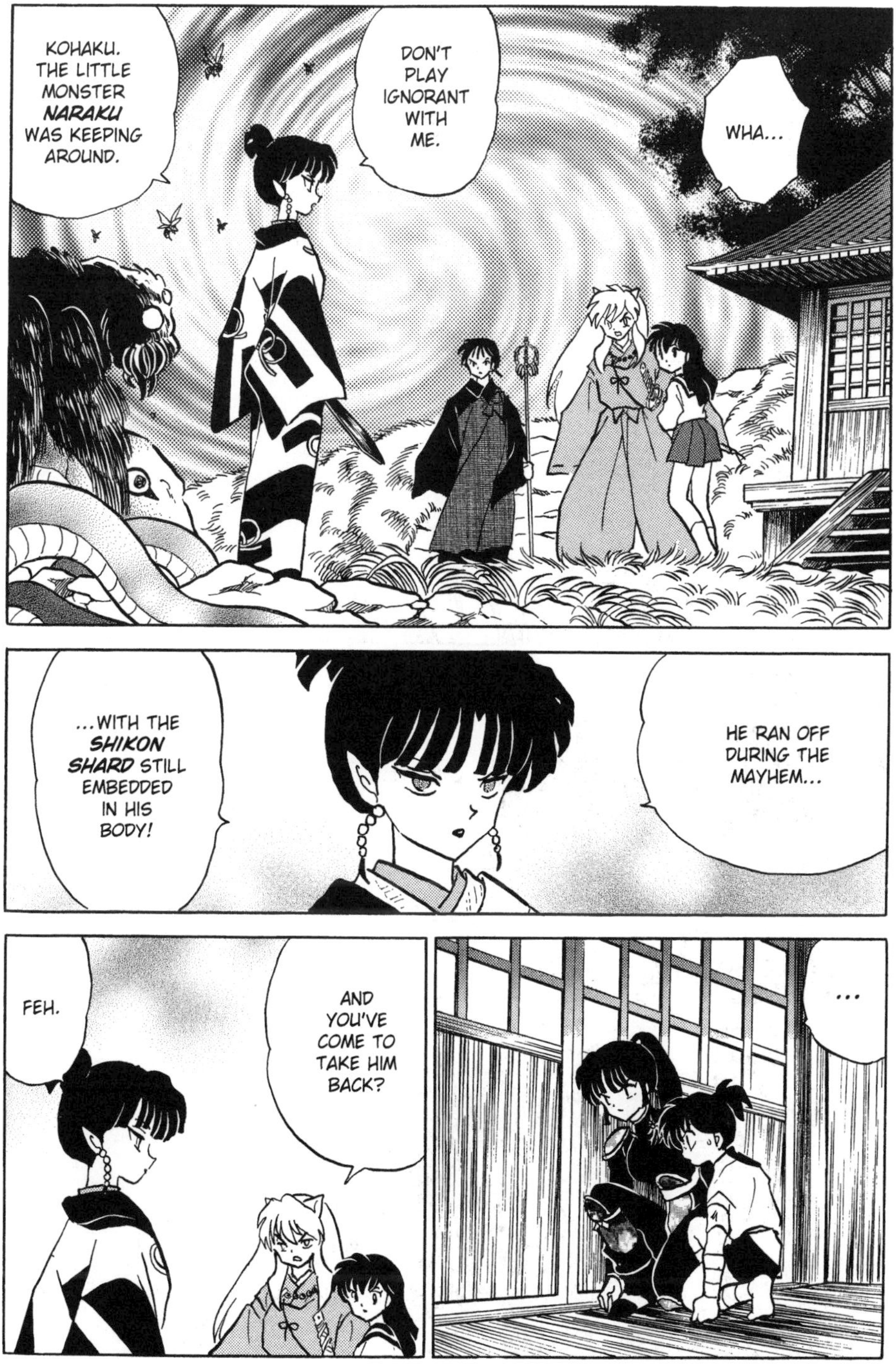
WHA...
DON'T PLAY IGNORANT WITH ME.
KOHAKU. THE LITTLE MONSTER NARAKU WAS KEEPING AROUND.
HE RAN OFF DURING THE MAYHEM...
...WITH THE SHIKON SHARD STILL EMBEDDED IN HIS BODY!
...
AND YOU'VE COME TO TAKE HIM BACK?
FEH.

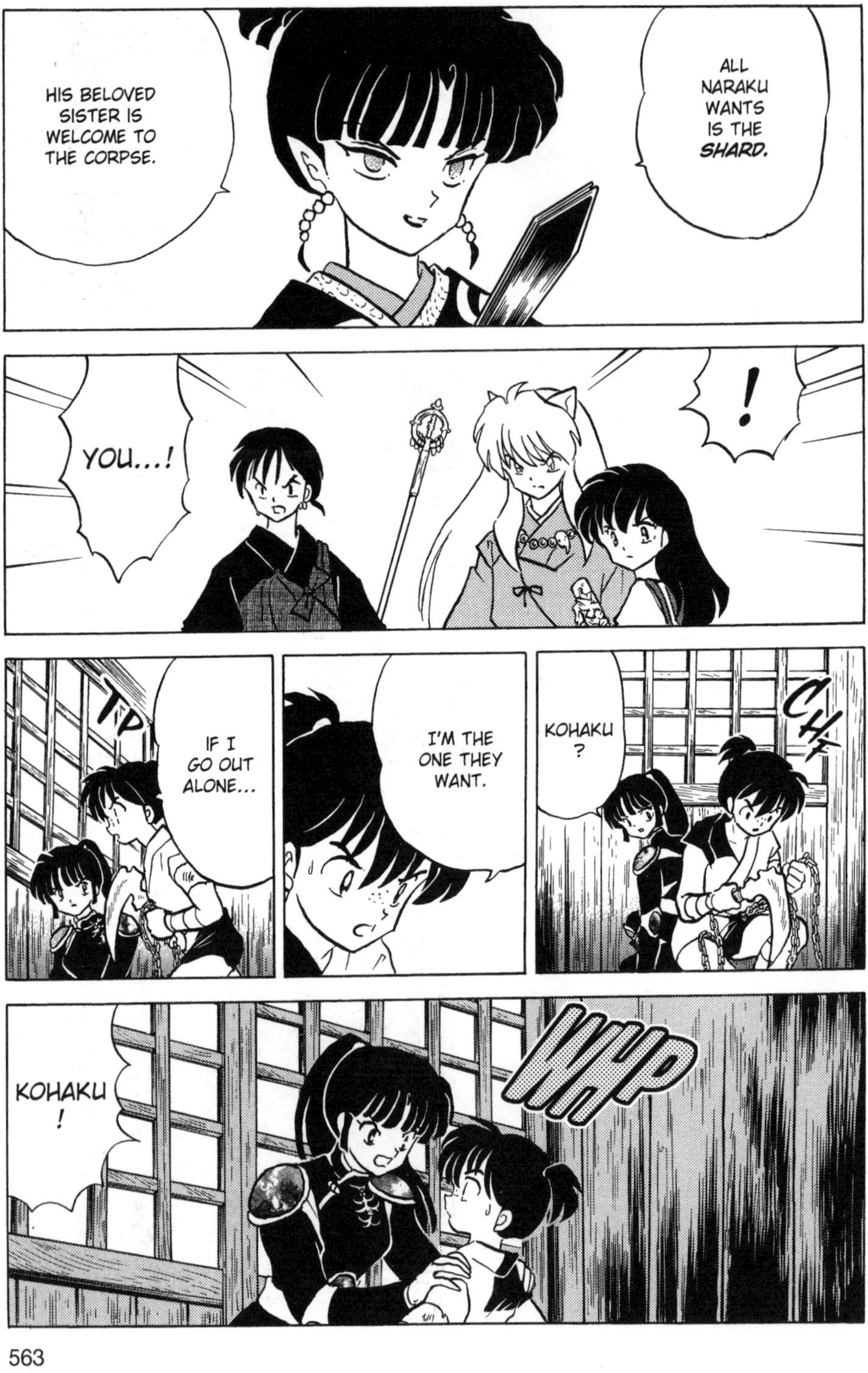
ALL NARAKU WANTS IS THE SHARD.
HIS BELOVED SISTER IS WELCOME TO THE CORPSE.
!
YOU...!
CHF
KOHAKU?
I'M THE ONE THEY WANT.
TP
IF I GO OUT ALONE...
WHP
KOHAKU!

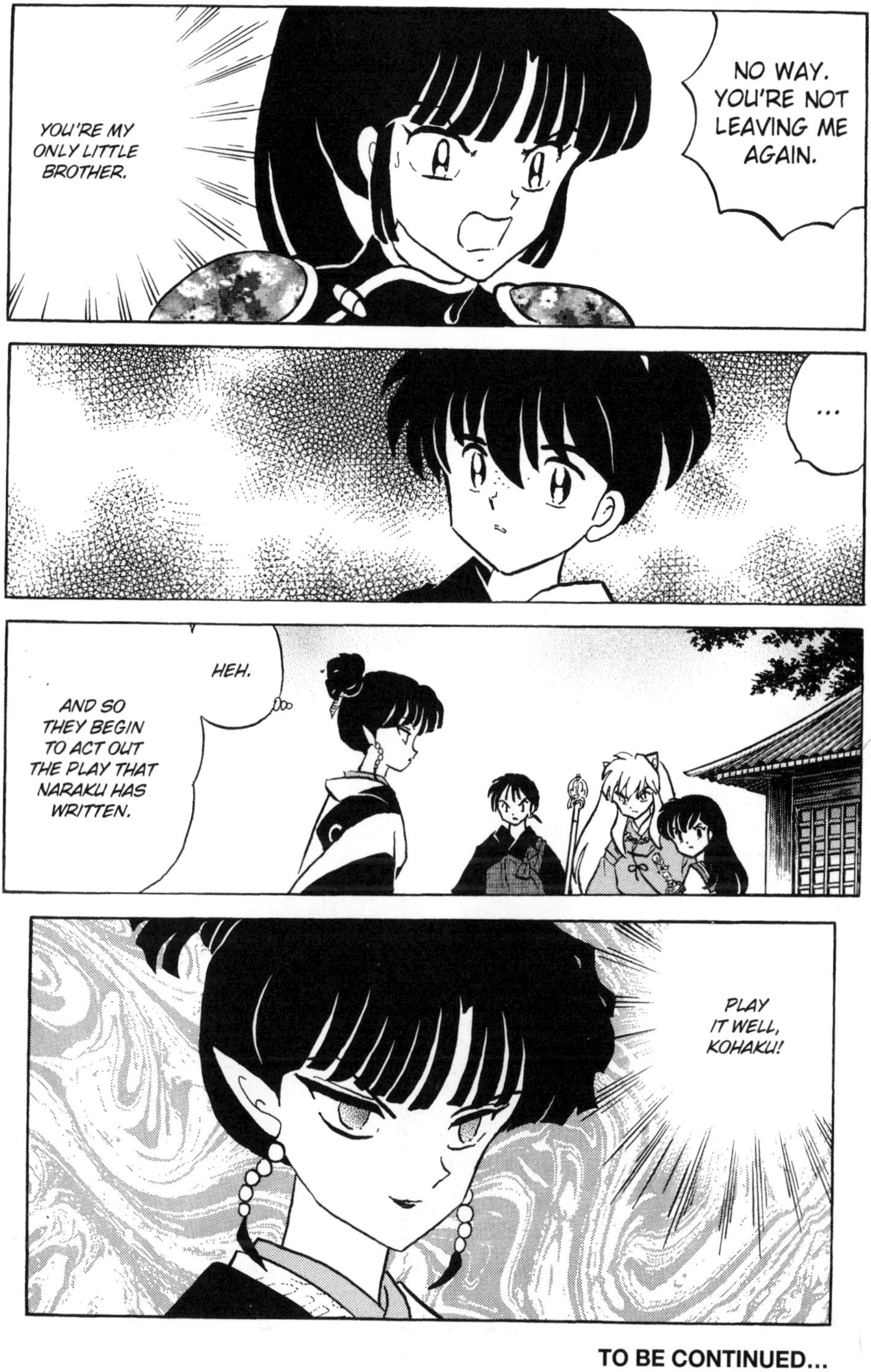
NO WAY. YOU'RE NOT LEAVING ME AGAIN.
YOU'RE MY ONLY LITTLE BROTHER.
...
HEH.
AND SO THEY BEGIN TO ACT OUT THE PLAY THAT NARAKU HAS WRITTEN.
PLAY IT WELL, KOHAKU!

TO BE CONTINUED...

Original Cover Art Gallery

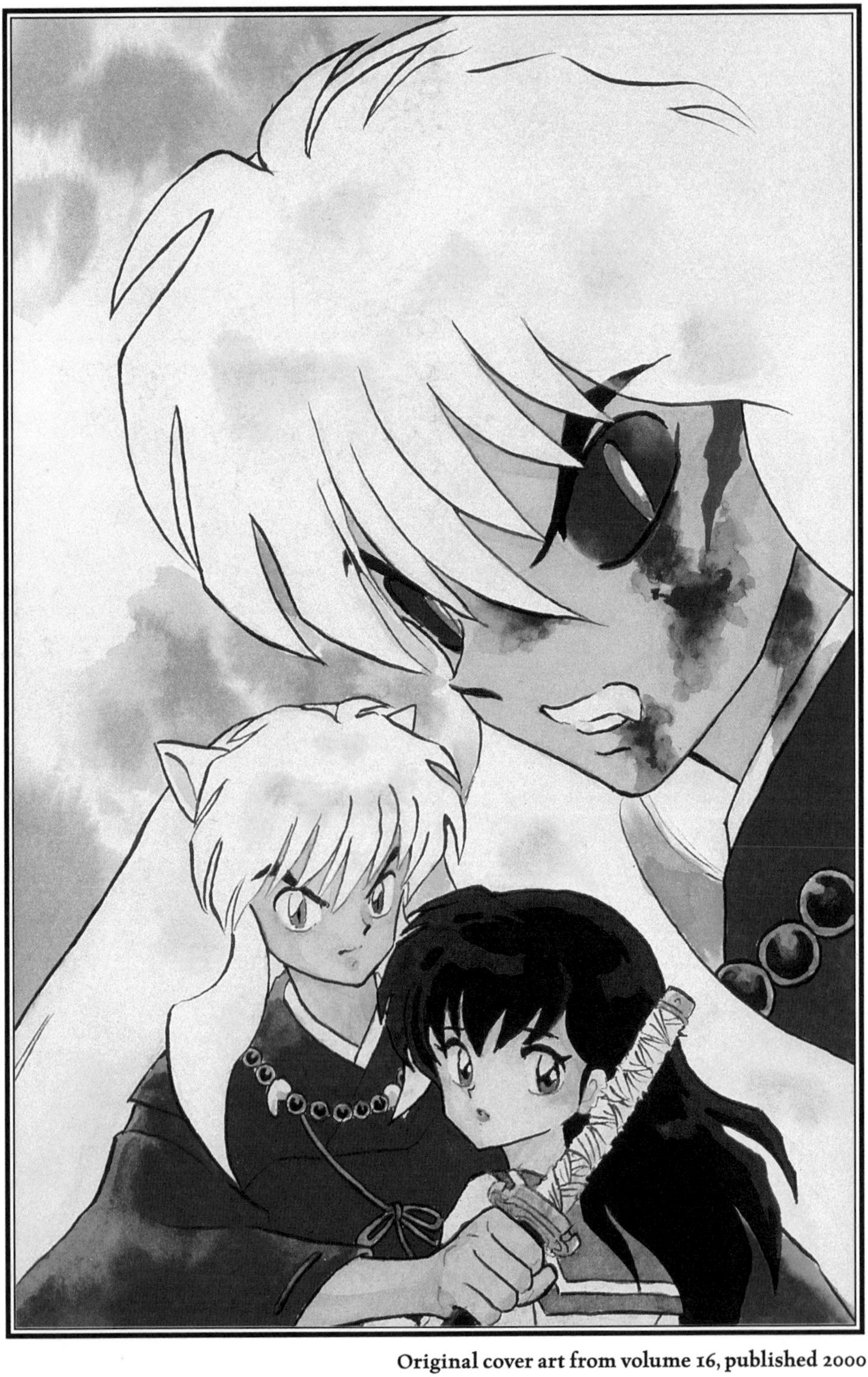

Original cover art from volume 16, published 2000

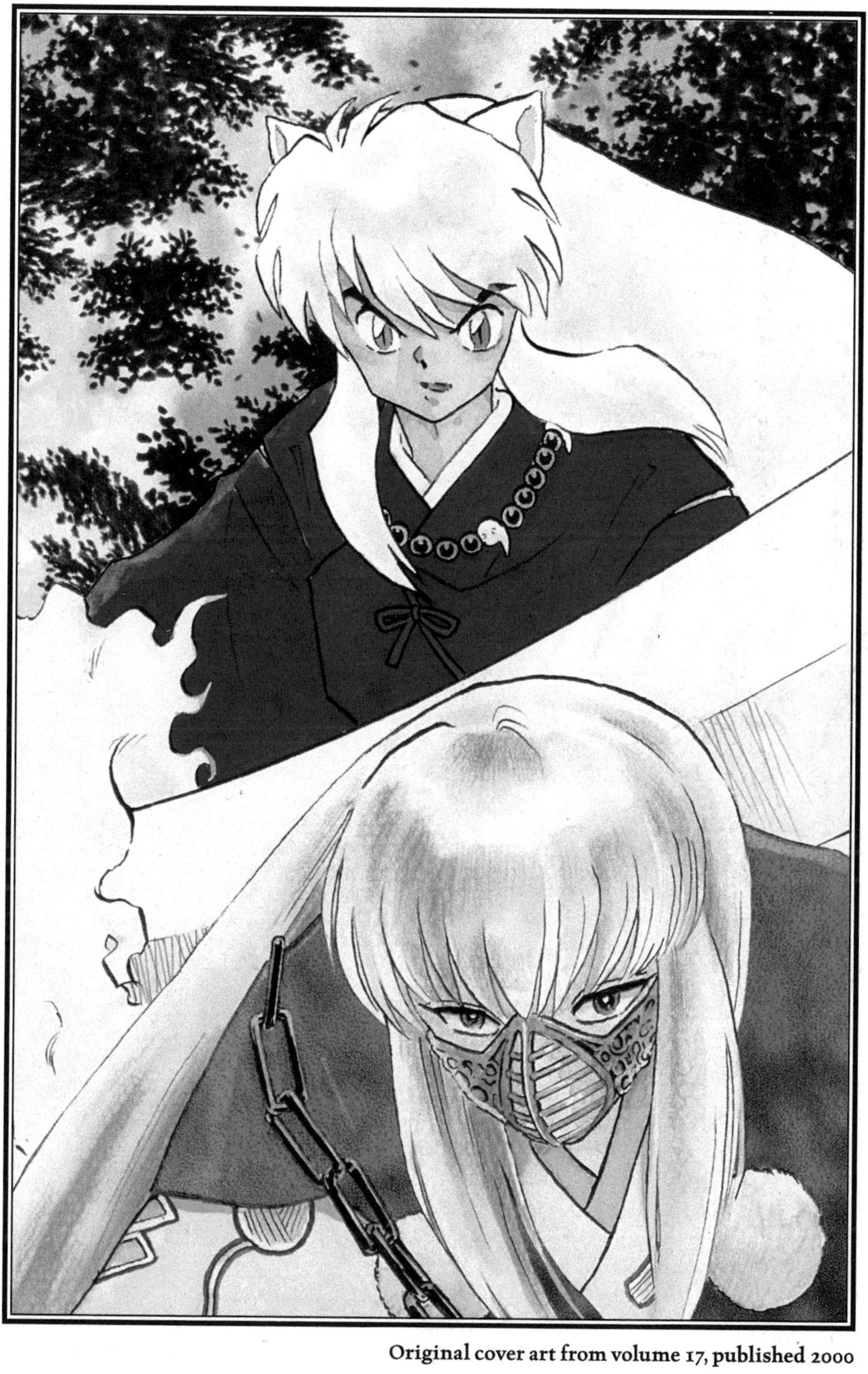

Original cover art from volume 17, published 2000

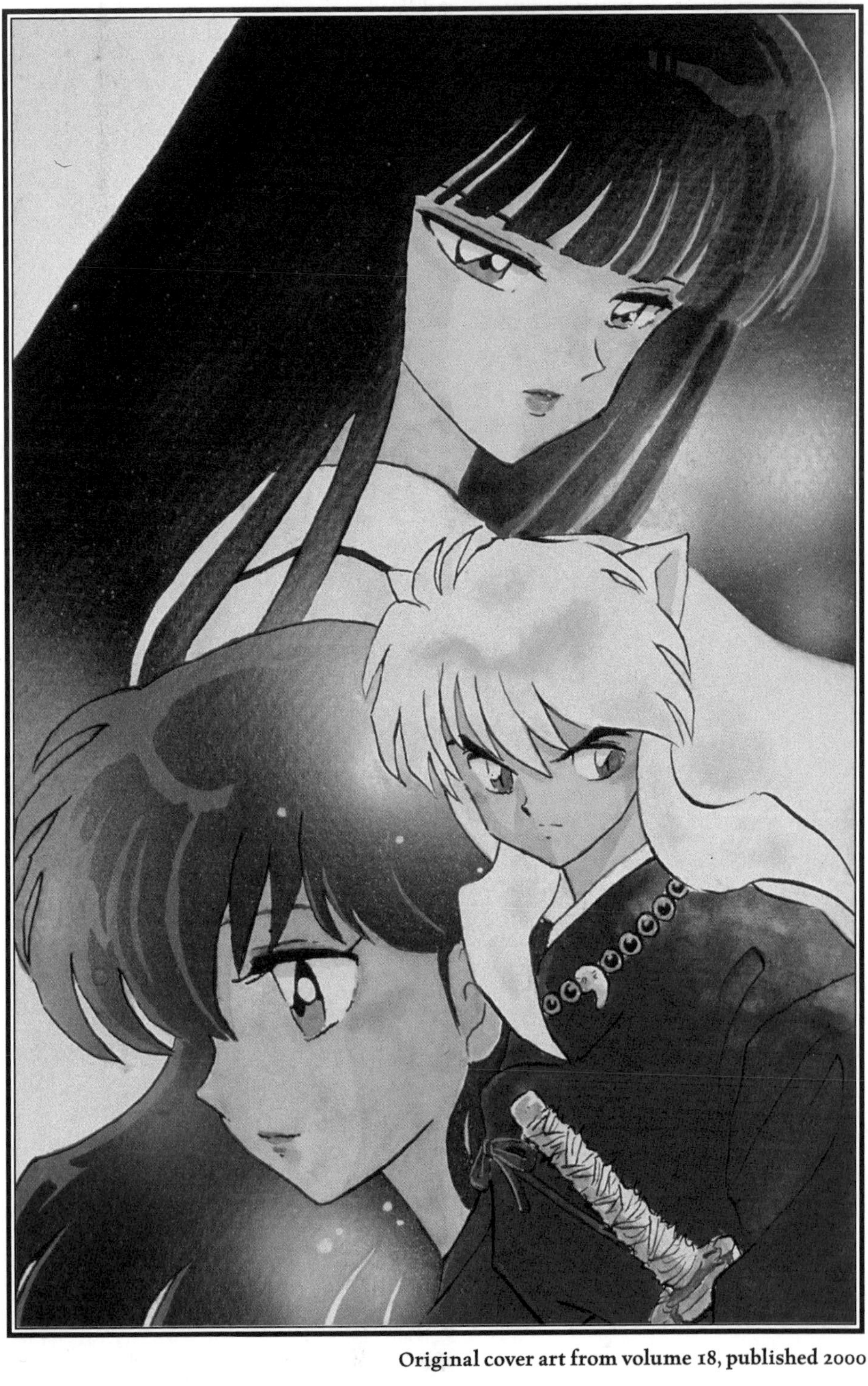

Original cover art from volume 18, published 2000

S0-AKM-098

Coming Next Volume

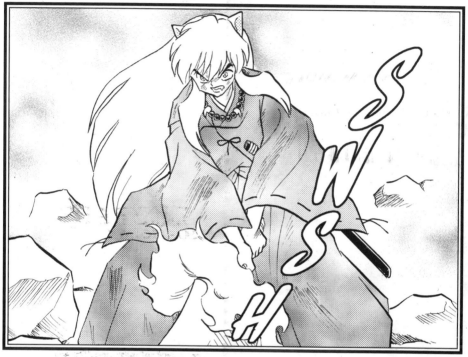

Kagome's friends each face difficult challenges as Naraku intensifies his efforts to gain complete control of the shards of the Shikon Jewel. Kohaku struggles to free himself from Naraku's grip, but doing so means facing up to the terrible deeds of his past. Then, as Inuyasha battles one enemy after another in his search to gain mastery over the heirloom blade Testusaiga, Kagome confronts Tsubaki, yet another pawn of Naraku's and one that may poison her soul. But even Naraku's servants scheme against him as Kagura tries to use Koga in an attempt to rid herself of Naraku's control. Then the coming of the new moon risks exposing Inuyasha's secret—how much has Kagura seen?